THE ENCYCLOPEDIA OF FOLK, COUNTRY & WESTERN MUSIC

IRWIN STAMBLER AND GRELUN LANDON

THE ENCYCLOPEDIA OF

FOLK, COUNTRY & WESTERN MUSIC

Second Edition

IRWIN STAMBLER

AND GRELUN LANDON

St. Martin's Press   New York

Encyclopedia of Folk, Country & Western Music
Copyright ©1983 by Irwin Stambler and Grelun Landon. All
rights reserved. Printed in the United States of America. No
part of this book may be used or reproduced in any manner
whatsoever without written permission except in the case of
brief quotations embodied in critical articles or reviews. For
information, address St. Martin's Press, 175 Fifth Avenue,
New York, N.Y. 10010

Library of Congress Cataloging in Publication Data

Stambler, Irwin.
  Encyclopedia of folk, country & western music.

  Bibliography: p.
    1. Folk music—United States—Dictionaries.
2. Country music—United States—Dictionaries.
3. Musicians—United States—Biography. 4. Country
musicians—United States—Biography. I. Title.
ML102.F66S7 1982   781.773'03'21   82-5702
ISBN 0-312-24818-0   AACR2

Design by Kingsley Parker

First Edition

10   9   8   7   6   5   4   3   2   1

CONTENTS

C   3

PHOTO CREDITS

INTRODUCTION AND ACKNOWLEDGMENTS

The massive increase in the size of this edition of *The Encyclopedia of Folk, Country & Western Music* compared to the first edition over a decade ago indicates the steadily growing popularity of these music fields. This is particularly noticeable on the country side where a rising tide of releases by country artists appear on the national pop charts as well as the country lists, and acknowledged country stars like Willie Nelson, Waylon Jennings, and George Jones prove able to fill large concert halls that normally cater to rock acts.

Part of the impetus for this trend comes from "progressive" country performers whose music (as Bill Ivey of the Country Music Foundation points out in his article in this book) has effectively popularized some of the down-to-earth attributes of traditional country music. At the same time, progressive country also embodies some of the aspects of rock 'n' roll. In fact, the success of country-bred rock superstars like Jerry Lee Lewis, Carl Perkins and, of course, Elvis, though it caused a temporary depression in the country field in the late 1950s and early 1960s, in time proved to be a positive factor by directing the interest of many young popular music fans toward the content of modern country. The interplay of musical forces from both sides of the fence led to the rise of many 1970s groups that provided a bridge between rock and country and, indeed, rock and folk. This is acknowledged in this Encyclopedia through entries for bands like Charlie Daniels, Marshall Tucker, the Eagles, and Alabama, whose offerings have found favor with both rock and country/folk audiences.

Over the past years since the first FCW edition, while the type of music generally described as folk hasn't gained the large scale airplay and associated record sales of the late 1950s-early 1960s "boom," neither has it disappeared. Folk music's fortunes, in truth, also have improved, though not as dramatically as for the genre's "country cousin." Most of the major folk festivals in existence at the end of the 1960s continue today, typically drawing sizeable crowds. At the same time, new festivals of folk and folk/country music continue to be organized in the United States and in other nations.

It is the authors' premise that there is a strong relationship between the major categories of folk, country and western music. If you were to place an elite group of country and folk authorities in one room to formulate what should be in an encyclopedia covering these disciplines and attempted to define what country and folk, or a combination of the two, really are, it would be wise to bring a sleeping bag, several changes of clothing, and survival rations for a long stay. In assembling this volume, we have tried to accommodate these viewpoints to some extent in order to provide a broad sweep of information that may not satisfy the specialist's position, but is intended to provide the reader with insight into the overall scope of the music, trends and personalities.

Thus there are entries for artists not only in what some would call the mainstream of folk, country and western music, but also such subgroups as folk rock, folk blues, country rock and bluegrass. Creative individuals—writers and performers alike—often tend to defy easy pigeonholing, which extends to the various word descriptions of specific forms of music. Historically there has been cross-pollination of music forms in the popular domain. Thus early country music, which often descended directly from ballads popular centuries ago in England, Ireland, and other places of origin, can fit into either folk or country categories. Many traditional country artists thus were given places of honor at the folk festivals that sprang up in the United States in the decades after World War II. Those festivals—as do folk festivals to this day—also featured the blues, both the "folk" and "country" types, since roots blues and even the specifically composed numbers of recent times fall into the folk idiom. At the same time, there are strong elements of the blues in country music history. Jimmie Rodgers, the man known as the "father of country music" (more properly, father of modern country music), drew heavily on blues elements in many of his classic songs, and more than a few of the major country stars since then similarly amalgamated some blues-related material into their repertoires.

To some extent, in selecting entries for this book, the authors considered performers not yet well known, but who seem likely to make important contributions later in their careers. This has been made more difficult recently because of some changes in artist exposure patterns. Some of this has been caused by changes in the way a performer is "sold" to an audience; for instance, the recording success of a Boxcar Willie or a Slim Whitman through unconventional marketing techniques (the use of sold-through-TV albums, rather than the conventional record store distribution pattern) poses a challenge to the slow-but-sure ascension of talented artists, formerly considered a typical trait of both the folk and country fields. Both were previously thought of as stable fields where an artist, having built up a following, might find his or her popularity dipping from time to time over the decades, but not dissipating completely as has been the more typical case in the pop field.

However, the country field, in particular, has become more sensitive to the impact of TV and radio. This, in turn, has brought patterns more in line with pop music, including rock 'n' roll, where a new talent can become famous and successful in a brief period of time, then fade completely from view. One example: the sudden slippage of disco music in public interest in the late 1970s caused hundreds of radio stations to abruptly switch to country music formats, but usually without the addition of knowledgeable country music staffs or record playlists derived from such expertise. Movies also are having an often unpredictable effect. The film Urban Cowboy focused attention on John Travolta, Gilley's Club in Pasadena, and the mechanical bull. Since then, the film inspired the opening of even larger country music clubs than Gilley's, such as Billy Bob's in Ft. Worth, Texas, where a real bull ring (seating capacity 500) is almost lost in the cavernous acreage under one roof. Symbolic of the continued blurring of lines is that it is possible to hear, at one time or another, country, rhythm & blues, jazz, or rock music, despite the avowedly country decor. (As an aside, the original mechanical bull from Gilley's is now part of the Country Music Foundation's collection in Nashville.)

In recent times, social scientists have tried to interpret the folk/country music content in terms of issues like drug abuse, social unrest, the late Equal Rights Amendment, medical breakthroughs and other such "buzz word" themes in an effort to analyze our culture as represented through our music. Taking Kris Kristofferson as an example, sophisticated attempts have been made to classify him as a performer and songwriter in one "slot" or another, either for "now" or "for the ages." Such an approach would seem a contradiction in terms for an artist variously acclaimed as a country, contemporary folk, rock, film and TV star.

The difficulty of achieving simple classifications tends to cause problems not only for outside observers, including reviewers, but also for the business links between artists and the audience—radio stations and record companies—a situation which, in turn, often has effect on the concert circuit. Since neither record sales nor radio ratings are barometers that now hold up in once easy-to-classify fields, they have to be regarded as popularity feedback and regarded in that context. In recent years, with many record or radio operations becoming divisions of conglomerate corporations, the executives of those organizations have become more comfortably attuned to a computer printout than the dynamics of a virtuoso on banjo or a Ralph Mooney slipping in an incredible lick on the pedal steel guitar. (This aspect is discussed in more detail in Bill Ivey's article).

Still, it could be clichéed that the more things change, the more they stay the same. At the same time that many country "name" artists were turning out watered-down or glossier recordings to enhance their crossover potential into the pop field, artists of more traditional bent like George Jones began finding new mass public favor. Also during the 1970s, the "western" part of the country & western equation, which was all but totally assimilated into the "country" category (the Academy of Country & Western Music, for instance, changed its name to Academy of Country Music), suddenly made a comeback.

Groups of young musicians, such as those who assembled under the band name Asleep at the Wheel, breathed new life into "western swing," along the way reviving worldwide interest in older practitioners, such as the veterans of Bob Wills' Texas Playboys. The other side of western music, once represented by such greats as the Original Sons of the Pioneers, Gene Autry, and Tex Ritter, also returned to the fore as evidenced by the *Grand Ole Opry*'s signing as regulars in mid-1982 a young group called Riders in the Sky. The latter, comprising Doug Green, Woody Paul and Fred LaBour, offers material and delivery clearly in the tradition of the Sons of the Pioneers in its heyday.

A word about the approach in assembling this book: the first step involved sending some six hundred questionnaires to individuals or groups selected for coverage. (In the case of deceased individuals, the questionnaire was sent to the estate or other representative). As much as possible of the data provided was used in the final entry. In many cases, the entry was based on direct interviews. Other background information was obtained from the literature and through material provided by music industry press personnel (unfortunately in these recession days the press information group is a greatly diminished breed), artists' agents and various industry organizations.

We might note that, compared to the first edition, there was greater reluctance on the part of many people to supply actual birth dates, a shyness that prevailed among both sexes. On the other hand, reflecting increased fan interest with a resultant increase in media coverage, many artists' careers were discussed in greater depth in many publications with what appeared to be greater accuracy and less "hype" than in the past.

As always in a project of this kind, bringing the work to completion depended in great part on the assistance and suggestions of many individuals and groups. Those to whom we are particularly indebted (including some cited in the first edition who are not listed here) include: Fran and Bill Boyd of the Academy of Country Music; Bill Ivey, President, National Academy of the Recording Arts & Sciences (NARAS) and Executive Director, Country Music Foundation; Ronnie Pugh and other staff members of the Country Music Foundation who provided research assistance on many occasions; Acuff-Rose Publications; Chris Farnon of NARAS; Edwards Memorial Foundation, University of California at Los Angeles; Hugh Cherry; Bill Anderson; Cliffie Stone; Jo Walker-Meador, Executive Director, Country Music Association; Stan Gortikov, President, and Stephen J. Traiman, Executive Director, Recording Industry Association of America; Maggie Cavender, Nashville Songwriters Association International; Art Fein; Michael Ochs (for his assistance on pictures and artist background); the trustees and board members of the Country Music Foundation whose contributions have meant so much for the development of country music—Wesley Rose, Irving Waugh, Emmylou Harris, Bob Kirsch, Jerry Bradley, Ric Blackburn, Ralph Emery, Pee Wee King, Roy Horton, Brad McCuen, Joe Talbot, Frank Jones, Bill Denny, Richard Frank, Jim Foglesong, Frances Preston, Connie B. Gay, Michael Milom and Bill Lowery; Todd Everett (whose record collection and recall proved very beneficial); Marion Charles (whose insight opened doors); Larry Scott; Cynthia Kirk; Biff Collie; Kyo Sharee; Susan Stewart; Richard Waldow; Muriel De Cunzo; Pat Thomas; Shelly Selover; Sue Sawyer; Heidi Robinson; Sharon Weisz; Mara Mikialian; Bryn Bridenthal; Jacki Sallow (for original pictures of several major artists); Sue Satriano; Barbara Wyatt; Teresa Leyva; Paula Batson; Kathy Brisker; Valerie Hayden, John Mankiewicz; Tommy Thomas (Palomino Club); Billy Bob Barnett (Billy Bob's); Connie Bradley; Susanella Rogers; Terry Cokes; Gene Bear; Bob Levinson and Levinson Associates; Bobbi Cowan; Beverly Magid and Solters & Roskin; Jim Halsey Co.; Jack McFadden and OMAC Artist

Corp.; and such record companies as CBS/Epic, MCA, Warner Brothers/Reprise, Warner/Curb, Elektra/Curb, Elektra/Asylum, United Artists/Liberty, Fantasy, Flying Fish, Rounder, A&M, RSO, Casablanca, and Capitol.

For their encouragement and patient forbearance, thanks also are due to Connie Stambler; Barrett Stambler; Leigh, Casey, Amy and Jim Sprague; Abe and Adam Seidman; Anne, Mark and Miranda Rose Berch; Jennifer, Michele, Chris and Jessica Kate.

Lyndon Stambler and Alice Siedman did some fine editorial research, and those entries prepared by Alice are indicated by the initials A.S

We also would like to express our appreciation for the yeoman efforts on this project by the staff of St. Martin's Press including Les Pockell, who kept a weather eye on it since its inception, and such others as Ina Shapiro, Christine Kinser, Kathleen Babcock and Cheryl Rae Glickfield.

Los Angeles, California, 1982
Irwin Stambler
Grelun Landon

COUNTRY MUSIC GOES BACK-TO-BASICS
WILLIAM IVEY*

During the early 1970s country music appeared to change very little; a monotonous continuation of the bland Nashville-Sound style that had dominated the 1960s, on the verge of a pop/country merger in which country music's unique character would be lost. However, the 1970s proved to be a pivotal time in the development of country music. Within this decade, women first came to play a major role in country music, and groups and group singing gained a prominence not enjoyed by vocal ensembles since the days before World War II. The 1970s witnessed an explosion of mass popularity for both country singers and songs. If the period was characterized at the outset by the bland, pop-style vocals of Ray Price and Faron Young, by the decade's end, Waylon Jennings, Willie Nelson, Emmylou Harris and even Ricky Skaggs had begun to return country music to its natural center. In fact, the 1970s witnessed a back-to-basics movement in country music that would have seemed impossible ten years earlier.

The commercial growth of country music in the 1970s can be charted by the number of country music radio stations. Though the concentrated efforts of the Country Music Association had increased the total number of full-time country radio stations from 81 in 1961 to 606 by 1969, the 1969 total more than doubled in the 1970s. By 1979, 1434 stations were full-time country, and nearly 1,000 more played some country material. This growth, however, was accompanied by painful wrangling within the country music scene, as the forces of progress, committed to increased sales and the "crossover" hit, did battle with those elements that prized the soul, the tradition, and the authentic values which had been country music's strength through the years.

The struggle in the 1970s between innovation and tradition should have surprised no one. The entire decade of the 1960s had been given over to integrating country music into the larger pop-music mainstream. Record producers like Chet Atkins and Owen Bradley had consciously utilized pop-music techniques of instrumentation and recording to develop a sound acceptable to both pop and country music audiences. It was in the 1960s that the use of string sections, brass, and background choruses on country records resulted in the "Nashville Sound" which brought fame to that southern recording center. These recording tech-

* Director, Country Music Foundation, Nashville, Tennessee, and President, National Academy of the Recording Arts & Sciences.

niques, combined with the rather pop-sounding vocal work of such artists as Jim Reeves, Patsy Cline, and Eddy Arnold produced a spate of hits in both the pop and country fields. The sound of country music moved a considerable distance away from that of the fiddle, banjo, and steel guitar that had characterized it for several generations.

Country-pop was the legacy of the 1960s and the 1970s dawned with some of the most pop-oriented recordings ever cut in Nasville. Ray Price's recording of "For the Good Times," a giant 1970 smash, was performed by a tuxedoed Price on the CMA Awards telecast in the fall of 1971. His image on screen—black tie, a handheld microphone, orchestral accompaniment—was vivid evidence of the radical changes brought to country music during the 1960s. The country singer in the cowboy costume, strumming a guitar and singing a mournful narrative in a nasal voice was gone, at least from the TV screen and from the airways of the thousand radio stations that had been converted by the creamy appeal of country-pop.

For many observers, the early 1970s foretold the demise of country music. It is a widely-held theory that country music had begun as a form of folk art; crude at times but rich in excitement and honest poetic expression, which over the decades had been diluted by contact with other musical styles, and undermined by the demands of the commercial marketplace. Each decade seemed to produce a country style closer to the pop mainstream, as instrumentation, song, texts, and vocal style moved away from country music's Appalachian roots. Critics saw the early 1970s as the end of country music and many pundits predicted that country music would not survive the decade but would, by 1975, merge with pop music and lose its distinct identity.

Certainly many hit records of the period supported this contention. In 1971 Ray Price had a hit with "I Won't Mention It Again," and Lynn Anderson had a smash with the pop-oriented "Rose Garden." In 1972 Faron Young recorded "It's Four in the Morning," and Donna Fargo had a crossover hit with "The Happiest Girl in the Whole U.S.A." Charlie Rich recorded "Behind Closed Doors" in 1973 and had another hit with "There Won't Be Anymore" in 1974. In 1975 Glen Campbell's "Rhinestone Cowboy" was one of the year's biggest records. None of these hits belonged to the country styles pioneered by Ernest Tubb, Hank Snow, Hank Williams, or Lefty Frizzell. To those connected with country music and Nashville in the 1970s, these crossover hits were proof that traditional country music was dying.

Not only did country music move toward pop during the 1970s, but pop artists began to record songs in a country vein. John Denver made the country charts with "Back Home Again" and had equal success with "Thank God I'm a Country Boy" in 1975. Olivia Newton-John hit with "Let Me Be There" and in 1975 Linda Ronstadt had successful records of country music standards including *Heart Like A Wheel.* The success of the Nashville Sound encouraged record producers and pop artists to adopt elements of country recording technique. In the 1960s a singer had to journey to Nashville if he or she desired a country flavor on a particular recording (many artists, including Bob Dylan, Joan Baez, and Perry Como made the Nashville trek). By the 1970s, however, the vocabulary of country music was known internationally, and country-style records could be cut anywhere: New York, Los Angeles—even London.

The dominance of country pop and the appearance of pop and rock artists on the country charts produced related reactions in the middle 1970s. A group of singers/songwriters (they would come to be known as the "outlaws") outspokenly rejected Nashville and the style of recording developed during the 1960s, the era of the Nashville sound. Foremost among the outlaws, Waylon Jennings and Willie Nelson rebelled against Nashville and what it represented in country music and focused their attempt to revitalize the country tradition on the city of Austin, Texas. Supported by an enthusiastic group of local musicians and by the student body of the University of Texas, Austin had developed, by the early 1970s, into one of the most vital music communities in the United States. Austin possessed open, nurturing audiences and a nightclub scene that fostered the development of new talent. It was to this environment that the outlaws fled.

The outlaws' complaints were legitimate. They sensed, first of all, that country music had drifted away from its traditions. They blamed the great record producers of the 1960s—the people who had done so much to change the music of a rural working class into a highly stylized commercial sound aimed at the maturing middle classes. Chet Atkins, Owen Bradley, Don Law, and other producers associated with the Nashville establishment were criticized for their authoritarian ways in the studio and their willingness to force country singers into a Jim Reeves/Eddy Arnold mold.

Such twisting of singers' musical styles had, in fact, occurred. Nashville studios in the 1960s were staffed by a handful of studio musicians who played on virtually every session, and records were produced by an even smaller handful of specialists employed by record companies. These producers and musicians had hit upon a formula for success in the early 1960s, and, by the end of the decade, that formula had become iron-clad. Country singers received standard accompaniments on all their recordings, and were encouraged to mold their singing toward the country-pop style.

By abandoning Nashville the outlaws tried to renounce the Nashville sound. They recorded in Texas, with their own bands, rather than professional studio musicians and frequently produced their own discs. They eschewed such Nashville innovations as string and horn sections. The result was striking. Outlaw recordings tend to sound sparse, for they usually employed only the same five or six musicians who played with the singer on the road. Their efforts sounded much like country records of the 1950s (though, of course, the sound quality was much improved). Outlaw records by Willie Nelson and Waylon Jennings, cut in the 1970s, exhibit a charming and often moving simplicity which links their work to such country pioneers as Hank Williams and Left Frizzell.

In addition to the outlaws there were other forms of resistance to the impending merger of country and pop music. Mainstream country acts (most of them associated with Nashville's *Grand Ole Opry*) responded to the trend by forming the Association of Country Entertainers (ACE), which represented the most organized response to the dramatic changes occurring within country music in the early 1970s. The sudden chart and radio dominance of such country-pop acts as Ray Price, Donna Fargo, and Charlie Rich threatened those entertainers who performed in a traditional country style. Suddenly in the early 1970s, such artists as Hank Snow and Ernest Tubb found their concert and recording audiences stolen by this new generation of entertainers. To compound their dismay, much of the music programmed on country radio was not played by country acts at all, but by such performers as Linda Ronstadt, John Denver and Olivia Newton-John. ACE recognized that the growth in country radio and the expansion of country music into an international phenomenon had been a very mixed blessing.

Though there were more country radio stations than there had been in the 1960s, they now programmed tight playlists (no more than 40 or 50 discs were viewed as "playable" at any one time) usually associated with pop and rock radio, selecting material to reach as broad an audience as possible. This meant that few records were played, and those that reached the airwaves were always of the country-pop variety. In fact, records by pop artists frequently topped the play lists of these so-called country stations. There was little room on country radio for new artists trying to break in, and almost no room for the traditional country entertainer whose appeal was primarily to a more limited country audience.

For the ACE membership, of course, airplay was a bread-and-butter issue. Radio airplay affected both the artist's ability to tour and the size of their fees for live appearances. Inability to achieve airplay limited record sales, and thus jeapordized the recording contracts of long-established stars. The careers of many country music greats were suddenly menaced. Competition with rock and other forms of pop music caused the country artist to find himself in a new world—competing for airplay on stations resistant to new acts and "hard country" sounds, and spending ever-increasing amounts of money to generate the elusive hit. ACE attacked the Nashville establishment from within by demanding that country radio acknowledge the mainstream country tradition and by trying to force Nashville to abandon the headlong pursuit of international acceptance and the pop-crossover hit.

To the observer involved in country music during the early 1970s, it appeared that the gloomiest prophecies were coming true. Country music was about to dissappear. After having evolved to a point where it was virtually identical to pop music, and after pop artists were successfully imitating country style and generating country hits, it seemed that the artistic tradition, begun in the 1920s, was about to end in a flurry of crossover hits and pop impersonations. However, the much-touted Austin revolt against Nashville and the campaign waged against country pop by ACE gradually directed country music away from the excesses of the 1960s. In many cases, the changes came too late to salvage the careers of some prominent entertainers who had lost bookings and recording contracts in the early 1970s. Ernest Tubb and Lester Flatt, among others were let go by major labels. Despite such casualties, country music was able to reshape itself, and the seeds that produced that change proved to have been present all along. Although Ray Price's "For The Good Times" symbolized country music's pop aspirations in the 1970s, Conway Twitty's hit "Hello Darlin'" was evidence that the mainstream style of country music was still alive. Though Twitty never achieved significant critical acclaim for his work, he was, in 1970, beginning a string of number-one records that would make him the most successful country singer of all time. During the same period, Merle Haggard wrote and recorded hit after hit in an uncompromising country style. Real country singers existed and an audience for their style could still be found.

There was, in 1970, another trend which would reshape country music: the emergence of the female vocalist. Anne Murray's hit "Snowbird," was one of the year's biggest records. Not only did "Snowbird"'s success foretell Murray's long career in pop and country music, but it introduced a decade during which female vocalists would become a vital part of the country music scene. Lynn Anderson, Donna Fargo, Tanya Tucker, Emmylou Harris, Dolly Parton and Crystal Gayle emerged in the 1970s. Even females who had begun their careers in the 1960s— most notably Loretta Lynn and Tammy Wynette—really peaked during the 1970s. Not only did women become increasingly important within the overall country music scene, but performers such as Emmylou Harris and Crystal Gayle helped shape and define the country music performance styles which would energize the end of the decade.

The increased popularity of singing groups was another 1970s trend that illustrated the revival of traditional country music. At the beginning of the decade, the Statler Brothers were virtually alone in the field of country-ensemble singing. By the end of the decade, the Oak Ridge Boys, the Kendalls, Riders in the Sky, the Gatlin Brothers Band, and Dave and Sugar had returned group singing to the prominence it had enjoyed in the 1930s, the era of the Original Carter Family.

Important as these changes in country style were, the 1970s lent even further significance to the remarkable resurgence of mainstream country performance styles later in the decade. While the early 1970s were dominated by country-pop, the end of the decade saw a back-to-basics movement. As RCA Vice President Jerry Bradley said, "It's all going back to fiddles and pedal steel guitar."

The change was a reaction to the 1960s, to the Nashville sound, and to the encroachment of popular music and pop singers. The outlaws pushed for real country music, though they were not able to move the recording industry from Nashville to Austin. (As early as 1974, Chet Flippo, *Rolling Stone* writer and supporter of the Austin movement, noted that it was time for Austin to ". . . put up or shut up . . ." as a recording center.) Austin's impact was nevertheless felt in Nashville, as singers began to produce their own albums and record with their own bands while still retaining their mass appeal. By 1976 some of the outlaws had also gained positions on the record industry's popularity charts. Waylon &

Willie's "Good Hearted Woman" was the top record of the year. In 1977 the top disc was Waylon's ode to the outlaw scene, "Luckenbach, Texas (Back to the Basics of Love)." Of course, the outlaws never quite really moved to Luckenbach, but they did "get back to the basics."

A back-to-basics movement of a different sort emerged from the circle of songwriters, record producers, and artists who surrounded Nashville production genius Jack Clement, who had forged a reputation as a brilliant maverick. (He had launched the recording career of Charley Pride.) In the 1970s Clement and his associates shaped the recorded sound of Crystal Gayle and Don Williams— artists who became major influences late in the decade. Unlike the outlaws, who derived a hard country sound by returning to recording techniques of the 1950s, Clement, Allen Reynolds, and others used professional studio musicians, but produced a recorded sound that was both modern and simple. Don Williams' early discs are masterpieces of understatement, employing sparse, country instrumentation (rhythm guitar, dobro guitar, electric bass, harmonica) and a subtle percussion sound that became a Williams trademark. Crystal Gayle, though she recorded some pop-oriented songs, was supported by simpler instrumentation than that found on her New York or Los Angeles recordings.

Though there were many different approaches to recording country music at the end of the 1970s, the result was often the same: a simplicity that avoided the pop cliches of the late 1960s and early 1970s. It thus came as little surprise when the major new country artist of the decade burst on the scene singing traditional country songs, recorded in simple country style. "Lucille" is as hard-country a song as can be imagined. It talks of drinking and marriage break-up and does it in the simplest and most direct language. Kenny Rogers' recording of the song is also straight country, utilizing simple, strong rhythm guitar as the main accompaniment. It is difficult to imagine a less likely smash crossover, but cross over it did, in the same year that Waylon Jennings hit with "Luckenbach, Texas. . . ."

In fact, *Billboard's* top four recordings of 1977 illuminated country music's new direction as clearly as Ray Price's "For The Good Times" had defined the decade's early years. "Luckenbach" was the year's number-one hit, followed, in order, by Crystal Gayle's "Don't It Make My Brown Eyes Blue," "Lucille," and the Kendalls' "Heaven's Just A Sin Away." Those top four recordings of 1977 contained the stylistic innovations that would revitalize country music through the late 1970s and into the 1980s. The return of "hard country" in the work of Kenny Rogers and the Kendalls, the revolt of the outlaws stated so clearly in "Luckenbach" and the newly-developed country style expressed in "Don't It Make My Brown Eyes Blue," pointed out the direction that country music would take.

These trends accelerated toward the end of the decade. In 1978 Waylon and Willie scored with "Mama Don't Let Your Babies Grow Up to Be Cowboys." In 1979 Kenny Rogers recorded another mainstream country single, "The Gambler." In the same year, Don Williams gained substantial success with

"Amanda." By 1980 the stage had been set for the full acceptance of traditional country music, and George Jones—premier honky-tonk singer—won both DMA and Grammy Awards. That Jones could win such establishment recognition was clear evidence that, although the music industry did not move to Austin, and though ACE did not reverse the country-pop trend in radio, the forces of reaction and revitalization had triumphed.

Many had believed in a straight-line evolutionary process in country music: a steady movement away from cheatin' songs, fiddles, and steel guitars toward the bland expression of tin-pan-alley pop. The 1970s showed clearly that it was possible for the roots of country music to reassert their importance. The artistic concerns of the outlaws and the commercial worries of the ACE membership helped pull country music back from a merger with pop. The return to the roots of country music did not blunt the music's commercial success. By 1980 more than 2400 radio stations programmed some country music, and country record sales had risen to their highest portion of total record sales ever. This success had been achieved in a more open artistic environment than that of the early 1970s. In 1982 George Jones was king, and in 1982 Ricky Skaggs, ex-Emmylou Harris band member and Ralph Stanley sideman, had a number-one chart record with—what else—a bluegrass cut.

A

ACADEMY OF COUNTRY MUSIC: Western-based country music industry organization, founded 1964. (Original name, Academy of Country & Western Music).

The concept of special awards for creativity in the entertainment field seems to have its strongest roots in California. Such events as the Academy Awards of the Academy of Motion Picture Arts and Sciences and the Grammy Awards of the National Academy of the Recording Arts and Sciences originated in the state. Thus the environment was right when a new series of awards for the country & western music field was established by the newly formed Academy of Country & Western Music in 1964.

The new organization grew out of discussions in 1964 between trade journal publisher Tommy Wiggins *(D.J.'s Digest)* and three other country music enthusiasts, Eddie Miller, Mickey Christiansen, and Chris Christiansen. Their original goal was to promote greater interest in country and western music in the western states and provide a framework for meetings and programs for the exchange of information about the field by interested parties. During initial organizational efforts, one goal was to provide forms of recognition for performers and executives in country & western music.

Interest was quickly forthcoming, leading to the holding of the first awards event in late 1964. Locale was the Red Barrel nightclub in the Los Angeles area. Wiggins' publication underwrote the evening and Tex Williams served as emcee. In 1965, a second awards dinner was held, sponsored by *V.I.P.* magazine.

As Academy membership increased, it was decided to form a continuing committee to handle future progress. A dues plan was instituted so that sponsorship of future awards affairs could be handled by the Academy itself. The first official awards show of the Academy was held at the Hollywood Palladium in February 1966.

By the time the second Annual Awards Dinner was held at the Beverly Hilton, Beverly Hills, California, on March 6, 1967, the Academy had elected its first officers: Tex Williams as president, Eddie Dean, vice president, Bettie Azevedo, secretary, and Herb Eiseman, treasurer.

Since that time, the Academy continued to expand its membership and activities. During the 1970s, it changed from a regionally oriented organization to a more national one in outlook. As part of the trend, the awards ceremonies became an annual feature of network TV, starting on ABC-TV in 1973 and switching to NBC-TV late in the decade. (For Award winners, see Appendix).

ACUFF, ROY: *Singer, fiddler, band leader (Crazy Tennesseans; Smoky Mountain Boys), emcee, songwriter, record and music industry executive. Born Maynardsville, Tennessee, September 15, 1903. First living member of the Country Music Hall of Fame, elected in 1962.*

Few would argue with Dizzy Dean's designation of Roy Acuff as "The King of Country Music." Embodying the soul and symbol of the *Grand Ole Opry* in the 1940s, Roy Claxton Acuff remained its most charismatic figure over the ensuing decades.

Giving little evidence of having much interest in a music career until he was in his late twenties, Roy, as a child, excelled in athletics. His talent was impressive: he won thirteen athletic letters in high school. While not starring on the playing field, he was holding the center of the stage. He recalled that he "acted in every play they [the high school] had."

After high school, Acuff played semi-pro baseball and had hopes of having a successful tryout for a major league baseball team when disaster struck. Playing in a game in Knoxville on July 7, 1929, he suffered a sunstroke and collapsed in the dugout. After a week, another fainting spell came and, following three months of rest, still another. When a fourth attack hit him during a round of golf, he was so ill he had to spend most of his time indoors for almost two years. Slowly he recovered his strength, and as he noted, "I had to pick me out a new career."

His father's collection of country records helped point the way. Roy spent many hours at home listening to the fiddling tunes of Fiddlin' John Carson and Gid Tanner and the Skillet Lickers, trying to emulate the masters.

By 1932, he seemed in excellent health again. But if it were not for a neighbor named Dr. Hauer, a patent medicine man, Roy might not have gone into music. He asked Roy to join his show, to sell something called "Moc-A-Tan." As Roy told Douglas B. Green of the Country Music Foundation, "There was three of us that got to do all the entertainment, and I got to play every type of character: the blackface, the little girl's part, the old woman's part, plus play the fiddle and sing. And I'd sing real loud on the med show, sing where they could hear me a long ways. Yes, I got a world of training."

The tour lasted from spring to early fall. When it was over, Roy formed a band, the "Tennessee Crackerjacks." In a relatively short time, they had a following in the Knoxville region and soon were being featured on local stations KNOX and WROL. By the time they were approached by American Record Company to cut some sides, they were one of the most popular groups in Tennessee and had changed their name to the Crazy Tennesseans. Their first session, which included an odd type of gospel song called "The Great Speckled Bird," took place in Chicago on October 26, 1936.

Even prior to that, Acuff had yearned to join the *Grand Ole Opry*. Several inquiries had received little encouragement. But in early 1938, star *Opry* performer Arthur Smith, a favorite fiddler with program fans, got into an argument with the show and was suspended. A replacement was needed in a hurry. Someone thought of Acuff and, on the rainy night of February 19, 1938, he and the band set out for Nashville, arguing among themselves about what material to offer.

The matter still wasn't settled when Roy opened their set on the Dixie Tabernacle stage in East Nashville with the fiddle tune "The Old Hen Cackled and the Rooster's Going to Crow." He was so nervous, he told Green, "I did an awful poor job of fiddling. I played back of the bridge about as much as I played in front of it." Then he turned to dobro player Clell Summey and told him to start "The Great Speckled Bird," a number the band had urged him not to use. Again he felt he wasn't at his best. When the band left for their next engagement everyone thought they'd ruined their big chance.

Acuff recalled, "I didn't hear anything for two weeks after we returned to Knoxville. Out of the blue I received a telegram from David Stone asking me if I would come and take a regular job. The mail had come in tremendous—bushel baskets full— and they sent them on to me in Knoxville. That night 'The Great Speckled Bird' really changed my life."

Before 1938 was over, Acuff had begun to make his mark on the *Opry* and on country fans across the country. His single of the old Carter Family success, "Wabash Cannonball," was one of the most popular releases of 1938. He caught the fancy of *Opry* fans so rapidly that within a year's time he had replaced Uncle Dave Macon, the original superstar of the show, as the top performer. In the 1940 Republic film *Grand Ole Opry*, Acuff was considered the star of the movie, although Uncle Dave and other longtime luminaries were featured. Acuff also held center stage in 1940 on the "Prince Albert" broadcast, the most prestigious portion of the *Opry* program.

During 1939, at the urging of *Opry* management, the name of Roy's band was changed to the Smoky Mountain Boys, a name that stayed with the band. Although early members like Clell Summey and bassist Ed Jones departed to be replaced by other musicians as the 1940s went by, the band makeup in the mid-1940s remained together for many years: Howard "Howdy" Forrester, Jimmie Riddle on harmonica and accordion, Pete Kirby (better known as Bashful Brother Oswald) on dobro, banjo, and vocals. Other members in the 1940s were Lonnie "Pap" Wilson, Jess Easterday, and Tommy Magness. By the 1970s, Forrester, Kirby, and Riddle still were in the fold, along with Gene Martin, Charlie Collins, and Onie Wheeler.

Roy's records were top country sellers almost every month throughout the 1940s. His top sellers of the period included "Wreck on the Highway" and "Fireball Mail" in 1942, and "Night Train to Memphis," "Low and Lonely," and "Pins and Needles (In My Heart)" in 1943. Things were going so well for him in the early 1940s that he expanded his activities into the publishing field, joining forces with Fred Rose to form Acuff-Rose Publishing in 1942. The company became a major force in country music development over the decades, and its staff of contract writers provided not only some of the finest country songs but many of the top-ranked performers as well.

During the 1940s and early 1950s, Acuff made dozens of singles and albums that were issued on the Vocalion, Okeh, or Columbia labels (Columbia bought out the American Record Company). Some of his Vocalion singles were "Steamboat Whistle Blues," "New Greenback Dollar," "Steel Guitar Chimes," "Wabash Cannonball," "The Beautiful Picture," "The Great Shining Light," and "The Rising Sun." His output on Okeh included "Vagabond's Dream," "Haven of Dreams," "Beautiful Brown Eyes," "Living on the Mountain," "Baby Mine," "Ida Red," "Smoky Mountain Rag," "Will the Circle Be Unbroken," "When I Lay My Burden Down," "Streamline Cannonball," "Weary River," "Just to Ease My Worried Mind," "The Broken Heart," "The Precious Jewel," "Worried Mind," "Lyin' Women Blues," "Are You Thinking of Me Darling," "Wreck on the Highway," "Night Train to Memphis," "Don't Make Me Go to Bed and I'll Be Good," and "It's Too Late to Worry Anymore."

Roy's recordings for Columbia those years were even greater in number than his combined total on Vocalion and Okeh.

His Columbia list included many of the songs listed above, plus such others as "Beneath That Precious Mound of Clay," "It Won't Be Long," "Branded Wherever I Go," "Do You Wonder Why," "The Devil's Train," "The Songbirds Are Singing in Heaven," "I Saw the Light," "Unloved and Unclaimed," "Mule Skinner Blues," "Not a Word from Home," "Waiting for My Call to Glory," "I Called and Nobody Answered," "Golden Treasure," "Heartaches and Flowers," "Tennessee Waltz," "Sweeter than the Flowers," "Polk County Breakdown," "I'll Always Care," and "Black Mountain Rag."

Since childhood, Roy had harbored thoughts of emulating his father's legal career. In the 1940s, he ran for governor of Tennessee on the Republican ticket, both in 1944 and in 1948. Had Tennessee been a state less dominated by the Democratic Party, things might have been different. As it was, though, Acuff lost both times and stuck to his musical career thereafter.

During the 1950s and first part of the 1960s, Roy was no longer able to penetrate the upper segments of the singles charts, but remained a fans' favorite on the *Opry* as well as on the county fair, rodeo, and concert circuits. Even if Roy himself wasn't dominating the charts, the output of Acuff–Rose was. Through 1967, that company's writers turned out 108 songs that made the top 10, including fifteen number-one records. That was more than twice as many top-10 successes as the next publisher, Hill and Range. During those years, Roy also diversified into other enterprises, operating Roy Acuff Hobby Exhibits, Dunbar Cave Park and Recreation Center near Clarksville, Tennessee. He also helped Fred Rose start Hickory Records and became a member of the Hickory recording roster in 1957. (His association with Columbia ended in 1952 and was followed by brief stays with Decca, MGM, and Capitol, before the Hickory alignment.)

Most of his album work from 1957 was for Hickory. Some earlier material was reissued on various labels in the 1960s, such as Capitol's *Best of Roy Acuff* in 1963, *Great Roy Acuff* in 1964, and *Voice of Roy Acuff* in 1965, and MGM's *Hymn Time* in 1962 and

Smoky Mountain Boys in 1965. He was represented on Pickwick in the 1960s by the album *How Beautiful Heaven Must Be.* Decca also issued material by Roy in a series of seven albums titled *All Time Country & Western Hits* issued at intervals from July 1960 to August 1966. His name also graced several Harmony Record LPs, such as *Roy Acuff* (3/58), *That Glory Bound Train* (7/61), and *Great Roy Acuff* (7/65).

His Hickory LPs of the 1960s included *American Folk Songs, Gospel Songs, King of Country Music, Once More, Songs of the Grand Ole Opry, The World Is His Stage,* all issued or reissued in July 1964; *Great Train Songs, Hall of Fame, Sings Hank Williams* (1/67); *Treasury of Hits* (7/69). Harmony issued the LPs *Waiting for My Call* in August 1969 and *Night Train to Memphis* in July 1970. Hickory issued *Roy Acuff Time* in 1970. Also released about that time was the Columbia album *Roy Acuff's Greatest Hits,* and on Hilltop, *Roy Acuff Country.*

Like most country stars during their heyday, Roy was on the road hundreds of days each year. His schedules included long overseas trips to entertain the U.S. armed forces. His first such effort was to Berlin during the 1949 Russian blockade and continued with shows in Korea in the 1950s and the Dominican Republic and Vietnam in the 1960s. Roy and the Smoky Mountain Boys also were featured in concerts in many European countries. The intensive tour grind came to a halt, though, on July 10, 1965, in an automobile accident that injured Roy and several band members. He returned to action on the *Opry* three weeks later, but cut back sharply on the road work, pruning his schedule to almost nothing by 1972, when he was nearly seventy years old. Roy continued to be a mainstay of the *Opry,* however, delighting countless fans throughout the decade of the 1970s. On the occasional *Opry* specials telecast on PBS, the show often included segments showing Roy happily presiding over impromptu jam sessions by *Opry* greats in his dressing room.

During the 1960s and 1970s, Roy's recorded output included a sizable number of remakes of earlier hits on Hickory. But he also included new numbers, such as his single "Back in the Country" in 1974. Many of those recordings, old and new, were included in the two-record *Roy Acuff's Greatest Hits, Volume 1,* issued by Elektra in 1978. In 1979, Elektra issued *Volume 2.*

Roy was nominated for the Country Music Hall of Fame in 1961 and his plaque was unveiled there the following year. It read, in part, "The Smoky Mountain Boy . . . fiddle[d] and sang his way into the hearts of millions the world over, often times bringing country music to areas where it had never been before. 'The King of Country Music' . . . has carried his troupe of performers overseas to entertain his country's armed forces at Christmas time for more than 20 years. Many successful artists credit their success to a helping hand and encouraging word from Roy Acuff."

ALABAMA: *Vocal and instrumental group. Personnel as of 1981: Randy Yeuell Owen, born Ft. Payne, Alabama, December 13, 1949; Jeffrey Alan Cook, born Ft. Payne, Alabama, August 27, 1949; Teddy Wayne Gentry, born Ft. Payne, Alabama, January 22, 1952; Mark Joel Herndon, born Springfield, Massachusetts, May 11, 1955.*

In the years following World War II, most of the names appearing on country music charts have belonged to solo artists, and to a lesser extent, duets. Very few bands have made the charts at all, and even fewer have reached the highest positions on the charts. Even those who have reached the top have failed to do so consistently. Alabama, in the early 1980s, seemed an exception to this trend, with a string of hit singles and albums, some of which also crossed over to the pop charts.

As its name implies, the band had its origins in Alabama. Randy Owen, Jeff Cook, and Teddy Gentry—the three cousins who are the band's primary members—were all born and grew up near Ft. Payne, Alabama, a locale where country music has strong roots. By the time the three cousins reached their teens, they were all interested in music and had learned to play various instruments. It would be a while, however, before they would perform together.

When the cousins first started jamming together around Christmas, 1969, it seemed doubtful that any of them would ever make music a career. At that time, Jeff was working for Western Electric, while Teddy was earning a living laying carpets, and Randy was still attending school. In their partnership, all three handled vocals with Randy singing most leads work. Instrumentally, Randy and Jeff played guitar and Teddy bass guitar. Another cousin, Jackie Owen, was the group's first drummer. They formally became a band at the start of the 1970s, after getting a job offer to play at the nearby Canyonland tourist park. Each weekend, Canyonland brought in an established star like Bobby Bare, Narvel Felts, and Jerry Wallace, and the band would back them, then play a one-hour dance set.

After a while, when no new opportunities for the band opened up, Jeff became discouraged and took a government job in Anniston, Alabama. However, Randy (having finished high school) and Teddy remained hopeful and moved there also, both taking day jobs as carpet-layers. The cousins kept working days and picking up night and weekend band dates until March 1973, when they moved to Myrtle Beach, South Carolina, where they found work playing six nights a week in local clubs for tips. Without a record contract at the time, the group cut its own records and hawked them to audiences from the stage.

They sent demo tapes to record companies during the mid-1970s without success until they finally gained the attention of executives at GRT Records, which issued their single "I Want to Be With You" in 1977. The disc only made lower-chart levels, but helped bring a contract with MDJ Records of Dallas, which issued several Alabama recordings starting with "I Wanna Come Over" in late 1979, a tune that made the country singles top 40. By then a new drummer, Mike Herndon, had joined the group to complete the foursome, still intact as of late 1981. In early 1980, the MDJ release "My Home's in Alabama" (written by Randy and Teddy) rose to the top 20.

That April, the group moved over to RCA Records, which soon released the single "Tennessee River" (written by Randy) and the debut LP *My Home's in Alabama.* Both became chart hits, with the single reaching upper-chart levels during the summer. Before 1980 was over, the group had its biggest hit ever, the single "Why Lady Why," which made the country top 10 in late fall.

The band continued its progress in 1981, beginning with the single "Old Flame," which rose to number one on country lists in April. Later in the year, Alabama had another top-10 single, "Love in the First Degree." Its 1980 debut LP, *My Home's in Alabama,* was still prominent on the chart throughout 1981, earning a gold-record award. The group's second album, *Alabama,* came out during 1981.

Meanwhile, the band was touring intensively, headlining in smaller clubs and opening for other, better-known acts in major venues. Alabama also gained a great deal of TV exposure, and was featured on Johnny Carson's *The Tonight Show* and the *Merv Griffin* show, among others. The band also performed on the 1981 Country Music Association's annual award show.

ALAN, BUDDY: *Singer, guitarist, songwriter. Born May 23, 1948, Phoenix, Arizona.*

It seems natural that the son of such illustrious country-music performers as Bonnie Owens and Buck Owens would make a name for himself in the field. He did—in fact, he made a new one, deciding against using his well-known last name. Instead he chose his first for his last name and his nickname for his first.

Growing up in Bakersfield, California, where his family had moved when he was a child, Alan was exposed to rock 'n' roll as much as to country & western music, even though Bakersfield had a much greater concentration of country artists than many other California cities. During his teenage years, people like Elvis Presley, Jerry Lee Lewis, and, later, the Beatles and the Rolling Stones were the music idols of many of Buddy's friends. When he began playing guitar seriously in his teens, theirs was the kind of music he tended to emulate. When he decided to assemble his own band at the age of fifteen, it was a rock group that played local shows and dances for several years.

It was not until his late teens that Buddy's interest in country music blossomed and helped him decide to become a full-time performer. He wrote the authors, "I grew up in Bakersfield, California, where I lived with my mother, Bonnie Owens, until I was seventeen. I moved to Arizona to go to school [Arizona State University] and became a disc jockey on a [Phoenix] country radio station. [In Arizona he also attended an electronics school and earned his First Class radio license from the FCC.] At that time I got a job with a country night club and, after traveling with the Buck Owens Show during the summer decided to try music at age twenty-one."

He continued to perform when he had the chance and also turned out original songs in the late 1960s. The die was finally cast when he became a regular cast member of his father's *All American Show*. From then on, he toured throughout the United States and in other countries, initially concentrating on the Owens series, but later, as his recording fame grew, headlining shows of his own. He also amassed numerous TV credits in the 1970s including, naturally, many appearances on *Hee Haw*.

Buddy signed with Capitol Records in the late 1960s and before long had a number of singles that made the national country charts. One of his early hits was "Cowboy Convention," a top-20 song in late 1970 that Buddy recorded with Don Rich, lead guitarist of Buck Owens' band, the Buckaroos. A number of his chart hits in the first half of the 1970s were his own compositions, such as "All Around Cowboy of 1964" in early 1974 (co-written with R. MacDonald). Some of his other chart-makers during 1974–75 were "I Never Had It So Good," "Chains," and "Another Saturday Night," the latter a remake of an old Sam Cooke hit.

One of his first albums on Capitol was *Wild, Free and 21*, released in 1969. This was followed in 1970 by *A Whole Lot of Somethin'* and in 1971 by a collaboration with Don Rich, *We're Real Good Friends*. In May 1976, Capitol issued the LP *Chains/Another Saturday Night.*

In the early 1980s, Buddy called Phoenix, Arizona, home. His total recorded output as of that time, he wrote, comprised "10 albums and 29 singles on Capitol. I also have had 41 songs recorded that I have written."

ALLANSON, SUSIE: *Singer, pianist, actress. Born Las Vegas, Nevada, March 17, 1952.*

Winsome Susie Allanson's waif-like expression and slim athletic build contrasted sharply in appearance with many of the reigning female stars of country music in the 1970s. But she could match many of them in the intensity of feeling she could impart to her vocal renditions in the modern country idiom, an ability that made her one of the fastest rising young artists in the field at the start of the 1980s.

Like another country artist from the Far West, Lynn Anderson, Susie was far more interested in horseback riding than music for much of her youth. As with Lynn, though, there was a strong country music environment around her from her earliest years. When she was in the first grade her grandmother taught her to play the piano, a skill she continued to upgrade. She also had a fine voice as a child and sang in church choirs and in school choruses.

But, she recalls, "When I was growing up, all I could think of was horses. My sister and I rode in rodeos every chance we got. I've retained that interest to this day [1979] and now raise champion quarter horses. But when I got older, I found there were other things in the world besides horses. Instead of riding at rodeos, I began singing at rodeo dances. I guess it was about that time I thought about singing a little more seriously."

A turning point for her came in 1970 when she was working as an usher for the *Merv Griffin* show, then telecast from Las Vegas. She heard that auditions were being held for a road company of the rock musical *Hair*. She tried out and made the cast, touring with the show for a year. After that, she auditioned and made the cast of the original U.S. company of another rock musical, *Jesus Christ Superstar*. She remained with that show eighteen months, during which she not only sang on the *Superstar* album, but also was a member of the film cast.

She moved to Southern California in the mid-1970s. When her work in *Superstar* was over, she looked around for other engagements in the entertainment field. One of the opportunities was an audition for a Bicentennial project, which turned out to be far more than a regular audition. The man in charge of it, Ray Ruff, was so impressed with her ability he not only took over her career on a full-time basis but also asked her to marry him. After that, Ruff, a veteran of years in the music industry, handled the instrumental arrangements and production of Allanson's recordings and personal appearances.

Their initial collaboration included the single "Baby Don't Keep Me Hangin' On," which Ruff first released on his own label, Oak Records, in early 1977. As it began to show signs of audience response, distribution was taken over by Warner/Curb Records in Los Angeles, which also signed Susie to a recording contract. The single reached upper-chart levels in August 1977. That was followed by a series of successful singles on Warner/Curb through 1978, including "Baby, Last Night Made My Day," a chart hit in late 1977, a remake of the old Buddy Holly song, "Maybe Baby," high on hit lists in 1978, "That's What Makes the Jukebox Play," on charts in the summer, and, finally, "We Belong Together," one of the top country hits of 1978. The song rose to number one on the charts in August and became the title song of Allanson's debut LP. The album, which also contained her earlier chart-makers, rose to number one on national country charts in the fall of 1978. At year end, Susie had another single, "Back to the Love," in the top 20.

In 1979, she changed her record alignment to Elektra, a sister company of Warner's, for the new Elektra/Curb label. Her debut on that label, in early 1979, was the single "Words," which rose to top-chart levels in a few weeks' time. In March 1979, she was represented by her debut Elektra/Curb LP, *Heart to Heart*, followed a few months later by the chart hit single "Two Steps Forward and Three Steps Back." At year end, "I Must Be Crazy" was on the

lists, remaining there through early 1980. During 1980, Susie switched from Elektra to a new recording association with Liberty/UA under the Liberty/Curb label. In the fall of the year, the single "While I Was Making Love to You" on that label was in upper-charts positions. Late in the year she had "Dance the Two Step" on the charts. Her 1981 Liberty/Curb charted singles included "Love Is Knockin' at My Door" in the fall.

From the late 1970s on, of course, she was a much sought-after guest for major TV shows. She also performed widely on the country & western circuit, appearing at major fairs, rodeos, and clubs across the United States.

ALLEN, REX: *Singer, guitarist, fiddler, actor, songwriter. Born Willcox, Arizona, December 31, 1924.*

Through his narration of countless Walt Disney nature films, and his appearances at rodeos, Knott's Berry Farm, and Disneyland, Rex Allen seemed to epitomize the voice of the American cowboy from the 1950s through the 1970s. A ranch hand and rodeo contestant in his early years, he appropriately gained the nickname of "Mister Cowboy." Although his efforts tapered off, he was still turning out albums and occasional singles in the late 1960s and early 1970s, adding to his many credits and chart successes over three decades.

Born and reared in Willcox, Arizona, Rex learned to rope and ride as a youngster and already was showing skills in local junior rodeos in his early teens. At eleven, he was given his first guitar and before long he was accomplished not only as a guitar player but as a fiddler. His fine voice began to be heard in western shows in his home state. His reputation grew rapidly, and, at thirteen, he was widely known as "that young cowboy with the amazing voice." Helping him to gain that designation was a series of engagements on radio, starting with his debut performance during the State Cattlemen's Convention. In high school, his music teacher also contributed to his career by entering him in a statewide singing contest, where Rex won first place.

For a while in his late teens in the early

1940s, Rex couldn't decide whether to concentrate on music or rodeo competition. He was above average at bulldogging and bronc riding and took part in a number of major rodeos. But in 1944, after he'd studied electronics for a time in California, he moved cross country to New Jersey, where he got his own show on Station WTTM in Trenton. During part of 1944 and 1945, besides performing on that show, he also could be heard on station WCAU in Philadelphia. His ability attracted the attention of the National Barn Dance in Chicago, which lured him to the Midwest in 1945. He remained a featured artist on the nationally broadcast show until 1950.

Luring him further west in 1949 was CBS's offer to do his own show. He finally made California his home base when Republic Pictures signed him in 1949 to start work on his debut film, The Arizona Cowboy. Throughout the 1950s, Allen fans were treated to a steady diet of new westerns that featured Rex and his horse, Koko. Before his association with Republic on the series ended, he was featured in thirty-five films. Meanwhile, Rex's CBS-TV show, Frontier Doctor, was a hit, ranked seventh nationally for the 1949–50 season, and remained a network favorite for a number of years.

His singing TV work in the 1950s included regular cast status on the Town Hall Party in Los Angeles and guest appearances on many network programs, including several on the Red Skelton Show.

His movie and TV activity continued in the 1960s and 1970s. Featured in the 20th Century-Fox film For the Love of Mike and Universal's Tomboy and the Champ in the 1960s, he also narrated more than eighty Disney Studios movies and TV programs from the early 1960s through the 1970s.

Rex signed with Decca Records in the late 1940s and turned out many singles and albums for the label in the 1950s. In 1953, "Crying in the Chapel" was a top-10 single on country & western charts. Among the albums he completed for Decca were the 1958 releases Under Western Skies and Mister Cowboy. In the early 1960s, he moved from Decca to Mercury and scored a top-10 hit in 1961 with

"Don't Go Near the Indians." He also recorded for Disney's Buena Vista label, which released his "16 Favorite Songs" in May 1962. His other LPs of the 1960s included Mercury's Faith of a Man and Rex Allen Sings and Tells Tales and, on Pickwick, Western Ballads. Though many of the songs on his various albums were traditional western ballads, such as "Old Faithful," "Streets of Laredo," "The Last Round-Up," and "On Top of Old Smoky," he often included some of his own compositions. By the end of the 1970s, his original songs numbered well over three hundred.

During the 1950s and 1960s, Rex played many engagements on the county fair and rodeo circuits. His contribution to modern rodeo in general was recognized by the Rodeo Producers of America and Canada in 1965 when it named him "Rodeo Man of the Year," the first entertainer to be given that award. In 1966, he was named Arizona Man of the Year and in 1968, he was elected to the Cowboy Hall of Fame, where he served as a member of the board of trustees in the late 1970s. As he said in 1973, "I love the personal appearance dates of a rodeo or fair more than anything else in my life. I love people and I love to be with people. I'm still a country boy at heart."

In the 1970s, though, he followed a more leisurely pace than he had in earlier decades, "hunting, fishing, boating, and trying to climb every hill in California." It was a period, too, when one of his sons, Rex Allen, Jr., was establishing himself as a major name in modern country & western music.

Allen continues to make a certain number of personal appearances a year, while also lending his distinctive western voice to movies, TV and commercials, and occasional new recordings. Among his LPs still in the active catalog in the early 1970s were Golden Songs of the West (Vocalion) and Touch of God's Hand (Decca).

ALLEN, REX, JR.: Singer, guitarist, songwriter. Born Chicago, Illinois, August 23, 1947.

Although Rex Allen had four children, only his namesake has directly emulated him. Rex Allen, Jr., has shown himself to be a worthy recipient of the family heritage, and a performer likely to have a career marked with almost as many honors as his illustrious father.

Not surprisingly, Rex, Jr., was infatuated with the entertainment field from early childhood. Raised in Southern California, he was taken to some of the western movie sets his father was working on throughout the 1950s. When he was six, he began to travel as part of his father's act on the rodeo, fair, and theater circuit.

Young Rex quickly developed good stage presence and began to learn guitar chords before he was out of elementary school. In junior high school he formed his first group, the Townsmen, which performed at school and local events. Later, he assembled Saturday's Chidren, with whom he gave a number of shows and also headlined on several TV programs.

During the mid- and late-1960s, Rex, Jr., continued to pursue his music career with mixed results, taking time out from these efforts to serve in the U.S. military. Later he decided he would make better progress in country music by moving to Nashville. Once there, he managed to gain a spot as a CBS-TV summer replacement show called *CBS Newcomers*.

At the end of the 1960s and in the early 1970s, he made a little progress in his recording efforts. Represented by the album *Today's Generation* on the SSS label, he turned out other recordings that appeared on JMI Records. He also continued to add to his performing experience on various tours and TV programs around the country.

However, it was not until he joined Warner Brothers Records in 1973 that he began to attract a following. His first single release on the label, "The Great Mail Robbery," was issued at the end of 1973 and showed up on the lower levels of the country charts in January 1974. Several months later, he markedly improved on that with his chart hit, "Goodbye." Both of those songs, as well as "The Same Old Way" and his version of the reggae song, "I Can See Clearly Now," were included in his debut LP, *Another Goodbye Song*. After much success in 1974, he had an equally impressive follow-up year with such

charted singles as "Never Coming Back Again" and "Lying in My Arms." His second Warner's LP, *Ridin' High,* which came out in 1975, included his excellent baritone treatment of several songs associated with his father, such as "Streets of Laredo" and "San Antonio Rose," as well as an original composition, "I Gotta Remember to Forget You."

In 1976 Rex achieved his first major hit with the song "Can You Hear Those Pioneers," (co-written with J. Maude.) The song reached the top 20 in June. In September, he had another top-20 single, "Teardrops in My Heart." His third LP on Warner Brothers, *Rex,* didn't make the country top 50, but the sales total showed a steady gain compared to earlier LPs.

Allen, Jr.'s, 1977 offerings included the summer chart single "Don't Say Goodbye" and his fourth LP, *The Best of Rex,* issued in September. The album, he noted, "wasn't intended to be a 'greatest hits' collection," which would have been a bit premature, "but a collection of the songs that I've loved best or the people I respect or have liked." It did, though, include some of his more successful numbers, such as "Two Less Lonely People," "Can You Hear Those Pioneers," "I'm Getting Good at Missing You," and "Don't Say Goodbye." Accompanying them were tracks like "Tumbling Tumbleweeds," "Cool Water," Merle Haggard's "Silver Wings" and "Today I Started Loving You Again." In September 1978, one of Rex's best singles was issued, his own composition "With Love." It achieved top-10 levels, as did the single "It's Time We Talk Things Over" in early 1979, co-written with J. Maude, and "Me and My Broken Heart" later in the year.

From the mid-1970s on Rex, Jr., was an increasingly important factor on the country & western concert circuit. As a featured artist, he often shared bills with the brightest names in the field, including Dolly Parton and Hank Williams, Jr. In many cases, he and his band were the headliners at rodeos, fairs, and in major auditoriums around the country. He also performed on almost all the important network country TV programs, including appearances on the *Grand Ole Opry.*

Rex began the 1980s in good style with such charted singles (on Warner Brothers) as "Yippi Cri Yi," "It's Over," and "Drink It Down, Lady" in 1980, and "Cup of Tea" and "Just a Country Boy" (the last written by him) in 1981. "Cup of Tea," a duet with Margo Smith, was in the top 20 nationwide in early 1981 and reached the top of some regional lists.

AMAZING RHYTHM ACES: *Founding members, 1972: Russell Smith; Butch McDade; Jeff Davis; Billy Earhart III. Barry Burton, James Hooker added shortly after. Burton left 1977, replaced by Duncan Cameron.*

Like many of today's "country" bands, the Amazing Rhythm Aces were initially difficult to classify. Their main successes were in the country genre, but the Memphis-based group combined country, rhythm & blues, rock, and gospel sounds. This posed an image problem for the group with potential fans. An additional problem was the band's tendency, in concert, toward a harder-edged, more R&B-oriented musical format than on records.

Lead singer Russell Smith agreed that too much diversity was always a problem, although in 1979 he still felt optimistic about the situation. "It's been a problem for us just as it's been for groups like Asleep at the Wheel. But somebody likes us. They may not know exactly what to call us, but they're buying our records. Our last album [the 1978 ABC release *Burning the Ballroom Down*] sold the most of any of our LPs. It was over 300,000 the last time I looked. As long as somebody still likes us and comes to see us, that's all that counts. I don't care what they call us as long as they don't call us bad."

The unfettered approach to music of the group's members, he noted, was central in the band's formation in 1972. It was then that Smith and drummer/percussionist Butch McDade first got together over a shared interest in blues singer B.B. King. "The reason the band came into existence is probably the same reason nobody knows what kind of music we play. When Butch McDade and I got things started we were disaffected musicians. We didn't want to play heavy metal in bars; we

didn't want to play disco; we wanted to play what we wanted to. So we kind of got together out of a dissatisfaction with other things going on and kept adding and dropping people until we got a group that fitted together with what we had in mind."

Among the initial additions who stuck with the band were bassist Jeff "Sticks" Davis, who had played in Otis Rush's blues band, and keyboard-player Billy Earhart. By the time the band adopted the name Amazing Rhythm Aces in 1974, it had expanded to include engineer/multi-instrumentalist Barry "Byrd" Burton and pianist James Hooker. Burton came aboard to help engineer the band's recording of Smith's composition "Third Rate Romance." Smith, the group's principal songwriter, came from a musical family and was trying to write songs almost as soon as he learned to play guitar. One of his compositions of the early 1970s was "Third Rate Romance," which Jesse Winchester included on his *Learn to Love It* album. When a number of other artists began to pick up the song, Smith and his group decided they should make their own recording of it.

The single was on the band's debut album for ABC Records, *Stacked Deck*. It made upper-chart levels on country lists as well as national pop lists. The LP also spawned a second single that made country charts, "Amazing Grace (Used to Be Her Favorite Song)." The album won generally favorable reviews, as did the band's second album, *Too Stuffed to Jump.* Their third album, *Toucan Do It Too* failed to attain the success of the first two, even though it contained some excellent original songs by Smith and McDade. In 1976, the Aces won a Grammy Award for Best Country Vocal Performance by a Group for Smith's composition "The End Is Not in Sight" from the third LP.

In the mid-1970s, the band maintained a busy touring schedule, often opening for noted country artists such as Willie Nelson and Waylon Jennings. The grind proved too much for Burton. Smith commented, " 'Byrd' just got tired. He got tired of touring. He didn't want to go out on the road as much as we do. He was older than the rest of us and all he wanted to do at this point was produce and play sessions. He finally got the chance to do that in Nashville and he took it. It [the split] was an amicable thing. We're still friends. He's in Nashville now playing a lot with Don Williams. We're satisfied with the present setup. He's going towards country & western and we're moving a little bit more rock 'n' roll, a little more blues and soul."

Burton was replaced by Duncan Cameron, who had been playing guitar and backing country bands since he was fifteen years old. He also had been a member of Dan Fogelberg's band, Fool's Gold. He made his first contributions to the group's fourth LP, *Burning the Ballroom Down*, on the charts in 1978.

For the next album, the Aces had a new producer. "We went to Jimmy Johnson of Muscle Shoals Studios," Smith noted. "Other things haven't changed. Actually, everything you hear on the new album is in the Amazing Rhythm Aces tradition. For instance, R&B and more rock-oriented music is stuff that we like to play on stage, but that hasn't been on our albums up to now."

The resulting 1979 ABC release, *Amazing Rhythm Aces,* had more R&B content, but also had a country-rock tune, "Lipstick Traces"; Cameron's country-rock ballad, "Homestead in My Heart"; and Smith's country-story song, "Rodrigo, Rita and Elaine." As good as any Aces collection, the album nonetheless failed to catch the public's fancy. In the early 1980s, Smith and McDade disbanded the group, at least temporarily. Smith signed as a solo vocalist with Muscle Shoals Sound Records, with his debut LP due for distribution by Capitol Records in 1982.

Based in part on a 1979 phone interview with Russell Smith by Irwin Stambler.

ANDERSEN, ERIC: *Singer, guitarist, harmonica player, songwriter. Born Pittsburgh, Pennsylvania, February 14, 1943.*

In the mid-1960s, when it was fashionable to compare every new folk artist to Bob Dylan, Eric Andersen was considered one of the foremost candidates for Dylan's folk mantle. Andersen, who in his writing and concert work steadfastly hewed to what might be called "old-school folk," was overshadowed by the resurgent rock movement of the period. However, he persevered and remained a favorite of the small but enthusiastic folk audiences of the late 1960s and 1970s, in a way symbolizing the weary-struggle-against-fate theme voiced in many of his compositions.

Born in Pittsburgh, Andersen grew up in Amherst, upstate New York. Influenced by the strong folk music movement of the mid-1950s, he started to learn guitar in 1957, and by his mid-teens often accompanied himself when singing folk songs in school shows. By the time he enrolled in Hobart College in New York at the start of the 1960s, he was an excellent guitarist and harmonica player as well. Before long he tired of college and dropped out to try his hand as a folk performer in the Boston, Massachusetts area.

His reputation grew and after working solo for a while he assembled his own group, The Cradlers, and made his mark on the folk circuit throughout New England. Performing in group concerts and folk festivals, he sometimes shared the bill with such early 1960s luminaries as Joan Baez, the Kingston Trio, and Peter, Paul and Mary.

In the mid-1960s Manhattan was his base of operations; he often appeared at major folk clubs in Greenwich Village. Besides his headline appearances, including several acclaimed concerts at New York's Town Hall, he was sought out by other artists to work as a sideman in various bands or as a session musician in recording studios. From the mid-1960s throughout the 1970s, he backed many top artists in every segment of pop music from folk through rock.

In 1964, he signed with Vanguard Records, making his album debut with *Eric Andersen* in May 1965, followed in April 1966 by *'Bout Changes and Things.* As a *Harper's* magazine writer noted, he was considered one of the most promising young performers in the Big Apple. "At the age of twenty-three, he is one of the mainsprings of the folk world. Tall, thin

. . . with high cheekbones like Rudolph Nureyev (the ballet dancer), he is what everyone who is eighteen in the village wants to look like."

In the late 1960s, he continued to perform not only in New York but across the United States, with occasional forays into Canada. During these years, he continued to add new songs to his repertory, averaging about forty compositions a year. His Vanguard albums of those years included 'Bout Changes and Things, a reissue of his 1966 LP, Take 2 (9/67), More Hits from Tin Can Alley, Country Dream, and a double-disc retrospective, Best of Eric Andersen. In 1969 he changed record companies, joining Warner Bros., which released Eric Andersen in December 1969 and Avalanche in the early 1970s. As he had in most of his previous recordings, Andersen arranged and produced his original works. He also turned out the Eric Andersen Song Book in those years and established his own music publishing company, Wind and Sand.

The Warner Bros. alignment was short-lived, and he moved to Columbia in 1972. His initial LP on that label changed the pattern for a time. Called Blue River (released in August 1972), it was one of his best efforts and made the national album charts, a rare accomplishment for a folk artist during those years. But bad luck prevented him from following up that success. He worked up material for a new album, but the master recordings were lost, and with them a wonderful opportunity to revitalize his career.

After that experience, he left Columbia and signed with Arista Records, which issued several of his albums in the second half of the 1970s, including Be True to You, Sweet Surprise, and The Best Songs. Throughout the decade he continued to appear in small folk clubs across the United States and sometimes abroad. In the mid-1970s, he acknowledged the changing times and included an electric bass guitar in his band arrangements. The emphasis remained, though, on acoustic instrumentation. Typically, he performed on an acoustic guitar with a harmonica brace around his neck and with one or two acoustic backing musicians.

ANDERSON, BILL: *Singer, guitarist, actor, songwriter, music industry executive, band leader (Po' Boys, Po' Folks). Born Columbia, South Carolina, November 1, 1937.*

In an article Bill Anderson wrote for the first edition of the Encyclopedia of Folk, Country, & Western Music, he pointed out that the country music business was just recovering from the "rock 'n' roll depression" when he first entered it. "They talked in 1960 about the 'good ole days' of country music. Backstage gab sessions among the entertainers were often about the days when 'old Webb' had twenty-one straight number-one songs, the least of which sold a quarter of a million records . . . of the days when 'Old Hank' was packin' 'em in singing 'Lovesick Blues.'

"I notice today, however, that I don't hear too much of that anymore. Our people today are too busy talking about the new Country Music Hall of Fame and Museum in Nashville that's attracting tourists by the thousands, of the record crowds . . . at the Grand Ole Opry . . . of the full-time country radio stations in New York, Chicago, Philadelphia, Los Angeles, Dallas, Atlanta, and just about everywhere else. And they're talking about the attendance records broken nearly every week [by country stars], about the syndicated country music television shows pulling top ratings in just about every city. . . ."

That was written at the end of the 1960s, and perhaps is even more appropriate today. Country music has endured and prospered. So has Bill Anderson, who was as successful in the 1970s as he was in the 1960s, and who played a vital role in the rejuvenation of country music.

Born in South Carolina, Anderson grew up in Georgia, the heartland of country music. He was already working on his guitar chording by the time the Andersons moved from Commerce, Georgia, to the Atlanta suburb of Avondale, where he attended high school. In his teens, he had his own country band and won a high school talent contest for one of his original songs.

He earned his B.A. from the University of Georgia in the late 1950s in journalism. During his college years, not only did he play in country shows in Atlanta and other

Georgia towns, he also had his own disc jockey program on local stations. Meanwhile, he kept writing country songs and tried to interest people in the country music field in performing them, even as he worked at newspaper jobs at the *Dekalb New Era* in Decatur and at the *Atlanta Constitution*.

In 1958, his first music breakthrough came with the hit single of "City Lights" by Ray Price. "That's What It's Like to Be Lonesome," another Anderson composition, made the national top 10 in 1959. At this point, Bill made a commitment to music and signed with Decca, the label for which he was still placing singles and albums on the country charts two decades later. (Decca merged with MCA, and the latter is the name found on his releases of recent years.) In late 1959, Anderson started touring in support of his recording efforts, and, more than twenty years later, he remains a major concert attraction not only in the United States but in Canada and many other nations.

His credits as a performer and songwriter snowballed as the 1960s went by. In 1960, he made top-chart levels with "Tips of My Fingers," and the late Jim Reeves hit, "I Missed Me." In 1961, Hank Locklin hit the charts with Bill's "Happy Birthday to Me," and Bill made the lists himself with "Walk Out Backward" and "Po' Folks." (The latter song provided the name for Bill's famous backing band, the Po' Boys.) Among other songs that became hits for Bill or other artists in the 1960s were "My Name Is Mud," "Mama Sang a Song," "I've Enjoyed as Much of This as I Can Stand," "8×10," "I Love You Drops," "Nobody but a Fool," and "Still." While Bill wrote or co-wrote much of his material, occasionally he recorded other writers' material, such as his 1964 hit single of Alex Zanetis' "Me."

In the years before the Country Music Association Awards, most honors came from trade magazines, DJ polls, or industry organizations such as Broadcast Music Inc. (BMI)—the music licensing agency to which Anderson belonged. Bill gained many honors from these, including Top Male Vocalist of the Year for 1963, Record

of the Year for 1963, and Top Songwriter of the Year for C&W in 1963, 1964, and 1965. He was still winning or placing high in those competitions in the 1970s. As of 1979, for instance, he had been honored as Male Vocalist of the Year five times, Top Duet of the Year for his work with Jan Howard, with whom he worked in the late 1960s and part of the 1970s, and chosen in a 1970s *Billboard* magazine poll as one of the "Three All-Time Greatest Country Music Songwriters." As of 1977, he had received forty-nine BMI songwriter awards, more than any other country-music composer on the organization's roster. When the CMA Awards program got underway, Bill naturally took part in many of the events, either as a performer on the nationally televised TV shows or a nominee in various categories.

In 1961, he became a regular cast member of the *Grand Ole Opry* and was still on the show as the 1980s began. During the 1960s, he appeared on just about every important country TV show, as well as on his own syndicated program, which was still going strong at the end of the 1970s. Among those featured in the regular cast during that decade were Mary Lou Turner, his duet partner from 1973 to 1979, singer-instrumentalist Jimmy Gately, and, naturally, the Po' Boys. The same cast plus (later renamed the Po' Folks) different guest stars was a major live concert attraction under the banner of the *Bill Anderson Show* throughout the United States and much of the world.

Anderson's other activities in the entertainment field ran the gamut from music publisher to film performer. Among his movie credits were *Country Music on Broadway, Forty Acre Feud, Las Vegas Hillbillies,* and *The Road to Nashville.* In the 1970s, he also owned his own radio station, KFTN in Provo, Utah, a full-time country-music channel.

In the 1970s there was no slowdown in Bill's recording accomplishments. He had a major hit in 1970 with his composition "Where Have All the Heroes Gone," also the title of a top-10 album. His other album releases of the late 1960s and early 1970s included *If It's All the Same to You* (with Jan Howard); *Love Is a Sometime Thing; Always Remember; Greatest Hits, Volume 2; That Casual Country Feeling.*

In the mid-and late-1970s, his chart hits included such original compositions as "I Still Feel the Same Way About You," "Country D.J.," "I Can't Wait Any Longer," and "Double S" (the last two co-written with B. Killen). His single hits of other writers' songs in those years included "Thanks" in late 1975, "Peanuts and Diamonds" in mid-1976, "Head to Toe" in the summer of 1977, and "Still the One" in the fall of that year. He recorded duets with Mary Lou Turner, including the top-10 hits "That's What Made Me Love You" in May 1976 and "Where Are You Going, Billy Boy" in the late summer of 1977. Among his chart LPs in the late 1970s were *Sometimes* (with Mary Lou Turner) in 1976, *Scorpio* and *Billy Boy and Mary Lou* in 1977, and *Love . . . And Other Sad Stories* in 1978. For his 1979 LP, *Nashville Mirrors,* he wrote seven of the ten songs, including the chart hit "More Than a Bedroom Thing." At the end of the 1970s, after two decades of activity, Bill could point to a total of close to forty albums, over fifty hit singles and tens of millions of records sold.

In 1980, he began a new phase of his career by signing up to emcee a new TV game show called *Funzapoppin.* The first shows were taped at Astroworld in Houston, with others planned to be taped at Opryland in Nashville. During the year, his charted singles for MCA included "Make Mine Night Time," "Get a Little Dirt on Your Hands" (written by Anderson, recorded as a duet with David Allan Coe), "Rock 'n' Roll to Rock of Ages," his composition "I Want That Feeling Again," and, in 1981, "Mister Peepers."

By 1980, Bill Anderson had accomplished just about anything that one could in the field of country music, except election to the Country Music Hall of Fame—and that is sure to come in due time.

ANDERSON, LIZ: *Singer, songwriter. Born Pine Creek, Minnesota, March 13, 1930.*

It was lucky for Liz Anderson that her husband was a car salesman. His contacts at the agency helped launch Liz on a songwriting career she might not otherwise have considered. And that, in turn, led to her becoming a singing star at a point in life when others might have thought more about behind-the-scenes work.

Liz grew up in a rural area of Minnesota near the Canadian border. Her birthplace, Pine Creek, she recalled as a "cross in the road" thirteen miles north of the town of Roseau, Minnesota. "I was born on a farm, though my father wasn't a farmer," she told *Music City News* (October 1967). "My folks were awfully poor and we were very, very religious. I can remember liking country music. We had a mandolin and when I was about eight years old we used to sing in church all the time. We also sang on street corners. I had a brother older than me and we used to harmonize, but he quit singing when he was about fifteen."

The family moved to Grand Forks, North Dakota, when Liz was thirteen. She attended high school there and met Casey Anderson. "He lived across the alley from me, but I didn't know him too well until he came home on leave one time while in the Navy. The only time I got to see him was when he was in the alley working on his cars—and I didn't like him because he was always so dirty looking. But he looked real handsome in that blue uniform."

The two were married on May 25, 1946, and within a few years had a young daughter named Lynn. In May 1951, they decided to head for California, where Casey meant to go to jet engine school. "But the way it worked out," he told *Music City News,* "is that we had a kid driving the truck and he busted an engine on us in Montana and when we hit California we were flat broke. So I started selling cars."

They first settled in Redwood City, but eventually moved to Sacramento, east of San Francisco, near members of Liz's family, and there, in 1957, Liz started writing original country songs. Sometimes when her sisters would come over to their house on weekends to socialize, everyone would sing songs, including some of Liz's.

Casey, impressed with his wife's writing skills, issued her a challenge a few years later that was to prove decisive. Being a member of the Sacramento Sheriff's Posse, which was planning to take part in the National Centennial Pony Express celebration, he suggested she write a song in honor of the Pony Express. She did, and her effort was named the official song for the event and earned her a Medal of Honor from the group.

These activities weren't lost on a friend Casey had made at work. Jack McFadden, then also on the sales force of the Chevrolet agency where Casey was employed, later became Buck Owens' manager. He spent time at the Anderson's home and heard some of Liz's country compositions. He liked "I Watched You Walking" and since he was dabbling in the country field on the side, asked if he could try to do something with it. He recommended it to Del Reeves, who recorded it for Slim Williamson's Peach Records label. The song achieved moderate regional success and encouraged Del to record more of Liz's work. He turned out another single on Peach, "I Don't Wonder," and when he was signed by Decca Records chose still another of her tunes, "Be Quiet Mind," for his initial sessions. The single became one of 1961's major hits, bringing both Del and Liz their first top-10 successes. The song also was the title number of Del's debut LP on Decca.

Interest in Liz's offerings naturally increased among country performers. In 1964 Ray Drusky made top-chart levels with her "Pick of the Week," which won a BMI award. A little later, Bonnie Owens came over to the Anderson's house, heard "Just Between the Two of Us," and recorded it with Merle Haggard. Haggard himself dropped by when he was appearing locally and became enthusiastic over a new song called "My Friends Are Gonna Be Strangers."

Liz recalled, "I remember telling Merle about some of the lines being so corny, like 'should be taken out, tarred and feathered,' but Merle said, 'No, leave it just like it is.' But it took him about a year to record the song and I thought he never was. He's a perfectionist, and he kept working until he thought we had it just right. . . .

'Strangers' opened the door for us in Nashville and we began to get more songs recorded. We made the 1965 disc jockey convention there and received a BMI award for the song."

The trip proved eventful in other ways. Chet Atkins of RCA Records had decided Liz had the potential to be a singing star, and she went into RCA's Nashville studios to work on her debut album. While the family was there, they also renewed acquaintances with Slim Williamson, who now headed Chart Records. Williamson expressed interest in signing the Andersons' pretty blonde teenage daughter, Lynn.

As country fans know, both Liz and Lynn since have made their mark on the field as top-rank vocalists. Liz's debut LP came out on RCA's Camden label in August 1966. Included in it was the song that became her first single release, "Go Now, Pay Later." In late 1967, Liz was represented with her first LP on the RCA label, *Cookin' Up Hits.* This was followed by a steady string of new singles and LPs throughout the late 1960s and the 1970s. Among her LP credits were *Game of Triangles* (recorded with Bobby Bare and Norma Jean), *Liz Anderson Sings Her Favorites, Like a Merry-Go-Round, Country Style, If the Creek Don't Rise* (12/69), and *Husband Hunting.* Lynn paid tribute to her mother in one of her albums, called *Songs My Mother Wrote.*

In the late 1960s, having gained enough rewards from country music to make it a full-time livelihood, Liz and Casey moved to Old Hickory Lake near Hendersonville, Tennessee. Casey took an increasing role in the music industry, helping to start the Andersons' own music publishing firm, Greenback Music. He also collaborated with Liz on a number of songs, including "The Fugitive," a charted single for Merle Haggard.

ANDERSON, LYNN: *Singer, guitarist, songwriter. Born Grand Forks, North Dakota, September 26, 1947.*

"Like mother, like daughter" is an expression that certainly tells the story of Liz and Lynn Anderson, who both became

Roy Acuff

Bill Anderson

Asleep at the Wheel, seated, front center, Lucky Oceans; second row, Link Davis, Jr., Ray Benson, Chris York, Chris O'Connell, Tony Garnier, LeRoy Preston, Bill Mabry; rear, standing, Danny Levin, Pat "Taco" Ryan

Eddy Arnold

Gene Autry (left) and pioneer record executive "Uncle Art" Satherley

Chet Atkins

highly regarded country performers and songwriters. It's very likely, in fact, that if Liz hadn't started placing some of her original songs with country artists in the 1950s, her daughter Lynn might never have made country music her vocation, particularly since Lynn grew up far from the heartland of country music in an era when rock 'n' roll was the mainstay.

While Lynn was still a small child, the family left North Dakota and moved to Redwood City, near San Francisco, in May 1951. By the late 1950s they were living in Sacramento, California, where her father, Casey Anderson, worked as an automobile salesman. There he met Jack McFadden, who dabbled in the country field in his spare time. Later McFadden helped Lynn's mother Liz place some of her songs with a variety of country performers.

Lynn enjoyed singing and dancing as a child, but her main passion was horseback riding. In high school, she was one of the top-ranked young horse-show competitors in California, winning over 100 trophies, 600 ribbons, two regional championships, a reserve championship at the Junior Grand National Horse Show at San Francisco's Cow Palace, and, in 1966, the title of California Horse Show Queen at the State Fair in Sacramento. Though she switched prime allegiance to music in the late 1960s, she never abandoned her interest in horses: living in Tennessee in the 1970s, she and her husband had their own ranch where they raised quarterhorses.

Lynn's early musical grounding (she learned guitar before she was in her teens) and home environment kept pulling her back towards a musical career in her late teens. At seventeen, she entered a singing contest sponsored by the *Country Corners* program on a Sacramento TV station. After her first year at American River Junior College, she got an offer to join the *Lawrence Welk* TV show in Hollywood—an opportunity too good to pass up.

She became a regular on the show in 1967 and also signed a recording contract with Chart Records, producing the album, *Ride, Ride, Ride* and a hit country single, "Too Much of You." Lynn received good responses from *Welk* show viewers, but her stay on the program was cut short by her marriage to R. Glenn Sutton on May 4, 1968. They set up housekeeping in Hendersonville, Tennessee, both to be closer to the "Country Music Capital," Nashville, and to Lynn's parents, who had earlier moved back East.

In the late 1960s, Lynn continued to turn out a steady series of well-received singles and albums for Chart, many of which became best sellers. Among her singles were "I've Been Everywhere," "That's a No-No," "Rocky Top," "Promises, Promises," and "Big Girls Don't Cry." Her Chart LPs included such titles as *Promises, Promises, At Home, Uptown Country Girl, Songs My Mother Wrote, I'm Alright, Greatest Hits, Lynn Anderson with Strings,* and *Songs That Made Country Girls Famous.*

At the start of the 1970s, Lynn signed a new contract with Columbia, which issued the LP *Stay There 'Til I Love You* in July 1970 and followed with *No Love at All* in September. But the real blockbuster arrived at year end with Lynn's single of Joe South's composition, "Rose Garden." It rose to the top of both country and pop charts and stayed there from the end of 1970 into early 1971. The album of the same title, released in February 1971, was equally successful, making Lynn a national celebrity. Besides earning her gold records from the Recording Industry Association of America for both single and album, the song brought in thirteen more gold records from different countries around the world. (That album, as well as the ones that succeeded it, all were produced by her husband, Glenn Sutton.) "Rose Garden" also brought Lynn a Grammy for Best Country Vocal Performance of 1970.

Throughout the 1970s, Lynn continued to be a vocalist and recording artist of the first rank in the country field. During most of the decade, she spent a good part of every year on the road with her backing group, The Country Store, performing in concert halls, fairs, and rodeos throughout the United States and abroad. In the early 1970s, President Nixon invited her to attend the Celebrity Breakfast in the White House. She also was featured on almost every major network TV program, including Johnny Carson's *The Tonight Show, Kraft Music Hall, The Ed Sullivan Show, Johnny Cash, Merv Griffin, Mike Douglas,* and *Dean Martin's Music Country.* In addition, she was a guest on dozens of specials as well as returning a number of times to appear on *Hee Haw* and on some *Grand Ole Opry* telecasts.

In the early 1970s, one of Lynn's records was chosen as the national theme song for the Christmas Seal Campaign. At that time, Lynn and her daughter, Lisa, then twenty-one months old, were depicted on a national Christmas Seal poster.

Among Lynn's Columbia LPs after *Rose Garden* were such releases as *You're My Man, World of Lynn Anderson, I've Never Loved Anyone More* (a chart hit in the fall of 1975), and *I Love What Love Is Doing to Me/He Ain't You,* on country charts in late 1977. Her chart hit singles of the mid- and late-1970s included "Sing About Love" in late 1974, "Smile For Me," "I've Never Loved Anyone More" in the fall of 1975, "I Love What Love Is Doing to Me" in the summer of 1977, "He Ain't You," a top-20 hit in late 1977, and "Last Love of My Life" in the fall of 1978. Her 1980 Columbia chart hits included "Even Cowgirls Get the Blues" in the summer and "Blue Baby Blue" late in the year.

ARNOLD, EDDY: *Singer, guitarist, song writer. Born near Henderson, Tennessee, May 15, 1918. Elected to Country Music Hall of Fame in 1966.*

Eddy Arnold once said, "I'm a Heinz 57 singer. I sing many different kinds of songs which mean something different to many different kinds of people." That facility, which included the ability to change his singing style and material to meet changing audience tastes, served him well in a long and eventful career. For decades he was a giant among country artists who was able to cross over into the general pop music field as well.

He rose to stardom from humble beginnings, hence his nickname, "The Tennessee Plowboy." His father was a sharecropper, and Eddy worked on the farm as soon as he was old enough to lend a hand. His parents enjoyed music; his father was an old-time fiddler and his mother was a guitarist and taught him the instrument when he was a boy. When he entered Pinson High School, he sang and played the guitar in school events. However, he had to leave high school in the early 1930s to help on the farm, and for a while, music was mainly a sideline. He still played for local functions, though, riding to and from the events on a mule with his guitar slung on his back. His income at the time came not only from music but from farming and a job as an assistant at a mortuary.

Gradually, his talent brought more and more chances to perform. In 1936, he made his radio debut on a Jackson, Tennessee, station. In the late 1930s, he performed for a while on station WMPS in Memphis, then went to St. Louis, where he worked in small night clubs and had a spot on a radio show. In 1942, he joined station WTJS in Jackson, Tennessee, and for six years was one of the audience's favorites. His growing reputation helped win him a contract with RCA Records in 1944, with whom, in 1946, he broke through with his first series of hits. (His first manager was Colonel Tom Parker, later Elvis Presley's manager.) His popularity snowballed from then on. From 1946 through 1952, it wasn't unusual for two or three of his records to be in the top 10 at the same time. He soon had star status on various country radio shows, including the *Grand Ole Opry.*

In 1948, he had no less than nine top-10 records, five of which ranked number one for several weeks each. Many of those he wrote or co-wrote. His 1948 output included "I'll Hold You in My Heart" (co-written with Horton and T. Dilbeck), number-one ranked "Just a Little Lovin' Will Go a Long Way" (co-written with Zeke Clements), and "Then I Turned and Walked Slowly Away" (written with Fortner). Other 1948 hits included number-one songs "A Heart Full of Love," "Bouquet of Roses," "Any Time," "Texarkana Baby," and top-10 hits "My Daddy Is Only a Picture" and "What a Fool I Was to Cry Over You."

The 1949 hits included such Arnold co-authored songs as "C-H-R-I-S-T-M-A-S,"

"I'm Throwing Rice at the Girl I Love," "One Kiss Too Many," and "Will Santa Come to Shanty Town." Other 1949 hits included number-one ranked "Don't Rob Another Man's Castle," "Show Me the Way to Your Heart," "The Echo of Your Footsteps," and "There's Not a Thing I Wouldn't Do for You." His 1950 hit roster included "Cuddle Buggin' Baby," "Lovebug Itch," "Mama and Daddy Broke My Heart," "Take Me in Your Arms and Hold Me," "Why Should I Cry," and "Enclosed, One Broken Heart."

As the 1950s went by, Eddy added to his list of best sellers with every passing year. In 1951, he had such number-one ranked songs as "Kentucky Waltz," "There's Been a Change in Me, " and "I Want to Play House with You." In top-10 ranks were "Heart Strings," "May the Good Lord Bless and Keep You," "Somebody's Been Beating My Time," and "Something New." The following year he scored with an original composition, "Easy on the Eyes," and such others as "Bundle of Southern Sunshine," "Full Time Job," and "Older and Bolder." His other hits of the 1950's included number-one ranked "Eddy's Song," "Mama, Come Get Your Baby Boy" (1953); "Hep Cat Baby," "I Really Don't Want to Know," "My Everything," "This Is the Thanks I Get" (1954); number-one ranked "Cattle Call," "I've Been Thinking," "Richest Man," "That Do Make It Nice," "Two Kinds of Love" (1955); "Trouble in Mind," "You Don't Know Me" (1956); and "Tennessee Stud" (1959).

During the 1950s, Eddy appeared at one time or another in every state in the union and a number of foreign countries. He was a featured guest on such network TV shows as *Arthur Godfrey's Talent Scouts, Milton Berle, Perry Como,* and *Dinah Shore.* He had his own TV show for several years on NBC and ABC networks and also starred in a syndicated TV series, *Eddy Arnold Time.*

The Arnold magic did not wither in the 1960s. He continued to tour widely and appear often on major TV shows. He also turned out several dozen chart hits during the decade. These included such top-10 hits as "A Little Heartache," "After Loving You," "Tears Broke Out on Me" (1962); "I Thank My Lucky Stars," "Molly" (1964); "Make the World Go Away," "What's He Doing in My World" (both number-one ranked hits) (1965); number-one ranked "I Want to Go with You," "The Last Word in Lonesome Is Me," "Tips of My Fingers," "Somebody Like Me" (1966); number-one ranked "Lonely Again" (1967); "Here Comes the Rain Baby," "It's Over," "Here Comes Heaven (1968). Eddy was voted the number-one male vocalist in country music in country polls for several years and almost always was in the top 5 or 10 in year-end ratings of *Billboard, Cash Box,* and *Record World.* In 1968, for instance, he was neck and neck with Glen Campbell for number-one album artist.

His singles success was matched by enormous album sales as well. Among his RCA LPs of the late 1950s and 1960s, most of them top-10 hits, were *Any Time, All Time Favorites, Chapel on the Hill, Wanderin', Dozen Hits, Praise Him, Praise Him* (1958); *Eddy Arnold, Have Guitar, Will Travel, Thereby Hangs* (1959); *More of Eddy Arnold, Sings Them Again, You Gotta Have Love* (1960); *Memories* (1961); *One More Time* (1962); *Country Songs, Cattle Call, Our Man Down South* (1963); *Folk Song Book, Eddy's Songs, Sometimes I'm Happy, Pop Hits* (1964); *The Last Word in Lonesome, I Want to Go with You; and My World* (1966). In 1967, when *Billboard* ranked him number-one country album artist, he had five charted LPs, including *Somebody Like Me, Best of Eddy Arnold,* and *Lonely Again.* In 1968, his top-10 LPs included *Everlovin' World of Eddy Arnold, Turn the World Around,* and *Romantic World of Eddy Arnold.* His 1969 releases included the LP *Warmth* (12/69).

He had a steady stream of albums on RCA in the early 1970s, though public interest seemed to slacken a bit. Among them were *Love and Guitars* (5/70), *Best of Eddy Arnold, Volume 2* (5/70), *Standing Alone* (9/70), *This Is Eddy Arnold* (two discs, 11/70), *Portrait of My Woman* (3/71), *Welcome to My World* (8/71), *Then You Can Tell Me Goodbye* (Camden, 9/71), *Loving Her Was Easier* (12/71), *Lonely People* (7/72), and *Chained to a Memory* (8/72).

Eddy's honors and milestones continued

to multiply in the 1960s and early 1970s. In 1966 he was elected to the Country Music Hall of Fame. His bronze plaque in the Nashville museum reads in part, "He has been a powerful influence in setting musical tastes. His singing, warm personality, and infectious laugh have endeared Eddy to friends and fans everywhere." On February 23, 1970, during his New York night club debut in New York's Waldorf-Astoria, RCA records presented him with an award to commemorate his reaching the 60 million-plus-mark in record sales. (As of the end of the 1970s, the total went past 70,000,000). That, RCA stressed, placed him among the top recording artists of all time. (Earlier, Arnold's night club debut in Los Angeles took place in October 1967 at the Coconut Grove.)

From the late 1960s through the 1970s, he performed before millions of people in person and on TV, including two appearances at New York's Carnegie Hall and many performances with major symphony orchestras. He hosted more than twenty TV specials, including a *Kraft Music Hall* Christmas Special in 1970. Besides emceeing seventeen *Kraft Music Hall* shows, he headlined a summer *Kraft Music Hall* series titled *Country Fair*. Other credits included acting as a guest host for Johnny Carson on *The Tonight Show*, cohosting the *Mike Douglas* show and narrating an NBC-TV special that presented a history of country music, *Music from the Land*.

His recording career seemed to hit a dry spell the first part of the 1970s. At least it was a dry spell for Eddy, though many country artists would have been happy to trade with him. While almost all his singles still made the charts, they tended to linger in the mid- or lower-chart levels, as was the case, for example, with the 1972 RCA release, "Lonely People," which only made it to the top 30s. A similar situation occurred in the mid-1970s after his almost three decades' affiliation with RCA was severed and he moved to MGM. On that label he had a series of moderate hits that included "She's Got Everything I Need" and "Just for Old Time's Sake" in 1974 and "Butterfly," "Red Roses," and "Middle of a Memory" in 1975.

In 1976, Eddy returned to RCA and soon showed the old magic still could be rekindled. He made the top 15 in mid-summer with "Cowboy" and in September had a top-10 hit with "Rocky Mountain Music/Do You Right Tonight." In 1977, he had a moderate hit with "Freedom Ain't the Same as Being Free." Late in 1978, the single "If Everyone Had Someone Like You" appeared on the lists and, in early 1979, rose to upper-chart levels. In early summer, he had another top-10 hit with "What in Her World Did I Do." Another 1979 hit single was "Goodbye," still on the charts in early 1980. He had another excellent year in 1980 with three more bestselling singles, "That's What I Get for Loving You," "Let's Get It While the Getting's Good," and "If I Ever Had to Say Goodbye to You."

ASLEEP AT THE WHEEL: *Vocal and instrumental group. Personnel (as of 1977): Ray Benson, born Philadelphia, Pa., March 16, 1951; Lucky Oceans (Reuben Gosfield), born Philadelphia, Pa., April 22, 1951; Chris O'Connell, born Williamsport, Md., March 21, circa 1953; Danny Levin, born Philadelphia, Pa., 1949; Pat "Taco" Ryan, born eastern Texas, July 14, 1953; Link Davis, Jr., born Port Arthur, Texas; other bandsmen, Floyd Domino, LeRoy Preston, Tony Garnier, Chris York, Bill Mabry. Roster as of early 1982: Benson, Oceans, O'Connell, Levin, Ryan, Preston, Domino, Garnier, York, Mabry.*

In the late 1950s and throughout the 1960s, the descriptive term "country music" was more fashionable than "country & western." But a rash of new bands came along in the late 1960s that brought the "western" back into "country," not the least of which was Asleep at the Wheel. The band considered Bob Wills and the Texas Playboys a major influence who, in turn, reciprocated with enthusiastic approval of the band's efforts to revitalize western swing.

Though the band's home base was centered in Austin in the mid-1970s, the Wheel's origins weren't in Texas. The founding members grew up in the Northeast, where the friendship between two Philadelphia suburban teenagers, guitarist-singer Ray Benson and pedal steel guitarist Reuben Gosfield (who took the stage name of Lucky Oceans) planted the seeds of the band. The two played in several local bands while attending high school in Springfield, Montgomery County, Pennsylvania. They kept in touch after going to college and later added a singer and drummer from Vermont named LeRoy Preston to their circle of friends. After finding another soulmate in Eastern-bred pianist Danny Levin, the foursome retired to a friend's ranch in West Virginia in 1970 to develop their blend of country, rock, and big-band swing. During the three months of rehearsals, Oceans came up with the group's name, reputedly while sitting in the outhouse.

Benson recalled, "We led a dual existence then—musically. Rather than a country-rock band, we were a country band and a rock band playing either hard-core country or genuine old-time fifties-style rock 'n' roll. We didn't mix the two." * The initial location was a 1500-acre ranch, but a run-in with the law required a move to a smaller forty-acre farm in Magnolia, West Virginia. From there the band went out to perform at local spots, including the Paw Paw Sportsmen's Lodge and the Moose Club. Typically the band makeup was rather fluid. Some musicians left and new members joined. One of the departees was Levin; one of the additions a high-school graduate named Chris O'Connell. Chris started as a backing singer and rhythm guitarist and in six months moved up front to share lead vocals with Benson and Preston.

As the band picked up skill and confidence, they began to perform in Washington, D.C., where they became almost a fixture in the city's music scene, usually as an opening act for groups like Poco and Joy of Cooking. Benson noted, "During 1970 and 1971, there was quite a little scene going on in the D.C. clubs. Emmylou Harris was getting her start there. So were Walter Egan and Bill and Taffy Danoff [cowriters of the John Denver hit "Country Roads" and later sparkplugs of the Starland Vocal Band]. We all played the same joints." *

One band that had musical tastes similar to Asleep at the Wheel was the Lost Planet Airmen, whose leader, George Frayne (stage name Commander Cody), suggested that San Francisco was a hotbed of activity. The Wheel decided to go there in late 1971. Chris O'Connell recalled that "except for the fact that we were starving it was really neat. There were 1,500 bands in the Bay Area and the Cody band helped out all they could, but we were still starving. We weren't even making a slight living. So we went on the road with country singer Stoney Edwards and made a worse living, except that we ate."

In 1972, keyboardist Floyd Domino was added, bringing considerable jazz and boogie woogie grounding to the dates the band headlined at the Longbranch Saloon in Berkeley, California. The group was slowly expanding its following and late in 1972 impressed United Artists executives enough to get a recording contract. The debut album was issued in March 1973, with little impact on the general public. Still experimenting with personnel, Benson and company welcomed another member— electric and standup bass player Tony Garnier.

Expanding its tour schedule during 1973, the group found a warm reception from Texas fans. This inspired it to shift headquarters again, this time to Austin, Texas, in February 1974. About the same time, the band gained a new contract from Epic, which led to release of its second LP, in September 1974, an album that, if it didn't make the charts, did expose a wider spectrum of people to the band's mixture of hardcore country, country rock, jazz, blues, and western swing. During 1974, Scott Hennige took over on drums while Preston concentrated on vocals and rhythm guitar. Danny Levin returned, this time stressing his fiddle and mandolin talents.

Still looking for a recording breakthrough, the group moved over to Capitol Records. This time Asleep at the Wheel hit paydirt. Its debut on Capitol, *Texas Gold*, which was released in August 1975, caught fire with country fans and rose into the top 10 on country LP lists while also showing up on national pop charts. The album spawned three singles that made hit charts in 1975-76: "The Letter That Johnny Walker Read," "Bump Bounce Boogie," and "Nothin' Takes the Place of You." The latter months of 1975 saw the addition of Bill Mabry on fiddle, allowing the band to emulate the famed twin-fiddle sound of the old Bob Wills group. Soon after, a third fiddle player, also adept on saxophone and accordion, came into the fold—Link Davis, Jr. From his father, Davis had inherited strong Cajun musical leanings, adding still another dimension to the Wheel's influences.

The Wheel's success proved to have an impact on the fortunes of the alumni of Bob Wills Playboys. A number of the old Playboys band, including Leon McAuliff, assembled to make a joint appearance with Asleep at the Wheel on the *Austin City Limits* series on the Public Broadcasting System. That, in turn, led to the Playboys making several new albums on Capitol.

Capitol, meanwhile, had proven a good recording home for Asleep at the Wheel. The group's second LP on the label, *Wheelin' and Dealin',* came out in July 1976 and showed up on both country and pop charts. Handling drums by then was Chris York, born in Ft. Worth, Texas, who previously had worked in a band led by Leon Rausch. That album, like the one before, provided three chart singles, a country swing version of the old big band hit "Route 66," "Miles and Miles of Texas," and "The Trouble with Lovin' Today." "Route 66" received a Grammy nomination in 1976; it was the band's second, *Texas Gold* having earned a nomination the year before.

The band expanded to eleven members before work began on the third Capitol LP. Pat "Taco" Ryan, from Tulsa, Oklahoma, added his saxophone and clarinet skills. The next album, *The Wheel,* which came out in March 1977, contained almost all band-written material, including the title track, which received a Grammy nomination. The album included the traditional fiddle tune "Ragtime Annie," which provided a fourth Grammy nomination. Soon after the LP came out, the constantly mov-

ing group was in Europe making its debut appearance overseas on a tour with Emmylou Harris. Just before going abroad, the band recorded some of its work for the Smithsonian Institution's Americana archives. In early 1978, the Wheel was named "Best Touring Band" in the Academy of Country Music awards.

Despite the increasing trappings of success, Ray Benson still felt the group was falling far short of its potential with record buyers. He told Jack Lloyd of the *Philadelphia Enquirer* in late 1977, "We can and we do play Western swing, but we also play hard-core country and Cajun music and there's the strong jazz influences you find in Western swing. I call it all good music. But it seems the average person's musical taste is not eclectic enough to relate to both George Jones and Count Basie." What he felt was needed "is to translate our American country, western, blues, jazz and Cajun roots into our own thing."

There was strong indication the group was indeed going in that direction with release of the album *Collision Course* in July 1978. The album contained elements of most of the diverse styles the band embraced, but these were closely integrated into a consistent musical and rhythmic pattern. And it did contain still more singles chart candidates, such as "Me You and Texas." The album sold well, but there was no indication of any change in pattern from earlier Capitol releases.

Deciding that more adjustment was needed, Benson announced a reduction in size. "Our eleven-person lineup has been trimmed to a fighting weight of eight. And I don't mind telling you the newly-reconstituted Asleep at the Wheel is the leanest, tightest, meanest, and most determined Asleep at the Wheel you've ever heard." *

The new alignment retained Benson, O'Connell, Oceans, Ryan, and Levin. Filling out the new cast was multitalented musician John Nicholas (guitar, piano, harmonica, mandolin, lead vocals) who previously had his own band in Boston and also had backed notable blues harmonica

---

* *From an interview with Irwin Stambler in 1979.*

player Big Walter Horton; stand-up bass player Spencer Starnes, who had worked with Michael Murphey; and drummer Fran Christina out of Nova Scotia. Though Link Davis, Jr., was no longer a full-time band member, he worked with the band from time to time as did saxophonist/fiddler Andy Stein.

ATKINS, CHET: *Guitarist, composer, singer, producer, record industry executive. Born Luttrell, Tennessee, June 20, 1924. Elected to Country Music Hall of Fame in 1973.*

It's hard to fit more than the highlights of Chet Atkins' illustrious career into a few pages—the many awards and honors presented him over the years alone could take up many lines of any encyclopedia entry. As an acknowledged all-time great guitarist, his instrumental technique has been studied and often copied, in part, by musicians in fields ranging from classical to rock. In the country field, besides having a hand in hundreds of important recordings—his own and those of the many others whose careers he helped to shape—he contributed to the growth of Nashville as the hub of that music. *Record World* editors noted, at one point, "No one person can honestly receive total credit for the phenomenal explosion of Nashville's music business. However, no individual has been more responsible for this growth than Chet Atkins."

He had the advantage of growing up in a home where music was almost a way of life, in the small town of Luttrell, twenty miles from Knoxville, in the Clinch Mountains of Tennessee. The son of a piano and voice teacher, Chet was only three years old when Jimmie Rodgers cut the first sides that were to revolutionize country music, but he soon fell in love with the Rodgers discs that were played on the family's old wind-up phonograph.

During that period, he already was interested in playing an instrument, but his brothers, Jimmy and Lowell, didn't want little Chet to play their guitar. Instead, he tried to master a fiddle. When he was nine, he traded an old pistol for a beat-up guitar, recalling, "I remember that deal well. It was one of the smartest I ever made. A lot of guitars have come and gone for me since then but it is the truth that I've been picking since I was nine."

By the time Chet finished high school he had acquired respectable proficiency on the guitar and got a job on station WNOK in Knoxville with the *Bill Carlisle Show*. He also filled in with a band called the Dixie Swingsters. He stayed in the Knoxville area for three years, then played jobs on the radio circuit as a solo act or sideman at WLW in Cincinnati, WPTF in Raleigh, North Carolina, WRVA in Richmond, Virginia, KWTO in Springfield, Missouri, and KOA in Denver.

His Missouri show started the chain of events that was to make him a Nashville legend. Steve Sholes, then RCA Victor's top country-music executive, heard Chet on a Mutual radio show that originated in Missouri. He liked Atkins' style, but couldn't find him for a time because of Chet's rapid changes in station affiliation. Meanwhile, Si Siman of KWTO had forwarded a transcription of one show to Al Hindle, who ran the custom-records business for RCA from a Chicago office. Hindle sent it along to Sholes in New York, who realized, after listening to it, that Atkins was the man he was looking for. Sholes quickly followed up, as Atkins remembered:

"By that time I had been fired in Springfield and was working KOA in Denver with Shorty Thompson and his Rangers. Steve called me and asked me if I wanted to record for RCA and I said sure. He mailed me a contract. A couple of months later on I mortgaged my car, borrowed some money, and went to Chicago, where I met Steve and we recorded—two sessions in one day; one morning, one afternoon—eight sides."

Considering the fact that Atkins almost never uses his voice anymore, it's interesting to note that five of the eight numbers had vocals. The vocals included, "I'm Gonna Get Tight," "Standing Room Only," and "Don't Hand Me That Line." Since then, Atkins has tried to locate and destroy all masters from those vocal efforts. The three instrumentals, "Canned Heat," "Bug Dance," and "Nashville

Jump," found favor with disc jockeys and got considerable airplay even if they didn't make any bestseller lists. In 1949, though, releases like "Gallopin' Guitar," "Main St. Breakdown," and "Country Gentlemen" started to bring the first wave of public acceptance that was to bring him the nickname "Mr. Guitar."

His first appearance on the *Grand Ole Opry* was in 1946 with Red Foley, but he didn't become a regular until several years later. In the late 1940s, Chet started working with the Carter Family and, with his recordings starting to come off RCA presses, he decided to settle in Nashville. In 1949, Sholes made Chet studio guitarist for RCA Nashville sessions and noted that his suggestions often improved the overall work of the musicians concerned. His executive talents were recognized on a more formal basis in 1953 when he was designated a consultant to Victor's Nashville operations. By then he was a featured artist on the *Opry,* which added him to its regular cast in 1950.

In 1957, Sholes made Chet a part-time producer, and later that year, when Steve was named head of pop A&R in Victor's New York offices, Atkins moved up to full-time manager. In the decades after, Chet presided over the growth of the studios from a few people to a large, multifaceted organization. In 1968, he was named Division Vice President.

Sholes said, "The hit artists Chet found for us include Don Gibson, Floyd Cramer, Connie Smith, Dottie West, and many others. [Among those others were Waylon Jennings and Bobby Bare.] Although I was lucky enough to bring Jim Reeves in, Chet did all the successful recordings with him." In fact, very few of the RCA artists in the country field (plus some pop stars) didn't at one time or another profit from Atkins' tutelage. At any given time, he supervised recording efforts of twenty-five artists on a roster that included such names over the years as Elvis Presley, Al Hirt, Eddy Arnold, Homer and Jethro, Perry Como, and Floyd Cramer.

Atkins always tended to downplay his producing role. "You hear about the successes, but we try to keep the failures—the duds—a trade secret. There is no sure-fire system for hits. What I do is listen a lot during a recording session and try to pick up some little something from the musicians playing on the session that might make the record more commercial. A lot of us producers have picked up reputations as specialists with the help of some musician who tried just a little harder, or experimented with an unusual sound."

Sholes once pointed to the elements of Atkins' style that first gained his attention. "Chet plays finger-style guitar. He doesn't pick, he just *touches* the strings, pushes down on them and lets the fingers up—except for his thumb and that's generally for the bass strings. He can play other styles too—Spanish, classical, everything else. But the style that first got me intrigued was his finger-style playing. I had never heard it before. There are few people who play that way now."

Atkins never let his executive responsibilities take him away from his first love—performing—for any extended period of time. Year after year, from the 1950s into the 1980s, he turned out his share of recordings either as a soloist or in conjunction with other artists or groups. His recording partners over the years included Floyd Cramer, the Boston Pops, Ravi Shankar, Merle Travis, Jerry Reed, and, in the late 1970s, Les Paul, and an outfit called the Chet Atkins String Quartet.

Restlessly experimenting over the years, he donated his guitar artistry to all kinds of musical formats in many different settings. Besides performing as a soloist with symphonies in the United States, he appeared in concert with classical groups in Europe. He proved he could play jazz as well as anyone on occasion, including an acclaimed appearance at the 1960 Newport Jazz Festival. In March 1961, he played for the Press Photographers' Ball before an audience that included President Kennedy. His engagements with the Boston Pops in the 1960s helped pave the way for many other country stars guesting with Arthur Fiedler and Co. (He cut two Red Seal albums with the Pops.) Among his early 1970s musical activities were a series of country engagements called The Music Masters in which he joined forces with Boots Randolph and Floyd Cramer. Throughout the decades, besides his countless appearances on *Opry* radio programs, Chet was a regular visitor to all manner of radio and TV variety shows ranging from Johnny Carson to the Grammy Awards programs.

His name often appeared in the winner's circle at Grammy events. His first Grammy came when the RCA album *Chet Atkins Picks the Best* was named Best Contemporary Instrumental Performance of 1967. He added another one for 1970 when his duet LP with Jerry Reed, *Me and Jerry*, was named Best Country Instrumental Performance. In 1971, the National Academy of Recording Arts and Sciences voters chose his "Snowbird" as Best Country Instrumental Performance. In 1976, still another Grammy came his way, this time for his collaboration with another guitar legend, Les Paul, on the LP *Chester and Lester*. Some of his recordings made the final five even if they missed the award itself, an example being his *Solid Gold '69* album.

Atkins' name often topped the list in various polls for top guitarists. Year after year, from the early 1960s throughout the 1970s, for instance, *Cash Box* named him Outstanding Instrumentalist. He won the *Playboy* poll four times as Best Guitarist and was highly ranked in surveys in other magazines and in polls held in other parts of the world. In 1972, he was honored by the National Council of Christians and Jews, which gave him its Humanitarian Award.

During his long career as a recording artist, Chet turned out dozens of albums. A partial list of his 1950s and 1960s LPs follows, all on RCA unless otherwise noted. Mid-1950s releases included *Sessions, In Three Dimensions, Stringin' Along,* and *Finger Style Guitar.* Late 1950s offerings included *Hi Fi in Focus,* issued in December 1957, *At Home* (7/58), *In Hollywood* (7/59), and *Hum & Strum Along.* Releases in the 1960s included *Mister Guitar* (1/60), *Teensville* (2/60), *Other Chet Atkins* (9/60), *Workshop* (2/61), *Guitar* (5/61–Camden), *Most Popular* (7/61), *Down Home* (3/62), *Caribbean*

Guitar (9/62), *Back Home Hymns* (11/62), *Our Man in Nashville* (2/63), *Guitar Genius* (5/63–Camden), *Travelin'* (9/63), *Guitar Country* (2/64), *Best* (6/64), *Progressive Pickin'* (7/64), *Reminiscing* (12/64), *My Favorite Guitars* (5/65), *Guitar Country* (11/65), *Picks on the Beatles* (5/66), *Best* (7/66), *Music from Nashville,* (8/66–Camden), *From Nashville* (11/66), *Guitar World* (4/67), *Picks the Best* (6/67) *Class Guitar* (11/67), *Chet* (12/67–Camden), *Solid Gold '69, Warmth* (12/69).

In the 1970s, Chet's album output didn't taper off even though it was his third decade on RCA. His releases included *Best, Volume 2* (5/70), *Love and Guitars* (5/70), *Standing Alone* (9/70), *Me and Jerry* (10/70), *This Is Chet Atkins* (11/70), *Portrait of My Woman* (3/71), *For the Good Times* (4/71), *Welcome to My World* (8/71), *Then You Can Tell Me Goodbye* (9/71), *Pickin' My Way* (10/71), *Chet, Floyd & Boots* (11/71–Camden), *Lovin' Her Was Easier* (12/71), *Nashville Gold* (4/72–Camden), *Now & Then* (11/72), *Picks on the Hits* (11/72), *The Atkins-Travis Travelin' Show* (1974), *Atkins String Band* (1975), *Chester and Lester* (1976).

Though better known as an album artist, Atkins turned out many singles over the years, a number of which made the charts. Among his 1970s charted numbers, for instance, were "Snowbird" in 1971, "The Night Atlanta Burned" (1975, with the Atkins String Quartet), and the 1974 hit, "Fiddlin' Around." He was still placing singles on the charts at the start of the 1980s, one example being "Blind Willie" in 1980.

In 1973, Atkins' preeminence in the country field was recognized by his fellow artists, who elected him to the Country Music Hall of Fame.

AUTRY, GENE: *Singer, guitarist, songwriter, actor, business executive. Born, Tioga, Texas, September 29, 1907.*

Few performers can live up to the cliché "he did it all," but if anyone has come close to being the all-around entertainer, Gene Autry has. After enjoying an immensely successful career as a singer, guitarist, actor, and songwriter for more than four decades, he was able to turn most of his attention toward running the vast business empire he had been building, a rare talent of a different sort.

As a youngster growing up in Texas and Oklahoma, Gene naturally heard cowboy songs and country music, but the idea of a music career hardly occurred to him. Upon graduating from high school, he took a job as a railroad telegraph operator in Sepulpa, Oklahoma. It was a night job with long, lonely hours between messages, so he bought a guitar and learned to play it in order to keep himself awake. One night, a stranger came in to write a telegram while Gene was playing. The man waited until he finished the song, then said, "Young feller, all I can say is that you're wasting your time here. You ought to quit and try radio." The name on the telegram sheet was Will Rogers.

Autry took Rogers' advice and soon gained a job with station KVOO as "Oklahoma's Singing Cowboy." He became quite popular and his reputation spread to other states. In 1927, he went to Chicago to cut his first record for a small, independent record company. Nothing happened with that record, but Gene kept trying. He went to New York and in 1929 was signed by recording pioneer Art Satherly to make several cowboy records, among the first such songs ever recorded, for the old American Record Company. Out of the first six sides he recorded for Satherly, Autry had one hit, "That Silver Haired Daddy of Mine," a song he had written himself. In succeeding years that record sold over 5 million copies.

Following the success of "Silver Haired Daddy," Autry went to Chicago, where he was given his own singing program on radio station WLS. (The call letters stood for "World's Largest Store"—Sears, Roebuck and Co.) In the four years that he stayed at WLS, Autry became one of the best-known singers in the Midwest, through such top hits as "Mexicali Rose."

In 1934, Gene was signed to act in his first film, a bit singing role in a Ken Maynard western, In Old Sante Fe. The picture's box-office success led to a chance to star in a serial, The Phantom Empire, a thirteen-chapter cliff-hanger. When this, too, did well at the box office, Republic Pictures, a new movie company, signed Autry to a motion picture contract. It was for Republic Pictures that he made what came to be known as the world's first singing western, Tumbling Tumble Weeds. Around the same time, another newcomer to the movies, John Wayne, was also making a picture for Republic, entitled Westward Ho. These two films were the first to be made under the Republic banner.

Gene rapidly became one of the most popular film stars of that era, a status enhanced by personal appearances throughout the 1930s in all parts of the world. These included another first, the initial appearance of a movie cowboy as star of the World Championship Rodeo in New York's Madison Square Garden. During the 1930s he was also honored by having the town of Gene Autry, Oklahoma, named for him. By the end of the 1950s he had been seen by untold millions in film audiences all over the world in eighty-two feature-length musical westerns; by 1968 the total exceeded one hundred.

At the same time that Autry was making one film after another, he also continued to write and record hit songs, such as "You're the Only Star in My Blue Heaven" and "Dust" in 1938, "Tears on My Pillow" and "Be Honest with Me" in 1941, and "Tweedle O Twill" in 1942.

On July 26, 1942, Autry enlisted in the Army Air Corps as a technical sergeant, thereby going from a salary of over $600,000 a year to one of around $135 a month. The wartime duties of the cowboy film star entailed serving as a flight commander and first pilot in the Far East and ferrying planes, cargo, and supplies to India, North Africa, and Burma. This occupation, however, did not stop him completely from writing songs or recording them; together with Fred Rose he wrote a song, "Mail Call Today," that sold over a million records during the war years.

After the war, Autry returned to Hollywood and resumed an even more dynamic career than before. For a time he continued to record for Okeh records and had hits such as "I'll Go Riding Down That Texas Trail," "The Yellow Rose of Texas," "Deep in the Heart of Texas," and "Maria Elena." He also continued to make motion pictures and started his own network radio show, *Melody Ranch,* which was to become the longest-running radio show for one sponsor (Wrigley's Gum). The television version of *Melody Ranch* remained on the air throughout the 1960s.

In the late 1940s, Autry signed with Columbia Records and proceeded to turn out dozens of records, many of which became all-time standards. Among these recordings were "Buttons and Bows," "Frosty the Snow Man," "Peter Cottontail," "South of the Border," "Back in the Saddle Again," "Tumbling Tumble Weeds," "You Are My Sunshine," and "Boots and Saddles." Among his largest hits were two Christmas records, "Here Comes Santa Claus" and "Rudolph the Red-Nosed Reindeer." As he told Claude Hall of *Claude Hall's International Radio Report:*

"After I came back here [from the war] I made a record that the first year sold a million and a half and that's after I'd been out of the record business five years. It was called 'Here Comes Santa Claus,' and I got the idea for the song—I wrote it with another guy. I was the Grand Marshal of the Hollywood Parade on Thanksgiving. I was riding down there, you know, the Grand Marshal and all the kids would say, 'Hey, here comes Santa Claus, here comes Santa Claus.' So I made a note of that and I got together with this guy and wrote the goddamned song 'Here Comes Santa Claus.'

"So the second year I was huntin' for another record, a Christmas record. And a guy from New York sent me a demonstration record, a demo, and I heard it. I played it several times but I didn't care a hell of a lot about it. So my wife said, 'I think that you ought to listen to that record you played called "Rudolph the Red-Nosed Reindeer." There's something about that thing that I like. It reminds me of the story of the ugly duckling—that line "They wouldn't let poor Rudolph join in any reindeer games." It's kind of cute.'

"I said, 'Well, what the hell.' I didn't have anything better so I recorded it. That thing sold two and a half million the first

year. . . ." Over the years that record sold around 7 million copies.

Autry's other records continue to sell and he still gets royalties from many of them. In the 1960s he had some best-selling albums, including *Greatest Hits* (Columbia, 1961); *Golden Hits* (RCA Victor, 1962); and *Great Hits* (Harmony, 1965).

During the 1950s, while continuing his career as an entertainer, Autry began an additional vocation as an investor and business magnate. He had actually bought his first radio station in 1942 when he enlisted in the service. He realized that he might not be able to sing and perform forever but that he could continue to make money if he invested wisely. When he returned from the war he continued to buy radio stations and also had the foresight to purchase television stations when that medium was still in its infancy. By 1962 he owned a chain of TV and radio stations and also established his own record firm, Challenge Records, and his own television production company, Flying A Productions. (In the early 1960s, he performed in a series of fifty-two half-hour TV shows for Flying A.) He had by this time also branched out his investments to include a hotel chain, a music publishing firm, and more.

Autry had always been an avid sports fan and he was eager to get a contract to broadcast Los Angeles Dodgers games over his radio station, KMPC. However, he was unable to obtain this contract as the Dodgers had committed their coverage to another station. So Gene, along with sportsman Bob Reynolds, decided to try to put together their own Los Angeles baseball club. In 1962, their bid for an expansion franchise in the American League was accepted, and the Los Angeles Angels were born. In 1966, the team moved to nearby Anaheim and became known as the California Angels. At long last, in 1979, Autry saw his team have a winning season, as the California Angels became the Western Division American League champions. —*A.S.*

AXTON, HOYT: *Singer, guitarist, pianist, songwriter. Born Duncan, Oklahoma, March 25, 1938.*

With his craggy features and strong,

broad-shouldered build, Hoyt Axton looked the part of a lumberjack, man of the soil, or football player. As it happened, he was a talented athlete in his early years. Although he developed into one of the major folksong performers and writers of the 1960s and 1970s, he never learned traditional ballads at his parents' knees. His background was urban, though his mother segued from her initial profession of teacher to a songwriter who helped make Elvis Presley famous and, in passing, changed her son's ideas of what he wanted to do with his life.

Hoyt and Johnny Axton were the two sons of Mae Boren Axton, who was teaching English and drama when her boys were little. In 1950, when Hoyt was ten, she turned her attention to writing songs with friends and musicians from the Jacksonville, Florida, area the Axtons then called home. She wrote a variety of songs from country to pop and, for a number of years, not much happened. But in the mid-1950s, she co-wrote a song called "Heartbreak Hotel" that came to the attention of a new young artist named Elvis Presley. The song, of course, became a smash, one of the best-selling singles of 1956 and one that was a major spark in bringing the rock revolution to fruition. The impact on Hoyt and Johnny Axton was as great as it was on millions of other teenagers of the era. In Hoyt's case it triggered the writing of his own original songs.

As Mrs. Axton wrote in the C&W magazine *Picking Up the Tempo* (February–March 1976), "Hoyt was in high school in Jacksonville, Florida, when Elvis knocked the props out from under the classy, but staid music industry—daring to be himself—and Hoyt and Johnny [who later went on to become an attorney] found themselves among the mushrooming number of Presley fans. Hoyt sang such Presley tunes as 'I've Got a Woman (Way Over Town)' in high school assembly and variety shows."

As a boy he had taken classical piano lessons although, as his mother noted, he didn't necessarily follow the music put before him: "Sometimes, to the dismay of his piano teacher, he would start playing the boogie in the middle of a lesson." He learned to play piano after a fashion but

the instrument he really took to in his teens was the guitar. He also liked sports and played on several high school varsity teams, and was good enough in football to get scholarship offers from a number of colleges.

"As a freshman football whiz at Oklahoma State University," Mrs. Axton wrote, "Hoyt entertained his friends by singing and picking his guitar. Hoyt left college for naval service, which was ironic, since he was trying to forego the demands of R.O.T.C.—and inadvertently chose a more demanding way of life in the Navy."

Meanwhile, Hoyt's musical tastes were changing. He found less and less interest in rock music and more in the growing folk music boom of the late 1950s. When he got out of the service, he began to travel around the coffee houses and small folk-club circuit of the West Coast, initially concentrating on venues in the San Francisco Bay area, then extending his performances to the northwest and south to Los Angeles, where he often was featured in the late 1950s and early 1960s in the prestigious Troubadour Club. He built up a small but loyal following during those years, though he didn't become a top star for several reasons. One was the fact that the East Coast "folk establishment" classed him as too "conservative" in outlook, apparently more because of his independence of mind, which kept him from blindly joining causes for the sake of joining, than any lack of humanity. A second reason, though, was his admitted fondness for excess in drink, romance, and high-speed driving.

The lack of nationwide attention didn't seem to bother him much. He went his own way, often hitchhiking from one job to another, playing engagements in many out of the way places, working with others who had the same outlook. He was continually writing new material. One of those songs, co-written with the late Ken Ramsey, was the 1962 "Greenback Dollar." The song was picked up by the Kingston Trio and became one of their major hits of the early 1960s.

Hoyt was offered a recording contract with Harmony Records in the early 1960s and had a series of albums issued on the label, including *Balladeer, Thunder 'n' Lightnin'* (5/63), and *Saturday's Child* (2/64). He continued to appear regularly at the Troubadour in the mid-1960s, as well as other folk clubs around the country, and more than a few pop and rock artists came to hear him sing. At one of those shows in 1964, a young musician named John Kay caught his act and was impressed by Hoyt's song "The Pusher." Later, when Kay formed his group Steppenwolf, which became one of the top rock bands of the late 1960s and early 1970s, "The Pusher" was a staple in the band's repertoire. It was included in four best-selling LPs and made top levels of the singles charts in the early 1970s. In the mid-1970s, the song was used in the soundtrack of the movie *Easy Rider.* Several other Axton songs also were featured by Kay, including one called "Snowblind Friend."

Other rock groups became interested in Axton's material. One band, Three Dog Night, arranged for Axton to go around the United States with them as their opening act during the 1969–70 period. The association provided unanticipated bonuses both for Hoyt and the group. During one concert series he played a new song called "Joy to the World" for Three Dog Night. The band recorded it and the single rose to number one on U.S. pop charts in early 1971 and also rose high on country lists. It was awarded a gold record by R.I.A.A. on April 9, 1971. Later, Hoyt's "Never Been to Spain" also brought the group a top-10 singles hit. At the time, Axton was recording for Capitol Records, which released his version of "Joy to the World" in the LP of that title recorded with the *Hollywood Living*

Room Band. Another Capitol LP of his that came out soon after was titled *Country Anthem.*

During the 1970s, Hoyt performed in concert throughout the United States and in many countries of Europe and the Far East. He shared the stage on occasion with such contemporary folk stars as Steve Goodman and John Prine. Goodman and Axton were featured on several shows presented on the Public Broadcasting System. Hoyt also was a guest on many major network and syndicated talk and variety shows. In the mid-1970s, he signed with A&M Records, which issued a number of his LPs in the mid- and late-1970s.

Though he tended to keep a low profile as far as his contributions to charitable causes were concerned, his mother emphasized that "a concern for people has always been foremost in his mind. He was affiliated with UNICEF and prisoners' work [a charter member of the Bread and Roses organization, founded by Joan Baez's sister, Mimi Farina]. He has been helping to care for three orphan children . . . and he and Linda Ronstadt recently did a benefit in Santa Fe, New Mexico, for needy Indians."

In the late 1970s, Axton's recordings came out on Jeremiah Records. Results of that affiliation included "Della and the Dealer" in early summer 1979 and the late 1979 top-10 singles hit, "A Rusty Old Halo." The latter was the title song of a chart hit album as well. In 1980, he added more charted singles on Jeremiah, including "Wild Bull Rider," "Evangelina," and "Where Did the Money Go."

B

BAEZ, JOAN: *Singer, guitarist, songwriter. Born Staten Island, New York, January 9, 1941.*

At the start of the 1980s, on the verge of her third decade as a major artist, Joan Baez sang, as she always had, to entertain and to inform, advocating nonviolence, whether her stand infuriated one side of

the political spectrum or the other. In the 1960s, she was condemned by one extreme for her efforts against the Vietnam War; in the late 1970s, many on the left objected vehemently to her concerts on behalf of the Vietnamese "boat people" and the Cambodian refugees.

Her lifelong fight for the underdog came

partly from her childhood days. She told Dan Wakefield (Redbook magazine, January 1967, p. 114), "My mother is Irish and my father, a physicist, is Mexican (born in Brooklyn, New York) and I grew up in Redlands, California, where there were a lot of Mexicans and Mexican kids were looked down upon. Though my father had professional status, I was still in a sort of no-man's land; the white kids looked down on me because I was part Mexican and the Mexican kids didn't like me because I couldn't speak Spanish. In the fifth grade, I started singing and playing the ukulele—it was a way of getting accepted. At first, my singing got me accepted on a kind of 'court jester' level—someone who was all right because she could entertain."

Actually, her parents, who liked classical music, had earlier tried to get her to take piano lessons, but young Joan was rebellious and refused. At twelve, she took up guitar, using an instrument bought from Sears, Roebuck. Her first fervor wasn't for folk music, but for the first wave of rock 'n' roll represented by artists like Elvis Presley and Bill Haley.

The family moved to the East Coast just after Joan graduated high school in Palo Alto, California, settling in the Boston area, since Dr. Baez had a teaching appointment at MIT. He took his daughter to Tulla's Coffee Grinder one night and Joan was entranced. Although she enrolled in Boston University's Fine Arts School of Drama, she began spending more and more time hanging around Tulla's, adding to her folk song repertoire. After a while, she knew enough songs to start performing on the folk circuit and began taking the stage at such spots as the Golden Vanity, Ballad Room, and Club 47. She became a local favorite, but didn't feel ready for bigger challenges, turning down a bid from Harry Belafonte to join his troupe.

A brief appearance at the Gate of Horn Club in Chicago resulted in folksinger Bob Gibson suggesting she appear at the 1959 Newport, Rhode Island, Folk Festival. (She came there in a Cadillac hearse with her name painted on the side.) Her name was not on the program but she won wild applause from the Newport crowd and became close friends with Odetta, the Weavers, and the Seeger family. Record offers came, but Joan turned them down, preferring to go back to Boston and spend her time singing in coffee houses. After another successful appearance at the 1960 Newport show, she felt more confident of her recording capability and signed with Vanguard.

Her debut LP, Joan Baez, came out in 1960, and, in a short time, Vanguard was surprised and pleased to find a steady stream of orders and reorders coming in from record dealers. By early 1961, Joan was becoming known all over the United States and she set off on what became a triumphal tour of college campuses and concert halls. From then on, even though Joan continually turned down lucrative offers for TV shows, movies, and nightclub engagements, she remained one of the favorite artists of millions of fans all over the world.

Actually, the fact that she imposed limits on herself—trying not to tour commercial venues more than two months a year and doing only one or two albums each year—probably contributed to her retaining star status even when rock music overshadowed the folk field in the mid- and late-1960s. She used her time away from the regular concert spotlight to polish material for her LPs and to give support to causes she believed in. She made many free appearances every year for charities, UNESCO, civil rights, and, in the 1960s and early 1970s, for anti-Vietnam war rallies. Sometimes she rejected offers that she felt conflicted with her principles. An example was her refusal to appear on the ABC-TV show Hootenanny in 1963 unless blacklisted artist Pete Seeger was invited. In April 1964, she informed the Internal Revenue Service she would not pay the portion of her 1963 taxes she felt would be used for the armed forces. (That November, the IRS responded by filing a lien against her for $50,000.)

Meanwhile, she had become known as the "Queen of the Folksingers." Her increasingly anti-establishment (or at least that's the way it seemed to her critics) activity antagonized some segments of society, but had little obvious impact on the size of her own musical audience. As she added to her catalogue, she continued to be one of Vanguard's most important artists. Her second album, *Joan Baez, Volume 2*, a two-record set issued in December 1961, was well received, as were such succeeding albums as *Joan Baez in Concert* (12/62), *Joan Baez in Concert, Part 2* (3/64), and *Joan Baez 5* (12/64). (Squire Records also released a *Best of* LP in January 1964, featuring Joan with Bill Wood and Ted Alevizos.)

During the increasingly turbulent mid-1960s, Joan still managed to turn out new albums, though much of her time was devoted to rallies, marches, and protests. Her mid-1960s offerings on Vanguard included *Farewell Angelina* (1965), *Noel* (1966), and *Joan* (1967). Among her activities in 1967, for instance, was a performance at an anti-war rally in Tokyo, organization of a draft card turn-in day and performance at a free concert before 30,000 people at the base of the Washington Monument (after being turned down in a concert request for DAR-owned Constitution Hall for her "unpatriotic activities"). In October 1967, she, her mother, and sister were jailed for demonstrating at the Armed Forces Induction Center in Oakland, California.

She worked closely during that period with a Stanford University activist named David Harris. In 1968, they married. Shortly thereafter, David was sent to jail for three years for refusing to register for the draft. While this turmoil continued, Joan's popularity with album buyers remained strong. The 1968 LP *Baptism* was on the hit charts for the last third of 1968 and her next release, *Any Day Now*, reached gold-record levels. In late 1969, her album in honor of her spouse, *David's Album*, came out and was on the charts for months. The year 1969 had its joys. One was the rousing welcome given her at the now legendary Woodstock, New York, Festival, during the summer (with her material included in the Woodstock set issued on Cotillion); another was the birth of a son, Gabriel Earl Harris, on December 2.

In 1970, Vanguard celebrated her first decade on the label with the retrospective two-disc set, *The First Ten Years*, on the charts from year end into early 1971. Early in 1970, she was represented by a new studio LP, *One Day at a Time*, on hit lists for most of the spring and summer. In 1971, the LP *Blessed Are* was in the top 20 late in the year, eventually earning a gold record, and her single release, "Let It Be," was a top-50 hit at the same time. In late 1971, her Vanguard LP, *Carry It On*, featured a cover showing her welcoming David home from prison. But hardly had the LP been completed than the two decided to separate.

Separation, in fact, seemed to be a theme in Joan's life at that point. In early 1972, she announced the end of her long association with Vanguard, signing with A&M Records. Ironically, even as she was leaving, Vanguard readied a new single of her version of The Band's "The Night They Drove Ol' Dixie Down." The single proceeded to go to number five on the pop charts for Joan's biggest singles hit ever. It stayed on the list for fifteen weeks, and, soon after it slipped off, her debut LP on A&M, *Come from the Shadows*, made the album lists. The LP essentially represented Joan's songwriting debut, with most of the material written either by Joan or sister Mimi Farina.

Her next LP was taped during a visit to Hanoi, capital of North Vietnam, in December 1972. She was there as a guest of that country's politically organized Committee for Solidarity with the American People. The massive bombardment at the time by U.S. planes played a role in the tone of what was to be her next A&M release, "Where Are You Now, My Son." It was a plea against war of any kind. As Joan said, "If my pacifism was ever going to be put to a test, this must have been the time. At the end of eleven days of bombing, I was only reconfirmed in my belief that right-wing violence and left-wing violence are the same, and if the human race cannot find a life-supporting substitute for them, we will exterminate ourselves."

The LP was on the charts several months in 1973. Vanguard issued the LP *Hits/Greatest and Others* the same year. Joan spent much of the year working to advance the organization called Amnesty International, dedicated to freeing political prisoners and ending torture. Also a member was the conservative exponent, William F. Buckley, Jr.

Though Joan didn't give up fighting for causes, she was able to relax somewhat and give more time to music after the Vietnam War ended. Her remaining LP for A&M toned down the "message content" with more emphasis on the joys of life or the problems of daily living. Those LPs comprised *Gracias a la Vida* (1974), sung completely in Spanish, *Diamonds and Rust* (1975), whose title song was issued as a single and became Joan's first completely self-penned hit, *From Every Stage* (1976), and *Gulf Winds* (1976). *From Every Stage* was a live LP based on her tour in the summer of 1975.

In the fall of the year Bob Dylan asked her to join his tour and she accepted. She and Dylan had been friends since the early 1960s, when Joan had helped bring the then-newcomer to national attention by adding him to a series of her concerts. The first phase of the Dylan series, called the Rolling Thunder Revue, got underway in November 1975. A second series of concerts was presented by the Revue in the spring and early summer of 1976. Her experiences on the tour provided the basis for several songs included in *Gulf Winds*. That 1976 release was her first LP having only songs by her and it also was her last recorded for A&M. By 1977 she had moved to Portrait Records, a label owned by Columbia Records.

Her debut on Portrait, *Blowin' Away*, came out in 1977. Meanwhile, A&M issued a retrospective titled *The Best of Joan C. Baez*. Joan toured in support of *Blowin' Away* as she did in 1979 for her next Portrait LP, *Honest Lullaby*. Issued in May 1979, it included more original songs, plus her renditions of numbers ranging from Jackson Browne's "Before the Deluge" to Bob Marley's "No Woman, No Cry." Joan's association with Portrait ended at the start of the 1980s.

In preparation for her 1979 album, she took voice lessons and noted, "It's so strange. I used to be a soprano, then all of a sudden I find I sing everything in a lower register. It's easier and smoother. But the higher register is really hard to get, so I have a voice teacher helping me to exercise the upper ranges. That's one thing I've never done before in my musical life . . . exercise my voice."

BAILEY, RAZZY: *Singer, guitarist, songwriter. Born Lafayette, Alabama, February 14, 1939.*

Traditionally, a prime motivation for country musicians to go into the field was to get away from the farm. So it might seem odd that music provided an incentive for young Razzy Bailey to join the Lafayette, Alabama, chapter of Future Farmers of America. However, it was simply that the local FFA had a string band.

From his early years, of course, farm life was what Razzy was used to, having been born and raised in rural areas of Alabama. Country music was a major source of pleasure and relaxation for the family. His father played guitar and banjo and often entertained family, friends, and neighbors in informal get-togethers. While the family lived in Five Points, Alabama, between Razzy's sixth and seventh birthdays, his father helped organize a Saturday night songfest at the house to which many neighbors came to join in the singing or play an instrument. Bailey remembered, "I sang along with the rest of the family, but the truth is, I was mostly just hollerin' back then." But he was becoming increasingly interested in music, not only traditional and popular country, but blues and other songs of black field hands, as well as the way they played bottleneck guitar and blues harmonica.

During those years he started to learn guitar. The first instrument his father gave him "was a used five- or six-dollar guitar with a neck so warped it looked more like a bow and arrow than a guitar." Razzy didn't care; he took some lessons from a school teacher and afterward kept practicing and picking up new chords and techniques on his own. By the time he was in junior high in the mid-1950s, he could play well enough to make the FFA string band. He continued with the FFA group into his high school years. When he was fifteen, the group took second place in a statewide contest held at Auburn University.

At fifteen he was one of the better instrumentalists around his home area and was getting the chance to work many other places besides with the FFA. As soon as he graduated high school he sought full-time work as a musician and got a job with a country band playing in a club located along the road between LaGrange and Columbus, Georgia. His hopes were high, but after four months, state closure of the highway forced the club to shut down and Razzy was out of work. Things were slow in the country field then and Razzy couldn't find an equivalent position. Discouraged, he decided he had to find regular day work to provide an income. For four years in the early 1960s, he essentially retired from music, working such jobs as delivery truck driver, insurance representative, and furniture seller.

Still, he didn't give up hope of returning to music. Besides picking up occasional spare-time gigs, he wrote original country songs. In 1966 he wrote "9,999,999 Tears," a song that was to have a major impact on his future. When Bailey took his material to Atlantic music executive Bill Lowery in the mid-1960s, that was the song he liked. Lowery arranged for a recording session where the backing group included such stellar musicians as Joe South, Billy Joe Royal, and Freddy Weller. The song didn't make the hit lists back then, but it marked a milestone that encouraged Razzy to try for a full-time career in music again.

In 1968 he formed a trio called Daily Bread, which gained a two-week booking in a club in Naples, Florida. The group was so well received that it was asked to extend the engagement. Before the trio departed the club, it completed six months as the regular house band. With that experience under his belt, Razzy was able to find a series of other jobs that kept the pot boiling while he worked on advancing his writing and recording efforts.

During the late 1960s and the first part of the 1970s, he turned out recordings of both originals and other writers' material for a number of labels, mostly small.

Among his discs were such songs as "Stolen Moments," "Dancing on Brimstone," "I Hate Hate," and "Peanut Butter." None of those brought him into the spotlight, though the last named was to prove a massive success for another singer, Dickey Lee. In the mid-1960s, he had the chance to do some recordings for MGM, and, while nothing much developed directly, the event brought Razzy's songwriting skills to the attention of a staff member named Joe Mascolo. It proved a pivotal meeting because when Mascolo later joined RCA he told singer Dickey Lee of the material.

Lee auditioned some of Razzy's songs and decided to record the over-ten-year-old "9,999,999 Tears." The song rose to number one on the country charts and Dickey and other country artists soon were asking for more of Bailey's output. Another relative oldie, "Peanut Butter," was recorded by Lee and moved to top-chart levels in late 1971.

As Razzy's songs became staples on hit lists, the doors opened for him to try to make it as a performer again. He signed with RCA, which started to issue some of his singles in 1978. One of them, "What Time Do You Have to Be Back to Heaven," showed up on the charts in August and remained almost to year's end, bringing Razzy his first recording success. He followed in early 1979 with another top-level single, "Tonight She's Gonna Love Me (Like There Was No Tomorrow)," and had such other hits during the year as "If Love Had a Face" and "I Ain't Got No Business Doin' Business Today."

His forward momentum continued as the 1980s began. His 1980s successes included such top-10 hits as "I Can't Get Enough of You"; "Too Old to Play Cowboy"; and "Loving Up a Storm," number one in October 1980. At the end of 1980, his single "I Keep Coming Back/True Life Country Music" showed up on the charts and moved to the number-two position in January 1981. Later in 1981 he had the top-10 hits "Friends/Anywhere There's a Jukebox" and "Midnight Hauler/Scratch My Back."

BAND, THE: *Vocal and instrumental group. Robbie Robertson, born Toronto, Canada, July 5, 1944; Richard Manuel, born Stratford, Ontario, April 3, mid-1940s; Garth Hudson, born London, Ontario, August 2, circa 1943; Rick Danko, born Simcoe, Ontario, December 9, circa 1943; Levon Helm, born Marvell, Arkansas, May 26, circa 1942.*

When the album *Music from Big Pink* (issued by Capitol Records in August 1968) became a bestseller months after it came out, it was truly the pot of gold at the end of the rainbow for The Band, a group that had almost literally wandered in the wilderness, unknown and often booed, for more than a decade. The event was an important milestone not only for rock 'n' roll but for country music as well since the orientation of many of the tracks, such as "The Weight" (featured on the soundtrack of the 1970 film *Easy Rider*), was toward country music, a trend continued in later hit LPs.

Outwardly it seems strange that a group composed mainly of Canadians should become known for Southern soul music. As some critics noted, the lyrics of one Band hit, "The Night They Drove Old Dixie Down," sounded as if the song had been a traditional tune from Civil War days. (In part, the lyrics went, "Virgil Cane is the name/And I served on the Danville train/ 'Til Stoneman's cavalry came/And tore up the tracks again/In the winter of '65, we were hungry and barely alive.")

But it turns out that all the members had been fans of country music in their early years and received additional exposure to country music when they were the backup group for country-rock artist Ronnie Hawkins in the early 1960s. Lead guitarist and songwriter Robbie Robertson recalls listening to country music when he was five years old and learning guitar and writing music not long after. He left high school to play with rock groups, including one of his own, in his home area of Toronto, Canada. In the late 1950s, he met Ronnie Hawkins and joined his band, the Hawks, touring much of eastern and northern Canada for several years.

Richard Manuel also grew up in a Canadian family that enjoyed country music. He started learning piano at nine and formed a band, the Revols, during his high school years in Stratford, Ontario. Ronnie Hawkins took a liking to his style when the Revols shared a bill with the Hawks, and later asked him to join the group.

Garth Hudson, born and raised in London, Ontario, recalls that his father "used to find all the hoedown stations on the radio, and then I played accordion with a country group when I was 12." He also became an excellent organist and used the organ as the central instrument in a rock group he formed in Detroit in the early 1960s after graduating from high school in Canada. In 1962, there was an opening for a keyboards player with the Hawks and he moved back to Canada to take it.

Rick Danko, bass guitarist and vocalist with The Band, began playing guitar, mandolin, and violin before starting high school and performed with local groups before he was in his teens. Like the others, he had been a country-music fan for a long time. He began listening to the *Grand Ole Opry* when he was five. Midway through high school he dropped out to concentrate on music and, at seventeen, joined the Hawks.

The only member of the group from the United States was drummer/vocalist Levon Helm. He listened to country stations as a boy in Arkansas, but also liked to play blues records, particularly those of Sonny Boy Williamson, a native of Marvell. In high school, he formed a rock group called the Jungle Bush Beaters. Afterward he joined fellow Arkansan Ronnie Hawkins as a member of the original backup group that worked with Hawkins at the end of the 1950s. When Ronnie decided to make Canada his home base, Helm agreed to remain with him.

As Robertson recalls about his days with the Hawks, "There were only three kinds of rock then: rhthym & blues, corny white rock, and rockabilly. We played rockabilly."

After a while, members of Hawkins' backing bands tended to tire of the format. The musicians who were to form The

Band left the Hawks and drifted south of the border to look for new directions in the United States. (After they left, others took their places in Ronnie Hawkins' band, which continued to be called the Hawks.) Their previous association caused Robertson and the others to get together to form a new group that played in small clubs along the eastern seaboard of the United States. In 1965, they got their first big break when Bob Dylan chose them to tour with him as his backing band.

"I didn't remember exactly how it happened," Robertson said. "I think we were in Atlantic City at the time. Dylan had heard of us, I guess. And we'd heard of him, but weren't into that kind of music and I didn't really know who he was or that we could play with each other at all. Then we jammed together and a lot of things happened. We've had a great effect on each other. Dylan brought us into a whole new thing and I guess he got something from us."

The group toured widely with Dylan, playing concerts in major cities all over the world, sometimes taking abuse from the audience. Dylan fans who hated the thought of his abandoning folk music for folk-rock took out their frustrations not by booing Dylan but by booing and heckling his supporting musicians.

In 1966, those engagements ended abruptly when Dylan suffered serious injuries in a motorcycle accident. He moved to Woodstock in upstate New York (site of the famed Woodstock Festival in 1969) and Band members moved there to be near him. Part of their efforts included working on some new songs with him and helping him to complete a film that had been started in Europe. The Band also went to work on some new material of its own, recording it in the Woodstock Playhouse during 1967-68. Those songs formed the basis for the 1968 debut LP.

The success of the album in late 1968 gave them a chance to be featured performers in their own right. In 1969, they gave memorable concerts in such places as San Francisco's Winterland, New York's Fillmore East, and, with Dylan, who approved of their solo efforts, in a "Tribute to Woody Guthrie" at New York's Carnegie Hall. The Band was featured in England's Isle of Wight pop festival.

The group's reputation grew with each new album. Its second LP, *The Band*, was issued by Capitol in November 1969 and its third, *Stage Fright*, in midsummer 1970. The latter two included songs that became Band classics, numbers like "Up on Cripple Creek," "The Night They Drove Old Dixie Down," "The Rumor," "The Shape I'm In," "Strawberry Wine," "All the Glory," "Just Another Whistle Stop," and "W.S. Walcott Medicine Show."

Both LPs easily went over gold-record levels. During 1971, the group's fourth LP, *Cahoots*, was released and quickly shot up to the national top 20. Though it stayed on the charts many months, it did not match the success of earlier LPs. In the fall of 1971, The Band was warmly greeted on one of its increasingly rare tours. Its first California concert in a year and a half took place in San Francisco's Civic Auditorium in late November. It was one of a series of concerts that served as warmups for appearances at New York's Academy of Music, in December, which provided the recordings for their first live album. Called *Rock of Ages*, it was issued in August 1972 and the two-disc set earned a gold record by year end.

During the summer of 1973, The Band was one of the featured groups at the rock concert held in Watkins Glens, New York, attended by an estimated 600,000 people, an even vaster audience than the one that had gone to Woodstock four years earlier. On October 29, Capitol issued album number six, *Moondog Matinee*, on the charts well into 1974.

At the beginning of 1974, Dylan and The Band teamed up once more for one of their landmark concert series of the 1970s. The coast-to-coast tour took them to forty cities around the United States and played to standing-room-only crowds in every venue. The tour played to 658,000 fans, but promoter Bill Graham announced that figure represented only a tenth of the more than 6 million ticket requests that came in by mail. The live LP made during the tour, *Before the Flood*, came out in the summer on

Dylan's label at the time (Arista Records) and received a gold-record award on July 8, 1974.

The Band, however, grew increasingly weary of touring and, in fact, members were becoming restless about the restrictions of group work. The group turned out new LPs from time to time, such as *Northern Lights/Southern Cross,* issued by Capitol in late 1975, and *Islands,* released on a new label, Warner Bros., some time after.

In mid-1977, the group announced it would go out on the road once more for one last tour, then disband. The cross-country series began in the east in the fall and ended with a gala banquet and concert in San Francisco in November 1977. The series was titled *The Last Waltz,* also the title of the LP issued in the spring of 1978, drawn from the music of the final concert. Besides The Band, it featured a galaxy of guests, including Dylan, Van Morrison, Joan Baez, Dr. John, Muddy Waters, and many others. During the summer of 1978, a film, *The Last Waltz,* directed by Martin Scorcese, which Robbie Robertson helped to assemble from films of the concert, was released and soon was recognized as one of the most effective pop-music documentaries ever made.

BANDY, MOE: *Singer, guitarist, band leader. Born Meridian, Mississippi, February 12, 1944.*

Since Moe Bandy's birthplace, Meridian, Mississippi, was also the hometown of the great Jimmie Rodgers, the Singing Brakeman, and since his grandfather worked with Rodgers on the railroad, young Moe naturally listened to a lot of Jimmie Rodgers' records. Since his parents were musically oriented and, for a time, his father had his own country band, it might have been expected Moe would think of music as a career goal from the start. As it happened, for many years he was more interested in bronco-busting and bull-riding and, had he made the big time, rodeo's gain would have been country music's loss. But at least he knew what he was singing about when he placed recordings like the fall 1981 hit single "Rodeo Romeo" on the charts.

"My dad plays guitar and sings," he related in 1979, "and my mother plays piano and sings so that's where I got started. I learned guitar when I was a kid. My dad taught me. I dropped it for a long time, then took it up again when I was nineteen. He wanted me to be a fiddle player too, so I started, but I never did pick that up again.

"We moved to San Antonio, Texas, when I was six and I grew up there. I entered Burbank High School in 1959, then I switched to East Central. I graduated from there in 1962. I played very little music until I got out of high school. What I was doing was rodeoing. I started when I was about ten and by the time I was sixteen I was entering rodeos all over Texas. I broke a lot of bones and made a little money, but not much. My brother did better. He's been in the top 10 for the last six years [as of 1979]."

Thus Moe, having little luck as a rodeo contestant, returned to picking guitar. He formed his first group, Moe and the Mavericks, in 1962. "I started playing local beer joints and honky tonks around Texas. It was a thrill. I just did it for fun at the start. I started in 1962 and did that for twelve years. I made several records on small labels—GP, Satin, Shannon, that didn't do any good." In order to survive, like so many other would-be musicians, he worked during the day (as a sheet-metal worker) and at night and on weekends he played as much as he could. His first single to come out during that period was the 1964 release "Lonely Lady" on Satin. It got little attention, and Moe and the Mavericks continued to perform as the house band on a local TV show, *Country Corner,* and to back up national touring acts.

In 1972, Moe found out that record producer Ray Baker was in San Antonio on a hunting trip, so he knocked on his motel room door and persuaded Baker to listen to some of Moe's tapes. A few weeks later, Baker called Bandy and said he would like to try producing something for him. Moe hocked his furniture to pay for the studio time, but nothing much happened with the recordings.

Baker decided to wait until he found the

right tune before trying again with Bandy. In 1973 he called Moe and told him to come to Nashville and bring some more money to pay studio expenses. This time Moe took out a loan, but the gamble paid off.

Bandy recalls, "Baker came up with 'I Just Started Hatin' Cheatin' Songs Today.' He made 500 copies on Footprint Records and started promoting it. The record broke nationally and it was picked up by GRC Records in Atlanta, Georgia." Within five weeks after GRC took over, the song was in the national top 5 of the country charts and Moe was on his way. He followed with more singles hits on GRC: "Honky Tonk Amnesia" in 1973; "It Was Always Easy to Find An Unhappy Woman" and "Don't Anyone Make Love at Home Anymore" in 1974; and, in 1975, "Bandy the Rodeo Clown," which he co-wrote with Lefty Frizzell. That song, he noted, with its echoes of rodeo life and his brother Mike's bull-riding exploits, "is one of my favorites. I like all of them though. They've been good to me."

Although he co-wrote that tune and wrote some others, like the early "Lonely Lady," he stresses that writing isn't his forte. "I've written a couple of songs, but mostly I've done songs by other writers. I'm just gonna try to keep it the way it is. What I do is traditional type country music. It's what I do best and I think there definitely is a need for it. Other than performing, though, I like all kinds of music."

Moe's "hard country" songs follow in the tradition of Hank Williams—songs about cheating and heartache performed with a straightforward delivery. Will Hardesty of Rocky Mountain Music Express describes his impact in this way: "What he does best is enough to make a listener able to smell stale beer and stale cigarette smoke, enough to make the listener hear the clink of glassware, the buzz of conversation and laughter, the shuffle of slow-dancing feet. It's enough to make you want a beer."

In 1975, Moe left GRC and signed with Columbia, still his label in the early 1980s. By then, he also had three albums released on GRC, *I Just Started Hatin' Cheatin' Songs*

Today (1973); *It Was Always Easy to Find an Unhappy Woman* (1974); and *Bandy the Rodeo Clown* (1975). On the new label, he picked right up where he'd left off with a steady string of top-10 hits. In 1975, he started the new series with the single "Hank Williams You Wrote My Life" and followed, in the second half of the 1970s, with the chart hits "The Biggest Airport in the World," "Here I Am Drunk Again," "She Took More than Her Share" (all 1976); "I'm Sorry for You My Friend," "Cowboys Ain't Supposed to Cry," "She Just Loved the Cheatin' Out of Me" (1977); "Soft Lights and Hard Country Music," "That's What Makes the Jukebox Play," "Two Lonely People" (1978); "I Cheated Me Right Out of You," "Barstool Mountain," "It's a Cheatin' Situation" (duet with Janie Fricke) (1979).

During 1979, Moe joined forces with Joe Stampley to form a highly successful duo. About its origins, he said, "Joe and I was in Europe together and Joe came up with the idea and I talked to my producer [still Ray Baker] and got it all together." The first result of the new alignment was the single "Just Good Ol' Boys," which rose to number one on country charts. The song also served as the title track for a hit album from which two more hit singles (in 1980) were culled, "Tell Ole I Ain't Here, He Better Get on Home" and "Holding the Bag." The success of their teamwork was indicated by their May 1980 selection by the Academy of Country Music as "Duo of the Year"; a choice seconded in October by members of the Country Music Association, who voted them the "Duet of the Year."

During 1980, Bandy continued his string of hit solo singles as well as his chartmakers with Stampley. Those included "One of a Kind," "The Champ," and "Yesterday Once More." He began 1981 with another duet top-10 hit, "Following the Feeling," this time with Judy Bailey, "Soon after, he combined with Joe again for the top-10 single "Hey Joe, Hey Moe." Other 1981 successes included the solo "Rodeo Romeo" and the duet, with Stampley, "Honky Tonk Queen."

From the mid-1970s on, Moe also was

represented on Columbia Records by albums that generally made upper-chart positions. His debut on the label in 1976, *Hank Williams You Wrote My Life*, was followed by such titles as *Here I Am Drunk Again* (1976); *I'm Sorry for You My Friend, Best of Moe Bandy, Volume 1, Cowboys Ain't Supposed to Cry* (1977); *Soft Lights and Hard Country Music, Love Is What Life's All About* (1977); *It's a Cheatin' Situation* (1979); *One of a Kind, The Champ* (1980). With Joe Stampley he completed such LPs as *Just Good Ol' Boys* (1979); *Holding the Bag, Tell Ole I Ain't Here* (1980); *Hey Joe, Hey Moe* (1981).

After becoming well known to country fans across the United States in the early 1970s, Moe maintained a hectic in-person and TV schedule to maintain fan rapport. He didn't become a *Grand Ole Opry* regular, but did guest on it a few times. "I played the *Grand Ole Opry* twice as of 1979 and it was really a great thrill," he enthused. "I first played it in 1974 and played it again last year. I'm on the road 250-300 days a year. I've been overseas twice—England the year before last and this April [1979]. In April I also appeared in Sweden and Holland. We're doing real well overseas, especially in England. In the U.S. I've played every state. I've had a band for about four years—the Rodeo Clowns—it's a six-piece group. When I'm not on the road, I still live in San Antonio."

Bandy quotes from 1979 interview with Irwin Stambler.

BANNON, R. C.: *Singer, guitarist, songwriter, disc jockey. Born Dallas, Texas, 1945.*

Over the years, musicians have been known to use the job of disc jockey as a stepping stone to performing success. Perhaps it's a sign of the times, though, that R. C. Bannon's first paid job in Nashville was as a discotheque DJ.

Bannon's road to Music City and eventual acceptance as an important part of the country music family was a circuitous one, beginning in Texas and wending its way through Seattle and Los Angeles. In his home town of Dallas, his father was active in local church affairs and R. C. sang in his family's Pentecostal church choir at the age of four. He continued to take part in gospel and hymn singing as he grew older, but increasingly his musical interests turned toward rock 'n' roll. By the time he got to high school, he was an above-average guitarist, and during his teens in the late 1950s and early 1960s, he organized several rock and soul bands.

After he moved to Seattle with his family in the mid-1960s, he not only performed in local night clubs but sang the "hymn of the hour" every morning on a local TV show. His main income, however, came from working as a disc jockey on a Seattle station.

After five years as a DJ, he decided to try for a full-time performing career again in Southern California and Las Vegas, opening for such country artists as Barbi Benton and Mayf Nutter. An important milestone was the chance to open for Marty Robbins during one of that *Grand Ole Opry* star's tours. Robbins was impressed enough with Bannon's singing and writing talents to suggest that R. C. move to Nashville. The latter demurred because "I knew the time wasn't right. I wasn't ready to compete with the 'big boys' in Music City."

Back in Los Angeles, Bannon kept honing his skills and seeking a recording contract from West Coast based record firms. In the mid-1970s he was signed by Capitol, but nothing much happened with the sides he made. In April 1976, Bannon belatedly took Robbins' advice and drove his Datsun pickup eastward to Tennessee. Musicians' jobs were hardly hanging from trees, so Bannon took what he could find—a record-spinning job at a Nashville discotheque for seventy-five dollars a week.

Meanwhile he kept seeking contacts in the country music industry, resulting in meetings with writer–performer Harlan Sanders. The two hit it off well. Sanders liked Bannon's songs and helped him get a job as a contract writer for Warner Brothers Music. From late 1976 on, an increasing number of artists included songs written or co-written by Bannon in their recording sessions. Among those who released singles of that material between

1977 and 1979 were Marty Robbins, Harlan Sanders, Ronnie Milsap, and Bobby G. Rice. During the summer of 1978, Milsap's "cover" of a song written by Bannon and John Bettis (included in Bannon's debut LP), *Only One Love in My Life*, became one of the year's best sellers. In mid-July 1978, the Milsap disc stood at number one on the *Billboard* charts. At year end, Bobby G. Rice's recordings of another Bannon song (co-written with Sanders and K. Westbury), "The Softest Touch in Town," rose to upper-chart levels.

During 1977, Bannon was signed to a recording contract by Columbia Records. His debut LP, *R. C. Bannon Arrives*, was released in March 1978. The album included four songs co-written by Bannon and John Bettis (who was a coproducer of the LP), one co-written with Sanders, "Southbound," one entirely by Bannon, "Rainbows and Horseshoes," and a Paul Anka song, "It Doesn't Matter Anymore." The last three were on country charts in 1977–78. At the end of 1978, Bannon was represented on the charts by the single "Somebody's Gonna Do It Tonight."

His 1979 chart singles included duets recorded with Louise Mandrell, such as "We Love Each Other." (They met at Nashville's Fan Fair in 1977 and married in 1979.) In 1980 his chart singles were mainly solo efforts such as "Lovely Lonely Lady," "If You're Serious About Cheatin'," and "Never Be Anyone Else."

In 1982, R. C. moved to RCA Records with Louise. His debut LP on RCA, *Me and My RC*, featuring six duet tracks, came out in early 1982.

BARBER, AVA: *Singer. Born Knoxville, Tennessee, June 28, 1954.*

Most teenagers in the 1970s took a dim view of their parents' tastes, particularly if they enjoyed the *Lawrence Welk* show. However, in Ava Barber's case, it was her mother's prodding to contact Lawrence Welk that helped launch Ava on the road to country music success.

Born and raised in Knoxville, Ava was exposed to all forms of music in her childhood, including a good dose of country and gospel. For a time, she joined her peer group in admiration of rock and soul artists. In elementary school, when the Beatles were the ruling favorites, she recalled chipping in money with some friends to buy new hit records of the English foursome and other pop stars. After learning the lyrics, she and the others would go around the neighborhood "putting on shows. I had one of those little True Tone record players and we'd act as if we were the Supremes, singing for anyone who would listen."

She had a good voice and made her professional debut at the age of ten, but things really didn't start moving strongly for her until several years later when she already was a dedicated country vocalist. Ava's first foray into the country-music field was as a cast member on the *Bonnie Lou and Buster Show*, syndicated to twenty TV stations around the country, when she was fifteen. The credits that resulted from being a cast regular helped bring other work during the four years she remained with the program. Nights and weekends, she often performed at barn dances and small clubs in her home region. She also made her first recordings on the local Dogwood Records label, which released the single "Atlanta, Georgia."

When Ava was in her late teens, her mother encouraged her to try for bigger opportunities. Her suggestion was that Ava send a sample of her work to Mrs. Barber's favorite, Lawrence Welk. Ava recalled, "I thought that was crazy. I'd never hear from him. He probably receives one hundred letters a day. Why should he even listen to my music and write me back. My mom said I didn't have anything to lose. So I did." She sent the material to Welk in the summer of 1973 and several months later received a reply indicating some interest. Ava sought Welk out when he was in Nashville shortly thereafter for a golf tournament. "He took me into a tent, sat me down at a piano and auditioned me. Mr. Welk said that he had a country show coming up that I would be perfect for."

By then Ava was married, and she and her band-drummer husband, Roger, pooled their resources and moved to Los Angeles. At first the going was rough because Welk's operation was hampered by a studio strike. Once that was settled, though, she joined the *Lawrence Welk* show in 1974 and was still the regular country vocalist at the end of the decade.

In the mid- and late-1970s, in addition to the *Welk* show she performed on many other major programs and in hundreds of in-person engagements. Among her credits are the Wheeling, West Virginia, *WWVA Jamboree; That Good Ole Nashville Music* TV show in 1975; *Pop Goes the Country,* 1978; *Hee Haw,* 1978; and *Grand Ole Opry* in 1978 and 1979. "I have worked many, many fairs during fair season and have traveled and sung in the largest concert halls all over the U.S. and Canada with the Welk organization. I also spent thirteen days in Germany doing country shows for military bases in 1978." Ava also was often a headliner in major Nevada hotels, and appeared usually at Harrah's Club in Lake Tahoe from 1975 through 1979.

Working with Welk also brought new luster to her recording career. Through Welk's association with Ronwood Records, part of the GRT Records Group, she signed with the label in the late 1970s. In 1977, this resulted in two charted singles, "Don't Take My Sunshine Away" and the top-20 hit "Waitin' at the End of Your Run." In 1978, she had an even bigger hit with Gail Davies' composition "Bucket to the South," which reached fourteen on the national country charts. She also was represented by two LPs in the late 1970s, *Country as Grits* and *You're Gonna Love, Love.* The title song from the latter was on mid-chart levels in the summer of 1978. In early 1981 she was represented on lower-chart levels by the Oak Records single, "I Think I Could Love You Better than She Did."

BARE, BOBBY: *Singer, guitarist, songwriter, actor. Born Ironton, Ohio, April 7, 1935.*

An outspoken advocate for trying new directions in country music, Bobby Bare sometimes raised the hackles of the traditionalists. But even the staunchest supporters of hewing to time-honored country-music formats had to admit Bobby was a tremendously talented per-

former and writer. As an innovator and a shrewd judge of talent who helped bring attention to a number of future superstars, he had a profound effect on his chosen field from the early 1960s into the 1980s.

Some of Bare's independence and toughness of spirit can be traced to the adversity of his early years. Born to a poor farm family in Ohio, he saw the death of his mother when he was five. Later, the family finances became so bad that his sister had to be given out for adoption. Bobby left school at fifteen to earn extra money for his family, toiling as a farm laborer and bundle-boy in a clothing factory for the next few years.

One of the few pleasures in his boyhood was music. He built a guitar for himself out of an old coffee can, a stick, and some string. After a while, he obtained a regular instrument and by his mid-teens was performing with a country band in the Springfield–Portsmouth section of Ohio. In the mid-1950s, he was still at it—working at other jobs during the day while picking up whatever work he could in music, in small clubs in Ohio and Kentucky and occasionally on radio and TV. He was already writing original material, some of which he included in his club appearances.

Still, as the late 1950s drew on, his career wasn't progressing very quickly. He switched his singing and writing efforts to rock and moved to the Los Angeles area, leaving for California with only twenty-five dollars in his pocket. Shortly after arriving in Los Angeles, he was drafted. The day before he entered the service, he made some demonstration tapes and sent them to Ohio-based Fraternity Records. That label issued a single of one of Bare's songs, "All American Boy," in 1959, and it became a major pop hit.

As it happened, Bobby had recorded it under the name Bill Parsons, so its success didn't lift him from anonymity. In fact, the record company sent another performer out under the Parsons name since Bare wasn't available. (Bobby had no claim to the song by then anyway, having sold the rights for fifty dollars.)

After his discharge in the early 1960s, Bobby rushed back to the rock field with his excellent voice and good guitar style. Among the artists he toured with in that period were the Dave Clark Five, Jay and the Americans, Roy Orbison, and the late Bobby Darin. However, Bobby soon decided to return to his first love, country music, but with a perspective that was innovative, combining his stylings with an emphasis on modern themes. Some of his offerings of the first half of the 1960s were precursors of such later trends as folk-rock and progressive country.

RCA's Chet Atkins was quick to recognize Bobby's great potential and signed him to the label in the early 1960s, where Bare recorded such songs as "Shame on Me," on the charts in 1962, and "Detroit City," which rose to number one on all major charts in 1963. The latter won Bobby a Grammy in the 1964 National Academy of Recording Arts and Sciences competition. In 1963, he had another big hit in "500 Miles From Home" and in 1964 provided such top-10 successes as "Four Strong Winds" and "Miller's Cave." He also made his film debut that year with a leading role in the Warner Brothers movie *A Distant Trumpet.* That didn't interfere with his musical progress, though; he showed up with the 1965 top-10 hit "It's Alright" and, in 1966, another of his classics, "Streets of Baltimore."

Meanwhile, Bobby helped further the careers of promising new artists. In the early 1960s, after hearing a then unknown named Waylon Jennings in an Arizona club, he brought him to the attention of Chet Atkins. As he recalled for an RCA biographer, " 'Chet Atkins, you gotta sign that boy up,' I said. 'I listened to Waylon Jennings last night at the club in Phoenix and he's one of the best I've heard in ages.' And I said, 'Yeah, I know I'm cuttin' my own throat because he's gonna be doing the same thing I'm doing . . . but he deserves to be on a major label.' And I gave him Waylon's phone number and he called him up and signed him."

It was the same thing that happened almost a decade later to another aspiring artist named Billy Joe Shaver. Shaver told *Music City News* (December 1977), "I guess I'd been in and out of Nashville for about 10 years with no luck. Then one day I walked into Bobby's publishing company. He told me flat out, he wasn't looking for any more writers, but I guess I musta looked kinda pathetic. He started to send me away, then he said I could leave a tape. But I didn't have any. My songs were all in my head. He said he'd listen to one song. By the time I was halfway through 'Restless Wind,' he'd signed me." In the mid-1970s, Bare was still working with Shaver, coproducing some of Billy Joe's albums on MGM.

Bobby also was an early supporter of other new writers and performers, including Mickey Newbury and Kris Kristofferson. One of his first singles released after he switched from RCA to Mercury Records at the start of the 1970s, for instance, was a Kristofferson composition, "Come Sundown." He also was quick to appreciate Shel Silverstein's writing skills, turning out his own version of the Dr. Hook hit, "Sylvia's Mother," on Mercury, reaching upper-country-chart levels in the fall of 1972. (Earlier that year his chart singles on Mercury included "What Am I Gonna Do.")

His enthusiasm for Shel's work led to a close collaboration between the two in the mid-1970s, sometimes as co-writers, other times with Shel providing songs especially for Bobby to record. For most of those years, Bobby once more had returned to the RCA fold. His chart hit singles of Silverstein's songs included "Daddy, What If" and "Marie Laveau" (the last named co-written by Shel and B. Taylor) in 1974; "Alimony" in 1975; "The Winner" in 1976; and "Red Neck Hippie Romance" in 1977. The two worked closely on one of Bobby's more ambitious projects of the 1970s, a two-record "concept" album released in 1975 titled *Bobby Bare Sings Lullabies, Legends and Lies.* Bobby hardly restricted his output to material provided by Silverstein. His chart successes in the late-1970s included such songs by other writers as "Put a Little Lovin' on Me" and "Dropkick Me Jesus (Through the Goalposts of Life)."

During 1976, Bobby switched labels to Columbia, which released his debut LP,

Bare, late in the year. Among those who made guest appearances on that Bare-produced LP were Waylon Jennings, Willie Nelson, Shel Silverstein, Dr. Hook, and Chet Atkins. In late 1978, he had his first major singles success on Columbia with "Sleep Tight Tonight, Goodnight Man" (by J. Silber and S. Lorber), which rose to number eleven on *Billboard* lists in early December.

Bare toured widely in support of his new Columbia releases as he had done for most of his illustrious career. By the end of the 1970s he had performed in all the states of the union and many other nations around the world. His European tours, in fact, went back to the early 1960s. In 1963, he was one of the first country artists to make a major swing through Germany and Scandinavia. His TV appearances in the 1960s and 1970s included most major country programs as well as such popular showcases as *American Bandstand, Mike Douglas,* and *The Midnight Special.*

Though his own songwriting efforts slowed down somewhat in the 1970s, his total of original compositions numbered in the hundreds.

Bobby began the 1980s with the charted single "Numbers" in January 1980. Among his early 1980s discs that reached high-chart positions were "Have Another Tequila, Sheila" (a Shel Silverstein contribution) and "Food Blues" in 1980 and "Willie Jones" and "Dropping Out of Sight" in 1981.

BEE, MOLLY: *Singer, actress. Born Oklahoma City, Oklahoma, August 18, 1939.*

Fame and fortune came to blonde, blue-eyed Molly Bee early. A national star in her teens, she was unable to cope with the pressures of success and at one point in the 1960s her career was imperiled by a five-year bout with pills and drugs. However, she finally recovered, returning to the country field in the mid-1970s.

As she told Ellis Nassour of *Music City News* (August 1975), "I've done it all! Radio, TV, movies, concerts, USO tours with Bob Hope, fairs, rodeos, summer stock, you name it. And lived to tell about it. Mine has been like six lifetimes rolled into one and I've had more hectic and wild experiences than almost any other in show business. And you know what? I wouldn't trade it for anything.

"I'm from Beltbuckle, Tennessee. Of course it's real. [Molly was born in Oklahoma, but spent her childhood in Beltbuckle.] You don't make up names like that. My family name is Beachboard. I've been singing ever since I can remember—from the time I used to ride our mule around the farm and yodel. We moved to Tucson (Arizona) where Mom took me to meet Rex Allen and said, 'Sing for him!' (She sang "Lovesick Blues" for him and, shortly after, the ten-year-old made her debut on his Tucson radio program.) I guess you could say he discovered me."

She moved to Hollywood with her family the next year and was soon signed for Cliffie Stone's *Hometown Jamboree,* where she remained until she was in her late teens. During those years she was asked to appear on national TV, starting with a job on the *Pinky Lee Show* when she was thirteen. After three years with Pinky, she was signed as a regular cast member on the *Tennessee Ernie Ford* daytime TV show for two years.

From then on, she was a featured guest artist on many other TV programs, including Tennessee Ernie Ford's nighttime TV show, *The Ed Sullivan Show, Roy Rogers, Jimmie Rodgers, Jackie Gleason, Jack Benny, Bob Hope,* and *Jimmy Dean.* In the late 1960s, she was a regular cast member of the nationally telecast *Swingin' Country* show, which also featured Roy Clark and Rusty Draper. She was in demand as well for personal appearances at fairs, rodeos, and night clubs across the United States and in a number of other countries. Among her overseas credits were tours of Japan and Europe, including well-received appearances in England's Wembley Stadium and Palladium. Her first personal appearance at Mesker Auditorium in Evansville, Illinois, broke a six-year attendance record—one of a number of such career high points during the 1950s and 1960s.

Her credits in the late 1950s and through most of the 1960s included numerous appearances in Las Vegas, which she still called a second home in the 1970s (when her actual residence was in Tarzana, California). She was featured often at such Vegas spots as the Thunderbird, Desert Inn, and Flamingo, and also in such 1960s venues as the Shamrock Hotel in Houston, Moulin Rouge in Los Angeles, Harrah's Club and the Mapes in Reno, Nevada, and the Crystal Bay Club in Lake Tahoe.

During the 1960s, Molly proved adept at musical comedy in addition to country singing. Her first role was in *The Boy Friend* at the Garden Court Theater in San Francisco's Sheraton Palace Hotel. She later starred with Alan Young in *Finian's Rainbow* at Melodyland, Anaheim, California, and with Buddy Ebsen, of *Beverly Hillbillies* TV show fame, in *Paint Your Wagon* at the Valley Music Theater, Woodland Hills, California.

Her recording career began with Capitol Records in the 1950s and continued on MGM Records in the mid-1960s. Her MGM releases included the album *It's Great* in October 1965, and *Swingin' Country* in March 1967. Among her successful singles of the 1950s and 1960s were "Single Girl," "I Saw Mommy Kissin' Santa Claus," "Losing You," "Hate to See You Go," and "Miserable Me."

She retired at the start of the 1970s, hoping to make her third marriage work. As she told Nassour, "I succeeded at everything else, but I'm the Zsa Zsa Gabor of the country music set." However, the happier side was that she had two daughters from that marriage, Bobbi Jo and Malia, whom she doted on. "If you call raising two girls 'retirement'—let's call it time off for good behavior."

In 1975, Molly felt her two girls were old enough for her to resume her country music activities. She signed with Granite Records, which came out with her debut LP on the label in the summer. Singles like "She Kept on Talkin'" made the national charts, indicating that Molly still was remembered by many of her long-time fans.

She told Nassour, "I've been away too long. I got lazy and wanted to enjoy life— some of the things I worked so hard for. I wanted to be with my kids. I never saved

my money—spent it all. And, stupid me, I guess, I always married for love, all three times. It was good to go back into the recording studio. The musicians may not think so. I'm a stickler and know my music. They were on the ball, though. Best of all, the record has been selling and two of the cuts made the charts."

BELAFONTE, HARRY: *Singer, actor, TV producer. Born New York, New York, March 1, 1927.*

With his great voice and matinee idol features, Harry Belafonte was a natural to succeed in the entertainment field. However, it took a number of years of struggle and experimentation before he discovered his true bearings. Once he did, he became a major artist and innovator in folk music, a fine actor in films and on TV, and a potent moral force in the civil rights movement.

Though strongly associated with West Indies-style folk music, Harry George Belafonte was born in New York and lived there his first eight years. He did have an authentic heritage of the Caribbean region, since his mother came from Jamaica and his father from the French-speaking island of Martinique. In 1935, his mother went back to Jamaica with Harry. He spent five years there, a period when he learned much about the island's music and culture.

By 1940, his mother took him to New York again, where he first attended parochial school, then George Washington High School in upper Manhattan. However, with World War II underway, he left in 1944 before graduating to enlist in the U.S. Navy. He spent several years in the service, then got a job as a janitor in a New York building in the late 1940s after receiving his discharge. A tenant gave him tickets to the play *Home Is the Hunter*. Impressed by the drama, Harry decided to use the G.I. bill to study acting.

He enrolled in Erwin Piscator's Dramatic Workshop. One of his roles called for him to sing, which led to his discovery by the owner of the Royal Roost, a Broadway nightclub, who offered Harry a two-week engagement. Harry's vocalizing brought such enthusiastic response that the engagement was extended to a twenty-week stay. More engagements followed, until Capitol Records finally gave him a recording contract.

Harry became dissatisfied with singing the pop songs of the day and, in 1950, decided to take a break. He decided that folk music, then enjoying the first stirrings of what was to turn into a boom in the late 1950s, suited him more. He joined some friends in opening a small folk spot in Greenwich Village where he hung around, listening to various folk artists and sometimes singing himself. He also made many trips to Washington to study the material at the Archive of American Folk Music. In the early 1950s, he had a considerable repertoire of American as well as West Indian folk songs and began working in an act with two guitarist friends, Millard Thomas and Craig Work.

The three opened at the Village Vanguard in New York for the familiar two-week stand, and once more Harry had to be held over. The show played to packed houses for twelve weeks. Harry and his friends went on to other engagements, including a highly successful one in New York's Blue Angel.

Some of Harry's film contacts were also interested in him, and he was invited to come to Hollywood to do his first film part, in *Bright Road*. Another opportunity came along back on Broadway for him to be a cast member of John Murray Anderson's *Almanac*. When it opened in New York in December 1953, Harry's singing of "Hold 'Em Joe' and "Acorn in the Meadow" stopped the show. Then in 1954 he won the lead role in Oscar Hammerstein II's musical version of the opera *Carmen* (with a black cast), titled *Carmen Jones*. Late in 1954, Harry added to his steadily growing reputation by touring the country in a revue called *Three for the Road*. Everywhere he went, critics and audiences were thrilled by his treatment of fourteen folk songs.

His talents weren't lost on record industry executives; during 1954, he signed with RCA, for whom he ultimately sold tens of

millions of records. Along the way, he also became the first pop music performer to sell over a million copies of a long-playing album.

The event that catapulted him to a mass-audience celebrity took place on June 23, 1955. Harry's singing of calypso and other folk songs on a CBS national telecast was one of the highpoints of the TV year and the beginning of a close association between Belafonte and the medium. He went on to guest on almost every major network variety or talk show. During the late 1950s and through the 1960s, he was featured a number of times on *The Ed Sullivan Show* and made a number of dramatic appearances on TV over the years including an acclaimed role in *General Electric Theater's* "Winner by Decision." During the 1960s, Harry added producing to his other credits, producing not only some of his own TV specials but hour-long shows on the subjects of black music, folk music, and black humor.

His 1950s film work included a movie version of *Carmen Jones* (his second film part) and the controversial 1957 *Island in the Sun* with its interracial romantic theme. At one point he formed a company to produce films, appearing in two movies under that arrangement, *The World, The Flesh and the Devil* and *Odds Against Tomorrow*.

He began to come into his own as a folk-music recording star during 1956–57. The initial impetus came from his unique renditions of calypso numbers such as "Jamaica Farewell," "Day-O (Banana Boat Song)," "Matilda," "Brown Skin Girl," and "Come Back, Liza." One of his first RCA albums, *Calypso,* earned a gold record and remained a bestseller for RCA for many years. Some of his well-received singles of the 1950s included the American-style folksong "Scarlet Ribbons," "Danny Boy," "Shenandoah," "Hava Nagela," and "When the Saints Go Marchin' In," all recorded during 1956; and "All My Trials," "John Henry," and "Mama Look a Boo Boo" (recorded during 1959).

From the late 1950s on, Harry was a giant in the personal appearance field. For decades, he set attendance records in major auditoriums and arenas the world over. After his initial debut at New York's Carnegie Hall in the late 1950s, he sold out the facility many times in later years. The same held true for Los Angeles' Greek Theater, where, during the 1960s, he became almost an institution, returning regularly at two-year intervals to post SRO signs for three-week periods. He cut back on his touring for much of the 1970s, but when he returned after a long absence to the Greek in mid-1979, he still attracted large audiences to his series of concerts.

During the 1960s, Harry was very active in the fight for civil rights. He took part in benefit concerts and freedom marches and in 1966 performed in Paris and Stockholm for the first European-sponsored benefit concerts for Dr. Martin Luther King, Jr. He was a member of the Board of Directors of the Southern Christian Leadership Conference and, after the tragic killing of Dr. King, served as chairman of the Martin Luther King, Jr., Memorial Fund. As a producer, he presented the much-honored drama by the late Lorraine Hansberry, "To Be Young, Gifted and Black," to New York audiences in 1969.

Over the years his creative and humanitarian efforts won him honors from many organizations, including the NAACP, City of Hope, and the American Jewish Congress. He was awarded an honorary Doctorate of Humanities by Park College in Missouri in 1968 and later the New York New School of Social Research awarded him a Doctorate in the Arts.

From the late 1950s on, he also accumulated many credits in television, including such firsts as being the first of his race to win a TV Emmy Award and the first black producer in TV. Among the specials he produced and starred in were "The Strollin' Twenties" on CBS and "A Time for Laughter" on ABC. He also starred in a number of annual TV specials on Canada's CBC.

Always a strong album artist, Belafonte mainly made hit lists with his LPs after the first surge of singles successes in the 1950s. During his close to two decades on RCA, he turned out dozens of albums, both studio and live. Among his releases were

Harry Belafonte and Mark Twain & Folk (early 1950s), Calypso (1955), An Evening with Belafonte and Songs of the Caribbean (mid-1950s), Love Is a Gentle Thing (4/59), At Carnegie Hall (two records, 9/59), Sings Blues (3/60), What a Mornin' (2/60), Swing Dat Hammer (5/60), Harry Belafonte Returns to Carnegie Hall (two records, 12/60), Jump Up Calypso (9/61), Midnight Special (5/62), Many Moods of Belafonte (11/62), Streets I Walked (7/63), Harry Belafonte at the Greek Theatre (two records, 4/64), Ballads, Blues and Boasters (11/64), An Evening with Miriam Makeba (7/65), An Evening with Nina Mouskouri (2/66), In My Quiet Room (7/66) Calypso in Brass (12/66), Harry Belafonte on Campus (7/67), Homeward Bound (1/70), By Request (5/70), This Is Harry Belafonte (two records, 9/70), Warm Touch (4/71), Calypso Carnival (12/71), and Belafonte Live (two records, 11/72).

As the 1970s went by, Belafonte's recording efforts became more of a sideline as he devoted more time and energy to other projects, including charitable work and films. His contract with RCA phased out and until the late 1970s, he had no arrangement for U.S. releases, though in 1979 RCA did put out a retrospective of some of his major hits, called Harry Belafonte—A Legendary Performer.

In the early 1970s, he teamed up on a film project with long-time friend Sidney Poitier, with whom he once had acted in the American Negro Theater. In that unusual western titled Buck and the Preacher, Belafonte played an aging "jackleg" preacher, Reverend Willis Oaks Rutherford. Harry showed a flair for satiric humor in a later 1970s movie called Uptown Saturday Night, where his role was a takeoff on Marlon Brando's portrayal of Don Corleone in The Godfather.

Harry signed a recording contract with CBS Records International in the late 1970s for material to be released outside the United States. The first of several late-1970s LPs for that label came out in 1977, titled Turn the World Around. In liner notes for the 1977 collection, he reiterated his belief in folk, as opposed to 'fad,' music. "As one crosses the length and breadth of this country each region reflects its own unique styles, whether it be in ways of dress, language, tastes in food, and, most significantly, in music. What most people are not aware of are the vast riches which can be found in America in what I call 'hidden' cultures. I believe the music of these hidden cultures is far richer and more reflective of what America really is than what is suggested by much of the music we hear blazing across the airwaves."

In 1981, there were indications Belafonte would have a resurgence of his entertainment activities in the new decade. He was featured on TV in a dramatic program about integration in reverse—the story of the first white student athlete (played by Bruce Jenner) to enter formerly all-black Grambling College. Belafonte played the part of Grambling's noted football coach, Eddie Robinson. During the year, Harry also completed a grueling seven-and-a half month concert tour that took him to major venues all across the United States. In August, his first album for Columbia for U.S. release, *Loving You Is Where I Belong*, was issued.

BELLAMY BROTHERS: *Vocal duo from Florida. David Bellamy, born September 16, 1950 and Howard Bellamy, born February 2, 1946.*

Brothers David and Howard Bellamy picked up years of experience in the bubbling country rock circuit of Florida, a state that produced such stellar groups as the Allman Brothers and Lynyrd Skynyrd. The Bellamys' music contained elements of blues, soul, and rock, though it evolved more toward a slick pop-country sound that made their recordings cross over readily between the two fields.

Howard recalled, "My father influenced me a lot. He played dobro and fiddle in a bluegrass band. He was pretty good too. I really liked the country music, so when I was thirteen years old, I picked up the guitar. Actually I did it only to accompany myself as a singer."

David also was a role model. When he was nine he began learning the accordion and became reasonably proficient. Later on, though, his interest in blues and soul music caused him to concentrate on playing keyboards. Even before he picked up an accordion, David was doing some writing. "I began putting words down on paper when I was eight. Oddly enough, though, I only wrote short stories and poems until I was seventeen. That's when I wrote my first song."

David was the first to play in a professional group when, in 1965, he became organ player for a soul group called the Accidents. "We played backup for people like Percy Sledge, Little Anthony and the Imperials, and various other black singers. Otis Redding was my favorite performer at that time. That's how I became involved in soul music. Those were fun days. I even had a go-go girl dancing on top of the organ."

In 1966, the Bellamys teamed up initially for an annual event in Tampa, Florida, called the "Rattlesnake Roundup," a popular festivity where "ranchers and farmers bring the rattlesnakes they've caught during the year and display them." For their part of the show, David held forth on accordion, Howard on guitar, and their father played the fiddle.

The brothers became members of a rock group called Jericho in 1968 that sometimes shared bills with such other performers as the Allman Brothers and Brewer & Shipley. "We played high school proms, assemblies, and small clubs," Howard noted. "When we worked with the Allmans, they also were starting out and we admired their music. We never dreamed that they would be as big as they became. After all, it's hard to imagine that kind of success when you're playing in a local coffee house called The Bottom of the Barrel." Major influences on their own developing sound, he stressed, included Paul McCartney and Brewer & Shipley.

The Bellamys were becoming interested in broader horizons as the 1960s came to a close. Howard had started writing original material "because I got tired of singing other people's songs." Their first recording efforts, however, in an Atlanta studio in 1969 proved disastrous. The results of the sessions were so poor, the group disbanded.

In the early 1970s, the brothers shifted their attention to studio work. They gained session assignments throughout the South, which helped them to polish their performing styles and increase their contacts. David recalled, "It gave us time to write. One day I wrote a song called 'Spiders and Snakes' and sent it to Phil Gernhard, who was producing Jim Stafford. Next thing I know, I'm on the phone with Stafford doing a rewrite." The Stafford single of the song became one of the top novelty successes of the mid-1970s, selling over 2 million copies.

That breakthrough brought a bid from Phil Gernhard and his associate, Tony Scotti, to handle the Bellamys as an act. The brothers moved their base of operations to Los Angeles, where they settled in to work on a new series of recordings. In early 1976, the single "Let Your Love Flow" was issued by Warner/Curb Records and quickly became a major hit on both country and pop charts. In the spring, their debut LP on Warner/Curb, titled *The Bellamy Bros.*, came out and also made upper-chart levels. Besides "Let Your Love Flow," which earned a gold-record award, it included another Bellamy offering that had been a regional hit, "Nothin' Heavy." For much of 1976, the duo and supporting bandmembers toured the United States and Canada to increase their name recognition. During the year, they were featured on many major network and syndicated TV shows.

Their second LP, *Plain and Fancy*, came out in 1977. Their 1977 tour schedule, in addition to dates all over the United States, included swings through Canada, England, the Scandinavian nations, and Germany. Their 1977 recording achievements, however, fell short of the previous year, which helped trigger a move to a new management alignment with former Loggins and Messina manager Todd Schiffman and to a new producer, Michael Lloyd. First fruit of that association was the May 1978 LP release *Beautiful Friends*, which provided several songs that made the charts—"Slippin' Away" and "Let's Give Love a Go." One of the elements that provided a thread between all three albums to that point was a

series of songs written by David dealing with the early days in the American West. The songs were "Rodeo Road" in the first LP, "Livin' in the West" in album two, and "Tumbleweed and Rosalee" in the 1978 release.

At the end of 1978, the Bellamys had a new single, "Lovin' On," that promised to provide their first big hit since "Let Your Love Flow." By early 1979, it was in the country top 20 on the way to rarefied top-10 levels. In the spring, the brothers scored a major hit with Don's "If I Said You Had a Beautiful Body Would You Hold It Against Me," which made number one on country lists in May 1979. Later it received a Grammy nomination. The song was included in their fourth Warner/Curb LP, *The Two and Only*. Their fifth album on the label, *You Can Get Crazy*, came out in January 1980.

During 1980, they had such major hits as "Sugar Daddy," "Dancin' Cowboys," and "Lovers Live Longer," all written by David Bellamy. Also on the charts in early 1980 was a holdover from late 1979, "You Ain't Just Whistlin' Dixie." In March 1981, the brothers had the number-one hit single "Do You Love As Good As You Look." Another bestseller during the year was "You're My Favorite Star."

BERLINE, BYRON: *Singer, fiddler, songwriter, band leader (Country Gazette, Sundance, L.A. Fiddle Band). Born Cornwell, Kansas, early 1940s.*

One of the finest fiddlers of modern times, Byron Berline has made his presence felt in everything from folk music to rock. The extent of his reputation can be assessed by the many first-rank artists who have enlisted his services for backing bands or session work: Bill Monroe, Doug Dillard, David Bromberg, Olivia Newton-John, Linda Ronstadt, Henry Mancini, Bob Dylan, the Rolling Stones, The Flying Burrito Brothers, and many others. Despite his backing of diverse artists, his first love remained bluegrass, an art form to which he contributed fine original compositions and inspired solo recordings.

Born in Kansas, but raised on a farm in Oklahoma, Byron took up fiddling as a child. As he told Michelle Pelick Kingsley for an article in *Frets* magazine (June 1979, pp. 34–36), "I guess I was five years old. My dad was a fiddle player and I had always heard music since the time I was born. I never played in any groups till I went to college, though. That was in the early 1960s. Folk music was popular back then and the local TV station was auditioning acts for a hootenanny program it was going to do. . . . They said they needed a bluegrass band, so some of us put a group together. I didn't know what bluegrass was, but this banjo player knew 'Cripple Creek' so we got us a bass player and a guitar player and learned 'Cripple Creek' for that show. We called ourselves the Cleveland County Ramblers because Norman [Oklahoma], where the college is, was in Cleveland County. After that we played for fraternity parties around campus. Sometimes we'd make money, sometimes we wouldn't, but we really didn't care."

Next, he performed for two years on a TV program sponsored by Garrett Household Furniture of Oklahoma City. After receiving his B.A. from the University of Oklahoma in 1967, Byron joined Bill Monroe's famous Blue Grass Boys. He remained with Monroe into early 1968, when his career was interrupted by the military draft. He was stationed at Ft. Polk, Louisiana, performing at the officers' club and for special events as well as in nearby clubs with a local bluegrass band.

While attending the University of Oklahoma, Byron had made the acquaintance of Doug Dillard, and the two had worked on a show at the school. Dillard was enthusiastic about Berline's fiddle-playing and, years later, was only too happy to renew acquaintances when Berline moved to Los Angeles after leaving the Army.

Byron arrived on the coast in July 1969 and became part of Doug's Dillard and Clark group, which gave way to Dillard and the Expedition. Berline was with the band until it broke up in 1971, and he still toured with Dillard on occasion in later years. Berline made a number of recordings with the Dillard organizations, including such LPs as *Pickin and Fiddling* and

Copperfields on Elektra and *Duelin' Banjos* on 20th Century Fox.

In 1971, Berline was assembling a band of his own that was named Country Gazette when he was asked to tour with the Flying Burrito Brothers. Among the members of the Country Gazette were bass player Roger Bush, guitarist Kenny Wertz, and a long-time friend from Oklahoma days, banjoist Alan Munde. The first recruit was Wertz, followed by Roger Bush. As Berline told Michelle Kingsley, "When Alan Munde joined the group a little later, it became the Hot Burrito Revue. We went to Europe with the Burrito Brothers a couple of times. Kenny, Alan, Roger and I didn't really get going as Country Gazette until 1972 though. I stayed with the Gazette until 1975. The last gig I did with them was a trip to Europe." Berline lent his talents to a number of Burrito Brothers' LPs during those years, including *Burrito Deluxe* and *Last of the Red Hot Burritos* on A&M Records.

Tired of touring, Byron decided to stay home with his family in Los Angeles after that to concentrate on writing, session work, and movie assignments. Throughout the 1970s, he was in much demand for film scores. Among the movies he provided music for were *White Lightning, Bound for Glory* (the story of Woody Guthrie), *The Longest Yard*, Bob Dylan's *Pat Garrett and Billy the Kid, Sometimes a Great Notion* (the film version of the Ken Kesey novel), and many others. One of his favorite efforts, he told *Frets* magazine, was *Sometimes a Great Notion*, particularly since Henry Mancini was the one who invited him to provide fiddle music for the Mancini score.

Berline decided that if he formed another band he would get away from a straight bluegrass format. "I had known [guitarist] Dan Crary for a while and I had met [bassist] Jack Skinner in Las Vegas a few years before; the two of them and a couple of other people happened to call me up right around the same time, so I said, 'Let's get together and do some picking.' That's how Sundance got started: Dan, Jack [banjoist], John Hickman [guitarist], Allen Wald and myself. We got a record deal with MCA but that meant a big promotional tour right at the end of the summer and on into the fall. Dan [professor of speech at Cal State University at Fullerton] couldn't go because he had to start teaching again. We had to get another guitar player, somebody to play rhythm, so we took Skip Conover, who played dobro and guitar. He was kind of an honorary member. The record, *Byron Berline and Sundance,* was cut in 1976. That was our only album."

The group remained active until the end of 1978, playing folk clubs and festivals around the country. The band reorganized in the fall of 1976 when Skinner left and was replaced by Vince Gill (who became a member of Pure Prairie League in 1979). Also added were drummer Mark Cohen and bassist Joe Villegas. The last change before the group's final phase was John Hickman's departure in January 1977. However, he and Berline remained close friends and by 1979 they and Dan Crary joined in forming a production company called BCH.

Though Sundance had been shelved by 1979, Berline didn't lack projects. Besides session work, he completed a new solo album called *Barn Dance* in mid-April and also completed another LP with a group called the L.A. Fiddle Band, comprising three fiddles, dobro, banjo, guitar, and bass. A small label called Takoma also prepared an album based on Berline's solo appearance at the small McCabe's hall in Santa Monica (a well-known gathering place for local folk musicians and enthusiasts) called *Live at McCabe's.* During the summer of 1979, Berline was again on the road as part of Doug Dillard's new touring band.

BIKEL, THEODORE: *Singer, guitarist, actor, linguist. Born Vienna, Austria, March 2, 1924.*

Theodore Bikel, the entertainment field's "renaissance man," has demonstrated many varied talents—from acting and singing to writing and executive skills—in a long and distinguished career. An excellent scholar, well-versed in many subjects, he is also proficient in seventeen languages.

Bikel was born in Austria, but his family fled to Palestine in 1938 and became British subjects. Theodore learned English and studied other languages with the goal of eventually becoming a teacher of linguistics. To help pay his expenses, he started working as a laborer on a communal farm. In his spare time, he was charged with directing and staging local pageants.

In 1943, he left the farm to join the Habimah Theater in Tel Aviv and later formed the Tel Aviv Chamber Theater with four other young actors. Within two years he had outgrown location production and went on to study at London's Royal Academy of Dramatic Arts. Soon his acting in little theater groups in London began to draw attention from others in the profession. Sir Laurence (now Lord) Olivier was impressed and signed Bikel for a part in the first European production of Tennessee Williams' *A Streetcar Named Desire,* which opened in London on September 27, 1947.

Bikel's work in that play helped bring movie offers within a few years' time. The first of a long series of supporting roles he essayed was that of a German sailor in the 1951 film *The African Queen.* (That same year he played a Russian officer in a hit London play, *The Love of Four Colonels.)* He added many more movie credits in the 1950s for both English and U.S. filmmakers. Among them were *Moulin Rouge* (1952); *Melba* (1953); *A Day to Remember, Love Lottery, The Little Kidnappers* (1954); and *Divided Heart* (1955).

In 1955, he made New York home base, where he still lived at the start of the 1980s. As in England, his main preoccupation was with the dramatic theater, but he always had been interested in music of various kinds from classics to folk, and he began to do an increasing amount of entertaining in the latter category. Since he had been collecting folk songs of all kinds from the many languages he studied, he was well positioned to take advantage of the steady growth of interest in the folk domain at the time.

However, the chance to perform on the New York stage had been the initial lure. His first show was a flop, but the second, *The Lark* (November 1955), was a critical success with much praise for his acting from reviewers. In December 1956, he made his TV debut in *Hallmark Hall of Fame's* "There Shall Be No Night." More film roles also came his way and he appeared in *Vintage, The Pride and the Passion,* and *The Colditz Story* (all 1957); and *The Defiant Ones* (1958), which brought him an Academy Award nomination for best supporting actor.

In the music field, Bikel signed with Elektra Records in the mid-1950s and began to record folk material for them. He gave his first solo concert in New York at Town Hall on October 5, 1958, before a capacity audience. Some of his songs were captured for the live album *Bravo Bikel,* released the next year by Elektra. From then on, when his schedule permitted he gave folk music concerts all over the United States and in several other countries. He also was a guest on many radio and TV shows in the late 1950s and throughout the 1960s. In the early 1960s, he had his own radio show, *At Home with Theodore Bikel,* on FM stations in New York, Los Angeles, and San Francisco.

A major musical milestone for him occurred in August 1959 when he was selected to play the lead role of Baron Von Trapp in Rodgers and Hammerstein's *The Sound of Music.* He was warmly praised by critics when the show opened on Broadway on November 16, 1959. He also was featured in the original cast album, released by Columbia in January 1960, a record that sold millions of copies. Later in the 1960s, he performed in other musicals, including the role of Tevye in a late 1960s production of *Fiddler on the Roof* in Las Vegas.

From the late 1950s through the 1960s, Elektra issued a series of LPs by him. Among them were *Actor's Holiday, Folk Songs from Just About Everywhere* (5/59), *Bravo Bikel* (11/59), *From Bondage to Freedom* (5/61), *Best of Theodore Bikel* (10/62), *On Tour* (4/63), *Folksinger's Choice* (5/64), and *Yiddish Theater & Folk Songs.* Other titles included *Folks Songs of Israel* and *Songs of the Russian Gypsy.* His association with Elektra ended in the latter part of the 1960s, but some of his material appeared on various labels thereafter. Among those albums

were *New Day* on Reprise (11/69), *Silent No More* (1972), and *Song of Songs,* a collection of Biblical material set to music.

During the 1970s, though he did some concert work, most of his activities in the entertainment field revolved around stage performances. In 1972 and 1974, he toured in the show *Jacques Brel Is Alive and Well and Living in Paris.* In 1972 he also played the role of Meyer Rothschild in *The Rothschilds.* In 1975, he appeared as the dramatist Chekhov in *The Good Doctor,* and in 1976 he toured in the title role of *Zorba.*

During his career, he has been active in many charitable and professional groups. For much of the 1970s, he held high executive posts in performers' organizations. He was elected president of Actors' Equity in 1973, a post he held until 1982, when actress Ellen Burstyn assumed the post. In 1977, he was appointed by President Carter to the National Council for the Arts.

BILL BLACK'S COMBO: *Instrumental group. Membership 1959–60: Bill Black, born Memphis, Tennessee, September 17, 1926, died, Memphis, Tennessee, October 21, 1965; Carl McAvoy, Martin Wills, Reggie Young, Jerry Arnold. Personnel as of 1982: Bob Tucker, Gil Michael, Billy Compton, Robert Gladney, Phil Munsey.*

Although the Bill Black Combo had strong country roots, it began as a rock band and remained that way throughout the 1960s and early 1970s. The group was founded by Bill Black, born and raised in Memphis, Tennessee, and already a highly regarded bass player by the late 1940s, well before he brought the group together. Along with guitarist Scott Moore, it was Black who backed Elvis Presley on almost all of his classic recordings of the mid- to-late 1950s.

In 1959, Bill decided to form his own band with the members who had worked with him on the Combo's first series of hits: Reggie Young on guitar, Martin Wills on saxophone, Carl McAvoy on piano, and Jerry Arnold on drums. The band offered a blend of rock and R&B in its releases. The singles "Smoke" (Parts 1 and 2) were propelled to the top of the pop charts in the United States and England and to number one on American R&B lists. In 1960, the band gained two more gold records for the singles "White Silver Sands" and "Josephine." Some of the group's early 1960s albums on Hi Records were *Saxy Jazz* and *Solid & Raunchy* in 1960; *That Wonderful Feelin'* in 1961; *Movin'* and *Record Hop* in 1962; and *Untouchable Sound* and *Greatest Hits* in 1963.

In the early 1960s, one of the personnel changes brought Memphis guitarist Bob Tucker onto the roster. In 1962, Bill Black relinquished leadership of the group to guitarist Tucker, who presided over the band's heavy worldwide touring schedule. After Bill Black died in 1965, Tucker gained an agreement with his widow that allowed Bob to keep the group going under its original name. Over the years, the group remained popular with pop audiences and also developed a strong following in country ranks. As of the 1970s, for instance, the band's managers estimated that about 75 percent of its personal appearances were in country shows or clubs.

Some of the Combo's repertoire over the years was in the country-rock vein, but in the mid-1970s Tucker decided to turn out material more country oriented. The first avowedly country LP, titled *Solid and Country*, was released in 1975. The record label remained the same as it always had been, Hi. One track, "Boilin' Cabbage," received so much air play that it was issued as a single and moved well up on country charts. This was followed by such other well-received singles as "Back Up and Push," "Fire on the Bayou," and a fall 1976 chart hit, "Redneck Rock." The group's achievements of 1975–76 won them the nod from *Cash Box* magazine in October 1976 as its Top Instrumental Group, Singles.

By the mid-1970s, the band's roster had changed completely from the makeup in the early 1960s. With Tucker on guitar, it was composed of Gil Michael on steel guitar and fiddle, Robert Compton on drums, and Phil Munsey on bass.

At the start of the 1980s, the group still had many LPs in the active catalogue of Hi Records. Those included *Award Winners; Memphis, Tennessee; Saxy Jazz; Solid and* *Raunchy; Untouchable Sound; Greatest Hits; Bill Black Combo Plays the Blues; Bill Black Combo Plays Tunes by Chuck Berry; Bill Black Combo Goes Big Band; More Solid and Raunchy; Greatest Hits, Volume 2; Solid and Country; World's Greatest Honky-Tonk Band;* and *It's Honky-Tonk Time*. Also available was *The Bill Black Combo* on Zodiac records.

BLAKE, NORMAN: *Singer, guitarist, dobro player, mandolinist, fiddler, songwriter, band leader. Born Chattanooga, Tennessee, March 10, 1938.*

A major name in the bluegrass revival of the 1970s, adept at playing many other folk and country styles, Norman Blake might well have been a superstar had he so desired. But he preferred to shun the mass audience, rejecting the musical compromises they required, and delighted his smaller but devoted following instead.

Blake, born in Tennessee and raised in Georgia, showed an early aptitude for music and could play several instruments by the time he was in his teens. When he was sixteen, he quit school to play mandolin with the Dixie Drifters. They debuted on radio on the *Tennessee Barndance* program on WNOX, Knoxville, and played on several other Southern stations the next few years.

In 1956, Norman left the band to team with banjo player Bob Johnson as the Lonesome Travellers. In the late 1950s, they added banjoist Walter Forbes and the threesome made two records for RCA. In 1959, Blake joined another group, Hylo Brown and the Timberliners, though he still did some work with Johnson, including several appearances on the *Grand Ole Opry* in Nashville.

At the start of the 1960s, Blake was drafted into the U.S. Army, stationed as a radio operator at the Panama Canal. He formed a bluegrass band called the Fort Kobbe Mountaineers, playing mandolin and fiddle. The group was voted the best instrumental group in the Caribbean Command, with Norman voted best instrumentalist.

After receiving his discharge, Blake went home to Georgia, where he found the main emphasis in pop music to be either rock 'n' roll or "Nashville-sound" country. He might well have become a top artist in either category, but his refusal to adapt his repertoire and performing technique in those directions drastically restricted his musical options. To earn a living he became a guitar teacher with as many as 150 students a week and played in a country & western dance band three or four nights a week.

His musical abilities were not lost on other members of the country field. June Carter of the Carter Family was particularly impressed by his instrumental skills and for a while he was a part of her road group. Later he performed with her and Johnny Cash as a regular on their 1969 CBS summer TV show.

During 1968–69, Norman did session work on Bob Dylan's *Nashville Skyline* album, issued in the spring of 1969. Later that year Norman moved to Nashville to join Cash's band for the TV series, playing guitar and dobro. Once based in Nashville, Blake's performing career took on new impetus. At the start of the 1970s he played guitar and dobro in Kris Kristofferson's first road band and also toured with Joan Baez, playing those instruments plus mandolin. He also helped on recordings of both those artists in the early 1970s.

From Kristofferson, Blake departed to become a member of John Hartford's Aero-Plane band. When that was disbanded, Norman stayed with Hartford for a year and a half as an accompanist. While working with Hartford, Blake recorded material for his first solo album, *Home in Sulphur Springs,* which came out on Rounder Records in the early 1970s. Keeping his hand in as a session musician, he contributed to the Nitty Gritty Dirt Band's *Will the Circle Be Unbroken,* one of the group's best-selling efforts, issued in 1973. He toured for nine months with the Red, White and Blue (grass) band, then plunged into a full-time solo career.

From the mid-1970s on, he was on the road constantly, performing in folk and country clubs and on the college concert circuit. After completing a second LP on Rounder, *Whiskey Before Breakfast,* he shifted to Flying Fish for such albums as

The Fields of November, Old and New (issued in 1975), *HDS Sessions,* and *Blackberry Blossom.* During those years, he was also represented on Takoma Records with *Live at McCabes* and on County Records with *Darlin' Honey.* In the late 1970s, Takoma issued another LP, *Directions.* Blake also recorded with other major folk and country artists, including Bryan Bowers on the *Album from Home* on Flying Fish; Doc Watson on *The Essential Doc Watson* on Vanguard; and Mason Williams on *Fresh Fish* on Flying Fish.

From 1974 on, Norman was joined by his wife, Nancy, who had been with the group Natchez Trace. She played mandolin, fiddle, and guitar in addition to cello. In 1978 the Blake group expanded to a trio with the addition of fiddler James Bryan, an old friend of Norman's. He had first recorded with Blake in 1975 on the *Old and New* album. During the 1970s, he had sometimes toured with such bluegrass greats as Bill Monroe and Bill's son, James Monroe. Bryan also filled in for Kenny Baker on the *Grand Ole Opry* during those years.

Blake told Art Coates of *Frets* magazine that he felt the trio combination gave increased depth to the music. "Our sound is a complete form with this instrumental combination. You've got the fiddle on top as a solo instrument with a high voice. The guitar takes care of the mid-range and the accompaniment for the fiddle, as well as being able to exchange solos with the fiddle; and they bolster each other up with harmonies, completing each other. Also, the guitar serves to accompany the vocals. Then Nancy's cello is on the bottom, playing the bass part and harmonies. It is a complete package, musically."

When Coats asked him to define his music, Blake replied, "I'd prefer not to see myself or our music labeled, but I'd have to say that our music falls someplace between British music and the old-time country music that is organic to this country. We're not copying British music and we're not playing old-timey music just for the sake of old-timeyness. Instrumentally, we could be related in some ways to jazz in concept, the way we play lines, not just chords. We play bass lines and progressions, some in simple form, but it's still not quite what might be played in country or bluegrass music forms. It's not purely traditional. We draw on all those things, which I guess puts us someplace in the ocean between Britain and the U.S."

In 1979, Blake and his group signed a contract with Rounder Records. The first product of the new association was the 1979 release, *The Rising Fawn String Ensemble.*

BLANCHARD, JACK, AND MISTY MORGAN: *Vocal and instrumental duo, songwriting team. Both born Buffalo, New York, Blanchard, May 8, 1941; Morgan, May 23, 1945.*

The joint career of Jack Blanchard and Misty Morgan seems preordained. Both were May babies born in the same Buffalo, New York, hospital, and both had parents named John and Mary, sisters named Virginia, and ancestors hailing from Ireland and Alsace-Lorraine. As they grew older, each demonstrated singing talent and learned to play keyboards and each followed the same general geographic route—from Buffalo to Tonawanda, New York, to Ohio, and finally to Florida. But neither became aware of all those coincidences until they met for the first time in Hollywood, Florida, about 1963.

Jack, born into a family of artists and musicians, felt a desire to perform even as a child. His initial training was on the piano, though over the years he added skills on synthesizer, slide guitar, dobro, and Hawaiian lap steel guitar. He already was performing in public in his teens and played in a variety of groups over the years, ranging from jazz to rock and country. However, in between engagements he worked at diverse occupations. "I drove trucks, worked in factories, dug graves, played professional hockey, and generally knocked around the country until I met Misty . . . then settled down somewhat," he informed the author.

Misty, who spent her early years in Buffalo before her family moved to Tonawanda (also in upstate New York), started taking piano lessons at nine. She kept that up for a year, then gave up formal instruction, but continued to practice and pick up new material on her own. (By the late 1970s, her keyboard talents extended to organ, clavinet, synthesizer, and string synthesizer.)

She performed with several small groups in the Tonawanda area before moving to Cincinnati, Ohio, in her late teens, where she played piano and sang at various night clubs. In the early 1960s, she headed south to Miami, Florida, where she got a job singing in a club in Hollywood, Florida, a block away from another night spot that featured Jack. The two became acquainted and not long afterwards became husband and wife.

However, it took a number of years before the two formed their own act. As Jack recalled, "It just happened that the band I was with broke up, so Misty and I decided to try it as a team. It was that or starve."

It proved a fortunate decision. Jack had had some success but no major hits. He had made a number of country recordings, including one on the Midas label called "The King of Hearts," which now is considered a collector's item. After the two teamed up in the late 1960s (with Misty changing her name from Mary for the new act), they began to place records on the charts, hitting the jackpot in 1970 with the million-selling single "Tennessee Birdwalk," number one on the charts for five weeks. In the fall of that year they had another single on the country lists for a number of months, their composition "You've Got Your Troubles, I've Got Mine," which brought them an ASCAP writing award. Their combined efforts for 1970 also resulted in all three trade magazines, *Billboard, Cash Box,* and *Record World* naming them Vocal Duo of the Year.

By then Jack had demonstrated the ability to write in other formats besides songs. From the late 1960s on, he wrote a newspaper column that appeared in the local paper of the city they chose for their residence, Orlando. Over the years, his output included a comic strip and three books dealing with the music field. Comedy routines became a part of Jack and Misty's stage act.

Over the period from the late 1960s into the 1980s, Jack and Misty turned out dozens of records of country-flavored material on such labels as Wayside, Mega, Epic, Phillips, RCA, VIK, and others. Their biggest success, "Tennessee Birdwalk," was issued on Wayside, a subdivision of Mercury Records. During those years, some thirty singles and two albums made the national country and/or pop charts. Among their singles successes were "Humphrey the Camel" (Wayside Records), which sold a half million copies and rose to number three nationally, and "Somewhere in Virginia in the Rain" (Mega), a top-10 hit. Some of their other releases that made upper-chart levels were "The Legendary Chickenfairy" (top 20, spring 1972 on Mega), "Down to the End of the Wine," "There Must Be More to Life than Growing Old," and "Just One More Song" (Epic, late 1973, early 1974).

After breaking through to national prominence at the start of the 1970s, the duo moved from lead-ins for country stars to headliners in their own right. Welcomed by audiences all over the United States and Canada, they also made many appearances on national television, including a number of guest spots on the *Mike Douglas* show and *Good Old Nashville Music.* They also were featured on several occasions on Dick Clark's *American Bandstand.* (Clark spoke admiringly of Jack's writing ability. "Jack Blanchard has one of the strangest [meaning in this case, unique] minds in the world. His thought processes and writings are one of a kind.") Among their other TV and radio credits were appearances on the *Robert W. Morgan Show, Pop Goes the Country, Music Hall America,* and many syndicated country programs.

The songs Jack and Misty wrote, either together or separately, provided chart hits for other performers in the country or pop fields over the years. This work brought a number of BMI citations for songwriting excellence.

BLUE SKY BOYS: *Brother vocal and instrumental duo. Born North Carolina, Bill Bolick, October 28, 1917; Earl Bolick, December 16, 1919.*

One of the great teams of traditional country music, the Bolick Brothers rank with such legendary artists as Uncle Dave Macon, Gid Tanner, and Jimmie Tarleton. Although their heyday overlapped the active periods of some of the most noted exponents of old-time mountain music, they were considerably younger than the others, and, indeed, folklorists who rediscovered the Bolicks after they had been out of the music field for over a decade were amazed to find the brothers still relatively young and robust.

Growing up in the hill country of North Carolina, the brothers were weaned on the country music of Gid Tanner and the Skillet Lickers and other great old-time fiddlers. Like many Southern families, get-togethers of friends and neighbors to sing and play favorite folk songs were a normal part of living. The brothers learned to play stringed instruments early, with Bill favoring mandolin and Earl mastering the guitar before they reached their teens. They gathered a repertoire of secular and religious songs from the 1920s and earlier decades.

In their early teens, they performed for local dances and social events in Hickory. Before long, word of their ability reached other parts of their home state. In 1935, they expanded their audience by joining the roster of station WWNC in Asheville, North Carolina. Within a short time they had a following throughout the state. Not long after, they cut their first sides on June 16, 1936. By the start of the 1940s, they were one of the most highly regarded country acts in the United States.

The boys were featured on many stations in the 1940s and made personal appearances in many parts of the South. In the late 1940s, they were regulars on station WNAO, Raleigh, North Carolina. They also continued to record during that decade and at the start of the 1950s. They recall recording 124 sides in all between 1936 and 1951. Typical of their material were the songs presented on the 1965 Capitol LP, *The Blue Sky Boys,* which included "Corrina, Corrina," "Jack o' Diamonds," "The Unquiet Grave," "Wild and Reckless Hobo," "Midnight Special," "Poor Boy," "Who's Gonna Shoe Your Pretty Little

Feet," and "Oh Those Tombs," (Capitol label).

By the early 1950s, when the tastes of the country audience had changed, the brothers refused to imitate the popular acts of the day and decided to retire from the music field. They settled down to regular day jobs and in a short time most people had forgotten about them.

However, there still remained a core of country fans who loved the mountain ballad tradition and a growing group of folklorists who wanted to preserve that type of music. Experts like Dr. D. K. Wilgus and Ed Kahn of UCLA's John Edwards Collection, for instance, collected the Bolicks' records and, after the resurgence in the popularity of folk music in the late 1950s and early 1960s, began to search for the duo.

Finally their search was successful, which renewed interest in the Bolicks' performances and their recordings. The initial results included release of a number of LPs, including *Blue Sky Boys* on Starday Records in December 1962, *Together Again!* on Starday (1/64), *Blue Sky Boys* on RCA's Camden label (3/64), and *Precious Moments* on Starday (3/64).

After turning down a number of offers to perform at festivals, they finally agreed to go on stage again at a fall 1964 concert sponsored by the University of Illinois Campus Folksong Club. Their offerings brought a standing ovation and pressure for other engagements. In 1965, the Bolicks were featured at the UCLA Folk Festival and the New York Folk Festival at Carnegie Hall. They also played at other festivals and gave a number of college concerts during the mid- and late-1960s.

In the 1970s, however, the brothers again sought privacy. As of the end of the decade, Earl worked at Lockheed–Georgia Division in Marietta and Bill earned his living as a postal inspector in North Carolina. The only album of their music available in the late 1970s was *The Blue Sky Boys* on the Bluebird label.

BOGGS, DOCK: *Singer, banjoist. Born Dooley, Virginia, February 7, 1898, died March 1971.*

"I was born February 7th, 1898, place of birth, Dooley, Virginia. Long time done away with. I was named after the 1st phisician ever was in Norton, Va. My dad nicknamed me 'Dock' and it has stuck with me ever since." *

It took retirement to bring Moran L. "Dock" Boggs to the forefront of the folk music revival of the 1960s. Many folk song experts had been enthusiastic about rare recordings made by this traditional Virginia mountain singer and banjo player decades earlier and wondered what had happened to him. As he later related, his wife had thought working as a miner a more honorable way to earn a living and to please her he had abandoned his music until he completed forty-one years in the mines in 1954.

Dock first heard folk music from his older brothers and sisters and other family members who played and sang the songs popular in the mountain areas. Dock joined in as soon as he was old enough. The banjo was the main instrument in the Boggs' home and Dock began to play it in traditional "knockdown or claw hammer style" (that is, with one finger and thumb) when he was twelve. At the same time, he started his long career as a miner.

Dock had been playing the banjo only a short time when he was introduced to a different way of playing. As he wrote in *Sing Out!* (July 1964, p. 32), ". . . My younger brother Rosco brought a colored man home with him one evening that used to be around Norton. I heard him play 'Alabama Negro.' He played with his forefinger and next finger—two fingers and thumb." From that time on, Dock developed that style of playing to a fine art.

Dock's banjo playing slowed down after he married in 1918. Though devoted to her husband, Mrs. Boggs had a religious upbringing in which secular music was considered sinful. Dock continued to play for his own enjoyment for most of the 1920s, though, and his ability gained much notice among people of his home area. Thus when representatives of Brunswick Records came to Norton in 1927 to look for

* *Letter to the author, August 21, 1968.*

country music talent, Dock was urged by friends to apply. He finally agreed to go to the tryout in the ballroom of the Norton Hotel. He played his favorite type of "lonesome songs": "Country Blues," "Down South Blues," and "Mean Mistreatin' Mama." The record executive signed him to record twenty-four songs, which he did during 1927 and 1928. The contract increased his wife's unhappiness, however, so after Dock completed his commitment, he agreed to put the banjo aside.

When Dock began to draw his miner's pension and Social Security in 1954, his wife's attitude had mellowed. There was no bar to his banjo playing and he took it up again, playing for friends and neighbors and also attending folk festivals throughout the region. The rising interest in traditional music among young urban artists eventually provided the groundwork for his rediscovery in the 1960s. Mike Seeger sought Dock out at a festival and encouraged him to expand his performing horizons.

Seeger brought word of Boggs' talents to the Eastern folk music establishment and set wheels in motion that led to Dock's participation in major folk music festivals. Seeger also helped line up a new recording contract for Dock with Folkways Records. Boggs' debut on that label, *Dock Boggs*, was issued in 1964. In March 1965, another LP of his recordings was issued on the Disc label. In December 1965, Folkways released *Dock Boggs, Volume 2* (with Mike Seeger). Earlier that year, Folkways also issued the album titled *Dock Boggs Interviews* (9/65), in which Boggs' responses to questions by Mike Seeger recalled the environment in which mountain music was performed before the rise of popular recording stars like the Carter Family and Jimmie Rodgers. Verve/Forecast released an album titled *Legendary Dock Boggs* in June 1966, and, in 1967, a third volume of Boggs' performances came out on the Folkways label.

During the mid-1960s, Dock covered much of the United States in concert appearances at folk clubs and on many college campuses. He also was featured at the Newport Folk Festival several times as well as at a number of other major folk festivals.

At the start of the 1980s, three of his LPs remained in Folkways Records' active catalogue: *Dock Boggs Interviews, Dock Boggs, Volume 2,* and *Dock Boggs, Volume 3.*

BOND, JOHNNY: *Singer, guitarist, songwriter, actor, music executive. Born Enville, Oklahoma, June 1, 1915; died June 12, 1978.*

In a career that spanned over forty years, Johnny Bond did just about all there was to do in the country & western field. He was an excellent musician, a pioneer in western film musicals, and, above all, a consummate composer of songs whose credits include such classics as "Cimarron," "I Wonder Where You Are Tonight," and "Tomorrow Never Comes."

As a child living on the family farm in Marietta, Oklahoma, where they moved a few years after his birth, he had his first exposure to country music. In his autobiography he wrote, "Just as far back as I can remember there was the old wind-em-up Victrola which gave out the sweetest sounds, the echo of which has never died. They lifted me up to watch the old 78 rpm records go around. Two of the most requested melodies were by some fellow singing 'The Prisoner's Song' and 'The Death of Floyd Collins.'"

As he grew up, he sometimes dreamed about the pleasures of making phonograph records "in a cool room" rather than sweating in the noonday sun in the fields. When he talked about show business, his family was aghast. "Show business?" said the home folks. "You mean money business!" But the die already was cast.

Bond recalled, "While in high school, about 1933, I had the good fortune to get into the brass marching band where I learned about music. As soon as I was financially able I blew the whole roll of 98¢ for a Montgomery Ward ukulele, with which came a booklet of self instruction. Fame and fortune were now within my grasp . . . so I thought.

"Upon graduation in 1934, I left home in a dust storm to stay with my brother and his wife in Oklahoma City. There I began broadcasting on local radio stations, wandering from this dance band to that, when Jimmy Wakely came along." The year was 1937 and Johnny became a part of the Jimmy Wakely Trio, whose goal was to make its way to Hollywood and try for work in the movies.

The year 1938 was an important one for Johnny. He composed "Cimarron," for one thing, and also met Tex Ritter, who was to be a close friend of Johnny's up to Ritter's death in the mid-1970s. In 1939, Bond got his first chance to appear in a movie, Roy Rogers' *Saga of Death Valley*. While Bond was in Southern California for that, he became acquainted with Gene Autry, the beginning of another enduring relationship.

"We were soon hired by Gene Autry to broadcast on the CBS *Melody Ranch Show* while [also] touring the country with him. [Since] singing westerns were being filmed in most of the studios we found little difficulty in landing a few here and there." Bond remained a member of the *Melody Ranch* cast until it finally closed down in 1954, and he worked with Autry on many other projects after that. In addition, he found time for other efforts, including appearances on the *Hollywood Barn Dance* from 1943 to 1947.

In 1940, he wrote another C&W standard, "I Wonder Where You Are Tonight," one of more than one hundred songs he wrote in the 1940s, including "Tomorrow Never Comes" in the mid-1940s. In 1942, he made his first film with Tex Ritter, the star of a series the two took part in for quite a few years.

His home base after 1940 was Southern California, where he resided until his death in 1978. He found plenty to occupy him as the decades went by. In 1953, he joined the cast of a locally televised program called *Town Hall Party*, remaining with it throughout the show's long lifetime. He also appeared on dozens of nationally televised programs in the 1950s and 1960s, including a number of Gene Autry projects. Although California was home, he toured all over the country during those decades. He had debuted on the *Grand Ole Opry* in the 1940s and often was a guest on the show in later times.

He also recorded a long list of singles and albums, from his initial contract with Columbia Records in 1940 to many releases on the Starday label in the 1960s. He scored one of his biggest hits in 1960 with the single "Hot Rod Lincoln," which went high on the national pop charts as well as showing up on country lists. In 1964, he recorded the song "Ten Little Bottles" at the disc jockey convention in Nashville in Studio C at station WSM, and the single became a top-10 hit the following year. Among the many albums Starday issued during the 1960s and up to the early 1970s were *Live It Up & Laugh It Up* (issued September 1962); *Famous Hot Rodders I Have Known; Song That Made Him Famous* (7/63); *Bottled in Bond* (11/65); *Branded Stock; 10 Little Bottles; 10 Nights in a Barroom;* and *Here Come the Elephants.*

In 1970, Johnny authored a book describing his thirty years with Gene Autry. Later in the 1970s, he devoted his attention to behind-the-scenes activities administering a number of music organizations, including Vidor Publications (which had been founded with Tex Ritter), Red River Songs, and Laredo Publications. He remained active in industry affairs though retired as a performer, and, in the mid-1970s, served as a director of the Country Music Association.

BONOFF, KARLA: *Singer, pianist, guitarist, songwriter. Born Los Angeles, California, 1952.*

A look at the song credits on the albums of many major folk and folk-rock stars of the mid-1970s often disclosed the name Karla Bonoff. People like Linda Ronstadt, Jackson Browne, Wendy Waldman, and Andrew Gold paid her that compliment (as did several country artists, including Emmylou Harris) and also suggested she had the talent to achieve hits of her own. That was, in fact, a major desire of Karla's, leading her to start her recording career in the late 1970s.

Building up experience toward that end for a relatively long time, she was exposed to music almost as soon as she could understand what was going on in the world around her. Her family loved music, particularly the classics, and her mother had trained as a classical pianist. Naturally, her mother started both Karla and her sister, Lisa, learning piano while they were still grade-school age. One deterrent, she recalled, was the stern manner of the outside teacher given the task of teaching them keyboard style.

Karla enjoyed the piano but was even more excited when someone gave her "an actual toy guitar." She went off by herself for hours perfecting her guitar technique. Naturally, some of the songs she mastered on the instrument were folk tunes. However, when she started to write original music at the age of sixteen, it was the piano that she used.

She already was interested in singing in her teens and for a while she and her sister formed a duo. They tried out some of their material on friends, then went on to dare the fates by going on stage to take part in amateur shows. In particular, they sang at a number of "Hoot Nights" at the Los Angeles Troubadour in the late 1960s and early 1970s—one of the premiere folk, folk-rock and rock clubs in the area. She told an interviewer, "It was fun. In those days Jackson Browne was doing Hoots, and so was James Taylor. It was an exciting place. You knew when you played there some one would hear you. It was really scary, though. I mean I used to completely freak."

However, as a duo the girls didn't seem to be making much progress. Lisa decided to concentrate on college work. Karla still wanted to pursue a music career, but it took a chance meeting with a musician named Kenny Edwards at a Transcendental Meditation meeting in 1970 to act as a catalyst. Edwards had been a member of the Stone Poneys, the group that gained some national prominence because of the young lead vocalist, Linda Ronstadt. By the time Kenny met Karla, the Stone Poneys had been out of existence for some time and he had played with several groups that hadn't gone anywhere.

The friendship between Kenny and Karla had a strong musical base, and before long they were part of a group called Bryndle. The other members since have gained attention as soloists: Wendy Wald-

man and Andrew Gold. The group gained a contract from A&M Records in the early 1970s and completed tapes for an album. But the album never came out and Bryndle broke up, with all four members going separate ways.

Waiting for something new to come along, Karla continued to write songs, a number of which Kenny was enthusiastic about. As Karla told *Fullerton Hornet* editor Chip O'Neal (December 3, 1976), "About three years ago, Kenny went to play in Linda's [Ronstadt] band and he took a cassette of 'Lose Again' to her. It almost went on Linda's *Prisoner in Disguise* album."

But while that was a disappointment, Karla's spirits soon rose when Linda selected "Lose Again" for her next LP, which turned out to be the phenomenally successful *Hasten Down the Wind*. Besides that tune, Linda included two others, "Someone to Lay Down Beside Me" and "If He's Ever Near." "Someone to Lay Down Beside Me" was issued as a single and made top-chart levels. Soon more of Karla's songs were being discovered by a wide range of artists, which helped open record company doors for her to try for a performing contract.

During 1976, she signed with Columbia and began work on her debut disc. That collection, produced by Kenny Edwards, was issued in March 1977 and verified her skills as vocalist and song interpreter even if it didn't threaten to outstrip any of Ronstadt's late 1970s releases. Linda, though, as well as Kenny and ace guitarist Waddy Wachtel, did session work on the album and Wachtel later accompanied Karla on many of the concerts she gave in support of the LP.

One of her problems, she agreed, was her relatively low volume of new songs. She told O'Neal, as far as inspiration is concerned, "I just sort of wait for it to happen. I wish I knew what it was because then I would write more. I don't get inspired very easily.

"When I write [lyrics] it comes out in a burst. Like I wrote 'Someone to Lay Down Beside Me' in about twenty minutes. I had the music and I just went and sat down and words just sort of came out and I went 'Oh, far out!' and it was there. That's the best way really. To just have it flow out of you. It's the least self-conscious way of doing it. It comes out more pure. But that kind of mood doesn't hit me too often."

She noted, "I had seven years to write the songs for my first album. I was living in a house with a piano in the garage, which sounds real romantic, but it was a very isolated existence."

It was slow going, but with a good reception for her first album, she did put together material for the next LP somewhat faster. That collection, called *Restless Nights,* was issued by Columbia in September 1979 and included such new songs by Karla, besides the title track, as "The Letter," "Only a Fool," and "Never Stop Her Heart" plus two co-written with Kenny Edwards, "Trouble Again" and "Baby Don't Go." Also included was the adaptation of the traditional "The Water Is Wide," on which Karla collaborated with Frank Hamilton and Pete Seeger. The album made the charts soon after its release and remained on them well into 1980.

BOONE, DEBBY: *Singer. Born Leonia, New Jersey, September 22, 1956.*

Heiress to a great family music tradition, young Deborah Ann "Debby" Boone proved she was a worthy torch bearer in 1977, when her recording of "You Light Up My Life" was a smash hit in both the pop and country fields. It was an achievement that symbolized both sides of her inheritance. Her father, Pat Boone, was one of the major pop stars of the 1950s (though his hit releases included a sprinkling of songs that made country lists) while her maternal grandfather, Red Foley, was one of the giants of modern country music.

Debby, the third of Pat's four daughters, spent her early years in New Jersey as her father rolled up a dozen gold records and was voted "Outstanding Singer in the World" by Britain's *New Musical Express* in 1959. Pat's increasing involvement in the movies caused him to move the family to the Los Angeles area during the 1960s, where Debby went to elementary school, high school, and college. When Debby was still a pre-teenager, she and her sisters often harmonized by themselves or with their parents. At the end of the 1960s, Pat and Shirley Boone decided their daughters had above-average talent and worked up an act in which all six participated.

In the late 1960s and early 1970s, the Boone family sang at places like Knott's Berry Farm, Magic Mountain, and Disneyland, all major amusement complexes in the Los Angeles region. They also appeared in concerts in other parts of the country and were featured on many network TV shows. The group made a number of recordings at the time, one of the first releases being *The Pat Boone Family* on Word Records.

During 1977, Debby, then twenty-one, signed a recording contract with Warner/Curb Records. One of the first fruits of that alignment was the single "You Light Up My Life" which quickly became the year's best-selling single and eventually was certified platinum (for over 2 million copies sold) by the Recording Industry Association of America, making it the only platinum single of that year. In December her debut album of the same title was certified gold by R.I.A.A.

In the Grammy Awards competition, Debby's name naturally figured prominently in final nominations. When the winners were announced in early 1978, she won the Grammy for Best New Artist of the Year and "You Light Up My Life" won the Best Song of the Year Award for writer Joe Brooks.

During 1978, Debby was a featured artist on almost every major TV music show and also appeared in concerts across the United States. Late in 1978, she again was represented on country charts with the single "In Memory of Your Love," though it didn't come anywhere near the level reached by "You Light Up My Life." In early 1979, another of her singles, "My Heart Has a Mind of Its Own," was on the country lists. Later in the year she made the country charts with "Everybody's Somebody's Fool."

Debby's standing with the country audience became stronger as the 1980s began. In the spring of 1980 she had the single

"Are You on the Road to Lovin' Me Again" vying for the number-one spot. Other times during the year she had such top-10 hits as "Free to Be Lonely Again" and "See You in September." At year end she had the single "Take It Like a Woman" on the lists and in early 1981 had the disc "Perfect Fool" high on the charts.

BOONE, CHARLES EUGENE "PAT":
Singer, actor. Born Jacksonville, Florida, June 1, 1934.

Pat Boone's reputation obviously derives from his phenomenal success as a pop singer in the 1950s and early 1960s, but he sang or recorded more than a few country tunes during his career and his name showed up from time to time on country charts. His roots, of course, were in country & western territory, and his wife was the daughter of country great Red Foley. In the 1970s, when his day as a pop star was long past, he still was able to achieve an occasional chart hit with country-style recordings.

Pat, who got his nickname from his parents, was descended from frontiersman Daniel Boone. His father, a building contractor, was working in Florida when Pat was born. The family moved to Donelson, Tennessee, then, when Pat was six, to Nashville. Pat was already singing in public in Nashville at ten. In high school, he retained his interest in music, but also excelled in other areas. He was a member of the baseball, basketball, and track teams and was president of the student body. By the time he met and proposed to Shirley Foley, he had his own show, *Youth on Parade*, on Station WSIX, Nashville. He and Shirley eloped during his freshman year at David Lipscomb College and moved to Denton, Texas, where Pat helped pay for his schooling at North Texas State College by running a show for WBAP-TV at a salary of $44.50 a week.

Denton TV fans began urging Pat to audition for *Arthur Godfrey's Talent Scouts*. He tried out in 1954 and was a winner, an achievement that soon brought Dot Records head Randy Wood to Texas to offer a contract. The first record, made in Chicago in February 1955, "Two Hearts, Two

Kisses," made the top 10, and Pat followed with his version of the R&B tune "Ain't That a Shame." The latter became a million seller, the first of over a dozen gold record singles Pat recorded. Among the others were "I Almost Lost My Mind," "Friendly Persuasion," "Love Letters in the Sand," and "Don't Forbid Me."

The enormous popularity of Pat's recordings caused the Arthur Godfrey program to offer him regular cast status. Pat took up residence in New Jersey, birthplace of daughter Debby (one of four daughters), and completed his education at Columbia University. About the same time, Hollywood beckoned and he took time out to go there to complete his first film, *Bernadine*, which was followed in 1957 by *April Love*. His record of the title song reached gold record status the same month the movie was released (December 1957). Through the early 1960s, he took part in a number of other movies for 20th Century Fox.

His activities in the mid- and late-1950s including hosting his own TV program, *The Pat Boone Chevy Showroom*, and writing a book, *Twixt Twelve and Twenty* (Prentice-Hall), which sold over 400,000 copies. Among the many awards he received in the late 1950s was the J.C. Penney Father of the Year designation in 1959 and selection as Most Popular Male Vocalist by both *Cash Box* and *Billboard* magazines.

From the mid-1950s to the late 1960s, he made dozens of albums for Dot Records, some of which provided tracks that found favor with country fans. A large segment of the country audience also enjoyed the many religious LPs Boone recorded. Among his LPs, his mid-1950s efforts include *Pat Boone, Howdy!* and *Hymns We Love*. Later 1950s collections were *Pat Boone Sings Irving Berlin* (issued 12/57), *Yes Indeed* (11/58), *Tenderly* (6/59), *Side by Side* (with Shirley Boone, 7/59), *Pat's Great Hits* (6/59), and *He Leadeth Me* (11/59). His 1960s output included *Pat's Great Hits, Volume 2* (2/60), *Moonglow* (4/60), *Great! Great! Great!* (4/61), *This and That* (7/60), *My God and I* (7/61), *Moody River* (8/60), *I'll See You in My Dreams* (4/62), *I Love You Truly* (2/63), *Days of Wine & Roses* (4/63),

Joan Baez   Moe Bandy

Harry Belafonte, Grelun Landon (standing), former manager Mike Merrick (1960s).

Harry Belafonte

Bobby Bare

The Bellamy Brothers

Bryan Bowers

Norman Blake and the Rising Fawn String Ensemble, l. to r., James Bryan, Nancy Blake, Norman Blake

Jimmy Buffett (right) jams with sax player Jimmy Hall

Original Byrds (mid-1960s)

Guess Who? (9/63), *Star Spangled Banner* (8/63), *Tie Me Kangaroo Down* (9/63), *Golden Hits* (11/63), *Touch of Your Lips* (3/64), *Ain't That a Shame* (6/64), *Lord's Prayer* (8/64), *Twelve Great Hits* (8/64), *Boss Beat* (11/64), *Near You* (1/65), *Blest Be Thy Name* (4/65), *Golden Era of Country Hits* (5/65), *1965* (10/65), *Great Hits of '65* (6/66), *Winners of Digest Poll* (12/66), *Memories* (10/66), *How Great Thou Art* (6/67), *Kaiser Bill's Batman* (7/67), *Golden Hits* (10/67). At the end the 1960s, he was represented by the LP *Departure* (7/69) on the Tetragramaphon label.

Pat's career slowed down to a walk in the mid-1960s, partly because he was financially secure and partly because of rock's dominance, but also, he admitted later, because of some problems with alcohol. By the late 1960s, his long association with Dot ended and he was almost unknown to new pop fans.

At the end of the decade he pulled things together and made a comeback. He organized his four daughters (Debby [see separate entry]; Cheryl Lynn, born in Denton, Texas, July 7, 1954; Linda Lee, born in New Jersey, October 11, 1955; and Laura Gene, born in New Jersey, January 30, 1958) into a vocal group and with his wife, Shirley, appeared on TV and as the Pat Boone Family at such venues as Disneyland and Knotts Berry Farm. The group recorded for a time on the Word label. As the 1970s went by, Pat was personally active as a performer, guesting on many TV shows, including a number of appearances on Johnny Carson's *The Tonight Show*. His face and voice also became familiar to TV viewers through his association with a series of TV commercials extolling the virtues of milk and, later, hot dogs.

He made a number of country recordings, several of which made the charts, including "I'd Do It with You" on the Melodyland label in the fall of 1975 and "Texas Woman" on Hitsville Records in the late summer of 1976. At the end of the decade, Pat was pointing with pride to the tremendous success of daughter Debby as both a pop and country vocalist. The Boone family still worked together on projects like their late 1979 network TV Christmas special. During 1980, his solo single on Warner/Curb, "Colorado Country Morning," was on country charts.

BOOTH, TONY: *Singer, guitarist, songwriter. Born Tampa, Florida, Feburary 7, 1943.*

There have been more than a few Floridians who grew up to become successful country music artists. In Tony Booth's case, if he hadn't headed for the far West to attend school that scenario might never have taken place.

Born and raised in Tampa, Florida, Booth played guitar in his teens, but his musical interests were oriented mainly toward pop and rock during that period. He enrolled as a music major at the University of New Mexico in the early 1960s, hoping to earn a teaching degree. But once a resident in the Southwest, he began to pay attention to the country music broadcasts on a number of local stations. Before long he was playing country songs at local clubs.

After a while, he decided he would try to make a living in the field and paid a lot of dues as the 1960s went by playing with country bands in a succession of Western towns. One of his first engagements was at the Caravan East in Albuquerque; from there he slowly worked his way toward the Coast playing such places as Mr. Lucky's in Phoenix, Arizona, and The Westerner in San Diego, California, before finally making his way to the major music industry center of Los Angeles.

By the time he arrived in Los Angeles, he was one of the better musicians in the field—good enough to become part of the regular house band at the best-known country night club on the West Coast, the Palomino in North Hollywood. His group regularly was voted the Best Non-Touring Band by the membership of the Academy of Country and Western Music in the early 1970s. The band usually played the top hits on the charts or country music standards, but sometimes some of Tony's original material was offered.

Eager to make his name on a broader scale, Tony went the usual route of sending demo tapes around and finally got a contract from MGM, for whom he made a number of recordings, including the album *On the Right Track,* issued in the early 1970s. Shortly thereafter he moved to Capitol Records, where one of his early singles, "The Key's in the Mailbox," rose to upper-chart levels in early 1972. He also was represented by an album of the same title. In late summer of 1972, he made the top-chart levels on the national country lists with the single "A Whole Lot of Something." His charted singles over the next few years included the songs "Lonesome 77203," "Happy Hour," and his version of Jim Croce's composition "Working at the Car Wash Blues," which was the title number of his sixth LP on Capitol, issued in the mid-1970s.

Booth's talents were recognized by the Academy of Country and Western Music in the mid-1970s with several nominations for Most Promising Male Vocalist. As the 1970s went by, he got the chance to perform before audiences much farther afield than North Hollywood as his concert work took him to all parts of the United States. He also was a guest on many network and syndicated TV programs from the early 1970s on.

BORCHERS, BOBBY: *Singer, guitarist, songwriter. Born Cincinnati, Ohio, June 19.*

In the annals of country music there is a "Singing Brakeman," "Singing Ranger," and even a "Singing Cop." Bobby Borchers fits the last description, although it wasn't a title he ever used in his act.

Bobby was born in Cincinnati and raised in other parts of southern Ohio and neighboring Kentucky, where he was exposed to a lot of country music played in the region. When he was twelve he got his first guitar, a Stella bought for ten dollars, and fashioned a makeshift strap from suspenders. Almost as soon as he mastered basic chords, he wrote his first song. In high school he continued to write, though most of the material he played with local groups came from the national hit charts.

Music was still a sideline when he was old enough to earn a living. Police work attracted him and by the late 1960s he was a member of the force in a Kentucky locale and playing country music in local clubs whenever he could get engagements for his spare time. As time went by, he yearned more and more for a music career and began to make contacts in the business.

One of his trips took him to Nashville in the early 1970s during the annual *Grand Ole Opry* Convention, where he met Kris Kristofferson. Borchers recalled, "He was hotter than a firecracker and I didn't know who he was. There I was, just a regular uncool person who comes to town." After cruising around convention events together, Kris became interested in Borchers' capabilities and after he listened to some of Bobby's compositions, suggested Borchers come to Nashville and try to make it as a writer. "If anybody else would have told me that, I would have thought they were handing me a line, but I took his word for it.

"I decided that I didn't want to be a hometown hero; I wanted to see if I could come to Nashville and make it with the big boys. I didn't want to wake up one day and ask myself if I could have made it if I tried—could I have made it if I'd gone to Nashville? Was I good enough?"

He moved to Nashville in 1971 and while he wrote songs, he made the rounds of Music Row firms—mainly with discouraging results. His "Jamestown Ferry" found its way to a rising new artist named Tanya Tucker, who turned it into a top-10 hit in 1972. After that, an increasing number of songs he wrote or co-wrote were recorded by such artists as Mickey Gilley, Barbi Benton, and Johnny Paycheck. Many of the compositions made their way onto hit lists. Among them were "Brass Buckles," "I Can't Keep My Hands Off of You," "Just Let Me Go to Texas When I Die," "Movie Magazine Stars in Her Eyes" (a chartmaker for Barbi Benton in September 1975), and the hugely successful "I'm the Only Hell My Mama Ever Raised" (co-written with M. Vickery and W. Kemp), a top singles hit for Johnny Paycheck in August 1977.

In 1976, Bobby signed with Playboy Records and during 1976–77 placed a series of singles on the charts, mostly of songs written by others: "They Don't

Make 'Em Like That Anymore," "Cheap Perfume and Candlelight," a national top-10 hit in July 1977, and "What a Way to Go," in the top 20 in the fall of that year. During the fall of 1977, Playboy released Bobby's debut LP, *Bobby Borchers.*

The next year, Borchers signed with Epic Records, resulting in such charted singles as "Sweet Fantasy," a top-20 hit in September 1978, and "Wishing I Had Listened to Your Song," moving upward on the lists in January 1979. Even as that took place, Bobby was represented in the top 10 by Tanya Tucker's version of "Texas When I Die." Later in 1979, he made the charts with the single "I Just Wanna Feel the Magic."

BOWERS, BRYAN: *Singer, guitarist. Born Virginia, August 18, 1940.*

The autoharp certainly isn't considered a virtuoso instrument by most people—unless someone like Bryan Bowers plays it. With his five-finger Bowers' picking style, he draws amazing melodic combinations from his carefully tuned autoharp, covering a range of material from Mozart to songs like "You Are My Sunshine," "My Bonnie Lies Over the Ocean," and "Will the Circle Be Unbroken." Not without reason, some reviewers have called him the world's best autoharpist.

With his broad shoulders and imposing height (6 feet, 4 inches), Bowers gives an appearance of a rugged individualist, but he is anything but immodest. As he told Art and Leota Coats for an article about him for *Frets* magazine (May 1979), "When people write [that he's the 'best'], I just want to ask them if they have ever listened to Mother Maybelle Carter, Pop Stoneman, Kilby Snow, or Mike Seeger. 'Best' is simply a matter of personal taste. My style of playing and technique are different and I can do a lot of things that other people can't or won't do, but there are people who can do things with the harp that I can't do. I think anyone who writes that I am the best should listen to some other good players, and then put that story back together with me in perspective."

Bowers grew up in Virginia and was exposed to some folk music, but didn't consider getting involved in it until he was in college. In high school his height earned him a place on the basketball team, and that, in turn, brought an athletic scholarship from Randolph–Macon College in Ashland, Virginia. Shortly after both of his parents died, he quit college—just three credits shy of earning his degree. "Almost by accident," he told the Coatses, "I picked up a guitar about that time. As I started picking around on it I began to feel better about myself and a lot of things." In fact, it banished suicidal thoughts from his mind. "Music saved my life!"

After fooling around with guitar, slide guitar, dulcimer, and mandocello, he was introduced to the autoharp in the late 1960s by a Virginia friend named Dr. Rollie Powell. He fell in love with it almost immediately. "The harp filled up the void that was in me. It felt spiritual, all-embracing." For the next few years, though he didn't give up the other instruments completely, he spent more and more time learning to play the autoharp, trying to master the art of tuning, the key to good autoharp performance.

In the early 1970s, he headed west and settled for a time in Seattle, Washington, singing with autoharp accompaniment in Seattle streets. After a year and a half, he loaded his instruments and other possessions into an old Chevy panel truck and drove back to the East Coast to try to work into the folk-club/coffee-house circuit. Unfortunately, while stopping to visit some friends in Pennsylvania, he unloaded his gear to repaint the truck. At that point, someone asked him to come down to jam with other friends in Washington, D.C., and while he was away a rainstorm ruined all his things.

Reduced to only the autoharp, he tried street singing in Washington, D.C., but citizens of the nation's capital proved to be close fisted with money. Things looked bleak, but he managed to get the owner of the Childe Harold Club in D.C. to let him play between sets of the scheduled artist for a little pay and some food. That kept him going for a while, and soon after he met the Dillards, who liked his work enough to take him along to a bluegrass concert where he got some additional exposure.

After that, more and more people became interested in his talents. The opportunities in the late 1970s to perform in folk clubs, on college campuses, and at major folk festivals increased. Among his festival credits were the Philadelphia Folk Festival, Culpepper (Virginia) Bluegrass/Folk Festival, and the Walnut Valley Festival in Winfield, Kansas. He also appeared as an opening act for both folk and rock artists, including a number of concerts with Merle and Doc Watson, in all parts of the United States. Whether appearing at the Bottom Line in New York or the Roxy in Los Angeles, before several hundred fans or in front of 15,000 people at a bluegrass festival, Bowers was able to create a rapport that had his entire audience singing along on songs like "Will the Circle Be Unbroken."

Despite his increasing number of adherents during the second half of the 1970s, it took almost to the end of the decade before he found his way onto records. One stumbling block was the lack of interest of large record companies in signing an autoharpist; the other was Bowers' perfectionist outlook. He preferred not to cut a record until he felt he could do one that met his personal standards. He finally signed with Chicago-based, folk-music oriented Flying Fish Records, which issued his debut LP, *The View from Home*, in early 1979. His second album was released by Flying Fish in the spring of 1980.

A major part of his success with the autoharp was the development of his special picking style. He described it to Art and Leota Coats in this way, "With the five-finger approach, I catch one string with the thumb, which would be the rhythm part, and play the high and low melodies and harmonies with the fingers." This was considerably different from the method favored by Mike Seeger and Mother Maybelle Carter, which, the Coatses note, "features primarily a back-and-forth strum with a melody note here and there."

BOYD, BILL: *Singer, guitarist, band leader (Cowboy Ramblers), disc jockey, emcee, actor, songwriter. Born Fannin County, Texas, September 29, 1910.*

An important figure in the "western" segment of country & western music, Bill Boyd sometimes suffered from a case of mistaken identity. He shared the same name as the famed cowboy film actor Hopalong Cassidy and, to add to the confusion, made a number of western films himself. However, if you added the descriptive "Cowboy Rambler" to his name, C&W fans immediately knew who was being referred to, though in truth his rambling never kept him away from his beloved home state of Texas very long.

Boyd had a legitimate cowboy background. Born and raised in ranching country, he learned to rope and ride at an early age on his father's stock farm and cattle ranch near Ladonia, Texas. As a boy, he often took part in family sings (he was one of thirteen children), initially accompanying himself on an old five-gallon paint drum; later his mother taught him the rudiments of guitar and banjo.

Bill performed for friends and at local functions in his teens, until he left for Dallas at nineteen to try to find work in the field. After a while, he joined a minstrel group called the Wolfe City Wanderers that got an audition on Station WFAA (from which nothing much resulted).

In 1930, however, Boyd got a job on another Dallas station, WRR, as a performer and sometime disc spinner. The combination proved fruitful, as he built up a sizable following and remained WRR's most popular artist and DJ for twenty-five years. After that, he switched to station KSKY, where his show was broadcast regularly for twelve more years.

While maintaining his radio work, Boyd became one of the country & western field's best-known band leaders, beginning in 1931 when he and associate Cliff Wilkins put together the Cowboy Ramblers band. He billed himself on his live radio show as Bill Boyd and His Cowboy Ramblers, and he had a hand in almost every aspect of the show: singing, leading the band, functioning as master of ceremonies, as well as producing the program and providing many of his own compositions. Among his output of songs were "Blues," "David's Blues," and "New Fort Worth Rag." Besides starring on radio, Bill and his band played for fairs and dances throughout the Southwest.

In 1934, Bill signed a recording contract with RCA Victor, which quickly resulted in the single "Ridin' on a Humpback Mule." The following year, he and his band turned out the most famous of the three hundred-plus recordings they made for RCA, the instrumental "Under the Double Eagle," a track still available in the 1970s on RCA's "Gold Standard" series. Among Boyd's releases from 1934 through the early 1950s on RCA and Bluebird labels were such songs as "Oklahoma Bound," "Homecoming Waltz," "Shame on You," "Don't Turn My Picture to the Wall," "Get Aboard That Southbound Train," "Old Fashioned Love," "New Spanish Two-Step," "The Train Song," "Southern Steel Guitar," "Drifting Texas Sand," "Lone Star Rag," "Pass the Turnip Greens," "Over the Waves Waltz," and "Jim's Waltz" (written by his brother Jim).

By the start of the 1940s, Boyd and his group were nationally known to country & western music fans from their recordings and personal appearances. Producers Releasing Corporation signed him in 1941 to star in a series of musical westerns: *Texas Manhunt, Raiders of the West, Rolling Down the Great Divide, Tumbleweed Trail, Prairie Pals,* and *The Sundown Trail.*

After he finished the sixth opus, however, America's entry into World War II caused PRC to cut back on its output and Boyd's contract was one of the casualties. Boyd then answered the call from the U.S. Treasury Department to help the war effort by performing in shows for the armed forces and in bond drives. He became part of the group of cowboy actors that was called the Western Minute Men. Besides Bill, the group was composed of Art Davis (Boyd's movie costar), Hoot Gibson, Ken Maynard, Tex Ritter, Johnny Mack Brown, and Ray Whitley. Boyd kept up that series of appearances during 1942 and 1943 before returning to his regular recording and band-leading operations for the rest of the 1940s.

He kept up a fairly active schedule of radio work coupled with stage shows throughout the 1950s. In the 1960s, he

started to taper off on his touring, restricting his in-person efforts to a scattering of concerts each year, a pattern he still held to in the early 1970s. In March 1969, he began a new disc jockey affiliation, signing to do an afternoon program on station KTER in Texas. The program continued on KTER into the 1970s, with the broadcast originating in a studio Boyd had built in his home.

BRAMLETT, BONNIE: *Singer, songwriter. Born Granite City, Illinois, early 1940s.*

With a musical background ranging from choir work to jazz and R&B, Bonnie Bramlett was well suited to be instrumental in bringing gospel rock to the fore at the end of the 1960s. For half a decade, she and then husband Delaney Bramlett inspired fervor and approval not only from a large segment of the music public but also from some of the biggest names in pop music. Although their reign as major stars ended in the mid-1970s, their work had considerable influence on future trends in both country and rock genres.

Born in Granite City, Illinois, and raised in the St. Louis area, Bonnie was first exposed to music through her family's church affiliation. "All the kids in church sang in the choir and I loved it. I did solos and my mother would get excited and encourage me. I never was bashful. Neither was my mother; she still calls me when she sees me on television."

In her mid-teens, she was an attractive, willowy blonde with a voice admirably suited to belting out R&B-type songs with rafter-shaking impact. She had, as she approached her high school years, become impressed with the blues and soul music she heard on the radio, and the idea of making a career of singing that kind of material began to appeal to her. She frequented blues clubs in the St. Louis area, listening to such talented black artists as Ike and Tina Turner and Albert King with the hope of getting to sing with some of them. "One night at a place called Teen Town I got up with Albert King's band and sang." Her ability impressed King and other members of the R&B community. "The Turners, Chuck Berry, Fontella

Bass—they were all really helpful to the younger ones like myself. They'd invite us over to sing and play."

For a time in the mid-1960s, she toured with a number of jazz groups, in addition to performing with local clubs. "After the Beatles made it, it was hard finding work as a rhythm and blues singer, so I started doing jazz. A lot of the guys in the bands didn't like me at first 'cause I'd show up with no charts [song arrangements] and they'd think I didn't know what I was doing. Until I started singing, that is." Among the jazz greats she worked with were Cannonball Adderley and Joe Zawinul, who later was the motivating force of the fusion group Weather Report.

For a time during those years, home base for Bonnie was Memphis, Tennessee, where she was much in demand as a backup vocalist for rock and soul groups during recording sessions. She supported many artists from Stax/Volt Records, and toured the country with the Ike and Tina Turner Revue as a white Ikette.

In the mid-1960s, a series of bookings in the Los Angeles area spurred her to move west. One night in 1967, when she was in a show at a club near the L.A. Airport called the Carolina Pines, she met a Southern-born country-rock musician named Delaney Bramlett. "I met Delaney seven days before we were married. He came over to see me and just never left."

Kindred musical spirits, the Bramletts embarked on a lengthy period of dues paying, organizing their own groups to play small clubs in the L.A. area, mainly in the San Fernando Valley. Rather than a fixed group of musicians, they depended on a loosely drawn pool. Bonnie noted, "That was how the concept of the Friends started. We'd go in the club where we had a gig and whoever came down would play." Word began to get around about their abilities and many well-known musicians sometimes dropped by to hear them play. On one occasion, they were engaged to perform at a private party and George Harrison of the Beatles came by and expressed his enthusiasm for their ability.

In 1968, the Bramletts signed with Stax Records, which issued their debut LP *Home*

that year. Not much promotion was given the album and the Bramletts moved to Elektra for one album that met a similar fate. But executives at Atco Records had been getting signals about their potential from people who had attended some of the Bramletts' club dates and bought their contract from Elektra. The success of the first Atco release, *Original Delaney and Bonnie*, proved the wisdom of their decision.

The caliber of musicians who joined the Bramlett band on concert tours helped cement their growing reputation. The first lead guitarist of the *Friends* turned out to be Dave Mason of Traffic rock group fame. When the English rock supergroup Blind Faith came to the United States for its debut tour (members included stars Eric Clapton on guitar and Ginger Baker on drums) in mid-1969, Delaney, Bonnie, and Friends shared the bill. Plans were made for the two groups to tour Europe in the fall, but Blind Faith broke up before then. The tour was altered so that Delaney and Bonnie headlined with Clapton as one of the Friends. For a time, European fans held Delaney and Bonnie responsible for Blind Faith's demise and the tour threatened to be a disaster. But as the series went on, the Bramletts and associates picked up steam and, after George Harrison joined them in England, the tour became a triumph. It also became the basis for the smash hit 1970 album, *Delaney & Bonnie & Friends on Tour*, one of the best-selling releases of the year.

The Bramletts added to their laurels near the end of 1969 when they made their debut with the original Plastic Ono Band in London on December 15, 1969, backing John Lennon and Yoko Ono.

In the early 1970s, the Bramletts ranked as major headliners at home and abroad, and toured to major cities all over the United States. Their repertoire ranged from new songs written by Bonnie, such as "Superstar" and "Never Ending Song of Love" to gospel-rock versions of Beatles songs to songs from blues, country, and R&B domains, including, for example, Woody Guthrie's "Goin' Down the Road Feelin' Bad." Their singles and albums regularly made the hit charts during those years. Among them were the LPs *To Bonnie from Delaney* (1970) and *Motel Shot* (1971) and the singles "Soul Shake" (1970), "Never Ending Song of Love" (1971), and "Move 'Em Out" (1972).

By 1972, the Bramletts were losing momentum, partly because of personal problems. They left Atco for Columbia, which issued their first LP on the label in March 1972. The collection made the charts, but was far less successful than earlier albums. Soon after, Bonnie and Delaney's marriage broke up and both pursued separate careers. Bonnie's debut solo LP on Columbia came out in July 1973, presenting a number of original compositions plus songs by several other writers. Neither that collection nor later albums seemed to catch fire with the music public.

In the mid- and late-1970s, Bonnie continued to keep active in the music field, doing some solo concerts as well as tours with other artists. She also was a session singer on a number of albums of those years. During the mid- and late-1970s she recorded several albums for Capricorn Records, *It's Time, Ladies Choice,* and *Memories.* At the start of the 1980s, she was affiliated with Muscle Shoals Sound Records and worked on a new LP scheduled for distribution by Capitol Records in 1982.

BRAMLETT, DELANEY: *Singer, guitarist, songwriter. Born Pontococ, Mississippi, circa 1940.*

Delaney Bramlett said it best himself in the early 1970s: "The kind of music that we're doin' ain't Nashville and it ain't Memphis. I think it's a country sort of gospel that folks've been doin' for a long time. It's the only music that I've ever really played." Although the Bramletts were no longer international stars by the mid-1970s, one could still hear some echoes of the music they helped pioneer in the recordings of artists like the Eagles, Jackson Browne, and Linda Ronstadt.

Delaney had been interested in music from his early years in rural Mississippi where he was exposed to both gospel and country influences. "I'll never forget that Christmas morning—I was eight—when I got up and found my mom had gotten me

a Playtime guitar. I just couldn't put it down all day.

"I kept workin' at it and I could play pretty well by the time I was in high school. Me and my brother John started in high school plays singing together. We kept right on singing in school, churches, anywhere there was a crowd."

In 1957, in his late teens, Delaney joined the U.S. Navy, where, stationed in Chicago, he played guitar in noncommissioned officers clubs. He played both country and rock, varying the emphasis to meet crowd interests. Invited to back up professional groups, he played with a number of touring rock or country artists, including the Everly Brothers.

In the early 1960s, after receiving his discharge, he moved to Los Angeles and did session work at various recording studios. He also worked in a series of bands on the country circuit, including groups that played the Saddle Club and the top-ranked Palomino Club. Still, as brother John noted, "Though he was with country bands, he was always playing a kind of rock style; he kept sneaking it in."

His inclination toward strongly gospel-and-country-flavored rock brought him to the attention of a group called the Shindogs, featured on the nationally telecast ABC-TV program *Shindig.* He joined the group, staying with them for several years. The next milestone came in 1967 when, working in a band playing at the Carolina Pines club near the Los Angeles Airport, he met Bonnie, who was part of the show. A week later they were married.

Soon after, the twosome began making plans for a new act. They started working in small clubs all over Los Angeles' San Fernando Valley, building up experience and a local following. They appeared regularly at a jazz-turned-rock club called the Brass Ring, and the people that came to hear them in the late 1960s included such stars as Jim Morrison of the Doors and Dave Mason of Traffic.

By 1969, after their first record effort, "Home" (on Stax Records), fell short, they began to have a more sophisticated sense of what they wanted to do musically. Their growing number of friends from the rock pantheon, which numbered not only Mason but Eric Clapton, George Harrison of the Beatles, and others, encouraged them to keep going. Mason, in fact, agreed to join their band as lead guitarist. When the English supergroup Blind Faith embarked on its first (and only) tour of the United States in mid-1969, Delaney & Bonnie were asked to be part of the show.

Delaney was surprised to find how much English rock giants like Clapton were interested in gospel country-type music. "When I first met Eric [Clapton], we got to talkin' an' y'all know it's funny. We're both into the same kind of music. We had almost the same exact record collection. We was both listenin' to the same kind of music."

By the fall of 1969, Delaney & Bonnie were getting ready for their first tour of Europe, initially intended to be another swing with Blind Faith. The band at the time included Mason on lead guitar, Delaney on rhythm guitar (and also lead vocals with Bonnie), Bobby Whitlock on organ, Jim Price on trumpet, Carl Radle on bass, and Jim Gordon on drums. That band, augmented overseas by Clapton and, for a series in England, with George Harrison, gained notoriety. The live tapes of some of the concerts provided tracks for the 1970 LP *Delaney & Bonnie & Friends on Tour*, which became a top seller. The LP was issued by Atlantic, to which the group had moved (after a brief stay with Elektra Records) in 1969.

With the success of the live album, Delaney & Bonnie ranked as one of the most respected new groups at the start of the 1970s. They followed with a series of hit LPs and singles (see entry for Bonnie) and were headliners in large auditoriums across the United States for several years. On some of those engagements, they joined forces with folk-blues artist John Hammond, Jr.

However, strains were growing in their marriage. Soon after their debut album on Columbia, *Delaney & Bonnie Together*, issued in May 1972, came out, they separated. For a time, Delaney went back to New York to work with John Hammond, Jr. Later he worked on some solo material, which

didn't achieve the same success as his collaboration with Bonnie. One result was the 1977 release on Prodigal Records, *Delaney Bramlett and Friends—Class Renuion*.

BRAND, OSCAR: *Singer, guitarist, songwriter, actor, author, emcee. Born Winnipeg, Canada, February 7, 1920.*

Best known in the music field, perhaps, for his series of "bawdy songs" recordings (which seem rather tame now), Oscar Brand's credits amount to a spectrum of careers. Besides his folksinging activities, he wrote many scripts for films and TV, authored several stage shows, and hosted a long-running radio program that helped introduce many important artists of the 1950s and 1960s.

He was born on a wheat farm in Canada, but moved with his family to Minneapolis, then to Chicago, and then to New York. He completed elementary school in Brooklyn and went on to graduate from that borough's Erasmus Hall High School in 1937. Because of the Depression and an interest in seeing more of the world, he worked his way across country as a farm hand the next few years, picking up more and more folk songs to play on the banjo that he carried with him.

He returned home and enrolled in Brooklyn College to work toward a B.A. with a major in abnormal psychology. World War II interrupted and he entered the Army. After his discharge in 1945, he decided to try to earn a living in music and toured as a singer with the *Herb Shriner Show*. But in late 1945, he gave that up and got a job with New York City's radio station WNYC as coordinator of folk music.

He also started his own program on WNYC called *Folksong Festival*, which remained a mainstay of Sunday evening radio for several decades. It provided a showcase for all types of folk music recordings and for live performances by everyone from Woody Guthrie and Pete Seeger to Bob Dylan. In the 1950s and 1960s, the show was rebroadcast overseas by the United States Information Service (USIS). In the mid-1960s, his government-sponsored show, *The World of Folk Music*, was broadcast every week over 1,880 stations.

As a performer, Brand appeared throughout the United States in almost every folk club, on many college campuses, and in many folk festivals, and during the 1960s, served as a member of the board of directors of the Newport Folk Festival. Besides doing concert work, he was a guest on many TV shows, ranging from *The Tonight Show* and *Today* to a number of early 1960s hootenannnies.

His TV efforts included scriptwriting and serving as musical director of a number of programs. In the early 1960s, he was musical director of NBC-TV's *Exploring Show*, which won the Peabody and Edison Awards for contributions to U.S. education. In 1966–67, he was both music director and head of the cast of NBC-TV's *The First Look*. In his original homeland, Canada, he also was active, performing as star and host on CBC-TV's weekly show *Let's Sing Out* from 1962 into the mid-1970s and, in the late 1960s, handling the same tasks on CTV-TV's weekly show *Brand New Scene*.

Among his TV output of scripts, narrations, and scores were contributions to "Invisible Journey," "The Farmer Comes to Town," Agnes de Mille's "The Gold Rush" on CBS-TV, Frederick Remington's "Bay at the Moon," and more than fifty scripts for the National Lutheran Council. He provided music, lyrics, and script material for several musicals, including the off-Broadway show *In White America* and the 1966 Broadway presentation, *A Joyful Noise*, which starred John Raitt. His writing credits include a number of books, such as *Singing Holidays*, published in 1957, and *The Ballad Mongers*, one of the basic histories of folk music in the United States. He also wrote forty-five movie scripts, some of which won him awards at the Venice and Edinburgh Festivals, as well as winning him Golden Reel, Valley Forge, and Scholastic film awards.

He made hundreds of recordings in a career that extended from the late 1940s into the 1970s. Most of those were of traditional folk songs or songs by other writers, but he also performed some of his own material. One of his earliest song hits was a toned-down version of a bawdy ballad titled "A Guy Is a Guy." Later, in the late 1950s and early 1960s, he specialized in singing such barrack-room numbers without any protective editing. His many albums were issued on a variety of labels, both major and minor. While most were recorded by him for the specific label, some were reissues.

His best known albums were the series of "bawdy" collections issued on the Audio Fi label from the late 1950s to the mid-1960s. These included *Bawdy Sea Chanties* (late 1950s), *Bawdy Songs and Backroom Ballads* (late 1950s), *Bawdy Western Songs* (2/60), *Bawdy Songs Go to College* (early 1960s), *Singa-Long Bawdy Songs* (10/62), and *Bawdy Hootenanny* (2/64), plus *Rollicking Sea Chanties* (5/62). He was represented on Elektra by such albums as *Wild Blue Yonder* (late 1950s), *Every Inch a Sailor* (2/60), *Out of the Blue* (5/60), *Boating Songs* (7/60), *Tell It to the Marines* (4/60), *Sports Car Songs* (10/60), *Up in the Air* (5/61), *Snow Job for Skiers* (1/63), *Songs Fore Golfers* (9/63), *Cough!* (10/63), *For Doctors Only* (10/63), and *Courting's a Pleasure*. On Folkways, he had such titles as *Election Songs of the U.S.* (2/61) and *Town Hall Concert*. His Tradition releases included *Laughing America, Pie in the Sky*, and *The Best of Oscar Brand*. Riverside Records issued a number of his albums, including *Give 'Em the Hook, Riddle Me This, Drinking Songs, Children's Concerts*, and *G.I.* Other albums included *Songs for Adults* on ABC (9/61), *Morality* on Impulse, *Songs for Fun* (with the Tarriers) on Decca (7/62), *Singing Holidays* on Caedmon, and *Brand X* on Roulette (early 1970s). One of his best LPs was *Oscar Brand and Jean Ritchie*, issued by the Archives of Folk and Jazz Music (3/67).

BRESH, TOM: *Singer, guitarist, songwriter. Born Chatsworth, California, 1948.*

Anyone who's been selected as a replacement for Roy Clark at one point in his career has to rank as an above-average artist. If Bresh hasn't quite achieved Clark's star status going into the 1980s, no one could say he wouldn't somewhere along the line.

Bresh, who grew up in California, entered show business almost as soon as he could walk. When only three years old, he could handle a country & western song well enough to take part in the musical shows at the Corriganville Movie Ranch in the desert near Barstow, California. While still a youngster, he also began doing feats of daring and was billed as "Hollywood's Youngest Stuntman." When he was old enough to start learning an instrument, he took up steel guitar for a time, but soon switched to acoustic. As he went along, continuing to perform in various country & western programs, he picked up additional pointers on guitar playing from country stars Tex Williams and Merle Travis.

In his teens in the early 1960s, he worked with a rock group called the Crescents. They made a number of recordings, one of which started to move up the charts, only to have its momentum checked by the onslaught of the Beatles and the "British Invasion."

In the mid-1960s, Tom decided to concentrate on the country field. A major opportunity came along when Roy Clark decided to leave a traveling show headed by Hank Penny. Bresh was signed on as Clark's replacement, a role he filled to everyone's satisfaction for years. After that, Penny retired and, for a while, Bresh became the show's headliner.

He next accepted a bid to operate a recording studio in Seattle, Washington, owned by Merrilee Rush. He also did some work in local clubs and recorded some of his own material, such as his early 1970s single "D. B. Cooper Where Are You?" (Kapp Records).

After that Bresh put together a new traveling country-and-western troupe, which he had to fold because of problems in lining up people he felt comfortable with musically. He moved back to Los Angeles and signed a new contract with MGM, one of the early results being the single "You're The Best Daddy in the World."

Not satisfied with his progress on MGM, he moved to a new association with Farr Records. His debut record on the label, "Homemade Love," became a top-10 country hit in mid-1976. He followed that

with still another major singles success, "Sad Country Love Songs," in the top 10 in late summer. Also on the charts by then was his LP *Homemade Love*. Those releases helped make him a familiar figure on the country circuit, as a guest on major TV shows, and as a headliner at clubs across the United States. Besides demonstrating singing skills, he also proved an excellent mimic whose impersonations included Howard Cosell and Charley Pride.

Before 1976 was over, Tom had received notice from most industry trade publications. In the *Cash Box* poll, he was voted the Top New Male Vocalist, Singles of 1976.

The time then seemed ripe for a move to a larger recording company and Bresh signed with ABC. He provided that label with a number of singles that made the charts, such as his compositions "Until I Met You" (on hit lists in the summer of 1977) and "First Encounter of a Close Kind," on lower-chart levels in late summer of 1978. Another chartmaking single in 1977 was "That Old Cold Shoulder." However, by the time Bresh was added to the ABC roster, the firm was having problems that eventually led to its sale to another record company. The situation tended to hamper promotion work on Bresh's releases and, while he had songs on hit lists, none reached the all-important (from a commercial standpoint) top rungs. Thus, by 1979, Bresh's tenure with ABC was ended.

BREWER & SHIPLEY: *Vocal and instrumental duo. Mike Brewer, born Oklahoma City, Oklahoma, 1944; Tom Shipley, born Mineral Ridge, Ohio, 1942.*

Mike Brewer and Tom Shipley, who individually cut their musical eyeteeth on the folk boom of the early 1960s, proved adept at surviving the collapse of that movement later in the decade. In fact, although they fled the big cities and retired to the "heartland" of the United States, they still managed to become major forces in pop music with their folk- and soft-rock efforts in the first half of that decade.

Brewer, born and raised in Oklahoma City, started playing guitar as a boy, with the full approval of his father, an artist who supported the family by working as a post-office supervisor. After high school, Mike Brewer set off to wander around the country working the then-thriving coffee house circuit. On occasion, his path crossed that of Tom Shipley, beginning an acquaintance that was to blossom into friendship later.

With the folk boom dying out, Mike moved to Los Angeles in 1966 to join a group whose members included a musician named Tom Mastin. Eventually Mastin and Brewer worked as a duo and won a recording contract from Columbia. But the arrangement didn't work out and the two went separate ways. After a brief period working with one of his brothers, Mike gave up performing for a while and signed a songwriting contract with Good Sam Music, an affiliate of A&M Records, in 1968.

As for Tom Shipley, he noted that his musical appetite was whetted as a child by his family's interest in "cowboy music." "I always liked that and the whole family used to sing, riding in the car or sitting around the house. Dad sang in the choir, my sister played piano, and I toyed with a trumpet. None of us had any formal training, but we had a lot of informal fun."

Tom did some singing in high school. As a student at Baldwin Wallace College in Ohio, he became interested in the folk music renaissance, learning acoustic guitar and polishing his singing. His early interest at school was ecology, but, he recalled, "I studied singing to help my head. Also I learned guitar and luckily at that time there were a lot of hootenannies where you could go and sing your song for people."

After graduating, he worked as house musician at a local club, performing both folk standards and occasionally some original material he was writing. Then he married, bought a trailer, and wandered first to California, then to Toronto with his wife, picking up whatever singing work he could find. "We went up to Toronto because I thought 'why not?' The folk scene was peaking everywhere and they were great. Of course it didn't stay like that be-cause nothing ever does, and when the clubs started to close, I came back to California."

The time was 1968 and one of the people he ran into was Mike. They found a mutual interest in the kind of material they were writing and decided to join forces. Mike noted, "I already had my publishing arrangement with Good Sam, but Tom didn't, so he linked with me in my deal and, after writing together for a year, we decided to form a total duo and perform our own material."

But they began to tire of the L.A. scene. "It was really a drag," Mike said. "It was really foreign to us to have to face it like a job, you know, just cranking out songs. We started to feel like a jukebox. And there wasn't anything personal happening with anyone. It wasn't fun. It wasn't making sense. It had to be fun. So . . . we split."

Eventually, the duo plus their families settled on a small farm in Missouri near Kansas City. Before they got there, though, Tom lived in a tent on a Hopi Indian reservation for a time, an experience which eventually led to such songs as "Too Soon Tomorrow" and "Song from Platte River."

From their Missouri retreat, the duo sallied forth at the end of 1969 and the start of the 1970s to perform in clubs throughout the neighboring states. At the same time, A&M, without their knowing it, issued an album of their material called *Down in L.A.* When they found out that the LP was made of old demo tapes for Good Sam that didn't show them at their best, they were far from happy.

But it did help bring their skills to the attention of some fans and indicated there was an audience out there for their songs. Stan Plesser of Good Karma Productions offered to manage their career. The duo accepted and soon had a recording contract with Kama Sutra Records. In early 1970, they went to San Francisco to work on their first album for that label, with Nick Gravenites as producer. The session musicians for the resulting LP, entitled *Weeds,* included violinist Richard Greene, guitarist Mike Bloomfield, and Nicky Hopkins on keyboard.

Weeds wasn't a blockbuster, but it did do moderately well for what Brewer & Shipley considered their first release. The group supported the LP with a series of engagements in major cities, including shows at the Bitter End in New York and the Troubadour in Los Angeles. Their next LP, *Tarkio,* came out in early 1971 and won highly favorable reviews. The single "One Toke Over the Line" quickly became one of the most-played new releases on radio. It moved into the top 10 and helped make *Tarkio* a strong entry on the album charts. The team now was one of the major acts in pop music and headlined concerts and festivals all over the United States. Brewer & Shipley also performed on a number of major network TV shows.

In late 1971, their third LP on Kama Sutra, *Shake Off the Demon,* coproduced by Brewer and Shipley, came out. It appeared on bestseller lists in early 1972, but did not approach the success of *Tarkio.* Their fourth and final album on Kama Sutra, also self-produced, was *Rural Space,* which came out in 1973 and appeared on hit lists for some weeks. However, its reception was even less strong than the previous one.

Figuring that a label change might help bring new momentum, the team left Kama Sutra and signed with Capitol. The debut on that label, an untitled LP just bearing the number *ST-11261,* came out in the mid-1970s. Among its contents were such new songs as "Look Up, Look Out," "Eco-Catastrophic Blues," the country-gospel "Fair Play," and folk-rock "How Are You?" It ranked with their best efforts to that point, but perhaps because of changes in the taste of their audience or problems with promotion, it made little headway in the marketplace.

BRITT, ELTON: *Singer, guitarist. Born Marshall, Arkansas, July 7, 1917; died McConnellsburg, Pennsylvania, June 23, 1972.*

One of the top stars of the country & western field during the 1940s and 1950s, Elton Britt (real name: James Britt Baker) literally sprang up from behind the plow to stardom. During World War II, his reputation was such that President Franklin D. Roosevelt sent Elton a personal invitation to perform at the White House.

Elton's half Cherokee Indian–half Irish background was symbolic of a country musical heritage. Though born in Arkansas, he was brought up in the Osage Hills of Oklahoma, where family sings were a tradition. His father was one of the top old-time fiddlers of Oklahoma and Arkansas. When Elton was still grade school age, his father bought him a five-dollar guitar from Sears Roebuck and taught him three chords. Elton continued to develop his singing and playing ability after that by listening to country & western records. Before he was in his teens, he occasionally entertained at local parties or dances.

In the early summer of 1932, some talent scouts came through the region looking for a real country boy who could sing and yodel. They were directed to Elton and found the fourteen-year-old plowing. They listened to him sing and promptly signed him to a year's contract with station KMPC in Los Angeles. Elton was rushed to California and in a few days was singing on his first radio program. Before the year was up, Elton had created quite a stir among local country & western fans and was soon featured on several network radio shows.

His following continued to grow, resulting in a recording contract with RCA Victor in 1937, where he turned out 672 single records and fifty-six albums in a relationship that lasted twenty-two years. In the 1960s he also recorded for several other labels, including Decca, ABC-Paramount, and Ampar.

During World War II, Elton became one of the nation's most popular recording artists, turning out a number of million-selling records: "There's a Star Spangled Banner Waving Somewhere" sold more than 4 million copies through the 1960s. His other top-10 hits included "Chime Bells" in 1948, "Candy Kisses" in 1949, and, with Rosalie Allen, "Quicksilver" in 1950. Some of his other successful RCA records were "Detour," "Someday," "Blue Texas Moonlight," "I'd Trade All of My Tomorrows," "I Hung My Head and Cried," "Roses Have Thorns," "Born to

Lose," "Cowboy Country," "Roses of Yesterday," "It Is No Secret," and "Oklahoma Hills Where I Was Born." His duets with Rosalie Allen included such songs as "Soft Lips", "Game of Broken Hearts," "Tennessee Yodel Polka," "Tell Her You Love Her," and "Cotton Candy and a Toy Balloon."

In 1948, Elton signed with Columbia Pictures for several films. His first one, in 1949, was *Laramie*. Later he also starred in such movies as *The Prodigal Son* for Universal International. During the 1950s and 1960s, Elton appeared on many network shows, including the *Grand Ole Opry*, WWVA *Wheeling Jamboree*, and the *George Hamilton IV* TV show. His LPs available in the 1960s included an RCA Victor album, *Yodel Songs*, and ABC-Paramount's *Wandering Cowboy, Beyond the Sunset*, and *I Heard a Cowboy Praying*. In 1968 he hit with the single "The Jimmie Rodgers Blues," released in April, the fortieth anniversary of Peer-Southern International Organization, publisher of Rodgers' songs.

BROMBERG, DAVID: *Singer, guitarist, pianist, banjoist, mandolinist, fiddle player, flutist, songwriter, record producer. Born Philadelphia, Pennsylvania, September 19, 1945.*

Said David Bromberg in the mid-1970s, "I figure that I'll get exactly as successful as I'm supposed to, no more, no less. I'm not going to fight it and I'm not going to grovel for it. I'm not going to act surly in order to preserve my anonymity or folklike status, and I won't eat dirt so that somebody will bill me in some special concert. I don't believe in that. The only time that I do get surly is when someone tells me how to do my music. That's *all* I've got. It's the sum total. I'm not married; I've got no kids; I spend my life on the road and I've no hobbies beyond playing guitar, fiddle, and mandolin. There's nothing else in my life, so don't mess with it." That single-mindedness helped make Bromberg one of the most respected session musicians in the country. It also helped bring him the respect of a small but loyal following for his performing efforts.

Born in Philadelphia but raised mainly in New York, Bromberg did not take up the guitar until he was bedridden with a bout of the measles when he was thirteen. Once he began, he took to the instrument with a passion, teaching himself by listening to records by people like Pete Seeger, the Weavers, Josh White, Django Reinhardt, and Big Bill Broonzy. He particularly recalls the album *Josh White Comes Visiting*, on which Big Bill Broonzy took part, as a major inspiration.

He continued to add to his instrumental repertoire while attending high school. After graduating he entered Columbia University to take courses in harmony and music theory, intending to become a musicologist. However, he found the musical environment in Greenwich Village too attractive. He started performing occasionally in small clubs and coffee houses and soon forsook college to work at his craft full time.

His first engagement in the mid-1960s was with Jerry Jeff Walker, of "Mr. Bojangles" fame, with whom he appeared for several years. He backed many other artists during those years, including Rusty Evans, Fred Neil, Screamin' Tony McKay, Tad Tuesdale, and Richie Havens. He told Michael Brooks of *Guitar Player* (March 1973), "The first time I was in the studios was either with Screamin' Tony McKay or Rusty Evans. I didn't get paid for it as it was just going in for the thrill of being able to record. And that's where I found out that studio situations are tricky and that recording is not always the same thing as playing."

He picked up session technique rapidly, though, and became one of the most sought-after studio musicians in the city. In the late 1960s and the 1970s, he supported artists from all segments of the pop music field, including albums with Bob Dylan, Jerry Neff, Tom Paxton, Carly Simon, Patrick Sky, Mississippi John Hurt, the Reverend Gary Davis, Ringo Starr, Chubby Checker, John Prine, Paul Siebel, John Denver, and many others. Through the mid-1970s, he participated in over eighty albums. He also tried his hand at producing during those years, including John Hartford's Warner Bros. release, *Aereo-Plain.*

One of his first road engagements in the late 1960s was as backing guitarist for a group called the Phoenix Singers. For a while after that, he played electric guitar with the Mojo Four during another concert swing.

At the start of the 1970s, Bromberg finally decided it was time to move to center stage. He had a chance to showcase his solo ability at the Isle of Wight pop festival in England and won resounding cheers from the massive audience. Columbia Records signed him soon after. His initial LP, *David Bromberg,* came out the following year, followed by *Demon in Disguise, Wanted Dead or Alive,* and, in mid-1975, *Midnight on the Water.*

The album contained some original compositions as well as his versions of a variety of music from traditional folk songs to jazz blues and rock-oriented material. His wide range of stylings was noted in the early 1970s by John S. Wilson, *The New York Times* jazz critic, who wrote, "David Bromberg fits no pigeon-holes. He is part of everything contemporarily musical. He is a product of blues, country, jazz, folk and classical music. . . . From his early success as a guitar virtuoso, Mr. Bromberg has developed into a brilliant entertainer."

Success had not occurred overnight, as Bromberg stressed to Michael Brooks. It came through "trial and error, because guitar playing doesn't come easy to me at all. Anything I do, I have to really work on. That doesn't mean that every solo I have is pat or anything, because I try to stay away from pat solos, as they're boring. But any amount of technique I have is really the result of a lot of hard work. Some people are just disturbingly brilliant on the guitar without much work, but with me, I have to practice and practice, just sitting down and getting locked into it."

After the mid-1970s, David parted company with Columbia and signed with San Francisco-based Fantasy Records. (Columbia issued the retrospective LP *Best of David Bromberg: Out of the Blues.*) In the late 1970s, Bromberg's releases on Fantasy included *Reckless Abandon, Bandit in a Bathing Suit,* and *How Late'll You Play 'Til?*

During the 1970s, Bromberg formed his own regular backing group, which he dubbed "The World's First Folk Orchestra." He noted, "The band just crept up on me. I started out with just a bass player. Wherever we played musicians I'd met on the road would come and sit in. Sometimes there would be ten musicians on the stage. It was very inspiring. I loved it! But then as we went along I began to miss certain guys. And by then I was making enough to afford to pay whoever I wanted to play with me." The band roster at the end of the 1970s comprised: Dick Fegy (fiddle, mandolin, guitars, banjo, string synthesizer), born Hartford, Connecticut, May 8, 1950; John Firmin (saxophone, clarinet, flute, percussion), born Anchorage, Alaska, April 20, 1947; George Kindler (fiddle, mandolin), born Washington, D.C., February 6, 1943; Curt Linberg (trombone), born St. Louis, Missouri, November 3, 1940; Lance Dickerson (drums), born Detroit, Michigan, October 15, 1948; Dan Counts (bass), born Roanoke, Virginia.

BROONZY, BIG BILL: *Singer, guitarist, fiddler. Born Scott, Mississippi, June 26, 1898 *; died Chicago, Illinois, August 14, 1958.*

Big Bill Broonzy was one of the greatest country blues performers of all time. As John Swenson of *Rolling Stone* noted, "Broonzy is the key transitional figure between the delta style of Robert Johnson and the electric Chicago blues of Muddy Waters." Sadly, he received little of that recognition during most of his lifetime. In fact, he was famous in Europe before more than a handful of Americans knew his name. Like so many folk-blues greats, Bill led a hand-to-mouth existence until his final years, though he managed to maintain his good nature and zest for living to the end of his days.

As one of a family of seventeen children, he knew hard work from his earliest years. His family wandered between Mississippi and Arkansas during the first fif-

---

* *Broonzy himself gave the year as 1893; after his death his twin sister produced a birth certificate giving it as 1898, the currently accepted year.*

teen or sixteen years of his life. In 1915, he farmed on a sharecropping basis, but gave it up in 1916 when drought wiped out his crops. During those years he picked up many songs, from spirituals to blues numbers, and, at ten, was inspired to learn some instruments. He built himself a fiddle from a cigar box and a guitar out of a goods box and began to teach himself some accompaniments for his vocalizing. After a while he was accomplished enough to play with a friend at picnics. Those informal dates included "two-stages"—picnics where the whites danced on one side of the stage and the blacks on the other.

During World War I he enlisted in the Army and went overseas in 1917. He returned home in 1919 and went to Chicago, where he got a job with the Pullman Company and perfected his guitar playing with veteran musician Papa Charlie Jackson.

The pattern of his life in the Windy City typified his life in general. He worked at various jobs to earn a living and gained his main enjoyment, and a little extra money, from part-time jobs in music. For much of the 1920s, he entertained at Saturday night "house rent" parties. One of his first original compositions of those years was a guitar solo called "Saturday Night Rub." He wrote fairly steadily afterwards, completing more than 350 compositions before his death. Among the many musicians he performed with in Chicago during the early phases of his career were Sleepy John Estes, Shorty Jackson, Blind Lemon Jefferson, Blind Blake, Lonnie Johnson, Shorty George, Jim Jackson, and Barbecue Bob.

In 1923, he made his first two records of his own material, "Big Bill Blues" and "House Rent Stomp." A friend wangled away the $100 he made on the records. He managed to hold on to some of the money he got for later efforts of the 1920s, such as "Date with an Angel Blues," "The Walking Blues," "Big Bill Blues No. 2," "House Rent Stomp No. 2," "Bull Cow Blues," "Milk Cow Blues," "Serve It to Me Right Blues," and "Mama Let's Cuddle Some More."

In the 1930s he found increasing work in Chicago nightclubs and made a number of records with various other bluesplayers on Champion Records. In 1932, he was in New York with one of several bands he organized and made a number of recordings on such labels as Vocalion, Oriole, and Melotone, including "Too Too Train Blues," "Worryin' You Off My Mind," "Shelby County Blues," and "Mistreatin' Mama Blues." Soon he was back in Chicago, where his old routine resumed. He made many more commercial recordings and worked as a performer fairly steadily, but got little money for those activities. To survive, he had to keep working at various menial jobs. His reputation was growing with folk fans, though, and in 1939, he was one of the stars of the "Spirituals to Swing Concert" at New York's Carnegie Hall.

Although the enthusiasm of folk fans for his talents brought opportunities for engagements in nonsegregated clubs and college concerts across the United States in the 1940s, the folk audience still was too small to allow him the luxury of concentrating on music. During the 1940s, he supported himself mainly by working as a cook, porter, molder, piano mover, and a half dozen other "trades." As the 1950s began, he didn't seem to be getting anywhere and, in 1950, considered giving up performing. But he had become part of a group formed by Chicago folk artist Win Stracke called I Come for to Sing (whose other founders were Studs Terkel and William Lane) that began to get a growing number of engagements thanks to the beginnings of the postwar folk boom. As demonstrated in the group's debut performance, sponsored by the Renaissance Society of the University of Chicago, its goal was to present a panorama of all types of American folk music. The group was welcomed by enthusiastic crowds on major college campuses across the United States.

This exposure helped bring Bill an offer to tour Europe in 1951. It was a triumphal concert series, marked by standing ovations and critical praise. Europeans were amazed to find that Bill was virtually unknown in the United States, but when he got home that began to change. He was featured on dates with many established folk artists, from Pete Seeger to his old friends Brownie McGhee and Sonny Terry, and he started to receive invitations to guest on radio and TV shows. He extended his overseas tours to Africa, South America, and the Pacific region, and kept on making new recordings. The sales of his available catalog began picking up. From 1953 on, his financial position improved to where he could live quite well on his music earnings. Unfortunately, by 1958, he was dying of cancer, finally passing away on August 14.

Bill had told the story of his life to Belgian writer Yannick Bruynoghe back in 1954, and the material was published in a book, *Big Bill Blues: Big Bill Broonzy's Story as told to Yannick Bruynoghe* (1955). An updated revision later came out in paperback (Oak Publications, New York, 1964).

Fortunately, his legacy remains in recorded form. By the late 1950s, his album catalog had begun to increase sharply with the release of such Folkways LPs as *Big Bill Broonzy Sings Country Blues*, *Big Bill Broonzy's Story*, and a 1959 blues album featuring Bill, Sonny Terry and Brownie McGhee. Two massive collections came out posthumously on Verve in October 1961, a five-record set called *Big Bill Broonzy's Story* and a three-disc set, *Last Session*. More releases came out in the next few years. Folkways issued *Big Bill Broonzy Sings* in May 1962 and Mercury issued a *Memorial* album in October 1963 and another titled *Remember Big Bill* in August 1964. Releases on other labels in the mid-1960s included *Big Bill Broonzy* on Scepter, *Big Bill Broonzy with Washboard Sam* on Chess, and *Big Bill Broonzy* on the Archives of Folk Music.

Continued recognition of Bill's importance as a performer and songwriter was indicated by the availability of his albums for decades after his death. At the start of the 1980s, all of his Folkways LPs remained in print. Some of his 1930s and 1940s recordings also were available in current catalog albums of other companies, such as *Big Bill Broonzy* on Everest Records;

Do That Guitar Rag and *Young Bill Broonzy* on Yazoo; *1932–42* on Biograph; and *Feelin' Low Down* and *Lonesome Road Blues* on Crescendo.

BROTHERS FOUR, THE: *Vocal group. Bob Flick, born Seattle, Washington; Michael Kirkland, born Everett, Washington; John Paine, born Wenatchee, Washington; Richard Foley, born Seattle, Washington.*

One of the most successful folk-pop groups of the 1960s, The Brothers Four played almost every college campus across the United States. They were naturally at home in this environment since their group name does not refer to direct kinship but to the fact that they met as fraternity brothers.

All four members of the group were born in the state of Washington between 1939 and 1940. They attended elementary and high schools in different sections of the state and then went on to the University of Washington at Seattle. Their choice of majors was varied, Bob opting for radio and TV production, Mike for pre-med, Dick for electrical engineering, and John for political science.

Their meeting resulted from their joining the same fraternity. As Mike reported in a Columbia Records release, "The guys at the fraternity house did a lot of singing, usually in a gang—no really worked-out arrangements. We decided to get together a small group, with maybe a little instrumental backing, just for fun. By Christmas time, we were performing some place or other every weekend." For their first professional date at Seattle's Colony Club in 1958, they received five dollars each.

In 1959, the group prepared a tape of some of their folk renditions and sent it to Columbia Records in New York. Company executives enthused over the demonstration and signed them in July 1959. A few weeks later, Columbia released the record *Greenfields*, which became one of the major national hits of the year and is still a standard. Later in the year, similar success was achieved by the group's first LP, also called *Greenfields*, produced by Bob Morgan.

In the 1960s, the Brothers became one of

the top national singing groups. In the 1961–62 season, their schedule included a ninety-day personal appearance tour of one hundred colleges. In 1962–63, their college tour ranged over two hundred campuses. In April of 1962, they had a wild welcome from crowds of admirers during their first tour of Japan.

One of their major hits of the early 1960s was *Green Leaves of Summer*. They were invited to sing it as part of the 1961 Academy Awards presentations, on network TV. Their TV appearances during the 1960s included most major network shows, including *Mitch Miller's Sing Along, Today, Bell Telephone Hour, The Pat Boone Chevy Showroom* and *Bob Newhart*. They were also featured a number of times over the years on *The Ed Sullivan Show*. Their agenda included nationwide concert and nightclub work. In New York, they were headlined several times at Basin Street East.

Their LP output for Columbia included *Brothers Four, Rally 'Round* (1960); *Brothers Four On/Off Campus, Roamin', Song Book* (1961); *Greatest Hits, In Person* (1962); *Cross Country Concert, Big Folk Hits, Brothers Four Sing of Our Times, More Big Folk Hits* (1964), *Honey Wind Blows; Try to Remember* (1965); *Beatles Songbook* (1966); *New World's Record* (1967). In the early 1970s, they were represented by the LP *1970* on Fantasy Records and *Great Songs of Our Times* on the Harmony label.

BROWN, JIM ED: *Singer, songwriter. Born Sparkman, Arkansas, April 1, 1934.*

When one of country fans' favorite singing groups, The Browns, broke up in 1967, it was feared the disbandment would leave a gaping hole in country ranks. However, in a short time, Jim Ed Brown showed he could do as well or better as a soloist than in the days he worked with his two talented sisters. Then, after close to a decade as a solo headliner, he added new luster to his career by teaming with Helen Cornelius in one of country music's most accomplished duos.

As a boy, Jim Ed was aware of country music from his early years, when listening to *Grand Ole Opry* broadcasts on Saturday

nights was a family ritual. Jim and his older sister Maxine sometimes sang along with artists like Roy Acuff or Ernest Tubb and often daydreamed about holding the spotlight themselves. They formed a duo while in junior high school and began to sing at local events, school functions, and square dances. Later, they sang regularly on station KCLA in Pine Bluff, Arkansas. Still it wasn't certain that Jim would make show business his main interest in life, although his sister Maxine was enthusiastic about that prospect. Jim Ed worked regularly in his father's sawmill and thought seriously about taking over its operation later on.

That consideration prompted Jim to enroll as a forestry major at Arkansas A&M, but after a year, he decided that music interested him more and moved to Arkansas State. When he and Maxine won first place in a talent show on Little Rock's station KLRA in 1953, they became regular members on the station's *Barnyard Frolic* program. Soon after, the twosome got the chance to record for Abbott Records, owned by Fabor Robinson, and turned out several excellent sides, including "Draggin' Main Street" and "Looking Back to See." The latter, one of their own compositions, was recorded in a session in which the backing group included Jim Reeves (then on the Abbott label) on rhythm guitar and Floyd Cramer on piano.

They expanded their following with a highly successful guest appearance on the *Louisiana Hayride* show in Shreveport. In 1955, after younger sister Bonnie joined to complete The Browns trio, they became featured artists on Red Foley's *Ozark Jamboree* out of Springfield, Missouri. That same year Jim Reeves, who had moved to RCA, brought them to the attention of RCA executives Steve Sholes and Chet Atkins, who soon signed the Browns for the label. Over a quarter century later, Jim Ed still was an RCA recording star.

This steadily brightening outlook slowed down for a time when Jim Ed was drafted into the Army. Another sister, Norma, filled in while he was away. Almost as soon as he returned, the tempo picked up. The trio recorded a song called

"The Three Bells" that became one of the top country hits of 1959 and also crossed over into the pop charts. The single, which sold over a million copies, made the group nationally known. They consolidated their new-found star status with a series of hit recordings in the early 1960s. During those years, they became familiar to both concert-goers and TV viewers through constant touring and guest appearances. Among the network programs on which they were featured were *The Ed Sullivan Show* and Dick Clark's *American Bandstand.*

From 1960 to 1963, when not on tour, the trio tended to their business in the supper club and catering service in Pine Bluff, Arkansas, when they became regular cast members on the *Grand Ole Opry.* The amount of touring they did was reduced, but Bonnie and Maxine wanted to spend still more time with their families and left the act in 1967.

Jim Ed set about developing his solo activities. From the start he showed he commanded a strong following in his own right. His initial releases on RCA in 1967 included "I Heard from a Memory" and the major hit "Regular on My Mind." Later on, he added such other 1960s best-sellers as "Pop-A-Top" and "The Enemy." He accepted a long engagement at the Sahara Tahoe's Juniper Lounge in Lake Tahoe, Nevada, in 1968, and from the late 1960s through the 1970s, Jim Ed remained a major headliner on the country music circuit.

His name rarely was off the singles or album charts for very long during the first half of the 1970s. His credits included the late 1970 top-10 success "Morning," which he reprised a few years later with the chart-making "Evening." Some of his other charted singles from 1970 through mid-1976 were "Sometime Sunshine" and "It's That Time of Night" in 1974; "Don Junior" and "Fine Time to Get the Blues" in 1975; and "Another Morning" in 1976. His album releases included, on RCA, *Just for You* (8/70), *Morning* (3/71), *Angel's Sunday* (7/71), and *She's Leavin'* (12/71) and on Camden, *Gentle on My Mind* (8/71).

In 1976, he started singing with Helen Cornelius, and one of their initial collab-

orations, "I Don't Want to Have to Marry You" rose to the top of the charts in late 1976 after they earlier had reached top-charts levels with the single "Born Believer." They placed several songs on the charts, including "If It Ain't Love by Now," a top seller for many months in the fall. In 1978, they scored a top-10 hit with "If the World Ran Out of Love Tonight" in the fall and came out with their version of Neil Diamond's "You Don't Bring Me Flowers," which rose to top-chart levels in early 1979. In May 1979, their single "Lying in Love with You" soared to number one on the national country lists and in the fall they had another hit with "Fools."

Jim Ed and Helen were featured on many major radio and TV shows in the late 1970s, from the *Opry* to *Hee Haw, Pop Goes the Country* and Dolly Parton's *Dolly.* In addition, they were hosts of their own syndicated TV program, *Nashville on the Road.* Several times in the late 1970s they were among the five finalists in CMA voting for Vocal Duo of the Year.

Brown wound up 1979 with "You're the Part of Me" on the charts. The song remained on them into early 1980. During 1980, he teamed with Helen Cornelius on such charted singles as "Morning Comes Too Early" and "The Bedroom." (By 1981, the duet had broken up.)

BROWNE, JACKSON: *Singer, pianist, guitarist, songwriter. Born Heidelberg, Germany, October 9, 1948.*

It might be said that Jackson Browne was to the 1970s what Bob Dylan was to the 1960s, not that their styles or songwriting approach were alike. But if Dylan was the premiere male solo folk-rock artist of the 1960s, Browne certainly could lay claim to that status for the next decade.

Browne, born in Germany, moved to Los Angeles with his family when he was three. He studied several instruments at an early age and was a proficient pianist and guitarist by his late teens. By then he also had demonstrated a budding talent for songwriting. In 1967, he went to New York City, where he worked at a number of local clubs through 1968, picking up experience but not making much headway in furthering his career.

He headed back to the West Coast in the late 1960s, where his reputation began to rise with his peers because of his songwriting skills. He also picked up some jobs as a sideman and session pianist in Los Angeles. He became friends with many other struggling young performers blending folk and country elements with rock, including Linda Ronstadt, J.D. Souther, and future Eagles' mainstay Glenn Frey.

In fact, for a while, Frey and Souther joined Jackson in his frugal sixty-dollars-a-month apartment in L.A.'s Echo Park district while all of them waited for the big break. Frey and Browne worked on song material together. One creation, "Take It Easy," was to prove highly important later on for the Eagles. Browne's version of the song was included in his For Everyman album. Browne began to make progress as a songwriter as artists such as Tom Rush, Linda Ronstadt, Johnny Rivers, The Byrds, and Brewer & Shipley recorded his material.

During that period, he made several attempts to make his way as a solo artist, but without notable success. However, in 1971, he finally struck paydirt when David Geffen signed him for Geffen's new label, Asylum Records. His debut LP, *Jackson Browne*, came out in October 1971 and gradually started getting considerable airplay across the country, particularly on FM stations. It made the charts in early 1972 and stayed on them for months, helping to spawn two hit singles, "Doctor My Eyes" and "Rock Me on the Water." Browne backed it up with a steady round of concerts that included tours with J.D. Souther and the Eagles in the fall. The Eagles had been Linda Ronstadt's backup band in the early 1970s, but finally went out independently after Browne assured Geffen of the group's potential. Their hit single in 1972 of Frey/Browne's "Take It Easy" propelled the Eagles to national prominence.

After 1972, Jackson never looked back. Though his album output was relatively sparse in the 1970s, every one contained a number of folk-rock gems, most of them completely written by him. Those songs plus other originals were often covered or introduced by other artists, among them Bonnie Raitt, Linda Ronstadt, Joan Baez, Ian Matthews, Gregg Allman, and Warren Zevon. In his concert tours, Browne surrounded himself with excellent musicians, including noteworthy talents like fiddler/pedal-steel player/guitarist David Lindley and lead guitarist Waddy Wachtel.

His second LP, *For Everyman,* came out on Asylum in the fall of 1973; the single "Red Neck Friend" made the charts. The album itself was on bestseller lists well into 1974. In the fall of 1974, he was represented by his third album, still one of his finest, *Late for the Sky,* which remained in upper-chart levels into 1975.

Though Browne continued an intensive concert schedule, it was close to two years before he completed another LP. (Unlike other "stars," Browne never disdained playing smaller venues and much of his concert work was on the college concert circuit with ticket prices set within a typical student's budget.) By the time the collection came out in late 1976, considerable anticipation had been built up among his now sizable following. Called *The Pretender,* the LP rose to the top five on the charts in December, having earlier earned a gold record award from the R.I.A.A. on November 15, 1976. His next release, *Running on Empty,* found even more favor with the public. It turned up on the charts almost as soon as it was issued in late 1977 and stayed on them throughout 1978 and part of 1979, bringing a platinum record award from the R.I.A.A.

During the 1970s, Browne remained a strong advocate of protecting the environment and saving endangered species, often giving fund-raising concerts for causes he believed in. At the end of the 1970s, he joined forces with Graham Nash in urging a stop to the proliferation of nuclear power. They helped assemble a number of concerts in 1979 both to express their opposition to and collect money to fight against the nuclear field. They were joined in 1979 by many rock and folk-rock artists in a series of concerts in New York's

Madison Square Garden that provided material for the two-record *No Nukes* live concert album.

BROWNS, THE: *Vocal trio. Maxine, born Sampti, Louisiana, April 27, 1932; Jim Edward, born Sparkman, Arkansas, April 1, 1934; Bonnie, born Sparkman, Arkansas, July 31, 1937.*

It was the fall of 1967 in Nashville and the annual WSM-Country Music Association disc jockey convention was in full swing. The Browns had just finished performing their spot on the *Grand Ole Opry* to a rousing ovation. Moments later the audience was stunned by the announcement that the group was breaking up. Bonnie, in tears, announced that after thirteen years with the family trio, she was retiring to spend all her time with her growing family. Maxine too, she said, had decided to follow the same route.

So ended the saga of one of the stellar country groups of the 1950s and 1960s, though fortunately not the Brown heritage, for Jim Ed went on to even greater fame as a solo performer. But the Browns left a valuable collection of singles and albums of their many hits, many of which remained prized possessions of their fans years afterwards.

The Browns' story began in Arkansas where Ella Maxine, Jim Ed, and Bonnie grew up on a 160-acre farm near Sparkman. All pitched in to help with the chores when they were young, and Jim Ed also spent a good many hours over the year helping his father run the family sawmill. Listening to country shows on the radio, particularly the Saturday night *Grand Ole Opry* show, was a favorite pastime that gave the Brown children a desire to sing and perform. Jim Ed and Maxine formed a duo, appearing in school shows and at local functions and square dances. In 1953, he and Maxine won a talent contest sponsored by station KLRA in Little Rock and joined the *Barnyard Frolic* show as regulars. Thoughts of running sawmills faded away for Jim Ed.

The duo had added considerable performing experience on local country stage shows and more prestigious broadcasts like the KWKH (Shreveport) *Louisiana Hayride* by the time sister Bonnie joined them in 1955. As a duo, Jim Ed and Maxine also had recorded a number of songs on Abbott Records, including their own composition "Looking Back to See." Once Bonnie completed the vocal blend, the Browns auditioned and won regular cast status on Red Foley's *Ozark Jamboree* in Springfield, Missouri. The same year friend Jim Reeves helped them get a contract with RCA Victor.

Things slowed down somewhat for the Browns when Jim Ed was called into the U.S. Army. His place was taken by another sister, Norma, who made some recordings on RCA with her sisters. However, neither those nor the ones initially made before Jim Ed left had made any major impact on the national country-music public as the late 1950s approached.

Things changed for the better when he returned to the group, with a song they liked called "Jimmy Brown." But they ran into problems finding the copyrighted music needed for legal clearance. The reason, it later turned out, was that the original song that came out in France was copyrighted under the title "Three Bells." In a phone conversation with Grelun Landon, then vice president of Hill and Range Songs, Inc., the Browns mentioned the song. Landon tracked it down and sent the necessary material to the trio in time for their next recording session. Almost as soon as their recording (the "Jimmy Brown" version) came out, it hit sales rates of 100,000 copies a week. In a short time the trio had its first million-seller and a national reputation.

Opportunities to appear in major venues all over the country arose for the group in the early 1960s, including *The Ed Sullivan Show* and Dick Clark's *American Bandstand*. In the midst of this prosperity, both Bonnie and Maxine got married. Soon after Bonnie's marriage, the Browns had more top-10 singles to smile about, such as their versions of "Scarlet Ribbons" and "The Old Lamplighter." The trio had its own supper club in Pine Bluff, Arkansas, from

1960 to 1963, then joined the cast of the *Grand Ole Opry* in 1963. From 1963 until mid-1967 the Browns not only were headliners at home but also were given warm welcomes by fans throughout the world, including Germany, Japan, and England.

Among the albums of their work issued on RCA were *Sweet Sounds* (11/59), *Town & Country* (5/60), *The Browns* (9/60), *The Browns* (2/64), *3 Shades* (3/65), *When Love Is Gone* (11/65), *Best of the Browns* (7/66), *Our Kind* (1/67), *Old Church* (8/67), and, on Camden, *I Heard the Bluebirds* (7/65) and *Big Ones* (6/67).

After 1967, Jim Ed remained the family member primarily active in the music field. Maxine did some solo recordings on a limited basis beginning in 1968, after signing with Chart Records.

BRUSH ARBOR: *Vocal and instrumental group from San Diego, California. Personnel: Jim Rice (vocals, guitar), Joe Rice (tenor vocals, mandolin, guitar), James Harrah, Mike Holtzer (drums), Dave Rose (bass, vocals). (Harrah temporarily replaced by Dale Cooper, mid-1970s. Yabe Obien added temporarily in 1977.)*

Although there are many folk and country enthusiasts in San Diego, the city isn't known as an incubator of new talent. Brush Arbor (named for the brush-covered shelters to protect revival meetings from the elements) was an exception. They started out as a local favorite in the early 1970s and became recognized as a top bluegrass and country & western band within a few years' time.

The inspiration for the band was brothers Jim and Joe Rice who handle, in Jim's case, lead vocals, primary songwriting, banjo, guitar, steel guitar; and in Joe's, tenor vocals, mandolin, and guitar. In a short time they worked up enough of a repertoire to begin to get engagements for events on local college and high school campuses. Soon after the brothers formed the band in 1972 with several other friends, they got a major boost by beating out some two-hundred other entries to win first place on local station KSON's *Country Star* talent show. This achievement helped gain them a spot on a special concert

bill that featured such country greats as Sonny James, Mel Tillis, and Bill Anderson. Word of their ability spread so rapidly that during the summer of 1972, Brush Arbor got the rare opportunity to appear at the *Grand Ole Opry*. The band also got a chance to perform on WSM's *Grand Ole Opry Gospel Hour* and the *Ernest Tubb Show*.

The group members of that initial period included, besides the Rices, James Harrah on lead guitar and vocals, Mike Holtzer on drums, and Dave Rose on bass guitar and vocals. During the next few years the group was featured at many spots in California, including Sea World, Knott's Berry Farm, Disneyland, and several folk and country festivals, and also toured with many major country artists. They were also featured on the *Dean Martin's Music Country* show in the summer of 1973 for five weeks, and in 1974, Johnny Cash asked the band to appear on his NBC-TV special.

Brush Arbor worked with Olivia Newton-John, Charlie Rich, Rich Little, Boots Randolph, Sammi Jo, Doug Kershaw, Mel Tillis, and Mac Davis in live appearances during the 1970s. They ended up their summer schedules with five-day concert series with the *Johnny Cash* show, and signed for repeat performances at the Golden Nugget Casino in Las Vegas, spending an average of twelve weeks a year at that venue.

The group signed with Capitol Records during 1972 and turned out two albums and several singles during the next few years. The LPs were *Brush Arbor* and *Brush Arbor 2*. Charted singles included the band's version of the old Creedence Clearwater Revival hit "Proud Mary" and an original tune, "Brush Arbor Meeting," that made the country top 40. The group moved to Monument Records, debuting with "Page One," released in mid-1976, followed by the LP *Straight* in 1977. By the time that album came out, there had been some changes in the band: James Harrah's place on lead guitar was taken over by Dale Cooper in the mid-1970s and the group added a sixth regular, Yabe Obien, on keyboards in 1977.

The band continued extensive touring and occasional TV work in the late 1970s. A guest appearance on the Canadian network show *Celebration* helped increase their audience in that country and also brought them in contact with Sam Lovullo, who produced not only *Celebration* but the syndicated *Hee Haw* show. One result was four appearances by Brush Arbor on *Hee Haw* during 1976 and 1977. The group was in Nashville during the summer of 1976 to finish its first Monument LP and guest on Johnny Cash's *Summer of 1976* show.

The group earned many honors during the 1970s. On a number of occasions they were voted one of five top bands in the Country Music Association and Academy of Country & Western Music polls. In 1973, they won the award in the Academy voting and received the trophy on a nationally televised program from Knott's Berry Farm. In 1974, readers of *Music City News* voted the band the second most popular bluegrass group in the United States.

BRYANT, BOUDLEAUX AND FELICE:

fiddler (Boudleaux); songwriting team. Boudleaux born Shellman, Georgia, February 13, 1920; Felice, born Milwaukee, Wisconsin, August 7, 1927.

Certainly one of the most successful and prolific husband-and-wife songwriting teams in popular music history, the Bryants contributed many standards both to rock 'n' roll and to country music. They have had the pleasure of seeing their compositions both old and new show up on hit lists from the 1940s through the 1980s.

Boudleaux, born in Shellman but raised in Moultrie, Georgia, had an excellent classical background. He began to study violin when he was five and continued until he was eighteen, with the goal of becoming a concert violinist. In 1938, he played a season with the Atlanta Philharmonic.

Then, in a violin-maker's shop, he met a man from Atlanta station WSB who needed a fiddle player for a country band. Having also played country music for his own enjoyment, Boudleaux took the job. He continued to perform as a country fiddler for several years, then joined a jazz band with which he toured much of the United States. In 1945, while playing in Milwaukee, he met Felice, an elevator starter at the Shrader Hotel, who was born and raised in Milwaukee.

Soon after that first meeting they were married, and after the wedding she traveled with him. Sometimes they made up country & western songs just for fun, and eventually decided to try to place some. In 1949, at the suggestion of a friend, performer Rome Johnson, they sent a song called "Country Boy" to Fred Rose of Acuff–Rose Publishing in Nashville. Rose bought it and Little Jimmie Dickens turned it into a hit. The next year, at Rose's suggestion, the Bryants moved to Nashville.

From then on, their songs rarely were absent from the hit charts. Many of the tunes made it on both country & western and popular charts. An example was "Hey Joe," a top-10 country hit for Carl Smith in 1953 and a million-seller for Frankie Laine in the pop domain. For some years the Bryants worked closely with Carl Smith. This resulted in such top-10 successes as "It's a Lovely, Lovely World," "Our Honeymoon," "Just Wait 'Til I Get You Alone," "Back Up Buddy," and "This Orchid Means Goodbye," the last named cowritten by Boudleaux and Carl.

In 1955, Eddy Arnold achieved hits with the Bryants' "I've Been Thinking" and "Richest Man." By the mid-1950s, the Bryants had begun to make their mark on the dynamic new field of rock 'n' roll. They were assigned to work with a rising young brother act, the Everlys. In 1957, this combination provided the Everlys with Bryant songs that made number one on both country and pop charts: "Bye Bye Love" and "Wake Up Little Susie." The following year, the Everlys were given two more number-one ranked songs, "All I Have to Do Is Dream" and "Bird Dog." In 1958, the Bryants were represented on country top-10 lists with Jim Reeves' version of "Blue Boy." From 1957 to 1960, the Bryants provided the Everlys with a number of other songs that made upper-chart levels, although not the very top.

In 1961, Boudleaux had a worldwide hit with an instrumental composition, "Mexico." The song won a gold record in Germany. After the Everlys signed with Warner Brothers Records and moved to Los Angeles in the early 1960s, the Bryants concentrated once again on country material. Some of their top-10 hits in the 1960s were the singles "Let's Think About Living" (performed by Bob Luman), "My Last Date" (Skeeter Davis, who co-wrote the song with Boudleaux), "Baltimore" (Sonny James), "I Love to Dance with Annie" (Ernest Ashworth), and "Rocky Top" (Buck Owens). The Bryants published most of the material they wrote through their own firm, House of Bryant, which was still a thriving business in the 1980s.

A sampling of the charted singles in the 1970s written by one or both of the Bryants includes "We Could" (by Felice, a hit single for Charley Pride in 1974), "Take Me as I Am (Or Let Me Go)" (Mack White, 1976), "Sweet Deceiver" (Christy Lane, 1977), "Penny Arcade" (Cristy Lane, 1978), and "Raining in My Heart" (Leo Sayer, 1978).

In late 1979, the Bryants tried a new tack by agreeing to record an album themselves for an English company. Called *Surfin' on a New Wave*, it was released in early 1980. Eight of the songs were new ones written for the LP. However, Boudleax noted, "We were going to do nothing on the album but new songs, but our two sons [Dane and Del] suggested we record some of the older things for identification purposes." The four "oldies" chosen were "All I Have to Do Is Dream," "Bye Bye Love," "Raining in My Heart," and "Rocky Top."

In 1981, Boudleaux provided Joe Stampley and Moe Bandy with the top-10 single composition "Hey Joe, Hey Moe."

BUCKLEY, TIM: *Singer, guitarist, banjoist, songwriter. Born Washington, D.C., February 14, 1947; died Santa Monica, California, June 29, 1975.*

Tim Buckley lived a scant twenty-eight years and never achieved the commercial heights that many expected of him. Yet he bequeathed much to posterity—fond memories of some great concert moments to many of his followers and nine albums, including many gems and innovations likely to influence music lovers and musical innovators in years to come.

Born Timothy Charles Buckley III in Washington, D.C., he spent his first ten years in Amsterdam, New York, then moved with his family to Anaheim, California. Buckley's reminiscenses of his early influences were given to interviewer Frankie Nemko *(Down Beat,* June 10, 1977). "I was only about twelve years old and I had probably five or six notes to my voice. I heard a recording of a trumpet playing things way up there. So I tried to reach those notes. Little Richard got them. It was like a falsetto scream. I'd ride my bicycle around the neighborhood screaming at the buses until I couldn't go any higher.

"Then one day I heard the opposite end, the baritone sax, waaaay . . . doooown . . . there. I said, 'There's gotta be a way to do that.'

"So I practiced, and I screamed, and I practiced some more, until I finally ended up with my five-to-five-and-a-half octave voice."

As he moved into his teens, he was attracted to various musical styles, from Hank Williams to Miles Davis. He taught himself to play banjo from listening to country and folk records, and then played local dates with a country band.

During his brief stay in college, his interests were beginning to shift toward poetry and folk-flavored rock. He started to collaborate with a close friend, poet Larry Beckett, on original songs. At first Tim supplied music, but before long he was creating songs of his own. Buckley formed an act with bass player Jim Fielder, later a member of the rock group Blood, Sweat and Tears, which played many of his songs at small clubs in the L.A. area. One of those shows was heard by drummer Jim Black of the Mothers of Invention, who told Mothers' manager Herb Cohen of Buckley's striking voice. Cohen followed up, and selected six of Tim and Larry's songs for a demonstration record.

He booked Buckley into New York's Night Owl Cafe during the summer of 1966 and sent the demo material along to Jac Holzman, president of Elektra Records. Even before Buckley appeared in New

York, Holzman had been so impressed by the advance recordings that he was ready to sign Tim. "I asked Herb to arrange a meeting, but I had made my mind up already. We spent a late afternoon together and my belief in Tim was more than confirmed." In a short time, Tim was in the studios back in Los Angeles working on his debut LP, *Tim Buckley*, released in October 1966. The album had a strong folk flavor that, as it happened, forced Buckley into a straightjacket he didn't want.

As Underwood, who was a sideman in Buckley's first band and had worked with him in the years to come, wrote in *Down Beat*, "Tim liked the melodic and harmonic flow of 'Valentine Melody,' 'Song of the Magician,' and 'Song Slowly Sung,' but for the most part, he later regarded this first effort as just that, a first effort, naive, stiff, quaky, and innocent. It was, however, a ticket into the marketplace. There, because he played an acoustic guitar and strummed, they called him a 'folk' singer, a misnomer from which he never freed himself."

The album didn't make any waves, although it did help bring increasing opportunities to perform on the college campus and rock festival circuit. His abilities attracted attention from many musical peers. George Harrison, for instance, urged the Beatles' manager Brian Epstein to hear a Buckley concert at New York's Cafe Au Go Go in April 1967.

In 1967, the follow-up album did much better—the title song, "Goodbye and Hello" showed up on national charts as did the antiwar song, "No Man Can Find the War." By then, Buckley was moving away from the cerebral world of Larry Beckett to concentrate on themes closer to his heart. Almost all the material on his third Elektra release, *Happy/Sad*, was by him. The album had much greater emphasis on jazz-related themes, including the song "Strange Feeling," which was patterned after Miles Davis' "All Blues."

However, Tim's creative restlessness alarmed Elektra officials, who felt he was abandoning the approach that promised to make him a major star. Rather than listen to the commercial pleadings, Tim went

still further afield in the album *Lorca*, where he was interested in developing music based on unusual sound and lyric patterns. Wrote Underwood, "The album, which was composed in 5/4 time, proved too experimental. It failed dismally with the public and also caused Elektra to drop him. When he essayed some of his new musical gymnastics in concert, he drew negative responses from unprepared critics and audiences."

Under pressure from management, he finally agreed to assemble some of his previously unrecorded songs in his earlier styles and turn out a new LP. The result was *Blue Afternoon*, issued on Straight Records in the early 1970s. "The performances were perfunctory," Underwood wrote. "Tim's heart was not in them, and it showed." The album was a failure. Undaunted, Tim went back to playing music his way. The result was *Star-Sailor*, in which most of the pieces return to the oddtime signatures—particularly 5/4— Buckley was exploring. The album, issued on Straight Records, didn't set the charts on fire, but it won praise from a number of critics, particularly in the jazz field. *Down Beat*, for instance, gave it a five-star rating.

However, the impact on his career was even more catastrophic than *Lorca*. Buckley found himself without a recording contract and, for legal reasons, unable to perform except on the q.t. "After two years," stated Underwood, "he was strapped in every way. He needed money. He desperately needed the idolatry recognition of his long-vanished public. He needed to record. He needed to feel like a man again. He needed to come back!" Buckley also needed to come back from the drug- and alcohol-dependency he had developed.

He seemed to be achieving his goal in 1973-74, when he signed with Warner Brothers. They released his three LPs, *Greetings from L.A.*, *Sefronia*, and *Look at the Fool*. He cut back sharply on drugs and alcohol and got the chance to hit the concert trail again. He found audiences interested in his modified mid-1970s folk-rock style. But in 1975, he once more was without a recording agreement. Watching him at the Starwood in May 1975, a *Los Angeles*

Times critic praised his supple, roaming voice and wrote, "Tim Buckley is a bona fide legend and no record company should be allowed to sign another country-rock act or heavy-metal group until he is back in the studios."

Time, though, was running out. Late the next month, returning home from an engagement in Dallas, he hit the bottle in the afternoon and then, visiting a friend, accepted some heroin. Said Underwood, "Buckley's system had been clean. The combined dosage of alcohol and heroin proved to be too much for him." Tim was pronounced dead at 9:42 P.M. the evening of June 29, 1975, in Santa Monica.

In his farewell in *Down Beat,* Underwood wrote, "Tim Buckley held hands with the world for awhile. He gave in fire and fury and perverse humor the totality of his life's experience, which was vast beyond his mere 28 years. . . . He had a beauty of spirit, a beauty of song and a beauty of personage that re-etched the face of the lives of all who knew him and of all who ever truly heard him. He burned with a very special flame, one of a kind. Bye, bye, baby. . . ."

BUFFETT, JIMMY: *Singer, guitarist, songwriter, band leader (Coral Reefer Band). Born Mobile, Alabama, December 25, 1946.*

"Someone once asked me, 'How can you write those real sensitive songs and then write those real trashy songs?' Well, I told him, 'Sometimes I feel real sensitive and sometimes I feel real trashy!'" Those comments at a 1977 concert, typical of the offhand manner Buffett usually affected, had as much truth as comic content. Buffett always wrote songs as the mood struck him, and much of his output was in a light-hearted novelty vein, such as his 1978 single, "Cheeseburger in Paradise." Underlying his humor was a deadly serious creative bent that provided some of the best songs in the progressive country-folk-rock genre.

Although he was born and bred in the South and was later to achieve a high standing with country fans, for a long time the music Jimmy said he liked the least was country. In his youth Jimmy rebelled against many of the conventional things he saw around him. As he told an audience at a mid-1979 concert, "After I finished school I had to bust out and taste the many things that had been denied me while I was growing up. I spent eighteen years in the Catholic school systems and anyone who's been there knows what I mean." Later, when he was an established performer, he listed his occupation on a biography form as "Professional Misfit."

Jimmy could play the guitar reasonably well by the time he finished high school, but didn't yet think of music as a way of earning a living. He entered college in Mississippi to obtain a degree in journalism, but the delights of New Orleans proved too strong. Folk music was still popular in the mid-1960s, and Jimmy began performing at local folk clubs there and in other Gulf Coast locales. He sang many well-known folk or folk-flavored songs, but also began to work up original songs.

He got married and completed college in the second half of the 1960s and, now determined to stay in the music business, moved to Nashville late in the decade to further his career goals, though he had no desire to move into country & western music. Once there, he got a job as a reviewer for *Billboard* magazine, found some performing work on the side, and managed to get a recording contract from Barnaby Records. That label issued two of his albums in the early 1970s, including *Down to Earth,* but neither of those made much of a dent in the marketplace.

After a while, he left *Billboard* and moved to Los Angeles, where he auditioned for the New Christy Minstrels. The management of that group had been interested in him since his first Barnaby release. Jimmy, more interested in drinking and toking with close friends, however, let the opportunity fall through.

From there he switched base to Key West, Florida, his favorite resting place from then on. In the late 1970s, when not on tour or in the recording studios, he was performing in local night clubs or sailing the Caribbean or Atlantic on his yacht *Euphoria II.*

However, for many months after he took up residence for the first time in Key West, he had to wage a continuing campaign to get a new record alignment. After a year of taking his demonstration material from company to company and talking to industry executives, ABC/Dunhill finally decided to take a chance on him. In mid-1973, his debut on the label, *A White Sport Coat and a Pink Crustacean,* came out. In his usual blunt way, he talked openly in one song of the supermarket raids he conducted to keep from starving: "Who's gonna steal the peanut butter/I'll get the can of sardines/Runnin' up and down the aisle of the Mini-mart/Stickin' food in our jeans." The album wasn't a smash hit, but it did gain enough attention for ABC to feel they might have a winner on their hands.

In 1974, Jimmy's live appearances in support of his new album, *Livin' and Dyin' in 3/4 Time,* brought growing approval from a still small but faithful group of fans. He also got the chance to write, score music, and act in the Frank Perry 1974 film *Rancho Deluxe.* Later he contributed to the 1978 film *FM* and to the preparation of the soundtrack for the Jack Nicholson vehicle *Goin' West.*

Jimmy continued to turn out new albums at a steady clip. In 1975, ABC issued *AIA* and in January 1976 released *Havana Daydreamin',* his most successful album to that point. The title song became one of his best-known numbers. In January 1977, the album that was to make him an international star, *Changes in Latitudes, Changes in Attitudes,* came out. In a few months it was well up on the charts, reaching top levels in both pop and country categories. The album was certified gold by R.I.A.A. in July and moved up to platinum by year end. During the summer of 1977, Jimmy also won a gold record for a single from the album "Margaritaville." By then he already had a growing catalogue of highly regarded songs, including such others as "Come Monday," "The Captain and the Kid," and "Door Number Three."

In March 1978, his sixth ABC LP, *Son of a Son of a Sailor,* came out and almost immediately showed up on the hit lists. In less than a month, on April 12, it was certified gold by R.I.A.A. Later in the year, a two-record live concert set, *You Had to Be There,* was issued. In mid-1979, he was represented by a new album, *Volcano,* one with a strong West Indies flavor, as befitted a collection recorded on the island of Montserrat, which was over gold-record levels by 1980. Other albums in his catalogue in the early 1980s included *Somewhere Over China* and *Coconut Telegraph.* Standing-room-only crowds greeting his 1979 and early 1980s concerts in all parts of the United States proved that Jimmy had arrived as a major artist.

BURGESS, WILMA: *Singer. Born Orlando, Florida, June 11, 1939.*

A city girl who grew up in Orlando, Florida, Wilma Charlene Burgess had a closer affinity to popular music than rural ballads for most of her early years. The catalyst that changed her viewpoint was a concert by Eddy Arnold in her home town. As the show progressed, Wilma became more and more excited about his renditions of his many country music standards. She started to memorize the lyrics of many of the country & western songs she heard on the radio. However, a music career was not in her plans when she enrolled as a physical education major at Stetson University in Florida.

Soon after she finished college, a friend who wrote country music asked her to go to Nashville to sing some of his songs for prospective publishers, in 1960. Charlie Lamb of Sound Format publications became more interested in her voice than the songs and brought her ability to the attention of some recording executives.

Owen Bradley, a Decca Records executive, agreed with Lamb's estimate and signed Wilma, who moved to Nashville. (Lamb became Wilma's manager.) She recorded a number of sides for Decca, several of which stayed on the charts for a number of weeks in the early 1960s. In 1967, she achieved a major milestone with her first top-10 single, "Baby." In 1968, she had two more successes with the singles "Fifteen Days" and "Misty Blue." The latter was the title song for her chartmaking

Decca album, *Wilma Burgess Sings Misty Blue*, issued in April 1967. That was her second LP on Decca, her debut, *Wilma Burgess*, having been issued in August 1966.

Another single that made top-chart levels in the late 1960s was "Tear Time," also the title song of an LP issued in January 1968. In 1969, she had the single "Parting" in upper-chart positions.

In the mid-1970s, Wilma left Decca (later MCA) and signed with Shannon Records, owned by Jim Reeves Enterprises. Under the supervision of Shannon executive Mary Reeves Davis (widow of Jim Reeves), Wilma made a number of recordings that made top country chart levels. Her releases included the solo single "I'll Be Your Bridge" and a number of duets with Bud Logan.

Logan, born in Harrisburg, Illinois, had been the leader of Jim Reeves' band, the Blue Boys. After Reeves' death, the band's name was changed to The Blue Boys featuring Bud Logan. (That act prepared some recordings for RCA in the mid-1960s.) Mary Reeves Davis had wanted to combine Logan and Wilma vocally for many years, but wasn't able to bring that about until Wilma was free to sign with Shannon. One of the results of her new alignment was a hit single with Logan in 1974 called "Wake Me into Love."

BURNETTE, DORSEY: *Singer, guitarist, songwriter. Born Memphis, Tennessee, December 28, 1932; died Woodland Hills, California, August 19, 1979.*

On October 12, 1979, a group of friends of Dorsey Burnette held a special benefit concert for his family at the Los Angeles Forum. Among those performing in honor of this gifted artist were Glen Campbell, Kris Kristofferson, Gary Busey, Delaney and Bonnie Bramlett, Johnny Paycheck, Roger Miller, and Tanya Tucker. The concert's advertisements called Burnette "The Father of Rock and Roll," which was a bit exaggerated, but there is no doubt that he contributed to the birth of that field just as he did over the years to country & western.

Memphis born and bred, Dorsey's first love as a boy was country music, as was the case for other family members, including his brother Johnny. As he told Lee Rector of the *Music City News* in 1975, as soon as he could drive a car and had some money in his pockets, "I used to drive all the way to Nashville every Saturday night to go to the *Grand Ole Opry.* I had been listening to it ever since I was just a little kid rolling around on the floor. My old man wouldn't miss that show for anything in the world."

The Burnette boys learned to play instruments at an early age and were playing for friends and in school events in their teens. In the early 1950s, they had their own country band and played dances and clubs in Arkansas, Louisiana, and Mississippi. Ruggedly built, Dorsey considered trying for a career in boxing. "I went to St. Louis as a pro fighter," he told Rector, "but it got to where I would come home and there would be blood coming from somewhere. I remembered how I picked that guitar, so I said, 'It's time to learn to pick a little better.' "

Still, Dorsey wasn't certain he should concentrate on music. For six years he worked to get his electrician's license. However, he found that he didn't enjoy crawling around in narrow passages in buildings "getting that fiberglass insulation down in your rear end where you can't scratch." But his electrical training did help when he and Johnny needed some money to tide them over between engagements. It helped in the early 1950s, when the brothers sought to score a breakthrough in New York. They finally got an audition for the *Ted Mack Amateur Hour* and won the show four straight times. "After that, we went on tour with the show playing banquets, Madison Square Garden and for President Harry Truman."

In 1954, the Burnettes were in Memphis working at Crown Electric Company, where Elvis Presley first worked after getting out of high school. Presley was a friend of theirs during those years, as was another Crown employee, guitarist Paul Burlison. Burlison and the Burnettes formed the Burnette Trio, which played local clubs when the chance came along. During those times their friend, concert promoter Preston Pierce, recalled to Art Fein of the *Los Angeles Times,* "Elvis used to call Dorsey and Johnny the Dalton Gang, for all the trouble they'd get into." Not long before Elvis cut his first record, he did a guest spot in a Trio show.

The Burnettes began making singles of their own in the mid-1950s, two of which have become classics: "Tear It Up" and "Train Keep a Rollin'." The former was revived by Britain's Yardbirds with great success in the mid-1960s and the latter was a major hit for the rock band Aerosmith in the late 1970s.

Becoming discouraged about chances of moving upward in the music field, the Burnettes moved to California in 1957. Back then, said Dorsey, "No one would listen to us in Memphis. We played a lot of times for our beer and passed the hats." But when they headed west, their fortunes changed. They decided to stress their writing talents and in short order became associated with Ricky Nelson, providing him with a series of songs that became smash pop hits, among them "Waitin' in School," "Just a Little Too Much," "Believe What You Say," and "It's Late."

At the start of the 1960s, the brothers returned as solo performers. In 1960, Dorsey made the charts with "Hey Little One" and "Tall Oak Tree." (In 1968, his close friend Glen Campbell turned out a single of "Hey Little One" that went past platinum-record levels.) Before long, Johnny was in the winner's circle with hits like "You're Sixteen" and "Dreamin'." However, in 1964, Johnny was killed in a boating accident, an event that left scars which remained with Dorsey for years afterward.

Dorsey's pop music efforts faltered in the mid-1960s and he began to concentrate on country-oriented songs, though initially without any marked impact on country charts. For a while in the 1960s, he had the house band at the Palomino Club, with one of his band members a then unknown named Johnny Paycheck. Other artists Dorsey worked with or socialized with during the 1960s and 1970s were Roger Miller, Delaney and Bonnie Bramlett, and Glen Campbell.

Dorsey continued to develop new mate-rial, and his ability as a singer and writer finally brought increasing attention from country fans. Between 1971 and 1977, he placed fourteen songs on the national lists. During the first half of the 1970s, those releases were on Capitol Records with chartmakers like "In the Spring," "Darling Don't Come Back," "Let Another Good One Get Away," and "I Just Couldn't Let Her Walk Away." He also was respected for his gospel songs, one of the most recorded of which is "The Magnificent Sanctuary Band." He recorded two albums for Capitol, "but they really didn't go like I would have liked to see them go." He moved to Melodyland Records in 1975 and soon had one of his best-selling country singles, "Molly I Ain't Getting Any Younger." He followed with three more charted singles over the next few years.

A comparatively young man, Dorsey seemed to be on the way to major acceptance as a country artist at the end of the 1970s. He had a lot of projects he was looking forward to in the summer of 1979; he had just signed a new recording contract with Elektra/Asylum Records and his debut single on the label, "Here I Go Again," was finding favor with country fans. He also was discussing a new show in Las Vegas designed to showcase his own hits and those of his brother. At that juncture, he was felled by a heart attack in his Woodland Hills, California, home on August 19.

The owner of the North Hollywood Palomino Club, Tommy Thomas, where Dorsey had performed many times in the 1960s and 1970s, mourned Dorsey's passing. He told Art Fein, "Dorsey was a great artist. In many ways he was ahead of his time. But no matter what stage of his career he was at, we'd always book him into our club. The man had a lot of friends."

BUSH, JOHNNY: *Singer, drummer, guitarist, songwriter. Born Houston, Texas, February 17, 1935.*

Unlike rock 'n' roll, the drummers in country music rarely become artists with widespread name identification. One exception to the rule is Johnny Bush, an excellent drummer and songwriter but only average on the instrument most identified with country music, the guitar.

Guitar, though, was the instrument he started on. "My dad taught me when I was nine and I haven't improved much since," he said in the early 1970s, "but I have no desire to be a guitar player. I want to sing."

Born and raised in Houston, in the heart of country & western music territory, Johnny continued to play guitar once he'd learned it, despite his reservations. During his teens he sang and played in school events and finally decided to make music his career. He gained his first paying job at the Texas Star Inn in San Antonio in 1952, handling rhythm guitar and vocals. The money he earned was scanty; to make ends meet, he worked a variety of day jobs. Meanwhile he sought as many night and evening music gigs as he could find.

After several years he decided to change his approach and took up drums. He turned out to be a much better drummer than guitarist and his luck seemed to side with the drums. He got a job in a small-time Texas band whose sidemen included another young artist named Willie Nelson. After the band broke up, Johnny was to hear from Willie again.

In the early 1960s things started picking up for Willie. Faron Young scored a triumph with Nelson's composition "Hello Walls," and in a little while Willie had his own hit single, "Touch Me." Soon Willie needed his own tour band and asked Johnny to come along as drummer. The tour lasted only a year, but when Willie disbanded the group he got Bush a new job in Ray Price's band. For three years in the mid- and late-1960s, Johnny toured all over the United States with Price, who included some of Bush's original songs in the band's repertoire and recorded "Eye for an Eye."

In the late 1960s, Johnny had a number of demos of his singing style circulating among record industry executives. The answers kept coming back "no," but Johnny had Willie Nelson in his corner. Willie responded to his longtime friend's request for help by paying for a recording session that produced a single and an album, both

called *Sound of a Heartache*. They were leased to Stop Records, which distributed them. The recordings found some response from country fans, enough to encourage further releases in the late 1960s and early 1970s. The result was several charted singles, such as "You Ought to Hear Me Cry," "You Gave Me a Mountain," and "Undo the Right." Several more LPs were issued during those years, including *You Ought to Hear Me Cry* on the Hilltop label, *Bush Country* on Stop, and, in 1972, a Starday LP, *Here's Johnny Bush*.

In 1972, Johnny was signed by RCA Records, which issued a number of singles and albums in ensuing years. Johnny's chartmakers on that label included "We're Back in Love Again" in late 1973 and "Toy Telephone/Tennessee to Texas" in the spring of 1974. By the late 1970s, Johnny's affiliation with RCA was severed and his releases came out on several small labels from then into the early 1980s. In 1978 his name showed up on lower-chart levels with "She Just Made Me Love You More" on Gusto Records. In 1979 he had similar results with "When My Conscience Hurts the Most" on Whiskey River Records and in early 1981 with his version of his composition "Whiskey River" on Delta Records. That song was published by Willie Nelson, whose own version of Bush's ballad long had been one of his concert staples as well as a best-selling single.

BUTLER, CARL: *Singer, guitarist, songwriter. Born Knoxville, Tennessee, June 2, 1927.*

Carl Roberts Butler discovered how to cram two successful performing careers into a lifetime: add your wife to the act. For more than a decade, he had had star status as a solo performer and songwriter. Then in 1962, he was joined by his wife, Pearl, to form an act that won them the nod in a disc jockey poll as the number-one new vocal team in 1963.

Carl was born and raised in Knoxville, Tennessee, a hotbed of country music activity. He followed the *Opry* and other country & western programs eagerly as a boy and learned to play guitar before he reached high school age. In 1939, he was accomplished enough for his first show date, picking for a square dance and singing between the sets. By the time he was graduated from Stair Tech High school in the mid-1940s, he had a number of engagements at local clubs and dances to his credit.

During the next few years he appeared in shows in other parts of the Southwest. He also was featured on radio on such stations as WROL and WNOX, Knoxville, and WPTF, Raleigh, North Carolina. In 1948, he was asked to join the *Grand Ole Opry,* the start of a long association with the show. He was featured on a number of TV shows in the 1950s, including appearances on WATE-TV and WBIR-TV in Knoxville.

In the 1950s, Carl moved ahead in the industry as both performer and songwriter. His own compositions were performed by such top artists as Roy Acuff, Carl Smith, Rosemary Clooney, Bill Monroe, and Flatt & Scruggs. He wrote some songs with Earl Scruggs, including "Building on Sand" and "Crying My Heart Out Over You." Some of Carl's other efforts included "If Teardrops Were Pennies," "My Tears Don't Show," "Crying Alone," "Grief in My Heart," "Loving Arms," "A White Rose," "I Like to Pretend," "So Close," "Hold Back the Dawn," "Guilty Conscience," and "Country Mile."

Carl's recording efforts began with a contract with Capitol in 1951. In 1953, he switched to Columbia Records. Among his recordings during the 1950s and early 1960s were "Borrowed Love," "Angel Band," "Walking in God's Sunshine," "Hallelujah," "We Shall Rise," "Only One Heart," "Through the Windows of Heaven," "Watching the Clock," "Cry You Fool, Cry," "If Teardrops Were Pennies," "Rivers of Tears," "I Know What It Means to Be Lonesome," "I Know Why I Cry," and "You Don't Steal Pennies from a Poor Man."

Close harmony had been long a private enjoyment of Carl and his wife, Pearl. In 1962, they decided to try their hand as a show business team. They soon had a top-10 hit of 1962, "Don't Let Me Cross Over." Now a hit act, they were featured on the *Opry* and such other network shows of the

1960s as Porter Wagoner's. They also appeared in a movie, *Second Fiddle to a Steel Guitar.* In 1964, they hit a new career high with another Carl Butler composition, "Too Late to Try Again." The song remained on the hit charts for many weeks, a good part of them in the number-one-ranked position.

Among Carl's LP total were such 1960s releases on Columbia as *Carl Butler* (1963), *Loving Arms* (1964), *Old and the New* (1960s), *Avenue of Prayer* (1967), and, on Harmony Records, *The Great Carl Butler Sings* (1966).

BUTLER, PEARL: *Singer, guitarist. Born Nashville, Tennessee, September 20.*

A husband-and-wife team hailing from Knoxville and Nashville would seem a natural for country & western music success. The combined backgrounds helped move Mrs. Pearl Butler frm the kitchen to front and center on the *Grand Ole Opry.*

Growing up in Nashville, young Pearl Dee Jones naturally had a youthful interest in country & western music. As a girl, she sang in school choruses but also enjoyed singing some of the *Grand Ole Opry* hits for her own pleasure. When she completed schooling in Nashville, she had both an excellent singing voice and a solid reputation as one of the best cooks in her class.

Later, she added to that reputation among country & western artists after her marriage to a young, rising performer, Carl Butler. For a good many years she remained in the background as Carl won his spurs as a top songwriter and musician. When Carl had time away from his profession, he and Pearl often took a busman's holiday, singing together at home or at family get-togethers. In the early 1960s, after Carl completed a new song called "Don't Let Me Cross Over," they decided to record it as a duet for Carl's label, Columbia.

The song became a top-10 hit of 1962, and the new team of Carl Butler and Pearl was on its way to regular status on the *Grand Ole Opry.* Carl and Pearl recorded such other well-received songs as "Forbidden Street," "I'm Hanging Up the Phone," "Just Thought I'd Let You Know," "We'll

Destroy Each Other," "Wrong Generation," "Little Mac," "Little Pedro," "Call 29," and "Same Old Me." In 1964, Carl wrote "Too Late to Try Again"; Carl and Pearl's recording became number one in the nation for several weeks in 1964.

The Butlers turned out a number of hit LPs during the mid-1960s, including *Don't Let Me Cross Over, Greatest Country and Western Hits,* and *Old and the New.* In nationwide demand for personal appearances, they performed in all fifty states between 1962 and 1967, as well as many parts of Canada and Europe. The Butlers also appeared in the movie *Second Fiddle to a Steel Guitar.*

Carl and Pearl were awarded the title of best new vocal team of 1963 in the annual disc jockey poll. In 1967, their many years of effort for the Salvation Army resulted in their receiving that organization's Meritorious Service Award.

Their record output dwindled in the 1970s, though they still had some active LPs such as the 1972 *Watch and Pray* on the Harmony label. They continued to do many live appearances throughout the decade.

C

CAMPBELL, GLEN: *Singer, guitarist, banjoist, actor, mandolin and bagpipe player. Born Delight, Arkansas, April 10, 1938.*

Perhaps Glen Campbell was born lucky, for he was the seventh son of a farmer who had also been number seven in his family. In any case, Glen's talent (and perhaps luck) has won him nearly every major honor that a singer/musician could win and has brought him a long way from his hometown of Delight, Arkansas.

The world of music first opened up to Glen at the age of four when his father, sensing his interest in music, ordered him a five-dollar guitar from a Sears Roebuck catalog. By the time he was six, Glen had begun to receive regional acclaim for his guitar playing. Listening to Django Reinhart and Barney Kessel albums helped him to develop his guitar technique. Before he was fourteen, Glen dropped out of school and began playing with a western band led by his uncle, Dick Bills, in Albuquerque, New Mexico. Glen toured the Southwest with his own band for a few years before heading for California in 1960 to find work as a studio musician.

While Glen's reputation as a skilled musician was growing, he was able to interest a local label in his singing. That led to the single "Turn Around, Look at Me," which was a minor hit in 1961. The record attracted enough interest so that Capitol Records offered him a contract. The first LP issued under that agreement was called *Big Bluegrass Special.* It came out in November 1962 credited to "The Green River Boys Featuring Glen Campbell." His single "Too Late to Worry, Too Late to Cry," title song of his second LP (Apri 1963) made the charts, but he failed to follow up with more hits in the next few years. Still in demand as a backing musician, he supported many stars, including such top celebrities as Frank Sinatra and Elvis Presley. At one point he even stood in for Brian Wilson, who was unable to travel on the Beach Boys' 1965 tour.

Meanwhile, Capitol still had faith in his singing potential, even though for a while his records didn't sell very well. In March 1964, the LP *The Astounding 12-String Guitar of Glen Campbell* was issued, followed in September 1965 by *Big Bad Rock Guitar of Glen Campbell.* Also issued were several singles, including "Universal Soldier" in 1965, which was a chart hit. Still, when his LP *Burning Bridges* came out in June 1967, he wasn't making much overall progress.

He finally achieved his big hit later in 1967 with "Gentle on My Mind," a John Hartford composition he had discovered when in Nashville. The song climbed to the top of the national charts and won Campbell Grammy Awards for Best Country and Western Performance and Best

Country Vocal Performance, Male. He followed with another blockbuster hit, "By the Time I Get to Phoenix," for which he won Grammy Awards for Best Vocal Performer, Male and Best Contemporary Pop Vocal Performance, Male, bringing his total to four Grammies in 1967. In 1968, the Country Music Association named him Entertainer of the Year. He was also named Top Male Vocalist by the Academy of Country and Western Music, as well as being honored by that organization for Album of the Year and Single of the Year ("Gentle on My Mind").

In 1969, Glen won even more awards and honors than in the previous year. In addition, he was now beginning to appear on television shows and in movies. His television career began when he hosted the summer replacement for CBS-TV's *The Smothers Brothers* show. In 1969, he won his own variety show, *The Glen Campbell Goodtime Hour*, which ran for four and a half years before he grew tired of the weekly grind and quit. The year 1969 also marked Glen's first motion picture appearance, with his boyhood idol, John Wayne, in *True Grit*. The following year he starred in the movie *Norwood*. Among his other movie credits was his 1974 appearance in *Strange Homecoming*, a made-for-television movie, with Robert Culp and Barbara Anderson.

Meanwhile, Glen continued to turn out hits that tended to appeal not only to country-music fans but to a wider-based audience as well. His gentle country-rock style propelled such songs as "Galveston," "Dreams of the Everyday Housewife," "Wichita Lineman," "Manhattan Kansas," "I'll Never Pass This Way Again," "Oklahoma Sunday Morning," "Sweet Dream Baby," "It's Only Make Believe," and "Try a Little Kindness" to the top of the national music charts.

After a few years with some minor hits but no major successes, Glen again scored a smash hit in 1975 with "Rhinestone Cowboy." He followed up with more huge hits, such as "Country Boy (You Got Your Feet in L.A.)," "Southern Nights," and "Sunflower." In late 1977, he had a hit with "God Must Have Blessed America"

and in 1978 he scored with "Another Fine Mess" and "Can You Fool."

From the late 1960s on, Glen's name appeared many times on album charts as well as singles lists. During 1968, he was awarded gold records by the Recording Industry Association of America for the Capitol LPs *Gentle on My Mind* (issued 8/67); *By the Time I Get to Phoenix* (11/67); and *Wichita Lineman* (11/68). In 1969, he won gold records for *Hey Little One* (3/68); *Bobbie Gentry and Glen Campbell* (9/68); *That Christmas Feeling* (10/68); *Galveston* (3/69); and *Glen Campbell Live* (8/69). Other late 1960s LPs were *A New Place in the Sun* (5/68) and *True Grit* (7/69).

In 1970 he received a gold record for *Try a Little Kindness* (1/70). Also on the charts that year were *Oh Happy Day* (4/70); *Norwood* (6/70); and *The Glen Campbell Goodtime Album* (9/70). In 1971 he earned a gold record for *Glen Campbell's Greatest Hits* (2/71). Other 1971 charted albums were *The Last Time I Saw Her* (7/71) and a duet collection with Anne Murray, *Get It Together* (11/71). In late 1972 he had the LP *Glen Travis Campbell* (10/72) on the lists. His Capitol LP releases of the mid- and late-1970s included *Arkansas; I Knew Jesus (Before He Was a Star)* (5/73); *I Remember Hank Williams* (10/73); *Houston (I'm Comin' to See You)* (4/74); *Reunion* (10/74); *Ernie Sings and Glen Picks* (5/75); *Rhinestone Cowboy* (7/75), a massive hit—like the title single, a gold record; *Bloodline* (4/76); *The Best of Glen Campbell* (10/76); *Southern Nights* (2/77) a number-one LP during 1977, bringing Glen his twelfth gold record album; *Glen Campbell Live at the Royal Festival Hall* (11/77); *Basic* (10/78); and *Highwayman* (10/79).

As of 1978, Glen had four gold singles, twelve gold albums, five platinum albums, and one double platinum album in the United States alone. He is also extremely popular in Great Britain and tours the United Kingdom regularly. In 1972 he gave a command performance for the Queen of England. He also hosts the Glen Campbell Los Angeles Open golf tournament, a major event on the PGA tour.

Glen finished up 1979 with the single "My Prayer" on lower-chart levels. During

1980 he had duets on the charts with Rita Coolidge ("Somethin' 'Bout You Baby I Like") and Tanya Tucker ("Dream Lover," issued on MCA label). In June 1980, Capitol issued the LP *Somethin' 'Bout You Baby I Like*, his thirty-seventh for that company and the last released while he still was on the Capitol roster. In early 1981 he had his first top-10 hit single in some time as "Any Which Way You Can," title song of a Clint Eastwood movie, rose to the top-10 on the Warner/Viva label. Soon after, the Capitol single "I Don't Want to Know Your Name" was in mid-chart levels. Another duet single with Tanya Tucker (with whom his name was romantically linked), issued on Capitol, "Why Don't We Just Sleep on It Tonight," was on hit lists in the spring of 1981. In the fall, he had a single on his new record label, Mirage, "I Love My Truck," on the charts for several months.

As with most artists of today, Glen Campbell's style is difficult to categorize. Basically, he blends country, folk, and jazz into a style that is uniquely his own. He has often referred to his music as "crock," a blend of country and rock. His tenor voice is sweet, not at all gruff or angry. His relaxed, country personality and humor have also contributed to his on-stage performance and to his overall popularity.
—A.S.

CARGILL, HENSON: *Singer, guitarist, emcee. Born Oklahoma City, Oklahoma, July 20, 1940.*

The story of Henson Cargill parallels that of many successful artists in all segments of pop music. The personable but persistent Oklahoman spent a lot of time playing small clubs and knocking on music industry doors before breaking through to "overnight" stardom in 1968. In 1967, hardly anyone knew his name; twelve months later he was a candidate for the most promising new artist of the year.

He grew up in Oklahoma City in a family with deep roots in the Southwest. Though his parents and relations weren't unfamiliar with country music, the general assumption was that Henson would follow in the footsteps of his immediate kin and find a career in such pursuits as ranching, law, or politics. He seemed headed in that direction when he studied animal husbandry for several years at Colorado State University, then returned to Oklahoma to work on the family-owned ranch full time. But meanwhile an early interest in country music grew into an obsession.

For a long time, it seemed to those closest to him that it would prove a vain effort. He worked a series of small clubs in his home state without making any decisive breakthroughs. He expanded his activities to include appearances in local shows and venues in other parts of the Southwest and West, gaining experience but not much more. Finally, in the mid-1960s he felt the time was ripe to move to Nashville and to try to move up in the country-music world.

He auditioned for almost every artist and repertoire person he could reach in his efforts to gain a recording contract. The months went by with only polite turndowns to show for his endeavors, until finally some of the people at Monument Records were impressed with his potential. He teamed with veteran producer Don Law, and one of the first songs they decided to record was one written by a blind young songwriter named Jack Moran, a combination that proved to be magic. The single "Skip a Rope" took country audiences by storm, rising to number one on the national country charts in 1968 and becoming, at year's end, the top-selling country release of the year. His debut album on Monument, with *Skip a Rope* as title track, reached top-chart levels. Before 1968 ran its course, Henson placed several more singles on the charts, including the top-10 "Row, Row, Row." He was represented by a few more charted singles in 1969, though none approached "Skip a Rope" in impact.

With his star on the rise, Cargill played major country venues all over the United States in late 1968 and early 1969. He also was asked to take over from long-time emcee Dean Richards as host of a revised version of the Avco Broadcasting *Midwestern Hayride*, originating from Cincinnati's WLWT-TV station. His premiere appearance as host of the program was on Saturday, August 2, 1969. Under a long-term contract, he continued to host the show into the 1970s, with the program running on the Avco network and in syndication as well. The latter version was telecast in many cities as *Country Hayride.*

Cargill's association with Monument, which included the early 1970s LP *Uncomplicated Henson Cargill,* ended at the start of the decade. He turned out an album on Mega titled *On the Road* and later had an album on Harmony label (10/72) called *Welcome to My World.* In the mid-1970s, he signed with the Atlantic Records country group and scored a hit in late 1973 and early 1974 with the single "Same Old California Memory." He also was represented by the album *This Is Henson Cargill Country.*

Like many artists, Henson found himself temporarily without a recording outlet in the mid-1970s when Atlantic decided to close down its country division. However, he had his concert work and master of ceremonies activities to keep him going, and in time he signed with another record firm. At the start of 1980, he had a new single, "Silence on the Line," on Copper Mountain Records, moving up the charts. Later in the year he placed "Have a Good Day" on them.

CARLISLE, BILL AND CLIFF: *Singers, instrumentalists, comedians, songwriters. Bill Carlisle, born Wakefield, Kentucky, December 19, 1908; Cliff Carlisle, born near Taylorsville, Kentucky, May 6, 1904.*

To sports fans, the name Carlisle means the famed Indian school for which Jim Thorpe played. The Carlisles of Kentucky were no relation to the school, but their star began to rise about the time Carlisle College went out of business. For more than three decades, the name Carlisle, as borne by Cliff and his younger brother, Bill, meant some of the best contributions to country music and country humor.

Both boys learned to play guitar during their school days in Wakefield, Kentucky. Clifford Raymond Carlisle preceded his brother at Ashes Creek Grade School, near Wakefield, attending from 1912 to 1915. William Carlisle began school about the time Cliff started his courses at Doe Run Grade School in Wakefield. Cliff went to Doe Run from 1916 to 1920 and then finished his schooling (1922) at Jacob's Addi-

tion Grade in Louisville, Kentucky, after the family moved there in 1921. By the time the family moved to Louisville, Kentucky, young Bill could take full part in Carlisle Sunday sings with his four brothers and two sisters. Cliff, by this time, was beginning to perform professionally. When Bill finished school some years later, he decided to follow in Cliff's footsteps and try for a career in country music. As the Carlisle Brothers, Cliff and Bill were featured on many shows in the Louisville-Cincinnati area from the late 1920s through the 1940s.

The brothers' first radio exposure was on station WLAP, Lexington, Kentucky, in 1931. They moved to a Louisville station in 1937. Over the next decade, though spending much time in their home region, they played throughout the Midwest and were featured for a time on a station in Charlotte, North Carolina.

One of the top hits of Cliff and Bill was "Fresh from the Country." Ths was also the title of their King LP album of 1959. In the late 1940s, the brothers began to go their separate ways, touring with their own groups at times, though still performing together at others. Bill was featured on station WSB, Atlanta, in 1949, and soon after formed a new group called The Carlisles.

The Carlisles soon became one of the most popular humorous groups in the country & western field. Their first radio engagement in Cincinnati, at the start of the 1950s, was avidly followed by local audiences. Their comic rendition of "Rainbow at Midnight" was soon turned into a national record hit. They followed up in the early 1950s with two more successes in the same vein, "No Help Wanted" and "Too Old to Cut the Mustard," both of which were written by Bill. After several guest appearances on the KWKH *Louisiana Hayride,* The Carlisles accepted a bid to perform on station WNOX in Knoxville. They added two top-10 hits to their earlier successes with "Is Zat You Myrtle" and "Knothole." Bill wrote the latter himself and the former in collaboration with the Louvin Brothers.

In 1954, Bill and The Carlisles were asked to join the cast of the *Grand Ole Opry.* The group remained major cast members for many years. After it disbanded, Bill was still an *Opry* regular in the 1960s. In 1966, his *Opry* audiences roared at his new hit, which became a top-10 national favorite, "What Kinda Deal Is This."

During his long career, Bill recorded for Bluebird, RCA Victor, Mercury, King, and, in the mid-1960s, Hickory. Some of his other songs on these various labels were "Rattlesnake Daddy," "I'm Rough Stuff," "Do You Need Any Help?" "Shake a Leg," "Business Man," "Gettin' Younger," "The Girl in the Blue Velvet Band," "Wedding Bells," "Maggie," "Rainbow Follows Rain," "Lost on a Sea of Sorrow," "Dollar Bill Mama Blues I and II," "Tramp on the Street," "Poor Man's Riches," "Skip to My Lou," "Old Joe Clark," and "I Hope You See the Same Star I Do." In 1967, Bill was featured on a Hickory LP, *Best of Bill Carlisle.*

Bill and the Carlisles recording efforts tapered off in the 1970s but the group was still active on the concert scene late in the decade.

CARTER, WILF (MONTANA SLIM): *Singer, songwriter, guitarist. Born Guysboro, Nova Scotia, December 18, 1904.*

Wilf Carter was a pioneer western singer, but he ws a true cowboy, no doubt about it. He has covered the rodeo circuit regularly and is in the Horsemen's Hall of Fame. He was brought up in Canadian ranch country, later shifting around from job to job, picking and singing.

After Merle Anderson hired him as a cowboy in 1924, Carter combined two professions into one. Anderson, who still entered a chuck wagon into the races at the Calgary Stampede each year into the early 1970s, was influential in encouraging Carter to entertain along the rodeo circuit.

Carter's radio experience started in Calgary (Ontario), Canada, in 1933, on CFCN. Shortly after another program for Radio Vancouver, he moved to New York for a CBS radio show. It was around this time that Bert Parks introduced him as "Montana Slim," which he adopted.

His recording career has been with Bluebird, Decca, and, in the mid-1960s, with

Don Pierce's Starday label in Madison, Tennessee. His repertoire was predominantly campfire-and-round-up-flavored—plaintive ballads and yodels with overtones of Jimmie Rodgers' influence.

"I'm Hittin' the Trail" and "Swiss Moonlight Lullaby" are among the five hundred-plus songs written by Carter. In the late 1960s, Wilf was in professional semiretirement, living in Winter Park, Florida. He kept his cowboy roots going with an interest in a Canadian ranching operation. A visit to New York to see Roy Horton of Peer-Southern Organization in 1967 resulted in a recording session that provided an LP, "Montana Slim–Wilf Carter," released on Starday.

In 1982, Carter was nominated as one of the candidates for election to the Country Music Hall of Fame.

CARTER FAMILY, THE ORIGINAL: *Vocal and instrumental group. Alvin Pleasant "A.P." Carter, born Maces Spring, Virginia, December 15, 1891, died Maces Spring, November 7, 1960; Sara Carter, born Wise County, Virginia, July 21, 1899, died Lodi, California, January 8, 1979; Maybelle Carter, born Nickelsville, Virginia, May 10, 1909, died October 23, 1978.*

On August 1, 1927, a historic event took place in the border city of Bristol, Tennessee. In the upper story of a three-story house at 410 State Street on the Tennessee side (the state line between Virginia and Tennessee runs down the middle of the street), Ralph Peer, RCA Victor talent scout, supervised the first recordings of the soon-to-be famed Carter Family. That period was doubly important, for the first cuts of another legendary artist, Jimmie Rodgers, were also being made.

The Carter Family had come down from their home in Maces Spring, Virginia, near Clinch Mountain, in response to an advertisement in *The Bristol Herald* offering auditions to local musicians. Johnny Cash described their trip to Bristol in a booklet accompanying a commemorative album released in 1979: "With a hearty country breakfast under their belts, the four [A.P., his wife, Sara, Maybelle and her husband, Ezra] loaded up into Ezra's old Hupmobile and headed for Bristol. Rains had swollen the Holsten River at a place where they were to ford it, and the Hupmobile stopped right in the middle of the river and refused to go any further. Long dresses were hiked up over the ladies' knees, and guitars and autoharps carried on their shoulders to the dry bank, as the men pushed, struggled, and tugged until they finally got the old car moving. Up on the bank they discovered another problem; there was a flat on the right rear tire. A.P., being the flat-fixer, got out the hand patch kit and quickly repaired the flat, pumped the tire up, and, with the instruments and the ladies aboard again, they made their way on to Bristol."

When the trio came before Ralph Peer for the audition, Peer was immediately impressed with them, especially with Sara's strong, pure voice. On those first recordings, Sara sang lead, while A.P. sang the bass line, Maybelle sang tenor harmony, and Maybelle and Sara played guitar and autoharp. The first six songs recorded that day, which were soon to make the Carter Family well known in many parts of the country, were "Bury Me Under the Weeping Willow," "Little Log Cabin by the Sea," "The Poor Orphan Child," "The Storms Are on the Ocean," "Single Girl, Married Girl," and "The Wandering Boy."

Long before this date, the Carter Family had been performing for church socials, school parties, and other local events. For A.P. and Sara, music was one of the prime pleasures they enjoyed together after their marriage on June 18, 1915.

Alvin Pleasant Delaney "Doc" Carter, or A.P., was the oldest of eight children born to Robert and Molly Bays Carter. Both of his parents came from musical backgrounds, but A.P.'s father gave up playing music when he got married because of his religious views. However, Molly Carter taught A.P. and his brothers and sisters the old ballads that had been handed down for years and years, many of which the Carter Family would later record.

When A.P. grew up, he left Virginia for Indiana, where he went to work for a railroad gang. However, after about a year, he missed his home on Clinch Mountain, and returned in 1911, selling fruit trees for a living. While he had been away from home, he had begun to write songs about his Clinch Mountain home and the life he had known there.

A.P. met Sara Dougherty on one of his many trips around the area selling fruit trees. According to family legend, she was singing "Engine One Forty-Three" and playing the autoharp when A.P. set eyes on her. Their romance blossomed and soon led to marriage.

Sara had learned to play the autoharp, a very popular instrument in those days, as a young girl and was quite skilled at it by the time she got married. A.P. played the fiddle although he was never confident of his ability. Both of them loved to sing and did so as often as they could, when A.P. was not busy working as a gardener or carpenter or farming or doing blacksmith work to supplement his income.

The third member of the group, Maybelle Addington, was added when she married A.P.'s brother Ezra in 1926. Like Sara, she had learned to play the autoharp as a child, and was well known in her hometown area of Scott County, Virginia, for her proficiency on the banjo and guitar. She had played with A.P. and Sara before her marriage to Ezra, but after their wedding she moved near Maces Spring, enabling her more time to practice with the now-complete group.

With the instrumental skill of Sara and Maybelle, the Carter Family was always in demand to perform at local events and get-togethers. Their vocal style was distinctive and innovative as well. As Johnny Cash wrote, "If you listen to the early hillbilly recordings, you find that, basically, the singers were barely singing over the instruments. The Carter style was built around the vocals and incorporated them into the instrumental background, usually made up of the basic three-chord structure. In essence, the Carter Family violated the main traditions of vocal and instrumental music, but in doing so created a whole new style and a whole new sound."

RCA apparently realized the innovative nature and potential for success of that new sound. A short time after Peer completed the first Carter cuts, RCA came back for more recordings. Those records sold well, so in May 1928 the Carter Family was asked to go to Camden, New Jersey, the recording center for the Victor Company at the time. They recorded eleven songs that May and twelve more in February 1929. Among the songs they recorded in those two sessions were some of the best-loved of Carter songs, "Wildwood Flower," "Diamonds in the Rough," and "The Foggy Mountain Top."

By the end of the 1920s, the music of the Carter Family was known from one end of the country to the other. In the 1930s, their fame continued to spread, resulting in many more record releases and personal appearances at country fairs and city auditoriums and on radio in many parts of the United States. Their popularity kept them together as a group even though increasing problems kept cropping up in the marriage of A.P. and Sara. They separated in 1933 and were finally divorced in 1939, but they continued to perform together until the early 1940s.

Among the many Carter recordings were such songs as "Keep on the Sunny Side," "Room in Heaven for Me," "Soldiers Beyond the Blue," "The Titanic," "Where the Sunset Turns," "False-Hearted Lover," "On the Rock Where Moses Stood," "The Homestead on the Farm," "On a Hill Lone and Gray," "Anchored in Love," "Meeting in the Air," "Pickin' in the Wildwood," "Worried Man Blues," "Gathering Flowers from the Hillside," "Forsaken Love," "You Are My Flower," "Western Hobo," "I Shall Not Be Moved," "Carter Blues," "Beyond the River," "The Wayworn Traveler," "Angel Band," "Dixie Darling," "Waves of the Sea," "Sunshine in the Shadows," "Bury Me Beneath the Weeping Willow," "Shall the Circle Be Unbroken," and "My Clinch Mountain Home." From their first session in August 1927 to their last record date on October 14, 1941, the original Carters recorded more than 250 songs.

Typical Carter Family songs that became country standards were their versions of "Wabash Cannonball" and A.P. Carter's original compositions, "I'm Thinking To-night of My Blue Eyes," "Lonesome Valley," and "Jimmy Brown the Newsboy."

In 1938, the Carters moved to Del Rio, Texas, to begin a series of broadcasts that lasted for three seasons over XERA, XEG, and XENT, Mexican border stations that broadcast 50,000 watts. Also taking part in some of the group singing by now were A.P. and Sara's children, Jeanette and Joe. In 1939, Maybelle's three daughters, Helen, June, and Anita, were added to the group. The Family stayed in Del Rio until 1941, when they moved to station WBT in Charlotte, North Carolina.

The Original Carter Family broke up in 1943, and the members went their separate ways. A.P. returned to Maces Spring, where he died in 1960. Sara moved to Angels Camp, California, with her second husband, Coy Bays, whom she had married in 1939. Maybelle formed a new act with her three daughters and moved to Richmond, Virginia, where they were featured performers on station WRVA from 1943 to 1948. Soon after this, they accepted an offer to join the *Grand Ole Opry*. In the 1950s, the girls went out in their own directions, but Maybelle remained a regular on the *Opry* for many more years and was later rejoined by daughters Helen and Anita.

The Original Carter Family was elected into the Country Music Hall of Fame in 1970, thus becoming the first group to be honored in this way. Maybelle and Sara were on hand to accept the award. Their commemorative plaque in the Hall of Fame building in Nashville, Tennessee, reads: "A.P. Carter, his wife, Sara, and his sister-in-law, Maybelle, played in one of the first commercial recording sessions at Bristol, Tennessee. For two decades they performed as an unbeatable team. Their songs became country standards, and some of A.P.'s original compositions are among the all-time greats. They are regarded by many as the epitome of country greatness and originators of a much-copied style."

Although the Carter Family ceased to exist as a group after 1943, some of their recordings always were in active record company catalogues in ensuing years. At the start of the 1980s, their available LPs included the following on RCA or its subsidiary label, Camden: *Fifty Years of Country Music, Happiest Days of All, Lonesome Pine Special, The Original and Great Carter Family, My Old Cottage Home, Smoky Mountain Ballads, Mid the Green Fields of Virginia,* and *More Golden Gems from the Original Carter Family.* Liberty Records offered *The Carter Family Album.* In the active Columbia catalogues in the early 1980s were *Three Generations, World's Favorite Hymns, Country's First Family,* and *Best of the Carter Family.* —A.S.

CARTER, MOTHER MAYBELLE: *Singer, autoharpist, guitarist, banjoist, songwriter. Born Nickelsville, Virginia, May 10, 1909; died October 23, 1978.*

The artistry of the Carter Family had become a living legend in both folk and country music circles by the end of the 1930s. For nearly four more decades, until her death in 1978, the Carter sound was kept alive by an original member of the group, the redoubtable "Mother" Maybelle Carter.

Born and raised in southwestern Virginia, Maybelle Addington began to sing traditional hill-country ballads almost as soon as she could talk. She learned to play both the guitar and the autoharp before reaching her teens and won much applause from friends and relations at local sings. She was fairly accomplished on the banjo and fiddle also.

Maybelle's guitar and autoharp playing styles were unique. On the autoharp, she picked out the melody with her thumb and finger picks rather than merely strumming across the harp while barring a chord, as was generally done in those days. Her son-in-law, Johnny Cash, described her guitar-playing style as follows: "What she did was play the melody on the bass strings while maintaining a rhythm on the treble strings, fingering a partial chord. Later she developed some intricate melody runs on the bass strings. Of course, such runs were not new, but they were used differently by Maybelle; they were being used not only as a part of the lead instrument, but as fills and also for the 'bottom' of the song. Throughout it all, the strong emphasis on the bass was a must, and this was gained in part by the use of a thumb pick and two steel finger picks. Later, this style was to be imitated to the note by literally thousands of guitar players."

Before she was out of her teens, Maybelle married Ezra Carter on March 23, 1926, and set up housekeeping with him in Poor Valley, Virginia, about twenty-five miles from Bristol, Tennessee. Ezra also came from a musical family. His brother A.P. and A.P.'s wife Sara were particularly skilled musicians, and in the mid-1920s Maybelle joined them to perform at many local events. On August 1, 1927 (see Carter Family, the Original), A.P., Sara, and Maybelle (Ezra came along, too, but did not perform) traveled to Bristol to answer an RCA Victor ad for recording talent. The results of the first records soon made the Original Carter Family the royalty of American country music. In the years that followed, Maybelle joined A.P. and Sara in nationwide tours and many more recording sessions in such places as Camden, New Jersey; Chicago, Illinois; New York City; Atlanta, Georgia; and Memphis, Tennessee.

In 1938, the Carter Family accepted a bid to broadcast a daily radio program on station XERA near Del Rio, Texas. Maybelle moved there with her family, which now included three daughters, Helen, June, and Anita. It was not long before all three were taking part in some of the programs, along with A.P. and Sara's children, Jeanette and Joe. The Carters stayed in Del Rio until 1941, when they all headed north again to a new show on station WBT in Charlotte, North Carolina.

The Original Carter Family broke up in 1943. A.P. and Sara had been divorced since 1939 and they now went their separate ways. Maybelle, however, formed a new Carter Family composed of herself and her daughters. Their first job together was with station WRVA in Richmond, Virginia. They broadcast a radio program there for five years, from 1943 to 1947. They then went to a station in Knoxville, Tennessee, in 1948, followed by a year in Springfield, Missouri, in 1949.

In 1950, Maybelle and the girls moved

to Nashville, where they became featured stars on the *Grand Ole Opry*. Along the way they had discovered a bright young guitar player named Chet Atkins, and when they went to Nashville, he came with them. Later on in the 1950s Helen and Anita left to get married and raise their families and June pursued a career of her own as an actress and singer. Maybelle continued to star on the *Opry* until 1967.

Among the songs Maybelle and her daughters recorded for Decca and Columbia Records were "Amazing Grace," "Wabash Cannonball," "Are You Afraid to Remember Me," "Wildwood Flower," "Gold Watch and Chain," "Blood That Stained the Old Rugged Cross," "Gethsemane," "How About You," and "Softly and Tenderly." They also treated *Opry* audiences to some of Maybelle's own compositions, such as "A Jilted Love," "Walk a Little Closer," and "Lonesome Homesick Blues." Their repertoire also included songs co-written by Maybelle, including "I've Got a Home in Glory, "The Kneeling Drunkard's Plea," "Don't Wait," and "A Rose-Covered Grave."

In the late 1960s and early 1970s, popular interest in country and traditional music increased. In 1967, Maybelle performed at the Country Music & Blues session of the Newport Folk Festival as well as many other concerts across the country, and she was always greeted with generous applause.

When Johnny Cash and his new wife, June Carter, became stars on their own television show at the end of the 1960s and in the early 1970s, Maybelle, Helen, and Anita got together once again and appeared on many of the weekly shows. From then on until her death in 1978, Maybelle enjoyed a period of acclaim that she well deserved as one of the artists who helped make country music what it has become today. In 1970 the Carter Family was elected into the Country Music Hall of Fame.

CARVER, JOHNNY: *Singer, guitarist, songwriter. Born Jackson, Mississippi, November 24, 1940.*

The country roots of Johnny Carver are about as basic as you can get. Early in his career, he would go from singing about rural life in country night clubs to milking cows on the family farm.

Born in a rural Mississippi region not far from the state capital of Jackson, he saw little of city life as a boy. His interest in singing began early and centered on religious music. As he told Dixie Deen of *Music City News* (January 1968), "I used to go with my aunts and uncles over to my grandmother a lot. We had a gospel singing quartet and we'd sing in neighborhood churches and some radio singing too."

He got his first guitar when he was twelve. "You must have heard the same story many times, but it really is true and my mother, who raised chickens, sold eggs, and gave me four dollars of her egg money. I paid her back by doing chores and mowing lawns."

Johnny persistently set about learning the instrument. He asked family friends to help him and tried to imitate some of the country artists he heard on the radio. The first song he recalled learning was Eddy Arnold's "Love Bug Itch" and after that he added many Hank Williams numbers. At fourteen, he gathered some school friends together and started his own band, The Capital Cowboys.

"Down in Jackson they have a lot of drive-in restaurants with curb service and during summer we would play at those places three or four nights a week." The group also appeared at the Kiddie Matinee presented at a Jackson theater. "This was good exposure for us because it was sponsored by a milk company and broadcast too."

After that, he lined up performing work with a local ice-cream company. "Every Saturday morning we would take a flatbed truck and travel to different cities in Mississippi. Then we would go to the stores selling this brand of ice-cream and we'd put on a show and draw a crowd.

"When I was about sixteen, we began to play some night clubs. My father was in insurance and traveled a lot, which meant my mother depended on me, being the oldest, to take over certain responsibilities.

So although my working in clubs didn't meet with their approval, I satisfied them that the experience would be good for me when I left home and began performing for a living."

When he was a senior in high school, he was performing six nights a week. His mother wasn't overly happy, but said, "Well, you can play music at night, but there's two things you have to do. You have to milk every morning and you have to go to church every Sunday." "That means that I would get home at two-thirty [A.M.], go to sleep and then be up again at five-thirty [A.M.] to milk. Now I could have very well-taken my turn at milking in the afternoon, but I believe my mother was putting me to the test. I did it because I loved to play music. . . ."

Once he was out of high school, Johnny set about in earnest to make his mark in the country field. He went on the road with his band and played clubs and fairs in many parts of the United States and Canada. By the mid-1960s, he had moved to Southern California, where he found a secure spot as leader of the house band at the Palomino Club in North Hollywood, then as now the top country nightclub in the area. He also was a regular performer on a country show telecast on a local Los Angeles station.

During those years, he naturally worked up demo tapes, finally placing a single with L.A.-based Imperial Records. The artists and repertoire person he worked with at Imperial, Scotty Turner, suggested Carver would be better off going to Nashville to record with Music City sidemen. After thinking it over, Johnny decided to quit his Palomino job and make the move. One of the first results was his debut LP on the label, *Johnny Carver*, issued in September 1967.

In Nashville, Carver found other outlets for his talents. He placed some of his original songs with other artists and, in late 1967, had the pleasure of seeing Roy Drusky's single of "New Lips" make the charts. He also went out on the road again, often as an opening act for people like George Jones and Connie Smith. His own recordings began to pick up momentum; in late 1967 and early 1968, he placed his single "Your Lily White Hands" on upper-chart levels. During those years, he also achieved a life-long dream by making his debut as a guest artist on the *Grand Ole Opry*.

In the late 1960s and early 1970s, he turned out more recordings for Imperial, a number of which did well on the charts. By the start of the 1970s, he had paid enough dues to rank as a headliner at most country music venues. In the early 1970s, he switched labels from Imperial to ABC and quickly became one of ABC's more successful country stars. When his country version of the pop hit "Tie a Yellow Ribbon Round the Ole Oak Tree" reached the top 5 nationally in June 1973, it represented the fourteenth straight single of his to make the charts up to then. Of those, seven had made the top 20.

He maintained a steady pace through the mid-1970s on ABC, making the charts with singles like "Tonight Someone's Falling" and "Country Lullaby" in 1974; "January Jones," "Strings," and "Starting All Over Again" in 1975; and, in 1976, one of his biggest successes, his top-10 single of Bill Danoff's "Afternoon Delight." The latter was in the national top 10 in September. In 1977, he had another top-ranked single, "Down at the Pool." Late in 1977 his single "Apartment" was on hit lists. However, his recording efforts seemed to cool down as the 1970s came to an end and his affiliation with ABC was phased out. In the early 1980s, his releases came out on minor labels. In 1980, the single of his composition "Finger Tips" made the charts on the Equity ER label. In 1981, the charted single "S.O.S." appeared on Tanglewood Records.

By the early 1970s, his concert work had taken him throughout the United States and Canada, as well as to a number of nations in the Pacific and Europe. By the late 1970s, he had returned to many of those venues several times over. He still had not achieved his goal of becoming a regular cast member of the *Opry* by the early 1980s, though he continued to guest from time to time and to appear on all the TV shows syndicated out of Nashville.

CASH, JOHNNY: *Singer, guitarist, songwriter, band leader (Tennessee Three). Born Kingsland, Arkansas, February 26, 1932.*

When Johnny Cash reached his "Silver Anniversary" as a recording artist in 1979, he could look back on a career that had all the elements of a classic romance novel. He had reached the heights, then plunged to the depths of seeming self-destruction, from which he was saved, in effect, by a woman's love and his own inherent toughness. Almost at the gates of hell, defeated by drug addiction and despair, he rose to become one of the most respected figures in country and popular music of the 1970s. Achieving more than that, he reflected an inner strength and strong religious faith that had an effect on millions of people the world over.

Some of the answers to the complex personality that for many years made him an erratic comet across the horizons of American music lay in the poverty and daily fight for survival of his youth. The Ray Cash family was proud, though bent by years of sharecropping, tragedy, and near tragedy. Johnny almost died of starvation in his infancy in Kingsland, Dyess County, Arkansas, a locale he called "just a wide place in the road." Life consisted of a dirt farmer's shack, five brothers and sisters, cotton patches to be hoed and weeded, and a fundamentalist bible rearing by a determined mother and a work-wearied father. Young John was hauling water for a road gang when he was ten and pulling a nine-foot cotton sack when he was twelve.

The family stayed together, but when Cash was in his early teens, another blow struck the sensitive boy. Sudden death claimed two brothers, leaving Johnny, Reba, Joann, and Tommy to work the fields with their parents. During those years Johnny already was showing signs of creative talent. He was writing songs by the time he was twelve, trying to emulate some of the country stars he sometimes heard on the radio. While attending high school he sang on radio station KLCN in Blytheville, Arkansas.

He seemed reluctant to break away from home, though. With the advent of the Korean War, Johnny enlisted in the Air Force and, after initial training, was assigned to Germany, where he worked as a military cryptographer. Since he found himself with a lot of time on his hands, he bought his first guitar; while learning to play it, he also wrote some new songs, including one of his future hits, "Folsom Prison Blues," inspired by the movie *Inside the Walls of Folsom Prison*. He recalled, "There wasn't much romance to the writing of 'Folsom Prison Blues.' I saw the movie, liked it and wrote the song. That's all there was to that."

After his discharge in the mid-1950s, Johnny settled in Memphis, Tennessee, where he scratched for a living as an appliance salesman and married his first wife, Vivian (they were to have a family of four girls). In his spare time, he took a radio announcing course as a gesture toward a more creative occupation. In Memphis, he met Luther Perkins, who played an amplified guitar, and bass player Marshall Grant. They got together and practiced with the ultimate objective of auditioning for Sam Phillips of Sun Records. The first material they brought to the record company was turned down as being too "country." But after Elvis Presley left for RCA, the label was more receptive to new talent. An audition with Phillips finally brought a contract, and the result of the first sessions of Johnny and the Tennessee Two was the hit single, released in June 1955, "Hey Porter," backed with "Cry, Cry, Cry." These were followed by "Folsom Prison Blues" and such top-10 hits in 1956 as "So Doggone Lonesome," "There You Go," and "I Walk the Line." All of those were Cash originals. He also made the charts with his version of the Rouse Brothers fiddle tune, "Orange Blossom Special."

Johnny by now was one of the most successful artists in Sun Records history. In 1957 he scored with such top-10 originals as "Train of Love" and "Next in Line" and a coauthored hit, "Home of the Blues." In 1958, Johnny had six top-10 hits, including two number-one ranked songs, "Guess Things Happen That Way" and "Ballad of a Teenage Queen." The other four records included songs he wrote or co-wrote: "You're the Nearest Thing to Heaven,"

"What Do I Care," "All Over Again," and "The Ways of a Woman in Love."

By now his first manager, Bob Neal, had booked Cash and the Tennessee Two into personal appearances throughout the country. (The band later became the Tennessee Three with the addition of drummer Bill Holland.) In 1958, Cash moved from Sun to the more affluent Columbia label, where his first release, his own song "Don't Take Your Guns to Town," sold past the half-million mark and stayed in the number-one spot on both pop and country charts for many weeks. His first Columbia LP, *Johnny Cash* (issued in January 1959) sold an impressive 400,000 copies. Sun released more of his material and had another top-10 single in 1959 with "Luther Played the Boogie." Columbia hit pay dirt with "Frankie's Man Johnny" and "I Got Stripes."

The pressures of his growing success were beginning to tell on Cash, however. Adding to that was his depression when his friend Johnny Horton died in an auto accident in late 1960. Outwardly, as the 1960s began, things seemed about as bright as could be. Cash was an established national favorite. He was featured on both country & western and major network pop variety TV programs and was able to fill large concert halls in all corners of the land. As the 1960s went by, he also became a favorite with folk music audiences, starring at many major folk festivals and performing in folk music clubs around the United States, Canada, and overseas.

In his private life, however, things were far from serene. He had become increasingly dependent on amphetamines and barbiturates, going on wild binges that made some of his friends and associates despair for his future. Sometimes he failed to show up for concerts or if he did show up was in poor form or pleaded laryngitis. The strain told on his marriage, resulting in a separation from his first wife by the mid-1960s. At the same time, he could do an about face and show the world a blaze of boundless energy and a driving desire to work almost around the clock on his career.

Those spurts of energy resulted in a continued outpouring of new compositions and recordings that included some of his most notable successes. His top-10 hits of the period included "Seasons of My Heart" (1960); "In the Jailhouse Now" (1962); number-one ranked "Ring of Fire" (1963); "Bad News," "It Ain't Me Babe," "The Ballad of Ira Hayes," number-one ranked "Understand Your Man" (a Cash original) (1964); "Orange Blossom Special," "The Sons of Katie Elder" (1965); "Happy to Be with You," "The One on the Right is on the Left" (1966); "Jackson," and "Guitar Pickin' Man" (1967). The last two were duets with June Carter, daughter of Mother Maybelle Carter of the Original Carter Family and the lady who helped change the course of Johnny's life.

June had been a member of Johnny's troupe since the early 1960s and performed with him in many memorable engagements, including the 1966 performance in Liverpool, England, that shattered the attendance record of no less a group than Liverpool's own Beatles.

June and Johnny became close and marriage seemed in the air, but June asked him to take steps to cure himself of his drug habit. Johnny agreed and, at June's urging, got together with Dr. Nat Winston, former head of the Tennessee Department for Mental Health, for an extended period of treatment. These sessions, coupled with Johnny's renewed interest in his Christian roots, succeeded. Cash no longer found it necessary to require chemical crutches to keep going, and his marriage to June in 1967 proved one of the happiest in the country music fellowship. From then on, they were almost inseparable in a family show that often featured June's sisters, Mother Maybelle, the Statler Brothers, the Tennessee Three, and a number of other excellent artists.

Johnny and June recorded such major hits in 1968 as "If I Were a Carpenter" and "Daddy Sang Bass." Johnny's TV appearances in 1967–68 won such fine response from critics and viewers that ABC gave him the chance to host his own summer replacement series in 1969. The show was hailed by sophisticated urban reviewers as well as "down-home" observers and resulted in a regular season version starting in January 1970.

The year 1969 was a halcyon one for Johnny. Not only was he "clean" of drug problems but happily married and recipient of all manner of awards. He received gold records for the LPs *Johnny Cash at Folsom Prison* and *At San Quentin* and the single "A Boy Named Sue." In the Country Music Awards, he won in every category in which he was nominated: Entertainer of the Year, Male Vocalist of the Year, Best Group (with June), Best Album *(San Quentin)*, Best Single ("A Boy Named Sue").

The TV show was renewed for the 1970–71 season and continued to be very popular, though its ratings declined somewhat. It might have gone on further, but it was caught in the "prime-time squeeze" caused by new Federal Communications Commission restrictions on network programming for those hours and was cancelled.

Johnny and June continued to be favorites on the concert circuit, both during and after their TV period. They filled major auditoriums in the United States, including shows at such places as the Los Angeles Forum and Madison Square Garden and Carnegie Hall in New York. They also performed before large crowds on several European tours and in other parts of the world as well. In November 1971, the Cashes fulfilled a long-time ambition by going to Israel to work on a film about Christianity and modern-day life in the Holy Land. Called *Gospel Road*, it originally was distributed by 20th Century-Fox but later was acquired by Reverend Billy Graham's World Wide Pictures, of Burbank, California.

That was not the only movie credit of Johnny's career. He costarred with Kirk Douglas in *A Gunfight* for Paramount Pictures, among others. He also had a number of TV acting credits, including a role in *Colombo* opposite Peter Falk in March 1974 and in the 1978 CBS-TV movie (also featuring June) *Thaddeus Rose and Eddie*. He hosted the mid-1970s ABC-TV special on railroad history, *Ridin' the Rails*, and in 1976, filmed his first television Christmas special, a show that became an annual event the rest of the decade.

Johnny continued to turn out a steady stream of singles and albums over the decade from 1969 through 1979, many of which made top country (and sometimes pop) chart levels. His singles included the Shel Silverstein novelty song "A Boy Named Sue" in 1969, "See Ruby Fall," backed with "Blistered" (1969); "What Is Truth," "Sunday Morning Comin' Down," "Flesh and Blood" (1970); "Man in Black," "Singin' Vietnam Talking Blues," "Papa Was a Good Man," "A Thing Called Love" (1971); "Kate," "If I Had a Hammer" (with June); "Oney," "Any Old Wind That Blows," "The Loving Gift" (with June) (1972); "Children," "Praise the Lord and Pass the Soup," "Allegheny" (with June) (1973); "Orleans Parish Prison," "Ragged Old Flag," "The Junkie and the Juicehead (Minus Me)," "Father and Daughter" (with Rosie Nix), "The Lady Came from Baltimore" (1974); "One Piece at a Time" (1976); "After the Ball" (1977); "I Would Like to See You Again", "It'll Be Her" (1978); "There Ain't No Good Chain Gang" (a number-one hit with Waylon Jennings), "I Will Rock & Roll with You" and "Ghost Riders in the Sky" (1979).

During his decades with Columbia, Johnny recorded dozens of albums, both secular and spiritual. Among his releases were *Ride This Train* (9/60), *There Was a Song!* (12/60), *Johnny Cash Sound* (8/62), *Blood, Sweat & Tears* (2/63), *Ring of Fire* (8/63), *I Walk the Line* (7/64), *Bitter Tears* (12/64), *Orange Blossom Special* (4/65), *True West* (9/65), *Mean as Hell* (3/66), *Everybody Loves a Nut* (6/66), *Happiness Is You* (11/66), *Carryin' On* (9/67), *Greatest Hits, Volume I* (9/67), *At Folsom Prison* (/68), *At San Quentin* (8/69), *Johnny Cash* (Harmony, 9/69), *Hello, I'm Johnny Cash* (6/70), *World of Johnny Cash* (two LPs, 7/70), *Jackson* (with June Carter, 8/70), *Walls of a Prison* (11/70), *Johnny Cash Show* (1/71), *Man in Black* (8/71), *Greatest Hits, Volume 2* (two LPs, 12/71), *Thing Called Love* (6/73), *Give My Love to Rose* (with June, 7/72), *America* (9/72), *Any Old Wind That Blows* (1973), *Ragged Old Flag* (mid-1970s), *The Junkie and the Juicehead (Minus Me)* (mid-1970s), *I Would Like to See You Again* (4/78), *Gone Girl* (late 1978), and

Silver (1979). His other Columbia albums included *Five Feet High and Rising, Johnny Cash's Children's Album, Johnny Cash Sings Precious Memories, Ballads of American Indians, Johnny Cash and His Woman, Sunday Mornin' Comin' Down, A Thing Called Love, Understand Your Man, Look at Them Beans, Strawberry Cake, One Piece at a Time, Last Gunfighter Ballad, The Rambler.*

During the late 1960s and in the 1970s, Sun Records also issued LPs of Johnny's earlier work on that label. Among these were *Get Rhythm, Living Legend, Johnny Cash—the Man, His World, His Music, Original Golden Hits, Volumes 1 and 2, Rough-Cut King of Country Music, Show Time, with the Tennessee Two, Singing Storyteller, Story Songs of Trains and Rivers,* and *Sunday Down South* (with Jerry Lee Lewis). Harmony Records also provided such albums as *Johnny Cash* (9/69) and *Johnny Cash Songbook* (10/72).

Cash recorded many religious albums over the years. Among these were *Hymns* (5/59), *Hymns from the Heart* (6/62), *Christmas, The Christmas Spirit, The Gospel Road* (1973), *The Holy Land,* and *The Holy Road.* In 1979, he dedicated his two-LP release *A Believer Sings the Truth* (issued on Cachet Records) to his mother, Mrs. Ray Cash, "who inspired me at the age of seventeen when she said, 'God's got his hand on you, son. Keep on singing.' "

His singles continued to show up regularly on the charts in the early 1980s. He began 1980 with another Waylon Jennings duet, "I Wish I Was Crazy Again," in high-chart positions. Other charted releases that year were "Bull Rider," "Song of the Patriot," and "Cold, Lonesome Morning." His 1981 charted singles included "Without Love" and "The Baron."

Although he was a firm believer, Johnny wasn't obtrusive about his religious feelings, respecting the beliefs of others. He told writer Patrick Carr in 1978, "I don't impose myself on anybody in any way, including religion. When you're imposing, you're offending, I feel. Although I am evangelical and I'll give the message to anyone that wants to hear it, or anybody that is willing to listen. But if they let me know they don't want to hear it . . . [i]f I think they don't want to hear it, then I will not bring it up."

His approach was not necessarily that of formal religion. He told Carr that while "the churches are full . . . the slums and the ghettos are still full, and for the most part, the church and the needy haven't gotten together yet. And until more people in the church realize the real needs of the people, and go out rather than going in . . . I mean, to go into church is great, but to go out and put it all into action, that's where it's all at. And I haven't seen a lot of action."

Cash himself followed that approach whenever he could. Early in his career, he established a practice of singing before prison groups, and at the end of the 1970s, he still made ten to twelve such appearances a year. He also contributed his services to various charitable services over the years.

Cash outlines his philosophy of life in his autobiography *Man in Black,* published in 1975 by Zondervan.

CASH, ROSANNE: *Singer, songwriter, actress. Born Memphis, Tennessee, May 24, 1955.*

If you want to break into the entertainment field, it helps to be the daughter of a superstar like Johnny Cash. That alone won't guarantee public favor, but Rosanne Cash proved by the early 1980s she had the ability to become a success in her own right.

A child of Johnny Cash's first marriage, she was born in Memphis, Tennessee, but moved to California in 1959 when Johnny settled the family near Ventura. In the early 1960s her parents separated, but her father kept in touch with the children. Rosanne attended grade and high school in Southern California; after getting her high school diploma, she joined her father's concert troupe. During her three years with the Johnny Cash show, she started as an assistant in the wardrobe department and later was promoted to backup singer and sometime soloist.

Wanting to figure out her own career goals, she went to England in 1976 and spent half a year in London before returning to the United States to enroll in drama classes at Vanderbilt University in Nashville, Tennessee. After a year there, she went back to the Los Angeles area to enroll in the famous Lee Strasberg Theatre Institute. She was still studying acting there when a 1978 demo tape she had made in Nashville (produced by Rodney Crowell) caught the attention of European-based Ariola Records. The company paid her way to Munich, Germany, to record an album slated only for European release.

That work, in turn, sparked interest in her by her father's record firm, Columbia. She signed a contract with Columbia in 1979. Assigned to produce the new LP was Rodney Crowell, whom she had married in early 1979. Titled *Right or Wrong*, that debut collection came out during 1980 and won both considerable favorable critical comment and audience interest. (Backing her on the album was a band called Cherry Bombs, whose members included Rodney Crowell, Emory Gordy, Frank Reckard, Hank Devito, John Ware and Tony Brown.) It spawned the 1980 hit singles "Couldn't Do Nothin' Right" and "Take Me, Take Me."

After that, Rosanne took some time off to have a baby before starting work on a second album the latter part of 1980. The new LP, *Seven Year Ache,* came out in February 1981. The title song was an original composition by Rosanne, as was another track, "Blue Moon with Heartache." The title song was issued as a single and moved to well within the top-20 by April. In the fall, another track from the album, Leroy Preston's "My Baby Thinks She's a Train," rose to number one on country lists. As she told interviewer Chet Filippo, it was a song almost left out of the sessions. "At first I didn't think I could sing that because of the octave changes. But I love it. Me and Rosemary [Butler] and Emmylou [Harris] did the harmonies like the Andrews Sisters going rockabilly."

CASH, TOMMY: *Singer, guitarist, band leader (The Tomcats). Born Arkansas, April 5, 1940.*

Tommy Cash has a fine, deep-toned voice reminiscent of Johnny Cash in his early recordings, and a relaxing stage manner. The fact that he's the brother of Johnny Cash helped open doors for him when he decided to become a full-time performer in the mid-1960s, but, by the same token, the relationship probably proved more a hindrance than an asset over the long haul. With his vocal ability, Tommy might well have made country music his career under any circumstances. Having to follow in the footsteps of someone who had become almost legendary presented, psychologically, a greater barrier than the normal obstacles an aspiring artist must overcome.

Like Johnny, Tommy experienced the deprivation of sharecropper farm life in Arkansas. The family, though, was close knit and one of its affordable pleasures was music. Tommy recalled that his first attempts at singing took place when he was three years old and his mother took him on her lap while she played the piano. Naturally, Tommy was exposed to country music and the church hymns and gospels that were sometimes sung by the entire family.

Though Tommy enjoyed singing, he didn't immediately follow Johnny into the field. While Johnny was starting to make a name for himself in the mid-1950s as one of the rising group of rockabilly singers presented on Memphis-based Sun Records, Tommy pursued work at local stations. By the late 1950s, he was doing well as a disc jockey on station KWAM in Memphis. When he was on military tour, instead of carrying a rifle he was assigned to spin records for the Armed Forces Network in Germany from June 1959 until May 1961. He returned to civilian life briefly, but when President Kennedy called up the reserves he found himself back in uniform again. He was sent to Fort Bragg, but managed to continue his music activities by getting a disc jockey position on station WFNC in Fayetteville, North Carolina.

He finally left the Army for good in 1962 and joined his brother Johnny's organization. Until 1965 he handled executive chores in Johnny's publishing company and doubled as a public relations representative. At the time, he noted, Johnny was "already a star but not yet a legend." After a while, Tommy became restless at doing behind-the-scenes work and decided to try for a singing career. His first recording session in January 1965 produced his initial single, "I Guess I'll Live," a milestone on one level, but far from a hit with the country-music audience. Undaunted, Tommy not only continued his recording efforts but, beginning in August 1966, started doing personal appearances. From then on, he had many engagements every year. By the end of the 1970s, his concerts had taken him to almost every major country-music auditorium in the country as well as night clubs and country fairs. For most of that period he made regular stops in Las Vegas, headlining shows there several times a year.

His recordings began to show up on the hit charts at the end of the 1960s, mostly on the lower levels, though sometimes in the top 10 or 20, on the Epic label. Things took a turn for the better at the start of the 1970s. As he wrote the author in 1980, "It is an unexplainable feeling when you have your first number-one record. My record of 'Six White Horses' achieved that in the charts in January of 1970. Followed by several other top-20 records including 'Rise and Shine,' 'So This Is Love,' 'That Certain One,' 'I Recall a Gypsy Woman,' etc." Among his other better-known releases were "Roller Coaster Ride," "Cowboy and the Lady," "There's More to Her than Meets the Eye," "Reach Out," "Take My Love to Rita," and "One Song Away."'

In the early 1970s he assembled his own band called the Tomcats, for both recording and concert work. The band name, he noted, "was a nickname I had when I was a baby." His early 1970s album releases include *Rise and Shine* in 1970, *Tommy Cash Country* in mid-1971, and *American Way of Life* in 1972. Tommy's recordings during the 1970s included both material from other writers and some original compositions. Though many of his efforts did reasonably well, as the late 1970s approached, he still lacked enough major hits for across-the-board recognition.

He noted, "It's easy in Nashville, with all the great songwriters, to find a good song, but it's difficult to find a great song and that's what it takes to get a monster record. First it's the song, then a good performance and arrangement for that particular song. Sometimes I envy guys like Gatlin and Conway—one of my goals is to write a great song."

Figuring that a change of scenery might bring results, Tommy signed with Monument Records in 1977, and his album debut on that label, *The New Spirit* (which included an updated version of "Six White Horses") was released in February 1978.

CATO, CONNIE: *Singer, guitarist. Born East St. Louis, Illinois, March 30, 1955.*

More than a few successful country stars became professional performers in their early years, leaving disadvantaged environments. Connie Cato, who was earning money as a singer in her mid-teens, had a sizable list of hit recordings to her credit before she reached her maturity.

As she told Lee Rector of *Music City News* (February 1976), her early memories were hardly euphoric. "I only went through the fourth grade. My past history is sort of blah. I lived with my real mother and a stepfather. She was always sick and I had to take care of her and raise my three . . . stepbrothers. I've never seen my real father. I remember when I was real young, when my mother couldn't do anything, I used to stand on a chair and iron, cook, and do the dishes."

As she grew up she worked whenever she could to put some money in her pocket. She also enjoyed listening to country music, though she didn't consider the possibility of making a career in music until a chance event changed her direction. In the early 1970s, she was sitting under a hair dryer in a beauty shop when she felt the urge to sing the country song "Ruby Don't Take Your Love to Town." The hairdresser was impressed and told Connie she ought to do something with her voice. A meeting was arranged with a man who needed a singer for a homecoming dance; after auditioning, Connie got the job.

She recalled, "I had to take two tranquilizers to do my first show. After that, the man who got me that job kept working with me." As she gained a little experience, Connie began to think about moving on to bigger and better things. One day she packed some clothes, took her guitar, and went out on the highway to hitchhike to Nashville. A truck driver picked her up and took her all the way to Music City. Once there she found a motel room in Murfreesboro, Tennessee, and started making the rounds of music offices. The first audition was at Mega Records and resulted in a turndown "because they felt I sounded too much like Dolly Parton."

More disappointments followed, but she finally won the attention of songwriter Curly Putnam (whose credits include "The Green, Green Grass of Home"). He had her cut a demo tape which he took to an executive named Happy Wilson who, in turn, took it to the Capitol Records home office in Hollywood. But while the tape found some favor, Capitol turned her down because they felt that at fifteen she wasn't ready to take on the rough and tumble routine of touring.

For a while, Connie gave up her bright hopes and went back home, where she took on an array of day jobs including working as a waitress and pumping gas, while picking up any singing jobs she could find. Capitol, though, hadn't forgotten her. A year later she was asked to go to Nashville by producer Joe Allison to work on some promising material they felt suited her talents. Her first two recordings were "How Come You Struck the Match," her initial single, which didn't have much impact on the country audience, and "Superskirt," which became a chart hit in the early 1970s. Her career was on its way. Through the mid-1970s, she placed such other hits on the charts as "Super Kitten," "Lincoln Autry," "Good Hearted Woman," and "Who Wants a Slightly Used Woman."

One of her biggest thrills as her career flourished in the first part of the 1970s was her *Grand Ole Opry* debut. As she relived the time she noted, "Ray Pillow brought me out. I was so excited I couldn't believe it. I jumped all over the place. I got to do three songs and you're only supposed to do one. People went crazy! I'll never forget it as long as I live."

She and Capitol parted company by the end of the 1970s. During 1980, she recorded material for MCA Records, one result being the charted single "You Better Hurry Home."

CHAPIN, HARRY: *Singer, guitarist, songwriter. Born New York, New York, December 7, 1942; died Long Island, New York, July 16, 1981.*

A singer/guitarist/songwriter whose original compositions incorporated musical elements ranging from folk to jazz and rock, Harry Chapin not only was a troubadour of modern times but also a bit of a pied piper. Besides entertaining audiences all across the United States, he often persuaded them to contribute to a variety of humanistic causes, ranging from campaigns to combat world hunger to funds to support the performing arts. Describing his code to one interviewer, he said, "Our lives are to be used and thus to be lived as fully as possible. And truly it seems that we are never so alive as when we concern ourselves with other people."

Born in New York's Greenwich Village in 1942, he was the son of a big band drummer whose credits included stints with the Tommy Dorsey and Woody Herman bands. It was a close-knit family and Harry and his three brothers all drew inspiration from their father's musical interests. One of Harry's early musical pursuits was singing in the Brooklyn Heights Boys Choir (after the family moved to the Brooklyn Heights section in the 1950s). Among his acquaintances in the choir was Robert Lamm, later of Chicago rock group fame.

The first instrument Harry learned was trumpet, but he later took up banjo and guitar. When he was fifteen, he organized a musical act with his brothers. The older one soon dropped music, but younger siblings Tom and Steve stayed with it and later were regulars in the band that accompanied Harry around the United States and all over the world. Their father, Jim, sometimes sat in with them when they were young and he too became a cast member of the Chapin troupe in the 1970s, when he often opened one of Harry's programs with his own Dixieland jazz group.

Harry had become enthusiastic about folk music during its boom of the late 1950s and early 1960s when he attended first the Air Force Academy, then Cornell University, where he studied architecture and then philosophy. In 1964, he decided he'd had enough of higher education and left school to join his brothers Tom and Steve and his father in a group called the Chapin Brothers that worked in Greenwich Village spots. The group recorded an album, *Chapin Music,* on Rockland Records, but disbanded when Tom and Steve went back to school.

Meanwhile, Harry was also trying his hand in the film field, first working as a film packer, loading reels into crates, then moving into film editing. By the late 1960s, he was making some of his own documentaries. One of his projects, completed with an associate named Jim Jacobs, was a documentary called *Legendary Champions.* It won a nomination in the Academy Awards competition for best documentary of 1969 and also received prizes at the New York and Atlanta film festivals. In the mid- and late-1960s, Harry also was writing original songs, mostly of the storytelling kind that were to become his trademark in the 1970s.

In 1970, his family resurrected the Chapin Brothers and got a contract to cut an LP for Epic. Harry provided the songs, though he didn't play in the group. Among the tracks on the LP were such numbers as "Dog Town," "Greyhound," and "Any Old Kind of Day," which later were re-recorded by Harry and became important parts of his repertoire. Not too much happened with the 1970 group, but the following year, Harry got back into action, assembling a new band that included his brother Steve. Instead of looking for paying engagements with others, Harry hit on the idea of renting the Village Gate in New York for a summer run. Critics praised their work and soon not only local fans were coming to hear them but record company executives as well. In late 1971, Harry signed a contract with Elektra, his

record company until the end of the 1970s.

In short order he had a single and album that made the national charts. The single, a story song called "Taxi" that drew on Harry's short-lived efforts to get a taxi driver's license in the mid-1960s, received considerable airplay despite its unconventional length of six minutes. His debut LP on Elektra, containing the song, was *Heads and Tales,* released in early 1972. Harry continued to build up a following across the world during 1973 and 1974 with the albums *Sniper and Other Love Stories* and *Short Stories.* The most played track from *Short Stories* was the hit single "W*O*L*D," a bittersweet view of the AM radio world through the eyes of an aging disc jockey.

His fourth album on Elektra, *Verities and Balderdash,* proved even more exciting. One of the tracks in it, "Cat's in the Cradle," was a telling indictment of a father who was more concerned about becoming a success in business than helping his son grow up. Both single and album soared past gold-record levels and verified that Chapin was a bona fide star even though his balladeering approach to music didn't fit neatly into any particular cubbyhole. At bottom, he essentially was a folksinger, but in a completely modern idiom.

In the mid-1970s, without abandoning his steady recording pace (which included two LPs, *Portrait Gallery* and *Greatest Stories—Live*), Harry ventured into other entertainment field areas. During 1974 he was working on a new musical, a multimedia concept show that opened on Broadway in 1975 under the title *The Night That Made America Famous.* The show was highly praised by reviewers and later was given two Tony nominations by New York theater critics. Two years later, this time across the country in Hollywood, a revue at the Improvisation Theater based on his music called *Chapin* achieved a seven-month run and later spawned similar productions elsewhere.

During the 1970s, Chapin kept up a hectic touring schedule that averaged two-hundred concerts a year all over the United States and in many other nations. His visits became annual events at many major venues, including the Greek Theater in Los Angeles. Besides his regular commercial shows, he also constantly crammed in benefit appearances for the many causes and charities he believed in. In the mid-1970s, for instance, he organized a series of Concerts for Africa to help aid victims of the the drought in sub-Sahara regions. In the summer of 1974, he gave three shows for that cause, in the Astrodome in Houston, the Los Angeles Forum, and Madison Square Garden, that helped raise over $6 million in relief funds. In fact, of the two-hundred annual concerts, typically half were benefits.

Another of Chapin's causes involved his efforts to eradicate hunger throughout the globe. He helped found the World Hunger Year, during which time he gave many benefit concerts, enlisting other artists to do the same, and lobbied House and Senate members and the president of the United States to pass a resolution for a governmental commission on world hunger. At many of his concerts, he told the audience he would remain after the show as long as necessary to sign autographs and talk to people donating money to whatever charitable enterprise he was working on at the time.

With that kind of schedule, he still managed to write new songs and turn out new albums, though it must be said that sometimes the pace appeared to be reflected in some loss in creative results. After his 1976 LP, *On the Road to Kingdom Come*, he provided material for a two-album set released in August 1977 called *Dance Band on the Titanic*. He had a theme running through the eleven songs on the latter, that the entertainment industry was sinking. However, the LP seemed far muddier and less interesting than his earlier releases. His next offering, *Living Room Suite*, issued by Elektra in June 1978, was in better form. Among those providing backing vocals were such diverse groups as the Persuasions, the Dixie Hummingbirds, and the Cowsills.

Though still a favorite with concert audiences at the end of the 1970s, Chapin's recording efforts seemed to be bringing diminishing returns when he left Elektra to sign a new contract with Boardwalk Records. By the end of 1980, though, that part of his career was on the upswing with the success of his single "Sequel," in upper-charts levels in December, and his Boardwalk LP of the same title, on the charts from late 1980 well into 1981.

"Sequel," as the title indicates, was a follow up to his earlier hit, "Taxi," in which the man and woman meet after ten years with their roles reversed—by then the one-time taxi driver is a success in the music field and the woman is divorced from her rich husband and working for a living. There is some irony in Chapin's comments to Paul Grein of the *Los Angeles Times* (December 6, 1980): "My wife has been kidding me that in another ten years I've got to write a new song called 'Hearse' and finally haul 'em off."

Unfortunately, Chapin's own life was abruptly ended in an automobile accident on New York's Long Island Expressway in July 1981.

Just before his passing he had expressed his concern over political trends in the United States to Andrew Epstein of the *Los Angeles Times,* though at the same time indicating optimism that the younger generations would in time improve things. (Chapin was somewhat political himself; in the 1980 elections he had campaigned for five Republican and nineteen Democratic congressional candidates, basing his support on their stands in favor of action to alleviate world hunger.)

"Frankly," Chapin said, "there's more potential movement out of this generation than there was in the '60s. The real question is whether America is going to use Reagan as an excuse to forget about things it already knows it should stand up for. When David Stockman [Reagan's budget director] says to America that there's no such thing as entitlement, it's giving us all an excuse to not feel guilty about them [the poor] and just be selfish. And we know that's nonsense. Because we know that Nelson Rockefeller, when he was born, was entitled to $400 million and somebody else was entitled to brain damage because of malnutrition.

"The scary thing about the current political situation is that it is allowing people to have a political excuse to go to sleep."

Soon after Chapin's death, there were indications that others would rally to his causes. Benefits were planned to collect funds for them as well as to salute his memory. His manager, Ken Kragen, announced establishment of a Harry Chapin Memorial Fund "to keep his work going and try to accomplish some of the goals he set."

CHARLES, RAY: *Singer, pianist, songwriter, band leader, record company executive. Born Albany, Georgia, September 23, 1930.*

"Soul is a way of life," Ray Charles once told a reporter, "but it is always the hard way." Ray should know, for he had a long uphill fight to develop his talent and overcome the hindrances of blindness (he wasn't born blind, but lost his sight in an accident when he was six) and racial prejudice. Despite those obstacles, Ray persevered and went on to become an acknowledged superstar, as gifted in capturing the essence of country & western songs as such other genres as R&B/soul, pop, rock, and jazz. And he managed also to remain singularly free from the bitterness and self-pity that might have accrued under the circumstances.

In general, Ray avoided social commentary, because, he once said, "My audiences have spent their hard earned money to get a few minutes entertainment. Everyone can see I'm black, so I guess I don't have to tell anyone about it."

But he didn't avoid the issue either. He took part in the civil rights protests of the 1960s and recorded some civil rights material, such as the 1970s LP *A Message from the People.* As he told Leonard Feather at the time, such a collection shouldn't have surprised anyone. "I was recording protest songs when it wasn't a popular thing to do. Back around 1961 I had one called 'Danger Zone,' and there was another one called 'You're In for a Big Surprise.' Some of the words were: 'I call you mister, I shine your shoes/You go away laughin' while I sing the blues/You think I'm funny and you're so wise/But baby, you're in for a big surprise.' Now that was years before the black

pride and black is beautiful songs came along, but it had the same sort of message."

He also recalled how his initial foray into country & western raised a few eyebrows. "But that first country & western album didn't indicate a change in direction any more than his new *(Message from the People)* album does. These are all simply additional directions." Such efforts were significant, not just for Ray but for other artists. His success in country music, for instance, was a breakthrough of sorts against bigotry that made the path of the great black country singer Charley Pride a little bit easier later on.

Ray was born in Georgia, but his first important move into show business took place in Seattle, Washington, where he headed his own trio in the 1940s. One of the members for a while was Nat "King" Cole, the first of many future stars who gained valuable experience in one of Ray's groups. In those years, rhythm & blues was just developing as an important force in the music world, and Ray soon became a major factor in that forerunner of soul and rock.

Ray achieved his first R&B singles hit in 1954 on Atlantic Records, "It Should've Been Me" and his first national chart hit, "I Got a Woman," the following year. From then on, Ray was rarely out of the spotlight as a concert artist, TV performer, and recording artist. His name was constantly on the R&B and pop charts throughout the 1950s with such singles as "Blackjack," "Come Back," "Fool for You," "Greenbacks," "This Little Girl of Mine," "Drown in My Own Tears," "Hallelujah I Love You So," "Lonely Avenue," "Mary Ann," "What Would I Do Without You," "Right Time" and "What'd I Say" (all on Atlantic).

In 1960 he moved from Atlantic to ABC/Paramount (though Atlantic kept reissuing album packages of his work throughout the 1960s) and promptly had such early 1960s hits as "Sticks and Stones," "Hit the Road Jack," "Them That's Got," and "Ruby." He also made the charts on Impulse Records with "I've Got News for You" and "Mint Julep." In

1962, he made his initial move into country, scoring three hit singles on ABC/Paramount that made both country and pop charts. These were "You Don't Know Me," "You Are My Sunshine," and "I Can't Stop Loving You," the last of which made number one on the bestseller lists and earned a gold-record award from the Recording Industry Association of America. From then on, country songs were a regular part of Ray's repertoire, with one or more often showing up on his new album releases throughout the 1970s and into the 1980s. (As an example, his late 1970s Atlantic LP release, *True to Life,* included soul/country versions of the songs "The Jealous Kind" and "I Can See Clearly Now." He had, by then, left ABC to become reaffiliated with Atlantic.)

His singles hits in the 1960s and 1970s came from an assortment of soul, rock, and country stylings. They included "Busted," "Don't Set Me Free," "No One," "Your Cheating Heart," "Take These Chains from My Heart," "Cryin' Time," "Together Again," "Let's Get Stoned" (a number-one-ranked hit), "Here We Go Again," "Don't Change On Me," and "Feel So Bad."

Ray's activities in the late 1960s through the early 1980s included his own record label (Tangerine) and music publishing firm. His home base was maintained in Los Angeles, California, but he was constantly on the road giving concerts all over the United States and in other countries. He was a featured guest on almost every TV show of consequence during those years, including many country-music programs. Among his credits in the latter category was as featured artist on one of PBS's *Austin City Limits* country-music shows in the early 1980s.

CHILD, FRANCIS J: *Folklorist, author, educator. Born Boston, Massachusetts, February 1, 1825; died Boston, Massachusetts, September 11, 1896.*

Harvard University isn't a strange place to be associated with folk music in the post-Korean War era. To many, though, it does seem odd to connect the austere image of the Harvard of the 1800s with the field. However, not only is this so, but it was at Harvard that the groundwork was laid for the worldwide folk scholarship of the current century.

The man responsible for this was a brilliant professor of English at Harvard, Francis James Child. Child's youthful goal was to go to the great university of his home town, which he achieved despite his father's meager income as a sailmaker. His obvious gift for learning won him a series of scholarships that brought a degree from Harvard in 1846. A few years later, in 1851, he was appointed Boylston Professor of rhetoric, oratory, and elocution. By the time he gained this position, he was deeply immersed in literature studies in Berlin and Gottingen, from 1849 to 1853. It helped establish his reputation as a scholar in Europe and eventually led to a book contract that changed his life.

In 1855, he increased his stature by editing a five-volume edition of the works of British poet Edmund Spenser. He was then asked to prepare a study of Anglo-Scottish ballads as part of a series covering British poets. The result was an eight-volume set, "English and Scottish Ballads," published in 1857–58. Child was not satisfied with the short period of time given him to prepare the material, particularly since he became intensely interested in the subject during his researches. From then on, his thoughts turned more and more to doing a proper study. Eventually, he was determined to spend years, if necessary, to compile a work covering all authentic old folk ballads.

He began to collect materials on ancient British folk music, increasing his efforts as time went on. He did not abandon his studies of English literature, however. In 1863, he wrote a famed treatise called "Observations on the Language of Chaucer." The university recognized his great contributions in 1876 by appointing him Professor of English. By this time, he had provided the university library with hundreds of manuscripts, song sheets, and other material on English and Scottish ballads. (He had secured a publisher for his projected new work in 1872.) This was to make Harvard one of the world's major repositories of information on folk music in later years.

From 1872 on, Child went at his task in earnest. He wrote to educators the world over for possible material and collected songs and verses from many states in the United States. His deep interest in the subject was from the standpoint of the poetry of the verses, for he was not deeply interested in music nor is there any indication he ever tried his hand at singing.

In 1882, the first part of his work was completed. Between this time and the mid-1890s, Child continued to sift and judge hundreds of songs to turn out a work that included only authentic material. He had completed the last of ten parts of the work before his death in 1896, although the final volume did not appear until 1898.

Shortly after, the total collection of 305 ballads, covering such titles as "The Elfin Knight," "Sir Andrew Barton," "Sir Patrick Spens," and "The Marriage of Sir Gawain," was published in five quarto volumes. The work was called *The English and Scottish Popular Ballads.* A cryptic note of Child #10, 20, 100, or whatever the case may be, after ballad references in the world's folk music literature testifies to the genius and effort of the great Harvard scholar.

CLANCY BROTHERS AND TOMMY MAKEM: *Vocal and instrumental group: Patrick, Liam, and Tom Clancy, all born Carrick-on-Suir, Ireland; Tommy Makem, born Keady, County Armagh, Ireland, 1932.*

The singing Clancy brothers and friend Tommy Makem formed one of Ireland's most likable and talented contributions to the American and international folk music scene from the 1950s into the 1970s. Their contributions went far beyond singing, embracing almost every area of entertainment from acting to management. The three Clancy brothers and Makem performed as a group from the mid-1950s to the early 1970s (though each had his own activities as well). In the late 1970s, the tradition was carried on by the twosome of Liam Clancy and Tommy Makem.

The first of the four to seek his fortune away from home was Patrick Clancy, oldest of the three brothers, but not of the nine children that made up the total clan in Tipperary. He enlisted in the RAF for two years and, from that activity as well as post-service civilian jobs, traveled to England, Canada, Wales, Venezuela, and India in the early 1950s. His occupations over three years included painter, insurance sales representative, welder, cab driver, diamond hunter, and actor. His acting hopes found fruition in the United States in the mid-1950s, where he found work with the Cleveland Playhouse and then on and off Broadway in plays by Yeats, O'Casey, and Synge.

His knowledge of Irish folk music was put to use editing and arranging songs for such New York-based firms as Folkways and Elektra Records. He became imbued with the idea of starting his own record company and finally saved enough to start Tradition Records. He soon signed people like Oscar Brand, Odetta, Josh White, Sr., and Carolyn Hester.

Soon after this, a second Clancy arrived—Tom. After serving in the RAF, Tom won attention in Ireland as a pop band vocalist. Acting appealed to him as well and he appeared with an English Shakespearean repertory company and in many Irish plays before going to the United States. Once in America, he emulated brother Patrick by finding work in summer stock and in New York productions. His acting career was hardly garden variety. Among his credits in several decades in the theater were appearances with Orson Welles in *King Lear,* with Siobhan McKenna in *St. Joan,* with Helen Hayes in *A Touch of the Poet,* and an award-winning portrayal of poet Dylan Thomas on CBS-TV's *Camera Three.*

Brother Liam also had an early love for the theater and took formal dramatic training at the National College of Arts in Dublin. After Pat started Tradition Records, he wrote Liam to be on the lookout for new material or artists. Liam then came across Tommy Makem.

He recalled, "It was . . . beyond that mystical border that separates the blessed subjects of the Queen from the Irish misfortunes that I first met Tommy Makem. I went to a Ceilidhe in Newry town one night in a big dance hall there. I was very embarrassed when the band leader announced, in the midst of the fun and the dancing, that this one poor chap was going to sing and not a person in the hall stopped talking or looked up at the stage. Your man wasn't fazed the slightest. He just sat down and started silently to work on his boot.

"One person looked up and then another, and in ten seconds you could hear a pin drop. Then when he had complete attention he began to sing 'O Me Name Is Dick Darby, I'm a Cobbler.' That was my introduction to Tommy. We both took the 'emigrant ship' to America the next year."

Makem's path to that dance hall began in County Armagh, where his family had a tradition of playing and singing Irish folk music. By the time he was five, he was on stage singing and acting with his parents. When he was in his teens, he had an excellent singing style and also could play a number of instruments. When Liam met him, he could handle banjo, guitar, pennywhistle, drums, piccolo, and bagpipes. In his teens, Tommy moved into the pop music field for a time before returning to the folk domain. At fifteen, he formed his own ceili, which translates as Irish country dance band. At seventeen, he had become well known in Ireland as a pop vocalist in the American style.

After Liam and Tommy crossed the seas together, Liam went into acting while Tommy stuck to music. Liam starred at the Poet's Theatre in Cambridge, Massachusetts, and went on to appear in New York in Frank O'Connor's *Guests of the Nation* and to perform with Julie Harris in stage and TV versions of *The Little Moon of Alban*. He also won excellent notices for his work in Brendan Behan's *The Quare Fellow*.

Makem's first notable engagement was at the Circle in the Square in New York's Greenwich Village. From there he went on to an acclaimed appearance at the Gate of Horn folk nightclub in Chicago. (Interestingly, perhaps influenced by the Clancys, he was also to establish himself as a talented actor in the late 1950s.) His reputation as a folksinger kept on growing and

reached a high point with a show-stopping set at the 1960 Newport, Rhode Island, Folk Festival.

The Clancys and Tommy Makem had sometimes gotten together in informal songfests and by the late 1950s had begun to develop a joint repertoire. Their first public outing took place at the Circle in the Square. The response was so good they were booked into the prestigious uptown nightclub, the Blue Angel. This led to engagements at major folk clubs across the United States, from the hungry i in San Francisco to the Village Gate in New York. From then on, the group was a fixture on the folk concert circuit in the United States and abroad until they disbanded.

During the 1960s, the three Clancys and Tommy were featured on almost every major TV show in the United States including *The Ed Sullivan Show, The Tonight Show, Arthur Godfrey's Talent Scouts,* and many others. Their overseas work included TV appearances on the BBC in England and on programs in Ireland, Europe, and Australia. In the early 1960s they played to sellout audiences at New York's Carnegie Hall, which led to a long-standing annual series of twice-a-year concerts there, in November and on St. Patrick's Day. As their careers blossomed, the foursome renewed ties with their homeland. In the 1960s, Pat bought a dairy farm in Carrick-on-Suir; Liam became owner of two pubs, The Jug of Punch in Kilkenny and Doolan's in Waterford; Tom returned to stage at the International Dublin Folk Festival in September 1967; and Makem bought a house on fifty acres of land in Dromiskin.

Once the Clancys and Makem were embarked on their singing careers it was natural for them to start making records for the brothers' company. They began in the late 1950s with *Rising of the Moon* and *Fill Your Glass* (6/59) and continued into the early 1960s with LPs like *Clancy Bros. & Tommy Makem* (9/61). In 1961, they signed with Columbia Records, which took over distribution of the last title. They followed with a series of albums on the label during the next decade that included *Hearty & Hellish, The Boys Won't Leave the Girls Alone* (1962); *In Person* (11/63); *First Hurrah!*

(4/64); *In Ireland* (3/65); *The Irish Uprising* (two discs, 1966); *Bold Fenian Men* (7/69); and *Flowers in the Valley* (3/70). They also were represented by several releases on the Harmony Records label, including *Green in the Green* (3/71) and *I'm a Free Born Man* (6/72). Several LPs also came out on Tradition, such as *Irish Folk Airs* (9/69) and *Irish Drinking Songs* (1970). From time to time, Tommy Makem, as he had throughout his career, turned out solo LPs. His late 1960s through early 1970s offerings included *Tommy Makem* and *Love Is Lord of All* on GWP Records.

As the 1970s went by, some of the Clancys became tired of the touring grind, but Tommy Makem continued a relatively heavy solo schedule. In the late 1970s, he and Liam Clancy formed a new team and found a warm reception for their fine performances wherever they went on the folk circuit.

CLARK, GENE: *Singer, tambourine player, songwriter, band leader (Dillard & Clark Expedition). Born Tipton, Missouri, November 17, 1941.*

As a charter member of The Byrds, Gene Clark played a pioneering role in the blending of folk and rock music. Indeed, some critics trace the beginning of the decline of that seminal group to his departure in 1966. In the years after that move, he continued to make contributions both to folk and to rock, though perhaps never achieving the dramatic impact of his brief stay with the band that made both Bob Dylan's "Tambourine Man" and the Pete Seeger biblically derived "Turn! Turn! Turn!" folk-rock classics.

Born in Missouri, Clark became interested in both folk and country music as a boy. His interest increased as he went through his teens, particularly in folk music, which had achieved widespread popularity during those years. He had an excellent voice that he sometimes showed to good advantage in local hoots or at Midwest folk clubs. In time, his desire to maintain a career in the genre led to an audition for Randy Sparks' New Christy Minstrels. Clark became a member of that highly successful, if not particularly

original, group and took part in its recordings of such hits as "Green, Green," "Saturday Night," and "Liza Lee."

The Minstrels' format seemed too restrictive for him after a while, and he jumped at the chance to join a new band being assembled by folk and jazz A&R person Jim Dickson in Los Angeles in 1964. The other original recruits of what were to become The Byrds were Jim (later Roger) McGuinn, and David Crosby, like Gene young veterans of the folk music scene. The approach the new band would have to its music was still a bit vague, Dickson told writer Derek Taylor, when he, Clark, McGuinn, and Crosby went to see the Beatles' film *A Hard Day's Night.* After viewing it several times, they were deeply impressed. Said Dickson, "We saw that these were not young punks. But real, vital people, with Lennon the catalyst for the exceptional attitudes and communicable magic of the Beatles. We felt that here there was something in popular music in which we could be proud to be involved."

When the five original Byrd members (the others were Michael Clarke and Chris Hillman) were settled in, the saga of that landmark group got underway. The goal was to combine folk roots with the melodic rock approach of the Beatles. It took a little while to put everything in proper order, but in 1965, with the overwhelming response to the single of "Mr. Tambourine Man" and the group's debut LP of that title on Capitol (issued June 21, 1965), the band found itself on the brink of stardom. That position became fact by the end of the year with completion of The Byrds' second LP, *Turn! Turn! Turn!* issued on December 6, 1965, which became a number-one record in the United States and many other countries soon after. Gene Clark contributed a number of lead vocals to both albums and also provided original songs like "It's No Use" for the band's concert repertoire.

By early 1966, fans around the world were clamoring to see the group; at that stage of development, they crammed in as many live appearances as possible to keep the momentum building. However, the frantic pace of plane and bus rides, one-night stands, and performance pressure began to take its toll. Those aspects, and some of the frustrations that went with having to mesh day after day with sometimes conflicting temperaments, finally caught up with Clark.

McGuinn told an interviewer, "Gene developed a tremendous fear of airplanes. . . . One day we were going to New York [from L.A.] to do a Murray the K special and Gene was on the airplane. I got there late, just as the thing was closing up. I always do. Gene was already freaked out and they were holding his arms. He got off and [later] decided to quit the group." When the band's third LP, *Fifth Dimension,* came out in mid-1966, Clark had not contributed to it.

After leaving the Byrds, Gene did some session work, then joined forces with Doug Dillard of the Dillards bluegrass group in a new band, the Dillard & Clark Expedition. It was a more folk-oriented band than The Byrds, though still with some rock flavor. The band completed two above-average albums at the end of the 1960s on A&M, the second one, *Through the Morning,* released in January 1970, and did some touring. However, despite critical approval, the group failed to catch on with the public and disbanded.

Meanwhile there were sporadic attempts to reunite the original Byrds. There also was a release of some early Byrds recordings on Together Records (produced by Jim Dickson) called *Preflyte,* which came out on July 29, 1969. The Byrds' reunion took place in 1973 when McGuinn and Clark were doing solo work and the others were momentarily at loose ends. It seemed a great idea and the quintet worked hard on new material, including two songs by Gene, "Full Circle" and "Changing Times," that feature mandolin-based bluegrass effects. (Clark, though, said "It's not country, it's acoustic.") The album came out on Asylum during 1973, supported by a Byrds tour, but the old magic somehow failed to return.

After that, Clark mainly stayed close to home, writing songs, doing some session work, and raising a family until the late 1970s. In early 1978, he and McGuinn

were signed to headline a show at the Roxy Club in Los Angeles. They were joined onstage by two other former Byrds in an impromptu get-together that brought spontaneous enthusiasm from the audience. The four decided to work together in more shows in San Francisco and other cities, and found similar warm responses.

Crosby had other plans, but McGuinn, Clark & Hillman decided to form a new band of that name. They signed with Capitol, which issued their first LP, *McGuinn, Clark & Hillman,* in early 1979. It wasn't a blockbuster hit, but it made a respectable showing, moving into the national top-10 album lists and staying on the charts for a number of months. A coast-to-coast concert tour that extended into the summer also indicated that there were many fans still very interested in what Clark and the others had to offer. However, though the outlook was promising, the pressures of touring still proved too burdensome for Gene. By the time the second LP came out in early 1980, the group name had changed to McGuinn and Hillman, featuring Gene Clark. Clark wrote and sang lead vocals on two excellent songs in the LP, but appeared only sporadically with the band in its concert work.

At the end of the 1970s, besides his band-related recordings Clark was represented in current album catalogues with several solo LPs. One of them, from Columbia, was titled *Collector's Series: Early L.A. Session.* Others provided more recent work—*White Light* on A&M and, on RSO, *Two Sides to Every Story.*

CLARK, GUY: *Singer, guitarist, songwriter. Born Beaumont, Texas, 1941.*

A painstaking poet songwriter of the so-called "Austin (Texas) School" of the 1960s and 1970s (whose members include Jerry Jeff Walker, Waylon Jennings, and Willie Nelson), Guy Clark has created a relatively small but significant body of classic songs. Rich in the imagery of people and places he's encountered from his youthful years in Texas to his slow progression along the way-places on the road to music industry success in Nashville, the heart of his repertoire is his own body of work.

One of his best-known tunes, "Texas—1947," harks back to the time when, as a six-year-old, Clark used to wait at the local railroad station to watch the first streamliner come through the small town he was living in. The boy puts a nickel on the track, old men leave games of dominoes or glasses of beer, and, the lyric goes, "You'd have thought that Jesus Christ himself/ Was coming down the line."

Another of his classic compositions dealt, as many Clark songs do, with one of the characters he knew in the bigger-than-life Texas environment. The song, "Desperados Waiting for a Train," deals with an oil-well driller, originally a Quaker from Pennsylvania, who decided to seek a permanent haven in his grandmother's West Texas hotel. Since the old-timer was down on his luck he wanted to pay for his keep by working as a handyman.

As Guy told Dale Adamson of the *Houston Chronicle,* "For some reason they just hit it off and she said 'OK.' And he stayed there. When I was a kid, growing up, he was just like a grandfather, except not really because he was still who he was: " 'He's a drifter and a driller of oil wells/ He's an old school man of the world/ Taught me how to drive his car/When he's too drunk to drive/He'd work and give me money for the girls.'

"I was around him a lot when I was a kid. Then we moved away from there—down to Houston, then to Rockport. The older I got, the less I saw him. So he seemed to change pretty drastically in later years.

" 'One day I looked up and he's pushin' 80/Got brown tobacco stains all down his chin./To me he's one of the heroes of this country/So why's he all dressed up like them old men?' "

Clark learned to play guitar as a boy, initially playing Mexican songs rather than country or folk melodies on the instrument. The goal of making a career in music eventually took him to Los Angeles in the 1960s. While he sought outlets for his musical efforts, he earned his living by working in the Dopera Brothers guitar fac-

tory. The product made there is the famous dobro guitar widely used in both country and pop bands in recent decades. The paycheck put groceries on the table not only for him but for his equally talented wife, Susanna.

He didn't make much progress in placing his songs there, but the city proved the inspiration for one of his most important compositions, "L.A. Freeway." While he was fighting the battle of traffic jams and exhaust fumes one night, he thought, "If I can just get off this L.A. freeway without getting killed or caught. . . ." It became the chorus for a song that eventually was made a hit by Jerry Jeff Walker.

The Clarks moved to Nashville in 1971, where Guy made the rounds of studios and publishing firms and Susanna turned out a growing body of original paintings. The going was slow, but more and more artists became aware of Guy's ability as a writer from 1971 to the mid-1970s. Jerry Jeff Walker was a particularly strong supporter, using one or more Guy Clark songs in almost every album from the early 1970s on. *L.A. Freeway* was the title track on one of those, an LP that also included Guy's "That Old Time Feeling." Walker used "Desperados Waiting for a Train" in the album *Viva! Terlingua,* one of Walker's best releases of the 1970s. In *Ridin' High,* Walker sang Guy's "Like a Coat from the Cold," a song Guy wrote specifically for Jerry Jeff in honor of the latter's marriage.

Other artists have covered Guy Clark songs, including the Earl Scruggs revue, the Everly Brothers, Jim Ed Brown, Rita Coolidge, Tom Rush, and David Allen Coe. In late 1975, Johnny Cash's version of "Texas—1947" made the country charts. Meanwhile, Susanna also was proving her prowess as a songwriter. At the same time the Cash single was gaining attention, good reaction was being voiced for Susanna's "I'll Be Your San Antone Rose," featured on an album by RCA singer Dottsy.

Though Guy Clark was signed to an RCA recording contract in the early 1970s, it took almost three years before that matured into an album. Clark, ever the perfectionist, didn't like some of the original recordings and insisted on reworking some of them. The album, *Old No. 1,* finally came out the end of 1975. It included his versions of already known songs like "Desperados," "Texas—1947," and "L.A. Freeway," as well as such other fine offerings as "Instant Coffee Blues" and "Rita Ballou." The album was one of the most impressive debuts in the country field of the 1970s, though it didn't do as well with the public as it deserved.

In 1977, Guy switched record labels, signing with Warner Bros. Again, he took his time in preparing the new release, which finally appeared in late 1978 under the title *Guy Clark.* He provided six originals of the ten songs in the album: "Fool on the Roof," "Fool on the Roof Blues" (despite the title, two different songs), "Fools for Each Other," the bluegrass track "The Houston Kid," "Comfort and Crazy," and "Shade of All Greens," the latter about "the late afternoon sun filterin' through the trees and the bushes out where I live. There's so many greens."

As Guy told Dale Adamson, "I write songs different every time. Sometimes the music comes first, sometimes the words come first. I don't have any set pattern to the way I write. I just try to get some sort of creative thing goin' and just follow it wherever it goes, whether it starts with the music or the lyrics or both at the same time.

"Sometimes I have to work at it really hard—like sit down and concentrate and work for days and days on a song. Sometimes it'll happen in 30 minutes, completely by surprise. There's just no real formula to it for me. But I do work at it. Both 'Texas—1947' and 'Desperados' are songs I worked on a lot, which may be obvious if you think they're well constructed. It took a long time to write those songs. But other songs, for example 'Old Time Feeling,' didn't take any time at all.

"When I write songs, I'm serious about writing them and I'm very self-critical. I don't just write a song to write a song. I really make sure I'm not just throwing away words or lines or something just to get a rhyme. It's got to make sense. It's got to hang together. . . . But I'm a singer, too.

I write 'em to sing 'em. I don't write 'em specifically for other people. I really enjoy singin' and playin'. That's all part of it as far as I'm concerned."

CLARK, ROY: *Singer, guitarist, banjoist, fiddler, songwriter, comedian. Born Meaherrin, Virginia, April 15, 1933.*

A multitalented individual, Roy Clark, with his corn-fed humor, would have the audience roaring with laughter and minutes later his superb instrumental artistry on guitar, banjo, or fiddle would have them rapt in attention. His instrumental skills proved adaptable to a variety of surroundings, from the madcap *Hee Haw* TV series to the concert halls of Russia or the stage of the Boston Pops.

He began his progress toward those accomplishments from his very early years in Virginia. His father, a sometime tobacco farmer, played in local groups, as did other relations, and his mother played piano. He recalled that "I was just a kid of about three when I discovered Dad's banjo and I naturally assumed it was a drum, something to pound on, which is exactly what I did. Well, I got straightened out pretty quick."

His father saw to it that the boy learned banjo techniques. An apt pupil, Roy began to impress those around him by his early teens. In the late 1940s, he entered the Country Music Banjo Championship and walked off with first prize. The next year he repeated, gaining an appearance on the *Grand Ole Opry.* By then he not only could play banjo, but the twelve-string acoustic guitar and fiddle as well.

At the start of the 1950s, he settled in Washington, D.C., where he worked as a sideman or soloist in country clubs. He became close friends with Jimmy Dean, who spotlighted Roy's talents when he had his own show in the early 1950s. Roy's growing reputation gained an additional boost when he guested on *Arthur Godfrey's Talent Scouts* in 1956, the first of several appearances with Godfrey. At the end of the decade, he joined forces with country star Wanda Jackson, working a number of engagements with her and also doing backing instrumentals on her recordings for

Capitol. One of the places he worked with her was Las Vegas' Golden Nugget. It was the start of a loving relationship between Vegas hotels and Clark, who headlined many shows there from the mid-1960s on. In the 1970s, in fact, he had a long-term contract to play the main showroom of the Frontier Hotel twelve weeks a year.

Roy's backing work for Wanda Jackson helped bring a solo contract arrangement with Capitol. In 1962 his album *Lightning* won above-average attention from both critics and country fans. In January 1963, he made his debut on Johnny Carson's *The Tonight Show* on NBC-TV. As the decade went by, he returned a number of times to the show. Many times in the 1970s and at the start of the 1980s, besides appearing as a guest artist from time to time, he also served as Johnny's guest host. The year 1963 proved important in other ways; Roy gained his first top-10 singles hit, "Tips of My Fingers," which became the title track for a hit LP issued in the fall. Throughout the mid-1960s, Capitol kept issuing new albums of his, including *Happy to Be Unhappy* in October 1964; *Guitar Spectacular* (12/65); *Lonesome Love Ballads* (3/66); *Stringin' Along* (6/66); *Roy Clark Live!* (on Tower Records).

Roy's activities continued along at a breakneck pace as the 1960s went by. Besides a steady diet of live engagements throughout the United States and in other countries, Roy often showed up on TV. Among his mid-1960s credits were the *Andy Williams Show, Jimmy Dean,* and a number of *Grand Ole Opry* radio and TV releases. In the mid- and late-1960s, he helped host the syndicated *Swingin' Country* show. At the end of the decade, he was asked to be cohost of a brand new series with Buck Owens called *Hee Haw,* a blend of corncob humor and contemporary country music. For its first two years of existence the show was presented on the CBS network. Though it got good ratings, CBS decided *Hee Haw* didn't fit its image and cancelled it.

But the show's producers decided to buck the odds and syndicate it themselves. Their gamble paid off, helped in part by the great rapport Clark had with viewers,

and *Hee Haw* not only remained alive but prospered. In 1978, in fact, with Clark still very much in evidence, the show celebrated its tenth anniversary. In the early 1980s, the program remained a staple on several hundred stations.

By the time Roy joined *Hee Haw* he had changed record labels, going from Capitol to Dot (continuing on the Dot roster after the operation was absorbed by ABC Records, which in turn was acquired by MCA). In the late 1960s and early 1970s, Roy's fans had plenty of new recordings to choose from, including such albums as *I Never Picked Cotton, Incredible Roy Clark, Magnificent Sanctuary Band, Best of Roy Clark,* and *Roy Clark Country.* He also had a number of hit singles, including the 1969 success "Yesterday When I Was Young," which sold over 250,000 copies and won him an Outstanding Country & Western Song Award from ASCAP. During the 1970s, he won more ASCAP Outstanding Country & Western Song Awards: "Then She's a Lover" (1970); "Riders in the Sky" (1973); "The Lawrence Welk Hee Haw Counter Revolution Polka" (1973); "Somewhere Between Love and Tomorrow" (1974); "Think Summer" (1976); "Heart to Heart" (1976); and "We Can't Build a Fire in the Rain" (1978).

During the 1970s, Roy added to his TV credentials with a bewildering array of TV specials including the *Mitzi Gaynor Special, Bell Telephone Hour* special, several Bob Hope specials, *The Captain & Tenille, Flip Wilson, Donnie & Marie* (Osmond) show, *Mac Davis* show, *Merv Griffin, Dinah!, Sammy and Company,* and even a role on the *Odd Couple* comedy series. He was in evidence at many awards events and served as cohost of the nationally televised Country Music Association 1976 show and the American Music Awards.

Starting in the late 1960s, his superstar status was given increased recognition. The West Coast-based Academy of Country Music named him Top Country Comedy Act for 1969 and voted him similar awards in 1970 and 1971. The Academy also voted him TV Personality of the Year for 1972 and Entertainer of the Year for 1972 and 1973. During that period—from

1969 to 1972—the readers of *Music City News* voted him number-one Instrumentalist. The Country Music Association also honored him many times, starting with election as 1970 Comedian of the Year. Later the CMA named him Entertainer of the Year for 1973 and, with Buck Trent, Instrumental Group of the Year for 1975. In 1974 he was dubbed Country Music Star of the Year (for 1973) by the American Guild of Variety Artists. In 1975, a star with his name on it was embedded in the Walk of Fame on Hollywood Boulevard.

In 1976, Roy was given the opportunity to make a three-week concert tour of the Soviet Union. He performed before standing-room-only crowds in Riga, Moscow, and Leningrad, and his bravura performance led to standing ovations and an invitation for a future return engagement. In honor of that achievement, the CMA named him its International Friendship Ambassador. During the summer of 1976, Roy performed with Arthur Fiedler and the Boston Pops Orchestra, a show screened several times afterward on the Public Broadcasting System.

Additionally his ABC albums of the mid-1970s often showed up on the country charts and sometimes crossed over to the pop charts. In mid-1974, for instance, his LP *The Entertainer* was a top-10 hit, as was his mid-1975 duo with fellow banjo player Buck Trent, called *Pair of Fives (Banjos That Is)*. In the fall of 1975, his *Greatest Hits, Volume 1* was in the top 15 and his late 1975 release *Heart to Heart* was on the country lists in early 1976. In 1977, his ABC album release *Labor of Love* also appeared on country bestseller lists.

These discs helped bring new acclaim from his peers. In 1976, the CMA voted Roy and Buck Trent the Instrumental Duo of the Year for a second time and in 1977 and 1978 named Clark Instrumentalist of the Year.

Roy closed out the 1970s with his MCA single "Chain Gang of Love" rising on the hit lists, moving into upper brackets in early 1980. Several months later he had the charted single "If There Were Only Time for Love." In 1981 he made the charts with such singles as "I Ain't Got Nobody" and "She Can't Give It Away."

CLAYTON, LEE: *Singer, guitarist, songwriter. Born Russelville, Alabama, October 29, 1942.*

Border Affair by Lee Clayton, one of the best country albums of 1978, underscored the great talent of Clayton, one of the finest songwriters in Nashville in the 1970s. His contributions to the repertoires of artists like Waylon Jennings, Willie Nelson, and Jerry Jeff Walker earned him the designation of "the outlaw's outlaw."

Born in Alabama but raised in Oak Ridge, Tennessee, Clayton grew up in a household that played old Jimmie Rodgers songs and recordings of Red Foley like "Peace in the Valley." Lee inherited his father's love for country music and became addicted to listening to Saturday-night *Opry* programs featuring artists like Roy Acuff, Hank Snow, and a wonderful newcomer named Hank Williams. He recalled, "My father once took me to the *Opry* when I was six years old. To this day I still remember the entertainers signing autographs in the alley at the stage door and the smell of Tootsie's as we walked in the back entrance."

His father gave him the choice of learning accordion or guitar when he was nine. He chose guitar and was given a steel guitar. "I took lessons for about one and a half years on the Hawaiian guitar. I couldn't stand it. They started making me try to learn notes. My mind wasn't ready for it then, though I understand its importance now." Still, he progressed enough to debut "on the radio one Saturday playing Leon McAuliffe's 'Steel Guitar Rag' when I was ten.

"I picked up the guitar again when I was sixteen and the folk wave hit with the Kingston Trio. I married my high school sweetheart six months before I graduated from the University of Tennessee, put my guitar away again and proceeded to become 'Mr. Normal.' That lasted about one year.

"One morning I was sitting in bumper-to-bumper traffic on my way to work when an airplane flew over me on the way to landing. I looked up and said to myself, 'F it, I'm gonna fly!' I loved my wife, but she was working on a Ph.D. in mathematics and I was headed for a degree in hanging out. Within a year we were divorced and I was in the Air Force [in late 1965] taking pilot training."

As it turned out, flying was not well suited to Lee's personality. In fact, after he was discharged in 1969, he never flew again. But the change of environment made him concentrate on music more. He played whenever he could and also turned to songwriting in earnest. As he told the author of this book, "The first song I consider a song I wrote probably in 1966. That was a long time ago and I don't even recall its title. When I got into writing and hanging around Nashville after leaving the service, I'd written about twenty-five. Friends in country music told me, 'Well, when you're really a good writer you'll throw away the first one hundred.' I wrote 'Ladies Love Outlaws' right about that time. Waylon Jennings recorded it in early 1972 around March and it became my first writing success."

Lee began to get attention as a performer that year, which he considered another major turning point. "I got to go back to Griffith Springs, Texas, to the first big country-music concert there. I found myself performing on the same bill with people like Roy Acuff, Tex Ritter, Willie Nelson, and Waylon. Billy Joe Shaver and I went in there unknowns and came out with national publicity. It was luck. The first night before the concert began the concert people gave a party for everyone involved with the program. I met writer Arnie Lewis from *Rolling Stone* and Annie Leibowitz, a photographer from the magazine. We hung out together all three days. When they went back they wrote about me and Billy Joe."

That helped get him a contract with MCA Records, which released his debut LP in 1973. The album proved a failure. "After one of the most grueling years of my life, I realized that neither myself nor my music was together. I had absolutely no idea what to do except to stop and think about it." He did so for most of 1974. But meanwhile, other artists retained great interest in his songwriting abilities. The result was that an increasing number of recordings of his originals came out as the mid-1970s went by, including Jennings' versions of "If You Could Touch Her at All" and "Memory of You and I"; Jerry Jeff Walker's offering of "Won'tcha Give Me One More Chance"; "Silver Stallion" recorded by Bonnie Koloc; and Hoyt Axton's track of "Whisper on a Velvet Night."

After a sojourn in Joshua Springs, California, in 1974, Clayton returned to Nashville, where he settled down on a farm outside town to continue writing while seeking ways to rejuvenate his recording career. In 1977, he signed a new agreement with Capitol, which issued the LP *Border Affair* in late 1978. In 1979, with glowing reviews for the album in his file, he returned with full vigor to work on a followup. He told us at that time, "On the new album I felt I went to a higher level of writing. The material is simpler in structure, closer to home in feeling—simple things are always harder, but I think it's the way to really express yourself musically." *

CLINE, PATSY: *Singer, pianist. Born Winchester, Virginia, September 8, 1932, died Camden, Tennessee, March 5, 1963.*

"I remember the last time I saw Patsy alive. It was in Nashville on a Thursday. That Thursday night, I went over to Patsy's house because she had some tapes she wanted me to hear from a recording session. At that session she cut 'Sweet Dreams.'

"I remember that while we listened to the tapes, Patsy embroidered a tablecloth. She did that to relax. Her little boy Randy was on a rocking horse, rocking very hard. I was worried that he'd fall off and get hurt, but Patsy said not to worry. That

* *Based partly on a 1979 phone interview with authors.*

night we made plans to go shopping when she returned from doing the benefit show in Kansas City for some disc jockey [Cactus Jack Call] who had gotten hurt in a wreck. . . ."

"On Sunday evening, March 6, 1963*, Patsy, Hawkshaw Hawkins, Cowboy Copas, and Randy Hughes, the pilot, were flying home from the Kansas City benefit in a twin-engine Comanche, when they ran into a storm near Dyersberg, near where I live today. On Monday morning I wondered why I didn't hear from Patsy. . . . Just then, I got a call from Patsy's booking agent, who told me she was dead. I said, 'Baloney, her and me is going shopping!' Then I realized it was true. . . . That just about broke me up, to think that someone as good as that was gone."

Thus did Loretta Lynn recall the last days of Patsy Cline in her autobiography, *Coal Miner's Daughter.* Her feelings of shock and loss were shared not only by Patsy's many friends and associates in country music but by the millions of people who had helped make her the logical choice not long before as "Top Female Singer."

Patsy, whose original name was Virginia Patterson Hensley, was often described as a child prodigy. When she was only four, she made her public debut by winning first prize in an amateur contest for her tap dancing skill in her home town of Winchester, Virginia. By the time she was in grade school, she was also exhibiting talent as a singer.

At eight, she started learning to play the piano. Knowledge of the basic patterns of music gained from her piano lessons helped improve her vocal efforts. While still in public school, she was a featured singer with her church choir and continued to sing with that group through her teens. She also sang in school plays and made some appearances in local clubs.

When she was sixteen, Wally Fowler of the *Grand Ole Opry* was starring in a touring show that played the Winchester Palace Theatre. Patsy managed to audition for

* The records show March 5 to be the correct date.

him and won a guest spot on the bill. Through his intervention, her parents helped her to go to Nashville to try to carve out a career in the country field. Initially, she made little headway with agents or recording executives, and earned a precarious living mainly working as a dancer in small clubs. Discouraged, she finally returned home to Winchester.

However, still harboring hopes of scoring a breakthrough in the entertainment industry, she auditioned and won a chance to appear on *Arthur Godfrey's Talent Scouts.* The song she chose for her debut on the nationally televised program was "Walkin' After Midnight." Her rendition on January 21, 1957, won an ovation from the studio audience and approval from followers of the program. She won first prize and soon after was given a recording contract by Decca, which released her single of the song. The record became a hit on both pop and country charts and Patsy at twenty-five was embarked on the road to stardom.

For a time in the late 1950s, none of her follow-up recordings approached the success of "Walkin' After Midnight," particularly in the country field, but in the early 1960s, she started to turn out releases that found widespread favor with country fans. During those years, she became a headliner on the country concert circuit as well as a regular cast member of the *Grand Ole Opry.* Her first banner year was 1961, when she had the top-10 hit "Crazy" and one of the top-selling singles of the year, "I Fall to Pieces," which went to number one on country charts. She turned out a number of excellent singles in 1962, including another number-one single, "She's Got You" and the top-10 "When I Get Through with You, You'll Love Me Too." In 1963, she had the top-10 singles "Faded Love," "Leavin' on Your Mind," and "Sweet Dreams (Of You)," the last-named release after her death. Among her early 1960s album releases were *Patsy Cline* (1/62) and *Sentimentally Yours* (10/62).

Since that tragic plane crash in early 1963, Patsy's voice continues to this day to beam forth from radio stations and home turntables. Soon after the tragedy, Decca issued a two-record set titled *The Patsy Cline Story* in August 1963. This was followed in 1964 with *Patsy Cline Portrait*; in February 1965 with *How a Heartache Begins*; and in May 1967 with *Greatest Hits*. Several releases came out on the Evergreen label, including *Golden Hits* (1963); *In Memorium* (6/63); *Patsy Cline Legend* (3/64); and *Reflections* (2/65). Album releases on other labels included, on Vocalion, *Here's Patsy Cline* (8/65) and *Great Patsy Cline* (8/69); on Metronome, *Gotta Lot of Rhythm* (8/65); and on Pickwick, *I Can't Forget You, Stop the World, Today, Tomorrow, Forever*, and *In Care of the Blues*.

In 1977, Loretta Lynn paid tribute to her friend's memory with her album *I Remember Patsy*. The LP included Loretta's versions of nine of Patsy's major hits and a conversation between Loretta and veteran producer Owen Bradley (who had been Patsy's producer), reminiscing about the late, great vocalist.

Patsy was elected to the Country Music Hall of Fame in 1973. The bronze plaque in her honor reads, in part, "Patsy will live in country music annals as one of its outstanding vocalists. . . . Her heritage of recordings is testimony to her artistic capacity. [Her] biggest hit, "I Fall to Pieces" . . . has become a standard. . . . Joined *Grand Ole Opry* 1960 . . . [which was the] realization of a lifelong ambition."

During the 1970s and into the 1980s, MCA Records, the successor to Decca, continued to maintain a number of Patsy's albums in its active catalogue and also issued repackaged collections of some of her work. As of late 1981, those comprised *Patsy Cline's Greatest Hits; Patsy Cline Showcase; Sentimentally Yours; A Portrait of Patsy Cline; Always; Here's Patsy Cline; The Patsy Cline Story;* and *Country Great*. Occasionally, reissued or re-engineered versions of her recordings appeared on singles charts, such as the MCA release "Always" in 1980 and the 1981 duet with the late Jim Reeves (issued on RCA), "Have You Ever Been Lonely." Actually, Patsy never recorded with Reeves. The single resulted from an engineering merger of two separate recordings of the same song by the two artists.

CLOWER, JERRY: *Comic. Born Amite County, Mississippi, September 28, 1926.*

Rural humor always has been an integral part of the country music scene, sometimes in the form of comic sketches delivered by bandsmembers, other times handled by stand-up comics the likes of Minnie Pearl and the Duke of Paducah. Maintaining the latter tradition in the 1970s was burly Jerry Clower, "The Mouth of Mississippi," whose wild anecdotes of goings on in his home region of Amite County kept his audiences howling with laughter, not only in the South but in all sections of the United States.

Clower depended for his impact on timing and histrionics. As he said, "I tell stories funny, not funny stories." His approach was described by Lawrence Buser. "Clower talks. He bellows. He wails. He waves his arms. He contorts his face. Puckers his lips. Furrows his brow. And does the best imitation of a chain saw that you ever heard. (Although 'Wah-wa-wa-wa-wa-wa' does not look like much when you read it, listen to Clower bring it to life in one of his stories and then look around for that tavern screen door the notorious Marcel Ledbetter, in a fit of anger, reduced to a twisted pile of wire and splinters.)"

As a farm boy growing up in Mississippi in the 1930s and early 1940s, Jerry gave little thought to a show business career. In his teens, he already was a two-hundred pounder who liked sports of all kinds. In his late teens at the tail end of World War II, he entered the service for several years, then played football at a local junior college and gained a full scholarship to Mississippi State University, where he considered becoming a pro football player. But the competition was tough and he opted for a regular job as a fertilizer sales representative for Mississippi Chemical Corporation in Yazoo City, joining the firm in 1954.

Somewhat in the tradition of the first *Opry* star, Uncle Dave Macon, Jerry developed his comic touch as a sideline and didn't move on to the commercial entertainment arena until well along in years. In fact, he worked up his repertoire of funny stories mainly to help his sales pitch. Over a decade and a half of selling fertilizer, he unconsciously polished and refined his delivery until he was more a performer than huckster. After a while, he began to expand his scope by giving some of his routines at company sales meetings and in front of local groups. In time, people began to urge him to do more with his talent. On the advice of a friend, he taped a "raccoon" story and submitted it to Decca Records (now merged into MCA Records) in the early 1970s.

In 1971 Clower met his manager, Nashville-based agent Tandy Rice. "Ever since . . . my life's been boiling just like a great big Alka-Seltzer."

With those steps under his belt, things began to move for Clower. Decca recorded his first album, *Jerry Clower from Yazoo City, Mississippi, Talkin'*, live (all his LPs through the late 1970s were recorded in that fashion, in line with his belief that he came across best that way). His appearances on the *David Frost Show* in New York and many other major TV programs helped to make the record a million seller. He quickly became a favorite with fans all over the country, and each succeeding album brought in new gold-record awards, including his second LP, *From the Mouth of the Mississippi*, followed by *Clower Power, Live in Picayune* (issued in 1975), and *The Ambassador of Good Will* (1976).

Clower soon was asked to become a regular on the *Grand Ole Opry*, where he still was a featured performer in the 1980s. His other activities included an appearance on a Walter Cronkite program on desegregation in the South and a starring role on the syndicated country music show *Nashville on the Road*.

He was particularly proud of the Cronkite program because he felt it showed the real progress achieved in integration in his beloved home town of Yazoo City. He acknowledged to Buser that his views in favor of tolerance and equality made him anathema to the Ku Klux Klan. "I find I fought a war to give a man the right to be a bigot if he wants to, but those same people don't want to give me the right not to be one. I'm a redneck, but I'm an educated redneck. I was taught that you should

never have your mind so made up that facts couldn't change it."

A Bible-reading Christian, he insisted to interviewers that he never drank, smoked, lied, cheated, or swore. As a lay minister and deacon of the First Baptist Church in Yazoo City, he often was called on to deliver sermons in his home church and elsewhere across the United States. His speaking engagements in the religious area included appearances with the *Billy Graham Crusade* and, on one occasion, serving as keynote speaker at the Southern Baptist National Convention in Miami, Florida.

At the start of the 1980s, Jerry continued to turn out new albums for MCA Records. In 1980, *Ledbetter Olympics* was released, followed in the fall of 1981 by *More Good 'Uns*.

COCHRAN, HANK: *Singer, guitarist, songwriter. Born Greenville, Mississippi, August 2, 1935.*

The name Cochran is familiar to both rock and country fans. To rock followers it brings to mind Eddie Cochran, a legendary figure whose "Summertime Blues" was almost an anthem for the teenagers of the 1950s. For country fans, the Cochran of note is Hank, writer of many classic songs and a talented performer in his own right. Oddly, both Hank and Eddie worked together for a time under the name The Cochran Brothers even though they were unrelated. Eddie died in 1960 after contributing some major rock hits; at the time, Hank was still unknown. Fortunately, he was active for decades afterward, still contributing to the country scene at the start of the 1980s.

Hank (original name Garland Perry Cochran), born in Mississippi, spent many of his early years in Tennessee. His parents died when he was a child and he was placed in a Tennessee orphanage. At ten he ran away from there and somehow managed to keep from returning, eventually making his way to Hobbs, New Mexico, where he had some relatives. While there, he earned a living as an oil-field hand. He also took his first steps toward a music career when an uncle taught him to play guitar. Many of the first songs he picked out on the instrument were Hank Williams songs that he had listened to on the radio. After a while, though, Cochran felt the urge to write original material and he had a fair number under his belt by the time he headed for California in the mid-1950s.

Continuing to earn money from manual work, he spent much of his spare time at a place called the Riverside Rancho. Some of the time he just hung around listening to the regular country artists. On occasion he got to sit in with some of them. He also met other aspiring young musicians, including Eddie Cochran. The two teamed up and worked together for several years before Eddie decided to concentrate on rock in 1958. Hank by then was gaining a reputation as a good sideman and became a regular on a country TV show in Stockton, California, called the *California Hayride.*

Hank's career was interrupted for a time when he was drafted into the Army and stationed at Fort Ord, California. His stay was fairly brief, and after his discharge he played for a time at the Fort Ord noncommissioned officers club. He was writing steadily by then and decided to try for a regular job. The result, at the end of the 1950s, was a job as staff writer with the California branch of Pamper Music Company at fifty dollars a week. His work was promising enough that within a year Pamper agreed to transfer him to its Nashville branch. He arrived there in October 1959. A few days after he reached Nashville, Skeets McDonald became the first Music City artist to record one of his numbers, "Where You Go I'll Follow." Another of the results of the move was a collaboration with Harlan Howard on a song called "I Fall to Pieces" that provided Patsy Cline with a number-one country hit.

In Nashville, Cochran hung out at a well-known club called Tootsie's Orchid Lounge, where he met other young hopefuls. One of them, with whom he forged a close friendship, was Willie Nelson. He thought so much of Willie's potential that when Joe Allison, then head of Liberty Records country-music division, offered Hank a recording contract, Hank urged them to sign Willie first. They did, but soon after added Cochran to the roster as well. Hank responded with several releases, the second of which, "Sally Was a Good Old Girl" (a Harlan Howard composition), remains a country classic.

But while Hank continued to perform in many major country spots as the 1960s went by, his main accomplishments remained in the writing field. He had a banner year in 1962, for instance, with such hits as Patsy Cline's version of "She's Got You," which reached number one nationally; Burl Ives' recordings of "A Little Bitty Tear" and "A Funny Way of Laughin'"; Eddy Arnold's single of "Tears Broke Out on Me;" and Shirley Collie and Willie Nelson's release of "Willingly." In 1963, he provided Ray Price with the country standard "Make the World Go Away" (two years later a number-one hit for Eddy Arnold) and George Jones with "You Comb Her Hair." Arnold earned a number-one singles hit in 1965 with Hank's "I Want to Go with You." In 1966, Jeannie Seely scored a top-10 hit with his "Don't Touch Me," a recording that was rewarded with a Grammy as well.

In 1964, Hank left Liberty and signed with RCA, which released a number of his albums during the mid-1960s, including the collection *Hits from the Heart.* However, though many of the recordings were excellent, Hank never was able to achieve star status as a performer during those years. He continued to be on the Pamper Music staff up to the time the firm was sold to Tree International in 1969. Other than the ownership shift, nothing changed much. In the 1970s, Hank penned new material under the Tree banner.

For most of the 1970s, Hank kept a relatively low profile as a performer. In 1977, though, he signed a new contract with Capitol Records. His debut LP on the label was *Hank Cochran—With a Little Help from His Friends.* The friends referred to included Jeannie Seely, by then his wife, Merle Haggard, Jack Greene, and Willie Nelson. Nelson's contributions included working with Hank on Cochran's song "Ain't Life Hell." On another track, Haggard joined Cochran in a tribute to Nelson titled "Willie," written by the album's producer, Glenn Martin. In 1974, he was inducted into the Nashville-based Songwriter's Hall of Fame.

In 1979, Willie Nelson got Hank to appear in the movie *Honeysuckle Rose,* in which Cochran sang "Make the World Go Away." On the hit soundtrack LP from the film, Cochran's tracks comprised that song plus a later composition, "I Don't Do Windows." While Hank was working on the movie, he and Willie agreed to go to Austin, Texas, for one of the *Austin City Limits* shows. Cochran served as the program's host; the show was first telecast in 1979 and repeated several times in later years.

Another outgrowth of those activities was Cochran's agreement to assemble a band of his own as the opening act for a series of Willie Nelson concerts during the 1979–80 season. In late 1980, Willie and Ray Price placed a duet single of Hank's "Don't You Ever Get Tired of Hurting Me" on the top rungs of the country charts. By then Hank had a new recording contract of his own with Elektra/Asylum Records; his first release with them was the November 1980 LP *Make the World Go Away.*

COCKBURN, BRUCE: *Singer, guitarist, pianist, dulcimer player, songwriter. Born Ottawa, Canada, May 27, 1945.*

Bruce Cockburn (pronounced Cōburn) has been hailed as one of Canada's foremost folk artists of current times, but he tends to back away from the description. He says, "I don't think of myself as a folksinger now and I never have. I do object to that kind of categorizing, though not strenuously. I don't feel my music fits any particular category. To me, folk music means music coming out of some identifiable tradition and Canada as a nation doesn't have any identifiable tradition except for the French one. I haven't tried to identify with that, so I don't consider myself a folksinger.

"I got the label because I showed up [during one career phase] playing acoustic guitar and playing solo. For the past few

years I've been working with a band and, in fact, I played with a lot of bands early in my career. I felt confined by the folk music label, because people feel that kind of music has nothing to do with today and, for me, my music has to do with today because I'm living today and writing about today."

Bruce grew up in Ottawa, where his interest in music intensified when he entered his teens. He started learning to play guitar when he was thirteen and took up the piano at seventeen. Later he mastered such other instruments as the dulcimer and wind chimes. "Early on, when I first was developing a finger-picking style on guitar, I was playing ragtime and ethnic blues. I was listening to ethnic styles from all over the world. I still do. But my style covers everything—classics, rock, jazz. I played in rock bands for years, played in jug bands a while and jazz—sort of avant-garde jazz. In school I played jazz and country music, among other things."

After getting his high school diploma, Bruce felt his calling would be music. "It wasn't so much of a decision, but sort of a nondecision. When I got out of school it was the only thing I could do."

After high school, he took off for Europe, where he earned a living by singing in the streets in such cities as Stockholm, Copenhagen, and Paris during 1963. Deciding to pick up more formal music training, he recrossed the Atlantic and enrolled in the famed Berklee School of Music in Boston, Massachusetts, in 1964. He studied composition and theory there from 1964 to 1967 and also played in jazz and blues groups in his leisure time. During those years, he spent part of his time in Canada and, in fact, never did accrue enough credits for graduation.

One of the things that lured him back to Ottawa was the chance to join a promising rock group called Children. The project fell apart after a short time and he moved around to several other bands for similar brief periods, including such groups as the Esquires, Olivus, Flying Circus, and 3's a Crowd. He recalled, "I was always committed to the bands at first, but often I would be the one in the end to break them up by leaving. I was discovering that I had to do my music by myself."

It was during that period he started to write in earnest. He says, "The first serious band I was in—this would be in 1965—was one in Ottawa that was into doing original material. Originally I wrote music for another guy's material and then got into writing words as well. During the next few years with a variety of bands I did more writing. None appeared on records that I know of. They weren't particularly good. It was a period of learning and growing."

In the late 1960s, he turned to the folk circuit, playing small folk clubs throughout Ontario. His performing ability and some of his original songs steadily added to his reputation with Canadian folk fans. One of his most acclaimed appearances of that period was at Canada's prestigious Mariposa Folk Festival.

At the start of the 1970s, he signed his first solo recording contract with Canadian-based True North Records, distributed by Columbia Records of Canada. A decade later, it remained his "home" label, though his recordings were handled in other countries on other labels. His debut LP, *Bruce Cockburn*, was issued by True North in May 1970 and was hailed by Canadian critics as a major event. Pete Goddard of the *Toronto Telegram*, for instance, called it "the best Canadian folk-music record of the year."

Over the next few years, more and more honors came his way in Canada as additional albums came out on True North supported by extensive tours of Canadian colleges, folk clubs, theaters, and occasional festivals. By late 1972, he had received Canada's equivalent of the U.S. Grammy, the R.P.M. Juno Award, as Top Folksinger, and two BMI songwriting awards. One of the latter was for the title song he penned for the movie 'Going Down the Road. Though he remained virtually unknown to U.S. listeners, his compositions began to be recorded by many well-known artists from both folk and country ranks. Early covers were made by Chet Atkins, George Hamilton IV, and Anne Murray,

and later, the list of those who favored his material grew to include Mary Hopkins, John Allen Cameron, Tom Rush, and many more.

His second album, *Sunwheel Dance*, was completed in 1971 and issued only in Canada. The next year Epic Records contracted to provide some U.S. distribution for his follow-up release, but still his inroads into the United States remained very small through his next four LPs of the mid-1970s. This began to change in 1976 when an agreement was concluded with Island Records for U.S. marketing. The first offering was the True North/Island 1976 LP *In the Falling Dark*. He made a number of appearances in American cities in support of the collection, including a fine showing in November 1976 at New York's Lincoln Center.

Many of his best known compositions were included in the double live collection, *Circles in the Stream*, issued in 1977. This was followed in September 1978 by a new studio album, *Further Adventures of Bruce Cockburn*, a package that presented ten of his compositions, ranging from the semicomic "Outside a Broke Phone with Money in My Hand" to such other varied styles as "Rainfall," "Laughter," "Bright Sky," "Red Ships Take Off in the Distance," and "Ship of Fools."

At the end of the 1970s, Bruce switched to Millenium Records, distributed by RCA, for U.S. marketing. His first release on that label was the album *Dancing in the Dragon's Jaws*, which not only was a Canadian bestseller but made the U.S. top 50 and remained on U.S. album charts for most of 1980. Commented Cockburn, "That definitely was my fastest seller to date. There may have been one other that sold as much, but it took longer. *Dancing in the Dragon's Jaws* took two months to go gold in Canada while the other one took five years."

His next album, *Humans*, was on U.S. charts the latter part of 1980, but didn't remain on them into 1981.

Bruce wasn't much worried about attaining ever higher sales. "I'm not really that concerned with the expansion or contrac-

Glen Campbell

The Original Carter Family,
l. to r.: Maybelle, Sara, A.P.

Roy Horton

Johnny Cash   Rosanne Cash

June and Johnny Cash

Ray Charles

Ray Charles and Johnny
Cash

David Allan Coe

Patsy Cline

Roy Clark

Judy Collins

Jessi Colter

Ry Cooder

Dick Curless

Country Music Hall of Fame, Nashville, Tennessee

tion of the audience. My main interest in terms of my career is that technically I want to do everything better—sing better, write better, play better, and do better shows. I'm not dissatisfied with the past, but there's always room for growth. As far as getting things across to people, I think there's been a sort of qualitative growth in recent years." *

COE, DAVID ALLAN: *Singer, guitarist, songwriter. Born Akron, Ohio, September 6, 1939.*

"From the time I was nine until just about three years ago," David Allan Coe said in 1970, "the longest I was 'free' at any one time was sixty days." It was, indeed, the truth that for twenty years of his life, Coe seemed an incorrigible jailbird and, in fact, toward the end of that period, it looked as though he might be put in the electric chair. He was one of those saved by the ending of capital punishment; his later achievements form a strong argument for a continuation of that trend.

Born in Akron, he was the product of an unhappy, broken home. He quickly developed an antisocial attitude, resulting in his initial experience with "rehabilitation." At nine, he was sent to a reform school in Albion, Michigan, the Starr Commonwealth for Boys. From then on, whenever he was released from reform school or prison, he always seemed to find some activity that would put him back behind penal walls. In his early years the offenses ranged from possession of burglary tools to car theft and later for offenses related to membership in various motorcycle gangs (including the Headhunters Motorcycle Club in New York). At fourteen he was sent to Boys Industrial School, at sixteen to National Training School for Boys, at eighteen to Chillicothe Reformatory, at nineteen to Lima State Hospital (for observation), between twenty and twenty-five a series of remissions to Ohio State Penitentiary, and from twenty-five to twenty-seven, Marion Correctional Institution.

* *Based on phone interview with Irwin Stambler, early 1981.*

While he was in Ohio State Penitentiary, he killed an inmate who made a homosexual advance to him. To fight the man off, Coe grabbed the wringer from a mop bucket and struck out twice, killing his assailant. Though self-defense might have been indicated, a convict is limited in his resources. Coe was sent to death row, where he awaited execution for three months. Oddly enough, he was joined there by his foster father, also sent up for murder. While there, the two wrote songs and poems together. Coe, during his years in prison, had managed to learn to play guitar. After capital punishment was abolished, both of them had their sentences commuted to life.

Things looked a bit brighter, though still hardly encouraging, as Coe was beginning to have a different outlook on life. He continued to write and work on new material. He also became increasingly interested in performing and soon was headlining penitentiary shows. All of these activities apparently helped persuade the parole board to give him another chance. In 1967, he was released from prison, already aiming for a show business career. (His foster father was set free some seven years later.)

He headed for Nashville in an old car. When he got there, Edgar Bayer wrote, "He had exactly one dime. He slept in his car, picked his guitar and sang for meals. Spent days knocking on doors trying to peddle some of the jail-written songs that sang of pain, death, narcotics, prostitution, prison, and love—long before others were putting such stark realism into songs."

Finally, things began to turn his way a bit. Music executive Shelby Singleton took him in hand and soon Coe's debut LP, *Penitentiary Blues,* came out on the SSS label. The album received some attention, though it was hardly a major success. During those years he also had the satisfaction of seeing two singles reach the top 40, "Tobacco Road" and "Two Tone Brown." In the early 1970s, he recorded for Plantation, and a sardonic comment on the travails of the Nixon administration, "How High's the Watergate Martha?" was taken note of in a number of national publications. Coe also gained his first regional singles hit with "Keep Those Big Wheels Running."

His songwriting eventually provided the major turning point in his career. During the early 1970s, more and more country artists were including Coe compositions in their repertoire. Then Billy Sherrill selected the song "Would You Lay with Me (In a Field of Stone)" for a Tanya Tucker session. The single became one of her greatest hits, rising to number one on all trade magazine country charts during 1973. That achievement naturally attracted industry attention to Coe, and major record companies began to talk with him about his future plans. Ron Bledsoe, CBS vice president for operations in Nashville, was particularly impressed and asked Coe to prepare demonstration recordings of some songs. Satisfied with those efforts, Columbia signed Coe and Bledsoe produced his first album, *The Mysterious Rhinestone Cowboy.* Issued in 1974, the album caught fire with both critics and fans and soon Coe and Bledsoe completed a second album for 1974 release, *The Mysterious Rhinestone Cowboy Rides Again.*

David turned out two excellent singles on Columbia in 1974, "Sad Country Song" and "If I Could Climb the Walls of a Bottle." They weren't massive hits, but his version of Steve Goodman's "You Never Even Called Me by My Name" reached the top 10 in September 1975. By then Coe was starting to receive recognition from both the country audience and his musical peers as he guested on most major radio and TV shows. He also sometimes shared bills with such other members of the "progressive" country movement as Jerry Jeff Walker, Willie Nelson, and Waylon Jennings. During the mid-1970s, David also made a number of appearances on the *Grand Ole Opry.*

Throughout the mid- and late-1970s he continued to turn out a steady series of singles and albums on Columbia, many of which made the charts. Among his LPs were *Once upon a Rhyme* (whose tracks included his version of "Would You Lay with Me in a Field of Stone)" and *Long-*

Haired Redneck, both issued in 1976. The last-named album's title song included such lines as "My long hair can't cover up my red neck/I've won every fight I've ever fought/I don't need some turkey/Tellin' me that I ain't country/Sayin' I ain't worth the damned old ticket that he bought. . . ." In 1977, Coe completed his fifth Columbia LP, *David Allan Coe Rides Again,* as coproducer with Ron Bledsoe, and continued in that capacity for *Tattoo* in 1977 and *Family Album* in 1978. His second 1978 album, *Human Emotions* (which dealt in part with the break-up of his marriage), was produced by Billy Sherrill.

His singles releases in the mid- and late-1970s included "Would You Be My Lady" (1975); "When She's Got Me (Where She Wants Me)" (1976); "Willie, Waylon and Me," coproduced by Coe, Waylon Jennings, and Bledsoe (1976); "Lately I've Been Thinkin' Too Much," "Face to Face," "Just to Prove My Love for You" (1977); "Divers Do It Deeper," "You Can Count on Me," and "If This Is Just a Game" (1978), all produced by Billy Sherrill.

In 1978, Coe's songwriting talents again came to the fore as Johnny Paycheck scored a smash singles hit with "Take This Job and Shove It." The record was nominated for a Grammy for Best C&W Song of the Year. Paycheck's name joined a long list of others who recorded Coe material in the 1970s, including Johnny Cash, George Jones, Charlie Louvin, Melba Montgomery, Billy Jo Spears, Del Reeves, Stoney Edwards, and Tammy Wynette.

Though now a celebrity in the 1970s, Coe didn't forget his earlier history. He gave concerts from time to time at prisons around the country. In addition, with two partners he set up a music publishing firm in the mid-1970s called Captive Music with the goal of providing a possible outlet for songs written by prison inmates.

In 1978, Coe's autobiography, called *Just for the Record,* was issued by Dream Enterprises with the credit line "written entirely by ex-convict David Allan Coe."

At the start of the 1980s, new Columbia singles by Coe continued to make the charts, such as the duet with Bill Anderson

"Get a Little Dirt on Your Hands" in 1980 and "Stand by Your Man" in 1981.

COHEN, LEONARD: *Singer, guitarist, songwriter, actor, author. Born Montreal, Quebec, Canada, September 21, 1934.*

"Like a bird on a wire/Like a drunk in a midnight choir/I have tried in my way/To be free." Those lines from one of Leonard Cohen's most famous songs, "Bird on a Wire," exemplify both his poetic lyrics and the credo that made him one of the standard-bearers of both the folk and folk-rock movements of the 1960s and the 1970s. Besides being included in his second solo album, it was the title of a documentary of one of his European tours and a major pop singles hit for rock star Joe Cocker.

His way with words preceded his foray into songwriting by many years. In fact, he already had a considerable reputation as a poet and novelist before he began adding music in the mid-1960s. Born and raised in Montreal, Canada, he began writing fiction and poetry at an early age and was considered a hugely promising serious writer when still in his teens. He was completing work toward his degree from McGill University in 1955 when his first book of poetry was published, a work that in a few years' time was rated one of the best such volumes of the decade. (Cohen later received an honorary L.L.D. from Dalhousie University in Halifax, Nova Scotia.) By the late 1960s, he had increased his total of poetry volumes to four: *Spice Box of Earth, Let Us Compare Mythologies, Flowers for Hitler,* and *Parasites of Heaven.* In the 1970s, two more volumes were published, *Selected Poems* and *Energy of Slaves.*

Poetry readings first brought him before live audiences. In 1957, he made his first tour of the States, reading some of his poems against the backdrop of music played by jazz pianist Maury Kay. Though he hadn't turned to writing songs then, he had been interested in folk music for a long time. He recalled that a friend's father, who had been a union organizer, taught him to play many folk songs and old union songs on the guitar. ("Only Socialists and Communists played the guitar

in those days," he quipped.) He also was a member of a group called the Buckskin Boys in Montreal in 1954, a "strictly amateur band that played country music." However, though he sometimes played the guitar to entertain himself or his friends, he didn't attempt to use it professionally until 1966.

In the early 1960s, Cohen increased his literary stature by writing two novels, *The Favorite Game* and *Beautiful Losers.* The first won him a worldwide cult following; the second focused worldwide attention on his home city of Montreal. The novels were published by McClelland and Stewart in Canada and Viking Press in the United States and eventually qualified as bestsellers. *Beautiful Losers* went over the 300,000-sold mark by the end of the 1960s. However, it took a 1967 documentary film about his life and works, prepared by the National Film Board of Canada, to really bring him large-scale attention at home. Called *Ladies and Gentlemen . . . Mr. Leonard Cohen,* the movie was released in 1967 as an Easter special on CBC. As a result of the film, he received several assignments to write themes or complete scores for NFB programs, including Derek May's *The Angel* and Don Owens' *The Ernie Game,* in which he also was a cast member.

Humanistic in outlook, Cohen is independent in thought and action. Much of his writings reflect his desire to find out for himself about events or situations that affect people's lives. Thus he tried drugs at an early age and rejected them. After comparing many religious beliefs, he concluded, "Our natural vocabulary is Judeo-Christian. That is our blood myth." In 1961, he visited Cuba after the Bay of Pigs debacle and, unlike many intellectuals from Canada and Europe, didn't automatically take Castro's side. As he stated in his poem *The Only Tourist in Havana Turns His Thoughts Home,* he left "not knowing which side to favor."

The event that triggered his move into music occurred in 1966 when he was in New York for a poetry reading. (By then, he had taken up residence on the Greek island of Hydra, where he lived off and on for much of the 1960s. After Hydra, he took up residence for a while in Nashville, Tennessee, before making Montreal home base once more in the 1970s.) CBS-TV approached him to do a program based on some of his readings that might also include some musical interludes. While in New York, Cohen attended a performance by Judy Collins, whose folk renderings inspired him to write some original songs of his own. One result was that she sang some of them in later programs, the beginning of a long association in which Judy tried to include at least one of Leonard's songs in each new LP. The first instance was in her LP *In My Life* (released February 1967), where she performed Cohen's classic "Suzanne" (a major hit for Noel Harrison in the mid-1960s) and "Dress Rehearsal Rag." Before long many other artists were discovering Cohen compositions.

Soon, with friends' urging, Cohen started to perform his material himself. In 1967 his efforts were well received at the Newport Folk Festival in July, at Expo '67 in Montreal, and with Judy Collins at the summer Rheingold Music Festival in New York. From then on, he made many tours of the United States and in other nations, including several extensive tours of Europe in the early 1970s.

Meanwhile he had been signed to a Columbia Records contract by the label's vice president for talent acquisition, John Hammond, Sr. His debut album, *Songs of Leonard Cohen*, was released on December 26, 1967. Among its contents were such classic compositions as "Suzanne," "Hey, That's No Way to Say Goodbye," and "Sisters of Mercy." The songs from that first album later were employed to provide a striking soundtrack score for the Robert Altman western *McCabe and Mrs. Miller.*

His second album, *Songs from a Room*, was released on March 17, 1969, and included such important tracks as "Bird on a Wire" and "You Know Who I Am." He performed some of the album's numbers before massive audiences in 1969 and 1970, including appearances in the latter year before wildly enthusiastic crowds at the Olympia Music Hall (Paris) in August and in front of over 100,000 people at England's Isle of Wight rock festival.

His first album of the 1970s was *Songs of Love and Hate*, issued on March 17, 1971, whose tracks included "Joan of Arc," "Famous Blue Raincoat," and his version of "Dress Rehearsal Rag." This proved to be one of his most commercial releases, making the U.S. hit charts in May 1971 and staying on them for most of the summer. His fourth LP and his first live album, *Live Songs*, came out on April 27, 1973. The recordings were selected from several different concerts between 1970 and 1972 and included such previously recorded songs as "Bird on a Wire," "Story of Isaac," "You Know Who I Am," "Nancy," and "Tonight Will Be Fine." New songs included "Queen Victoria," "Please Don't Pass Me By," and "Passing Thru," which was issued as a single in 1973. His fourth (fifth over-all) studio LP, *New Skin for the Old Ceremony*, was issued on October 4, 1974. In support of the album, he embarked on his first tour of the United States in five years and one that extended into 1975. As it happened, the LP was his last on the Columbia label for some time.

The next Cohen album didn't appear for two years and when it did it was on a new label, Warner Brothers, and with a new collaborator. His new co-worker was the wildly unlikely choice of Phil Spector, the boy wonder of rock 'n' roll in the early 1960s. The two were introduced by a mutual friend—Cohen's lawyer—Marty Mahchat. The two found a creative chemistry developing and not long after their first meeting were getting together in Spector's Southern California mansion (sometimes considered more a fortress than a home) to work on songs combining Cohen's lyrics and Spector's melodies.

Things went surprisingly well during that phase and fifteen new songs were assembled in a short period of time. However, it became rougher when recordings got under way. As Cohen told Janet Maslin for an article in *The New York Times* (November 6, 1977), "I'd heard he was a genius who knew how to make records—I had no idea of the ordeal of a session with him. I never thought I would give up that much control. I didn't even know when [the record's various tracks] were being mixed—I never heard the mix and I don't approve of it. The mix is a catastrophe. No air. No breath. It's like what he has become himself. He doesn't know how to let a situation breathe. Let alone a song.

"But it's very hard to fight him—he just disappears. He was in possession of the tapes. His bodyguard took them back to his house every night. I knew he was mad, but I thought that his madness would be more adorable, on the ordinary daily level. I love the guy, but he's out of control. Finally, I just said let the thing go."

The LP, *Death of a Ladies' Man*, came out in late 1977. As might be expected, it aroused a storm of praise and criticism from critics, some suggesting it was a disaster, others considering it one of the year's best. The collection, on first hearing, certainly didn't seem in line with what one expected creatively from either individual. Though it found considerable audience interest in Europe, where Cohen has had a much bigger following than his home continent, it gained little public support in the United States.

Still, it has many elements that promised to make it a collector's item in future years. Cohen perhaps described it best: "There's nothing I like about it—but it may be a classic."

In 1979, Cohen returned to the Columbia fold with a new album, *Recent Songs.* Jennifer Warnes supervised the vocal arrangements and sang with Cohen on several tracks.

COLLINS, JUDY: *Singer, guitarist, songwriter, pianist. Born Seattle, Washington, May 1, 1939.*

One of the brightest newcomers to the then thriving folk music field in the early 1960s was a slender, beautiful, blue-eyed young singer named Judy Collins. She burst on the Greenwich Village folk scene like a meteor and, in a short time, her dazzling vocal treatment of traditional folk songs and the new folk compositions of Dylan, Paxton, Ochs, and others made her the talk of critics and folk audiences across the country. She proved to have flexibility and resilience as well, retaining an important place in both folk and pop in later years, despite the recurrence of personal problems and the periodic impact of new pop music forms—British 1960s rock, heavy metal, punk, etc.—on the record-buying concert-going public.

Although Judy became a celebrity at the start of the 1960s, she hardly was an overnight musical convert. Her interest and training in music went back to her early years. Show business, in fact, was part of the family heritage. Her father was a radio personality, and thus there was a lot of moving about. Soon after Judy's birth, the family relocated from Seattle, Washington, to Boulder, Colorado, then to Los Angeles. Judy showed an interest in music early on and, at five, in Los Angeles, she began classical piano. She picked up technique so rapidly she was considered a prodigy and her teachers predicted she might have an important career in the classics. Her studies continued when she was settled in Denver, Colorado, where her family finally found a permanent home base. It was in that city that, as a protégé of conductor Dr. Antonia Brico, she made her public debut at thirteen in a performance of Mozart's *Concerto for Two Pianos.*

But she was starting to pay attention to other, more popular forms of music. Folk music particularly enthralled her. It better suited her nature than the early wave of rock then being brought to the fore by Elvis Presley, Bill Haley, and their confreres. When she was sixteen, she took up the guitar, considering it a better instrument to accompany her new repertoire of folk songs. For several years, she mainly sang for her own pleasure or to entertain friends or school audiences. At nineteen, she decided to try for broader exposure. She auditioned for a job at a Boulder nightclub. As she told Donald Mullen of UPI in April 1967, "The manager said, 'I hate folk music. I'm sorry your audition was such a great success, because the demand is so popular I'm going to have to hire you for $100 a week. . . .' "

For a while at the end of the 1950s, she played in her home region. As time went on, though, she gradually began to appear in coffee houses and folk clubs in other parts of the country. The hub of folk music activity at the time was New York, so she headed east at the start of the 1960s. Once there, it didn't take long for her talents to become widely noted by other young artists and by talent hunters for record companies. By 1961 she was under contract to Elektra Records, then an independent, with whom she still remained at the start of the 1980s (by which time it was part of the Warner Communications conglomerate).

Her debut LP, *Maid of Constant Sorrow,* came out on Elektra in October 1961. An excellent initial effort, it found favor with a sizable number of folk adherents, though it came nowhere near gold-record levels. That was the way it was to be for most of Judy's releases in the 1960s, but considering the subsidence of the folk boom in the middle part of the decade, she did manage to do quite well.

Her concerts increasingly were eagerly awaited events in New York and elsewhere. Appearances at such major venues as New York's Town Hall and Carnegie Hall in the mid-1960s brought standing-room-only results. Similar receptions greeted her in medium- and even large-size auditoriums not only all across the United States but in Canada and throughout Europe. Meanwhile, Elektra continued to release new albums at the rate of about one a year in keeping with her desire to take her time and strive for maximum quality in each new group of recordings. Her second LP, *Golden Apples of the Sun,* came out in October 1962 and *Judy Collins No. 3* in January 1964. In October of that year, her first live album was released, *Judy Collins in Concert.*

Taken from her appearance at New York's Town Hall on March 21, 1964, it demonstrated her still-strong emphasis on traditional folk material, something she was to change in coming years. Among her offerings were "Hey Nellie Nellie," "The Lonesome Death of Hattie Carroll," "Coal Tattoo," "Wild Rippling Water," "Tear Down the Walls," and "Winter Way."

During those years, like most young folk artists, Collins was actively involved in the civil rights movement. She often contributed her services to fund-raising events and also participated in marches in behalf of various civil rights causes. Though not quite as strident as Joan Baez or Bob Dylan, she still was proud of her efforts. As she noted in 1967, "I don't have the young rebel image. I'm trying to make statements as a woman. My message is in my music—what one woman is doing. One of my new songs is 'The Dove.' It says war is wrong. You have to answer 'yes.' There's no way to say 'yes . . . maybe.'"

As her albums continued to come forth, the content began to shift away from heavy folk orientation toward new, more sophisticated songs, both in the modern folk and pop vein. This was evident after *Judy Collins' 5th Album,* issued in November 1965; in such late 1960s releases as *In My Life* (11/66), *Wildflowers* (11/67), and *Who Knows Where the Time Goes* in November 1968, the last two of which sold well over gold-record-award levels. Another trend in the late 1960s was inclusion of a sprinkling of original compositions by Judy. Apparently she had taken to heart the criticism of her failure to do anything but interpret other writers' songs.

Judy also began to have chart-making singles during those years. One of them, "Hard Lovin' Loser" in 1967, was followed with her first blockbuster single, her 1968 rendition of Joni Mitchell's "Both Sides Now." The record won a Grammy Award for best single of 1968. In 1969, Collins had another vintage year with such singles as "Chelsea Morning," "Turn, Turn, Turn," and "Somebody Soon." She continued her chart inroads in the early 1970s with such hits as "Amazing Grace" in 1971 and "Open the Door (Song for Judith)," an original composition, co-written with actor Stacy Keach, in 1972.

Also on the album charts in the early 1970s were such releases as *Recollections,* issued in July 1969, *Whales and Nightingales,* released in November 1970, and *Living,* issued in November 1971 and on the charts well into 1972. By then, though, there already were signs of some difficulties in her private life, sometimes rumored, but previously not obvious in any change in her performing work. She announced she was taking a sabbatical for all of 1972 and planned to write a book. She was represented on the charts, though, by a May 1972 reissue of some of her early material, *Colors of the Day.* In January 1973 she released an album, *True Stories and Other Dreams,* which reflected her extensive feminist involvement of the time.

Collins began to try her hand at writing when she prepared some autobiographical material for the *Judy Collins Songbook,* published in the late 1960s. She was offered writing assignments by *Redbook* and *Ms.* magazines; for the latter, she decided to do an interview with her former teacher, Dr. Brico. A friend suggested filming the interview and Judy enlisted the aid of Jill Godmilow for that. The resulting material caused them to pursue the matter further as a documentary dealing with Dr. Brico's life and particularly the frustrations of trying to gain acceptance as a female conductor in a male-dominated field. The film, *Antonia: A Portrait of the Woman,* was issued in 1974 to excellent reviews and has since won many honors. It was chosen to open the American Filmmakers Series at New York's Whitney Museum, was named by *Time* magazine as one of the ten best films of 1974, was nominated for an Oscar in the Best Documentary category, and won the Christopher Award and the Independent Film Critics Award.

Her relative inactivity extended for a few years, then she went back into the studios to work on a new LP that was released in March 1975, called *Judith.* One of the tracks on the album was her sensitive version of Stephen Sondheim's "Send in the Clowns." Released as a single, her recording was recognized as the classic handling of the ballad and since has been one of her best-known numbers. The album won a gold-record award in November. In the voting for the 1975 Grammies, the single reached the final five nominees for best female vocal effort.

She finished another LP, *Bread and Roses,* which was released in August 1976, but then once more returned to the sidelines, although one single, "Special Delivery," received substantial airplay. (Elektra did, however, release an excellent double album retrospective, *So Early in the Spring:* *The First Fifteen Years,* in July 1977.) She remained there until early 1979, when she again was ready to tour in support of a new album, *Hard Times for Lovers* (which featured nude photos of Judy on the cover), released by Elektra in February. She told interviewers at the time that the mid-1970s had been particularly traumatic for her, with the onset of depression about her goals and personal relationships. As she said to Dennis Hunt (*Los Angeles Times,* February 16, 1979), she went into hiding at the end of 1976. "I didn't have an album out. . . . This is my first album since 1976. I've been taking it easy for a while. Last year [1978] was a quiet year, my first quiet year in many years and I desperately needed it."

She recalled when *Judith* came out, "I was having tremendous personal problems then. It was difficult to balance what was going on professionally with what was going on in my personal life. There was too much drama happening on the personal level for me to see anything clearly. It was a very painful time in my life and I can't really say that the pain has all disappeared."

However, she felt she had mastered her problems and was ready to go forward. "There has been a 180-degree shift in my perspective. . . . It's maturity. Maturity comes with age and I'm happier now than I've ever been, so aging does have its rewards."

Nonetheless, there were some anxious moments for her fans. Rumors persisted that she had lost much of her vocal effectiveness. This was given further credence by a near-disastrous vocal effort on NBC's *Saturday Night Live* in early 1979. She was better but still below par on a later appearance on Johnny Carson's *The Tonight Show.* However, she sounded in good voice on *Hard Times for Lovers,* and she held a concert series in which her voice, if somewhat more limited in range than in earlier years, returned to the purity of tone and clarity that always had been Judy's trademark.

During 1981, she worked on a new album, which she coproduced with Lewis Hahn, titled *Times of Our Lives,* released in January 1982.

COLTER, JESSI: *Singer, pianist, songwriter. Born Phoenix, Arizona, May 25.*

Jessi Colter's stage name seems appropriate considering her association with the progressive country "outlaw" movement in the mid- and late-1970s. Her original name was Miriam Johnson, but when she became an entertainer she modified the name of a great-uncle of her father's, an outlaw and counterfeiter named Jesse Colter.

The sixth of a family of seven children, she grew up in Phoenix under strong gospel influence. "I started taking piano lessons when I was about six or seven. Because my mother was a minister and an evangelist, I grew up spending a lot of time in church and by the time I was eleven, I was playing piano in church." She recalls that by then she already had decided to make singing and writing her life's work. Five years later, she started singing professionally.

"When I was sixteen, I met Duane Eddy. I guess that's where it all started. My sister Sharon, who married Jack Clement [a major producer, performer, and songwriter], found out that Duane Eddy was looking for a singer to produce a record with. And she managed to set up an audition for me. Our family was strict, so my brother had to smuggle me out of the house because the audition was at a bar."

Duane liked her and "we recorded in Phoenix and Duane did some overdubbing in Los Angeles and finally the record came out on the Jamie label. . . . Nothing happened with the record." But Jessi toured with Eddy and married him several months later. The marriage brought her to Beverly Hills for a while and Jessi cut back on her music activities to raise a family. The marriage ended in divorce after seven years. Later she was to marry Waylon Jennings.

The two originally met in Phoenix while Waylon was starring at a club called JD's. She went over some of her songs with him and the two recorded a duet in a local studio. Waylon kept in touch with her and finally proposed. After the wedding, he got her a contract with RCA. She did an album and some singles were released, but again nothing resulted from it.

She continued to do some backing vocal work and write new songs while her career languished for a while. Then she got the chance to sign with Capitol Records, an alliance that resulted in the crossover national singles hit "I'm Not Lisa" and the gold-record album *I'm Jessi Colter* in 1975. The single actually was somewhat cloying, but other tracks on the album verified that Colter had a fine, flexible voice and the ability to project a range of emotions with strong impact. "I'm Not Lisa" was one of the five songs nominated for the 1975 Grammy for Best Country Vocal Performance, Female, and Jessi also was nominated for the songwriter's Grammy for Best Country Song.

Before 1975 was over, Colter could point to other songs on the country singles charts: "You Ain't Never Been Loved (Like I'm Gonna Love You)" and "What's Happened to Blue Eyes," the latter a top-10 success in October. She kept it up in 1976 with "I Thought I Heard You Calling My Name" early in the year (from her second Capitol LP, *Jessi*) followed by such other chartmakers as "Without You" and a duet with Waylon, "Suspicious Mind." Later in 1976, her album *Diamond in the Rough* not only made the country charts but, as had been the case with her debut album, went well up in the pop top 100.

During that year, RCA released one of the landmark albums in recent country history, a collection of songs by Jessi, Waylon, Willie Nelson, and Tompall Glaser called *Wanted: The Outlaws*. The album was an exciting showcase of what progressive country is all about and caught the fancy of both country and non-country fans alike. As of the late 1970s, the album remained a steady seller and a country record setter, having earned R.I.A.A. certification for well over a million copies distributed. The extensive concert series that Waylon, Jessi, and Willie (sometimes with Glaser as well) offered in support of the album remains among the most memorable of the mid- and late-1970s.

In the late 1970s, Colter slowed down a bit; although her singles and albums still showed up on the charts, they tended to stay on country lists rather than cross over.

Her fourth Capitol LP, *Miriam,* appeared on country lists in the summer of 1977. In the fall of 1978, her fifth album, *That's the Way a Cowboy Rocks and Rolls* (produced by Waylon and Richie Albright) suggested a change in musical direction. In her late 1978—early 1979 concert tour in support of the LP she was backed by her husband's band, The Waylors. Her next album effort was one for RCA with Waylon that was released in 1980. Called *Leather and Lace,* it passed RIAA gold record levels (in the fall of 1981). In 1981 she went into the studios to work on her first solo LP for Capitol since 1978. Called *Ridin' Shotgun,* it was scheduled for release in early 1982.

CONLEE, JOHN: *Singer, guitarist, song-writer. Born Versailles, Kentucky, August 11, 1946.*

In September 1978, with prospects for star status in the country field looking up, John Conlee played things close to the vest, driving his old 1973 Plymouth Fury and keeping his budget for stage outfits low. Having observed the pop field for years as a DJ, he thought he was on the right path. As he told Jack Hurst of the *Chicago Tribune,* "If somebody walked in right now and said 'I can make you a pop star,' I'd thank 'em and tell 'em to move along. You can't count on pop. It's nothing to have two, three, or four hits in pop and never be heard of again. There's more longevity to country, and I want to establish myself there."

Of course, John's outlook was colored by his country roots. Born on a 300–400-acre farm in Versailles, Kentucky, he helped his father raise tobacco and tended the hogs, cattle, and other animals while growing up. Before he was nine, he was taking guitar lessons, and he kept up an interest in pop and country music in his teens. He didn't consider making a living at it, though, and instead took a 180-degree turn, becoming an embalmer and working at the trade for six years after finishing high school. In his mid-twenties the entertainment field still beckoned, so he quit the funeral home and sought work in radio. Having worked briefly on three stations in his home area, in Fort Knox,

Elizabethtown, and Versailles, he then moved on to the country-music capital, Nashville, in 1971, where he joined station WLAC-FM (which later changed to WKQB). He remained there as a pop music DJ for most of the 1970s.

The Nashville environment seemed to revive his interest in country music. After a few years, he began trying his hand at songwriting with other station members, including fellow DJ Dick Kent, who later became his manager, and George Baber. Kent achieved the first milestone for John by bringing him together with ABC/Dot Records' head, Jim Foglesong, for whom John played some of his new material from time to time. In 1976, ABC/Dot was impressed enough by Conlee's progress to give him a recording contract. This led to some singles releases that brought in three regional hits during 1976–77, "Back Side of Thirty," "Let Your Love Fall Back on Me," and "The In Crowd." While having some minor hits is better than no success, it wasn't enough to induce John to give up his DJ efforts.

That changed in the spring of 1978 when he wrote a song called "Rose Colored Glasses" with George Baber, a song the Nashville *Banner* described as "hard core country about this poor guy who is in love with a two-timing girl and deludes himself into thinking she's true." The single of the song came out in late spring and by August had not only been on the charts most of the summer, but made it into the top 10.

In early June 1978, the record had already done so well that ABC was clamoring for an album and Conlee decided the time was ripe to depart the station. By September he was touring on weekends to booked engagements from Ohio to Texas and by mid-November had another single, "Lady Lay Down," in the country top 20 moving toward the topmost levels. Although things looked good, John shunned premature optimism. "To keep the ball rolling we have to keep having hit singles as strong or stronger than 'Rose Colored Glasses.' When we have a couple more of those, I guess we can throw a big celebration."

However, before long he had to agree there was good reason for optimism. "Lady Lay Down" remained on the best-seller lists into 1979 and by mid-January was number one in the United States. ABC came out with a reissue of "Back Side of Thirty" in the spring and it went into the top 5 in May. By the end of the year, on ABC's successor, MCA Records, he had another chart single, "Baby, You're Something," which made it to the national top-10 in February 1980. His other top-10 hits of the year were "Friday Night Blues," "Before My Time," and "She Can't Say That Anymore." His 1981 hits included "What I Had with You" and "Miss Emily's Picture."

COODER, RY: *Singer, guitarist, banjoist, mandolinist, songwriter. Born Los Angeles, California, March 15, 1947.*

Restless, innovative, with almost unlimited musical curiosity, Ry Cooder always seemed to be exploring a different area of music with every new recording or concert series. One moment he was playing avant garde rock, the next roots blues, then country & western, even jazz. For those who kept pace with him, he often helped illuminate overlooked musical corners with striking results, though his refusal to be typecast tended to put off many fans and members of the musical establishment. Although he was regarded as a true superstar by his musical peers (after his debut solo album came out in 1970, *Rolling Stone* called him "the finest, most precise bottleneck guitar player alive today, as well as the reviver of the lost art of blues mandolin"), his following remained a musical minority for most of his career.

Born and raised in Southern California, he recalled receiving his first guitar when he was three, a Sears Silvertone tenor four-string. After a while, he began trying to play along with some of the artists on his parents' folk music records. "They bought me a Josh White album when I was eight. That was the first blues I ever heard. I learned all his runs, spent hours with him." When Ry was ten, his father bought him a six-string Martin guitar and tried to set up a series of lessons, but young Ry didn't like the teacher's instructions and dropped out.

For several years he taught himself whatever new material he picked up until, at thirteen, he became enthralled with Appalachian finger picking. Looking for a teacher of that type of playing, he was led to what was then the center of folk music in Los Angeles, the Ash Grove. As noted in his biographical material for Warner Brothers Records, "Whenever there was a pretty good player [at the Ash Grove] I'd sit in the front row and watch. If someone like [Reverend] Gary Davis was in town, I'd talk to him, go where he was staying, give him five dollars and get him to play as much as he could while I watched. About a month later, I'd find that I'd start to remember how he did things.

"They used to have party nights at the Ash Grove, when people would get up out of the audience and play. And it seemed like when I was sixteen I was good enough and somebody said 'Get up! Get up!' and they pushed me on stage. I got up and was so scared I was petrified. I played and sweated and people laughed and clapped." He began to play more often at the club and in 1963 formed an act with folksinger Jackie DeShannon. However, it proved a failure.

Meanwhile, Ry was expanding his musical skills, learning the banjo and also becoming involved in the traditional blues bottleneck style of guitar playing, in which he used a three-inch neck from a bottle on his little finger to produce a ringing, sliding tone. To perfect his technique, Ry spent hours listening to records by Delta blues bottleneck experts, playing them over and over until he was satisfied he had mastered every inflection.

"Sometime around 1964 or 1965, Taj Mahal showed up in Los Angeles. He was real raggedy and I was raggedy, so we got together and went to the Teenage Fair in Hollywood and sat in a booth for Martin Guitars and just played Delta blues. It was hard and it was good." The two became friends and started a rock group called the Rising Sons. The band won some attention from local appearances and was supposed to record an album for Columbia, but it was never completed. The band broke up and Taj and Cooder went separate ways.

The next affiliation Ry formed was with a performer and songwriter named Don Van Vliet, better known as Captain Beefheart. On the surface it seemed an unlikely alliance—the Zappa-ish Beefheart and the folk-oriented Cooder. However, Cooder, always interested in new musical forms, proved an excellent session person for Beefheart's first LP. Ry arranged two songs for the collection, "I've Grown So Ugly" and "Rolling and Tumbling." Cooder did other session work in the late 1960s, including some with Paul Revere and the Raiders. He also got an assignment in England working on the score for a film called *Candy*. While there, he did some backing work for the Rolling Stones' *Let It Bleed* album.

Back in the United States, he did a number of other session jobs and, with the help of friends Van Dyke Parks and Lenny Waronker, finally gained a solo record contract from Warner/Reprise in 1969. The two friends coproduced that LP, *Ry Cooder*, which came out in October 1970 to well-deserved critical acclaim. In that collection, Ry demonstrated his superb finger-picking skills on "Police Dog Blues." Also presented were songs like "Alimony" and "How Can a Poor Man Stand Such Times and Live," a fiddle tune by country musician Blind Alfred Reed.

Cooder was paired with Captain Beefheart's Magic Band in a 1971 cross-country concert tour in support of both artists' new albums. The concerts produced a lot of publicity but not much buyer response to Cooder's LP. Things changed for the better in that regard with his second release, *Into the Purple Valley*, which made the pop charts in 1972. It was even more strongly received overseas, particularly in Holland, where it earned a gold-record award. Cooder played mandolin and bottleneck to good effect on such traditional numbers as "How Can You Keep on Moving" and "Billy the Kid." Other tracks included Leadbelly's "On a Monday" and a mid-1940s commentary, "F.D.R. in Trinidad."

Cooder continued to examine different aspects of American history in his 1973 album, *Boomer's Story*. The numbers presented ranged from his version of "Rally 'Round the Flag" to one titled "President Kennedy." On one track, "Maria Elena," he demonstrated his ability to play classical-style guitar. On his next LP, Cooder emphasized gospel-style music. Several tracks were in that vein, including "If Walls Could Talk" and "Jesus on the Mainline." However, other kinds of music were included, ranging from an upbeat "Ditty Wa Ditty," to which jazz pianist Earl "Fatha" Hines contributed, to such ballads as "Tattler" (co-written by Cooder) and a folk-flavored version of Burt Bacharach's "Mexican Divorce."

In the mid-1970s, Cooder traveled to two widely separate areas to study and work with important but little-publicized instrumentalists. In one direction he sought out Hawaiian slack-key guitar expert Gabby Pahinui to learn his techniques and do some jamming with him. Besides introducing some slack-key stylings into his own work, Ry also arranged for Warner/Reprise to release an album of Pahinui's performances in the United States. At other times, Ry went east to Austin, Texas, to examine the accordion skills of Flaco Jimenez. As with Pahinui, Cooder not only spent time playing impromptu sessions with Flaco, he also took instructions on duplicating Jimenez' style on the accordion.

Both these influences were incorporated in Cooder's fifth Reprise album, *Chicken Skin Music*. Slack-key was emphasized on such tracks as "Yellow Roses," "Chloe," and "Always Lift Him Up" (in some cases by Pahinui, in others by Ry), and Jimenez provided accordion backing on such tracks as "Stand By Me" and "He'll Have to Go" (the last named an old Jim Reeves country hit).

In 1977, Cooder put together a show featuring a merging of Tex–Mex and gospel sounds with instrumental backing provided by Jimenez and four other Tex–Mex musicians, and vocal support from three black gospel singers. The entourage, called the Chicken Skin Revue, played clubs, campus halls, and theaters around the United States and in Europe. Again, he found greater attention overseas than at home, with his European concerts spurring sales of the *Chicken Skin Music* LP to hit levels in both Germany and Holland. The tour spawned his sixth LP, the live *Show Time*, recorded during a Chicken Skin Revue performance in San Francisco.

His next LP, released in May 1978, departed completely from all his earlier offerings. Called *Jazz*, it stressed some of the early jazz material from the 1920s and early 1930s with particular emphasis on the work of Bix Beiderbecke. Some of the other material derived from the stylings of guitarist Joseph Spence, whom Cooder visited in his native Bahamas. In 1979, Ry explored other aspects of jazz and pop in his LP *Bop 'Til You Drop*.

COOLEY, DONNELL CLYDE "SPADE":
Singer, fiddler, band leader. Born Pack Saddle Creek, Oklahoma, December 17, 1910; died Oakland, California, November 1969.

When western swing got a new lease on life in the 1970s, two names tended to spring to mind from the past—Bob Wills and Spade Cooley. Thanks to the alumni of Wills' old band, the Texas Playboys, his memory remained alive. But Cooley's star had descended earlier and much more precipitously than his Texan contemporary and there was no band left to remind country fans of his one-time greatness.

For much of Cooley's life his story was one of an American Dream-like rise from rags to riches. He was born to an impoverished family in Oklahoma and was taken to Oregon when he was four, where his father, John, and mother, Emma, hoped for a better life. The change wasn't particularly successful—Spade once noted, "I was born poor and raised poor." However, it did bring about the boy's first exposure to music training. His father liked to play fiddle and made friends with a man who taught the instrument. One time when the two were playing together, the friend noted young Donnell imitating them and offered to give the boy lessons. The lessons were of classical, not country, music and later Cooley played violin and cello in his school orchestra.

As Spade grew older, when he wasn't helping on the farm, he earned spare money by playing country fiddle for local dances and parties. He still followed that routine when his family moved to a new farm near Modesto, California, when he was twenty. Longing to get away from farm work, Cooley went to Los Angeles and hung around small country-music clubs. Unsuccessful, he returned to Modesto and found a job performing for fifteen dollars a night at a local club. He was a sideman with several local bands in the early 1930s, but was down on his luck once more when he made a second foray to Los Angeles in 1934.

This time the pendulum swung his way. After scrounging a living as best he could for a time, he met Roy Rogers. Because Spade resembled Roy, this eventually led to a job as a stand-in when Roy became a featured actor in Republic Pictures' westerns. That gave him a reasonable income that he supplemented by working with various bands around the city.

At the start of the 1940s, he had established a reputation as an excellent fiddler with bands that played the Venice Pier Ballroom in Venice, California. The management suggested he form his own band and, when he did, he became a crowd favorite. The exposure led to a recording contract that soon produced a hit single, "Shame, Shame on You." The song became Cooley's theme song.

As the World-War-II years went by, things got better and better for Spade. (He had gotten his nickname many years before from his prowess as a card player.) His record releases came out steadily and sold well and his band soon became one of the best-known groups in Western swing. The group left the Venice Pier for a successful run at the Riverside Rancho, then moved to the even more highly regarded Santa Monica Ballroom. Spade and the band also gained nationwide attention from their appearances in a number of movies including *Chatterbox, The Singing Bandit, The Singing Sheriff, Outlaws of the Rockies,* and *Texas Panhandle.*

Spade also was well positioned for the next entertainment revolution, the rise of television. He was given the opportunity to head his own show on station KTLA, the first commercially licensed TV station in Los Angeles. Called *The Hoffman Hayride,* after the sponsor, the Hoffman Company (which produced TV sets), it began in 1947 and quickly became the top-rated program in the area.

As Bruce Henstell noted in *Los Angeles* magazine ("How the King of Western Swing Reached the End of His Rope," June 1979), "Soon Cooley was calling himself 'the King of Western Swing,' and western swing became the name for the odd music he, and Bob Wills before him, played. Los Angeles loved Spade Cooley, and in the late 1940s, 75 percent of the receivers in Los Angeles were tuned each Saturday night to 'The Hoffman Hayride.' As the show's director recalled, 'Even Milton Berle couldn't compete with it on the coast.' "

However, the pressures of staying on top began to tell on Spade. In the early 1950s he was sidelined for a while by the first of a series of heart attacks. Competing programs also began to make inroads into his TV show's popularity . He tried various remedies, including replacing his old band with a new all-women aggregation. That didn't work, however, and he soon disappeared from the home video screen. He still was able to command a following as an artist, performing at various venues in and around California during the mid- and late-1950s.

Meanwhile, however, his performing frustrations were aggravated by his personal ones. He had a drinking problem that tended to become worse as the years went by. He also had marital problems. During the 1950s, his second marriage disintegrated and he and his wife separated. But Spade couldn't stop seeing her, on the one hand talking of divorce but on the other hand harboring forlorn hopes of reconciliation. This dragged on for some years, then blew up in tragic fashion in July 1961 when an argument with his wife led to her death in a scene witnessed by their fourteen-year-old daughter.

After a trial sensationalized in the newspapers, Cooley was convicted of murder and sentenced to life in prison. During the trial he suffered another heart attack and afterwards was sent to a medical detention center at Vacaville rather than a high-security prison. In prison, he seemed to find himself again. He calmed down and spent much of his time helping other inmates learn to play musical instruments or performing for them. The outlook was for a favorable response from the Parole Board when his case was due for review in 1970.

Before then, taking his excellent behavior into consideration, the Vacaville authorities gave him permission to go to Oakland, California, for a few days to take part in a benefit concert.

Henstell wrote in *Los Angeles* magazine, ". . . the fifty-nine-year old Cooley played before a crowd of 3,000 and was greeted warmly, at least by those who looked beyond the lingering memory of the murder. He thanked the crowd and the authorities 'for the chance to be free for a while.' Then he went backstage. There, speaking with friends, he slumped over from yet another heart attack. The show had been a triumph for Spade—but it was his last. The King of Western Swing was dead."

COOLIDGE, RITA: *Singer, pianist, band leader (Dixie Flyers), songwriter. Born Nashville, Tennessee, May 1, 1944.*

The daughter of a Baptist minister and a school teacher, born and raised in the South, Rita Coolidge started with a heritage of gospel and country music. As she grew up, she added an affinity for the blues and rock 'n' roll that helped make her one of the favorites of audiences ranging from pop to folk and country in the 1970s.

She started singing in her father's choir when she was two and continued to add to her choir experience until she was in her teens. Her parents saw to it that she learned to play the piano at an early age. When she was fifteen, she moved to Florida with her family, where, after graduating from high school, she enrolled in Florida State University as an art major. She began her pop music career in college to help pay her school expenses.

As she told England's *New Musical Express* (April 14, 1973), "It was in college that I first started working clubs with groups. Before that I'd sung in church choirs with my two sisters. We played a lot of fraternity parties at the University of Florida and at Florida State. In college I also worked with a kind of folk-rock group—an acoustical group—then when I left school, I went to Memphis and started working for Pepper Records for a year, and eventually cut a record for them."

Actually, her original goal in taking the job with Pepper was to earn more money to help pay for a master's degree. "Thought I'd work for a year, but at the end of it, I was hooked."

While she was in Memphis, she became friends with Bonnie and Delaney Bramlett and Leon Russell. When they decided to move to California to try to expand their careers, she went with them. "I tried to get out of my record contract in Memphis because California was so much more exciting and inspirational. So I was hung up with legal hassles for a year and a half.

"During that time, I worked with Delaney and Bonnie [she sang backing vocals on their debut album on Elektra] and did background [vocals] in Los Angeles. I finally got out of the contract—and then ended up in Mad Dogs and Englishmen."

Prior to that noteworthy concert tour, she worked on album projects with Russell and Joe Cocker in 1969–70. When they organized the Mad Dogs project, they saw to it that she had a featured spot in the show. She won standing ovations in many concerts in the United States and Europe during 1970 for her performance of the Leon Russell–Delaney Bramlett composition "Superstar." The association with Russell in those projects was something of a reunion since she had worked closely with him in the mid-1960s.

Russell's respect for Rita was emphasized by the song he wrote in her honor, "Delta Lady." She told the New Musical Express, "I was with Leon for a long time and not too long before we split he wrote the song. Joe Cocker cut it first [it was a top-10 hit in 1969 for him]. When I went over to sing on Joe's session, it was the first time I'd seen Leon since we had parted ways. I guess I became the Delta Lady—and when I got on stage people would scream, do 'Delta Lady,' do 'Delta Lady.' No—I don't do 'Delta Lady.' "

In the latter part of 1970, Rita signed with A&M Records as a solo performer. Her debut LP, Rita Coolidge, was released in early 1971. Among the superstars who worked as session artists for the album were Leon Russell, Steve Stills, Graham Nash, Clarence White, and Booker T. Jones.

For her tour in support of the album, Rita brought in a band called the Dixie Flyers. Most of its members were playing as a session group in Memphis when she asked them to join her. The band included Marc Benno and Charlie Freeman alternating on lead guitar, Mike Utley on organ and piano, Tommy McClure on bass, and Sammy Creason on drums. The Memphis sidemen flew to Los Angeles in early spring, rehearsed briefly with Rita and Benno, then debuted in several clubs in England. The group was to back Rita in many excellent concerts across the United States and Europe during the next year. Among the songs Rita offered were Neil Young's "I Believe in You" (a singles hit in Canada), Van Morrison's "Crazy Love," and such others as "Whole Lotta Shakin' Goin' On" and "Blues Power."

The debut LP did fairly well, but her career began to gain momentum with the second release in late 1971, Nice Feelin', which appeared on the charts by year end and stayed on them into 1972 amid reviews in many publications hailing her as a new star. In the fall of 1972, her third LP, The Lady's Not for Sale, appeared and was a chart hit from late 1972 into 1973. During this time, Rita's relationship with Kris Kristofferson was developing. The two first met in an airport in 1971 and spent more and more time together, eventually developing their own stage act and later becoming husband and wife. Both included a considerable amount of country-oriented material in their act, which helped bring them the opportunity to be cast regulars on the NBC-TV 1973 summer show Music Country (the replacement for the Dean Martin show).

During 1973–74, Kris and Rita recorded

two albums together, one on his label of those years, Monument, titled *Breakaway,* the other on A&M, *Full Moon.* The latter, issued during 1974, remained on the charts many months and earned a gold record on October 20, 1975. *Breakaway,* issued the end of 1974, was on the charts for a number of months in 1975. Rita continued to add solo LPs to her credits, though, including *Fall into Spring* and the 1975 release *It's Only Love.*

Throughout the mid- and late-1970s, Kris and Rita made many tours through the United States and throughout the world, when their schedules permitted. One of the rare periods of inactivity for Rita occurred when she gave birth to their child, Casey, in the mid-1970s. Kris, of course, had an extremely busy acting career in films during the 1970s, but still managed to find time for extensive concert work with his wife.

Things hit a plateau for Rita during 1975–76, but she soon rectified that with her 1977 album, *Anytime . . . Anywhere.* Released by A&M in early 1977, the LP presented some of her most effective vocal efforts, including many strong country-influenced songs. The album stayed on the charts the balance of the year, much of the time in the top 20 or top 10 and by fall had surpassed platinum-award levels. She achieved several singles hits during the year as well, including her version of Boz Scaggs' "We're All Alone," in the top 20 in the fall. In the summer of 1977, she had one of the year's top singles with her gold record "(Your Love Has Lifted Me), Higher and Higher."

She continued right along in 1978 with her hit LP *Love Me Again,* from which the late-1978 charted single "Love Me Again/ The Jealous Kind" was taken. Released during the spring, the album passed gold-record levels in the summer. In early 1979, she and Kris had another LP on the charts, *Natural Act.* However, things had started to deteriorate in their marriage and before 1979 was over, they had separated.

At the start of 1980, Rita had a new solo LP, *Satisfied,* on lower-chart levels. At the same time, she had the disc "I'd Rather Leave While I'm in Love" on the singles charts. Later in the year her duet with Glen Campbell (issued on Capitol Records), "Somethin' 'Bout You Baby That I Like," was on the lists. In early 1981, her A&M single "Fool That I Am" was on lower-chart levels.

COOPER, STONEY: *Singer, fiddler, songwriter. Born Harman, West Virginia, October 16, 1918; died Nashville, Tennessee, March 22, 1977.*

The husband-and-wife team of Stoney and Wilma Lee Cooper for decades ranked as one of the best practitioners of traditional country music in the United States. They were held in high repute during a long career together both by country-music peers and by folk music experts. An example of the former was their long reign as featured members of the *Grand Ole Opry* cast and the latter, their selection in 1950 by the Music Library of Harvard University as the most authentic mountain singing group in the United States.

Dale T. "Stoney" Cooper was born and raised on a farm near Harman, Randolph County, West Virginia, in the famed Clinch Mountain region. He received considerable background in hill country music, music which in many cases could be traced back to Elizabethan folk music, from his own family. At an early age he learned to play the fiddle and, when he was twelve, taught himself the guitar as well. By the time he finished school, he was one of the more accomplished performers in his age group. For a time he was a member of a group called the Green Valley Boys.

One of the best-known local groups during those years was the singing Leary Family. At the end of the 1930s, Stoney joined that group and performed with them at church functions and on radio programs. He soon became fond of young Wilma Leary and she assented to his marriage proposal. They stayed with the family group for a time, then decided to strike out as a separate act.

They gained singing jobs on several stations in the late 1930s, starting in Fairmont, West Virginia, and continuing to Harrisonburg, Virginia, and Wheeling,

West Virginia. However, income from performing wasn't enough to meet their bills, particularly after a daughter, Carol Lee, was born. To meet expenses, for a time Stoney had to work for a beverage company.

Things picked up in the early 1940s as the Coopers found jobs outside their old area. They played on a variety of stations during those years, including ones in Grand Island, Nebraska; Indianapolis, Indiana; station WJJD in Chicago; Blytheville, Arkansas; and Asheville, North Carolina. Besides radio, the Coopers took part in whatever concert work they could line up. Still, while they lived in Chicago in the mid-1940s, Stoney worked in a defense plant in Gary, Indiana, for a time.

In 1947, the Coopers moved back to West Virginia as regular cast members on the famed *WWVA Jamboree* in Wheeling. The Coopers remained on the *Jamboree* until 1957, starring on the Saturday-night show broadcast nationally from the Virginia Theatre several times a month on the CBS network. Backing the Coopers on those programs was their band, the Clinch Mountain Clan. In 1957, the Coopers and their band heeded the call to join the *Grand Ole Opry* and moved their home base to Nashville. Stoney remained an official member of the *Opry* for the rest of his life.

During the 1950s and 1960s, the Coopers spent a good part of every year on the road appearing at almost all major fairs and other country venues all over the United States one or more times over that period. Their live appearances included several overseas tours. Helping to increase their audiences was a series of successful recordings, including many that were original compositions. In 1959, they scored one of their biggest recording breakthroughs with three top-10 hits on the Hickory label, "Come Walk with Me," "There's a Big Wheel," and "Big Midnight Special." In 1961, they had another top-10 hit with a revival of Dorsey Dixon's "Wreck on the Highway." Among their other successes were Wilma's singles "Legend of the Dogwood Tree" and "Walking My Lord Up Calvary's Hill."

Some of their other recordings included "The Golden Rocket," "West Virginia Polka," "Just for a While," "How It Hurts to Be Alone," "Please Help Me if I Am Wrong," "I Want to Be Loved," "Cheated Too," "Each Season Changes You," "Thirty Pieces of Silver," "This Crazy, Crazy World," "Walking My Lord Up Calvary's Hill," "Tramp on the Street," "Rachel's Guitar," "Diamond Joe," "The White Rose," "Not Anymore," "We Make a Lovely Couple," "Row Two, Seat Three," "This Thing Called Man," "Is It Right?" "Come Walk with Me," and "Canadian Reel."

The Coopers credits from the late 1960s to the mid-1970s included appearances on the network show *Anatomy of Music* and on a number of Canadian CBC network programs, including *This Is My Country* and the *Tommy Hunter Show*. They also appeared in the movies *Country Music on Broadway* and *W.W. and the Dixie Dance Kings*. In October 1976, Stoney received the honorary degree of Doctor of Christian Music from Victory Institute of Lewistown, Ohio. Stoney's last recordings with Wilma were for the Gusto Records LP *Wilma Lee and Stoney Cooper Sing The Carter Family's Greatest Hits*.

Stoney kept an intensive schedule of *Opry* work until the early 1970s, when failing health forced him to restrict his activities. He had a series of attacks that hospitalized him for various lengths of time over a period of four years. He had been in the hospital for some weeks when he passed away on March 22, 1977. Only a few days earlier, for the last time he heard his wife sing on the *Opry* when she dedicated the old A. P. Carter song "Little Darling Pal of Mine" to him on the Saturday-night broadcast.

COOPER, WILMA LEE: *Singer, guitarist, banjoist, organist, songwriter. Born Valley Head, West Virginia, February 7, 1921.*

Considered one of the finest traditional artists in post-World War II country music, Wilma Lee Cooper was heir to a family heritage in gospel and balladry that went back many generations. With her husband, Stoney Cooper, she continued to perform new and old songs in the folk style of the country idiom for decades and, after his retirement and death, went her own way as a solo artist.

Born Wilma Lee Leary in Valley Head, West Virginia, she was fated to join her musical parents in the Leary Family gospel group, one of the best known church-singing groups in the hill country. As soon as she was old enough to carry a tune, she joined the other members of the family, comprising several generations, in entertaining at church get-togethers and regional folk and country festivals. Her first public performance came when she was five. From then on, she sang regularly with the Leary Family on many radio and church programs. In 1938, the group was featured at a national folk festival sponsored by the nation's first lady, Mrs. Eleanor Roosevelt. The group, not restricted to only immediate family members, included a boy from Harman, West Virginia, named Stoney Cooper. Not long after he joined the troupe, Wilma accepted his proposal of marriage.

Wilma had not been sure she would make music her life's work and completed high school and went on to earn a B.A. degree in banking from Davis & Elkins College in Elkins, West Virginia. But marriage to Stoney helped insure that music, not banking, would be her main concern. While she was completing her schooling, the Coopers stayed with the Leary Family. By the start of the 1940s, however, they started their own act. They performed at some local events and then got work singing on a station in Fairmont, West Virginia. From there they went on to perform on stations in Harrisonburg and Wheeling, West Virginia.

In the mid-1940s, with a growing family, they tried their luck outside their home region, doing some concert work and singing on a variety of stations, including Grand Island, Nebraska; Indianapolis, Indiana; station WJJD in Chicago; Blytheville, Arkansas; and Asheville, North Carolina. More often than not during those years, Stoney had to supplement family income with jobs in other fields.

While staying in Chicago, he worked at a defense plant in nearby Gary, Indiana.

In 1947, the first important breakthrough came. They got the chance to join the regular cast of the *WWVA Jamboree* in Wheeling, West Virginia. It was a year in which they also got their first record contract with a major label. For a decade they were featured artists on various WWVA shows and were headliners from 1954 to 1957 on the prestigious Saturday-night *Jamboree* that was broadcast over many stations throughout the East and Midwest. In 1957, they moved to the highest rung on the country-music ladder, regular cast status with the *Grand Ole Opry*. (They had occasionally guested in previous years.) The Coopers moved to Nashville, remaining there the rest of their careers. From the late 1950s to the end of the 1960s, the Coopers were often away from home on extensive tours of the folk and country circuit. Their travels, accompanied by their band, the Clinch Mountain Clan, took them at one time or another to all fifty states, Canada, and many Western European nations.

During the Coopers' long career, they recorded for a number of labels, including Columbia, Hickory, Decca, and Gusto. Many of their songs were written by Wilma Lee or Wilma and Stoney. Among those were "Cheated Too" (1956); "I Tell My Heart," "Loving You," "My Heart Keeps Crying," (1957); "He Taught Them How" (1958); and "Heartbreak Street," "Tomorrow I'll Be Gone," and "Midnight Special" (1959), all on Hickory. The last-named song was a top-10 hit for the Coopers in 1959, a banner year that also brought two other top-10 hits, "Come Walk with Me" and "There's a Big Wheel."

After another major hit in 1961 with their version of the old Dorsey Dixon classic, "Wreck on the Highway," the Coopers rarely had any releases that went past mid-chart levels. They retained a sizable following, though, and were warmly welcomed by crowds at state and county fairs and during their part of the *Opry* Saturday-night program. In the mid-1970s, failing health sidelined Stoney, but Wilma remained an *Opry* regular backed by the Clinch Mountain Clan. Just before Stoney's death, Wilma dedicated a song to him on an *Opry* show, the Carter Family's "Little Darlin' Pal of Mine."

Considered one of the finest country and bluegrass artists, Wilma was asked to provide material for a number of folk music collections over the years, initially with Stoney and later as a solo artist. Some of her recordings were made for the Library of Congress Archive of American Folk Music and Harvard University's Library of Music. In the 1970s, the Smithsonian Institution in Washington, D.C., asked her to appear at Baird Auditorium, where her live performance was recorded for the Institution's Archives of the Performing Arts Division. In July 1974, at the Institution-sponsored folk festival, she was honored as "First Lady of Bluegrass" as part of a series of "Women in Country Music." Over the years, she was named an honorary colonel by many state governors, including John J. McKeithen of Louisiana in 1961, George Wallace of Alabama in 1964, and Edwin W. Edwards of Louisiana in 1975.

She recorded on many lables in the 1970s, including Rounder and Gusto. Typically, these releases contained one of her favorite singles hits, "The Legend of the Dogwood Tree."

In 1979, Wilma, assisted by daughter Carol Lee and the Clinch Mountain Clan, was one of the featured acts on the "Bluegrass Spectacular" TV show telecast nationally over the U.S. Public Broadcasting System. Going into the 1980s, she remained an *Opry* star and continued to maintain a sizable touring schedule as well.

CORNELIUS, HELEN: *Singer, guitarist, songwriter. Born near Hannibal, Missouri, December 6, 1941.*

The supreme glory of Hannibal, Missouri, lies in its inspiration to native son Mark Twain for such creations as Huck Finn and Tom Sawyer. But now a part of the town's spotlight rests on one of its modern day celebrities, Helen Cornelius. In the mid '70s, Helen took her place as one of the fastest rising newcomers in the country music field.

Her childhood was spent on the family farm near Hannibal and, aside from the inevitable chores, a prime facet of the life of Helen and her seven brothers and sisters (she was the next to youngest) was music. She recalled, "When I was very little, my dad listened to the *Grand Ole Opry* on Saturday nights, even if it couldn't come in clearly. My brothers always had country bands and we had a great big front porch where they'd set up out there and play music all afternoon on Sundays."

As a small girl during the first half of the 1950s, she demonstrated an effective singing voice that she blended in with some of the other children in the family. She and two sisters did so well as a trio that their father began to arrange for them to take part in country shows in Missouri and nearby states. Often this involved driving long distances in the family car. "He really didn't have the money to take us," Helen noted, "but he always found a way, even in blizzards." During those early years, Helen also began to learn to play the guitar.

Helen continued to polish her performing style as she continued through elementary school and into high school. She appeared in school events and sang at local dances and parties. Sometimes she entered amateur and semiamateur contests in Missouri and other nearby states. During her high school years, she also appeared on a number of radio and TV shows in the region. To take part in one amateur contest in the 1960s, she traveled to Quincy, Illinois. She won the contest and one of her prizes was the opportunity to audition for the *Ted Mack Amateur Hour.* However, the show's talent coordinator was present at Quincy and was so impressed by her work he decided she could go on the Ted Mack program without auditioning.

When Helen took her turn on the *Amateur Hour* a short time after, she proved a top vote getter for that phase of the competition. She returned for later stages of the show and won twice more. Her achievements in the preliminaries made her eligible for the grand finals. But the Ted Mack program was in its period of decline and was canceled before the finals took place.

The exposure, however, was more than enough to give Helen's career some upward momentum. She appeared in shows throughout the Midwest in the mid-1960s, initially working with a band, later as a vocalist accompanying herself on guitar. Her performing career wasn't opening the way to major success, however, and in the late 1960s, she decided songwriting might be more productive. "I read every music magazine and article I could get my hands on. I decided writing songs was a way to get into the business. I listened to the radio, studied the female voice and wrote for them."

For a year she polished her writing skills, writing original material without submitting anything to music executives or music publishers. When she felt ready, she selected some of them and made a demo tape. The tape eventually was submitted to Columbia-Screen Gems, where it soon caught the attention of company officials. The result was a songwriting contract and, before long, first placement of the songs with important country vocalists. Oddly, Columbia-Screen Gems closed down in the mid-1970s, as had the Ted Mack TV show. But now, with a track record, it was relatively easy for Helen to gain a contract from MCA Music after she sent a new demo tape to executive Jerry Crutchfield. In this case, he enthused over her vocal ability as well as her writing talent and came back with a suggestion for sending the tape to some recording companies. Elated after he phoned her about the matter, she recalled, "I went over to the piano and sat down and played all the songs I'd sent him on the tape."

The first releases of singles of her material came out in 1970 and, by the middle of the decade, many well-known artists had added her compositions to their catalogs. Among those who recorded some of her songs were Lynn Anderson, Barbara Fairchild, Jeannie C. Riley, Connie Smith, Skeeter

Davis, Charlie Louvin, LaCosta, Dottsy, Bonnie Guitar, and Melba Montgomery.

Crutchfield's efforts won her a chance to record for Columbia Records. She went to Nashville and cut two songs. Neither of those songs came close to being hits, but another Nashville music industry official, John Ragsdale of Duchess Music, became interested. Helen provided him with another demo tape, which he presented to RCA producer Bob Ferguson. Ferguson agreed both songs and voice were promising and added her to the RCA roster. Her debut single on the label came out soon after—"We Still Sing Love Songs in Missouri."

Ferguson also produced long-time country star Jim Ed Brown and suggested that Helen and Jim would make an excellent duo. He brought them together in early summer of 1976 to record their initial duet, "I Don't Want to Have to Marry You," written by F. Imus and P. Sweet. The song made the charts in mid-summer and rose to number one on *Billboard, Cash Box,* and *Record World* charts in August and September. The success of the song brought a fast acceleration to Helen's career. As it moved to top levels in August, she made her debut on the *Grand Ole Opry* the same week she joined Jim Ed Brown's road show, and became a cast regular on the syndicated TV show *Nashville on the Road.* That month she and Jim also completed work on their first duet LP for RCA.

In 1977, Helen and Jim Ed continued to demonstrate rapport with the country audience. During June they had the top-10 single "Born Believer" and followed that in the fall with another hit, "If It Ain't Love by Now." Their credits also included a hit album, *Born Believer.* At the Country Music Association Awards that October, they were among five finalists in the duo category and when the final votes were tabulated, won the award as Vocal Duo of the Year. Although they didn't win in 1978, they again were among the five finalists for a year in which they placed a number of singles on country charts, including "If the World Ran Out of Love Tonight," a top-10 hit in September. Their recording of the song also won a Grammy Award nomination. In early 1979, Helen and Jim Ed's version of Neil Diamond's "You Don't Send Me Flowers Anymore" was moving toward the top of the charts. Both these songs were included in their early 1979 album release, *Jim Ed Brown and Helen Cornelius.*

Her success with Brown didn't make Cornelius lose sight of her goal to make it as a solo artist as well. In late 1978 she made progress in that direction with the hit single "Whatcha Doin' After Midnight?" In 1979, her chart singles included "It Started with a Smile."

During 1980, she teamed with Jim Ed Brown for such charted singles as "Morning Comes Too Early" and "The Bedroom."

COUNTRY GAZETTE: *Vocal and instrumental group. Original members, early 1970s, Byron Berline, Kenny Wertz, Roger Bush.*

The growth of the West Coast-based country genre at the end of the 1960s and start of the 1970s that embraced bands like Poco, Flying Burrito Brothers, and the Eagles also helped spawn the bluegrass revival of the 1970s. One offshoot of the country-rock movement, for instance, was the Country Gazette, a band that gained initial exposure as part of the Flying Burritos show and later went its own way on the folk circuit during the mid-1970s.

The first incarnation of Country Gazette comprised Byron Berline on vocals and fiddle, Kenny Wertz on vocals and guitar, and Roger Bush (earlier a member of the Kentucky Colonels bluegrass band) on bass and guitar. The threesome toured with the Burritos in 1971–72, performing as sidemen on some Burritos numbers and also doing their own set. After the Burritos disbanded, Berline sparked continued activity of the band (with various alignments of musicians) on the country and bluegrass circuit. Banjoist Alan Munde also played a major role in the second phase of Country Gazette.

The band got the chance to record for United Artists in 1972. The result was the LP *Traitor in Our Midst,* issued that year and still in the United Artists catalog at the end of the decade. Later in the 1970s,

Country Gazette was represented by the *Country Gazette Live* LP on Antilles Records and one titled *Out to Lunch* on Flying Fish Records.

By the late 1970s, the group had disbanded and Byron Berline was working as a soloist and a member of the Doug Dillard Band. (See also Berline, Byron: Burrito Brothers, Flying: Dillard, Doug.)

COUNTRY GENTLEMEN, THE: *Vocal and instrumental group. Personnel in early 1960s: Charlie Waller, born Jointerville, Texas, January 19, 1935; John Duffey, born Washington, D.C., March 4, 1934; Eddie Adcock, born Scottsville, Virginia, June 17, 1938; Jim Cox, born Vansant, Virginia, April 3, 1930.*

From its inception in the late 1950s to the start of the 1980s, the Country Gentlemen ranked as one of the most popular bluegrass bands in the United States. Its concerts, featuring the group's trademark, "on-the-mark triple harmonies," were among the most consistently exciting in the field. The group attracted a following ranging from dyed-in-the-wool bluegrass fans to mainstream country and some soft-rock adherents.

Considering its many musical achievements, it may come as a surprise that the group was born by accident. Its genesis occurred when a mutual friend asked Charlie Waller, then working in Baltimore, and John Duffey, then at station WFMD, Frederick, Maryland, to fill in for a sick musician at a date in the Baltimore area on July 4, 1957. The two enjoyed playing together and decided to continue their musical association.

Before their paths crossed, Waller and Duffey had become proficient on guitar many years earlier. Waller, though born in Texas, went to Los Angeles with his family while still a child. When he was ten, he obtained a fifteen-dollar guitar and learned to play. By the time he met Duffey, he was an accomplished instrumentalist with a leaning toward bluegrass style.

Duffey grew up in the Washington, D.C., area, mainly in nearby Bethesda, Maryland. When Duffey was seventeen, a neighbor persuaded him it would be worthwhile to play guitar, and before long he was demonstrating his skills for friends and playing informally with other musicians.

After becoming friends, Waller and Duffey expanded the group to a trio by recruiting Jim Cox as banjoist and bassist in early 1958. Raised on a farm in Virginia, Cox began playing the banjo before he was in his teens. In June 1960, another Virginian, Eddie Adcock, was added, lending a stronger bluegrass tone to the group. Adcock learned to play the mandolin at twelve and became a regular on a gospel program on station WCHV, Charlottesville, Virginia, in his teens.

With the addition of Adcock, the group soon began to win attention from the burgeoning folk music audience of the early 1960s. The Country Gentlemen became familiar figures on the folk club, college auditorium, and folk festival circuit. Helping to move things along was their recording activities, initially on Folkways Records, which issued such early 1960s LPs as *Audience Participation* and the two-record *Country Gentlemen* (December 1960). Later in the 1960s, Folksways followed up with *Country Gentlemen, Volume 2, Volume 3,* and *Volume 4.* Some of their work also came out on Starday in the 1960s, including the LPs *Bluegrass* (July 1962) and *Country Gentlemen* (1965). Some of the group's LPs on other labels in the 1960s and 1970s were *The Country Gentlemen* and *Remembrances and Forecasts* on Vanguard and *Live at Roanoke* on Zap Records.

From the late 1960s on, the band's main record affiliation was with the Rebel label. Albums issued by Rebel in the late 1960s and early 1970s included *Bringin' Mary Home, The Traveler, Play It Like It Is, New Look, New Sound, One Wide River to Cross, Best of the Early Country Gentlemen,* and in 1972, *Sound Off* and *The Award Winning Country Gentlemen.* Another early 1970s release was *The Gospel Album,* which emphasized some fine vocal harmonies by the band members. Other mid- and late-1970s releases on Rebel were *Yesterday and Today, Volumes 1, 2* and *3,* and *Joe's Last Train.*

The Country Gentlemen persevered through the downturn in American interest in bluegrass during the latter part of the 1960s and were in a position to benefit from the rebirth of widespread activity in the 1970s. The group appeared at many of the annual festivals that thrived in the 1970s in places such as Telluride, Colorado, and Bean Blossom, Indiana, and often was featured at the bluegrass-week concerts in Nashville.

COUNTRY MUSIC ASSOCIATION: *Industry trade organization, based in Nashville, Tennessee.*

One of the important forces behind the growing popularity of country & western music from the start of the 1960s is the Country Music Association. The CMA was formed in 1958 by industry executives and artists to promote this form of music and try to combat the temporary depression caused by the rise of rock 'n' roll. In November 1958, a series of meetings led to the organization's formation with an original leadership of nine directors and five officers. Connie B. Gay was elected to the first two-year term as CMA president with Wesley Rose, president of Acuff-Rose, as CMA board chairman.

At the first annual meeting in November 1959, the board of directors was increased to eighteen and officers to nine. The meeting confirmed the continued work of Mrs. Joe Walker as executive secretary. The membership was divided into nine categories: Artist–Musician, Artist–Manager, Booker, Promoter, Agent, Ballroom Operator, Composer, Disk Jockey, Music Publisher, Radio–TV and Record Company Personnel, Trade Publication Representative, and Non-Affiliated. Each category is entitled to elect two board members; the board, in turn, appoints the officers.

Functions of the CMA include promoting country & western music worldwide, conducting industry surveys to provide useful data to members, and informing members of industry news. The most ambitious project of the CMA was establishment of the Country Music Hall of Fame (see Country Music Hall of Fame), in which CMA offices are now located.

COUNTRY MUSIC HALL OF FAME AND MUSEUM: *Building in Nashville, Ten-*

nessee, housing plaques of members elected to Hall of Fame and collections of exhibits, historical data, and other items of interest.

In 1967, an impressive monument to country music was opened to the public at 700 16th Avenue South, Nashville, Tennessee. The structure was the culmination of years of work by the Country Music Foundation toward a repository of information about the field. The idea for the center had been proposed by the Country Music Association in 1964. Funds had been collected from country artists, music fans, firms, and others.

The building, since expanded, consisted of a modernistic barn-shaped center section flanked by two flat wings. A "Walkway of Stars" led up to the center entrance, consisting of brass emblems with names of leading country artists on them embedded in concrete blocks. The right wing housed a fifty-seat theater in which films on the history of country music and videotapes of major artists are shown. The other wing includes the "Artists' Gallery," a series of pictures of famous performers below which are earphones for listening to some of their recordings.

The hall also houses other exhibits of importance: a library of tapes, books, films, recordings, and publications, and material from the John K. Edwards Memorial Foundation, a collection of information about country & western music considered one of the foremost of its kind in the world.

Each member elected to the Hall of Fame is represented in the center hall with a bronze plaque giving biographical data and including an image of the person. Selection of Hall of Fame members is by annual vote of a committee of approximately one hundred members selected by the Country Music Association.

The Foundation is administered by a full-time staff of scholars, educators, and museum and library professionals. More than 500,000 visitors a year from throughout the world pass through the exhibits, including nearby Studio B where all-time country greats recorded in the past.

The Foundation is the foremost organization in dealing specifically with country

music, and in a larger sense speaks for the legitimacy and importance of all American folk and popular music forms through active participation in national museum, library, and arts associations. It has become the advocate for all forms of commercial, popular, and folk music and continues to argue in every forum for the equality of all artistic endeavors.

The first six members of the Hall of Fame included three living artists, Ernest Tubb, Roy Acuff, and Tex Ritter, and three deceased, Jimmie Rodgers, Hank Williams, and Fred Rose. (For complete list of Hall of Fame members, see Appendix.)

CRADDOCK, BILLY "CRASH": *Singer, guitarist, bandleader. Born Greensboro, North Carolina, June 16, 1939.*

When Billy "Crash" Craddock came onstage in baby-blue form-fitting slacks and matching sequined shirt, there was no mistaking the Elvis Presley-style touch of sensuality. Nor could you miss elements of rock, from Elvis through Charlie Daniels, in the arrangements offered by his brightly garbed band. But neither was there any doubt that Billy was, first and foremost, a country artist in basic form and content, albeit of the new breed that came to the fore in the 1970s.

Commenting on his approach, he told a reporter in 1977, "We country artists need the young audience. I love country music and I tried to record straight for fifteen years before I struck the fans with 'Knock Three Times.' I do country-rock now and it's because my fans won't accept me doing 'hard' country. It seems that after you get a hit record in one pattern, the fans sort of expect it."

Billy, one of ten children of a poor rural family, grew up on a farm near Greensboro, North Carolina, and recalls that Hank Williams was his first idol. He played a make-believe broomstick guitar as "accompaniment" before an older brother, Clarence, began giving him lessons on a real one when he was eleven. Soon after, he mowed an aunt's lawn for almost three months to earn the money to buy his own instrument from a local pawnshop.

When he was high school age, he and another brother, Ronald, were competent enough as "pickers" to win a local talent contest thirteen weeks in a row. Later they enlisted two friends for a rockabilly band called the Four Rebels. Taking a break from music, Billy was a running back on the high school football team, bringing him the nickname "Crash."

After a talent scout for Columbia Records caught the Rebels' act one night, Billy was signed and told to come to Nashville during 1959. He was naturally elated, but it proved a preface to a soul-searching letdown. "They tried to make another Fabian out of me. You've got to realize that back then there was pop and then there was country. There was no blend of the two like there is today. They wanted me to be a pop singer, but there was a great deal of country in my style. It just didn't work." The singles issued by Columbia fell flat at home, but strangely three songs became top-10 hits in Australia.

That wasn't enough to save the situation and Billy, discouraged, returned home. For most of the 1960s, he did shows in his spare time in North Carolina and neighboring states and worked in the construction field for his main income. At first fellow workers who heard of his Columbia contract gave him a hard time. "They would say, 'Hey, Crash! What the hell are you doing here? I thought you were some kind of big recording star.' I had to develop a pretty good sense of humor."

His luck finally turned again in 1969. A pharmaceutical salesman named Dale Morris caught a Craddock set in a local hall and was impressed. Still, it was hardly an overnight rise in fortune. It took almost two years for Morris and producer Ron Chancey to form a label called Cartwheel Records before Craddock got the call to Nashville once more. He cut the single "Knock Three Times," which amazingly gained enough exposure to reach number one on country charts in 1971. The team followed with two more hits, "Ain't Nothin' Shakin'" and "Dream Lover" (Craddock later named his band the Dream Lovers), after which ABC bought out Cartwheel to gain Billy's services.

Billy supported his recordings with concert tours that drew enthusiastic audiences representing almost every age group. From 1971 through 1977, he had seventeen singles that made the country top 10 on Cartwheel/ABC, including nine that reached number one. Among those were "Knock Three Times," "Dream Lover," "Ruby Baby," "Sweet Magnolia Blossoms," "Walk Softly," Easy as Pie," and "Broken Down in Tiny Pieces." ABC released nine albums of his, all of which made the country charts. Some of his records also crossed over to the U.S. pop charts as well.

In the fall of 1977, Billy left ABC for Capitol Records. The first release from the new alignment was the album *Billy Crash Craddock*. With Dale Morris as producer, the album demonstrated again Billy's "hybrid" format, ranging from a version of Bobby Goldsboro's "Rock and Roll Madness" to the Lester Flatt arrangement of the country classic "Rollin' in My Sweet Baby's Arms." The debut Capitol single "I Cheated on a Good Woman's Love" found favor with country fans in 1978, bringing Billy his eighteenth top-10 country single. Also on the hit lists that year were "I've Been Too Long Lonely Baby," "Don Juan," and "Hubba Hubba." In 1979, he added such top-10 credits as "If I Could Write a Song as Beautiful as You," "Robinhood," "My Mama Never Heard Me Sing," and the charted single "Til I Stop Shaking." His 1980 charted singles included "I Just Had You on My Mind" and "Sea Cruise."

As of 1982, the band comprised Charlie Waller on guitar, Robert Yates on bass (born Big Rock, Va., April 30, 1935), James Gondreaux, on mandolin (born Wakefield, R.I. on July 3, 1946) and Richard Smith on banjo (born Syracuse, N.Y., October 4, 1943).

CRAMER, FLOYD: *Pianist, organist, songwriter. Born Shreveport, Louisiana, October 17, 1933.*

During the 1960s and 1970s, while Chet Atkins held the unofficial Nashville title of "Mister Guitar," his contemporary Floyd Cramer was regarded as "Mister Keyboards." The similar designations to some extent reflected career interactions. It was

Chet who first induced Floyd to come to Nashville, where the two often worked together on their own albums or on tour and backed recordings of other artists. And both contributed immeasurably to the post–World War II development of the Nashville sound.

Floyd showed countless young keyboard players how to achieve a characteristic country feel on piano and organ by adapting traditional guitar techniques used by people like Mother Maybelle Carter to keyboard playing. He described his approach, based on a method of slurring notes, in this way: "The style I use mainly is a whole-tone slur which gives more of a lonesome, cowboy sound. You hit a note and slide almost simultaneously to another. It is a sort of near-miss on the keyboard. You don't hit the note you intend to strike right off, but you 'recover' instantly and then hit it. It is an intentional error and actually involves two notes. The result is a melancholy sound."

Cramer was born in Shreveport, but his family moved to a small Arkansas sawmill town called Huttig where he grew up. He seemed to enjoy music almost as soon as he could walk and talk: "My parents told me that they saw in me an early love for music which was the reason they got a used piano when I was five. I was the only child and that old piano, which I learned to play by ear, became an inseparable companion."

When he was in high school, he played in school groups and also began to perform at dances and in local clubs. After finishing high school in 1951 he went to Shreveport to audition for the popular KWKH *Louisiana Hayride*. He got the job and soon was working on the show with people like Webb Pierce, Jim Reeves, and Faron Young. He toured with some of the *Hayride* stars, including Reeves and the immortal Hank Williams. Later, he was on the *Hayride* when a young performer from Mississippi made his debut—another musical giant, Elvis Presley. Floyd also backed Presley on concert dates in the early 1950s and later played for many Presley recording sessions as well as several of his movie soundtracks.

During his years in Shreveport, Floyd backed many early recording efforts of future stars at Shreveport's Abbott Records. He also got the chance to cut his first solo record on Abbott and did a number of sides for the label in 1953–54.

On occasion, he went to Nashville for session work between 1952 and the end of 1954; while there he became acquainted with Chet Atkins. Chet was enthusiastic about Floyd's piano skills and urged him to move to Nashville to help out in sessions Chet supervised as part of his production duties at RCA and to cut original recordings on the label. In January 1955, Floyd complied and for decades after became what amounted to an institution on the country-music scene. During those years, not only was he the keyboards bellwether in that field, but like Chet Atkins, he demonstrated he was equally at home playing just about every kind of pop music and some classical material as well.

Starting in the 1950s, Floyd was constantly on the go, touring all over the United States and in many other nations. At the end of the 1970s, he still had a rugged schedule of appearances in concert halls, including many annual performances as a soloist with major symphony orchestras in pop concerts, clubs, and music theaters. During the 1970s, one of his notable series was called the Masters Festival of Music, where he headlined with Chet Atkins and Boots Randolph throughout the United States and Canada.

In the mid-1950s, he became a regular on the *Grand Ole Opry* and was often featured on nationwide *Opry* radio and TV programs for decades thereafter. Just a few of his network TV credits in the 1960s and 1970s were Johnny Carson's *The Tonight Show*, a Perry Como TV special, *Kraft Music Hall*, several appearances on *The Ed Sullivan Show*, *Jimmy Dean*, *Johnny Cash*, *Roger Miller*, *Merv Griffin*, and *Hee Haw*.

RCA began issuing albums and singles of Floyd's work in the mid-1950s, mostly recordings of songs written or made famous by others, but also a certain number of originals. In 1960, he scored his first major record success with his composition "Last Date," one of the top-selling country singles of the year. He followed up shortly after with another hit, "On the Rebound," and later in his career had a third major success with "Fancy Pants."

His albums remained a staple item in RCA's catalog. While few of them made rarefied top-chart levels, almost all found a steady market with Cramer's following, which cut across many of the arbitrary lines between pop music classifications. His yearly album output averaged two to three and covered all kinds of material, from country and pop songs to blues, jazz, ragtime, musical comedy, and movie themes. As of early 1979, his total of LP releases on RCA Records was forty.

Among them was an annual series called *Class of . . .* in which Cramer capsulized most of the top hits of the preceding year. The series began with the *Class of '65*, issued in September 1965, and was followed regularly by collections generally released in September or October of each year. Besides those, his RCA list included such albums as *Blues*, issued in March 1960, *Late Date* (1/61); *On the Rebound* (5/61); *Pianist* (10/61); *Floyd Gets Organ-ized* (4/62); *Sing Along* (3/63); *Comin' On* (10/63); *Floyd Cramer* (3/64); *Best of Floyd Cramer* (8/64); *At the Console* (8/64); *Hits* (4/65); *Magic Touch* (5/65); *Big Ones* (3/66); *Here's What's Happening* (2/67); *Floyd Cramer Plays Monkees* (5/67); *Night Train* (8/67); *Country Piano/City Strings*; *Plays Country Classics* (2/68); *More Country Classics* (12/69); *Floyd Cramer with Music City Pops* (6/70); *This Is Floyd Cramer* (two records, 8/70); *Sounds of Sunday* (7/71); *Almost Persuaded* (8/71); *Floyd Cramer Date* (3/72); *Detours* (4/72); *Superhits* (1/79).

During his long career, Cramer received many awards and was nominated often in Country Music Association polls. He was among the five finalists for Instrumentalist of the Year nine times from 1967 through 1981. One of his more coveted awards was received in November 1974 while he was appearing in the Festival of Music at Opryland, USA. Chet Atkins was presenter of the Metronome Award, annually given to an individual who contributed most to the development of "Music City"—Nashville. Said Atkins, "This met-

ronome serves a dual purpose, it marks your fifteenth year with RCA Records . . . and it'll help you keep time."

CREACH, PAPA JOHN: *Singer, violinist, songwriter. Born Beaver Falls, Pennsylvania, May 28, 1917.*

In a career that spanned the decades from swing to rock, Papa John Creach proved adept at almost every kind of music, from an early interest in classics through jazz, R&B, and blues to the acid-rock of the Jefferson Airplane. As part of the Airplane offshoot, Hot Tuna, and as a solo artist on that group's record label, Grunt, he played all manner of material, from traditional folk tunes like "Danny Boy" to low-down blues and blues-rock, with a freshness and enthusiasm that belied his years.

John first picked up a violin belonging to an uncle when he was eleven or twelve in Pennsylvania. "My uncle started helping me to play," he told Diane Gardner of Grunt Records in 1971, "showing me the fundamentals on it, the notes and scales and so forth. Then I started practicing scales. After that I studied with my sister Ruth because by that time she was doing very well. She was playing overtures—classical music—piano. So that made it just right for me because I had someone who could accompany me."

When he was eighteen, his family moved to Chicago, where he continued in the classical vein for a time. "I was a guest artist with the Illinois Symphony Orchestra one time. I studied with the symphony orchestra down at the musicians' union and we had all the pros. We were doing concerts different places, and my sister and I were playing popular tunes, what they call, like "Am I Blue," at the time. But I didn't really get serious about jazz until I got a basic foundation on the violin because the violin is an instrument that the more basics you have on it, the better for you: the scales and positions and bowing techniques. I started out to study a little theory and harmony. When jazz came out and blues—well, there wasn't any rock at the time, but rhythm and blues, more or less—I kept on playing and got with different people and got little odd jobs which encouraged me to make a little money at being a musician."

In the late 1930s, he joined a trio, the Chocolate Music Bars, that played for six years in various hotels in the Albert Pick chain. In 1943, the trio began working clubs and lounges outside the chain. In 1945, Creach moved to California and started a group he called the Johnny Creach Trio (bass, guitar, and violin) that played the Chi Chi Restaurant in Palm Springs for a time and also traveled throughout the United States and Canada. Starting in the late 1940s, John began working with many of the greats of the jazz, R&B, and blues fields, performing material that often was derived from the folk-blues tradition.

"I traveled all out around Memphis and through that area with R&B bands. See, my buddies are Roy Milton, Eddie 'Cleanhead' Vinson, T-Bone Walker, Joe Turner, Jimmy Rushing. I traveled with Roy Milton down to Memphis and then down to Mississippi and then back."

But California remained his main base in the 1950s and 1960s. He worked in several movies, including Dick Haymes' *Cruising Down the River* and *Blue Gardenia*, whose stars included Anne Baxter, Ann Sothern, and Nat "King" Cole. In the 1960s, he teamed with an organist to perform regularly at the Dinner Horn Restaurants in Newport Beach and Balboa, California. The job lasted four years, until he went on to work with a group that called itself the Shipmates. That band provided music for passengers taking the SS Catalina steamship between Los Angeles Harbor and the city of Avalon on Catalina Island. He remained in that situation for about five years.

Late in the 1960s, he stopped his channel voyaging to work as a single in Los Angeles clubs. "We had other artists, but I had my own show. In the Parisian Room in Los Angeles. I stayed there for two and a half years and after that I met Joey Covington [in 1971]. I had met him a good while back, but we had never gotten together.

"I met him at the musicians' union and

he was looking for somebody and I was looking for somebody, too, to play with. I guess it was about two years lapsed in between that. Then one time, he calls and said he was in Jamaica with the 'Planes' and he said let's get together. I said, 'Yeh.' And so after that he said Marty Balin was with him and they all stopped by my house. I put on a good pot of my corn bread and stuff which Joey loves and they discussed all the possibilities of me coming up to San Francisco to do some kind of recording bit.

"So once I went and played with Jefferson Airplane and the whole group at the Winterland Auditorium. And then I guess I went over pretty good and they said why not just make the tour and I stayed with them after that."

John's violin expertise, both on acoustic and electric violin, became a feature of the Airplane's act. He also was one of the first outside artists to be signed by the record company the group established for itself, Grunt. His debut LP, *Papa John Creach*, came out in 1971, made the hit charts late in the year, and remained on them into 1972. The album contained a range of material, from new songs written just for the LP, such as the blues shuffle "Papa John's Down Home Blues" (co-written by John with R. H. Spotts), to his treatment of such classic songs as "St. Louis Blues" and "Danny Boy."

Backing John on some tracks were members of Hot Tuna, a group formed by Airplane charter members Jorma Kaukonen and Jack Casady to play material that didn't fit in the acid-rock confines of Airplane sets. Kaukonen told an interviewer, "It was stuff I'd been doing before—with more traditionally oriented folk roots, finger picking stuff." Some of the material was written by Hot Tuna members, the rest was "old traditional stuff arranged so we can play it. The Reverend Gary Davis is a large source of our material."

Papa John seemed a natural for the group. He became a key member, remaining with Hot Tuna for a number of years in the mid-1970s. For most of that period, the band comprised Kaukonen, Casady, Creach, and first Covington, then Sammy

Piazza on drums. Creach played in major venues all over the United States as a member of Hot Tuna and also helped record several of the group's albums.

After a while, though, Creach began to long for his old jazz roots. He left Hot Tuna and worked as a solo artist in jazz clubs and festivals during the second half of the 1970s.

CROCE, JIM: *Singer, guitarist, accordionist, songwriter. Born Philadelphia, Pennsylvania, January 10, 1942; died Natchitoches, Louisiana, September 20, 1973.*

The countless times that Jim Croce's voice has beamed forth on rock and folk radio programs have brought acclaim far surpassing anything that accrued in his short lifetime. It is generally agreed that had he lived, this sensitive, highly creative folksinger turned rock artist might have become one of the brightest stars of the 1970s.

He grew up in south Philadelphia, where his initial musical training began with the accordion at age six. It was not until he was eighteen, working in a toy store, and playing the blues in his spare time that he bought his first guitar, a twelve-string. He became reasonably proficient on it while attending Villanova University, where he was emcee of a three-hour folk and blues show on the school radio station. While folk and blues were his primary interest, the various bands he formed during his Villanova years (he graduated in 1965) played everything from rock to folk and pop ballads. He was a warm, gregarious individual and made many lasting friendships during his college years, including one with Tommy West, later of the team of Cashman and West.

He loved music, but for a while after he left college it was mainly a sideline. One of his first jobs was selling ads for a black rhythm & blues station. After that, he began a series of jobs as a laborer. On one of these, he broke a finger with a sledge hammer, but he was able to regain the ability to play guitar by developing a picking style that didn't depend on the finger. In 1966, he got married and with his wife, Ingrid, worked at a summer camp in Pine Grove, Pennsylvania teaching guitar and ceramics. In the fall he began a teaching job at a ghetto junior high school in south Philadelphia.

It wasn't easy, but Jim persevered until he and Ingrid decided to go to Mexico under a fellowship grant she received to study Mexican pottery. When they returned to the United States in 1967, they heeded the suggestions of Tommy West to put their folk music ability to work and soon were performing in coffee houses and small clubs in the New York area. They also managed to get a recording contract with Capitol, which issued the LP *Jim and Ingrid Croce*, a disc that quickly sank without a trace.

At the end of the 1960s, the Croces moved onto an old farm in the Philadelphia area and lived a hand-to-mouth existence during 1969 and 1970. Jim eked out a meager living by working at a series of odd jobs, but at one point was forced to pawn his collection of guitars to make ends meet. He finally found a reasonably steady job as a truck driver, and composed new songs on his many long hauls to occupy his mind. When he had a half dozen completed that he liked, he recorded them on a tape cassette that he submitted to Cashman and West, who increasingly were more concerned with management than their performing activities.

Cashman and West liked the demo and arranged for Jim to record some of the songs at the Hit Factory studios in New York in the fall of 1971. ABC Records signed him, and Jim completed enough tracks for an album in early 1972. His debut LP, *You Don't Mess Around with Jim*, came out in the spring. Both title song and album made the charts after a while, and while they didn't zoom right to the top, the reception was promising. In the fall of 1972, another single from the album, "Operator," gained considerable airplay and also appeared on national pop lists. There was eager expectancy among many critics for his follow-up LP. When that collection, *Life and Times*, came out in early 1973, it confirmed that Croce was indeed a writer and performer with rare gifts. The album sold much more briskly than the first one and a single from it, "Bad, Bad Leroy Brown," became one of the top hits of 1973, reaching number one on U.S. charts in July.

All seemed going well with Croce's career as he took off on a summer tour in support of his album. He had just completed a standing-room-only concert in Louisiana and was on his way in a private plane to the next one-night stand when fate stepped in. Something malfunctioned on takeoff and the plane hit the ground and burst into flames near Natchitoches. Even as his lifeless body lay in the wreckage, articles were appearing in three different music trade magazines hailing him as the next American superstar. As West told a reporter, "Jim became a star just three weeks before he died."

Instead of ending things, the shock of the accident caused millions of fans to realize what they had lost. Somewhat like what occurred with Jim Reeves, the country star who also died in a plane crash, years afterward reissues of old recordings or new releases of previously unreleased recordings resulted in a series of posthumous hits. The first impetus affected his already issued records. Elliott Abbott of BNB Associates, his management firm, told Jack Hurst of the *Los Angeles Times* (June 9, 1974), "His first album had sold about 10,000 or 50,000 and the second about 230,000 or so when he died." By mid-1974, both were over the half-million mark.

Soon after Croce's death, his single "I've Got a Name" moved into the top 10. Later in 1973, "Time in a Bottle" rose to number one. (The latter is a song whose hauntingly ironic lyrics include the prophetic words, "There never seems to be enough time to do the things you want to do. . . .")

The Croce impact continued unabated into 1974. Early in the year, his seventh singles release on ABC, "I Have to Say I Love You in a Song," appeared on the charts, remaining for well over four months and rising to number one at one point, earning a gold-record award. During the year, the *Don Kirshner Rock Concert* show devoted an entire ninety-minute concert to Croce. A seven-minute movie of Croce performing was used on the show

and also presented on other TV programs, including several in Europe.

At intervals in the mid- and late-1970s, Croce's recordings were released in various album combinations. Unlike Reeves, who had been recording for quite a few years before he died, Croce's catalogue was much more limited so that, by the late 1970s, there was nothing available for new singles. Abbott told Hurst, "The last album was finished eight days before the crash and he hadn't recorded other things that are being held in the can. What he had done was it. That's all there is."

CROSBY, STILLS, NASH & YOUNG: *Vocal and instrumental group. David Crosby, born Los Angeles, California, August 14, 1941; Stephen Stills, born Dallas, Texas, January 3, 1945; Graham Nash, born Lancashire, England, 1942; Neil Young, born Toronto, Canada, November 12, 1945.*

The names of Crosby, Stills, Nash, and Young, in various combinations—solo, duos, trios, or quartet—bulked large on the pop music scene from the late 1960s into the 1980s. Their contributions included some of the finest folk-rock material of the period and some of their original compositions fit into all pop categories, from rock to folk and country.

By the time the members came together in Los Angeles at the end of the 1960s, all of them had impressive credits behind them. David Crosby, of course, had been a founding member of The Byrds, with whom he remained from 1964 to 1968, and, before that, had been a singer-guitarist on the folk music circuit for five years. Steve Stills and Neil Young, who helped form the landmark rock group Buffalo Springfield in the mid-1960s, first became acquainted when they were members of a folksong group called the Au Go Go singers in 1964. Young's earlier history (see separate entry) included his own rock band as a teenager in Winnipeg, Canada, followed by several years as a folksinger on the coffee house circuit. Stills, born in Texas but brought up in many different places by parents whose work kept them constantly on the move, already could play many instruments, from guitar to piano to drums, by his teens and was finding some work as a performer during his high school years. Later, after winning some local attention appearing in folk clubs while attending the University of Florida, he dropped out of college to concentrate on a show business career.

Graham Nash, raised in Lancashire, England, already had a stage act called the Two Teens with a friend named Allan Clarke while in grammar school. At fifteen, in 1957, they became the youngest artists to appear at a well-known English venue, the Manchester Cabaret Club. After several other group affiliations in the late 1950s and early 1960s, in 1963 the two founded a vocal and instrumental group called The Hollies, which became one of England's top rock groups (and was still active in the 1980s). With Nash as the main songwriter and lead singer, the group scored many major hits in the 1960s. When he announced he had decided to leave the group in 1968, fans flocked to his last shows with the band, including the standing-room-only farewell show at London's Palladium on December 8, 1968.

By then, Nash already was rehearsing new material with the first Crosby, Stills, Nash & Young alignment, Crosby, Stills & Nash. The origins of that threesome were described by Ellen Sander (Hit Parader, September 1969): "It all started one late summer afternoon in a picturesque house in Laurel Canyon [Los Angeles]. Crosby was preparing material for a solo album after having left the Byrds. Nash, still with the Hollies, was visiting, and Stills, after the breakup of Buffalo Springfield had been sitting around and staring at the side of a mountain trying to decide what to do next between playing sessions. Goofing around in the California living room, they all began to play and sing together. And they loved it immediately and they talked about making an album and boy, it was going to be a hassle with each of them contracted to a different record company. Music biz wunderkind, David Geffen, a twenty-six-year-old funky imp, was called in to move minds and signatures around to make it possible, no small feat, mind you, but he did it and then some."

The three went to England in the fall of 1968 to compose new songs and rehearse while Nash closed out his career with the Hollies. They then flew back to L.A. to record their debut LP, Crosby, Stills & Nash, which came out on Atlantic Records in the spring of 1969. The record, still one of the best in folk-rock annals, included Stills' seven-minute long "Suite Judy Blue Eyes," "Helplessly Hoping," "49 Reasons," and "Bye Bye Baby"; David Crosby's lament for Senator Robert Kennedy, "Long Time Coming"; Graham Nash's "Lady of the Island" and "Marrakesh Express"; and a song by Crosby, Stills, and Paul Kantner of Jefferson Airplane, "Wooden Ships."

The LP spawned several hit singles and earned a gold record before 1969 was over. The trio's concerts also were among the most welcomed appearances of the year. By the time the members were ready for a second album, Neil Young had agreed to join the loosely organized operation. The first offering of Crosby, Stills, Nash & Young, Deja Vu, came out on Atlantic in the spring of 1970, matching the first one almost song for song in quality. It too was a success, rising to number one on U.S. charts in May and finding similar response all over Europe. The top-10 single "Woodstock," written by Joni Mitchell, was drawn from this LP. A year later the quartet had another number-one hit, the LP 4 Way Street, a live album. The band played before huge audiences all over the United States and abroad during 1971, including a memorable concert at New York's Carnegie Hall.

However, the individuality of the four superstars was beginning to cause strains. By 1972, Neil Young had dropped out of the alliance to concentrate on solo work and, though efforts were made from time to time during the 1970s to get him to take part in some reunion efforts, he kept on his own way. Stills, too, had his separate projects to work on during the mid-1970s, though he did return for trio work late in the decade. Besides Deja Vu and 4 Way Street, one other LP was issued of Crosby, Stills, Nash & Young recordings, a "best of" collection titled So Far.

In the mid-1970s, Crosby and Nash

worked together steadily as a duo, making several extensive tours during that period. One of their albums, *Crosby and Nash,* came out on the old Crosby, Stills, Nash & Young label, Atlantic, but most of their releases were issued on a new label affiliation, ABC. Their first ABC release, *Wind on the Water,* was one of the best folk-rock collections of 1975 and a top-10 hit in November 1975. They followed with two more ABC LPs, *Whistling Down the Wire* and *Crosby & Nash Live.*

Steve Stills returned to the fold briefly for the 1977 Atlantic Records LP, *CSN.* (Neil Young had been invited to take part, but reportedly backed out at the last minute.) The trio toured in support of the album in 1977 and the sold-out signs in major auditoriums across the United States testified to the artists' standing with the mass audience. The album was in the top 5 on U.S. charts during the summer of 1977 and earned a gold-record award from R.I.A.A.

However, following that flurry, the group broke up once more, with even Crosby and Nash giving up collaboration, at least for the last part of the 1970s. Nash turned most of his attention to solo work (with his solo LPs coming out on Warner Bros. during 1979–80) and cooperation with Jackson Browne on environmentalist issues. Those efforts included appearances by Nash and Browne in a concert series to raise funds to fight nuclear energy. One of those concerts formed the basis for a two-record album *No Nukes,* issued on Elektra at the end of 1979.

CROWELL, RODNEY: *Singer, guitarist, drummer, songwriter, record producer. Born Houston, Texas.*

One of the most promising of the new, creative individuals who started to have an impact on country music in the 1970s, Rodney Crowell had made his mark in several ways by the early 1980s. His original songs provided major hits for a number of artists; his production efforts brought new faces to the fore (including Rosanne Cash, who became his wife in 1979); and his potential as a performer and recording artist became evident.

Born and raised in Houston, Texas, Rodney gained considerable incentive toward a music career from his family environment. Both of his grandfathers were musically inclined—one was a church-choir leader and the other a bluegrass banjoist. One of his grandmothers played guitar and his father had performed in bars and honky tonks as a sideline when the chance arose. The first instrument Rodney decided to play departed somewhat from family tradition. He took up drums at eleven and later, in his teens, worked with several local rock groups. However, he liked country music and became increasingly interested in the field as progressive country began to make its mark in the early 1970s. By then, he already was writing original material and also had developed skill as a guitarist in addition to his drum work.

At the start of the 1970s, he went to Nashville to try to further his songwriting efforts. He managed to gain the ear of Jerry Reed, who took him on as a writer. During that two-year association, Jerry recorded some of Rodney's songs. Meanwhile Rodney was making other contacts and friends, such as songwriter Guy Clark, whom he cited later as a major influence on his work, and producer Brian Ahern, who worked closely with Emmylou Harris.

When Ahern brought Crowell to Emmylou's attention she was strongly impressed with Crowell's writings. From the mid-1970s on, many of Crowell's songs showed up on her albums, including "Amarillo," "Til I Gain Control Again," "You're Supposed to Be Feeling Good," "Tulsa Queen," "Leaving Louisiana in the Broad Daylight" (co-written with D. Cowart), and "I Ain't Livin' Long Like This." Rodney also became a member of her Hot Band, playing guitar with that group for two and a half years from 1975 to 1977.

In the fall of 1977, Rodney left that group to devote more time to his new record agreement with Warner Brothers and to do more production work. His debut LP on Warner Brothers, *I Ain't Livin' Long Like This,* came out in July 1978. It contained six originals and three by others, including an old Dallas Frazier song, "Elvira," which was the first single release.

Commenting on the project, Crowell said, "I'm not a pure country songwriter, but I think I'm a good country singer. On the album I tried to isolate different elements. For instance, there are straight-out country songs as well as straight-out rock songs. I've tried to stay close to my roots and at the same time give the songs a contemporary feel. Some of my own personal favorites are the title track and a tune Emmylou's recorded, 'Leavin' Louisiana in the Broad Daylight.' I'm also partial to 'Elvira.' "

His judgment couldn't be faulted. Although the songs didn't reach the top for him or Emmylou, all three became number-one hits for others. The Oak Ridge Boys had a number-one single with "Elvira" in 1981; before that they had gained a number-one hit with "Leavin' Louisiana in the Broad Daylight" in February 1980. In March 1980, Rodney could point to writing or co-writing two number-one hits in a span of two months as Waylon Jennings' version of "I Ain't Livin' Long Like This" made the top spot.

In the early 1980s, though, as Rodney's performing career moved forward it didn't seem far-fetched to see him singing his own way to a number-one record later in the decade. His second LP, *But What Will the Neighbors Think*, issued by Warners in February 1980, was a fine collection with such Crowell originals as "Here Come the '80s," "It's Only Rock 'n' Roll," and "The One About England." Equally impressive was his third LP on Warner Brothers, *Rodney Crowell*, released in the fall of 1981, which quickly moved onto the national country charts. At the same time, a single from the album, his composition "Stars on the Water" moved toward the top-20 on singles lists.

Rodney continued to add to his impressive production credits as well. In the early 1980s he helped his wife, Rosanne, achieve a major hit with the album *Seven Year Ache* and produced such other excellent collections as Bobby Bare's *As Is* and Guy Clark's *South Coast of Texas*.

CURLESS, DICK: *Singer, guitarist. Born Fort Fairfield, Maine, March 17, 1932.*

Country music has had a strong following throughout the history of Maine. The state has supported a number of homegrown artists in local clubs, but few have gone on to national prominence. An exception is Dick Curless, whose deep baritone voice and trademark eye patch often graced major country venues from the stage of the *Grand Ole Opry* to the fair and rodeo circuit from the mid-1960s on.

Curless grew up in New England, but his boyhood was spent in the woods and fields of Maine. As a child, he often worked in the potato fields with his brother for upward of ten hours a day during harvest season. One of the main joys of his family was music. His father played guitar and his mother, piano and organ; on weekends Dick and his brother often joined them in family songfests. Before Dick was in his teens, he had also learned to play guitar reasonably well.

He already had some experience performing at local events when his family moved to Massachusetts. When he was sixteen, he gained his own radio show in Ware, Massachusetts, billed as *The Tumbleweed Kid.* He already had his heart set on a country-music career when he finished high school. "My parents gave me some money for graduation and I was supposed to go up to New York City with my class. I spent it instead on a cowboy outfit, a real fancy one. Figured I'd see New York later on. Never did feel much at home in the city."

He quickly got a job with a local band and soon convinced the leader there were greener pastures in his beloved Maine. "I told him about the hunting and fishing and all those trees and that one-nighter route just waiting to be taken by a good group." In 1950, Dick and the band, called the Trail Blazers, moved to Bangor, the same year he met his wife-to-be, Natalie.

He was beginning to get some attention beyond Maine for his singing ability when he was drafted into the Army. It looked like a step backward, particularly when he later was sent to Korea. "They must have been hard up. I had a bad eye, heart trouble, been married six months and my wife was pregnant. I went to Korea." It proved a fortunate assignment, since he was sent as a performer, not a soldier. As the *Rice Paddy Ranger*, he became a favorite with the troops through his show on the Armed Forces Korea Network. One of his songs that was particularly popular was "China Nights."

He was discharged in 1954 and returned to Maine, where he took up the grind of one-night stands coupled with some radio and TV work. In 1955, he got the chance to headline the opening show at Bangor's new nightclub, the Silver Dollar Ranch House. He remained the featured artist there for a year, but illness forced him to retire from entertaining for a while. Late in 1956 he returned to action and in 1957 once more was hired by the Silver Dollar. During this run, he was asked to audition for the *Arthur Godfrey's Talent Scouts* program. That was enough of a lure to get him to the big city of New York, where his version of Merle Travis' "Nine Pound Hammer" brought first prize and a number of appearances on the TV show. "The Godfrey show really got me started—took me to places like Las Vegas and Hollywood. It was one of my best breaks."

However, his happiness proved short-lived. A series of personal problems, including a recurrence of physical ailments, and little luck with his record efforts resulted in his returning to Maine. He bought a truck and for most of 1958 earned his living in the logging business.

Feeling better after that, he tried to pick up his music career once more. His first engagement was in a place called the Hotel Belmont, after which he went on to play a number of other hotels and clubs in and around Maine. In 1960 he made another effort to make the national scene, traveling to Hollywood to audition for a film part. That was supposed to be followed by a West Coast tour. He hardly had settled in when Hurricane Donna hit the eastern seaboard. He called his wife only to have the phone call abruptly stop after a scream. Unable to make further contact, he rushed home. He found that everyone was all right; a tree had crashed into the living room and knocked out the phone.

He had lost another chance for new opportunities, however. He began to believe it wasn't fated for him to achieve stardom. For the next four years he kept up the routine of working local clubs and resort hotels without thinking too much about the world beyond New England.

He was resigned to being a big fish in a small pond when he formed a close friendship with Dan Fulkerson, a copywriter in a Bangor radio station. In his spare time, Dan wrote country songs and he talked Dick into paying for a record of his composition "A Tombstone Every Mile." The single was released on their own label, Allagash (they also put out sheet music by their own Aroostook Music Corporation), and it began to gain airplay. This led to an offer from Capitol's Tower Records subsidiary to buy the master and also sign Dick to a recording contract. The Curless-Fulkerson team soon was working on new material to follow the 1965 success of "Tombstone." Before 1965 was over, Curless had a second chart hit, "Six Times a Day." In 1966, they could point to a third charted single, "Tater Raising Man," followed in 1967 by "Travelin' Man."

Dick's debut LP on Tower, *Tombstone Every Mile*, was released before the end of 1965 and was followed by a number of new LPs as the 1960s went by, including *Dick Curless at Home, Soul, Travelin' Man, Dick Curless* (July 1966) and *All of Me*.

In 1966, Dick was voted the best new country singer of 1965 in two different disc jockey polls. During 1966, he also was signed as a regular member of the Buck Owens *All American Show* and traveled with the troupe all over the United States and to Europe and the Far East. "Those were good times—particularly the shows at Carnegie Hall and the Hollywood Bowl. Eventually, though, I figured I'd better get back to doing my own kind of music again and it seemed Nashville was the best place to do it."

Curless ended his work on Buck's show after two years and soon was booked solidly for shows, session work, and a movie project in which he recorded the soundtrack of the film *Killers Three*, which starred Merle Haggard and Dick Clark. Once more overwork took its toll and in 1968 he collapsed one day in Atlanta.

Back to Maine he went. "[I] went off in the woods, set up camp—no electricity, no refrigerators, plumbing, nothing but 16 million acres of elbow room. Didn't see anybody, didn't want to see anybody. Had to start wearing this patch—never could see out of two eyes, but the strain got so bad that I couldn't see much at all. Right eye was interfering with the vision I had in the left."

Once more the peace and quiet restored his health. In 1969 he signed a new recording contract with Capitol, which issued his debut on the label, "Hard, Hard Travelin' Man," soon after. Though Curless had decided to cut back on his efforts somewhat and spend more time with his wife and family, it was only a matter of degree. He continued to tour in the 1970s and also took on such other jobs as heading a publishing company, recording company, and talent agency.

His Capitol LP releases in the early 1970s included *Doggin' It,* issued in February 1971, and *Comin' on Country.* Capitol also reissued *Travelin' Man* and an album titled *Stonin' Around.* His singles releases included "Big Wheel Cannonball"/"I Miss a Lot of Trains," "Hard, Hard Travelin' Man"/"Winter's Comin' on Again," "Drag 'Em Off the Interstate, Sock It to 'Em J.P. Blues"/"Drop Some Silver in the Juke Box," and "Juke Box Man"/"Please Buy My Flowers."

D

DALE, KENNY: *Singer, drummer. Born Artesia, New Mexico, 1951.*

From his earliest years, Kenny Dale recalled having an infatuation with music, a singlemindedness that lasted all through his school years and on into adulthood. For someone with a minimum of talent, such perseverance can lead to failure and depression, but fortunately Dale proved to have singing ability and stage presence to go with his desire for a career in entertainment.

He claims that he was concentrating on music before he was old enough to carry on a conversation. "People used to feel sorry for my parents because they thought something was wrong with me. I used to sit in the back seat of our car with my fingers stuck in my ears and make sounds. Then I'd rock back and forth and jump around to the rhythm I was hearing. It was my way of making music for myself."

Listening to records or music on the radio was a major pleasure during his childhood and teen period in Texas. His first entry into the band area came relatively late, all things considered, and he made it by working as a drummer. "I didn't even know what a swing beat was at first, but I landed my first job in Houston with Terry and the Rounders by telling them I could play."

Singing, though, was what he wanted to do. After working with bands for a time he went up to Fiddlin' Frenchie Burke and asked for the opportunity to do some vocals. Stage fright caught up with him and he forgot the words partway through the song. However, Dale persisted in seeking another chance and finally proved his ability to Burke as well as other band leaders and club owners in town. He performed with Burke and did some comic routines in his show a number of times.

Dale then organized his own group, Love Country, and began to get engagements in bars and clubs in all parts of Houston. He also put together demo tapes in hopes of moving into the recording end of things. In 1974, he completed his debut single on a local label, a remake of a hit called "Patches." He followed with more singles on small labels, including "Somebody Help Me Get to Houston" and "Bluest Heartache of the Year." The last named, released on Earthrider Records, went to the top of the hit lists in Houston and gained attention from disc jockeys in

that town and several other Southwest locales. The single did well enough to persuade executives from Capitol to buy the
master and release the number nationally.
The result was a top-10 hit for Kenny Dale
in 1976 and a contract with Capitol.

By the time Kenny went into the studio
to record his debut LP on Capitol, he was
playing concert dates well beyond Texas.
The release of the album *Bluest Heartache* in
mid-1977 did nothing to stop the trend.
Album tracks included Willie Nelson's
"Crazy," Mickey Newbury's "An American Trilogy," "Misty," and a new song,
"Shame, Shame on Me (I Had Planned to
Be Your Man)." The latter came out as a
single and made upper-chart levels in late
summer of 1977.

Kenny continued to add to his credits as
a performer and record artist in the closing
years of the 1970s. In the fall of 1978, he
had a major hit with the single "Two
Hearts Tangled in Love" and in early summer of 1979 made the top 20 with "Down
to Earth Woman." Later that year he had
the top-20 hit "Sharing." In 1980 he placed
the singles "Let Me In" and "Thank You
Ever Lovin'" on upper-chart levels and
had the single "When It's Just You and
Me" on bestseller lists for a number of
months from late 1980 into early 1981.

DALHART, VERNON: *Singer, songwriter.
Born Jefferson, Texas, April 6, 1883; died Sep-
tember 18, 1948. Elected to the Country Music
Hall of Fame in 1981.*

Though it remained for the original Jimmie Rodgers and the Carter Family to provide the impetus for the rise of country
music to a major force in American popular music, some of the seeds already had
been sown by Vernon Dalhart, the first
country music "recording star." After recording his first country hits in 1924, he
went on to record hundreds of country oriented numbers in the 1920s and 1930s on a
variety of labels and with various pseudonyms.

Though born and raised in Texas (real
name Marion Try Slaughter), he was
not initially interested in "down home"
music. He had a good voice and had some
thoughts in his teens of an operatic career.

Eventually, he went to New York to take
professional vocal lessons and, while there,
became impressed with the growing popularity of record discs. His first release appears to have been on the Columbia label
in 1916 titled "Just a World of Sympathy."
However, that disc received little public attention. Dalhart himself considered his
first "real recording" as the result of a successful audition for Thomas A. Edison
which led to the famed inventor's signing
Dalhart as a recording artist for Edison
Diamond Disc. His first Edison release, in
August 1917, was "Cain't Yo Hea'h Me
Calling Caroline."

From then until the early 1920s, Dalhart
turned out many recordings of light opera
or then-popular music stylings. That type
of material did well for a time, then sales
of his discs began to drop. Looking for
something new to restore his fortune, he
decided to try some "hillbilly" tunes. He
initially selected a cover record of "The
Wreck of the Old Southern 97," already
released by another performer. For the
other side of the single, he recorded (on
August 13, 1924) an old poem, recently set
to music, called "The Prisoner's Song."
The latter, after the disc was issued by
Victor Records (his label at the time) in
November 1924, became a major hit and
remained a favorite for many years with
the record-buying public. At his death in
1948, an obituary in the *New York Daily
News* claimed some 25 million copies of
"The Prisoner's Song" had been sold.

"The Prisoner's Song" is considered to
be the first million-selling country record; Dalhart is supposed to have earned
$85,000 in royalties from it while it was
in print. In the years that followed, Dalhart had great success with other country
type recordings, such as "Molly Darlin',"
"The Letter Edged in Black," "The Death
of Floyd Collins," "Golden Slippers,"
and "My Blue Ridge Mountain Home."
Though many of the records were issued
under the name Vernon Dalhart (a name
he formed from the names of two Texas
towns), he employed more than one hundred pseudonyms. Among them were: Bob
White, Jeff Calhoun, Tom Watson, and
Mack Allen.

Dalhart, who early on saw the potential for "hillbilly" music, also was an early success on radio. During the 1930s, he was well known to many listeners for his radio work under still another pseudonym, "Sam, the Barbasol Man."

In 1981, Dalhart was elected to the Country Music Hall of Fame.

DALTON, LACY J.: *Singer, guitarist, songwriter. Born Bloomsburg, Pennsylvania, circa 1947.*

In Lacy J. Dalton's saga, there are sufficient periods of struggle and poignancy to befit a potential future queen of country music. She persevered through years of hard work in occupations like charwoman and short-order cook to support herself and her family; a tragic accident that killed her first husband; and years of thwarted efforts as a songwriter and rock vocalist. Success finally arrived at a time when most people would have given up in despair. With more years of accomplishment in the field to match Lacy's achievements in the early 1980s, it's a story one can easily envision gracing movie screens with an impact similar to Loretta Lynn's "Coal Miner's Daughter."

Lacy, whose original name was Jill Byrem, wasn't a coal miner's daughter: her grandfather had been a farmer near her birthplace of Bloomsburg, Pennsylvania, fifty miles north of the state capitol of Harrisburg, and her father was a guide on a private hunting preserve. Although typical music interests of people in the area ran to pop music, polkas, and some blues, both her parents, she recalled, were interested in "real down-home country music."

Although she had a good voice, Dalton envisioned becoming an artist during her teens. After graduating from high school, she enrolled as an art major at Brigham Young University in Utah. She went there, she told Eric Siegel of the *Baltimore Sun* (April 6, 1980), because "the tuition for the school was real low. I was cleaning toilets from three to seven in the morning in the campus art department to put myself through school. I got more out of that than I did out of school."

She stayed a semester and a half, then dropped out to work fitfully as a folksinger in Salt Lake City. "I used to sing these old protest songs and bore everyone to death." She moved on to Minnesota for a while, then back to Bloomsburg, where she decided that folksinging wasn't her forte. By then she was increasingly interested in rock, particularly the folk- and country-rock blends. She decided to break with her old environment and headed for California, where she soon helped form a rock band in the Santa Cruz area. The time was the late 1960s and the region below San Francisco was a hotbed of activity of new bands hoping to emulate the breakthroughs achieved by rock bands such as Jefferson Airplane and the Grateful Dead.

For three years, she fronted a group called The Office. She told Siegel, "It was a pretty good band. . . . At one point, I had offers from just about every major record company. But they told me I'd have to drop my band. I was very stupid and loyal. I told them to forget it. But it worked out for the best. If I had signed [a recording contract] then, I would never be the singer I am today."

By the early 1970s, the band had broken up, but the memory lingered on in more ways than one. Lacy had married the group's manager, John Croston, and now pursued her career as Jill Croston. As the 1970s went by, she did achieve a local reputation in and around Santa Cruz, performing with a wide variety of groups, from rock to soul and jazz, and gaining some attention for her original songwriting efforts. Meanwhile, her responsibilities had increased.

For one, not long after her marriage, her husband died from the results of a freak swimming-pool accident. She told Mike Greenblatt of the *Aquarian* (April 16, 1980), "It was a very unusual accident. He was pushing up off the bottom of the pool. Another guy was doing the backstroke and my husband hit his head, as he came up, into this guy's back. As a result, my husband was paralyzed from the neck down for three months until he died."

The tragedy left her with a young son to support. She told Siegel, "A week after [the accident], I found out I was pregnant. I hadn't planned it. But I realized I'd never be able to have another child with this man. So I decided to have the baby [Adam Croston, nine years old at the time of the interview].

Jill Croston had hopes that music might pave the way to a better life for herself and her son, but for a long time this proved just wishful thinking. She managed to keep active in the field performing various kinds of material, but most of her income came from more mundane efforts. For several years just before her late 1970s breakthrough in country music, for instance, she worked making crepes in an all-night Santa Cruz restaurant. As she told Greenblatt, "When you play music in California, where there are more musicians than people, you just expect to be poor for a very long time. If you're lucky enough to get a break, that's great; if you don't, then it's back to the artichoke factory or something."

But she was one of the lucky ones. The wheels started turning in 1978 when she cut an album with a range of material from soft rock to country in a Santa Cruz garage studio. She sold three to four thousand copies herself in Northern California and also sent free copies to people she hoped might help expand its promotion. One copy went to attorney friend David Wood, a one-time country disc jockey. Wood was particularly impressed with the country numbers and contacted Jill to arrange for some demo tapes. He then sent the package to Emily Mitchell, artists and repertoire executive with CBS Records. After a consultation with top CBS producer Billy Sherrill, Mitchell offered a contract. Sherrill recalled it was the songwriting aspect that impressed him. "There are a lot of good singers out there, but there aren't that many good writers. I think her potential is to the top of the country thing and beyond. I don't think there's any limit to what she can do. She's got the talent. I just hope the timing is right."

Indications were that the timing was right. Her debut single, "Crazy Blue Eyes," co-written by her and M. McFadden, spotlighted a smoky, husky, powerful voice that captivated most critics (a vocal quality

the newly renamed Lacy J. Dalton attributed to the rigors "of singing psychedelic rock for fifteen years") and enough fans to make it a top-20 chart hit in the fall of 1979. In early 1980, she followed with another top-20 single, her version of the Redd Stewart–Pee Wee King standard, "Tennessee Waltz." Her debut LP, *Lacy J. Dalton,* came out early in 1980 and was on the bestseller lists in March. (Besides her two hit singles, it also included one of her trademark compositions, "Are There Any Cowboys Left (In the Good Ol' U.S.A.)." Soon after, she had another charted single, "Losing Kind of Love" (co-written with M. Sherrill) that made the top 15 in June. In the fall, the massive promotional backing of Columbia and her intensive touring schedule paid off in the top-10 hit single "Hard Times." The song was the title track from her second album, issued in September 1980. It was a chart hit as well, befitting a notable year in which Lacy's rewards included being named by the Academy of Country Music as the most promising new vocalist (presented at the awards show in May 1980).

At the end of 1980, she had another single on the charts, "Hillbilly Girl with the Blues," for which she wrote both words and music, which entered the top 10 in early 1981. Later in the year she had the single "Takin' It Easy" (co-written with M. and B. Sherrill) at number two on *Billboard* lists.

DANIELS, CHARLIE: CHARLIE DANIELS BAND: *Vocal and instrumental group. Personnel as of mid-1970s: Charlie Daniels, born Wilmington, North Carolina, October 28, 1943 (vocals, fiddle); Joel "Taz" DiGregorio, born Worcester, Massachusetts (keyboard); Tom "Bigfoot" Crain, born Tennessee (guitar); Charlie Hayward, born Alabama (bass); Fred Edwards, born California (drums); Don Murray, born Maryland (drums). Charlie Marshall replaced Murray on drums in 1978.*

The 1970s saw the rise of "raunch & roll," a blending of blues, country music, and rock made popular by bands with strong Southern roots. One of the bellwethers of that movement was the Charlie Daniels Band, organized and led by a good-natured, massive giant of a man (6 feet, 4 inches tall and built like a football tackle) who could play country fiddle (backing friends like Willie Nelson) or rock guitar with equal dexterity.

Charlie grew up in rural North Carolina and started playing music at a very early age. He recalled "I don't know when the desire came to be a musician, but I had it since I can remember. My family wasn't musical. My father [who worked in a local lumber mill] played a little harmonica, that's all. When I was in my early teens [in the late 1940s] I got around with some guys who had experience with instruments. I started playing guitar when I was about fifteen, then learned mandolin and switched over to fiddle. The chords on a mandolin are about the same as those on a fiddle, so after a year and a half or so, I got into fiddle playing.

"We had a little bluegrass band in my home area around Wilmington, North Carolina. We called ourselves the Misty Mountain Boys. But there weren't any honky tonks. I lived in a dry county. We played square dances, school proms, things like that. There wasn't any rock 'n' roll when I began, but I got into that later about the time when Elvis came along. I never knew him, though he recorded a song of mine."

For a while, music was a sideline and Charlie worked days in the creosote plant where his father and grandfather were employed, while playing nights with a band in Jacksonville, North Carolina, near Camp Lejeune. "That's where I started playing professionally. When I decided to work in music full time [when he asked to be laid off at the creosote plant instead of a black employee who had a family to support] I drifted up the country to Washington, D.C. We'd switched to playing almost all rock and top-40 songs by then—Presley, Fats Domino, Bill Haley, Chuck Berry.

"It was the same band that turned into the Jaguars. We had two guitars, bass, and drums. Originally we called ourselves the Rockets. We went up there [to D.C.] in 1958 and 1959 and played about three years off and on. We made our first trip to California during that time and had jobs in

Oklahoma, Kansas, Florida, Texas—all over the United States. In 1959 we went through Fort Worth, Texas, and cut our first record. Actually, the band got its name there. I met a guy named Bob Johnston who was a local record producer and we cut a tune called 'Jaguar' that came out on Epic. After that we changed our name to Jaguars."

While Daniels wandered around the nation during the first part of the 1960s playing his mix of Southern rock, country, and blues, Johnston progressed along the Columbia Records ladder until he became one of its main producers working out of Nashville. "Bob brought me to Nashville. He said, 'Why don't you come down and see if you can do it as a studio musician, songwriter, what have you.' By then I had one song hit to my credit, 'It Hurts Me,' that Elvis recorded in 1963. I got seriously involved in songwriting in the late 1950s. The first one was "Does Your Conscience Bother You?" Full of clichés. But it never got recorded. But since the CDB started I'm proud of everything we've got on record. In some of the earlier recordings, I'm prouder of the songs than the performance."

The move to Nashville proved rewarding. Daniels spent four years as a studio musician, earning a substantial living. He also was exposed to a wide variety of musical stylings. He supported such diverse artists as Bob Dylan, Al Kooper, Pete Seeger, Leonard Cohen, Ringo Starr, and Flatt and Scruggs. "I liked working with Dylan. He was always a gentleman to me. I contributed to albums like *Nashville Skyline, Self Portrait,* and *New Morning.*" Charlie also toured as part of Cohen's backup band in the late 1960s.

After a while, Charlie tried his hand as a producer. He was particularly involved with the Youngbloods and produced what is still considered that band's best LP, *Elephant Mountain.* When Jerry Corbitt left the group, Charlie produced two solo albums of Jerry's for Capitol. In turn Corbitt produced Daniels' debut album, also on Capitol.

"That first [and only] 1971 Capitol album was essentially a solo Charlie Daniels and we did it mostly with studio musicians. Then I put a band together and started doing concert business." He averaged 250 touring days a year for the rest of the 1970s and early 1980s.

By 1972, Daniels had changed labels to Buddah, a firm more closely associated with bubble gum or soul than Southern blues/country-rock. But his efforts on the five LPs issued on Buddah's Kama Sutra label, which began with the excellent *Te John, Grease and Wolfman* in 1972, helped establish the CDB as a first rank Southern country-rock group. The single "Uneasy Rider" from the *Honey in the Rock* album first placed the band on the charts. As he says, "That was perhaps the most unlikely hit song I've ever written or recorded."

It was Charlie's fourth Kama Sutra LP, *Fire on the Mountain* (LP three, *Way Down Yonder*, contained the CDB song "Whiskey"), that finally brought a full measure of success to the CDB. "When that came out in 1975, it was a turning point for me as important as the Presley song." The LP, which includes such tracks as "No Place to Go," Charlie's impassioned performance of the classic fiddle tune "Orange Blossom Special," and the CDB's signature song, "The South's Gonna Do It Again," brought the CDB its first gold record. Before moving to a new contract with Epic, Charlie made his *Night Rider* album (issued in 1976) for Buddah, which also showed up on the charts. The CDB roster at the time, besides Charlie, included Tom Crain on guitar and vocals, Charlie Hayward on bass, Joel DiGregorio on keyboards, and Fred Edwards and Don Murray on percussion. In 1978, Murray was replaced by Charlie Marshall.

The switch to Epic (which issued some of his old Buddah masters) didn't seem to hurt Charlie's reputation. His first two releases for Epic in 1976–77, *Saddle Tramp* and *High Lonesome*, both moved to upper levels of national charts. His third Epic LP, *Midnight Wind*, also made the charts, though it did better on country lists than pop ones.

One of Charlie's favored achievements in the mid-1970s was establishing the annual Tennessee Jam, a country rock festival hosting many foremost Southern rock bands held every April in Nashville. In 1978, Epic released a two-record set of live recordings from the third and fourth Tennessee Jams.

Charlie and his band had one of their most productive periods during 1979–80. They turned out the album *Million Mile Reflections*, whose tracks contained the stirring fiddle tune "The Devil Went Down to Georgia." That combination provided the CDB with its biggest successes ever. Both single and album went over gold-record levels. The LP still was on the charts well into 1980 and had earned a platinum-record award. Charlie earned three awards in Country Music Association voting for 1979, announced on the network TV show in October 1979 and, when the Grammy winners were disclosed in February 1980, the CDB won the trophy for Best Country Vocal Performance by a Duo or Group for "The Devil Went Down to Georgia." On the nationally televised Grammy Awards show, the Daniels Band performed the song.

Charlie and his group closed out 1979 with another hit single, "Mississippi." In 1980, their charted singles included "Behind Your Eyes," "Long Haired Country Boy," "In America," and "The Legend of Wooly Swamp." In early 1981, the group had "Carolina (I Remember You)" in upper-chart brackets.

About his band and his approach to music, Daniels said, "I think it's anybody's individuality that sets them off. I think the most important thing in any profession is being yourself and doing it your own way. We don't follow fads or trends, don't rush out to record disco or punk rock just because it's hot. We just record what we feel is best for us. I feel if the CDB is unique, that would be the reason why.

"The fact that there's no particular trend today is good for me. I can't just lock in on one style of music. I'd hate to think I'd never play another rock song, blues, jazz or what have you, because that's all of what we—the whole CDB—are. I don't think the genre is as important as the quality."

DAVE AND SUGAR: *Vocal group. Original personnel, 1976: Dave Rowland, born Anaheim, California, January 26; Jackie Frantz, born Sidney, Ohio; and Vicki Hackeman, born Louisville, Kentucky, August 4. Frantz replaced in 1977 by Sue Powell, born Gallatin, Tennessee. Hackeman replaced in 1979 by Melissa Dean, born Lancaster, Kentucky. Powell replaced by Jamie Kaye, early 1980.*

One mark of the stature of a country artist is the number of important new names in the field that spin off from the artist's performing troupe; thus Charley Pride's stature in the 1970s was embellished when his alumni, the increasingly successful vocal and instrumental trio, Dave and Sugar, started to make a name for themselves.

The group's organizer, Dave Rowland, brought a wealth of performing experience to his new endeavor. Music was an important part of his life, going back to his early years when he began to learn his first instrument. Over a period of time he added skills in such diverse instruments as piano, trumpet, drum, bass guitar, and lead guitar, though it was only the latter he usually employed in the Dave and Sugar act. After being drafted into the Army in the 1960s, he won the attention of Special Services and, during his years in uniform, was a vocalist for a seventeen-piece band, trumpeter with the 75th Army band, and a leading actor in four theatrical productions. He claimed the distinction of being the only soldier to be given a theatrical scholarship by the Army's entertainment division.

His background includes graduation from the Stamps School of Music in Texas, where he also was a member of the Stamps Quartet. With the Stamps gospel group, he became part of Elvis Presley's touring show. He said, "Elvis was the first great thing to happen in my entertainment life. I don't have to read books that talk about him because I was there. We were good friends, and I feel fortunate that I got to know Elvis and work with him."

After about a year with the Stamps group, he left to join the Four Guys quartet which toured with Charley Pride and also appeared regularly on the *Grand Ole Opry*. After a year, though, problems arose concerning artistic directions and Rowland had to leave. "I had just bought a new home, a piano and a new car and suddenly—no job. I became singing waiter at Nashville's reknown Papa Leone's Italian restaurant. That definitely was not enough, so I decided to form my own group. I put together a progressive country-rock group, Wild Oates, but it still wasn't successful."

He then got the idea for a trio with talented, personable female artists. "The first day I held auditions, I knew the combination was magic. It was a great look and a great sound. There was nothing like it in country music." In short order he had his new act ready and gained a spot with the Charley Pride show.

The original lineup comprised Dave, Jackie Frantz, and Vicki Hackeman, who was the wife of lead guitarist Ron Baker of Charley Pride's Pridesmen band. Ohio-born Jackie was a member of the group when it became a name act in its own right. She sang on the initial recordings the trio made for RCA, including its first major chart hits, before leaving to be replaced by Sue Powell in 1977.

Vicki, who spent her early years in Louisville, Kentucky, later moved to West Palm Beach, Florida, with her parents. Much of her musical activity during her high school years there revolved around singing in her local church choir and in the high school choral group. However, as she progressed through her teens, she switched to pop music and was part of a trio that won first place in a statewide contest.

She extended her singing work to radio and TV, first in West Palm Beach and later in Chicago. During the 1970s, she worked for a while with a group called The Dallas Star and also, at one time or another, performed on stage with such well-known pop artists as Bob Seger, Buddy Miles, Cactus, the Association, and Crazy Horse.

Sue Powell was born in Gallatin, Tennessee, but grew up in Sellersburg, Indiana. Both her parents were interested in music; her father built his own recording studio and her mother was a vocalist. When she was only seven, she debuted in country shows in the Louisville area and within a year her father had recorded her first record. It didn't lead to an overnight raid on the country audience, but Sue had plenty of time. Her first major milestone came at the age of thirteen when Brenda Lee's stepfather, Jay Rainwater, heard her sing in Nashville and sought the right to manage the young blonde vocalist's career. This led to her first regional singles hit, "Little People," which went to number three on Lousiville-area country charts.

Eventually, the paths of Rowland, Hackeman, and Powell came together under the Charley Pride banner in the mid-1970s. With the increasingly enthusiastic reception the trio received as an opening act, Rowland became confident they could go further still. With Pride's help, they auditioned for RCA and were given the opportunity to make their initial recordings on the label during 1975. The trio's first single release, their version of Shel Silverstein's "Queen of the Silver Dollar," made the trade magazine country charts in late 1975 and remained on them for twenty weeks—well into 1976. At one point, the record made it into the top 20.

It was a harbinger of better things to come. Recalling his approach to the second single, "The Door is Always Open," Rowland said, "I suggested since we were going after the 'group' sound anyway, that we start with the chorus and hit 'em over the head with it." The device worked, the song moved to the rarefied environment of number-one on U.S. country lists during the summer of 1976. Before the year was over, they had still another number-one single, "I'm Gonna Love You." In 1977, their debut album also rose to number one and stayed in the top 20 for twenty weeks.

The group continued to tour widely during 1977 and 1978, sometimes headlining their own show at clubs like the Los Angeles Palomino and other times working on the Pride tour. They made an impact overseas as well, including well-attended concerts in Japan, Australia, England, Ireland, and Scotland. By then all of them lived in Dallas, Texas, home base for Pride's organization.

Their chart hits in 1977 included "That's the Way Love Should Be," a top-10 hit in late summer, and "I'm Knee Deep in Loving You," in upper-chart levels at year-end. In 1978, they added to the list with "Don't Throw It All Away" in the summer and "Tear Time," a chart hit in the autumn.

In 1979, there was another change in Sugar when Vicki Hackeman left and was replaced by Melissa Dean, born in Lancaster, Kentucky, and raised in Louisville. The revamped trio was still a popular act on the country concert circuit and on TV. At the end of 1979, the group had a top-5 hit with "My World Begins and Ends with You/Why Did You Have to Be So Good," which remained on the charts into early 1980.

During 1980, the trio had such charted singles as "New York Wine and Tennessee Shine" and "A Love Song." In early 1981 they placed "It's a Heartache" in upper-chart positions. *New York Wine and Tennessee Shine* was the title song of an album issued by RCA in May 1980. In January 1981, RCA issued the LP *Greatest Hits.*

By early 1981, Dave and Sugar had left RCA and signed with Elektra/Asylum. Their debut single on the new label, "Fool by Your Side," came out in April 1981 and the debut Elektra/Asylum LP, *Pleasure,* in May 1981. By then the trio comprised Dave Rowland, Melissa Prewitt, and Jamie Kaye.

Based partly on a 1978 interview with Irwin Stambler.

DAVIES, GAIL: *Singer, guitarist, songwriter. Born Broken Bow, Oklahoma, April 4, 1948.*

Gail Davies is often compared to such artists as Linda Ronstadt and Joan Baez, and few would argue, as she began to gain attention in the country field in the late 1970s, that she might achieve superstardom in the 1980s. She has a supple, effective voice and one aptitude neither Ronstadt nor Baez can claim—she is a highly gifted songwriter as well as performer.

By the time Patricia Gail Dickerson was born in the late 1940s in Broken Bow, Oklahoma, her father had been playing guitar for many years. As she recalled, "He learned his first three chords from Ernest Tubb." Her mother had a fine voice and liked singing; like her husband she was a country fan.

When Gail was five, her parents separated and her mother took Gail and her two brothers to the state of Washington. The event later formed the subject of one of Gail's songs, a big hit for singer Ava Barber in the late 1970s called "Bucket to the South." The lyrics went, in part, "My dad was quite a guitar man/Pickin' in his country band/He trifled with a woman/ And broke my mother's heart. . . ."

Gail spent the rest of her childhood in Washington. Her mother remarried a man named Davies whom Gail eulogized in her song "Soft Spoken Man." The Davies household was far from affluent, but there always were plenty of country records on hand and Gail grew up doting on the music of people like Hank Williams, Carl Smith, Patsy Cline, and Webb Pierce. When she was nine, she started harmonizing with her brother Ron. Their early singing was in the country vein but that changed when they hit their teens. "All I'd ever listened to all my life was country music. When I reached high school, however, that was the Beatles Generation. That was what was happening. So I left country music for the Beatles."

She and Ron kept working together, but this time doing rock material. When she was fifteen, the two of them worked with rock groups at local functions. She was still going strong and was something of a local celebrity when she finished high school. Offered the chance to tour with a rock band, she accepted; starting in the mid-1960s, she was on the road almost constantly for the next nine years.

In the mid-1970s she got fed up with traveling and decided to stay put for a while. She had married a jazz musician who hated country music ("I had to learn to sing jazz just to maintain my marriage status quo") and they made their home in Los Angeles. For a while she organized her own rock group to play local dates, but gave that up when she ran into trouble with her vocal cords and had to take it

easy for a while. About the time she hit that roadblock, her marriage also broke up.

With time on her hands until her voice healed, she started concentrating on writing original songs, perhaps inspired by her now successful songwriter brother Ron. (Among his successes was "Long Hard Climb," a hit for Helen Reddy, and "It Ain't Easy," ditto for Three Dog Night.)

As her voice got better, she began to return to the performing area, doing some backing vocals when she could get assignments. She had decided to return to her roots by then and her primary efforts were aimed at moving into the country field. She made a number of friends in the country artist fraternity and, from time to time, backed such people as Ronee Blakely, Hoyt Axton, and Roger Miller. One of those who thought highly of her ability in those years was Paul Williams, who was still a struggling writer at the time. She recalled, "He told me he had a great song for me once and sat down at my piano and played me 'Rainy Days and Mondays.' This was right before he hit it big—and I passed on it. . . . I passed on it!"

At times the going got rough and, to help pay the rent, Gail entered contest nights at L.A.'s main country nightspot, the Palomino Club. She won all but one contest, but those achievements didn't seem to further her career. "People told me my singing was too traditional for the L.A. scene! 'Try Nashville,' they said. So I finally got to Nashville [in 1975] and they told me 'Your style is nice, but it just isn't country enough.' "

Back in L.A., Gail kept active with her session work and songwriting. A solo record contract seemed as far off as ever when in 1978 she got married again. Her new husband was Richard Allen, also a songwriter and an executive with Screen Gems based in Nashville. She finally became a resident of Music City and the relocation proved fortunate. Not long after, she gained the attention of Tommy West (of the Cashman and West duo), vice president of Columbia's record affiliate, Lifesong, who finally signed her. His enthusiasm for her vocal and writing talents was encouraged by the changing guidelines for country material.

It was, in fact, as a result of people like Ronstadt and Emmylou Harris, with whom she was to be compared, that her opportunity came along. "I think Linda's coming along, and then Emmylou and other people, has opened it up for people to just play music. Before there were a lot of lines and walls, and a lot of the walls have come down."

Her LP *Gail Davies* came out in November 1978 (distributed by Columbia's Epic Division) and proved one of the most exciting debut releases in country music in recent years. (It was preceded in late summer by her hit single of Mel Tillis' "No Love Have I," in the top 30 in August). Most of the tracks were Gail's own compositions, including "What Can I Say," "Grandma's Song," "Bucket to the South," "Soft Spoken Man," "Someone Is Looking for Someone Like You," and "It's No Wonder I Feel Blue." She also added renditions of three old country tunes chosen from her mother's files; one of those, "Poison Love," gave her another chart hit single the last months of 1978. During the spring and early summer of 1979, she added to her credits the best-selling single of "Someone Is Looking for Someone Like You," on the charts for over four months.

Before 1979 was over, Gail had departed Lifesong/Epic Records for Warner Brothers. One of her first successes under the Warner's banner was "Blue Heartache," in the top 30 by mid-December 1979 and in the national top 10 in mid-January 1980. Later in 1980 she had the top-10 hits (on Warner Brothers) "Like Strangers" and "Good Lovin' Man." In 1981, she expanded her top-10 laurels with "I'll Be There (If You Ever Want Me)" in the top 4 in February, "It's a Lovely World," and "Grandma's Song," written by her.

DAVIS, DANNY: DANNY DAVIS AND THE NASHVILLE BRASS: *Horn player, arranger, band leader, artists and repertoire executive. Born Randolph, Massachusetts, April 29, 1925.*

One of the major trends in the country field starting in the late 1960s was increasing flexibility in both musical content and instrumental arrangement. This trend coincided with a steady growth in "crossover" records, records made by country performers that not only were hits in that field but also rose high on pop charts in the original version. An individual who was influential as an artists and repertoire executive and musical innovator was Danny Davis, whose successful introduction of brass to country caused the National Academy of Recording Arts & Sciences to set up a special category covering the format.

Davis explained his feelings on the matter to Bill Williams of *Billboard* in 1968 just after his initial effort at a new country sound, *Danny Davis and the Nashville Brass,* was released on RCA (where he had been in A&R for several years previously). "The music," he noted, "is more orchestral. Country writers are using more involved chord changes . . . but not so much that it ceases being simple, which is its charm. . . . Country listeners have accepted both more strings and a 'more legitimate' vocal background than in the past. . . . By that I mean something more involved and meaningful than do-wahs and simple two-part harmony. It complements the song. There is some acceptance, too, of horns, but this is coming more slowly."

He pointed out, at the time, that more artists were accepting backing arrangements with a horn or two at each session. Even long-time traditionalists had done an album with a French horn on a track. Of course, in the 1970s, the country audience indicated it had no objection to horns and reeds as long as they provided valid insights into the music. Davis, naturally, both led and profited from that with a steady series of well-received recordings of his group.

Davis had far from a "down home" upbringing. He grew up in Boston, where classical music was a family tradition; his mother was an operatic vocal coach. He demonstrated ability as a trumpet player at an early age and progressed rapidly. At fourteen, he became a trumpet soloist with the Massachusetts All State Symphony Orchestra. But like many young Americans, the siren call of popular music overcame his initial classical grounding. In his case the call came during the big band era. When he was fifteen in 1940 and a student at the New England Conservatory of Music, Gene Krupa offered him a job and he took it. Later on he became a member of name bands headed by Bob Crosby, Hal McIntire, Art Mooney, Freddy Martin, and Bobby Byrne.

After years as a sideman, Danny moved into A&R and, in 1965, joined RCA to handle production chores in New York. There he worked with Lana Cantrell and Nina Simone on their debut albums on the label, as well as others. He and Chet Atkins had known each other since the early 1950s, and when Chet suggested Danny would be a good addition to the Nashville staff, Davis moved there, receiving the title of Executive A&R Producer. After working with many major country artists, Danny became enthusiastic about the idea of adding a brass sound to his music and got Atkins to okay the idea of recording some material with a new band.

The release of his first two albums, *The Nashville Brass Featuring Danny Davis Play Nashville Sounds* in November 1968 and *More Nashville Sounds* in 1969, created a sensation. The latter album inspired N.A.R.A.S. to set up the new category of Best Country Instrumental Performance, for which the Brass were awarded a Grammy for 1969. Danny's fourth LP (the third was *Movin' On*, issued in December 1969), *You Ain't Heard Nothin' Yet* (June 1970), earned him a Grammy in the same category for 1970.

Nor was the band being ignored by the Country Music Association. The Nashville Brass was voted the Best Instrumental Band of the Year in 1969, 1970, and 1971. Other awards flowed in too. In 1970 the band was named Best Instrumental Group in *Billboard's* Annual Country Music Awards as well as Most Programmed Band and Top Up and Coming Band in the *Cash Box* country disc-jockey poll. *Record World* also voted it best country instrumental group in 1970. In 1971, all three major trades, *Billboard, Cash Box,* and *Record World* named the Brass the Best Instrumental Group.

And the Brass didn't wear out its wel-

come as the 1970s went by. The group kept turning out new albums, such as *Down Homers, Somethin' Else, Super Country,* and *Dream Country,* and nationally was almost a perennial nominee in country music polls of all kinds. In 1980, the group joined Willie Nelson for a series of recordings of his compositions that spawned such joint singles hits as "Night Life" and "Funny How Time Slips Away." The group was featured on most of the CMA Awards telecasts during the 1970s and early 1980s and appeared on a wide range of network TV shows, including Johnny Carson's *The Tonight Show, Johnny Cash, Hee-Haw, Red Skelton Show,* and *Mike Douglas.* Its numerous in-person shows included engagements in major cities across the United States (and overseas) and regular visits to Las Vegas showcases.

One of the awards Davis treasured, since Nashville was his adopted home throughout the 1970s, was an award from the city of Nashville for his contributions both to music and the city.

By the start of the 1980s, Davis and his group had become an institution in the country field, overcoming the early fears that the move to big-band country sounds might sound the death knell of the music. Davis early had stressed his belief that applying more formal music structures would not cause a drop in the creativity of country artists. "Native talent will keep things from going too far. Country won't sophisticate itself out of the market. It still is close to earth."

DAVIS, REVEREND GARY: *Singer, guitarist, banjoist, songwriter. Born Clinton, Laurens County, South Carolina, April 30, 1896. Died New York, New York, May 5, 1972.*

A towering figure in blues and gospel history, Gary Davis during his many years of performing served as an inspiration and a musical model for countless younger artists. Generations of singers and instrumentalists, black and white, incorporated some of his techniques and some of his songs into their own acts. For much of his life, though, he was more intent on using his talents to save people's souls than to win acclaim.

Raised in rural South Carolina, he began

singing gospel and blues songs while still a small child. Although he was sightless when he started to build a reputation as an artist with blues and folk music fans, he was not born blind, as was the case with many black troubadours of the early decades of this century. But he did have an almost inborn love of music, and before he was in his teens he could sing and play guitar and banjo so well that he often was asked to perform at corn-shuckings, barn-raisings, and buck-and-wing dances.

He continued to improve his performing style and increase his musical repertoire. During his teens in the early 1920s, he already was bent on making music a career. As the decade went by, he traveled all through North and South Carolina and into Tennessee picking up whatever work he could as a blues singer. His lifestyle paralleled that of most of the black artists of the period. Money was scarce and places to perform relatively few and far between. He sang and played on street corners at times, on other occasions in low-down bars and sometimes bawdy houses. It was a rough environment and a person had to be handy with fists and sometimes more dangerous weapons to survive. Reportedly it was during one unfortunate incident that Davis lost his sight.

To cure the profound depression that swept over him after his loss, he turned to religion. He stopped singing blues and concentrated on hymns and gospels. He also began to develop a skill in preaching. He decided to study for the ministry in the early 1930s and was ordained in 1933. After that he sang and preached in churches throughout the Southeast, though not as a regular pastor of a particular congregation.

He returned to his musical wanderings, often teaming up with other famous names in blues and folk annals. Among the artists he worked with in the 1930s and 1940s were Blind Boy Fuller, Bull City Red, and Sonny Terry. In line with his new outlook on life, Davis mostly sang gospel and folk songs, though he occasionally was willing to do some blues as well.

Still essentially an itinerant performer, he settled in New York in the 1940s. His base of operations usually was Harlem, where he eked out a living in the usual way—performing or preaching on street corners, sometimes obtaining small amounts of money begging. After awhile, though, things improved. For one thing, he got opportunities to preach in Harlem churches. At the same time, his skills as a folk artist gradually became known to an increasing circle of people in the thriving New York folk environment of the 1950s. As the decade went by, Davis was asked to perform on the growing number of small folk clubs in the city and in other parts of the Northeast. Soon he also was a familiar figure at the burgeoning circuit of folk festivals. He became an honored performer at the best-known folk festival of them all, Newport, where audiences loved his intricate five-string banjo and acoustic guitar accompaniment to his hoarse, gritty voice. In dark suit, white shirt, wearing a hat and dark, wire-rimmed spectacles, he seemed the living personification of the folk-blues and gospel genre.

Helping to expand his reputation not only to other parts of the United States but to many other nations as well were the series of recordings issued by various small folk labels. Most of them, such as *Little More Faith,* issued on Bluesville in December 1961, and *Pure Religion,* released on Command label in July 1964 (available on the Prestige label in the 1970s), contained gospel songs and hymns, though with strong blues intonations in the vocals and instrumental work. Among his other albums were *Blind Reverend Gary Davis* (Bluesville, October 1962); an album of the same title put out by Prestige Records in May 1964; *Singing Reverend,* issued by Stimson, in which he is joined by Sonny Terry; and *Guitar & Banjo,* issued by Prestige in the 1970s.

In the 1970s, his new recordings were released on Kicking Mule Records, Berkeley, California. Among his LPs on the label were *Ragtime Guitar, Lo I Be With You Always, Children of Zion,* and *Let Us Get Together.*

Throughout the 1960s and 1970s, he toured widely; while hardly affluent or anywhere near as well known as even a middle-level rock star, he had enough of a following to be reasonably comfortable.

The days of begging or singing on street corners at least were past. During those decades he appeared in folk clubs, at festivals, and on college campuses across the United States. He also became a favorite in England. In the 1960s, he was part of the Blues and Gospel Caravan that attracted large audiences in many English cities. In the early 1970s he went there to give a number of performances on his own, including a show-stopping set at the Cambridge Folk Festival in 1971.

DAVIS, JIMMIE H.: *Singer, guitarist, songwriter, educator, public official. Born Quitman, Louisiana, September 11, 1902,. Elected to the Country Music Hall of Fame in 1972.*

When TV viewers watched Senate majority leader Robert Byrd perform on the *Grand Ole Opry* in 1979, it seemed an unusual event. But Byrd, in truth, was following in a tradition of blending music and politics of long standing in country annals, a tradition that embraced such notable individuals as Roy Acuff, who ran for governor of Tennessee several times, Texas Governor W. Lee O'Daniel, and, of course, the two-time chief executive of Louisiana, as well as country superstar, Jimmie Davis.

Davis, born and raised in rural Louisiana, where his home town was Beech Springs, grew up in an environment where singing country music and gospels was an integral part of day-to-day living. He formed an early fondness for "the warm living songs of the cowboys and farmers and country folks." He learned to play guitar as a boy; by the time he began high school in Beech Springs he already had a considerable repertoire of songs, though at the time music seemed only a pleasant sideline.

He earned his B.A. degree from Louisiana College in Pineville in the early 1920s and from there completed a master's degree at Louisiana State University in Baton Rouge in the mid-1920s. Later in the decade, he was hired as a professor of history at Dodd College. In the meantime his musical efforts, particularly in the gospel field, continued and his reputation expanded well beyond his home state. By the late 1920s, he was giving gospel concerts at church meetings and at various religious centers all over the Southwest.

In the 1930s, he became more active both politically and musically. He was the holder of several public posts during the decade, including a year and a half as a public service commissioner and a period of time as a criminal court clerk. But it was as a performer of gospel and secular country material that he became well known. As the decade progressed, he spent more and more time on the road performing his country and gospel stylings before audiences all over the United States. Many of the songs he performed were original compositions, including "You Are My Sunshine" and "It Makes No Difference Now." Both songs became favorites of the Oklahoma Singing Cowboy, otherwise known as Gene Autry, who released singles of them that undoubtedly would have risen to number one on the charts—if there had been any hit charts in those years. As it was, they helped make Autry an international star. Both songs have been recorded by hundreds of artists over the decades since Davis wrote them and are among the classic songs of American music history.

By the end of the 1930s, though, Davis had acquired a national following that rivaled that of Autry's in size. He was a headliner on the country concert circuit and featured on national radio programs. He turned out dozens of records from the late 1930s through the 1940s on the RCA Victor label. He had a role in the movie *Louisiana,* released by Monogram Pictures in 1944.

During this time a yearning to make a name for himself in politics was in the back of Jimmie's mind. His musical achievements made his name familiar to almost everyone in his home state, which was no small help in his bid to gain the nomination for governor on the Louisiana Democratic ticket in 1944. He combined discussions of state problems with musical entertainment and won the post. He completed his first term as governor in 1948 and returned to the entertainment field, though with greater emphasis on gospel material than popular-style country songs. It was a pattern that continued throughout the 1950s, when his religious activities brought him many awards, including, in 1957, the American Youth Singers Award as Best Male Sacred Singer.

First for RCA and, in the 1950s and 1960s, for Decca Records, Jimmie turned out a great many sacred and secular recordings. Among his single releases were such songs as "Suppertime," "Lord, I'm Coming Home," "Get on Board," "Aunt Susan," "Honey in the Rock," "The Great Milky Way," "Alimony Blues," "You've Been Tom Cattin' Round," "Somewhere There's a Friend," "The Lord Has Been Good to Me," "Take My Hand, Precious Lord," "Worried Mind," "I'm Bound for the Kingdom," "Columbus Stockade Blues," "When I Prayed Last Night," "I Won't Have to Cross Jordan Alone," "There's a Chill on the Hill Tonight," "I Hung My Head and Cried," and "Down by the Riverside." He also recorded his own version of his classics "You Are My Sunshine" and "It Makes No Difference Now" as well as such other originals as "Doggone That Train," "Someone to Care," "When It's Roundup Time in Heaven," "When We All Get Together Up There," and "I Dreamed of an Old Love Affair" (the last two coauthored).

Among his 1950s albums on Decca were *Someone to Care* and *You Are My Sunshine.* He also recorded many gospel albums for that label, including *The Door Is Always Open* (issued in 1958), *Hail Him with a Song* (1959), *No One Stands Alone* (1960), *Watching Over You* (1961), *How Great Thou Art* (1962), *Beyond the Shadow* (1963), *Near the Cross, Highway to Heaven, Hymn Time, Songs of Faith, Suppertime,* and *Sweet Hour of Prayer.* In the early 1970s, he was represented in the Decca catalogue by such Christmas albums as *It's Christmas Time Again* and *Going Home for Christmas.*

Growing political upheaval in Louisiana at the end of the 1950s brought about another chance for Jimmie to enter the political arena. Amid cross-currents of racial strife and arguments about the Long family political machine, Davis entered the primary and won out over several adversaries. As Democratic nominee, he had no trouble in winning the governorship. Once

again his music work came to a halt while he ran the affairs of the state from 1960 to 1964. As his term drew to a close, he was represented by a new release on Decca in 1964 called *Jimmie Davis Sings.*

In the years after he stepped down from office for the second and last time, he maintained a relatively low profile. He was active in church endeavors but, in effect, retired from any major country music involvement. Many performers, both veterans and newcomers, however, included some of his songs in their repertoire.

Jimmie's contributions to country music were recognized when he was nominated as a candidate for the Country Music Hall of Fame by Country Music Association members in 1968. In 1972, he received the required number of votes for election. As the bronze plaque in his honor installed in the Hall of Fame in Nashville states, "His humility, deep felt responsibility to his audience and winning way with a song has brought much 'sunshine' to gospel and country music."

DAVIS, MAC: *Singer, guitarist, songwriter, actor. Born Lubbock, Texas, January 21, 1941.*

Though most of Mac Davis' reputation was made in the pop music domain, there was no gainsaying his Texas roots. A good share of his popularity always lay with country fans and many of his recordings showed up on country charts over the years.

Davis' early upbringing in west Texas had many of the basic elements of a country background. He spent much of his time on his uncle's ranch, and his early musical experience was derived to a great extent from the church. His first public singing efforts were in a church choir as a boy. Later he sang in local choirs in high school. However, his teen years coincided with the rise of rock and he became increasingly interested in the kind of music typified by artists like Elvis, Jerry Lee Lewis, and Carl Perkins. By then Davis was playing guitar and working with teen groups in his home area.

Later he moved to Atlanta, Georgia, where he worked days for the Georgia State Board of Probation and attended night classes at Georgia State University. His thoughts turned strongly to music, though, and he spent his spare time hanging around clubs or recording studios picking up contacts and trying to further his songwriting efforts. At the start of the 1960s he formed his own rock band and worked at college dances and private parties in Atlanta and vicinity. In 1961, though, he gave that up because, he said, "I had this image of being a rock'n'roller at the age of thirty-five, trying to make a buck."

Management, he decided, was the way to go. He found work as Atlanta district and regional manager for Vee-Jay Records, which he held until 1965. He moved over to a wider ranging job at Liberty—setting up local offices for the label throughout the South. (Liberty later became United Artists Records.) He did well enough for the company to bring him to Hollywood to head its music publishing operation, Metric Music.

Since he had continued to build up a backlog of original songs during previous years, Davis began to show some of them to record company executives and performers. In 1967-68 two releases of his material made the charts: Lou Rawls single of "You're Good to Me" and Glen Campbell's release of "Within My Memory."

Even more important, Davis' work caught the attention of his idol of his high school years, the King of Rock himself, Elvis Presley. Presley and his manager Colonel Tom Parker chose several Davis songs that Elvis sang in 1968, including one that made upper-chart levels, "A Little Less Conversation." Elvis next asked Mac to give him some new songs for his first recording session in many years in Tennessee. Among the material Davis turned over was a song about the deprivations of black life, "In the Ghetto." The song became a top-20 hit for Elvis in 1969 and, after Davis started his own singing career, a staple in his repertoire. Davis and Presley teamed up on still more hits in 1969-70: "Memories" and "Don't Cry Daddy."

Presley wasn't the only artist prospering with Mac's songs, some of which were published under such pseudonyms as

Scott Davis and Mac Scott Davis. Hit releases of his material at the end of the 1960s and in the early 1970s included O. C. Smith's versions of "Friend, Lover, Woman, Wife" and "Daddy's Little Man"; Bobby Goldsboro's single "Watching Scotty Grow" (written about Davis' son from his first, brief marriage); and Kenny Rogers and the First Edition's rock hit, "Something's Burning." Other credits Davis achieved in those years were the preparation of music for the first Presley TV special and for two of Elvis' movies and the composition of five songs for the Glen Campbell film, Norwood.

At the start of the 1970s, Davis decided to come out from behind the scenes and make his way as a soloist. A series of appearances on Johnny Carson's The Tonight Show and the David Frost Show in 1970–71 got things rolling and from then on he was a frequent guest on all manner of major network shows. He also became a headliner at Las Vegas show spots and played major hotels and night clubs regularly in the United States and abroad throughout the 1970s.

He signed with Columbia Records in the early 1970s; his label debut, Mac Davis: Song Painter, came out in mid-1971. That same year he had two chart singles, both written by him, "Beginning to Feel the Pain" and "I Believe in Music." The latter did well in both pop and country markets. In 1972, he scored heavily with his single, "Baby, Don't Get Hooked on Me," number one on the U.S. pop charts in September and a gold-record award winner (September 20, 1972). The album of the same title was in upper-chart levels the last four months of 1972 and well into 1973, earning a gold record in May 1973. Earlier in 1972, he had made the charts with his second album, I Believe in Music, and the single "Everybody Loves a Love Song." In spring 1973, he again made album charts with the LP Mac Davis. Other hits of the mid-1970s were "Smell the Roses" and "One Hell of a Woman."

Most of his pop hits also did well on country lists. In fact, he was still placing songs on the country charts when his pop momentum seemed to be slowing down.

Among his singles that made country lists in the mid-1970s were "Burning Thing" (co-written with M. James) and "I Still Love You (You Still Love Me)," both in 1975; "Forever Lovers," a top-20 hit in May 1976; and his composition "Picking Up the Pieces of My Life" in the summer of 1977.

During the mid- and late-1970s, Mac continued to be a popular in-person act and one of the more successful music industry hands at TV specials. For a while in the early part of the decade he had his own variety show, which gave way to a series of specials on NBC. His 1977 Christmas special, *I Believe in Christmas*, ranked sixth in the Nielsens and his first (of two) 1978 specials in May of that year also did well with viewers. During the year, he signed a new contract with the network for two specials a year for the next three years, bringing his association with NBC to nine years, the longest association of that kind for any artist.

His recording career languished somewhat in the late 1970s. By the start of the 1980s he had moved from Columbia to Casablanca Records, accompanied by an upsurge of buying interest among country fans. In the spring of 1980 he had a top-10 hit single, "It's Hard to Be Humble," an original composition that provided the title track for a best-selling LP. Later in the year he added such top-10 singles hits as "Let's Keep It That Way" and his own composition, "Texas in My Rear View Mirrow." In 1981 his singles successes included "Hooked on Music" and "You're My Bestest Friend."

Mac made his movie debut as a Don Meredith style quarterback in the 1979 movie *North Dallas Forty*. The following year he played the male lead in the film *Cheaper to Keep Her*.

DAVIS, SKEETER: *Singer, songwriter. Born Dry Ridge, Kentucky, December 30, 1931.*

One of country music's foremost female vocalists for decades, Skeeter Davis was noted for her treatment of religious songs. In the 1970s, though she still sang her usual repertoire of secular songs, she often took part as a singer of sacred material in programs of such well-known evangelists as Oral Roberts.

Growing up on a farm in Kentucky, the eldest of seven children, Mary Frances Penick (Skeeter's original name) loved to listen to the folk/country/gospel songs presented by the Original Carter Family on their radio programs. As she got a little older, she also stayed up nights to hear the many hours of the *Grand Ole Opry*, sometimes dreaming that one day she herself might become a member of the show.

When she reached her teens she began to take steps to realize her goals. She enjoyed singing with one of her close friends, Betty Jack Davis (born Corbin, Kentucky, March 3, 1932), and, in time, formed a duo with her. Calling themselves the Davis Sisters, they performed at small clubs in Lexington, Kentucky, then broke into radio in 1949 on station WLAX of that city. In the next few years they were featured on WJR Detroit, WCOP and WKBC-TV, Cincinnati, and WWVA (home of the *WWVA Jamboree*) in Wheeling, West Virginia.

The good reception their efforts received in those locales encouraged the women to go to New York to try for a recording contract. Their audition at RCA brought a contract from company executive Steve Sholes in the early 1950s. His judgment was verified with the success of their single *I Forgot More than You'll Ever Know*, which went to number one on the country charts. Tragedy struck on August 2, 1953; while returning to Cincinnati from an appearance on WWVA, the women's car was struck by another that had crossed over the dividing line. Betty Jack was killed and Skeeter critically injured. Skeeter's recovery was slow, complicated by her shock over the loss of her friend. At times she despaired of returning to the entertainment field. But her many friends urged her not to give up and finally she resumed her career in 1954, teaming up with Betty Jack's sister, Georgia.

By 1955, she decided she wanted to work as a solo artist and began to record new material under the watchful eyes of RCA Nashville A&R executive Chet Atkins. She also steadily added to her experience in the mid-1950s by touring with the *RCA Caravan of Stars* and also working with such other artists as Eddy Arnold and Elvis Presley.

Her rapid progress was taken note of in 1958 when she was named Most Promising Female Country Vocalist in the *Cash Box* magazine survey. In 1959, her growing audience provided her with a top-10 hit, *Set Him Free*. The song received a Grammy nomination for that year, the first of five such nominations she was to achieve between then and 1972. In 1960, she had another major hit with the single "I'm Falling Too," followed by such top-10 successes as "Optimistic" in 1961; "Where I Ought to Be" in 1962; "I'm Saving My Love" and "The End of the World" in 1963; and "Gonna Get Along Without You Now" in 1964. Some of her other singles hits of those years were "Dear Judge," "Am I That Easy to Forget," "I Can't Stay Mad at You," "He Says the Same Things to Me," and a song she co-wrote, "Homebreaker." In 1964, "He Says the Same Things to Me," brought a second Grammy nomination and her 1965 chart hit "Sunglasses" brought a third. Her 1963 smash hit "(It's Not) The End of the World" rose to the top of the pop as well as country charts, which resulted in her first gold-record award from the Record Industry Association of America. It also helped bring such honors as the *Music Reporter* Award for Entertainer of the Year and *Music Vendor* Award for Top Female Vocalist of the Year.

By then she had realized one of her girlhood fantasies for some years, having been named a permanent member of the *Grand Ole Opry* cast in 1959. The same year Skeeter also joined the troupe of her longtime idol, Ernest Tubb.

In the mid-1960s, she continued to add to her laurels with such singles as "Somebody Loves You" in 1965 and "What Does It Take (To Keep a Man Like You Satisfied)" in 1967. The former brought her the Peter DeRose Memorial Award and the latter a fourth Grammy nomination.

Throughout the 1960s and most of the 1970s, she was on the road much of each year performing at fairs, rodeos, and on the country theater and club circuit throughout the United States and Canada.

She appeared in major cities of Europe and journeyed on occasion to such far-off places as Indonesia and Japan during her career. Among her trophies were platinum records for some of her recordings from South Africa and Norway. Featured on network TV shows, during the 1960s and 1970s her credits included such programs as *The Steve Allen Show*, Dick Clark's *American Bandstand*, *The Jimmy Dean Show*, *Mike Douglas*, the Oral Roberts Specials, *Dean Martin's Music Country*, *The Midnight Special*, and *Hee Haw*.

In the 1970s, Davis continued to place songs on the hit lists, though not with the frequency of the 1960s. One of her major hits was "One Tin Soldier" in 1972, which brought a fifth Grammy nomination. In late 1973 and early 1974, the single "Don't Forget to Remember" was on the charts. During the 1960s and 1970s, Skeeter received a number of awards as a songwriter and/or music publisher from both BMI and ASCAP. Among her efforts so recognized were "Set Him Free," "My Last Date (With You)," "There's a Fool Born Every Minute," and "Bus Fare to Kentucky."

Her recording work on RCA between 1953 and the mid-1970s encompassed more than sixty singles and thirty albums. Some of those were duets with such artists as Bobby Bare, Porter Wagoner, and George Hamilton IV. Her album titles included the Fortune Records releases *Hits with the Davis Sisters* and *Jealous Love* and such RCA/Camden LPs as *Songs* (issued 1/60), *Skeeter Davis* (3/61), *End of the World* (5/63), *Cloudy* (12/63), *I Forget More* (8/64), *Let Me Get Close* (12/64), *Tunes For Two* with Bobby Bare (4/65), *Written by Stars* (8/65), *Blueberry Hill* (Camden, 9/65), *Best of Skeeter Davis* (8/65), *Skeeter Sings Standards* (1/66), *Singin' in the Summer Sun* (7/66), *My Heart's in Country* (1/67), *Hand in Hand* (6/67), *Skeeter Davis Sings Buddy Holly* (8/67), *What Does It Take* (11/67), *Place in the Country* (5/70), *Easy to Love* (Camden, 5/70), *Skeeter* (5/71), *It's Hard to Be a Woman* (10/71), *Foggy Mountain Top* (Camden, 11/71), *Love Takes a Lot* (1972), *Bring It on Home* (3/72), *Skeeter Sings Dolly* (8/72).

From the mid-1950s on, Skeeter lived in

the Nashville area. As of the beginning of the 1980s, home was a 300-acre farm in Brentwood, Tennessee.

DEAN, JIMMY RAY: *Singer, guitarist, accordionist, pianist, harmonica player, songwriter. Born near Plainview, Texas, August 10, 1928.*

During the 1970s, Jimmy Dean probably was better known to most people for pork sausages than his entertaining. Still, he continued to keep his hand in with a series, in-person appearances, and TV work. His hectic pace of the 1960s, when he had been one of the stellar country artists who often captured the attention of the broader popular audience with his recording and TV efforts, had slowed down a bit. Still, he proved he hadn't lost his touch in the 1970s and placed several more singles on the charts.

Dean sometimes recalled the straitened circumstances of his childhood when his mother, who was the family's sole support, ran a barber shop in their small Texas town to keep things going. As soon as Jimmy, who was born Seth Ward, was old enough to help, he had to pitch in and work on local farms. As he told Edith Efron of *TV Guide* (January 4, 1964), "Oh, I was a hardworkin' little boy. Pullin' cotton, shockin' grain, cuttin' wheat, loadin' wheat, choppin' cotton, cleanin' chicken houses, milkin' cows, plowin'. They used to laugh at my clothes, my bib overalls and galluses, because we were dirt poor. And I'd go home and tell mom how miserable I felt being laughed at. I dreamt of havin' a beautiful home, a nice car, an' nice clothes. I wanted to be somebody."

His mother wasn't able to provide him with material things but she taught Jimmy the piano when he was ten. Naturally talented, Jimmy not only picked up the piano rapidly, he soon taught himself to play a succession of other instruments—guitar, accordion, and harmonica.

Still, music seemed a sideline for a long time. When he was sixteen he went into irrigation engineering for a while, then gave that up in favor of a two-year enlistment in the Merchant Marine. After completing his sea-going hitch, he signed on with the Air Force. During those years, he used his musical skills as a source of spare-time income. Stationed at Bolling Air Force Base outside Washington, D.C., he formed a group called the Tennessee Haymakers with three friends and played in service clubs and local honky tonks. After he was discharged in 1948, he continued his musical routine.

Several years later, impresario Connie B. Gay agreed to represent Jimmy. In 1952, Gay sent him on a tour of U.S. bases in the Caribbean. Jimmy and his new group, the Texas Wildcats, then were placed on station WARL, Arlington, Virginia. In 1953, the group gained a national reputation with the singles hit, "Bummin' Around."

By 1955, Jimmy had his own TV show, *Town and Country Time*, on WMAL-TV. It soon was expanded to *Town and Country Jamboree* and was syndicated to other parts of the country. The success of the show led to a CBS contract for a network morning spot called *The Jimmy Dean Show*, which debuted April 8, 1957. The show gained excellent audience response, but no sponsors. In 1958, an afternoon network show from New York was planned, but a dispute arose and Jimmy quit the project.

For the next few years, Dean concentrated on live appearances around the United States and on turning out records under a Columbia Records agreement. In 1961, while on a plane to Nashville for a recording session, he tried writing his first song. The result was the massive gold-record winning hit, "Big Bad John." After that, he made the charts again with a variation on the theme, "Dear Ivan." In 1962, he followed with the hits "The Cajun Queen," "P.T. 109," and "Gonna Raise a Ruckus Tonight." Also a chart hit that year was his LP titled *Big Bad John*.

His recording achievements helped him win a new TV show contract, this time from ABC. The show was a feature of afternoon TV from 1963 into 1966. An hour-long nighttime version aired from 1964 to 1966, attracting an audience of millions, but still not enough for good Nielsen ratings. Besides hosting his own show, Jimmy was a frequent visitor on other major programs, including *The Ed Sullivan Show, The Pat Boone Chevy Showroom, Hollywood Palace,* and many country syndicated programs. He toured widely, starring at such places as Harrah's Club in Reno, Valley Music Hall in Salt Lake City, Circle Star Theatre in the San Francisco Bay area, Shoreham Hotel, Washington, and many others. His mid-1960s activities also included a tour with the Icecapades. By then he had switched record affiliations from Columbia to RCA. Among his chartmakers in the mid-1960s for RCA were "Stand Beside Me" in 1966 and "I'm a Swinger" in 1967.

His album output on Columbia, besides *Big Bad John*, included *Hour of Prayer* and *Jimmy Dean Portrait* in 1962, *Everybody's Favorite* in 1963, and *Songs We Love* in 1964. Some of his material appeared on other labels, including *Favorites* on King in 1960 and *Television Favorites* on Mercury in 1965.

In 1967, he made his LP debut for RCA with *Jimmy Dean Is Here*. Also issued during the year was *Most Richly Blessed*. He continued to record for Victor through the early 1970s with such releases as *At Harrah's Club* (late 1960s); *Dean of Country* (6/70); *Country Boy & Country Girl* (12/70); *Everybody Knows* (7/71); and *These Hands* (12/71).

In the mid-1970s, Jimmy recorded on the GRT/Casino label. One result of that affiliation was the best-selling single "I.O.U." which was awarded a gold record by the R.I.A.A. on May 20, 1976.

DELMORE BROTHERS, THE: *Vocal and instrumental duo, songwriters. Alton Delmore, born Elkmont, Alabama, December 25, 1908; died Nashville, Tennessee, July 4, 1964. Rabon Delmore, born Elkmont, Alabama, December 3, 1910; died Athens, Alabama, December 4, 1952.*

Long-time favorites on the *Grand Ole Opry* and on country music programs on WLW, Cincinnati, and other stations, the Delmore Brothers provided some of the all-time standards in the country field, numbers like "Beautiful Brown Eyes" (co-written by Alto and Arthur Smith) and "Blues Stay Away From Me," a joint composition of Alton and Rabon. The brothers also rank high in the bluegrass pantheon and formed the nucleus of one of the most famous quartets in country music history,

the Brown's Ferry Four, a group whose members included, at various times, such notables as Grandpa Jones, Red Foley and Merle Travis.

Both brothers were farm bred and sang for pure enjoyment when their boyhood chores were through. They learned to play the fiddle at early ages and, in their teens, entered many fiddle contests in their local area. Later, they mastered guitar and became highly proficient on that instrument as well.

After playing for some years for local events, the boys auditioned for Columbia Records in 1931. It was their first time before a microphone and proved the start of an illustrious recording career. Soon affter, they were signed by the *Grand Ole Opry* and they debuted on the program in 1932. They remained regulars on the *Opry* from 1932 to 1938. In the late 1930s and throughout the 1940s, the brothers were heard on many other stations, including WPTF, Raleigh, North Carolina; WFBC, Greenville, South Carolina; WAPI, Birmingham, Alabama; WIBC, Indianapolis, Indiana; WMC, Memphis, Tennessee; KWHN, Ft. Smith, Arkansas; and WLW, Cincinnati, Ohio. They became particular favorites of midwest audiences through their many years association with WLW.

From the 1940s into the 1950s, the brothers were represented on King Records. Their output on the label included many original compositions; before Rabon's untimely death in 1952, they wrote a total of over 1,200 songs together or separately (some of the latter co-written with other writers). Their King singles output included: "Prisoner's Farewell," "Sweet, Sweet Thing," "Midnight Special," "Why Did You Leave Me, Dear," "Don't Forget Me," "Midnight Train," "Freight Train Boogie," "Boogie Woogie Baby," "Harmonica Blues," "Barnyard Boogie," "Used Car Blues," "Peachtree Street Boogie," "Take It Out On the Captain," "Fifty Miles to Travel," "Shame On Me," "Calling to that Other Shore," "The Wrath of God," "Weary Day," "Blues Stay Away From Me" (a top-10 hit in 1949), "Pan American Boogie," "Trouble Ain't Nothin' But the Blues," "Blues You Never Lose," "I

Swear by the Stars," "Sand Mountain Blues," "Life's Too Short," "I Let the Freight Train Carry Me On," "Please Be My Sunshine," "Field Hand Man," "Gotta Have Some Lovin'," "Everybody Loves Her," "Lonesome Day," "The Girl by the River," and "There's Something 'Bout Love." Their output included several sides with Grandpa Jones, including "Darby's Ram" and "Take It Out on the Door."

Besides "Blues Stay Away From Me" and "Beautiful Brown Eyes," their best known career successes included "Brown's Ferry Blues," "Freight Train Blues," and "Born to be Blue."

The Delmores were among the nominees in 1981 for consideration for election to the Country Music Hall of Fame.

DENNY, SANDY: *Singer, songwriter. Born England, January 6, mid-1940s; died London, England, April 22, 1978.*

Sandy Denny, before her career was tragically cut short, established herself as one of England's foremost folk and folkrock artists in the 1960s and early 1970s.

As a child growing up in England, she bore the impressive full name of Alexandra Klene Maclean Denny. Obviously too long for a theater marquee or for fans to commit to memory, the nickname Sandy proved a better choice as she made her way as a performer in later years. Reaching her teens in the late 1950s, she was influenced by both the blues-based skiffle movement and the burgeoning folk scene at home and abroad. With a fine voice and the ability to relate emotionally to the content of her material, she first impressed friends and schoolmates and, in the 1960s, patrons at the small folk clubs that flourished throughout England.

In the mid-1960s, inspired in part by the rise of folk-rock in the United States under the aegis of people like Dylan and the Byrds, a parallel trend developed in England. Sandy, though considered one of the best young folksingers in her homeland, gave up the folk circuit to join larger groups, starting with a brief stay with the Strawbs and followed, in 1967, by membership in Fairport Convention. The latter band was started in London's Muswell Hill

section by five young folk musicians, including lead guitarist/vocalist Richard Thompson and guitarist Simon Nicol. Sandy was not a founding member—the original group had Judy Dyble as female lead singer—but the group reached its creative peak during her years with it.

She joined Fairport, a band that blended elements of traditional English folk music with modern folk and rock material and arrangements, when the group was working on its second album. That LP, under the title *Fairport Convention,* eventually became the band's U.S. debut release on A&M Records in 1969. She toured widely with the band in the late 1960s and at the start of the 1970s received effusive praise from critics for concerts in Europe and at a number of venues across the United States. Contributing both as a performer and a songwriter, some of her songs ranked among Fairport's most successful numbers. Their next two albums, *Unhalfbricking* and *Liege and Lief* were among the best in the folk/folk-rock genre.

At the start of the 1970s, she left the group to form a new band with musician Trevor Lucas, whom she later married and worked with in a mid-1970s reorganized version of Fairport. The new group, called Fotheringay, turned out one LP called *Fotheringay* that was released in the United States by A&M. Neither the album nor the band seemed particularly inspired and, by 1971, Sandy had decided to try for a solo career.

The first of four solo LPs, *The North Star Grassmen and the Ravens,* came out in 1971, followed in 1972 by *Sandy* and in late 1973 by *Like an Old Fashioned Waltz.* The first two came out in the United States on A&M and the third on Island Records. Those LPs, and particularly the first two, were excellent offerings that won deserved acclaim from critics in England and the United States. Besides some ear-catching original songs of hers, she also did ample justice to Dylan with such fine tracks as "Down in the Flood" on the first LP and "Tomorrow Is a Long Time" on the second.

Though her solo work brought her star status at home, she still remained a cult figure among U.S. fans. She rejoined Fairport Convention in the mid-1970s, working on two new albums with the revamped group and taking part in a cross-country concert series in the United States in 1975. The new albums did not match the quality of her earlier Fairport work, but she continued to demonstrate her ability as a show-stopper in the concert appearances.

She returned to solo work in the late 1970s to try to further extend her audience. However, those hopes were dashed as a result of a fall down a flight of stairs in the spring of 1978. She was staying alone in a friend's apartment in London at the time and did not go for treatment. The head injuries caused by the fall did not seem to trouble her at first, but a week after the accident she collapsed in a coma. She was taken to St. Mary's Hospital and never recovered consciousness. Her death, on Friday evening, April 22, 1978, was found to have been the result of a cerebral hemorrhage.

DENVER, JOHN: *Singer, songwriter, guitar player, actor. Born Roswell, New Mexico, December 31, 1943.*

Few musical artists are able to draw listeners from people of all ages and all musical tastes. John Denver is one of the few who can do so. At the peak of his success, his music was played on country stations as well as on rock and middle-of-the-road channels and his fans were said to range in age from three to ninety-nine.

Henry John Deutschendorf, Jr. (Denver's real name) was the son of an Air Force officer who was constantly being transferred to new locations. From Roswell, New Mexico, where he was born, the family moved to Tucson, to Oklahoma, to Japan, back to Oklahoma, and back to Tucson. While in Tucson for the second time, John's grandmother gave him an acoustic guitar and he started taking lessons. When the family moved again, to Montgomery, Alabama, John, who was now in the ninth grade, found that his guitar-playing ability attracted attention and soon people started seeking out his friendship.

A year later, John's family moved again,

this time to Fort Worth, Texas, but he no longer had to be the lonely new kid in school, a role he had played so many times before. He immediately started meeting people by singing in a church choir and by bringing his guitar to school. For a time, John's family stayed in Forth Worth, and John found himself being asked to perform with local rock bands and to play at school proms and parties.

After running away from home to California for a short while, Denver, frightened and confused, returned to Texas. He graduated from high school and enrolled at Texas Tech in Lubbock as an architecture major. But soon he found himself spending more time making music than studying. Folk music was in vogue at that time (the late 1950s and early 1960s) and he became an avid fan of folksingers such as Joan Baez, Tom Paxton, Peter, Paul and Mary, and the Chad Mitchell Trio, and sang some of their songs at local coffee houses and at college hootenannies.

Meanwhile, John's grades were slipping, which meant friction with his parents. At the semester break of his junior year, he dropped out of school, and, for the second time in his life, headed for California. This time he reached Los Angeles with more confidence than before. He got a job as a draftsman and spent all his spare time trying to break into the music business.

After a year of floundering, John got his first big break when he sang at Leadbetter's night club, a folk music center located in West Los Angeles near the University of California, Los Angeles (UCLA). The club's owner, Randy Sparks, who was also the founder of the New Christy Minstrels, told John that he liked his voice and that he wanted him to work as a regular performer at Leadbetters's, marking the turning point in his career.

John became a member of the Back Porch Majority, a Sparks-supervised group which acted as a sort of "farm club" for the New Christy Minstrels. But soon the Back Porch Majority became a successful group in its own right, with Denver singing several solos that were often well received by the audience. However, he felt that the Back Porch Majority was a dead end street, so he auditioned for and won a job at a club called the Lumbermill in Phoenix.

Before he moved to Phoenix, John heard that Chad Mitchell was leaving his trio and was looking for a replacement. He sent a tape and was called for an interview in New York with the Trio's management. Despite the fact that 200 to 300 other people were competing for the job, Denver was selected. He toured with the Trio for nearly four years, during which time he began to develop as a successful songwriter.

John had done some songwriting before joining the Chad Mitchell Trio, but his efforts were sporadic and he often took eight or nine months to finish a song. One of those songs, "Leaving on a Jet Plane," he wrote in one evening in 1966, as he related in an interview in January 1971, "while holed up in a Washington, D.C., hotel room. You see, we [the Chad Mitchell Trio] were always being invited to parties. I was never the type to play around on the road and time after time I'd be the only guy at these parties without a girl. This time I decided I'd had it with that. When the others left for the party, at eight, I got a pound of salami and a six-pack of beer and my guitar and locked myself in my room. When they came back about midnight, I had eaten the salami, drunk all the beer and written 'Jet Plane.'"

The Chad Mitchell Trio began to include "Leaving on a Jet Plane" in their stage act. Peter, Paul and Mary heard the song, liked it, and recorded it on an album in 1967. However, the song did not become a hit until 1969, when the girlfriend of a disc jockey in Denver, Colorado, talked him into playing the song over and over again on the station. The song caught on and became one of the top hits of 1969.

Meanwhile, the Trio was going through changes and suffering from tensions between the various members. Joe Frazier left to go more deeply into rock music and Mike Kobluk eventually left the Trio in part because of personality clashes with Denver. John reorganized the group with new members David Boise and Mike Johnson. Chad Mitchell sued to remove his

name from the group since none of the original members remained, but Denver pointed out that he had assumed $40,000 worth of debts from the old group, and that the suit would prevent him from continuing to pay it off. Mitchell dropped the suit. Denver paid off the debts and then changed the name of the group to Denver, Boise and Johnson.

In 1969, Mike Johnson decided to leave the group. At that point, John decided to disband the Denver, Boise and Johnson group and to try his luck as a solo artist. With the support of his wife, Anne Martell, he went to Aspen, Colorado, where he began to perform at local ski resorts. He was well received and was invited to perform at the Cellar Door in Washington, D.C.

During this time, he met Jerry Weintraub, a rising managing expert then working out of New York. The two got along well and Weintraub took over management of Denver's career. He placed Denver as a guest artist on several shows, such as *Merv Griffin*, and also got him a recording contract with RCA.

Denver's first album was entitled *Rhymes and Reasons* and was released in the fall of 1969. The LP contained his version of "Leaving on a Jet Plane" as well as the title song, also an original Denver composition. (Most of the material, however, was written by other writers.) The album received good reviews but failed to hit the charts, as did his next two RCA albums, *Take Me to Tomorrow* and *Whose Garden Was This*. "Aspen-glow" on the *Take Me to Tomorrow* LP was one of Denver's few original compositions in these years.

John's first recorded hit was co-written with Bill and Taffy Danoff, whom John ran into at the Cellar Door in Washington. The husband and wife songwriting team, also performing under the name Fat City, were having trouble completing a song. Denver already featured one song they had written for him in his act, entitled "I Guess He'd Rather Be in Colorado," which he later recorded on his *Poems, Prayers and Promises* LP. They got together and finished the song, "Country Roads," before the night was over.

John recorded "Country Roads" for his then upcoming album, *Poems, Prayers and Promises*. The single was released in early 1971 and climbed to the number-fifty position on the charts, the highest a Denver single had ever reached. However, he and Weintraub were not satisfied with reaching number fifty. They pushed the song through performances on talk shows and by getting maximum radio coverage. The plan worked and the song moved up to the number-one position. Before 1971 was over, Denver had his first two gold-record awards, one for the single "Country Roads" and the other for the album, *Poems, Prayers and Promises*.

Denver's next album, entitled *Aerie*, was released in November 1971 and included his composition "Eagle and the Hawk," originally written for a TV special. *Aerie* also featured other original compositions such as "Friends with You" and "Aspen in Starwood," in which Denver sang the praises of his new home in Colorado, where he and Anne settled permanently in the early 1970s. Although not an instant bestseller, *Aerie* was met by good reviews and sales soon picked up. The album was certified gold by the R.I.A.A. on January 10, 1972.

John took some time off from doing concerts in the United States to do a series of telecasts for BBC II in England. The idea was to improve his performing ability in front of TV cameras. His increased skills in this area were soon made evident when Denver returned to the United States. In 1972 and 1973 he appeared on numerous talk and variety shows. He also hosted *The Midnight Special*, a late-night ninety-minute musical show on NBC, on which he not only sang some of his songs but also held discussions with other entertainers about the importance of getting young people to register to vote. This "special" *Midnight Special* show received the highest rating ever scored by an early morning TV show as well as excellent critical appraisal. Among Denver's other television endeavors was "Bighorn," his first prime-time special, which emphasized the importance of ecology.

John's sixth album, *Rocky Mountain High*, was released in late 1972 to great critical acclaim. The title song was released as a single and soon climbed to the top of the charts. The album also featured "Goodbye Again," "Season Suite," and "Paradise." The LP was soon certified gold by the R.I.A.A. and reached unofficial platinum status by May 1973. His next album, *Farewell Andromeda*, contained the hit single "I'd Rather Be a Cowboy" and was certified gold on September 3, 1973.

Denver continued to use the television media to boost the sales of his records. In 1973 he wrote the score for the TV drama *Sunshine*, one of the most highly acclaimed television shows of that year. Part of the score included the original composition "Sunshine on My Shoulders," first introduced on the *Poems, Prayers and Promises* LP. The song was reissued on his next album, *John Denver's Greatest Hits*, which was certified gold within two weeks of its release in November 1973. The song "Sunshine on My Shoulders" received such enormous airplay that it was issued as a single in early 1974 and was certified gold by the R.I.A.A. not long afterward.

In early 1974, Denver made some television appearances. He played a dramatic role on the TV series *McCloud* in February 1974. During that period, he served as guest host on *The Tonight Show*, standing in for Johnny Carson. He continued to produce occasional television specials in the mid-1970s.

To coincide with a countrywide concert tour in the summer of 1974, RCA issued a new LP, *Back Home Again*. The album included the Denver compositions "Annie's Song," "Matthew," "Sweet Surrender," and "This Old Guitar," as well as songs by other writers such as "Grandma's Feather Bed" and "Thank God I'm a Country Boy." The album was certified gold within a week of its release. In addition, the Governor of Colorado, John Vanderhoof, declared the week of June 24–30 as "Welcome Back Home Again John Denver Week" and proclaimed Denver the poet laureate of the state.

As always, John's albums continued to sell. The single "Annie's Song" was certified gold by R.I.A.A. The *Back Home*

Again LP was said to be "going platinum" less than a month after its release. The song "Sweet Surrender," featured in a new Disney movie, *The Bears and I*, was released as a single in December 1974, becoming a hit although not a bestseller. Denver won his fourth gold-record award for a single for "Back Home Again" in January 1975.

The year 1975 proved to be a year in which John Denver truly reached the heights of his profession, and was generally agreed to be the number-one-selling record artist in the United States. His album, released in February 1975, *An Evening with John Denver*, a two-record set based on his 1974 concert tour, included five songs never previously recorded by him: "Summer," "Annie's Other Song," "Today," "Boy from the Country," and "Pickin' the Sun Down." His older songs, such as "Thank God I'm a Country Boy," were even more popular. This song was released as a single and was certified gold by the R.I.A.A. in June 1975. Denver's *Windsong* LP was released in October 1975 and had "gone gold" before the year was out. So did both sides of the single release from the album, "I'm Sorry" and "Calypso," a song celebrating the undersea explorer Jacques Cousteau. Another single from that album, "Fly Away," also became a chart hit. His 1975 Christmas album, *Rocky Mountain Christmas*, was certified gold almost as soon as it was released. His earlier albums, *Back Home Again* and *John Denver's Greatest Hits*, remained on the national hit lists throughout 1975, with the latter album reaching a total volume of over 5 million units by December 1975, thereby becoming one of the biggest-selling albums in pop music history.

Among the many kudos received by Denver in 1975, one of the greatest was undoubtedly being named Entertainer of the Year by the Country Music Association, perhaps the most prestigious award in all of country music. He accepted the award via closed circuit satellite relay from Australia, where he was doing a concert tour.

The naming of John Denver as Entertainer of the Year was somewhat unusual

for the CMA, as he is not a "hard-core traditional" country singer. Actually, the bespectacled, shaggy-haired entertainer has remained a folk music singer throughout his career, which is what he started out to be, despite his considerable popularity with country and rock fans.

After 1975, Denver's hit productivity declined somewhat. He continued to do TV specials, however, and he appeared in the movie, *Oh, God!* with George Burns in 1977, receiving mostly positive reviews for his performance. The movie was a box-office smash. Denver returned to the pop hit charts in 1979 with his single, "Downhill Stuff," from his album *John Denver*. As evidence of his continued popularity and respect as an all-around entertainer, he was asked by the record industry to serve as host of the annual televised Grammy Awards in 1979. In the early summer of that year his single "What's on Your Mind/Sweet Belinda" (the first was one of his compositions, the second by Steve Gillette and D. MacKechnie) was on the country charts for two months. At year end his LP *A Christmas Together* (with the Muppets) was on country album lists. In 1980, his album *Autograph* was on both pop and country charts. His 1981 chartmakers included the country single "The Cowboy and the Lady" and the pop hit album *Some Days Are Diamonds*.—A.S.

DeSHANNON, JACKIE: *Singer, songwriter, actress. Born Hazel, Kentucky, August 21, 1944.*

As befits one who early trumpeted the greatness of Bob Dylan and was a pillar of strength in the folk movement of the 1960s, Jackie DeShannon seemed to personify the words of "We Shall Overcome" by bouncing back from low points in her career with renewed vigor.

Born in Kentucky (named, Sharon Myers), she spent most of her early years in Chicago, where she made her public debut in a nearby town at the age of six. Her talents matured rapidly and at twelve she had her own radio show on a station in southern Illinois. Even at that stage, she was writing original songs, compositions good enough for Imperial Records' head

Lew Chudd to seek her out and sign her to a recording contract for his Los Angeles-based firm.

By the start of the 1960s, this association prompted a relocation to Southern California, from where she sallied forth to become one of the better-known performers in the pop and folk field throughout the decade. She became a favorite of fellow artists from every segment of pop music. In her many concert engagements of those years she appeared with such stars as Glen Campbell, soul singer James Brown, Harry Belafonte, and many others from both folk and rock fields. At some of the folk festivals she appeared in, she shared the program with people like Bob Dylan and Joan Baez. In the mid-1960s, the Beatles sought her out to join on one of their tours. She also had close rapport with the Byrds, who included one of her compositions, "Don't Doubt Yourself Babe," on their landmark first album.

By the time the Byrds' first album came out, Jackie already had placed several singles on the charts, starting with "Faded Love" in 1963, followed the same year by "Needles and Pins" and, in 1964, with "When You Walk in the Room." In 1965, she gained her initial gold-record singles award for her version of Burt Bacharach's "What the World Needs Now." Meanwhile, others besides the Byrds were profiting from her original compositions, including Brenda Lee, who made top chart levels with "Dum Dum," the Searchers, with the hit "When You Walk in the Room," and Marianne Faithfull, with a mid-1960s winner, "Come Stay with Me."

Her Liberty/Imperial album releases in the mid-1960s included *Jackie DeShannon* in November 1963, *This Is Jackie DeShannon* (11/65); *In the Wind* (1/66); *Are You Ready for This* (12/66); *New Image* (7/67); and *For You* (12/67). Though she turned out many pop-oriented records in the early and mid-1960s, most of her offerings were in the folk vein. Particularly with college students, she was considered a major folk artist and played to capacity crowds on campuses around the United States.

She also was no stranger to TV, appearing on many programs, including *The Ed Sullivan Show,* the *Andy Williams Show,* and the *Johnny Cash* show. Her TV work expanded to include acting roles in the second half of the 1960s, including guest appearances on *My Three Sons, Wild, Wild West,* and *The Name of the Game.* In 1970, she had a cameo role on the Screen Gems TV movie *Hide and Seek.*

Her singing efforts seemed to flag a little as the 1960s drew to a close. A move to Atlantic Records helped lead to the success of her 1969 single of her composition "Put a Little Love in Your Heart." The song was one of the major pop hits of the year, earning DeShannon a gold record and bringing invitations to appear on the supper club circuit in such gilt-edged places as San Francisco's Fairmont Hotel and New York's Copacabana. The song's success helped push the LP *Put a Little Love in Your Heart* over gold-record levels. She finished up 1969 with another single, "Love Will Find a Way," on the charts.

However, her image as a shallow club singer disenchanted many of her younger fans, reflected in a poor reception to her early 1970s college tours. She stressed to *Los Angeles Times* writer Richard Cromelin (December 4, 1977) that she never felt her songs lacked depth. She claimed they actually were similar in approach and content to the material that made Carole King a national favorite in the mid-1970s.

"I think if I had been more consistent in stringing things together, I might have made a little more sense. I just was not able to do that. I think I was ahead of a lot of what was to come. Sometimes when you're a pioneer in something you have to pay a little bit.

"I'm kind of grateful that it did happen that way. I think it really has helped me grow and find myself because maybe one does become comfortable with a certain kind of success. I was never interested in just being comfortable. I was trying to move along. I was trying to feel what was coming."

After things slowed for her in 1970, she moved to Capitol Records, which issued her debut single on the label, "Keep Me Warm," in June 1971. That recording also represented Jackie's debut as a producer.

Her first Capitol LP, *Songs*, came out in mid-1971 and won some attention, but not as much as her next, *Jackie*, in 1972, which made upper-chart levels. A number of her singles showed up on national charts that year: "Only Love Can Break Your Heart," "Paradise," and "Vanilla Olay." Her total song catalog by then was over the 500 mark, including songs co-written with such people as Randy Newman and the lead guitarist of the Led Zeppelin, Jimmy Page.

In the mid-1970s, despite the 1975 release on Columbia of a first-rate album, *New Arrangement*, Jackie's career again hit some soft spots and she gave up touring for a while to concentrate on writing. In late 1977, she reemerged with a new album on Amherst Records titled *You're the Only Dancer*. A single from the album, the composition "Don't Let the Flame Burn Out," made the hit lists, the first single to do that for several years.

Looking back over her career, she told Cromelin, "I've learned a lot from my low periods and I've been able to come out of them and make them work for me. You can sit here and say that this wasn't done right or that wasn't done right, but you can waste a lot of energy doing that. I really don't dwell on the negative aspects. Maybe I have too much Walt Disney in my eyes. Basically I think I'm a pretty positive kind of person. . . . Maybe I'm feeling how everybody else is feeling . . . that there's a lot of good in people, that you can make things better if you yourself get better, that you are the master of your own destiny. As I say, maybe it's a little too much Walt Disney, but I'm basically just a simple person."

In the early 1980s, DeShannon's recording career was in the doldrums, but some of her songs provided hits for others. One example was the single of her "When You Walk in the Room," recorded by Stephanie Winslow, which made the country top 30 in 1981.

Even more striking was "Bette Davis Eyes," co-written by Jackie and Donna Weiss. A smash hit for singer Kim Carnes in 1981, it won Grammies for Record of the Year and Song of the Year.

DEXTER, AL: *Singer, guitarist, organist, songwriter. Born Jacksonville, Texas, May 4, 1902.*

One unique song sometimes can give a form of immortality to its creator, even after the writer's name has become dim in most people's memory. This is the case with "Pistol Packin' Mama," still familiar to millions of people who haven't the slightest idea that Al Dexter and his Texas Troopers once were among the best-known acts in the country & western field.

Dexter, born Albert Poindexter in Jacksonville, Cherokee County, Texas, was already acquiring musical experience before there was such a thing as the *Grand Ole Opry*. He learned to play guitar in his teens and was taking part in school events in 1917. Besides guitar, he learned the organ, which he sometimes played in local church services. As a result, his first efforts as a songwriter took the form of a series of hymns, the first titled "Going Home to Glory." As he reached adulthood, he became increasingly interested in playing with small local groups at square dances and parties and was already writing secular songs for some of those bands in the 1920s.

In the early 1930s, the impact of the Depression forced him to take a new look at his means of livelihood, which was housepainting at the time. Because he loved writing and singing songs and because regular work was increasingly hard to find, he decided to focus on music as a full-time occupation and formed a band called the Texas Troopers. By then the impact of Jimmie Rodgers and the Carter Family had built more interest in the music industry for country & western musicians. The goal of any group, then as now, was to break into the recording end of the field. In 1934, Dexter and his group managed to place some releases on a local label that won attention from East Texas fans. That success was a strong selling point for a contract from a major label, and before long the band's stylings were reaching wider audiences on the Vocalion and Okeh labels.

Some of the recordings were original compositions by Al. In a short speech in 1971 marking his induction into the Nash-

Charlie Daniels

Lacy J. Dalton

Gail Davies

Danny Davis

The Dillards (early 1980s)

John Denver

Dr. Hook: l. to r., Rik Elswit, Rod Smarr, Ray Sawyer, John Wolters, Dennis Locorriere, Billy Francis, Jance Garfat

Bob Dylan

ville Songwriters Hall of Fame, Dexter recalled trying to find satisfactory recording arrangements. "It was 1935 and times were not so good. The record company said they could not pay much royalty on records [that] sold for sixteen cents wholesale then, but I said I would take it as 'I'm not doing much anyway now.' "

During the 1940s, Dexter was considered one of Columbia Records' top artists thanks to such hit singles as "Honky Tonk Blues" and "Rosalita." The latter, written in 1942, became a favorite of audiences at his live appearances, but was kept off the air for a long time because of the contract dispute embroiling BMI, ASCAP, and the nation's radio stations. When the matter was settled, his record company advisors counseled Dexter to write a new song for the "B" side of "Rosalita." The song he came up with was "Pistol Packin' Mama," a recording that swept the country and made Dexter one of the best-known performers of the mid-1940s. Among the awards given him was one from the Juke Box Operators Association naming him the leading artist of 1946.

With "Pistol Packin' Mama" as the pièce de résistance, Dexter remained a favorite of country & western audiences in nightclubs, county fairs, and rodeos from the late 1940s through much of the 1950s. Though he made many other recordings during those years, some of which did quite well, none ever approached the impact of his one superhit. (Some of his other records were "Guitar Polka," "Car Hoppin' Mama," "One More Day in Prison," "Down at the Roadside Inn," "Triflin' Gal," "Little Sod Shanty," "Alimony Blues," and "Sundown Polka.")

During the 1950s, Al cut back on traveling and concentrated most of his entertainment efforts in his own nightspot, the Bridgeport Club in Dallas. Increasingly, as the years went by, he devoted more of his time to motel, real estate, and federal savings and loan operations than to music. After the 1950s, he essentially was retired from songwriting and recording, though an occasional album of his material came out. In 1962, Harmony Records issued an LP titled *Pistol Packin' Mama,* and in the early 1970s, a similarly titled album was available on the Hilltop label.

On October 11, 1971, he was officially named a member of the Songwriters Hall of Fame in Nashville. Estimating that the total number of songs he had written was somewhere around 300, he declared himself happy with his accomplishments: "I had my share of hits. I have had some dogs too."

DICKENS, LITTLE JIMMY: *Singer, guitarist, songwriter. Born Bolt, West Virginia, December 19, 1925.*

Nicknamed "little" for his four feet, eleven inch build, Little Jimmy Dickens was only diminutive in physical size. His energy and vocal skills galvanized country audiences year in and year out (including the hit song, "I'm Little but I'm Loud") and he remained a favorite for decades. In 1978, he celebrated thirty years as a regular cast member of the *Grand Ole Opry* with no indication of slowing down afterward.

Born and raised in rural West Virginia, he went on to enroll at the University of West Virginia. By the time he was in his teens he had learned to play guitar and entertain friends with country songs old and new. When he was seventeen he auditioned at station WILS, Beckley, West Virginia, and won his first commercial job. He called himself Jimmy the Kid and worked with Johnny Bailes and His Happy Valley Boys. His early efforts included performing on another West Virginia station, WMNN in Fairmont.

After serving his apprenticeship locally, he moved further afield in the mid-1940s and began to sing on his own rather than as a member of a group. He toured many of the eastern and midwestern states and performed on several Midwest stations including WKNX, Saginaw, Michigan; WING, Dayton, Ohio; and WLW in Cincinnati. During the late 1940s, he signed with Columbia Records and began to turn out singles that showed up on country hit lists in various parts of the East, South, and Midwest. Coupled with personal appearances on the country fair and nightclub circuit, he began to build a growing reputation among country fans. In 1948, he was sufficiently well known for the *Grand Ole Opry* to ask him to become a regular cast member.

In 1949, he had his first top-10 country single with the Columbia release "Take an Old Cold Tater." His second major hit, "Country Boy," became one of his trademark songs ("I'm a country boy/A good old fashioned country boy/I'll be behind the ol' grey mule/When the sun comes up on Monday"). In 1950, he had two more top-10 singles with "A-Sleeping at the Foot of the Bed" and "Hillbilly Fever." Some of his other popular recordings were "Just When I Needed You," "My Heart's Bouquet," "Out Behind the Barn," "Conscience," "I Can't Help It," "Lovin' Lies," and "Salty Boogie." The original songs in his repertoire included "Sea of Broken Dreams" and "I Sure Would Like to Sit a Spell with You."

From the late 1940s through the 1960s he turned out a number of albums for Columbia. These included *Little Jimmy,* issued in December 1957, *Big Songs of Little Jimmy Dickens* (1/61), *Behind the Barn* (11/62), *Handle with Care* (4/65), *May the Bird of Happiness Fly Up Your Nose* (late 1965), and *Greatest Hits* (11/66). *May the Bird of Happiness* was his all-time bestseller on Columbia, rising to number one on country charts. He also had a number of LPs on the Harmony label, including *Old Country Church* (3/65), *Best of Little Jimmy Dickens* (5/64), *Little Jimmy Dickens* (3/65), and *Ain't It Fun* (6/67).

In the 1970s, the rise of "progressive" country and country rock tended to limit the audience of the more traditional artists like Jimmy. His long-time ties with Columbia ended by the end of the 1960s. However, he retained a sizable following in many parts of the United States and in other countries as well. Maintaining a busy schedule of in-person appearances throughout the 1970s, at the start of the 1980s he still was on the road an average of 150 to 200 days a year, and he still was a featured artist on the *Grand Ole Opry.*

DILLARD, DOUG: *Singer, banjo player, guitarist, band leader (Doug Dillard Band).*

Born East St. Louis, Illinois, March 6, 1937.

For much of the 1970s, many bluegrass fans wondered "Whatever happened to Doug Dillard?" The group he had founded with his younger brother, Rod, was very much in evidence at concerts and festivals, but Doug's name was conspicuously absent. It turned out Doug had been active in other phases of the entertainment field; at the end of the decade he returned to the recording front with a new solo LP produced by his brother.

The Dillards' interest in country and bluegrass music went back to their early years growing up in a rural area just south of Salem, Missouri. Both could play bluegrass style on instruments by the time they were in their teens, with Doug particularly proficient on banjo. The brothers performed at local and school events in the mid-1950s and wrote original material. In 1958, when Rodney was a senior at Salem High School, the brothers went to St. Louis and recorded their first number, an instrumental they wrote jointly called "Banjo in the Hollow."

In the years that followed, they assembled their own bluegrass band and, in 1962, moved west to Los Angeles to improve their musical fortunes. Once there, they actively sought a record contract and, in time, landed one with Elektra. Their debut on the label, *Back Porch Bluegrass,* came out in July 1963. Doug remained a key member of the band for two more albums, *The Dillards Live—Almost* and *Pickin' and Fiddlin',* and also appeared as a regular (with the Dillards) on the *Andy Griffith Show.* For three years, the members performed on the show under the name of the Darlin Family. (For more details, see the Dillards entry).

In 1968, Doug, who wanted to try other musical directions, left the Dillards to tour with the Byrds. When their tour was completed, he joined with ex-Byrd Gene Clark to form a new country-rock band called the Dillard and Clark Expedition. The band, which completed an album for RCA and placed a single on the charts, was well regarded by critics, but unfortunately was ahead of its time.

Afterwards Doug applied himself to a

broad spectrum of show business activities. From the late 1960s on he did considerable session work and was involved in many recordings made in the 1970s. Among his credits were work on the soundtracks for such movies as *Vanishing Point, Bonnie and Clyde,* and the Woody Guthrie biography, *Bound for Glory.* During the 1970s, he also worked as an actor or musician on many TV dramatic and variety shows, on TV commercials, and in a number of movies. He was part of the cast of Bette Midler's movie, *The Rose,* released in the fall of 1979.

After keeping a relatively low profile in musical efforts for many years, Doug returned to the personal recording scene and organized a new band in the late 1970s. Kicking off that phase of his career in 1979 was a "gospel-grass" LP called *Heaven,* issued on Flying Fish Records. His new "Doug Dillard Band featuring Byron Berline" comprised himself on banjo, Byron Berline on fiddle and mandolin, Billy Constable on acoustic guitar, and Joe Villiegas (a Sundance alumnus) on bass. Before 1979 was over, the band had demonstrated its musical prowess at clubs all over the United States, including the Palomino in Los Angeles and the Lone Star in New York, and at major folk festivals, including the Jim and Jesse Third Annual Mid-America Bluegrass Convention and the Telluride (Colorado) Country and Bluegrass Festival. The band's set at Telluride was recorded under Rodney Dillard's supervision for a planned 1980 release.

The Jim and Jesse event, which took place in the Dillards' home region, was memorable for the brothers in a number of ways. August 8, 1979, was proclaimed Dillard Day by the mayor of their home town of Salem, Missouri. At a special event that Wednesday, everyone was treated to a Dillard family reunion in which Doug, Rodney, and other members of the family and band members old and new took part, an event taped for presentation on NBC-TV's *Real People.*

DILLARDS, THE: *Vocal and instrumental group. Personnel, early 1960s: Douglas Flint "Doug" Dillard, born East St. Louis, Illinois,* *March 6, 1937; Rodney Adean "Rod" Dillard, born East St. Louis, Illinois, May 18, 1942; Roy Dean Webb, born Independence, Missouri, March 28, 1937; Mitchell "Mitch" Jayne, born Hammond, Indiana, July 5, 1930. Doug Dillard left 1968, replaced by Herb Pedersen. Paul York added 1968. Pedersen replaced by Billy Ray Latham, 1971. Jayne replaced by Jeff Gilkinson, mid-1970s. Latham replaced by Doug Bounsall, 1977.*

Bluegrass has had several spurts of popularity since it was introduced on the national level by Bill and Charlie Monroe and the Bluegrass Boys in the 1930s. One of those "revivals" took place in the late 1950s and early 1960s as part of the folk boom and another in the 1970s as part of the "progressive" bluegrass period. Missouri's pride, the Dillards, participated in both revivals .

The founders of that band, Douglas and Rodney, were born across the river in Illinois, but their family home was in Salem, Missouri. Playing country and bluegrass music was a tradition in the Dillard clan, and both the father and grandfather of the boys played stringed instruments. While Doug and Rod still were in elementary school they began playing bluegrass on guitar and banjo. In their teens, first Doug and later Rod played at local events with friends and schoolmates. Doug, five years older than Rod, continued to perform whenever he could after graduating from school.

By then the brothers were writing original material and looking for ways to further their musical careers. In 1958 they went to St. Louis and found a backer for their first recording efforts. One of their first discs was a song co-written by the brothers called "Banjo in the Hollow." Working with them at the time were such other young musicians as John Hartford (fiddle), Joe Noel (mandolin), and Buddie Van. The Dillards won support in the late 1950s from their friend, Mitch Jayne, then a disc jockey on Salem station KSMO. Mitch played their new record on the radio a number of times.

Jayne, who played banjo and bass, joined the boys in playing local school events, square dances, and other functions.

Soon after, a fourth member, Dean Webb, mandolinist, was added. The group extended their efforts to playing folk clubs and coffee houses in various parts of Missouri and nearby states in the early 1960s. In 1962, they decided to try to make the "big time" by journeying westward to Los Angeles.

Once in Los Angeles they followed the usual routine of working small clubs, making demo tapes, and looking for a recording opportunity. That came when Elektra Records' officials gave them a contract. Their first album was released in July 1963 under the title *Backporch Bluegrass.* This was followed in November 1964 with the LP *The Dillards Live—Almost* and a year or so later by the album *Pickin' and Fiddlin'.*

During that period, a talent agent found them a job acting and playing music on the *Andy Griffith Show* on TV. For three years the band members played the roles of the slow-witted Darlin Family on the nationally televised program. Their skit showcased their excellent bluegrass playing for the national audience.

The group, meanwhile, had become somewhat controversial with bluegrass purists, who were upset that the band used electronically amplified instruments at one of the bluegrass festivals they appeared at in 1964. The Dillards, however, persisted in playing the music their own way. (In the 1970s, though, the band stressed acoustic rather than electronic offerings.) Later on, the band committed another heresy by adding a drummer to the roster.

In 1968, Doug left (see separate entry) and was replaced by guitarist-banjoist Herb Pedersen. That same year, the group added Paul York on drums. The reorganized band continued to tour widely and record for Elektra, turning out *Wheatstraw Suite* in 1968 and *Copperfields* in 1969, the group's final offering on Elektra.

Pedersen departed in 1971 to form his own group, Country Gazette, and his place was taken by Billy Ray "Hot Rod Banjo" Latham, who took part in the band's first and only recording for Anthem/UA Records, *Roots and Branches,* issued in 1972. The Dillards then moved to Poppy Records, which released the LP *Tribute to the*

American Duck in 1973. Soon after, Jayne departed and Jeff Gilkinson (bass, harmonica, cello) came aboard.

The Dillards kept active in the mid-1970s, performing in country and bluegrass festivals, folk clubs, and on college campuses across the United States and Canada, though their recording activities were at a standstill. The band made occasional TV appearances, as well, including a PBS *Live from Wolf Trap* (near Washington) concert.

By the late 1970s, interest in bluegrass, which had increased slowly but steadily throughout the decade, reached a new high, with many bluegrass night clubs springing up in all parts of the United States and even overseas. All of this helped the Dillards' fortunes improve and brought a new contract with Flying Fish Records. Their debut on the label was the LP *The Dillards and the Incredible L.A. Time Machine,* released in 1977. Soon after, the band had another change when Latham left and was replaced by Doug Bounsall (electric guitar, banjo, fiddle). One of the first projects Bounsall took part in was the direct-to-disc album, *Mountain Rock,* issued on the Crystal Clear label.

In 1979, the band recorded its second LP on Flying Fish, *Decade Waltz.* Helping on this was Herb Pedersen, who, besides playing acoustic and electric guitar and banjo and contributing on vocals, mixed the final LP. Among the songs in the album were Pedersen's "Easy Ride," Bounsall's "10 Years Waltz," Jeff Gilkinson's "Gruelin' Banjos," and the Rod and Homer Dillard and Paul York collaboration on "Greenback Dollar." Besides performing at such festivals as the Telluride (Colorado) Country and Bluegrass Festival and the Jim and Jesse Third Annual Mid-America Bluegrass Convention, the band joined in the Dillard's reunion in Salem, Missouri, in August. For that event, the mayor of Salem proclaimed August 8 "Dillard Day." The reunion brought together not only former band members and close associates such as John Hartford and Byron Berline, but four generations of Dillards, ranging from seventy-eight-year-old Homer Earl Dillard, Sr., on fiddle to his grandson, eighteen-year-old Earl Dillard, on banjo. The proceedings were recorded for later release as a live album on Flying Fish. The reunion also was taped for presentation on NBC-TV's *Real People* program in the 1979–80 season.

DION: *Singer, guitarist, songwriter, band leader (the Belmonts, Streetheart Band). Born the Bronx, New York, July 18, 1939.*

A fair number of successful artists have moved from rock to folk-rock or country music, but few have moved from the rock to the folk genre. Dion is one of the latter, a major star in the early phases of rock'n'roll who later made his mark as a respected folk artist in the late 1960s. In the late 1970s, turning back to rock, he made some excellent recordings that never seemed to get enough exposure to allow him to regain his stature with new generations of rock fans.

Dion, born and raised as Dion DiMucci in the Bronx, New York City, shared his peer group's enthusiasm in the mid-1950s for such rock pioneers as Elvis, Bill Haley, and the Coasters. He formed his own group, Dion and the Tamberlaines, which made one hit single, "The Chosen Few," and then broke up. Soon after, he emerged as lead singer of a new foursome, Dion and the Belmonts, whose other members were Fred Milano, Carlo Mastangelo, and Angelo D'Aleo. (The backing trio's name came from Belmont Avenue in the Bronx.) In May 1958 the group had a hit single, "I Wonder Why," and was on its way to becoming a featured act on the rock concert circuit.

During 1958, the group hit the pop charts with the singles "No One Knows" and "Don't Pity Me." In 1959, it made the United States top five with one of its best-known releases, "A Teenager in Love," and followed with lesser hits, "Every Little Thing I Do" and "A Lover's Prayer." The next year was a good one as well, producing Dion and the Belmonts' all-time best-seller, a remake of the old pop hit "Where or When," plus such other chartmakers as "When You Wish upon a Star" and "In the Still of the Night."

By late 1960 Dion was getting restless and began a solo career with the hit single "Lonely Teenager." He had several minor hits, such as "Little Miss Blue" in 1960 and "Havin' Fun" and "Kissin' Game" the first half of 1961, then hit pay dirt with "Runaround Sue." That release on Laurie Records made hit lists in October 1961 and rose to number one in the United States and many other nations, providing Dion with a multimillion-seller. His next release, "The Wanderer," also topped the million mark, rising to number two in the United States in 1962. The reverse side of that single, "The Majestic," also made the charts.

He had a number of other chartmakers on Laurie in 1962–63 before accepting a bid from Columbia. He started the new alignment with a major hit, "Ruby Baby," in early 1963. Dion also made the pop lists with such 1963 releases as "This Little Girl," "Be Careful of Stones That You Throw," "Donna the Prima Donna," "Drip Drop," and the 1964 remake of Chuck Berry's standard, "Johnny B. Goode." During those years, he also was represented by a number of album releases, many of which made upper-chart levels. His LPs of the period included, on Laurie, *Dion and the Belmonts* (4/60), *Wish upon a Star* (10/60), *Alone, Runaround Sue,* and *Lovers Who Wander,* and, on Columbia, *Prima Donna* (12/63).

In the mid-1960s, the impact of the Beatles and other British groups began to overwhelm the more simplistic "old-timey" U.S. rock of the previous decade, like Dion's. Dion continued to turn out new material and to appear in concerts around the United States and abroad, but his name rarely showed up on bestseller rosters. He left Columbia and moved on to ABC without any noticeable improvement. Meanwhile, Laurie released a number of albums, mainly retrospective ones, in the mid-1960s, including *Greatest Hits, Vol. 1, Greatest Hits, Vol. 2* (10/66), *15 Million Sellers* (10/66), *Together, with the Belmonts* (10/66), and *Dion Sings to Sandy* (10/66). His initial LP on ABC, *Together, with the Belmonts,* came out in March 1967.

During this time, Dion was reexamining his career, exposing himself to other styles of music—urban and country blues. Originally only a singer, he had begun to learn guitar in the early 1960s, inspired by his new interest in folk and folk-blues. He moved to Miami, Florida, in the mid-1960s, where his circle of friends included a number of writers in the modern folk tradition, such as Fred Neil. Besides adding the songs of some of those people to his repertoire, he spent a lot of time writing songs of his own.

In 1968, once more working with Laurie Records, he recorded a song by Dick Holler, "Abraham, Martin and John," an expression of the emotional trauma of the time in 1968 following the assassinations of Dr. Martin Luther King and Senator Robert Kennedy, and recalling the killing of President John F. Kennedy. The single, certified gold by the Recording Industry Association of America on January 13, 1969, focused new attention on Dion, who was once more a featured artist on the concert circuit and on TV. Some of his original compositions also began to be recorded by other artists, including "Purple Haze," though none did as well as "Abraham, Martin and John."

Disagreements over creative directions led to his leaving Laurie once more, this time for Warner Brothers. His first release on the label was the late 1969 *Sit Down, Old Friend,* a folk- and blues-oriented collection that included a song he had written against the use of drugs, "In Your Own Backyard." He made several more albums on Warner Brothers in the early 1970s, such as *You're Not Alone* and *Sanctuary,* generally receiving critical praise but not much public support.

For a while in the mid-1970s, not too much was heard from Dion, but in the late part of the decade he surfaced once more with a new rock backing band called the Streethearts. With that group, he turned out a fine album in 1978 titled *Heart of Saturday Night,* which several critics hailed as one of the overlooked gems of the year.

DIRT BAND, NITTY GRITTY DIRT BAND (name changed to Dirt Band in 1976): *Vocal and instrumental group. Original personnel, 1965, included Jeff Hanna, born De-*troit, Michigan, July 11, 1947, and Bruce Kunkel, born Long Beach, California, circa 1948. Members as of late 1960s: Hanna; John McEuen, born Long Beach, California, December 19, 1945; Jimmie Fadden, born Long Beach, California, March 9, 1948; Ralph Taylor Barr, born Boston, Massachusetts; Leslie Steven Thompson, born Long Beach, California; Chris Darrow, born California. Darrow replaced Kunkel in 1968. Barr replaced in 1971 by Jim Ibbotson, born Philadelphia, Pennsylvania, January 21, 1947. Band roster, mid-1970s, reduced to Hanna, McEuen, Fadden, and Ibbotson. Ibbotson left mid-1976; John Cable and Jackie Clark added.*

The Nitty Gritty Dirt Band, which renamed itself the Dirt Band in 1976, went through many changes in fortune and personnel over the years, but its core members, Jeff Hanna, John McEuen, and Jimmie Fadden persevered and saw to it that the band's blend of folk, country, and rock continued to delight fans into the 1980s. In 1977, the Dirt Band was invited to tour the Soviet Union as a move to open that nation up to "rock music."

The band's origins were in Long Beach, California, where two high school students, Bruce Kunkel and Jeff Hanna, began getting together to play guitar and sing folk songs. After a while they brought in three other friends and formed a group called the Illegitimate Jug Band, the title reflecting the fact that it played jug band music without a jug player. After Kunkel and Hanna graduated from high school, the band reorganized into what was to soon be the Nitty Gritty Dirt Band. That group added four other Long Beach associates of Kunkel and Hanna: Jimmie Fadden (autoharp, harmonica, jug, washtub bass, tuba, trombone); John McEuen (five-string banjo, fiddle, accordion, guitar, steel guitar, vocals); Leslie Thompson (guitar, bass, mandolin, vocals); and Ralph Taylor Barr, born in Boston but who moved to Long Beach at eleven (guitar, vocals). Hanna, born in Detroit, but transplanted to Long Beach with his family in 1962, handled lead guitar and washboards and some writing. Kunkel handled vocals, guitar, and writing.

The band began its professional career in 1966 under the guidance of Bill McEuen, John's older brother, who had been a disc jockey and had established a good reputation as a producer of rock and R&B records by the mid-1960s. As manager, he helped gain initial dates in small clubs and coffee houses. Soon the group moved up to support roles in concerts featuring such stars as Nancy Wilson, Joan Baez, and Bob Newhart. At the same time, McEuen won a record contract from Liberty Records. The band stayed with the label after it was absorbed by United Artists and still was on the roster at the end of the 1970s.

The group's first single release, "Buy for Me the Rain," came out in 1967 and quickly became a major hit. When the band's debut LP *The Nitty Gritty Dirt Band* also rose high on the charts, the band was widely recognized as one of 1967's most promising new groups. Besides the hit track, the album contained a potpourri of stylings, ranging from updated versions of folk songs like "Dismal Swamp" and "Candy Man" to Bruce Kunkel's folk-flavored composition "Song to Jutta" to such wild numbers as "Hard Hearted Hannah," "I Wish I Could Shimmy Like My Sister Kate," and "Crazy Words, Crazy Tune."

The follow-up LP, *Ricochet*, issued in November 1967, was arguably as good as the group's debut effort, but it didn't sell as well. The same held true for other albums issued by Liberty in 1968 and 1969. As the decade came to a close, U.S. audience interest tapered off, though a faithful core of fans remained.

Meanwhile, Kunkel left the band in 1968 and was replaced by Chris Darrow. In 1971, Barr moved on and Philadelphia-born Jim Ibbotson took over drums, bass guitar, accordion, and piano. Ibbotson, who earned a degree in economics from DePauw University in Indiana, previously had performed with such bands as the Arista-Tones, The Warf Rats, the Evergreen Blue Shows, and the Hagers.

The Liberty album *Uncle Charlie and His Dog Teddy* started getting major airplay in late 1970 and made the charts from November of that year until the following fall. A single from the album, the band's

version of Jerry Jeff Walker's "Mr. Bojangles," began to gain attention, reaching the top 10 on the pop charts and doing well on country lists as well. By the spring of 1971 it had sold almost a million copies. Those new successes brought the group engagements in theaters and clubs all over the United States and a popularity that far exceeded that of its early years. Hanna said happily, "We're finally beginning to make a comfortable living, which is a nice change."

In mid-1971, the band had another singles hit with the Kenny Loggins song "House at Pooh Corner." In early 1972, United Artists released the LP *All the Good Times*, which featured sparkling renditions of Hank Williams' "Jambalaya" and the Cajun song "Diggy-Liggy-Lo." A single of "Jambalaya" made the charts in 1972, as did the singles "Some of Shelley's Blues" and "I Saw the Light." The latter record was a country hit in which the band was joined by Roy Acuff. There also was a strong country flavor to many of the tracks in the band's next album, *Will the Circle Be Unbroken*, issued in late 1972 and on the charts through mid-1973.

By the mid-1970s, the band had moved home base from California to Colorado, where much of its material was recorded throughout the decade. From there, the group sallied forth each year for extensive tours that took it to a wide range of venues, from college auditoriums and folk clubs to medium- and large-size halls across the United States and, on occasion, overseas. At times John McEuen worked as a solo performer (see separate entry on McEuen) but always returned to the fold for band concerts and recording work.

Opening for a number of concerts of the band in the mid-1970s was a promising comedian named Steve Martin. Later, after Martin became a superstar, he still returned as a surprise guest from time to time to play banjo duets with McEuen. During a Dirt Band appearance at the Los Angeles Music Center in February 1978, Martin came on stage unannounced and delighted the audience by debuting his song "King Tut" with the band. Later in the year the song became a novelty hit.

In mid-1976, the band celebrated its tenth anniversary, shortening its name to Dirt Band and shifting from a quartet to a quintet. When Jim Ibbotson left he was replaced by two musicians, John Cable on guitar and vocals and Jackie Clark on guitar and keyboards. Both took part in the debut LP under the new name, issued in September 1976, titled *Dirt, Silver and Gold,* followed a year later by *Dirt Band.*

The group's landmark tour to the Soviet Union in early summer 1977 was hailed by some as the first break in the Russian "rock barrier." Talking about the origins of that unprecedented concert series, John McEuen told a reporter, "We were playing a concert in Washington, D.C. last year [1976] when there apparently were some representatives of the Soviet Union in the audience. Later we got a call that they would like for us to play the Soviet Union. After that it was up to the Soviets and the Americans to make the arrangements."

The tour extended from one end of the Soviet Union to the other, including concerts in Armenia and Riga, Latvia. One of the objections of the band members to arrangements was the tight security that insulated them from the ordinary people. What little contact they did have disclosed that most people had never heard of them until the tour began.

Although all concerts were sold out, audience response was relatively sedate until the band played Yerevan, Armenia. McEuen reported, "The Yerevan people were more like the ones back home. During our last performance, they packed 5,700 people into an outside stadium that was supposed to hold 4,000. We heard there were several thousand outside. Someone even threw in a tear gas canister which caused some excitement."

The group closed out the decade with the LP *Stars & Stripes Forever* in 1978 and *An American Dream,* released in mid-1979. The title song of the latter, issued as a single in early 1980, was on country charts for a number of weeks.

DIXON, DORSEY: *Singer, guitarist, songwriter. Born Darlington, South Carolina, October 14, 1897; died Plant City, Florida, 1968.*

Dorsey Murdock Dixon was one of the most talented of the older generation of country-music artists and writers. His song "Crash on the Highway" is one of the standards of country music and one of the all-time hits of Roy Acuff. Dorsey and his brother Howard also formed one of the oft-remembered teams of the 1930s, The Dixon Brothers. (Howard was born in Darlington, South Carolina, June 19, 1903, and died March 24, 1961.)

Despite this, Dorsey gained little but enjoyment from his music. He was born too soon, and his active career came at a time when there was little money in the country field. In fact, though many of his songs were widely played, he had sold the rights and received no additional royalties in most cases. He spent almost his entire life as a mill hand, able to devote more than a few hours a day to music only in his years of retirement.

Dorsey Dixon was one of seven children of a textile mill family. His father worked for the Darlington Cotton Manufacturing Company as a steam engine operator, and the children followed suit; Dorsey's older sister started work for eight cents a day as a spinner in the mill at the age of eight. Dorsey was a bit luckier; he started there at age twelve.

But though life was hard, the family was close knit and happy. Music was a prime way of adding meaning to their life and Dorsey learned spirituals and hill country ballads from his mother from the time he was five. Dorsey got his first guitar when he was fourteen and quickly taught himself to play. He also learned to play the fiddle from a local teacher and soon performed at local Sunday schools. In his later teens, he teamed with his brother Howard to play duets in the Rockingham movie theater.

During World War I, Dorsey worked as a railway signalman on the Atlantic Coast Line in Darlington. When the war ended, he returned to mill work and remained a mill hand from 1919 to 1951. His jobs over the years took him to Lancaster and Greenville, South Carolina, and East Rockingham, North Carolina. In 1947, he also worked for a time in a New Jersey rayon plant before going back to southern mills. In 1951, he left the mills and worked in a munitions factory in Baltimore.

Over these years, Dixon continued to develop as an artist and writer. During the 1920s, he and his brother played at many local dances and affairs, but never for pay. In the late 1920s, Dorsey finally began to write some of his own music. One of his first efforts (1929) was "The Cleveland Schoolhouse Fire," originally a poem that his mother and brother began to sing to an old country tune. In the early 1930s, Dorsey and Howard met the legendary Jimmie Tarleton when he worked briefly in East Rockingham, from whom they learned many new tricks with the guitar.

The Dixon Brothers branched out into show business in 1934 by appearing on J. W. Fincher's *Crazy Water Sunday Night Jamboree* over station WBT in Charlotte. This led to a record date with RCA Victor two years later, the first of five such sessions between 1936 and 1938. The brothers recorded more than sixty songs during this period, but their income was still not enough to permit working as full-time artists. Some of the Dixon songs of this period were later turned into national hits by other performers.

For a long time, the Dixons settled back to their work in the mills. Occasionally a song showed up on the country hit charts with Dorsey's name on it. In the 1960s, he was rediscovered, this time by folk music collectors. He was asked to appear at the 1963 Newport Folk Festival. He listened to some of his songs performed by others and sang some himself. In the years that followed, he sang at a number of folk concerts as well as returning to Newport several times. Among the songs he presented were "Weave Room Blues" and "Will the Circle Be Broken."

His 1963 Newport performance was presented on the Vanguard LP *Old Time Music at Newport.* He also recorded an LP for Piedmont Records in 1963. In November 1963, and the following January, he provided thirty-eight songs for the Library of Congress American Folk Song Archive. In 1966, Testament Records released a new Dorsey Dixon album called *Babies in the Mill.*

DR. HOOK: *Vocal and instrumental group: Dennis Locorriere, born New York, June 13 (vocals, guitar); Ray Sawyer, born Chicksaw, Alabama, February (vocals, guitar, percussion); Jance Garfat, born California (bass, vocals); Rik Elswit (lead guitar, vocals); John Wolters, born New Jersey (drums, vocals); Billy Francis, born Mobile, Alabama (keyboards, vocals); Bob "Willard" Henke, born Pennsylvania (guitar, vocals).*

Dr. Hook, the shortened name for the seven-man group of Dr. Hook and the Medicine Show, has a reputation for their zany on-stage antics and the often offbeat delivery of the madcap lead singers, Ray Sawyer and Dennis Locorriere. Their country-rock aggregations are one of the most successful of the late 1970s and early 1980s.

The story of Dr. Hook's formation begins with Ray Sawyer, the group member known for wearing a black eyepatch and cowboy-style clothes. Sawyer started playing guitar in southern honky-tonks when he was fourteen. As he says, "I must have played all the clubs from Houston to Charleston until I decided I was going insane from too much beans and music, and gave it up. I saw a John Wayne movie and proceeded to Portland, Oregon, to be a 'logger' complete with plaid shirt, Colk boots, and Pike pole. On the way my car slipped on the road and the accident left me with the eye patch I now wear. When I recovered I ran straight back to the beans and music and vowed, 'Here I'll stay.' "

Sawyer got together with keyboard player Billy Francis, and they worked in clubs together from Alabama up the East Coast to New Jersey. As Sawyer relates, they "stopped in a little place called Transfer Station near Union City. It was where buses stopped on the way between New York and Philadelphia and there was all these little bars to capture passengers taking a rest stop. We went to work with a band in one of those bars. . . . At that time we had a drummer, another guitarist and then Dennis came in and played bass."

In the words of Dennis Locorriere, "Transfer Station was near where I grew up. I loved music and I just went there and floated around—played drums or other things. That's how I met Ray. He asked if I could play bass [guitar] and I said yes," although he didn't play bass very well, he stayed with the now three-man group. They continued to play the New Jersey bars and occasionally made tape demos for people promising to make them stars. One man was particularly insistent, so they gave him a tape of two of their songs and a Bob Dylan song.

According to Dennis, "He took it along with him, but had second thoughts. He was in this New York office building and met someone he knew in the industry in the elevator. He told the other guy, 'I've got this group in New Jersey who are too crazy for me' and gave him the tape. The fellow who got the tape was Ron Haffkine, who became our manager and still is."

Haffkine was at that time musical director of the film *Who Is Harry Kellerman and Why Is He Saying These Terrible Things About Me?* starring Dustin Hoffman. Songwriter-folksinger-cartoonist-author Shel Silverstein, a long-time friend of Haffkine, had written the score for the movie. When Haffkine heard the tape of Dr. Hook, he felt that they would be the right group to sing the soundtrack, so he brought Silverstein to the New Jersey club and signed the group to appear in the movie and sing the theme song, "Last Morning."

Before the film was done, Haffkine got the group its first recording contract, with Columbia Records. As Ray Sawyer recalls, "We wasn't signed to any contract after we started on the Kellerman job so Ronnie went in and got a hold of Clive Davis and got us to do an audition for him. When he brought us there we didn't know who Davis was. I was fresh up from Alabama and I didn't know Davis was really a big wheel. We went in with two guitars only. The whole band was there, though, and our drummer took the waste basket and turned it upside down and beat on it and Dennis danced on the table. If we knew how important Davis was maybe we wouldn't have been so informal, but he liked us."

Silverstein continued to give Dr. Hook songs to record and introduced the group to two more musicians who soon became members, Jance Garfat and Rik Elswit. Not long afterward, John Wolters also joined

the band as did George Cummings, who left the group in 1975. Dr. Hook had several large hits with the Silverstein compositions "Freakin' at the Freakers Ball," "I Got Stoned and I Missed It," and "Penicillin Penny." The group continued to flourish during the early 1970s both as a recording act and as one of the most varied, often zany, live acts in business. Two of the Silverstein-penned songs, "Sylvia's Mother" and "Cover of the Rolling Stone," hit the top of the pop charts and became gold records.

During the economic recession of 1973–74, the group was in a lull, and in 1974 found themselves completely broke and declared bankruptcy. They held a meeting of the band, their management, and their road crew, and everyone decided to stick with the band. They pooled all their money, $400, rented a cheapie studio for ten dollars an hour, and recorded an album, called *Bankrupt*. Capitol Records signed Dr. Hook to a contract and agreed to distribute the record. (They had previously dissolved their contract with Columbia when they declared bankruptcy.) After the first single release from the album, "Millionaire," went nowhere, Capitol released "Only Sixteen," Dr. Hook's remake of the old Sam Cooke song, and the song caught on with both country and pop audiences and earned the group its third gold record. Meanwhile, in 1975, guitarist Bob "Willard" Henke, originally a stand-in for Rik Elswit, was added to the group.

Dr. Hook's second Capitol LP, *A Little Bit More*, released in April 1976, climbed to the country top 20 as well as the pop charts, where it remained for nine months. The album contained smash hits "A Little Bit More" and "A Couple More Years" as well as a huge country hit, the love ballad "If Not You." In January 1977, Ray Sawyer released his first solo album, which was predominantly country in flavor.

Dr. Hook continued its streak of hits to the end of the 1970s and into the early 1980s. The LP *Pleasure and Pain* became a bestseller in 1978–79, reaching platinum sales levels. From it came two singles that reached upper-chart levels on both country and pop lists: "Sharing the Night Together" and "When You're in Love with a

Beautiful Woman." In 1980, the group had a top-10 hit with its single "Sexy Eyes" from the 1979 LP *Sometimes You Win.*

During 1980, the band was widely acclaimed during its tour of Japan and Europe, as had occurred previously whenever it ventured abroad. In fact, over the years, the group had done better in the international marketplace with many of its releases than at home. By the end of the 1970s, it had already accumulated thirty-five or forty gold records internationally, far more than won in the United States. Other 1980 activities of the band included a TV special presented on England's BBC and the recording of a live LP. In October 1980, the band affirmed it had moved from Capitol Records to Casablanca Records, which released the LP *Rising* and the debut Casablanca single "Girl Can Get It" shortly after.

The goal of Dr. Hook's members, Ray Sawyer stresses, is to entertain. "We don't get insulted when someone tells us they don't take our music seriously. That's like McDonalds getting upset if you put ketchup on their hamburgers. We're in pop music and no one should take this kind of music seriously. . . . But I will say this. We have had more fun at it than anyone—the Rolling Stones—the Beatles—you name it."–A.S.

Based partly on a 1978 interview.

DONOVAN: *Singer, guitarist, songwriter, arranger. Born Glasgow, Scotland, February 10, 1946.*

An artist who will always be remembered for his anti-Vietnam war songs during the heyday of the folk movement of the 1960s, Donovan P. Leitch was an idealist who finally became disillusioned with society's increasing apathy.

The son of working-class parents in Glasgow, Scotland, Donovan spent his first ten years in the Gorbals area of the city, one of the roughest in Scotland. In 1956, his family moved to the outskirts of London, where he developed an interest in art and learned to play the guitar. "At school, the teachers thought I was a little strange because I wrote a lot of fear and horror

stories and drew sketches for them. One of them was about this man who got locked in a drain when it rained."

In college he continued his art studies until, after a year, his money ran out. With a friend, Gypsy Davy (who was later to figure in some of his songs), Donovan began to wander all over England, hitching rides on trucks and beachcombing. "We weren't working out the problems of the world," he writes, "we were letting our days fill us with strange encounters. We didn't talk much, but we moved fast a lot." During the months on the road, Donovan spent a good deal of time writing stories and folk-flavored songs.

Settled in London in 1964, he lived in a small basement flat and began to take his tapes around to music industry people. He was asked to perform on the top British Broadcasting Company pop music show, *Ready, Steady, Go;* audience response was so favorable he was signed for two more appearances.

Soon after, he turned out a single of his song "Catch the Wind," which rose to number two on the English charts and is still a favorite with folksingers. Two more hit songs, "Colors" and "Universal Soldier," followed, making the hit charts all over the world. His first two LPs, *Catch the Wind* and *Fairytale,* also created a stir.

In 1965, he appeared at the Newport Folk Festival, making his U.S. debut and creating a sensation. Similar encomiums and standing-room-only shows followed him throughout the 1960s and into the early 1970s, when he came to be considered a superstar and the perfect symbol of the flower children movement. When that movement phased out in the 1970s, Donovan's career seemed to wane with it.

His contract with Epic in 1966 marked his first U.S. label affiliation. "Sunshine Superman" was his debut on the label, a best-selling single and the title of a charted LP. Although some of the media tended to focus on his "message" songs, the compositions in the *Sunshine Superman* LP, and many of his later LPs, covered such topics as children, love, fairy tales, beaches, and a girl who entangles her hair in a Ferris wheel.

For a large part of the late 1960s, it was rare if Donovan didn't have an album or single on the bestseller lists. His single "Mellow Yellow," issued the end of 1966, sold over a million copies and earned a gold record. His album of the same title, released in March 1967, was on the charts, as were several of his releases on the Hickory label. The latter, comprising material issued in Europe before Donovan signed with Epic, included *Catch the Wind, The Real Donovan,* and *Donovan* (all issued in January 1967). Also a chart hit was his third Epic release, a two-record set titled *Gift from a Flower to a Garden* (February 1968). His other Epic albums of the late 1960s and early 1970s included *Barabajagal* (10/69), *Open Road* (9/70), and *Wear Your Love Like Heaven* (1971). In a situation similar to Hickory's, Janus Records issued several LPs in the early 1970s, such as *Hear Me Now* and the two-record set *Donovan P. Leitch.*

Donovan's TV credits during the 1969–70 season included several segments of *The Smothers Brothers Comedy Hour* and an appearance on the Everly Brothers summer replacement show in 1970. Afterward his personal appearances began to taper off, as did most of his activity, though he did place a single or two on the charts, including "Celia of the Seals" in 1971. During 1970–71, he also had a contract with Warner Brothers to write the music and screenplay for a film combining live action and animation. Among the films he contributed to in the 1970s were: *If It's Tuesday, It Must Be Belgium; The Pied Piper;* and *Brother Sun, Sister Moon.*

Even at the start of the 1970s, Donovan's occasional live concerts showed he still had a strong following, but as the early 1970s went by he phased concert work out almost completely. Little was heard from him for several years until Epic came out with the first LP in a while of all original new songs, *Cosmic Wheels.* Another new collection followed, *Essence to Essence.* However, both LPs did much more poorly than earlier releases.

His next LP, *7–Tease,* which came out in late 1974, did not seem to reverse the trend, so he went on tour and finally ended his affiliation with Epic. The reason he had stayed away for the past three years, he told Dennis Hunt of the *Los Angeles Times* (December 1974), was that "I was disillusioned with the 1960s. I was also disgusted with the music business. I got so disgusted with all of the rotten aspects of it that I had to get out.

"Music and business just don't seem to mix. It's hard to be an idealist and just want to make good music and not get trampled on by all the ruthless people who just want to make money. That's why artists freak out, run away, get sick or do anything to escape.

"Recently I came to terms with this business and decided to work with it instead of against it. I've cooled down somewhat. It may be a mistake. I don't know yet."

DOTTSY: *Singer. Born Seguin, Texas, April 6, 1954.*

Dottsy Brodt started her singing career at the age of twelve, appearing at a district firefighters' convention in her hometown of Seguin, Texas. She was an immediate hit. After that, she found herself in demand to sing at local clubs, talent shows, variety shows, and conventions.

At a hotel managers' convention in San Antonio, Texas, Dottsy met the man soon to become her manager, Happy Shahan, who realized she had a great deal of talent and asked to meet her.

Shahan took Dottsy to meet another of his protégés, Johnny Rodriguez. Johnny liked her singing and asked her to appear with him at an upcoming rodeo in Austin. Soon afterward, she obtained an RCA Records recording contract with Shahan's assistance.

Dottsy's first RCA single, "Storms Never Last," was released in April 1975. The young blue-eyed blonde-haired singer embarked on a promotional tour that took her from New York to California, visiting record stores, radio and television stations, and newspapers. Her efforts paid off, and "Storms Never Last" became a top-10 hit. She followed with another top-chart single, "I'll Be Your San Antone Rose," which led to her first album, *The Sweetest Thing.*

Dottsy's rich voice continued to turn out hit singles, such as "It Should Have Been Easy" in late 1977; "I'm All Right (I Just Had You on My Mind)" in 1978; and "Play 'Born to Lose' Again" and "Slip Away" in 1979. Dottsy's recording of "Storms Never Last," which was written by Jessi Colter, impressed her as well as her husband, Waylon Jennings. In 1979 Dottsy teamed with Jennings on the top-10 single "Trying to Satisfy You."

However, Dottsy had objectives in life beyond performing. She purposefully cut back on her entertainment activities in favor of continuing her education. Her particular goal was to learn how to work with autistic children, an occupation she moved into full time by the beginning of the 1980s.

DRAKE, PETE: *Pedal steel guitarist, songwriter, music industry executive. Born Atlanta, Georgia, October 8, 1932.*

Pete Drake's innovativeness was a significant contribution to the resurgence in the use of the pedal steel guitar in bands and recordings in both pop and country music. It is difficult to believe that a few decades ago the instrument was almost unheard of.

Pete, born and raised in Georgia, initially learned to play acoustic guitar. An avid listener to the *Grand Ole Opry* radio program, he fell in love with the lap steel work of Jerry Byrd when he was eighteen. A used steel instrument at an Atlanta pawn shop cost him $33, and he essentially taught himself to play it. As he told Douglas Green in *Guitar Player* (September 1973), "I took one lesson, but I'd get records and sit around playing to them. That's how I really got started. This was around 1949 or 1950. Then when Bud Isaacs came out with a pedal guitar on 'Slowly' by Webb Pierce, that shocked everybody wondering how he got that sound. I guess I was the first one around Atlanta to get a pedal guitar. I had one pedal on a four-neck guitar. . . . I made it myself. . . . I was playing in clubs all around Atlanta, then right after that I formed my first band. . . . I had some pretty big stars working with me back

then: Jerry Reed, Joe South, Doug Kershaw was playing fiddle, Roger Miller . . . and country singer Jack Greene was playing drums.

"And we got fired because we weren't any good. I was on television for three and a half years, but we kind of wore ourselves out and I decided to move on to Nashville."

The Nashville move came in 1959; for a while Drake worked only sporadically. The style of pedal steel he'd developed in Atlanta didn't find favor at first, so he played conventional Nashville style. In mid-1960, Drake reverted to his old technique, using a C6th tuning on a session for Carl and Pearl Butler. Country artist Roy Drusky heard about it and asked Drake to use the same approach on a song he was doing for Decca. The result was the number-one hit "I Don't Believe You Love Me Any More." After Pete backed George Hamilton IV on another smash single, "Before This Day Ends," the "Pete Drake Style" became a Nashville trademark.

Later in the early 1960s, Drake gained new attention for his "talking guitar" efforts. The idea for the approach came to Pete from watching Alvino Ray do something similar in a Kay Kyser film. He told Douglas Green the way it works: "You play the notes on the guitar and it goes through the amplifier. I have a driver system so that you disconnect the speakers and the sound goes through the driver into a plastic tube. You put the tube in the side of your mouth then form the words with your mouth as you play them. You don't actually say a word. The guitar is your vocal chords and your mouth is the amplifier. It's amplified by a microphone."

The first record on which Pete applied the technique was Roger Miller's "Lock, Stock and Teardrops" on RCA. Although the single didn't do too well, Jim Reeves achieved a top-level hit when Pete used the talking guitar on "I've Enjoyed as Much of This as I Can Stand." By then Drake had done some solo recordings on the Starday label with regular pedal steel methods, including "For Pete's Sake." Mercury Records executives suggested he do some talking steel work, and the result was the smash hit single "Forever," which sold over a million copies in 1964. The album of that title, issued on the Smash label in June 1964, was a chart hit as was the follow-up *Talking Steel Guitar* (January 1965). Still another LP on the same theme was *Talking Steel Singing,* released in May 1965.

Throughout the 1960s and into the 1970s, Pete continued to be represented by new guitar albums, though he got away from the talking guitar emphasis after the mid-1960s. Some of his later LPs included *Fabulous Steel Guitar* on Starday and *Pete Drake Show* on Stop Records.

Though his solo work didn't often appear on bestseller lists after the mid-1960s, his instrumental talents continued to be in demand not only in the country field but in many other segments of pop musicals well. As he noted in *Guitar Player,* "The steel wasn't accepted in pop music until I had cut with people like Elvis Presley and Joan Baez. But the kids themselves didn't accept it until I cut with Bob Dylan. After that I guess they figured it was all right. I did the *John Wesley Harding* album, *Nashville Skyline,* and *Self Portrait.* Bob Dylan really helped me an awful lot. I mean, by having me play on those records he just opened the door for the pedal steel guitar, because then everybody wanted to use one."

Among the people who became enamored of pedal steel were the members of the Beatles. George Harrison brought Pete to London for a week to do session work on his album *All Things Must Pass.* Later Ringo Starr came to Nashville, where Drake performed and helped produce a number of country-rock and blues numbers by the Beatles drummer.

The interest in Pete's stellar musicianship never slackened as the 1970s went by. During his discussions with Green in 1973, for instance, he noted at one point that he contributed instrumental material on fifty-nine of the top seventy-five albums on the *Billboard* hit lists. In the mid- and late-1970s, he had his pick of countless recording sessions. His widening influence on the music field in general could be seen in the many top-rated pop and country bands in

the 1970s that included a pedal steel player on their roster. Many of those musicians traced some of their performing techniques on the instrument to careful analysis of Drake records or in-person efforts.

Drake received many honors over the years from various polls of top instrumentalists. His name often showed up on year-end lists in major music industry trades and he was nominated many times for various categories in both CMA and Grammy competitions.

DRIFTING COWBOYS: *Vocal and instrumental group, originally Hank Williams' band: Don Helms, born Alabama, Bob McNett, born Pennsylvania, Hillous Butram and Jerry Rivers, both from Nashville, Tennessee.*

To help him in what was to become his brief but creatively rich glory years, Hank Williams assembled a band called the Drifting Cowboys, a group that backed him on some of his most famous recordings. A quarter century after his death, the original members of the band reassembled and found a wide audience for their renditions of Williams' repertoire. Their live performances made many onlookers feel a palpable link to the career of one of the greatest innovators in country—and pop music—history.

The band assembled initially on July 14, 1949, Rivers told Kelly Delaney for an article in *Music City News* (June 1979, p. 23). "We met together for the first time up at WSM and ran through some songs with Hank. When Hank first began to hit on records, this brought him to Nashville and the *Grand Ole Opry.* As did most of the acts of that day, Hank decided to form a band around him to do everything—recording, tours, everything from that point on. He picked the name that he had used on some occasions previously, the Drifting Cowboys."

Steel guitarist Helms' association with Williams went back to 1943, when both lived in Alabama. "With the exception of two years I was in the service, I was with him off and on for eleven years until he died." For a while Helms joined another band during Hank's days with the *Louisiana Hayride* in Shreveport, Louisiana, because the pay was better. When Williams was invited to join the *Opry*, though, Helms agreed to go back with him.

McNett met Hank in Shreveport, where the Pennsylvania-born electric guitarist was a member of Patsy Montana's band. However, she broke up her group in time for him to accept a bid from Hank to come to Nashville. That city was home base for the other original bandmembers, Butram and Rivers.

At one point, fiddle player Rivers had turned down a bid to join Hank in Shreveport, preferring to stay in Music City. In the interim, he played with various *Opry* artists, including the Talking Blues Boys and Jam Up and Honey. He tried working as a duo with performer Benny Martin but that failed, and he was between jobs when Hank called to say he was forming a new band in line with his *Opry* affiliation. When Hank indicated he was looking for a bass player, Rivers recommended another Nashville sideman and session player, Hillous Butram.

Soon after the band got together, they and Hank could point to a number-one national hit, "Long Gone Lonesome Blues." In the short period of time left to Williams, the band basked in the glow of a series of hits, all now classics, including "Your Cheatin' Heart," "Cold, Cold Heart," "I'm So Lonesome I Could Cry," "Jambalaya," and "Hey Good Lookin'," as well as new recordings of some of Hank's earlier successes, including the 1949 number-one hit "Lovesick Blues."

But it was a trying period, during which Williams seemed intent on destroying himself. His unpredictability helped contribute to some changes in the group. In 1952, Butram left to take a job with the *Hank Snow Show* and was replaced by Cedric Rainwater Watts. Soon after McNett departed, going back to Pennsylvania to open a country-music park. Sammy Pruett took over on electric guitar.

Reminiscing, Rivers told Kelly Delaney, "None of us, including Hank, never even thought about thirty years from then—that Hank's impression on the business would be as much or more than Ernest Tubb,

Cowboy Copas, Red Foley, all these people who were big before Hank. So none of us considered what he was accomplishing was any bigger than what they had done."

When they heard Hank had died on January 1, 1953, Rivers added, "It was a shock. It had to be [but] to me it wasn't a big, big surprise—like how in the world could this possibly happen. It wasn't that kind of shock. Personally, because of the way his life had turned, especially in the last six months of it, you didn't have to do a whole lot of wondering about how he could get into a situation like that. We had a lot more good experiences with Hank than we had bad, but we also had some real bad experiences with him."

Helms, who also stayed with Williams to the end, agreed. "The last several months before Hank died was the period where we were kind of thrown at a loss, because of the circumstances under which he left the Opry. It was a temporary leave of absence. He had some personal problems and his drinking had become more frequent. He needed to take some time off, get his head straight and come back. Well, we had all just bought homes and cars, and I just couldn't see under those circumstances pullin' up and goin' to Louisiana or Montgomery. I didn't know if he'd be back next week or next month."

The band members went separate ways until 1977, when Butram's involvement in a series of country movies made in Nashville sparked a reunion. Acting as talent coordinator for one of them, a film called *That's Country* that featured Lorne Green, he brought the original Drifting Cowboys together to work in the project. One thing led to another and soon the group was working on many fronts, from radio to records.

One of the first efforts was a series of radio shows hosted by Grant Turner of WSM, an announcer long involved with the *Opry*. Soon the Drifting Cowboys got the chance to record an album on Epic, *A Song for Us All*, issued in 1978. During 1978, their single "Ragmop" made the country charts. The band was a natural choice for the first annual "Hank Williams Memorial Show" broadcast over station WWVA in Wheeling, West Virginia, in 1978. Before 1978 was over, their new credits included two appearances on Ronnie Prophet's TV country program telecast over the Canadian Broadcasting Company network and a set at Nashville's annual Fan Fair, which later was part of a TV presentation on the U.S. Public Broadcasting System. Some of the material from those performances was used to provide a 1979 live LP release, *The Best of the Drifting Cowboys*.

They continued to have a busy schedule in 1979. Besides appearing at a number of U.S. venues, the group went on a twenty-five-show tour of Britain during early summer. They also accepted an invitation to appear in a special performance honoring Hank Williams' contribution to American music sponsored by the Smithsonian Institution in Washington, D.C., in March 1980.

DRIFTWOOD, JIMMY: *Singer, guitarist, fiddler, banjoist, songwriter. Born Mountain View, Arkansas, June 20, 1917.*

A true representative of the American folk heritage, Jimmy Driftwood grew up in the hill country of Arkansas, where he almost unconsciously fell into a pattern of listening for and preserving traditional songs from his early years. As a collector of rural music and a gifted songwriter who sometimes wrote brand new songs in the folk tradition and other times expanded on earlier themes, he made important contributions to both folk and country movements in the United States over his many active decades.

As a boy named Jimmy Morris growing up in the Ozark Mountains, the major form of entertainment during his childhood was when his family and neighbors gathered round and played and sang songs whose roots went back to Elizabethan times. Before long Jimmy was taking part in the vocals and starting to learn how to play some of the instruments. His favorite instrument, one he remembered fondly all his life, was a homemade guitar given him by his uncle Morris. It was made, he once

said, of "fence-rail, ox-yoke and bedstead." By the time Jimmy was nearing grade school age, he not only could handle the guitar quite well but also mastered banjo and fiddle.

Jimmy's first educational lessons were in a one-room schoolhouse in Mountain View. Later he completed three years of high school at a Mountain View school, then finished his senior year at nearby Marshall. In those years, even a high school degree was quite an attainment and, after receiving it, Jimmy embarked on a career as a teacher in rural Arkansas schools. Finally, after ten years, in the late 1940s, he earned a B.A. with honors from Arkansas State Teachers College in Conway.

During the 1940s, he took part in many folk festivals in his home area, including several appearances at the Ozark Folk Festival in Eureka Springs. During this period more and more musicologists and other academics were increasingly going through rural regions with notebooks and tape recorders to further their collections of traditional music. The contacts that Jimmy made helped bring his talents to the notice of folk fans outside the South and Southwest. In the 1950s, Jimmy began to take part in festivals and concerts in many other sections of the United States.

During the folk boom of the later 1950s, record executives at major labels sought out talented artists. As a result, Jimmy got the chance to sign with RCA Victor, which issued his debut LP, *Newly Discovered Early American Folk Songs*, in June 1958. Among the tunes in the collection were "Unfortunate Man," "Fair Rosamund's Bower," "Soldier's Joy," "Country Boy," "I'm Too Young to Marry," "Pretty Mary," "Sailor Man," "Zelma Lee," "Rattlesnake Song," "Old Joe Clark," and "Battle of New Orleans." The latter, an updated version of a folk tune Jimmy had discovered in his musical searches, caught the ear of country artist Johnny Horton. Horton turned out a cover record of it that became a major hit of 1959, rising to number one on country charts. Driftwood was represented by his own single of that song in the late 1950s, which also did reasonably well. Soon other country artists were recording some of Jimmy's material. In 1959, Eddy Arnold scored a top-10 hit with Driftwood's "Tennessee Stud."

During the 1960s, Jimmy steadily expanded the range of his performances, but in between engagements he always returned home to his beloved Arkansas, where during the 1960s he had a career as a high school principal. There he continued to work with friends and folk adherents throughout the region to collect and preserve local folk material. One vehicle he helped found to further those aims was the Rackensack Folklore Society. He also helped start the Arkansas Folk Festival in 1963 and served as its director for many years. Besides taking part in that festival, he often was invited to other folk gatherings all over the world. He was a featured performer at many of the Newport Folk Festivals during the 1960s, and some of his work was included in Newport Folk Festival albums issued by Folkways and Vanguard.

Jimmy never concentrated his efforts on the commercial country-music circuit, though he always was highly respected by many country fans and leading country artists. During the 1960s and 1970s, he was a guest many times on the *Grand Ole Opry* and, indeed, some of his recordings were included in the RCA 1964 set *Stars of the Grand Ole Opry*. A highlight of many of his appearances was his playing of the unusual instrument called the "picking bow" or "mouth bow," one of many special instruments in a collection he assembled over the years.

Most of Jimmy's recorded output was released in the 1960s, including the RCA album, *Songs of Billy Yank*, issued in March 1961, the United Artists LP *Festival of Carnegie Hall*, and several albums on Monument Records, his label of the mid-1960s. Among the latter were *Jimmy Driftwood*, issued in March 1964, *Down in the Arkansas* (1965), and *Best of Jimmy Driftwood* (August 1966). In later years, he had recordings on minor folk labels.

Jimmy didn't stray far from Arkansas much in the 1970s, but he still played occasional folk festivals in various locales. From time to time he also took part in country reunion shows in Nashville, Tennessee.

DRUSKY, ROY: *Singer, guitarist, songwriter, disc jockey, band leader (The Loners). Born Atlanta, Georgia, June 22, 1930.*

At the start of the 1980s, Roy Frank Drusky was in his third decade as one of the most respected regulars on the *Grand Ole Opry*. Considering his achievements in the music field, one would not expect that in his late teens he wanted to earn his living either as a professional athlete or in the veterinary field.

Not that he wasn't exposed to musical influences in his early years as a child in Atlanta. His mother was a church pianist for twenty years and tried to get him interested in piano lessons when he was a boy. But baseball and other sports caught his fancy early and he resisted her efforts successfully. As starting second baseman on the school baseball team, he dreamed of some day becoming a major leaguer.

After graduating from high school in the mid-1940s and attending the University of Georgia for a while, he signed for a two-year hitch in the U.S. Navy, which it turned out to be the open-sesame to his future country music leanings. While aboard the cruiser U.S.S. *Toledo* in the Pacific, a number of his shipmates used to get together in the evening for some "pickin' and singin'." Roy was part of the audience to start with, but the more he heard, the more he wanted to be a participant. He recalled, "We were docked in Seattle, Washington, one day and I bought a seventeen-dollar guitar from a pawn shop. Each night when the fellows would perform on ship I would sit next to this guy who could really play and study how he moved his fingers. After they stopped playing, I'd go down to my bunk and practice making the same sounds he did."

Still, after his discharge in 1950, he went back and enrolled in Emory University as a veterinary medicine major. He still loved sports, but had given up that idea after a four-day tryout at the Cleveland Indians training camp. Meanwhile he dropped by to visit an old friend who had a couple of guitars on hand and the two started jamming a bit. "It felt good," said Roy, "and we really had a ball. So we decided to get together the next weekend. Before long two other fellows joined our 'Sunday Afternoon Living Room Band.' "

In 1951, for a lark, the group entered a talent contest sponsored by station WEAS (now station WGUN) in Decatur, Georgia. The prize was a regular show on the station and Drusky's band walked off with the laurel. Under the name the *Southern Ranch Boys,* the program became a favorite with WEAS's local listeners. The station asked him to become a featured announcer and disc jockey. Soon he also added two weekly TV shows on station WLWA in Atlanta to his activities and fronted a band in personal appearances throughout the local area.

After doing that for several years, Roy accepted an offer in 1955 to join station KEVE in Minnesota as a disc jockey. He also got the chance to headline at a major club in the area, the Flame Club. He already had shown signs of becoming a major recording artist. In 1953, he had a hit on Starday called "Such a Fool," which led to a contract with Columbia.

By then he was writing a lot of original material. Some of the great artists at the Flame Club brought word of Drusky's talents to Nashville. Before long, other artists were considering some of his songs for their own sessions and Roy was traveling between Minnesota and Nashville to try to further both writing and recording sides of his career. In the late 1950s, Webb Pierce suggested to executives of his record firm, Decca, that they issue a Drusky single of Roy's composition "Alone with You." Roy's version did well, but a Faron Young cover did even better, reaching the top 10 during 1958. Decca recommended he take up residence in Nashville and Roy complied. Before the 1950s were over, the move brought an invitation to join the *Grand Ole Opry* (1958). More than two decades later, that association was still going strong.

From the start of the 1960s into the 1980s, his reputation with country fans

was equally firm as he racked up dozens of chart hits both with his own performances and as supplier of hit songs to other artists. In 1960, he made the top 10 with his releases of two original songs, "Another" and "Anymore." In 1961, he co-wrote two more hits for himself on Decca (with V. McAlpin and J. Felrod), "I Went Out of My Way" and "I'd Rather Loan You Out." He also made top levels with his version of another writing team's song, "Three Hearts in a Tangle." In 1963, he had a hit with the single "Second Hand Rose." In 1964, he switched from Decca to Mercury and soon had another top-10 hit with Bill Anderson's "Peel Me a Nanner." In 1965, he scored his first number-one single, "Yes Mr. Peters," written by S. Karliski and L. Kolber, and recorded as a duet with Priscilla Mitchell. In 1966, he made upper-chart levels with "White Lightning Express" and added another top-10 feather to his cap with the single "World Is Round." In 1967, he had three singles on the charts for Mercury, though none gained the top 10.

The song "White Lightning Express" was the title song for a country & western film in which Roy appeared. He also starred in two other C&W films of the mid-1960s, *Forty Acre Feud* and *The Golden Guitar.*

Besides leading his band, The Loners, on extensive tours across the United States and in many other nations during the 1960s and 1970s, Drusky also worked at other aspects of the music business. Among other things, he handled production chores for a number of artists, including such people as the Coquettes, Brenda Byers, Bill Goodwin, and English performer Pete Sayers. In addition, he helped set up and, for a time, directed the Nashville office of the music licensing firm known as SESAC. He also headed his own music publishing firm, Funny Farm Music. Besides his regular *Opry* appearances, Drusky was a familiar figure on many TV country shows over the years. At times he hosted his own nationally telecast programs.

Roy had dozens of albums to his credit from the late 1950s into the 1980s. His late

1950s and early 1960s efforts were on Decca, including *Anymore,* issued in September 1961, and *It's My Way* (12/62). In 1964, he debuted on Mercury with the album *Songs of the Cities* (3/64), followed by such others as *All Time Hits* (7/64), *Yesterday's Gone* (10/64), *Pick of the Country* (1/65), *All Around the World* (6/65), *Love's Eternal Triangle* (9/65), *Great Roy Drusky Songs* (10/65), *Greatest Hits* (1/66), *Song Express* (3/66), *Roy Drusky with Priscilla Mitchell* (8/66), *In a New Dimension* (10/66), *If the World Stopped Livin'* (2/67), *Roy Drusky Now* (11/67), and *I Love the Way You've Been Lovin' Me* (late 1960s). Some of his recordings were issued by other labels, such as Vocalion *(Roy Drusky—4/65—*and *Country Special)* and Hilltop *(El Paso).*

He started the 1970s in fine style with a top-10 singles hit in late 1970, "All My Hard Times" and an equally successful LP of the same title on Mercury. However, the rest of the decade's record's proved considerably less exciting than the previous one's. Changes in record companies failed to cause a reversal of the situation. As a recording artist for Capitol in the mid-1970s and Scorpion in the late 1970s, he placed songs on the charts, such as "Close to Home" on Capitol in early summer of 1974 and "Betty's Song" on Scorpion in mid-1977, but none made high chart levels. Still, he didn't lack for things to do. He remained one of the best regarded and most popular interpreters of country songs old and new through the 1970s and into the 1980s, whose concerts still drew sizable crowds in the United States and elsewhere.

DUDLEY, DAVE: *Singer, guitarist, songwriter. Born Spencer, Wisconsin, May 3, 1928.*

The truck driver as folk hero was one of the phenomena of the 1960s and 1970s and Dave Dudley was one of the first progenitors of the trend with his series of truck-driving songs. His material, related to both folk and country domains, was recognized by the organizers of the Newport Folk Festival of 1967, who invited Dudley as a featured performer.

Dave grew up in Stevens Point, Wisconsin, where, when he was eleven, his father bought him a guitar. Dave managed to learn to play the instrument by watching Saturday performances at the local Fox Theater. Still, his main preoccupation was baseball. He was a star baseball pitcher in his teens with high hopes of a pro career. After the six foot, two inch Dudley completed high school he played semi-pro ball before he suffered an arm injury that invalided him home. While recovering he realized that the arm might never be good enough for him to make a success as a ball player.

So he was receptive when a neighbor who worked at station WTWT suggested he come down and spend some time there. One morning, Dave dropped in on disc jockey Vern Shepherd, who had just bought a new guitar. Dave picked it up and began to play along with the records Shepherd was spinning. The latter liked Dave's style and asked him to come down the next morning to sing live on the program—and a new career was born.

In the fall of 1950, Dave was given a morning show of his own on WTWT. His fan mail grew, and the next year he moved on to head a new DJ and singing show on station KBOK, Waterloo, Iowa. In 1952, he moved again, this time to KCHA in Charles City, Idaho.

In 1953, Dave went a step further by forming his own trio. For the next seven years, the Dave Dudley Trio played nightclubs and lounges in most of the Midwest states. Audience response generally was favorable, but nothing sensational happened. In 1960, Dave disbanded the group in Minneapolis and soon after, formed a new group, the Country Gentlemen, for a new nightspot called the Gay Nineties Club. The band, not to be confused with the bluegrass group of the same name, consisted of three other musicians and a woman vocalist. He gained enough of a following in the city to earn a disc jockey spot on station KEVE. He also was hired as master of ceremonies for a new country format featured at the Flame nightclub.

Dave's career seemed to be taking a turn for the better, but just at that point he was hit by a car after finishing work at the Flame on December 3, 1960. The injuries were serious; he was restricted to bed for six months. For another six months after that, he was only able to work a little each week. Other people had taken over the jobs he once held and it seemed Dave's musical career might go the same way as the athletic one.

But he decided to make one more try. He bought time at a local recording studio to cut a number called "Six Days on the Road," given to him by a friend from Decca Records. He took the dubbing to a friend named Jim Madison, who supplied records for jukeboxes. Madison recognized that the song might be a natural for placement in the many truck stops that dotted major highways. The song came out on Soma Records at a time when Dave was away from home on a trip to the Dakotas. It began to find favor both in jukeboxes and on country radio programs. When Dudley returned from the trip, he found that he suddenly was becoming known from coast to coast.

This time, he was ready to take advantage of his good fortune. He made the charts with several more songs on small labels, including a top-10 hit in 1963, "Cowboy Boots," on the Golden Wing label. In 1964, he moved up to the majors in the record field when he signed with Mercury Records and made top-chart levels with the singles "Mail" and "Last Day in the Mines." With a new four-piece backing band called The Roadrunners, he guested on most major national TV country shows and also was presented on the *Grand Ole Opry* radio program. In 1965, he added two more top-10 hits, "Truck Drivin' Son-of-a-Gun" and "What We're Fighting For." For the rest of the 1960s, he always had two or three singles on the charts during each year. In 1968, his singles credits included the top-10 hit "There Ain't No Easy Run" and two other chartmakers.

He was represented by a number of LPs on Mercury during the 1960s. His debut on the label, *Dave Dudley*, came out in June 1964, followed by *Travelin'* (10/64) and *Talk of the Town* (1/65). Other mid-1960s albums included *Dave Dudley* (9/65), *Star Spangled Banner* (3/66), *Greatest Hits* (1/66), *Lonelyville* (8/66), *Free & Easy* (1/67), *My*

Kind of Love (6/67), and *Dave Dudley Country* (11/67). His Mercury LPs of the late 1960s and early 1970s included *Best of Dave Dudley, George & the North Woods* (1/70), *Pool Shark, Listen Betty,* and *Original Traveling Man* (1972).

Coming into the 1970s, Dave continued to place recordings on the country charts, but with declining frequency. In the mid-1970s, his long association with Mercury came to a close. With his many past hits to his credit, Dave retained a sizable following at home and abroad and continued to headline shows in nightclubs and on the state and country fair circuit throughout the decade.

In the late 1970s and early 1980s, Dudley recorded some songs for smaller labels. An example was the single "Rolaids, Doan's Pills and Preparation H" on Sun Records, which was on the charts for a number of weeks in the late summer and early fall of 1980.

DUNCAN, JOHNNY: *Singer, guitarist, songwriter. Born Texas, October 5, 1939.*

A big (six feet four inches), ruggedly handsome Texan, Johnny Duncan always hears comments about his resemblance to Kris Kristofferson, but his voice sounds like that of the late Jim Reeves, a traditionally oriented country vocalist. Duncan's boyhood heroes included early country stars but, a child of his times, he also emulated the approach of people like Waylon Jennings and Willie Nelson. Appropriately, his first giant success was with one of Kristofferson's songs. One of the most popular artists of the mid- and late-1970s, most of the hits Duncan wrote or performed fell somewhere between traditional and progressive.

Duncan, born and raised in Texas, was encouraged to take an interest in music from his earliest years. His mother liked to play guitar and she began to teach Johnny the instrument as soon as he could handle it. Other young relations, such as his cousins Jimmy and Dan Seals, were also influential. Jimmy was to team up with Dash Crofts to form the late 1950s rock group "The Champs," and later to make a new career for themselves as the folk/

country-rock team of Seals and Crofts. In the 1970s Dan Seals made star status as half of the England Dan and John Ford Coley team.

In his teens, Duncan worked local events with his mother. He recalled, "We used to have these country dances. We'd ice a No. 3 washtub full of Pearl beer and honk all night, my mother playing guitar and my Uncle Moroney playing the fiddle."

After finishing high school in the late 1950s, Johnny entered Texas Christian University, where he studied English and speech for a while. But he kept up his music interest, by then adding some rock to his schedule. Though his idols at the time were Chet Atkins and Merle Travis, for a while he dabbled in the pop genre by working with the Buddy Holly organization.

That phase of his career began in 1959 when he moved to Clovis, New Mexico, site of the recording studios of Norman Petty, who had been Buddy Holly's sound engineer as well as collaborator on a number of Buddy's songs. Clovis was Duncan's locale until the early 1960s.

Recalling those years for Mary Ellen Moore of Country Music magazine (April 1977), Duncan stated, "Jimmy Gilmer and the Fireballs—remember them? I was out there with them and they tried to record me as a pop singer. [Petty] said I had a smooth voice. We went to London and did 4,900 violins and all that and got back and naturally nothing happened with it, and Petty came in—this would've been around '63—and he said, 'Johnny, you act like you're not happy, maybe Nashville would be a good idea.'

"Well that's all he had to say, because I'd already had my sights on Nashville. These are my people here. This is where it's at."

Duncan had worked as a DJ in the Southwest before moving to Music City. However, he wasn't a major disc spinner, and for two years, to make ends meet, he had to do some work as a bricklayer as well. He was performing whenever he could as well as writing original songs. Among his appearances was a spot on an

early morning TV show on station WSM hosted by Ralph Emery in 1966. Fortunately for Johnny, a Columbia Records executive caught the show and asked Duncan to come and see him. This quickly led to a recording contract. "It was the biggest day of my life," Duncan later said.

The contract did not bring overnight success, but it did bring his recordings to the attention of Charley Pride, who liked his material and recorded a number of his songs. Duncan also got the chance to work with Pride on concert tours. Meanwhile he was building up a following of his own, but at a frustratingly slow pace. As he told Moore, "We'd have songs that would hit the top 20, the top 15 and disc jockeys have known me since the late 1960s, but we never seemed to put it together, Columbia Records and I, until Billy Sherrill and I got together."

Before Duncan and Sherrill combined forces, Johnny had a respectable, if not sensational, track record. Among the many singles he placed on middle- or upper-chart levels in the first part of the 1970s, for instance, were "Let Me Go" in late 1970, "Fools" in the spring of 1972, "The Pillow" in the spring and summer of 1974, and "I Don't Love Her Anymore" in the summer of 1975. His first LP on Columbia, Johnny One Time, came out in July 1969 and was followed by a duet LP with June Stearns in November 1969. His next release was "There's Something About a Lady" in July 1971. He followed that a while later with an album titled Sweet Country Woman, whose title track was an original Duncan composition that provided one of his more successful singles. Some of his other compositions that he turned into chart successes were "Charley Is My Name," a song about a fling with a cocktail waitress named Charley he met in the Western Place club in North Dallas, and "Jo and the Cowboy," based on a relationship with a girl he met while commuting between Nashville and the farm he owned in Granbury, Texas. "Jo and the Cowboy," which he co-wrote with Larry Gatlin, reached the upper-chart levels in late 1975, its popularity a harbinger of the massive success that was soon to follow. Contributing to the impact of the 1975 hit was the vocal backing of Jamie Fricke.

"I really think 'Jo and the Cowboy' got their attention at Columbia," he told Mary Ellen Moore, "because I had just asked to be released from the label. It just wasn't happening, and I said let me try something else. [Columbia] wanted to do another record, so Larry Gatlin and I recorded 'Jo and the Cowboy.' He suggested Janie sing the lines in there because the lines belonged to a girl." After that, Janie backed Duncan on a series of blockbuster hits that made him a country superstar.

Next a series of recording sessions were planned by Johnny and Billy Sherrill. During early 1976, while Duncan was driving back from Texas to Nashville, he heard Kris Kristofferson singing his composition "Strangers" on the radio. Enthusiastic about the song, Johnny brought it to producer Sherrill's attention when he got to Nashville, and soon after, Sherrill, Duncan, and Janie Fricke were in the studios recording it. Released as a single, "Strangers" proved to be one of the hottest releases of the year. It began moving up the charts in May, and, in June, rose to number one in the nation. The same team quickly followed with two straight additional number-one hits, "It Couldn't Have Been Any Better" and "Thinkin' of a Rendezvous." While some of these were on the charts, Duncan also had a charted album, *The Best of Johnny Duncan*, which was in the top 5 in September 1976.

As the 1970s went by, Duncan continued to add to his impressive credits with a series of new singles successes. In the summer of 1977, "Song in the Night" was in the top 5 as was "Come a Little Bit Closer" (with Janie Fricke) later in the year. In 1978, he had another number-one hit in the early part of the year, "She Can Put Her Shoes Under My Bed (Anytime)," and another top-5 song in September, "Hello Mexico." In early 1979, he was represented on the lists by the single "Slow Dancing." During the last months of 1979, his single "The Lady in the Blue Mercedes" was in upper-chart positions.

His album releases in the second half of the 1970s included *Johnny Duncan* in 1976,

Come a Little Bit Closer in 1977, *The Best Is Yet to Come* and *Johnny Duncan's Greatest Hits* in 1978, and *See You When the Sun Goes Down* in 1979.

From the mid-1970s on, Duncan had no trouble filling his engagement schedule for either TV or live appearances. Before the decade was over, he had performed in all parts of the United States and overseas as well. He also was featured on the *Grand Ole Opry* over those years, including on appearance in September 1976 when he won rousing applause for his offering of "Strangers."

Johnny began the 1980s in impressive fashion. In early 1980 he had the hit single "Play Another Slow Song" and followed that with the summer success "I'm Gonna Love You Tonight (In My Dreams)." He closed out the year with the chart hit "Acapulco." In 1981, he placed several singles on the lists, including "All Night Long" in the fall.

DYLAN, BOB: *Singer, guitarist, pianist, harmonica player, songwriter. Born Duluth, Minnesota, May 24, 1941.*

From songs of social consciousness such as "The Times They Are A-Changin' " and "Blowin' in the Wind" to songs about his new-found faith in Christianity, Bob Dylan's music has sparked controversy and set trends. Refusing to be classified in any specific political or artistic posture, he has written about whatever strikes his fancy, restlessly probing one area of popular music, then moving on to another. His frequent shifts in musical style and subject matter have often outraged and confused some of his fans, yet he always managed to find favor with a large segment of the record-buying public.

The legendary Bob Dylan was born Robert Allen Zimmerman, and he grew up in the mining town of Hibbing, Minnesota. Although at one time he professed to have been a rebellious teenager, often running away from home, he later disavowed these stories. Actually, according to his more recent interviews, he had a fairly normal childhood that did not change direction until his freshman year at the University of Minnesota. During the six months he spent at college, Dylan did some singing at the campus coffee house and changed his name from Zimmerman to Dylan, in reverence to one of his favorite poets, Dylan Thomas. He also was to become influenced by Woody Guthrie and in fact, when he left school, traveled to visit the dying Guthrie at Greystone Park Hospital, New Jersey. He managed to get to see Woody, and the two became friends.

Dylan remained in New York, where he began to try to make his living in folk music. After a brief difficult period, he was discovered by Columbia Records' executive John Hammond, who heard him by accident during a rehearsal session of another folk artist. Hammond set up Dylan's first recording sessions. His first album, *Bob Dylan*, was released in 1961 and was followed by other folk-oriented LPs, *Freewheelin' Bob Dylan* (7/63) and *The Times They Are A-Changin'* (4/64). These albums met with rave critical reviews and remained on the bestseller lists for many weeks.

At the same time, Bob was appearing at various coffee houses in New York City. The critics raved about his work, and he soon became a focal point of the short-lived folk music boom of the early 1960s. The dozens of folk songs he composed during this time that became all-time standards included such compositions as "Blowin' in the Wind," "The Times They Are A-Changin'," "Masters of War," "Don't Think Twice, It's All Right," "Mister Tambourine Man," "Spanish Harlem Incident," and "Chimes of Freedom." Some of his songs helped propel other artists to stardom, as "Blowin' in the Wind" did for Peter, Paul and Mary and "Mr. Tambourine Man" did for the Byrds.

With the folk music boom on the wane, Dylan's songs began to veer more toward a blend of folk and rock elements. He now employed wildly upbeat arrangements and intricate but hard-to-understand lyrics that sometimes seemed written more for the sound and imagery of the words. These albums—*Another Side of Bob Dylan* (10/64), *Highway 61 Revisited* (11/65), *Bringing It All Back Home* (6/65), *Blonde on Blonde* (6/66)—had considerable influence on that period's

rock revival. His first single release to make U.S. charts was "Subterranean Homesick Blues," which made the lists in April 1965. Later in the year, he had a major hit, "Like a Rolling Stone," which reached number two. His other bestsellers of the 1960s were "Positively 4th Street," "Can You Please Crawl Out Your Window," "Rainy Day Women Nos. 12 & 36," "I Want You," "Just Like a Woman," "Leopard-Skin-Pill-Box Hat," "I Threw It All Away," "Lay Lady Lay," and "Tonight I'll Be Staying Here with You."

In 1966, Dylan suffered a near-fatal motorcycle accident and spent several years recuperating, away from the public eye. When he resurfaced musically at the end of the decade, he had once again switched his musical style to a blend of country & western and rock 'n' roll music with lyrics dealing generally with more basic, simple themes than his earlier songs. His best-selling Columbia albums, *Nashville Skyline* and *John Wesley Harding* helped spark the growing trend toward the merging of country, folk, and rock that was still going strong at the beginning of the 1980s.

In the 1970s, Bob Dylan embraced many different themes and causes in his songs and tried several different musical styles. Although many music critics felt his recordings in the early 1970s were not up to his earlier quality, his fans made up their own minds, propelling such albums as *Self-Portrait* (8/70), *New Morning* (12/70), and *Greatest Hits, Volume 2* (1/72) (*Greatest Hits, Volume 1* was issued in June 1967) onto the bestseller lists.

If many people were concerned that Dylan had lost his sense of political concern, he demonstrated over and over again that this was not so. He expressed outrage over the death of George Jackson in San Quentin in his song "George Jackson." He also performed at a concert in the support of the new nation of Bangladesh at Madison Square Garden in New York in 1971. This concert was organized by George Harrison and resulted in a three-LP album, *The Concert for Bangla Desh*, which featured a number of tracks by Dylan. In 1975, he performed at a concert dedicated to freeing Rubin (Hurricane) Carter, an ex-boxer serving a life sentence for murder. Dylan felt he was falsely accused of this crime and wrote one song, "Hurricane Carter," specifically for the concert to free him.

All in all, however, the Bob Dylan of the 1970s was much more concerned with personal feelings and relationships than the Dylan of the 1960s. He expressed this himself in one song from his 1974 album, *Planet Waves*, whose lyrics include such lines as "It's never been my duty/To remake the world at large/Nor is it my intention/To sound a battle charge."*

The 1970s also witnessed Dylan's involvement in modes of communication other than music. A stream-of-consciousness-style book he had written, *Tarantula*, appeared in print in 1970, and in 1973 he published his own authorized text, *Writings and Drawings by Bob Dylan*, which contained lyrics to most of the songs he had written up through 1971 and also included some album notes he had written and some drawings he had made. In 1973, Dylan made his acting debut in the movie *Pat Garrett and Billy the Kid*, directed by Sam Peckinpah and also starring Kris Kristofferson. The soundtrack album, which included Dylan's "Knocking on Heaven's Door," was issued by Columbia in July 1973. This actually marked Dylan's third movie effort. His first appearance had been in *Don't Look Back* (released in 1967), a documentary about a British tour with Joan Baez. A book of the dialogue from the film was a bestseller in the late 1960s. His second movie was actually intended as a TV special. Called *Eat the Document*, it was completed in the late 1960s but was turned down by ABC (which sued for return of advances) as not professional enough.

Dylan tried his hand at film-making once again in 1978 with *Renaldo and Clara*, which Dylan starred in, wrote, directed, and coedited. Robert Hilburn, pop music critic for the *Los Angeles Times*, typified most critics' reaction to the movie when he wrote: "Bob Dylan will hopefully make a

better film some day than *Renaldo and Clara*, but it's doubtful that rock's most acclaimed songwriter will ever make a more fascinating one. At once mocking and reinforcing his own almost mythical pop status, Dylan has crammed enough provocative symbolism into this nearly four-hour production to keep Dylan-cologists aflutter for years."

The film featured Dylan as Renaldo, his ex-wife Sara as Clara, and Ronee Blakely and Ronnie Hawkins as Mr. and Mrs. Dylan. Joan Baez appeared as a teasing reminder of the rumors about Dylan's decade-old romance with her. One of the film's scenes showed Dylan and poet Allen Ginsberg visiting the tombstone of novelist Jack Kerouac, affirming that one's art is all that will survive. In addition, a great deal of concert footage (forty-seven songs) was included in the film.

Meanwhile, Dylan continued to do what he is most famous for, write songs and sing them. From 1974 until the end of the decade, he demonstrated conclusively that he still had the talent and originality that had taken him to the pinnacle of the rock 'n' roll pantheon in the 1960s.

For a brief period, his recordings appeared on the Asylum label. After his recording contract with Columbia expired in late 1973, he organized his own firm, Ashes and Sand, with distribution to be handled by Asylum Records. Plans for this new operation dovetailed with his decision to return to the concert stage after a long hiatus.

When Dylan announced that he would make a coast-to-coast tour in early 1974, a deluge of mail-order requests hit box offices across the nation. Bill Graham, producer of the concerts, estimated that 6 million orders came in, roughly ten times the 658,000 seats available. The lucky chosen who got seats went away happy. Dylan sang many of his old standards but also introduced new songs from his upcoming Asylum debut album, *Planet Waves*.

He was backed by The Band, a rock group he had discovered in Atlantic City, New Jersey, in the mid-1960s and that later went on to become a highly regarded

© 1974, Ram's Horn Music, Inc.

American musical aggregation in its own right in the late 1960s. The use of The Band, therefore, not only provided Dylan with fine backup musicianship but supplied further continuity with Dylan's past, for he had been backed by The Band on his last tour eight years earlier. The live album resulting from the 1974 tour, *Before the Flood* (Asylum Records), climbed onto the hit charts and stayed there for many weeks.

In 1975, Dylan continued to build on the momentum he had gained the year before. He had meanwhile returned to the Columbia fold, which remained his label into the 1980s. His *Blood on the Tracks* LP became a bestseller. Robert Hilburn described that album as follows: "The 10 songs on *Blood on the Tracks* (Columbia PC 33235) represent a variety of styles (acoustic, electronic, folk, blues, rock) and themes (tenderness, anger, sarcasm, humor, affection) that we've associated with Dylan's music over the years.

The album's most arresting song—one that reflects the stinging intensity of "Like a Rolling Stone"—is "Idiot Wind." Like so many of Dylan's songs, it contains a variety of crosscurrents and can be interpreted on several levels, but its most persistent theme is a sense of being disappointed or betrayed. The song reflects the kind of direct, unguarded emotional outburst that is at the heart of much of Dylan's most interesting work. . . ."

Dylan also had a surprising best-selling album on Columbia in 1975, *Basement Tapes,* surprising because the two-LP set had actually been recorded eight years earlier. The album set was the long-awaited legitimate, professionally prepared tracks made from bootleg magnetic tapes of Bob Dylan and The Band that had circulated many years before. Even though eight years had elapsed since the tapes were made, the songs stood the test of time so well that many fans and critics felt the LP was probably the most exciting rock release of the year. *The Basement Tapes* was ranked number one in the *Village Voice* 1975 Jazz & Pop Critics Poll, in which thirty-eight music critics were allowed to divide one-hundred points among ten 1975 American-released LPs.

In the fall of 1975, Dylan embarked on an "informal" tour of some small New England cities, playing mostly in small, 2,000- to 3,000-seat auditoriums. The tour was called the Rolling Thunder Revue, and, although Dylan was always the focal point and main attraction, the concerts featured a number of other excellent musicians, who stepped forward at various times in the concerts to do solo performances. Among the members of the supporting cast of the Rolling Thunder Revue were Bobby Neuwirth, Roger McGuinn, Ramblin' Jack Elliott, guitarist Mick Ronson, Ronee Blakeley, T-Bone Burnett, Rob Stoner, and Scarlet Rivera. During this tour, Dylan introduced a few songs from his next album, *Desire,* which was released in January 1976.

Desire was received favorably by most music critics, further evidence that Dylan had indeed returned to the top of the rock heap. The album's songs could be seen as an overview of the major themes of Dylan's previous work, from social protest ("Hurricane"), to affection for the underdog ("Joey," about slain underworld figure Joey Gallo), to many different views about romance and man-woman relationships ("One More Cup of Coffee," "Oh, Sister," "Sara"). Dylan wrote all the music, but the lyrics to seven of the album's nine songs were co-written with Jacques Levy.

Dylan devoted much of his time in the next two years to the making of the aforementioned film, *Renaldo and Clara.* His next musical appearance was in 1978 with a new Columbia album, *Street Legal,* which sold well but seemed lightweight for Bob Dylan. His new songs incorporated Latin rock, reggae, and soul styles, the result of which was a more top-40 pop-oriented sound than usual. Dylan gave a week-long series of concerts at the Universal Amphitheater in Los Angeles in June 1978 before he embarked on a wide-ranging tour of Europe. He surprised his fans by playing totally new, almost unrecognizable versions of his old hits, such as a reggae-flavored rendition of "Don't Think Twice" and a soul-flavored version of "Just Like a Woman."

The next year Dylan did another unexpected about-face. His new album, *Slow Train Coming*, indicated that he had been converted to Christianity. If anything could surprise Dylan's fans after all his previous changes in attitude and musical style, it was his new incarnation, for the Jewish-born rock poet had always seemed to be something of a cynic. However, as Gregory Reese and David Sperling pointed out in a column in *The News World*, "Dylan's exhortations are certainly at odds with the "do your own thing" mentality of the '60s. But in a curious way, the album is true to Dylan's origins—in fact, this LP may be more pure Dylan than anything he's put out in a long time. Dylan has traditionally railed against hypocrisy, materialism and corruption—the religious themes only serve to intensify the message."

Whatever his fans thought of Dylan's conversion, many soon concurred that his new-found faith added power to his music. His voice seemed stretched by a new force. In addition, Dylan went beyond his own personal conversion and probed new aspects and applications of the morality implied in the embracing of Christianity. In "When You Gonna Wake Up," he expresses the idea that America is a great country but warns that we must "strengthen the things that remain," "wake up" to the corruption around us, and focus on a new set of values. Early in 1982, Bob Dylan publicly renounced his conversion to Christianity and committed himself to Judaism once more.

In August 1981, Dylan's twenty-fourth album issued by Columbia, *Shot of Love*, was released. Some of the songs from the LP were included in his summer tour of England and the Continent, a series of concerts that played to standing-room-only crowds. In the London segment of the tour, in July, he performed for six nights at a club in Earl's Court before capacity crowds of 20,000 people each night. In connection with these activities, he recorded a special, limited-edition promotional piece, *The Bob Dylan London Interview*, intended mainly for radio station use. (The world premiere broadcast of the interview was on station WNEW-FM in New York on July 27, 1981.) In it, he had some scathing words for trends in the recording industry: "The record business has changed—because when I went in in the 1960s everybody made records the same way I did, no matter who you were, the Beatles, Rolling Stones, Animals, Byrds. And you were *somebody* before you went in and made the record. You earned it. You paid enough dues to make a record. Now, people don't pay no more dues. They expect to make a record right away without anybody even hearing them."—A.S.

E

EAGLES, THE: *Vocal and instrumental group. Original personnel, 1971–1974: Don Henley, born Gilmer, Texas, July 22, circa 1947; Glenn Frey, born Detroit, Michigan, November 6, circa 1948; Randy Meisner, born Scottsbluff, Nebraska, March 8, circa 1946; Bernie Leadon, born Minneapolis, Minnesota, July 19, circa 1947. Don Felder added early 1974, born Florida, circa 1948. Leadon replaced in 1976 by Joe Walsh, born Cleveland, Ohio. Meisner replaced in 1979 by Timothy B. Schmit, born Sacramento, California.*

From the mid-1970s to the start of the 1980s, the Eagles held sway as one of the great rock bands of the decade. But while rock was the group's forte, they blended elements of folk and country into many of their songs, which had an impact on musicians in both of those genres over the years. While heir to the mantle of such landmark country-rock bands as Poco and the Flying Burritos, the Eagles achieved a rapport with the mass audience far beyond those groups and turned out consistently high-quality recordings that maintained their position as a superstar band throughout the 1970s.

In fact, as Glenn Frey, who teamed with Don Henley as the primary writers for the band, pointed out, they learned from the problems of pioneer country-rock groups. He told Cameron Crowe of *Rolling Stone* magazine, "We had it all planned. We'd watched bands like Poco and the Burrito Brothers lose their initial momentum. We were determined not to make the same mistakes. This was gonna be our best shot. Everybody had to look good, sing good, play good and write good. We wanted it all. Peer respect. AM and FM success. Number one singles and albums, great music and a lot of money."

The Eagles evolved from the folk and country-rock movement that sprang up in Southern California in the late 1960s and early 1970s. None of the four founding members were native Californians, but all eventually settled in Los Angeles because of the musical environment. The closest to a native was Bernie Leadon, who was born in Minnesota, but moved to San Diego with his family at ten and lived there until his father got a job in Gainesville, Florida, when he was seventeen. An interest in folk music caused him to learn guitar and banjo before he reached his teens; among the groups he played with in high school was one headed by Chris Hillman called the Scottsville Squirrel Barkers. Leadon continued to play with local groups in Florida in the mid-1960s before heading back to Los Angeles in 1967, where he worked with a series of groups in the late 1960s beginning with one called Hearts & Flowers and followed by a stint with the Dillards and then the Flying Burritos.

Meisner's career began in his teens with local groups in the Midwest. Later he was a founding member in Los Angeles of Poco, with Richie Furay and Jim Messina. Besides performing with Poco, he did session work from time to time, which brought him in contact with people like Leadon and Linda Ronstadt. Though he played a lot of country-oriented material, he had less an interest in it than other original Eagles. He told Crowe, "No, I don't go along with everything they say or do. For example, I'm probably the only one who loves funky rock 'n' roll, trashy music and R&B. And I don't agree with some of our images either. But Don and Glenn have it covered. I guess I'm just very shy and nervous about putting myself on the line. They're used to doing that."

Glenn Frey grew up in the more frenetic pace of urban Detroit. As soon as he was old enough to gain a certain amount of freedom from parental control, he developed two main interests, girls and music. He listened to rock music and went to concerts at the city's Olympia Hall, including two performances by the Beatles. He recalled later that he began to dream about holding the spotlight as rock superstars did, which led him to take up the guitar. Detroit then was the center of Motown's soul music empire, but other bands were coming along as well, such as the Bob Seger System. Frey learned at which studio Seger recorded and began to frequent it. "Seger was cool. I was never in his band, but he liked me and let me come to some of his sessions when he was recording four-track. He let me play maracas, an' on one song he let me play acoustic guitar." (Later, in 1979, Seger and Frey collaborated on material for the Eagles *The Long Run* LP.)

Frey didn't work with Seger, but managed to find his way as guitarist into a number of other groups, such as the Mushrooms, the Subterraneans, and the Four of Us. After enrolling in college, he dropped out over his parents' objections and took off for Los Angeles. "The whole vibe of L.A. hit me right off. The first day I got to L.A. I saw David Crosby sitting on the steps of the Country Store in Laurel Canyon, wearing the same hat and green leather bat cape he had worn for "Turn! Turn! Turn!" To me that was an omen. I immediately met J. D. Souther who was going with my girlfriend's sister and we really hit it off. It was definitely me and him against whatever else was going on."

Souther and Frey formed a folk-rock duo called Longbranch Pennywhistle and got a contract with Amos Records, for whom they did a debut LP. For a while, the twosome shared an apartment in L.A. with Jackson Browne, one result of which was a Browne-Frey collaboration on a song called "Take It Easy."

A legal dispute with Amos Records sidelined Frey and Souther and led to their spending some time hanging out at a club called the Troubadour, where Frey eventually became acquainted with another habitué, Don Henley. Henley, born and raised in Texas, liked to play drums, but wasn't sure of his career direction while attending college in Linden, Texas. He finally heeded the advice of an English teacher at college that music suited him best and he headed for the "big time" of Los Angeles.

He had formed a band in high school called Shiloh and he took that nucleus along with him to California. The band made some inroads in the L.A. music club scene, but nothing dramatic. Frey meanwhile was trying to use some of his songs as a wedge for a solo career and got the chance to play some for David Geffen, then manager of Joni Mitchell and Crosby, Stills, Nash & Young and later president of Asylum Records. (In the 1980s he had his own label, Geffen Records.) Geffen discouraged the solo approach and told Frey to join a band. Heeding this, Frey accepted a job with Linda Ronstadt. The band needed a drummer, which caused Frey to look up Henley. The two proved highly compatible. "The first night of the Ronstadt tour," Frey recalls, "we agreed to start our own band."

The band, in effect, took shape around them. Ronstadt's manager, John Boylan, brought in Randy Meisner on bass guitar when Randy left Rick Nelson's group and also recruited Bernie Leadon on lead guitar. Much as The Band had gone on from being Dylan's support group, the Eagles took shape and eventually left Ronstadt. As The Band has done with Dylan, the Eagles have appeared on joint concert bills with Linda over the years.

Henley points out that they didn't walk out on Linda Ronstadt, but told manager Boylan of their goals. Both Boylan and Linda, while hating to lose them, he stresses, were sincere about not wanting to stand in their way.

The group, helped by a strong recommendation from Jackson Browne, got Geffen as their first manager. The latter provided expense money so they could move to Aspen, Colorado, to rehearse, write songs, and polish their act in local clubs. Meanwhile, Geffen got Frey a release from Amos Records and lined up a recording contract with Asylum. In early 1972, he arranged for them to go to England to work on their debut LP under the direction of veteran producer Glyn Johns, who had supervised LPs by groups like The Who, Rolling Stones, and Led Zeppelin. The first fruit of their efforts was the single "Take It Easy," issued in early summer and soon getting healthy airplay. In July 1972, the first album, *The Eagles*, came out.

Soon after, the band began an extensive tour, mainly as an opening act, in support of the recordings. The critical response to the album was mostly positive, although some of the reviewers from eastern U.S. centers tended to shrug it off as lacking in social commentary. And even though only a cursory listening to the LP showed the group could play a diverse array of musical styles, some critics just bracketed it as another typical country-rock band. But concert audiences were the final judge. They liked what they heard and the album did well, moving onto the charts soon after its release and staying there into 1973. The album also was the source of two more charted singles, Henley-Leadon's "Witchy Woman" and the Henley-Frey "Peaceful Easy Feeling."

In 1973, the band went back into London's Olympia Studios to work on album two. It was an ambitious project, a concept album with all the songs tied into the theme of the rise and fall of the Doolin-Dalton gang of wild west fame. Called *Desperado*, it came out in the spring of 1973 and made the charts in April where it stayed for much of the year, though it wasn't "instant gold." Some of the singles made the national top 40—"Outlaw Man" and "Tequila Sunrise"—but none was close to being a smash hit. The essentially lukewarm reception to the LP stirred unease among some admirers, who feared the Eagles might go the way of Poco and the Burritos. Adding to that were reports of internal dissension and, later, of arguments with Johns about the next LP.

In fact, after working with Johns on two songs, "You Never Cry Like a Lover" and "Best of My Love," in London, the Eagles decided to finish the album in L.A., returning in early 1974 to line up a new producer. Almost at the same time, the band switched from Geffen to Irving Azoff for management. But all ended well. With Bill Szymczyk moving in as producer, the resumed album work went smoothly. In the process, the band found a fifth member, Florida-born session guitarist Don Felder, one of the best slide guitarists in pop music. Said Frey, "He just blew us all away. It was just about the best guitar work we'd ever heard." When the album, *On the Border*, was released by Asylum on March 22, 1974, it was announced that Felder had become the Eagles' fifth member.

During the spring, the album became a bestseller and easily went past gold-record levels. Turnaway crowds thronged Eagles' concerts and the band now was accepted as a major group with staying power.

Rumors persisted about internal problems as the months went by and no follow-up LP appeared. However, there was some exaggeration, Azoff told the authors at the time. "There was a lot of give and take on the fourth album just as there is on the next one and the one before that. But I wouldn't call it fighting. It's sort of like the President can veto a bill. Any one of the band can do it on a new piece of material. It's a matter of rounding out, of finishing off the rough edges. Obviously, success has mellowed them some. They feel an obligation to the music field to maintain quality. Even more than before, they all want to take their time. To us melodies, lyrics and vocals all are really—and equally—important. And that's why we say the Eagles are the Beach Boys of the 1970s."

The new album bore him out. Called *One of These Nights*, it is arguably one of the finest pop collections of the decade. Released June 10, 1975, it went gold in a few weeks' time and went well past plati-

num levels not long afterward. The initial single, "Lyin' Eyes," by Henley and Frey, was a number-one hit, and the LP produced such other singles successes as "Hollywood Waltz," by Henley, Frey, and Bernie and Tom Leadon; and Meisner, Henley, and Frey's "Take It to the Limit."

By the end of 1975, though, Leadon indicated he had become tired of the touring grind and the pressures of big-band life and wanted out. His place was taken in early 1976 by Joe Walsh, also managed by Azoff, an excellent guitarist, singer, and songwriter, who had been a member of the James Gang rock group and later a successful solo artist. His LP *The Smoker You Drink, the Player You Get* was a top-10 hit in 1974. Perhaps feeling a bit nervous about the shift, Asylum released the retrospective LP *The Eagles: Their Greatest Hits* on February 17, 1976.

However, once Walsh took hold, the Eagles soared even higher. The new LP, *Hotel California*, came out at the start of 1977, an album that combined unique insights with first-rate musicianship on every track. Among the singles hits culled from it were gems like the title song and the Joe Walsh-penned "Life in the Fast Lane." The LP was number one for some time on the pop charts and still in the top 10 in the summer, also making inroads on the country charts during the year.

The group toured in support of the LP, then took another hiatus as work got underway on the next collection. Another personnel shift was on the agenda. Randy Meisner departed during 1979 to seek a solo career, and his place was taken by bass guitarist Timothy B. Schmit. The Sacramento, California, native had worked with local bands while in high school and while he worked for a degree in psychology at Sacramento State College. He opted for music, however, and became a longtime member of Poco prior to his Eagles' affiliaton.

The new lineup's next album was issued by Elektra/Asylum in October 1979. Called *The Long Run*, it had many tracks up to previous Eagles' standards but several that fell short. The public, however, was happy to have new Eagles songs, and the

LP rose to number one in the United States at the end of 1979, staying in that exalted spot for most of January 1980. In a wide-ranging concert tour during late 1979 and early 1980, the band proved it still was one of the most exciting live bands in pop music.

In late 1980, the album *Eagles Live* was issued and quickly made the album chart's top 10, where it remained into 1981.

In early 1982, with Henley and Frey working on solo albums, it was announced that the Eagles had disbanded.

EDWARDS, JOHN, MEMORIAL FOUN-DATION: *Collection of country & western (plus some folk) material, maintained at the University of California at Los Angeles.*

Until establishment of the Country Music Hall of Fame in Nashville, probably the most complete collection of country & western material in the United States was housed in the Folklore and Mythology Center at UCLA. The late John Edwards' compilation of records, tapes, correspondence, photographs, and biographical and discographical material is the heart of the collection.

Edwards established himself as one of the major authorities on country & western music of the period 1923–1941 mainly through correspondence. Ironically, he was a native of Australia who never visited the United States to talk to performers or record companies in the country & western field. By 1960, he had gathered together more than 2,000 78-rpm records of the earlier period as well as a number of magnetic tapes. In addition, he had documented many important facts about the careers of pioneer performers in an accumulation of letters to and from the performers, their acquaintances, and music industry executives. His collection included taped interviews with many of them.

Born in 1932, John Edwards died in an automobile accident near his home in Cremorne, Australia, on December 24, 1960. In his will he requested that his collection be sent to the United States to be used for scholarly purposes. The material was shipped to his designated trustee and friend, Eugene W. Earle, then in New Jersey. In 1962, Earle arranged for the collection to be located at UCLA. Though the Foundation is housed on the campus, it is supported solely by outside contributions.

The John Edwards Memorial Foundation, Inc., was chartered as an educational, nonprofit corporation in California on July 19, 1962. Initial charge of the collection was given to folklorist Dr. D. K. Wilgus, who served as secretary of the Foundation. A graduate student at UCLA when the material arrived, Ed Kahn, also became closely associated with the Foundation, where he held the titles of treasurer and executive secretary. Other initial Foundation directors included Earle as president, Archie Green, first vice president, and Fred G. Hoeptner, second vice president.

Additions to the Foundation included almost 10,000 records from the combined holdings of all the directors. Other collections were added over the years, including in the mid-1960s one comprising 487 song folios. Various publications and industry mementos, including musical instruments of several important performers, have also been contributed.

Foundation goals include continued collecting of new material, archiving, cataloging, and indexing the old and new information, and publishing and distributing scholarly articles on various aspects of the field. Other goals are "To sponsor and promote field collections of such music, to stimulate academic research in this area, and to instruct and educate the public to the value of such music as part of its cultural heritage."

The importance of the Edwards collection was recognized by the Country Music Foundation when its new Nashville building was opened. A grant was given to the Foundation to copy the original material for a second Edwards collection in Nashville.

EDWARDS, STONEY: *Singer, guitarist, pianist, fiddler, songwriter. Born Seminole, Oklahoma, December 24, circa 1930.*

Country music usually is thought of as white people's music, but the truth is there always has been a strong interaction between the rural music played in both black and white communities. Many of the elements Jimmie Rodgers, the father of modern country music, incorporated in his material derived from his association with black laborers on the railroad. There always have been black followers of country music; it's only been in recent years that black artists have found a forum for their country artistry. After Country Charley Pride blazed the initial trail, others have followed, most notably O. B. McClinton and Stoney Edwards.

Born and raised in a rural area of Oklahoma, Edwards came of a considerably mixed heritage. On his mother's side, his ancestry was Negro and Indian, on his father's a combination of Negro, Indian, and Irish. He had plenty of chores do on the small farm he grew up on, especially after his father left and he had to help support his five brothers and two sisters. He did it until he was thirteen. As he told Glenn Hunter (*Country Music*, March 1976), "Runnin' corn liquor and helpin' to take care of them, I was only able to go up to the third grade. Later, I was too old. I was plum' shamed to go back to school. I still don't know how to read and write."

By the time he was thirteen, Stoney could play several instruments and had long been a country-music fan. He developed that liking during many childhood trips to relatives in North Carolina. He had a "bunch of uncles," he told Hunter, who would "sit around in a ring and pick, and I'd put right down in the middle of 'em. I had them to help steer my interest to Bob Wills and the *Grand Ole Opry*. I remember even back then I wanted to sing on the *Opry* so bad I could taste it."

For a time, in his teens, Stoney was reunited with his father in Oklahoma City, where he earned money working as a dishwasher. After a while he got restless and began to move around the country, going to Texas with an uncle, returning home for a time, leaving again, working at a variety of jobs ranging from janitor and truck driver to cowboy. In the mid-1950s, he made his way to California, where he met a girl named Rosemary, married her in 1954, and settled down to raise a family in the San Francisco Bay area. He found steady work for the next decade and a half, brought home a reasonably good paycheck, and kept at music only as a spare time activity.

That was the pattern until a near fatal mishap changed everything. It occurred in 1969 when he was working as a machinist in a shipyard in Richmond, California, and received a severe case of carbon dioxide poisoning. Though it was discovered in time, the after-effects were severe, requiring hospitalization. It affected his memory so that, for a time, he didn't even recognize his wife. He finally regained his strength and went back to the shipyard, only to suffer another accident that broke his back. This time, the doctors said he had to give up anything involving heavy physical labor.

At one point during those disasters, Stoney thought it might be best if he left so that his wife, at least, could go on welfare or find someone who could support the family better. He told Hunter, "I had my bag packed one night and was ready to leave when my little girl came in with this ole windup toy I'd bought her. She said, 'Daddy, if I can't go, how come you get to go?' Well, I just put my bag down and went to my room and wrote my first song, 'Two Dollar Toy,' before I went back to bed."

It was a harbinger of things to come. Stoney wrote more songs and played his guitar more in succeeding months. (Although he plays a number of instruments, he prefers not to use any of them on stage.) In 1970, he had an invitation to perform in a benefit show for Bob Wills in Oakland, California. He arrived a little late and almost wasn't allowed to take part, but a singer named Tony Rose insisted he take part of his set. After Stoney did "Mama's Hungry Eyes," an attorney in the audience was impressed enough to suggest he audition for Capitol. A week later he'd completed a demonstration recording and soon after was signed by the label.

His first album came out in March 1971, called *Stoney Edwards: A Country Singer*, and included such tracks as "Poor Folks Stick Together," "An Old Mule's Hip," "A Few of the Reasons," and his composition "The Cute Little Waitress." Stoney backed the album with an exhaustive concert tour, a pace of several hundred appearances a year at clubs, county fairs, and other country venues he kept up throughout the 1970s.

He was hardly an overnight success, but slowly he began to gain a following and his records started dotting the charts. Occasionally, as with "Hank and Lefty Raised My Soul" in 1973 and "Mississippi You're on My Mind" in the mid-1970s, he made the upper-chart levels. About "Hank and Lefty," a song by Dallas Frazier and A. L. Owens in praise of Hank Williams and Lefty Frizzell, Edwards told about going into a small bar in Nashville in 1973 to see Frizzell in a corner crying over the recording that was playing on the jukebox.

"Later this guy told me he'd overheard Lefty say, 'Why, that song's a tribute to me . . . and here I didn't think nobody cared a shit about me anymore. And wouldn't you know . . . it had to be a black man.'" Hunter noted that Stoney was asked whether he took offense. "Hell no," he roared, "that was a compliment."

Among the other singles by Edwards that made the charts in the 1970s were "She's My Rock," "Two Dollar Toy," "Daddy Bluegrass" (in early 1974), and "Love Still Makes the World Go Round" in the spring of 1976, all on Capitol. In 1978, Stoney was on a new label, JMI, for which he still provided a number of chart singles, including "If I Had to Do It All Over Again." By the start of the 1980s he was on a new label, Music America, for which he placed the single "No Way to Drown a Memory" on mid-chart levels during the summer of 1980 and "One Bar at a Time" in the fall of the year.

ELLIOTT, RAMBLIN' JACK: *Singer, guitarist. Born Brooklyn, New York, August 1, 1931.*

A cowboy from Brooklyn? This seems a little incongruous, but it is perhaps no more so than a matador or flamenco dancer from the same territory. Elliott is indeed from the big city, as are many others of the urban folk movement of the 1950s and 1960s. However, most critics agree that his music has the true flavor of the plains and the hills.

As Elliott told interviewer Bill Yaryan (*Sing Out!* November 1965, p. 16), "People [in the United States would] . . . just laugh their heads off at the idea of a kid from Brooklyn singing cowboy songs. So I invented this Oklahoma thing to keep 'em quiet. Said I was born on a ranch."

Elliott gained his initial interest in cowboys from watching countless movie westerns in his home town. Though born Elliott Charles Adnopoz, son of a doctor, he began to think of himself as "Buck Elliott" by the time he was high school age. When he was sixteen, he ran away from home to join Col. Jim Eskew's rodeo. His family notified the authorities and Buck was sent home two months later. He finished high school in Brooklyn and went on to college, first to the University of Connecticut and later to Adelphi College in New York. Along the way, he had learned to play guitar and sang cowboy songs whenever he had the opportunity.

The urge to escape was too great for Jack to finish school. He left Adelphi and moved to Greenwich Village. Here he moved in coffee houses and folk music circles. In 1951, this led to a meeting and start of a warm friendship with Woody Guthrie. Guthrie was impressed with Elliott's talent and invited the young man to stay with the Guthrie family in the Coney Island section of Brooklyn. The two played and sang for hours each day and Elliott learned many of the fine points of combining guitar playing with other folk instruments.

When the Guthries moved to the Topanga Canyon area of Los Angeles, Elliott went there too. Here he met many other major folk artists, including Bess and Butch Hawes, Guy Carawan, and Derroll Adams. Elliott gained his first professional experience in Southern California at Knott's Berry Farm, acting and playing guitar in the Farm's covered-wagon-encircled amphitheater. He also worked as a "faith-cured cripple" for local revival meetings.

When Elliott met and married actress June Hammerstein, he decided to take her suggestion to go to Europe. His association with Guthrie helped pave the way for acceptance by European audiences. He became a major favorite in England in the mid-1950s, which soon resulted in a recording contract with Topic Records. During 1956 and 1957, the Elliotts traveled throughout Europe, appearing in concerts and major clubs and starring on TV. They appeared on Alan Lomax's show "In the Big Rock Candy Mountain" and, joined by Derroll Adams, played to enthusiastic audiences at the Blue Angel in London and later at the Brussels World's Fair.

In 1958 the Elliots returned to California but went back to England in 1959. Elliott was then featured on a European tour with the Weavers and Pete Seeger. After his triumphal reception overseas, Elliott once more tried his hand in his home country. This time his engagement at Gerde's Folk City won critical and popular acceptance throughout the United States. In the years that followed, Elliott became a favorite with U.S. audiences in concerts across the country. He also played at most major festivals in the 1960s, including several appearances at Newport.

By the mid-1960s, Elliott's name appeared on LPs on several labels. On Prestige, he turned out *Guthrie Songs* (1961); *Country Style Ramblin' Jack Elliott* (1962); and *Hootenanny* (1964). His output on Monitor included *Ramblin' Cowboy* and *Jack Elliott Sings Guthrie and Rodgers*. In 1964, he was featured on Vanguard label with *Jack Elliott*. His other 1960s albums included *Talking Woody Guthrie* on Delmark Records (5/66); *Songs of Woody Guthrie* on Prestige (6/67); and *Jack Elliott* on the Archives of Folk Music. At the end of the decade he signed briefly with Reprise Records, resulting in such LPs as *Bull Durham Sacks*.

During the 1970s and into the 1980s, Elliott performed regularly on the folk music circuits, appearing mainly in small clubs and on college campuses around the United States and in other countries. An exception to that routine occurred in the mid-1970s when, as a member of Bob Dylan's Rolling Thunder Revue, Jack performed across the United States before crowds ranging from several thousand to tens of thousands. With rock 'n' roll on the ascendant, recording opportunities for folksingers were very limited. The only "new" album of his to come out in that period, and that one was composed of previously unreleased recordings from the 1960s, was the 1976 Vanguard two-record set, *The Essential Jack Elliott*. The LP contained one original by him, "Guabi Guabi," plus a number of traditional folk songs ("House of the Rising Sun," "Buffalo Skinners," "Sadie Brown") and songs by modern folk writers, such as Bob Dylan's "Don't Think Twice, It's Alright"; Woody Guthrie's "Ramblin' Round Your City"; Derroll Adams' "Portland Town"; and Jesse Fuller's "San Francisco Bay Blues."

Besides that LP, his albums still in print at the start of the 1980s included *Hard Travelin'* on Fantasy; *Jack Elliott* on Evergreen; *Jack Elliott* and *Ramblin' Jack Elliott* on Prestige; and *Songs to Grow On* (Woody Guthrie children's songs) on Folkways.

Although people not too familiar with Elliott's work tended to think of him as a singer of traditional material or the songs of others, particularly Woody Guthrie, he took pains to correct that image in answering questions posed by *Guitar Player* magazine (October 1974). He replied, "I have always created my own sources, but I still sing Woody's songs. While a lot of people don't think I'm imitating Woody, I still feel I am in a way, you know, like he's looking over my shoulder. [Onstage] I do a lot of Woody's songs, a lot of Dylan's songs, and once in a while I'll make up a song onstage."

As to how he uses the guitar in the latter instance, he told *Guitar Player*, "I don't plan it. I just get my fingers rollin' on the guitar, and the strings are rollin'. It usually happens when I'm not paying attention to it. Just when I think I'm gettin' lost."

That kind of improvising, he pointed out, depended on audience rapport. "It just depends. Sometimes when I get an uptight audience, one that's bugging me, I can't really relax and get into myself so I just do the traditional showbiz set. Then the only way I can get loose enough to create in a loose way is to try to relax. But other times it gets outrageously improvisational."

ELY, JOE: *Singer, guitarist, band leader, songwriter. Born Amarillo, Texas, circa 1947.*

From Joe Ely's appearance you can tell he's been through a lot of hardship, with a background of riding the rails and being stranded broke and alone in strange towns and cities. He wears old, beat-up cowboy boots and a large rangerider's hat, and he walks with the gait of someone used to the saddle.

"I was born in Amarillo, Texas," he says, sitting sprawled on a couch with his boots propped up on a motel room table, "about half a block from Route 66. I kinda grew up there and moved to Lubbock when I was about eleven. Not a whole lotta difference—one's a wheat town and one's a cotton town. My folks weren't interested in country music at all. There was always a piano, so there was a lotta music. Sorta church gathering music. My grandfather was always with the choir."

He was started out on the classics. "I started taking violin lessons in the second grade. Then I started taking steel guitar lessons around the fifth or sixth grade. A guy going door-to-door offered them. That didn't last too long. After a while the violin looked less and less appealing. So I turned to guitar. I found guitar was more of a total instrument. You could carry it around and use it to accompany yourself.

"Even though my folks weren't into country, growing up in the Panhandle of Texas I was kinda surrounded by it from the moment I popped out of the womb. I was also listening to some rock 'n' roll on the radio too. Guess that's why when I started writing there turned out to be a bit of rock in a lot of my songs. Of course I was influenced by all the early rockers like Bo Diddley and all, but I also was listening to country people like Jimmie Rodgers and bluesmen like Robert Johnson.

"I went to school in Lubbock. Not too long, but long enough to realize I didn't have any place in high school. I was playing in clubs when I was about fifteen or sixteen. There for a while I was playing

solo and then got a little band together at the end of junior high school. We played wherever we could—mostly rock 'n' roll. By then I knew a lot of old country standards too, y'know.

"For a while I was washin' dishes in a fried chicken place and playin' in a band, tryin' to carve out somethin' between the two. I was about seventeen when I ended up playin' in clubs in ole Fort Worth and Houston and a little bit around Dallas. After that I turned up in Los Angeles, of all places."

The event that catapulted him on the way there was a brush with a Houston club manager. The latter got mad because Joe missed a performance and pulled a gun, threatening to have some club bully boys beat him up. "It scared the hell out of me. I ended up pooling all my money with another guy for a oneway plane ride to L.A. Someone had stolen my guitar before I left and I was broke and only had a few bucks to my name.

"When we got outta the L.A. airport we only had five or six dollars and we ended up walking to Venice Beach to save money. We didn't know where we was. Kind of spin-the-bottle kind of journey. All I had was this old amplifier. I had an extra shirt or two in the bottom of it. It was my only possession."

Out on the beach, Ely found a man with an old guitar and managed to buy it for five dollars. That, in effect, put him back in business. He still has the guitar. In fact, it nestled in an old rundown case at one side of the motel room. For some years after that, Ely lived from hand to mouth, working odd jobs, playing for coins in the streets, picking up gigs here and there, knocking about.

"I started doin' a lot of hard travelin' goin' coast to coast with points in between. Those old freight yards in San Bernardino [California]—if you could find a brakeman who wouldn't pull the wool over your eyes you could get from L.A. to Amarillo in two to three days."

Riding the rods, besides getting him from one place to another, also gave him time to make up songs. "I guess I really started writing in the late 1960s and early 1970s. 'Cause more and more, that was the only thing I really had that moved me—playing, singing, and racking up songs. Along the way, no matter how I traveled, there was a lot of dead space in between some of those towns and music filled it in."

As the years went by, he kept "movin' on," even ending up in Europe at one point. "After a while, I kinda got burned out on California. I kept goin' back and forth between L.A. and Austin, Lubbock, and San Francisco. I kinda came back to Texas to be back home. I was workin' a little bit with a band in Austin when I just took off and went to New York with a friend.

"This friend of mine knew of a Texas bunch of people who were doing a thing with Joseph Papp's [New York] Shakespeare Theater. Sort of a Texas revue. My friend was a painter who was supposed to do a mural for the show and I was supposed to be his assistant. But he met Johnny Winter in our hotel and split back west with him, leavin' me at loose ends. I kind of asked the guys in the revue—like I had nowhere to go—so I said, 'I can do lights, a little guitar, anything.' They put me up and I had three squares.

"Right after I joined them, they got an offer to go around Europe to all the festivals. So that sounded like a good place to go. I took off with them. Stayed over there about five months. That was about 1970. When that finished I came back to Texas again and kept shuttlin' between there and New York. There was different groups I got together with, playing some, laying around waitin' for work other times."

During one of those early 1970s dry spells, he was in Albuquerque, New Mexico, and, on the spur of the moment, joined Ringling Brothers Circus. "It just happened to be there and I walked up and asked for a job. I ended up taking care of some animals. I had two horses, one called Omar, the other King. We went round and around with the world's smallest horse. I think it also was the world's meanest. I still got scars where he bit me. Then there

were the llamas—they used to spit at me." Ely spent about three months with the circus before an injury sidelined him. "Finally I got kicked in the ribs and bid my farewell—enough is too much.

"I ended up pickin' pears and green chilis in New Mexico for a while. Knockin' around like that was beginning to get to me, though. I went back to Lubbock and got this band together. By then [in the mid-1970s] I had a lot of songs in my head. A lot written down, but a lot I just carried around in my memory."

Among the friends Ely renewed contact with was a West Texas songwriter-performer named Butch Hancock, whose material often is found on Joe's LPs. "Anyway, I got a band together with a guy named Jimmy Gilmore and we had a saw player named Steve Wesson and a mandolin player named Tony Pearson—an acoustic band. We just kinda got together and did some of my songs, and Butch's and Jimmy's. We went to Nashville—some guy on a radio station took the band there. We did a tape, but I didn't like the whole deal that was offered so I didn't sign. Turned out my hunch was right; nothing much ever happened to that material."

Back in Texas, though, word about Ely's potential was beginning to float around the music field, which eventually led to his signing with MCA Records. "I kinda got with them by accident. A new band kinda got together and we made a few tapes for our own satisfaction—just to have 'em because of the songs we worked up. The Gonzo Band—Jerry Jeff Walker's band—gave Jerry a copy of the tape. One of the MCA guys heard it and came out to Lubback to hear us play at an old club [The Cotton Club] and he and some others were around again when we were in another town the next week. Things just started comin' together. Other music people began kickin' things around with us. But MCA just got together with us and worked out somethin' we both could live with."

Ely began recording material for MCA in late 1975; his debut LP, *Joe Ely*, came out January 10, 1976. The album created considerable excitement among pop music critics but fell far short of hit status. Although the signs were good, Ely's next LP didn't arrive until two years later, which caused a certain loss of momentum with the public. (Called *Honky Tonk Masquerade,* it was issued February 13, 1978.) Joe toured widely in support of it and his reputation grew, but hardly at a breakneck pace. In early 1979, his third LP, *Down on the Drag,* was released with suggestions that the time might be nearing for Joe to take his place with Willie, Waylon, and Jerry Jeff as a mainstay of the progressive country movement.

One of his problems was his unique, hard-to-categorize style, which combined often unusual lyric themes with varying blends of country, rock, and blues musical elements. This tended to confuse radio programmers; rock music selectors thought his material too "country," while country programmers had the reverse viewpoint. The resulting lack of airplay had the effect of making him a cult figure. This situation still held sway in 1981, when he came out with two more fine albums, the studio LP *Musta Notta Gotta Lotta,* issued by MCA in early 1981 and the live album *Live Shot,* released in the fall. His concert work continued to excel. An example was his set at the California State University at Long Beach Banjo, Fiddle & Guitar Festival in April 1981, where an audience of 7,000 initially unfamiliar with him ended up rewarding his performance with thunderous applause.

Still, it seemed that if the Goddess of Success were to claim Ely, she would have to do the pursuing. As he said, "I don't think about success. I never set success as a goal. I just set out to make music and that's what I've done. What I'm doin' now is all I can concern myself with. That in itself keeps me goin'. I woulda laid it down a long time ago without that. Music is my whole life. Sometimes I lay down the guitar for a while and take off, but I always come back to it.

"Of course, it's a lot different now than playin' at a truck stop on some highway for coffee and a hamburger. But when it comes down to it, it's about the same. I still drink coffee and I still eat hamburgers."

Based on an interview with Irwin Stambler, March 1979.

ENGLAND DAN AND JOHN FORD COLEY: *Vocal and instrumental duo, band leaders, songwriters. England Dan born McCarney, Texas; Coley born Dallas, Texas.*

There are more than a few things in the backgrounds of England Dan and John Ford Coley that might seem a bit contradictory. Dan Seals isn't from Britain, but Texas, as is Coley. Nor does the nickname indicate sophisticated roots; in fact, Dan comes from a small town and was weaned on country music. (Coley, though, is a city boy from Dallas whose parents saw to it that he took classical piano lessons.) Nor do they look like a pair of bookends physically. Dan, a head taller than his former partner, could pass for a football lineman while Coley looks—well—like a piano player.

But the two blended together well musically, as they proved with such hits as "I'd Really Love to See You Tonight," "It's Sad to Belong," "We'll Never Have to Say Goodbye Again," and "Love Is the Answer." Again, there is some contradiction because, while those successes are in the soft country or folk-rock mold, the main emphasis throughout much of the team's career was on fast paced rock 'n' roll or rhythm & blues. Indeed, there was some difference between the song arrangements on their albums and the group's typical stage approach. Coley told the authors, "On stage, the music often varies quite a bit from the album. We have a good rock band and we get more into that and R&B for a live audience. We use a lot of dynamics more than any particular style of music, because we don't care to do the same thing night after night. What we play must also be interesting to us."

Still, 1970s tempos were mellower than the high voltage rock the two performed when they first worked together. "Our collaboration started off in 1964 in high school," John recalled. "Dan was playing in a band that was already established and I was doin' absolutely nothin'. They needed a piano player because they'd just lost a guitarist and didn't want another one."

By then Dan, like many youngsters in the South, had switched from country music traditions to no-holds-barred rock. (He grew up in a small town, but was taken to Dallas when he was nine by his mother, who had separated from his father.) "I was into country music from about four until I was nine. I played with a family group. We still have strong country music ties. I have a half-brother who opens for Boots Randolph, my cousin is country singer Johnny Duncan, and a good friend of ours from Dallas, country singer Janie Fricke, backed us on our first two albums."

However, Dan's first idol was his older brother, Jimmy Seals, of the present superstar team of Seals and Crofts. Jimmy first led a successful rock group called The Champs. "I didn't have anything to do with the Champs," Dan stressed. "When they hit, I was in the fifth grade. But I followed their progress with a lot of interest."

Coley stated, "When Dan and I were first in a band together, we didn't like each other. Actually, it wasn't like a close knit family. Very few of the guys in that band hung out together."

"But after six to eight months," said Dan, "we began writing some songs together and that started the whole thing.

"Meanwhile the band was changing," added Coley. "Originally it was a rock 'n' roll group, then it moved over into soul and then into acid rock. Dan and I got tired of that. We were writing softer stuff. At times, we even opened for our group with acoustic guitars.

"We went out on our own in 1969," Dan related. "Started playing clubs in Dallas. We went under the name of Coley and Wayland—my full name is Dan Wayland Seals—and the music field was into a sort of folk-related era then. James Taylor was doing well, acoustic guitars were being used a lot. We played in the vein of Taylor, Carole King, Cat Stevens, and at the start of the 1970s like an artist who was

beginning to gain some notice, Elton John. We got to tour with Elton in 1971. That was our first major break. He took us to England. We were the warmup group. We opened the show for him.

"But we had the England Dan tag before that," said Coley (who had changed his name from John Edward Colley to John Ford Coley, feeling Ford had a tougher sound and Coley was less likely to be misspelled). "We just made it up because we couldn't use Seals and Coley because of Seals and Crofts. It's a twist for us to use that nickname, in a way, because the English fans really love Texans."

Naturally, the duo wanted a recording contract. "We finally went with A&M Records in 1971," Dan noted. "The first time we approached them, we got thrown out. But we had producer Lonnie Shelton in our corner. At the time, we were appearing at a little club in Pasadena, California, called the Ice House. Sandy, the light and sound manager, ran off a tape of our act. We cut it up into three songs a reel and started taking those tapes around to record companies."

After the first A&M rejection, Shelton took a tape to company head Herb Alpert. "Herb took it back and listened to it while he was shaving one day and said to his staff, 'Get 'em out here.'"

A contract was signed, but, Dan recollects, "We cut two albums for A&M [*Fables* and *I Hear the Music*] and started on a third. But neither of us were too happy about the way things were going by then. Both sides agreed it wouldn't be good to stay together."

Dan and John felt pretty depressed and disillusioned. "We quit the business for a year and a half," Dan said. "We got more active in our religion, the Baha'i faith. We didn't give up public performing altogether during that hiatus, but we only worked small clubs from time to time and otherwise did Baha'i music shows called Firesides two to three times a week.

"It was fun, too," remembered Coley. "We could go out and play our music and not have any pressure. We could take time and write new material. That lifestyle helped us get a new perspective on ourselves and what we wanted from life, because what we'd been through before had just about wiped us out emotionally."

After a while, the twosome felt better about themselves and their career possibilities. Coley stated, "I feel our music took on a more positive attitude because we looked at things differently."

"We also started looking more outside ourselves," said Dan. "We started doing other people's music besides our own. The songs that made our career turn around mostly were by other writers."

So in 1975, the duo felt they were ready to try again. "We submitted our first demo to Atlantic," Coley said. "Doug Moore of that organization heard it through the walls when someone else played it. He rushed in and said, 'I've gotta have that record,' and that's how it happened."

The result was the team's 1976 gold-record single, "I'd Really Love to See You Tonight" (written by Parker McGee) and the highly successful debut album on Atlantic's small subsidiary label, Big Tree, *Nights Are Forever Without You*. The title song of that LP also was a chart hit. The duo and their band proved it wasn't a fluke with a fine second effort, *Dowdy Ferry Road* in 1977, which provided the singles hit "It's Sad to Belong." The latter was in the number-one position on *Billboard's* "Easy Listening" charts for five straight weeks and was one of the reasons most music trade magazines voted them the Top Duo for 1977.

In 1978, in support of their third album on Big Tree, England Dan and John Ford Coley made several tours of the United States and also made their headline debut in the Los Angeles Roxy nightclub. During the year, they also opened for Three Dog Night in a series of sold-out concerts in Japan. In the summer of 1978, Dan and John had another number-one easy-listening single, "Never Have to Say Goodbye Again." Dan noted, "Jeffrie Comanor wrote it and it's his first big hit. Before, he had so many flip sides of successful songs by others he was called 'King of the B sides.' When it went number one, he called me and he sure was happy."

The team kept its batting average at 1.000 in 1979 with a fourth straight best-selling LP, *Dr. Heckle and Mr. Jive*. Included in the collection was their version of the Todd Rundgren composition "Love Is the Answer," which not only rose to the top of the easy-listening charts but made the top 10 in the national pop charts too.

Despite this success, behind the scenes strains were beginning to grow between the partners that led to the break-up of the act by 1980. Before going separate ways the duo recorded the soundtrack album *Just Tell Me You Love Me*, issued by MCA Records in August 1980. Included in the LP were such original compositions (co-written with Bob Gundey) as "Part of Me, Part of You," "Never, Never Night," and "Movin' on Down the Line."

Based partly on a 1978 interview with Irwin Stambler.

EVANS, DALE (MRS. ROY ROGERS):
Singer, actress, songwriter. Born Uvalde, Texas, October 31, 1912.

The first family in western entertainment in the decades just after World War II were Mr. and Mrs. Roy Rogers. Dale and Roy, both artists of the first rank, have contributed more than their share in humanitarian and religious activities.

The western outlook was natural to Dale, who was born and spent part of her girlhood in Texas. Later, her family moved to Osceola, Arkansas, where she attended high school and demonstrated a talent for singing. After a brief marriage (1928–30) to Thomas Frederick Fox, she went on to concentrate on a career as a vocalist.

During the 1930s, she gradually worked her way to the top as a popular singer, and was featured on a number of radio stations in such cities as Memphis, Dallas, and Louisville. In the late 1930s, she became vocalist with Anson Weeks' band, then one of the top organizations in Chicago. Her growing reputation resulted in a hit engagement at the Chez Paree Night Club in Chicago in 1940. That year she also was signed as a singer on a weekly CBS show called *News and Rhythm*. As the 1940s went by, she was a guest star on many major radio shows and vocalist on the *Edgar*

Bergen–Charlie McCarthy network show.

Next came the chance to get started in films. In 1943, Dale made her Hollywood debut in *Swing Your Partner*. This was the first of her many movie roles over the next twenty years. Her picture credits from 1943 on included *West Side Kid, Here Comes Elmer, Hoosier Holiday, In Old Oklahoma, Yellow Rose of Texas, My Pal Trigger, Sunset in El Dorado, Bells of San Antonio, Bells of Coronado, Pals of the Golden West,* and *Don't Fence Me In.* Most of the films were with Roy Rogers, whom Dale had married in 1947.

In the 1950s, the team of Roy Rogers and Dale Evans had become number one in the western field. They were starred on the *Roy Rogers* show, which was one of the top-rated shows on NBC-TV for a number of years. In addition, they were featured at many rodeos and other major shows across the country, which continued into the 1980s, long after the show had ended. They often helped entertain New York audiences during the World's Championship Rodeo in Madison Square Garden. Their international popularity was well demonstrated by rousing receptions from audiences during their first tour of the British Isles in 1954.

Dale and Roy turned out many records during the 1950s for RCA Victor. Some were of songs composed by Dale, such as "The Bible Tells Me So," "Aha San Antone," and "Happy Birthday Gentle Savior." They were also represented in the 1960s by a long-time RCA Victor LP bestseller, *Dale Evans and Roy Rogers,* and a Capitol LP of religious songs. In addition to songwriting, Dale found time to write several books, including *Angel Unaware* and *Spiritual Diary.* She also turned out a number of articles for national magazines during the 1950s and 1960s.

The Rogerses won acclaim during the 1950s and 1960s for their charitable work and for their dedication to children. They adopted and raised a large family of their own. Over the years they received many awards for their efforts, including the Masquer's Club's George Spelvin Award for humanitarian service in 1956, the National Safety Council's public interest award, and citations from the American Red Cross,

National Association for Retarded Children, Muscular Dystrophy Association, National Nephrosis Foundation, and many religious denominations.

After Roy suffered a heart attack in the early 1970s, both he and Dale took a brief respite from the entertainment field. Before long, when Roy had recovered his strength, the two resumed a certain amount of career activity, but on a much reduced scale compared to earlier times. However, they picked up the pace somewhat as the decade drew to a close. In the early 1980s, their career had something of a renaissance, as they were featured guests on many network TV shows, both country and general variety. They also were asked to do a number of commerical endorsements of various products, so that their faces peered forth from billboards, magazine ads, and on TV spots. They continued to make their home in Apple Valley, where they continued to operate the Roy Rogers Museum. (See also Roy Rogers.)

EVERLY BROTHERS: *Vocal and instrumental team, solo artists after mid-1973. Both born Brownie, Kentucky; Don, February 1, 1937; Phil, January 19, 1939.*

Taking their cue from Elvis Presley, who was their early idol, the Everly Brothers had an impact on pop music in the late 1950s and early 1960s almost as great as Elvis'. Their country-rock recordings of those years affected the styles of many rock stars of the 1960s, both in the United States and abroad. Among their fans of the late 1950s in England, for instance, were future members of the Beatles and the Animals. Their performances also had an impact on young folk and country artists, which prompted Bob Dylan to say, at one point, "We owe those guys everything. They started it all." After the brothers parted company in 1973, their activities centered more and more on the straight country field rather than rock.

The boys had an impeccable country background. Their parents were Ike and Margaret Everly, country/gospel artists well known to Southern and Midwestern audiences from the 1930s into the 1950s. The boys learned to sing many country standards at an early age and learned the rudiments of guitar as soon as they could hold an instrument. When Don was eight and Phil six, they made their first public appearance on radio station KMA in Shenandoah, Iowa. After that, the boys regularly joined their parents on performing tours each summer.

After their parents retired just following the boys' graduation from high school, the brothers decided to keep going on their own. They moved to Nashville, playing the local clubs and waiting for their first break. It was the mid-1950s, and traditional country music was reeling from the success of rockabilly artists like Elvis and Jerry Lee Lewis. In 1956, the brothers got their first record contract with Columbia Records (but were dropped by that label within a year). In making the rounds of music publishers looking for new material, they met the songwriting team of Felice and Boudleaux Bryant at Acuff–Rose (through music publisher, Wesley Rose). The Bryants played them a new composition, "Bye Bye Love," which the Everlys decided to record. A close association with the Bryants and Rose started that lasted many years and resulted in a series of hits, many of which have become standards and have since been recorded by many artists besides the Everlys in both the pop and country fields. The new disc was released on the Cadence label.

"Bye Bye Love" rose to number one on country and pop charts in 1957. The brothers soon provided Cadence Records with another smash success with the Bryants' "Wake Up Little Susie." The brothers soon were featured on most American TV shows, including *The Ed Sullivan Show* and Dick Clark's *American Bandstand.* They had another excellent year in 1958 with such hits as "All I Have to Do Is Dream," "Bird Dog," and "Devoted to You," all by the Bryants and recorded on Cadence, and "Cathy's Clown," which marked a move to Warner Brothers Records. "Cathy's Clown" also signaled the brothers' emergence as songwriters, a talent they underlined in 1959 when they had a top-10 hit with their composition "Til I Kissed You." Their names continued to appear regularly at the top of the hit lists at the end of the 1950s and start of the 1960s, some of the

releases material previously recorded on Cadence and some on Warner Bros. Their top-20 hits included, on Cadence, "Problems" in 1958; "Take a Message to Mary" in 1959; and "Let It Be Me" and "When Will I Be Loved" in 1960. On Warner Bros. their successes included "So Sad" in 1960; "Ebony Eyes," "Don't Blame Me," and "Walk Right Back" in 1961; and "Crying in the Rain" and "That's Old Fashioned" in 1962.

During those years, the duo also turned out a series of LPs, most of which made top-chart levels. On Cadence, their retrospective *Best of the Everly Bros.* was a bestseller. Their early 1960s albums on Warner Bros. included *It's Everly Time, Date with the Everly Brothers, Top Vocal Duet, Instant Party, Golden Hits,* and *Great Country Hits.*

The brothers moved to Los Angeles in the early 1960s, but their career slowed down soon after, partly because Don enlisted in the Marine Corps. While he was away in the mid-1960s, the Everlys still were represented in the music field by a series of LPs issued by Warner Bros. Among them were *Rock 'n' Soul* (5/65), *Gone, Gone, Gone* (3/65), *Beat 'n' Soul* (10/65), *In Our Image* (5/66), *Hit Sound* (4/67), and *Everly Brothers Sing* (9/67).

The brothers began working together again in the late 1960s. They were guests on many shows, including the *Johnny Cash* show and *Glen Campbell Goodtime Hour,* and made a number of appearances on *The Smothers Brothers Comedy Hour.* Concert and club audiences welcomed them in many cities, although they were unable to regain the massive following that had been theirs a decade earlier. In both TV and live work, they demonstrated greater self-assurance and polish than ever before, showing a gift for comic repartee not evident in the past. Eventually they were invited to host their own CBS-TV summer replacement series in 1970.

Their albums sold well enough for companies to keep issuing new ones, though sales did not approach gold-record levels any more. Among their releases of the early 1970s were *Everly Brothers Greatest Hits* on Epic Records; *The Everly Brothers Show* on Warner Bros.; *Chained to a Memory*

Joe Ely

Ramblin' Jack Elliott

The Eagles

Fairport Convention: l. to r., Dave Mattacks, Richard Thompson, Dave Pegg, Simon Nicol, Dave Swarbrick

The Eagles

Donna Fargo

Freddy Fender

Dan Fogelberg (left) and Tim Weisberg

EPA/David Gahr

Flatt & Scruggs, Earl Scruggs (top), Lester Flatt.

Steve Forbert

Janie Fricke and Johnny Duncan

Columbia/Norman Seeff

(Harmony Records, 5/70); and *End of an Era* (two discs, Barnaby Records, 5/71). In 1971, the Everlys' agreement with Warners ended and they signed with RCA. Their first RCA LP, *26*, was well received critically, but did not catch on with the public. The same held true for their *Stories We Could Tell* LP.

But the brothers retained a strong following, as indicated by the fact that they still could fill medium-size concert halls and pop and country clubs all over the world. However, there were increasing strains on the team—differences of opinion on creative directions and rising unhappiness about continuing to follow a well-trodden path. This feeling was indicated, for example, in Don Everly's early 1970s composition, "I'm Tired of Singing My Song in Las Vegas." Phil also showed a desire to go his own way by recording a solo album on RCA in 1973.

The brothers finally announced they were breaking up in mid-1973, announcing they would give their final concert together at Knott's Berry Farm's John Wayne Theater, Buena Park, California, on Saturday, July 14, 1973. As Don said at the time, "It's over. I've quit. I've been wanting to quit for three years now and it is finally time to just do it. I'm tired of being an Everly Brother. I still like to sing 'Bye Bye Love' sometimes, but I don't want to spend my life doing it. I've got to find something else." Later, he added, "The Everly Brothers died ten years ago."

Phil, who had stormed out of the first of three final shows that night, leaving Don to do the last two alone, noted in early 1974 that the decision to end the duo was his brother's, but it probably was inevitable. "It was simply a case of growing in different directions—musically, philosophically, politically—and add to that the normal, all-American brother-to-brother relationship, compound that by being together almost constantly for fifteen years and you have a general idea of what went on. . . . There is some bitterness, yes. We do not see each other—but then you can't really say that we're on bad terms. That would seem to be a contradiction, but it's the only way to describe our relationship today."

Phil was the first to strike off on a new tack. In early 1974 he inaugurated a syndicated rock program called *In Session*, a combination talk and music program that he hosted. He also began touring as a solo artist, playing many major country music clubs, and was still doing so at the start of the 1980s. In mid-1975, one of his compositions, "When Will I Be Loved," provided a best-selling single for Linda Ronstadt. Other songs he wrote or co-wrote showed up on the charts now and then, including one called "Better than Now" (co-written with T. Slater) issued as a single by Dewayne Orender at the end of 1978. Phil continued to turn out new recordings of his own, including the 1979 LP *Living Alone*. In late 1980 and early 1981, his single of his composition "Dare to Dream Again" (issued on CBS/Curb Records) was on the country charts.

Don also continued doing stage shows and records from mid-1973 on, though with less intensity than Phil. Much of his activity took the form of behind-the-scenes work. As with Phil, he was represented on the hit charts from time to time with other artists' recordings of his songs. Among those were Connie Smith's chart-making singles of "Til I Kissed You" and "So Sad (To Watch Good Love Go Bad)" in 1976 and a new version of the latter made by Steve Wariner in mid-1978. In 1976, Don had the single "Yesterday Just Passed My Way Again" (on Hickory Records) on the country charts for a number of months.

F

FAHEY, JOHN: *Singer, guitarist, songwriter. Born Cecil County, Maryland, February 28, 1939.*

John Fahey's guitar techniques and original compositions have had an important impact on the styles of many better-known artists in fields ranging from folk to rock. He himself, while highly respected by his musical peers, has gained only a relatively small following. That galling relative anonymity has been caused by his refusal to compromise his musical goals to meet the requirements of the commercial music industry.

He was born and raised in Takoma Park, Maryland, near Washington, D.C., and learned several instruments as a boy. His first leanings were toward classical music, but that changed by the time he was in his teens. As he told Michael Brooks of *Guitar Player* (April 1972, p. 20), "I was frustrated. I had been playing clarinet in a school band and was interested in orchestras and symphonic music, but I couldn't maintain my interest playing clarinet. I've always wanted to improvise and write things, more than I wanted to play them." His frustration eased when he turned to a new instrument. He writes, * "At the age of thirteen I bought a seventeen-dollar Sears guitar. I did it so I could entertain girls in the park." As he told Brooks, "All learning guitar was was a couple of kids who showed me some chords. I never had a teacher. I did get a chord book, though, and I also made up some chords. You know, a lot of the chords I play, I don't even know what they are. If I stopped to analyze what I play, though, it would take all the fun out of it."

The music he plunged into at that point was country & western. He writes, * "My influences, from radio, were Hank Snow, Eddy Arnold, Bill Monroe, Stanley Brothers, Wilma Lee and Stoney Cooper, Roy Acuff, the Delmore Brothers, Merle Travis, Chet Atkins, Hank Thompson—and Sam McGee. My main idol was Sam McGee of the *Opry!* I always tried (and try) to play like him, but never can make it."

He also listened closely to country records by Eddy Arnold ("I Really Don't Want to Know"), Hank Williams, and Bill Monroe. The Monroe recordings caused Fahey to spend a lot of time perfecting his bluegrass technique. He also began to try his hand at writing original material from those early teen years on. He traced this interest in blues and other Black music to a visit to Baltimore in 1957 when he came across a record by Blind Willie Johnson called "Praise God I Am Satisfied."

He told Brooks, "The first time I played it, it made me sick, so I put some Bill Monroe on the phonograph. But that sound kept coming back to me. Like five minutes later I just had to hear Blind Willie again. So I listened to it again and started crying. I thought it was the most beautiful thing I had ever heard."

That experience inspired him to make a number of trips through southern states searching for rare recordings of both blues and traditional country material. He began some of those swings while in his teens and continued his searches in his twenties, including an extensive tour with Henry Vestine, who later became a member of the Canned Heat rock group.

Through all those years, Fahey continued his schooling, finishing high school and going on to college. He always found plenty of time for his musical activities, spending time practicing guitar and playing occasional dates in small folk clubs on an amateur level. His first major professional appearances came during the summer of 1964 in Boston, where he was paid $200 a week for a stay at a club called the Odyssey. After that, he told Brooks, "I stayed around Boston that summer of 1964 playing most of the places there, little dives like the [Club] 47 and all in all didn't get along with the people there that well.

So I moved to Berkeley, then on down to Los Angeles."

By the time Fahey got to Berkeley, he had amassed enough college credits to start working on a doctorate. He entered the University of California at Berkeley as a philosophy student, but didn't take to it. As a result he switched to the University of California at Los Angeles to work on a Ph.D. in Folklore and Mythology. That effort was just getting under way when he was asked to perform at the major Berkeley folk venue called the Jabberwock, an important feather in his cap in the folk field.

Fahey's main objective in entering UCLA was to "write an empirical thesis on a blues singer or the blues. I wanted to 'de-romanticize' wherever it was called for. I mean, all these guys had big romantic legends built up around them, so I went down to try and get the facts." The subject he chose was blues singer Charley Patton, and the completed thesis was published by Studio Vista Ltd. in London.

John continued to perform in local events in California when he got the chance and also gave some consideration to expanding his recording efforts. At one point, he decided to produce a record of his stylings on his own and sold his motorcycle to pay for pressing a hundred copies. During the mid-1960s, he established his own label, Takoma (named after his home town), which essentially was a mail-order operation based in Berkeley. Among the discs he put out in those years were a four-record set titled *John Fahey* issued in October and November 1966 and one titled *Days Have Gone By* in October 1967. He also was represented by the album *Transfiguration of Blind Joe Death* on the Riverside label.

His talents came to the attention of the major folk-oriented recording firm Vanguard, which signed him in 1967. The association helped bring about an intensive series of concerts by John in folk clubs and on college campuses across the United States in support of his Vanguard releases. However, neither party seemed to feel comfortable under the arrangement and soon John returned to doing his record work on his own. Among his late 1960s

and early 1970s releases on Takoma were *Death Chains, America,* and *Voice of the Turtle.* His most popular albums, he reports, both on Takoma, were *Best of John Fahey, 1959-1977* and *The New Possibility—Christmas Album,* the first of which had sold 70,000 copies as of 1980, and the second over 200,000 copies.*

Fahey also issued albums by other young artists he respected. One of those was Leo Kottke, whose debut LP on Takoma came out in 1970. (Fahey's path crossed that of Kottke when John performed at the Scholar Coffeehouse in Minneapolis.) Later, when Kottke moved to Capitol Records, he included a number of Fahey compositions in his various releases. Fahey also handled production chores on many Kottke Capitol releases.

Some of Fahey's stylings came out on Reprise Records in the 1970s, including the 1972 album *Of Rivers & Religions.* John's pattern during the decade remained pretty much as it always was. He lived modestly in Santa Monica, California, much of the time and received warm welcomes from admiring audiences in college auditoriums, small folk music concerts, and occasional festivals.

Expressing some of his methods and frustrations, he states, "I write most of my songs and I play, don't write them down (I can't read or write music. Do it all by ear.) There's one thing about the guitar drives me nuts. I can't get over this year [1980]. I'm rated number 13 on the *Playboy* magazine poll of pickers. But I can play better than Atkins or any of them except Sam McGee. [Besides performing and recording] I am an A&R man with Chrysalis. I would love to make a record someday in Nashville." *

* From letter to the authors, 1980.

FAIRCHILD, BARBARA: *Singer, songwriter. Born Knoebel, Arkansas, November 12, 1950.*

Most youngsters don't make a career choice until their late teens, but Barbara Fairchild seemed to sense music was her destiny almost as soon as she was out of the cradle. She was singing in school shows before she was high school age and had her first recording contract at fifteen.

She first appeared on stage at the age of five in her home state of Arkansas when she sang "Here Comes Peter Cottontail" and "Easter Parade" in the local school's talent contest. She didn't win then, but seven years later took top honors and received a prize of ten dollars.

Her parents moved the family to St. Louis, Missouri, when she was thirteen. In high school there, she pursued her dream of becoming a successful singer. At fifteen, she achieved her first milestone on that path when she gained a recording contract with Norman Records. That led to release of the single "A Brand New Bed of Roses."

Later on, impatient with the way things were progressing, Barbara and a friend, Ruby Van Noy, decided to go to Nashville to see if they could attract some attention from the major record labels or publishing companies with some of their original compositions. They managed to meet publisher Jerry Crutchfield, who listened to their music. He liked one song, but told them to go back to St. Louis and write at least six more songs equally as good. Buckling down to work, Barbara soon was ready to return—with fifteen new songs instead of six. Crutchfield was impressed; he signed her to a writing contract with Kapp Records.

Convinced she also had a future as a performer, he had her audition for Billy Sherrill, vice president and top record producer at Columbia Records' Nashville office. Sherrill nodded approval and she soon had her first singles out on Columbia, "Love Is a Gentle Thing" (issued March 1969) and "A Woman's Hand" (7/69). In 1971, she had three more singles, one of her composition "A Girl Who'll Satisfy Her Man" (1/70) and such others as "Find Out What's Happening" (6/70) and "Loving You Is Special" (11/70). Her debut album came out in the fall of 1970, originally titled *Someone Special* and later retitled to *Love Is a Gentle Thing*. In the early 1970s, she added more singles and albums to the list, including a number of new original compositions: the singles "What Do You Do" (3/71); "Love's Old Song" (6/71); "Color My World" (11/71); "Thanks for the Memories" (4/72); and "A Sweeter Love" (9/72); plus such LPs as *The Barbara*

Fairchild Way (retitled *Love's Old Song)* and *A Sweeter Love* (issued in the fall of 1972).

A song from *A Sweeter Love* provided a major breakthrough in Fairchild's career. Up to late 1972, she had placed some releases on the charts, but nothing had penetrated the bestseller levels. In 1972, however, disc jockey Joe Clemmons at station WPLO, Atlanta, played a cut from *A Sweeter Love* called "The Teddy Bear Song." The number of subsequent requests he received for the song was phenomenal. He got word of this to Crutchfield, who relayed it to Columbia. The song was issued as a single in November 1972 and quickly began moving up the charts. In early 1973, it reached the number-one position nationally. It also crossed over to the pop charts. Ever since then, the song has continued to receive frequent airplay on country stations.

After that, most of Barbara's releases of the mid-1970s found considerable favor with country record buyers. Among her follow-up singles were "Kid Stuff" (7/73); "Baby Doll" (12/73); "Standing in Your Line" (5/74); and "Little Girl Feeling" (10/74). Her mid-1970s album releases included *Kid Stuff* and *Standing in Your Line*. Her Columbia recordings later in the decade included "For All the Right Reasons," on singles charts in the fall of 1977, and the 1978 album *This Is Me!*

During the 1970s, Fairchild performed across the United States on the country nightclub, fair, and rodeo circuit. She also made many appearances on TV, including the *Bill Anderson Show, Billy Walker Show, Jim Ed Brown Show,* and *Good Old Nashville Music.* Her songwriting efforts also prospered. (In the mid-1970s she was under contract to MCA Music). Among the many artists who recorded some of her material were Loretta Lynn, Liz Anderson, and J. David Sloane.

By the end of the 1970s, Barbara and Columbia came to the parting of the ways. In late 1980 and early 1981, she had a new duet single (with Billy Walker on Pad Records) on country charts.

FAIRPORT CONVENTION: *Vocal and instrumental group, all members born in England. Original members, 1966: Simon Nicol, born*

Muswell Hill, London; Richard Thompson, born London; Judy Dyble; Ashley Hutchings; Martin Lamble, died 1969. Ian Matthews added in 1967. Dyble replaced by Sandy Denny in 1967. In 1969, Hutchings and Lamble replaced by Dave Pegg, Dave Mattacks, and Dave Swarbrick. Matthews and Denny left at start of 1970s. Group makeup in 1970: Thompson, Nicol, Swarbrick, Mattacks, and Pegg. Thompson left early 1971. Denny returned during 1975. Denny died 1978.

A group whose history encompasses an intricate web of shifts and changes in personnel and stylings, not always to its benefit, Fairport Convention nevertheless ranks as one of the finest and most underrated bands in modern folk/folk-rock music. Its blending of elements of traditional English folk music with twentieth-century folk and rock provided new songs by various band members as well as new interpretations of English folk tunes and the writings of people like Bob Dylan and Joni Mitchell.

The original band in 1966 was composed of a group of young English folk-oriented musicians: vocalist Judy Dyble, lead guitarist Richard Thompson, bass guitarist Ashley Hutchings (who provided much of the band's original material), rhythm guitarist Simon Nicol, and drummer Martin Lamble. Thompson, one of the key members, whose musical interests ranged from folk to jazz and classics, was the son of a North London police officer. Just before helping to start the new band, he worked for a time as a stained glass apprentice. Nicol, born and raised in Muswell Hill, played not only fine rhythm guitar but innovative autoharp as well. His house in Muswell Hill, called "Fairport," is where the group first started and provided the band's name.

During 1966 and 1967, the original quintet slowly began building up a reputation at home, playing small folk and rock clubs in the London area. At first without a recording contract, the band gained recognition by word of mouth on the underground circuit, with rumors of their potential even reaching across the Atlantic to American fans. By 1968, though, their manager and producer, Joe Boyd, lined up a record deal with an English company,

which led to their debut LP titled, in England, *What We Did on Our Holidays.* During that period, Judy Dyble left to form her own group and her place was taken by a superbly talented vocalist and writer, Sandy Denny, whose contributions to the band included some of its most favored songs, such as "Who Knows Where the Time Goes." By the end of the 1960s, the group had an American label, A&M, which released its debut LP in the States, *Fairport Convention,* in August 1969.

That album remains today a classic of the folk-rock genre worldwide, as does the next A&M release, *Unhalfbricking.* Those LPs showcase Denny's vocal skills and Thompson's work as singer and lead guitarist. The group supported those albums with critically praised concerts in England and the United States in the late 1960s. An important member of those tours was guitarist-vocalist Ian Matthews, who soon after left to form his highly successful Southern Comfort group (whose output included the top-10 1971 folk-rock hit "Woodstock").

Meanwhile, other changes kept occurring, both through intention and accident, in personnel and musical approach. In the spring of 1969, a tragic car accident cost the life of drummer Martin Lamble. His place was taken by Dave Mattacks, who previously had worked with English big bands for three years. During 1969, Ashley Hutchings decided to start a band of his own; the remaining members chose bass guitarist Dave Pegg as a replacement. Pegg had played with Ian Campbell's band for a year and, before that, had worked with several pop bands in the English Midlands. Also joining in 1969 was vocalist-violinist Dave Swarbrick, who had been a major folk figure in England for years, much of it in partnership with guitarist Martin Carthy. Swarbrick initially was only supposed to do some session work on the *Unhalfbricking* LP, but his style seemed to fit so well with the band's material he was asked to join full time.

The group's next LP, *Liege and Lief,* was devoted to updated versions of English traditional songs. One of the best tracks featured Sandy Denny's vocal on "Matty

Groves." Like the earlier LPs, the album rose to upper-chart levels on English charts. In that phase, besides the three LPs, the group also had a hit single called "Si Tu Dois Partir."

By early 1970, Sandy Denny had departed, leaving, for the first time, an all-male group comprising Thompson, Nicol, Swarbrick, Mattacks, and Pegg. Still, the group continued to maintain its position as one of the most interesting folk-rock aggregations and was warmly received during a U.S. tour in the summer that included a featured spot in the Philadelphia Folk Festival in August. In the autumn of 1970, the band played to capacity audiences during an extensive tour of England.

The band continued to turn out new albums that increasingly stressed the use of electric instruments. The next release on A&M was titled *Full House*. Richard Thompson, who worked on that LP, went his own way by early 1971. The next album was recorded by the remaining four members, who also toured widely in 1971, giving concerts throughout the United States, England, and continental Europe.

The band continued to tour and record during the next few years with Swarbrick taking over as lead vocalist and Simon Nicol doing lead guitar work, but the new albums, such as *Babbacombe Lee and Nine,* did not have the impact of earlier ones. In 1975, there was hope for rejuvenation when Sandy Denny rejoined. She took part in two sets of recordings that were issued on Island Records and gave her usual impressive vocal stylings during tours of Europe and, in late summer of 1975, the United States. However, the results still were less than breathtaking, particularly since the new material was weaker than the band's early favorites. By 1976, Sandy struck off in other directions once more, leaving Fairport Convention in disarray.

FARGO, DONNA: *Singer, guitarist, songwriter. Born Mt. Airy, North Carolina, November 10, 1949.*

It seemed ironic for a woman who became famous through a song titled "The Happiest Girl in the Whole U.S.A." and who seemed to personify that description for much of the 1970s to suddenly come face to face with crippling disease while she was still youthful and vigorous. But Donna Fargo faced up to multiple sclerosis in the late 1970s and learned to cope with it and carry on in the entertainment field with good grace.

It was a field she hadn't really thought of entering until well into her twenties. As a child growing up in Mt. Airy, North Carolina, she had sung some solos in the Baptist church her family attended, but that didn't suggest any career goals. Instead, after completing high school, she enrolled at High Point College, where she completed work on her teaching credentials. After graduation, she went to California, where she got a job as an English teacher.

The turning point in her life came when she met a man named Stan Silver, who was a musician and a hopeful music-industry executive. Stan, later to become her record producer and her husband, taught her to play guitar and, when Donna began composing her own songs, criticized them as well as encouraged her to keep writing. While still teaching in high school, Fargo started performing as a country artist in local California clubs on weekends and during holidays. The response was usually quite favorable; eventually she decided to go into music full time, with the advice and assistance of Stan Silver.

She didn't become a star overnight. Indeed, she spent several years working in small clubs and perfecting her writing skills. She said later, "I wasn't ready for success and fate saw to it I didn't get the success right away. For that I'm actually glad."

In the early 1970s, she made a series of demonstration records, which finally caught the attention of Dot Records executives. Now success was almost overnight. Her 1972 single "The Happiest Girl in the U.S.A." was literally a smash, rising to number one on country charts and crossing over to become a pop hit too. Eventually the single went platinum and won a host of awards for her: Academy of Country Music Award for Single Record of the

Year, a Grammy for Best Country Vocal Performance, Female, and the Robert J. Burton Award from BMI for Most Performed Song of the Year (1972 and 1973).

She quickly proved it wasn't a fluke with a string of singles that rose to the top of the country charts: "Funny Face," "Superman," and "You Were Always There," with "Little Girl Gone" reaching the number-two slot.

After a few years of recording on the Dot label, Donna switched to Warner Brothers. Her first album for Warners, *On the Move* (issued in the spring of 1976), featured her hit song "It Do Feel Good" as well as other original compositions like "Sing for My Supper" and "Song with No Music" and an assortment of songs by other writers. Commenting on her writing approach at the time, she said, "I try to write all the time. I can never tell when an idea will strike me. When I have an album to do, though, I usually discipline myself. I lock myself in a room at home and start composing. I don't come out until I've got a handful of new songs. Most of the original songs for *On the Move* I've written over the last six months. 'Sing for My Supper' was co-written about two years ago, but I wrote new lyrics to it recently. I do that often: rewrite older songs. It's not that hard for me to write, but I'm kind of a perfectionist. I do think my songs convey a pretty consistent attitude."

Having established herself as a fine country artist when singing her own compositions (in "traditional" country style based on the twangy, relatively unpolished nature of her voice), she began to make hits out of other writers' songs. Her remake of the old standard "Mockingbird Hill," released in 1977, made it onto the top 10 on the country charts. Later that year, "Shame on Me," from the album of the same name, also entered the top 10. (The LP *Shame on Me* followed her second Warner Brothers LP, *Fargo Country*, issued in early 1977.) Donna also had a major hit in 1977 with an original composition, "That Was Yesterday." The song was entirely spoken, rather than sung, and it dealt with the conflicting emotions involved in daydreaming about a past love, a

kind of "almost love" that never blossomed. During 1978, Fairchild had top country chart hits with "Do I Love You (Yes in Every Way)" and "Another Goodbye," both written by others.

In early 1978, everything seemed to be going extremely well for her. Her career was flourishing in every way. She was being featured on almost every major TV country variety show and some general talk/variety programs as well. In the mid-1970s she hosted her own syndicated TV variety show for several years. Her extensive tours and nightclub engagements (including an engagement in Las Vegas with Charlie Rich) won good audience response. But in the summer of 1978 she didn't feel quite right. She checked into a hospital in Santa Barbara, California, for a checkup. The tests showed her to have multiple sclerosis, a progressive, degenerative disease of the nervous system. Among possible symptoms are numbness, loss of coordination, pain-filled spasms, and paralysis.

She was despondent about the future for a time, then turned to religion for help. She said, "I always believed in God and went to church as a little girl, which I think is reflected in some of my songs. But I've gotten much more serious about it now. It's been a kind of gradual growth for me the past few years, though I certainly don't have it perfected yet. But I came to the realization through this disease that you eventually come to the end of yourself. You realize how helpless you are by yourself, that there has to be something in life bigger than you are. Now I read the Bible and I listen to faith-building tapes, especially tapes by Kenneth Hagin, a minister in Tulsa. I've found a lot of comfort in the reading and the tapes—in fact, they probably have saved my life." Later, after she resumed her career, she signed with MCA Records' Songbird label to record some religiously oriented albums.

After resting for some months, Donna felt ready to pick up the threads of her life. She was determined to follow her doctors' orders as much as possible, observing carefully regulated diet plans, finding out as much as she could about M.S. and its causes, and taking time for exercises to keep her body in as good condition as possible. With husband Stan she planned touring and TV schedules that would provide good audience exposure but without one-nighters requiring long bus rides between engagements.

Her recordings continued to show up on country lists, with 1979 providing such best-selling singles as "Somebody Special" and "Daddy." Her LP *Dark Eyed Lady*, on the charts the latter part of 1978, remained on them into 1979. In 1980 she made the lists with singles like "Walk on By" and "Seeing Is Believing." In the fall of 1981 her single "Jacamo" was moving up the charts.

FARINA, MIMI: *Singer, guitarist, songwriter. Born California, April 30, 1945.*

There were more than a few emotional hurdles Mimi Farina had to overcome in achieving a career in folk music. One of those involved trying to avoid the long shadow of her older sister, Joan Baez, who already was a superstar when Mimi was just developing momentum for her own vocal efforts. But even more traumatic was the tragic death of her young and creatively dynamic husband, Richard Farina, in 1966, when she was only twenty-one. Somehow, Mimi found the inner capacity to cope and develop her own identity as a performer and writer.

She was born in California, but, like sister Joan, traveled to many different places. Her Mexican-born father, who held a doctorate in physics and worked for the United Nations, took his family with him on his many assignments. He and his British-born wife both liked music and encouraged their children's interest in it. In Mimi's case, she learned to play piano and violin. Later, when the family settled in the Boston area during the late 1950s, she was attracted by the folk music enthusiasms of the time to add guitar playing to her skills. Joan, of course, was old enough to start performing in some of the small folk clubs in Boston and environs, but Mimi, still in her early teens, sang and played for her own pleasure or for friends.

For a time in the early part of the 1960s,

while her sister established herself as one of folk and pop music's brightest stars, Mimi went to Paris. There, she recalled, her approach to folk music and guitar stylings was influenced by the methods of local street musicians.

Among the other Americans she met there, she was particularly attracted to the musician and writer Richard Farina, whom she married in 1963. Joan Baez gave a fond capsule portrait of him in her foreword to his posthumous book *A Long Time Coming and a Long Time Gone.* "He was my sister Mimi's crazy husband, a mystical child of darkness—blatantly ambitious, lovable, impossible, charming, obnoxious, tirelessly active—a bright, talented, sheepish, tricky, curly-haired, man-child of darkness."

The two seemed eminently compatible, both as a married couple and as a striking performing and writing team. Among the songs they unveiled to delighted folk fans in their brief span of concerts, with Mimi handling guitar and Richard dulcimer, were such originals by Richard as "Pack Up Your Sorrows," "Children of Darkness," and "Birmingham Sunday." Besides appearing in major cities all over the United States and Canada in 1964 and 1965, they gave memorable performances at a number of folk festivals, including a sensational debut at the 1965 Newport, Rhode Island, Folk Festival.

The Farinas signed with Vanguard Records in 1964 and their debut LP, *Celebration for a Grey Day*, came out in June 1965. This was followed in March 1966 by *Reflections in a Crystal Wind*. A third album, *Memories*, came out after Richard's death and later Vanguard issued a retrospective, *Best of Mimi and Richard Farina*.

The glowing promise of their association came to an abrupt end in 1966 when Richard was killed in a motorcycle accident on his birthday. For many months Mimi was unable to decide about continuing in the music field. Gradually, however, she put the tragedy behind her and began to try to reestablish her career on a solo basis. In 1967, she won heartfelt applause from Newport Folk Festival attendees for her first appearance there since her 1965 event with Richard.

In the late 1960s, Mimi settled in California, where she joined a troupe of political/social satirists called the San Francisco Committee. She found that acting with that improvisational group was excellent therapy for the depression she still was fighting. She started writing new songs and began thinking about doing more singing work again. However, she still felt the need for an artistic partner, a need met for a time in the early 1970s by Tom Jans.

Recalling those events for interviewer Robert Beers in 1971, Jans said, "I was singing by myself in California and Mimi was looking for someone to sing with. She was writing songs at that time, about a year ago. I was singing at a little club, and some people from the Institute of Nonviolence asked me to come up and have dinner. That's when I met Joan and through Joan I met Mimi."

The two found common ground as writers and performers and developed a new act that included some of their own song collaborations. Mimi told Beers, "In the beginning, writing was something to do. Something to do to keep from not doing anything. Then it became more creative, and then singing together started to kind of work. And it was listenable and fun. But to set out to be a songwriter. I don't know how someone could do that. To decide 'I'm gonna write songs that are gonna sell,' I don't know how that can be done. And yet it is, all the time."

Jans noted, "The reason why we write is to tell people that even if you are lonely there are ways of fighting your way out of it. Fighting your way out of depression and being able to relate to each other better."

The result of their efforts was a joint album, *Take Heart*, issued by A&M in 1971, and a cross-country concert tour. The album itself was not that impressive, though, and critical appraisal of their stage show was less than ecstatic. In 1972, Tom and Mimi decided to go separate ways as performers. But the partnership did seem to give Mimi more confidence in her own ability, a way station that allowed her to become psychologically aware that she could make her own way in music without needing another person as a crutch. For the

next few years she toured extensively as a solo artist with many major folk performers, including Hoyt Axton, Phil Ochs, Gordon Lightfoot, Arlo Guthrie, Kenny Rankin, Mose Allison, and Leo Kottke. When not working in larger venues with such artists, she often headlined her own set at smaller folk clubs and on college campuses.

In 1973, she began to work on a solo album for A&M. When the Arab oil crisis caused temporary panic in the record field, Mimi left A&M, feeling that they were using the crisis as an excuse to hold back on her recordings. Returning to the San Francisco area, for a time she channeled her efforts into beginning a new organization called Bread & Roses, a nonprofit operation to provide free entertainment to people in hospitals, prisons, and convalescent homes in Marin County. After spending much of her time for several years to set up the program, she gradually turned more attention to her music.

By the late 1970s, she resumed a relatively heavy concert schedule. Some of her appearances were with the Gordon Lightfoot concert series. In her headline concerts at colleges, folk clubs, and folk festivals, she often was accompanied by Banana, a multitalented musician who earlier had been a charter member of the Youngbloods folk-rock group. She continued to write new songs, some of which were included in late 1970s albums by her sister and by Judy Collins. At the start of the 1980s, she was preparing material for a new solo LP.

FELICIANO, JOSÉ: *Singer, guitarist, banjoist, organist, mandolinist, harmonica player, pianist, harpsichordist, bongo and timbales player. Born Lares, Puerto Rico, September 10, 1945.*

The dark glasses José Feliciano always wears symbolize his blindness, but his musical achievements demonstrate how much better he can "see" than many people blessed with perfect sight. (Actually, though legally blind, he can see slightly. As he told an interviewer in 1980, "Apart from when I go to bed, I never take [the dark glasses] off because I can see better with them on.") As an interpreter of Latin songs for the Spanish-speaking people of the Americas and of music in many languages for English-speaking U.S. audiences, he established a reputation as one of the most talented folk and pop performers of the 1960s and 1970s.

Recalling his early years, he stated, "I am proud of where I come from. I derive a lot from my origins. I was born . . . in Lares, Puerto Rico. It's about three hours away from San Juan. When I was four years old, my family—my father, my mother and the nine surviving boys out of the eleven my mother gave birth to—came to New York."

By the time this move took place, little José already had shown some musical promise. He recalls his earliest musical experience at three, when he accompanied an uncle by tapping on a tin soda-biscuit can. Later, in the mainland United States, he started teaching himself the accordion but soon switched to guitar. As he grew up he added many other instruments to his repertoire. Some of those talents, he noted, surfaced while he attended various schools for the blind, where several music teachers gave him some pointers in classical and other musical genres.

His father, a shipping clerk, encouraged José's interest in music but tried to make his son concentrate on Spanish material. José made his first public appearance at El Teatro Puerto Rico in Spanish Harlem when he was nine. While he performed, he remembered, "My father had to pick me up because it was so crowded no one could see me, and the audience stood up and screamed with joy." He continued to perform at local events for no pay, often entering and winning talent shows, until he was thirteen, when he became a full-fledged professional.

In the early 1960s, he began to gain a following among folk music fans in New York with his renditions of both Spanish and American folk songs. In 1963, he was appearing at Gerde's Folk City in Greenwich Village when an RCA executive came to watch the show and was greatly impressed by the seventeen-year-old's poise and impact. José was signed by RCA, but for his first five years on the label, most of his recordings were in Spanish for release to the Latin American market.

Meanwhile José added to his laurels with a show-stopping performance at the Newport Folk Festival in Rhode Island in the summer of 1964. During the mid-1960s, he toured all over the world, performing in England, the Continent, and throughout Central and South America. He established himself as a favorite with the Latin nations, underlined by the tumultuous welcome given him at major events like the Mar Del Plata Festival in Buenos Aires, Argentina. He also was the star of his own syndicated Spanish language TV program during those years, which was top rated all over Latin America.

He already was one of the most popular recording artists south of the border when he began to make inroads in the U.S. record market. The first breakthrough came in 1968 with the hit LP *Feliciano* and his top-selling single of the Doors' rock hit, "Light My Fire." At the time he had two hit singles and three LPs on RCA's International label on Latin American hit charts. The singles were "La Copa Rota" and "Amor Gitana" and the LPs *Sombras . . . Una Voz, Una Guitarra* (recorded in Argentina); *Mas Exitos, de José Feliciano* (recorded in Argentina and Mexico); and *La Voz y la Guitarra de José Feliciano* (recorded in Venezuela and Argentina).

By the end of 1968, he was recognized as a first-magnitude star by almost every segment of the U.S. population. Helping to bring that about were several more hit records and a wide range of personal appearances. He was featured on TV and radio talk shows and on such programs as ABC-TV's *Close-Up* and on the first Bing Crosby TV special of the 1968–69 season. He also signed to sing the title song for Gregory Peck's film *McKenna's Gold* and won a standing ovation from the audience that attended his Las Vegas debut shows in August 1968. The reception he received brought a return engagement there in October. (Just before the latter series, he was the center of controversy for a time because of his "Spanish soul" rendition of "The Star Spangled Banner" before the fifth game of the baseball World Series in Detroit.)

Other highlights of that eventful year included a rousing reception from over 10,000 people of Puerto Rican descent at a festival in New York during the summer and standing-room-only concerts late in the year in Madison, Wisconsin; Cleveland, Ohio; Chicago, Illinois; and Phoenix, Arizona.

It was more of the same in 1969, and his popularity carried over strongly in the 1970s. He starred on almost every major TV show on American networks and was often featured on the most popular programs elsewhere in the world. During the late 1960s and early 1970s, he was the star of several of his own TV specials on U.S. networks. During the 1970s, he headlined concerts in prestigious places all over the world, including a number of appearances at venues like the Greek Theater in Los Angeles, London Palladium, and Paris Olympia. He also was a soloist on several occasions with major symphony orchestras.

He placed several more singles besides "Light My Fire" on upper-chart levels in the late 1960s, such as "Hitchcock Railway" and "Hi Heel Sneakers." However, in the 1970s, his main successes were as an album artist. Among his charted LPs were *Souled Out* and *Feliciano/10 to 23* in 1969 and *Alive-Alive-O,* issued the end of 1969 and a top-40 entrant in January 1970. During the summer of 1970, his album *Fireworks* appeared on the charts, featuring the medley "Susie Q" and "Destiny," on the singles charts for a few weeks in July. Late in 1970, his Christmas album *Feliz Navidad* came out, the title song receiving much airplay. From then on, it was a standard number for the Christmas season. In the summer of 1971, he had a chart hit LP, *Encore,* and at year end had a highly ranked single, "That the Spirit Needs." The LP of that title was on the charts from late 1971 to early 1972. In the spring of 1973, his album *Compartments* was on the hit lists for several weeks.

He had several more LPs on the charts in the mid-1970s, but things slowed down with record buyers and his association

with RCA came to an end. In the late 1970s, he did not record for any major label. At the end of the 1970s, his albums still in RCA's active catalogue included *And the Feeling's Good, Compartments, For My Love . . . Mother Music, Encore! José Feliciano's Finest Performances, Feliciano!, Fireworks, José Feliciano, Just Wanna Rock 'n' Roll, Feliciano/ 10 to 23.* He also had an LP on Private Stock Records, *Sweet Soul Music.* However, his achievements still were noteworthy. As of the start of the 1980s, he had attained worldwide record sales of $68 million and earned thirty-two gold records.

He continued to be a popular attraction both as a concert artist and TV guest into the 1980s and to find time, as he had in the past, for an average of twenty to thirty charity concerts a year for organizations serving the blind.

FELTS, NARVEL: *Singer, guitarist, songwriter. Born near Bernie, Missouri, November 11, 1938.*

The story of Narvel Felts essentially is that of country music in the post-World War II decades. A farm boy, bred to the country tradition, he was briefly captured by the rock revolution in the mid-1950s, then returned to the fold to help spark a country-music rebirth in the 1960s and 1970s.

Born and raised on a Missouri farm, he "never lived in a town until I got married and had a home of my own." (Home base for Narvel, in the 1970s, was hardly in a metropolis—he and his wife, Loretta, and their two children lived in Malden, Missouri.) In his early years, the first artist who made an impression on Narvel was Ernest Tubb. Recalling his youthful fondness for Tubb's "Walking the Floor Over You," he said, "I used to wonder what his girl friend was doing on the floor and why the Texas Troubadour was walking over her."

As a boy, Narvel had a good voice, but he was shy and practiced singing *Grand Ole Opry*-type songs when he could get off by himself. He wanted to have his own guitar, so at fourteen he picked cotton to earn enough to buy a $14.98 instrument from the Sears' mail-order catalog, a familiar step in many a country musician's biography. In 1956, he had developed enough self-confidence to compete in a high school talent show, but by then rock had become a musical force and the song he sang was Carl Perkins' "Blue Suede Shoes." He won the contest, which led to a spot on the Saturday morning program on radio station KDEX in Bernie. He soon became a regular member of the backing band for singer Jerry Mercer, playing bass guitar. When Mercer left, Narvel took over as band leader.

Felts began to expand his activities in the music field. He made his way to Memphis, where he did some session work at Sun Records. Among other aspiring young rockabilly artists at the time were Charlie Rich and a performer named Harold Jenkins, who soon after gained a national reputation as a rock recording star under the name Conway Twitty. Felts meanwhile picked up work in clubs and shows in the South and Midwest for a while as a rock singer, then as a member of the country circuit.

He did some recordings for Sun, then gained a contract from Mercury that was not particularly productive. Later on in the 1960s, he signed with a small company, Pink Records, and finally began to have a certain amount of success, mainly as a regional artist but occasionally with national chart songs such as "Honey Love" and "3000 Miles." Though he sang a variety of material from blues to country and country-rock, most of his recording efforts in the 1960s were aimed more at the pop audience than country, with only desultory success.

By the time he came to Nashville in 1970, under contract to Hi Records, he had become increasingly determined to concentrate on the country field. It took a while for things to come together properly, but finally in 1972 he and an old music industry friend, Johnny Morris, worked out a management agreement and Morris, in turn, helped set up an independent label called Cinnamon. Within a year's time Narvel was on the way from second-level performer to national recognition. The first breakthrough was the top-5 single "Drift Away" in early 1973. Later in the year he made the top 20 with "All in the Name of Love." In 1974, he scored still another top-10 singles hit on Cinnamon, "When Your Good Love Was Mine." In addition to those, he had several other releases that showed up on lower-chart levels.

Considering the unusual quality of Felts' voice, it was surprising it had taken him a decade and a half to finally establish himself. One reviewer remarked, "The voice that one hears when Narvel opens up is very much like a roller coaster, but a smooth one. It gradually goes soaring up the scale, then swoops down low, all with an easy, understated grace. After he hits a very high note, he usually kicks it even higher. If Narvel had been as agile as his voice, he would have been a world-class gymnast."

Felt's achievements on Cinnamon naturally brought intense interest from major record companies. In 1975, this resulted in his signing with ABC Records. With the release of his debut recordings on the label, it was obviously a good move for both parties. Throughout the mid- and late-1970s, Felts' name was rarely absent from either singles or album charts in the country field and some of his releases also crossed over to the national pop charts as well. Among his charted singles in the late 1970s were "I Don't Hurt Anymore" in 1977, "One Run for the Roses" in 1978, and "Everlasting Love" in early 1979. Soon after ABC was absorbed by MCA Records, he had the single "Moment by Moment" on the hit lists in the summer of 1979. However, he didn't remain on the MCA roster into the 1980s. As of late 1981, MCA maintained five of his previous ABC albums in its active catalogue: *The Touch of Felts, Narvel, Inside Love, One Run for the Roses,* and *Greatest Hits, Volume 1.*

FENDER, FREDDY: *Singer, guitarist. Born San Benito, Texas, June 4, 1937.*

"My real name is Baldemar G. Huerta. I was born in the south Texas valley border town of San Benito. I'm a Mexican-American, better yet, a Tex–Mex. I just picked my stage name, Freddy Fender, in the late fifties as a name that would help my music sell better with 'gringos.' Now I like the name.

"Music was part of me, even in my early childhood. I can still remember sitting on the street corner facing Pancho Dalvin's grocery store, plunking at my three-string guitar. It didn't have a back on it, but it sure sounded pretty good to me. Music kept a lot us happy, even when it was hard for our mama to put beans on the table. We began migrating up north as farm workers when I was about ten. We worked beets in Michigan, pickles in Ohio, baled hay and picked tomatoes in Indiana. When that was over came cotton picking time in Arkansas. All we really had to look forward to was making enough money to have a good Christmas in the 'valley,' where somehow I'd always manage to get my mother to buy me a guitar if the old one was worn out.

"When I was sixteen, I dropped out of high school and joined the Marines for three years. I got to see California, Japan, and Okinawa; but mainly I got my point of view from the time I spent in the brig. It seemed that I just couldn't adjust myself to such a disciplined way of life. I always liked to play the guitar in the barracks and to drink, so much so that sometimes I forgot where or who I was."

Thus the early saga of Freddy Fender in his own words. He wasn't much different from many other Chicano youngsters growing up in the difficult environment of the Anglo-Saxon–dominated United States. But there was opportunity for those with unusual talents. In Freddy's case, it took almost twenty years before he achieved stardom.

He had chosen music for a career when he returned home from the service in the 1950s. He played local beer joints and dances and began making a name for himself in the Mexican-American community with a series of all-Spanish discs that were top sellers in Texas and nearby Mexican regions. It was obvious to him, though, that the road to major success lay elsewhere, and he began to cut some Tex–Mex rockabilly songs. In 1959, this paid off with two songs, "Holy One" and "Wasted Days

and Wasted Nights," which found an audience far beyond Texas borders and suggested that Freddy might be on the path to national acclaim. In 1960, he had another hit, "Crazy, Crazy Baby," but his hopes turned to ashes on May 13, 1960.

"I was busted for grass in Baton Rouge, Louisiana. I'm not bitter, but if friends ask, I still say that the three years I had to spend in Angola State Prison were a long time for a little mistake." He was released in July 1963 but found it wasn't possible to pick up where he'd left off. He got gigs, sang for most of the 1960s (to 1968) at Papa Joe's on Bourbon Street, in New Orleans, but he couldn't get his recording career back in gear. "I played music there with such cats as Joe Berry, Joey Long, Skip Easterling, and Aaron Neville."

In 1969, he went home to the San Benito Valley feeling it might be time to look elsewhere for his main vocation. He got a job as a mechanic "and played music on weekends, getting $1.60 an hour and $28 a night picking." He picked up his education again, taking the examination for a high school diploma, then taking college courses as a sociology major for two years.

In 1974, some musician friends suggested he contact producer Huey Meaux, who had a label in Houston called Crazy Cajun. His audition for Huey clicked and they cut a country song called "Before the Next Teardrop Falls." It became a local hit, and Dot Records, a subsidiary of ABC Records, bought national rights. The song became a gold-record single, crossing over from country to pop charts in 1975, and Freddy's debut album of the same title did likewise. Before the year was over, Freddy had two more chart hits, the single "Secret Love" (a country remake of an old Doris Day vehicle) and his second album, *Are You Ready for Freddy*.

After all those years of obscurity, Fender was a national celebrity, starring on TV variety shows and singing one of the songs on the *Grand Ole Opry* stage during the Country Music Association awards telecast. In early 1976, at the Grammy Awards, Freddy received a nomination for Best Country Vocal Performance, Male, and

"Before the Next Teardrop Falls" (written by Vivian Keith and Ben Peters) was nominated for Best Country Song.

Freddy has remained a featured country artist since then, though without the equivalent of the blockbuster year he had in 1975. His country following remained strong, as demonstrated by his appearance on hit charts regularly, including such top-10 singles as "You'll Lose a Good Thing" and "Living It Down" in 1976; "If You Don't Love Me (Why Don't You Leave Me Alone)" and "The Roses Came/Sugar Coated Love" in 1977 and "I'm Leaving It All Up to You" in 1978. Freddy's albums on ABC were *Freddy Fender, Before the Next Teardrop Falls, Are You Ready for Freddy, Rock 'n' Country, Since I Met You Baby, If You're Ever in Texas, Your Cheatin' Heart, If You Don't Love Me, The Best of Freddy Fender, Swamp-Gold,* and *Tex-Mex.*

In 1979, Freddy began recording for Huey Meaux's new record label, Starflite, distributed by Epic Records. His debut LP on Starflite, *Texas Balladeer,* was issued in June 1979. During 1980, he had such Starflite singles as "My Special Prayer" and "Please Talk to My Heart" on country hit lists.

Starting in the late 1970s, he also became interested in acting and screenwriting. His acting credits during those years included playing the role of General Pancho Villa in *She Came to the Valley* and a part in a show titled *Tijuana Donkey.*

Summing up the way things turned out overall, he said, "I always said the Old Man upstairs was shooting craps for me. Well, he finally rolled a seven."

FLATT, LESTER RAYMOND: *Singer, guitarist, songwriter, band leader (Foggy Mountain Boys, Nashville Grass). Born Overton County, Tennessee, June 28, 1914; died Nashville, Tennessee, May 11, 1979.*

The split of the long-time duo of Flatt & Scruggs into two separate units in the 1970s didn't bring either man the level of success achieved during their long association. However, both remained major figures in the country-music field, and Flatt continued to receive a warm welcome

at concerts and festivals throughout the United States up to his death in 1979.

Tennessee remained his home for his entire life. He started learning the guitar as a boy, following the traditional "old-timey" style then popular in country music. For a long time, however, music was a sideline and Lester earned a livelihood working in textile mills. He steadily improved his guitar skills as the 1930s went by, performing with local groups when the opportunity arose.

Encouraged by friends to widen his horizons, he turned professional in 1939 and soon after made his radio debut on station WDBJ in Roanoke, West Virginia. In the early 1940s, he was increasingly interested in bluegrass-style music, working with many other young musicians who favored that style, including Mac Wiseman. In 1944, he was added to the roster of the most famous bluegrass group in the nation, Bill Monroe's Blue Grass Boys. He remained an important part of that band through the mid-1940s, touring all over the United States and appearing regularly on the *Grand Ole Opry.* In 1945, another talented instrumentalist joined Monroe, a super banjo player named Earl Scruggs. The stage was set for the emergence of the most famous bluegrass act since the appearance of Monroe's band, a group that helped expand bluegrass from an essentially regional styling to a nationally recognized art form.

Flatt & Scruggs decided to join forces in 1948. In a short time they had a featured segment on Mac Wiseman's *Farm and Fun Time* show on station WCYB, Bristol, Virginia. Their popularity rose rapidly and they went on to star in bigger and bigger locales. They also signed their first recording contract with Mercury Records before the 1940s were over. Though they only stayed with Mercury for a few years, one of the songs they recorded was Earl's "Foggy Mountain Breakdown," one of their trademark hits, which was adopted for the name of their band, the Foggy Mountain Boys. In 1951, they switched from Mercury to Columbia, an association that provided big rewards both to the label and the group, even after the team disbanded in 1969.

During the more than twenty-year lifetime of the team of Flatt & Scruggs, the duo became what amounted to ambassadors of country music to the U.S. mass audience and to the world. Many of the dozens of albums and singles released by Columbia rose to upper levels of both country and pop charts. Among their massive hits were the theme song for *The Beverly Hillbillies,* "The Ballad of Jed Clampett," as well as the themes for *Petticoat Junction* and for the film *Bonnie and Clyde.* In 1953, they became regular members of the *Grand Ole Opry* and still were featured artists on the show when they came to the parting of the ways. (For more details, see Flatt & Scruggs entry.)

During their long association, both contributed not only important compositions and classic recordings but also innovations in bluegrass style. In Flatt's case, he popularized a guitar approach called the "Flatt Lick." As Lee Rector described it in *Music City News* (October 1973), "It consists of a run on the guitar that comes at the end of most every verse and chorus or however else it can be slipped in and can be adapted to almost every bluegrass song: boom, diddle, dum-di-dum-doom."

The breakup of Flatt & Scruggs was attributed to differences about future musical direction. Scruggs, influenced by his sons, preferred moving toward a blend of country and rock, while Flatt preferred staying with more traditional stylings. The announcement of the separation was made in early 1969, and that March, Flatt announced he would continue to appear at the head of the Foggy Mountain Boys on the *Martha White* TV show. (Martha White Flour was a long-time sponsor of Flatt & Scruggs.) However, objections from Scruggs at the use of that band name led to Flatt's adopting a new name, the Nashville Grass.

For the next decade, Flatt and his group had a regular segment on the *Grand Ole Opry,* which they opened and closed with the "Martha White Theme Song." Ensconced in his large tour bus, Flatt took his band all across the United States to solo concerts and as part of country and bluegrass festivals, typically covering 10,000 miles a month to keep engagements, some booked as much as a year in advance. The program usually included many of the songs made famous by Flatt & Scruggs.

The band lineup in 1973–74 included Charlie Nixon on dobro, Marty Stewart (then only fourteen) on mandolin and flattop guitar, Johnny Johnson (previously with Ernest Tubb) on bass, Haskell McCormick on five-string bano, and Paul Warren on fiddle. Warren's association with Flatt went back to the Foggy Mountain Boys band.

Flatt recorded steadily from 1969 to the late 1970s, initially on RCA and later for other labels. Many of his recordings in the early and mid-1970s were joint efforts with his old friend Mac Wiseman, with whom he also appeared on the *Opry* and in many concerts throughout the United States. His RCA LPs included *On Victor* (issued June 1971), *Lester 'n' Mac* (8/71), *Kentucky Ridgerunner* (3/72), and, again with Wiseman, *On the South Bound* (8/72).

By the mid-1970s, Flatt could look with joy at a steady revival of interest in bluegrass music among young music fans, which he helped spark with an increasing number of concerts on college campuses. Throughout the 1970s, roughly two thirds of all his in-person appearances were on college campuses.

Lester remained in harness almost up to his last days. His health began to fail, though, when he underwent successful open heart surgery in 1975, then had to return to the hospital the next year for removal of his gallbladder. Stubbornly refusing to give up, he was back heading his band soon after. In November 1977, he again was sidelined by a brain hemorrhage, but rebounded once again to charm *Opry* fans in March 1979. It was a short-lived respite. On April 23 he fell ill once more and entered Baptist Hospital in Nashville, finally dying on Friday, May 11.

Commenting on Flatt's career afterward, Earl Scruggs told an Associated Press reporter, "His record speaks for itself as far as his playing and singing. He's going to be missed for a long time by a lot of people. He just had a talent that people enjoyed. He was blessed with a good following. We had a lot of good memories together."

The previous February, Flatt indicated he had had a fulfilling career. "We should be proud of being able to accomplish what we set out to do. We wanted to be in a field to ourself. We had a sound all our own. There always will be somebody to carry [bluegrass] on. It's been good for us since it started. They've quit playing it on radio and maybe this is good for us. This way, the festivals draw people to hear it." Bluegrass, he was sure, would never die.

FLYING BURRITO BROTHERS: *Vocal and instrumental group. Personnel as of 1968: Gram Parsons, born Winterhaven, Florida, November 5, 1946, died Joshua Tree, California, September 1973; Chris Hillman, born Los Angeles, California, December 4, 1942; Sneeky Pete Kleinow*, born South Bend, Indiana, circa 1935; Chris Ethridge; Popeye Phillips. Lineup as of late 1969: Parsons, Hillman, Kleinow; Bernie Leadon, born Minneapolis, Minnesota, July 19, circa 1947; Michael Clarke, born New York, New York, June 3, 1944. Sneeky Pete replaced by Al Perkins, 1971; Parsons by Rick Roberts, 1971. Other members during 1971–72 included Byron Berline, Kenny Wertz, and Roger Bush.*

In the late 1960s, the idea of blending country with rock won many converts among veteran performers of the decade. However, the idea, which flowered in the mid-1970s with such bands as Asleep at the Wheel, Marshall Tucker Band, and the like, was ahead of its time in the 1960s. Bands that blazed the trail, such as Poco and the Flying Burrito Brothers, found little outlet for their recordings on major radio stations and, while they found an audience of sorts, never gained enough exposure to succeed. After the fact, many of the early recordings of groups like the Burritos have gained the reputaion of classics.

The Burritos evolved in California with a strong flavor of the folk-rock pioneers. Two of the original Burritos in late 1967 had been Byrds members: songwriter/guitarist/bass player Chris Hillman and vocalist/songwriter/keyboard player/guitarist Gram Parsons influenced the group's move toward country-rock recordings. Joining them initially were Chris Ethridge (vocals, bass, piano, songwriter), Sneeky Peter Kleinow* (pedal steel guitar), and Popeye Phillips (drums). The five members constituted the lineup on such early records as "Hot Burrito #1" and "Hot Burrito #2," both included on the band's debut album on A&M Records, *The Gilded Palace of Sin.* Two of the LP tracks, "Sin City" and "My Uncle," were excellent examples of songs that, as one critic noted, "bridged the gap between country music and contemporary rock." Also notable from that period were such songs as "Wheels," "Christine's Song," and "Do Right Woman."

Almost from the start, the Burritos personnel kept shifting. A particular problem for a while was drums, when Phillips' spot was taken briefly by such others as Jon Corneal, Sam Goldstein, and Eddie Hoh. The situation was resolved to everyone's satisfaction in 1969 when original Byrds' drummer Michael Clarke, who had worked with a band called Dillard and Clark after leaving the Byrds, agreed to join up. Clarke remained as drummer until the group finally broke up in 1972. Another change in 1969 was the departure of Ethridge, whose place was taken by Bernie Leadon, who had worked with Clarke in Dillard and Clark and then was a backing musician for Linda Ronstadt. Leadon, of course, later was a founding member of the Eagles.

Despite lack of airplay and major concert exposure, the roster of Parsons, Hillman, Leadon, Kleinow, and Clarke did seem to make some progress with the music public during late 1969 and into 1970. The group completed a second LP, *Burrito Deluxe,* and added such songs as "God's Own Singer," "If You Gotta Go" (a Dylan song), "High Fashion Queen," "The Train Song," Merle Haggard's "Sing Me Back Home," John Loudermilk's "Break My Mind," and "Close Up the Honky Tonks." Things seemed to be picking up a little in

---

* *Kleinow's nickname has variously been spelled Sneeky and Sneaky.*

1970, when unfortunately Parsons, whose charismatic vocals formed a large part of the appeal at the time, was sidelined by injuries from a motorcycle accident.

The layoff seemed to dampen Parsons' ardor about the band. He returned for a while, then left for good in 1971. His place was taken by Rick Roberts, who had been added to the group in the summer of 1970 after Parsons' accident. Roberts also inherited Parsons' songwriting mantle, providing a number of originals featured by that group in its final phases, such as "Did You See" and several tracks on the band's third album, *The Flying Burrito Brothers*. That album was supposed to include one of the relatively rare compositions by Kleinow, a showcase for his pedal steel talents called "Beat the Heat," but the song was omitted in the final mix. During 1971 and 1972, the band appeared in a series of concerts all over the United States, mostly on college campuses but with some engagements at places like Bill Graham's Fillmore theaters in New York and San Francisco and the Aquarius in Hollywood.

Before 1971 was out, the Burritos had a new pedal steel player, Al Perkins, who took over the seat from Sneeky Pete. Things were becoming increasingly desperate for the band as 1972 began. The group was not without some chart success, but the records that made it never went far enough up the ladder to make the band a household name. Bookings were slim and spirits tended to go down. However, the group reorganized with Perkins handling pedal steel and guitar. (Perkins, a fine musician who could play a number of different instruments, came to the Burritos from a group called Shiloh.) A trio of bluegrass artists from a band called Country Gazette were added: Kenny Wertz (vocals, guitar), Byron Berline (vocals, fiddle), and Roger Bush.

The 1972 edition of the Burritos naturally offered a blend of bluegrass, country, and rock that provided some new luster to its reputation. But that still wasn't enough to save the situation. In mid-1972, the group gave up the ghost. Ironically, there were already strong indications that the potential audience for the Burritos kind of music was increasing. The band's final album, *Last of the Red Hot Burritos*, had made inroads on the national charts.

The band's growing stature after the fact was demonstrated anew in 1974 when A&M issued a two-record set of their work titled *Close Up the Honky Tonks*. Besides containing tracks of many of the band's best-known previous recordings, the album presented many previously unreleased songs (but songs that the band played in live concerts), which, besides the title song, included "Beat the Heat," "Did You See," "Break My Mind," and Burritos versions of the Beatles' "Roll Over Beethoven," the Everlys' "Wake Up Little Susie," the Bee Gees' "To Love Somebody," and Gene Clark's "Here Tonight." That album set sold considerably better than some of the releases made when the band had been functioning.

Perhaps encouraged by that, some of the members of the earlier group brought it back to life in the mid-1970s. One such incarnation included original members Kleinow and Ethridge, ex-Byrd Gene Parsons, and newcomer (to the Burritos) vocalist/songwriter Gib Gilbeau. A contract with Columbia Records led to some new LPs: *Flying Again* and *Airborne* (the latter with another ex-Byrd, Skip Battyn, among the band members). The new albums lacked the originality and spark of earlier releases, but the band did find it still had fans out there during concert tours in the late 1970s. Gilbeau noted, "We found that we were real popular overseas, particularly in Europe and Japan."

Still, the rewards were too meager to justify keeping the band together. Once more, the Burritos were saved in the nick of time. Recalled Gilbeau, "We were about to give up the Flying Burrito Brothers as a group when I met John Beland [vocals, guitar, songwriter] at a Christmas party [in 1979]. We started talking about the group and how I really didn't want to see it fold. Somehow I believed that if it had taken a broader musical direction, or still could, we could keep it alive. John and I decided to get together and do some writing, and when we had put some tunes together, we presented them to the other members.

They were agreeable to give our new direction a shot and a demo ensued which got us the deal with Epic/Curb Records."

The core of the 1980s incarnation was Gilbeau, Beland, and the sole remaining original Burrito, Kleinow. Under the new name of the Burrito Brothers, the band had the debut Epic/Curb LP *Hearts on the Line* in release in January 1981. It soon spawned several singles (of songs written by Gilbeau and Beland) that made the country charts: "She's a Friend of a Friend" in early 1981 and "She Belongs to Everyone but Me" in the fall.

FOGELBERG, DAN: *Singer, pianist, guitarist, songwriter. Born Peoria, Illinois, circa 1951.*

Dan Fogelberg sometimes sounded somewhat like the Eagles in his mid-1970s recordings. The comparison is apt since both he and they were part of the Southern California-based folk and country-rock movement of that decade and also were represented by the dynamic Irv Azoff. But the point is that Fogelberg alone could sound like the entire Eagles group because he was adept at so many instruments and modern recording methods could put separate tracks of his work together to form what amounted to a one-man band.

Music was a long suit in Dan's family, so it's not surprising he finally chose it for a career. His father was a band leader and his mother a singer in his home town of Peoria. They saw to it that he took piano lessons as a child, and his grandfather, after whom Dan is named, gave him an acoustic slide guitar. He played in a variety of bands in elementary and high school and, at fourteen, started writing original material. At the same time, he also developed an interest in painting that eventually became his major when he enrolled in the University of Illinois in the late 1960s. He left school after two years, however, because "I saw it was going to be tough to make a living out of painting."

He worked in various groups until he became friends with an eager young entrepreneur named Irv Azoff. They headed to California, where Azoff got his charge a contract with Columbia Records. Dan's debut album, *Home Free*, was recorded in

Nashville, where Dan had settled on a farm in an outlying area. While waiting for his recording career to take off, he earned a good living as a session musician in Nashville studios, backing such artists as Randy Newman, Eric Andersen, Buffy St. Marie, Roger McGuinn, Michael Stanley, Joe Walsh, and Jackson Browne.

Walsh returned the favor soon after by producing Dan's second album, recorded mainly in Los Angeles. Session musicians on the effort included Glenn Frey, Don Henley, and Randy Meisner of the Eagles, Graham Nash, Kenny Passarelli (later lead guitarist for Hall and Oates), and many others. Called *Souvenirs*, the album established Fogelberg as an important addition to the folk/country-rock scene after its release on Epic/Full Moon label in October 1974. The album spawned one of Dan's relatively rare singles hits, "Part of the Plan."

Fogelberg made a point of expressing his dissatisfaction with the industry's stress on singles. He told Dennis Hunt of the *Los Angeles Times* (March 7, 1978), "Record companies still tell you that you can't make it if you don't have a hit single, but me and a few others are proving them wrong. I have an FM-based audience and could care less about AM radio. I'll take an AM hit if it comes along, of course, but I'm certainly not going to go after one."

By the time that discussion took place, Fogelberg had two gold records, one for *Souvenirs* and the second for *Captured Angel*, issued by Full Moon/Epic in October 1975. The latter album presented an even more relaxed tone and a more poetic interest in nature that reflected Dan's move from Tennessee to a house in the Rocky Mountains near Denver. Fogelberg not only played most of the instrumental tracks on *Captured Angel*, but provided backing vocals and handled the production chores himself.

In line with his attitude about setting his own goals and timetables, Dan took a while before finishing his fourth LP, *Nether Lands*. The album's songs tended to be more introspective than much of his earlier work and dealt in part with his view on the rites of passage from adolescence to adulthood. The album, released in the spring of 1977, moved onto the charts soon after and remained on them throughout the summer. By late summer, in the steady fashion typical of audience response to his work, it passed gold-record levels and later went on to be certified platinum by the Recording Industry Association of America.

In 1978, Dan teamed up with flutist Tim Weisberg for a new series of recordings. As Fogelberg noted in the liner notes, "This album constitutes a collaboration, experimental in nature, between Tim and myself. It is an attempt for both of us to move outside our own recognizable boundaries and try new directions—new forms of music which we rarely get to explore on our own. It is a chance to stretch, an opportunity to grow, and a hell of a lot of fun."

The album didn't fully achieve all of those goals, but it proved a finely crafted, very listenable blend of elements of jazz, folk, and even hints of classical music. The general public expressed approval of the effort by pushing *Twin Sons of Different Mothers* into upper-chart levels a short time after its release in August 1978. By the end of the decade, the LP won a platinum record award from the R.I.A.A. His next solo album, *Phoenix*, was released on Full Moon/Epic in November 1979 and by early 1980 was in the top-5 spot on national charts. (It too passed platinum levels in the early 1980s.) At the same time, the single "Longer" from the LP (written by Dan with Robert Putnam and Marty Lewis) also was a top-5 success. His next album, *The Innocent Age*, came out in August 1981 and went platinum by the fall.

FOLEY, CLYDE JULIAN "RED": *Singer, guitarist, harmonica player, songwriter, variety show host. Born Blue Lick, Kentucky, June 17, 1910; died Fort Wayne, Indiana, September 19, 1968.*

The words on the bronze plaque in the Hall of Fame in Nashville sum up Red Foley's career best: "One of the most versatile and moving performers of all time. He could make you pop your fingers to "Chattanooga Shoeshine Boy" . . . choke back a tear with "Old Shep" . . . or look to your God with "Peace in the Valley." A giant influence during the formative years of contemporary country music and today a timeless legend."

Indeed, Red Foley left a generous legacy to country-music enthusiasts in the form of the many recordings that are still highly regarded years after his death and still readily adapted by contemporary performers. His achievements as performer and writer bulk large in country music annals; at the time of his election to the Hall of Fame, for instance, he ranked fifth on the all-time list of country recording artists with thirty-one top-10 singles, including five that reached the number-one position.

As a boy in Blue Lick, Kentucky, Foley liked to go off by himself to his favorite blackberry patch and play the old battered guitar that his father bought him when he was six. Later, when his family moved to Berea, his father, who ran the general store, stocked harmonicas, which fascinated young Clyde. All of them were broken in before they were sold.

In high school, Foley excelled in track and basketball, winning several trophies and ribbons, but he felt a singing career was more promising than one in sports. His mother hired a vocal coach, which proved wearing for the boy; he decided to go along singing his own way.

Under the circumstances, his family was surprised when he won a local Atwater-Kent singing contest and was invited to Louisville to compete for state honors. When the seventeen-year-old came out on the "big city" stage to sing the hymn "Hold Thou My Hand, Dear Lord," he developed a case of the butterflies and had to start the song over three times, before he finally made it through. His excellent final treatment and unconscious showmanship so charmed the judges and audience that he won first prize.

In 1932, Foley entered Georgetown College, in Georgetown, Kentucky, where he continued to perform when he got the chance. During his first semester, a talent scout for WLS in Chicago spotted him and signed him for the fledgling *National Barn Dance* program.

In Chicago, Foley became enthralled by the blues and folk music often played on the radio. The thirties was a time when many unknown, talented black artists were flocking to the city and playing exciting new music in the streets and small clubs. Flat-top guitars played Hawaiian style with the neck of a broken bottle, washtub steel bands, the soul sounds of a population on the move—all of these sounds and sensations were absorbed by young Foley. Many of his major successes of future years were to reflect a blending of roots blues and the country and gospel heritage of his childhood.

Red's reputation in the country field developed rapidly in the mid-1930s, as did his ambitions to do bigger and better things in the genre. In 1937, he took a giant step forward when he originated the Renfro Valley radio show with John Lair. Two years later, he was the first country artist to have a network radio show, *Avalon Time*, which costarred comic Red Skelton. Strings of one-nighters, fair dates, theater engagements, and other personal appearances put Foley into gear for later recording success with Decca Records, which eventually signed him to a lifetime contract.

During the 1940s, such singles as "Foggy River" and "Old Shep" helped establish Red as one of the top country names. In 1948, he added the top-10 single "Tennessee Saturday Night" and finished the decade with a banner year in 1949, turning out such top-10 bestsellers as "Blues in My Heart" (co-written by Foley and Carson), "Candy Kisses," "Sunday Down in Tennessee," "Tennessee Border," and "Tennessee Polka." He then roared into the 1950s by dominating the country charts the first year of the new decade with no less than eight top-10 hits, including two number-one releases, "Birmingham Bounce" and "Chattanooga Shoe Shine Boy." The latter, one of his trademark songs thereafter, was recorded in Nashville in Owen Bradley's studios—a converted garage—and contributed to Red's total of 24 million records sold by the end of the 1960s. His other 1950 hit singles were "Choc'late Ice Cream Cone," "Cincinnati

Dancing Pig," "Just a Closer Walk with Thee," "M-I-S-S-I-S-S-I-P-P-I," "Our Lady of Fatima," and his composition "Steal Away."

The pace slowed a bit after that, but it was a rare period through the mid-1950s when a Foley release wasn't on hit lists. His 1951 credits include the top-10 singles "Alabama Jubilee," "Hot Rod Race," and "Peace in the Valley." In 1952, he had the number-one hit "Midnight" and a top-10 single, "Too Old to Cut the Mustard," the latter with *Grand Ole Opry* sidekick Ernest Tubb. (Red became a regular on the *Opry* in the 1940s.) In 1953, his top-10 successes were "Don't Let the Stars Get in Your Eyes," "Hot Toddy," "No Help Wanted No. 2," and "Shake a Hand." In the mid-1950s, Red teamed with Kitty Wells as a featured duo, resulting in the 1954 top-10 single "One by One." In 1955, Red and Kitty scored with "As Long as I Live" and Red had solo hits with "Hearts of Stone" and "Satisfied Mind." In 1956, he and Kitty had the top-10 hit "You and Me." In the late 1950s, as rock music affected the country field and new performers came to the fore (some given a boost by Red himself on his country radio and TV programs), Red's string of chartbusters came to an end. Some of his releases still showed up on hit lists, but didn't rise to the very top rungs.

For quite some time Red was very active in television. For six years in the 1950s, his *Ozark Mountain Jubilee*, nationally telecast on ABC, was one of the major showcases of country music. Many future stars got their first exposure to large audiences on the Springfield, Missouri-based show. In 1962, Red was costarred with Fess Parker on an ABC-TV series, *Mr. Smith Goes to Washington*.

Throughout the 1960s, Red kept on the go making personal appearances across the United States and Canada. From his home base of Nashville in the 1960s, he handled the packaging of his own show for national distribution.

During his long career, Red recorded dozens of albums besides his extensive singles releases. Among them on Decca were *Red & Ernie Tubbs* (mid-1950s), *Sou-*

venir Album (mid-1950s), Red Foley Story, Beyond the Sunset, He Walks with Thee (10/58), My Keepsake Album (3/59), Let's All Sing (4/59), Let's All Sing to Him (9/59), Company's Comin' (7/61), Golden Favorites (4/61), Songs (with the Jordanaires, 4/62), Dear Hearts & Gentle People (1962), Red Foley Show (3/63), Songs Everybody Knows (8/65), Songs for the Soul (4/67), and, posthumously, Songs of Devotion. A number of his LPs came out on Vocalion label, including I'm Bound for the Kingdom (6/65), Red Foley (11/66), and Memories and I Believe (with the Anita Kerr Singers, 8/69).

Foley remained a dedicated entertainer to the end of his life, a year after he had been elected to the Country Music Hall of Fame. He passed away of natural causes September 18, 1968, after taking part in two Grand Ole Opry shows.

Other members of his family continued the Foley heritage in country music in later years. His daughter Betty already had been a well-known country artist from the early 1950s. A decade after his death, one of his grandchildren, Debby Boone, established herself as a fine singer of both pop and country songs.

FORBERT, STEVE: *Singer, guitarist, harmonica player, band leader, songwriter. Born Meridian, Mississippi, December 15, 1954.*

The new wave of folksingers of the late 1970s tended to avoid the emphasis on traditionalism of previous generations in favor of a flexibility in both style and content. Steve Forbert was a typical exemplar of the trend, a balladeer who, like Bob Dylan, wrote his own folk songs and blended several elements of music, including rock, blues, and country.

Forbert was born and raised in Meridian, Mississippi: as he proudly told the authors, "I'm from Meridian, the home of the Jimmie Rodgers, the father of country music. When I was a kid I went to five or six of the memorial concerts for him in Meridian. I don't get home much now, but I do go when I have some time."

At the same time, he also knew he shared the birthright of another Mississippian, the long-time King of Rock, Elvis

Presley. He lists both Presley and Rodgers as influences, along with Dylan, various Delta blues artists, Chuck Berry, Woody Guthrie, Van Morrison, and Neil Young.

Recalling his musical saga, he noted, "I started playing guitar at the age of eleven, although prior to that I'd played plastic guitar and trash-can drums in my first band, The Mosquitos." He continued to play with a variety of groups, mostly rock oriented, from elementary school through two years of junior college. When, in 1976, he headed to New York, folk and folk-country–flavored rock were his main formats.

"Hen White's Auto Store in Meridian went out of business and I lost my job as a truck driver/warehouseman that year. So I got on a train and took a ride to New York and took a room in the YMCA on 23rd Street and began to check it out." Steve performed any place he could, finding jobs in Manhattan venues like the Other End, Kenny's Castaways, Folk City, The Bells of Hell, and The Cornelia Street Cafe or in outlying spots such as the Harmony Coffee House in the Bronx, the Rainy Nighthouse in Queens, and The On tap Bar in North Bergen, New Jersey.

He also wasn't hesitant about singing in the streets to earn money. He described one such performance in the song "Grand Central Station, March 18, 1977" in his debut album: "Grand Central Station/It wheels and it deals/The crowds rush and scramble . . . And I did some singin' and I played some guitar/Down near the doorway."

Oddly, Forbert's breakthrough didn't come from street singing or his folk club dates but from appearances at CBGBs, the center of punk rock in New York in the mid- and late-1970s. He opened for a number of superheated rock bands at CBGBs, and his singing impressed the management team of Danny Fields and Linda Stein. That alignment led to his signing a record contract with one of Columbia Records' labels, Nemporer, on April 10, 1978. His debut LP, *Live on Arrival*, appeared in the fall of 1978, amply demonstrating his ability to write sensitive, insightful lyrics and music covering a gamut of tempos from thoughtful pieces like "Goin' Down to Laurel" and "Tonight I Feel So Far Away from Home" to rousers on the order of "Big City Cat" and "You Cannot Win if You Do Not Play."

Surprisingly, the LP made headway with the music audience despite rock's dominance and during the first part of 1979 it was a top-100 album for months. Doors opened in the concert field and he played not only small folk and rock clubs but a fair number of medium-size halls toward the end of the year.

By the time his second album, *Jackrabbit Slim*, came out in the fall of 1979, he already had name recognition with many disc jockeys and fans. Many of the songs from the LP got considerable airplay across the United States, numbers like "Wait, I'm in Love with You" and the autobiographical "January 23–30, 1978." (The latter deals with a trip home in which he understood that he no longer could be a part of small town life: "Sunday morning/The church bell rings/The organ plays and the choir sings/Where am I while the preacher speaks?/Dreamin' dreams between my sheets . . . asleep.")

The album matched the debut collection in quality, though some critics felt the orchestration was becoming too intricate for folk-style material. He told the authors, "There really wasn't more orchestration on the second album than on the first. We added a couple of girl singers and, a couple of times, had a horn section, but that was all. The approach was different. The second one is like a living room record as against a street concert. People say it's more lush, but that's not true. There are no overdubs; it was done live just like the first one."

He was asked about the emotional effect of playing for steadily growing audiences instead of on New York street corners or in Grand Central Station. "It still feels a lot the same," replied the skinny, curly-haired artist. "I get up and play or sing either way. About the only thing that's different is I'm on the road a lot more. I still live in New York, but I don't get there very

much. In 1979, I was touring for nine months and the rest of the time I was in Nashville and Springfield, Missouri, rehearsing my new tour band.

"I would like to spend more time playing before East Coast crowds. I play a lot in New Jersey; that and Philadelphia are my favorite spots. I really love Philadelphia because, for some reason, the chemistry between me and the audience is great."

Did he ever think about the perils of fame; did he worry about losing his identity if he became a mass audience idol? "It's a strange trip, a very strange trip. But I want to grow. I want more people to hear my music."

In the fall of 1980, his third LP, *Little Stevie Orbit*, came out on Nemporer and made the national charts for several weeks.

FORD, TENNESSEE ERNIE: *Singer, songwriter, disc jockey, actor, emcee. Born Bristol, Tennessee, February 13, 1919.*

The trademark of Ernest Jennings "Tennessee Ernie" Ford was a relaxed air combined with the soothing tones of his deep bass voice. His portrayal made him one of the most popular performers first in country & western and then in the overall popular entertainment market. In the several instances when Ford left top-ranked TV programs to spend more time with his family, he found a national audience waiting to verify his star status on his return to the limelight.

Born and raised in Tennessee, Ernie spent many of his boyhood hours listening to country & western musicians, in person or on the radio. He was particularly interested in radio and, during his high school years in Bristol, spent many hours hanging around the local station. He won his first job as a staff announcer in 1937 at ten dollars a week, and discovering that he had a first-rate voice, he went on to study at the Cincinnati Conservatory of Music in 1938. Returning to the announcing field in 1939, he worked for stations in Atlanta and Knoxville from 1939 to 1941.

Enlisting in the Air Corps soon after Pearl Harbor, he became a bombardier on heavy bombers and later spent two years as an instructor. Stationed in California, he met and married a girl named Betty Heminger and decided to settle there after the war. He found a job as a DJ on a San Bernardino station after his discharge.

He then moved on to an announcing spot with country & western station KXLA in Pasadena. There he struck up a warm friendship with veteran band leader Cliffie Stone, who had a show on the station. Ernie occasionally joined Cliffie's quartet in a hymn.

After a while, Cliffie asked Ernie to join his Saturday night program and also saw to it that Capitol Records auditioned Ernie. Capitol signed the newcomer and results were fast in coming. In 1949, Tennessee Ernie had two singles in the top-10 country & western charts, "Mule Train" and a song he wrote with Cliffie Stone, "Smokey Mountain Boogie." The following year things were even better, as Ernie recorded such top-10 hits as "Anticipation Blues," "I'll Never Be Free" (duet with Kay Starr), "The Cry of the Wild Goose," and "Shotgun Boogie." The last-named was an Ernie Ford original that remained number one nationally for many weeks.

In short order Ernie became a network radio figure, with his own shows on CBS and ABC from 1950 to 1955. During these years he continued to turn out top-10 hits, including "Mister and Mississippi" (1951); his own composition, "Blackberry Boogie" (1952); "River of No Return" (1954); and "Ballad of Davy Crockett" (1955). In 1955 he recorded a song by his friend Merle Travis that eclipsed anything he had done before, called "Sixteen Tons." This record became number one in both country & western and national polls and made Tennessee Ernie Ford an almost legendary figure. Through 1967, more than 4 million copies of the record had been sold.

By the end of 1955, Ernie was featured on his own daytime show on NBC-TV. This won such enthusiastic audience response that NBC started a new nighttime series in September 1956, starring Ernie. Sponsored by Ford Motor Company, the show was consistently among the top-rated during its five-year existence.

In 1961, Ford left TV to move to northern California and spend more time with his wife and sons on a ranch-style home in Portola Valley, forty-five miles from San Francisco. Ernie also spent much of his time in succeeding years building up his cattle ranch at Eagleville, California.

After a year away from TV, Ernie signed for a new weekday show with ABC-TV, starting in April 1962. Ernie's personal magic quickly moved it to the top ranks of the polls, where it stayed until his three-year contract was up in 1965. Once again Ernie returned to Portola Valley and vicinity.

Continuing to give selected public appearances, in May 1965 he played to a sell-out audience at the new Melodyland Theater near Disneyland. The following year, he signed for four more engagements at in-the-round theaters in the Los Angeles and San Francisco regions.

The pattern remained essentially the same from the late 1960s into the early 1980s. Ernie maintained a relatively low key schedule, doing occasional club or stage appearances but having no intensive touring operations. He was a guest on many major TV programs during those years, including some work as a presenter or host on some of the awards shows, particularly those of the Country Music Association.

Ernie continued to turn out albums on Capitol Records until the mid-1970s. In 1974, his *25th Anniversary* album came out, a two-record set that later was reissued as two separate albums still in the Capitol catalogue at the end of 1981. His long association with the label came to an end in August 1976 with the release of his LP *For the 83rd Time*. After that, the only new titles on the Capitol list were reissues of older material. Over the years, his religious albums were particulary well received, exceeding 10 million sales by the start of the 1970s. His only Grammy Award was for a gospel LP *(Great Gospel Songs)*, which was named the Best Gospel or Religious Recording of 1964. He received six R.I.A.A. gold-record awards for gospel albums.

Among his album releases from the late 1950s into the early 1970s were *Hymns;*

Spirituals; Nearer the Cross (1958); Gather Round; Friend We Have (1959); Sing a Hymn, Sixteen Tons (1960); Come to the Fair, Civil War Songs South, Hymns at Home (1961); Sing a Hymn with Me, Sing a Spiritual with Me, I Love to Tell the Story, Favorite Hymns (1962); This Lusty Land, Tennessee Ernie Ford, We Gather Together, Long, Long Ago (1963); Great Gospel Songs, Country Hits (1964); World's Best Loved Hymns, Let Me Walk with Thee (1965); My Favorite Things, God Lives!, Wonderful Peace (1966); Aloha, Faith of Our Fathers (1967); Our Garden of Hymns (1968); Holy, Holy, Holy (1969); America the Beautiful, Everything Is Beautiful, Sweet Hour of Prayer/Let Me Walk with Thee (two-record set), Abide with Me, and Folk Album (early 1970s). In the early 1970s, Ernie also was represented on the Pickwick label with the two-record reissue set, Tennessee Ernie Ford.

At the start of the 1980s, his LPs still in the active Capitol catalogue included Spirituals, Hymns, Sweet Hour of Prayer, 25th Anniversary, America the Beautiful, Best of Tennessee Ernie Ford, Book of Favorite Hymns, Country Hits . . . Feelin' Blue, Great Gospel Songs, Nearer the Cross, Let Me Walk with Thee, Make a Joyful Noise, Precious Memories, Sing His Great Love, Star Carol, and Story of Christmas. On Word Records, he also had the album He Touched Me.

FORD, WHITEY, "THE DUKE OF PADUCAH": Comedian, instrumentalist (banjo, mandolin, harmonica), emcee. Born DeSoto, Missouri, May 12, 1901.

"I'm goin' back to the wagon, these shoes are killin' me!"

If any sentence can be said to be immortal in the country field, it's this tag line of one of the greatest of all rustic comedians, The Duke of Paducah. Although he delighted audiences for decades on network shows with his humor, his career covered many years as a pioneer musician in the country & western field.

Benjamin Francis "Whitey" Ford was born in Missouri, but when his mother died when he was only a year old, he was sent to live with his grandmother in Little Rock, Arkansas. He grew up in Little Rock and was interested in music, though no more so than any other boy growing up in

an area where singing old songs and playing the banjo or guitar was common. With the country's entry into World War I, young Ford ran away from home to enlist in the Navy in 1918. He stayed in the service for four years.

While a sailor, he became more interested in music and perfected his playing on the banjo. When he got out in 1922, he decided to go into the music field, starting his own Dixie Land Jazz Band. During the 1920s, he toured widely with the band and with all kinds of other organizations, including medicine shows, tab shows, stage shows, burlesque shows, and dramatic tent shows. Late in the decade, he teamed with Bob Van in a banjo act on the national vaudeville circuit.

When vaudeville began to wane, Ford joined one of the first major country & western bands, Otto Gray's Oklahoma Cowboys. His experience with Gray led to a bid from a young up-and-coming radio singer in Chicago. The singer was Gene Autry, who asked Ford to join his group on WLS, Chicago, as emcee, comic (with Frankie Marvin), and banjoist. Once on WLS, Ford also was one of the first cast members of the new WLS Show Boat, which later became the famed network WLS Barn Dance. Ford teamed up with Bob Van in a banjo duo on the Show Boat. During these years, he also acquired the nickname "The Duke of Paducah" while performing on station KWK, St. Louis, Missouri.

Ford left WLS before the Barn Dance went network. The reason was a chance to emcee on a new program called Plantation Party over the NBC network. On the show, Ford was almost a one-man gang. As The Duke of Paducah, he was the star comic. In addition, he wrote the entire show and helped work out most of the details of each performance. For nine years, he delighted audiences across the country with his stand-up humor and deft handling of a show that featured many of the top country artists in America. His work on Plantation Party started a personal gag library that eventually totaled over a half million jokes catalogued under 455 different subjects.

The Duke's association with Plantation

Party came to an end in 1942, when he left for an overseas trip entertaining the nation's armed forces. After his lengthy tour, he came back to the United States to find that his agent had booked him for three guest appearances on the *Grand Ole Opry.* The audience at Nashville yelled and thundered their approval, as did the radio listeners with stacks of mail. The result was a long-term association between the *Opry* and The Duke that lasted for sixteen years. During these years, he was featured in personal appearances in major shows and theaters throughout the United States. He also was often asked to speak before church groups, college and high school student groups, and at men's clubs.

At the end of the 1950s, The Duke decided to give up the weekly routine of a network TV show. However, he continued to tour, making from 150 to 200 personal appearances a year. He also appeared on many TV shows during the 1960s, including the *Opry,* the *Red Foley Show, Gary Moore, The Jimmy Dean Show,* and the *Porter Wagoner Show.* He also found time, in 1963, to make his second movie, *Country Music on Broadway.* His first, some years earlier, was *Country Farm.*

In the early 1980s, he was among the nominees for the Country Music Hall of Fame.

FRAZIER, DALLAS: *Singer, guitarist, trumpeter, songwriter. Born Spiro, Oklahoma, October 27, 1939.*

Among his country-music peers, Dallas Frazier was known to be an extremely important force in the field. His name has shown up time and time again on the hit charts, but mainly in fine print. Though he is a polished singer and instrumentalist, his most important contributions have been behind the scenes as one of the top country songwriters of the 1960s and 1970s.

Dallas was born in Oklahoma but raised in a farming area near Bakersfield, California, then as now a hotbed of country-music activity. By the time Dallas was twelve he had learned to play several instruments. When he took first place in a talent concert sponsored by Ferlin Husky,

Husky quickly offered the youngster a job with his touring troupe, traveling all over the United States. Ferlin brought Frazier's talents to the attention of Capitol Records and the company gave Dallas a recording contract.

Cliffie Stone, then heading the country operations at Capitol, was impressed with Frazier and soon brought him in as a regular cast member of his TV show, *Hometown Jamboree.* Frazier soon became a favorite with Los Angeles audiences, taking part in the show as a soloist and often teaming up to do duets with another young star of the *Jamboree,* Molly Bee. By this time Frazier was writing music steadily. He was still in his teens when he turned out his first smash hit, the novelty song "Alley Oop." The latter made the top 10 on the pop charts and also showed up on country lists during 1957. It has since been revived successfully several times by various pop and rock artists.

After Cliffie disbanded his show in the late 1950s, Dallas move to Nashville. There he continued to work as a performer on radio and TV while steadily expanding his song output. Other artists gradually began to incorporate some of his compositions into their repertoires, though it took a while before Dallas really hit pay dirt. His first true banner year as a songwriter was 1966, when he provided three of the year's best-selling songs: Jack Greene's version of "There Goes My Everything" rose to number one on national country charts, while Connie Smith had a top-10 hit with "Ain't Had No Lovin'" and George Jones did likewise with "I'm a People." In 1967, George Jones made the top 10 with Dallas' "I Can't Get There from Here," and in 1968, Dallas' top-10 successes included George's single of "Say It's Not You" and Connie Smith's release of "Run Away Little Tears." Some of Frazier's other songs recorded by major artists in the 1960s were "Georgia," "Elvira," "Hawg Jaw," "Soakin' Up the Suds," and "Timber I'm Fallin'." By the end of the 1960s, Frazier had written over 300 songs.

He kept adding to his total throughout the 1970s. Among his chartmakers in 1974, for instance, were "Baptism of Jesse," co-written with Sanger Shafer and recorded by Johnny Russell, "Ain't Love a Good Thing," a top-10 hit for Connie Smith, and "Freckles and Polliwag Days," co-written with D. Owens and a success for Dallas' old mentor, Ferlin Husky. The following year proved another fine one for Dallas, starting off with charted singles such as "The Way I Lose My Mind" (co-written with S. D. Shafer), recorded by Carl Smith; "Champagne Ladies and Blue Ribbon Babies" (co-written with A. L. "Doodle" Owens), a moderate hit for Ferlin Husky; and "Then Who Am I" (co-written with D. Owens), a number-one hit for Charley Pride. Later in the year, Dallas' name showed up in the writing credits for "The Fiddlin' of Jacques Pierre Bordeaux" (written with A. L. Owens), released by Frenchie Burke, and "Big Mable Murphy," recorded by Sue Thompson. In 1976, Frazier's charted songs included Roy Head's version of "The Door I Used to Close" (written with E. Montgomery) and Leon Rausch's recording of "That's the Trip I've Been On" (co-written with S. D. Shafer).

In the early 1980s, Frazier's list of credits continued to grow. Gene Watson had a top-10 hit with "14 Karat Mind" (co-written by Frazier and L. Lee) as one example. One of the best singles of 1980 was Emmylou Harris' version of his "Beneath Still Waters." In the spring of 1981, the Oak Ridge Boys made a new recording of one of Dallas' old compositions, "Elvira," and gained a number-one record on country charts as well as placing the single on pop charts.

During the 1970s, though Dallas did some concert and TV work, his main emphasis was on songwriting. In the early part of the decade, he was represented by a series of solo recordings on RCA Records, such as the LPs *Singing My Songs* (issued 7/70) and *My Baby Packed* (9/71). During the 1970s, more than a few artists released albums in which only songs written by Frazier were included.

FRICKE, JANIE: *Singer, guitarist. Born South Whitney, Indiana, December 18, 1950.*

For a time, Janie Fricke could have claimed the title of "Queen of the Country Session Singers." She backed so many major artists during one period in the mid-1970s it sometimes seemed that every other single released in the country field had her voice somewhere in the background. Between that and singing jingles for commercials and radio station announcements, she did so well financially that she hesitated to give it up in favor of a solo singing career. Fortunately for country fans, she decided to give up her anonymity, soon becoming one of the brightest new stars in the country music firmament in the late 1970s.

Janie was born into an Indiana farm family and grew up on her father's 400-acre farm near South Whitney. Her mother was a piano teacher who also played the organ. Janie recalled, "By the time I was eight years old I would sing while mama played the organ." Some of her early singing experience came from singing hymns solo or in duets with her older sister in the church the family attended. However, she said, "I would never sing hymns the straight way. I'd always kinda jazz them up or sing them in a folk style."

Janie was interested in secular music as well. In high school she liked the folk style of people like Joan Baez and Judy Collins and the middle-of-the-road rock offerings of Neil Diamond. She sang at school events and local functions, accompanying herself on guitar after her father taught her how to chord when she was fifteen. When she went off to attend the University of Indiana in the late 1960s, she used her musical talents to earn money to help pay college expenses. Between her sophomore and junior years she spent some time in Memphis, Tennessee, where she made as much as $300 a week singing jingles and radio station call letters.

After receiving her degree and a teaching certificate in 1972, she headed for Dallas, where she again did commercial vocals. After a year there, she went to Los Angeles to try to get work as a session vocalist. However, the doors didn't open on the coast, so she returned briefly to Memphis, then continued on, in 1975, to Nashville. It proved a much more receptive environment for her talents than the other stopping places. In a short time she was providing anonymous vocals for commercials for such companies and products as United Airlines, 7-Up, Coors Beer, and Pizza Hut. Her schedule of recording sessions also filled up rapidly. During 1976 and 1977, she backed many of the best-known artists in the country field, including Tanya Tucker, Ronnie Milsap, Billy "Crash" Craddock, Lynn Anderson, Mickey Gilley, Tommy Overstreet, Dolly Parton, Zella Lehr, Crystal Gayle, Barbara Mandrell, Donna Fargo, England Dan and John Ford Coley, and Johnny Duncan. With Duncan, she backed three straight number-one singles of 1976-77, "Stranger," "Thinkin' of a Rendezvous," and "It Couldn't Have Been Any Better."

The producer of those smash hits, Columbia vice president and top producer Billy Sherrill, didn't have to be hit with a brick to realize that Fricke had something special to offer creatively. He offered her a contract, an opportunity thousands of hopefuls would give their eyeteeth for, but Janie hesitated. She said, "I had to be coaxed to sign because I didn't want to give up the security of singing jingles and back-up for so many artists. But after a lot of discussion, plus the added incentive of getting to work with Billy Sherrill, I decided to give it a try."

The answer came almost immediately—and it was positive. Her first solo single on Columbia, "What're You Doin' Tonight," made the top 20 in late 1977. At the same time, she had another hit single with Johnny Duncan (this time with her name on the record), "Come a Little Bit Closer." She followed with three more hit solo singles in 1978, "Please Help Me (I'm Falling)," "Baby It's You," and "Playin' Hard to Get" (the last-named on the charts into early 1979). Those four initial solo hits plus "I'll Love Away Your Troubles for Awhile" all were culled from her first two LPs on Columbia, *Singer of Songs* (her debut LP) and *Love Notes*. In addition, in late 1978, she had a number-one hit single with Charlie Rich on Epic, "On My Knees."

Her accomplishments brought widespread recognition from the music industry as well as the public. Both *Billboard* and *Cash Box* magazines voted her the Top New Female Vocalist of 1978. In 1978 and 1979, the members of the Country Music Association nominated her for Female Vocalist of the Year. In 1979, the reader's poll of *Music City News* named her the Best New Vocalist of the Year.

Janie finished up 1979 with the single "But Love Me," from her third album, *From the Heart*, moving up the charts to reach upper levels in early 1980. Another song from the album, "Pass Me By (If You're Only Passing Through)," moved high on the charts in the early summer of 1980. Later in the year, she had a top-15 duet with Johnny Duncan, "He's Out of My Life." At year end, her single "Down to My Last Broken Heart," from her fourth album, *I'll Need Someone to Hold Me When I Cry* (issued October 1980), was on the charts, rising to number one on some lists in January 1981. In the spring of 1981, the single "Pride" was on the charts and in the fall the title song from album four was in the top 5. In September 1981, her fifth album, *Sleeping With Your Memory*, was released.

Starting in the late 1970s, Janie began to accrue a growing list of concert and TV credits. As an opening act, she appeared with stars like Ronnie Milsap, Kenny Rogers, Eddie Rabbitt, Charley Pride, and the Statler Brothers. By special request in the early 1980s, she also performed for President Ronald Reagan and his guest President Lopez Portillo of Mexico at Camp David. Her TV appearances through the early 1980s included *Dinah and Friends*, *The John Davidson Show*, *Mike Douglas*, *Merv Griffin*, *Dance Fever*, and a Showtime cable TV special, *Women in Music*.

FRIEDMAN, KINKY (RICHARD): *Singer, songwriter, band leader. Born Palestine, Texas, October 31, 1944.*

All art forms offer some resistance to bold, innovative new artists and country music is no exception. So when Kinky Friedman and His Texas Jew Boys started performing in small country nightspots, they often ran into severe criticism of their outrageous songs and on-stage performances. The group's name alone was enough to raise eyebrows among many country-music fans.

The leader of the band, "Kinky" (Richard) Friedman, graduated from the University of Texas as a psychology major, after which he joined the Peace Corps. After spending three years in Borneo, he returned to the United States. First he settled in Austin and soon afterward formed the first incarnation of his Texas Jew-Boy band. Within this framework, Kinky could express the self-mocking persona and humor of a Jew from Palestine, Texas. The fact that the name of the group is a spoof on Bob Wills and His Texas Playboys is in itself quite significant, in that it expresses a willingness to make fun of as well as to embrace the almost sacred Texas institution of country music as epitomized by Bob Wills.

In 1973, after two years of trying, Friedman finally found a record company (Vanguard) to release his first album, *Sold American*. Among the songs on that LP were "Sold American," "Ride 'Em Jewboy," "Let Saigons Be Bygones," and "We Reserve the Right to Refuse Service to You," about the hostility a Jewish longhair encounters in a redneck cafe. Several lines from this song are "Take your business back to Walgreens,/Have you tried the local zoo./You smell just like a Communist,/You come through just like a Jew."

Later in the song, the longhair is rebuffed in a synagogue ("Your friends are all on welfare/You call yourself a Jew.")

Friedman followed with another Vanguard album that featured such songs as "Homo Erectus," "Something's Wrong with the Beaver," and "They Ain't Making Jews Like Jesus Anymore." In his on-stage performances, Kinky came across as an old-style Texas country band leader except that he wore Stars of David and mezuzahs around his neck. He also used some four-letter words on stage, which old-time Texas country band leaders would only use off-stage. This curious blend of elements proved to be extremely controversial, and the band occasionally got kicked off the stage and had subsequent perform-

ances cancelled. Of course, such incidents also gained a lot of publicity for the Texas Jew Boys.

A sign that the times had indeed been changing was evident when Kinky Friedman and His Texas Jewboys were invited to appear at the *Grand Ole Opry*. In late 1975 and early 1976, the group toured with Bob Dylan's Rolling Thunder Revue, a loose-format tour in which several different artists performed along with Dylan in concerts across the United States.

In 1976, Epic Record Company signed Friedman and his band to a recording contract. Their first album was entitled *Lasso from El Paso* and included such cuts as "Lady Yesterday," "Dear Abbie," "Asshole from El Paso," and "Mens Room L.A."—A.S.

FRIZZELL, LEFTY (WILLIAM ORVILLE):

Singer, guitarist, songwriter. Born Corsicana, Texas, March 31, 1928; died Nashville, Tennessee, July 19, 1975.

When Lefty Frizzell died, people revered him as one of the grand old men of country music. Yet he was comparatively young, only forty-seven. His image, though, was one of a country-music traditionalist, whose biggest period of success had occurred two decades earlier.

He was only five years old when Jimmie Rodgers, the father of modern country music, died, but his family treasured the Rodgers recordings for years to come. As a boy in Texas, Lefty learned to play the guitar to the tunes of Rodgers and his immediate successors to country royalty, Ernest Tubb and Roy Acuff.

The Frizzell family was very transient. Lefty's father was an oil well driller who moved from field to field throughout Texas. When the Frizzells were living in El Dorado, Texas, in the late 1930s, young William Orville auditioned and gained a featured spot on a children's program on station KELD. He kept up his musical activities as the Frizzells changed locales again and was playing country fairs and local dances by the time home was in Greenville, Texas, in 1943. A few years later, Frizzell was working the bar and club circuit in Waco and Dallas and winning a reputation as one of the better young country singers and pickers around.

He also proved handy with his fists, at one point entering local Golden Gloves' competition. He didn't end up as a champion but he did gain his nickname for his wicked left hook.

In the late 1940s, appearing for the most part in clubs in West Texas and New Mexico, Lefty had decided music would be his role in life. He worked up some demonstration recordings with Dallas agent Jim Beck, who took them to Nashville. Columbia producer Don Law was impressed and asked Lefty, at the time appearing in clubs in Big Springs, Texas, to come to work on his debut releases on the label.

Those first releases, both written by Frizzell, were "I Love You a Thousand Ways" and "If You Got the Money, Honey, I've Got the Time." Issued as opposite sides of one single, both songs made the country top 10 in 1950. Both, of course, have since been recorded by many other artists as well. In 1951, Lefty achieved a banner year, mostly with songs he either wrote or co-wrote. That year, two songs reached number one on country charts: "Always Late" (co-written with B. Crawford) and "I Want to Be with You Always" (co-written with J. Beck). Other 1951 top-10 hits were "Look What Thoughts Will Do," "Mom and Dad's Waltz" (both Frizzell compositions), and "Travelin' Blues." The last named was a track on one of Lefty's early album successes, Songs of Jimmie Rodgers, which was later reissued on the Harvard label in 1960.

In 1952, Lefty turned out four top-10 songs, "Don't Stay Away," "Forever," "Give Me More, More, More" (co-written with Ray Price), and "I'm an Old, Old Man." At one point, those four songs provided him with the unusual achievement of having four of the top-10 country singles at the same time. Oddly, none of the four made it to the number-one position.

After 1952, though, things quieted down noticeably for Lefty. Though he recorded many singles that made the national country charts, some of which made the top levels regionally, he didn't have a single top-10 success until the end of the decade.

In 1959, he broke the drought with the single (by Wilkin and Dill) "Long Black Veil." Part of the problem, of course, was the onset of rock 'n' roll, which had severe repercussions on the country field in the mid- and late-1950s, particularly for artists who objected to changing their styles just to increase commercial appeal.

Frizzell, however, remained a major stage attraction on the country fair and package show circuit not only throughout the 1950s but the 1960s as well. From the early 1950s he was a regular member of the Grand Ole Opry and made many guest appearances on other major country-music radio and TV shows. In 1964, Frizzell reminded the industry of his still strong rapport with the country audience when his single "Saginaw, Michigan" (by Don Wayne) rose to number one nationally, giving him a career total of thirteen top-10 songs and three number-one hits.

Columbia continued to release albums by him into the 1960s. These include One & Only Lefty Frizzell, issued October 1959; Saginaw, Michigan (5/64); Sad Side of Love (12/65); Greatest Hits (7/66); Great Sound (10/66); and Mom and Dad's Waltz (7/67). In those recordings, as indeed in all his work right up to the end, Frizzell maintained the same singing and picking style he always had used. It was a straightforward country approach with lyrical phrasing and delivery that has had considerable influence on new performers over the years.

In 1973, his long, mutually beneficial association with Columbia Records finally came to an end. A short time after, he signed a new recording agreement with ABC Records and went into the studios in Nashville to prepare new material. Before his debut album could come out on ABC, though, he suffered a massive stroke at his Nashville home on July 19, 1975. He was rushed to Memorial Hospital but failed to rally and died at 11:20 P.M. that night.

FULLER, JESSE: *Singer, guitarist, harmonica player, "fotdella" player, songwriter. Born Jonesboro, Georgia, 1896; died Oakland, California, January 30, 1976.*

Most of Jesse Fuller's life was a fight for

survival. He never knew his father and his mother gave him away to another family when he was only six or seven. Yet, instead of becoming bitter or despairing, he eventually became a folk-blues artist with a message of hope and beauty for several generations of fans.

When he was seven or eight, staying with a family named Wilson near Macedonia, Georgia, he evinced his first musical interest when he made himself a mouth bow. Soon after, he made a simple guitar. Though not yet ten, he made his way to Saturday night dances and learned to play many songs by observing the performances of various musicians.

He finished the third grade before running away from the Wilsons when he was ten. Later, in his 1964 composition "Drop Out Song," he urged other youngsters not to follow his example but rather to see that they got good educations. Still, he was street-wise and, as his nickname of later years, "Lone Cat," suggested, independent. In the years after leaving the Wilsons, he got by in various ways. He grazed cows, worked in a buggy factory, did housework, delivered groceries, worked in a chair factory in Brunswick, Georgia, laid track on the railroads, and sometimes made extra money by singing on street corners. He attended minstrel and other shows when he could, picking up songs he could play on guitar or harmonica.

His roster of occupations continued as he reached his late teens. At eighteen, he was a wood chopper and a few years after worked for a junkman in Griffin, Georgia. In his early twenties, he finally left the South, going to Cincinnati where he worked on a street car for a while. Then he joined the Hagenback Wallace Circus, where he was a canvas stretcher. World War I had just ended when the circus went through Michigan and Jesse earned what for him was a sizable amount of money playing his guitar in the streets for the returning troops.

When he was twenty-four, he hopped a freight and went to California, which became home from then on. He worked shining shoes near the gate of the United Artists Studio in Los Angeles. Leading film

actors, including Douglas Fairbanks, Sr., liked him. Fairbanks, in fact, got Jesse bit roles in several movies, including *East of Suez, Thief of Bagdad,* and *Hearts of Dixie.* Director Raoul Walsh later financed a hot-dog stand for Fuller, but Jesse left that for a job on the Southern Pacific Railroad.

In the 1930s, he relocated to Oakland and vicinity, working as a construction worker days and playing occasional pick-up music dates at night. His musical activity gradually increased until, by the late 1940s, both jazz and folk artists in the San Francisco Bay area often sought him out.

In the early 1950s, he began to play steadily at a small club in San Francisco called the Haight Street Barbecue. He also opened a small shoeshine stand on College Avenue in Berkeley, which attracted many folk music fans. They enjoyed hearing him play both traditional folk material, mostly blues, and some of his own originals, which, after 1954, included the "San Francisco Bay Blues." During those years Fuller also devised a new kind of instrument he called a "fotdella." Essentially a one-man-band rig, it included a right foot pedal to operate a hammer against an arrangement of seven piano strings, a left foot pedal to run a high-hat cymbal or a washboard, and a harness to hold a harmonica and kazoo. While sitting amidst all this, he also played a six- or twelve-string guitar with his hands.

Helped by close friend folksinger Barbara Dane, Jesse's career began to blossom in the late 1950s. He and Barbara were featured at the Ash Grove in Los Angeles in 1958 and also performed at other folk venues in the state. In 1959, he went to the Monterey Jazz Festival uninvited, was set up outside the stands by Festival Director Jimmy Lyons, and vied with major jazz acts as a highlight of the program.

Things got even better for him in the 1950s. He got the chance to perform at an increasing number of festivals, concerts, and coffee houses. As the decade went by, he delighted audiences in all parts of the United States. He created a sensation in England in 1966, starring twice with legendary rock groups—the Rolling Stones and the Animals.

Some of his songs were played by rock 'n' roll bands as well as by folk performers. Peter, Paul & Mary sold many records of their single of his "San Francisco Bay Blues" and the song was recorded by dozens of other folksingers over the years. Jesse himself was represented by several albums titled *San Francisco Bay Blues,* one on Prestige Records that came out in February 1964 and another of that title on GTJ label that came out shortly afterward. GTJ (Good Time Jazz) issued one of Fuller's first collections, *Jesse Fuller,* which came out in August 1958, and followed that with the LP *The Lone Cat* in May 1961. His singing and playing also were offered on the Folk-Lyric Records' release *Greatest Negro Minstrels* (11/63). His mid-1960s releases included *Favorites* on Prestige (5/65) and *Frisco Bound* on Arhoolie Records (7/67). Also among his LPs was the World Songs LP *Jesse Fuller Working on the Railroad.*

By the start of the 1980s, though folk artists still included some of his songs in their repertoire, little of Jesse's recorded work was still available. A few albums of his 1960s work continued to be offered by small record companies, an example being Fantasy Records' *Brother Lowdown,* a repackaging of Fuller's Prestige recordings, and *The Lone Cat* on GTJ.

FURAY, RICHIE: *Singer, guitarist, songwriter. Born Yellow Springs, Ohio, May 9, 1944.*

Richie Furay, in the late 1960s, was one of the first to combine rock with folk and country music. His experiments helped pave the way for such performers of the 1970s as the Eagles and Jackson Browne.

In his home state of Ohio, Richie was attracted to folk music at the start. He learned guitar at eight and continued his musical pursuits through high school and into Otterbein College, in Westerville, Ohio. In the early 1960s he moved to New York and joined a folk group called the Au Go Go singers. The group performed on television and recorded one album for Roulette Records. Later, another aspiring musician named Steve Stills joined the group for a while until the unit broke up. Stills went to Los Angeles soon after and

Richie followed. As Furay recalled, "Stephen had convinced me that there was a scene going on in L.A., and so I really came out to join him. But whatever was supposed to be happening wasn't and Stephen and I wound up trying to get something going together, just the two of us. Then we ran into Neil [Young], who neither of us knew was in town and he had [bassist] Bruce Palmer with him. And, eventually, drummer Dewey Martin showed up."

The result was formation of the Buffalo Springfield in April 1966, a legendary group that created a classic body of rock material (with some folk flavor) in three albums recorded during only two years and one month of existence. At the end, of the founding members only Furay remained, trying to hold the band together with Jim Messina, Palmer's replacement. Their association produced a milestone in music history when, during the recording of "Kind Woman," they used a pedal steel guitar. Played by Rusty Young, it is considered the first time that that country music standby was used in a rock context. Since then, pedal steel became commonplace on hundreds of records by various groups.

In the late 1960s, Messina, Furay, and Rusty Young started a new band in the country-rock vein, the first to make major inroads in the rock field with that kind of format. The band first took the name Pogo after the cartoon, but threatened with a lawsuit by the strip's creator, changed it to Poco. Besides those three, the initial group included George Grantham on drums and Randy Meisner on bass. Meisner was to go on to work as a backing musician for Linda Ronstadt in the early 1970s by way of becoming a founding member of the Eagles. The band's debut album came out on Epic in 1969 and did reasonably well. It was followed in the early 1970s by *Deliverin'* and four others.

As Furay told Dennis Hunt of the *Los Angeles Times,* things didn't work out as well as he'd hoped. "I know the country-rock label hurt Poco. We couldn't get any AM airplay and we didn't get much FM play. After six albums with Poco I saw there weren't going to be any hits so I left. Now it seems silly to be that hung up on getting a hit. When I finally got a gold record [Buffalo Springfield never achieved any either], I saw it wasn't the great thing I thought it would be."

Richie had his hit LP after leaving Poco in 1973 to become part of a group with former Byrds' bassist Chris Hillman and songwriter-musician John David Souther. The first Souther-Hillman-Furay release on Elektra gained the gold. The second album wasn't as effective. In addition, just after it was finished, Richie injured his hand while chopping wood near his home in Colorado and was sidelined for many months. When he was healthy again, he decided to concentrate on a solo career. He organized the Richie Furay Band to record a new LP, released under the title *I've Got a Reason* on Asylum Records in the summer of 1976. The collection essentially stressed a middle of the road commercial rock approach. As Furay said at the time, "There's only one song on the album that is sort of country-rock. I hate the country-rock label. I don't want to be limited by it."

Still, the album wasn't an exceptional effort. Furay, after touring for a few months with the group, became dissatisfied and disbanded it. In early 1977, he started preparing material for the first album to be released solely under his name. When it was issued in March 1978, it proved to have more of Richie's earlier folk coloration in its material than the previous LP. Overall, it was lighter in tone than his albums of the Poco or Springfield years. Of the title song, he noted, "It's just a good-time rock and roll, with probably more of a Poco-feel than anything else on the album." Indicating a possible new direction were several songs with rhythm & blues emphasis, one an oldie by Doc Pomus and Mort Schuman, "This Magic Moment," the other a new Furay piece (cowritten with Tom Stipe), "You Better Believe It."

G

GARFUNKEL, ART: *Singer, actor. Born Newark, New Jersey, November 5, 1941.*

Certainly one of the great folk/folk-rock teams of all time, the duo of Simon and Garfunkel set new standards for their art form in the 1960s before going separate ways at the start of 1970s. Though Simon was more active following the split, Garfunkel also made his mark on the entertainment field as a soloist, an actor, and a recording artist.

Art recalls that he first began singing at age four, after his father brought home a wire recorder. "That got me into music more than anything else. Singing and being able to record it." In sixth grade his interest in music was still strong when he met a boy named Paul Simon in their elementary school in Queens, New York. (Art was born in Newark, but spent much of his childhood and teens in Queens.) Before long, the two were singing in school events—mostly popular songs of the day.

Through their high school years, they were interested in the 1940s-style pop songs still dominating the field in the early 1950s. "Then rhythm and blues . . . rock 'n' roll came along." The two began developing material in those genres. "We practiced in the basement so much that we got professional sounding. We made demos in Manhattan and knocked on all the doors of the record companies with our hearts in our throats. Just a couple of kids."

Under the pseudonyms of Tom (Art) and Jerry (Paul), they actually did make an impact on the pop field in the mid-1950s. A single called "Hey School Girl" made lower-chart levels in 1956. The duo appeared on Dick Clark's *American Bandstand* and were added to some of the multiartist rock shows playing eastern theaters.

The outlook seemed promising, but Art

decided not to take a chance on the vagaries of show business. "I left and went to college. . . . I was the kid who was going to find some way to make a decent living." He enrolled at Columbia University with a major in art history and minors in architecture and education, eventually getting his B.A. in the early 1960s.

But he didn't abandon singing. He turned out some solo singles and rejoined Simon to sing at a Queens fraternity house (Simon was going to Queens College) in 1962. That led to a decision to try to find more joint engagements. At the end of their sophomore year, they played Gerde's Folk City in Greenwich Village, and a Columbia executive who heard the act offered them a contract. Those recording sessions provided the material for their debut LP, *Wednesday Morning, 3 A.M.,* which came out in 1964.

Most of the songs on the album were provided by Simon. As Garfunkel noted, "Up until then we sang and wrote rock 'n' roll songs together . . . but suddenly one of us could write poetic folk songs. I really connected with that . . . so the rejoining, after several years, was on the basis of the two of us as singers and Paul as the songwriter. People always asked why I didn't write songs. It was because Paul was so good. It seemed foolish to go for equal time."

The debut album, finally, after another brief separation, brought them national acclaim, primarily through the success of the song "Sounds of Silence." From mid-1965 on, Simon and Garfunkel rapidly became one of the most esteemed singing teams in the United States and the world. (For more details, see separate Simon and Garfunkel entry.) They still were at the peak of their careers when they both decided they wanted to try new creative directions.

For Garfunkel, one of his initial goals was to be an actor. His work with director Mike Nichols on the soundtrack of *The Graduate* led to the chance for featured roles in the major films *Catch 22* and *Carnal Knowledge.*

Meanwhile, Columbia was urging him to record some new solo material. He finally got back into the studio in 1972 and began work on what was to be the 1973 debut solo LP *Angel Clare.* Among the artists who backed him on various tracks were Paul Simon, Jerry Garcia, J. J. Cale, Larry Knechtel (of Bread), and Jim Gordon. The album tended toward the sophisticated ballad side, but had folk elements as well. One of the tracks, "All I Know," written for him by Jimmy Webb, became a chart hit, as did the album.

He followed that with the album *Breakaway,* which proved even more successful after its release in 1975. Three of the songs made the hit charts: his update of the old pop ballad "I Only Have Eyes for You," the title track, and a new song written by his old partner, Paul Simon. The two recorded it together and it was included not only on *Breakaway* but also on a new Simon solo album. The two also made a rare joint appearance to sing the song on a *Saturday Night Live* telecast.

In early 1978, his third album, *Watermark,* was issued, an album in which most of the material was written for Art by Jimmy Webb. Garfunkel handled production himself in the famous Muscle Shoals Studios in Muscle Shoals, Alabama. Discussing his approach, he stated, "In the past, I would have saved vocals for last. I would start with guitar and piano and build from there. This time I brought my voice down lower. I'm more a baritone tenor [as compared to the mainly high tenor stylings used on his previous two albums]. I wanted to stand there at the mike and sing the song."

To support the new album, in 1978 Garfunkel agreed to do his first tour since the farewell concerts of Simon and Garfunkel in 1970. In 1979, he completed another album, *Fate for Breakfast,* issued by Columbia in March. At the time the LP came out, Art was working on his third movie, *Bad Timing,* which costarred Theresa Russell and Harvey Keitel.

During the summer of 1981, Art and Paul Simon celebrated their reunion by giving a free concert in New York's Central Park that drew an audience estimated at half a million people. That didn't necessarily mean the two artists meant to give up solo work, as indicated by the release of Art's fifth solo album for Columbia, *Scissors Cut*, issued in August 1981.

GATLIN, LARRY: *Singer, guitarist, songwriter, band leader (Gatlin Brothers Band). Born Seminole, Texas, May 2, 1948. Band members, both born Texas: Steve Gatlin, April 4, 1951; Rudy Gatlin, August 20, 1952.*

Larry Gatlin's name may be the best known of his family, but he is always quick to point out the contributions made by his younger brothers Steve and Rudy. Together they make up the Gatlin Brothers Band, from the mid-1970s on one of the most successful stage and recording acts in country music.

Music always had been a family affair for the brothers. They first performed together when Larry was six years old in a gospel group singing at family and church get-togethers. Their father worked as an oil driller and moved from job to job, taking his family with him wherever he went. One year the Gatlins lived in eight different towns.

Religion and music helped keep the family together during those rootless years. Finally the Gatlins settled in Odessa, Texas, and whenever gospel groups such as the Blackwood Brothers or the Statesmen came to town, the whole family would go to see them. Meanwhile the brothers kept singing together during their elementary and high school years, eventually performing on a weekly TV show in Abilene, Texas, for two years. Larry already was showing some interest in songwriting, writing religious lyrics to the melodies of popular songs. The brothers had other interests as well, including sports. Larry was an excellent athlete in high school and won a football scholarship to the University of Houston.

When he entered the university, it marked the first time he and his brothers went separate ways. When Steve and Rudy went to college, they enrolled in other schools. At the time, Larry harbored thoughts of eventually going into journalism or perhaps becoming a lawyer. The incident that changed his career direction was a 1971 job attempt that failed. While in school, he heard that the Imperials gospel group would be backing Elvis Presley and needed a baritone. He auditioned for the position and, although he didn't get it, the Imperials were sufficiently impressed with his singing to ask him to work with them for a month during a later Las Vegas engagement with Jimmy Dean. On the bill at the time was Dottie West.

Recalling that occasion, Larry said, "I started writing [songs] in 1971. I was out in Las Vegas trying for a job with the Imperials. I didn't get the job, but I sat around Dottie West's dressing room writing songs. She said, 'When you get home, why don't you send some to me,' because she had a publishing company. So I did and she liked them—rags to riches."

Larry's songs tend to take the form of short, short stories or vignettes, perhaps reflecting the fact that he was an English major at the University of Houston. He recalled, "I used to write short stories in college. I remember writing one titled 'I, a Handball,' that the teacher gave me an 'F' for. It was about a handball split up in a wastebasket talking enviously about its first cousin, the basketball, and second cousin, the football. Those cats were making a big splash and the handball was small, black, and discarded. I thought anyone could see it wasn't really about a handball at all and all the instructor could say was 'I don't understand it.' Maybe I'll try my hand at short stories again later on, but I think I'm really best suited to writing songs."

Dottie West certainly agreed about his songwriting skills. Of the eight songs he sent her, she recorded two, "Once You Were Mine" and "You're the Other Half of Me," and also helped get others recorded. She also furthered Larry's career by sending him plane fare to come to Nashville and continue his writing. When he got there, she also set about opening doors for him as a performer. She played one of his tapes for Kris Kristofferson, who in turn told Fred Foster, President of Monument Records, about the talented young writer-performer. By the time Foster offered a contract, Larry had influenced his brothers to come to Nashville so that all three worked on the debut LP on Monument, *The Pilgrim*, which was released in January 1974. In preparation for that collection, Larry had written a hundred songs before he had ten which he felt were good enough for his first album. Among those was his first country hit, "Penny Annie," a song whose theme he hoped would provide the basis for a movie as of the early 1980s.

All of his subsequent albums contained one or more songs that became hit singles. His second LP, *Rain Rainbow*, featured the hit single "Delta Dirt." His third album, *Larry Gatlin with Family and Friends*, provided "Broken Lady," which reached number one on country charts in 1976 and also won a Grammy Award. Next came the album *High Time* from which came Larry's number-one single, "Statues Without Hearts."

Larry and the Gatlin Brothers Band's fourth Monument album, *Love Is Just a Game*, contained "I Don't Wanna Cry," which hit number one on the *Cash Box* country charts in August 1977. "I Just Wish You Were Someone I Love," from the same album, hit number one in early 1977. Their bestselling fifth album, *Oh ! Brother*, was preceded by the number-one hit single "Night Time Magic" and also included the top-10 hit, "Do It Again Tonight." Larry and his brothers were represented on the charts in late 1978 and early 1979 with the single "I've Done Enough Dyin' Today." They continued their string of hits into 1980 with the number-one hit singles "Midnight Choir" and "I'm Taking Somebody with Me when I Fall." Also on the singles charts in 1980 were "All the Gold in California" and "We're Number One." All those 1980 discs were on a new label, Columbia, to which Larry and his brothers shifted in late 1979. Their album debut on the label, *Straight Ahead*, came out in late 1979 and made both country and pop charts, showing up on them in 1980 as well. In 1981, Larry and his brothers had several more Columbia singles on the charts, such as "It Don't Get Better than This" and "What Are We Doin' Lonesome."

From the mid-1970s on, the group performed across the United States and in many other countries. Their popularity was particularly high in England, where Larry was the subject of two BBC-TV specials. Their TV credits included almost every major country-music show as well as numerous network and syndicated talk shows. The Gatlins performed on several Country Music Association and Grammy Award TV programs and, over the years, their names appeared as finalists in several categories in those competitions as well as those of the Academy of Country Music, in which Larry and his brothers were big winners in 1980, walking off with awards for Top Male Vocalist, Best Single, and Best Album.

The secret to the Gatlin brothers' success lies in the consistent quality of the lyrics and music of their songs, almost all crafted by Larry, which often elicit response from listeners. For instance, Larry received mail objecting to the refrain of the song "Midnight Choir," which asks, "Do they have Mogen David in heaven/ Dear Lord, we'd all like to know/Do they have Mogen David in heaven, sweet Jesus/ If they don't, who the hell wants to go?" Larry, who is against hard drugs and violence, does not believe in being sanctimonious about it. In this case, as he replied to critics, he was expressing the feelings of the people involved, not his own.

"When I write a song, I try to put myself in the position of the people I'm writing about. I try to look at it with compassion and hope that telling the truth will allow listeners to draw common sense conclusions. I had people condemn me for writing lines like not wanting to go to heaven, but that was the skid row derelicts talking, not me."

As it happens, the inspiration for the song was far removed from skid row. "We were eating in this Chinese restaurant in Saginaw, Michigan, and walked outside stuffed and happy. I said, 'Man, if they don't have Chinese food in heaven, I don't want to go.' It just stuck in my head. It was too good a line to lose. I couldn't get to sleep until I used it and the song just wrote itself."

Larry is quick to point out that the success of "Midnight Choir" indicates that most listeners did understand what he was trying to illustrate. He also expresses pride in responses describing the positive impact of some of his songs on people's lives. As an example, one girl wrote to tell him that listening to one of his songs on the radio snapped her out of a near-suicidal depression. In another case a mother wrote to say that "Penny Annie," about a girl whose life is destroyed by drug addiction, gave her daughter the strength to refuse to join others in her sorority in trying heroin. He called the family, who lived in Iowa, and asked how things were going. "I wanted to speak to her daughter, who wasn't there at first, but who came in while I was still on the phone. I talked to her and she told me all was going well."

One hint he has for aspiring songwriters is to listen as well as observe. "I try to be a very good listener. The ability to listen is a very important asset for someone who writes songs. I feel I'm maturing as a human being and a songwriter. I realize the same thing ties us all together—men and women, boys and girls—it's humanness. I try not to moralize, but I believe in caring and I hope it shows in my songs."—A.S.

Larry Gatlin quotes from 1980 interview with Irwin Stambler.

GAYLE, CRYSTAL: *Singer, songwriter. Born Paintsville, Kentucky, Jaunary 9, 1951.*

Crytal Gayle hardly sounds like the typical country singer of several decades ago. Then again, the different musical styles of country and pop have increasingly faded into each other as country music has become accepted by a wider audience than ever before. By the same token, the influence of rock has become more acceptable in country circles. Indeed, Crystal has played an important role in the growing popularity of country music. Her dramatic, almost operatic, vocal style makes her more like an American version of the late French balladeer, Edith Piaf, than the more traditional country style of her older sister, Loretta Lynn.

Crystal's life, too, has been a blend of country and city influences. Born Brenda Gail Webb (later renamed Crystal Gayle when she started her recording career), she was the youngest of the eight children born to Ted and Clara Webb and spent much of her childhood in Wabash, Indiana. Loretta, the second eldest of the children, spent her entire youth in rural Butchers Hollow, Kentucky, only 400 miles away from Wabash, but an entirely different environment. Crystal's father, Ted Webb, an ex-coal miner, was a victim of black lung disease and had trouble finding work, so her mother, Clara, supported her children through a series of jobs. Ted died in 1959, and Clara eventually remarried; she and her husband lived in Wabash in the same house she bought before two of her daughters became famous singers.

Sister Loretta was married by the time Crystal was born, and while Gayle was growing up, Lynn was making her way up the rungs to country-music stardom. As a teenager, Crystal listened mainly to pop and folk music, yet she sang country songs with her family on weekends in church and for charity benefits. As she told one reporter, "Wabash just wasn't a country-music town. It was always a big thing in my life, but you know how some people used to think about country music: even if they liked it in the privacy of their homes, they were ashamed to admit it, because they didn't want to be looked down upon."

After Crystal graduated from high school, she started touring with Loretta, also signing on her sister's record label, Decca (now MCA). Crystal recorded a song written by Loretta, "I've Cried the Blues Right Out of My Eyes," which was a minor hit, making number 23 on the country charts. Loretta coined her new name, Crystal Gayle, so as not to duplicate the name of Brenda Lee, also on the same label. The name was derived from a hamburger chain, Krystal's, in business around Nashville. Despite her hit and her new name, Gayle was unhappy with MCA. She felt they didn't promote her enough and saw her only as Loretta Lynn's baby sister, so she signed with United Artists in 1972. By then she had also married her high school sweetheart, Bill Gatzimos.

At United Artists, Crystal teamed up with producer Allen Reynolds, who had also been responsible for refining Don Williams' laid-back country style. Reynolds helped Crystal to define her own taste and style, and soon after things began to happen for her. Her first United Artists single, "Restless," reached the top 40 on the charts.

Crystal's renown kept growing with each new album she recorded. Her first UA album, *Crystal Gayle*, contained three country hit singles, "Beyond You," "Wrong Road Again," and "This Is My Year for Mexico." Her second album, entitled *Somebody Loves You*, contained the hit single, "Somebody Loves You" and Crystal's first number-one hit, "I'll Get Over You." Her third album, *Crystal*, included "One More Time," "Do It All Over Again," and "Never Miss a Real Good Thing." This album was her first to show some pop crossover potential.

By this time, many country fans had taken note of Gayle's talent. She had already been named "Outstanding Female Vocalist" in 1976 by the Academy of Country Music. With the release of her fourth album, *We Must Believe in Magic*, in mid-1977, Crystal truly achieved nationwide recognition. Her single from that album, "Don't It Make My Brown Eyes Blue," climbed to number one on both country and pop music charts. The album reached platinum status in February 1978, the first recording by a female country artist to sell more than a million copies. Crystal was named Best Female Country Singer by the Grammy Awards, the Academy of Country Music, and the Country Music Association.

Following these successes, some of Crystal's cuts from previous albums were re-released. In addition, she re-recorded a song from an earlier album, "Ready for the Times to Get Better," and earned herself another number-one country hit.

Crystal's fifth album, *When I Dream*, contained the hits "Talking in Your Sleep," "Someday Soon," and "Why Have You Left the One You Left Me For." The Country Music Association named her Best Female Vocalist in 1978, for the sec-

ond year in a row. During 1979, she added to her list of top-10 singles on UA with releases like "What Have You Left the One You Left Me For" and "When I Dream." At year end, "Your Old Cold Shoulder" was moving up the lists, reaching the top 10 in early 1980.

By 1979, the strikingly beautiful singer with knee-length hair had become an internationally known star. She appeared on all the major variety shows as well as on several specials, such as the Lou Rawls special, the Osmond Brothers special, and Bob Hope's "Road to China" television show, for which she went to the People's Republic of China during the summer of 1979. She also had her own special on CBS, the first for any female country vocalist.

In 1979, Crystal switched from the UA label to Columbia. When she moved, she took producer Allen Reynolds with her, who had been a major contributing factor to the continual success of her record releases. Her debut album on Columbia, *Miss the Mississippi*, came out during 1979 and went gold soon after its release. It provided such hit singles as "Half the Way," "It's Like We Never Said Goodbye," and "The Blue Side." "It's Like We Never Said Goodbye" became her first number-one single on Columbia, reaching that pinnacle in April 1980. Late in 1980, the single "If You Ever Change Your Mind" was in the top 10. Her 1981 hits included "Take It Easy" and "The Woman in Me." Her charted albums during 1980–81 included, on UA/Liberty, *Classic Crystal* and *A Woman's Heart* and, on Columbia, besides *Miss the Mississippi*, *These Days* and *Hollywood, Tennessee*. During 1981 she worked with Tom Waits on the soundtrack for the Francis Ford Coppola film *One from the Heart*, released in early 1982.

In an interview with Dennis Hunt of the *Los Angeles Times*, Gayle revealed that she consciously chose to record softer, more middle-of-the-road-type songs than her sister, Loretta Lynn. "If I sang real country like she does," Crystal said, "the country audience would never accept me. They'd all say I was trying to copy her. The kinds of songs she sings don't suit me, anyway.

You have to be sort of hard to sing hardcore country. I wouldn't be convincing singing that stuff."

GENTRY, BOBBIE: *Singer, guitarist, songwriter. Born Chickasaw County, Mississippi, July 27, 1944.*

In early July 1967, six violin players, two cellists and a pretty, blue-jeaned guitar-carrying young woman entered Capitol Records' Studio C in Hollywood. The group recorded a song written by the woman and shown to Capitol artists & repertoire executive Kelly Gordon only a few days before. Within a few weeks after the session, the previously unknown woman had a worldwide reputation as the song, "Ode to Billy Joe," became number one on both pop and country charts in the United States and a worldwide sensation.

The song, which also became the theme for a motion picture of the same name in the 1970s, has become a classic. One of Bobbie Gentry's primary creative credits, the song was the first of many that were to have a marked impact on the pop and country field in the late 1960s and early 1970s.

Bobbie Gentry wrote the country/delta-blues melody to the song from memories of her childhood in Mississippi's delta region. She was born there and spent her early years in rural settings. When she was six she went to live with her grandparents in a farmhouse in Chickasaw County, Mississippi, without indoor plumbing or electricity. Her grandparents, sensing the child's musical interest, traded a cow for an old piano when Bobbie was seven.

She taught herself to play by imitating the methods of the local church pianist, who played mostly on the black keys. Bobbie remembers using those keys as the basis for her first composition, penned when she was seven and called "My Dog Sergeant Is a Good Dog," later to become part of her nightclub act.

When she was thirteen, Bobbie's family moved to Palm Springs, California, which was to become home. In her teens, she took up a number of other instruments, including guitar, vibraharp, banjo, and bass fiddle. She continued to spend time writing music and at one point got a job performing in a local country club.

After graduating from Palm Valley High School, she enrolled at the University of California at Los Angeles to major in philosophy and took on occasional club dates as an entertainer to help finance her education. After a while, she decided to focus on music, studying musical theory, composition, and counterpoint at the Los Angeles Conservatory of Music. During those years, she performed with several small theater groups and also worked as a dancer in Las Vegas, Nevada, for a time.

She built up a backlog of original songs and began to show them to record companies, finally achieving her 1967 Capitol session. When "Ode to Billy Joe" became a million-selling single, she incorporated many other songs based on the rhythms of her original home area into the debut LP, such as "Chickasaw County Child," "Lazy Willie," "Papa Won't Let Me Go into Town with You," and "Tuesday's Child." The album, *Ode to Billy Joe,* came out in November 1967 and made the charts soon after, remaining there into 1968 and bringing Gentry a second gold-record award. In the voting of the National Academy of Recording Arts & Sciences for 1967, Bobbie won three Grammy Awards: Best New Artist, Best Contemporary Female Solo Vocal Performance, and Best Vocal Performance, Female. The Academy of Country and Western Music also named her the Most Promising Female Vocalist of 1967.

For the rest of the 1960s, Bobbie established herself as an international star. Besides appearing in concerts all over the United States and Canada, she was featured in person and on TV in England, Holland, France, Germany, and Australia. She was invited to appear at Italy's San Remo Song Festival and won the Italian Press Award for her performance of "La Siepa."

The same year, 1968, she was featured on "Tom Jones' Radio Special" on the BBC and was so well received there and as a guest on several TV shows that she was offered her own program. Beginning in 1968, she was hostess and star of the *Bobbie Gentry* TV series for BBC, an annual series that remained on the BBC through the early 1970s. The series was expanded to other overseas markets in 1971. At home, Bobbie also became a familiar TV figure, starring in three 20th Century–Fox specials and cohosting a CMA Awards show, a Grammy Awards show, and a number of other programs. In 1969, she was asked to host the weekly *Bobbie Gentry Show* on Armed Forces Radio, a program still featured during the first part of the 1970s.

In 1968, she recorded a duet LP with Glen Campbell, *Bobbie Gentry and Glen Campbell*, that caught the music public's fancy. It rose high on pop and country charts and earned both artists a gold-record award in 1969. Her work with Glen resulted in a number of successful singles, such as "Let It Be Me," which earned a Country Music Association Award in 1970, and a new version of an Everly Brothers' hit, "All I Have to Do Is Dream," which earned a silver disc as a bestseller in England in 1970. Among her other solo releases of the period were the LPs *Touch 'Em with Love* (8/69), *Bobbie Gentry's Greatest!* (12/69), *Fancy* (1970), *Sittin' Pretty/Tobacco Road* (1970), and *Patchwork* (4/71).

Bobbie continued to maintain a hectic schedule as performer, writer, and manager of several business enterprises, including her own production and publishing company, Gentry Ltd. However, she cut back on her work as public interest in her recordings appeared to fade and, by the late 1970s, her association with the music field mainly took the form of behind-the-scenes efforts.

GIBBS, TERRI: *Singer, pianist. Born Augusta, Georgia, June 15, 1954.*

Terri Gibbs was born blind, but she also was born with talent that compensated—to an extent—for her misfortune. She gave evidence of this when only three by demonstrating the ability to pick out tunes on the piano. As she grew older, she continued to improve her keyboard skills until she was an excellent player in her teens. By then she also had acquired experience singing in public, initially performing gospel songs in local churches.

From the last years in elementary school on, Terri was showing determination to shape a musical career. She entered a number of talent contests, some of which she won, and took part in school shows and events in elementary and high school. In the early 1970s, when she was eighteen, she went to Nashville to make her first demonstration recordings, but wasn't able to win the attention of country-music recording executives.

Before she was twenty, she was a member of her first professional band, Sound Dimension. Soon after, in 1975, she formed her own group in Augusta, Georgia. She got an engagement for the new group at the Steak and Ale Restaurant in Augusta. It proved to be more than a fly-by-night relationship. Five years later, at the start of the 1980s, she was still the featured attraction in the restaurant's lounge, playing three sets a night during which she typically sang about fifty songs each evening.

Hoping to go beyond that, Gibbs periodically sent new demo tapes to record companies in Nashville. For a long time that only brought silence or polite rejections. But in 1979, one tape came across the desk of Nashville-based songwriter-producer Ed Penney. He liked Terri's voice, but found her address either had been accidentally left off or had fallen off. Fortunately, soon after a second demo tape from Terri came to him, this time with a return address.

Terri came to Nashville to make her first recordings under Penney's direction. One of the songs in the session, written by Penny and co-writer J. Gillespie, was called "Somebody's Knockin'." It became the title song of her first album as well as her debut single. Both were released in the fall of 1980 by MCA Records. Disc jockeys picked up on the song and before long it was on the country charts, moving up to the top 20 by year end and moving into the top 10 in January 1981.

Both single and album were impressive first efforts. In April 1981, they provided the basis for Gibbs' selection by the Academy of Country Music as the Top New Female Vocalist. More honors followed: in the *Music City News* poll in June she was one of the finalists for Most Promising Female Artist of the Year; *Record World* in July named her its Most Promising Female Vocalist of Adult Contemporary Music and ranked her third in the top 10 of adult contemporary female vocalists; the Country Music Association nominated her in three categories in the 1981 awards competition, including those for Female Vocalist of the Year and Single of the Year. In September 1981 she got the chance to make her first appearance on the *Grand Ole Opry*. That same month saw the release of her second MCA album, *I'm a Lady*.

In the CMA Awards voting, announced in October, she proved to be the first winner in a new category, the Horizon Award.

GIBSON, BOB: *Singer, guitarist, folk music collector. Born New York, New York, November 16, 1931.*

As a solo performer and part of the Gibson and Camp folk song team, Bob Gibson had considerable impact on the U.S. folk music movement. As a collector of a number of previously obscure folk songs of Ohio and the Midwest, he also enhanced other artists' repertoires.

Gibson himself was not a native of the Midwest. He was born and raised in New York City, which, by the time he was in his teens, was the center of thriving folk music activity spearheaded by people like Pete Seeger, Woody Guthrie, Leadbelly, Oscar Brand, and Burl Ives. Listening to folk music broadcasts and recordings inspired Gibson to develop skills on guitar and five-string banjo and to learn a number of folk songs. By the late 1940s, he was performing in folk clubs and in folk music concerts.

Like many young folk enthusiasts of the period, he started to go off on collecting trips, ferreting out authentic folk ballads, especially in the Midwest. Thus one of his first albums, on Stinson Records, titled *Folksongs of Ohio,* included such songs as "Katey Morey," "Ohio River," "There Was an Old Woman," "Workin' on a Pushboat," and "Father Grumble."

By the mid-1950s, Bob was ranked as one of the best new folk artists. Following his initial TV appearance in 1954 on a Cleveland station, he performed on several network shows in succeeding years. He also gave a notable concert at New York's Carnegie Hall, which was the basis for a live LP issued by Riverside Records. His concert selections demonstrated a wide-ranging repertoire with material not restricted to Midwest origins. Among his offerings were "Sail Away Ladies," "Michael Row the Boat Ashore," "Marry a Texas Girl," "Day-O," "Go Down to Bimini," "Wheel-a-Matilda," "Good News," "When I Was Single," "You Must Come in at the Door," "Alberta," "The Erie Canal," and "John Riley."

Riverside Records issued two other albums by Gibson in the 1950s, *Offbeat Folk Songs* and *I Come for to Sing*. In 1959 he signed with Elektra; his debut album was *Ski Songs,* followed in June 1961 with the album *Yes I See.*

At the start of the 1960s, he and Bob Camp (later known as Hamilton Camp) became one of the most popular acts on the folk music circuit. They played before sizable audiences in folk clubs, coffee houses, and college auditoriums all over the United States. They were featured on the Elektra album *Bob Gibson and Bob Camp* issued in December 1961.

As the resurgence of rock in the Beatles era pushed folk music into the background again, Gibson and Camp decided to go separate ways. Camp was more interested in combining folk with rock while Gibson preferred the more traditional approach. Elektra released another Gibson LP at the start of 1964 titled *Where I'm Bound.* Later it issued a solo LP titled *Hamilton Camp* (December 1964) Camp, who worked with various rock artists during the 1960s, had an album on Warner Brothers, issued in February 1968, called *Here's to You.*

Compared to his status in the days of the folk music boom, Gibson had a relatively low profile from the mid-1960s on. He continued to perform on the folk club circuit and on the college concert scene and also appeared at a number of folk festivals over the years. At the start of the 1970s he was represented on Capitol Records with the LP *Bob Gibson.*

In 1976, Gibson and Camp reestablished

their duo and began to appear at small folk clubs like McCabe's in Los Angeles. The songs they offered were in a more modern vein than in their previous association, examples being Camp's rendition of a song once in the repertoire of the group Quicksilver Messenger Service, "Pride of Man," and Gibson's offering of Shel Silverstein's "You Should Have Seen Me in 1961." The latter recounted the saga of many of the leading lights of the early 1960s folk boom who were idolized by fans back then but who never adapted to changing times.

GIBSON, DON: *Singer, guitarist, songwriter. Born Shelby, North Carolina, April 3, 1928.*

A common witticism in Nashville in the 1960s and 1970s was that if an artist badly needed a new hit record, the best approach was to listen to some old Don Gibson albums. A tribute to Don Gibson's songwriting ability, the approach worked for many performers—some who needed new hits and some who already were at the top of the heap. As for Gibson, though his career as a writer reached its zenith in the late 1950s and early 1960s, his efforts as a recording artist and sometime performer— using both original material and that crafted by others—continued along at a steady, if not spectacular pace throughout the 1960s, 1970s, and into the 1980s.

Growing up in North Carolina, Don showed an aptitude for music in his early years, learning to play guitar before he finished grade school and, before he was in his teens, singing at local events. At fourteen he turned professional and gained experience, during the mid-1940s, working on country shows at many radio stations in the South.

Just after World War II ended he moved to Knoxville, Tennessee, where he soon was featured on the WNOX *Tennessee Barn Dance* and the *Mid-day Merry-Go-Round.* By the mid-1950s, he was one of the best-known performers in the area and received the key to the city from the mayor in acknowledgment.

Don had expanded his audience somewhat in the early and mid-1950s with recordings that sometimes were local or regional hits. His major successes, however, came in the songwriting area. Increasingly, both Knoxville and Nashville artists looked to him for important new material. His first major credit came in 1956 when Faron Young gained a top-10 hit with Don's "Sweet Dreams," ever since one of the classic country songs. Two years later Kitty Wells had similar success with "I Can't Stop Loving You."

Meanwhile, Wesley Rose of Acuff–Rose Publishing Company had seen him perform at a Knoxville club and brought his talents to the attention of RCA Victor. The company signed Don to a long-term contract in 1957. The following year he scored three national country hits with his own compositions, a top-10 single "Give Myself a Party" and two number-one songs, "Blue, Blue Day" and "Oh Lonesome Me." Now a national celebrity with country fans, he was asked to join the *Grand Ole Opry* in 1958.

Gibson closed out the 1950s in style with two more top-10 hits, "Don't Tell Me Your Troubles" and "Who Cares." He moved into the 1960s with a top-10 original in 1960, "Just One Time," and in 1961, his own recorded hit of "Sweet Dreams." In 1961, he also made the top 10 with another writer's song, the H. David–P. Hampton "Sea of Heartbreak." In 1962, Kitty Wells made the top 10 with Don's "Day into Night" and Don also made it with two more of his own songs, "I Can Mend Your Broken Heart" and "Lonesome Number One." In 1963, he didn't have any top 10 releases, but Patsy Cline scored a top-10 hit with Don's "Sweet Dreams." After a rare year with no top-ranked songs or records in 1964, Don returned in 1965 with "Watch Where You're Going" and in 1966 with "(Yes) I'm Hurting." But the late 1960s proved disappointing, with only one or two chart-making releases and no major hits. This situation, in turn, ended his association with RCA. He moved to Hickory Records, which helped spark a renewal of his career in the 1970s.

From the late 1950s to the start of the 1970s, Gibson provided material for several dozen albums on RCA or its subsidiary label, Camden, many of which made the album charts. Among those LPs were *Lonesome Me* (6/58), *No One Stands Alone* (2/59), *That Gibson Boy* (11/59), *Look Who's Blue* (6/60), *Sweet Dreams* (2/61), *Girls, Guitars* (9/61), *Some Favorites* (7/62), *I Wrote a Song* (10/63), *God Walks Hills* (6/64), *Blue Million Tears* (Camden, 3/65), *Best of Don Gibson* (8/65), *Too Much Hurt* (12/65), *Fabulous Don Gibson* (Harmony, 1/66), *Don Gibson with Spanish Guitars* (7/66), *Hurtin' Inside* (Camden, 11/66), *Great Songs* (12/66), *All My Love* (8/67), *King of Country Soul* (1968), *All Time Country Gold* (8/69), *Great Don Gibson* (with the Jordanaires, 10/70), *Best of Don Gibson, Volume 2* (3/70), *Lovin' Lies* (Camden, 5/70), *I Walk Alone* (Camden, 8/71).

Almost as soon as Don signed with Hickory (then part of the MGM organization), his name began to appear on the singles charts with regularity, for the most part with material written by others. Among his early 1970s chartmakers were "Someway" in late 1970; "Touch Your Woman," a top-10 hit in the spring of 1972; "I Think They Call It Love," a duet with Sue Thompson, in the summer of 1972; and the top-5 success that summer, "Woman (Sensuous Woman)." In the mid-1970s, his charted singles included "Snap Your Fingers" and "One Day at a Time" in 1974; "I'll Sing tor You," "(There She Goes) I Wish Her Well" (written by Don), "Oh How Love Changes," sung with Sue Thompson, and "Don't Stop Loving Me" (by Gibson) in 1975; and, in 1976, "Doing My Time." In the late 1970s, he made the charts with releases like "If You Ever Get to Houston (Look Me Down)" and "When Do We Stop Starting Over" in 1977; "The Fool" and "Oh Such a Stranger/I Love You Because" in 1978; and "Any Day Now" in 1979. His releases from 1977 to 1979 were on the ABC/Hickory label.

Gibson also recorded many albums during the 1970s, including *Don Gibson* on MGM and, on Hickory, *Hits, Hits, Don Gibson Way, Perfect Mountain, Don Gibson Sings Hank Williams,* and *Country Green.*

During his long career, Gibson naturally traveled extensively, appearing at one time or another in all fifty of the United States and many foreign countries. Besides his many years on the *Opry,* he also was featured on countless radio and TV programs over the years. During the 1970s, he cut down on his travel schedule, though he still was making occasional swings across the United States at the end of the decade. In keeping with his low-key approach to performing, he refused to assemble his own band for such appearances, preferring to use various "house" bands. This approach indicated that he always valued his writing ability more highly than his entertaining efforts.

The lasting nature of his work was underscored by the way some of his 1950s compositions provided 1970s hits. In 1974, a then newcomer named Ronnie Milsap scored a number-one success with Don's 1959 song "Legend in My Time," an achievement that helped win him the CMA Award as Best Male Vocalist of that year. In 1975, Emmylou Harris earned a number-one country hit with the venerable "Sweet Dreams." In 1981, the hit single of his "One More Time" by Tompall and the Glazer Brothers played a role in making the reunion of the famous group successful.

In the early 1980s, Don formed a new recording affiliation with Warner/Curb Records. One of the first products of that was the 1980 charted single "Sweet Sensuous Sensations."

GILLEY, MICKEY: *Singer, pianist, songwriter. Born Natchez, Louisiana, March 9, circa 1937.*

Entertainment history is full of stories about talented individuals who confront the problem of sounding almost exactly like someone already famous—Sinatra doubles, Presley sound-alikes, and so on. Some of those unfortunates make a precarious living mimicking the one lucky enough to come first; most sink without a trace. Mickey Gilley, however, beat the odds.

Gilley's problem was that both in vocal style and piano technique he seemed for a long time like a carbon copy of Jerry Lee Lewis. It wasn't all that surprising, since the two were first cousins: Gilley's mother Irene was the sister of Jerry Lee's father

Elmo. Jerry Lee was several years older, but the two were almost inseparable as children, along with a third cousin named Jimmy Swaggart, who went on to become a famous radio and TV minister. (Mickey was born in Natchez, Louisiana, but grew up in Jerry Lee's home area of Ferriday.) The three all became interested in playing the piano and, though they came from poor families, their parents managed to get them instruments. In Gilley's case, his mother saved money from the eighteen dollars a week she earned as a waitress to get her son a piano when he was ten or eleven.

It was the mid-1960s and blues and boogie woogie were in vogue in the black community while country music was the staple of most white Southerners. The three boys fell in love with boogie woogie, though, and crept into a place in the black section of town called Haney's Big House to listen to the music and pick up the infectious piano rhythms. By the time they were in their teens, all three could play pretty well, but only Jerry Lee thought of it as the basis for a career.

In 1954, Gilley had pretty well forgotten about the music field. He had gotten married and settled in Houston, where he worked in the parts department of an engineering firm. In 1956, he heard one of Jerry Lee's initial releases on Sun Records, "Crazy Arms," and after getting over his first excitement began to try to move in that direction himself. Soon he cut his first record at the Gold Star Studio in Houston amid dreams of glory. As he admitted later, the record was awful.

However, though success didn't smile on him, he had gotten the show business bug. He kept polishing his piano playing and began to get more session work in local studios, including one owned by Huey Meaux, the "Crazy Cajun," who later was instrumental in Freddy Fender's climb to fame. He began to pick up work in clubs and bars in the latter 1950s, including stints in New Orleans, Biloxi, the Azalea Grille in Mobile, Alabama, and an extended stay at Ray's Lounge in Lake Charles, Louisiana. He cut more sides for a series of small labels and moved up a

notch to Dot Records, where he gained some attention for the single "Call Me Shorty." However, by the time he decided to make Houston home base again in 1959, his recording efforts essentially were failures. Things took a slight upturn later in the year when he scored a local hit with his version of a Warner Mack success, "Is It Wrong?"

But that proved to be a flash in the pan. Audiences seemed to feel that one Jerry Lee Lewis was enough. In the meantime, Gilley developed into a personable live performer with a strong local following. He earned a reasonable salary working in a series of clubs, beginning with the Ranch House in 1959 and continuing in popular spots in an outlying area of Houston on the Spencer Highway. That was the way things went throughout the 1960s, despite another regional hit single, "Lonely Wine," in 1964. For most of the decade he was featured at Houston's Nesadel Club.

At the start of the 1970s, he changed his pattern, teaming up with a friend named Sherwood Cryer to open their own club, Gilley's, in Pasadena, Texas. The club prospered, featuring Mickey Gilley and his Rocking Piano. Mickey branched out some, hosting his own shows on local TV. Every now and then, he got restless, though, and made an effort to gain recognition outside the Houston area. His similarity to Jerry Lee didn't bother the Houston populace, who made Mickey one of their favorite entertainers, but it tended to work against him with record companies, disc jockeys, and the wider public. Thus when he got the chance to record an album for GRT in the early 1970s, he consciously tried to change his style. He went so far as to refuse to play the piano at all during the sessions.

As he told Peter Guralnick for a *Country Music* article, "I let it bug me to the point where it just about drove me nuts, man. I didn't want to sound anything like Jerry Lee at all, even though I knew that the type of music that he played was the type of music that I feel."

That effort came to naught too and, by 1974, Gilley had just about abandoned hope of national attention. Then a strange series of events catapulted him into the limelight almost before he knew what happened. The catalyst was the request by the ticket taker at Gilley's for Mickey to record a song she loved, "She Calls Me Baby," for local juke box distribution. He agreed and, needing something for the "B" side, put in a song that had been a hit for George Morgan called "Room Full of Roses." In preparing the song, Mickey decided to overdub some steel guitar on his recording. But the engineer, in mixing the material, made the steel guitar much louder than Gilley thought proper.

As he told Guralnick, when he heard the final version of the single he had mixed emotions. "I liked "She Calls Me Baby" and thought to myself, well, I finally got something. Then I flipped the record over. All I could hear was that damn steel guitar. The echo was just bounding off the walls. I called up the engineer. I said, 'Why's it so loud?' He said, 'Man, I just mixed it the way I felt it.' 'Well, I said, 'I'm just going to have to remix it. This is terrible.' I went and got the tape. I actually cued the tape up, then I said, 'Hey, I don't want to take the time to mess with this. It's just a local record; it's only going to be played on the local jukeboxes.'"

Once the single came out, "Room Full of Roses" swept Houston. Smelling victory at last, Gilley flew to Nashville to try for a major record tie-up. Everyone turned him down and he was just about to give up again when he thought about one last possibility, the newly established Playboy label. He took a plane to California, where the company's executives agreed to take a chance. The song turned out to have as powerful an influence on the national country audiences as on Houston. By early spring the single was on the national charts and before long Mickey had his first top-10 hit. This was only the beginning. He followed up with the single "City Lights," which came out at the end of 1974 and quickly zoomed to number one on the charts. Simultaneously, the album of the same title was making a similar move so that in February, Mickey's name dominated both the album and singles charts.

From then on, Mickey was on the move

to the top echelons of the country field. He was featured on just about every major TV show, beginning with the *Grand Ole Opry* and extending to nationally telecast country and pop programs. Though Houston remained his main stamping ground, other pianists appeared at Gilley's while Mickey performed in the major stops on the country-music personal appearance circuit.

Meanwhile, Mickey's name rarely was missing from the charts in the mid- and late-1970s. Among his chart singles during that period were "Bouquet of Roses" and "Roll You Like a Wheel" (a duet with Barbi Benton) in 1975; "Don't the Girls All Get Prettier at Closing Time" and "Bring It on Home to Me," both top-10 hits in 1976; the number-one "Honky Tonk Memories" and "Chains of Love" in 1977; and "Here Comes the Hurt Again" and "The Song We Made Love To" in 1978. Mickey's Playboy chart albums included *Overnight Sensation* in early 1976; *Gilley's Greatest Hits, Volume 1*, in the top 10 in August 1976; and *First Class*, a top-10 hit in the summer of 1977. By the late 1970s, he signed with a new label, Epic.

Mickey still found time to appear at his own club in the late 1970s and into the 1980s, and Gilley's prospered whether he or some other country star headlined. The club was selected as the setting for John Travolta's film *Urban Cowboy*, that was issued in 1980. Gilley and his band were given prominent parts in the film score and their contributions were included in the soundtrack LP that was released in April 1980.

His late 1970s and early 1980s chart singles on Epic included "Just Long Enough to Say Goodbye" and "My Silver Lining" in 1979: "A Little Getting Used To," on the lists from late 1979 to early 1980; "True Love Ways" and "That's All That Matters to Me" in 1980: and "A Headache Tomorrow (Or a Heartache Today)" and "Lonely Nights" in 1981. Also a bestseller was the single "Stand By Me," issued by Asylum Records during the summer of 1980. His 1980–81 chart hit Epic LPs included *Encore* and *That's All That Matters to Me*. Epic issued his LP *You Don't Know Me* in July 1981.

GIMBLE, JOHNNY: *Singer, fiddler, mandolinist, banjo player, songwriter. Born near Tyler Texas, May 30, 1926.*

For decades most of Johnny Gimble's instrumental contemporaries knew that he was one of the greatest fiddle players Texas had ever produced. His name, however, wasn't very familiar to most followers of country & western music most of that time, though the sounds of his fiddle (and other instruments) could be heard on the hit records of many artists over the years. All that changed in the mid-1970s when Johnny, helped by a revival of interest in western swing bands, suddenly found himself in the spotlight as a solo performer.

Born and raised in Texas, Johnny showed ability as a musician at an early age and could play several instruments by the time he was in his teens. At the age of sixteen, he played banjo for a group headed by Bob and Joe Shelton. At the end of the decade, in 1949, he got the chance to join one of the foremost western swing bands in history, Bob Wills' Texas Playboys. Again he wasn't recruited as a fiddler but as a mandolinist.

In his years with Wills, which extended well into the 1950s, he established himself as a first-rank fiddler. Besides playing fiddle and other instruments, he also wrote a number of original songs, some of which were recorded by the Playboys. By the time Gimble's years with Wills came to an end, he had an impressive reputation with important artists in both country and pop music and with record producers. During the 1960s and early 1970s, when he wasn't working as a sideman with various tour bands, he had a busy schedule of session work in major studios in Nashville and other major music industry centers. In his fiddle playing, he demonstrated amazing versatility on not just one type of fiddle but two. One of those was a four-string instrument he called "Ole Red," the other with five strings, he just referred to as his "Five."

This pattern might have continued throughout the 1970s except that Bob Wills, who had been semiretired for some years, conceived a new record project. He wanted to reform his Playboys band for new versions of some of his most famous songs. But this wasn't to be just any band; he wanted to assemble what he considered the best of all those who had been in the band over the decades of its existence. The fiddle players he wanted were Keith Coleman and Johnny.

The project got under way, but only part of the sessions was completed when Wills was incapacitated by a stroke. The remaining members went on to finish the recordings, which later provided the basis for the multi-LP set *For the Last Time*. Meanwhile, Leon McAuliffe and Leon Rausch, who had taken over the band's reins after Wills was stricken, eventually agreed to some new stage work by the band. In October 1975 (by which time Wills had died), the group won a standing ovation when it made a guest appearance at Nashville's Exit-In club with Asleep at the Wheel. That, in turn, paved the way for further concert work in early 1976 and a decision to make some new band recordings for Capitol.

Gimble continued as a featured artist with the all-star group during those events and was a member of the band for its 1976 studio sessions for the new Capitol LP. Meanwhile, he had received additional notice for some of his solos in a Capitol release in August 1976 (*Bob Wills and His Texas Playboys in Concert*) prepared from tapes of old radio programs. This activity brought him renewed attention from members of the Country Music Association, who voted him Instrumentalist of the Year in the CMA Awards competition, results of which were announced on a network TV show in October 1976.

As a result, he began to get offers from recording executives to cut some solo albums of his own. By the time the new Playboys studio LP came out in August 1977, titled *The Late Bob Wills' Texas Playboys Today*, he had taken leave of the band to work on the new solo material. He turned out two LPs during the year, one on Capitol called *Fiddlin' Around* and another on Lone Star Records called *Johnny Gimble,*

Texas Dance Party. Both albums still are considered prime examples of "old-timey" Texas fiddling.

In the late 1970s, Gimble headlined a number of shows of his own on the country-music circuit. He also continued to back some of the superstars of the period, such as Willie Nelson and Waylon Jennings. During 1979–81, for example, he was a member of Nelson's tour band, which played before large crowds in major venues all over the United States.

GOLDSBORO, BOBBY: *Singer, guitarist, ukulele player, songwriter. Born Marianna, Florida, January 18, 1941.*

Like many modern country artists, Bobby Goldsboro made his initial impression on the pop field before making country his primary interest. He probably provided almost as many hit records for other performers with his compositions as he achieved with his own releases, but his biggest success came with a song by another, Mac Davis' "Watching Scotty Grow."

Bobby, born in Marianna, Florida, learned to play guitar copying the styles of artists like Elvis Presley and Carl Perkins. After his family moved to Dothan, Alabama in his mid-teens, he formed a band with some friends called The Webs. After Bobby graduated high school and enrolled at Auburn University, in Auburn, Alabama, the band was still together, playing for school events and local parties.

After completing two years of college, Bobby decided to make music his career. His father reluctantly gave him the go-ahead to leave Auburn to try music full time, but with the agreement that Bobby would go back to get his degree if he made no progress after a year.

Fortunately, soon after that, a friend' lined up an audition for Bobby's band with Roy Orbison, who hired them as his backup group for a concert tour. The arrangement extended to two years, during which time Roy and Bobby became close friends and collaborated on a number of songs, a collaboration that continued after they went separate ways as performers.

Beginning a career as solo vocalist in the early 1960s, Bobby signed a recording contract with Laurie Records. His single "Molly" made the charts in December 1962 and stayed on lower levels until early 1963. Later that year, he left Laurie to sign with United Artists, which issued his debut album, *Bobby Goldsboro,* in July 1964. At about the same time, he had his first major singles hit with "See the Funny Clown." He followed with a series of chartmakers on pop lists, some of which also appeared on country charts, including "Little Things," "Voodoo Woman," "Broomstick Cowboy," "It's Too Late," "Blue Autumn," and "Can't Stop Loving You." Many of those were title tracks on his mid-1960s album releases, which included *Loving You* (issued 1/65), *Little Things* (6/65), *Broomstick Cowboy* (3/66), *It's Too Late* (5/66), *Blue Autumn* (1/67), *Solid* (4/67), *Romantic, Soulful* (10/67), and *Our Way of Life* (1968).

As the mid-1960s progressed, Bobby increased his stature as a performer, headlining shows in nightclubs and concert halls around the United States and making many guest appearances on major TV shows. In 1968, his career reached new heights with his hit single of Bobby Russell's "Honey." The single reached number-one position on both pop and country charts and was one of the ten biggest selling singles in the country field in 1968. Sales of the disc reached platinum levels. The song was so popular internationally that Bobby flew to England to re-record the song in several foreign languages. During the year his LP *Honey* also was on both pop and country charts many months. That achievement, plus his placing two other singles on country hit lists ("Autumn of My Life" and "The Straight Life") resulted in *Billboard* ranking him in the top-20 country artists of the year.

In 1970, Bobby made the album charts with the LPs *Bobby Goldsboro's Greatest Hits* and *Muddy Mississippi Line* and repeated that success in 1971 with *Come Back Home* and *We Gotta Start Lovin'.* That year he had a singles hit to match "Honey" with "Watching Scotty Grow," a song written by Mac Davis about his son. The song

Larry Gatlin and the Gatlin Brothers Band

Crystal Gayle

Bobbie Gentry

Don Gibson

Mickey Gilley

Epic/Larry Williams

Terri Gibbs

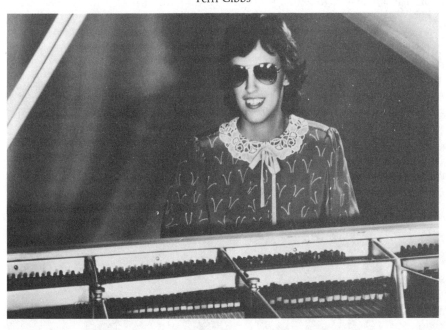

David Grisman

Steve Goodman

David Grisman Quintet: l. to r., Mark O'Connor, Mike Marshall, David Grisman, Darol Anger, Bob Wasserman

Arlo Guthrie

Woody Guthrie and Leadbelly

Pete Welding

brought Bobby top-10 attention on both pop and country charts. Also on the charts in 1971 was his single "And I Love You So."

In 1972, Bobby had another banner year, placing such singles as "California Wine," "Danny Is a Mirror for Me," "Poem for My Lady," and "With Pen in Hand" on the charts. The last named, an original composition, also was a major success for Vicki Carr and was recorded by many other artists during the 1970s. As of the mid-1970s, over seventy-five performers had offered their versions of "With Pen in Hand." In 1973, Bobby's name again was on top-chart levels with his single "Summer (The First Time)." Other notable Goldsboro releases during the late 1960s and the 1970s were "Autumn of My Life," "The Straight Life," and "I'm a Drifter."

His United Artists recordings of the mid-1970s included the country chart single "I Believe the South Is Gonna Rise Again" in the spring of 1974 and the major hit "A Butterfly for Bucky" in top-chart positions in the summer of 1976. One of his last album releases on United Artists was the 1976 *10th Anniversary* collection. Soon after that came out, Bobby ended his long association with the label and moved over to Epic Records.

His releases on Epic in the late 1970s provided several singles that made lower-chart levels, such as his composition "The Cowboy and the Lady" in mid-1977. However, as the decade came to a close he was still looking for recordings that could capture the public fancy as his earlier releases often had done.

At the start of the 1980s, Bobby joined the newly established CBS/Curb label and things seemed to take a turn for the better. In late 1980, he made upper-chart positions with the single "Goodbye Marie." In early 1981, his single of his composition "Alice Doesn't Love Here Anymore" did well with record buyers as did another 1981 single written by him, "The Round Up Saloon." A number of other artists also had good luck with some of his songs in the early 1980s, including Brenda Lee's 1980 top-10 single of "The Cowgirl and the Dandy."

GOODING, CYNTHIA: *Singer, guitarist, folk music collector. Born Rochester, Minnesota, August 12, 1924.*

One of the most familiar voices to New York radio audiences in the late 1940s and early 1950s was that of Cynthia Gooding. Often heard on Oscar Brand's folk music show on the New York City station WNYC, she also had her own radio folk music show for a good number of years.

Cynthia's schooling began in Minnesota and then extended to several private schools in the Midwest and Canada, including Laurel School for Girls in Cleveland, Lake Forest in Illinois, and Branksome Hall in Toronto. When she had completed high school, she decided to go to Mexico instead of to college. Up to this time, Gooding had little interest in folk music. South of the border, however, she was taken with the beauty of Mexican folk music. She learned guitar playing along with Spanish and soon began collecting some of the local songs. Her abilities were recognized by folk enthusiasts in Mexico City and she was featured on the city's station XEW in 1945.

In 1947 she returned to the United States and settled down in New York. By then she had decided to try for a career in folk music. The first positive result was an engagement at the Soho Club in Greenwich Village. She was so well received that she stayed for a year. As her talents became well known to radio audiences, invitations for recitals came from many parts of the country.

Marriage and a family caused her to cut down on her activities in the 1950s and 1960s, but she managed to give hundreds of recitals over the years in all the eastern and many midwestern states, and some in Mexico. Her skill in languages led to a varied repertoire that included songs from Spain, Portugal, Italy, Turkey, and Mexico as well as old American and English ballads.

Her linguistic talents merged well with those of another accomplished specialist, Theodore Bikel, on their Elektra LP, *A Young Man and a Maid.* Songs in the album include: "Coplas," "Parle Moi," "Greensleeves," "Laredo," "Mi Jaclito," "Haj Pada

Pada," and "A Meidl in di Yoren." Other LPs by Cynthia Gooding are *Faithful Lovers and Other Phenomena; Italian Folk Songs; Mexican Folk Songs; Turkish, Spanish, and Mexican Folk Songs;* and *Queen of Hearts* (early English folk songs).

GOODMAN, STEVE: *Singer, guitarist, banjoist, songwriter, record producer. Born Chicago, Illinois, July 25, 1948.*

During the 1970s, Chicago was the center of a mini folk boom. A number of very talented young artists and songwriters attracted growing attention not only from an enthusiastic (though relatively small) group of local folk adherents but also from many established performers who enjoyed visiting folk clubs like the Earl of Oldtown to catch the work of promising newcomers like Bonnie Koloc, John Prine, and Steve Goodman. Their work didn't spark any folk revival along the lines of a decade and a half earlier, but they did have an impact on the national scene at times. Steve Goodman, in particular, won music industry respect in 1972 when Arlo Guthrie's single of Steve's now-classic "City of New Orleans" made top-chart levels.

Goodman was born and raised in Chicago, the son (as he fondly recalled in his 1977 tribute to his father after his father's death) of a warm-hearted used car salesman. In his early years, Steve enjoyed the first wave of rock stars, but by the time he picked up his first guitar at the age of thirteen, it was 1961 and folksingers like Pete Seeger, Bob Gibson, and Bob Dylan were all the rage. As Steve moved through high school, his interests expanded to the work of earlier folk greats such as Woody Guthrie and the roots blues often played in Chicago black area clubs. Country music also was an influence, particularly the work of the great Hank Williams.

When Steve graduated from Maine Township East High School in the mid-1960s, his repertoire already was beginning to include some original compositions to go with the other folk and country songs he liked to sing. In the late 1960s, he had pretty much decided that he would try to earn his keep as a professional musician. Steve found the pickings meager, as might be expected in the folk song environment of those years. However, he found it possible to survive until better days came along by earning a side income writing radio commercials.

As he told Rick Ansorge of the *Chicago Lakes Countryside* (March 16, 1978), it came about unexpectedly. "I was playing in the Earl [of Oldtown] about ten years ago and was on the bill with a group called John Garbo's Banjo Rascals. One of the people in that group worked with an ad agency and talked me into coming down and singing one of those jingles for sixty bucks. It was for Dial Deodorant." He worked other such jobs for small amounts of money. "But then all of a sudden I did this Maybelline Blushing Eye Shadow spot and I got three hundred bucks for it. I didn't give it another thought, but a few months later it went on the air and they sent me a check for $1500. This was in January of 1970."

Shortly afterward came the marriage to his wife, Nancy, and, as it happened, the birth of "City of New Orleans." After their marriage, they went to visit Nancy's grandmother in the South and the train ride inspired Goodman to begin writing a song mourning the decline of railroad transportation.

In 1971, Goodman's career took an upward swing. Steve was on a double bill in Chicago with Kris Kristofferson. Paul Anka, he recalled for Ansorge, "was singing one of Kristofferson's songs in his nightclub act so he came to see him play on his night off. In the process he heard me play and paid for some demo sessions in New York." The result was a contract from Buddah Records. Kristofferson lent a hand by producing that debut LP for Steve. The album, *Steve Goodman,* came out in 1971 and earned some fine reviews, but not much else. However, it helped bring more engagements for Steve, particularly on the collegé circuit. Ever since then, Goodman's good-humored style and relaxed stage presence have won him so many followers that, for most of the 1970s, his concert income rather than record sales kept him afloat.

More important, the debut album contained "City of New Orleans," which caught Arlo Guthrie's interest. Guthrie's version became a gold record in 1972. Goodman noted Guthrie "slowed it down a bit, changed one of the chords and read the words so good that I learned the song."

Goodman's second Buddah LP, *Somebody Else's Troubles,* was issued in 1972. Steve's peer group respect was indicated by the people who helped out on the album. Besides such friends as Jimmy Buffett and John Prine, the credits include the name Bob Landy, an anagram for Bob Dylan. The release, though a good effort, didn't do much better than the first one. Problems between Goodman and the record company then kept him on the recording sidelines for two years afterward. When the situation finally was resolved, Steve moved to Elektra/Asylum, which issued his first effort for that label, *Jessie's Jig and Other Favorites.*

Still, though both critical and audience acceptance was better than before, Goodman was more successful as a songwriter than a performer. During the summer of 1975, country star David Allen Coe had a single of Steve's, "You Never Even Call Me by My Name," which rose high on the country charts. In April 1976, Steve's second Elektra/Asylum LP, *Words We Can Dance To,* came out. Coproduced by Steve and sometime co-writer Steve Burgh, the album included such highly listenable tracks as "Unemployed," "Old Fashioned," "Can't Go Back," and "Death of a Salesman." The album did somewhat better with the buying public, indicating that Steve was slowly widening his following. In October 1977, his next LP, *Say It in Private,* was issued, providing probably his best collection to that point. The songs ranged from a tongue-in-cheek "tribute" to the late boss of Chicago, "Daley's Gone," a Goodman version of Hank Williams' "Weary Blues from Waiting," and one of soul star Smokey Robinson's "Two Lovers," plus a fast-moving folk-country commentary co-written with John Prine, "The 20th Century Is Almost Over."

Backing Steve on that album as well as several tracks on the other two Elektra/

Asylum albums was country great Jethro Burns. In a series of concerts in support of the 1977 LP, Goodman and Burns blended their talents in fine fashion. Burns (of the famous comedy team of Homer and Jethro) not only backed Steve on many songs but provided some of the major highlights with solo work on the mandolin.

Besides his performing and writing efforts, Goodman also did some record production work during the 1970s. A good example of his expertise was John Prine's 1978 release, "Bruised Orange," the latter's debut on Elektra/Asylum and one of the best folk/folk-rock releases of 1978.

Steve's next solo LP on Elektra/Asylum was *High and Outside,* which came out in February 1979. On one track, "The One That Got Away," Steve was joined in duet by Nicolette Larson, a song recorded just before release of her first solo album. In October 1980, his LP *Hot Spot* was issued by Elektra/Asylum, a collection that turned out to be his swan song on that label.

GOSDIN, VERN: *Singer, guitarist, mandolinist, banjo player. Born Woodland, Alabama, August 5, 1934.*

One night in 1977 a nervous newcomer to country-music acclaim prepared to make his debut on the *Grand Ole Opry.* Vern Gosdin had first imagined himself on the *Opry* stage close to four decades earlier and had just about given up hope years before. But in the country field, there often is room for a second chance.

As he told writer Sanford Brokaw, "I used to listen to the *Opry* religiously every Saturday night down on our farm in Woodland, Alabama. There was no TV, so it was important. There were thirty-nine knobs and only two of them worked. The reception wasn't too good either. I had to go outside and jiggle the ground wire. Even then, I put one ear against the speaker so I could hear.

"There were many Saturday nights I went to sleep listening to the *Opry* and dreaming of being right there. By the time I was eight, I was a big fan of the Louvin

Brothers. I really liked their harmonies. This, of course, has been a big influence on my singing."

Those harmonies were emulated by Vern and two brothers, who started singing gospel songs in their church and then became regulars on the Gosdin Family gospel show on WVOK radio in Birmingham, Alabama, in the early 1950s. Vern moved to Atlanta, Georgia in 1953, where he sold ice cream to support himself while he sought work as a country artist. His next move was north to Chicago in 1956, where he ran a country-music nightclub, the D&G Tap, for several years. During that time, he continued to hone his bluegrass oriented style as a multitalented musician and a strong-voiced singer.

The big time in country music or music in general obviously wasn't Chicago, so in 1960, Vern headed west to California to join brother Rex in a bluegrass group called the Golden State Boys. In the early 1960s, Vern and Rex switched to a group called the Hillmen, led by a young California-bred bluegrass musician, Chris Hillman. But the folk boom was fading and Chris moved into rock after a while as a founding member of the folk-rock supergroup, the Byrds. The friendship between Chris and the Gosdins remained, which later led to Chris and another ex-Byrd, Clarence White, recording Vern's song "Someone to Turn To" for the soundtrack of the film Easy Rider.

Meanwhile, Vern worked as a session musician in the mid-1960s and tried to break into the recording field. He was signed for short periods with a variety of labels, including Liberty, Capitol, Metromedia, Era, and Bakersfield International with varying degrees of success. Vern and Rex continued to stress their traditional bluegrass sound, which was favored by many Byrds, including Gene Clark. This led to Gene teaming with them for the 1966 album Gene Clark with the Gosdin Brothers, where the sidemen included such names as Chris Hillman and Michael Clarke from the Byrds, Leon Russell, Doug Dillard, and Glen Campbell.

The Gosdins recorded some sides for the small Bakersfield International label during that period, one of which, "Hangin' On," caught fire with country DJs and made it up to eighteen on the charts. (The song, like Vern, had a second time around.) The Gosdins seemed on the brink of country stardom, particularly when they moved over to Capitol in late 1967. They worked up an album called Sounds of Goodbye that included an excellent song by Vern's wife, Cathy (they since have divorced), called "Till the End." However, things slowed down for the brothers as the decade came to an end and they broke up the act.

Discouraged, Vern went back to Georgia and settled in Atlanta to raise his family. He opened a glass and mirror business that did reasonably well and relegated music to a spare-time avocation. That's the way things stood for close to a decade. Then, one day in 1976, producer Gary Paxton, a friend from Vern's years in Los Angeles, called from Nashville. "I ran into your brother Rex today," Gary said. "I told him I was looking for someone to record the old 'Hangin' On' as a single. Would you like to do it?"

Vern admits he was skeptical, but the pull of the music field was still too strong to refuse. He recorded several songs under a new pact with Elektra Records. The debut single wasn't "Hangin' On," but "Yesterday's Gone," which, with Emmylou Harris singing harmony, made the top 20. "Hangin' On" followed with equal success, finally making Vern begin to feel he might make it to the top after all those years. Still, for a while he refused to tour, staying in Atlanta to keep his business going. (Later he turned it over to his sons to operate.)

In June 1977, his debut LP came out on Elektra, named after the title track, Till the End, which found the favor that had eluded it in 1969, making it into the country top five and helping the album to attain a similar position. Other songs from the album were issued as singles and showed up on the charts: "Mother Country Music" in October 1977 and "It Started All Over Again" in January 1978. In early 1978,

Vern was back in the studios recording *Never My Love*, released in the spring and almost immediately a hit, as was the title track. In March, Rex rejoined Vern for a new round of concert dates. It was just like old times—only better.

Vern finished up the decade with several more chart hits on Elektra, including singles like "Break My Mind," in the top 15 in late 1978, and, in 1979, "You've Got Somebody, I've Got Somebody" and "Sarah's Eyes." In the early 1980s, he left Elektra for Ovation Records. One of his initial recordings on Ovation was "Too Long Gone," on the singles charts in early 1981.

GRAND OLE OPRY: *Weekly variety show, originating from station WSM, Nashville, Tennessee.*

In the days of vaudeville, the goal of all performers was to play the New York Palace Theater. During the years of Palace greatness, another institution was beginning to take hold in the South. An appearance on the *Grand Ole Opry*, a radio program broadcast from Nashville, Tennessee, was to become the goal of all hopefuls in the country & western field. Although the *Grand Ole Opry* was a radio program, it bore a strong resemblance to the Palace shows. From its early years, the *Opry* was performed before live audiences and, after 1941, in its own auditorium, the Ryman Auditorium in downtown Nashville, (where it remained until the early 1970s when it relocated to its present home, Opryland).

The show began under a different name on November 28, 1925. It was called the WSM *Barn Dance* and was founded by George D. Hay, known as the "Solemn Ol' Judge" (See separate entry for Hay, George D.) The first performer on the program—broadcast for about an hour starting at 8 P.M., Saturdays, from Studio A of WSM in Nashville—was a bearded fiddler, Uncle Jimmy Thompson, accompanied by his niece, Mrs. Eva Thompson Jones. (Uncle Jimmy died at age 83 on February 17, 1931.) When the show later shifted to WSM's Studio B, it became known as the *Grand Ole Opry*.

Hay was credited with coining the new name. The *Barn Dance* followed a broadcast of the NBC Symphony Orchestra originating from New York City and, one evening, Hay introduced his show with the words: "From here on out folks, it will be nothing but realism of the realistic kind. You've been up in the clouds with grand opera, now get down to earth with us in a . . . shindig of *Grand Ole Opry!*"

During 1926, Uncle Dave Macon joined the cast, and soon became the first performer to achieve national stardom through the *Opry* broadcasts. He remained a featured artist with the show until his death in 1952, by which time the program had expanded to occupy most of the evening hours on WSM with the greatest names in country music taking part. Over the years, the *Opry* has continued to grow in stature while maintaining its position at the center of the country & western field. Since its inception, the program has showcased almost every country artist of any prominence as guests or regulars, including almost all the country performers listed in this encyclopedia.

The *Opry* can't claim the honor of being the first of its kind. Earlier examples of the same kind of format included a barn dance program broadcast on station WBAP, Ft. Worth, Texas, on January 4, 1923, and the *National Barn Dance*, which began its run on station WLS, Chicago, Illinois, in 1924. But long after the others had gone off the air, the *Opry* was still in existence as the acknowledged mecca of the major stars of the country & western field. After the rise of television, the *Opry* stage was used not only for *Opry* radio broadcasts, but also as the setting for countless country music specials and syndicated country TV shows. The first telecast of an *Opry* show took place on September 30, 1950.

The *Opry* had several temporary homes before it settled down to its many decades in the Ryman Auditorium. These included the Hillsboro Theater, the East Nashville Tabernacle, WSM's Studio C, and the War Memorial Building. When the program moved to Ryman in 1941, long lines of people assembled every Saturday for the show that began at 7:30 P.M. and continued until midnight. By the 1960s, the outside of the theater had been turned into a replica of a big red barn with the words "Grand Ole Opry" spelled out in large white letters.

As the 1960s drew to a close, WSM management (the station has been owned by National Life and Accident Insurance Company throughout the *Opry's* history) decided the time had come to consider building a new home for the show. A study contract was issued to Research Associates, Los Angeles, the firm that had planned Disneyland, for a new combined auditorium (4,000 seats) and tourist center to be named Opryland. A site for the new theme park was chosen outside Nashville. Opryland opened officially on April 27, 1973. The last Saturday night *Opry* performance from the Ryman Auditorium took place on March 9, 1974, after which all performances were scheduled for the new Opryland.

GRAPPELLI, STEPHANE: *Violinist, pianist, composer. Born Paris, France, January 26, 1908.*

To ardent followers of jazz, the name Stephane Grappelli signifies the finest in jazz violin. Most folk or country fans probably wouldn't even recognize the name. But many folk and even country violin players of post-World War II decades would acknowledge a strong debt to Grappelli, whose techniques have enlivened the styles of such people as Richard Greene and David Grisman. Grappelli himself occasionally has included some folk-based material in his albums and concerts, more often from American sources (particularly blues) than European.

Born and raised in Paris, Grappelli demonstrated great promise in the arts as a child. At the age of six, his family arranged for him to take lessons in dance from Isadora Duncan. Before Stephane was in his teens, his father presented him with a three-quarter-size violin that he learned to play partly from watching street violinists. His violin playing already was excellent when he entered his teens, and he had already learned to play piano. When he was fourteen, he worked in a pit band in the era of silents at a Paris movie theater. His interests at the time were in the general run of pop music of the period as well as classics, but when he heard some of Louis Armstrong's early recordings in the 1920's, he noted, "that changed my destiny."

By the end of the 1920s, he was well on the way to becoming one of the most acclaimed musicians among the jazz set in France. For part of the decade, he was pianist in the best-known French show band of the time, Gregor and His Gregorians. At the start of the 1930s, though, he was becoming restless and looking for ways to express his own musical tastes to a greater extent. In 1931, another major milestone occurred when he met the legendary French jazz guitarist, Django Reinhardt. Three years later, they formed what was to become the top jazz aggregation of Europe—and one that made many friends in the United States—the Quintet of the Hot Club of France.

His career naturally was sidetracked by World War II, but his reputation with jazz fans around the world was substantial by then and his efforts after peace returned added to his luster. Up to the summer of 1969, however, American enthusiasts only were able to hear him on recordings. That year he made his first trip to the States to appear in Rhode Island at the Newport Jazz Festival. His performance did nothing to tarnish his standing as a superior instrumentalist, a position he held throughout the 1970s, although he was in his sixties. Leonard Feather observed in the *Los Angeles Times,* "He remains one of the two geniuses of the jazz violin (Joe Venuti would surely agree). Grappelli is a total virtuoso and a legitimate artist."

Though Grappelli made other visits to the United States during the 1970s, he concentrated most of his activity in Europe. Although he recorded more than ninety albums through the end of the 1970s, few were made outside his home area. An exception was the 1977 *Uptown Dance,* recorded in New York and issued by Columbia in 1978. His playing included many of the flourishes that influenced both folk and jazz violin players.

Discussing his skills, Whitney Balliett of *The New York Times* wrote, "Grappelli's playing is often called 'elegant' and so it is. But there is more to it than that. It has, at its best, a controlled ecstasy. It is fluid, yet structured. Grappelli is a superb melodist; that is, he can play a song 'straight' while subtly so altering its melodic line that its strengths double. And he is a tireless improvisor. At fast tempos, he often gives the impression that he is carrying on two solos at once."

Grappelli himself often emphasized his belief that his approach to playing was based on individualism. At one point, he told Don Bacon for an article in *Coda*, "I've been inspired by orchestra and by black music, but never by instruments. Of course, I've had some musical loves in my life, like Bix Beiderbecke, at the piano, Art Tatum, and so many other good people. But I was never influenced by an individual, not even Joe Venuti."

Talking about his renowned gift for improvisation, he said, "Improvisation—it is a mystery, like the pyramids. You can write a book about it, but by the end no one still knows what it is. Mostly I improvise on the chords of people playing behind me. The better the chords, the better I play."

In 1979, Grappelli came to the United States to tour with mandolin notable David Grisman and his group.

GRAY, CLAUDE: *Singer, guitarist, band leader. Born Henderson, Texas, January 26, 1932.*

Claude Gray is called "a man you have to look up to" by his manager, referring both to his successful career as a hit comedy record artist and his height. At six feet five inches, he certainly deserves his nickname, "The Tall Texan."

When he was not so tall, growing up in Henderson, Texas, he still bent over to listen to the family radio when such programs as the Saturday night *Grand Ole Opry* were on. In those days, he looked up to the stars of country & western music and did his best to emulate them. In high school, while other boys spent all their spare time in sports activities, Claude learned to play guitar and began to per-

form at local events. In the late 1950s, he played many clubs and radio stations in the South and Southwest, slowly building up the experience he needed to break into the big time.

He signed his first major recording contract with Decca about this time. In 1960, after several successful records, he hit the top-10 national list with "Family Bible." The following year he moved to Mercury and scored with two more top-10 recordings, "I'll Just Have a Cup of Coffee, Then I'll Go" and a song provided by a new young songwriter, Roger Miller, "My Ears Should Burn." Another Gray hit of this period was "Mean Ole Woman."

In the 1960s, Claude settled in Nashville and appeared on most of the major TV shows produced there. He was, naturally, a frequent guest on the *Grand Ole Opry*. His tours during these years took him to all parts of the United States and Canada. In the mid-1960s, he returned to his old label, Decca. The second time around proved a good one, providing Claude with an all-time bestseller, "I Never Had the One I Wanted."

The year 1966 marked the organization of Claude's first band. Called The Graymen, it comprised Buck Evans on bass, Terry Bethal on steel guitar, and Bob Taylor on drums. The group backed him on his 1968 hit, "Night Life."

In the 1970s, Claude's recording efforts slowed down, though he remained active on the concert circuit. In the late 1970s, some of his material came out on the Granny White label.

GREENE, JACK: *Singer, guitarist, drummer, songwriter, band leader (The Jolly Giants). Born Maryville, Tennessee, January 7, 1930.*

A number of performers got their seasoning in Ernest Tubb's band, the Texas Troubadours. Perhaps the most notable is Jack Greene, called "The Jolly Giant" because of his height (over six feet) and personality, who sprang to stardom from the band.

Born and raised in Maryville, Tennessee, Jack started to learn guitar when he was eight and was still attending school when he was featured on two daily shows of his own on a home-town station. In his teens, he varied his musical routine by becoming proficient on drums.

By the late 1940s, he was living in Atlanta, Georgia, where he played guitar and sang with a group called the Cherokee Trio. The other members were standup bass player L. M. Bryant and fiddler Speedy Price. In 1950, he joined a group called the Rhythm Ranch Boys as a drummer and guitarist. The group started to pick up a following in the region, but that phase of Jack's career ended after a year when he entered the U.S. Army. The Army soon sent him to Alaska, where he spent much of 1951, and then back to Colorado the following year to be a member of the Special Drill Squad at Camp Carson.

In 1952, he received his discharge and returned to Atlanta, where he soon signed on with a group called the Peachtree Cowboys. For a decade, the band worked the southern states, often serving as a house band for local clubs.

Jack's turning point came in June 1962, when Ernest Tubb had an opening for a skilled musician in his band. Tubb was impressed by Greene's versatility—the fact that he could perform on drums and guitar and also handle either lead or backing vocals with equal skill—and Greene won the job. The association with the Troubadours gave Jack exposure to Tubb's legion of fans and the chance to play regularly on the hallowed Grand Ole Opry radio program. The contacts he made on the Opry led to one of his first chances to take the spotlight. Dottie West had recorded a song with Jim Reeves a little before that superstar perished in a plane accident. She enlisted Greene's aid to take the male part on "Love Is No Excuse" on an Opry show in 1964.

During his stay with the Troubadours, Jack gradually received more and more opportunity to showcase his talents. Besides taking several solos on some show segments, he got the chance to sing lead on several recordings. In the mid-1960s, Decca released a band album titled Ernest Tubb Presents the Texas Troubadours, and one track, Jack's vocal of "The Last Letter," be-

gan to get airplay on country stations across the land. Public clamor for a single of the number became so great the record company released one. The single swiftly moved into the top-chart positions and Jack was catapulted from the band into stardom. Ensuring that status was the success of a string of hit singles from late 1966 into 1968.

The first of those was Hank Cochran's "Don't You Ever Get Tired of Hurting Me?" Next came his version of Marty Robbins' "Ever Since My Baby Went Away." But topping all of those was his single of Dallas Frazier's "There Goes My Everything," which became a number-one country hit. Jack noted that his wife, Barbara, had liked the song and tried several times to get him to record it. She commented, "It laid around the house for a couple of years and then one day he just decided to do it." During 1967, Greene had another number-one hit, "All the Time," to further solidify his reputation as a great new star.

At the end of 1967, on December 23, he received a special Christmas present—he was chosen as a regular cast member of the Opry. When he made his first appearance as a solo artist in front of Opry mikes, his introduction was given by long-time mentor Ernest Tubb. Jack's achievements were recognized by those voting in the Country Music Association's first annual awards competition that year. He was named Male Vocalist of 1967 and also awarded top spot for Single of the Year and Album of the Year (for There Goes My Everything). The song also was voted Song of the Year.

In addition to those honors, Jack also was given two Grammy nominations for 1967. Another highlight of the year for him was taking part in the Macy's Thanksgiving Day Parade. As part of that effort, he sang his hit song before NBC-TV cameras in front of the New York department store.

Jack continued to make top-chart levels in 1968 with such singles as "What Locks the Door" and "You Are My Treasure." Besides his Opry chores, he was on the road constantly in the late 1960s, headlining shows in major country venues all over the United States and Canada. At the end of the decade, he started doing a series of duets with Jeannie Seely that also caught the fancy of country audiences. Jeannie became a regular member of Greene's touring show, still one of the most popular on the country circuit over a decade later. That standing held true for the Greene and Seely segment of the *Opry*, which was still going strong at the start of the 1980s.

Greene continued to place songs on the charts in the early 1970s, though things slowed down for him after that. Among his charted singles were "Something Unseen/What's the Use," a top-20 hit in late 1971, "If You Ever Need My Love," in top-chart levels in the spring of 1972, and "What's Wrong with Our Love," a hit duet with Seely in the late summer of 1972.

Jack's debut album, *Jack Greene*, was issued by Decca in February 1967. Among his other LPs of the late 1960s were *All the Time* (8/67), *Jack Greene* (1/68), *I Am Not Alone*, and *Statue of a Fool* (8/69). Among his early 1970s album releases were *Lord Is That Me, Jack Greene with Jeannie Seely, Greatest Hits, There's a Whole Lot About a Woman*, and *Jack Greene Country*.

Jack and Decca/MCA parted company during the 1970s. In 1979 he signed with a new label, Frontline Records. His debut single for Frontline, "Yours for the Taking," was on country charts in early 1980 and was the title track for his debut album on the label. Later in the year he had such other charted singles as "Rock I'm Leaning On" and "Devil's Den."

GREENE, RICHARD: *Singer, violinist, mandolinist. Born Beverly Hills, California, circa 1945.*

One of the finest folk and country fiddlers of the 1960s and 1970s, Richard Greene at one time or another proved his ability to excel in every form of violin playing from classical to rock. He easily could have earned his living in either field and, in fact, had he concentrated on rock might have built up a mass following. However, always an individualist, he ended up performing the kind of music he enjoyed even if that meant performing mainly before small but "tuned-in" audiences.

Born and raised in Beverly Hills, California, Greene demonstrated phenomenal musical talent as a young child. His classically inclined family saw to it that he started taking violin lessons when he was five, a regimen he began to chafe over as he grew older. As he said, "I quit as soon as I was tall enough." It was that early grind that influenced his decision to turn away from classics later on.

In high school, though, he kept up the classical routine, and was named concertmaster of the Beverly High orchestra in his sophomore year. He was beginning to turn his attention to folk music, however, listening to recordings of some of the folk artists of the late 1950s and early 1960s and doing some exploratory playing of that material in his spare time. His interest in folk music grew when he enrolled in the University of California at Berkeley, and when he was eighteen he was a member of a mountain-music trio on campus.

Increasingly, he looked to folk and country music as his career direction. Helping him move that way was an association with fiddler Scott Stoneman of the Stoneman Family, who introduced him to bluegrass. In a short time, Greene mastered mandolin and bass guitar and was a member of a folk group called the Greenbriar Boys. He spent a while with them, then moved on to a prestigious association in Nashville in the mid-1960s with the Father of Bluegrass, Bill Monroe. Another young urbanite who was in Monroe's group during Greene's tenure was Massachusetts-born guitarist Peter Rowan.

Greene stayed with Monroe for a year, then left to join one of Jim Kreskin's Jug Band alignments. Richard toured the country with the Jug Band and performed on several albums (he had previously made some records with Monroe and the Greenbriar Boys). He also did session work and, at one point in the late 1960s, wrote the score to a critically acclaimed movie titled *Riverrun*. He stayed with the Jug Band until it disbanded in the late 1960s. After that occurred, Greene settled in San Francisco for a while, doing some solo work and writing new material.

His San Francisco sojourn was interrupted by a call from Andy Kulberg to join the new band he was forming, called SeaTrain. Kulberg was aware of Greene's talents and felt sure Greene could play inspired rock-oriented music as well as he did folk, blues, and country. In fact, a prime objective of the new band was to blend those elements of music. Greene, in turn, encouraged Kulberg to bring Peter Rowan in as a founding member.

Greene became a SeaTrain band member in late 1969. After the band rehearsed for a time, they began to work up demonstration tapes and pick up engagements in various parts of the United States. Signed by Capitol at the start of the 1970s, the band went to England to record its debut LP on the label, *SeaTrain,* issued in early 1971. A second album, *Marblehead Messenger,* came out later in the year. Both made the national charts for many months and demonstrated Greene's technique of deftly blending his violin work in with the ensemble playing of the entire band.

Still, while Greene won applause as one of the music field's finest rock violin players, he was becoming restless with the genre. In 1972, he left SeaTrain in favor of concentrating for a while on solo performances in the folk-country vein.

During the mid-1970s, he took part in several band efforts in what might loosely be called experimental folk-bluegrass. One of those was the Great American Music Band, formed in 1974 by Greene and mandolin virtuoso David Grisman with Taj Mahal performing on string bass. The blend of jazz, bluegrass, folk, and blues favored in the band's repertoire pointed the way for Grisman when he organized his David Grisman Quintet a few years later. Greene and Grisman also joined forces with Peter Rowan for a time in the bluegrass-oriented group, Muleskinner.

GRISMAN, DAVID: *Mandolinist, mandocellist, guitarist, saxophonist, composer, band leader (David Grisman Quintet). Born Hackensack, New Jersey, 1945.*

There are some musicians who can weave their way in and out of a series of bands of varied styles without appearing to be out of place in any of them. Such a one is David Grisman, whose career took him from classics to folk to rock to bluegrass to an amalgam of his own that combined elements of jazz with touches of several other genres.

Born in Hackensack, New Jersey, and later raised in Passaic, New Jersey, Grisman could play a number of stringed instruments in his teens as well as saxophone and piano. His piano teacher, he recalled, told him the mandolin "wasn't a real instrument." Nonetheless, after he finished high school in Passaic and enrolled at New York University, he took the mandolin along and played it in various folk ensembles, including a stint with the Even Dozen Jug Band, where he met such artists as Maria Muldaur and John Sebastian.

For a time he moved to the San Francisco Bay region in the mid-1960s, where his musical acquaintances included guitarist Jerry Garcia, who hadn't yet made his international reputation. In the late 1960s he heeded a call to go cross-country to Boston to join a new group formed by Peter Rowan called Earth Opera. In the mid-1960s, Rowan had been a fiddler and backing vocalist with Bill Monroe's Blue Grass Boys, but the goal in setting up Earth Opera was to play rock 'n' roll–type material. The band made its concert and record debut in early 1968 (the debut LP came out on Elektra) and won some attention as the year went by from tours of the United States and Canada. It had several regional hits and considerable critical praise. However, faced with dwindling reserves, at the end of 1968 it disbanded.

For a while Grisman and Rowan went different ways, both doing session work and playing with other groups for several years. By 1973, they had joined forces once more in a bluegrass-oriented band called Old and in the Way, whose members included Jerry Garcia, by then the famed lead guitarist of the Grateful Dead (playing acoustic guitar in this case). Another member of the group was fiddle virtuoso Vassar Clements. The band played a number of concerts in various parts of the United States, including a 1973 set at the Boarding House in San Francisco that was taped for the live LP *Old and in the Way,* released by Rounder Records. During the 1970s, Grisman and Rowan also were the featured artists of another bluegrass band called Muleskinner. Whereas Grisman had been featured on saxophone in the Earth Opera days, with the bluegrass groups he rarely played an instrument other than mandolin. His work was recognized by folk and bluegrass adherents as some of the finest mandolin playing of modern times.

Another mid-1970s project of Grisman's was the group called The Great American Music Band, formed in 1974 with violinist Richard Greene. (Greene also worked with Grisman and Rowan in Muleskinner.) Among the musicians who performed with that band were Taj Mahal (who played string bass) and composer John Carlini.

In addition to his band work in the mid-1970s, Grisman continued to do some session work and also wrote film scores. Among his movie credits were scores for *Big Bad Mama, Capone, Eat My Dust,* and *King of the Gypsies.*

In 1976, the first version of the David Grisman Quintet made its debut. He assembled a group that stressed instrumental music, featuring, besides his mandolin playing, Tony Rice on guitar plus a stand-up bassist and one or two fiddles. The music the band performed, much of it written by Grisman, was strongly jazz flavored, but not easily typified. Grisman later commented, "Words like jazz, rock-fusion or crossover bluegrass don't really mean anything. I'd just as soon call it 'Dawg Music,' after a nickname I've been stuck with, than refer to it as anything else." The band's debut LP, released on Kaleidoscope Records in 1977, was called *The David Grisman Quintet* and sold over 80,000 copies, surprisingly good for a release on a small label. In the late 1970s, the group switched to Horizon Records, distributed by the major Warner Brothers record firm.

Some of the band's numbers were by French jazz greats, an example being the Grisman Quintet's version of "Minor Swing," written by the late jazz guitarist

Django Reinhardt and jazz violinist Stephane Grappelli. That number, along with new compositions, was presented in the group's debut LP on Horizon Records, *Hot Dawg,* issued in mid-1979. Grisman wrote or co-wrote five songs on the album, including "16/16," "Dawgology," and "Janice."

At the end of the 1970s, the Grisman Quintet performed in jazz clubs, some folk venues, and, at times, as an opening act for rock bands at places like the Universal Amphitheater in Los Angeles. Among the band's credits in 1979 was an appearance on Johnny Carson's *The Tonight Show.* Another high point of 1979 was a number of concerts in which Stephane Grappelli, in one of his relatively rare visits from France, performed with Grisman's group. At the time, the band comprised Tony Rice on guitar; Darol Anger on violin, violectra, cello, and mandolin; Todd Philips on bass; and Mike Marshall on mandolin, guitar, and violin. (Anger, Philips, and Grisman all contributed article material to Grisman's publication, *Mandolin World News.*)

By the time Grisman's new album, *David Grisman—Quintet '80* came out in July 1980, the band's makeup had changed somewhat. Rice and Philips had left, with Mark O'Connor (guitar, violin) and Rob Wasserman (bass) taking their place. Two months after the new LP had come out, it was voted the best album of the year by readers of *Frets* magazine. In the same poll, Grisman was voted the top mandolin player, beating out thirty-three other nominees. Grisman's talents were also recognized in an article in *Newsweek* (November 10, 1980), in which he was dubbed the "Paganini of the Mandolin."

GUITAR, BONNIE: *Singer, guitarist, songwriter, record producer. Born Seattle, Washington, March 25, early 1930s.*

The U.S. Pacific Northwest doesn't come to mind as an incubator of native country-music talent. Still, like all sections of the country, it always has had a sizable audience for the art form that has supported a number of local artists and provided a training ground for many young country performers from other parts of the nation. At times, though not too often, some home-grown talent has made it to the national level, the most noteworthy example in post-World War II decades being Bonnie Guitar.

Bonnie, who grew up in Seattle, showed an interest in music as a young girl and, by the time she was high school age, could play several instruments, including the guitar. One of her friends liked her work and helped her prepare a demonstration recording that eventually was submitted to a Hollywood firm. The firm asked her to record a single and several other recordings in the 1950s, issued on Fabor Records.

However, Bonnie wasn't satisfied with the way things were going and gambled on establishing a record company of her own. She started the label, called Dolton Records, in her home area during the mid-1950s and began turning out some of her own discs. Not averse to adding other artists, whether in the pop or country genres, she signed a trio of Washington teenagers that caught her attention. The group, known as the Fleetwoods, had a pop single titled "Come Softly to Me" that made the national pop charts in 1958 and earned a gold-record award in 1959. In 1959, the Fleetwoods had an even bigger hit, still considered a pop classic, "Mr. Blue," and added several other lesser hits in the early 1960s. Bonnie's contributions were considerable. On the group's initial recordings she handled production and also played guitar, including a classical guitar sound that provided a striking conterpoint to the pop vocal.

Even as she worked with the Fleetwoods, Bonnie was considering offers to sign with other labels as a country artist. She finally accepted a bid from Dot Records and joined their roster in the late 1950s. Her efforts for the label included two 1959 albums, Whispering Hope (issued in February) and the May release, Moonlight. In 1960, she had a major hit with a single of her composition "Dark Moon," which remained in the country top 40 for many weeks. In December 1960, Dot issued her album of the same title. As her country career picked up momentum, Bon-

nie found it difficult to attend to the needs of her own label and sold Dolton.

As the 1960s went by, she continued to make the charts with new singles and was represented by a steady series of new LPs on Dot. They included Two Worlds of Bonnie Guitar (5/66), Miss Bonnie Guitar (10/66), Award Winner (6/67), and Affair! (9/69). During a particularly productive period in the late 1960s, she had five records on top chart levels, three in 1967 and two in 1968. The 1968 output included the top-10 hit "I Believe in Love."

In the 1960s, she became well known to country audiences around the nation from constant touring as a headliner or part of a country-music show "package." For much of the decade she toured with the Eddy Arnold show. Arnold paid tribute to her at one point, noting how much the fans at his concerts enjoyed her work: "Her songs are so eagerly accepted by the public because they're so honest and straightforward." Arnold himself recorded some of her compositions, as did many other first-rank country performers.

Bonnie's album catalogue in the late 1960s and early 1970s included Night Train to Memphis on the Camden label and Allegheny on Paramount. Though most of her 1960s LPs were on Dot, some of her material appeared on other labels, such as Favorite Lady of Song on Pickwick and Bonnie Guitar Sings on Hamilton (November 1966).

In the early 1970s, Bonnie recorded some material for Columbia, including the 1972 chart single "Happy Everything." At the start of the 1980s, she was affiliated with 4-Star Records; her 4-Star single of her composition "Honey on the Moon" was on country charts in the spring of 1980.

GUTHRIE, ARLO: *Singer, guitarist, pianist, songwriter. Born Coney Island, Brooklyn, New York, July 10, 1947.*

Most biographies of Arlo Guthrie tend to emphasize his links to his illustrious father, Woody. But the truth is that while he carries on the folk music tradition of the Oklahoma balladeer, to most of his fans he is the distinguished Guthrie and

Woody a shadowy figure from past decades. Critics also tend to bracket Arlo with the protest era of the 1960s, but he rose to prominence in the latter part of the decade and has generally stressed optimisim and hope for the future rather than the cynicism or despair that gripped many folk artists in the mid-1960s.

He expressed those views as long ago as 1968, when he had just gained national attention from his 1967 success, "Alice's Restaurant." (The song won initial acclaim at the 1967 Newport Folk Festival, though it was the title track from his debut LP on Warner Bros. released in June of that year.) He told a reporter, "I'm not really politically minded in my songs. The songs are sometimes about politics, have things about politics in them, but the songs aren't political at all. Because they don't say to choose one politic or another. No one ever can be a spokesman for someone other than himself . . . and I'm a spokesman for myself."

He noted that "the music has changed from being against a lot of things to being for a lot of things. They're just different things. So this is why the protest thing has died, because people happen to be for things instead of against things."

Arlo's positive outlook spurred him to get married and raise a family despite the specter of Huntington's chorea, the scourge that killed his father and reappeared in several of Woody's offspring. When he married Jackie Hyde in Stockbridge, Massachusetts, in October 1969, he was relaxed and confident. He later told a reporter that while he had a 50 percent chance of developing the disease, his children would only run half the risk. "That gives them a 75 percent chance for safety. No matter how you cut it, that's pretty good odds."

The musical odds worked out well for Arlo as he closed out the 1960s and came into the 1970s commanding growing respect as both an interpreter of new and old songs (mostly folk, but with forays into country and rock on occasion) and a writer of new ones, usually with a strong strain of humor, as in "The Motorcycle Song" and "Pause for Mr. Clause." In 1969, he was featured at the legendary Woodstock concert in upstate New York in August, where he won an ovation for the song "Coming into Los Angeles." It was included in his third Warner/Reprise album, *Running Down the Road*.

In the early 1970s, he maintained his momentum, building up a following that cut across generation and stylistic lines with albums like *Washington Country* and *Hobo's Lullaby*. The last named contained Arlo's version of the Steve Goodman modern folk composition, "City of New Orleans," which made the pop charts to become Arlo's biggest hit to date and has become a classic since then. In the mid-1970s, Arlo became more closely involved with a long-time friend of the Guthrie family, Pete Seeger. The two often appeared on the same bill and, after a while, collaborated on a series of concerts that presented, in effect, a history of folk music (including traditional country and the blues) from Revolutionary times to the present.

Arlo's increased emphasis on traditional folk material was demonstrated on such mid-1970s albums as *Last of the Brooklyn Cowboys* and *Peter Seeger/Arlo Guthrie Together in Concert*. *Last of the Brooklyn Cowboys* included several tracks featuring Irish jigs and reels performed by Irish fiddler Kevin Burke and several country songs ("Lovesick Blues," "Miss the Mississippi and You") with backing provided by Buck Owens' Buckaroos. His next album, *Arlo Guthrie*, was a more contemporary collection that contained such tracks as "Presidential Rag" and "Won't Be Long!"

Arlo's eighth solo album, *Amigo*, was issued on Warner/Reprise in 1976. Its tracks included such Guthrie originals as "Grocery Blues" and "Massachusetts," plus Arlo's version of an old Rolling Stones hit, "Connection." During 1977, while Arlo was touring with his excellent new group called Shenandoah, his first retrospective disc was released. *The Best of Arlo Guthrie*, issued in the fall of the year, included, besides "Alice's Restaurant" and "City of New Orleans," such tracks as "Cooper's Lament," "Darkest Moment" and a re-recording with additional comedic lines of

"The Motorcycle Song," called "The New Motorcycle."

Arlo's tenth Warner's LP, *Arlo Guthrie with Shenandoah*, was released in the fall of 1978. The album included traditionally oriented folk numbers such as "Tennessee Stud," "Buffalo Skinners," and "St. Louis Tickle," as well as a nineteen-minute version of a Guthrie saga called "The Story of Reuben Clamzo & His Strange Daughter in the Key of A." Shenandoah, which comprised David Grover on guitar and banjo, Carol Ide on guitar and percussion, Steve Ide on guitar and trombone, Dan Velika on bass, and Terry A. La Berry on drums (all five members also handled vocal support), provided adequate backup but was not as effective as in live shows.

His album *Outlasting the Blues*, released in June 1979, also featured Shenandoah. Later that year, his early composition "The Motorcycle Song" was featured in an animated short film titled *No No Pickle*. Peter Starr, who produced that picture, also featured Guthrie material in a semi-documentary movie, *Take It to the Limit*, about professional motorcycle racing, that won a Silver Venus Medallion at the 1979 Houston International Film Festival.

In February 1981, Arlo and Pete Seeger again joined forces in a new two-record set issued on Warner Brothers titled *Arlo Guthrie and Pete Seeger—"Precious Friend."*

GUTHRIE, WOODY: *Songwriter, singer, guitarist. Born Okemah, Okfuskee County, Oklahoma, July 14, 1912; died Queens, New York, October 3, 1967.*

In his songs and legend, Woody Guthrie has remained a living part of America's folk music heritage more than a decade after Huntington's chorea claimed his life in 1967. Young folksingers still perform his Dust Bowl Ballads and other classic compositions, as earlier generations did in the 1970s and during Woody's lifetime. Reissues of his recordings continue to appear in record stores and his story has been told in books, including his autobiography, *Bound for Glory*, and the 1977 film of the same name.

Such a legacy seems appropriate for a man whose family helped settle this land,

and whose own love for his country was enshrined in his great composition, "This Land Is Your Land." Guthrie was born of pioneer stock in Oklahoma when it was still referred to as Indian territory. His father, Charles Edward Guthrie, came from Texas and brought to the family a background of pioneering, prize fighting, and guitar and banjo playing with several cowboy bands.

After marrying Nora Belle Tanner, Charlie Guthrie settled down to run a trading post and then a real estate office, which was prosperous for a while, since it coincided with the first oil boom in Oklahoma. Thus, in Woody's early years, he was surrounded by folk music from his parents, grandparents, neighbors, from Negro singing, and even from the many Indian villages in the region. At four, Woody himself started singing and continued to follow this lodestone for nearly the rest of his life.

As Woody reached high school age, things disintegrated at home when his father's real estate business failed, his sister died in a coal oil stove explosion, and his mother had to be committed to the state asylum. All of this contributed to Woody's dropping out of school. He learned to play harmonica and, when he left home at age thirteen or fourteen, he used it for entertainment and to pick up extra money during his traveling.

After his father moved back to Texas, Woody "hit the road down south to Houston, Galveston, the Gulf and back, doing all kinds of odd jobs, hoeing fig orchards, picking grapes, hauling wood, helping carpenters and cement men, working with water well drillers. . . . I carried my harmonica and played in barber shops, at shine stands, in front of shows, around the pool halls, and rattled the bones, done jig dances, sang and played with Negroes, Indians, whites, farmers, town folks, truck drivers and with every kind of a singer you can think of." (*American Folksong/Woody Guthrie*, Oak Publications, New York, 1961, p. 3.)

Later he wandered north to Pampa, Texas, where his father's half-brother Jeff taught him to play guitar. The two played at many local events and later had their own magic show. After marrying the first of three wives, Mary Jennings, Woody took off for California and worked as a painter during the day and a singer in saloons at night. By now he not only was collecting songs but writing them as well. For most of his life, he wrote one or two songs almost every day, resulting in an estimated total of more than a thousand published compositions winnowed from an even greater mass of material. (It should be noted that, like many folk artists, Guthrie often put new lyrics to folk melodies. A believer in the folk tradition that true folk songs evolved over many generations through the changes and additions of many individuals, he always expressed opposition, in later years, to the restrictions of copyright laws.)

In California, he joined with a woman named Maxine "Lefty Lou" Crissman in an act called Woody and Lefty Lou. They gained a regular spot on radio station KFVD in Los Angeles. After a few years, Woody's restless nature took him to Tijuana, Mexico, where he performed on station XELO. After that he returned to KFVD for a time as a solo performer.

During the trying years of the Depression and the drought and dust storms of his native Southwest in the 1930s, Woody vagabonded through the West and Southwest. Touched by the pressures and troubles of ordinary people, he became strongly supportive of unions and left-wing organizations, donating his talents performing before union groups, migratory workers, and other victims of hard times. Their problems showed up in a steady stream of new compositions.

In the late 1930s, he moved to New York, where he met many other folk artists, including a youngster named Pete Seeger who soon was joining him in concerts. Among other things, he wrote for the Communist *Daily Worker* and performed on the folk circuit throughout New England and other eastern states. An important contact was made with folk song collector Alan Lomax, who asked Woody to come to Washington, D.C., to record some of his music for the Library of Congress Archive of Folk Song. Woody re-

corded enough material, many of them original songs, for twelve records called *Dust Bowl Ballads*. Not only did Woody record songs, he also took part in taped conversations with Lomax about those years and his approach to writing and collecting. Those albums remain the most important focal point of Guthrie's life and art. Returning to New York, he received many opportunities to perform on radio and sang on such major shows as *Pursuit of Happiness, Cavalcade of America, Back Where I Come From,* and *Pipe Smoking Time.* He also performed on the *Music Festival* series broadcast over New York City's station WNYC.

After a sojourn in California and at the Bonneville Dam, he returned to New York, where he joined with Lee Hays, Pete Seeger, and Millard Lampell in a group called the Almanac Singers. During the early 1940s, the group toured the country, sometimes appearing in commercial concerts, other times performing at union meetings, radical meetings, and occasional charitable affairs. Among the songs in their repertoire were "Union Maid," "Talking Union," "Get Tree Behind Me Satan," and "Union Train a Comin'," as well as traditional folk songs and originals by various members.

With World War II under way, Woody entered the U.S. Merchant Marine with two other folk song friends, Cisco Houston and Jimmy Longhi. He was torpedoed twice during those years, sang and collected material from the British Isles to Russia, and composed still more songs. Just before the end of the war he was briefly drafted by the U.S. Army.

After the war ended, Woody returned to the New York area and resumed his singing activities. By then he had been divorced for a long time from Mary Jennings and had settled down with his second wife, Marjorie, a dancer who had worked with Martha Graham, in Brooklyn, New York. Among the children of that union was a son who would carry on the family musical tradition, Arlo Guthrie. In the years after 1945 until illness disabled him, Woody performed as a soloist and in concerts with almost all the best-known folksingers of those years, from Leadbelly to

Seeger and the Weavers. He also agreed to record for Moses Asch's Folkways Records and proceeded to provide material for dozens of albums from the late 1940s through the 1950s. Among the many songs he recorded for Asch were such titles as "Goin' Down the Road," "Boomtown Bill," "I Ain't Got No Home in this World Anymore," "Tom Joad," "Jack Hammer John," "The Ballad of Pretty Boy Floyd," "Billy the Kid," "When the Curfew Blows," "Sharecropper Song," "Electricity and All," "Pastures of Plenty," and many more.

In his lifetime, he was represented by a series of LPs, mostly on Folkways, but some on various other labels (some reissues of earlier material). Among the albums available in the early and mid-1960s were *Bound for Glory, Dust Bowl Ballads, Ballads of Sacco and Vanzetti* (2/61), *Woody Guthrie Sings,* with Leadbelly (and others) (5/62), all on Folkways; *Bed on the Floor* (8/65), *Bonneville Dam* (12/66), on Verve/Forecast Records; *Dust Bowl Ballads* (RCA Victor, 7/64); *Library of Congress Recordings,* on Elektra (three discs, 12/64); *Folk Songs by Woody Guthrie and Cisco Houston,* and *Guthrie, Terry and Stewart* on Stinson Records; *Woody Guthrie,* Archive of Folk Music (1/66).

By the 1960s, Woody was seriously ill with Huntington's chorea, a hereditary, degenerative disease of the muscles for which no known cure exists. Even as legions of young folksingers hailed him as the symbol of the folk music boom of the late 1950s and early 1960s, Guthrie himself had to withdraw from the activities he loved so much. Among those who sought-out the bed-ridden artist in the early 1960s was a young college dropout from Minnesota named Bob Dylan. Though Guthrie

had never heard of Dylan, Guthrie accepted his presence in his room at Greystone Park Hospital and the two became friends. In the years following, Dylan joined other friends and former associates in keeping Guthrie's songs and name before the public.

The end came for Guthrie in October 1967 in a physical sense, but his career had been thwarted by his illness for almost the entire decade. In the years after his death, he was honored by many memorial concerts, from New York's Carnegie Hall to the concert halls of California. In the 1970s, his widow, Marjorie, helped organize a number of concerts to raise money to support medical research on Huntington's chorea.

Meanwhile, reissues of his material continued to appear, such as Tradition Records' *Early Years* and the Folkways LP *Poor Boy: 13 of His Folk Songs.* When the film biography of his life came out in the late 1970s, it also set off a flurry of releases. Among his albums still in current catalogues at the end of the 1970s were RCA's *A Legendary Performer* (retitled from the 1964 *Dust Bowl Ballads* release); *Cowboy Songs, Folk Songs by Woody Guthrie and Cisco Houston* on Stinson; *Early Years, Legendary Woody Guthrie* on Tradition; *Immortal Woody Guthrie* on Olympic Records (University of Washington); *Woody Guthrie* on Evergreen; *Woody Guthrie* on Warner Bros; *Library of Congress Recordings* on Elektra; and, on Folkways, *Poor Boy, Dust Bowl Ballads, This Land Is Your Land, Woody Guthrie Sings Folk Songs, Woody Guthrie Sings Folk Songs, Volume 2,* and three albums of songs for children—*Songs to Grow On Volumes 1, 2 and 3.*

H

HADDOCK, DURWOOD: *Singer, guitarist, fiddler, songwriter, music publisher, disc jockey. Born Lamesco, Texas, August 16, 1934.*

Durwood Haddock's career had plenty of ups and downs, but he always managed to pick himself up from the "downs" to

make more than a few important contributions to the country field as a writer and performer.

He was born in rural Texas in Fannin County. "The place I was born, Lamesco, used to be two stores and a shed. Now it's one store and that's closed. It's just a wide place in the road. But when I was growing up, I lived all over Texas, sometimes with my folks and sometimes with an aunt. I moved around from farms to cities. I really wasn't a farm boy, but I was around a farm enough so I didn't want to live there—then. But now [1980] I finally got back down to it and I have my own farm in Lamesco."

He had an interest in country & western music from his early years. "As long as I can remember I've been involved in it. Country music and the radio business were the only things I occupied myself with once I was on my own."

Still, though he could play several instruments by the time he finished going to Dennison High School in Texas in the early 1950s, he didn't think of performing as a way to make a living. "I went to radio broadcast school in Tyler, Texas, and took one of those cram courses for about a year. When I finished, I caught a Greyhound Bus to a job at station KSRY in Seymour, Texas. I worked there a week and got fired. We didn't have the automatic equipment of today; you put the records on and played them yourself. I didn't bother looking at the records, I just put 'em on and they didn't take kindly to hearing Bing Crosby's "White Christmas" in the middle of July.

"Then I went off playin' fiddle in southern Oklahoma honky tonks, real spit-on-the-floor beer joints. We played for the kitty; sometimes it was real good and sometimes not so hot. When it was real good, the manager took part of it, like 90 percent. Then I went to West Texas and my first real professional job at the Odessa Danceland. I got sixty dollars a week which wasn't bad money in 1954. Played the club for three months and then the audience fell off and we got fired. I've been fired a whole lot in my career. Then we went to a place forty-four miles away called Kermit, Texas, stayed another three months and made some records for 4-Star. We decided we'd go on the road and set the world afire and, of course, we didn't.

"In nineteen and fifty four I met a man named Eddie Miller in Kermit. We got together and wrote some material. We came up with the title 'There She Goes' because it was West Texas and there was a lot of oil operations. I had the first record. It was recorded on a radio station in West Texas. It didn't do anything. But in 1955, Carl Smith had a cover record on Columbia and it was on the charts a long time. A lot of people have recorded it since then; Jerry Wallace had a top-10 hit with it. Just recently [1980] I went to see the movie *Coal Miner's Daughter* and it was the lead song in it. It's also in the album.

"Anyway, I went down to Denison, Texas, and started a 15-minute program and did some club work in West Texas. I got into the broadcast business at KFST in Ft. Stockton; worked there three months and got fired because I was the highest paid employee at fifty dollars a week and they decided they couldn't afford that. Then I went to Odessa and worked the news car there. Got fed up with that because I seen too many accidents and killings on that beat. I left for a station in Monahan and left there for KERV in Kermit, Texas. I found a home at KERV. I stayed there from 1957 into 1962 as a jack-of-all-trades. I was a DJ, managed the station, did sales, and just about everything else. All that time I worked in clubs on weekends and made some records, including a few that made the charts.

"I had my first chart record on United Artists in 1962 called 'Big Night in My House, [Haddock wrote the song]. It was a top-30 hit, then the label dropped me. Hard to figure this business out. We just formed our own label, Eagle International, and had two charted singles, 'How Are Things in Your City,' which was top 50 in 1963, and 'Our Big House,' on the charts in 1964–65. Then I cut two records for Monument that came out in 1966–67, 'Wait'll I Get My Hands on You' and 'Newest Thing in Night Life.' "

During those years, Haddock did a lot of personal appearance work. In 1962, he decided to form his own band and, having left KERV, he toured with the group all over the Southwest until 1968, "when I went to Nashville and decided to form a music publishing company and I've been there ever since.

"In 1968, I left Monument and went

with Metromedia Records. I cut a god-awful record—I didn't write it—'When the Swelling Goes Down' and Willie Nelson's 'Gotta Get Drunk and Sure Do Dread It.' That last one never charted, but it did good in the juke boxes. The last thing with them was 'East Bourbon Street.' It didn't chart, but it made some good airplay money for me. Then I didn't have anything much until I was back on Eagle International and made the charts with 'Big City Girl' in 1971."

In the early 1970s, Haddock made several singles for Caprice Records. That included "You Gotta Do a Little Puttin' On" and a top-50 release, "Angel in An Apron." "Then I did one called 'It Sure Looks Good on You,' which was never officially released 'cause we had a falling out and I left.

"I was a little disgusted with the field for a while and didn't do any recording. I began doing things on my own label again. I put out one called 'The Perfect Love Song' that did reasonably well, and another company, Country International, got a license and distributed it and it was on the charts on that label as well as Eagle. I got an ASCAP award for that song.

"Since then I've mostly been writing and getting things ready to go in the 1980s. It's hard to find good material from other writers. If it's really good, the big stars get first crack and if it isn't it doesn't pay to try it yourself. So I'm workin' up new material myself, doing some promotion work, and just keepin' busy."

Based on an interview with the authors, May 1980.

HAGGARD, MERLE: *Singer, guitarist, band leader (The Strangers), songwriter. Born Bakersfield, California, April 6, 1937.*

When Bakersfield, California, gained the reputation of "Nashville West" in the 1960s, a major reason was its native son, Merle Haggard. A rugged individualist, uncompromising in his creative efforts, he had an emotional flair that rarely failed to deeply affect his audiences. Though he became a superstar during the 1960s and 1970s, he always called Bakersfield home.

Merle's formative years, which formed the basis for many of his classic songs, were fraught with difficulties and traumas. The problems and poverty that beset his family at the time gave rise to an angry teenage rebellion that for a while seemed likely to destroy his life before it really got under way. It took a strong will for someone who, as Merle wrote in one song, "turned twenty-one in prison" to reverse his direction and set a positive example later on for his own children as well as millions of other young people.

His parents were victims of the Dust Bowl in Oklahoma during the Depression. Like thousands of other southwesterners in 1934, the Haggards en route to California found themselves mired in the so-called Hoover Camps so well depicted in John Steinbeck's *The Grapes of Wrath.* Merle's father finally found a low-echelon job on the Sante Fe Railroad and his mother milked cows. Still, it was a hand-to-mouth existence, and the family was living in a converted boxcar in Bakersfield when Merle was born in 1937.

The family's fortunes were improving in the 1940s until, when Merle was nine, his father died. The boy reacted bitterly, becoming increasingly wild as he approached his teens. Later, in the 1960s, he ruefully recalled the period with such moving songs as "Mama Tried" and "Hungry Eyes."

When he was fourteen, he ran away from home and spent much of the next half dozen years picking up odd jobs, wandering around California, occasionally resorting to petty crimes. Again, some of those activities turned up in songs such as "Workin' Man Blues," "Sing Me Back Home," and "The Bottle Let Me Down."

During all of this time his love for country music grew. At home he had listened to country programs on the radio, and, while he was on the road in his teens he continued to listen to the recordings of people like Jimmie Rodgers, Bob Wills, and Lefty Frizzell. After a while, he began to pick out some of these songs on the guitar.

His musical repertoire proved to be a sustaining force when, in 1957, he was convicted on a burglary charge and sent to San Quentin Prison for an extended period. Once in prison, exhorted by a brother to pull himself together, Merle slowly found a new path for himself. Part of the time he worked in the textile mill and took courses that promised the equivalent of a high school diploma. He also put his musical talents to work, first to entertain some of his cellmates, then as a member of the warden's country band. Merle began to think about trying to make a career in music once he returned to the outside world.

In 1960, after two years and nine months behind bars, having proved himself an exemplary prisoner, he was given his parole. He went home to Bakersfield to seek work as a musician. His auditions were impressive and he started working the many bars and nightclubs frequented by country fans in and around Bakersfield. Word of his talents started to circulate, leading to better assignments, including the opportunity to perform on local TV programs.

During the early 1960s, his contacts with the burgeoning Bakersfield country music operations expanded rapidly. He did some session work for established country artists and started looking for a recording alignment for himself. Among those he met was a fine female vocalist named Bonnie Owens, who originally came to Bakersfield as Buck Owens' wife (the two became estranged by the mid-1960s). Merle and Bonnie began to work together and, in 1964, had a moderate hit with the release "Just Between the Two of Us" on Tally Records.

That success caused Capitol Records to sign both of them in 1965, a pivotal year for Merle: he formed his own band, the Strangers, scored his first national top-10 hit, and married Bonnie Owens. Although he had already written quite a few original songs by then, either by himself or with Bonnie, his first breakthrough single was of a Bill Anderson song, "(From Now on All My Friends Are Gonna Be) Strangers." The title provided the name for his band.

His debut Capitol LP, also titled *Strangers*, issued in October 1965, was a top country LP of the year. The album featured five of his own songs, including one that made upper-chart levels, "I'm Gonna Break Every Heart I Can." For Merle's follow-up LP, he was joined by his wife, Bonnie. Called *Just Between the Two of Us,* issued in May 1966, its title number was a remake of their earlier regional hit. His next solo LP, *Swingin' Doors* (November 1966), also was a bestseller as was the single of its title song, a Haggard composition. Besides that release, his singles output for 1966–67 included "The Girl Turned Ripe," "The Longer You Wait," "I'm a Lonesome Fugitive," "Someone Told My Story," "I Threw Away the Rose," "Loneliness is Eating Me Alive," "You Don't Have Very Far to Go," "Branded Man," and "The Bottle Let Me Down." The last two, both written by Merle, were top-10 hits, as was "I Threw Away the Rose." "I'm a Lonesome Fugitive" did even better, rising to number one on national country lists and establishing Merle as a major new star with fans in all parts of the union. The song was the title tune of his third solo LP on Capitol, released in April 1967.

In recognition of his achievements, the western-based Academy of Country & Western Music named Merle and Bonnie the Best Vocal Group of 1965 and Merle the Most Promising Male Vocalist of 1965 and, in 1966, repeated the Top Vocal Group accolade. They won for a third time in a row in the 1967 voting.

To support their rising esteem with country fans, Merle, Bonnie and the Strangers made many coast-to-coast swings of the United States from the mid-1960s on. They also starred on many top TV shows of the mid-1960s, including *The Jimmy Dean Show* and *Swingin' Country.*

In the late 1960s, Haggard's stature in the country field continued to increase rapidly as he turned out a stream of excellently crafted singles and albums. Among the LPs were *Branded Man* (10/67), *Sing Me Back Home* (2/69), *CloseUp* (7/69), *Portrait* (10/69), and *Okie from Muskogee*. The single "Okie from Muskogee," a litany in favor of old-time American virtues and against pot smokers and hippies, capped his 1960s efforts and made him a familiar figure to pop fans as well as country adherents. The song rose to number one on country charts, as did the album of that title, and was high on pop lists as well. The pro and con controversy that eddied around him for a while, he agreed, indicated "I had more than just a song on my hands." He also had a near sweep of the top awards announced at the 1970 Country Music Association festivities, winning the award for best single and album for "Okie . . ." and also being named Top Male Vocalist and Entertainer of the Year.

Taking the stir in stride, Haggard went his own way, turning out new albums and singles as the 1970s progressed and staying on the road with the Merle Haggard Show a good part of each year. Though he did occasional TV guest spots, he avoided attempts to have him front his own TV series, as he told Jack Hurst of the *Chicago Tribune* (June 7, 1979): "How many ways can you shoot a guy standing with a guitar? How many unique things can you find about a man singing?

"We do concerts. That's the way I support a band. And I have to have a band to make good records. If I sell out, so to speak, on a TV screen, people won't have any reason to come to the concerts. It starts a deterioration of the whole deal."

There seemed to be some proof of his concept in the consistency with which he made the charts throughout the 1970s. He began with such early 1970s singles hits as "Fightin Side of Me" and "I Can't Be Myself/Sidewalks of Chicago" in 1970 and "Grandma Harp" and "It's Not Love (But It's Not Bad)" in 1972 and LPs like *Fightin Side of Me, Hag,* a two-record set, *Sing a Sad Song/High on a Hilltop, Someday We'll Look Back, Tribute to the Best Damn Fiddle Player (Bob Wills), Let Me Tell You About a Song, Best of the Best,* and *Land of Many Churches.* The latter was a two-disc set recorded with the Carter Family and the Strangers.

His singles hits of the mid-1970s included the smash hit "If We Make It Through December," which rose to number one the end of 1973 and stayed there into early 1974, the top five "Things Aren't Funny Anymore" in the spring of 1974, and such top-10 or top-5 successes as "Kentucky Gambler," Movin' On," "It's All in the Movies," and "The Roots of My

Raising" in 1976. All of those were Haggard originals except for "Kentucky Gambler" (by Dolly Parton) and "The Roots of My Raising" (by Tom Collins). In 1977, Merle ended his long association with Capitol and joined MCA Records. There was little change in the pattern with record after record reaching the upper-chart levels, sometimes to be joined by Capitol releases of earlier material.

In mid-1977, he had a top-5 hit on MCA with a combination of his song "Ramblin' Fever" and an old standard, "When My Blues Moon Turns to Gold Again." Several months later he made topmost levels with his song "From Graceland to the Promised Land" on MCA and "A Working Man Can't Get Nowhere" on Capitol.

Although his career seemed to be going smoothly enough during that period, his personal life was in turmoil once more as his marriage to Bonnie came apart. By the end of the 1970s, the two were appearing on stage together, but the split, Haggard told Hurst, hadn't been easy. "No, it wasn't friendly. I don't think there's ever been a friendly divorce. But I think that everybody cooled off, seeing it wasn't something I was doing as a personal insult, I think she understood.

"We still have an obligation to the fans, I think, to appear together. You don't go out on the street corner and find a Bonnie Owens—someone who knows every song I ever wrote and is totally experienced in what I'm trying to do. We're talking about the right arm here."

So it was that when the bitterness had worn off, Owens was back on the road with Haggard in the late 1970s. The introduction ran, "This is my ex-wife and very dear friend, Bonnie Owens."

Typical songs on the program in the late 1970s were such hits as "It's Been a Great Afternoon," "The Way It Was in '51" (on Capitol, with the Strangers) and "The Bull and the Bear" from 1978 and "Red Bandana/I Must Have Done Something Bad" from 1979. "The Bull and the Bear" in record form was a duet with Leona Williams, who also co-wrote the tune with Merle. Leona, who had her own shows to give, had become the new Mrs. Haggard.

During 1979, a new facet of Haggard was revealed. He proved himself a fine actor in a number of segments of the NBC-TV multipart drama *Centennial* (a James Michener story). Haggard indicated he would probably do more acting in the future, but music remained his first love.

Merle closed out the 1970s and came into the 1980s with a steady stream of hits. The single "My Own Kind of Hat/Heaven Was a Drink of Wine" was on the lists at the end of 1979 and stayed there into 1980. During 1979 his charted LPs included *The Way It Was in '51* on Capitol and, on MCA, *Serving 190 Proof* and *I'm Always on a Mountain When I Fall*, the latter originally issued in 1977. In 1980, he had the top-10 singles hit "The Way I Am" on the charts early in the year, followed by such others as "Bar Room Buddies" (a duet with film star Clint Eastwood), "Misery and Gin," and "I Think I'll Just Stay Here and Drink." "Bar Room Buddies" was on Elektra Records, the rest on MCA. His LP *Serving 190 Proof* stayed on the charts from 1979 into 1980. Late in the year he had another charted LP, *The Way I Am*. In early 1981, his composition "Leonard" on MCA provided one of the year's best selling country singles. Soon after he had another top-10 single, a duet with Johnny Paycheck of his composition "I Can't Hold Myself in Line," released on Merle's new record label, Epic. In the fall, he had the Epic release "My Favorite Memory" in the top 5 and moving toward number one.

HALL, TOM T.: *Singer, guitarist, songwriter, author. Born Olive Hill, Kentucky, May 25, 1936.*

In the future, Tom T. Hall, whose career in the entertainment field got its initial impetus from his songwriting abilities, may be remembered most for the songs he penned. The unique quality of that body of work gave rise to his nickname, "The Storyteller." But he also has had a remarkable record as a singer, starting in the late 1960s, placing many singles and albums in the country top 10 and some in the number-one position.

He began life as the sixth child in a family of ten born to a Kentucky minister and his wife. He naturally listened to pop and country music during his formative years, but he didn't think of making music his profession at the time. When he attended Roanoke College in Virginia, his goal was a career in journalism. Among his favorite authors were Mark Twain, Sinclair Lewis, and Ernest Hemingway.

For a while, though, it looked as though he might opt for a military career. He spent eight years in the U.S. Army, stationed in Germany part of that time. When he returned to civilian life, he eventually made his first move into the music field by working as a disc jockey on a Roanoke radio station. He had become increasingly interested in writing songs by then and he soon started submitting them to Nashville publishers. One publishing executive, Jimmy Key, liked Tom's work and suggested he move to Music City. Once there, Tom settled in as a contract writer for a starting salary of fifty dollars a week. Before long artists were beginning to record some of his material. The first to release a recording of one of Tom's songs was Jimmy C. Newman with his version of "D.J. for a Day." From then on, new recordings of Hall's compositions came out regularly, either performed by other artists or by Tom himself. From the mid-1960s into the early 1980s, Tom earned one or more BMI songwriting awards each year, along the way being inducted into the Nashville Songwriters Hall of Fame.

At the outset, Tom T. was reluctant to become a recording artist; he never had thought of singing as his strong point. However, after he signed with Mercury Records in 1967, his viewpoint changed and his output of singles and LPs over the next decade and a half was one of the highest among country artists. Through early 1981, those efforts resulted in eleven singles that rose to number one. It was a song recorded by another that really brought him to prominence, though. The song, "Harper Valley P.T.A.," had lain dormant for a year before Jeannie C. Riley decided to put it on vinyl. When she did, in 1968, the result was phenomenal. The record sold over 6 million copies and, as evidence of its lasting popularity, was dramatized as a popular movie in 1978 and became the basis for a TV series in the early 1980s. The song's success also opened doors right away for its author. Within a few months after the record hit, songs written by him occupied as many as six spots on the country charts. It also helped pave the way for his success as a singer.

The songs he placed on the charts himself, or that made upper levels in versions by other performers, typically were based on incidents or observations drawn from his life. The story behind "Harper Valley P.T.A.," for instance, Tom T. said, was based on an actual event that had occurred in his home town during his youth. His "The Year That Clayton Delaney Died" was written about the man who helped inspire him to become a musician; and "Old Dogs, Children and Watermelon Wine" tells about an old black man he met while getting drunk in a Miami, Florida, bar during a Republican presidential convention.

Many of his songs deliver a message along with a story. This is the case with the above-mentioned songs as well as such hits as "The Ballad of 40 Dollars," which deals with hypocrisy, "Margie's at the Lincoln Park Inn," about temptation, and "Faster Horses," which suggests that the meaning of life is "faster horses, younger women, older whiskey and more money." More involved narratives are presented concisely yet evocatively in compositions like "Salute to a Switchblade," "Ravishing Ruby," and "Ode to a Ground Round." Still others are poems, in effect, ultimately simple yet touching, such as "I Love," a list of things the writer loves (such as "winners when they cry, losers when they try"). Other songs are just plain fun, such as "I Like Beer," in which he states over and over again that he likes to drink beer. In "Country Is," Tom T. defines the meaning of country through its conflicting images, and in "Sneaky Snake," he sings a children's story set to music.

During his stay with Mercury Records, from 1967 to 1977, Tom T. turned out one or more LPs every year. These include *Homecoming, Witness Life, One Hundred Children, In Search of a Song, We All Got Together,*

And . . . , The Storyteller, Tom T. Hall's Greatest Hits, For the People in the Last Hard Town, Songs of Fox Hollow, Rhymer and Other Five and Dimers, Country Is, I Wrote a Song About It, Tom T. Hall's Greatest Hits, Volume 2, Faster Horses, Magnificent Music Machine, and *About Love.* A sampling of his chart hit singles on Mercury in the 1970s includes "Day Drinkin' " (with Dave Dudley, 1970); "Me & Jesus," "The Monkey That Became President" (1972); "Ravishing Ruby" (1973); "I Love," "This Song Is Driving Me Crazy," "Country Is" (1974); "I Care/Sneaky Snakes," "Deal," "I Like Beer" (1975); "Faster Horses (the Cowboy and the Poet)," "Negatory Romance" (1976); and "It's All in the Game" (1977).

In 1977, Tom T. left Mercury and signed with RCA, remaining with that label until 1981. His debut LP on RCA was *New Train . . . Same Rider.* It was followed by such others as *Places I've Done Time* (late 1978) and *Ol' T's in Town* (1980). His charted singles on RCA included "What Have You Got to Lose" (1978); "There Is a Miracle in You," "You Show Me Your Heart (and I'll Show You Mine)," "Son of Clayton Delaney (1979); and "The Old Side of Town/ Jesus on the Radio (Daddy on the Phone)," "Soldier of Fortune," "Back When Gas Was Thirty Cents a Gallon," "I'm Not Ready Yet" (1980).

During the 1970s, Tom T.'s face became quite familiar to TV viewers from his guest appearances on many country and pop shows as well as some specials of his own. He also made many concert appearances on the fair and rodeo circuit and in major venues, including a very successful show at New York's Carnegie Hall. His honors included nominations to various categories over the years in the Country Music Association awards competition and the receipt of a Grammy in the early 1970s for Best Album Notes (1972), written by him for his *Greatest Hits* LP. As of the early 1980s he was a regular cast member of the *Grand Ole Opry* and also host of his own syndicated TV program, *Pop Goes the Country,* filmed at Nashville's Opryland.

His early interest in journalism was revived once he achieved success in music, with opportunities to do some prose work.

During the 1970s he wrote two books, *How I Write Songs, How You Can* and *The Storyteller's Nashville*, the latter a combination of autobiography and a review of Nashville's development as a major force in pop music. As of early 1981, Tom T. also was at work on his first novel, under contract to Doubleday.—A.S.

HAMBLEN, STUART: *Singer, band leader, songwriter, actor, emcee. Born Kellyville, Texas, October 20, 1908.*

Tall, broad-shouldered, ramrod straight throughout his life, Stuart Hamblen looked the part of a rough and rugged cowboy. Indeed, the role was an authentic one. Born and raised in cowboy country in Texas, he learned to ride and rope as a child and later spent a number of years on the rodeo circuit. Appropriately, he contributed greatly to western lore with his musical skills and acting talents. However, he also tried to live up to the hard-living image of the old-time cowboy, which got him in considerable trouble until he fell under the spell of Billy Graham in 1949 and eventually was converted to Christianity and a new approach to life from the mid-1950s on.

As a teenager, Hamblen enjoyed listening to western ballads and had built up a repertoire of songs by the time he enrolled in McMurray State Teachers College in Abilene, Texas. Still, he thought music would be a hobby as he worked for his B.A., an activity he took time out from every now and then to take part in rodeo events. However, the urge to sing and write songs proved too strong and he began to take music courses and think about a possible career in the field.

In 1928, he made his way to the Victor Talking Machine Company, forerunner of RCA Victor, in New Jersey, and recorded some songs. Later he decided there might be more opportunity on the West Coast and moved to Southern California, which was to be his home from then on. Once there, he made contact with other young western artists and others in the music field. After doing some work as a sideman he established his own group to perform on a local station. For a good many years

he was featured on several stations, including NBC's Los Angeles outlet, KFI. One of the groups he worked with in those years was a western swing band, the Beverly Hillbillies, that gained considerable local repute. During the 1930s and 1940s, Hamblen hosted a number of popular radio shows, including *Covered Wagon Jubilee* and *Lucky Stars.*

Those decades were the heyday of the western movie, and Hamblen was a natural. He had parts in many such films of the 1930s and 1940s, but always seemed to end up as the villain. Among the people who "foiled" his evil deeds were Gene Autry, Roy Rogers, and Bob Steele. Hamblen's portrayals were not far from the truth; he made the headlines many times for getting into brawls, shooting out street lights, or other escapades.

He told James Brown, for an article in the *Los Angeles Times* Calendar section (April 4, 1976), "I'd always been a rough man, but my big problem was not being able to leave the booze alone. My daddy was a Methodist minister and I guess I was the original juvenile delinquent. I just loved to fight too and I suppose I got thrown into jail a few times. I remember old Sam Hoffman. He was one of my sponsors on the radio, and every time I'd get into trouble, Sam'd have to come and bail me out. He never could understand why I did those things. But I guess I was the only cowboy he knew."

However, Hamblen always had another side, that of a charming, very talented artist, who made many contributions to the progress of country & western music. During the 1940s, he had a growing number of recordings to his credit on Columbia, many presenting songs he wrote. Some of those were covered by other artists as well. In 1949, he scored a major national country hit with his single of his composition "But I'll Be Chasin' Women." In 1950, he made the country & western top 10 again with "(Remember Me) I'm the One Who Loves You." Besides Stuart's Columbia disc, Ernest Tubb made the charts with his version on Decca.

In 1949, a turning point in Hamblen's life occurred: he attended a Billy Graham prayer meeting. Graham's words had a steadily growing influence on him. Several years after, Hamblen embraced Christianity, quit the bottle, and retired from radio and films, though he still kept up his songwriting and recording activities. In 1952 he ran for President of the United States on the Prohibition Party ticket, though he did not garner many votes.

His biggest triumph in the music field was just around the corner. In 1954, his song "This Old House" became one of the biggest sellers of the year, with his single reaching upper-chart levels in the country field and Rosemary Clooney's version going to the top of the pop lists.

Hamblen recalled for James Brown how the song came into existence. "I always wanted to write music and for me, it could be anywhere. I can be up in the mountains, by a stream, and all of a sudden a tune will come into my head.

"I wrote 'This Old House' that way. I was in the mountains and found this old prospector dead in his cabin. I saw curtains, so that meant a woman had been there. I saw kids things lyin' around. And they were all gone now. The old man was alone. That triggered the song—'Ain't a gonna leave this house no longer/I'm gettin' ready to meet the Saints'—I wrote down the lyric on a brown paper bag. Oh, I guess it took me about thirty minutes or so to finish it."

In 1955, another Hamblen song was in the top 10 with the success of Hank Snow's version of "Mainliner." During those years, Hamblen turned out such other successful songs as "It Is No Secret," "Open Up Your Heart and Let the Sun Shine In," and "The Lord Is Counting on You." Hamblen compositions include "Golden River," "My Mary, Little Old Rag Doll," and "You Must Be Born Again."

Among his many recordings were such other titles as "Lonesome Cowboy," "Be My Shepherd," "Beyond the Sunset," "When the Lord Picks Up the Phone," "A Few Things to Remember," "Friends I Know," "Got So Many Million Years," "Desert Sunrise," "Whistler's Dream," "Sunny Side of the Mountain," "Oh How I Cried," "I'll Be Gone," "Hell Train," "That'll Be the Day," "This Book, My Brother," "Old Pappy's New Banjo."

Some of his many albums over the years were still current at the end of the 1970s. Among his LPs were the 1959 Coral LP, *Remember Me* and the 1961 Columbia release, *Spell of the Yukon.* Kapp Records also issued the LP *This Old House* in 1966. His religious LPs included the 1962 Columbia album *Of God I Sing* and several on RCA Victor, such as *Grand Old Hymns, It Is No Secret,* and *Beyond the Sun* (the last named issued on Camden).

Hamblen and his wife, Susie, sometimes collaborated on various projects. In the late 1950s, they cohosted a TV show on a local Los Angeles station and Susie also helped out in the religious radio program that Hamblen taped at home for most of the 1970s, called *Cowboy Church of the Air.* (Home at the time was the seven-and-one-half-acre estate once owned by Errol Flynn. The Hamblens lived there many years before putting it on the market at the end of the 1970s.)

Before doing the program, Hamblen had essentially been retired, though he often took time out to speak to religious and charitable groups as well as youth organizations around the United States. In 1971, the general manager of station KLAC, Bill Ward, offered Hamblen a Sunday morning period for a religious program. Hamblen told Brown, "Here I'd been retired, just huntin' and fishin' and livin' the good life. And I'd been doin' all of that speaking and singin' in every prison I could. So when Ward came along and asked me if I'd like to do this radio show, well, it was somethin' I wasn't too sure about. But then he said that I could reach more people on the radio in one week than I could traveling around the country for a year. That's what convinced me."

Almost a decade later, at the start of the 1980s, the *Cowboy Church* still was being broadcast every Sunday morning at 9:05. "But the one thing I want to make clear is I'm no preacher. We tell stories instead of sermons. And we don't accept donations even though some people, bless 'em, choose to send money. I just say thank you and send it right back."

Though their public appearances were limited for most of the 1960s and 1970s, Hamblen and Susie regularly took part in the Tournament of Roses Parade on New Year's Day. On January 1, 1980, the Hamblens rode their horses past the TV cameras as they had been doing for many years.

HAMILTON, GEORGE IV: *Singer, guitarist, songwriter. Born Matthews, North Carolina, July 19, 1937.*

George Hamilton IV, although his name was present on hit charts plenty of times in his long career, did not have as many top-10 hits as other major country artists. Instead he will be remembered as someone who helped make music fans all over the world aware of the delights of country music, an effort which earned him the unofficial title of the International Ambassador of Country Music.

Country, of course, was George's first love, a natural consequence of growing up in North Carolina. But it was rock and pop that first made his reputation when he sallied forth from college in 1956 to hit the national charts with "A Rose and a Baby Ruth," also the title song of his best-selling debut album on ABC that was released in March 1958. He followed with several other teenage favorites, such as "High School Romance" and "Why Don't They Understand."

By 1959, a combination of a slowdown in his pop career and a desire to concentrate on country stylings led to his moving to Nashville, where he started a new career phase as part of RCA Victor's country roster. In the early 1960s, he soon became a first-rank performer in the field, turning out such chart singles as "If You Don't Know I Ain't Gonna Tell You," "Before the Day Ends," "Ft. Worth, Dallas or Houston," "Truck Driving Man," and, in 1963, the number-one country hit "Abilene." RCA found cash registers clicked for his albums as well; LPs such as *Abilene* (released 10/63), *Ft. Worth, Dallas or Houston* (12/64), *Coast Country* (3/66), and *Steel Rail Blues* showing up on country charts. Asked to join the *Grand Ole Opry* early in the decade, he remained a cast member throughout the 1960s.

In the mid-1960s, George began to take increased interest in folk music, particularly the modern compositions being turned out by a gifted group of artists from Canada. As he told Jan Otteson of *Music City News* (January 1978), "For me . . . it started in 1965 when I was playing at the Horseshoe Tavern in Toronto. There I heard a record on the radio by Gordon Lightfoot. I wasn't aware of him then; I figured he was some Canadian Indian. But I really liked his sound. It seemed to be a perfect marriage of folk music and country music. When I met Gordon and we became good friends, he introduced me to people like Joni Mitchell, Leonard Cohen, and Ian and Sylvia and I found out how many great songs those people had written. I became infatuated with their music."

Hamilton's folk leanings became evident in his late 1960s releases. In March 1967, for instance, RCA issued his LP *Folk Classics,* followed by *Folksy* in September of that year. In 1969, his preoccupation with Canadian folk and country work culminated with the RCA release *Canadian Pacific,* a collection in which Hamilton performed only songs by Canadian writers, including a number by Lightfoot. The album wasn't a blockbuster with U.S. fans, but found favor with Canadians and people in England, Europe, and elsewhere and continued in the RCA catalogue in the 1970s. He dubbed his move in that direction as part of an attempt to expand the horizons of country music, a direction he described as "thinking man's country."

Hamilton's career took on its broad international flavor as the 1970s began. He had his start, he told Jan Otteson, in mid-1969, when he was invited to a concert in England. "That's when I attended the first Wembley Music Festival in England. And even though I didn't get paid for it, I liked it a lot and went back the following year. Then a guy from the BBC decided to put me in a BBC television series over there. From there, a Canadian TV producer named Mannie Pittson happened to see the show and asked if I would do a syndicated television show for him in Canada."

The idea made sense to George. He resigned from the *Opry* in 1971 and moved back home to Matthews, North Carolina.

That shift allowed him to spend more time with his family and made it easier for him to organize his new international show. He and Pittson agreed that the program, which was to be taped mainly in Canada, would feature primarily north of the border talent. The concept, claimed to be the first internationally syndicated country-music show, rapidly found favor overseas. By the end of 1977, it was presented on outlets in the United Kingdom, Ireland, South Africa, New Zealand, Hong Kong, Canada, and, starting in 1978, Australia.

In 1974, Hamilton added another laurel to his international work, becoming the first country-music artist to perform in the Soviet Union and Czechoslovakia. The Russian authorities were pleased with his kind of music (which did not grate their political nerves the way rock tended to do) and later invited such others as Tennessee Ernie Ford and Roy Clark to tour.

Later on in the 1970s, though Hamilton didn't give up his foreign concerts and telecasts, he decided to reestablish his credentials with the home audience. He signed with ABC/Dot in the United States, the label he had originally gained fame with in his pop days, and Anchor Records in England. His first LP in this series, *Fine Lace and Homespun Cloth,* came out in early 1978. The songs chosen were by such writers as Larry Kingston and Shel Silverstein, and the treatment emphasized by Hamilton and his producer, Allen Reynolds, was in the folk-country vein. This Hamilton defined as meaning "lots of acoustic guitars and a strong rhythm section rather than the hard-core country music that's dependent upon steel guitars and fiddles. Allen, I feel, cuts a commercial country record . . . but they go beyond that. They're distinctive and always fresh sounding."

His frank goal was to stress "sounds with a M.O.R. [middle of the road] appeal," an approach at odds with the progressive country concept of grittier material. Hamilton, however, always stressed his belief there was nothing wrong with good M.O.R., since it promised to meet the tastes of a broad spectrum of tastes and age levels.

When ABC/Dot was merged into MCA Records, George signed a new agreement with them. The first album on the MCA label was *Forever Young,* issued in 1979. Meanwhile, Hamilton continued to add to his overseas credits. In 1976 he served as emcee of the first "International Festival of Country Music," held in Sweden, and served in the same capacity for subsequent events in Finland (1977), Norway and Holland (1978), and Germany (1979). He continued his association with England's Wembley country music festival. From 1969 into the early 1980s, he was featured in the event all but three years. In 1979, he became the first American country singer to have a British summer season, appearing at the Winter Gardens Theatre in Blackpool.

An example of Hamilton's intellectual approach to his profession was his analysis of the roots of country music and his understanding of its relation to centuries-old traditions in the British Isles. He stressed to *Music City News,* "I get a big kick out of taking the music that originally had its roots in places like England and Ireland back to the descendants of its originators. To me, I feel like I'm putting something back into my art form."

HAMMOND, JOHN PAUL: *Singer, guitarist, songwriter. Born New York, New York, November 13, 1942.*

"My father tried for a year to talk me out of being a musician, but I wasn't afraid. You know, if you're not afraid you got nothin' to lose. And you can't lose anything anyway, losing is just a lesson."

John Hammond's father, John Hammond, Sr., was a jazz musician credited with discovering such greats as Bob Dylan, Benny Goodman, Billie Holiday, and Count Basie during his years as a Columbia Records executive. His son, though, went his own way to become a major force in the blues evolution, both "pure" and rock, during the 1960s and 1970s.

Young John, born and raised in New York City, naturally was exposed to music and famous music personalities from his earliest years. His parents separated when he was five, which probably contributed to the stuttering problem that plagued him much of the time. He sought some solace in music, particularly after he was sent to private school when he was thirteen. He told Jim Crockett, in an article in *Guitar Player* (March 1973), "That time away from home, between 1956 and 1959, was a very lonely one for me. All I could do was create my own fantasy world." One of his pleasures was playing slide guitar, which he took up in 1956, though he didn't think about making music his life's goal at the time.

At seventeen, after high school, he gained an art scholarship to a school in Maine where he roomed with David Getz, who later was drummer in the band called Big Brother and the Holding Company, which worked with Janis Joplin. Getz's interest in Hammond's collection of old blues records and blues singing style planted some of the early ideas of a change in emphasis for John. When Hammond was eighteen, he enrolled briefly at Antioch College in Ohio, but the folk boom was still flourishing and John finally decided to leave school and make his way as a performer. He played the coffee-house circuit around the United States, building up his confidence and getting enough attention when he returned to the New York–Boston area to gain a recording contract from Vanguard Records in 1962. His debut on the label, *John Hammond*, was released in 1963.

Eagerly awaiting the album's issuance, he was invited to the 1963 Newport Folk Festival blues workshop. To be included in a group that contained such legendary black blues singers as John Lee Hooker, Sonny Terry, Brownie McGhee, and Mississippi John Hurt was a fine compliment to a young white singer. He acquitted himself well, and his blues talents were further underlined when his initial LP came out. Leonard Feather, in *Down Beat*, March 12, 1964, described a test where he played John's track "Mean Old Frisco" for jazz great Fletcher Henderson. Said Henderson, "That's beautiful. Sounds like Brownie McGhee and Sonny Terry. . . . I don't think anybody today would be able to duplicate this, because they haven't lived this way."

Hammond continued to polish his reputation in the mid-1960s with coffee-house and club engagements plus occasional TV appearances, and with a series of follow-up LPs on Vanguard. Those included *Big City Blues* in 1964, *So Many Roads* in 1965, *Country Blues* in 1966,. and *Mirrors* in 1967.

He himself always was creatively restless, and during those years he became interested in electric blues and blues-rock. He became enamored with Ronnie Hawkins' backup group, later to gain fame as The Band, before they worked with Bob Dylan. At one point when the group was in New York, he asked Robbie Robertson, Garth Hudson, and Levon Helm to back him on an album. Rounding out the group was harmonica player Charlie Musselwhite and pianist Mike Bloomfield. The album, called *Source Point*, was too different from his normal blues approach for Vanguard, which refused to issue it right away. He cut a second LP on which he played electric guitar with a backing group that included Robbie Robertson on lead guitar and Bill Wyman of the Rolling Stones on bass guitar. That too was shelved for some years until it finally came out as *I Can Tell*.

Hammond's frustration over those efforts caused him to leave Vanguard and sign with Atlantic Records. He completed three albums on Atlantic in the late 1960s, including one called *Southern Fried*, recorded in Muscle Shoals, Alabama. Duane Allman of the Allman Brothers Band played lead guitar on a number of tracks in that LP.

Among John's projects in the 1970s was completion of a soundtrack for Dustin Hoffman's 1970 film, *Little Big Man*, still a staple on network TV. He switched to his father's old label, Columbia, at the start of the decade. The first result of that alignment was *Source Point*, issued in March 1971, followed in 1972 by the album *I'm Satisfied*.

Hammond's instrumental ability won attention as the years went by, as indicated by his inclusion in *Guitar Player*'s 1973 artist issue. His electric technique, Jim Crockett noted, was highly unusual. "Since he is self-taught . . . he picks the acoustic with the thumb and index finger, occasionally adding the middle finger for more inticate licks. This is exactly what he does on electric too. No flatpick, just a plastic thumb pick and a National metal fingerpick. "My hands are a wreck," he says, "calluses everywhere because I play every day. I really couldn't tell you how I actually play all the things I do. When I'm lost in a song, the guitar just comes."

He told Crockett of a technique called "popping" notes learned from Robbie Robertson. "You pick the note with the nail, then right after that you touch the string with the thumb to get a harmonic, then you bend the note at the same time."

He stressed he had no regrets about going into music, though the financial rewards certainly fell far short of typical rock idols. "I've achieved all my original goals. I've been around the world a couple of times. I've played with all my idols, like Son House, Muddy Waters, Howlin' Wolf and they love me. I've made a lot of mistakes, but that's how I am. If there are mistakes to be made, I'll make the worst ones. I wasn't dumb, I just wanted to see it all. For me, the toughest times are when I'm not active."

HANK THE DRIFTER: *Singer, guitarist, songwriter. Born Taunton, Massachusetts, September 2, 1929.*

One of New England's relatively few contributions to the country & western field, Hank the Drifter, as the pseudonym indicates, was a fan of the late Hank Williams from his early years. Since his voice turned out to closely resemble that of his idol, his career was based largely on that similarity.

His real name was Daniel Raye Andrade and he was born and raised in Massachusetts. He learned to play guitar by his teens and later joined a group called The Hayshakers. With Andrade as lead singer, the band entered amateur contests throughout New England and proved just about unbeatable. After the Hayshakers won fifteen straight first prizes, Andrade parlayed it into a fifteen-minute weekly show on station WPEP in Taunton. From there he moved on to a somewhat bigger market, sponsored as Hank the Drifter by the *New Bedford Times* on station WNBH in that Massachusetts seacoast city.

After a while he wandered farther afield, ending up in Texas, where he struck roots

in the 1950s and still resided (in Houston) in the 1970s. His appearances in the Lone Star State in the late 1950s and early 1960s included the *Corns a Poppin'* program on radio station KTRH, the *Big D Jamboree* in Dallas, and the *Cowtown Hoedown* in Ft. Worth. He continued to perform at county fairs, rodeos, and the like in Houston and other Texas cities throughout the 1960s and appeared on both radio and TV in the area.

During those years, he recorded for New England Records and also was featured on Canadian discs issued on the Sparton and Quality labels. Almost all the releases were original compositions, including such songs as "All These Things You Can't Erase," "I'll Never Say 'I Do' Again," "Hank Williams Is Singing Again," "Hank, You're Gone but Not Forgotten," "Cheaters Never Win," "Don't You Lock Your Daddy Out," "I'm Crying My Heart Out for You," "Bill Collector Blues," "Cold River Blues," "Why Did It Have to Be Me?" "You're Paying for It Now," "I'm Gonna Spin My Wheels," and "Painted Dolls."

HARDIN, TIM: *Singer, guitarist, songwriter. Born Eugene, Oregon, 1940; died Los Angeles, California, December 29, 1980.*

A singer with a unique vocal style that influenced many new artists in folk and pop music in the late 1960s and early 1970s, Tim Hardin suffered from the minority status of the folk field in terms of receiving widespread recognition for his performing ability. However, many people who wouldn't have known his name were quite familar with many of his excellent compositions, which provided hits for artists ranging from Joan Baez to such rock stars as Bobby Darin and the Youngbloods. At one point, Bob Dylan paid him an oblique compliment by issuing an album in 1968 called *John Wesley Harding,* the name of a legendary outlaw who was an ancestor of Tim Hardin.

Music was part of Tim's more immediate heritage. Both his parents were musically inclined. His mother, in particular, developed a major national reputation in the classical field. Both of his parents studied music in school and both earned master's degrees in the field. His mother, Molly Small Hardin, ranked as one of the world's most accomplished female violinists, and, when young Tim was growing up in Oregon, she served as concertmaster of the Portland Symphony Orchestra. His father tended to favor more popularly oriented music, having played in jazz bands during his school years and while serving in the Navy. However, he turned to selling real estate rather than the arts as his main vocation.

During Tim's childhood and teens, many notables in the classical world visited the Hardin home. He recalled that the family "once had boiled salmon with the Budapest String Quartet out there on our porch."

Tim's musical inclinations didn't start to take shape until his high school years. "I started fooling around with the guitar in high school and I sang in the Eugene high school choir. I never thought of going to college, really, in my life. If you've got any kind of talent, man, it just resticts you."

After high school, in the late 1950s, Tim enlisted in the Marines as the way to strike out on his own. The military occupied most of his next four years, first involving duty in Cambodia and Laos followed by two years in the reserves. When he was off duty, Tim kept improving his guitar playing and also added to his store of folk songs. After he completed his hitch, he headed across the United States to Cambridge, Massachusetts, where he soon became an important part of the still-burgeoning folk scene. He became a favorite of Boston fans from his appearances at local coffee houses and small clubs. Increasingly he introduced some of his original songs into his act.

In 1966, Verve Records signed him and issued his debut LP on the Verve/Forecast label, *Tim Hardin*, in September 1966. Close to a year later, his second album, *Tim Hardin II*, came out in July 1967. Two months later another release, *This Is Tim Hardin*, came out on Atco Records, an album he had recorded in the early 1960s but reportedly, by the mid-1960s, did not want released. Meanwhile, other artists were beginning to turn out recordings of

some of Tim's writings, including such well-known tunes as "If I Were a Carpenter," which provided a hit single in 1966 for Bobby Darin and later for Johnny Cash and his wife, June Carter, and "Reason to Believe," covered by dozens of well-known performers over the years, including Rod Stewart in 1972. During the late 1960s, many of Hardin's compositions were written in his new home, Woodstock, in upstate New York, where his paths crossed those of people like Dylan and The Band.

In the late 1960s, Verve/Forecast issued such other LPs as *Tim Hardin 3 Live in Concert* and *Tim Hardin 4*. In August 1969, Verve/Forecast turned out a retrospective of his earlier records, *Best of Tim Hardin*. He also was represented on MGM Records with an album called *Tim Hardin*. In 1968, he signed with a new label, Columbia, which issued his first LP, *Suite for Susan, Moore and Damian* in April 1969. Among his other releases on Columbia were *One, All in One*, and *Bird on a Wire*, released in August 1971.

His albums didn't make national charts, though Hardin maintained excellent rapport with folk adherents, including many critics. One of them wrote, "I wear out Tim Hardin's records as fast as Billie Holiday's. I suppose that's because Tim and Billie experienced pain so hurtingly and have so hauntingly made it a musical experience."

In the late 1960s and at the start of the 1970s, Hardin toured widely both in the United States and abroad. His concerts graced the stage of many colleges and clubs and concert halls in almost every major U.S. city. Indicating his standing with his musical peers, at many venues the audience included some of the best-known entertainers in the music field, past and present.

Hardin was frustrated by the rather limited attention he received in his homeland and at the fact that his songs tended to provide hits for other performers rather than himself. In 1971, he moved to England, where he remained for seven years. During that period he concertized in England and on the Continent, occasionally taking time out to record new material, such as the 1973 album *Nine* for Island Records, later issued in the United States in 1971 on Island's Antilles label.

In the late 1970s, Tim returned to the United States with renewed optimism about finding his audience at home. In April 1980, his path crossed that of old friend Don Rubin, in the 1960s Tim's executive producer and music publisher during his association with Verve/Forecast Records. As Rubin told Len Epand, public relations director of Polygram Records (recalled by Epand in notes for Hardin's posthumous album on Polygram), the two planned a new project. "It was like a dream come true. . . . He had returned to make a comeback here in the U.S. We immediately set about the task of preparing a new album. He had written ten new songs for the project and we began recording the LP, a never to be completed LP due to his untimely death."

In the same month that the music world lost John Lennon, Hardin was found dead of a drug overdose in Los Angeles. In early 1981, Polygram issued the *Tim Hardin Memorial Album*, at the time the only album of Hardin recordings in print. The tracks, all of his own compositions, mostly were culled from his first two Verve/Forecast LPs, with two from *Tim Hardin 4*. They were "If I Were a Carpenter," "Black Sheep Boy," "Misty Roses," "Green Rocky Road," "How Long," "Don't Make Promises," "Smugglin' Man," "Hello Baby," "Reason to Believe," "How Can We Hang On to a Dream," "Lady Came from Baltimore," and "It'll Never Happen Again."

HARGROVE, LINDA: *Singer, guitarist, songwriter. Born north Florida, February 3, 1951.*

Over the past few decades it hasn't been unusual for a southern-bred male singer to get started in rock 'n' roll, then switch over to become a success in the country field. On the female side, the trend has tended to go in the other direction, but Linda Hargrove is an exception.

Linda, who grew up in north Florida, was started on piano lessons while a young child and also displayed a promising voice as a church choir member. But as she moved along in years, she identified more with rock and pop than either country or gospel. At the ripe old age of ten, she taught herself guitar and in high school, at fourteen, began writing pop songs with a friend "just for our own amusement." At sixteen, she was playing in local rock bands. In her first year at Troy State University, Troy, Alabama, where she won a music scholarship to play the French horn, she dropped out and tried to get work as a pop musician.

It was the late 1960s and, as she recalled, "Rhythm and blues and blue-eyed soul was what was happening in north Florida at the time, so that was what we were playing." She was writing songs steadily by then, some of which were picked up by a local band that got a recording offer from Nashville. She went along in case any work was needed on the seven compositions of hers the band planned to tape. Though she hadn't been consciously writing country music up to that point, she liked the Nashville scene and moved there during 1970.

For a while, not much happened. She took her songs around to music executives and made little progress for many months. She finally got a hearing from Billy Robinson, husband of singer Sandy Posey, and the result was that Sandy recorded one of Linda's songs for an Epic session. Pete Drake, pedal steel expert, was a backing musician at the 1971 session, and he thought Linda's writing was promising. Soon after, he gave her a writing contract. Linda also did session guitar work at Drake's studios, usually on rhythm guitar, and also learned to run the control console for Drake's sixteen-track tape system.

She worked with many artists, both from pop and country fields, including Tommy James, Mike Nesmith, Bobby Bare, Mac Davis, Jackson Browne, Waylon Jennings, and Tom T. Hall. Some of them also recorded some of her compositions, as did such others as Lynn Anderson, B. J. Thomas, Leon Russell (who used two of Linda's songs in the album *Hank Williams Is Back)*, Billie Jo Spears, and Olivia Newton John. During the summer of 1975,

Johnny Rodriguez released a single of her song "Just Get Up and Close the Door" that soared to number one on the country charts. The song served as the title track for a Rodriguez LP that also made top-chart levels. Lynn Anderson also gained a major chart hit with Linda's "I've Never Loved Anyone More."

Before those achievements, Hargrove recorded two albums for Elektra Records that hadn't done very much. In 1975, she signed with Capitol, which released her debut LP on the label, *Love, You're the Teacher*, in 1976. The album wasn't a smash hit, but it did show up on the charts briefly, indicating that Linda was developing a following among country fans. For the balance of the 1970s, Linda had a number of singles on the charts, such as "Love Was (Once Around the Dance Floor)" and "Fire at the First Sight" (both written by her) in 1976 and "Mexican Love Songs" in 1977 (co-written with Pete Drake). During the late 1970s, Capitol issued another LP of hers, *Impressions*.

HARRIS, EMMYLOU: *Singer, guitarist, songwriter. Born Birmingham, Alabama, April 12, 1947.*

When Emmylou Harris was in high school, she wrote to her current idol, Pete Seeger, saying that she always wanted to sing folk songs but didn't know if she could because she hadn't suffered enough. As she told Robert Hilburn in an interview in the *Los Angeles Times*, "You know how it was in the folk era, you had to have had a real hard time to be valid." Seeger wrote back telling her not to worry about that. Her fans must be grateful that she did not get discouraged from pursuing success as a singer and musician.

Success, however, as is usually the case, did not always come easy. Emmylou was born and raised in Birmingham, Alabama. Coming from the South, she was certainly exposed to country music, but her first love was folk music. She entered the University of North Carolina as a drama major, but after a year and a half, she dropped out and headed for New York. There she sang folk music in small clubs and tried to win herself a record contract.

Unfortunately, folk music was considered passé and Emmylou received only rejections from the record companies.

In 1969, she was signed by Jubilee Records. She was pregnant when her first album was released (her marriage later ended in divorce). She didn't like the album, and when her daughter was born, retired temporarily to live with her parents in Washington, D.C. But by the following year, she had already begun singing in Washington, D.C., clubs, backed by a folk-country band. While she was appearing at the Cellar Door, the Flying Burrito Brothers saw her perform. They asked her to join their band, but a week later Emmylou discovered that they were breaking up.

However, it was through the Burrito Brothers that Emmylou met Gram Parsons, who was to have a lasting influence on her singing as well as, indirectly, a hand in the success she was later to enjoy. Harris was introduced to Parsons, an ex-Burrito member, by Burrito Chris Hillman late in 1971. Parsons had been looking for a female harmony singer, and he asked Emmylou to help him on his first album. She sang with him on that album, *GP*, later toured with him in the spring of 1973, and helped him on his last album, *Grievous Angel*.

Soon after, Gram Parsons died what may have been a drug-related death. Emmylou was saddened by his sudden demise and returned to Washington, D.C., for a time to play in small clubs, to write songs, and to organize her own band. Meanwhile, some people at Warner Bros. records had heard her on Parson's albums and had been impressed with her singing. She signed a record contract with them in mid-1974. Backed by several of Elvis Presley's musicians, she recorded an album, *Pieces of the Sky*, which was released in early 1975. As with all her future albums, this one contained a wide assortment of material. One cut from the album, a simple song previously recorded by the Louvin Brothers, "If I Could Only Win Your Love," became a number-one country hit. The album, too, reached number one on the country charts and also placed high on the pop charts.

Emmylou proved that she could do it again with the release of her next album, *Elite Hotel*. The big hits from the album were "One of These Days" and "Sweet Dreams," an old Don Gibson composition. However, every song on the album was capable of becoming a hit, from the upbeat "Amarillo," co-written by Emmylou with Rodney Crowell, to a beautiful country version of the Beatles' "Here, There and Everywhere," to the three songs written by her mentor, Gram Parsons: "Wheels," "Sin City," and "Ooh Las Vegas." Her clear, high-timbred voice blended perfectly with her accompanying musicians, who often provided a bluegrass-sounding background, adding a new dimension to every song on the album. The album won Emmylow a Grammy Award for Best Country Vocal Performance, Female, for 1976.

Luxury Liner, her next LP, was of the same high caliber. The standouts were her chart hits, "You Never Can Tell," a Chuck Berry rock hit of the 1950s, "Making Believe," which had been a 1955 hit for Kitty Wells, and a more recent country tune, Susanna Clark's "I'll Be Your San Antone Rose." Her next album, *Quarter Moon in a Ten Cent Town,* continued to prove her remarkable consistency and quality. It provided her with two top hits, "To Daddy," written by Dolly Parton, about a woman, ignored by her husband and family, who decides to leave home once her children are grown, and the poetic "Easy from Now On," written by Carlene Carter and Susanna Clark. *Quarter Moon* was one of five finalists in the Grammy competition for Best Country Vocal Performance, Female, of 1978.

Emmylou closed out the decade with still more chart-making singles in 1979: "Too Far Gone," "Save the Last Dance for Me," "Blue Kentucky Girl" and "Play Together Again, Again," the last named a duet with Buck Owens. She was represented on the album charts with two more LPs, *Blue Kentucky Girl* and *Profile/Best of Emmylou Harris,* both still on the lists at the start of the 1980s. *Blue Kentucky Girl* provided her with her third straight Grammy finalist nomination for the Best Country Vocal Performance, Female.

By the beginning of the 1980s she ranked as a superstar who appealed to audiences ranging the spectrum from folk and country to pop. Her concerts drew capacity crowds to college auditoriums and major venues in the United States and abroad. A program based on one of her concerts was presented several times on PBS-TV.

In the early 1980s, still recording for Warner Brothers (though there were reports of some strain in that relationship in 1981), she continued to have great rapport with record buyers and high respect from most critics. Among her 1980 offerings, all her singles made the country top 10 and most reached number one. The latter included her version of a Dallas Frazier song, "Beneath Still Waters," her haunting rendition of the old standard, "Wayfaring Stranger," and a duet with Roy Orbison, "That Loving You Feeling Again." Her 1979 single, "Blue Kentucky Girl," was still on the charts in 1980 and she also had a top-10 hit with Paul Simon's "The Boxer." Her early 1980 LP *Roses in the Snow* was on the country charts for most of 1980 and still on them in 1981, as was the case for the LP *Light of the Stable,* issued in late 1980 for the Christmas season. Her 1981 top-10 singles included "Mister Sandman" and a duet with Don Williams, "If I Needed You." In late 1981, her LP *Evangeline* was in the top 10.

In the late 1970s and early 1980s, her list of honors from her peers continued to grow. She often was one of the finalists in various categories not only on the Grammy Awards but also in voting for awards of the Academy of Country Music and the Country Music Association, and finished as top vote getter a number of times. In the October 1980 nationally telecast CMA Awards ceremony, at which she was one of the presenters, she was named the Female Vocalist of the Year for 1980. Her 1981 duet with Don Williams, "If I Needed You," was a finalist in the Grammies for Best Country Performance as a Duo or Group with Vocal.

As Robert Hilburn said of Harris in an article in the *Los Angeles Times,* ". . . the difficult thing in discussing Harris is fully describing her talent without stepping over the bounds of credibility. . . . [I]t's hard to imagine how Harris can move through the various strains of country music—from traditional to progressive, ballad to honky-tonk, from heartbreak to celebration—with such purity and evocativeness."—A.S.

HART, FREDDIE: *Singer, guitarist, band leader (The Heartbeats), songwriter. Born Lochapok, Alabama, December 21, circa 1928.*

To paraphrase Jim Croce, "You don't mess around with Freddie." He's seen it all and proven his mettle from farm hand to bouncer to country singer through decades of hard knocks and tough breaks, always persevering until luck turned his way.

Freddie began life as one of a poverty-ridden sharecropper family that was always on the move from one farm to another in Alabama. Before he was five, he was picking cotton, corn, or peanuts, as did all of the fifteen children in the family at one time or another. Even then, he was beginning to have a feel for country music and a longing to be on the *Grand Ole Opry.* When he was five, his Uncle Fletcher fed those dreams a bit by making him a home-made guitar from a long wooden cigar box, using coil wire from a Model T Ford for the strings. Little Freddie twanged it at times, used it as a sand truck at others. As he got a little older, though, the music side became more important and several times he ran away from home before he was twelve, telling his family, when he was picked up and returned, that he'd actually been on the *Opry.*

At twelve, his parents decided he was too rebellious and sent him off to a Civilian Conservation Corps (CCC) Camp. When he was fourteen, in 1942, with World War II raging, he got his mother to help fake his age so he could enlist in the Marines. He took part in the island-hopping Pacific campaign and, when he was in quieter surroundings, performed sometimes in various service clubs.

After the war, he came home hoping to make a career in music, but it wasn't that easy. He earned a haphazard living at all sorts of jobs: logging, pipelining, a steel worker in the Texas oil fields, and for a

while, a bouncer in the lawless, rugged gambling town of Phoenix City, Alabama. In the late 1940s, he washed dishes for a time in Hempstead, New York, and managed to work for a while in a small band with Bud Wilson.

He did get to Nashville every now and then, and in 1949 met the great Hank Williams. He toured briefly with Williams, mostly as a sort of country roadie, but learned a lot about writing from the master. As he told *Country Music* magazine, Hank advised him, "Don't just put down a line 'cause it rhymes. There's always a right line, and none better. And when you write and sing a song, write and sing it like it was the last one you were ever going to do." He also recalled that Williams told him, "You'll make it, but you have to believe in yourself, or nobody else can believe in you."

The next year, Freddie was in Phoenix, Arizona, working in a cotton seed mill, when he got to meet Lefty Frizzell. By then Freddie was stressing his writing skills. George Morgan had recorded one of Hart's songs in 1949 and Wayne Rainey, a close friend of Frizzell's, was considering doing another one. That connection helped Frizzell decide to take Freddie on as a sideman. Freddie worked with Lefty until 1952, when Hart got his first recording contract with Capitol.

Excitement ran high for Freddie when his debut single, "Butterfly Love," came out in 1952. Although it didn't set the world on fire, Freddie was getting recognition as a songwriter. In 1953, he became a regular on a country music show called *Town Hall Party,* which also featured such present or future superstars as Johnny Bond, Johnny Cash, and Tex Ritter during Freddie's stay from 1953 to the time the show ended in 1956.

But Freddie wasn't making it to stardom as the 1950s and 1960s went by. "I had good songs," he told *Country Music,* all the time. But I never could make it to the top. I never had the big hit that you so desperately need. The Big Success. I had 'Keys in the Mailbox' in 1957 and 'Loose Talk' [released on Capitol in 1954 and eventually covered by some fifty other artists]. I was writing some songs for other people. Lots of people. I wrote the other side of Patsy Cline's 'I Fall to Pieces.' But I knew I hadn't made it. I was making a living, but I wasn't known real big. Freddie who?"

He did become well known enough in the early 1960s to finally get a bid to appear on the *Grand Ole Opry*. But it was an anticlimax. "I prayed for so long. I tried for so many years. I tried too hard, I guess, because by the time it happened and I was right up there, well, I guess I had just about dreamed it all out of me. Not that I didn't love it—it's still one of the most important goals for any country singer, you know."

Meanwhile, Hart moved around, both as a performer and recording artist. He left Capitol and recorded for Columbia, Monument, and Kapp. Some songs made the lower-chart levels, but the blockbuster escaped him. In 1969, he returned to Capitol, which released his first album effort for them, *The New Sounds of Freddie Hart*, in 1970. That album fell flat and Capitol had just about decided to cast him out when the final album on the contract, *California Grapevine*, was issued in the fall of 1971. Freddie admits it was the low point of all low points. After eighteen years of persistence and struggle, he was finally starting to feel he might not make it.

He was saved in story-book fashion. A disc jockey at station WPOL in Atlanta, Georgia, fell in love with a track on the LP called "Easy Loving." He played it constantly, other stations picked up on it, and suddenly the song made the country charts that September and went all the way to number one. It also crossed over to the pop charts and got up to fifteen. Capitol hastily retitled the album from *California Grapevine* to *Easy Loving*, and the LP became a top-10 hit in late 1971. Freddie followed with a string of number-one singles during 1972 and 1973 and "presto," after two decades of effort, he was an "overnight sensation."

For the rest of the decade, Freddie's name was rarely absent from country lists. In early 1976, the single "Warm Side of You" was in the top 10 and the album *The*

First Time was moving up the charts. In May, he was represented by the single "She'll Throw Stones at You" and the LP *People Put to Music*. In the fall, he had the chart single "That Look in Her Eyes." The following year he had chartmakers like *The Pleasure's Been All Mine*, both a single and an album of the same title, and a single titled "The Search." In the fall of 1978, his Capitol single "Toe to Toe" was on the lists.

By the start of the 1980s, Hart had departed Capitol and signed with Sunbird Records. His charted singles on that label in the early 1980s included "Sure Thing" and "Roses Are Red" in 1980 and "You Were There" in 1981.

HARTFORD, JOHN: *Singer, guitarist, banjoist, fiddler, songwriter. Born New York, New York, December 30, 1937.*

A strong-willed individual, John Hartford gave up what looked like a sure-fire route to stardom as a pop artist to return to the environment he loved best—performing folk-country music with a bluegrass flavor and spending a good part of each year as a Mississippi riverboat pilot. "I was always very careful to make sure I would do exactly what I wanted to do. If I achieved some success I always wanted to be ready to buy back the limits so I wouldn't work just for the money. Like CBS offered me a detective series in the late 1960s, but I didn't want to be known as a detective."

He was born in New York, where his father, who was studying to be a doctor, was completing his internship. When he was two weeks old, the family moved back to St. Louis, Missouri. "Missouri is home. My family on both sides was from Missouri. My mom and dad used to square dance. I always did like square dance music. I was listening to the *Grand Ole Opry* on the radio every Saturday from the time I was a little boy."

John fooled around with various instruments in his early years before concentrating on the banjo and fiddle in his early teens. "I started with a four-string banjo, then made it into a five string. We drilled a hole and added the string. The thing that really turned me on was hearing Flatt & Scruggs when I was about fourteen. I loved Earl Scruggs playing bluegrass and I also was greatly influenced by Stringbean.

"I've always kinda known things on guitar. I always just played on other people's instruments. I never had one of my own until 1965. I liked to play fiddle almost as far back as I can remember. I kinda picked it up myself. A friend named Dr. James Gray, a state fiddle champ, showed me a lot of stuff and I also used to play with an old fiddler named Goforth in St. Louis."

His interest in country music continued as he progressed through high school. "I started to play professionally during those years. The music I loved was bluegrass. I had a band that did all the Flatt & Scruggs hits, as well as Don Reno, Red Smiley, Bill Monroe material. Occasionally we'd do a Roy Acuff song, but rearranged. I went to Washington University in St. Louis for a while in 1959–60, but I didn't finish. There didn't seem to be any need for it. I was either gonna be a boat pilot [he notes his first work on a steamboat was in 1947] or a musician and college wasn't much use in either case."

After leaving school, he worked at a number of jobs, including commercial artist (some of his drawings adorn the covers of his Flying Fish albums), steamboat deck hand, and radio announcer. He continued to play for small affairs or his own pleasure, but music seemed fated to be more a sideline than a primary occupation.

The years went by and, apart from marriage and the birth of a son, nothing dramatic took place. He had a few minor credits in the recording field in the first part of the 1960s. "I had a record out on the Marlo label and one on the Shannon label out of St. Louis." Then in the mid-1960s, he decided to try his luck in Nashville. He told an interviewer, "I was working in southeast Missouri at the time and I wasn't doing too well, moneywise, and I thought, well, you only live once, and a guy can starve to death as easily in Nashville as anywhere else and have more fun doing it, so I just packed up my wife and my little boy and moved to Nashville."

Drawing on his announcing credits, he got a job on a Nashville station. He began trying to place his original songs with a publisher. That effort finally won the attention of the Glaser Brothers, who added his name to their talent agency list and began playing some of his demo tapes for record company executives. The result was a contract for John with RCA. (Up to then, his last name was Harford, but it was decided that adding a "t" made it a catchier sounding appellation.)

Under the supervision of Chet Atkins, he recorded a number of his own songs. The first single release, in 1966, was of "Tall, Tall Grass" and "Jack's in the Sack." In July 1966, his debut LP on RCA came out, called *John Hartford Looks at Life*. It included such original compositions as "Eve of My Multiplication," "When the Sky Begins to Fall," "I Shoulda Wore My Birthday Suit," "Corn Cob Blues," "Today, Front Porch," and "Like unto a Mockingbird."

His songs won attention from other artists. The Glaser Brothers cut their versions of some of his songs in the late 1960s as did George Hamilton IV, Waylon Jennings, Jack Greene, Patti Page, Billy Grammer, and many others.

In 1967, his second LP came out, titled *Earthwords and Music*, with a song of John's titled "Gentle on My Mind." As 1967 came to a close, artist after artist covered the song. It provided a multimillion-selling smash vocal version for Glen Campbell and an instrumental hit for Floyd Cramer. Years afterward, the income from the song helped Hartford maintain his musical independence. (Reportedly he still was receiving about $170,000 a year in royalties in the late 1970s.)

Hartford now was on the way to becoming a national celebrity. His next LP in early 1968, *The Love Album*, made the pop charts and John was given a contract by CBS-TV to help prepare a summer replacement for *The Smothers Brothers Comedy Hour* (on which he had appeared during the regular season). In 1969, he was a featured performer on the *Glen Campbell Goodtime Hour* TV show.

He continued to do more recordings for

RCA, including the LPs *The Housing Project, Gentle on My Mind, John Hartford,* and *Iron Mountain Depot* (issued August 1970). They didn't do too well, partly he felt, due to lack of label support. He then switched to Warner Bros., for whom he did two albums that came out in the early 1970s, *Aereo-Plain* and *Morning Bugle,* then seemed to fade from view as far as the general public was concerned. He was intent on going his own way, a route that included development of his own folk music act and concentration on achieving more status as a professional Mississippi steamboat pilot. By the late 1970s he had earned a Coast Guard license for vessels up to hundred gross tons and had piloted the paddle-wheeler Julia Belle Swain in the annual Louisville Derby Days Steamboat Race. His goal was to pass the examination for a first-class pilot's license.

"After I left Warner Brothers," he notes, "I didn't record for several years. Then I decided I was ready to start again and I was looking around for some big label to go with when I was approached by Flying Fish [a Chicago company]. That was a decision, but it was kind of in line with my success through smallness approach, so I went with it."

The first result of that was the 1976 album *Mark Twang,* as the title indicates an album with a lot of the flavor of steamboating and the Mississippi in it plus his usual emphasis on bluegrass. In the Grammy Awards voting announced in early 1977, it was named Best Ethnic or Traditional Recording. (Hartford previously had won two Grammies in 1967 for "Gentle on My Mind": Best Folk Recording and Best C&W Recording.) It was the first of a series of unique recordings on Flying Fish that included such albums in the 1977–79 period as *Nobody Knows What You Do, All in the Name of Love, Headin' Down into the Mystery Below,* and *Dillard-Hartford-Dillard.*

In the last half of the 1970s, Hartford became one of the favorite artists of the traditional country and folk music audiences and his solo concerts at folk venues across the country usually were sold out. His material ranged from familiar square dance tunes and such fiddle classics as "Orange Blossom Special" to his many original songs about his life and times.

A feature of his act was the clog-dancing routine (on a three-fourths-inch plywood platform) that accompanied many of his songs. He said of that in 1979, "I added that clog routine about four years ago. It kind of evolved. I started jogging in place to music just to get some exercise. Before I knew it I was doing it while I was playing and singing on stage. It's just a case of one thing leading to another."

In the late 1970s and early 1980s, he rarely used other musicians in his act, but sometimes combined with other artists. "I work with different groups like the Dillards and the New Grass Revival. We'll each do a set of our own, then do a set together. It's an exciting time because bluegrass is doing pretty well again with a lot of involvement in it. It's certainly the main kind of music I play and it's good to see good young artists coming along to keep it going."

Based partly on an interview with Irwin Stambler, fall 1979.

HAVENS, RICHIE: *Singer, guitarist, songwriter. Born Brooklyn, New York, January 21, 1941.*

Following in the activist tradition of many modern-day folk artists, Richie Havens carried his commitment to peace and love, so much a part of the message of the Woodstock generation of the late 1960s and early 1970s, into the late 1970s and early 1980s, not only through his singing but also through practical activities in which he was engaged.

Havens grew up in the Bedford-Stuyvesant area of Brooklyn, which is now a black ghetto area but was then racially mixed and not as poverty-ridden. He was the eldest of nine children born to his piano-playing father, who worked as an electroplater in a factory, and to his churchgoing mother, who worked in a bookbinding plant. As a youth, Richie sang in church as well as on street corners with other neighborhood children. By the time he was fourteen, he had organized a group called the McCrea Gospel Singers.

At that time, Havens regarded singing as mainly for fun. He had his hopes set on becoming a surgeon. He was a very good student at Franklin K. Lane High School; however, he dropped out just before graduation. As he told one interviewer, "I loved school. I mean, here was this one big building with a lot of people in it. But we used to laugh a lot and they'd never let us laugh. I liked learning too, but I couldn't see any reason why I had to go over something I already knew. You know, we'd go over a lesson a week and then on Friday, the teacher'd say, 'It's time for review.' I said, 'Why?' I already knew it. So I quit! It was just time to go I guess. I've always known when it was time."

When he was seventeen years old, Richie felt it was time to leave home. For a few years, he held a variety of jobs. Eventually, he made his way to Greenwich Village, where he supported himself by painting portraits of tourists during the daytime and spent most of his nights hanging around the coffee houses that were springing up in the Village in those years. In the coffee houses he heard such artists as Len Chandler, Dino Valenti, and Paul Stookey, who later became a member of the group Peter, Paul and Mary. Richie was inspired to try singing.

Around this time, Havens bought himself a guitar and taught himself how to play it. He developed an unorthodox open-E tuning that allowed him to play chord patterns that were not possible with more conventional tunings. This new style of tuning was later used by other folk and blues singers.

Havens started singing at local Village clubs and slowly developed a devoted underground following, although at that time his pay often came exclusively from passing a basket around. In 1965 he joined a touring show for the Ford Motor Company, which starred such artists as Nina Simone, Herbie Mann, and Mongo Santamaria. Finally, in mid-1966, the Verve/Folkways label signed him to a recording contract. His first album, *Mixed Bag*, was released in the fall of 1966 and added to his growing reputation although it did not make the hit charts. Richie's second album, *Something Else Again*, led to bookings at some of the more important clubs and concert halls across the country, including the Fillmore West, New York's Cafe Au Go Go, and Expo '67 in Montréal, Canada, as well as at numerous college campuses.

In 1968 Havens was asked to be one of the performers at the Woody Guthrie Memorial Concert at New York's Carnegie Hall. His performance received a standing ovation. Word of this spectacular concert led to a booking on Johnny Carson's *The Tonight Show*. When he finished singing on that show, the audience response was so deafening that Carson, on the spot, asked Havens to return the next night.

For the rest of the 1960s, Havens performed at many folk and rock concerts in the United States and abroad. One of these was the legendary Woodstock music festival in 1969. There, Richie's energetic performance delighted the Woodstock crowd of half a million, and when the film of the concert was released a year later, he became a worldwide star.

The years following Woodstock found Havens turning out several albums that became chart hits. His contract with Verve expired in 1970 and he signed with the Stormy Forest label, a branch of the MGM group. His first two albums for Stormy Forest, *Mixed Bag* and *Stonehenge*, appeared on the national charts. His LP *Alarm Clock*, released in late 1970, climbed onto the hit lists in January 1971 and stayed in the top 100 for several months. His single "Here Comes the Sun" became a top-40 hit, Havens' only top-40 single to date.

Havens continued to place albums on the charts, however. *Great Blind Degree* was on the bestseller lists from late 1971 through early 1972. His double album *On Stage* made the charts in September 1972 and stayed there through early 1973. In the summer of 1973, the LP *Portfolio* appeared on the hit lists. Other of his hit albums were *The End of the Beginning* and *Mirage*, both issued by A&M Records.

As always, Havens continued to perform at concerts, about which he once said, "I don't rehearse—never have and probably never will, mainly because I don't have to.

I have always considered the spontaneous the best reality, so as a rule it never mattered—I never really thought about it. This approach was very naturally acquired. . . . So as I live I practice life and that's as spontaneous as I can be. . . ."

Havens' music hearkened back to the peace theme of the Woodstock years in 1978. After watching Anwar Sadat's televised visit to Jerusalem, he wrote a song, "Shalom, Salaam Aleichum." Both Egypt and Israel invited him to visit their countries. He did so and performed his song at the embassies of both countries, which resulted in a number-one hit in Israel as well as an ecstatic response from both sides of the Suez Canal.

In addition to working toward universal understanding and social change through his music, Havens has carried out other projects, some having nothing to do with music. For example, he has been working on creating and improving an undersea museum for children and a traveling exhibit on whales and whaling. Both the North Wind Undersea Museum and the "Right to Live" exhibit aim to teach young children about the importance of preserving the ocean and sealife through proper ecology.

In recent years, Havens also starred in a film, *The Boss's Son,* with Rita Moreno and worked on a stage musical, *Electric God,* based on the life of the late rock guitarist Jimi Hendrix. As of the early 1980s, he remained an avid painter and sculptor and exhibited his art work in shows across the country.—A.S.

HAWES, BESS LOMAX: *Singer, guitarist, mandolinist, songwriter, folklorist. Born Austin, Texas, January 21, 1921.*

In the 1960s, the effect of the Lomax clan on folk music spanned the country. On the East Coast, Alan Lomax continued ably to carry on the tradition of his father, John, by collecting folk songs from all over the world and lecturing on folk music at leading universities. Across the continent, in Santa Monica, California, his younger sister, Bess Hawes, ranked as one of the foremost unofficial authorities on folk music in the West.

Bess naturally grew up in an environment conducive to musical scholarship. Her father had established a reputation as one of the foremost collectors of folk material in the nation and, in general, enjoyed the arts. However, when she was old enough to participate in musical activities, he had left university work to become an official in a Texas bank. Thus she had more exposure to classical music than to folk material during elementary school.

Her family started her on piano lessons and she showed excellent potential as a pianist. By the time she was ten, she had received intensive training in the classics and in basic music theory. Then several hard blows changed the course of all the Lomaxes. Just as the Depression began to erupt, her mother's death sent Bess to a boarding school in Dallas. In 1932, the effects of the Depression caused cutbacks in the banking field and her father was laid off.

While Bess continued her studies in Dallas, her father and brother Alan embarked on new careers in folk music collecting, based on a book contract from The Macmillan Company. Bess proved a precocious student, walking off with honors at school. At fifteen, she was able to enter the University of Texas.

By now, folk music was a way of life with the Lomax family and Bess met many of the great artists discovered by her father, including Leadbelly and the Gant family.

In 1937, she left Texas to join her family, now living in Washington, D.C. She worked on transcribing material from field recordings for her father and brother's second book, *Our Singing Country.* When her father remarried soon after the book was finished, he took her along to Europe on his honeymoon. To keep busy on the trip, Bess bought a second-hand guitar for fifteen dollars and taught herself to play it. By the time the journey was over, she already had mastered part of the art of guitar playing.

When the family settled down in the United States once more, Bess enrolled at Bryn Mawr College. She soon met many of the folk music artists then living in New

York and was welcomed as a talented artist and kindred spirit. Among those with whom she sometimes performed in folk music gatherings were Pete Seeger, Butch Hawes, Earl Robinson, Woody Guthrie, and Burl Ives. Soon a new, somewhat amorphous singing group was formed, called the Almanac Singers. She became a part of it and later married one of the group members, Butch Hawes. During these years, she learned a second stringed instrument, the mandolin, with the great Woody Guthrie as her teacher.

When World War II caused the Almanacs to break up, Bess decided to help the war effort by joining the Office of War Information. She served with the Music Division, helping prepare material for broadcast to Europe and the Near East.

After the war, she and husband Butch Hawes moved to Boston. An informal songfest she gave at a nursery school attended by one of her children resulted in requests from parents for guitar instruction. She then set up her first class and was on the way to a reputation as one of the best folk music teachers in the country.

While in Boston, Bess took an active part in political campaigns. For one of these she wrote "The M.T.A. Song" with Jacqueline Steiner. The song later was made into a national hit by The Kingston Trio.

In the 1950s, when the Hawes family moved to California, she found herself in as much demand as ever as a music instructor. She also was sought out by many major folk artists when they traveled in the West and received many invitations to perform at both West Coast and national festivals. She accepted many of these, traveling east to Newport for several Folk Festivals in the 1960s. In addition, she was featured at the Berkeley and UCLA Folk Festivals and at other local concerts and festivals in Los Angeles, San Diego, and Newport. Throughout the 1950s and 1960s, she was also much in demand for appearances at coffee houses, concerts, and theaters in many parts of the country.

She continued to increase her stature as a teacher, joining the faculty of San Fernando Valley State College. As an instructor in anthropology, she advanced to the rank of associate professor by 1968. In the 1960s, she took on additional teaching responsibilities as a member of the summer faculty of the folk music workshops at Idyllwild School of Music and the Arts, Idyllwild, California.

During the 1970s, she continued to take part in folk music events and appeared in various venues on the folk circuit.

HAWKINS, RONNIE: *Singer, guitarist, band leader (the Hawks). Born Huntsville, Arkansas, January 10, 1935.*

Known as "Mr. Dynamo" to his fans, most of whom are Canadians, Ronnie Hawkins has had an impact, if somewhat indirect, on folk and country rock trends in the 1960s and 1970s. His own recordings often are classics of the genre, though known primarily only to a cult following in the United States. Some of the musicians he recruited for his backing groups went on to much wider fame, however. The most notable, of course, is The Band.

Hawkins was born and raised in Arkansas and was strongly influenced by gospel and country & western in his youth. However, like many others who reached their teens in the 1950s, he was swept up in the early rock revolution spearheaded by Elvis and other country-rock stars. He himself played a role in that development, working in the mid-1950s in local groups headed by such important artists as Carl Perkins and Conway Twitty. He wanted to make his own name known and formed his own rock group in Arkansas before he moved on to Memphis, Tennessee, where he was featured in a number of local clubs in the late 1950s.

Failing to make enough progress in expanding his career options there, in mid-1958, he took his band north of the border to Canada. He was impressed with the enthusiasm with which his then all-American group was greeted by young Canadians, but was not yet ready to remain there. (His band members included Will "Pop" Jones on piano, Jimmy Ray Paulman on guitar, and Levon Helm on drums.) On the way home from Canada in April 1959, the band stopped in New York and auditioned for Roulette Records. This led to Ronnie's first major recording efforts, which provided such singles as "Forty Days," "One of These Days," and "Mary Lou," the last a top-10 R&B hit. All of those were on his early 1960 debut LP, *Ronnie Hawkins and the Hawks*. The same band, plus James G. Evans on bass, was featured on Ronnie's next album, *Mr. Dynamo*.

The swing through Canada had made Ronnie eager to concentrate his live appearances there. When he decided to transfer his base of operations to that country, many of the musicians from the United States stayed home. He took Levon Helm back with him and recruited the balance of his new band from Canadians. It was this band that, after some changes, became the forerunners of The Band. As the Hawks, they backed him on such early 1960s Roulette releases as *Folk Ballads* and *Songs of Hank Williams*. The album titles emphasize the influences in Hawkins' repertoire. Robbie Robertson of The Band, looking back to his early years in Hawkins' band, noted, "There were only three kinds of rock then: rhythm & blues, corny white rock and rockabilly. We played rockabilly."

As the 1960s went by, the sidemen who were to become The Band left one by one to try their luck in the United States. Meanwhile, Hawkins simply added new musicians to maintain the supporting cast he needed. In 1965, when the five one-time Hawks were becoming acquainted with Dylan and other folk-rock stars, Ronnie continued to reign as one of Canada's most popular entertainers. He always seemed to have an unerring sense of a musician's potential, and if The Band was the only group of ex-Hawks that became major stars, some of his other former associates showed great potential even if they missed the top bracket. A case in point is the Crowbars, a major contender for rock honors in the early 1970s.

Though Ronnie had a number of hits in Canada, his releases rarely made much headway in the United States. He recorded for various labels in the 1960s and 1970s, including several releases in the early 1970s on Phil Walden's Cotillion Records (based in Atlanta, Georgia). His efforts for Cotillion included the early 1970s LPs *Ronnie Hawkins* and *Hawk*. One of his singles releases, "Down in the Alley," made U.S. pop charts in 1970.

The success of The Band in the late 1960s and early 1970s helped spark some renewed interest in his abilities, and he was well received in a number of U.S. concerts during those years. Roulette reissued some of his early 1960s material in 1970, titled *Best of Ronnie Hawkins, with The Band*.

From time to time during the mid- and late-1970s, Ronnie took part in rock concerts or on TV pop music specials. In November 1977, he was one of the guests at the final concert of his one-time support group, The Band, in San Francisco. He contributed to the album release of that last Band hurrah, *The Last Waltz*, and also could be seen in the excellent movie of the event, also titled *The Last Waltz*, that appeared in 1978. He also played the role of Bob Dylan's father in the 1978 Dylan film release, *Renaldo and Clara*.

HAY, GEORGE DEWEY: *Editor, reporter, announcer, radio station executive. Born Attica, Indiana, November 9, 1895; died Virginia Beach, Virginia, May 9, 1968.*

Few people have had a greater impact on the national development of country & western music than the man known as "The Solemn Ol' Judge." His insight into the potential of this form of entertainment led to the start of two of the landmark programs in the field, the *National Barn Dance* and the *Grand Ole Opry*.

In his teens, Hay began work in the real estate business. He worked for a number of firms in real estate and general sales until 1920. That year he gained a job as a reporter with the Memphis *Commercial Appeal*. The paper branched out into the infant field of radio, setting up station WMC, one of the pioneer stations of the South. Hay doubled in brass by spending part of his time as radio editor for WMC. In 1923, he suddenly gained a national reputation when he scooped the world with news of the death of President Warren Harding. Within a year, he moved north to Chicago as chief announcer for station WLS.

By now Hay was convinced of the bright future of the medium. He looked for other avenues for his talents, and eventually started a show called the *WLS Barn Dance,* later known as the *National Barn Dance.* Before long, the *Barn Dance* had a top national rating, and a country-wide poll by *Radio Digest* resulted in Hay's being named as the top announcer in the United States.

In the fall of 1925, Hay was invited to the dedication of a new 1,000-watt (75-mile range) station in Nashville, which went on the air on October 5, 1925. While in Nashville, Hay was offered the job of director of the new station, WSM, by its owners, the National Life and Accident Insurance Co. (The company still owns WSM.) A month later, he accepted and moved south again.

The continuing success of the *WLS Barn Dance* made Hay consider a similar show for WSM, but he took no action for a while. Part of his duties involved conducting studio tours; he became fascinated by the anecdotes on fiddle music related by one visitor, eighty-year-old Uncle Jimmy Thompson. This gave Hay the incentive to inaugurate the *WSM Barn Dance* with Thompson as the star. At 8 P.M., November 28, 1925, Thompson fiddled and Hay emceed a sixty-five-minute program. The *Barn Dance* was established as a regular WSM feature.

WSM, an NBC network affiliate, carried a number of programs originating in New York. One such was the *NBC Symphony Orchestra.* In the scheduling, the *Symphony* preceded the *Barn Dance.* One night not long after the *Barn Dance* began, Hay introduced the program with this historic bit of dialogue: ". . . From here on out folks, it will be nothing but realism of the realistic kind. You've been up in the clouds with grand opera; now get down to earth with us in a . . . shindig of Grand Ole Opry!" In January 1926, the show's name officially became the *Grand Ole Opry.*

Hay expanded the *Opry,* adding more performers, including Uncle Dave Macon in 1926. Macon, a singer-banjoist, added variety to the hoedown fiddles and jug and string bands. He was for many years the leading artist of the show. Other acts Hay introduced in the early years were Paul Warmack and his Gully Jumpers, George Wilkerson and his Fruit Jar Drinkers, the Dixie Dew Drop, Arthur Smith and his Dixie Liners, Sam and Kirk McGee, and The Delmore Brothers.

Before long, the *Opry* was extended to three hours of local programming. Hay, as emcee, brought the show to a close with a steamboat whistle. He literally "blew the whistle" indicating the end of another *Opry* radio segment in the middle of a rousing performance that went on for many minutes after the *Opry* was off the air.

Hay was instrumental in having the station designated a clear-channel station in 1929, and was successful in gaining approval for a maximum power jump to 50,000 watts in 1932. This signal strength permitted WSM to blanket the South and Midwest. Listeners were able to hear the *Opry* as far north as Canada. Through the 1930s and 1940s, Hay continued to recruit new talent and encourage trends that resulted in the emergence of name performers from *Opry* bands, including such artists as Roy Acuff and Eddy Arnold. He evolved formats and types of entertainment now standard throughout the country-music field.

In 1951, he retired to live with a daughter, Margaret, in Virginia. In 1966, he made a triumphal return to Nashville to celebrate his election to the Country Music Hall of Fame. From retirement until his death in May 1968, in Virginia Beach, Virginia, he remained on call and on the WSM payroll.

HAYS, LEE: *Singer, songwriter. Born Little Rock, Arkansas, 1914; died upstate New York, August 26, 1981.*

If it weren't for the Depression, Lee Hays might never have become a folksinger. In fact, he later said he had never even heard the words "folk song" until leaving the South and coming to New York in his early twenties.

He was exposed to folk music, though, in his youth. The son of a Methodist minister, he started grade school in Arkansas and graduated from high school in Georgia. Other children in the family went on to college, but the Depression thwarted Lee's ambition to continue his education. Affected by the hardships he saw around him, he became an ardent unionist during the early 1930s. He tried to help organize a union among southern sharecroppers.

He enjoyed singing, which was one factor that helped in his decision to move to New York in 1936. Once in the East, he became interested in folk music and began to sing with local groups. His bass voice won the attention of many first-rate folk artists and over the next four years he sang with many of them, including Woody Guthrie, Leadbelly, Burl Ives, Josh White, and Pete Seeger.

In 1940, when Seeger was instrumental in founding the Almanac Singers, Lee Hays was one of the first to join. Surprisingly, his work with this group provided his first income from folk singing. The group, one of the legendary ones of folk music, performed before college students, union groups, and folk music fans all over the United States before it was broken up by World War II. Recalling those days for Sing Out! magazine in 1979, he said, "All across the country, wherever we stopped, we'd pick up the local vibes, and we'd make up a song about Cleveland, or Chicago, or wherever we were."

When Seeger returned from the service after the war, he and Hays tried to revive the Almanacs, but gave that up. Instead they laid the groundwork for the better-known group, The Weavers, starting in 1948. The original members began singing informally in Seeger's Greenwich Village basement (other members were Ronnie Gilbert and Fred Hellerman) before auditioning successfully for Decca Records in 1949. The group, whose name Hays is credited with thinking up, soon was on the way to pop music renown with hits like "Goodnight Irene" and "On Top of Old Smoky." Lee remained with The Weavers as a performer and a collaborator on many hit songs throughout the group's existence.

(See separate Weavers entry). One of the most famous Hays-Seeger compositions is "If I Had a Hammer," a hit for the Weavers and covered over the years by many other recording artists.

During the early 1950s, investigations of "Communist subversion" by the U.S. House of Representatives Committee on Un-American Activities (which led to disbandment of The Weavers for three years), Hays as well as Pete Seeger was called to testify. Hays later said, "It was a frightening experience. Pete actually got handcuffs clamped on him and got hauled off for a few hours."

Hays' association with The Weavers continued through 1963, when the group broke up permanently after a farewell concert that December at Chicago's Orchestra Hall. The four original members later came together in November 1980 for a final concert celebrating the twenty-fifth anniversary of their famed 1955 concert at New York's Carnegie Hall.

By then Hays was in failing health. His legs had been amputated several years earlier because of diabetes. He spent most of his last years in his home in upstate New York, where he died after a heart attack on August 26, 1981.

To the end he believed folk music would remain a vibrant force despite its being overshadowed by rock and other pop forms after the early 1960s. In his 1979 interview with Sing Out! he noted its impact on antinuclear rallies. "I have a feeling that the folksong tradition is so strong that when they're needed, they arise. They come up out of the earth. And the fact that it was an anti-nuke rally doesn't make them any less valid because they're not being sung at a labor rally."

HEAD, ROY: Singer, guitarist. Born Three Rivers, Texas, January 9, 1943.

Here's a story that might sound familiar. A young singer gains a reputation as a rock star, runs into problems, messes up his life with "fast living" and, after a hiatus, comes back to a second career as a country artist. It could fit Johnny Cash or it could describe the saga of Roy Head, except that Roy probably fell farther and

Freddie Hart

George Hamilton IV

Emmylou Harris

Lightnin' Hopkins

Mississippi John Hurt

Stuart Hamblen and his "Gang" during a 1930s broadcast. Cliffie Stone plays stand-up bass at left.

1930s promotion picture for Stuart Hamblen and his group

Merle Haggard

John Hartford

Homer & Jethro (mid-1960s)

took longer to beat the odds and win his second chance.

Head was born in Three Rivers, Texas, and grew up in Crystal City, near the Mexican border. The family was far from affluent. In fact, his parents scratched a bare living from farm work and home "was a one-room shack with a toilet. The other kids used to poke fun at me until they found I was pretty handy with my hands. When I was a small boy my brothers used to bet money on me. They used to pit me against all the Mexicans' little brothers to get money to take their chicks to the show." Head's reputation as a battler remained with him for most of his career and all too often, until he reformed in the 1970s, he responded to challenges.

Coming from Texas, naturally he received a strong exposure to country music. He told Dale Adamson of the *Houston Chronicle* (May 8, 1976) that he recalls performing when he was nine with his older brother Donald. "My first country song was 'Old McDonald'! . . . I wore chaps and we did a show in San Antone. I thought I was killin' 'em out there."

But by the time Roy was in his teens and attending San Marcos High School, R&B and rock were the rage and Roy gravitated in that direction, as did many other young southern and southwestern performers. After finishing high school, where he worked in a furniture factory on weekdays and played in local bands on weekends, he moved to Houston to further his career. While trying for his first break in music, he earned money at such tasks as car seller and a vendor of Bibles door-to-door.

He made progress in his main goal, though, getting the opportunity to record and score a regional hit in 1958 with the song "Baby, Let Me Kiss You One More Time." The song was widely played throughout the Southwest, and Head was featured in R&B/rock shows as the 1950s gave way to the 1960s. He had some other local successes with his band, The Traits, such as "One More Time," and then really hit paydirt with a rocking single titled "Treat Her Right." The song rose rapidly on national charts and seemed headed for

the prestige of number one in the United States in 1965. But the British Invasion got in the way. As Head told Harold Fuller of *The News World* (February 22, 1978), "It never really got to the top. The Beatles killed it with 'Yesterday.' I'll never forget that. I kept looking at it [the song] every week thinking it's gonna do it."

The song just missed the top spot. Though it reputedly sold in the millions, Head never got a gold-record award. He told Adamson, "I don't really know why. It was just one of those unfortunate things. I don't want to say anything bad about anybody because I don't know exactly what happened. We [Gene Curtis co-wrote the song] didn't register with BMI—or, we did register it, but somehow it didn't ever get to BMI. So we never got credit for it."

But that was the least part of Roy's worries. His band objected to the travel requirements of becoming national favorites. They wanted Roy to remain in Houston with them and only work on weekends. Roy went on the road without them. Then, as he told Leon Beck of *Rambler* (December 2, 1976), "they sued me for six/sevenths of everything that I recorded, plus television, movies, whatever I was lucky to get into. They thought they were right. I can't put them down for their beliefs."

The case was settled a year and a half later, but then Roy ran into voice problems. He had developed nodes on the cords from his style of R&B singing. "I was a James Brown freak. Every five seconds I had to scream." After the operation, his doctors warned him to rest his voice for a while. When he finally did return to music in the late 1960s, "I was just like a cube of ice," he told Beck. "You get cold in this business you just forget it, especially with rock 'n' roll. If you're not on top of the market constantly, you're a dead loser."

Head hit the skids and found it almost impossible to find work for a while because of his dissipation. He had decided to go into the country field, but club owners "didn't want a drunk who had turned to country music. They thought it was a joke." Roy seemed to have run out of people to try when he came to Lee Savaggio, operator of the supper club Club Savaggio in Houston. Savaggio recalled, "He was down on the world, thinking it was the world's fault, not his own. He used whiskey like most people do, as a crutch, and people just wouldn't hire him because he would get to drinking and do a lot of fighting."

The two struck it off together and Lee took over reshaping Head's career. Roy recalled to Adamson, "I worked at Savaggio's a year and a half straight, not going anywhere and Sundays doin' benefits. It was hard."

However, it worked. Head began to develop a following among Houston country fans and a better image in the music industry. Savaggio helped line up a recording contract with a small label named Shannon and Roy began to gain attention with singles like "Most Wanted Woman," "I'll Take It," "Baby's Not Home," "Bridge for Crawling Back," and "One Night with You." The audience response to those recordings aroused interest from ABC/Dot Records, which signed him shortly after Christmas in 1975. (ABC/Dot also leased the rights to reissue some of his Shannon material.) In early 1976, his debut LP on ABC, Head First, came out along with the single "The Door I Used to Close." The latter rose to the national country top 10 and the album also did well.

The signs continued to be positive as his follow-up releases won generally similar responses. His second LP on ABC, A Head of His Time, also rose to upper-chart levels, as did his 1977 release, Tonight's the Night. As the title song suggested, Head has never completely abandoned the other kinds of songs he sang in the first phase of his career. Besides that cover version of the Rod Stewart hit, the album included three songs by Dennis Wilson of the Beach Boys in addition to more country-based songs like "Pieces of My Life."

Roy's new-found fame found him on the road constantly, but he didn't knock it. "A lot of people don't get that second shot at success," he told Adamson, "and, y'know, the only thing that kept me goin'—even when I finally got into just workin' bars before I went to country music—was my ability to be a good visual act

on stage. I think when people go out, they want to be entertained. And I've always had a good visual thing. I do the flip splits, the mike work and the razzle dazzle stuff. I wear those outfits that, when the lights hit, it shines all over everywhere. That's different to the country people, particularly the hard core country folks."

Roy had a number of charted singles on ABC/Dot in the late 1970s, such as "Julianne" and "Come to Me" in 1977 and "Tonight's the Night" and "Love Survival" in 1978. When ABC was purchased by MCA Records in 1979, Roy didn't make the transition to the new company. At the start of the 1980s, he was on the Elektra roster briefly, turning out such singles as "The Fire of Two Old Flames" and "Drinkin' Them Long Necks," which showed up on country charts but didn't reach uppermost levels. In 1981, he moved to Churchill Records. In the fall of the year his single "After Texas" on that label was in middle-chart positions.

HESTER, CAROLYN: *Singer, guitarist. Born Waco, Texas, circa 1937.*

There were few lists of suggested basic albums of folk music of the mid-1960s that did not include one by Carolyn Hester. It was not just her material that was impressive but her vocal ability as well. As New York Times critic Robert Shelton stated in a rave review following her first New York concert in the early 1960s, "Miss Hester has a vocal range from rooftop soprano to stunning chest tones."

Besides talent, Hester showed a great amount of feeling for folk songs, reflecting her southwestern upbringing. A distant relative of President Lyndon Johnson, she was born and spent much of her youth in Texas, where she was exposed to many folk and country-music influences. She began to sing first for her own pleasure and then for small gatherings during her teens.

By the late 1950s, Carolyn was able to take advantage of the folk song boom by singing at coffee houses in various parts of the country. Like many other young folk artists of the period, she found her way to New York at the start of the 1960s. Before long, she had scored with local audiences and had a growing reputation with other folksingers. During the first two years of the decade, she sang at most of the folk clubs on the national circuit. She also received bids to appear in college concerts, and by early 1962, she had been warmly welcomed at the University of Texas, University of Virginia, Yale, Harvard, and elsewhere.

In June 1961, her first LP, *Carolyn Hester,* was issued by Tradition Records. This was well received by folk fans and led to a contract with Columbia Records. Her first Columbia LP, *Carolyn Hester,* issued in June 1962, created a national sensation. She was rewarded with ecstatic reviews in all the music trade magazines and in many national newsstand publications, including *Time* and *Hi-Fi Stereo Review,* which compared her favorably with Joan Baez.

During 1962, Hester was the only native American artist invited to perform at Scotland's Edinburgh Festival. While there, she was asked to appear several times on the British Broadcasting Corporation network. She also toured most of the important British folk clubs. She returned to the United States to continued accolades on campuses and in concerts in many major auditoriums. Her English tours resulted in an invitation from the British government to take part in a sponsored tour of Russian cities in 1963.

During the mid-1960s, Carolyn appeared in many parts of the United States and Canada. Her engagements included several major folk song festivals. In 1965, she was featured on a Dot Records LP, *That's My Song.*

In the early 1980s, Carolyn resided in the Los Angeles area, making rare appearances on the folk circuit. She was active with her husband, David, in an ethnic club-restaurant which featured foods of all nations, folk dancing, and singing.

HILLMAN, CHRIS: *Singer, bass guitarist, mandolinist, songwriter. Born Los Angeles, California, December 4, 1942.*

A talented musician, Chris Hillman perhaps never quite gained the respect he seemed to merit from the popular audience. But he had a major impact on a wide range of trends in post-1960 pop music, including folk-rock, country rock, and blends thereof, and even on some of the musicians involved in the bluegrass revival of the 1970s. He was well regarded by fellow musicians, including Bob Dylan, who told a *Rolling Stone* reporter in 1969, "I've always known Chris, you know, from when he was with the Byrds. And he's always been a fine musician. . . ."

Although born in Los Angeles, Chris spent much of his boyhood in the cattle-raising country of northern California. Country & western music was favored there and young Chris also found it to his liking. During these years, he began to pick out folk and country songs on instruments like the guitar and mandolin. He also, in his teens, found work as a cowboy.

During the late 1950s and early 1960s, Hillman was part of the very active bluegrass scene in California. For a while he headed his own band, called the Hillmen, for which he handled some vocals and bluegrass mandolin. But the resurgence of rock had its impact on folk musicians all over the country in the early 1960s, and Hillman, like many others, started looking for other musical outlets. His major chance came in mid-1964, when a Los Angeles music impresario, Jim Dickson, was assembling a new band. Hillman became part of a quintet that soon took the name the Byrds. That group, of course, after its smash 1965 hit of Bob Dylan's "Mr. Tambourine Man," became one of the most acclaimed bands of the decade.

Hillman, who handled backing vocals and bass guitar, was a mainstay of the Byrds until 1968. He, new addition Gram Parsons, his cousin Kevin Kelly, and leader Roger McGuinn recorded the group's first country & western–oriented LP (on Columbia) in Nashville that year, *Sweetheart of the Rodeo.* Soon after that, Hillman and Parsons left to form their own country-rock band, the Flying Burrito Brothers.

The Burritos, whose debut LP came out on A&M Records in mid-1969, was a little ahead of its time. Certainly one of the landmark country rock-groups (see separate entry), it never quite broke through to major stardom. It set the stage, though, for the onset of a new wave of folk/country-rock bands, headed by the Eagles.

After the original Burritos finally disbanded in 1972, Hillman moved on to other associations. For a while he was a member of Stephen Stills group, Manassas. In the mid-1970s, he aligned himself with two other excellent folk-rock musicians to form the short-lived Souther-Hillman-Furay group. The band turned out two LPs on Elektra, but conflicting creative goals and an injury to one-time Buffalo Springfield star Richie Furay brought things to an end.

In 1978, an accidental reunion of two original Byrds, Roger McGuinn and Gene Clark, set the stage for Hillman's next step, though Chris didn't know it at the time. McGuinn told a *Newsday* reporter (February 23, 1970), "I was at the Troubadour in Los Angeles for [its] 20th anniversary party. Gene Clark and I felt some of the magic come back." They tried working together again at another local club with good results and then set up a tour of the Southwest which they asked Hillman to join. He did, and the response was enough for them to establish a new band, McGuinn, Clark & Hillman. A fourth founding Byrd, David Crosby, joined in on some shows but his then current co-worker Steven Stills talked him out of joining. By then, the other original Byrd, drummer Mike Clarke, was with another successful band, Firefall. (Actually, the five original Byrds had reassembled briefly in 1973, but the chemistry hadn't been right.)

The new trio signed with Capitol and started work on an album the second half of 1978. As part of their effort to change the band's image from classic Byrds style, more original material was provided by Hillman and Clark than McGuinn. In the Byrds' heyday, McGuinn had been chief writer. Among Hillman's contributions to the new album, issued in early 1979 and simply titled *McGuinn, Clark & Hillman*, were three original songs. By 1980, Clark had dropped out as a regular member, though he did contribute some vocal work to the second Capitol LP. During 1980, McGuinn and Hillman toured as a duo.

HINTON, SAM: *Singer, guitarist, dulcimer player, educator, marine biologist. Born Tulsa, Oklahoma, March 21, 1917.*

When Sam Hinton graduated from high school in Crockett, Texas, he received two books, *American Reptiles* and Carl Sandburg's *American Songbag*. The gifts were to symbolize his lifelong combination of careers as a distinguished scientist and part-time folksinger.

During his boyhood days in Oklahoma and Texas, Sam spent long hours exploring the wonders of nature in his rural surroundings. When he wasn't studying the wildlife and botanical features or going to school, he often sang for pleasure, by himself or with family and friends in local get-togethers. "During my youth," he recalls, "I always sang. It wasn't until I went to college that I found out it was folk music."

This discovery came in 1934, when Sam entered Texas A&M College as a zoology major. Sam remained at Texas A&M for two years, supporting himself with a variety of jobs, including singing, painting signs, and selling snake venom to an eastern manufacturer. The venom came from sixty water moccasins that he maintained as a zoological hobby. In 1936, Sam entered and won a *Major Bowes Amateur Contest* and left school to travel throughout the country with one of the Bowes troupes.

During the next two years, Sam sang his folk songs in forty-six states and throughout Canada. Finally tiring of traveling, he moved to Los Angeles and enrolled as a zoology student at UCLA in 1939. Again, singing came in handy to help pay tuition, as did another of Sam's skills, science illustrator. Not long after settling down in Los Angeles, Sam gained a part in the long-running musical comedy *Meet the People*. Joining Sam in the cast were such soon-to-be famous individuals as Nanette Fabray, Virginia O'Brien, Doodles Weaver, and Jack Gilford.

At UCLA, Sam met and married Leslie Forster, an excellent violinist and soloist with the university's a capella choir. Leslie provided Sam with his first introduction to the more formal aspects of music.

After earning his B.S. in zoology from UCLA in 1940, Hinton accepted a position as director of the Desert Museum in Palm Springs, California. He left there in 1943 to accept a post as curator of the aquarium and museum at the University of California's Scripps Institution of Oceanography at La Jolla. This was the start of a long relationship between Sam and UC San Diego that was still going strong in the 1970s. In 1964, he was appointed to the post of assistant director for the entire university system of the Office of School Relations. This job permitted him to combine his talents as educator, biologist, and singer, since he represented the university in discussion's with high schools, junior colleges, and other institutions of learning. During such sessions, he described the university system for prospective students and often sang some of his folk song repertoire.

In 1947, Sam made his first recording for the Library of Congress Archive of Folk Song, *Buffalo Boy and the Barnyard Song,* an album of Anglo-Irish songs and ballads. In 1950, he made his first commercial recording, "Old Man Atom," for Columbia Records. Among his other singles in the early 1950s were "The Barnyard Song" (two songs, 1952); "Country Critters" (four songs, 1953); and "The Frog Song," and "The Greatest Sound Around" (1954), all of which were for Decca Records' Children's Series.

Sam turned out his first LPs in 1952, *Folk Songs of California and the Old West* on Bowmar Records and nine songs for the two-record RCA album *How the West Was Won.* Besides singing in the RCA album, which also featured Bing Crosby, Rosemary Clooney, and Jimmy Driftwood, Sam worked with Alan Lomax and Si Rady in selecting and arranging the material. His other LP credits on Decca include *Singing Across the Land* (1955); *A Family Tree of Folk Songs* (1956); and *The Real McCoy* (1957). In the 1960s, Sam was featured on such LPs as *American Folk Songs and Balladeers* (Classics Record Library, 1964); *Newport Folk Fes-*

tival, 1963 (Vanguard); and, on Folkways Records, *The Songs of Men, Whoever Shall Have Some Peanuts* (1961), and *The Wandering Folksong* (1967).

In addition to his performing chores, Hinton taught a number of courses at the University of California at San Diego over the years, mostly in the Extension Division. From 1948 on, he taught courses in biology and folklore and, in 1962 and 1967, special courses on folk music on educational TV. (In 1967, he signed to prepare thirteen half-hour shows on folk music for the National Educational Television [NET] network.)

From 1958 into the 1960s, he provided a continuing newspaper feature, *The Ocean World,* for the San Diego *Union.* He also coauthored two books on oceanology with Joel Hedgpeth, *Exploring Under the Sea* (Doubleday) and *Common Seashore Animals of Southern California* (Naturegraph).

Sam was also featured as a lecturer in his chosen subjects in many parts of the country, as well as receiving many engagements for campus folk song concerts. From 1957 on, he was featured every year as performer and discussion leader at the Berkeley, California, Folk Festival. Throughout the 1970s and into the early 1980s, Hinton continued to perform in folk venues and to take part in major festivals.

He continued to believe in the enduring nature of folk material despite the breaking of the folk song boom in the mid-1960s. "The *Variety* headline 'Folk Music Is Dead' made no sense to me," he once said. "In the 1930s, songwriters used themes from Tchaikovsky, Chopin, and other classical composers. When that era disappeared, you could just as well have written the headline 'Classics Are Dead.' "

HOLCOMB, ROSCOE: *Singer, banjoist, guitarist, songwriter. Born Daisy, Kentucky, 1913.*

Were there a Folk Music Hall of Fame, Roscoe Holcomb undoubtedly would be in it. For those dedicated to preserving traditional southern mountain music, his name evokes memories of some of the finest performances of such material ever presented on stage or records. Still, his national exposure was brief; for most of his life only people in local areas of Kentucky were aware of his talents.

He was born and spent almost his entire life in the mountain region near Hazard, Kentucky, a long-time hotbed of mountain music, but perhaps better known for certain family feuds and for contention between coal miners and their often oppressive employers. Roscoe was introduced to music almost as soon as he could talk. Almost every week friends and relations would get together and play banjo, guitar, fiddle, and dulcimer as a form of relaxation. One of his earliest memories was listening to someone play the mouth harp. As a child he would sometimes walk to outlying farms to hear an expert on the harmonica.

By the time he was ten he had already learned to play the banjo. He was given a homemade banjo by his brother-in-law that lasted him many years. Soon after, he began to accompany a local fiddler. In a year's time, he learned to play and sing some 400 songs. He continued to learn new ballads, work songs, and square dance numbers as he grew up, sometimes adding new verses to them. When he was in his teens, he could play the guitar and other stringed instruments as well as the banjo.

His schooling, as was not unusual in his region, was scanty. He began working on local farms as a boy. After a while, he became a coal miner, his main occupation most of his life. When work in the mines was slow, he often worked on the railroads setting timber.

He kept up his music in his spare time. Between World War I and World War II, he built up a major reputation locally as a square-dance musician. He recalled those days for John Cohen (*Sing Out!* April-May 1966, pp. 3–7). "I've played for square dances 'til the sweat dripped off my elbow. I used to play for square dances a lot. Used a bunch of us get out, maybe we'd go to a party somewhere and after the party was over the moon'd be a-shinin' bright, you know, and we'd all go back home and going up the road, somebody'd start his old instrument, guitar or banjer or some-

thing or other, and just gang up in the middle of the road and have the awfulest square dance right in the middle of the highway."

Roscoe was religious and he felt increasingly guilty about playing. The "regular" Baptists, to which he belonged, considered secular music sinful. During the late 1920s, spurred on by his wife, he laid his instruments aside and stopped playing for some ten years. However, by the time World War II began, he was playing again.

He kept mining coal until the mines shut down due to competition from petroleum and other fuels, a situation that began to be reversed in the 1970s. He subsisted in the 1950s mainly by working at odd jobs. In 1959, John Cohen, a folk music collector and then a member of the New Lost City Ramblers folk group, heard about Roscoe and sought him out. One of the first results was Roscoe's debut album on Folkways Records, titled *Mountain Music of Kentucky.* One of the best tracks was a song Holcomb had constructed from earlier ballads called "Across the Rocky Mountain."

Cohen and Holcomb became close friends. Cohen wrote a number of articles about Roscoe for various folk publications in the early and mid-1960s and was inspired to start work on a documentary about Holcomb and his environment. The project got under way in 1962, and the film, *The High Lonesome Sound,* was issued in 1964. Folkways released an album of the same title. Later Holcomb completed a third LP in conjunction with another mountain singer, titled *The Music of Roscoe Holcomb and Wade Ward.*

Once Holcomb's skills became known, opportunities arose for personal appearances in folk concerts and festivals all over the United States. Among his credits during the mid-1960s were performances at the Newport Folk Festival, University of Chicago Festival, UCLA, University of California at Berkeley, Cornell, and Brandeis. In 1965–66, he toured Europe as a member of the Festival of American Folk and Country Music troupe.

Holcomb had considerable impact on

many of the young folk artists of the 1960s. Bob Dylan was one of his strong backers, calling *The High Lonesome Sound* album one of his favorites. By the end of the 1970s, that LP, which presented some interview material collected by Cohen as well as some of Holcomb's musical work, was the only album still in Folkways' current catalogue.

HOMER AND JETHRO: *Vocal and instrumental duo, comedy team; Jethro, born Knoxville, Tennessee, March 10, 1920; Homer, born Knoxville, Tennessee, July 27, 1920, died Chicago, Illinois, August 7, 1971.*

For three decades, the team of Homer and Jethro reigned as the finest comedy duo in country music. Their humor was universal, as demonstrated by their ability to rouse gales of laughter in audiences ranging from rural country-fair crowds to sophisticated assemblages in Las Vegas, Chicago, and other major cities. Their flair for satirizing all kinds of pop music from pop ballads to Hank Williams' songs tended to hide the fact that both artists were accomplished instrumentalists as well.

Both Homer, whose real name was Henry D. Haynes, and Jethro, real name Kenneth C. Burns, were born and raised in Knoxville and started learning to play stringed instruments as boys. However, their association wasn't a planned step but an accidental byproduct of their early attempts to break into show business.

Jethro recalled the circumstances for an interviewer from the *Gibson Gazette* in 1971 (Volume 11, Number 1). "It all began in 1932 at Radio Station WNOX, Knoxville, Tennessee. We were contestants on an amateur program. I was doing a guitar and mandolin duet with my brother and Homer was working with a trio. We were twelve years old. And backstage before the show we had a little jam session goin'. The program director, Lowell Blanchard, heard us playing so he picked Homer, me, my brother and another kid and put the four of us together as a quartet. We appeared in the contest and he disqualified us before we started and gave us jobs on the radio station as staff musicians.

"We called ourselves The String Dusters. It was sort of a real pop, swinging group. Later the same guy that gave us the jobs gave us the names Homer and Jethro. Homer and Jethro was just kind of a thing we did for kicks."

By that he meant that the two boys used to clown around off-stage burlesquing popular songs, doing the lyrics "straight" but in a comedy bluegrass approach. Blanchard liked the routine so much he began to work it into the String Dusters set in WNOX's *Mid-day Merry-Go-Round*. The comedy worked so well, Homer noted, "We broke the group up in 1936 and started doing Homer and Jethro full time. That's when we started doing strictly comedy."

The boys remained on WNOX until 1939, when they decided it was time to seek new surroundings. They auditioned for the *Renfro Valley Barn Dance* in Renfro Valley, Kentucky, and quickly became cast regulars, appearing on both CBS and NBC network shows during their two years on the program. In 1941, they were considering an offer from the *Plantation Party* in Chicago to become cast regulars when both were drafted into the Army and went off in different directions. Homer went into the Medical Corps and saw service in the Pacific while Jethro eventually ended up in Europe.

After their discharge, the duo reunited in Knoxville in 1945 and soon moved on to become part of the *Midwestern Hayride*. Homer told the *Gibson Gazette*, "We went to Cincy in 1945 to radio station WLW. We worked on the staff there with a lot of good guys: Chet Atkins, Rosemary Clooney, Merle Travis, and a number of other good musicians. We were there for about two and a half years and then we were fired." Jethro continued, "WLW was, at that time, owned by the Crosley Corporation and they had always gone heavy on country music because it was popular. Then they sold out to Avco. Well, the first thing Avco did was to bring in an efficiency expert and he just fired everybody he could find. In one week he fired Homer and Jethro, Rosemary Clooney, Chet Atkins, Merle Travis, and Roy Lanin."

The stay at WLW was valuable to the duo both for increased audience exposure and the team's first major record contract. They were signed by King Records, and during their work for the label from 1946–48, they turned out five albums and such hit burlesque singles of popular songs as "Five Minutes More," "Over the Rainbow," and "Symphony."

After leaving WLW, Homer and Jethro toured the United States with their own tent show for about six months, then returned to WNOX before going on to join the new Red Foley show on KWTO in Springfield, Missouri. They joined a cast that included Chet Atkins, Slim Wilson, and the Carter Family. Jethro recalled, "That was probably the most fun we ever had anywhere. It was very relaxed. Everybody went fishin'. We had a motto up there that 'We Never Let Work Interfere With Our Fishin'." During that period, the duo was sought out by Steve Sholes of RCA Records, which resulted in a recording contract that led to a long association and many major hit releases.

In 1949, the late orchestra leader Spike Jones persuaded the duo to join his management/booking company, Arena Stars. Homer noted, "We went on the road with Spike Jones in 1949. While we were in Chicago [in 1951] the *National Barn Dance* people came to us and asked us if we'd come down and perform at the *Barn Dance* in between shows. As a result of this, the Program Director offered us a job. Spike let us out of the contract with no problems. So we did the *Barn Dance* show every Saturday night and during the week we worked the *Don McNeil Breakfast Club.* We left the *Barn Dance* in 1958." The move to the *Barn Dance* also resulted in the team permanently relocating to the Chicago area. At Homer's death, he resided in Lansing while Jethro still called Evanston home at the end of the 1970s.

Even before joining WLS, Homer and Jethro had made their mark on the national country and pop charts. In 1948, they made the top 10 with their side-splitting version of "Baby, It's Cold Outside," recorded with June Carter. They followed with more singles hits in the early 1950s,

scoring their biggest success in 1953 with "Hound Dog in the Winter." Their RCA LPs of those years included such titles as *Worst of Homer & Jethro* (1958) and *Life Can Be Miserable* (1959). The year after they left the *Barn Dance*, they made the singles charts with "The Battle of Kookamonga." That effort won them a Grammy Award for the Best Comedy Performance of 1959.

At the end of the 1950s and throughout the 1960s, Homer and Jethro concentrated on personal appearances in major cities across the United States and Canada. They were a little hesitant about their debut in Las Vegas, and considered changing their act. Finally, noted Homer, "We went out there on opening night and our opening line was "We are Homer and Jethro, we're not brothers . . . my brother is living.' And you would have thought it was the funniest thing that had ever been said." Jethro added, "We did these old things that we were doing back in the 1930s and just tore the place up. We did so well that the second night instead of being the supporting act, we were the headliners. The papers would say, 'The funniest material ever heard on the Strip was by two hillbillies over at the Thunderbird.' "

The team returned to Vegas many times as they did to many other entertainment centers. They also made repeat appearances on such major 1960s TV shows as Johnny Carson's *The Tonight Show, Dean Martin's Music Country,* and, in the late 1960s, the *Johnny Cash* program, where they guested eight different times.

During the mid-1960s, the team probably gained as much attention from the TV viewing public for its wild commercials for Kellogg's corn flakes as for its other activities. The duo was featured on both radio and TV in those commercials for four years.

Meanwhile, RCA continued to release a steady stream of new albums during the decade, including *At the Country Club* (1960); *Songs My Mother Never Sang* (4/61); *At the Convention* (5/62); *Playing Straight* (1962); *Zany Songs of the '30s* (1963); *Ooh! That's Corny* (1963); *Confucius Say* (1964); *Go West* (8/64); *Fractured Folk Songs* (12/64); *Tenderly* (6/65); *Old Crusty Minstrel* (1/66);

Best of Homer & Jethro (2/66); *Any News* (7/ 68); *Wanted for Murder* (12/66); *Homer & Jethro* (3/67); *Songs for the 'Out' Crowd* (5/ 67); *Nashville Cats* (7/67); and *Somethin' Stupid* (11/67). Releases on the Camden label in the 1960s included *Strike Back* (6/62); *Humorous Side of Country Music* (9/63); *Songs to Tickle* (5/66).

The team continued to give concerts and turn out new recordings into the early 1970s. Just before Homer died of a heart attack during the summer of 1971, the duo completed an album with its Nashville String Band called *Strung Up*. The emphasis with the String Band, of course, was to play the music straight rather than for laughs. However, the team didn't ignore comedy with 1971 takeoffs on such songs as "Help Me Make It Through the Night" and "The Good Times."

Asked about the reaction of writers to Homer and Jethro's antics, Homer told the *Gibson Gazette*, "People used to come to us and say, 'You shouldn't butcher a Hank Williams song because what would Hank think?' Well Hank, he told us one time, that he didn't think a song was a success until it had been butchered by Homer and Jethro. [They turned his "Jambalaya," for instance, into "Jam-Bowl-Liar."] And he gave us written permission to do any song he had ever written."

It took Jethro a while to get over Homer's untimely passing but after a while he returned to the music field, though at a less hectic pace. During the mid- and late-1970s, he worked closely with Chicago folk artist Steve Goodman, backing Steve on most of his recordings and touring with him to many major cities.

HOOKER, JOHN LEE: *Singer, guitarist, songwriter. Born Clarksdale, Mississippi, August 22, 1917.*

A versatile, enduring artist, John Lee Hooker continued to exert an influence on many phases of popular music from the post-World War II years into the 1980s. His blues stylings over the years covered just about every facet of the field from traditional country blues to rhythm & blues with excursions into rock 'n' roll. His willingness to try such a wide variety of art forms has resulted in his being damned by some folk and blues purists as "uneven" and "opportunistic," but Hooker never paid much attention to such carping. Overall, while demonstrating an ability to survive in often difficult times, he carved out a justified reputation as one of America's greatest blues and folk-blues artists.

He was born and spent his early years in a region that produced many of the legendary names in country blues. The first wave to gain recognition included people like Sonny Boy Williamson, Mississippi John Hurt, and Big Bill Broonzy. Those artists were sometimes looked upon as old fashioned by the next generation, which encompassed such artists as Muddy Waters and Hooker.

Singing folk blues was a living, everyday tradition in John Lee's home area. In an environment where few children had the chance for much schooling or to do much else but work in the fields or at odd jobs, music was one of the few pleasures of life. Recalling his early years, Hooker told Jim and Amy O'Neal in an interview for *Living Blues* magazine (autumn 1979), "Well, I never did have a hard time 'cause my dad had a big farm down there. But I know it was rough. I didn't experience it 'cause I left there when I was fourteen, 'cause I was playin' music when I was twelve or fourteen. And I ran away from home. My dad came and got me. I run off from my dad and I went to Memphis. I stayed around two months. I was workin' at a motion picture show, the New Daisy, and then goin' to school when I could."

Hooker noted he always used the style of guitar playing he acquired as a boy, a style called "percussive, with stomping chords slashed out, often laced with walking bass lines." Although he knew many great delta slide guitar–style players (guitar turned to an open chord, fretted with a bottleneck or metal sleeve on one finger), he never mastered that approach. He told the O'Neals, "My style come from my stepfather, Will Moore. The style I'm playing now, that's what he was playing. And nobody else plays that style. I got a style nobody else don't have."

At seventeen, John was on the road

again, this time with no one pursuing to take him home. First stop was Memphis. "Didn't nobody know me. Me and B.B. [King] and them, we just messed around there. But B.B. stayed there for a while. Me and B.B. and Bobby [Bland] we were playin' around Memphis, for house parties there. . . . We'd go over [to West Memphis] and party all night and mess around. And a lot of clubs, they wouldn't let me in—they usually wouldn't let us in 'cause we wasn't old enough."

Hooker then settled in Cincinnati for a while, moving there when he was about eighteen. He worked at various day jobs and performed his music wherever he could, for house parties or small clubs, often for little or no money. "I stayed there about three years, but I didn't get no break and I left there."

Eventually, with the onset of World War II and the opening up of better paying jobs in the North, Hooker became part of the black migration that settled in Detroit in 1943. The pattern was much the same as before. He worked for a time as a hospital attendant, then in an automotive plant, while singing and playing his music in bars and at parties. But eventually Detroit proved lucky for him, bringing him together with "Bernie Besman and Elmer Barber, this Jewish guy and this black cat. And this black cat, he had that record store there in Detroit—him and Bernie was really good friends. Bernie Besman had this big, big distributor. It was downtown."

Barber heard Hooker play at a house party and was impressed. He approached John about making records and arranged a meeting between Hooker and Besman, for which John brought a demo of some songs. As Hooker told the O'Neals, after hearing the demo, one of them said, " 'Man, I tell you, you got somethin' different, ain't nobody else got. I never heard a voice like that. Do you want to record?' I said, 'Yeah, but I've been jived so much, I don't know if y'all just puttin' me on.' They said, 'No, no, kid. We're not puttin' you on. You're really good. You written them songs on there?' I said, 'Yeah. You know, 'Boogie Chillen,' 'Hobo Blues,' 'In the Mood'—I had all that on the dub.' "

Hooker accepted and in a few weeks in late 1948 recorded the songs that came out on his first single, "Boogie Chillen," backed with "Sally Mae." Originally made for the Sensation label, the disc was turned over to a larger company, Modern Records, for distribution. The record became a massive hit in the blues field in 1949, staying at the top of the sales lists for months. Soon Hooker decided to quit his day job and go on the road, aided by Besman, still a close friend decades later. He demonstrated that he wasn't a one-hit artist by recording more songs that became favorites with blues fans around the country on Modern Records—"In the Mood for Love," "Hobo Blues," "Crawling King Snake."

During the 1950s, with stepped-up popular interest in both R&B and rock 'n' roll, his name became increasingly well known both in the United States and abroad. Many of his old 1950s records had dramatic impact on the English rock stars of the 1960s, from the Animals to the Rolling Stones. Hooker ran into problems with Modern Records on matters of royalties, which triggered his working for many other labels under a variety of pseudonyms. Thus he used such names as Texas Slim and John Lee Cooker in recording for King Records; Johnny Williams on Staff and Gotham, as well as John Lee on Gotham; Delta John on Regent; John Lee Booker on Chance, Gone, and Deluxe labels, and Johnny Lee on some Deluxe releases; Birmingham Sam & His Magic Guitar on Savoy; The Boogie Man on Acorn; and Sir John Lee Hooker on Fortune. Though most of his output in the 1950s was on singles, there were occasional albums released, one of the best being *John Lee Hooker Sings the Blues* on King.

In 1955, he signed an exclusive recording contract with Chicago-based Vee Jay Records and remained on the roster until that company ran into financial problems in 1964. (After several years with Vee Jay, though, his name began to turn up on other labels, though some of those releases were reissues of older material.) Among the albums issued by Vee Jay were *Burnin'*, *I'm John Lee Hooker, Travelin'* (1961); *Folklore*

(1962); and *Big Soul, Best of John Lee Hooker* (1963). One of his most successful LPs came out on Riverside Records in 1969, at the height of the folk boom.

The folk movement of the late 1950s and early 1960s embraced country and folk-blues artists and John Lee Hooker gained a new following that cut across racial lines. He was invited to perform at the 1960 Newport Folk Festival in Rhode Island and became an important figure on the coffee house/folk club circuit. To fit the "folk image," he cut down on the amplification he used for his guitar playing or simply used an acoustic instrument.

Meanwhile he was becoming known as an influence on English rock musicians. The Animals, for instance, recorded his song "Boom Boom" and other bands included some of his material in their repertoire. In 1965, he was enthusiastically received by English fans when he toured the country as part of a blues package. While there, he recorded an album with an English blues-rock group called the Groundhogs. The English fans were especially responsive to his ability as a harmonica player. At times he would put his guitar aside and play the mouth harp. However, by the 1970s, he rarely played harmonica and almost no records are extant in which he plays that instrument.

From the start of the 1960s on, Hooker became primarily an album artist rather than a singles performer. Throughout that decade and the next, he almost always had a number of LPs in the active catalogue, as usual, on a bewildering list of labels. Many were repackages of earlier recordings, but there always were some new ones added. His early 1960s LPs, other than Vee Jay's, included *Don't Turn Me from Your Door* on Atco; *John Lee Hooker* on Galaxy; and *Great Blues Album* on Fortune. Later in the decade his new material included an LP with the Muddy Waters Band with Otis Spann on piano. Album releases from the mid-1960s to the early 1970s included *Alone* on Specialty Records, *Big Band Blues* on Buddha, *Coast to Coast Blues Band* on United Artists, *Endless Boogie* on Tradition, *Simply the Truth* on Bluesville, and *That's Where It's At* on Stax.

Throughout the 1960s and 1970s, John

continued to be busy as a live performer, going on the road much of each year to play clubs, festivals, and college concert halls. During the 1970s, when he made his home in California rather than Detroit, he performed more in the South, the West, and parts of Canada than in the Midwest and Northeast. However, he still made swings to all parts of the country at times, as was the case in 1971 when he toured with the blues rock group Canned Heat in support of a double-disc LP set called *Hooker 'n' Heat,* an album that was on the national charts for months.

In the 1970s, he was asked by Bonnie Raitt to join her in a number of concerts and in 1977 he was a featured artist in a *Tribute to the Blues* program at New York's Paladium, a show that also included Foghat, Paul Butterfield, Muddy Waters, Johnny Waters, and Honeyboy Edwards. One of his 1977 concerts, at the Keystone in Palo Alto, California, was recorded for a live album later issued on Tomato Records. He was a long-time idol of the Rolling Stones: Mick Jagger sang one of his numbers in a scene from the 1970s movie *Performance.*

In the summer of 1980, he appeared in the film *The Blues Brothers,* starring *Saturday Night Live* alumni John Belushi and Dan Aykroyd.

HOPKINS, SAM "LIGHTNIN' ": *Singer, guitarist, songwriter. Born Centreville, Leon County, Texas, March 15, 1912; died Houston, Texas, February 1982.*

"Twenty-one years ago, I went to Louisiana to get me a mojo hen and I got me a wife with it. I'm going to try to go back again soon. I might just end up with two wives. . . ." "It's not worth singing [the song, 'My Babe'], but I'll guitar to it. . . ." These song introductions alternately intrigued and convulsed a packed house at Los Angeles' Ash Grove in March 1967. The man delivering them and singing such original comic lines as "I tiptoed to her window just to see how sweet she snored" and others that etched many of the grim facts of life of ghetto living was one of the legendary names in blues history, Sam "Lightnin' " Hopkins.

He had come a long way from the days

of poverty and singing for his supper on street corners or in nondescript bars, but when he delivered some of his country blues, the audience knew he hadn't forgotten the rough spots of his life. Indeed, though he had been a consummate artist for decades, he only began to gain recognition from a broad cross section of his native land at the start of the 1960s.

He was born in a rural section of Texas not far from Houston. There wasn't much chance for schooling for a black child in those years, much less any formal musical education. When he wasn't doing farm chores, he spent a lot of his spare time in his youth teaching himself guitar and picking up song material from listening to farm workers or sneaking into local bars. He was still earning most of his small income from farm labor in the mid-1940s, playing an old beat-up guitar on evenings or weekends mostly for the edification of family and friends.

One of those friends, fortunately, realized Sam's talent deserved a wider audience. The friend got Sam a new guitar and urged him to move to Houston, where there was more opportunity for a performer. Hopkins at first resisted the idea; he had tried Houston in the late 1930s when he went there with his cousin Alger "Texas" Alexander, a one-time successful blues singer. The trip proved a disaster. Music jobs were almost impossible to find and Sam had to work on the Missouri-Pacific Railroad tamping ties while whatever money he got from music came from singing in the streets. He hustled back to Centreville after a few months.

The next trip proved more rewarding. Sam was singing on a place called Dowling Street that was to later become essentially his headquarters when Lola Anne Cullum, a scout for the Los Angeles blues label Aladdin, spotted him. She set up an audition in Los Angeles, which Hopkins traveled to accompanied by pianist Wilson Smith. Aladdin executives liked the duo, who made twelve recordings in their first sessions in 1946. When the first discs were released, a record company official gave the twosome nicknames for more oomph, calling Hopkins "Lightnin'" and Wilson "Thunder." The newly born "Lightnin'"

was getting homesick, though. He made some more recordings for Aladdin in 1947, but then moved over to Gold Star, a Houston label.

Back home in Houston, he left for other locales as little as possible during the late 1940s and 1950s. He made plenty of recordings—hundreds, in fact (by the end of the 1970s, various estimates were that the total number of songs he had recorded was anywhere from 800 to over 1,000)—during the 1950s, some of which took him to major eastern and midwestern cities for sessions, but almost all his live performances were in Texas. During the 1950s he held forth for long periods of time at small clubs in Houston, particularly on Dowling Street. As he said at one point, "Here in Houston I can be broke and hungry and walk out and someone will buy me a dinner. It ain't like that in a strange place where you don't know no one."

And it was true, in the 1950s, that few people in the mass audience knew who he was, though many blues experts were aware of both his prodigious recorded output and the fine quality of just about every effort. He did have a following in the black community around the nation, sometimes providing enough response for some of his singles to become moderate ethnic hits. With the growing interest in folk blues in the 1950s, Sam was occasionally enticed away from Texas to concerts in other sections. Meanwhile, his catalogue of LPs kept growing (even if none showed up on or came close to making the national charts). Among the dozens of albums released in the 1950s were the two-record set, *Lightnin' Hopkins and the Blues* on Imperial; the two-record *Lightnin' Hopkins* on Time Records; *Lightnin' Strikes* on Vee; *Lightnin' Hopkins* on Folklore (1959); and *Goin' Away, Gotta Move Your Baby*, and *Greatest Hits* on Bluesville.

In 1959, a folklorist named Mack McCormick sought Sam out, determined to bring his abilities to the attention of the growing number of Americans caught up in the "folk boom." One of his first projects was a hootenanny held in Houston's Alley Theater that featured Hopkins. That appearance was so well received that two more concerts followed. McCormick now looked farther afield and soon Hopkins was receiving ovations from integrated audiences at the University of California in Berkeley and at Carnegie Hall in New York. Hopkins' debut at Carnegie, which occurred on October 14, 1960, was on a bill that included such promising newcomers as Bob Dylan and Joan Baez and the veteran performer Pete Seeger. From there, Hopkins soon got the opportunity to do an extended engagement at the Village Gate in New York that solidified his newfound (and long overdue) recognition as one of the most compelling artists in the blues/R&B genre. From then on his reputation grew to worldwide proportions and the invitations to perform kept him on the move much of every year to clubs, theaters, and auditoriums across the United States and other parts of the world (although he gained considerable fame, he never achieved material gains anywhere near those of a typical pop star).

His 1960 discovery period extended to TV. On November 13, he was brought into the New York studios of CBS to tape a workshop called *A Pattern of Words and Music*. During the 1960s and 1970s, he appeared on a number of other TV programs, mostly made for the Public Broadcasting System. One of his other efforts of that period was the album produced by critic Nat Hentoff for Candid Records called *Lightnin' Hopkins in New York*, which included a number of his original compositions. The LP later was reissued in the mid-1970s by Barnaby Records as part of its great performance series. By the time Hopkins started the project with Hentoff, two new LPs on the Tradition label had come out in 1960, *Autobiography in Blues* in April and *Country Blues*, in March, as well as an album on Herald, *Lightnin' & the Blues*, issued in June 1960.

Throughout the 1960s, almost every year resulted in two or three LP releases or more, sometimes representing reissues of earlier material. (Some of his collections were reissued a number of times.) Main sources of his material included Bluesville, Arhoolie, Prestige, and Verve. His Bluesville releases of the 1960s included *Lightnin'* (6/61), *Blues in My Bottle* (2/62),

Walkin' This Road by Myself (9/62), *Lightnin' & Co.* (2/63), *Smokes Like Lightnin'* (8/63). His Verve (later Verve/Forecast) LPs included *Fast Life Woman* (3/62), *Roots* (8/65), *Lightnin' Strikes* (2/66), *Something Blue* (6/67). Among Arhoolie titles were *Lightnin' Sam Hopkins* (9/62), *Early Recordings* (2/64), *Lightnin' Hopkins with the Chambers Brothers and Barbara Dane* (10/66). Prestige releases included *Hootin' the Blues* (6/64), *My Life in the Blues* (two discs, 8/65) and *Soul Blues* (4/66). Other 1960s credits included *Lightnin' Strikes* on Vee Records, *First Meeting* (5/64) on World, *Best of Lightnin' Hopkins* (7/67) on Tradition, and *Blue* (12/67) on Jewel.

Among his available LPs in the early 1970s were such additional titles as *Gotta Move Your Baby*, recorded with Sonny Terry on Prestige; *Keeps on Rainin'* on Supreme; and *Lightnin' Hopkins* on Trip.

During the 1960s and 1970s, Lightnin' took part in a number of major folk festivals over the years. He also kept up a round of concerts at folk clubs and on college campuses, though he always avoided leaving Houston as much as possible.

HOUSE, SON: *Singer, guitarist, songwriter. Born Clarksville, Mississippi, March 21, 1902.*

A seminal figure in the history of country blues, Eddie "Son" House had an enormous impact on many far better-known musicians, both black and white. Even the relatively limited recordings available today, made for the most part when he was past his prime, affirm that his open-tuned, gutty, bottleneck guitar playing ranks at the top of that performing style. Though his live performances had become legendary by word of mouth among folk and blues artists, most of whom never had heard him play, for long periods of time nobody knew where he was or, indeed, if he was still alive. Fortunately, the folk boom of the 1960s resulted in his rediscovery and appreciation by new generations of fans.

Born in rural Mississippi but raised in Tallulah, Louisiana, his mother was a strict churchgoer and forbade Son to touch the guitar or sing blues. Son did sing with the church choir, however, wherever his family lived at the time. Son's father, Eddie House, Sr., who had separated from his mother when Son was young, played bass horn, later becoming a church deacon and, like Son's mother, giving up secular music.

At the start of the 1920s, Son's mother died and he made Clarksville home base. He worked at odd jobs there and in neighboring states, plowing, picking, and chopping cotton and, for a time, tending cattle.

In 1927, while in Matson, Mississippi, he heard two musicians named Willie Wilson and Reuben Lacy and was inspired to take up the guitar. In 1928, he bought an old one for $1.50 and had Wilson fix it up and show him some chords. In a little while, Son could play his first song, one learned from Wilson, "Hold Up Sally, Take Your Legs Offa Mine." Wilson thought he showed much promise and asked Son to work with him that Saturday night.

Soon Son had developed a distinctive style of his own and was building a backlog of songs, both from listening to other musicians and writing new ones himself. He began to play regularly on the Saturday night circuit and in 1930 crossed paths with that of blues musicians Willie Brown and Charlie Patton. The latter had made several recordings for Paramount Records in Grafton, Wisconsin, and when the company asked him to do some more, took Brown and House along with him.

During those sessions, House recorded several solos, including "Preachin' Blues," "Black Mama," and "Mississippi County Farm" and two with Brown, one of them "Clarksdale Moan." He recalled meeting the legendary Blind Lemon Jefferson in Grafton, where the latter also was doing some recordings. Son was paid forty dollars for his efforts and went back to Mississippi to play for more house parties and in local "jook joints." Paramount liked his work and asked him to travel to New York later on, but by then Son was married and settled down and didn't want to make the long trip. He did make more recordings, however, in 1932, for Spears Phonograph Company in Jackson, Mississippi, recording several originals, including "I Had a Dream Last Night Troubled Me."

Afterward, he concluded his commercial recorded work and gave up playing for local affairs for some time while he concentrated on earning a living at nonmusical jobs. The music industry lost sight of him, but in 1942 Alan Lomax sought him out in Robinsonville, Mississippi, twenty miles south of Memphis, Son's home from the late 1920s to the early 1940s. At the behest of Lomax, House recorded a number of songs for the U.S. Library of Congress Archive of Folk Song.

In 1943, Son moved to Rochester, New York, where he worked for a short time in a defense plant, then as a rivet-heater in a boxcar shop of the New York Central Railroad, and finally as a porter in the railroad's Buffalo operation. Later, Willie Brown moved to Buffalo and the two friends occasionally played together.

House remained with the New York Central for over a decade. He was living in upstate New York when the collecting team of Nick Perls, Dick Waterman, and Phil Spiro caught up with him. On Father's Day, 1964, they found the "long-lost" artist and began to record some of his music. Afterward, they spread the word that House was alive and well, and opportunities started to come along for House to appear as a featured artist on the folk circuit. One of his first live performances was at the 1964 Newport Folk Festival in Rhode Island. Among the songs he played there and at other festivals and college or folk club concerts in the mid-1960s were "Death Letter Blues," "Empire State Express," and "Pearline." He was sought out by folk authorities not only for his music, but also for reminiscences of such important blues figures as Patton, Willie Brown, Robert Johnson (who was strongly influenced by House), Ma Rainey, and others.

House began to record again, completing such albums as *Mississippi Delta Blues* on Folkways and *Blues from the Mississippi Delta* on Verve/Forecast, the latter released in August 1966. In January 1966, Columbia Records released the LP *Father of the Folk Blues*, still in the catalogue at the end of the 1970s. Also still in print at the start of the 1970s was the LP *Son House* on Arhoolie Records, comprising the recordings made under Alan Lomax's direction in 1942. The songs recorded by Nick Perls and his co-workers were available on the Blue Goose label, titled *Real Delta Blues*.

HOUSTON, CISCO: *Singer, guitarist, songwriter. Born Wilmington, Delaware, August 18, 1918; died San Bernardino, California, April 29, 1961.*

Gilbert "Cisco" Houston was regarded by his fellow artists as one of the greatest American balladeers as well as one of the finest human beings. His great legacy to folk music has been understood clearly only in the years since his untimely passing.

His close friend and long-time traveling companion Woody Guthrie once wrote for Folkways Records, "In my own mind, I see Cisco Houston as one of our manliest and best of our living crop of ballad and folksong singers. He is showman enough to make the grade and to hold any audience anywhere and at any time, I like Cisco as a man. I like him as a person, and as a fun loving, warmhearted, and likeable human being."

Cisco was born in the Baltimore area but spent only a few years there. His family came from the Carolinas and from Virginia. As a small boy, he heard his grandmother sing folk melodies. When he was just reaching school age, his family moved to Los Angeles, where he learned to play the guitar before graduation from high school.

Finishing school in the Depression-ridden 1930s, Cisco took his guitar and began his lifetime of wandering. He worked at many odd jobs, first in California and then in Colorado. For a good period in the late 1930s, he was employed as a cowboy on western ranches and learned firsthand many traditional cowboy songs. On several occasions, he sang in local clubs and on radio stations in the western region.

In his wanderings, Cisco met or was sought out by many folk musicians. Among them were Woody Guthrie, Huddie Ledbetter, and John Jacob Niles. In the late 1930s and early 1940s, Guthrie and Cisco toured through many states together, singing at small gatherings, union meetings, and small clubs. On several occa-

sions, Cisco traveled to New York, meeting among others, Moses Asch, later the founder of Folkways Records.

Despite poor eyesight, Cisco managed to enlist in the Merchant Marine during World War II, surviving three separate torpedoings of ships he was on. During these years, Cisco reached ports throughout the world; in each he picked up new material for his folk repertoire.

After the war, Cisco settled for a while in New York, then moved to Hollywood. He increased his performing pace, singing with many of the most gifted artists in the folk field. Besides working with Ledbetter in the late 1940s and again teaming with Guthrie, Cisco sang with such others as John Jacob Niles, Burl Ives, and Lee Hays. He performed on two of the first LPs issued by Moe Asch's new company in 1948.

Throughout the 1950s, Houston continued to perform before audiences across the nation. He was featured in concerts on college campuses, in churches, in leading nightclubs, and in such places as New York's Town Hall and Madison Square Garden. During the 1950s, he was seen or heard on radio and TV, including the American Inventory program and folk music programs broadcast by Mutual Broadcasting System.

In 1959, Houston toured India under the sponsorship of the State Department and the American National Theatre and Academy. In June of the following year, he served as emcee for the CBS program *Folk Music, U.S.A.*

During these years, Cisco turned out recordings for many labels, including Folkways, Stinson, Disc, Coral, Decca, and Vanguard. Releases of his performances continued at a steady pace after his death. His Folkways LPs included *Lonesome Valley, Railroad Songs, Cowboy Songs, Hard Travelin', Cisco Houston Sings, Songs of the Open Road,* and *Songs to Grow On.* In 1960, Vanguard issued its first Houston LP, *Cisco Special.* In later years, it issued *Songs of Woody Guthrie* (1961) and *I Ain't Got No Home* (1962). In 1964, Disc issued an LP, *Legacy of Cisco Houston.*

Over the years, Houston showed himself to be a talented songwriter and arranger as well as performer. Some of his compositions, such as "A Dollar Down," "Bad Man Blunder," and "Ramblin' Gamblin' Man," were included in a commemorative song book, *900 Miles, the Ballads, Blues and Folksongs of Cisco Houston,* issued by Oak Publications in 1965.

In 1960, Cisco developed cancer and died in a hospital in San Bernardino, California. His passing at forty-two was mourned not just in obituary columns but with the more positive tribute of songs to his memory, such as "Fare Thee Well, Cisco" by Tom Paxton, "Cisco Houston Passed This Way," by his protégé Peter La Farge, and "Blues for Cisco Houston" by Tom McGrath.

At the start of the 1980s, a number of his LPs were still in print, including: on Folkways, *Cisco Houston Sings American Folk Songs, Cowboy Ballads, Hard Travelin',* and *Railroad Ballads; Cisco Houston* on Evergreen; *Cowboy Songs* (with Woody Guthrie) on Stinson; and, on Vanguard, *I Ain't Got No Home* and *Cisco Houston Sings Songs of Woody Guthrie.*

HOUSTON, DAVID: *Singer, guitarist, songwriter. Born Bossier City, Louisiana, December 9, 1937.*

He might well have become a wealthy homebuilder or insurance salesman, but luckily David Houston got a phone call in the early 1960s that opened the door to his long-hoped-for entree to the country-music majors. The result has been a loss for industry but a gain of countless hit recordings for the country field.

Houston, whose ancestors included both General Robert E. Lee (his mother's maiden name was Lee) and Sam Houston, was born and raised in Bossier City, Louisiana. Both his parents liked music, and the great pop singer of the 1920s, Gene Austin (whose trademark song was "My Blue Heaven") was a close friend of his father's. Austin could perceive talent in David even when David was a small child and encouraged the Houstons to start him on singing lessons at four years of age. David also learned to play the guitar, taking lessons from an aunt who taught music, and later

added the piano to his instrumental skills. By the time he was twelve, he had become fond of country music and even auditioned for Horace Logan, producer of the *Louisiana Hayride.*

A while after David's initial appearance on the show, when he was in his teens, he became a regular cast member. Although he was not in the national spotlight, the show provided him with important contacts for the future. One of those was talent manager Tillman Franks. As Houston recalled, "I met Tillman through Slim Whitman who was then on the *Louisiana Hayride* and I was still in high school at the time. Not much happened then, but eventually Tillman put me in the business."

After graduating from high school, Houston attended Centenary College in Shreveport, Louisiana for a few years. However, he didn't find college work to his liking, so he left and joined his father and brother building houses in the Bossier City area. "I sold insurance for awhile too," he told the *Music City News* (October 1973) "and was singing around in local clubs and things like that. One day [in the early 1960s], Tillman called and asked if I could still sing and I told him I didn't know, but hoped I could. He told me he had a song he liked and we went over to Tyler, Texas, and recorded 'Mountain of Love.' He carried it to Nashville and played it for Epic Records and I've been with Epic ever since."

"Mountain of Love" proved a mountainous hit when it was issued in 1963, staying on country charts for sixteen weeks and reaching top-10 levels. That and other chart singles caused major music business trade magazines to vote him Most Promising Country Performer of 1964. In 1965, his efforts included an even bigger hit, "Livin' in a House Full of Love" and he topped that the following year with a gold-record, million-copy single, "Almost Persuaded." Among other releases that made the charts in the mid- and late-1960s were "Loser's Cathedral," "Chickashay," "One if for Him," "Sweet, Sweet Judy," "The Ballad of the Fool Killer," and "Already It's Heaven."

Among his 1960s album releases were

his debut LP, *New Voice from Nashville, Greatest Hits,* and *David.* In the early 1970s, his LP output on Epic included *Baby, Baby* (issued 5/70); *David Houston* (9/70); *World* (7/70); *Wonders of the Wine* (10/70); *Woman Always Knows* (7/71), *Greatest Hits, Volume 2* (10/71), and *The Day Love Walked In* (6/72). In the early 1970s, David also teamed up with Barbara Mandrell for a series, some of which were included in the album *A Perfect Match* (released 10/72).

During the first part of the mid-1970s, David continued to place new releases regularly on the country lists. In 1974, he had the top-20 selection "Lady of the Night" early in the year and also had such well-received singles as "I Love You, I Love You," recorded with Barbara Mandrell, and in the summer, "The Same Old Look of Love." In 1975, his chart singles included "I'll Be Your Steppin' Stone" in the summer and a duet with Calvin Crawford, "Sweet Molly," in the fall.

However, during 1975 and 1976, his releases didn't find the response of his earlier efforts. In 1977, Houston's new releases came out on Starday, including the chart single "Aint' That Lovin' You Baby." In mid-1978, he had a single on Colonial Records on the charts, "Waltz of the Angels." By year end he switched again, this time to Elektra/Asylum. At the end of 1978, he had a new single, "Best Friends Make the Worst Enemies," moving upward on the country lists.

During the summer of 1979, he had another Elektra single in the top 40, "Faded Love and Winter Roses." By year-end, though, he had left that label and had the single "Here's to All the Too Hard Working Husbands" out on the small Derrick label. In 1980 he moved again, this time to Country International, turning out such charted singles as "You're the Perfect Reason" and "Sad Love Song Ladies."

During his long career, Houston crisscrossed the United States many times and also was featured in a number of overseas shows over the years. He also appeared on many nationally broadcast programs, including prestigious ones like the *Grand Ole Opry* and *Hee Haw.* Through it all, Bossier City remained the place he always called home.

HOWARD, HARLAN: *Songwriter, singer, publisher. Born Harlan County, Kentucky, September 8, 1929.*

Although born in fabled Harlan County, Kentucky, young Harlan was raised in and around Detroit, where his parents moved when he was two years old. Their background and the wattage power of WSM's *Grand Ole Opry* into Detroit provided the boy with country-music indoctrination.

His idol, Ernest Tubb, indirectly taught Howard how to write lyrics. Tubb would sing on the *Opry* and Howard would attempt to write down the lyrics, his quick ear retaining the melodies. There were gaps in the lyrics and he would fill them in, add new verses, and get a sort of Ernest Tubb song as a result. This led him to try writing his own songs, using the earthy three- and four-chord structures of his favorite writers, Tubb, Fred Rose, Floyd Tillman, and Rex Griffen.

Four years with the paratroopers followed his graduation from high school; it was at Fort Benning, Georgia, that his buddies taught him to pick the guitar. On Friday nights, he would head directly for Nashville with a buddy, hitchhiking both ways. Sometimes the luck of the thumb was sour and they would report back to the base late for Monday's roll call.

Following his army tour, Howard worked at various jobs in Michigan, Tucson, and finally Los Angeles. It was there that he met Johnny Bond and Tex Ritter, both of whom took an interest in his writing, and had their firms publish his songs. (In Los Angeles, he also met an aspiring young singer who soon became his wife. Jan Howard was to become an important country artist in the 1960s with many of her hit records Harlan's songs.) This was in the late 1950s, a period that saw Wynn Stewart, Buck Owens, Bobby Bare, Skeets McDonald, and others trying their luck on the California country nightclub and recording circuit.

Stewart made the first recording of a Howard song, "You Took Her Off My

Hands," for Capitol Records, under Ken Nelson's direction. Not long after Columbia's Don Law recorded Charlie Walker with "Pick Me Up on Your Way Down," Howard's first recognized national hit. These were followed with Kitty Wells' "Mommy for a Day" and Ray Price's "Heartaches by the Number," which hit the pop charts with a cover record by Guy Mitchell.

With royalty money coming in nicely, Howard decided to go where the hits were being cut. In June 1960 he moved to Nashville. The first of his 400-plus recordings was made there, and in both 1961 and 1962 he was awarded *Billboard's* top country & western songwriter award.

Howard kept up correspondence with country disc jockeys and artists, regularly covering recording sessions in the various Nashville studios, the *Grand Ole Opry*, and other pipelines of the business. In 1964 he started his own publishing firm, Wilderness Music Publishing Company.

His BMI award hits include: "Mommy for a Day," "Pick Me Up on Your Way Down," "Heartaches by the Number" (1959); "Above and Beyond (the Call of Love)," "Three Steps to the Phone," "I Don't Believe I'll Fall in Love Today," "Odds and Ends (Bits and Pieces)," "Under the Influence of Love," "I Fall to Pieces," "I Wish I Could Fall in Love Today," "Heartbreak USA," "The Blizzard," "Foolin' Around" (1960); "Don't Call Me from a Honky Tonk," "You Took Her Off My Hands," "Busted," "Second Hand Rose (Second Hand Heart)," "You Comb Her Hair" (1963); "Your Heart Turned Left" (1965); "I Won't Forget You," "I've Got a Tiger by the Tail" (1964); "Streets of Baltimore," "Evil on Your Mind," "It's All Over (But the Crying)" (1966).

During the 1960s, Harlan made some recordings of his own, such as the 1966 Monument Records album *Harlan Howard* and such RCA LPs as *Mr. Songwriter* (1967) and *Down to Earth* (1968). He also had an early 1970s release on Nugget Records, *Silent Majority*. However, his performing career remained secondary to his writing activities, particularly since he didn't like touring and was an avid fisherman. For many years he lived in Madison, Tennessee, with Jan and the couple's three sons, but Harlan and Jan separated during the 1970s.

In the early 1980s he remained active on the Nashville recording scene, administering his copyrights and encouraging young talent in both the performing and writing areas.

HOWARD, JAN: *Singer. Born West Plains, Missouri, March 13, 1932.*

For decades after the late 1950s, the surname Howard often appeared on country charts. In bold face it was associated with singer Jan Howard, in fine print with songwriter Harlan Howard. Often both names appeared in connection with the same song, because many of Jan's hits were written by Harlan. For a long time it was a husband-and-wife partnership; although the two separated in the 1970s, for career purposes Jan retained her married name.

The idea of a music career seemed remote when Jan was growing up in West Plains, Missouri. However, she did enjoy listening to country & western music and sang along with records and radio programs as she reached her teens. She began to perform at local affairs, and in time moved to Los Angeles to try to further her musical background.

In California, she met an up-and-coming songwriter named Harlan Howard. It wasn't long before she became Mrs. Howard and settled down to raise a family that after several years of marriage consisted of three boys. Harlan made use of her singing ability on some demonstration records of new songs. There were plenty of listeners for these discs, for by this time Harlan was one of the most successful songwriters in the business.

One recording executive was as impressed with Jan Howard's voice as with the song. In short order, Jan had a part-time career as singer and recording artist. For Challenge Records, she turned out a number of hits, such as "Yankee Go Home," "The One You Slip Around With," and "A World I Can't Live In." Her ability was recognized by the jukebox operators of America, who selected her as the Most Promising Country & Western Female Vocalist for 1960. Shortly after, she received similar awards from *Billboard* and *Cash Box*. The year 1960 also was one in which the Howard family took up residence in the Nashville area, a region Jan still called home in the early 1980s.

In the 1960s, she was featured on a number of network TV and radio shows, including appearances on the *Grand Ole Opry*. As her home schedule permitted, she also made personal appearances in many states and overseas. She made many recordings during the decade, including many releases that found favor with record buyers. One of her early-1960s credits was the Wrangler Records LP, *Jan Howard*. In the mid-1960s she signed with Decca Records. Among her successes on the label was the 1966 nationwide top-10 single, "Evil on Your Mind," (written by Harlan). It also served as the title song for a 1966 Decca LP. Among her chart singles in 1967 was the hit "Roll Over and Play Dead." During the year Decca released the LP *Bad Seed*. Her 1968 output included *This Is Jan Howard* and the chart hit LP *Count Your Blessings, Woman*. Her 1968 singles successes included a duet with Bill Anderson, "For Loving You," and her solo "Count Your Blessings, Woman." In 1969 she made singles charts with songs like "When We Tried" and "My Son." Her duet work with Bill Anderson at the end of the 1960s and start of the 1970s brought two Country Music Association nominations for Best Vocal Duo in 1968 and 1970.

Her late 1960s and early 1970s albums on Decca included *For God and Country, If It's All the Same to You,* and *You Rock Me Back to Little Rock*. Among her early 1970s chart singles was the 1970 "The Soul You Never Had." By the mid-1970s, Jan's affiliation with Decca had ended. Later in the decade she recorded on the Con Brio label.

HUBBARD, RAY WYLIE: *Singer, guitarist, songwriter, band leader. Born Hugo, Oklahoma, November 13, 1946.*

In some ways, the song "Up Against the Wall, Redneck Mother" could serve as the anthem for the progressive country movement in Texas in the 1970s. Even if Ray Wylie Hubbard had no other claim to fame, writing that song made him an important figure in modern country music annals.

Although primarily associated with Texas in most people's minds, he was born and spent his early years in Oklahoma. However, when he was in his teens his family lived in Dallas, where he attended high school. He recalls, "Michael Murphey, B. W. Stevenson, and Larry Croce all went to the same high school. When I was a junior, Michael was a senior, B. W. a sophomore and Larry a freshman. Michael was in a folk group so I got in with it and then formed my own folk group. We played mostly assemblies and there was a coffee house named the Rubaiyat. I started playing there. Artists like Jerry Jeff [Walker] and Ramblin' Jack Elliott came there.

"I finally got a Martin B-18 and that made it official. I sang Kingston Trio–type songs, then got into Woody Guthrie, Cisco Houston–type material. After high school, some of us went to Red River, New Mexico. We had no leader. Just three high school kids formed a group, two guitars and one bass. We opened a family nightclub. We'd come back to Texas and go to college, then go back summers to play in our club. I was an English major at the University of Texas at Arlington and North Texas State University."

Red River, he notes, was roughly halfway between Austin, Texas, and Denver, Colorado. Many artists on the folk circuit, including Jerry Jeff Walker and Michael Murphey, would stop off in Red River while traveling to dates in the big cities. "They'd stop off at our place and we'd put 'em up for the night." During those years, Hubbard says, he sang quite a few original compositions by Murphey. "Primarily when I started I did a lot of his songs. He was a great influence on me.

"I started writing songs myself right after college. Except a lot of the songs I write aren't real commercial. The hardest thing for me to do is sit down and write a song like that. Most of mine aren't typical.

I wrote about things like a liquor store holdup and red-neck mother—I don't really know how that came about. I began it when I was up in Red River in a place called the B Bar D Bar. Originally it was kind of a pretty song."

The song, once started, seemed to develop a life of its own. "My bass player started playing bass for Jerry Jeff and sang 'Red Neck Mother' for him. It didn't have a second verse so Jerry Jeff called me on the phone from the studio. I made up a second verse on the phone, so the song makes no sense to me whatever." (By then, in mid-1973, Hubbard had left Red River and was working as a singer and acoustic guitarist in Texas clubs. He recalls, "I really got into country at the start of the 1970s. In 1970–71, I started to assemble my own band to play some Texas spots.")

Hubbard also began searching for a recording alignment in the early 1970s. He was signed to a recording contract by Atlantic, but that arrangement bore no fruit. Soon after, he moved over to that firm's sister company, Warner Bros., which did release an album by Hubbard in 1974. Unfortunately, nothing much happened with it. He did have a bit more success as a songwriter. A number of his songs were recorded by other artists in the mid-1970s, including his old high school associate Larry Croce, and such others as Sammi Smith, Bobby Bare, and the New Riders of the Purple Sage.

Interest in his writings was induced by the success of Jerry Jeff Walker's version of "Red Neck Mother." The song was included on Walker's 1973 LP, Viva Terlingua. Jerry Jeff's single of the song moved to the top levels of the country charts and, before long, other artists were turning out cover versions.

Hubbard still was looking for a recording breakthrough in the late 1970s. A hopeful step was the signing of a contract with Willie Nelson's Lone Star Records in 1978. Hubbard's LP on the label, Off the Wall, came out in the fall, featuring Hubbard's own treatment of "Red Neck Mother" and such other songs as "Bittersweet Funky Tuesday" and "Freeway Church of Christ." Other than Hubbard's cult following, the LP made little sales progress.

At the start of the 1980s, Hubbard and his band were doing reasonably well on the country circuit, but that all-important recording pact still eluded him. "We keep makin' demos and sendin' 'em out," he said in the fall of 1980. "With luck we'll get a contract with a major record company one of these days. Right now, 'Red Neck Mother' is about the only thing I'm known for. It's hard for me to write songs for other people. Waylon [Jennings] asked me to do some for him, but I kinda write when the spirit moves me and, as I said, they're usually strange songs.

"Actually, I had a million seller that nobody knows about. It's called 'Nutty Boggy Banjo Man' and it's the flip side of the Larry Croce single that has 'Junk Food Junkie.'"

Based on interview with Irwin Stambler and Grelun Landon, fall 1980.

HUNLEY, CON: Singer, pianist, guitarist, songwriter. Born Knox County, Tennessee, April 9, 1945.

Most country stars end up being adopted Tennesseans, but with all the activity centered on Nashville, it stands to reason a certain amount of talent would be homegrown. One of the more promising native sons of the late 1970s, Con Hunley, combined a powerful singing voice with an excellent keyboard style that made him a prospective candidate for major stardom in the 1980s.

Born and raised in Knox County, Con was part of a family where country and gospel music were strong favorites. His family not only was strongly religious but was one of the better-known gospel groups in the region. Almost as soon as he could talk, Con started learning gospel songs and performed in churches all over Knox and surrounding counties in his childhood and teens.

As he grew up, Con became interested in singing and playing country music. His first idol was Chet Atkins, and he dreamed of becoming a guitar master. However, he discovered he was limited as a guitar player. "It didn't take long to discover that another Chet Atkins I wasn't." He turned his attention to piano with much greater success. After he learned the basics, he began to study the techniques used by keyboard experts like Charlie Rich, Ray Charles, and Jerry Lee Lewis. "I particularly found I could really get into the singing of Ray Charles, a man who sings with more soul than anyone in the world."

He already was playing with groups in his home area in his high school years and later got a regular job at the Indian Rock Night Club in Knoxville. "My first gig paid twelve dollars and I thought I was rich," he recalled. After that, he was asked to join the Gene Hammock Band, remaining with it as a sideman for a year before leaving to enter the U.S. Air Force. He kept up his musical activity in the service, though, playing almost continually in a band up to the time of his discharge.

His next step was Knoxville, where for a time it looked as though music might not be his calling after all. Hunley went to work in a mill, but the lure of show business proved strong and he soon quit to make his way as a performer. He gained a club job again, this time at the Corner Lounge. His singing and piano work began to gain attention from Knoxville country fans, among whom was a stockbroker interested in entering the record business. He established a label called Prairie Dust Records in Nashville and signed Con as his first artist.

Con began recording a series of songs, mainly consisting of his own compositions. During 1976–77, Prairie Dust issued five singles of Hunley's: "Misery Loves Company," "Loving You Is a Habit I Can't Break," "Pick Up the Pieces," "I Will Always Remember That Song," and "Breaking Up Is Hard to Do." He quickly established a strong rapport with the country audience. Four of the songs made the charts, with "Breaking Up Is Hard to Do" showing strongest when it moved into middle-chart levels in the summer of 1977.

Feeling the time was ripe for a move to a major label, Con and his management arranged for a showcase performance for top executives at George Jones' Possum Holler

Club in Nashville. This brought five bids, from which Con selected Warner Bros. His debut release, "Cry, Cry Darling," made the charts in early 1978 and was followed by "Weekend Friend," which was on upper-chart levels in the summer as was "You've Still Got a Place in My Heart" later in the year. In early 1979, he added another chart single to the list, "I've Been Waiting for You All My Life." In March 1979, his debut LP on Warner Bros., *Con Hunley*, was released. At the start of 1980, he had the top-20 single "I Don't Want to Lose You." By the spring he had a new chartmaker, "You Lay a Whole Lot of Love on Me." Later in the year his single "They Never Lost You" was in the top 20. In 1981, he had the best-selling singles "What's New with You" and "She's Steppin' Out," and the LP *Don't It Break Your Heart*, issued in the fall of 1980, was still on the charts part of the following year.

HURT, MISSISSIPPI JOHN: *Singer, guitarist, songwriter. Born Teoc, Carroll County, Mississippi, March 8, 1892; died Grenada, Mississippi, November 2, 1966.*

In July 1963, the audience at the Newport Folk Festival in Rhode Island saw a "ghost." It was a legendary seventy-two-year-old artist who had dropped from sight thirty-five years earlier and had been thought to have died many years before. As soon as the crowd heard his thrumming one-two guitar beat and vibrant baritone voice, they knew Mississippi John Hurt was very much alive and deserving of the praise for his few recordings of many years ago. His performance was considered a highlight of the Festival and, in appreciation, the event organizers gave him a new guitar.

Hurt's interest in music began early. His mother gave him a $1.50 Black Anne guitar as a present when he was nine and in a short time he taught himself to play some tunes. Avalon, Mississippi, where he remained almost his entire life, was in a remote part of the state and he had little contact with the blues musicians who wandered through other parts of Mississippi. As he told one interviewer, he developed his own guitar style. "I taught myself to play the guitar the way I thought a guitar should sound."

As he grew older, he learned as many songs as he could from the field hands and other workers in his area. He played for enjoyment, earning his normal meager living from odd jobs. At one time or another, he worked as a field hand picking cotton and corn, worked cattle, spent time on the Mississippi River, was a railroad hand, and, in the 1930s, was on the WPA payroll.

Though he received little money, he played at many local dances and celebrations from the early days of the century on and occasionally picked up new material from both white and black itinerant singers who passed through Avalon. In the 1920s, he was able to listen to some of the new crop of country records turned out by many eastern companies. He was greatly interested in the songs of fellow Mississippian Jimmie Rodgers (many of them "white blues") that began to gain attention throughout the South after 1927. In addition to using songs from other sources, Hurt sometimes wrote his own, including the murder ballad "Louis Collins," "Coffee Blues," and "Chicken."

Until 1928, practically no one had heard of him outside of Carroll County and a few nearby counties. In that year, Okeh Records recording director, Tommy Rockwell, was touring Mississippi looking for country artists. Two white musicians suggested he see Hurt. Rockwell did and was impressed enough to bring him to Memphis for a recording session. Hurt was paid $240 plus expenses for making eight recordings. Two of these, "Frankie" and "Nobody's Dirty Business" were released. They sold so well that Rockwell arranged to bring Hurt to New York. On December 21 and 28, 1928, Hurt recorded such songs as "Louis Collins," "Candy Man Blues," "Spike Driver Blues," "Stagger Lee Blues," and "Avalon Blues."

Hurt went home to Avalon, his career seemingly on the verge of taking off. However, the Depression caused sharp cutbacks in sales of blues and country records and people forgot about him. He followed his established pattern of hard work and

leisure-time performing for the next three decades. After World War II, growing ranks of folklorists heard his old recordings and wanted to find him, but no one could recall his whereabouts. Many folk song enthusiasts searched for him without success and finally concluded he had died.

Then blues collector Tom Hoskins of Washington, D.C., realized the possible significance of the song "Avalon Blues." He went to the town in 1963 and, sure enough, found the lost balladeer. He talked John into going to Washington with him. In a short time people were thronging to see him at the local Ontario Place Coffee House. Later that year, at Newport, he achieved a national reputation. In the twilight of his life, Mississippi John was a celebrity sought out for engagements in folk clubs, festivals, and college concerts across the United States. In the few years left to him, he crowded many such performances into his schedule (always returning home to Mississippi, however), singing and playing guitar with obvious relish. In the summer of 1964, he repeated his success at the Newport Folk Festival. (His performances were included in the Vanguard album sets covering both the 1963 and 1964 Festivals.)

Soon after Hurt's rediscovery, he began to make new recordings. The first new LP, produced by Piedmont Records in 1963, was titled *Presenting Mississippi John Hurt: Folk Songs and Blues*. A second LP, *Worried Blues*, was turned out by Piedmont in October 1964. After that Vanguard recorded additional material, both live concert work and studio sessions. Unfortunately, John's health began to fail, as was evident in his final studio sessions for Vanguard in 1966. He passed away in Grenada, Mississippi, in November of that year.

The greater part of Hurt's modern LPs came out after his death and, in fact, there were more of his albums still in record company catalogues at the start of the 1980s than were available during his lifetime. Among them, most originallly issued in the late 1960s, were such Vanguard titles as *Mississippi John Hurt—Today* (1/67), *The Immortal Mississippi John Hurt, Last Sessions*, and *The Best of Mississippi John Hurt*.

The last-named was recorded live during a 1965 college concert and included such songs as "Coffee Blues," "Chicken," "C.C. Rider," and "Candy Man." Among the tracks included in *Mississippi John Hurt—Today* are "Louis Collins" and "Beulah Land." Also available at the start of the 1980s was the Biograph Records release *Mississippi John Hurt—1928—His First Recordings.*

HUSKY, FERLIN: *Singer, guitarist, comedian, songwriter, disc jockey. Born Flat River, Missouri, December 3, 1927.*

Simon Crum, Terry Preston, Ferlin Husky—these are all the same person, an excellent example of a successful musical split personality. So well did Husky develop the rural hayseed character of Crum, in fact, that at one point many country music fans accepted Crum as a separate individual. (Ferlin also spelled his last name Huskey on early recordings.) But whether singing straight country songs under his real name or comic ones as Simon Crum, Ferlin won enough favor to fashion a career that endured from the end of the 1940s into the 1970s.

Not only did he use different names at times, he also kept people guessing about his birthplace. It is officially given as Flat River, but biographies also list it as either Hickory Grove or Cantrell, Missouri. The reason is simple. Ferlin was born on a farm located at almost equal distances from all three small towns.

Brought up on the guitar and fiddle music of local dances and parties, Ferlin learned to play the guitar as a child. His musical skills, however, did not get him started in the entertainment field; rather it was his ability as an announcer. He made his way into radio with a series of disc jockey jobs during the second half of the 1940s, eventually landing at a station in Bakersfield, California. The booming country club scene in Bakersfield inspired him to increase his performing activity. He felt that Husky sounded wrong for a performer, so he assumed the name of Terry Preston for his various club engagements at the end of the 1940s.

Things developed well enough for him to put together his own touring country show in the early 1950s, sometimes recruiting new cast members by holding talent contests in the Bakersfield region. Meanwhile, he varied his announcing chores by introducing a new, comic philosopher character as part of his show. Simon Crum quickly caught on with the audience, so much so that Husky's first recording contract with Capitol was to do several sides as Crum.

Once on the Capitol roster, he soon had the chance to record "straight" country songs in the early 1950s, still using the pseudonym Terry Preston. One of those was a duet with Jean Shepard. The song, "Dear John Letter," became a number-one national hit in 1953. That year, Ferlin wrote a tribute to his idol, Hank Williams, who had just died tragically. The song, "Hank's Song," was released under his own name and its success brought about the permanent retirement of "Terry Preston," though not Simon Crum. Simon continued to be a mainstay of Husky's stage act the rest of his career. Before 1953 was over, he teamed with Jean Shepard for another top-10 hit, "Forgive Me John."

From then on, Ferlin ranked as a "name" country performer, and his live appearances, backed by his band, the Hush Puppies, took him all over the United States and Canada several times over from the mid-1950s through the 1970s. He was featured on most of the major radio and TV country-music programs of those decades. In 1957, he showed his versatility by playing a featured dramatic role in a *Kraft TV Theater* play. In 1958, he made his movie debut in *Country Music Holiday*, with Faron Young and Zsa Zsa Gabor as costars.

The year 1957 proved to be his best year since 1953. He re-recorded a song he originally had done in 1952 as Terry Preston. The 1957 version of ("Since You've) Gone" became one of the biggest country singles of the year, rising to number one on the national charts. Ferlin had a second major hit that year with the top-10 single "Fallen Star." In 1958, his alter ego Simon Crum burst on the nation with a top-10 single of Ferlin's comic composition

"Country Music Is Here to Stay." After placing some other songs on lower-chart levels at the end of the 1950s, Husky began the next decade with his third number-one bestseller, "On the Wings of a Dove."

Although he continued to be a popular favorite on the concert circuit, including some overseas appearances, Ferlin didn't make the top-10 bracket for most of the 1960s. However, he found a second wind the latter part of the decade. In 1967, for instance, he had three songs on the hit lists, including a top-10 single, "Once." In 1968, he again had three chart-making singles, including two top-10 hits, "Just for You" and "I Promised You the World." In the early 1970s he placed more singles on the charts for Capitol Records, including "How Could You Be Anything but Love" in 1972, but his overall results declined.

In 1973 he parted company with his long-time label, Capitol, and moved to ABC Records. At the end of 1973 and the beginning of 1974, his single "Rosie Cries a Lot" was on bestseller lists, making it into the top 20. He followed with such other mid-1970s charted releases as "Freckles and Polliwog Days" in the summer of 1974 and "Champagne Ladies and Blue Ribbon Babies" in early 1975, both written or co-written by Dallas Frazier, a discovery of Husky's talent contests back in the early 1950s.

During his long career, Husky naturally had a great many albums to his credit, most on the Capitol label. His output on Capitol from the late 1950s through the mid-1960s included *Ferlin Husky and His Hush Puppies, Boulevard of Broken Dreams, Born to Lose, Ferlin Husky,* and *Ferlin Husky's Favorites* in 1959; *Gone* in 1960; *Walkin' and Hummin', Memories of Home* (1961); *Some of My Favorites* (1962); *Heart and Soul of Ferlin Husky, Hits of Ferlin Husky, Simon Crum* (1963); *By Request* (1964); *True, True Lovin'* (1965); *Songs of Music City, I Could Sing All Night* (1966); *What Am I Gonna Do?* (1967). His Capitol releases of the late 1960s and early 1970s included *That's Why I Love You So Much, Your Love, Your Sweet Love Lifted Me,* and *One More Time.* He also was represented on several other labels, essentially by reissues, such as *Easy Livin'* and *Ferlin Husky* on King Records in the late 1950s, *Old Opry Favorites* on Pickwick (mid-1960s); and *Green, Green Grass of Home* on Hilltop. In the mid-1970s, he also turned out several LPs on ABC Records.

I

IAN AND SYLVIA: *Vocal and instrumental duo, songwriters. Ian Tyson, born British Columbia, Canada, September 25, 1933; Sylvia Fricker (Mrs. Tyson), born Chatham, Ontario, Canada, September 19, 1940.*

The gifted team of Ian and Sylvia spearheaded Canada's contribution to the folk movement of the 1960s and became one of the favorite acts of American folk audiences in the mid-1960s. For a time late in the decade their career floundered when folk fans objected to their new-found interest in country music. However, they went on to become important in the Canadian TV field during the 1970s.

Sylvia Fricker grew up in the small farming community of Chatham, Ontario.

Her father worked in the appliance department of an Eaton's store and her mother taught music. When Sylvia was old enough, she joined the choir at the Holy Trinity Anglican Church where her mother was organist and choir leader. Mrs. Fricker gave her daughter lessons on piano until, when Sylvia got older, her tastes in music tended away from the classical and waltz music her parents admired. She preferred trying to catch the far-off signals at night of an R&B program on a Detroit radio station.

During her high school years she made few friends, and from the ages of fifteen to eighteen worked summers at a local agricultural operation hoeing beans, picking tomatoes and berries, and the like. As she told interviewer Larry LeBlanc, "I wasn't too popular in high school. I very rarely went out. By the time I was starting to go out, I was working. I was always interested in music and English literature, the logical combination."

Her interest in music took the form of learning guitar (her first instrument sported a red and white image of a cowboy lassoing a cow) and picking out English and American folk songs from library books. She began to have the feeling that she had to go elsewhere. "You didn't stay there if you had any kind of feeling that there might be something better in life. I'm not putting down the town because it's a great place to grow up in until you're about thirteen . . . but it's a lousy place to be an adolescent in. I wanted to be a folk-singer from about the time I was fifteen. I decided I'd finish high school, if that's what everybody wanted, and then I'd go and do my own things."

For a year after graduation, Fricker worked at a jewelers in Chatham and traveled to Toronto when she could to try to break into show business. The commute was too trying, so she found a job in a Toronto clothing store. In Toronto she met another aspiring artist, Ian Tyson, with whom she formed a part-time partnership in the fall of 1959, working with him at a place called the Village Corner while doing her own solo sets on Thursday nights at the Bohemian Embassy.

Tyson had come to Toronto via a route that began in far off British Columbia in Canada's western region. Born and raised on a farm in that province, Ian dropped out of school in his teens to work at various jobs while adding to his store of folk music. For a while he was a farmhand, then a rodeo performer. As he wandered across Canada, he sometimes picked up spare change playing his guitar and singing at small clubs and coffee houses. His other jobs during those years included working as a commercial artist and lumberjack.

Ian told LeBlanc that when he first started singing with Sylvia, he was puzzled, "She was very standoffish. She was

unique. I didn't know what to make of her. Nobody did. She was very different, a loner, original, very introspective, very shy, very small-town, very green. But you could see she wasn't going to be small town very long."

Sylvia recalled that the team's approach to music "wasn't intellectualized. Ian did the lead. I did the harmonies, and he played guitar. Ian would learn a song and sing it until I worked out a harmony. We got along well. We didn't make any demands on each other during the early period. We would rehearse together, which in those days was unheard of. Everybody just fooled around on their own. If they worked with somebody, maybe they got together for an hour or so before they went onstage. Ian and I would rehearse three or four times a week."

The two decided to work together full time in 1961 as they found a steadily growing following in Toronto. That year they also gave their first U.S. concert, in Columbia, South Carolina. "It was at a cotillion ball," Sylvia reminisced. "Girls in hoop skirts, their partners from a nearby army base, plus terribly lost young soldiers that none of the girls would associate with. They didn't dig us. They found us a little raw. They wanted the Kingston Trio. Our music had a mountain flavor to it. They said, 'I don't want to hear that stuff. My grandmother sings it. That's not folk music.'"

To try to reach a wider audience, the duo moved to New York in the early 1960s, where artist's manager Albert Grossman agreed to handle the act. (When they first went there, they lived in separate places, but in 1964 decided to marry.) Grossman brought them to the attention of the leading folk music label of those years, Vanguard, which gave them their first major recording contract. Their debut LP, *Ian and Sylvia*, was issued in September 1962 and brought the first stirrings of interest. Soon after, inspired by the example of Bob Dylan (whom Grossman also managed for a long time), the partners decided to try to write original material. One of the first results was Ian's "Four Strong Winds," the title song of their second Vanguard LP (issued April 1964) and still often re-recorded. Sylvia's first composition, "You Were on My Mind," is another standard, which provided a best-selling single for the group We Five in the 1960s.

By the time the duo's album *Northern Journey* came out in September 1964, they were considered major folk stars all over the United States. Earlier that year, their popularity with New York fans had been demonstrated by a standing room only concert at Town Hall. During 1964 and 1965, Ian and Sylvia played before enthusiastic audiences in all parts of the United States and were featured in major folk festivals at home and abroad.

During those years, besides presenting more of their own compositions, they were instrumental in showcasing material of other talented writers from Canada. Their LP *Early Morning Rain*, for instance, issued in July 1965, had several Gordon Lightfoot numbers, including the title track. They also were among the first to promote the songs of Joni Mitchell. Their other Vanguard LPs of the mid-1960s included *Play One More* (5/66) and *So Much for Dreaming* (4/67).

Problems arose for them during 1965–66. After giving birth to their first child, Clay, Sylvia developed severe vocal problems. At loose ends during her pregnancy and after, Ian tried working as a solo performer, including appearances at The Riverboat in Toronto and in Dayton, Ohio.

Sylvia eventually recovered and they returned to their duo activities, but with increasing emphasis on country-related material. They signed with a new record firm, MGM, which released *Lovin' Sound* in June 1967. The single of the title track failed to catch fire, however, though appearances at folk venues during the year didn't indicate any major loss of popularity with their folk following.

Meanwhile, Vanguard had complained that their contract requirements weren't fulfilled and that another album was due. For that the Tysons went to Nashville to record a series of tracks, many of which featured what LeBlanc refers to as "extended, instrumental, free-form country jazz." That album was appropriately titled *Nashville.* It was followed by one in a similar vein on MGM titled *Full Circle.*

Enthusiastic about their new musical directions, the Tysons assembled a new show called The Great Speckled Bird, which they took on the road at the end of the 1960s. Once more they were ahead of the times. Audience reaction, to say the least, was negative. The fans felt they were being forced to hear country music when they bought tickets for a folk concert. Sylvia recalled, "People even got up and walked out. They would have a violent reaction to the steel guitar. They'd walk out on the first bars that the steel player would hit."

Undaunted, they persevered, and in 1970 seemed to turn the corner. Their set was warmly received at the Atlanta Festival and at a series of concerts across Canada. One notable performance took place in Calgary, where a standing ovation was given a rousing version of "Will the Circle Be Unbroken" in which the Tysons were joined by Bonnie and Delaney Bramlett and Rick Danko of The Band.

Now they looked forward to release of the debut *Great Speckled Bird* album on Ampex, an LP produced by Todd Rundgren. The album flopped, however, and, after another series of poorly received concerts, the show was disbanded.

The Tysons were again dispirited and wondering what course to follow when the Canadian Broadcasting System asked Ian to host a show called *Nashville North,* which soon became the *Ian Tyson Show.* The program became a top-ranked show on Canadian TV for most of the 1970s. Sylvia was a regular cast member on the program, though she didn't perform on every weekly show.

She told LeBlanc, "Ian having had his TV show for five years really gave me a breather. I had money coming in, but I really did not have to give myself full-time to the television show. The period gave me a lot of time to decide what I wanted to do. I started out in a lot of different directions. Not in any visible way, but with a lot of different possibilities."

In the mid-1970s, she got an offer she couldn't refuse—to host her own show on

CBC radio called *Touch the Earth*. The program featured a blend of folk, country, and pop music. Later it was groomed for TV. Sylvia also was signed to a new solo recording contract by Capitol EMI of Canada, her debut LP on the label being *Woman's World*.

IAN, JANIS: *Singer, guitarist, pianist, songwriter. Born New Jersey, April 7, 1951.*

With her Orphan Annie-like mop of hair and slight, four foot ten inch figure, Janis Ian gives an impression of being very young indeed. And it is true that Janis is unusually shy for a performer. But in her creative persistence and the body of the excellent work she's turned out, she stands tall.

Her association with music goes back to her earliest years. "I started with classical music at two," she recalls with a shadow of a smile. "I lived in New Jersey until I was thirteen and then my family moved to Manhattan. I started writing songs at twelve. My early influence included Billie Holiday, Edith Piaf, and Odetta."

For most of her childhood, her family was constantly on the move. During her first fifteen years she lived in thirteen different places in New Jersey and New York. She attended a variety of public schools before entering New York's High School of Music and Art. Her musical efforts, she later noted, "were the only things that kept me going as long as I did without totally freaking out. School was always absurd . . . but then the whole fame thing was happening and I was going to a school where most of the teachers were frustrated musicians—they didn't like it."

Janis had started singing for school events, then had performed in small New York folk clubs. By that time she was well versed in piano and acoustic guitar. In 1966, her efforts led to a recording contract from Verve/Forecast, which soon found itself with a major—and controversial—hit of her own composition, entitled "Society's Child." Objections to the song were prompted by its story of a doomed love affair between a white girl and a black boy. Compared to many of the popular hits of the late 1960s and 1970s, it seems in retrospect as mild as its folk song melody.

The success of the song made the sixteen-year-old a national celebrity. During most of 1967, Janis maintained a hectic schedule of engagements at concerts and in clubs across the country. She achieved a chart hit with her debut LP on Verve, *Janis Ian*, issued in January 1967. That was followed in January 1968 by the album *For All Seasons*.

Then Janis gave up her entertaining efforts for a while. Many factors contributed to her dropping out: the pressures of touring, family problems, a love affair, bad business deals. She made Philadelphia, Pennsylvania, home for the late 1960s. She said, "I retired for a while. I just got very bored with performing, so I stopped doing it. It was basically the same thing night after night. I did the same things, the same show. It becomes very predictable.

"It is true that I was struggling to put together a 'ruined life,' but it was of my own making. I don't regard that period as disastrous. I did a lot of reading (particularly writers like Rimbaud, T.S. Eliot, and Camus' *Notebooks*) and a lot of absorbing."

But in the 1970s, the urge to create new material took hold again. The comeback began in earnest in 1971, when she moved to California and purposefully set about learning classical orchestration and techniques of scoring while also writing a growing number of new songs. After several ups and downs, this brought her to new heights with the superb 1975 album *Between the Lines*. "I felt more mature, that I had more insight. I feel the songs are better now and I'm a better singer so the whole thing becomes more interesting. It isn't easy. It's hard work. The reasons I came back to the music field comes down to this: I was writing songs that I liked and I wanted to record them."

She signed with Capitol, and her debut LP on that label came out in March 1971, accompanied by her first tour in a number of years. The response was mixed. Her performances were excellent, but her new songs fell short. Critic Richard Cromelin echoed many reviewers when he wrote in the *Los Angeles Times* (July 16, 1971): "Her most glaring defect is her writing. Her tunes are pretty, if forgettable, but her lyrics . . . lack both facility and depth."

After doing several albums for Capitol, Ian signed a new contract in the mid-1970s with Columbia. Her first album on the label, *Stars*, had good spots, but nothing to bring her to creative prominence. Then came *Between the Lines*, an album whose songs in some ways harked back to Janis' early glory years, describing problems and relationships of young lovers. The album included such gems as "When the Party's Over," which recorded the singer's despair, tinged with hope, at the prospects of finding a loving companion, and "At Seventeen," a song that touched on the oft-felt feelings of inadequacy of a teenage girl.

The album and its related singles won a rash of nominations in the 1975 Grammy Awards. Discussing the TV program on which she sang "At Seventeen" and won two awards, including Best Pop Vocal Performance, Female, she noted, "That whole thing was great. I don't know if I'd like to perform again under that much pressure; it's pretty nerve-wracking. I wouldn't mind winning again. It's always nice to win.

"At the time, I figured since I'd been nominated for five Grammies I'd probably win something. Then when we won the engineering award [Best Engineered Song—Non-Classical: Brooks Arthur, Larry Alexander, and Russ Payne, engineers], I figured that was it. Winning another was frosting on the cake."

Janis continued to turn out new albums on Columbia the rest of the 1970s. Most made the charts for a number of months, but none repeated the blockbuster impact of *Between the Lines*. Still, all probably deserved better home exposure than they received, particularly since Ian did not stand pat but continued to experiment in subject matter and approach. This seemed apparent, certainly, to overseas record buyers. Her 1976 LP, *Aftertones*, earned a gold record in Canada and a platinum award in Japan, for example. The single "Love Is Blind" from the album rose to number one in Japan. It stayed there for twelve weeks, the first time that had been achieved by an American solo artist. Good audience response also greeted her extensive debut tour of Europe in 1976.

In the 1977 album, *Miracle Row*, she introduced touches of Latin style rhythms.

"The 'Miracle Row' influences essentially come from New York's Columbus Avenue," she noted. "They're Puerto Rican rather than Latin. I thought it deserved a better reception—oh well, win some, lose some." Again recognition came from other nations. The LP was certified gold in Canada and Holland and platinum in Japan. One result of that rapport was Janis' first Japanese tour. In other activities for 1977, Janis wrote music for the movie *Betrayal*.

In 1978, her album *Janis Ian* presented some of her best writing since *Between the Lines* and won a share of critical praise, though only moderate public support.

In 1979, Columbia issued her LP *Night Rains*, which she coproduced with Ron Frangiapane. The album attested to her tremendous appeal to audiences outside the United States. It was certified gold in England and Canada and reached platinum levels in Holland, Israel, Japan, Australia, Belgium, and South Africa. Her song "Fly Too High" was chosen as the theme song for the Casablanca Filmworks production *Foxes*. During the year she also wrote and recorded the theme song "Here Comes the Night" for the movie version of the Sylvia Plath book *The Bell Jar*.

She had no new releases in 1980, a year mainly occupied in concert tours of England, Europe, and Australia. In May 1981, the two-hour ABC-TV *Special of the Week*, "Freedom," which starred Mare Winningham and Jennifer Warnes, featured six songs written by Janis. Two of those, "Dear Billy" and "Sugar Mountain," were included in her seventh Columbia LP, *Restless Eyes*, which was issued in June 1981.

Based partly on an interview with Irwin Stambler in 1979.

INCREDIBLE STRING BAND, THE: Vocal and instrumental group. Original members, 1965, both born in Glasgow, Scotland, Robin Williamson and Clive Palmer, with Mike Heron, born Glasgow, added soon after. Reformed as a duo of Heron and Williamson in late 1966. Expanded to quartet, start of 1970s, with addition of Rose Simpson and Christina McKechnie. Simpson replaced by Malcolm LeMaistre in 1971; McKechnie by Gerard Dott in 1972.

One of the most innovative folk groups of the 1960s and early 1970s was Scotland's Incredible String Band, whose repertoire is often described as avant garde folk music. Although its various members all had early experience as part of the folk movement in Britain, the music they typically played as a group bore little obvious resemblance to the normally accepted folk music of Scotland, England or the United States Their influences were as diverse as the thirty different instruments its members played, many from remote portions of the globe, incorporating elements of medieval music, Scottish Highland music, American blues, and, in particular, oriental or Arabic music.

The founding members of the group were born and raised in Glasgow, Scotland. The original Incredible String Band was a duo of Robin Williamson and Clive Palmer, considered among Scotland's finest folk musicians in the early 1960s. They started working together in 1965 in Palmer's Incredible Folk Club (hence the name) in Glasgow. Soon after, they added Heron, who, like them, could sing well, play the guitar and a number of other instruments, and write unusual original songs.

By mid-1966, the trio was finding a steadily growing audience in England and had completed its first record releases. Nonetheless, the three friends decided to part company for a while and sought new musical insights through travel, with Clive going as far as Afghanistan and Robin spending several months in Morocco. When the artists reunited, their new material reflected their recent experience, incorporating instruments like the oud, finger cymbals, tamboura, and other instruments of North African and Middle Eastern origins.

Although Palmer contributed material and ideas, he didn't want to return to the concert circuit at the time, so the Incredible String Band reformed as a duo of Heron and Williamson. In November 1966, they made their first concert appearance outside Scotland as a team, sharing a bill with Judy Collins and Tom Paxton at London's Royal Albert Hall. The audience

responded enthusiastically, and word of the duo's talents was brought back to the United States by Judy and Tom, which helped generate interest for the duo's initial concert work in the United States in 1967 at the Newport Folk Festival.

Heron and Williamson were signed by Island Records, which later assigned U.S. distribution rights to their recordings to Elektra Records. The first result was the LP *Incredible String Band,* issued in June 1967. That collection won some attention, but it was only a preliminary to the excitement created by the duo's second LP, *The 5,000 Spirits or the Layers of the Onion.* After its release in 1968, the album made England's top 10; it didn't do nearly as well in the United States, but it did establish the team as a respected part of the folk and pop genres and brought a strong cult following in the States.

Even more impressive was their next LP, *The Hangman's Beautiful Daughter.* The influences in the various tracks ranged even further afield than usual for the team, sometimes embracing themes with Arabic flavor and, at others, such inputs as spirituals and even some Gilbert and Sullivan.

At the start of the 1970s, the group expanded to a quartet with the addition of Rose Simpson (guitars, vocals) and Christina McKechnie (vocals, acoustic guitar, organ, piano), who are simply referred to in album credits as Rose and Licorice. In January 1971, Rose Simpson left and was replaced by Malcolm LeMaistre (bass guitar, hand drums). In late 1972, Licorice left and was replaced by Gerard Dott (clarinet, saxophone, piano, organ, banjo, violin, percussion, xylophone). Dott was an old friend of the original members, having attended the same school as Heron as a boy in Scotland and later was a member of a skiffle group whose roster included Heron and Williamson at one time or another.

The various changes didn't affect the band's capabilities, judging from continued strong response from the band's adherents in the early and mid-1970s. The focus of the music continued to be on Heron and Williamson, who composed most of the songs and demonstrated their instrumental diversity. The group provided

Elektra with new recordings at regular intervals the first part of the 1970s, spawning such LPs as *Wee Tam, The Big Huge, Changing Horses, I Looked Up, U,* and *Relics. Relics* was a two-disc set of some of the band's most notable songs, including tracks from the first three Heron–Williamson sets.

While the Incredible String Band maintained a small but devoted following among U.S. folk and pop fans, their albums never became bestsellers. Elektra gave up distribution in early 1972, and Warner Brothers took over. The first LP on the Warner/Reprise label was *Earthspan* in 1972 followed in 1973 with *No Ruinous Feud.*

By then there were signs that Heron and Williamson were becoming somewhat restless with group work. Heron, for instance, started doing some solo work, in 1970 completing his first solo LP, *Smiling Men and Bad Reputations,* issued by Elektra.

The group may not have threatened the U.S. top-10 album list with its albums, but it remained a concert favorite from the late 1960s to the mid-1970s, with enough drawing power to fill medium-size halls in many major U.S. cities rather than just small folk clubs. Its popularity was even greater at home, where it could pull large crowds to the most prestigious venues. The response to its 1973 British tour included a standing-room-only concert at London's Royal Festival Hall.

As the 1970s went by, both Heron and Williamson did an increasing amount of separate work. In the mid-1970s, they decided to break up the band, at least temporarily. In the late 1970s, Williamson began to turn out a new series of solo recordings.

IVES, BURL: *Singer, guitarist, actor. Born Huntington Township, Jasper County, Illinois, June 14, 1909.*

In the world of music, Burl Ives is considered, first and foremost, one of the most talented folksingers of the twentieth century. And he is more than that. Not only had his recordings of country music done well enough to reach the uppermost levels of the country charts, his recordings also could be found on national pop charts at times. Additionally, he's a compiler of folk

song books and one of the more accomplished actors of his generation.

Burl likes to be regarded for his folk efforts, but he demurs at being described as a classical folk artist. As he told a reporter in 1978, "I've never defined what a folk song is exactly. But now I think I do know what a folksinger is. It has to do with the country, the soil. Now you take Leadbelly—he was a folksinger, born and raised in the country and he sang like it. I was born in the country, on the Illinois prairies, and moved to the big city at age twenty-four. I sing folk songs, but I'm not a complete folksinger. I have a foot in both camps, don't you know."

Still, there's no doubt his upbringing was in the folk tradition. His English-Irish ancestors came to the New World in the 1600s with farming in their blood, as it was for his parents, Frank and Dellie Ives, who were tenant farmers in Illinois. They sometimes sang old-time songs for their son, named Burl Icle Ivanhoe Ives, as did his grandmother, Katie White. His first public performance was before an old soldiers' reunion when he was four. A gifted banjoist, he performed in school shows when he attended Newton High School. But for much of his teens music took a back seat to sports as Burl starred as a fullback on the high school team. In fact, he decided to be a physical education major at Eastern Illinois Teachers College after graduating from high school in 1927, figuring on later becoming a football coach.

But wanderlust gripped him after two years in college, and he left to roam around the United States and Canada, picking up money to keep going from odd jobs or occasional musical efforts. As he drifted across the land, seeing new places and gaining all sorts of experience, he taught himself guitar and picked up new ballads as he went along. After several years he settled down for a time to attend Indiana State Teachers College in Terre Haute, earning some of his tuition singing folk songs on a local station. He dropped out once more to work at various tasks, including a spell as a pro football player, before settling in New York in 1937. Taking vocal lessons at New York University, he also attended Juilliard and concentrated on entering the entertainment field full time.

His first entree was through the theater. After playing summer stock at Rockridge Theater, Carmel, New York, in 1938, he made contacts that brought a small role in Rodgers and Hart's *The Boys from Syracuse*. Roles in other Broadway plays followed, and, in the meantime, he got a foothold in music by appearances at the Village Vanguard. After several guest shots on New York stations, he got his own program on CBS in 1940, where he soon had millions of people singing along on numbers like "Bluetail Fly" and "Foggy Dew." The title song for the show also became something of a nickname for Burl: *The Wayfarin' Stranger*. The program prospered until he entered the Army in 1942. Before he received his discharge in 1944, he performed in Irving Berlin's service musical, *This Is the Army*.

Back in civilian life, he resumed his acting and singing career with a vengeance. Among his credits in the period from 1944 to 1949 were the Donaldson Award for Best Supporting Actor in the 1944–45 Broadway season; a sold-out debut concert in New York's Town Hall in late 1945; his initial movie appearance in the western *Smoky* in 1946; and his initial record releases (1949) on the Decca label, which included three albums (Volumes 1–3) of *Ballads & Folk Songs*. Prior to his signing with Decca he recorded for Columbia, which reissued albums of his material at various times in the 1950s and 1960s.

He was so well known by the late 1940s that he got the opportunity to write his autobiography, titled *Wayfarin' Stranger*, which was published by McGraw-Hill in 1948. Most of his later efforts in the book field involved folk song collections. The first of those, containing 115 songs, came out in 1953. For much of the early 1950s, Ives was in California on acting assignments. In 1954, he returned to Broadway for one of his most acclaimed roles, that of Cap'n Andy in a revival of *Showboat*. The next year he played his most memorable role, that of Big Daddy in Tennessee Williams' *Cat on a Hot Tin Roof*. It was a role he recreated on film for the 1958 movie that also starred Elizabeth Taylor and Paul Newman.

As he told an interviewer in 1978, he didn't consider the role autobiographical. "There's littler of me in it than people might suppose. Fact is, I'm the opposite to the Big Daddy that Tennessee Williams wrote. I'm soft spoken. Don't talk overly much. Don't yell and holler at people."

He stressed the role wasn't written with him in mind. "How it happened, I got into a brawl one night in a saloon in Greenwich Village. Elia Kazan, a great director, saw me put out a couple of hecklers and figures there was some Big Daddy in me, just lyin' dormant. And out it came. People still do call me Big Daddy, but to me, inside, I'm no Big Daddy at all."

Throughout the 1950s he kept up his movie work and folk recordings. Among his movie efforts, a notable high was his 1958 work in *The Big Country*, for which he was awarded an Academy Awards Oscar for Best Supporting Role. His Decca albums of the 1950s included *Folk Songs Dramatic and Humorous, Songs of Ireland, Down to the Sea in Ships*, and *Old Time Varieties* as well as many others. Some of his 1950s Columbia releases included *Sings Songs for All Ages* and *More Folksongs*.

With the onset of the folk boom in the late 1950s and early 1960s, Burl was in more demand than ever for concerts and appearances on radio and TV folk music shows. He also tried his hand at country-flavored material in the early 1960s, and in 1962 hit the top of the country charts with three top-10 singles on Decca; "A Little Bitty Tear," "Call Me Mr. In-Between," and "Funny Way of Laughin'." The last of those earned him a 1962 Grammy Award for Best Country & Western recording.

The song also was the title song for a chart hit LP in 1962, a year in which Decca also issued the LPs *Sunshine in My Soul* and *Songs of the West*. Later in the decade, some of his Decca LPs were *Burl*, issued April 1963; *Singin' Easy* (10/63); *True Love* (7/64); *Pearly Shells* (1/65). Columbia issued the LP *Return of the Warfaring Stranger* in August 1960 and *Wayfaring Stranger* (1/65). At the end of the decade he returned to the label for the album *Softly and Tenderly,* issued in December 1969.

During the 1960s and 1970s, Ives did some film work, returned to Broadway in 1967 for the short-lived drama, *Dr. Cook's Garden,* and amassed a considerable number of credits for TV, including his own series, *O.K. Crackerby,* and the role of lawyer Walter Nichols on *The Bold Ones.* Although his career slowed down in the 1970s, he made occasional guest appearances to sing on network TV programs and was an award presenter on one of the Country Music Association Award telecasts. In the mid- and late-1970s, his familiar countenance also greeted TV viewers in a number of TV commercials.

During that decade, he spent much of his time at sea sailing, his favorite pastime. He also owned a 225-year-old stone house in Ireland. As he said in 1978, "Ireland is the only other country except the States that I feel comfortable in."

J

JACKSON, STONEWALL: *Singer, guitarist, songwriter. Born Tabor City, North Carolina, November 6, 1932.*

"Stonewall" sounds like a nickname but in Stonewall Jackson's case it's his given name. His father named him after the famed Confederate general, though the latter's real name was Thomas Jonathan. Be that as it may, Stonewall lived up to his name by becoming a hard man to move from the hit charts from the late 1950s to the start of the 1970s.

Jackson's early road was not an easy one. His father died when he was two years old, and young Stonewall was brought up in the southern part of Georgia. When he was ten, he traded his five-dollar bike for an old guitar, one of the important steps in his life. Gradually he figured out the fingering for some of the chords and began to play. Before long he was singing some of the songs he heard on the radio and on records. In a few years, he went beyond this and started to make up his own songs. Some of these, such as "Don't Be Angry" and "Black Sheep," later became hits for him.

When he was seventeen, he signed up with the Navy and entered the submarine service. One of his stations was Norfolk, Virginia, where he bought his first good guitar. He played whenever he could and was asked, on several occasions, to entertain the crews. In 1954, he was discharged and headed home to Georgia, determined to make a career in music.

He continued to write songs and began to figure out how to get started in show business. The obvious goal was the country-music capital, Nashville, but he needed a stake. For the next two years he worked on a farm in the summer and logged during the winter. Finally he had enough money saved for the trip to Nashville and headed there in 1956.

He quickly went to the studios of Acuff-Rose Publishing Company to make some sample records (dubs) of his songs. He intended to take these around to stars of the *Grand Ole Opry* in hopes that they would record them. While they were being prepared, Wesley Rose heard them being played and was quick to ask who had done them. Rose called Jackson and said he had arranged an audition with the talent directors. They listened to Jackson and signed him to a long-term contract. Shortly after, Jackson found himself putting his signature to a contract with Columbia Records.

Audiences took to the newcomer right away. Within a short time, he was known to people across the country from his TV appearances. In 1958, he scored his first top-10 hit, "Life to Go." He followed with the 1959 number-one-rated "Waterloo." The song not only became a top country & western hit but made the national pop charts as well. As a result, he was starred three times on Dick Clark's coast-to-coast *American Bandstand* program.

Jackson continued his winning ways in 1960 with "Why I'm Walkin'." In 1962, he had two bestsellers in "A Wound Time Can't Erase" and "Leona." In 1963, he hit with "Old Showboat" and in 1964 with his own composition, "Don't Be Angry," and the number-one best-selling "B.J. the D.J." Jackson's hits also included "Mary Don't You Weep" and "I Washed My Hands in Muddy Waters."

His early LPs on Columbia included his debut album, *Stonewall Jackson,* in 1959: *Sadness in a Song* (1962); *I Love a Song* (1963); *Trouble and Me* (1965); and *Stonewall Jackson's Greatest Hits* (1966). In 1966, he also was represented on Harmony Records with the LP *The Exciting Stonewall Jackson.* In 1967, he scored another top-10 success with "Stamp Out Loneliness." He also turned out a best-selling LP with this title that included such other songs as "Promises and Hearts," "You Can Check on Me," "The Wine Flowed Freely," and "A Man Must Hide to Cry." He scored another chart hit in 1967 with his LP *All's Fair in Love 'n' War* (issued in 1966).

In the late 1960s Stonewall's recording successes tapered off. Though he placed singles on the charts (for example, two in 1968 and three in 1969), none reached the topmost levels. His album output on Columbia remained high into the early 1970s, including such titles as *Stonewall Jackson Country* (1967); *Tribute to Hank Williams* (1969); *Real Thing* (1970); *Stonewall Jackson at the Grand Ole Opry* and *Me and You and a Dog Named Boo* (1971); and *Stonewall Jackson's World* (1972). Though Stonewall kept active on the concert and TV circuit in the 1970s with his band, the Minutemen, for most of the decade he was not affiliated with a major record company.

In early 1981, First Generation Records issued an album of his recordings as part of its new Opry Stars series.

JACKSON, WANDA: *Singer, guitarist, songwriter, band leader (the Party Timers). Born Maud, Oklahoma, October 20, 1937.*

"I was lucky. I made a decision. I chose

a career and I was able to follow through with it. I've been performing since I was thirteen. I didn't have that agonizing, frustrating wait for the right place, the right time like so many performers."

That's the way Wanda Jackson summed up her early years for an interviewer in 1971. She also stressed she was fortunate in other ways, over the years. "My father always went on the road with me, driving, making all the arrangements, handling all the management. And then I married—well, I've never had to go it alone. I don't know that I could have done it myself. My parents actually made so much possible for me. My father, Tom Jackson, he probably could have been a pretty big star in country music. Somehow he just never had the chance. There was the Depression, then I was born. He never got a break, but he did so much for me. And my mother, she made my costumes, gave me encouragement, they really helped."

By the time Wanda was born in the small town of Maud, fifty miles southeast of Oklahoma City, her father earned a living by working at any odd jobs he could find. In his younger years he had played piano with small bands in Oklahoma. In 1941, like many others from the region, he put his family in their old car and headed to California for a better life, bucking a dust storm part of the way. In Los Angeles, he learned the trade of barbering and three months later moved north to Bakersfield. Once settled there, one of his early projects was to save enough money to buy his little daughter a guitar. He gave her the instrument in 1943 and soon spent many of his spare hours teaching her to play. He didn't have to urge her to practice; she loved the instrument. As her mother later recalled, "Wanda wasn't like other children after the guitar came into her life. Our problem was never to get her to practice—it was getting her to stop. She never wanted to quit practicing and as a result, we sometimes missed out on a full night's sleep."

When Wanda was nine, her father encouraged her newfound interest in the piano. He helped her learn to read music and pick out melodies on the keyboard.

Even in those years, Wanda was beginning to make up songs of her own.

When Wanda was twelve, the Jacksons moved to Oklahoma City where Tom got a job selling used cars, a trade he followed many years later. Soon after, Wanda started attending classes at Capitol Hill High School. The school was only two blocks from station KLPR, which ran a weekly talent program. Wanda and her friends began to attend some of the shows until Wanda got up enough nerve to try out herself. She did so well the station gave her a fifteen-minute daily program of her own, quite a plum for a thirteen-year-old. Before long that gave way to a half-hour program that was one of the most popular country shows in Oklahoma City and remained so during most of Wanda's teenage years.

When she was in her junior year in high school, another major break occurred. She was leaving the station after finishing a show when she was called to the phone. A voice on the other end said, "Hello Wanda, this is Hank Thompson." After she recovered from the shock and responded, Hank continued, "I'm calling because I have a song I'd like for you to record with my band—if you're interested."

Thus, almost effortlessly, she was offered the first step to national recognition. She accepted the offer and recorded several songs, including a duet with the lead singer from Thompson's Brazos Valley Boys, Billy Gray, titled "You Can't Have My Love." The song soon became a major national country hit of 1954 on the Decca label, and Wanda was asked to sign with the label as well as join the band on a tour of the Northeast.

However, she demurred at becoming a full-time performer until she finished high school. She returned home, finished her senior year, and headed back onto the tour circuit for the 1955–56 season. The artist she toured with in those years was a young Mississippian, soon to set the world of entertainment on its ear—Elvis Presley.

Meanwhile, Hank Thompson had told one of the best talent agents in the country field, Jim Halsey, about her. Halsey listened to her records, watched her perform, and agreed with Thompson's evaluation. In 1956, Jackson signed with Halsey's agency and he soon arranged for a new recording contract with Capitol Records, an association that was to last into the 1970s. He also set up her debut in one of the Las Vegas night spots, the first of many such Nevada appearances. From the mid-1950s into the early 1970s, Wanda remained a favorite with Vegas audiences, who watched her shows in places like the Golden Nugget, Silver Nugget, and Show Boat. She also was a headliner in Reno hotels over the years as well as country venues in major cities across the United States.

During the late 1950s and throughout the 1960s, she placed many singles and albums on national charts. Though not a prolific writer, she still wrote a number of her greatest hits herself. Some of her songs were written for other artists, an example being "Kicking Our Hearts Around," a major hit for Buck Owens that won her a BMI award and was a top-10 single for Hank Thompson as well. Two of her originals that she turned into top-10 singles in 1961 were "Right or Wrong" and "In the Middle of a Heartache." She actually had written "Right or Wrong" while "in a daydreaming mood" in 1959. She hadn't considered it anything special at the time, but two years later, artists and repertoire executive Ken Nelson of Capitol heard her humming it one day and asked her to record it. She told interviewer Ben Townsend in the mid-1960s, "It likely will become a standard [at the time, versions by various artists had brought total sales to over a million] and to think, I never had intentions of putting it on a record."

Among her other hits of the 1960s were such singles as "Let's Have a Party," "Little Charm Bracelet," "Happy, Happy Birthday," "Just Call Me Lonesome," "Candy Man," "Stupid Cupid," "There's a Party Going On," "Heartbreak Ahead," "Making Believe," "The Box He Came In," and "Fujiyama Mama." The last named became a major hit in Japan and brought large audiences out to hear her when she toured that country. In 1965, she had a major hit in Germany with a single she sang in Dutch called "Santo Domingo." The record edged the Beatles out of the number-one spot on German lists. All of that made her one of the first truly international country stars.

As she recalled, "You know, I've recorded in German, Dutch, and Japanese. I've had top hits in Germany and Japan, and I don't speak any of those languages. I've been told that I shouldn't try to learn them because it might ruin my natural accent and inflection—you know, if I'm trying to translate each word as I sing. I guess what it all comes down to is the feeling— the feeling, the mood of a song is the same no matter what the language."

Wanda married an IBM programmer named Wendall Goodman in October 1961 in Gainsville, Texas, and her new husband took over the management of her career. In the 1960s, besides accompanying Wanda on concert tours all over the world, Wendall also packaged her syndicated TV show called *Music Village.* Backing Wanda in all those efforts was her band, the Party Timers. In the mid-1960s, the band members were Mike Lane of Tyler, Texas, lead singer; Tex Wilburn of Henderson, Texas, lead guitar; Al Flores of Liberal, Kansas, electric bass; and Don Bartlett of Liberal, Kansas, drums.

From the late 1950s into the early 1970s, Capitol released several dozen albums by Wanda, many of which made the country charts. Among those were *Day Dreaming,* issued in September 1958; *Rockin' with Wanda* (1960); *Right or Wrong* (12/61); *Lovin' Country Style* (6/62); *Wonderful Wanda* (10/62); *Love Me Forever* (7/61); *Two Sides of Wanda* (3/64), a major hit and nominee for a 1964 Grammy for best country LP; *Blues* (6/65); *Wanda Jackson Sings* (2/66); *Salutes the Country Music Hall of Fame* (11/66); *You're Always Here* (11/67); *Happy Side* (1968); *In Person* (12/69); *The Many Moods of Wanda Jackson* (1969); and, in the early 1970s, *Country!, Woman Lives for Love, I've Gotta Sing,* and *I Wouldn't Want You Any Other Way.* Besides all those releases on Capitol, she had a few on the Hilltop label, including *Leave My Baby Alone* and *We'll Sing in the Sunshine.*

Though she spent major parts of most years on the road, Jackson and her husband still found time for family life. Home was in Oklahoma City, where they raised a son and a daughter in the 1960s and 1970s. From the mid-1970s on, Wanda shifted much of her attention to religious activities, including taking part as a performer in a number of evangelical tours. In the late 1970s she recorded on the Word label.

JAE, JANA: *Fiddle player. Born western United States, circa 1942.*

Although by the 1970s country fans had become accustomed to the idea that a guitar virtuoso like Chet Atkins or a banjo great like Roy Clark could play anything from country to classics to good effect, the fiddle somehow seemed different. But Jana Jae showed that whether you called it a fiddle or a violin, she could hold her own with country groups, bluegrass groups, symphony orchestras, or even jazz combos.

In Jana's case, from her earliest years she drew on family influences embracing both country and classical sides of the musical spectrum. Her maternal grandfather played country fiddle on his Colorado farm and her parents were classical violinists. It was while her mother and father were studying violin at New York's Juilliard School of Music that she also began to play.

As she told John Northland for an article in *Country Music* magazine (May 1980, pp. 43–44), "I started playing when I was 2½ years old. Mother always worked with me during the day, she always played right with me, and that made it fun. But I was scared of my dad because he would come in and be very strict. I remember bursting into tears in our New York City apartment—I must have been about four—because I didn't have 'Mary Had a Little Lamb' down, and I knew he was gonna be real mad at me. But anyway, they really did work with me. I'm sure it was good that it was demanding. . . ."

That same year, when the family went to Colorado on vacation, her grandfather started showing her how he did country and square dance music. Later, after her parents divorced, her mother took her to live at Jana's grandparents' house, where she learned more and more country & western material to go with her classical repertoire. She told Northland, "Grandpa didn't play for a living, but he would just play every night at home, every single night. He insisted on playing in the kitchen, because that's where the acoustics were best, and grandma played with him on a piano right outside the kitchen."

As Jana grew up, she continued to work on both sides of her musical heritage. In her teens, after her mother married again and settled in Fruitland, Idaho, she played in high school orchestras and added to her classical knowledge at summer music camps in Puerto Rico and in Michigan. After graduating from high school, she was a classical music major at a woman's college in Denver and also spent a year in Vienna. All the while, she played country music for pleasure in her spare time, sometimes joining friends and classmates in informal groups.

Her main goal at the time was to become a music teacher. Soon after finishing her college studies, she married another teaching hopeful and moved with him to Redding in northern California. They both found teaching jobs, though Jana took time out to start a family. (She had three children in the 1967–70 time period, sons Chris and Matt and daughter Katy.) A few years after Katy's birth, she and her husband separated.

By then she already was giving some thought to a performing career. She told Northland, "I knew I didn't want to teach school forever and I loved playing. It just made sense for me to play. I started working in a bluegrass band that played in an old hotel outside Redding. Dentists, doctors, hippies, everybody in the world came out there. It was a little ghost town sort of thing, real quaint. We had such good success that we stayed together [in 1974]. . . . And all that time, I was really enjoying the bluegrass, but not making enough money to support myself and the kids."

During those years, Jae sometimes performed in places other than Redding. In

particular, she traveled to the National Fiddling Championships in Weiser, Idaho, during the summer and demonstrated her fiddling skills. The result was a victory for her in the women's division in both 1973 and 1974.

A major turning point occurred during 1974 when Buck Owens and his group were in the Redding area for a show. Buck heard Jana play and was impressed enough to ask her to sit in on his concert and join Buckaroos fiddler Don Rich in doing "Orange Blossom Special." Soon after that, Rich was killed in an auto accident, a tragedy that caused Owens to cut back on personal appearances for a time.

When he began reorganizing the band in early 1975, he remembered Jana and asked her to join his band. She agreed and, from then through part of 1977, she toured throughout the United States and abroad with the Owens' show. "It felt like I'd been dropped into the middle of a new world, but musically it was okay. I was getting real good crowd reactions and I knew Buck was pleased. I was really intrigued by the whole thing, and I was learning all the time, just by watching what was going on around me."

However, the arrangement broke up through a strange set of events. When she worked up an instrumental album of Owens' songs, Jana ran into conflict with his organization, which wanted her to arrange any recording contract through them. When she objected, she was fired. Still under contract to the Owens show, she was unable to perform elsewhere. After five months, she sought out Owens to try to resolve matters. The odd result of that was that they decided to get married. In rapid succession came two efforts at annulment, first by Buck, then Jana, a short reconciliation and, finally, a divorce.

Despite the wild proceedings, some measure of career rapport evolved, with Jae later performing again on the Owens-Roy Clark *Hee Haw* TV program. She also embarked on a solo career in the late 1970s, headlining her own act on the country-music circuit with occasional side trips to take part in both country and jazz festivals, the latter including performances at the Montreux Jazz Festival in Switzerland. In reordering her life at the end of the 1970s, she moved her family from the West Coast to a new home in Tulsa, Oklahoma.

JAMES, SONNY: *Singer, guitarist, songwriter. Born Hackleburg, Alabama, May 1, 1929.*

When somebody asked performer Hugh X. Lewis in 1976 whether he'd heard Sonny James' Columbia album set, *200 Years of Country Music* (a cavalcade of the nation's folk and country music from its birth to modern times), Lewis quipped, "No, I didn't realize he had been in the business that long." An observer might have responded that Sonny hadn't; it just seemed like it. From the standpoint of artistic longevity, "The Southern Gentleman" maintained a position as a major country star from the 1950s into the 1980s, ranking in the top 10 of best-selling album artists for much of that time.

Sonny, whose real name was Jimmie Loden, was born and raised in Hackleburg, Alabama. However, even as a small child he spent a lot of time on the road. Born into a show business family that toured throughout the South, he was only four years old when he made his stage debut with his parents and sister Thelma in a folk contest in Birmingham, Alabama. They won first prize before an audience that included singer Kate Smith, who, legend has it, gave little Sonny a silver dollar and predicted a great future career in the entertainment field. Before many more years had passed, he could play the guitar and sing occasional solos with the troupe. By the time he was in his teens, he had more hours of performing experience behind him than many artists in their twenties. He already had performed on a number of country radio shows before he reached high-school age.

In the early 1950s, his career was interrupted by fifteen months of military service during the Korean War. He kept his performing skills polished by singing before other servicemen or, on occasion, before Korean orphans. He had quite a few hours to kill when he was off duty and he put some of the time to good advantage by writing some original songs.

After his discharge in 1952, he returned to the United States fair and country nightclub circuit and began to look for ways to further his career. During his musical travels, he had become friends with Chet Atkins and visited Chet in Nashville for some advice. Chet introduced him to Capitol Records' producer Ken Nelson, for whom Sonny played some of his material. Nelson liked James' style as well as his compositions and recommended that Capitol sign him. As often happened with Nelson finds, it was the beginning of a long and rewarding relationship.

Sonny didn't achieve overnight stardom. His initial releases on Capitol had only moderate success, at best. In 1957, he scored his first big hit with his top-10 pop recording of "First Date, First Kiss, First Love." He followed with an even bigger success, his now classic "Young Love," which rose to number one on the pop charts and made the country top 10 as well. In 1962, Dot turned out a hit LP of Sonny's, also titled *First Love*. For a while, Sonny spent more time starring in pop and rock concerts than in the country field.

Then things slowed down for several years. He toured widely and remained a top favorite with audiences in the late 1950s and early 1960s, but didn't crack either the pop or country top 10 until the mid-1960s. By then he had settled down to a career as a country artist. And, from the mid-1960s on, he was a top country star with one release after another moving onto top-chart levels.

One of his first achievements in that period was a song he coauthored with Bob Tubert, "You're the Only World I Know." The song reached number one on country lists and remained there for weeks. Since then it has been recognized as a country standard and has been recorded by many other artists. Sonny also had a second hit, in 1964, his top-10 version of Felice and Boudleaux Bryant's "Baltimore."

In 1965, Sonny again had a number-one hit, "Behind the Tear," and a top-10 success in "I'll Keep Holding On." The following year provided still another number-one song, "Take Good Care of Her," and the top-10 hit, "True Love's a Blessing" (co-written with Carole Smith). In 1967, he added such number-one ranked singles as "I'll Never Find Another You" and "Need You." His other hits of those years included "The Minute You're Gone" and "Room in Your Heart." In 1968, he had one of the biggest country singles of the year, "A World of Our Own," and reached top-chart levels with "Heaven Says Hello." In 1969, he had the number-one hit "Only the Lonely." His other number-one singles of the late 1960s included "Running Bear" and "Since I Met You Baby." He started the 1970s with another number-one hit, "It's Just a Matter of Time."

Sonny duplicated his singles success with a number of album hits on Capitol. These included *The Minute You're Gone* (1/64), *You're the Only World I Know* (1/65), *Behind the Tear* (12/65), *True Love's a Blessing* (6/66), *Till the Last Leaf* (8/66), *Best of Sonny James* (11/66), *I'll Never Find Another You* (1967), *World of Our Own* (1968), *Best of Sonny James, Volume 2* (1/69), *Close-Up* (two discs, 8/69), and *Astrodome Presents Sonny James in Person* (10/69). Other LPs of the late 1960s–early 1970s period were *Bright Lights, Big City, Empty Arms, Here Comes Honey Again, My Love/Don't Keep Me Hangin On, #1,* and the double album *You're the Only World/I'll Never Find Another You.* Hilltop Records also issued one of his collections, titled *Timberline.*

From the late 1950s through the 1970s, Sonny's stage appearances took him to all fifty states several times over and to many other nations, backed by his own band, the Southern Gentlemen. During those years, he was featured on a wide variety of TV and radio shows, including a number of guest spots on the *Grand Ole Opry* plus such other shows as *The Jimmy Dean Show, The Ed Sullivan Show, Bob Hope, Tennessee Ernie Ford, The Pat Boone Chevy Showroom, Star Route, Music Scene,* and several 1970s appearances on *Hee Haw.*

During the 1960s, Sonny took part in several motion pictures. These included *Second Fiddle to a Steel Guitar, Las Vegas Hillbillies* (with Jayne Mansfield), and the 1967 *Hillbilly in a Haunted House,* which starred Basil Rathbone and Lon Chaney.

Sonny gathered a number of honors and awards, particularly in the 1960s. In the 1965 National Academy of Recording Arts and Sciences voting, he had three Grammy nominations. He won the *Record World* magazine Record of the Year Award in 1965. In 1966, he won the Number One Artist rating from *Record World,* and *Billboard* ranked him in the top five country artists (male) for the year while *Cash Box* ranked him number three for 1966. He finished high in those polls the next few years and, in 1969, *Billboard's* survey once again named him as number one artist.

Sonny's activities during the 1970s, besides his normal performing and recording routine, extended to music publishing and producing records of other artists. In that role, he supervised preparation of material for three albums by Marie Osmond, including the hit single "Paper Roses."

He continued to extend his list of chart-hit singles from the start of the 1970s to the end of the decade. His early 1970s successes on Capitol included "Endlessly," number one for weeks at the end of 1970, the top-10 "Only Love Can Break a Heart" in early 1972, the number-one ranked "When the Snow Is on the Roses" in September 1972, and "Surprise, Surprise" in early 1974. By the start of 1974, Sonny's long association with Capitol had ended and he had signed with Columbia Records. In short order he had a bestseller, "Is It Wrong (For Loving You)," number one on the country lists in May 1974. In 1975, he had such top-10 winners as "A Little Bit South of Saskatoon" (co-written by Sonny and Carole Smith), "Little Band of Gold," and "What in the World's Come Over You?" In mid-1976, he had the top-10 single "When Something Is Wrong with My Baby" and, in the fall, the equally successful "Come on In" (co-written by Sonny and Carole Smith). In mid-1977, his remake of the old Jimmie Rodgers classic "In the Jailhouse Now" rose to number fifteen and he also had a hit later in the year with "Caribbean." He closed out 1978 with the charted single "Building Memories" on Columbia, which made top-chart levels in early 1979.

During 1979, Sonny made another label change, leaving Columbia for Monument. His first charted single on that label was "Hold What You've Got," which was in the top 40 in the spring of 1979.

JANSCH, BERT: *Singer, guitarist, songwriter. Born Glasgow, Scotland, November 3, 1943.*

Though not as well known as the Beatles, Bert Jansch ranks with them as one of the foremost products of the English pop-music scene in the 1960s. As a writer and performer, he influenced the development of folk-rock and "modern" folk at home and abroad, starting in the mid-1960s and continuing into the early 1980s.

He was born in Glasgow but grew up in Edinburgh; his father was Austrian and his mother Scottish. Recalling his early years to Mark Humphrey (*Frets*, March 1980, pp. 18–23), he said, "When I was a kid, the first things I heard were people like Elvis Presley and Little Richard. That was very early. My interest in guitar started then. I did have piano lessons when I was about seven; they went on for six months. My mother couldn't afford to keep them up, which is why I didn't continue them. I actually tried to make guitars when I was nine or ten; in fact, the second one I tried to make was even playable, and I learned to chord a D on it. . . . But it wasn't until after I left school that I started to earn enough money to buy a guitar." (Among other things, he worked for a while as a gardener.)

His departure from school occurred when he was fifteen, a period when he also began hanging around a local folk club called the Halwff (Scottish for "meeting place"). For a while, he learned guitar from two of the coowners, Jill Doyle and Archie Fisher. He told Humphrey, "About six months later, Jill and Archie left the club, and there was no one to continue with the lessons. Being the most advanced player there, I ended up giving the guitar lessons myself. I never even contemplated singing.

They were usually Woodie Guthrie songs, with some Big Bill Broonzy, Brownie McGhee and Leadbelly. It was some time after that that I plucked up enough courage to actually sing in front of an audience. I got into performing because there was a pub down the road that used to have folk music and—being very poor at the time, and not earning enough money from the guitar lessons—I found that if I got up and did two or three numbers, everybody would buy me a beer."

In his late teens, influenced by folk music friends Clive Palmer and Robin Williamson (founders of the Incredible String Band), Bert finally branched out beyond Edinburgh, starting with a journey to Morocco. After returning home, for a while he went back and forth between London and Scotland, increasing his contacts in the folk field and adding to his performing credits at folk clubs in both places. By then he already was writing original material. He recalled writing his first song, "Green Are Your Eyes," when he was about seventeen.

By the mid-1960s, he had a growing reputation as one of England's best young folk artists. In 1965, his first solo album, *Bert Jansch,* came out (available in the 1980s on Transatlantic Records of London), followed soon after by his second LP, *Jack Orion.* During that period, Jansch was rooming with another young folk musician, John Renbourn, and they made an album together released by Transatlantic in the mid-1960s under the title *Bert and John.* For a time, the two ran their own folk club in London's Soho district, called the Scot's Hoose. Among those who frequented or performed at the club were friends and associates like Jacqui McShee and Danny Thompson, who soon were to join Bert and John in the folk-rock group Pentangle.

Jansch and Renbourn founded Pentangle in 1967, and over the next half dozen years the group achieved considerable success as a recording and performing group on both sides of the Atlantic. (See separate Pentangle entry). The band still was held in high regard around the world when it disbanded in 1973. The reason for this step,

Jansch told Humphrey, was essentially a desire for new creative opportunities. "We'd all had enough by then. We had gone around the world about five times; it was literally like three-month tours at a stretch; then a week off and another two-month tour somewhere else. Also, the manager at that time had a policy of sending us out by ourselves to do two-hour shows. We never met any other musicians, because there was nobody else on the bill. It became so insular and you do need to play with other people and meet other people."

In the mid-1970s, Bert turned out more solo recordings, such as the *Rare Conundrum* LP issued on Kicking Mule Records of Berkeley, California, and toured England and the Continent with various backing musicians. Preparing for one tour of Scandinavia, he found himself in need of a new fiddler and on the advice of a member of the road crew contacted Martin Jenkins. The artistic rapport proved excellent, and the new duo of Jansch and Jenkins became a featured act on the concert circuit from the late 1970s into the early 1980s. Adding a third member, bassist Nigel Smith, they formed the group Conundrum.

Jenkins, born in London in 1946, brought skills not only as fiddler but also on guitar, mandolin, and mando-cello. In his teens, he had a rock band, but later became interested in folk music, which held his attention in the mid-1960s. For some years he was a central figure in a band called Dando-Shaft that finally broke up in 1972. In the mid-1970s, he was part of a folk-rock band from Newcastle, England, called Hedgehog Pie. It was just after that group broke up that he got the invitation from Jansch that led to their collaboration in the late 1970s. Among the projects Jansch, Jenkins, and Nigel Smith worked on at the start of the 1980s was a joint effort between Conundrum and the amateur Cambridge Symphony Orchestra. Jenkins also supported Jansch on the instrumental album *Avocet.*

In the early 1980s, Jansch had a number of albums still in print on the Transatlantic label. Besides a number of Pentangle col-

lections and the solo LPs noted earlier, he was represented on Transatlantic by such solo releases as *It Don't Bother Me, Nicola, Birthday Blues,* and *Rosemary Lane.* On U.S.-based labels, Vanguard offered some of his work with John Renbourn on an album titled *Stepping Stones,* while Kicking Mule, besides *A Rare Conundrum,* also had the LP *The Best of Burt Jansch* in its active catalogue.

JENNINGS, WAYLON: *Singer, guitarist, songwriter, band leader (the Waylors). Born Littlefield, Texas, June 15, 1937.*

In the 1970s there was what amounted to a revolution in country music. In what was called "progressive country" by some and "outlaw music" by others, a new dimension was added to the field based on songs that more closely reflected the mores and trends of an urbanized, industrialized society. The leaders of the "revolt"—though they didn't consciously set about to organize a new movement—were two tough, talented Texans, Willie Nelson and Waylon Jennings. Though their careers developed in different ways, appropriately the two became close friends and joined forces for some of the pivotal developments that helped make the "new country" music a force whose impact extended far beyond conventional country & western audiences.

Though both Jennings and Nelson were bona fide superstars by the end of the 1970s, it had taken many years for them to achieve those reputations. Jennings' potential for stardom was agreed upon by many people in the country-music industry when his initial RCA recordings came out in the mid-1960s. But for close to a decade he did not fulfill those predictions and seemed to almost fight the idea. He failed to show up for interviews, was hard to pin down on tour plans, and, at least in the view of promotion people trying to expose his name or new record for press or radio coverage, was unpredictable and erratic. Added to that was the fact that Waylon wrote or selected songs—and performed them—as he pleased without bending to the "establishment" ways of the Nashville hierarchy. In time, though, both audiences and the industry came around to his way of thinking and Jennings became more than a favorite; he became a legend.

Jennings grew up in Littlefield, Texas, where much of the population enjoyed country & western music. As a child, he showed a deep interest in music and already had begun to learn guitar chords before he was in his teens. At twelve, he began hosting his own disc jockey show on a home-town station, emphasizing pop records rather than country discs. Throughout his teens he spun records and occasionally sang for local audiences. He also hosted local talent shows and made personal appearances in towns in his part of Texas. By the time he was seventeen, he was paying more attention to country & western material and he became a DJ on a country-music radio program.

By the time he moved to Lubbock, Texas, in 1958, to continue his DJ career in a more populous area, he had become a fan of Elvis Presley and the new rock movement. In Lubbock, he became acquainted with many of the young Southwest musicians eager to follow in Elvis' footsteps, sometimes playing backup guitar in local bands. Buddy Holly, already on the way to national stardom, liked Waylon's work and asked him to join his band as electric bass player. For the rest of 1958 and the beginning of 1959, Jennings toured with Holly. He was part of Holly's troupe the fateful day in early February 1959 when the group was to split up en route to an engagement, part taking a private plane, part going by bus. Jennings was supposed to take the plane, but he gave up his seat as a favor to another artist, J. P. Richardson (The Big Bopper). On February 3, 1959, the plane crashed in a field near Fargo, North Dakota, killing all aboard.

Saddened and shaken, Jennings returned to Lubbock and resumed his career as a DJ and part-time musician. The Holly mystique contributed to an enhanced respect and helped to some extent in his efforts to upgrade his performing status. One result was that he began to make records for small companies in the region. As time went by, he thought of himself more as a performer and less as a DJ.

In the early 1960s, Jennings went west,

settling in Phoenix, Arizona. He formed his own band, called the Waylors—still his group's name at the start of the 1980s—and played a combination of country & western and rock 'n' roll, a blend that at the time sounded discordant to many musicians in both fields. But audiences seemed to like it, at least in Phoenix. The group won lengthy engagements at nightclubs in Phoenix and neighboring Scottsdale and Tempe. In a short period of time Waylon and the Waylors were being featured in one of the largest nightclubs in the region, J.D.'s in Phoenix.

It was there that Bobby Bare, one of RCA Records' rising lights at the time, caught the show in 1964 and immediately sent word back to Chet Atkins in Nashville about Jennings' striking vocal sound. Atkins followed up, sought out Waylon, and signed him to an RCA contract in 1965. The first three recording sessions produced the singles "That's the Chance I'll Have to Take," "Stop the World and Let Me Off," and "Anita You're Dreaming," discs that made respectable showings on the charts and marked Jennings with country DJs as a promising new artist.

With his career seemingly on the way to the heights, Waylon moved to Nashville in April 1966. Once there, he and Johnny Cash, separated from his first wife and not yet married to June Carter, became roommates. As might be expected, some wild escapades resulted, but also some creative rapport that strengthened the innate individualism of both parties. Waylon, though he was a guest on the Opry in the mid-1960s and thrilled audiences in the Ryman Auditorium and in radioland with his gruff, powerful voice, was not the kind of artist most of the Nashville powers of the day were comfortable with. He didn't shrink from singing rock numbers if they pleased him—his version of the Beatles' "Norwegian Wood" was a mild hit in the mid-1960s—and he wore faded jeans and nondescript sports shirts rather than flamboyant rhinestone-studded pseudo-cowboy suits. If the country establishment looked askance at Waylon, the feeling was mutual, as he later took note of in compositions like "Nashville Bum."

He toured widely in the mid-1960s and

found strong support from segments of local audiences across the United States. He also played engagements in many parts of Canada and even performed in Mexico. During those years, besides playing the *Opry* several times, he guested on a number of TV shows, including ABC-TVs *Anatomy of Pop*, the *Bobby Lord Show*, *American Swing Around*, and Carl Smith's *Country Music Hall*. He also found time to appear in a movie, *Nashville Rebel*.

And he continued to turn out a steady flow of recordings. His singles of the period included "Dark Side of Fame," "Where I Went Wrong," "Look into My Tear Drops," "Norwegian Wood," "I Wonder Just Where I Went Wrong," "Time to Bum Again," and "That's What You Get for Loving Me," the last named a top-10 hit in 1966. He had reasonably good years in 1967 and 1968, making upper-chart levels in 1967 with the singles "Mental Revenge" and "Green River" and in 1968 with "Walk on Out of My Mind," "Only Daddy That'll Walk the Line," and a duet with Anita Carter, "I Got You." His debut album, *Waylon Jennings*, came out in April 1966 on RCA and was followed by titles like *Leavin' Town* (11/66), *Nashville Rebel* (1/67), *Ol' Harlan* (4/67), *Love of the Common People* (9/67), *One and Only* (12/67), *Country Folk* (with the Kimberleys, 9/69); and *Best of Waylon Jennings* (7/70). His work with the Kimberleys brought a 1969 Grammy Award for Best Country Performance by a Duo or Group for "MacArthur Park."

By the start of the 1970s, though, despite those and other credits, Waylon was not considered a first-rank star by most country industry people. He was still essentially a cult figure with an enthusiastic, but limited, following. His recordings often made the charts, but rarely the highest level and none had reached number one. (It was ironic that in mid-1975, when Jennings was on the verge of reaching superstar status, his wife, Jessi Colter, came out with her first single on Capitol, which rose to number one on country charts).

Doggedly, Waylon went on his own way and, in fact, went even further in what was to be known as "modern country" with his own writings and with presentation of the

work of avant garde country writers like Kris Kristofferson, Billy Joe Shaver, and Mickey Newbury. His new repertoire of material began to take shape in his *Singer of Sad Songs* LP (12/70) and developed rapidly in such follow-ups as *The Taker/Tulsa* (1971), *Cedartown, Georgia* (9/71), *Good Hearted Woman* (3/72), which first presented that Willie and Waylon classic title song, "Ladies Love Outlaws" (10/72), *Lonesome, On'ry and Mean* (1973), and *Honky Tonk Heroes* (1973). (All the songs but one on *Honky Tonk Heroes* were written by Billy Joe Shaver.) Some of those contained top-20 singles hits, such as "The Taker," in the top 15 in late 1970, and "You Ask Me To" (co-written by Jennings and Shaver) in the top 15 in late 1973, early 1974.

More important, his new material found favor with young fans both in the country and pop fields. Waylon was received with riotous applause and cheers at a broad spectrum of venues, such as The Bottom Line and Max's Kansas City in New York; a set presented in a Grateful Dead concert show at San Francisco's Kezar Stadium in May 1973 (where the 20,000 fans gave him a standing ovation); SRO concerts at Los Angeles' Troubadour in 1973 and 1974; a set at Willie Nelson's Dripping Springs Festival in Texas on July 4; and many other country and pop nightspots around the United States.

The indications continued to multiply that Jennings' refusal to compromise his musical principles was beginning to bear fruit. Sales of his albums, which had not been his strong point previously, began to rise. His early 1974 release, *This Time*, rose to upper country album chart levels in the spring and stayed there for many weeks. His *Ramblin' Man* LP (issued in late 1974) and *Dreaming My Dreams*—one of his finest collections (issued in the summer of 1975)—made the top 10. And then came *Wanted: The Outlaws* (issued at the start of 1976), one of the landmark albums in the entire pop/country field of the 1970s.

The LP was a combination of eleven previously released recordings by Waylon, Willie Nelson, Tompall Glaser, and Jessi Colter. (Jessi had married Waylon in 1974.) The album became a runaway hit, rising into the country top 10 in February

1976 and moving into the number-one position for many weeks. The LP also became a top-10 hit on the pop charts as well. It remained on country charts for years (occasionally slipping out of the top 50 only to return again), selling several million copies to become the all-time best-selling country album.

An RCA official speculated about the reasons to Bob Hilburn of the *Los Angeles Times* (April 6, 1976): "The only thing I can figure is there were a lot of people curious about all they had read or heard about the so-called 'outlaws' of country music—particularly Waylon and Willie—and they decided to take a chance on the package rather than buy a whole album by one of the artists. The important thing in this album is that it may then encourage people to go back into some of these artists' earlier works."

It did do that, but far more important, it focused wide attention on the artists' new work and consolidated the respect already building for Waylon. (Just before *The Outlaws* started to become a hit, Waylon was voted Best Male Vocalist for 1975 by the members of the Country Music Association.) Waylon's new albums almost routinely rose to top-chart levels. Thus *Mackintosh & T.M.* (issued early 1976) made the top 20, followed by two straight number-one solo album releases, *Are You Ready for the Country*, number one in September 1976, and *Ol' Waylon*, number one in mid-1977. Both albums held the number-one spot for a number of weeks each.

Waylon wasn't doing badly on singles charts either in the mid-1970s. He had a hit in early summer 1974 with his song "This Time" and made the top 10 in 1975 with "Rainy Day Woman/Help the Cowboy Sing the Blues"; "Dreaming My Dreams with You," and "Are You Sure Hank Done It This Way/Bob Wills Is Still the King" (the latter three Jennings compositions). In early 1976, his duet with Willie, "Good Hearted Woman" made number one and was followed by such 1976 top-10 hit singles as "Can't You See" and a duet with Jessi Colter, "Suspicious Minds."

At the start of 1978, RCA released the LP *Waylon & Willie,* arguably one of the best releases of 1978 and the 1970s as a whole. The album was number one on country charts for weeks and made the national pop charts top 10 in the United States and many other countries. Well over a year later, the album was still on the charts. Part of the time, it was joined on the charts by Waylon's solo LP, *I've Always Been Crazy,* issued in the fall of 1978 and number one from November into December. During much of 1979, a new *Greatest Hits* album of Waylon's was on the charts and was in the number-two spot in December. In late 1979, Waylon's next LP, *What Goes Around Comes Around,* was issued by RCA and already was number two on country charts in January 1980.

Jennings' name rarely was absent from singles lists either from the late 1970s into the 1980s. In the summer of 1977, he had the top-10 hit "Luckenbach, Texas" and late in the year had a major hit with "The Wurlitzer Prize," combining material by B. Emmons and Chips Moman with some by Jennings. In mid-1978 he had a number-one hit with Johnny Cash, "There Ain't No Good Chain Gang." That record was issued on Cash's Columbia label. In September 1978, he had a number-one single with his composition "I've Always Been Crazy." At year end, he had a single (of two of his songs) moving up from the number-five spot, "Don't You Think This Outlaw Bit's Done Got Out of Hand/Girl I Can Tell." His 1979 chart hits included "Amanda," "Come with Me," and another Johnny Cash duet (issued on Columbia), "I Wish I Was Crazy Again." He also helped Hank Williams, Jr., write and record a tribute to Hank's legendary father.

He began 1980 with another best-selling single, "I Ain't Living Long Like This" (written by Rodney Crowell) that reached number one in March. His other hit singles in 1980 were "Clyde," "Come with Me" and "Theme from the Dukes of Hazzard." Waylon's rendition of the last named song, which he wrote, always opened that hit TV comedy series. His charted albums in 1980, three of which had been on the lists for one to two years or more, were *What Goes Around Comes*

Around, Greatest Hits, Wanted: The Outlaws, and *Music Man.* In early 1981 he teamed with wife Jessi for the hit single "Storms Never Last," written by her. Late in the year, another of his compositions, "Shine," was his vehicle for another best-selling release.

By the start of the 1980s, Jennings had made his mark not just on country but on pop music as well and seemed likely to have an influence on generations of writers and performers to come. And he had done it on his own terms, as is generally true for any pioneering artist. He expressed his pleasure at the breakthroughs of the 1970s to Bob Hilburn of the *Los Angeles Times* in this way, "There has been a big change in country music. At one time, it was considered too far out if you had a minor chord in a song. We've moved a long way since then." And he summarized his response to purists in another interview: "Instruments don't make country. We're entitled to a heavy rock beat if it complemented our songs. Or if we want to use a kazoo played through a sewer pipe, that's all right, too. Why should we lock ourselves in?"

JIM & JESSE: *Vocal and instrumental brother act, band leaders (the Virginia Boys). Both born Coeburn, Virginia; Jim McReynolds, February 13, 1927; Jesse McReynolds, July 9, 1929.*

For much of its history, bluegrass has tended to command the attention of an enthusiastic but relatively small segment of the music public, hence the descriptor bluegrass underground. The McReynolds brothers, Jim and Jesse, remaining true to their hill-country roots, were part of the underground movement in its early stages and remained stalwarts through the boom times of the early and mid-1960s, the "recession" of the late 1960s and early 1970s, and the bluegrass revival of the mid- and late-1970s. The brothers and their group remained favorites of purists, who applauded the fact that their instrumental work always was acoustic, but the McReynoldses always moved with the times and their repertoire ranged from classic mountain ballads to bluegrass versions of all manner of modern pop music.

The brothers had been brought up in the bluegrass-country tradition. Their mother and father were talented musicians and often played for dances and get-togethers in their home in Virginia's Clinch Mountain region. Their grandfather was one of the best fiddlers in southwestern Virginia and made some early recordings for RCA Victor.

The boys learned to play stringed instruments in their early days on the family farm. When they reached their teens they began to sing at local gatherings, with Jesse playing mandolin and Jim the guitar. They made their radio debut in 1947 on station WNVA, Norton, Virginia, where they remained until 1952, when they moved to station WVLK, Lexington, Kentucky. They had made some records for Kentucky Records at the start of the 1950s, which helped bring a contract from Capitol Records in 1952.

With new recordings coming out on a major label and a growing reputation with country fans in general and bluegrass adherents in particular, the outlook seemed quite promising. However, the brothers suffered a dislocation when Jesse was called into service during the Korean War. He served for two years, including a year in Korea. While overseas, he met Charlie Louvin, and the two performed together for the troops in Korea.

After Jesse was discharged in 1954, the brothers set about making up for lost time. They became regulars on the *Tennessee Barn Dance* on station WNOX, Knoxville, and also were featured on CBS's *Saturday Night Country Style.* The following year they joined the *Swanee River Jamboree,* Live Oak, Florida, and also had a daily show on station WNER in Live Oak. In 1957, they moved again, this time to the *Lowndes County Jamboree* in Valdosta, Georgia, which remained home for many years. Their Virginia Boys, at the time, were Alfred Donald "Don" McHan, Robert Clark "Bobby" Thompson, and fiddling great Vassar Clements.

Because of the association of bluegrass with folk music, the boom times in the folk field in the late 1950s and early 1960s brought Jim & Jesse increasingly into the national spotlight. They were featured in a growing number of major folk festivals and headlined on their own on the folk club and college concert circuit. In 1963 they made their first appearance at the Newport Folk Festival in Rhode Island and returned again in 1966.

In 1962 the group changed record labels and signed with Columbia/Epic. Their debut on Epic, *Jim & Jesse*, was issued in April 1963. This was followed by a series of LPs over the years that included *Bluegrass* (11/63); *Country Church* (11/64), *Y'All Come* (6/65); *Berry Pickin in the Country*, a collection of bluegrass versions of Chuck Berry R&B/rock songs (1/66); *Sing unto Him* (10/66); *Diesel on My Tail* (8/67); *Sainting the Louvin Brothers* (7/69); *We Like Trains* (3/70). In the early 1970s, they had some releases on Capitol, such as *Freight Train* (4/71) and *20 Country Classics.*

In 1964, Jim & Jesse and the Virginia Boys were asked to become cast regulars on the *Grand Ole Opry* (they had been guests a few times before). This prompted a move to Nashville and the brothers and their families (the boys married sisters) settled on the Double JJ Ranch in Gallatin, Tennessee. Their 1965 credits included a guest spot on the *American Sing Along* TV show and their first appearance on a TV version of the *Opry* (taped in November 1965, but not shown nationally until January 1966). The group later appeared on other *Opry* TV programs, most presented on PBS, in the late 1960s and in the 1970s.

In the mid-1960s, Jim & Jesse had one of their most productive periods in terms of chart hits. They hit the singles lists with such records as "Memphis" and "Johnny B. Goode" in 1965, the top-10 "Diesel on My Tail" in 1966, and "Thunder Road" and "Tijuana Taxi" in 1967.

In the late 1960s, the brothers worked on their own syndicated TV series, *Country Music Carousel*. In the early 1970s, they started turning out a second syndicated TV series, *The Jim & Jesse Show."* Although bluegrass record sales were shrinking, there was no lack of opportunities in the live performance field. The duo and their band were on the road over 200 days a year as the 1970s began, performing at bluegrass festivals, state and county fairs,

and nightclubs around the country. They also made some overseas tours. The brothers had visited all of the states in the 1960s, and they repeated that cycle several more times in the 1970s. Among the festivals they performed at during the 1970s was the Bean Blossom, Indiana, event hosted by the Father of Bluegrass Music, Bill Monroe. During the decade they returned to Bean Blossom a number of times to play enthusiastically received sets.

In the late 1970s, the bluegrass field found new life, attracting a growing number of new adherents from both high school and college segments of the U.S. population. Many new festivals sprang up, such as the one in Telluride, Colorado, and the McReynoldses and their band at one time or another were featured in almost every one. In 1977, Jim & Jesse started their own annual bluegrass and country festival, generally held in early or mid-August, which was still going strong in the early 1980s. In the fall of 1979, their group was featured on a special TV show called "Bluegrass Spectacular," telecast over PBS from the *Grand Ole Opry* auditorium in Opryland Park near Nashville, Tennessee. At one point, Jim, Jesse, and the Virginia Boys backed the renditions of Bill Monroe and his Blue Grass Boys.

The Virginia Boys in the late 1970s included Jesse's son Keith on bass, Joe Meadows on fiddle, and Garland Shuping on banjo. Jesse continued to excel both on his mid-range lead vocals and in demonstrating his special style of mandolin playing called "McReynolds crosspicking." He was supported by Jim's high, piercing tenor, though on occasion Jim sang lead, as did Keith McReynolds. Typically, the group offered several originals by the brothers, such as Jesse's "Dixie Hoedown" and "Cotton Mill Man" and Jim's "Cash on the Barrelhead." Other songs played in a late 1970s or early 1980s set might range from traditional ballads to spirituals, driving bluegrass instrumentals, or bluegrass versions of recent country hits.

Examples of songs played on late 1970s programs were "Better Times a-Comin'," "Then I'll Stop Goin' for You," "Sweet Little Miss Blue Eyes," "Little Old Log

Cabin," "Blue Ridge Mountain Blues," "I Wish You Knew," "Heartbreak Mountain," "Last Train to Clarksville," "Border Ride," "Cumbanchero," "Iron Mule Special," "Mockingbird," "Lee Highway Blues," "Under the Double Eagle," "River of Jordan," "How Great Thou Art," "On the Wings of a Dove," "When the Wagon Was New," "Hard Hearted," "Ashes of Love," "Westphalia Waltz," "Dark as a Dungeon," "Knoxville Girl," "Old Slewfoot," and Hank Williams' "Mansion on the Hill." From the mid-1970s on, one of the band's most popular numbers was its version of John Prine's "Paradise," a song that told of the destruction of the hill country environment by the coal companies.

JONES, GEORGE: *Singer, guitarist, songwriter, bandleader (The Jones Boys). Born Saratoga, Texas, September 12, 1931.*

A performer's performer, George Jones was often cited as the favorite artist of many of the best-known names in country music. Equally appreciated by the public, he was a major star in the mid-1960s, and continued to be one of the most successful country entertainers into the 1980s. When he wasn't reaching the top levels of hit charts as a soloist in the 1970s, he usually was teaming with Tammy Wynette on highly successful duet recordings.

He was born and raised in Texas and was a devotee of country and gospel music as a young boy. Both his parents were musically talented: his mother was a church pianist and his father liked to play the guitar as a form of relaxation from his work as a pipefitter. The Joneses encouraged their son's interest in music and gave him his first guitar when he was nine. In a few years George learned to play it well and entertained at church socials and other local functions.

In his late teens, George joined the Marines during the Korean War. After being discharged, he headed home to Texas, where he found a job as a house painter. Though at first he didn't think of music as a way of earning a living, word of his talent led to increasingly important professional engagements. The turning point

came when veteran music executive H. W. "Pappy" Daily became interested in the young artist. Daily, then starting the Houston record firm of Starday, signed George for the label in 1954, starting a long and close association between the two men.

Soon after, George cut his first single for the label, "There Ain't No Money in This Deal." The record lived up to its name, but George and Daily persevered. In 1955, their persistence paid off when Jones scored his first major hit on Starday with the top-10 "Why Baby Why," a song he co-wrote with D. Edwards. The song's success helped bring a bid for him to join the *Grand Ole Opry* in 1956. George was happy to accept, though he continued to call Texas rather than Nashville home. His new status was recognized by Starday with his debut album, *Grand Ole Opry's New Star*, which also was the record firm's first LP release.

George turned out a number of other chartmakers for the label, such as "You Gotta Be My Baby," before switching to Mercury Records. His first top-10 hit for the new label was "Treasure of Love," in 1958. In 1959, he scored with "Who Shot Sam," which he helped to write, and achieved his first number-one national hit with his version of Sheb Wooley's "White Lightning."

By 1961, he had moved on to his third record affiliation, United Artists, for whom he turned out a string of hits during the first part of the 1960s. The first of these was his original composition, "Window Up Above," in 1961. In 1962, he had a number-one hit, "She Thinks I Still Care," as well as the top-10 successes "Aching, Breaking Heart" and "A Girl I Used to Know." His 1963 hits for UA were "Not What I Had in Mind," a duet with Melba Montgomery, "We Must Have Been Out of Our Minds," and "You Comb Her Hair." He added more top-10 hits in 1964 with "The Race Is On," a song that also rose high on the pop charts, "Where Does a Little Tear Come From?" and "Your Heart Turned Left."

When Pappy Daily started his new company, Musicor, Jones signed with him and provided the label with a series of top-10-

charted singles in the mid- and late-1960s. They included "Take Me," "Things Have Gone to Pieces," and "Love Bug" in 1965; "I'm a People" (1966); "You Can't Get There from Here" (1967); and "As Long as I Live" and "Say it's Not You" (1968). He also made upper-chart levels with "Flowers for Mama" and "4033."

During the late 1950s and throughout the 1960s, Jones was one of the major concert attractions on the country circuit, backed by his band, the Jones Boys. On the road for several hundred days a year, he appeared before audiences in all parts of the United States and Canada and made several overseas tours as well. Though he cut back a bit on his hectic stage work in the 1970s, he continued to be a major attraction wherever he went. His TV engagements included almost all of the major country shows of the 1960s and 1970s, such as *The Red Foley Show*, *The Jimmy Dean Show*, *Johnny Cash*, *Hee Haw*, and others. He was a guest on the *Grand Ole Opry* a number of times in the late 1950s and during the 1960s before he became a cast regular in 1969. He also found the time to take part in two movies in the 1960s.

For a long time Jones resisted the blandishments of Nashville and continued to live in a split-level ranch home in Vidor, Texas, with his second wife and two children (Jeffrey and Brian) during the 1960s. (His first marriage, in 1950, from which he has a daughter, Susan, ended in the early 1950s. He married his second wife in 1953.) In the 1970s, after that marriage broke up and he married Tammy Wynette (in 1968), he settled in Music City.

During the 1950s and 1960s, George completed a great many albums for the four labels he worked with during that period. The Starday catalogue included *Crown Prince of Country*, issued 10/61, *Fabulous Country Music Sound* (4/62), and *Greatest Hits* (4/62). Mercury LPs included *George Jones Sings* (1/60), *Country Church Time* (1960), *Country & Western Hits* (7/61), *Greatest Hits* (11/61), *Sings from the Heart* (9/62), *Ballad Side* (11/63), *Duets Country Style* (1/63), *Novelty Side* (6/63), *Great George Jones* (3/64), *Blue and Lonesome* (7/64), *Salutes Hank Williams* (8/64), *Number 1 Male*

Singer (11/64), and *Heartaches and Tears* (3/65). His United Artists releases the first part of the 1960s included *Best of George Jones* (10/63), *Grand Ole Opry* (1/64), *More Favorites* (4/64), *Sings Bob Wills* (4/63), *What's in Our Heart* (1/64), *Sings Like the Dickens* (10/64), *I Get Lonely* (12/64), *Bluegrass Hootenanny* (5/64), *The Race Is On* (5/65), *King of Broken Hearts* (10/65), *Trouble in Mind* (4/65), *Blue Moon of Kentucky* (4/66), *Golden Hits* (10/66), *Golden Hits, Vol. 2* (5/67), and *Young George Jones* (10/67), plus such others as *Great George Jones, My Favorites, New Favorites, Hits of Country Cousins*, and *Homecoming in Heaven*. His releases on Musicor from 1966 through 1969 included *I'm a People, Old Brush Arbor, Love Bug, Mr. Music, New Hits with the Jones Boys, I'll Share My World with You, My Boys, Songs of Leon Payne, Where Grass Won't Grow, Will You Love Me on Sunday*, and *With Love*. In the early 1970s, Musicor issued *Best of George Jones* and *Double Gold George Jones*. He also had albums on various other labels, such as *Color of the Blues* and *Seasons of My Heart* on Nashville, *Country Memories* on Sun; *Heartaches by the Number* on Hilltop, and *Sixteen Greatest Hits* on Trip.

RCA Records issued a number of George's albums under a distribution arrangement in the early 1970s, but his singles and albums continued to come out on other previous labels. In 1970, Musicor had several hit singles of his, including the year-end success "A Good Year for the Roses." RCA released a string of Jones' LPs during 1972–73, such as *First in the Hearts of Country Music Lovers* (3/72); *I Made Leaving, Country Singer, George Jones and Friends*, and *Poor Man's Riches* (all 8/72); *Best, Volume 1* (7/72); *Four-O-Thirty Three, Take Me*, and *Tender Years* (11/72).

During 1971, by which time George was having great success teaming up with his wife, Tammy Wynette, as one of the foremost country duets, he signed a long-term contract with Tammy's record firm, Epic. His first duet single with Tammy was "Take Me" backed with "We Go Together," released in 1971; it also marked his first release on Epic. He was still on the Epic roster at the start of the 1980s and still turning out chart-making singles and LPs.

His Epic solo album debut was *George Jones,* issued in June 1972. However, he already was represented on the label with some of his duets with Tammy, included in their album *We Got Together,* a chart hit in early spring of 1972. In September, he and Tammy had another hit LP, *Me and the First Lady.* In late 1974, RCA issued the *Best of George Jones, Volume 2,* which was on the country album charts well into 1974. Later in the year, George had a top-20 hit with the Epic LP, *We're Gonna Hold On.* Among his other charted Epic albums of the 1970s were *Golden Ring* (with Tammy Wynette) in 1976, *All the Greatest Hits, Volume 1,* in early 1977, *Bartender Blues* (1978), and *My Very Special Guests* (late 1979–early 1980).

His other Epic albums included such generally excellent offerings as *Grand Tour, Memories of Us, Picture of Me, The Battle, Alone Again,* and *I Wanta Sing.* A number of the latter were autobiographical or semiautobiographical, dealing with the breakup of his marriage to Tammy Wynette; in particular, *The Battle,* one of his most impressive albums, dealt with the final stages of the relationship. After the separation, previously recorded duets by the two artists continued to be released, resulting in a number of hit singles. By the end of the 1970s, Jones' total of album releases on all labels was approaching 100.

George's rapport with the country-music audiences was proven again and again throughout the 1970s; his solo singles, as well as his duets with others, were constantly on the bestseller lists. In 1972, for instance, he had a top-10 solo hit with "We Can Make It" and a duet top-10 success, "The Ceremony," with Tammy Wynette. Both discs were on Epic as were almost all his other chartmakers from then on. Among those were "Once You've Had the Best" in 1974, "God's Gonna Getcha for That" (with Tammy Wynette) and "Memories of Us" in 1975; "The Battle," "You Always Look Best (Here In My Arms)," "Golden Key" (with Wynette), "Her Name Is . . ." (1976); the number-one ranked "Near You" (February 1977 with Wynette) and top-10 "Southern Califor-

nia" (with Wynette, August 1977); "Put 'Em All Together and I'd Have You" (1977); "I'll Just Take it Out in Love" (1978); and "Maybelline" (with Johnny Paycheck, late 1978, early 1979).

Despite his many achievements, by the late 1970s George's life was in a shambles. As do many entertainers, he had used alcohol regularly as a crutch to alleviate the tensions, frustrations, and boredom of the performing grind. As his private problems mounted, so did his drinking, until he had become an alcoholic. Things reached a climax as the decade came to a close. Not only had his marriage to Tammy ended in divorce, his financial status plummeted and he had to declare bankruptcy. Increasingly he became unreliable as a performer, often failing to appear for scheduled concerts. During 1979, his doctors warned him that if he didn't stop drinking not only his career but his life was in danger. Heeding the message, he checked into a clinic in Alabama for a month for an alcoholism cure.

The result was a new upsurge in his interest in living and in his musical reputation. After returning home from Alabama, he recorded a new album, *I Am What I Am,* which was one of his best collections. The LP became his best-selling album ever and was on the charts from 1980 into 1981. One song from the LP, "He Stopped Loving Her Today," released by Epic in the spring of 1980, rose to number-one in early summer. Later in the year, George had another number-one single with "I'm Not Ready." Meanwhile, the passions between George and Tammy had cooled. They announced in February 1980 that they would perform together again. Their first duet in several years had been recorded in January 1980 ("Two Story House") and released on February 12 by Epic. Jones and Wynette debuted the song on Johnny Carson's *The Tonight Show* and also took part in Johnny Cash's "25th Anniversary Special." In the fall, George and Tammy had another hit single, "A Pair of Old Sneakers."

Jones had received many honors during his long career. In 1956, all the major music trade magazines voted him Most Promising Artist of the Year. He was among the finalists a number of times in the voting for best male vocalist by the Country Music Association and the duet of Jones and Wynette was among the five finalists for vocal group of the year for most of the 1970s. Despite that, at the start of the 1980s, most of his entertainment industry peers felt he had never gained the recognition he merited. But all of that changed dramatically in the early 1980s.

In the CMA 1980 voting, he was a major winner, receiving the awards for Male Vocalist of the Year, Song of the Year and Single of the Year (the last two for "He Stopped Loving Her Today"). At the Grammy Awards in early 1981, he won for Country Song of the Year ("He Stopped Loving Her Today") and similar approval was given by members of the Academy of Country Music, voting him Male Vocalist of the Year and naming "He Stopped Loving Her Today" Song of the Year and Single of the Year. In the annual *Music City News* Cover Awards in 1981, he was named Male Artist of the Year.

During 1981, his recording and concert work continued to prosper. Capacity audiences greeted him from coast to coast. (Members of his band, the Jones Boys, at this time were Rob Watkins, lead guitar and vocals; Mark Dunn, drums; Ron Gaddis, bass guitar and vocals; Tommy Keller, steel guitar; Steve Payne, keyboards; and Lorrie Morgan, backing vocals.) His album *I Am What I Am* earned a Recording Industry Association of America gold record, the first such in his career. In early 1981 he had the hit singles "You Better Move On" (a duet with Johnny Paycheck) and "If Drinkin' Don't Kill Me (Your Memory Will)" and later in the year made the top-10 with "Still Doin' Time." Also on the charts in late 1981 was his new album, *Still the Same Ole Me*. In October 1981, he won three more awards from the CMA, including being named Male Vocalist of the Year for the second straight time.

Reviewing the turnaround in his fortunes, George told Robert Hilburn of the *Los Angeles Times* (Calendar section, March 8, 1981), "When you're young, you take most things for granted—the money, the attention, the fans. But I can appreciate it all now. I'm older and I know what it is to have it all slip away. For a while, I didn't even know if I'd be alive much longer— much less be on stage. I'm a very lucky man."

JONES, GRANDPA: *Singer, banjoist, guitarist, fiddler, comic. Born Niagra, Henderson County, Kentucky, October 20, 1913.*

When the new *Hee Haw* program debuted on CBS-TV the summer of 1969, the headliners were Roy Clark and Buck Owens, but contributing mightily to the success of the program was the inimitable Grandpa Jones with his relaxed down-home humor and driving banjo solos. When *Hee Haw* celebrated its tenth anniversary as one of the most successful syndicated country-music shows, Grandpa still was gracing each telecast with skill and exuberance, a favorite figure with country audiences as he had been for over forty years.

Born Louis Marshall Jones in Henderson County, Kentucky, he started his music career at eleven when he surreptitiously practiced on a workman's old guitar on his family's farm. Enthralled by the experience, he persuaded his older brother to purchase a guitar, and then diligently tried to master it.

By the time the family moved to Akron, Ohio, in the late 1920s, he could play quite well. In 1929 he entered a talent contest promoted by Wendell Hall at the local Keith Albee theater. He won first prize, fifty dollars in gold pieces, and used it to buy a new guitar that he soon employed in a series of radio station jobs. From the end of the 1920s through 1935, he performed on radio stations in Akron and Cleveland. In 1935, he made a major step forward when he joined the group headed by veteran folk-country artist Bradley Kincaid to appear on the *National Barn Dance* over station WLS, Chicago. Besides that, he played on programs broadcast over station WBZ in Boston, Massachusetts, and WWVA, Wheeling, West Virginia, during 1935–36.

When Jones became associated with Kincaid, he sounded very old on the radio, though he was only twenty-three, and people started writing the *Barn Dance* about him, asking his age. As a result, he formed a new act as "Grandpa." He put on special makeup, used a false, bushy moustache (when he was older he was able to grow a grizzled one of his own) and affected old-time clothes, including large galluses and high boots. In addition, he now concentrated on banjo pickin' instead of the guitar. In 1937, with his own band, he debuted in Wheeling, West Virginia. The billing read "Grandpa Jones and His Grandchildren."

The audience went wild, as audiences still were doing four decades later. His style captured a rustic enthusiasm that conveyed the rural and pioneer spirit to people from all walks of life. It was described glowingly by Ed Badeaux, associate editor of *Sing Out!* in the December–January 1963–64 issue. "Grandpa plays the banjo not with just his hands and arms, but with his whole body. His footwork is as intricate as that of a prize fighter or ballet dancer, and is executed while he is both singing and playing the banjo. When he comes to a banjo solo, the neck of his banjo jets straight up in the air and he arches his body to get the drum as close to the microphone as possible. During his songs, he dances, does stationary road work, and takes frequent jumps and kicks to emphasize and reinforce the humor in his songs."

Grandpa took his new act to Cincinnati in 1938 as part of the cast of the new WLW *Boone County Jamboree.* He continued to delight radio listeners and live audiences from his WLW base until 1944, when he went into the Army. He ended up in Munich, Germany, after the war in Europe was over, where he played on the Armed Forces Network.

After his discharge in 1946, he returned to the States and soon accepted an offer to join the regular cast of the *Grand Ole Opry.* Decades later he still was one of the *Opry's* most-loved artists. During the late 1940s and into the 1950s, he made many trips to entertain U.S. troops overseas. During one of those tours while the Korean War was raging, he took part in thirty-four shows in fourteen days before 38,000 soldiers. One

performance was given within 200 yards of the front lines.

Through the 1950s and 1960s, Grandpa continued to tour widely. Most of his appearances—usually part of a package show—were on basically country-attraction circuits—theaters in the South and Southwest, county fairs, rodeos, etc. However, he also was well received in many major cities outside the South over the years. By the start of the 1970s, he had appeared in all fifty states and given concerts in many foreign nations as well. His wife, Ramona, accompanied him on his tours, adding her talents on fiddle and other instruments to the act.

During the 1950s and 1960s, Grandpa was an honored guest on almost every important country TV program, network or syndicated. His exposure on TV increased markedly when he became a regular on *Hee Haw* from 1969 on. His contributions included taking part in a variety of skits—such as the cornfield one-liners, the barber shop routine, and the hillbilly segment in which all the performers delivered their rural humor from supine positions. The spotlight often fell on one of his patented banjo solos during the program while at other times he joined Roy Clark and other pickers for banjo band performances.

During his long career, many songs became associated with Grandpa, including "Old Rattler," "Old Rattler Treed," "Old Rattler's Pup," "Good Ole Mountain Dew," "Eight More Miles to Louisville," "Going Down Town," and his version of the Lonzo and Oscar hit "I'm My Own Grandpa." All of those and many others were recorded by him over the years, sometimes more than once. His recordings were released on various labels, including King, Monument, Decca, Vocalion, and Nashville.

Grandpa was represented in record catalogues with dozens of releases from the start of the 1950s to the end of the 1970s. His LPs on the King label included such collections as *Gospel Songs* (issued 4/63), *Other Side of Grandpa Jones* and *Rollin' Along* (early 1960s), and *Do You Remember These Songs* (9/63). His Monument releases included *Rafters Ring* (4/62), *Yodeling Hits* (early 1960s), *Real Folk Songs* (9/64), *Grandpa Jones Remembers the Brown's Ferry Four*, (he was a member of that quartet during one phase of his career), *Everybody's Grandpa* (mid-1960s), and *Hits from Hee Haw* (1/70).

His LPs on other labels included *An Evening With Grandpa Jones* on Decca (8/63); *15¢ Is All I've Got* on Nashville (early 1970s); *Pickin' Time* on Vocalion (late 1960s), and *Grandpa Jones Lives* on Harmony (9/72).

One of the most memorable events for Grandpa occurred in October 1978. During the Country Music Association awards show telecast throughout the United States, he was called up on stage to watch the unveiling of the plaque commemorating his election that year to the Country Music Hall of Fame. In 1978 and 1979, he contributed part of his memorabilia, including some of his banjos, for use in his exhibit at the Hall of Fame museum in Nashville.

JONES, TOM: *Singer, drummer. Born Pontypridd, Wales, Great Britain, June 7, 1940.*

Over the years since World War II, many artists from the British Isles have shown an interest in country music. The Rolling Stones, several members of the Beatles, and pop star Tom Jones all tried their hand at country songs; in Jones' case, a cover record of a country hit helped make him an international star.

Born Thomas Jones Woodward, he strayed very little from his home in south Wales for the first quarter century of his life. His vocal efforts began as a boy in his church choir and later with the school choir at Treforrest Secondary Modern School. At sixteen, his formal schooling ended and he married his wife, Linda, soon after. He brought home money from an assortment of jobs that included builder's laborer, glove cutter, and, at night, popsinger. After learning to play drums and working with local groups for some years, he formed one of his own. By 1963, he had gained a local following for his group, called Tommy Scott and the Senators. In one of the local clubs in 1964 songwriter/record industry executive Gordon Mills heard him.

Mills told Bob Hilburn of the *Los Angeles Times* (Calendar, June 6, 1971, p. 41), "A friend persuaded me to go along and listen to this group because I had just left a singing trio myself to set up in songwriting and management. The first few bars were all I needed to hear—they convinced me that here was a voice which could make him the greatest singer in the world. It's strange, but Tom always had a feeling that some day, someone would come by the club and hear him. He didn't take the traditional step of going to London to be discovered."

Mills took over as Tom's manager and had him change his name, reputedly because of the success of the movie *Tom Jones*. It took some effort, but Mills finally got Tom a recording contract. (One objection was that "he moved like Elvis Presley.") After his first single failed, Tom recorded one of Mills' compositions, "It's Not Unusual," and gained a number-one chart hit in England in 1965. A series of singles hits followed, including "Little Lonely One," "What's New Pussycat," "With These Hands," and "Thunderball," and Tom became a featured performer on the nightclub circuit and on British TV.

Still, things took a turn for the worse when his recordings lost momentum during 1966. Then Jones heard Jerry Lee Lewis' recording of the country hit "Green, Green Grass of Home" and decided to do it himself. The recording, on the Parrot label (a subsidiary of London Records), moved to number one in England in three weeks. Later it became a hit in the United States, helping to pave the way for stardom in the States. In the years that followed, Tom added a number of other country songs or country-flavored numbers to his repertoire.

The success of "Green, Green Grass of Home" started a virtual avalanche of hit singles and albums over the next half decade. During 1968, he followed up with such songs as "Delilah" and "Help Yourself" and earned gold records in 1969 for the singles "Love Me Tonight" and "I'll Never Fall in Love Again" and the LPs *Help Yourself, Tom Jones, Live, Tom Jones Live in Las Vegas,* and *This Is Tom Jones.* In the early 1970s, he made top-chart levels in both the United States and England with the singles "Till," "Can't Stop Loving You," "Resurrection Shuffle," "She's a Lady," "Puppet Man," and "Lazybones" and the albums *I (Who Have Nothing), Tom Jones Sings She's a Lady, Close Up,* and *The Body and Soul of Tom Jones.*

He was a guest on major TV programs in the United States and England many times during the late 1960s and throughout the 1970s and had his own TV show in 1969–70. Guests on his program ranged from rock stars to country artists, and Tom himself included his versions of country numbers on a number of shows. He became a favored artist on the nightclub circuit all over the United States, Europe, and the Far East from the 1960s on. Lucrative offers from the glittering show palaces of Las Vegas came his way and he performed there at regular intervals. Though his name didn't appear on the hit lists too often the second half of the 1970s, his status as a major in-person draw continued to be impressive into the 1980s.

By the end of the 1970s, it was estimated that his overall sales of recordings worldwide, both singles and albums, was well past the 100 million mark.

JORDANAIRES: *Vocal group. Personnel as of the 1960s: Gordon Stoker, born Gleason, Tennessee, August 3, mid-1920s; Hoyt Hawkins, born Paducah, Kentucky, March 31; Neal Matthews, born Nashville, Tennessee, October 26; Ray Walker, born Centerville, Mississippi, March 16.*

Some of the most often heard voices in the music field belong to the artists who make up the Jordanaires. Each year, millions of records are sold that include their members. However, a good part of this is incognito, for the Jordanaires often provide vocal support for solo artists. From the group's founding in 1948 in Springfield, Missouri, through the 1970s, it backed such artists as Marty Robbins, Don Gibson, Elvis Presley, Kitty Wells, Patti Page, Ricky Nelson, Connie Francis, Tennessee Ernie Ford, and Gene Pitney.

As with most groups, the composition of the Jordanaires varied over the years. As of 1967, the basic quartet consisted of Gordon Stoker, first tenor, born in Gleason, Tennessee; Hoyt Hawkins, baritone, pia-

nist, bassist, born in Paducah, Kentucky; Neal Matthews, second tenor, born in Nashville, Tennessee; and Ray Walker, bass, born in Centerville, Mississippi.

Stoker, one of the first members of the group, learned piano in his youth before spending three years in the Air Force during World War II. He attended Oklahoma Baptist College in Shawnee, Oklahoma, and then majored in psychology and music at George Peabody College in Nashville. While attending Peabody he also worked as a piano accompanist on the *Grand Ole Opry* station, WSM. This eventually led to his role with the Jordanaires, starting in 1949.

Hawkins also went to the Jordanaires via George Peabody College, joining the group in 1950. In the 1930s, at the age of ten, he had begun singing in a family quartet over station WPAD in Paducah. Two years in the Army preceded his enrollment in Peabody.

Matthews, who learned to play guitar at thirteen, served in the Army during the Korean War. Then came a stint at Belmont College in Nashville as a psychology major. In 1953, he joined the Jordanaires.

Walker came to the group with a background that included twelve years as a radio announcer and solo and quartet singer. During his days at David Lipscomb College in Nashville, he sang in a quartet with a fellow undergraduate, Pat Boone. In 1958, he became the fourth member of the Jordanaires. (For some supporting work, the Jordainaires occasionally added the voices of Millie Kirkham and Dolores Dinning.)

The Jordanaires started as singers of barbershop songs and spirituals. They performed in many cities in Tennessee and surrounding states, rapidly winning acceptance and, in 1949, a bid from the *Grand Ole Opry.* The group extended their popularity to the national level in 1956 by winning on the *Arthur Godfrey's Talent Scouts* program. That same year, they started a long association with Elvis Presley by providing vocal harmony for "I Was the One."

Their work with Elvis included many movies, starting with the 1957 *Loving You.* In the late 1950s and 1960s they were featured on many network TV shows, including *The Ed Sullivan Show, The Steve Allen Show, Tennessee Ernie Ford, The Tonight Show,* and *American Bandstand.* Their soundtrack credits, as of 1967, totaled twenty-nine films.

Over the years, the Jordanaires collected many awards, including those for background accompaniment for such hits as "Battle of New Orleans" and "Big Bad John." In early 1965 they won a Grammy for best religious album of 1964 for their work with Tennessee Ernie Ford on *Great Gospel Songs.* Their popularity in the 1960s was international. In 1965, they were rated fifth most popular group in Europe; in 1966, they were rated sixth in Europe.

Some of their recordings were released on Columbia Records in the 1960s, such as *The Jordanaires* (April 1966). In the early 1970s, they had the album *Monster Makers* on Stop Records.

JOY, THE: *Vocal duo. Toni Brown, born Madison, Wisconsin, November 15, 1938; Terry Garthwaite, born Berkeley, California, July 11, 1938. Brown and Garthwaite also headed the group Joy of Cooking.*

Both individually and as joint artists, Toni Brown and Terry Garthwaite rank among the most versatile and talented musicians and songwriters to emerge from the pop music environment in the Berkeley, California, area in the late 1960s. Although they are responsible for some first-rate work, they never seemed to have received the widespread recognition they merited, partly because of prejudices against female band musicians and partly because their offerings covered a very wide range of styles—from folk and country to rock and jazz.

Both women became interested in music in childhood and went on to accrue considerable academic credits. Toni was born in Wisconsin but spent most of her childhood in the Boston, Massachusetts, area, where she began taking piano lessons at six, later picking up the ukulele at nine and guitar at fourteen. Although she studied classical piano for nine years, her first strong musical attachment was for country music. She recalls writing "simple little country songs" at nine or ten. After starting college at the University of Colorado, she transferred to the Boston Museum of Fine Arts to study painting and then enrolled at exclusive Bennington College, Vermont, from which she was graduated in 1961.

She credits a poetry reading by beat poet Lawrence Ferlinghetti with arousing her curiosity about California. After leaving Bennington, she headed to Berkeley, where she soon became a member of a country string band called the Crabgrassers. She wrote a number of original songs for the group, as well as others she recorded herself during a brief association with Arhoolie Records.

Terry Garthwaite was born and raised in Berkeley. "I fooled around on the piano when I was a kid. And then I began taking guitar lessons—classical, a little flamenco, and a little folk. My first exposure to the blues feeling was from an older friend, Rob Sterling, who had a rough voice and a real intimate style. He was a big influence." In her preteen years, she leaned toward folk music, enjoying people like Odetta, Leadbelly, Josh White, and Brownie McGhee and Sonny Terry. Later, though, she enjoyed rock groups and jazz singers.

During her teens she started performing as a folk singer in small coffee houses, a practice she continued after entering the University of California at Berkeley. After two years, she left to spend a year in England and when she returned, the music climate in Berkeley had changed dramatically. "When I got back to the Bay Area, the music scene was really exciting—the Airplane, Janis Joplin, a whole new atmosphere." Terry now wanted to play rock 'n' roll rather than folk, and sharing that interest was a new-found friend, Toni Brown.

The women decided to try to defy the unspoken tradition of rock music by forming what they hoped would be the first successful group to be headed by women. The result was Joy of Cooking, a band that deserved to be considered among the top rock groups of its era but that never quite gained the following it needed for stardom. After almost four years of playing small clubs on the rock circuit, interspersed with some work as an opening act for other bands, Garthwaite and Brown finally managed to win a recording contract from Capitol Records. The band's debut LP, *Joy of Cooking*, was issued by Capitol in 1970. Most of the songs were written by Toni, though a couple were provided by Terry. The band makeup featured Terry on lead vocals in all but two songs plus lead guitar and clarinet with Toni playing keyboards, steel guitar, kalimba, and doing some vocals. The other members were Terry's brother David on bass and acoustic guitar, Fritz Kasten on drums and alto sax, and Ron Wilson on percussion and harmonica. For the next LP, *Closer to the Ground*, issued in 1971, David Garthwaite was replaced by Jeff Neighbor. There were strong folk and country elements in that LP, such as "New Colorado Blues," and even more on the group's third LP, *Castles*, issued in 1972, which included the country song by Toni "Don't the Moon Look Fat and Yellow" and Terry's folk-rock composition "Home Town Man."

In 1973, Brown and Garthwaite went to Nashville to record an all country-style LP titled *Cross Country*. Backing them on the eleven tracks, eight written by Toni and two by Terry, were such fine musicians as Dennis Linde, Kenny Malone, and Vassar Clements. This material, the liner notes state, was a "side trip" while the rest of Joy of Cooking was laying down tracks for the next band album. However, that LP never came out. Toni had decided to leave to concentrate more on writing and, though Terry reorganized Joy of Cooking, it was too much of an uphill fight to keep it going.

Both of the women, though, soon were represented by new solo efforts. In 1974, MCA Records released Toni's *Good for You, Too*, a country/folk-oriented collection mainly written by her. In 1975, Terry's offering appeared on Arista. Called

Terry, it stressed R&B/soul and rock–type material. Her many musical interests were underscored a short while later when she contributed to a jazz collection (a direct-to-disc production) called *San Francisco Ltd.*, released on the Crystal Clear label, in 1976.

In 1977, the two artists joined forces once more in a duo called The Joy. The result was an album on Fantasy Records that combined the influences of both—Brown's country leanings and Braithwaite's jazz/blues/rock—in varying proportions to provide such fine tracks as "Feel like Heaven," "Snow," "Beginning Tomorrow," and "On the Natch," among the best offerings the team had turned out.

Both indicated, though, that while they would continue to work together, they also intended to continue to pursue their individual careers as well. Thus, in 1978, Terry's second solo LP, *Hand in Glove*, came out on Fantasy, including seven originals by her in its ten tracks. Terry also was thinking about writing a book "for singers that would include interviews with professionals, a how-to section including exercises and techniques and some of my own personal history." Some of the material, she noted, could be based on her work teaching singing and improvisation in the 1970s at the Blue Bear and Family Light Schools.

At the end of the 1970s, both Toni and Terry combined career efforts with raising their own children in Marin County. Toni, whose household included her husband, John, and five-year-old son Jody (as of 1979), stressed, "It's real interesting to me that, traditionally, women artists in any medium have not had children. I do think that it's possible, though it takes a lot of working out, the right mate, the right balance of energy, and so on. There's a lot being written about that now and I know I'll be writing more about the whole family scene—it's a subject that needs to be delved into."

Wanda Jackson and the Party Timers (mid-1960s)

Waylon Jennings

Sonny James

After performance at the Bottom Line in New York, early 1980s, George Jones poses with Linda Ronstadt (left) and Bonnie Raitt

Kingston Trio (early 1960s): l. to r., Bob Shane, John Stewart, Nick Reynolds

K

KEITH, BILL: *Singer, banjoist, pedal steel guitarist, songwriter. Born Massachusetts, early 1940s.*

In terms of banjo innovations, the two artists who contributed most in the post–World War II decades were Earl Scruggs and Bill Keith. If Scruggs' advances helped bring about a surge in bluegrass banjo interest in the late 1940s and during the 1960s, Keith's efforts laid the groundwork for the evolution of such new forms as "newgrass" and "jazzgrass" in the 1970s.

Bill, who grew up in Brockton, Massachusetts, near Boston, was interested in the banjo during his high school years in the mid-1950s. Initially he played tenor banjo in local dixieland groups, but the thriving folk music atmosphere of those years soon caught his attention. He was particularly impressed with the banjo styles of Earl Scruggs and Pete Seeger, though he didn't really set about to master those methods until he was attending Amherst College in Amherst, Massachusetts, in the late 1950s. He purchased a used five-string banjo for fifteen dollars as well as Pete Seeger's book, "How to Play the Five-String Banjo," in the fall of 1957 and learned the basics of both Seeger's and Scruggs' techniques before he started to experiment with variations of his own.

Meanwhile, he had found a kindred spirit in guitarist Jim Rooney, also attending Amherst, who liked folk and bluegrass music. The two began to jam together and soon formed a duo to play in local coffee houses and in campus shows. They also made other contacts in the music field, including a promoter named Manny Greenhill who helped them form a folk music organization called the Connecticut Valley Folklore Society. Those activities led to a series of concerts in many college areas of New England in which Keith, Rooney, and other college folk groups took part. During one of those late 1950s concerts, Keith unveiled the first version of his own picking style (the tune was called "Noah's Breakdown"), which later became known as chromatic banjo playing. In years to come, that invention had as great an impact on the banjo field as the earlier Scruggs style.

Comparing the two approaches, Keith told Roger H. Simonoff (*Frets* magazine, March 1980, pp. 32–27), "I would say that the basic difference between [his approach] and the regular Scruggs style is that [in chromatic banjo style] the hands are working together in a much higher degree of cooperation. . . . When you play chromatically, you're playing pretty much note for note, whereas in the regular Scruggs style, it's more apt to be lick for lick. One of the big differences in the way the left hand is used is that you're using different kinds of chord positions than are used in the regular Scruggs style. And, of course, you use open strings, so very often you're fretting on the second string and the first string is open, or you're fretting on the third string and the second string is open. . . ."

In addition to developing a new playing technique, Keith also developed new banjo components, such as a special tuner. In that case, he worked with a fraternity brother of Rooney's named Dan Bump. Bump suggested forming a banjo company in 1963, and Keith suggested they needed some kind of innovation to set such an operation apart. Between them, they decided an improved tuning peg would make sense, and the result of their work was a system incorporating the pitch-changer function into the peg. He told Simonoff, "Earl Scruggs had come up with his own cam-type pitch changers, . . . but those involved drilling holes in the peghead for installation. We felt the advantage of ours was that you could just substitute one for an existing peg." Later they showed the design to Scruggs, who was so impressed he joined them in producing Keith-Scruggs tuners in the mid-1960s. Dan Bump eventually set up his own firm in Putney, Vermont, to turn out Keith tuners.

Keith and Rooney continued to perform

whenever the chance arose, including an appearance at the Newport Folk Festival. They also managed to get a recording agreement with Prestige that resulted in 1963 distribution of their 1962 album, *Livin' on the Mountain*, which included debut renditions of two of Keith's best-known instrumentals, his version of "Salty Dog Blues" and "Devil's Dream." By 1964, Keith was banjoist for Jim Kweskin's Jug Band. After completing his studies at Amherst, Keith moved to Washington, D.C., for a while to study banjo-making methods from an expert named Tom Morgan. Rooney also migrated there and, through Morgan, the duo met bluegrass musicians Red Allen (guitar) and Frank Wakefield (mandolin), who asked Keith to become banjoist of their group, the Kentuckians. During that period, Manny Greenhill was promoting some of the Flatt & Scruggs concerts. While that famed team played Baltimore, Greenhill introduced Scruggs and Keith. Earl needed someone to do banjo tablature for a new book on the five-string banjo he was working on and asked Bill Keith to come to Nashville to help out.

Keith agreed, his work eventually appearing in the book, *Earl Scruggs and the 5-String Banjo*, when it was published in 1968 by Peer International. His stay in Nashville had other ramifications. Backstage at the *Grand Ole Opry* one night, he was overheard playing "Devil's Dream" by the Father of Bluegrass, Bill Monroe. Monroe brought Keith (whom he called Brad) into his Bluegrass Boys, an association that lasted about a year. Said Monroe, "There's not a banjo picker in the country that can beat Brad!"

Keith had too many interests to remain in the group and left to pursue them on his own. Over the years, he did session work, spent some time as banjo player for the Woodstock Mountain Review, did solo sets, such as the one at the 1967 Newport Folk Festival, wrote new material, and continued to refine both his chromatic style and banjo innovations. He also found time to perfect his performance on another instrument, pedal steel guitar, at one point dropping the banjo for a while.

He never dropped his friendship with Rooney. Throughout the 1970s and into the 1980s, they often toured together, playing the folk music circuit in the United States and Canada. Together or separately, they also made a number of trips to Europe; France, in particular, held Keith's work in high esteem. Besides his concert work, Keith also devoted considerable amounts of time to banjo workshops in many parts of the United States. When the magazine *Frets* began publication in the late 1970s, he was one of the charter columnists on banjo techniques.

Although Keith took part in many recording sessions during the 1960s and 1970s, only a limited number were albums featuring only his work. One of his solo LPs available at the start of the 1980s was Rounder Records' *Something Bluegrass*. Other album releases on which he was represented were, on Rounder, *Banjoland* and *Mud Acres—Music Among Friends;* on Musigrass-Diffusion, *Banjo Paris Sessions;* on Ridgerunner, *Muleskinner* and *Jazzgrass;* on MCA, *Bluegrass Time*.

In the 1970s, though he could play many styles of bluegrass, Keith made considerable contributions to the general classification of progressive bluegrass. He told Simonoff, "I think people generally will admit that there's a difference between newgrass and traditional bluegrass and I think the difference is the material that's dealt with. These days, there is a higher percentage of material that has more complicated harmonies in it. Also newgrass, jazzgrass, and what I call fusion music are taking bluegrass instrumental styles and playing other kinds of music, including jazz and old standards. . . . There's more of a variety of chords. In fact, you get into this kind of variety when you include more notes in the chord that you're playing (than in 'traditional' chording)."

KENDALLS, THE: *Vocal and instrumental duo. Royce Kendall, born St. Louis, Missouri, September 25, 1934; Jeannie Kendall, born St. Louis, Missouri, November 13, 1954.*

In the 1970s, Royce Kendall and his daughter, Jeannie, became one of the most successful father and daughter vocal teams in the history of country music. Their success, he noted, was the result of "persistence and hard work," though at times they could not be sure if they would stay in the entertainment business or settle back and make a more secure living in the barber/beautician field.

For Royce, his interest in country music went back a long way. He told Dolly Carlisle for an article in *Country Music* magazine (March 1980, pp. 19–21), "I'd been playing [guitar] ever since I was about eight, me and my brother. For a long time I didn't do anything with it, didn't even pick up a guitar for several years."

Like a magnet, he always seemed to be drawn back to music, to make some effort to move ahead as a performer. For a while, for instance, he worked with a country group while he was in the U.S. Merchant Marine. At one point in the late 1950s, he went to California to work with his brother. He told Carlisle, "We did a TV show in California a couple of years with Cal Smith and Hank Cochran. That was before Hank wrote any songs and before Cal had anything. . . . We didn't stick together very long. We went back to St. Louis and he stayed in California. Then I didn't do anything in music for a long time."

In St. Louis, he went to barbering school and settled down to work at his trade while his wife, Melba, developed a following as a beautician. During the 1960s, while daughter Jeannie was growing up, Royce and Melba concentrated on their trade, opening their own shop which did quite well financially.

Jeannie, who recalled seeing her father on TV as a little girl, liked music, though she didn't think of it as a possible career for most of her early years. Though she enjoyed all kinds of music, she showed a preference for folk and country. Among the artists whose records she listened to were Glen Campbell, Jerry Reed, and John Denver. She recalled that the turning point probably came when she was in her mid-teens. "Daddy [would] sit down in the house and play the guitar and we just started singing together for our own enjoyment. Neighbors, friends would say 'you ought to go cut a record.' "

The Kendalls decided to move ahead when a friend, with whom they had attended a *Grand Ole Opry* show in Nashville, urged them to record. Back in St. Louis, Royce and his wife got together about $1,300 and he and Jeannie went into a local studio and made some sides. After that they set up a small mail-order operation to try to sell them. At the same time, they sought and found work as a performing team in local St. Louis clubs.

All of that activity came to the attention of a St. Louis disc jockey who was impressed enough with their work to set up a contact with producer Pete Drake in Nashville. One of the first results of that association was a remake of John Denver's "Leavin' on a Jet Plane." Issued on the small Stop Records label, the song did surprisingly well, reaching the national top 20 in the mid-1970s. The Kendalls did two more singles on Stop, "Two Divided by Love" and "You've Lost That Lovin' Feeling," which also made some chart inroads.

Now attracting notice from larger record companies, Royce and Jeannie agreed to sign with ABC/Dot Records. However, once they had joined that label, they found that company executives wanted to feature Jeannie. Neither of the Kendalls was too happy with that development.

Royce told Dolly Carlisle, "They thought I was too old. But the thing she didn't like about it was they put her in a studio with six background singers."

Added Jeannie, "It was totally useless. I wasn't really allowed to sing in my own style. They were trying to make me into a female Tommy Overstreet. By the time they got finished with my voice, it wasn't me at all. They were trying to make something out of me that they thought the folks would like."

Finally, they left ABC and sought other outlets, and kept in form working the country club and concert circuit. In 1976, they caught the ear of Brian Fisher, heading the new country-music operation for Ovation Records. Enthusiastic about their potential, Fisher signed them and soon had them in the studio working on several songs. The first single was called "Makin' Believe," but it was overshadowed by a version made by another artist. In mid-1977, Fisher and the Kendalls had high hopes for a new single called "Live and Let Live." However, once promotional copies began to reach disc jockeys, they found more interest in the "B" song, "Heaven's Just a Sin Away." Airplay for the latter multiplied rapidly and by late August 1977 it debuted on the national charts. Three months later it was in the top 10 and by the end of October was number one in the United States. The song also was the title song of the Kendalls' debut LP on Ovation, which also rose high on the charts in the fall of 1977 and remained in the top 40 all through 1978 and well into 1979.

The Kendalls soon proved it was not a temporary breakthrough. In 1978, they placed more songs on top-chart levels, such as "Pittsburgh Stealers," "It Don't Feel like Sinnin' to Me," and "Sweet Desire," the latter an original composition by Jeannie Kendall. The single "Sweet Desire/Old Fashioned Love" was issued in the late summer of 1978 and rose to number one by late November. It was included in their second LP, Old Fashioned Love, on best-selling album charts from early 1978 into 1979. In 1979, Jeannie and Royce added to their credits with the singles hits "I Had a Lovely Time," "Happy Together," and "Just Like Real People," the last named the title song for their third Ovation album. They opened 1980 with still another top-10 single, "You'd Make an Angel Wanna Cheat," included in their fourth album, issued in early 1980, The Heart of the Matter.

During the late 1970s, the Kendalls gained many honors in various polls and competitions. They received nominations in both Country Music Association and National Academy of Recording Arts and Sciences votings. In 1977, the NARAS members awarded them the Grammy for Best Country Vocal Performance by a Duo or Group for "Heaven's Just a Sin Away." Among a number of trade magazine awards were several from Billboard, including the 1979 award for Top Country Duo, Singles.

As their careers had moved ahead in the 1970s, the Kendall family had closed down the St. Louis shop and moved to Tennessee. By the late 1970s, all lived in Hendersonville, Jeannie with husband Mack Watkins, lead guitarist in the Kendalls' band, whom she married in 1978.

The Kendalls continued to be one of country music's more successful acts at the start of the 1980s. In 1980, besides "You'd Make an Angel Wanna Cheat," noted earlier, they had the hit singles "I'm Already Blue," "I Don't Do like That Anymore/Never My Love," and "Put It Off Until Tomorrow." Their 1981 hit singles included "Heart of the Matter" and "Teach Me to Cheat." Their album Best of the Kendalls was on the charts almost as soon as it came out in late 1980 and remained on them for much of 1981.

KENTUCKY COLONELS: *Vocal and instrumental group. Original members: Clarence White, Rowland White, Billy Ray Latham, Roger Bush.*

A resurgent interest in bluegrass music was one facet of the folk music boom of the late 1950s and early 1960s. Though Bill Monroe, Flatt & Scruggs, and other veteran bluegrass musicians were part of the scene, young musicians formed new groups in all parts of the United States. The ferment spread to California, where one of the first new bands to come along was the Kentucky Colonels, organized in the late 1950s by Rowland White.

To complete the original quartet, Rowland recruited his brother Clarence on lead guitar, Billy Ray Latham on banjo, and Roger Bush on bass and guitar. Playing fast-moving versions of traditional bluegrass, country, and old-timey gospel music, plus some original material of its own, the band became a favorite with country and bluegrass fans the first part of the 1960s. The group played bluegrass and folk festivals around the United States and also headlined many shows on the coffee house circuit. The band made a number of recordings in the early 1960s, including the LP Kentucky Colonels issued on World Records in July 1964.

A combination of conflicting views on musical directions among members and the overshadowing of the folk movement by Beatles-inspired 1960s rock caused the group to break up in 1965. The members went in different directions, working as sidemen with folk and rock groups or doing session work. In 1968, Clarence White joined the reorganized Byrds, remaining with them as lead guitarist into the early 1970s. Rowland went to Nashville, where, at one time or another, he was a member of Bill Monroe's Blue Grass Boys and Lester Flatt's band (after the breakup of Flatt & Scruggs). Latham and Bush joined the group formed by Doug Dillard and Gene Clark in the late 1960s, the Dillard and Clark Expedition. Later Bush was a mainstay of Byron Berline's 1970 bluegrass band, the Country Gazette. Latham was with the Dillards' group from 1971 to 1977.

There were sporadic attempts at reinstituting the Colonels. In August 1970, for instance, Clarence White, Latham, and Bush joined forces (aided by several other sidemen) as part of a "Country Jamboree" series at the Los Angeles Ash Grove. In 1973, the Whites reunited for what was to be a highly acclaimed Swedish tour under the name the New Kentucky Colonels. With the reviving interest in bluegrass in the mid-1970s, the way seemed open for an important new phase in the Colonels' career, but this was short-circuited by the untimely death of Clarence White.

The Swedish tour was the basis for a live album issued by Rounder Records titled *The White Brothers (The New Kentucky Colonels)*. Two other albums of the Colonels' work were available at the end of the 1970s, both made from tapes recorded in the 1960s, one on Takoma Records called *Livin' in the Past* and the other on Rounder, *The Kentucky Colonels*.

KERSHAW, DOUG: *Singer, fiddler, guitarist, songwriter. Born Louisiana, January 24, 1937.*

The Cajun sound developed by the descendants of French Canadians forcibly relocated from Canada to Louisiana centuries ago has become an important part of modern country music. Many artists have contributed to the growing influence of this music form, but no song has typified the genre better than Doug Kershaw's "Louisiana Man."

For Kershaw, who grew up in the bayou country in Louisiana, it was part of his natural heritage. The main language spoken in his house was French—he didn't start to learn English until he went to school—and the music played at family get-togethers mainly consisted of Cajun folk songs. As a child, Doug recalled going fishing and muskrat-trapping with his father in the back country of his home state.

Doug learned to play fiddle and guitar at an early age and helped introduce his younger brother Rusty (born February 2, 1940) to Cajun and country music when Rusty became old enough to pick it up. Although there were other children in the family, Rusty and Doug seemed to hit it off best musically. They practiced together and by their teens in the mid-1950s were good enough to become regular cast members on the *Louisiana Hayride* in Shreveport. They began turning out records that first made local charts and then began to gain wider attention. One result was the opportunity for the brothers to join the *Grand Ole Opry* in 1957.

That they moved to the *Opry* in a year with a seven in it seemed significant to Doug. He told La Wayne Satterfield of *Music City News* (October 1969), "It is really amazing how the number seven is constantly popping up in my life. You know I was on the Johnny Cash premier show [in the late 1960s] which was shown on television on June 7th. I recently taped a guest appearance on Hank Williams, Jr.'s television show and on the seventh take it was right. The first money I ever made was seven dollars."

Other events that fitted in included that he started school at seven, that his father killed himself that year, that Doug was the seventh child born in his family, that he signed a longterm writer's contract with BMI in 1967, that his solo recording contract was with Warner Bros. Seven Arts, and that "Louisiana Man" was the seventh song he wrote.

The two brothers interrupted their performing careers in 1958 when both volunteered for the Army at the same time. They reasoned that they were going to be drafted anyway and by enlisting together they insured they would get discharged together. That's what happened in the early 1960s and, for a time, the duo picked up as if nothing had intervened. In fact, they soon had their all-time biggest single with the release of "Louisiana Man" in 1961. The record made the top 10 in the country field and also won considerable favor from pop and folk fans too. The song, of course, has become Doug's signature song, one he has played countless times on almost every major TV show in the United States and in live concerts throughout the world.

The team of Rusty and Doug remained together for several more years after the success of "Louisiana Man" and for a while in the 1960s had several more hits on Hickory Records (which issued the LP *Rusty and Doug* in July 1964). In the mid-1960s, the brothers broke up the team after a career in which over 18 million of their records were sold.

As a solo artist, Doug continued to receive an enthusiastic welcome from pop and country fans throughout the late 1960s and into the early 1980s. However, though some of his releases made the charts he never was able to duplicate some of the recording achievements of his earlier years. His album releases on Warner Bros. sold steadily if not spectacularly. Among those LPs were *Cajun Way*, issued in late 1969, and such 1970s releases as *Spanish Moss, Doug Kershaw, Swamp Grass, Devil's Elbow, Douglas James Kershaw, Mama Kershaw's Boy, Alive and Pickin', The Ragin' Cajun,* and *Louisiana Man*. All of those still were in Warner Brothers' active catalogue at the start of the 1980s. While Doug also had a number of singles issued on the label during the 1970s, some of which made lower-chart levels, only "It Takes All Day (To Get Over Night)," from *The Ragin' Cajun* LP, became a major success.

KILGORE, MERLE: *Singer, guitarist, songwriter, disc jockey, actor, music industry executive. Born Chickasha, Oklahoma, August 9, 1934.*

As a performer, writer, and executive, Merle Kilgore had both direct and behind-the-scenes impact on the development of country music in the decades after World War II. He achieved a number of hits as a singer and contributed to the success of other artists by providing them with successful songs or, in some cases, with initial encouragement to move ahead in the country field.

He was born in Oklahoma, but his family soon moved to Shreveport, Louisiana, where he learned to play guitar at an early age and was awarded his first stint as a disc jockey on station KENT in Shreveport. This was the first of a number of DJ positions on such other Louisiana stations as KNOE, Monroe, and KZEA, Springhill. While in his teens, he also started to establish a reputation as a performer with Louisiana fans and already was writing original material that he included in his act. Before long, other artists were playing some of his songs, too.

While still in high school, he was added to the cast of the *Louisiana Hayride* on KWKH, Shreveport, at the time almost as important as the *Grand Ole Opry* in the country field. An excellent guitarist by then, he accompanied many of the best-known performers on the show. In 1952, he also was featured on station KFAZ-TV in Monroe. He continued to perform on the *Hayride* while starring on KFAZ from 1952 to 1954. The year 1952 also brought his first guest spot on the *Grand Ole Opry* and on the *Big D Jamboree* in Dallas.

At first, after finishing high school, Merle decided to continue his education, entering Louisiana Tech in 1952. He stayed in college a year, then left in 1953 to work days for the American Optical Company while pursuing his musical career in the evening. In 1954, he achieved major success with his composition "More and More," a national hit for such disparate artists as Guy Lombardo and Webb Pierce. The response to that number encouraged him to concentrate all his efforts on the music field from then on.

Throughout the rest of the 1950s, he maintained a full schedule, appearing on the *Hayride* regularly, at country night-clubs throughout the region, doing his DJ chores, and writing steadily. Among the songs for which he wrote both words and music were "It Can't Rain All the Time" and "Seeing Double" (1954); "Funny Feeling" (1955); "I've Got a Good Thing Going" (1958); "Tom Dooley, Jr.," "Hang Doll" (1958); and "Baby Rocked Her Dolly," "It Will Be My First Time," and "Jimmie Bring Sunshine" (1959). In 1959, he had a singles hit with "Dear Mama" and also provided Johnny Horton with a best-selling song, "Johnny Reb."

Merle also co-wrote songs with a number of others over the years. His 1950s collaborations included such songs as "Everybody Needs a Little Loving" (1955); "Take the Last Look," "The Wild One" (1957); "Swing Daddy Swing," "Little Pig," "Change of Heart," "You Don't Want to Hold Me," "Old Enough to Love," "We're Talking It Over" (1958); and "I Took a Trip to the Moon." One person he penned some numbers with in those years was a Springhill teenager named Joe Stampley, who hung around the studios where Kilgore was a DJ. He encouraged Stampley and helped line up his first record contract. Eventually, Stampley became one of country music's top stars of the 1970s.

Kilgore moved into the 1960s with a major hit, in the U.S. country top 10 during 1960, his composition "Love Has Made You Beautiful," on Starday Records. (During the 1950s, he recorded for D Records and Imperial.) Two years later he teamed with Claude King to write "Wolverton Mountain." King's single of the song was a number-one hit on Columbia Records in 1962 and the tune has since been recorded by dozens of other artists. In 1963, Merle co-wrote another classic, this time with June Carter. Titled "Ring of Fire," the song was a smash hit for June's future husband, Johnny Cash, rising to number one on country charts and doing well on the pop charts, too.

Merle continued to perform widely on concerts and on TV as the 1960s went by. His engagements included appearances at the Hollywood Bowl in California, New York's Carnegie Hall, and as a headliner of a number of shows in Las Vegas and Reno. Although not placing his own recordings in the top 10 after 1960, he kept turning out discs that sometimes made lower-chart levels. Until the mid-1960s, he was associated with Starday, which issued the LP *Merle Kilgore,* in January 1964. He was represented on Mercury briefly, including the LP *Merle Kilgore* issued in January 1966. For a time, in the mid-1960s, he signed with Epic Records, then, in 1968, was affiliated with Ashley Records.

One of his first recordings for Epic was "Nevada Smith," the title song for a western film in which he starred. Before that, he had begun his acting career on film in *Country Music on Broadway.* His six foot, four inch frame lent itself well to western casting, and his mid-1960s credits included a leading role in *Five Card Stud,* in which Debbie Reynolds had the female lead.

Among Merle's other activities, he headed several music publishing firms during the 1960s and continued to spend much of his time in behind-the-scenes work in the 1970s. There were still occasional releases of his material in the early 1970s, such as the Hilltop LP *Ring of Fire.* By the latter part of the decade, he was without a recording contract, but continued to do live shows and was still headlining programs on the state and county fair and country nightclub circuit at the end of the 1970s.

KING, B.B.: *Singer, guitarist, songwriter. Born Ita Bena (near Indianola), Mississippi, September 16, 1925.*

It's lucky that B.B. King never worried all that much about personal schedules or he might not have attained the eminence in blues and rock that he eventually achieved. Though considered one of the major interpreters of country blues, he really didn't focus full attention on that genre until he left his native delta blues region. And he didn't gain recognition as a star until he was in his forties, and then as a favorite of young rock fans who generally didn't pay too much attention to artists of that advanced age.

Riley B. King was born on a cotton plantation near Indianola, Mississippi, in the heart of the Delta, but at the age of four, when his parents separated, his mother took him to a hilly section of the state. Life was no easier there: as soon as young Riley could do farm work, he was out doing chores and earning whatever he could to help out. Plenty of blues were being sung and performed in Negro ghetto areas, but his mother, an ardent churchgoer, warned him against paying attention to it. She took him to church regularly, where he sometimes sang in the choir, and she saw to it that no profane blues material was played in their home.

When he was nine, young Riley's mother died, and he had to work full time for a tenant farmer, chopping and hoeing cotton. He got a little schooling in, but not much, over the next six years. When he was fourteen, his father found him and took him back to Indianola. He still had to do farm work, but he was back within a family circle and could go to school somewhat more regularly. Equally important, he was directed toward the delights of the guitar. An uncle taught him some basic chords and soon after, the then fifteen-year-old bought one for eight dollars. He rapidly gained mastery of the instrument and then formed his first group, a gospel quartet.

When World War II came along, he went into the Army, resulting in his first intensive exposure to the blues. In a black company, he picked up blues songs and guitar techniques from some of his mates and had a reasonably large repertoire by the time he was discharged in the mid-1940s. However, back with his family blues was not allowed, so when he could, he went off to sing on street corners, sometimes making more in a day than he made in a week as a farm laborer. B.B. began to realize that music offered a possible escape from the drudgery of farm work.

In 1947, he hitchhiked to Memphis, Tennessee, where a cousin of his, now legendary blues artist Bukka White, lived. Bukka put him up and gave him pointers on both the blues and the music field. Eager to get ahead, King first got work as a free-lance performer singing commercials on black station WDIA. After a while, he developed contacts with club owners and began to find work under the name Riley King, the Blues Boy from Beale Street, which he soon changed to Blues Boy King and finally to its present form, B.B. King. This helped open the door to a job as a disc jockey in 1948, which, in turn, he employed to develop his recording career.

The recording executives B.B. met in the course of his DJ work provided the entrée to his first recording contract, in 1949, with RPM Records. He started turning out material on the label, one of which, "Three O'Clock Blues," made the national R&B lists in 1950.

Throughout the 1950s, King was represented by singles or LPs on RPM or its subsidiary labels, Crown and Kent. Those sold well enough to satisfy the company but never enough to gain any sizable royalties for King, a situation not helped any by the low ninety-nine-cent selling price of the records on drugstore racks. Among his many recordings were such titles as "Nany, You Lost Your Good Thing Now," "Five Long Years," "Every Day I Have the Blues," "Did You Ever Love a Woman," "Crying Won't Help You," and "You Upset Me, Baby." To keep going, during the 1950s and early 1960s, B.B. played the chitlin' circuit, small clubs and run-down theaters in ghetto sections of town.

He achieved what could be called a cult following in folk and rock fields, but not enough to make him a "name" artist. He didn't have the brash aggressiveness of people like Chuck Berry and Little Richard that let them fight the odds to cash in on the white-led rock boom. At the same time, his complex and polished blues style made folk purists damn him as "too commercial," a judgment later reversed in part, but that managed to keep him out of the folk resurgence of the late 1950s and early 1960s. His situation in the early 1960s is well summarized by a line from one of his songs, "I've been a good man, although/ I'm a poor man—understand?"

In the early and mid-1960s, the tide turned with the rise of the Beatles, Rolling Stones, and other British supergroups who were weaned on roots blues and greatly admired blues artists of all kinds. The Stones and other young artists praised King's talents and occasionally included some of his material in their shows. Soon American musicians followed suit, particularly Mike Bloomfield, who copied some of B.B.'s techniques and spread the word of King's superb guitar work to other musicians.

Even before that, King's star had started to rise at home. ABC-Paramount gave him a contract in 1961, but legal entanglements cropped up and he couldn't record for the label until 1963. From 1963 on, though, he was one of the company's most dependable artists, turning out one or more albums a year that came out on ABC or its subsidiary label, Bluesway. Close to two decades later, he still was on the ABC roster and moved with the label to MCA when the latter bought out ABC in 1979. (Over the years, of course, some of his work came out on other labels, either as reissues bought from ABC or re-releases of earlier recordings.)

His 1960s LPs included *Mr. Blues* (issued 9/63); *Live at the Regal* (3/65); *Confessin' the Blues* (1/66); *Blues Is King* (3/67); *Lucille* (10/68)—Lucille, it might be noted, is B.B.'s name for his guitar; *Blues on Top of Blues* (3/68); *Live and Well* (1969); and *Completely Well* (1969).

The success of the "British Invasion" of the 1960s paid off in steadily increasing prominence for B.B. as the decade went by. He got the chance to share bills with some of those bands at major festivals and major venues. In late 1966, for instance, he was asked to play the prestigious Fillmore West in San Francisco and won ovations from standing-room-only audiences. He returned both there and to the other Bill Graham emporium, New York's Fillmore East, before those clubs were shuttered in the early 1970s. His career moved ever faster as the late 1960s approached. In 1968 he made what amounted to a triumphal tour of England and Europe and later earned glowing reviews for an engagement at New York's Village Gate. In 1969, besides a number of appearances on network TV programs, he performed at the Newport Jazz Festival and the Texas International Pop Festival and joined the Rolling Stones on their late 1969 coast-to-coast U.S. swing.

As the 1970s got under way, King was an established star. He began the decade in fine fashion with a gold-record single, "The Thrill Is Gone," from the 1969 LP *Live and Well*. In 1971, he had two hit albums, *Indianola Mississippi Seeds* and *Live at Cook County Jail*, both on the charts much of the year. By then long overdue honors were starting to come his way. At the end of 1970, the *Guitar Player* magazine poll named him Top Blues Guitarist of the Year. He won the 1970 Grammy for Best R&B Vocal Performance—Male for "The Thrill Is Gone."

In 1972, he had another premiere year, placing nine singles and albums on the charts. Among those singles were "Ghetto Woman," "Ain't Nobody Home," and "I Got Some Help I Don't Need." His album hits included *B.B. King in London, Live at the Regal, Guess Who?,* and *L.A. Midnight*. In 1973, he had another hit single, "To Know You Is to Love You" and the late 1974 album release of his duet work with Bobby Bland, *Together for the First Time,* was a chart hit well into 1975 and earned a gold-record award on February 28, 1975. His album efforts won the *Ebony* Music Awards for Best Blues Album two years in a row, in 1975 and 1976. Later in the 1970s, he gave a series of twenty-two concerts in the USSR, the first major tour of Russia by an American blues/blues-rock artist.

His late 1970s album releases included a series of collaborations with the Crusaders. The first resulted in the ABC LP *Midnight Believer*. The next one, *Take It Home,* in which King, the Crusaders, and Will Jennings wrote all the material, was his first issued on MCA Records, in July 1979. In 1981, he had two more LPs on MCA, *Live: Now Appearing at Ole Miss* and *There Must Be a Better World Somewhere.*

KING, CAROLE: *Singer, pianist, songwriter. Born Brooklyn, New York, February 9, 1942.*

Carole King had what amounted to two phenomenal careers in pop music embracing two different decades. In the 1960s, she formed a songwriting partnership with

Gerry Goffin that provided dozens of superhits in the R&B/soul-rock vein. In the 1970s, as a writer and performer, she played a pivotal role in the development of a softer, more reflective sound in pop music, a sound closer to folk music than the more strident compositions of her earlier years.

Carole was born and raised in Brooklyn, New York, where jazz, swing bands, and the last stages of romantic ballads dominated the pop music field in her childhood. In her teens, she veered away from most of that, influenced by the new rock revolution represented by people like Bill Haley, Elvis Presley, and Fats Domino. As she progressed through high school, she delved a little deeper than her classmates into the roots of rock, finding a strong interest in the still submerged rhythm & blues stylings that were mainly restricted to the black population.

By the time she finished high school, though, R&B groups were beginning to show up regularly on the U.S. hit charts. She had started writing pop songs by then, some in the R&B format. After marrying a young lyricist named Gerry Goffin, she became part of a writing team that soon won the attention of New York publishers. By the time she was twenty, she and Gerry already had a reputation as songwriting greats of the future.

Their first massive success came with the Shirelles' recording of "Will You Love Me Tomorrow" in 1961. Soon they had another top-10 hit with the Drifters' single of "Up on the Roof." And more Goffin and King compositions proved winners for an ever-widening group of artists. Among their credits were such titles as "I Wasn't Born to Follow," "No Easy Way Down," "Child of Mine," "Eventually," "Hi-De-Ho," "Natural Woman," "Locomotion," and "Snow Queen." "Locomotion" provided a million-copy hit for Little Eva and was a fruitful number for several reissues by other artists in the late 1960s and 1970s. "Hi-De-Ho" in time became a major hit for the late 1960s group Blood, Sweat & Tears. Other hits of the early and mid-1960s included the Chiffons' version of "One Fine Day," the Drifters' "Some Kind

of Wonderful," Bobby Vinton's and Tony Orlando's releases of "Half Way to Paradise," Maxine Brown's "Oh No, Not My Baby," the Righteous Brothers' "Just Once in My Life," Gene Pitney's "Every Breath I Take," Dusty Springfield's "No Easy Way Down," and many more.

In the early 1960s, Carole tried her hand at singing some of the Goffin-King songs. Several discs made the charts, the most successful being the 1962 hit "It Might as Well Rain Until September." However, Carole preferred to take time out to raise a family rather than pursue the pressure-laden route to pop stardom.

The Goffin-King writing partnership continued to be highly productive until they ran into problems with their marriage. The two finally divorced, after which Carole went into semiretirement to concentrate on looking after her two young daughters. In the second half of the 1960s, that goal led her to move to the Los Angeles area. She kept on writing songs, though she didn't do much else in the music field for the first part of her stay in California. While she collaborated with various writers in the late 1960s, including Toni Stern and musician Charles Larkey, who became her second husband, much of her new material was completely self-penned.

In 1968, she formed a group called City with Charles Larkey and Danny Kortchmar, the latter a close friend and sometime associate of James Taylor. King had known record company owner Lou Adler since 1963 and he agreed to sign the group. His firm, Ode Records, issued an LP by City, but it was a failure. In the meantime she had been introduced to James Taylor by Kortchmar and Taylor urged her to go on as a solo artist.

She finally agreed and was buoyed by a good reception at several West Coast concerts and the faith expressed in her by Adler. Her first album, *Writer: Carole King*, was issued at the start of the 1970s and had a reasonably good, if not sensational, reception. The next one, however, provided the turning point. Titled *Tapestry*, it was released in early 1971 to coincide with a national tour in March and April on the same bill as James Taylor. So well were both album and tour received that by mid-year, people were clamoring for her to headline. The album provided such major hit singles as "It's Too Late," backed with "I Feel the Earth Move," and "You've Got a Friend." The last named also was recorded by Taylor and became a singles hit for him and a staple in his concert repertoire.

Tapestry was a sensation, making its way to number one on U.S. charts during 1971. Still on the charts in late 1976, it had sold over 13.5 million copies, to become one of the all-time best sellers. In the voting for the Grammy Awards for 1971, King won no less than four trophies, one for Album of the Year, one as Best Pop Female Vocalist, one for Song of the Year (songwriter's award) for "You've Got a Friend," and the fourth for Record of the Year for the single "It's Too Late." Before 1971 was over, Carole had added another gold-record award to her collection for her third Ode solo LP, *Carole King Music*. That was her second gold-record album award in 1971, *Tapestry* having been honored by the R.I.A.A. on June 7 and *Carole King Music* on December 9.

She continued to place records on the charts as the 1970s went along and, while the totals were far less than the blockbuster levels of *Tapestry*, all her Ode collections reached gold-record status. Her LP *Rhymes and Reasons* gained the award on November 1, 1972, followed by *Fantasy* on June 26, 1973, *Wrap Around Joy* on October 16, 1974, and *Thoroughbred* on March 25, 1976.

Always jealous of her privacy, Carole cut back on her live appearances sharply after the banner year of 1971. She did give concerts, but only at widely spaced intervals. In between she stayed behind the scenes, spending as much time as she could with her family, which, by the early 1970s, included another daughter born to her and second husband Larkey. That approach probably tended to cut down on the potential sales totals of her new albums, but she never felt that was the overriding concern of her life. It was a theme she was to emphasize in her 1977 album whose title song, written by Carole and musician Rick Evers, was *Simple Things*. As she said, "Simple things mean a lot to me."

The album represented a change in affiliation. In late 1976, she announced she had severed relations with Ode, though Ode stated it would still have several LPs of her work in release. In December 1976, she signed with Capitol Records, which set up a new label, Avatar, for her material. *Simple Things*, her first Avatar/Capitol LP, came out during the summer of 1977 and was certified gold by the R.I.A.A. in September. King finished out the decade with two more LPs for Capitol, *Welcome Home*, issued in May 1978, and *Touch the Sky*, issued in May 1979. She began the 1980s with an LP called *Pearls* (on Capitol label), which contained her versions of Goffin-King songs that had been major hits for other artists in the past.

KING, PEE WEE: *Singer, accordionist, band leader, songwriter, publisher, booking agent. Born Wisconsin, February 18, 1914.*

Raised in Wisconsin and later a permanent resident of Louisville, Kentucky, Pee Wee King probably will always be best known as co-writer of "Tennessee Waltz," though his activities and contributions to country and western music embrace a multitude of accomplishments. But his 1946 composition not only provided hit records for Patti Page and a number of other artists, it became the state song of the residence of the *Grand Ole Opry*, a show on which Pee Wee also starred for over a decade with his Golden West Cowboys.

King, whose original name was Frank Anthony Kuczynski, grew up in Milwaukee in a family that valued music. His father, who played ocarina and fiddle for dances and parties in northern Wisconsin, encouraged him to play instruments. Before young Frank finished at Bay View High School in 1932, he already was playing public dates as a fiddler and accordionist. In 1932, he studied mechanical drafting at Vocational Trade School in Milwaukee, but music was too enticing. When the call came to join the cast of the WRJN *Badger State Barn Dance* in 1933, he jumped at the chance.

He formed his own band, which originally played some country and square dance material but began to add western-style music, particularly after Gene Autry asked him to bring his band to the *Gene Autry Show* in Louisville, Kentucky, in 1934, the city Pee Wee later chose as home. He recalled in the CMA *Country Music Close Up* in May 1976, "So I got into the Western end of the business. But I cut my eyeteeth on what they call country music by listening to a band led by Clayton McMichen."

By the mid-1930s, King had named his band the Golden West Cowboys, a famous name in country music annals, whose alumni include such greats as Ernest Tubb and Eddy Arnold. The band joined the *Midday Round Up* on station WNOX in Knoxville, a show Pee Wee (who at five feet seven inches was the shortest member of the group) headed for a number of years even while he and his band became regulars on the *Grand Ole Opry*. They were asked to perform on the *Opry* in 1936 and were regulars from 1937 until the late 1940s. Besides the band's *Opry* work, it was featured in country shows from one end of the United States to the other and, though the group was generally back in Nashville on weekends for the *Opry*, in between it was constantly on the move from one one-night-stand to another.

Pee Wee not only was building a national reputation with country fans with his group's sound, but was also steadily turning out a growing list of original songs, some of which became band standards in the 1940s. The song that was to become his prime trademark finally reached fruition in 1946, though it had been in the repertoire after a fashion for years before that.

The catalyst was Henry Ellis (Redd) Stewart, who had joined the group in the early 1940s as a multitalented sideman (guitar, fiddle, piano). As King recalled for the *Country Music Closeup*, it occurred while

Stewart and Pee Wee were sitting in the band's luggage truck during a tour. "It was a Friday night in 1946 and the luggage truck was the easiest place to concentrate on listening to the radio. Bill Monroe's 'Kentucky Waltz' was playing on the radio. Redd said, 'You know, it's odd; we make a living in Tennessee, but nobody's ever written a Tennessee waltz that we know of.' And so we took the old melody that we were using as our theme—the 'No Name Waltz'—and Redd started writing the lyrics on the back of a matchbook cover. And we kept putting it together, putting it together."

But it wasn't until some time later, 1948, in fact, that "Tennessee Waltz" swept the nation. By then King had a show of his own on station WAVE and WAVE-TV in Louisville, which he began in 1947 and continued heading until 1957. The year was 1948 and singles of the song by King, for several years an RCA recording artist, and Cowboy Copas made the country top 10. But the version of the song by popular singer Patti Page did even better, reaching number one on the national pop charts.

He continued to add to his credits as the 1950s went along, making the charts with such singles as "Slow-Poke," one of his originals that reached number one in 1951, "Silver and Gold" in 1952, and "Bimbo" in 1954. Many more of his compositions showed up on country charts throughout the 1950s and in the 1960s, either recorded by him or other performers. In the early 1960s, for instance, Jo Stafford had a major pop hit with Pee Wee's song "You Belong to Me." In 1964, he had a top-10 country hit with another of his classic compositions, "Bonaparte's Retreat," a song that has served as a basis for hit singles for quite a few others since then.

As of the mid-1970s, his total compositions exceeded 400. From 1950 through 1955, his group had a stranglehold on the best country band title, being named to that spot throughout that period by both *Billboard* and *Cash Box* magazines.

King remained active on the movie scene, too, from the late 1930s into the 1950s. His initial appearance was in Gene

Autry's *Gold Mine in the Sky*, and he took part in other films by Autry as well as working with such other western movie notables as Johnny Mack Brown and Charles Starrett.

Pee Wee's TV show was televised nationally from Louisville from 1955 to 1957 and later he had similar coverage from Cleveland on ABC. In fact, in the late 1950s and early 1960s, for a while King had four major television shows going at the same time. In 1962 he decided the grind was too rugged and gave up all of them, though he continued to make personal appearances. His recording activities also slowed down in the 1960s. His association with RCA had ended in 1959 when he moved to Todd Records. In the mid-1960s he made some recordings for Starday.

He formed a new band in 1967 as part of "Pee Wee King's Country-Western Hoedown," which performed on station WMAS-TV in Louisville. In 1969, he disbanded that group and essentially retired from the active performing side of things. He remained active on the business side, though, packaging country & western shows throughout the 1970s for engagements across the United States and Canada. The main emphasis was on providing shows for the county fair circuit.

King's contributions to country & western music for over four decades were recognized by his peers in 1974, when he was elected a member of the Country Music Hall of Fame. King, a long-time supporter of industry organizations, was named to a two-year term as a member of the CMA Board of Directors in October 1975 and currently serves on the board of the Country Music Foundation.

KINGSTON TRIO, THE: *Vocal and instrumental group. Bob Shane, born Hawaii, February 1, 1934; Nick Reynolds, born Coronado, California, July 27, 1933; Dave Guard, born near San Francisco, California, October 19, 1934. Guard replaced by John Stewart, born San Diego, California, in 1941. Original trio disbanded in 1967 with new versions of the trio revived (separately) in the 1970s by Nick Reynolds and Bob Shane. Founding members Reynolds, Shane, and Guard reassembled in late 1981.*

The Kingston Trio often was disparaged by the "serious" members of the folk boom of the late 1950s and early 1960s as being, in effect, opportunistic. The Trio, they said, was essentially a pop group that happened to sing folk or folk-flavored material rather than an authentic folk group. But the fact remained that the Trio had a hand in making the American mass audience aware of the pleasures of folk music, and its enormous success provided an environment that allowed all types of folk artists to prosper for a time.

Two of the original threesome grew up in Hawaii; Dave Guard and Bob Shane learned to play ukuleles and sometimes sang Hawaiian songs together while attending Punahou School in Honolulu. Their paths didn't cross that of Nick Reynolds until they came to the San Francisco Bay area to attend college, Bob enrolling at Menlo College to major in business administration and Dave working his way through nearby Stanford University as an economics major. (Both earned B.A. degrees in their specialties in the mid-1950s.) Nick, the son of a Navy man, was born in Coronado, but lived in many different places during his youth. By the time he enrolled in Menlo College in the early 1950s, he could play guitar well, having been tutored at the start by his father, who also played the instrument.

Reynolds and Shane, both business administration students, became friends and started casually singing pop and folk songs for the fun of it. Soon they brought in Bob's friend Dave Guard to form a group that picked up spare income performing for college events. Still, they didn't think of making music a career at first. In fact, after graduation, Shane went home to Hawaii and worked in business for a time. But inspired by the growing public interest in folk material, they decided to re-form their act and try for a professional career. They performed at a college hangout near Stanford called the Cracked Pot, being paid essentially in free beer and meals. A San Francisco publicist named Frank Werber heard them and was so impressed he used a table napkin as paper for a contract that all signed one night. The group decided a distinctive name was needed and they chose "Kingston Trio" because calypso was in vogue then and "Kingston" sounded both collegiate and calypso.

They spent months polishing their act before debuting at the well-known cellar club of San Francisco, the hungry i. That 1957 engagement lasted a week. They won polite applause, but nothing to suggest their future superstar status. Then they moved across the street to another famous cellar spot, the Purple Onion, and things started to jell. By the end of the first week, audience response had picked up to the point that their engagement was extended a week, then another, until finally their stay extended to seven months. Other well-received dates followed in such San Francisco spots as Facks II and the hungry i. With their reputation starting to build, the boys took off across country to star in places like Mr. Kelly's in Chicago and the Blue Angel and Village Vanguard in New York.

In January 1958, the Trio signed a long-term contract with Capitol Records and also began considering overtures from major concert venues and from TV. One of their first major milestones was an appearance in both acting and singing roles in a Playhouse 90 TV program, "Rumors of the Evening." In June 1958, their debut album, The Kingston Trio, appeared. The record did fairly well, but its main impact proved to be one track titled "Tom Dooley." Released as a single late in 1958, it began to receive widening airplay until it finally rose to the top of the charts. In January 1959, it passed the million-copy mark, bringing the group its first gold-record award. The Kingston Trio by then was nationally known and on the way to becoming one of the most popular acts in the world in 1959 and the early 1960s.

("Tom Dooley" was thought at first to be a traditional ballad. One of the approaches the Trio favored was to sing updated versions of public-domain songs, often with new lyrics that could permit copyrighting of the song. As it happened, a long drawn-out lawsuit eventually demonstrated the song was the contemporary creation of a hill-country artist named Frank Proffitt.)

The group quickly showed that "Tom Dooley" wasn't a one-shot success by turning out a series of singles and albums that rose high on the hit charts. In 1960, they earned gold records for their first album, The Kingston Trio, and the followup Kingston Trio at Large in April and added two more awards in October for the LPs Here We Go Again and From the hungry i. In June 1961, their album Sold Out won another gold record. Also doing well on the charts those years were such songs as "Tijuana Jail," "M.T.A.," "Molly Dee," and "Green Grasses." The last two songs were written by a close friend, John Stewart, who had become a primary arranger for the group. When Stewart decided to switch from rock to folk performances at the start of the 1960s, the Trio members helped him form his folk trio, called the Cumberland Three.

In the spring of 1961, the Trio went on a highly successful tour of Australia, New Zealand, and Japan. Things were going well outwardly, but Dave Guard was becoming restless. He wanted to go his own way and finally decided to leave after the tour. The other two members asked John Stewart to be Guard's replacement. As Reynolds said, "John was a natural. He's not only a talented performer and a swinging musician, but he has that great quality of contagious enthusiasm that means so much to our performances."

The changeover went smoothly and, if anything, the Trio's shows seemed to achieve a new vitality. The band took cognizance of new trends in the folk field by including songs from Bob Dylan in its repertoire, making the charts with its version of "Blowin' in the Wind." Stewart continued to add new compositions of his own like "Song for a Friend." By the mid-1960s, typical concerts included such other songs with which the group had become identified as "Lemon Tree," "Raspberries, Strawberries," "A Worried Man," Pete Seeger's "Where Have All the Flowers Gone," the Hoyt Axton–Ken Ramsey composition "Greenback Dollars," Ed Mc-

Curdy's "Last Night I Had the Strangest Dream," the Woody Guthrie opus "Reuben James," Rod McKuen's "Two-Ten, Six-Eighteen," and Billy Edd Wheeler's "Ann." Sometimes included were folk-flavored songs from the musical theater such as "They Call the Wind Maria" and "The Merry Minuet."

Still, the inroads of the "British Invasion," and the rock resurgence it spawned, affected the group's status by the mid-1960s. Trio records made the charts, including gold-record attainment for the LP *String Along* in June 1962 and *The Best of the Kingston Trio* in September 1963, but more and more the releases tended to only go as high as mid- or lower-levels. The group continued to be a top-rated act and could bring out sizable audiences on cross-country tours of the United States and on swings through Canada, Europe, and the Far East, but it seemed obvious that the Trio's main glory days were behind them. As the latter 1960s came into view, both Shane and Reynolds were getting a little tired of the grind and Stewart was becoming increasingly eager to try to succeed as a solo artist. (The road proved to be much longer than he imagined. Solo stardom escaped him until the end of the 1970s.) In 1967, the group decided to disband and its *Farewell Album* was released by Capitol that year.

In the 1970s, Bob Shane decided to organize a new version of the Kingston Trio but without any of the other charter members taking part. The group toured widely the second half of the 1970s, mostly playing vintage Trio material, though with occasional new songs like "Aspen Gold." Besides playing small-to-medium-size clubs, the groups also made some TV appearances, including a mid-1979 set by Shane's group on the nationally televised *Mike Douglas* show.

In late 1981, the original members of the Trio, Reynolds, Dave Guard, and Shane, reunited for their first performance together since 1961. The performance was given at Six Flags Magic Mountain amusement park near Los Angeles and was taped for presentation later on PBS. There was

some talk of making it a continuing association, but nothing came of it. (Also taking part were John Stewart and Shane's associates of the 1970s-early 1980s group.)

The first new album of Kingston Trio recordings in some years—essentially remakes of early Trio hits—was issued on a new label, Xeres Records, in early 1982, titled *The Kingston Trio—25 Years Non-Stop.* The group making that LP contained Shane, George Grove, and Roger Gambill, the latter two having performed with Shane for over six years.

KOTTKE, LEO: *Singer, guitarist, harmonica player, songwriter. Born Athens, Georgia, September 11, 1945.*

A master of the twelve-string guitar, Leo Kottke ranks as one of the foremost performers on the instrument in the world, certainly one of the top two or three in the United States. He has devoted some of his playing efforts to classical-style music, but by far the largest portion of his material, whether in the form of his own compositions or other writers' offerings, falls in the category from folk to the fringes of soft rock. His folk influences include traditional country tunes and bluegrass.

Kottke was born in Georgia and later moved with his family to Muskogee, Oklahoma, where he spent his high school years. He told an interviewer, "I got into folk music when I was pretty young, listening to people like Burl Ives, the Kingston Trio, Jimmie Rodgers. In high school I started paying attention to people like Pete Seeger, Don Reno, Red Smiley."

His musical interests inspired him to learn an instrument and the guitar was naturally the one that seemed apt for the range of music he liked, though he also learned the harmonica along the way, as well as trombone and violin. He told Colman Andrews that he had learned to sight-read the bass clef during his school years to help in his trombone playing. "I played trombone for eight years; I used to like 'Londonderry Air,' that sort of thing. And I played violin for three years and flute for a month."

He learned to play guitar just by fooling

around with the instrument. "I just sort of picked it up. I'm definitely self-taught. Which has some disadvantages. Like the fact that I've played for myself so long that I've neglected to learn a lot of stuff I should know. Scales, even. . . . I'd like to take a vacation for a year or so and study seriously with a good teacher."

In the mid-1960s, Kottke went north to Minnesota to attend college. He spent some time at St. Cloud State in St. Cloud, Minnesota, but his involvement with music made it difficult for him to keep up with his regular class work. By 1968, he had given up college and was working bars and coffee houses to pay for his room and board. After a while, he settled down to a regular weekend job at the Scholar Coffeehouse in Minneapolis, and slowly word of his skills on six- and twelve-string guitar began to circulate among folk and pop fans in the area.

In 1969, his debut album came out on the small, local Oblivion label. Called *12-String Blues*, it was initially produced in an edition of only 1,000 copies. A slightly larger pressing was made of his next release, essentially a re-recording of the Oblivion material, which came out on another Minnesota label, Symposium. Feeling that his ability deserved a wider audience, Leo began looking around for another possible outlet. He heard of the Takoma Records label headed by another fine guitarist named John Fahey, whose travels occasionally took him to the Scholar Coffeehouse for an engagement. "John sounded like the right guy, so I sent him some tapes."

Fahey concurred that Leo had considerable potential as a guitarist, though he wasn't impressed with Leo's voice. Thus Leo's 1970 debut on Takoma contained thirteen instrumentals. The album was titled *6- and 12-String Guitar*. Feeling that the door of opportunity was opening, Kottke moved to the Los Angeles area to be closer to the centers of musical activity. For a while, though, not too much happened. Takoma was a mail-order company, so Leo spent a lot of time as a glorified messenger boy. He told Tim Murtha of *Rolling Stone*

(August 29, 1974), "I used to pack them up in boxes and take them down to the post office, tiptoe through the turtle shit on John Fahey's porch. John is probably the best friend I'll ever have."

A turning point in his career, he recalled, was when an individual named Denny Bruce sought him out and became his manager. Bruce helped line up a growing number of dates at clubs in and around Los Angeles and also brought him to the attention of Capitol Records. His debut album on the label came out in 1971. Called *Mudlark*, it included such tracks as the instrumental "Eight Miles High" and a collaboration with Kim Fowley called "Monkey Lust." In a series of club dates in support of the LP, he thrilled critics and fans alike with his lightning skill on the twelve-string and his powerful bottleneck slide work. Despite his friend Fahey's thoughts about his voice, he demonstrated an excellent ability to win audience attention with his occasional vocal efforts.

His 1973 album, *Greenhouse*, did nothing to lower his reputation. It included two tracks that remained among the most popular he recorded, one his version of a Paul Siebel folk song, "Louise," the other a Ron Nagle composition, "From the Cradle to the Grave." Those songs as well as his performance of country star Tom T. Hall's "Pamela Brown" were key elements of the vocal part of his act in the mid-1970s. Also included in the LP was his composition "The Spanish Entymologist," in which he interwove parts of such songs as "Jambalaya," "Pretty Redwing," and "Tumbling Tumbleweeds."

As his name became more widely known among folk and pop fans throughout the United States and overseas (in 1973 he won rousing ovations from concertgoers in Europe—particularly in Germany), Kottke decided he could keep a career going outside the Los Angeles region. So he packed up and moved back to Minnesota from Pasadena. He got the chance to put together his own program to be presented at the Tyrone Guthrie Theater in Minneapolis, which became an annual event in that city in the 1970s. His 1973 appearance there was the basis for his third Capitol release and his first live album. In 1974, his fourth release, *Ice Water*, became his top-selling collection, selling in the neighborhood of 200,000 copies.

His next album, *Dreams and Other Stuff*, issued in early 1975, was recorded and mixed in the Sound 80 Studios in Minneapolis, where he had done work on much of his previous Capitol releases. The collection marked a return to the instrumentals-only policy of his earlier LPs. By the time the album came out, his talents had received attention from a broad cross section of the mass media from several pieces in *Rolling Stone* to a feature story in *People*. However, despite all the publicity, Leo tended to go his own way, writing the kind of material he wanted and not trying to change his style for possible million-selling recordings.

He made several more albums for Capitol in the mid-1970s before parting company with the label. (In November 1978, Capitol put out a *Best Of* retrospective.) As the 1970s came to a close, he recorded for Chrysalis Records (his debut on Chrysalis, *Leo Kottke*, was issued in 1977) and continued to perform in smaller venues throughout the United States and in other countries, either holding the stage himself or with only a small backing group.

KRISTOFFERSON, KRIS: *Singer, guitarist, songwriter, actor. Born Brownsville, Texas, June 22, 1937.*

A multitalented individual, Kris Kristofferson could achieve brilliant results in varied entertainment fields when he concentrated on his work. The problem was that at times he seemed to spread himself too thin and that, combined with some of his personal problems, caused phases of his career—particularly in songwriting and live concert work—to be distinctly erratic. But taken as a whole, his work in country music provided some of the finest original songs ever written.

The son of a two-star general, Kris moved to many different places during his childhood and youth, a pattern that contributed to a somewhat disjointed feeling at times. Born in Texas and having spent some of his childhood years in the South, he gained a natural affinity for country songs, though for a time he was more interested in pursuing a literary career than a musical one. He did learn guitar and could play quite well by the time he enrolled in Pomona College in Claremont, California. There he demonstrated considerable athletic ability, lettering in football and soccer, an achievement that helped make him a candidate for a Rhodes scholarship at Oxford University in England. The scholarship calls for both academic and athletic prowess and Kris was a fine student of literature, at one point winning the top four out of twenty prizes in the *Atlantic Monthly* collegiate short story contest. At Oxford, one of his major efforts was the study of the work of William Blake.

When he began his work there in the late 1950s, his primary aim was to become a novelist. However, by the time he completed his work, he felt depressed about his abilities. When he returned to the United States at the start of the 1960s, he had no real idea of what career to pursue. He had started to write songs, but was uncertain of their quality and soon took one way of dropping out: he enlisted in the U.S. Army and spent most of the first half of the decade in uniform. He became an officer, going through Ranger school, parachute jump school, and pilot training. He enjoyed flying and became an excellent pilot, specializing in helicopters.

However, in other ways, it was a destructive period for him. He told an interviewer in 1970, "For a time in the Army I quit writing. I nearly ended up destroying myself. I was drinking all the time, doing all kinds of reckless things. I totaled two cars and had four motorcycle accidents. But I had to write. I could no more not write than I could not breathe. It is a part of me." Unfortunately, a craving for alcohol also seemed to be a part of him and was to plague his career a number of times in the future.

After leaving the service in 1965, he toyed with the idea of accepting an appointment to teach English literature at West Point. But he had felt the pull of songwriting and decided to settle in Nashville and try to make the grade in that field. It was to prove a four-year, often desperate operation. He moved into a tenement and made the rounds of publishing houses, meeting with consistent turndowns. To stay alive and, by the end of the 1960s, support a wife and two children as well, he took any work he could find, including night janitor at Columbia Records Studios and day bartender at Nashville's Tally-Ho Tavern. Both jobs had the advantage of providing contacts with the country-music industry, the Tavern being a hangout for many established and aspiring songwriters. At times during those years he earned money by working as a laborer or flying helicopters to offshore oil rigs in the Gulf States area. Eventually, the strain proved too great for his marriage and a separation ensued.

Some of his experiences were reflected in his hit songs of later years. His loves and hitchhiking days are recalled in "Me and Bobby McGee": "Busted flat in Baton Rouge/Headin' for the trains/Feelin' just as faded as my jeans." The loneliness of the slum years appears in one of the songs from his 1971 hit LP, *The Silver Tongued Devil and I*, where, in "To Beat the Devil," he sings of the days when "Failure had me locked on the wrong side of the door . . . no one stood beside me but the shadow on the floor."

In 1969, Kris's persistence finally paid off. A long-time admirer of Johnny Cash, he practically lived outside the studio where Cash's network TV show was being taped. He pestered anyone of note who came there to look at his material, and finally Roger Miller gave in and agreed to consider it. Roger decided to record "Bobby McGee," which became a country hit and encouraged cover releases by many other artists from both pop and country genres.

Cash himself became a fan of Kristofferson's, featuring such songs as "Sunday Morning Comin' Down" on his show, referring to Kris as one of the new, great talents, and having Kris as a guest several times in 1969 and 1970. Johnny's single of "Sunday Morning" became a hit in 1969. Meanwhile, Janis Joplin decided to include her styling of "Bobby McGee" in her new and, as it turned out, last album. The single became one of the major pop hits of 1969, selling over a million copies and earning a gold record. It brought similar success to her LP *Pearl*.

By 1970, Kris was considered one of country music's most promising artists for the 1970s. That year the *New York Times* (July 26, 1970) ran an article noting that he was "the hottest thing in Nashville right now—and if you're hot in Nashville, man, you're hot everywhere." He had signed with Monument Records in 1969 and in June 1970, his debut LP on the label, *Me and Bobby McGee*, came out. That year, too, many artists eagerly checked out his new songs to turn out covers. Many of them recorded his "Help Me Make It Through the Night," but it was Sammi Smith who had the number-one selling version. The Nashville Songwriter's Association recognized his achievements by voting him Songwriter of the Year in 1970. In 1971, he got his first Grammy Award for "Help Me Make It Through the Night," voted Best Country Song.

During 1970, Kris worked on his first film score, for Dennis Hopper's *The Last Movie*. On June 23, 1970, he made his first professional appearance as a performer at a "name" club, the Los Angeles Troubadour. It was the first of countless live concerts which took him to every state in the union and many other parts of the world during the decade. From the early 1970s on, most of those shows also featured Rita Coolidge, who became Mrs. Kristofferson.

His concert work the first part of the 1970s was excellent, but for a time in the mid-1970s, he seemed to become dispirited, partly because of an increasing preoccupation with movie acting. Late in the decade, starting with his tours of 1977, he seemed to find renewed interest in working in front of an audience. Part of his problem, he told an interviewer in August 1977, had been the continued use of liquor as a crutch. He claimed his resurgence was due to cutting back on that: "It feels weird out there. I mean I have to get used to singing sober again. It's like singing in the daylight or something. But it's coming."

Kris's own single of "Bobby McGee" finally became a chart hit in September 1971, helped by the success of a new LP, *The Silver Tongued Devil and I*, which made the charts in July 1971. Joining those favorites was a new single, "Loving Her Was Easier (Than Anything I'll Ever Do Again)," which became a bestseller during that summer. In 1972, he gained a gold record for "The Silver Tongued Devil" and had two new albums on the charts, *Border Lord* and *Jesus Was a Capricorn*, plus another chart single, "Josie." In 1973, he had another singles hit with "Why Me, Lord" (backed with "Help Me"), and he also released the single "Jesse Younger" backed with "Give It Time to Be Tender."

There was a gap of almost two years before he had any new albums. In 1974, he was represented by *Spooky Lady's Nightmare* and *Breakaway*, which contained some interesting material but seemed to indicate a creative slowdown from his earlier work. Things picked up a bit with his 1975 LP, *Who's to Bless and Who's to Blame*, but regressed once more in 1976 with *Surreal Thing*. He continued to turn out LPs regularly as the decade went by, with most of the releases on Columbia. However, very little of his new work in the second half of the decade measured up to what he had done the previous five or six years. Among the albums were the soundtrack from his starring vehicle (with Barbra Streisand) *A Star Is Born* in 1976, a "best of" release, *Songs of Kristofferson* in 1977, *Easter Island* in 1978, and *Shake Hands with the Devil* in 1979. *Easter Island* was the most disappointing of all his collections, little in any of the original work coming close to such earlier classics as "Bobby McGee," "The Pilgrim," "Chapter 33," or any of dozens of previous triumphs. But the quality seemed to improve markedly in his 1979 LP, indicating that better things might be in store in the 1980s.

One reason for the slump in songwriting was perhaps traceable to his movie work. There he had proven himself one of the finest new actors to come along in the 1970s. His initial major film breakthrough was in the movie *Pat Garrett and Billy the Kid*, released in mid-1973. He played Billy in the movie, which costarred Bob Dylan. From then on, a long series of movies came out featuring his talents as both a dramatic and comic actor. They included *Cisco Pike, Alice Doesn't Live Here Anymore, Bring Me the Head of Alfredo Garcia, Blume in Love, Vigilante Force, The Sailor Who Fell from Grace With the Sea, Semi-Tough* (costarring Burt Reynolds and giving some opportunity for Kris to use his athletic skills), *Convoy, A Star Is Born, North Dallas Forty, Heaven's Gate*, and in 1981, *Rollover*, with Jane Fonda. He won a number of awards for acting, including being named Best Actor by the Foreign Press Association for *A Star Is Born*.

During the mid- and late-1970s, Kris recorded many duets with Rita Coolidge, including such singles as "Rain" backed with "What 'Cha Gonna Do" in 1974; "Lover Please" backed with "Slow Down," and "Sweet Susannah/We Must Have Been Out of Our Minds" in 1975. Kris and Rita won two Grammy Awards for Best Vocal Performance by a Duo, the first in 1973 for "From the Bottle to the Bottom" and the second in 1975 for "Lover Please."

By the end of the 1970s, his marriage to Rita Coolidge had gone sour and they separated. Late in 1979, Willie Nelson turned out an album of Kristofferson songs, and the two toured together during the 1979–80 winter concert season. At the start of 1980, Kris's single "Prove It to You Just One More Time" was on country charts. In the early 1980s, Columbia issued his LP *To the Bone*. In early 1982, after the drastic early 1980s recording industry recession caused most labels to reduce their backlists, only that LP, *Easter Island*, and *A Star Is Born* remained in print.

L

LA COSTA: *Singer, songwriter. Born Seminole, Texas, December 12, 1951.*

The saga of La Costa closely parallels that of Tanya Tucker for much of their lives, which isn't surprising since both are the daughters of Mr. and Mrs. Beau Tucker. However, the similarity changed for a while in the early 1970s when Tanya became a major country star while La Costa concentrated instead on school work. Tanya was the younger of the two but led the way for La Costa eventually to achieve success in the country field.

Actually, according to the way La Costa remembers it, she was the one who first suggested that music would be a "good fun career." As children growing up in Wilcox, Arizona, where the family moved from Texas, the girls enjoyed singing together. They liked the Lennon Sisters and country music and both fantasized about becoming the "Lennon Sisters of country music." The girls did sing in local shows in their home area, though once La Costa (her real first name) reached her mid-teens, she did a lot of solo work, including taking part in local talent shows and, with a fine figure to go with her blonde hair and blue eyes, also finishing well in a number of beauty contests.

Going through high school in the late 1960s with little sister Tanya not yet trying to scale the musical heights, La Costa considered an education more important than music. She did well enough in high school to receive a scholarship for music from the Fine Arts Department of the University of Arizona. She started there, then switched to Cochise College, in Douglas, Arizona, where she finished with an associate degree. After completing school, she began working as a medical records technician, settling for a time in the Phoenix area.

At the same time, she began to start singing again in local clubs and contests, picking up the title Miss Country Music Phoenix along the way. She obviously was making some headway in her career when sister Tanya suddenly came to the forefront in the country music field with a series of hits that began with "Delta Dawn" in 1972. That breakthrough both served as encouragement to La Costa and also made her a more attractive gamble for other record companies. She had married Darrell Sorensen a few years before and he and her father, who served as her manager, helped arrange a contract with Capitol Records in the spring of 1974. She decided to use only her first name to minimize comparisons between herself and Tanya.

Her first single, released in 1974, was "I Wanta Get to You," which demonstrated that La Costa had the vocal skills necessary for country success. The song gained enough attention to make the charts, as did her next single, "Get on My Love Train," which also made the country hit lists—though it didn't have the stratospheric rise typical of most of Tanya's releases of that period—and became the title track of her debut album. In 1975, she was represented in the country top 40 with the singles "Western Man" and "This House Runs on Sunshine." In early 1976, she had a best-selling single, "I Just Got a Feeling."

Her second album, *Lovin' Somebody on a Rainy Night,* was unveiled during the spring of 1976, as was a single of the same title that appeared on the charts in May and rose to the upper levels by early summer. Her third Capitol LP, issued in 1977, was titled *Lovin' Somebody,* with the title song, "Lovin' Somebody on a Rainy Day" culled as a single. She had several more singles and LPs issued on Capitol in the late 1970s, but these made relatively little headway with record buyers. In the summer of 1980, she had a moderate singles hit in "Changing All the Time," the title song for an album that turned out to be her last on Capitol. (It was still on the active list in 1982.) In early 1982 she signed a new contract arrangement with Elektra/Asylum Records.

LANE, CRISTY: *Singer. Born Peoria, Illinois, January 8, early 1940s.*

As Cristy Lane recalls it, she never intended to become a music business personality. If anyone had told her when she was in high school that she would get up and sing in public one day, she would have been paralyzed with stage fright. Her husband, however, changed that.

Growing up in Peoria, Cristy Johnston had a normal childhood. Though she was one of twelve children, her parents managed to provide a loving and reasonably comfortable home. Cristy had conventional goals as a girl, looking forward to having a home of her own and children. That's the way it turned out for a while; she married Lee Stoller at the end of the 1960s and settled down in Peoria to raise a family. (The Stollers now have three children.)

But one of the things Cristy enjoyed doing from time to time was singing along with records, and her husband became enthusiastic about her vocal abilities. A salesperson by profession, Lee started to think about ways of taking advantage of his wife's talent. He wanted her to gain experience singing in public, but it took a lot of persuasion before Cristy went along with the idea.

As she told interviewer James Albrecht of *Country Style* magazine, "I was an extremely shy person. It took Lee a long time to bring it out of me. He was getting me up in different clubs trying to bring me out of my shyness. It was really a terrifying thing for me to get up in front of people. A couple times I'd back out and he'd get mad at me. So I kept right on doing it."

In 1968, Lee sent a tape of his wife's material to the talent coordinators of the *WLS Barn Dance* program in Chicago. "They called me back," Cristy said, "and asked if I could be on the show. I about dropped dead."

Lane was becoming accustomed to show business, however, and with the *Barn Dance* experience to savor she began to perform on the country nightclub and fair circuit in the Midwest. Soon she and Lee opened their own club in Peoria, Cristy's Inc. With Cristy as the house singer, it became a favorite with country fans. Things went so well at the first club that they opened a second nightspot in East Peoria.

Lee dreamed of still wider recognition of his wife's singing. The logical place to go to do that was Nashville, so, in 1972 they sold their nightclub business and moved to the country music capital, which they quickly discovered was not waiting with bated breath. Lee made the rounds of record companies with demo tapes, arranged auditions for Cristy, and discussed various custom-record arrangements. However, either little interest was expressed or the companies that seemed inclined to sign her would not commit themselves to providing enough promotion support.

Cristy told Albrecht, "One executive told me that I had no chance, that I should go back to Peoria. And at some companies my husband was told, 'Why don't you leave her down here by herself and we'll straighten her out.' "

Finally, Lee decided to set up his own record company, LS Records, in the mid-1970s. The odds against any small label succeeding are tremendous, but Stoller was confident he had an artist who could buck those odds. It took hard work and perseverance, which, by 1977, started to produce results. In the summer of that year, Cristy's name began to appear on the charts. The single "Sweet Deceiver" made the top 50. Her debut LP, *Cristy Lane Is the Name*, released in 1977, proved a bonanza of top-10 songs. From late 1977 to the fall of 1978, four singles of material from the LP made the national top 10: "Let Me Down Easy," "Shake Me I Rattle," "I'm Gonna Love You Anyway," and "Penny Arcade." The last named was in the top 10 in September 1978.

Her second album on the LS label, *Love Lies*, came out in late 1978. In a short time it spawned the single "I Just Can't Stay Married to You," on the charts the end of the year and in the top 10 in early 1979. In the early summer, another single, "Simple

Little Words," made top-chart levels. Meanwhile Cristy found friendly audience response in nightclub and fair dates across the United States. She made several appearances on the *Grand Ole Opry* and was a guest on all the major syndicated country TV shows of the late 1970s. During 1978, the Academy of Country & Western Music named her the Top New Female Artist.

During early 1979, Stoller began considering an offer from United Artists to handle Lane's recordings. The agreement was concluded later in the year with all of her LS material transferred to UA. Her debut album on the label, *Ask Me to Dance*, came out in early 1980. When it appeared, a single from her *Love Lies* album, "Come to My Love," was in the top 20.

In April 1980, her UA single "One Day at a Time" appeared on the charts, moving steadily upward until it reached number one in the United States in June. Other chart hits for the year were "Slippin' Up, Slippin' Around" and "Sweet Sexy Eyes." In 1981, her releases came out on the UA Liberty label, including hit singles like "I Have a Dream" and "Cheatin' Is Still on My Mind."

One thing she noted proudly to Albrecht was that her marriage had endured despite the stresses of entertainment success. (At the start of the 1980s, the Stollers celebrated their twentieth anniversary.) Maintaining a proper home life was the key, she stressed. "That's one thing that's kept us together. When he's at the office or I'm there, that's it—just business. But when we come home, everything is left outside the door. And we just carry on from there."

LARSON, NICOLETTE: *Singer. Born Helena, Montana.*

During the 1970s, the West Coast country and folk-rock movement brought many excellent female singers to the fore, starting with Linda Ronstadt and continuing as the decade passed with the rise of artists like Bonnie Raitt, Karla Bonoff, and Nicolette Larson. Most of them weren't natives of the coastal states—Nicolette Larson was born in Helena, Montana, and grew up mainly in the Midwest—but they gravitated to the region where groups like the Buffalo Springfield in the 1960s and artists like Jackson Browne and the Eagles in the 1970s were blazing new pop music trails with their blending of country and folk elements with mainstream rock.

During much of her childhood, Nicolette moved at fairly short intervals because her father's job with the Treasury Department involved many transfers. However, by the time she was of high school age, the family had found a permanent home in Kansas City. Her mother once had aspirations of becoming a professional singer, but that seemed to have little impact on Nicolette in her growing-up years. "I took piano lessons and listened to the Beatles, like most kids," she recalled, but didn't really envision herself making singing a career.

She still didn't have that in mind after finishing school and moving to San Francisco. However, she got a job as a production secretary with the Golden State Country/Bluegrass Festival, which brought her in contact with many local bay area musicians, some of whom were interested in rock as well as bluegrass. She did have a good voice, though, and some of her newfound friends began to encourage her to make use of it professionally. Before 1975 was over, she was doing just that in bay area bars and clubs with a group called David Nichtern and the Nocturnes. (During the mid-1970s, Nichtern provided Maria Muldaur with the song "Midnight on the Oasis," which gave a strong boost to her solo career.) After a while, Nicolette moved to Los Angeles, where she got work backing Hoyt Axton for a time. From Axton, she moved on to a job as vocalist with Commander Cody and the Lost Planet Airmen, with whom she toured many U.S. cities.

While that was going on, more and more people in the industry were talking about the vocal skills of this new artist. Increasingly, when she wasn't on the road she got recording assignments to back major performers. Among the sessions she worked from 1976 to 1978 were those for Jesse Colin Young, Gary Stewart, and Emmylou Harris. During those years she also formed strong friendships with Harris, Linda Ronstadt, and Mary Kay Place, whose interest in country music sparked a similar enthusiasm in Larson.

The association with Ronstadt proved decisive in her career. "I used to hang out over at Linda's a lot," she told an interviewer. "You know, just singing together. That's where I met Neil Young." It was somewhat of a symbolic merger of old and new folk/country-rock trends, since Young's background went back to the folk movement of the first part of the 1960s and extended into the folk-rock amalgam of the 1970s. Besides that, Neil had been a founding member of Buffalo Springfield. Impressed with the harmonies achieved by Linda and Nicolette, he asked them to do backing vocals on some of the tracks for his next album. On that LP, *American Stars 'n' Bars*, the group performed under the name of the Bullets.

The work with Young increased the already mounting interest in Nicolette by his record firm, Warner/Reprise. She was signed by the beginning of 1978. Before sessions on her debut LP got under way, she went to Nashville to work with Neil on his next album, *Comes a Time*. She told a Warner Bros. interviewer, "We had a great time. The album is really almost like a duet. I sang on almost every cut and really had a chance to cut loose. Neil just told me to sing whatever I wanted, and that's exactly what I did."

When that LP came out in late 1978, Nicolette's vocal contributions played a significant part in making the collection one of the freshest offerings by Young in the late 1970s. One of the tracks was Neil's composition "Lotta Love," which also was featured on Larson's debut album, *Nicolette*, issued in late 1978. Among other songs given the Nicolette treatment on her LP were Sam Cooke's "You Send Me," "Rhumba Girl" by Jesse Winchester, country writer Bob McDill's "Come Early Morning," and a new tune by J. D. Souther and the Eagles' Glen Frey, "Last in Love." *Nicolette* quickly joined *Comes a Time* on upper-chart levels. In early 1979, it also achieved gold-record level, amid predic-

tions that Nicolette was a prime candidate for best new artist of 1979. Helping that image was the stage presence she displayed in the cross-country concert tour in support of the LP.

Nicolette's second Warners LP, *In the Nick of Time*, came out in the fall of 1979 and was on the pop charts into early 1980. Unfortunately, it didn't measure up to the quality of her debut collection. After thus falling victim to what is sometimes dubbed "the second-album jinx," Larson recovered some of the lost ground with an improved third LP, *Radioland*, issued by Warners in the early 1980s.

LEADBELLY: *Singer, guitarist, songwriter. Original name Huddie Ledbetter. Born near Mooringsport, Louisiana, January 21, 1885*; died New York, New York, December 6, 1949.*

He was, simply, larger than life. Somehow escaping the ravages and impact of oppression and prejudice, he had a monumental impact on pop music the world over. Sure of his ability and proud of his bull-like strength, calling himself the "King of the Twelve-String Guitar," he was a legend in his lifetime. His saga went on afterward, in performance of his songs by countless other artists, in reissues of his recordings, in the creation of myths of his life and times, and in plays and movies about his life.

His early years are shrouded in some degree of mystery. He himself said he was born on a farm in the Caddo Lake district near Mooringsport, Louisiana, and it's pretty certain he grew up there, but one east Texas historical society claims his true birthplace was in the Lone Star State. Wherever he was born, Louisiana was home and a rugged one, where he was out working the fields with other blacks as soon as he was able. Similarly, his date of birth is also uncertain. Leadbelly gave January 21 as his birthday in talks with John and Alan Lomax in the mid-1930s, but it isn't certain that's the true date. His year of birth is variously given as 1885 and 1888.

While he was growing up he was ex-

* *Date open to question.*

posed to Negro work songs, hymns, and the thrum of voodoo drums. His Uncle Terrill gave him a concertina when he was barely past toddling stage, and before long Huddie (pronounced Hew'-dee) could pick out many melodies on the instrument. A few years later his father gave him a guitar, which became his pride and joy. In his teens, when he left home to wander through the countryside playing at local affairs or on street corners, he almost always had a guitar in his hands or slung over his shoulder.

In the years near the turn of the century, Huddie spent much time playing for coins in the street for his daily bread. He sang songs he had picked up in his travels and others that he had made up on the spot. By the early years of the century he had grown into a tall, muscled strongman, and he was able to find work during the day in construction or cotton picking. He picked up his nickname during those years, but there are various stories of its origin. It's said by some that he was given it by field hands because he was so powerful, and by others that he got it from knife-wielding opponents who said his stomach muscles could fend off knife blades. Another version is that he received it from whorehouse occupants for his sexual prowess. (The latter is the one used in the 1970s movie of his early years.)

Ledbelly had what amounted to a Jekyll-Hyde nature. He could be a pleasant companion, full of humor and good nature, but if antagonized or whipped up by liquor, he could be extremely violent. The latter facet of his personality kept him in trouble—and prison—much of his life. His towering talent, however, saved him from obscurity.

His wanderings took him across Louisiana and into Texas. In 1917 in Dallas, he met another since-famed folk musician, Blind Lemon Jefferson. They teamed up to play for coins on street corners or for better pay in the brothels of East Dallas. One story has it that Huddie took a bus driver's holiday one night at a traveling carnival. While moving along the midway, he is said to have come upon a man playing a twelve-string guitar. Falling in love with the sound, the story goes, he spent the

night listening to the man play, then went out and bought himself one the next day. However, Frederic Ramsey, Jr., writing in Sing Out! (March 1965), states that Leadbelly actually had learned to play the instrument some years earlier.

The pattern from the World War I years through the early 1930s was the same; Leadbelly was constantly getting into scrapes that landed him in prison more often than not. In between he wandered around playing his guitar and singing songs like "Pick a Bale of Cotton" or "Good Night Irene" for whoever would listen. He was working in Shreveport, Louisiana, whorehouses during the first World War and sometimes making his way to towns in Texas. During that period he got caught for killing a man in one of his numerous fights and was tried for murder. He was committed to a Texas prison called Harlem on May 24, 1918, and remained there until early 1925.

At Harlem, an all-black unit no longer in existence but then located near Sugar Land, just outside Houston, Leadbelly composed one of his most famous songs, "Midnight Special." The words "Let the Midnight Special/shine its everlovin' light on me" referred to the prison myth that if the light from that train from Houston shone on an inmate he would be freed.

A major—and true—part of his legend springs from Harlem. As Alan Lomax said, "He'd perform his way into more compassionate treatment." His wonderful singing and playing got him better assignments on work gangs and finally gained his release, which resulted from a visit to the penitentiary by Texas Governor Pat Neff. After hearing Leadbelly sing, including a song where he interpolated the words "If I had you, governor, like you have me/I'd open the doors and set you free," Neff did indeed grant a pardon. Leadbelly left the prison on January 15, 1925.

He resumed his former life, scrapes and all. The inevitable denouement caught up with him in 1930 in Louisiana. He almost killed another man and was sent up to the rugged Angola prison in the Bayou State. Again he survived, easing his burdens with songs, sometimes picking up new material from the other prisoners. While he was in Angola, he was fortunate in being befriended by the folk song collector, Dr. John Lomax. Lomax came to the penitentiary in 1932 to collect songs for the Library of Congress Archive in Washington and was amazed at Leadbelly's repertoire and musical ability. Huddie not only recorded a number of his trademark numbers for Lomax, together they also prepared a plea for freedom to be given to the state governor. This time, Huddie's music failed to move the state executive; Governor O. K. Allen turned down the appeal.

However, Lomax went back east to enlist support from friends and other folk song collectors, a campaign that finally won Leadbelly a good-conduct release in 1934. Huddie arrived in New York later that year, carrying a beat-up green guitar held together with a piece of string. His first performances in the city in January 1935 brought strong praise from both critics and fans. He followed that with an equally acclaimed concert at Harvard University. There was no doubt in anybody's mind that a talent of immense proportions had been brought forward.

The Leadbelly legend was beginning to blossom, but the man himself still was flawed. As John Lomax's son, Alan Lomax, told Jeff Millar, "He had a terrible violent nature. He drove my father's car for him and my father handled his bookings and when he didn't have whiskey in him, Leadbelly could be a good companion. But when he was drunk or suffering the effects of a hangover, he was unapproachable. He finally pulled a knife on my father in the late 1930s and my father got shuck of Leadbelly after that. I'm positive Leadbelly was guilty of everything he went to prison for and other things he got away with. There's no telling how many people he killed."

On stage, however, he could do no wrong. From the mid-1930s to the end of his life, audiences eagerly awaited his appearances not only throughout the United States but all over the world. He went to those concerts in relative style, staying in comfortable motels rather than sleeping

in the streets as he once did. And he was on the same bill or sang with many of the greatest names in folk music, people like Sonny Terry, Brownie McGhee, Josh White, Cisco Houston, Big Bill Broonzy, Woody Guthrie, and Pete Seeger. He was featured on network radio shows as well, and his music became available on records that captured permanently, if not necessarily perfectly, his renditions of songs like "Good Night Irene," "Gray Goose," "Midnight Special," "Whoa Back Buck," "Easy Rider," "Keep Your Hands Off Her," "Fannin Street," "Rock Island Line," and a great many others. Still, for all his activities in the last fourteen years of his life, he never gained much financial return.

Though he mellowed considerably under less stringent circumstances, he never reformed. In fact, in 1949, the year in which he died, he was jailed briefly in New York on assault charges. His growing overseas reputation brought the offer of many engagements in Europe. He went there to give a series of concerts in the fall of 1949. While in the midst of the tour, he came down with a disease that caused his muscles to atrophy. The symptoms became intense in Paris, and he went back to New York for treatment at Bellevue Hospital. There was nothing doctors could do to save him; he died in the hospital on December 6.

His great legacy has been reflected in the popularity of his songs ever since then. His own recordings have been reissued on various labels over the years. Among those available in the 1960s were *Leadbelly Sings* (with Guthrie, Josh White, and others), issued on Folkways Records in May 1962; *Ledbetter's Best* (Capitol, 1/63); *Midnight Special* (RCA Victrola, 9/64); *Goodnight Irene* (Allego, 11/64); *Play-Party Songs* (Stinson); *Memorial* (four discs, Stinson); *Leadbelly Legacy* (Folkways, four 10-inch discs); *Last Session* (four discs, Folkways); *Library of Congress Recordings* (two discs, Elektra); *Take This Hammer* (Verve/Folkways, 9/65); *Leadbelly* (Archive of Folk Song, 1/66); *Hands Off Her* (Verve/Folkways, 2/66); and *From the Last Sessions* (Verve/Folkways, 3/67). Coming into the 1970s, the pattern continued with additional reissues, such as

Legend on Tradition Records, *Leadbelly* (11/70) on Columbia Records, and *Shout On* on Folkways.

In 1974, a film crew under director Gordon Parks went on location in central Texas to start work on a film dealing with part of the Leadbelly saga. The movie, called *Leadbelly*, dealt only with the artist's life from 1908 through 1934 and, as its writers admitted, wasn't necessarily historically accurate. The completed movie, which was affected by executive changes in Paramount Pictures, initially was shown mainly in black areas and was not released to wider distribution until early summer of 1976. The script for the film was written by Marc Merson, who noted that the emphasis on Leadbelly's early days dealt with the fact that "his struggle [then] was not to make music, but simply to stay alive."

Summing up Ledbelly's troubled life, Alan Lomax said, "Women and liquor, that was his problem. My father got him to marry his girl, Martha Promise, and that settled him for awhile, a week or two, but that was all. He called himself 'the twelve-string champion guitar player of the world,' and I guess he was. I never heard anybody who could play it better. He loved being the best. He wanted to stay the best as long as he was alive."

LEE, BRENDA: *Singer. Born Conyers, Georgia, December 11, circa 1945.*

For someone whose management indignantly denied she was a country singer in the 1960s, diminutive Brenda Lee hasn't done badly at all in the 'down home' field in the 1970s. At the time, of course, Brenda had been a rock star for years even though only in her early twenties. But it would have been surprising if, coming from Georgia, she didn't have a strong feel for country music; in fact, a look at her career shows she first made major inroads into her music career as a protégé of the great Red Foley.

Her interest in music began very early. When Brenda was only three, her mother recalled, she could hear a song twice and start singing it almost letter perfect. When Brenda was five she sang "Take Me Out to the Ball Game" at a local spring festival

and won a first-prize trophy. Her singing ability continued to progress rapidly. Her mother took her to auditions for show business engagements while Brenda was in the beginning grades in elementary school. When the girl was only seven, she won a regular slot on the *Starmakers' Revue* radio show in Atlanta. That exposure caused the producers of *TV Ranch* on Atlanta's WAGA-TV to offer some guest spots on that program.

In early 1956, Red Foley's manager, Dub Albritten, took over direction of her career. She started sharing bills with Foley and was so well received that Dub soon lined up appearances for her on such nationally televised shows as *The Steve Allen Show*, *The Ed Sullivan Show*, *Bob Hope*, *Red Skelton Show*, and *Danny Thomas*. Record executives quickly began clamoring for her services and she soon signed with Decca Records. On July 30, 1956, she began her first recording session in a Nashville studio. A decade later, at twenty-one, she had completed a total of 256 sides for that company. Recalling that first encounter, producer Owen Bradley said, "She was so small. But I remember when we started on the first take all of a sudden she yelled, 'Stop, stop, he missed a note,' and she pointed straight at the bass player. The bass player had missed a note and no one else had caught it."

The initial recording proved to be a major hit in the fall, "Rockin' Around the Christmas Tree." It was only the beginning. In short order she turned out such pop hits as "Sweet Nothin's" and "I'm Sorry." By the end of the 1950s she was accepted as a pop music superstar, a position she maintained well into the 1960s, when, for five consecutive years, both *Billboard* and *Cash Box* named her the Most Programmed Female Vocalist. From the late 1950s thrrough mid-1960s she performed in night clubs, major auditoriums, and concert halls the length and breadth of the United States and also was a favorite of overseas audiences. Her European engagements began soon after she started recording for Decca with a long series of concerts at the Olympia Music Hall in Paris. Naturally, she also was featured on almost every major TV show at home and abroad.

Among the many albums released by Decca were *Grandma, What Great Songs*, issued in September 1959, *Brenda Lee* (8/60), *This Is Brenda Lee* (1/61), *All the Way* (9/61), *Emotions* (5/61), *Sincerely* (4/62), *Brenda, That's All* (12/62), *All Alone Am I* (4/63), *Let Me Sing* (1/64), *By Request* (7/64), *Versatile* (7/65), *Top 10 Hits* (4/65), *Too Many Rivers* (11/65), *Bye Bye Blues* (5/66), *10 Golden Years* (7/66), *Coming on Strong* (1/67), *Reflections in Blue* (12/67), *Memphis Portrait* (late 1960s).

After her marriage to Ronald Shacklett in 1963, she cut back on her music activity in favor of having a family. Her first child, a daughter named Julie Leann, was born in 1964 and a second daughter, Jolie, in 1969. Although Brenda was maintaining a relatively low profile in the latter 1960s, she showed that her performing skills still were formidable with the chart-making "Johnny One Time," a Grammy Awards nominee in 1969.

Starting in the early 1970s, Lee began to shift her musical focus away from pop and toward country. Most of her pop releases had made country charts in years past and country fans proved even more enthusiastic about her new material. In 1971 she placed "Is This Our Last Time" on country charts and followed in 1973 with "Nobody Wins" and "Sunday Sunrise." In 1974, she had a series of top-5 hits: "Wrong Ideas," "Big Four Poster Bed," and "Rock On, Baby." In 1975 she placed two more singles on country charts, "Bringing It Back" and "He's My Rock," and in 1976 added two more credits, "Find Yourself Another Puppet" and "Takin' What I Can Get."

In January 1978, Brenda switched to the Elektra/Asylum Records label, her first single for that company issued in May. The songs on it were "Could It Be I Found Love Tonight" backed with "Leftover Love."

Brenda's association with Elektra proved a brief one; by late 1979 she was recording for MCA Records. By year end her single "Tell Me What It's Like" was on the charts and in January 1980 it moved into the top 10. In April of that year, another single,

"The Cowboy and the Dandy," was in the top 15. Also on the bestseller lists during the year were "Don't Promise Me Anything" and "Broken Trust," the latter in the top 10 in late fall. In 1981, Lee had still more charted singles on MCA, such as "Every Now and Then" and "Only When I Laugh."

LEE, DICKEY: *Singer, guitarist, songwriter. Born Memphis, Tennessee, September 21, 1943.*

It seems appropriate that Dickey Lee achieved a top-10 hit with the single "Rocky" in 1975, since, like the hero of the film, he had been a fighter at one time. In his career, too, he was a battler, which helped make him one of the major country artists of the 1970s.

Lee was born and raised in Memphis, where both the blues and country music were prime favorites. Although it was a hotbed of pioneer rock activity when Dickey was in his teens in the mid- and late-1950s, he gravitated to country during that period. In fact, his first public appearance was as a leader of a three-piece country group he formed to compete in his high school's amateur show. After that, the band entered a number of talent contests in its home area and won several of them. Feeling more confident about his musical potential, Dickey and his associates went to Southern California during one summer vacation in the late 1950s and auditioned for a radio station in Santa Barbara. This resulted in their getting a fifteen-minute daily spot for a while.

During those years, the group got a hearing at Sam Phillips Sun Records and made some singles for that highly influential company. One of those became a local hit—Lee's first brush with fame.

He also was good with his fists and received a partial sports scholarship for boxing from Memphis State University. His fighting credits included winning the welterweight championship of his home city.

However, Dickey decided music had more to offer him than the ring. He became increasingly active as a professional musician in the mid-1960s, working hard both as a songwriter and performer. In the second half of the 1960s, he came into his own with a series of records that appeared on either country or national pop charts or both. Among these were "I Saw Linda Yesterday," "Laurie (Strange Things Happen)," "The Girl from Peyton Place," and his million-seller, "Patches." In the late 1960s and into the 1970s, many artists from both the pop and country fields recorded some of his songs, including Connie Francis, Gene Simons, Jerry Lee Lewis, and George Jones.

In 1971 he signed with RCA Records, which issued his debut single "Charlie (My Whole World)" during the year. Later in 1971, a follow-up single, "Never Ending Song of Love" rose high on the charts as did his debut album of that title released in January 1972. For the rest of the decade, Dickey had one or more songs on the country charts every year. Among them were such singles as "Busiest Memory in Town," a top-40 single in early 1975; "Rocky," in the top 5 in the fall; "Makin' Love Don't Always Make Things Grow" in the summer of 1976; and "Virginia How Far Will You Go" in the summer of 1977. In the fall of 1977, he had another top-chart hit with his single "Peanut Butter" and in 1978 was represented by the singles "My Heart Won't Cry Anymore" in the summer and "It's Not Easy" in the fall.

During the 1970s, Lee made his home in Nashville, not too far from his original home area. He pointed out that the blues and soul side of Memphis had flavored his approach to music, though not enough to make him move away from country. He chose country, he said, "because it's the kind of music where you can sit down by yourself and entertain people without having to have an orchestra or fifty electric amps behind you. To me good country is soul!"

At the end of the 1970s, Dickey's affiliation with RCA ended; by the start of the 1980s he recorded for the Mercury label. During 1980 he had several Mercury singles on the charts: "Don't Look Back," "Workin' My Way to Your Heart," and "Lost in Love." In 1981, his output included the chart single "I Wonder if I Care as Much."

LEE, JOHNNY: *Singer, guitarist, trumpeter, songwriter. Born Texas City, Texas, July 3, circa 1945.*

In early 1981, Johnny Lee won or was nominated for best new artist in many polls. It was an honor many country music fans in Houston considered long overdue, for he had been a favorite there for close to a decade.

Lee was a Texan born and bred. His birthplace was Texas City and he grew up on a dairy farm in Alta Loma in east Texas. He spent a lot of time as a boy listening to music on the radio while he milked cows. He didn't tune to country stations, though; his idols were people like Fats Domino, Jerry Lee Lewis, Elvis Presley, and Chuck Berry. "Rock 'n' roll was my favorite. I thought country music was too twangy then."

In high school he organized his own rock band, Johnny Lee and the Road Runners, in the early 1960s. The group won a local Future Farmers of America talent contest and went on to place first in the statewide finals. The group became well known to teenagers at the time, playing school events and local dances in and around Texas City. Johnny wrote some of the songs the band played, such as one that won some local attention, "My Little Angel."

After finishing high school, he spent four years in the Navy in the mid-1960s, including a tour in Vietnamese waters. After his discharge, he "bummed around California for awhile."

Finally, he went back to Texas to try to pick up his musical career. By this time, he had found increased interest in country music, though he was happy to work any type of gig he could find. His wanderings took him to Pasadena, Texas, where Mickey Gilley held forth as the featured entertainer at the Nesadel night club. Lee made up his mind to seek work in Gilley's backing group.

As he related for a 1980 Elektra/Asylum press release, "I was playing around the area and I finally got to meet this Mickey Gilley guy I'd heard so much of and always admired. 'Lonely Wine' had been one of my favorite songs in high school, but I was too young to go [where Gilley was performing], so I'd never seen him perform live back then.

"Anyway, I met him and I said, 'Mickey do you remember me? I was on the Larry Kane TV show in Galveston with you.' Well, that was an outright lie, of course, but Mickey was busy, you know, and he wanted to be nice, so he said. 'Uh . . . yeah, yeah, I think I remember you, but I can't remember what you did on the show.'

"I told him a few more lies and said, 'Man, I'd be honored if I could sit in with you.' He said, 'Sure, go ahead,' and I did. I sat in for about a half-hour, talking and singing, and the people really liked me. So, every now and then, I'd go out and sit in with him. Finally he offered me a job playing trumpet and singing with his group at the Nesadel. That was the start, and I've been with him ever since."

Eventually, Lee said, he told Gilley of the original deception and the latter laughed about it. By then Johnny was a member of Mickey's band at his own nightspot, Gilley's, which opened in 1971. Lee remained a sideman while Gilley finally broke through from local luminary to national superstar. Johnny had similar hopes for himself, though, like Mickey, he had to pay a lot of dues before those dreams came true.

In the early 1970s, he had a local hit on a small label titled "Sometimes" that was picked up for national distribution by ABC/Dot Records. For a while, Johnny took leave of Gilley's band to try to make his name nationally as a solo artist. However, the ABC connection didn't work out and Johnny returned to Mickey's group. In the mid-1970s, he got a new chance when he signed with GRT Records (this time, however, he didn't give up his part in Mickey's show). This resulted in a number of recordings that became major regional hits in Texas, such as "Red Sails in the Sunset," "Ramblin' Rose," "Dear Alice," and "Country Party" (the latter a country version of Rick Nelson's "Garden Party"). Some of the GRT singles made the national charts; "Country Party" made the top-15 in the summer of 1977. However,

the blockbuster hit needed for national stardom eluded him.

The turning point came with the filming of the John Travolta film *Urban Cowboy* at Gilley's. Johnny Lee not only performed with the Gilley Band, he also did a solo vocal for the soundtrack, "Lookin' for Love." Elektra/Asylum, which issued the *Urban Cowboy* soundtrack LP, was impressed with the airplay given the song and issued it as a single on the Full Moon/ Asylum label. The single became one of the top hits of 1980, reaching number one on country charts in September and also gaining the top levels on pop charts. Later in the year, Johnny followed with another number-one single, "One in a Million."

In support of those releases, as well as his 1980 debut solo LP, *Lookin' for Love*, Johnny toured widely either as a coheadliner with Mickey Gilley (including engagements with the Urban Cowboy band in major venues in Reno and Las Vegas, Nevada, and at New York's Copacabana nightclub) or as headliner. He also was a guest on major country and general variety TV shows and acted as a presenter at major music industry awards events.

In 1981, the Academy of Country Music named him Best New Artist and, in a 1980 year-end poll by *Ampersand* magazine, "Lookin' for Love" was named Favorite Country Single.

Johnny maintained his momentum in 1981, starting the year with the hit single "Pickin' Up Strangers," which reached number three nationally in April. He followed with another number-three success, "Prisoner of Hope." Indicative of his status was his opening of his own club, Johnny Lee's, down the road from Gilley's in Pasadena. In the summer, he and the Urban Cowboy band taped a special on the PBS-TV *Austin City Limits* series. Soon after, his second Full Moon/Asylum LP, *Bet Your Heart on Me*, was issued (September 1981). The title song was in the top-five singles list in November.

LEE, JONI: *Singer. Born Arkansas, circa 1957.*

The tradition of family involvement remains strong in country music, so people in the industry weren't too surprised when Joni Lee's name appeared on the hit charts in the mid-1970s. She is the older daughter of superstar Conway Twitty, who had a direct hand in her successes. (Her younger sister, Kathy, also performed briefly in the 1970s.)

Joni spent her early years in Arkansas, but moved to Oklahoma City in the 1960s, where her father began the country phase of his career with a show on a local TV station. By then, Joni already had made her public debut, having come on stage to sing at the Phillips County Fair in Arkansas when she was four years old. She grew to be a very comely girl in her teens and divided her career activities in high school between modeling and entertainment efforts. She took grooming and related classes and also took singing and dancing lessons. The latter efforts paid off when she was fourteen, helping her to win the international "Miss Charm" pageant. She used the name Joni Lee rather than try to capitalize on the family name.

During those years she entered a number of beauty pageants and also worked as a model in many style shows, again as Joni Lee. She also was voted football queen, at one point, by her high school's squad. Later on, in the mid-1970s, when she wasn't taking part in fashion shows in Oklahoma City, she was serving as a judge in various competitions. Those activities caused the Oklahoma City Times to vote her one of the top-10 women in Oklahoma news.

She still was interested in music and in 1975 got together with her father to record the song "Don't Cry Joni." Issued as a single by MCA Records, it rose to number one on the country charts and was one of the best-selling records of 1975. Afterward she was offered the chance to do some solo recordings. For that, Conway wrote "No Tears for Joni." The single became a top-5 hit in early 1976.

Lee appeared on a number of network TV shows in the mid-1970s with her father or as a soloist. She also appeared in a number of concerts around the United States with the Twitty show. By the late 1970s, though, she decided to retire, at least temporarily, from the entertainment field in favor of marriage and raising a family.

LEHR, ZELLA: *Singer, dancer, circus performer. Born Burbank, California, March 14.*

One might joke that for a good part of her early country-music career Zella Lehr was spinning her wheels.

The wheels actually should be singular, referring to the unicycle Zella was taught to ride as a young child by her father, descendant of a long line of circus performers. In fact, members of the Lehr family tree were part of the show business scene back in seventeenth-century England. When Zella was a baby, her family, which included her parents and two brothers, lived in Burbank, California. But her father already had plans for a new act in which the children would take part that involved, besides cycle riding, rope spinning, juggling, singing, and dancing. Before Zella was elementary school age, the Lehrs had removed to Europe, where they became regulars on the circus circuit.

In the United States, Lehr Senior loved country music, an interest he passed along to his daughter. But she didn't use any country material when she made her singing debut in the family act in England at the age of six. She was adept at the other skills in the act as well, an act that became very successful in European vaudeville and that was also presented in parts of Asia during the 1960s.

Zella might never have changed performing directions had not her father died. After that happened, the rest of the family returned to the United States, where the act disbanded. Left on her own, Lehr settled in New York, where she began to find work on TV commercials and as a vocalist in small clubs in the New York area. At first she stayed away from country for the most part, but when the chance came to appear at the Flamingo Hotel in Las Vegas, she decided to assemble an act based on country material. She and her group did well enough at the Flamingo to add more engagements in hotels both in Vegas and Lake Tahoe. She began to expand her reputation after that with a series of appearances on major TV shows. At one point she caught the attention of the producer of *Hee Haw* by coming into the office riding a unicycle. Besides that important country showcase, Zella sang country ballads on such general audience programs as *The Steve Allen Show, Rosie Grier Show,* and *The Real Tom Kennedy Show* in the 1970s.

During the mid-1970s, Lehr appeared in clubs and at fairs and country concerts in many parts of the United States. For a while in those years, she turned out some recordings for Mega Records, with only indifferent success. An engagement in Nashville in mid-1977 proved an important turning point. Executives from RCA Records attended one of her sets and decided she had a promising country style. She answered that challenge with a series of releases that made national country charts in the late 1970s. Her first RCA single quickly found the mark. A recording of Dolly Parton's composition "Two Doors Down" reached number five on the country charts in late 1977. She followed with three more charted singles, "When the Fire Gets Hot" in the summer of 1978, "Danger, a Heartbreak Ahead" in September and October 1978, and "Play Me a Memory," in early 1979. Later in the year she had such singles as "Only Diamonds Are Forever" and "Love Has Taken Its Time" on hit lists. The latter reached the top 30 in early 1980. Other RCA charted singles in 1980 were "Rodeo Eyes" and "Love Crazy Love." In 1981, Zella switched labels, joining Columbia. For her new label she had the single "Feedin' the Fire" in the top 20 in the fall.

LEWIS, BOBBY: *Singer, guitarist, lutenist, songwriter. Born Hodgenville, Kentucky, May 9,*

Many devotees of the folk roots of country music play relatively offbeat instruments like the dulcimer or autoharp. However, not many in the mainstream of modern country music wander far from such staples as guitar and banjo. One who created a niche for himself with a relatively special instrument was Bobby Lewis, usually billed as "The Artist Who Plays the Lute." (The lute, of course, in its early forms was an ancestor of the guitar.)

Not that the lute was Lewis' first instrument. As a child in Hodgenville, Kentucky (which lays claim to being the birthplace of Abraham Lincoln), he focused his attention on the guitar, an instrument featured on the *Grand Ole Opry* and local country broadcasts and played by many people in his home area. His brother, Jack, taught him some basic chords on a borrowed guitar when Bobby was nine, and soon thereafter his father bought the boy his own instrument.

By the time he reached high school he was one of the better musicians in his town. He also became interested in other instruments, which led to his mastering the lute. He followed the usual route of working with local bands, gradually expanding his scope to perform on country shows in large towns and cities. He sang many of the current hits by established artists but also added some originals of his own to his repertoire.

In the 1960s, he began to make strong progress toward the natural goal of any country musician, an invitation to appear on the *Grand Ole Opry.* His initial recording of an original composition called "Sandra Kay" gained enough popularity for Bobby to debut on the Nashville scene. After his first appearance on the *Opry,* he returned a number of times as a guest from the mid-1960s to the end of the 1970s. He also appeared on many nationally televised programs and sometimes was the headliner on such shows as Ernest Tubb's *Midnight Jamboree* and Nashville's *WSM Barn Dance.*

During the mid-1960s, Bobby signed with United Artists, which released his debut album, *Bobby Lewis,* in October 1966. He followed that with a series of albums, including *How Long?* issued in June 1967; *World of Love* (1/68); *Things for You and I* (10/69); and *Best of Bobby Lewis, Volume I* (1970). Although he had trouble cracking the top 10 during his stay with UA, Bobby recorded many singles that made the regional or national charts from the mid-1960s to the early 1970s. Among some of his better-known releases of the 1960s were "Forty Dollars a Week," "Crying in Public," "Perfect Example of a Fool," "Why Me?," and "Six Days a Week and Twice on Sundays."

Bobby hit a dry spell in the first part of the 1970s that led to his leaving UA. As he told Stacy Harris of *Music City News* (October 1973), "I was with United Artists Records for eight and a half years and we stayed on the national charts consistently up until about two years ago. Then we had changes in our producers and some other things I don't want to go into, but I felt at this point it was time that I made a change."

The result was a move to Ace of Hearts Records in mid-1973. Bobby emphasized he had no intention of changing his style and, in fact, noted that one of his first recordings for the new label, "Too Many Memories," underlined this. "You know, back in '69, '70 and '71 I had songs like 'From Heaven to Heartache' and 'Love Me and Make It Better.' 'Too Many Memories' is in the pattern of those songs and I certainly hope it's going to put me right back up there again. . . . I was lucky enough to be nominated for a Grammy Award [for 'From Heaven to Heartache'] in 1969 for Best Country Male Performance."

His faith in "Too Many Memories" proved justified. It made it into the country top 20 for a number of weeks in late 1973 and remained in the top 30 in early 1974. In early summer 1974, he had another single on Ace of Hearts on lower-chart levels, "Ladylover" (co-written by Lewis and G. Kennedy), and in mid-1975 had a mild hit with "Let Me Take Care of You." Bobby's fortunes dipped a bit in the second half of the 1970s, but by the end of the decade he was on upper-chart levels with a single on Capricorn Records called "She's Been Keepin' Me Up Nights."

LEWIS, HUGH X.: *Singer, guitarist, songwriter. Born Cumberland, Kentucky, December 7, 1932.*

There were many times when Hugh X. Lewis despaired of ever making his livelihood from music. He had loved singing country songs from his early years and was good enough to begin to get occasional jobs in local bars and clubs in his teens, but the years went by and he had to work regular day jobs to pay the food and rent bills. His perseverence and writing skills finally gave him the chance to leave the coal mines and find fame and fortune in Nashville in the mid-1960s.

Born and raised in the coal mine region of east Kentucky, he learned to play guitar as a boy and dreamed of one day charming audiences from the stage of the *Grand Ole Opry's* Ryman Auditorium. Those hopes rose a little higher when he made his professional debut at a club in Cumberland when he was seventeen. After he was graduated from high school, though, his family couldn't afford to pay his way while he tried to compete in the rough and tumble world of show business. Hugh got a job in the coal mines and relegated music activities to weekends and other days off.

Still he made some progress. He became a regular member of a weekly TV show on a Johnson City, Tennessee, station. On Saturdays he made the trip to Knoxville to perform on the *Tennessee Barn Dance* in the mid- and late-1950s. Meanwhile he was giving his employers a full day's work for a day's pay. He was made foreman at the U.S. Steel mine in Lynch, Kentucky, in 1959. In the early 1960s, he kept up his dual careers, slowly building up a reputation with his fellow performers for his singing and guitar playing on WSAZ's *Saturday Night Jamboree* in Huntington and the prestigious *Ernest Tubb Show* in Nashville.

Hugh also was building up a backlog of original compositions, but he was moving along in years. It seemed as though he had to make the break or resign himself to regular nine-to-five work the rest of his life. In 1963, he quit his job with U.S. Steel and moved to Nashville. He made the rounds of record companies, publishers, and agents and finally won the backing of music industry executive Jim Denny, who predicted great things for the thirty-one-year-old. Unfortunately, Denny died soon after, but his prophecy proved true. Several performers became interested in Lewis' songs, the first major breakthrough coming in 1964 with Stonewall Jackson's recording of "B.J. the D.J." The song rose to number one on the national country lists and also provided hits, as time went by, for Kitty Wells and Carl Smith.

Stonewall Jackson recorded a number of other Lewis songs in the mid- and late-1960s and made the charts with such singles as "Not My Kind of People" and "Picket Sign." Throughout the second half of the 1960s and in the 1970s, many other artists recorded Hugh's material. Among them were Carl and Pearl Butler, who turned out singles of "Just Thought I'd Let You Know" (also recorded by Leon McAuliffe) and "Make Me an Offer;" Jimmy C. Newman, who made the charts with "Recipe for a Broken Heart;" Carl Smith, who hit with "Take My Ring Off Your Finger;" Mac Wiseman, who recorded "Heads You Win, Tails I Lose;" George Morgan, who added "One Rose" to his list of successes; and Ray Pillow, a beneficiary of Lewis' "The First Chance I Get."

Lewis, of course, didn't want to remain on the performing sidelines. In 1964, he signed a recording contract with Kapp Records and achieved his first chart single, "What I Need Most," late that year. More charted singles ensued, which led to release of his debut LP, *Hugh X. Lewis,* in March 1966. This was followed by such albums as *Just Before the Dawn* in November 1966 and *My Kind* in October 1967. At the end of the decade, Hugh moved to GRT Records and placed a number of singles on the charts, such as "Blues Sells a Lot of Booze" in late 1970. By late 1978, he was recording for Little Darlin' Records and made the charts with "Love Don't Hide from Me." Some of his other recordings were "Out Where the Ocean Meets the Sky," "Talking to a Bottle," "Too Late," "Looking in the Future for the Past," and "This Makes Us Even."

During the 1960s, he finally achieved his goal of appearing on the *Grand Ole Opry.* He also headlined shows in clubs and at county fairs all over the country and was a guest on most major country TV programs in the 1960s and 1970s. During that period,

Hugh also got the chance to take part in two country-music movies, including the feature-length color film *Forty Acre Feud.*

LEWIS, JERRY LEE: *Singer, pianist, songwriter. Born Ferriday, Louisiana, September 29, 1935.*

One evening in early 1979 at the Palomino Club in Los Angeles, the emcee was singing the praises of the headliner, a relatively new female performer. He barely got out the words "I'm going to present one of the great country performers of the day" when Jerry Lee Lewis stood up in the audience and shouted "I'm the greatest." To the consternation of the host, he rushed on stage, sat down at the piano, and quickly worked the audience into frenzied excitement. It could never be said "The Killer" lacked confidence. And not without reason; in more than two decades as a performer, he cut a wide swath as a superstar, first in rock 'n' roll, then in his original proving ground, country music.

Jerry was born and raised in the small town of Ferriday, Louisiana, where gospel and country music were part of the natural environment. Though blues was considered off limits, Jerry and his childhood friends, including cousin Mickey Gilley, sometimes sneaked into local honky tonks. Jerry showed an early aptitude for the piano and did well enough while still small that his father, Elmo, took the boy around to perform in small shows in neighboring towns. At the time, Jerry Lee played the keyboards ensconced on the back of a flatbed truck. Besides playing in such surroundings, Jerry, as he grew older, also performed in gospel meetings and church programs.

His early love of the blues helped inspire an interest in the outburst of rockabilly material that began to have an impact on the music scene in the mid-1950s. In 1956, he moved to Memphis and became a session pianist for a time, backing artists like Carl Perkins and Billy Lee Riley. In the wake of selling Elvis Presley's contract to RCA, Sun was in the market for new talent and Jerry was quick to seize the opportunity. With such originals as "End of the Road" and "Crazy Arms" in

1956, he earned a recording contract and soon was out on the road gaining attention from his work with touring rock shows. With his wild actions—kicking the piano bench across the stage, waving the microphone as he played piano with the other hand, and jumping on top of the piano—he set off shock waves of enthusiasm among young onlookers.

In 1957 he started to hit his peak with the smash single "Great Balls of Fire," which became a worldwide hit and earned him his first gold record. Late in the year he came out with another blockbuster, "Whole Lotta Shakin' Goin' On," which went gold in early 1958. During that period he placed other songs in top-chart levels, including "Breathless" and "High School Confidential." The last named was the title song of his first movie in which he sang the song from the back of a flatbed truck.

In 1958, though, his soaring fortunes plummeted abruptly when word got around that he had married his thirteen-year-old second cousin, Myra (the marriage lasted thirteen years). That wasn't startling to many in the South, where early unions often occured. In fact, Jerry had married originally when he was only fourteen. But it shocked the rest of the nation and the world. When the story broke he was en route to a tour of England. The condemnation there was so great the concerts were canceled. The situation was only a little less bleak for him back home.

For the next half dozen years, he fought to keep his career afloat. He had some minor successes on Sun during that period, including the singles "John Henry," "Carry Me Back to Old Virginny," and "What'd I Say," and made another movie appearance in the 1960 film *Young and Deadly*. But he seemed relegated to a minor role in pop music from then on.

However, national mores were changing and the events of six years ago were ancient history to most fans. In 1964, with Sun in the doldrums, Jerry Lee switched to Smash Records and suddenly found his career rejuvenated. His first releases in March 1964 and January 1965 (both titled *Jerry Lee Lewis*) and *Rock Songs* in June 1965 all were aimed at rock fans. But the al-

bums sold much better in the country field. Of course, country always was one of the elements in Lewis's stylings and by the mid-1960s, many youngsters in the South had adopted country rock as part of their own culture. So without changing his approach too much, Jerry Lee set his cap in that direction and soon was doing quite well.

His new direction was indicated by the title of his January 1966 Smash LP, *Country Songs*. After that album, his LPs did steadily better over the last half of the decade. He followed it with such releases as *By Request* (1/67), *Return of Rock* (8/67), *Soul My Way* (1/68), and one of the best-selling country LPs of 1968, *Another Place, Another Time*. His singles sales also were moving along nicely. The title song of the latter album moved high on the charts, and he achieved another top-10 hit in 1968 with "What's Made Milwaukee Famous (Has Made a Loser Out of Me)." Other chart hit singles of the late 1960s were "She Even Woke Me Up to Say Goodbye," "To Make Love Sweeter for You," and "She Still Comes Around (to Love What's Left of Me)."

Jerry's in-person success moved right along with his recording achievement. In the late 1960s, he headlined shows before both rock and country audiences all over the United States and the world. He starred in such diverse places as plush hotels (including major Las Vegas spots), college campuses, county fairs, and large auditoriums. In 1969 and into the early 1970s he was a prime drawing card in the rash of rock 'n' roll revival shows that were presented in the United States and abroad. Another milestone for him occurred in 1968 when he starred in the role of Iago in a rock version of Shakespeare's *Othello* presented at the Los Angeles Music Center.

In the 1970s, albums of his kept coming out on several labels. When he still was on Smash in the late 1960s, some of his earlier work was reissued by Sun. In 1970, Jerry switched to Mercury Records and, naturally, Smash turned out some recordings of his after he had left the label. Among his Sun releases of the late 1960s and early

1970s were *Ole Tyme Country Hits, Volumes 1, 2, and 3, Monsters, Rockin' Rhythm & Blues, Taste of Country, Original Golden Hits, Volumes 1, 2 and 3,* and *Golden Cream of Country.* The latter made the country top 10 in May 1970. Two Sun singles also brought him top-10 laurels in 1970, "One Minute Past Eternity," which rose to number two in January, and "I Can't Seem to Say Goodbye," number seven in June. At year end, another Sun single, "Waiting for a Train," was high on the lists.

He also had a top-10 single on Smash in early 1970, "Once More with Feeling." Among the Smash LP releases of 1969 and the early 1970s: *Hall of Fame Hits, Volumes 1 and 2* (7/69), *Together* (with Linda Gall, 12/69), *She Even Woke Me Up to Say Goodbye,* and *Best of Jerry Lee Lewis.*

The move to Mercury didn't seem to slow him down. One of his first releases on the label, the LP *Live at the International in Las Vegas,* was issued in the fall and on the charts soon after. Also well received were such 1971 releases as *There Must Be More to Love than That, Touching Home,* and *Would You Take Another Chance on Me.* He also had a series of singles hits during those years: "There Must Be More to Love than This," number three on country charts in September 1971, "Touching Home," in the top 10 in June 1971, "Would You Take Another Chance with Me" backed with "Me and Bobby McGee," on the top 10 in late 1971, and "Chantilly Lace/Think About It Darlin'," number two in April 1972. In 1972–73, his Mercury album hits included *The Killer Rocks On* and *The Session.* Among the singles he placed on the charts were "Lonely Weekends," "Turn on Your Love Light," "When He Walks on You," and "Who's Gonna Play This Old Piano."

In the mid- and late-1970s, Jerry's name continued to make the charts with singles efforts for Mercury. These included "Drinking Wine Spo-Dee-O-Do," "Boogie Woogie Country Man" (mid-1975), "Don't Boogie Woogie" (early 1976), "Let's Put It Back Together Again" (top 20, September 1976), "Middle Age Crazy" (top 10, late 1977), and "I'll Find It Where I Can" (top 15, July 1978).

Besides a breakneck series of concert dates numbering in the hundreds each year, Jerry still found time for other tasks, including an appearance in the 1978 movie, *American Hot Wax.* In that movie, a biographical vignette of part of the career of rock impresario Alan Freed, Lewis played himself and was a major attraction both for film goers and purchasers of the original soundtrack album.

Early in 1979, Jerry made another record company move, switching to Elektra Records. His debut on the label, *Jerry Lee Lewis,* was recorded in Los Angeles, the first LP he had cut outside Nashville in some time. Released in March 1979, the album offered a combination of rock and country songs, including a previously unrecorded Bob Dylan song, "Rita May," that Dylan had offered to Lewis. In the early summer, Jerry Lee had a top-20 single from the collection, "Rockin' My Life Away/I Wish I Was Eighteen Again." A single of the title song from his second Elektra LP, *When Two Worlds Collide,* was in the top 20 the same month the album was released, February 1980. The album showed up on country charts during the summer. Another song from the LP, "Honky Tonk Stuff," was on singles lists in the summer. In September 1980, his third Elektra album came out, *Killer Country.* Lewis' version of the pop music standard "Over the Rainbow," from that album, provided him with a top-10 hit in November 1980.

The next year started auspiciously with another top-10 hit, "Thirty Nine and Holding." However, by the middle of the year, Lewis was in the hospital amid fears for his life. Many rumors circulated about his condition after he entered Memphis Methodist Hospital South complaining of stomach pains. In surgery it was discovered that he had a two-inch tear in his stomach lining "and related complications." After the surgeons repaired the damage, he was in intensive care for some time before it was announced in August that he was off the critical list and on the way to recovery.

By the fall, he was already becoming restless about his enforced inactivity, a feeling he made clear to several interviewers. At the start of 1982, he had regained enough strength to resume some of his performing work. In February he received an ovation from the audience at the 24th Annual Grammy Awards when he came on stage to take part in a televised piano duet with Mickey Gilley before the two cousins handled their chores as presenters of some of the country music Grammies.

LIGHT CRUST DOUGHBOYS, THE: *Vocal and instrumental group, formed early 1930s with many different alignments of musicians during its decades of existence. Early members, 1931–32: Bob Wills, Milton Brown, Durwood Brown, Clifton "Sleepy" Johnson, and Herman Arnspiger.*

One of the legendary names in country & western history, the Light Crust Doughboys, claims so many different alumni it almost could provide material for an encyclopedia of its own. The two individuals most closely associated with its initial phases, Bob Wills and W. Lee "Pappy" O'Daniel went on to carve national reputations for themselves, Wills' as leader of the famed Texas Playboys (see separate entry) and O'Daniel as the politician who used his country & western background to help win him the governorship of Texas.

Recalling the origins of the group, Texas Playboy alumnus Leon McAuliff said, "Bob Wills in about 1931 came to Ft. Worth, just himself and a guitar player [Herman Arnspiger]. He met a fiddler named Milton Brown (Milton Brown [1903–1936] and his brother, Durwood, were the central figures in a landmark western swing band called Milton Brown and His Musical Brownies) and they went on radio station KFJZ as the Wills Fiddle Band. They first got their show sponsored by the Aladdin Lamp Co. Called themselves the Aladdin Laddies. They were so popular they got themselves sponsored on a network of radio stations called the Texas Quality Network, whose members included WBAP in Ft. Worth, KPRC in Houston, and WOI in San Antonio. The company that sponsored them was the Burris Mill and Elevator Company that manufactured Light Crust Flour. That's

where the Light Crust Doughboys name came from." *

In getting that sponsorship, Wills approached O'Daniel, who then was on the sales staff of Burris. O'Daniel was born in Malta, Ohio, on March 11, 1890. His family later moved to Kingman, Kansas, where he finished his schooling and began working as a flour seller for local firms in the early 1920s. In 1925, he moved to Ft. Worth and got a job with Burris Mills. After Wills approached him in 1932, O'Daniel was receptive to the idea and initially sponsored the newly named group on KFJZ. In 1933, the group, by then already a favorite with Ft. Worth audiences, moved to WBAP, performing daily at 12:30 P.M.

Wills didn't stay with the band too long after that move. McAuliff notes, "Milton and Bob went separate ways. Bob went to Waco and started the band he called Bob Wills and the Playboys. In the summer of 1933 he moved to Oklahoma for a short stay and then on to Tulsa where, in 1934, the group finally took the name Bob Wills and the Texas Playboys." *

Meanwhile the Light Crust Doughboys kept going, with O'Daniel taking the helm as master of ceremonies. Brown's place was taken by fiddler Clifford Graves from Kentucky, and others were added to round out the band. The Doughboys made several recordings for RCA Victor before Wills left, but the bulk of the group's output came afterward when O'Daniel arranged a recording contract with Vocalion. Among the songs recorded for that label from 1933 to 1935 were "Beautiful Texas," "On to Victory Mr. Roosevelt," "Bluebonnet Waltz," "Texas Breakdown," "Memories of Jimmie Rodgers," "Doughboys' Rag," "Texas Rose," "Saturday Night Rag," "Gangster's Moll," "When It's Roundup Time in Heaven," "Alamo Waltz," "My Pretty Quadroon," "Carry Me Back to the Lone Prairie," "Milenburg Joys," "Old Rugged Cross," "The Cowboy's Dream," "Kelly Waltz," and "She's That Old Sweetheart of Mine."

O'Daniel's association with the group

---

* *Interview with Irwin Stambler, 1979.*

ended in 1935 when he resigned from Burris to form his own firm, Hillbilly Flour Company. Later on, when he entered politics, he and the Doughboys performed during his speeches and rallies, a move that helped win him the election and a technique later used by another country entertainer turned politician, Jimmie Davis, to score a similar victory in neighboring Louisiana.

Eddie Dunn took over from O'Daniel as emcee. He previously had a group of his own whose members soon took on Doughboys raiment: Marvin Montgomery, Dick Reinhart, Bert Dodson, and Muryel Campbell. His tenure was short, though. In 1936, the leadership of the group went to Cecil Brower.

Despite the personnel shifts, the band continued to be a mainstay of station WBAP programming into the 1940s. The situation changed in 1942 when Burris Mills canceled its advertising support. A new sponsor, Duncan Coffee Company, came aboard, and the Doughboys became the Coffee Grinders. Under that name the band kept going through the World War II period, but after the war was over it was decided to go back to the original name even without Burris' sponsorship since the Doughboys name had become famous in its own right.

The band of that name continued to survive in one form or another for over two decades afterward. Besides doing radio and TV work in the 1950s and 1960s, the group also continued to give live sets at various clubs around the United States and on the fair and rodeo circuit. None of those efforts, though, ever returned the group to the position it held in its heyday from the early 1930s through the early 1940s.

LIGHTFOOT, GORDON: *Singer, guitarist, pianist, songwriter. Born Orillia, Ontario, Canada, November 17, 1938.*

Starting as a folksinger-songwriter, Gordon Lightfoot never really abandoned his first love, though he often combined folk elements with rock to good effect during a long and eventful career. Even in the early 1980s, when the folk boom of the late 1950s and early 1960s was only a fleeting memory for most music observers, he commanded respect from a large segment of the music public, embracing almost all ages.

Gordon was born in the small town of Orillia, eighty miles north of Toronto. During his late teens, he spent summers playing in bands and driving trucks in northern Ontario. In 1958, after finishing high school, he went to Los Angeles to study piano and orchestration at a since-departed music school, Westlake College. For a time he earned money at such behind-the-scenes jobs as arranging, copying music, and writing and producing commercial jingles.

"Then in 1960, I started to listen to some people like Pete Seeger and Bob Gibson. That's when I got interested in folk music and that's when I started to play guitar. Ian and Sylvia [a Canadian folksong team] were friends of mine from before and we used to hang out at the folk clubs and coffee houses. I just started singing folk stuff. I used to get up on stage and play and sing like everybody else. Ian turned me on to the guitar because he was so adept with flat pick. The style of Bob Gibson also affected me a great deal.

"Actually, I'd written some songs before then, but they didn't have any kind of identity. I wrote thirty or forty songs up until the time I started to write stuff that I could do on stage. Then the writing explosion started with Bob Dylan and Phil Ochs and Tom Paxton and everybody else who followed them and I started to get a point of view and that's when I started to improve." Gordon went back to eastern Canada in the early 1960s and "sang in a lot of bars in and around Toronto."

In the early 1960s, Lightfoot began recording for a Canadian label, Chateau, and had a number of hits in his homeland. The first was "Remember Me" and was followed by others on various local labels, including "I'm Not Saying," "Spin, Spin," "Go Go Round," "The Way I Feel," and "Black Day in July." But it was performances of some of his songs by others that really focused attention on him in the United States. Ian and Sylvia hit with "For

Lovin' Me" and "Early Morning Rain" and, later, Peter, Paul and Mary did even better with a single of the latter song. Albert Grossman, who managed both those acts, took over as Lightfoot's manager and got him his first major U.S. contract, with United Artists, which issued his debut album on the label in 1966, titled *Lightfoot.*

Over the next three years, UA followed with such others as *The Way I Feel, Did She Mention My Name, Back Here on Earth,* and *Sunday Concert.* In 1969, Gordon changed record companies, moving to Warner Bros., which issued nine of his albums through 1978, making a total of fourteen on United States labels in all.

The move seemed to bring new vitality to Lightfoot's work. The debut album on Reprise, *Sit Down Young Stranger,* was released in April 1970 and was on the charts for many months of that year and later reappeared on them in early 1971. His second album on the label, *If You Could Read My Mind,* did better than that, moving into the national top 20 in the spring and providing a major hit single of the title song. In mid-year, his next release, *Summer Side of Life,* also appeared on the hit lists. A little later, *Classic Lightfoot* was issued, which also did well. For a while, that LP and the two previous releases were on the national lists at the same time. One of the Warner releases was the 1975 retrospective, *Gord's Gold,* a two-LP set that collected the many memorable songs Lightfoot had written and recorded during his first United States recording decade. These included "Cotton Jenny," "If You Could Read My Mind," "Carefree Highway," "Canadian Railroad Trilogy," and "The Last Time I Saw Her."

His career by then was in excellent shape, but for a time in the early 1970s he appeared to lose some momentum. For instance, his two albums of 1972, *Don Quixote* and *Old Dan's Records,* while certainly above average in many ways, still seemed weaker than most of his previous work. But in late 1973, Gordon returned to top form with the album *Sundown,* one of the year's best that also provided him with a gold-record award for the title song. This was followed over the next few years by

the aforementioned *Gord's Gold* and another well-crafted new collection, *Summertime Dreams,* both of which moved high on national charts and earned gold records. In 1977, he was represented by the album *Cold on the Shoulder,* certainly equal in quality to those albums and, in 1978, by *Endless Wire.*

Endless Wire had such highlights as the folk-rock title song, the up-tempo country-flavored "Hangdog Hotel Room," the ballad "If Children Had Wings," and a fine remake of his 1969 composition, "The Circle Is Small." In the late 1970s, as he had done for most of his career, he toured widely in support of his new album, drawing capacity crowds for most concerts.

Gordon started off the 1980s with a new album on Warner Brothers, *Dream Street Rose,* issued in March 1980 by Warner Brothers. The title song was issued as a single and appeared on country charts in the summer of 1980. His next LP, *Shadows,* was released by Warner Brothers in January 1982.

LIMELITERS, THE: *Vocal and instrumental trio. Louis Gottlieb, born Los Angeles, California, 1923; Alex Hassilev, born Paris, France, July 11, 1932; Glenn Yarbrough, born Milwaukee, Wisconsin, January 12, 1930.*

Witty bassist Lou Gottlieb, who earned a Ph.D. in musicology from UCLA, was the spokesman of the literate folk group, The Limeliters.

The group was formed in 1959 in the Cosmo Alley coffee house in Hollywood. Each artist had been working as a single supper club and coffee house act, though Yarbrough and Hassilev had been associated in running a club in Aspen, Colorado, called the Limelite. A few years earlier, Yarbrough had been engaged by the club and became a regular performer there. In time, he and Hassilev joined to buy the lease and run the club themselves.

Hassilev, born in France of Russian parents, had been brought to the United States as a boy. By the time he met Yarbrough, he was trying for a career as an actor, having spent some years working in off-Broadway productions. In 1959, Alex got a part in a horror movie in Hollywood and

Johnny Lee

Jerry Lee Lewis

Gordon Lightfoot

Lonzo & Oscar

Loretta Lynn

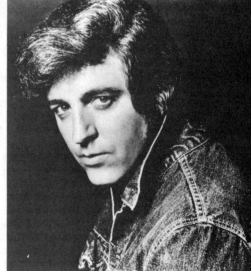

Bob Luman

Charlie Louvin

took a singing job at the Cosmo Alley to help pay expenses. Later that year, Glenn came to town and sang with Alex. Gottlieb heard them perform one night and suggested they make it a trio.

Gottlieb, by this time, had considerable professional experience. He had been one of the original Gateway Singers, a top folk group of the 1950s, but left after three years to complete work on his Ph.D. He had already gained a major reputation as an arranger. During the early 1960s he sometimes provided song arrangements for other acts, including "Miss Bailey" and "Good News" for the Kingston Trio.

The three men agreed to start work after Glenn and Alex finished their Cosmo Alley run in late July 1959. They based their name on the title of Glenn and Alex's Aspen club. Combining Gottlieb's arrangements and droll comic interludes with Yarbrough's lyric tenor and Hassilev's command of several languages, they moved to San Francisco to become a smash hit at the hungry i basement nightclub. Their repertoire included such songs as "Gari Gari," "When I First Came to This Land," "The Monks of St. Bernard," "Ya Se Murio el Burro," "The Cumberland Mountain Bear Chase," "Rumeynia, Rumeynia," "The Hammer Song," "Have Some Madeira, M'Dear," "Molly Malone," and the show-stopping comic renditions of "The Ballad of Sigmund Fraud," "Charlie, the Midnight Marauder," and "Mama Don't 'Low."

From that time until the group disbanded in the mid-1960s, they were featured on radio and TV and in concerts throughout the United States and the world. These included extended engagements at the Blue Angel, Roundtable, and Village Vanguard in New York and Mister Kelly's in Chicago, and a concert with Eartha Kitt at the Hollywood Bowl. The group also toured the country with Shelley Berman, Chris Connor, and George Shearing; joined Johnny Mathis in a show at the Greek Theater in Los Angeles; and formed an act for a time with comedian Mort Sahl.

The group signed with RCA Victor Records soon after its formation. Limeliter LPs were still finding a wide audience after the group had ceased performing. The list of titles included *The Limeliters* (1960); *Tonight in Person, Slightly Fabulous* (1961); *Sing Out, Children's Eyes, Folk Matinee* (1962); *Our Men in San Francisco, Makin' a Joyful Noise, 14 14K Folk Songs* (1963); *More of Everything, Best of the Limeliters, Leave It to the Limeliters* (1964); and *London Concert* (1965).

LINDSEY, LAWANDA: *Singer, songwriter. Born Savannah, Georgia, January 12, 1953.*

In country music it hasn't been all that uncommon for performers to achieve popularity in their early years. This has been partly because, for many families, finding such skills in children offered a way out of hand-to-mouth existence or, in other instances, because show business was a way of life for the family group. In LaWanda Lindsey's case, by the time she was born her father already had been working in the country-music field for many years. When she was five, she began working with his band. Thus, when she signed her first major recording contract at fourteen, she had close to a decade of performing experience behind her.

As she recalled to LaWayne Satterfield of *Music City News* (August 1975), "I started out singing with my father, Lefty Lindsey and The Dixie Show Boys, when I was five years old. Then I went through a period of being more interested in the boys than I was singing, but I soon got over that.

"When I was about nine years old my father gave up the band. But in 1964, Connie Smith became my idol and my interest in singing became the most important thing. At that time, Daddy re-formed his old band and our show was LaWanda Lindsey and The Dixie Show Boys. We worked for two years at this barn dance every Saturday night in a little town just outside Savannah. I was really rich in those days. I made five dollars every Saturday night and blew it all at Woolworth's Dime Store on Monday morning.

"My dad owned a country radio station in Savannah and they would do remote broadcasts each Saturday. One Saturday, during a remote from a store, Conway Twitty's business manager heard me. He was in the area and drove by to meet me. He talked to my father about getting me a recording contract. After the show we went down to the radio station and I recorded four songs. He and my dad brought the tape to Nashville and I was signed by Chart Records. . . . My first record was 'Beggars Can't Be Choosers' by Liz Anderson."

After her initial singles began to find good response from the public, LaWanda became a featured performer on many of the top-ranked radio shows and telecasts. Among her credits as the 1970s went by were a number of appearances on the *WWVA Jamboree* in Wheeling, West Virginia and the all-important *Grand Ole Opry*. Her talents were also highly praised by Buck Owens and Roy Clark of the syndicated *Hee Haw* show, who welcomed her as a guest on several occasions. Still other guest spots during those years were the *Bill Anderson Show* and the *Wilburn Brothers Show*.

During the late 1960s and early 1970s, Chart issued twenty-one singles by Lindsey alone or as part of a duet with Kenny Vernon. A number of those made the country charts, with one duet release, "Pickin' Wild Mountain Berries," reaching highest chart levels. From 1970 through 1973, Chart issued four albums of LaWanda's, including *LaWanda Lindsey, Swingin' and Singing My Song, Pickin' Wild Mountain Berries* (with Kenny Vernon), and *We'll Sing in the Sunshine*.

In the mid-1970s, Lindsey and her family moved from Nashville to Bakersfield, California. The move westward signaled a new alignment with Buck Owens' management organization, Omac Artist Corporation. A new recording arrangement was set up with Hollywood-based Capitol Records, which issued her first single on the label, "Today Will Be the First Day of the Rest of My Life," soon after. This was followed by the singles "Sunshine Feeling," "Hello Trouble," "Hello Out There," and "I Ain't Hangin' Round," all of which showed up on the national top-50 country lists during 1973–74. Her debut album on Capitol, *This Is LaWanda Lindsey,* was released in June 1974. Among her 1975 sin-

gles releases was "Goodtime Baby," which, she noted, marked her thirty-seventh single release: "I have had thirty-seven singles and never had a record that wasn't on all three trade magazine charts."

During the first half of the 1970s, LaWanda wrote a number of original compositions, though most of her successful recordings were of material supplied by others. Her work impressed established country artists, including Lynn Anderson, who recorded Lindsey's "Wave Bye Bye to the Man" in the mid-1970s.

LOCKLIN, HANK: *Singer, guitarist, songwriter, public official. Born McLellan, Florida, February 15, 1918.*

To go from a farm boy chopping cotton to a star of the *Grand Ole Opry* is not unusual in country-music lore. To do this and then return and win an election as mayor of one's home town, though, is much rarer.

Henry Locklin had little idea of becoming mayor of McLellan, Florida, when he hoed and chopped cotton on his family's farm in the 1920s. He did like to sing country songs, though, and, when he was ten, gathered enough small change for a down payment on a guitar from the local pawnshop. Although the monthly charges were only $1.50, he found this sum hard to come by and the guitar was repossessed.

Managing to learn a lot about playing the instrument before returning it, Hank persevered and finally got another one, on which he worked out some of his early compositions. He began to take part in local dances and sings, moving on to win a number of local contests when he was in his teens. In the 1930s, he performed as often as he could, but times were tough in those Depression years, and he ended up earning his keep working on road projects of the government Works Project Administration.

Lockin refused to give up his hopes for a successful musical career. This stubbornness finally paid off with more important dates and his first radio engagements, on Florida stations WCOA, Pensacola, and WDLP, Panama City. His star continued to rise with appearances in other cities in the

South and air shots on such stations as WALA, Mobile, Alabama; KLEE, Houston, Texas; and KTHS, Hot Springs, Arkansas.

Hank really began to move after World War II. He joined the cast of KWKH *Louisiana Hayride* in Shreveport soon after that show began. By the early 1950s, he was one of the audience favorites and had signed a record contract with Decca. He moved for a time to Four Star, the label of his first major record hit, the 1953 "Let Me Be the One." Soon after, Hank became a regular on the *Grand Ole Opry* in Nashville and signed a long-term contract with RCA Victor.

From the mid-1950s on, Locklin rapidly became one of the top artists in country music. He scored a top-10 hit in 1957 with "Geisha Girl" and followed up in 1958 with "It's a Little More like Heaven" and his own composition, "Send Me the Pillow You Dream On." In 1960, his version of Don Robertson's standard, "Please Help Me, I'm Falling," was number one nationally for many weeks. His other best-sellers of the early 1960s were "Happy Birthday to Me" (1961) and "Happy Journal" (1962).

During the 1950's and 1960's, Hank was represented by many successful LPs. These included two King LPs, *Best of Hank Locklin* and *Encores, Hank Locklin* on Metro (1965), *Born to Ramble* and *Sings Hank Locklin* on Pickwick, and the Wrangler label's *Hank Locklin Favorites*. His RCA Victor output included *Foreign Love* (1958); *Please Help Me* (1960); *Happy Journey, Hank Locklin, Tribute to Roy Acuff* (1962); *This Song Is for You* (Camden), *Ways of Life* (1963); *Irish Songs, Sings Hank Williams* (1964). *Sings Eddy Arnold* and *My Kind of Music* (Camden) (1965); *Once Over Lightly, The Girls Get Prettier, Best of Hank Locklin, Gloryland Ways* (1966); *Bummin' Around* (Camden), *Nashville Women, Send Me the Pillow* (1967); *Bless Her Heart* (late 1960s); *Country Music Hall of Fame* (1968).

Among the songs Locklin recorded in addition to those above are: "Living Alone," "Foreign Car," "Border of the Blues," "I'm a Fool," "Goin' Home All by Myself," "The Rich and the Poor," "How Much," "She's Better than Most," "The Same Sweet Girl,"

"Born to Ramble," "Fraulein," "Hiding in My Heart," "Anna Marie," "Blues in Advance," "My Old Home Town," "Seven Days," and the 1968 hit "Country Music Hall of Fame."

Over the years, Hank's personal appearances took him to all fifty states, Canada, and Europe. He guested on many major TV shows in the 1950s and 1960s, including ABC's *Jamboree U.S.A* In the early 1960s, Hank returned to his home town of McLellan to live, and soon was elected mayor. To complete a boyhood dream, he established his residence on the rambling "Singin' I. Ranch," which incorporated the cotton field in which he'd once worked as a child.

Hank continued to be affiliated with RCA in the early 1970s. His LPs included: *Hank Locklin with Danny Davis and the Nashville Brass* and *Candy Kisses* (Camden) (1970); and *First 15 Years* (1971).

LOGGINS AND MESSINA: *Vocal and instrumental group. Kenny Loggins, born Everett, Washington, January 7, 1948; Jim Messina, born Maywood, California, December 5, 1947. Band personnel as of 1973: Al Hirth, Jon Clarke, Michael Omartian, Larry Sims.*

Offering a mixture of old-timey rock, folk- and country-rock, Loggins and Messina became a favored group of a large segment of the pop music audience in the mid-1970s. Long after the group's dissolution, the original material, written primarily by the two principals but sometimes by other band members or associates, was often recorded and re-recorded by other artists.

Loggins came to the band with a background in folk and rock (see Loggins, Kenny) while Messina's roots were country and rock. Jim was born in California, but moved to Texas with his family when he was five, where he began to learn guitar. He recalled, "Between the time I was five and ten, I watched a lot of musicians play on television. While watching, I learned to play their chords. I really knew at that time that I wanted to be a musician."

Most of the music he listened to was country & western, an influence evident in his work with Poco and Loggins and Messina. (In the first LP that Loggins and Messina recorded, one of Jim's contributions was the song, co-written with Al Garth, "Listen to a Country Song.") However, when Jim's family moved back to live in the Los Angeles area beach community of Manhattan Beach, the then-twelve-year-old Messina "discovered" rock. At thirteen, he joined his first rock group and played professionally while he completed his high school years in a new locale, Colton, California.

After graduating high school, he embarked on a career that mixed session work with learning to become a recording engineer. For several years he pursued the latter job at various Los Angeles studios, including Harmony Records, Audio Arts, Wally Heider, and Sunset Sound. In 1967, he was asked to join the legendary Buffalo Springfield, then already nearing the end of its brief mercurial career. One of his contributions to the group was to produce their last LP, *Last Time Around.*

After the Springfield broke up, he joined forces with Richie Furay to found a new band called Poco, oriented toward blending country and rock. Messina performed with Poco for several years (see Poco), leaving formally in 1971 when he decided to join forces with Kenny Loggins.

The two really hadn't planned such an alignment. Loggins had signed with Columbia Records as a solo artist and Messina, who had continued to do a lot of production work with various artists besides his band commitments, was asked to handle that chore on the new LP. Once Loggins and Messina set to work, though, they found they hit it off well as musicians and that each contributed original songs the other liked. As the sessions proceeded, they found themselves with a good band sound from such sidemen as horn players Al Hirth and Jon Clarke, keyboards player Michael Omartian, and bassist Larry Sims. A chance appearance at the Troubadour nightclub in Los Angeles in February 1972, resulting from the club's last-minute need to fill an opening-act gap, proved decisive. The audience loved the group's set and gave them an ovation that proved to equal the reception for the feature act. With the album becoming more and more a joint project between Loggins and Messina, they decided to keep things that way.

The first LP, *Kenny Loggins with Jim Messina Sittin' In,* was issued during 1972 and proved a hit, moving to top-chart levels not once but twice over a span from mid-1972 into 1973. The collection contained many songs that quickly became staple items in Loggins and Messina concerts: Kenny Loggins' "Danny's Song" and the Loggins and Messina version of Kenny's "House at Pooh Corner" (previously a hit for the Nitty Gritty Dirt Band), plus Jim Messina's "Peace of Mind" and a contribution from Kenny's brother Dan (co-written with Don Lottermoser), "Vahevala."

The group's second LP, *Loggins and Messina,* issued in late 1972, was an even greater success. The album rapidly moved to the top of the charts, earning the band a gold-record award before year end and remaining on the hit lists well into 1973. The group added another hit single to its collection with the album track "Your Mama Don't Dance." The song was nominated for a Grammy Award as Best Song of 1972 and Loggins and Messina played it as part of the network TV awards program in March 1973. That same month, the team had another single high on the charts, "Thinking of You," and followed that in the fall with another chart hit, "Ain't Gonna Change My Music." Between early 1973 and late 1974, Columbia released two more albums, *Full Sail* and a live LP, *On Stage.*

In late 1974, the group had another album on the charts, *Mother Lode.* That LP earned a gold-record award on November 25, 1974, and remained on the charts into 1975. However, the duo seemed to be losing some of its creative fire. Its next album, *So Fine,* issued during the summer of 1975, and *Native Son,* issued the beginning of 1976, had some interesting tracks, but overall didn't have the spark of earlier releases. Both were on the charts for many months, but mainly in middle or lower levels. Kenny Loggins also was becoming restless about resuming his solo career, and the combination of factors led to the group's phasing out before the end of 1976. Columbia issued a "greatest hits" album that year titled *The Best of Friends.* Later it released another retrospective album, *Finale.*

LOGGINS, KENNY: *Singer, guitarist, songwriter. Born Everett, Washington, January 7, 1948.*

When you've been part of as eminently successful a team as Loggins and Messina, you aren't surprised when people shake their heads in doubt about the wisdom of sallying forth to try a solo career. Kenny Loggins, however, was certain he could do as well as a soloist as part of a team, emphasizing in the summer of 1977, "I love being on my own. It's been very exciting. It's very difficult to put the whole thing into words. Just the feeling of being responsible for your own fate and having the direction of your life in your own hands is the ultimate goal for an artist and I'm enjoying the hell out of it.

"I don't expect to do more work with Jim [Messina] at this time. But we keep in touch and we may help each other out now and then if it seems of value to do it. For instance, there may be a song he might be the right guitarist for or he may want me to help on one of his songs. But otherwise I don't see us reforming as a team."

At the time Kenny said that his solo career was still touch and go. His debut album was finding a reasonable reception from record buyers, but it didn't seem quite as strong as some of the Loggins and Messina efforts. But Kenny persevered, turning out successively more impressive albums until, by the end of the 1970s, the folk music alumnus had retained most of the old Loggins and Messina following and added a sizable number of new enthusiasts as well.

He was born in Everett, Washington, but moved first to Seattle, then to Alhambra, California, with his family. He started to learn the guitar in seventh grade, and in high school and early college his musical preference was folk music. When he was a sophomore in college, he joined a folk group. However, as time went by, he became more and more rock-oriented, although usually retaining elements of folk music in both his performing style and songwriting approach.

As he said in the late 1970s, though he hadn't considered himself a folk artist for many years, it still affected his approach to music. "I can't escape from my folk roots because it's a part of me. I remember when I showed [arranger] Bob James the material for my solo debut album and I'd sing and he'd write down notes and chords that totally were blowing my mind, he kept laughing as he did it. The reason, he said, was that he couldn't write the musical phrases down the same way I did it because I used folk phrasing 'and that was unwriteable.' His jazz roots interpreted what I was doing as folk while folkies would interpret it as rock."

In the late 1960s, Kenny's goal was to succeed in the rock field. He joined two rock groups during those years, one called Second Helping, which recorded on Viva Records, and the other Gator Creek, which did some tracks for Mercury. Neither band made any waves with the public at large and Kenny left Second Helping in 1969 to concentrate on writing and, he hoped, a solo effort.

Soon after, he got a writing contract with ABC Wingate Publishing. One of his compositions for that firm was the delightful "House at Pooh Corner," which became a major hit for the Nitty Gritty Dirt Band. The song later became a staple of Loggins and Messina shows and still is included in a typical Loggins concert.

In September 1971, Columbia Records executives were impressed sufficiently with his writings and performing potential to give him a recording contract. Jim Messina was assigned to produce Kenny's first solo effort, but as the sessions proceeded, Messina became involved in the performing as well as producing end. By the time the album was issued in early 1972, it bore the title *Kenny Loggins with Jim Messina Sittin' In.* The album became a major hit and also was the launching pad for one of the duo's most famous singles, "Danny's Song," which also was a top-10 hit in a cover version by Anne Murray.

The tremendous acceptance of the Loggins and Messina team caused Kenny's solo career to recede into the background for a while as the group turned out a series of best-selling albums and singles in the mid-1970s and also became a headline concert act. (For more details, see Loggins and Messina).

However, by 1976, the group's popularity began to fade. Part of the reason was the lack of striking new songs for the duo's repertoire, perhaps reflecting a loss of enthusiasm on Kenny's part at being a team member rather than soloist. The slowdown in audience interest, whatever its cause, helped make Kenny and Jim decide to try new directions.

This time Loggins was determined to go all out to make his solo ambitions pay off. Besides spending as much time as possible in writing and recording new material, he stressed performing before as many people as he could reach. "This is my shot and I'm taking it seriously. Part of my philosophy is giving 100 per cent of your effort in the things that mean something to you creatively and that means going out and working in front of the public."

Part of his approach in the early phases of this campaign was to open for many of the shows of the Fleetwood Mac rock group. He was aware he could fill medium-size or small venues on his own as a headliner, but he took the approach that, in the long run, it would pay off more handsomely if he took second billing in order to showcase his talents to the massive audiences for Fleetwood Mac shows. He noted in 1977, "Mostly I've been opening for Fleetwood Mac, including two nights earlier this summer [1977] in Madison Square Garden in New York. I had to make a decision whether to be the headliner in 3,000–5,000 seat halls or opening for Fleetwood Mac in 15,000 to 17,000 capacity auditoriums. I know I only have so much time to show people who I am and what I do. It made sense to do the Fleetwood thing and hopefully turn a lot more people on to my music."

The strategy worked. His debut 1977 release, *Celebrate Me Home*, didn't shoot up to the top of the charts, but it did stay in middle levels for a long time, selling steadily all the time. Eventually, the album went over the 500,000 copy mark to earn Kenny a gold record. His rising prestige with the music public was reinforced with the release of his second LP, *Nightwatch*, in the summer of 1978. Different somewhat in tone and content, indicating that Kenny was not afraid to experiment with new musical and lyrical material, the LP moved into top-chart levels in a few month's time and, before the year was out, had gone past platinum-award totals. His third solo Columbia album, *Keep the Fire*, was issued in the fall of 1979 and reached gold-record levels in early 1980. His fourth LP, *Alive*, came out in the fall of 1980 and earned a gold record even faster, passing that milestone before the year was out.

Discussing his approach to songwriting, he stated, "Essentially, it requires self-discipline. I find that creativity, inspiration will come into the room if I open the door. If I don't, if I don't work at it, it rarely arrives on its own. I wrote some things with the Bergmans [Alan and Marilyn Bergman, winners of several Academy Awards for movie songs] and Alan says songwriting is more perspiration than inspiration. I rather think at this point in my life it's more inspiration for me, but I feel there's always at least a small degree of perspiration.

"That's particularly true of my lyrics much of the time. Every once in a while I'll write a song and lyrics and music will be born almost simultaneously, but usually the music comes first and I wait until that moment comes when the lyrics fall into place. An example is my song 'Why Do People Lie?' from my 1977 solo album. I sat down four times after I wrote the music before the words came. I had a feeling about it; I felt I knew subconsciously what the theme would be, but it took several tries before it came. Then the fourth time I knew somehow the timing was right and the lines just came to me. I feel you're only a vehicle; the song writes itself and you have to wait for it to come out. It's wonderful, but it's scary too."

Based in part on an interview with Irwin Stambler, July 1977.

LOMAX, ALAN: *Singer, author, folk music collector. Born Austin, Texas, January 15, 1915.*

The name Lomax is almost synonymous with folk music scholarship in the United States. First the late John A. Lomax and then his son Alan provided the dynamic force that helped make the Archive of Folk Song of the Library of Congress one of the most comprehensive in the world. The Archive itself has been of major importance for many scholars as well as folk artists who built up much of their repertoire from browsing through the collection. In addition, the discovery or rediscovery of many greatly talented artists is directly traceable to the survey tours of John and Alan Lomax.

Alan spent most of his boyhood in Texas, where he was exposed to many folk songs in his home environment. He went to grade school in Austin and later attended a college preparatory school in Dallas. In 1933, he went on his first collecting tour as an observer and sometime helper to his father. The trip made him a confirmed folk music collector in his father's image. Soon after the trip was over, the Lomaxes moved to Washington, D.C., where John Lomax began his monumental work of collecting folk music material for the Library of Congress.

Now that the family was based in the East, young Alan enrolled at Harvard. After one year, though, he went back to Texas, entering the University of Texas, from which he was graduated in 1936. Returning to Washington, he settled down as assistant curator of the Archive in 1937. That year he spent three months in Haiti recording Haitian songs and dances.

In the next half dozen years (he left the Archive in 1942), Alan recorded new and established artists both in Washington and on field trips. Among those with whom he worked were Vera Hall, Horton Barker, and, in 1939, the great Leadbelly. During 1939, he also recorded famous jazz pianist Jelly Roll Morton and began a new folk music series for Columbia Broadcasting's School of the Air, called *Wellsprings of America.* Alan played recordings of old and

new artists, discussed folk music aspects, and sang some songs himself.

During World War II, Alan was active in government-sponsored morale programs. In 1943 and 1944, he worked for the Office of War Information, and in 1944 and 1945 with the Army's Special Services section. When the war ended, he accepted an invitation from Decca Records to serve as its director of folk music. His selections helped make the Decca catalogue one of the strongest in the field in the late 1940s and early 1950s.

Lomax continued to collect and classify folk material in the post–World War II era, augmented with a 1947 Guggenheim grant. He continued his broadcast work with a 1950 program for Mutual Broadcasting, *Your Ballad Man Alan Lomax.*

In 1958, Tradition Records issued an LP featuring Lomax's voice called *Texas Folk Songs.* Among the album numbers were "Billy Barlow," "Ain't No More Cane on This Brazos," "The Dying Cowboy," "My Little John Henry," "All the Pretty Little Horses," "The Wild Rippling Water," "Black Betty," "Rattlesnake," "Eadie," "Long Summer Days," "Sam Bass," "Lord Lovell," and "Godamighty Drag."

Lomax remained active in the 1960s as an artist and scholar. He performed at a number of festivals, including Newport. He also helped in the direction of some of these, an example being his service as a member of the board of advisors of the American Folk Festival at Asheville, North Carolina. He was one of the founding members of the Newport Folk Foundation and served on the Board of Directors of the Folk Festival for several years starting in 1963. In the 1960s, Kapp Records produced another album of Lomax singing, *Folk Song Saturday Night.*

Over the years Lomax also wrote many books and articles, both scholarly and of popular interest. He worked on a number of books with his father, including *American Ballads and Folk Songs* (1934); *Cowboy Songs and Other Frontier Ballads* (revised edition, 1938); *Negro Folk Songs as Sung by Leadbelly* (1936); *Our Singing Country* (1941); and *Folk Song, U.S.A.* (1947). With Sidney Robertson Cowell he compiled the *American Folk Song and Folk Lore* regional bibliography in 1942. In 1960, Alan was represented by *The Folk Songs of North America in the English Language.*

His activities in the 1950s and 1960s included lecturing on folklore at such schools as New York University, Columbia University, University of Indiana, University of Chicago, and the University of Texas. From 1951 to 1957, he served as editor for the Columbia Records World Library of Folk and Primitive Music (seventeen-volume set). Beginning in 1963, he started a comprehensive study in comparative musicology, work he was still engaged in as of 1969. His activities continued along similar scholarly lines in the 1970s. (See also Hawes, Bess Lomax; Lomax, John Avery)

LOMAX, JOHN AVERY: *Folklorist, folk music collector, educator. Born Goodman, Mississippi, September 23, 1875; died Greenville, Mississippi, January 26, 1948.*

The name Lomax is a pioneer name in many ways. Lomax ancestors were among the first settlers of the nation and of the Southwest. One of the descendants of this hardy family, John Avery Lomax, helped preserve the musical heritage of pioneer days while pioneering the new areas of American folklore scholarship of the twentieth century.

Born in Mississippi and raised in the Southwest, John Lomax had an ear for folk ballads of the hills and plains from his very early years. When he reached his teens, he began to collect some of this material, listening to farmers, itinerant musicians, and cowboys near his home. He scrawled their lyrics down on an assortment of papers, including the backs of envelopes and pieces of cardboard and wrapping paper. By the time he was in his late teens, he had a considerable pile of those odd-looking manuscripts.

In the mid-1890s, he gathered his belongings, making ready to enter the University of Texas at Austin. In among his clothes and some tattered textbooks was his collection of song material. He had no way of knowing that collecting this kind of material was almost unheard of in academic ranks in those years. At the university, he had occasion to show the notes to one of his English professors, Dr. Morgan Callaway, Jr. Dr. Callaway glanced through them and suggested they were of little value.

The disappointed Lomax filed them away and went on to gain his B.A. in 1897. Moving toward a career as an English instructor, he attended a number of schools over the next decade. He took some courses at the University of Chicago in 1903 and 1906 and also continued to attend the University of Texas, receiving his M.A. in 1906. He then moved north to Harvard, having received an Austin Teaching Scholarship to work toward another master's in American literature (1907). In one course given by Barrett Wendell, he received an assignment to bring in examples of native literature. Lomax dug out his old files and this time won the whole-hearted attention of his teacher.

Wendell introduced young Lomax to the nation's first-ranked folklorist, George Lyman Kittredge. Kittredge shared Wendell's enthusiasm and both supported further collecting by Lomax. From then on, collecting was an important part of Lomax's life and, in time, the lives of his children. Helped by a Shelden Traveling Fellowship, he went back to the Southwest. There he spent three years on its backroads with an Ediphone recording machine to make on-the-spot cylinders of folk melodies.

He returned to the East and, after several rejections, got a publisher. The firm of Sturgis and Walton agreed to produce a book with 122 song texts, eighteen with the music. Included in the book was a letter in praise of Lomax's work from Theodore Roosevelt, who had been shown the manuscript by Lomax during a Frontier Day Celebration in Cheyenne, Wyoming. Published in 1910, Lomax's *Cowboy Songs and Other Frontier Ballads* was a landmark that compared with the publication in the previous century of Francis James Child's ballad books.

Lomax continued to follow the usual pattern of collectors, earning a living in other ways and pursuing new material in his spare time. From 1903 to 1910, for instance, he held the title of Associate Professor of English at Texas A&M College. From 1910 to 1917, he was Secretary of the University of Texas in Austin.

For a while, from 1925 to 1932, he varied his pattern by entering the banking business. Although still interested in folk music, his bank work kept him from spending much time on it.

In 1933, he finally embarked on another major collecting tour, this time with his seventeen-year-old son, Alan. The Depression, which resulted in the failure of his bank, was the reason for the tour. To make ends meet, John signed a contract with a publisher for a folk song book. He and Alan built a 350-pound recorder into the back of their car and garnered hundreds of new songs.

These were published by The Macmillan Company in 1934 under the title *American Ballads and Folk Songs*. The raw material collected on the trip was sent to the Library of Congress in Washington. It so impressed Library officials that John Lomax was asked to come to Washington in 1934 as Honorary Consultant and Archivist, Curator of the new Archive of Folk Song.

During the 1930s and 1940s, John and Alan built this collection up into the most impressive in the world. Thousands of songs were added either through field trips or folk artists brought to Washington. In time, Alan succeeded his father as curator.

In the years between 1934 and his death, John gained a worldwide reputation. He continued to write books on folk music subjects, many with Alan, and lectured before learned and lay groups. The final fruits of his labors were a new public awareness of the importance of folk material and the use of the collection as a basis for growth by new folk artists who came to the Library to help increase their knowledge of the field. (See also Hawes, Bess Lomax; Lomax, Alan)

LONZO AND OSCAR: *Vocal and instrumental comedy duo. Original members: Ken Marvin, born Haleyville, Alabama, June 27, 1924, and Rollin Sullivan, born Edmonton, Kentucky, January 19, 1919. Marvin replaced in mid-1940s by Johnny Sullivan, born Edmonton, Kentucky, July 7, 1917, died Nashville, Tennessee, June 5, 1967. Sullivan replaced in 1967 by Dave Hooten, born St. Claire, Missouri, February 4.*

Down-home humor always has been an important part of country music; one of the most famous teams in that tradition is that of Lonzo and Oscar. From the 1940s to the end of the 1970s, there always was a duo of that name on the *Grand Ole Opry*, though with several changes in personnel over the years.

For much of Lonzo and Oscar's history, the duo was a brother act—John Sullivan taking the part of Lonzo and Rollin Sullivan that of Oscar. The team didn't start as a brother act, though, nor did it end as one.

The Sullivan brothers, oddly enough, were working together prior to the birth of Lonzo and Oscar. Both born in Edmonton, Kentucky, to a poor rural family, the boys were working at family chores and then odd jobs from their early years. Country music was a prime form of relaxation and both Sullivans took to playing and singing such material when still quite young. By the time they were in their teens, Johnny could play both bass fiddle and guitar and Rollin was a fine mandolinist. They already were performing in small clubs in their home area by the end of the 1930s.

Just before the United States entered World War II, the Sullivans made their radio debut on station WTJS, Jackson, Tennessee. There were a lot of other excellent country artists performing on WTJS programs, including Ken Marvin and Eddy Arnold. Marvin and Rollin Sullivan got together to form the original duo, with strong encouragement from Arnold. It was Eddy, indeed, who suggested they call themselves Lonzo and Oscar, with Marvin serving as Lonzo. Ken and Rollin made the first recordings under that title, though Johnny contributed by writing some of the original material with Rollin. It was one such collaboration, a comic number called "I'm My Own Grandpa," that made the duo's reputation in the mid-1940s. Marvin and Rollin made the original single, though later on Rollin and Johnny did their own version.

Things were moving quite well for the duo—they were invited to become cast regulars on the *Grand Ole Opry* in 1942—when the Sullivan brothers both entered the armed forces. By the mid-1940s, they were mustered out and Rollin and Marvin resumed their association. For a time, the comic act plus Johnny was part of a band that was featured on station WAVE, Louisville, Kentucky. In 1945, Ken Marvin retired from the music field and Johnny Sullivan took over as Lonzo. For a time, the brothers were part of the Eddy Arnold group, an association they ended in 1947, the year they also became full *Opry* cast members under the Lonzo and Oscar banner.

During the late 1940s and through the 1950s and most of the 1960s, the Sullivans toured widely with their own show. Among the members of the show over the years were many *Opry* stars, including Cousin Jody, Cousin Luther, Smokey Pleacher, and Tommy Warren. Besides personal appearances in all fifty states and in many other nations, Lonzo and Oscar had many TV credits. These included twenty-four films of their own show for TV, guest spots on *Kate Smith, The Ed Sullivan Show,* and *Dave Garroway,* and featured spots on most major country syndicated and network TV programs.

The team recorded on many labels over the years, including RCA, Decca, Starday, their own label, Nugget, and starting in 1967, Columbia. Their singles included such songs as "If Texas Knew What Arkansas," "My Dreams Turned into a Nightmare," "I'll Go Chasin' Wimmun," "Ole Buttermilk Sky," "My Adobe Hacienda," "Julie," "Hearts Are Lonely," and "Movin' On." Among the many originals they recorded or included in their act were "You Blacked My Blue Eyes Too Once Often," "Last Old Dollar," "There's a Hole in the

Bottom of the Sea," "I Don't Forgive No More," "Take Them Cold Feet Out of My Back," "Cornbread, Lasses and Sassafras Tea," and "She's the Best I Ever Saw."

Their LPs included *Country Comedy Time* on Decca; *Lonzo and Oscar* (1961) and *Country Music Time* (1963) on Starday; and *Country Comedy* on Pickwick. The original Ken Marvin and Rollin Sullivan recording of "I'm My Own Grandpa" was included in the RCA mid-1960s collection *Stars of the Grand Ole Opry.*

The team temporarily was dissolved when Johnny Sullivan died in June 1967. Several months later, it was reactivated when Dave Hooten took over the part of Lonzo. The new team went back into action both on the *Grand Ole Opry* and on the concert circuit and was still finding a sizable country following for its satirical offerings over a decade later.

LOUDERMILK, JOHN D.: *Singer, banjoist, bass fiddle player, mandolinist, trombonist, cornet player, organist, fiddler, songwriter, record producer. Born Durham, North Carolina, March 31, 1934.*

There's no doubt that John D. Loudermilk ranks among the most prolific and creative of country-music writers, with over 700 original compositions to his credit at the start of the 1980s. Many of those songs paved the way to stardom for a number of performers. A look at his career shows that he might well have become a superstar of stage and TV had he wanted to.

His parents were hard-working, family-oriented people who saw to it that their son got a better educational grounding than they'd received. His father, a carpenter who helped build the chapel at Duke University in Durham, John's birthplace, couldn't read or write. As soon as John mastered those fundamentals in school, his father started taking the boy down to the grocery store on Saturday afternoons to endorse his paychecks.

While John grew up, his family had to move constantly, though always staying in the same general area. He recalled the many times his mother had to pack up pasteboard cartons that the moving van took to a new locale. In all, there were nineteen such moves within the same school district before John finished high school and entered junior college.

By then he already had considerable experience as an entertainer. As a child he had enjoyed singing in church, where the accompaniments ranged from stringed instruments, horns, tambourines, and a bass drum to hand clapping. He remembered, too, the pleasure he got as a boy while taking his Saturday night bath in a galvanized wash tub placed next to the kitchen stove within listening distance of the radio, which carried the *Grand Ole Opry* show. When he grew older he became a member of the Salvation Army Band, where he learned to play just about every instrument imaginable, from fiddle to horns to banjo and guitar. It was in church as a youngster that he made his first public appearance, joining his mother to play and sing "Life's Railway to Heaven."

He already had considerable stage presence before he was in his teens. When he was eleven, he made his singing debut on radio and soon had his own show on a Durham station. When he was twelve, he entered and won a place on the Capitol Records Talent Contest in Charlotte, North Carolina, a show whose host was the now legendary Tex Ritter.

John continued his interest in music in his high school years, a period when he was expanding his purview to include not only country but many other categories, from the classics to rhythm & blues. Among the artists whose work he admired during those years were Eddy Arnold, Jimmy Reed, Andre's Segovia, Ivory Joe Hunter, Fats Domino, and Lloyd Price. He also was strongly influenced by the writings of the philosopher-poet Kahlil Gibran, which inspired him to write a number of poems of his own.

John got a job on TV station WTVD in Durham, where his activities included painting sets and also working as a part-time bass fiddler in the *Noon Show* band at the station. By then he already was experi-menting with not only poetry but original melodies. He came to the *Noon Show* one day in 1955 with a poem he'd set to music and played it on the air. Not only did the song, "A Rose and a Baby Ruth," elicit delighted letters and phone calls from viewers, it also brought a call from a local record producer named Orville Campbell who wanted to have another young singer, named George Hamilton IV, record it. The result was a smash hit that rose to number one in the United States in 1956 and became a springboard to industry renown for both Hamilton and Loudermilk.

At the time, Loudermilk had not considered music as a career. In fact, he left to study at Campbell University in Buies Creek, North Carolina. While there he wrote a second landmark song called "Sitting in the Balcony," which became his debut effort as a recording artist. The single gained some attention but, more importantly, it was picked up by a previously unknown rock artist named Eddie Cochran, whose version of the song in 1957 became his first massive hit. Loudermilk's main concern now was what to do about a spate of contract offers from New York and Nashville publishers. His life was changing in many other ways as well. While back in Durham he met a Duke University music major named Gwen Cooke who in time agreed to marry him. They were, in fact, married in 1959 in the same Duke chapel his father had helped to build.

Loudermilk eventually aligned himself with Jim Denny and Cedarwood Music, Inc., and moved to Nashville, where, besides writing a steady flow of fine songs, he also recorded a number of albums for RCA in the 1960s under Chet Atkins' guidance. (During these years, he also shifted his writing efforts from Cedarwood to Acuff–Rose Publications.) Some of his songs helped George Hamilton IV's transition from the pop field to country stardom in the 1960s, including such often covered numbers as "Break My Mind" (also a major hit later for Anne Murray), "Blue Train," and "Abilene." From the early 1969s into the 1980s, those or other Loudermilk compositions were recorded by just about every famous or near-famous artist in the country & western field and often became hits for pop performers as well. Among his oft-recorded songs are "Talk Back Trembling Lips," "Waterloo," "Sad Movies," "Norman," "Paper Tiger," "From Nashville with Love," "Thou Shalt Not Steal," "Bad News," "I Wanna Live," "Ma Baker's Little Acre," "Torture," "Big Daddy," "Tobacco Road," "Then You Can Tell Me Goodbye," "Ebony Eyes," "The Little Bird," "It's My Time," "Indian Reservation," "Googie Eye," and "Windy and Warm."

During the 1970s, Loudermilk became interested in the field of ethnomusicology and its relationship to contemporary record production. As a result of his studies, he gave many lectures at folklore society meetings and at colleges on the contributions of people like Pete Seeger and Jimmie Driftwood to all phases of music. Most of his limited amount of personal performances in that decade were at various folk and country music festivals in the United States and Europe.

Besides writing and recording, he also did a certain amount of production work in the 1960s and 1970s. One of his credits included handling production on the first recordings of the Allman Brothers Band at the end of the 1960s.

Among his honors are a Grammy Award, a Manny Award from the National Songwriters Association International, dozens of gold records for hit versions of his songs by various artists, and a similar large number of BMI citations for top-rated compositions. At one point, his career also was the basis for a series of TV specials telecast on the British Broadcasting Corporation. He also served on the board of directors of the National Academy of Recording Arts & Sciences (sponsoring organization for the Grammy Awards) and was elected to the board of directors of the Country Music Association of America for two different terms, the second one for the years of 1979 and 1980. He also was inducted into the Nashville Songwriters Association's International Hall of Fame.

LOUVIN, CHARLIE: *Singer, guitarist, songwriter. Born Rainesville, Alabama, July 7, 1927.*

The Louvin Brothers were one of the premier acts of country music for more than a decade and a half; when they split up in 1963, some wondered whether they could achieve equal success as soloists. For Charlie, still a *Grand Ole Opry* star at the start of the 1980s, the answer was a resounding "yes!" and the same probably would have proven true for Ira had he not died in a tragic accident.

The brothers grew up as members of a farm family in Henegar, Alabama, and spent many a backbreaking day as boys working in the cotton fields and doing other farm chores. Country music naturally was one of their interests as they grew up and both started picking out chords on guitars before they reached their teens. Charlie, the younger of the brothers by three years, recalled that their entry into the music business occurred "sort of accidentally" when he was sixteen. The duo won an amateur contest in Chattanooga, Tennessee; first prize was a radio program on station WDEF broadcast daily at 4 A.M. To make the show, the brothers worked first shift in a cotton mill, their mill earnings being their major revenue at the time. During the mid-1940s, they began to find additional jobs playing small clubs, country fairs, and the like, finally reaching the point where they could concentrate on performing alone.

As their reputation increased with local fans, the brothers began to look further afield, with a record contract a primary goal. Their first association was with Decca, which only released one recording; then in 1949 they signed with MGM. The MGM effort seemed promising at first, but later releases failed to continue the momentum and the contract lapsed in 1951.

One event that contributed to that downturn was the Korean War, which claimed Charlie's services in the Army for a time at the start of the 1950s, leaving Ira behind to try to keep things going as a single. In 1951, Charlie was back in Tennessee, trying to revive his career with Ira. The team's mentor, Fred Rose of Acuff–Rose Publishing, who had set up the MGM deal for them, sent some of their material to Capitol (the brothers had been writing original songs for some years), where producer Ken Nelson agreed that they had great potential. When he sought them out, their careers had slid to the point that they were working in a Memphis, Tennessee, post office and only playing an occasional weekend date.

The Louvins soon turned out the first of the more than 100 singles they made for Capitol, a label Charlie remained with into the 1970s and that Ira recorded for until his death in 1965. As the early and mid-1950s went by, the team became steadily better known to country audiences and disc jockeys through intensive live and radio performances and the release of a series of well-regarded singles and albums. In 1955, they were asked to become cast regulars on the *Grand Ole Opry* and the Nashville area became home.

Among the duo's hits were three top-10 singles in 1956, "Hoping That You're Hoping," "I Don't Believe You've Met My Baby," and "You're Running Wild." In 1959, they had a top-10 single with "My Baby's Gone." Some of their original compositions that made upper-chart levels, if not the top 10, were "When I Stop Dreaming," "The Weapon of Prayer," and "I Take the Chance." The brothers had twenty albums in the late 1950s and early 1960s, about half of which were sacred. The team received many honors and topped many polls, during one period being voted Most Programmed Sacred Group and Most Programmed Duet by the nation's country & western disc jockeys for five straight years.

In 1963, Charlie decided he wanted to see if he could make it as a solo act. As he recalled, "You know how it is. After so much time you get too close, can't accept criticism anymore." The move soon proved wise for him; one of his first releases, "I Don't Love You Anymore," became a major hit, reaching the top 10 in 1964. He followed with many other singles that made the top 20 or better, including

"Less and Less," "Think I'll Go Somewhere and Cry Myself to Sleep," "You Finally Said Something Good," "Off and On," and a major hit of 1965, "See the Big Man Cry, Mama." (Of his philosophy on hits, he once said, "I've never strived to be number one, but I sure do love being in the top twenty. There's not as many people shooting at you if you're not number one. It's more comfortable.") However, he never disdained a top-10 hit, and "See the Big Man Cry" not only rose high on the lists, it also was nominated for a Grammy.

Charlie's debut solo LP on Capitol, *Charlie Louvin*, was issued in March 1965, followed soon after by *Many Moods of Charlie Louvin* (2/66); *Lonesome Is Me* (7/66); *I'll Remember Always* (3/67), a tribute to his brother; *I Forget to Cry* (10/67), and several more late 1960s LPs, including *Will You Visit Me on Sundays, The Kind of Man I Am,* and *Here's a Toast to Mama.* In September 1970, Capitol issued his tenth solo album, *Ten Times Charlie.* At the end of the 1960s and in the early 1970s, Charlie teamed with Melba Montgomery for a series of duet recordings, including the albums *Something to Brag About* and *Baby, You've Got What It Takes.*

Over the years Charlie continued to add to his catalogue of original compositions, many of which provided chart-making recordings for other artists besides himself. At the end of the 1970s, artists like Emmylou Harris were including some of the songs written jointly by Charlie and Ira or by Charlie alone in best-selling albums. Reviewing his writing efforts in the early 1970s, Charlie noted, "I've written forty or fifty since Ira died; must have done over 500 together."

Charlie remained a major attraction on the country-music circuit from the mid-1960s throughout the 1970s, appearing in shows all over the United States. He also gave a number of concerts in Canada and other countries of the world over the years. Besides that, he was featured on many TV and radio programs, including guest spots on such 1960s programs as *Porter Wagoner Show, Bill Anderson Show, Bobby Lord Show, Wilburn Brothers Show, Flatt &*

Scruggs, and *American Swing Around* and such 1970s shows as *Hee Haw* and some of the PBS telecasts of the *Grand Ole Opry*.

He ended his long affiliation with Capitol in the mid-1970s and signed a new contract with United Artists. Among the UA singles he placed on the charts were "You're My Wife, She's My Woman" and "It Almost Felt like Love." In 1980, he celebrated twenty-five years as a regular on the *Grand Ole Opry* and continued to appear on the show into the early 1980s.

LOUVIN, IRA: *Singer, guitarist, songwriter. Born Rainesville, Alabama, April 21, 1924; died near Jefferson City, Missouri, June 20, 1965.*

The Louvin Brothers were so closely associated with each other for so many years in the minds of country fans that as the past faded into history many assumed their breakup was due to the untimely death of Ira in a car accident. Actually, the brothers had agreed to go their separate ways sometime before, though there's no doubt that Ira's passing had a near-shattering impact on Charlie.

The brothers grew up together on the family farm in Alabama, where they both worked long hours in the fields as boys. By the time they were in their teens, they had moved to Tennessee with their family, where they still helped do chores and sang and played guitars and other stringed instruments in their spare time. By his late teens, Ira had married and was working in a cotton mill with Charlie to help support his wife when the first chance to go into music came along. The brothers won a talent contest in Chattanooga, Tennessee, in 1943, which brought the opportunity to have their own daily program on station WDEF in the early morning.

That effort came to a halt when both entered the service in the mid-1940s. After being discharged, they got back together and won regular cast work on the WNOX, Knoxville, *Mid-day Merry-Go-Round.*

Their recording career began with one release on Decca, which didn't do much. In 1949, Fred Rose of Acuff–Rose Publishing brought them to the attention of MGM Records. Their material on MGM got off to a promising start, but that was interrupted when Charlie was called back to the Army during the Korean War. When he returned home in 1951, the brothers had to start almost from scratch. Both worked in the U.S. Post Office in Memphis and moonlighted as entertainers. They were following that routine when the chance came to sign with Capitol in 1951. Before long, some of their singles began to make lower-chart levels and jobs opened up on country network radio shows. By 1955, they had established their talents to the point that the *Grand Ole Opry* asked them to come on as regular cast members.

By the late 1950s, the brothers had a number of albums to their credit, including *Tragic Songs of Life*, *Nearer My God to Thee*, *Ira and Charlie* (released 2/58), *Family Who Prays* (2/59), and *Satan Is Real* (10/59). Their early 1960s LPs included *My Baby's Gone* (7/60), *Encore* (8/61), *Weapon of Prayer* (7/62), *Keep Your Eyes on Jesus* (1/63), and *Current Hits* (6/64).

The duo had four top-10 singles hits in the 1950s: "Hoping That You're Hoping," "I Don't Believe You've Met My Baby," and "You're Running Wild" in 1956, and "My Baby's Gone" in 1959. In the early 1960s, they placed a number of singles on the charts, but none approached the success of those earlier releases. That situation probably played a role in the increasing disagreements between the brothers that finally made them decide to split up in 1963.

Ira developed his own show and began playing road dates as a soloist in 1963. Also part of the show was his wife, Florence, who sang under the professional name of Anne Young. It was while Ira and Florence were on the way back to Nashville from an engagement in Jefferson City, Missouri, on Father's Day 1965 that they were killed in a head-on collision on a Missouri highway. Ira was buried at Harpeth Memory Gardens on Route 100, fifteen miles west of Nashville.

Ira had been working on a solo album before his death that was issued posthumously by Capitol under the title *Ira*

Louvin in December 1965. Several Louvin Brothers' albums were issued or reissued by Capitol in later times, including *Thank God* (7/65) and *Great Roy Acuff Songs* (12/67). The LP *Ira and Charles* also came out on the Metro label in February 1967.

Ira's memory was kept alive by his brother, who often devoted part of his concerts to some of the songs he and Ira had been known for. Many of the over 500 songs Ira and Charlie wrote together were included in albums or singles issued by other country artists in the late 1960s and on through the 1970s into the 1980s.

LULU BELLE AND SCOTTY: *Vocal and instrumental duo, songwriters. Myrtle Eleanor Cooper Wiseman (Lulu Belle), born Boone, North Carolina, December 24, 1913; Scotty Wiseman, born Spruce Pine, North Carolina, November 8, 1909; died Gainesville, Florida, February 1, 1981.*

The comedy and singing of the husband and wife team of Lulu Belle and Scotty was one of the highlights of the country-music scene from the early 1930s to the 1950s. At one stage of their careers, they vied with stars of the *Grand Ole Opry* for national attention as headliners of the rival *National Barn Dance* show broadcast nationally for decades from station WLS in Chicago. Apart from their performing efforts, some of the songs written by Scotty or co-written by Scotty and Lulu Belle rank as classics in country and folk music and have been recorded and re-recorded over the years by many other artists.

Both were natives of North Carolina. Scotty grew up in the Spruce Pine region, where he learned many traditonal songs from his friends and family. During his years at Altamont High School, Crossmore, North Carolina, he perfected his instrumental style on guitar and banjo. Although he performed in his spare time, his goal was a teaching career. With that in mind, he attended Duke University during 1927–1928, then entered Fairmont State College in West Virginia in 1929, earning his B.A. in 1932.

Meanwhile, Wiseman added to his performing experience. In 1927 he made his radio debut on station WRVA in Richmond, Virginia. During his college years in Fairmont, he sang and played as a regular performer on station WMMN. That brought the opportunity to join the cast of the *National Barn Dance* in Chicago. It was too good to pass up, so he accepted the offer in 1933 and moved to the Windy City. There he met another North Carolinian named Myrtle Eleanor Cooper who soon became Mrs. Wiseman. Myrtle was born in Boone and also enjoyed singing the traditional country songs of her home area from her girlhood. By the time she was a teenager, she had learned to play guitar and progressed from performing for friends or in school events to more extensive musical efforts in the late 1920s. For a while, she earned her primary living as a shoe clerk, her entertainment work essentially a sideline. In 1932 she auditioned and made the *National Barn Dance* and was a regular cast member the year before Scott Wiseman joined the show.

It wasn't too long after the team of Lulu Belle and Scotty debuted on the *Barn Dance* that they were on the way to becoming favorites of the program's nationwide audience. In 1933, Scotty wrote a song called "Home Coming Time" that became one of their first big hits the following year. It was the forerunner of many major hits on such labels as Conqueror, Vocalion, Bluebird, Brunswick, Vogue, Mercury, and KaHill. In the 1930s and 1940s, their best-known singles included "Whipperwill Time," "Mountain Dew," "Empty Christmas Stockings," "Time Will Tell," "In the Doghouse Now," "My Heart Cries for You," and "Have I Told You Lately That I Love You."

"Mountain Dew," a great country comedy classic, was co-written by Scotty and Bascom Lunsford in 1935. Other songs that he wrote or co-wrote (some with Lulu Belle) included "Empty Christmas Stocking" (1938); "Remember Me" (1940); "Time Will Tell" (1945); "You Don't Love Me like You Used to Do," "Tell Her You Love Her," "That New Vitamin E" (1946); "Don'tcha" (1947); "That Old Bible" (1953); "Tender He Watches over Me" (1954); "Between You and Me" (1955); and "Come as You Are" (1957). His most famous song was

"Have I Told You Lately That I Love You," recorded by well over a hundred artists over the years.

During the 1930s and throughout the 1940s, the fame of the team (who became known as "The Sweethearts of Country Music") spread far beyond Chicago as network broadcasts of the *Barn Dance*, personal appearance tours, and records made them national figures. For many years, besides performing on the *Barn Dance*, where they were regular cast members from 1933 to 1958, they had their own highly rated radio show on WLS, *Breakfast in the Blue Ridge*. For a while in the early 1940s, they starred on the *Boone County Jamboree* on station WLW, Cincinnati, which later became the *Midwestern Hayride*. In 1949, back in Chicago, they were featured on station WNBQ-TV, an association that lasted until 1957.

The duo were guest stars on many major shows in the 1950s, including the *Grand Ole Opry* in 1950 and 1952 and Red Foley's *Ozark Jamboree* in 1957–58. They also were guests on many major variety TV programs over those years, including an appearance on *The Steve Allen Show* in 1955. The team also made several movies over the years, including *Harvest Moon* (1938), *Country Fair* (1939), *Village Barn Dance* (1940), *Swing Your Partner* (1942), *Hi Ya Neighbor* (1943), *National Barn Dance* (1943).

The Wisemans were beginning to tire of the performing grind in the mid-1950s. Scotty began taking courses at Northwestern University, Evanston, Illinois, for an advanced teaching degree. He received his master's in 1958 and he and Lulu Belle moved back to North Carolina soon after, settling in Spruce Pine, where Scotty taught speech at Spruce Pine College. They announced they were in semiretirement from the entertainment field. They still did some concertizing, particularly during college vacation periods. It was not until the 1960s that they sharply curtailed those endeavors and made only occasional appearances. They were still represented on records as of the mid-1960s, when Starday issued such LPs as *Lulu Belle and Scotty* (1963) and *Down Memory Lane* (1964).

In the 1970s, the Wisemans were drawn out of show business retirement from time to time for special occasions, such as the annual Fan Fair Reunion in Nashville, sponsored by the Country Music Association and *Grand Ole Opry*. From their set at the 1975 event, their performance of "Have I Told You Lately That I Love You" was included in the album of the show issued by CMA's Foundation Records.

During the 1970s, Scotty continued with his teaching activities while Lulu Belle became interested in politics. In the mid-1970s, she was elected to the North Carolina House of Representatives.

In 1980, Lulu Belle and Scotty were nominated for the Country Music Hall of Fame. Sadly, not long afterward, in February 1981, Scotty died of a heart attack in Gainesville, Florida.

LUMAN, BOB: *Singer, guitarist, songwriter. Born Nacogdoches, Texas, April 15, 1937; died Nashville, Tennessee, December 27, 1978.*

Historically, the country music audience takes a long view of artists who find favor. Certainly this proved true for Bob Luman, whose career was disrupted several times but who found fans ready to applaud both old and new achievements each time. In the end, it was fate that brought an untimely end to his career, not audience indifference.

For Bobby Glynn Luman, listening to the *Grand Ole Opry* on the radio Saturday nights was as natural as breathing during his childhood in Nacogdoches, Texas. Not only was the program a favored one in his family, but his father also was a fine fiddler, guitarist, and harmonica player who enjoyed performing country songs for friends and family, though he earned his living as a school custodian. As Bobby grew up, his father started him out on stringed instruments, which the boy could play reasonably well by the time he was ready for high school.

Young Luman's radio interests extended to athletics. In his preteen years he looked forward to hearing the Friday night fights on his battery radio, and as he progressed to his teens became skillful at playing a number of sports. After the family moved to Kilgore, Texas, he became a star on the

Kilgore High baseball team, good enough to attract the attention of major league scouts.

But he kept up his musical interests, organizing his own band that played first for school events and later in local clubs. More and more, he leaned toward making music his career, although he was offered tryouts by several baseball clubs. After graduating from high school, he won a talent contest in Tyler, Texas, which proved a springboard to other successes and engagements, culminating in the chance to join the *Louisiana Hayride* in the mid-1950s. He became a featured artist on the show, while his growing reputation and industry contacts led to new opportunities, including the chance to work in the film *Carnival Rock* and appearances in stage shows at Las Vegas' Showboat Hotel, which headlined such artists as Johnny Cash and Tex Ritter.

Still, though he made some progress, his career didn't seem to be moving ahead fast enough for him in the late 1950s. Warner Bros. had given him a contract, but the recordings he turned out for them didn't fare very well. He had another chance to sign a baseball contract and was on the verge of joining the Pittsburgh Pirates organization when a meeting with the Everly Brothers changed things. After attending one of his shows, they came backstage and expressed confidence in his potential. Since they were major stars at the time, it was strong incentive for Bob to make another try. They suggested he record one of Boudleaux Bryant's songs, "Let's Think About Living." The result was a smash hit that rose to the top levels of both country and pop charts in 1960. When Luman followed this with another hit single, "The Great Snowman," his future in country music seemed assured.

However, his momentum was slowed by a draft notice from the armed services. Though he wasn't away from the public spotlight too long, when he returned to the performing scene in the mid-1960s, he found it hard to duplicate the successes of the early 1960s. Luckily, fans remembered him and he kept up a steady round of engagements on the country-music circuit even without top-10 singles. In 1965, he

achieved one of his boyhood dreams by becoming a regular cast member of the *Grand Ole Opry*.

In the mid-1960s, he made some recordings for Hickory Records, including the 1967 album *Bob Luman*, but with minimum response from record buyers. In the late 1960s, though, he moved to Epic Records and almost immediately the outlook got brighter. In 1968, one of his first singles on Epic, "Ain't Got Time to Be Unhappy," brought him his first major hit in years. The song also became the title track for his debut LP on Epic, which came out in 1968. For the next decade, Luman remained one of Epic's most popular artists, one who regularly turned out albums and singles that made national country charts.

From the mid-1960s on, Luman had his own stage show, which headlined many fairs and rodeos across the United States and overseas. Among his overseas milestones in the late 1960s and in the 1970s were a twenty-eight-day tour of Britain, Scotland, and Ireland; annual ten-day tours of U.S. military bases in Germany; being the first country act to play the San Jeronimo Hilton, San Juan, Puerto Rico, and Germany's Big Apple nightclub; and an acclaimed series of concerts in Japan. With his four-person backing group, the Stones River Band, he also was featured on many major TV shows over that period, including the *Johnny Cash* show, *Hee Haw, Good Old Nashville Music, Del Reeves Show, Bill Anderson Show, Dean Martin's Music Country* and, in Canada, the *Ian Tyson Show* and *Nashville North*.

Among Bob's chart singles in the late 1960s and early 1970s were such songs as "Woman Without Love," "Come on Home and Sing the Blues to Daddy," "Maybellene," "Is It Any Wonder That I Love You," and "I've Got a Woman." In the mid-1970s, he could point to successes like "When You Say Love," "Lonely Women Make Good Lovers," "Neither One of Us," "Still Loving You" (top 10 in early 1974), "Just Enough to Make Me Stay," "Let Me Make the Bright Lights Shine for You," "Proud of You Baby," and "Shame on Me." In the latter 1970s, he continued in good form with "A Satisfied Mind," a chart hit in early 1976, "The Man from Bowling Green," and "How Do You Start Over," in early and late summer, respectively, of 1976; "I'm a Honky Tonk Woman's Man" in late summer of 1977, and, in the fall of 1977, a top-20 hit, "The Pay Phone."

His Epic albums after his 1968 release, *Ain't Got Time to Be Unhappy*, included *Still Loving You, Come on Home and Sing the Blues to Daddy* (issued 8/69); *Getting Back to Norma* (6/70); *Is It Any Wonder That I Love You* (7/71); *A Chain Don't Take to Me* (1/72); *When You Say Love* (6/72); *Neither One of Us* (8/73); *Lonely Women Make Good Lovers, Bob Luman's Greatest Hits* (mid-1970s); and *A Satisfied Mind* (late 1975).

Luman's career ended in late December 1978. He came down with pneumonia and entered Nashville Hospital on December 19, four days after an appearance on the *Opry*. Though placed in the critical care unit, he failed to rally and died on December 27.

M

MACGREGOR, MARY: *Singer, pianist, organist, violinist, songwriter. Born St. Paul, Minnesota, May 6, 1948.*

Petite Mary MacGregor, possessor of a fine two-octave voice, was one of the pleasanter additions to the music scene in the late 1970s. With the sweeping success of her single "Torn Between Two Lovers," she generally was identified with the country or pop segments of the music field, though much of her background was in the folk domain and the initial impetus toward solo stardom was provided by folk stalwart Peter Yarrow of Peter, Paul and Mary.

Growing up in St. Paul, Minnesota, Mary showed relatively little interest in either folk or country music in her early years. Her family enjoyed classical music and she started receiving classical piano lessons at the age of six. Her loyalty to Bach, Beethoven, and Brahms didn't lessen as she went through elementary school and into high school even though her peer group preferred people like Elvis, the Beatles, and the Beach Boys. In high school, she continued her classical leanings, playing violin in a string ensemble.

But Mary was slowly becoming more oriented to other kinds of music and began to shift her emphasis after entering the University of Minnesota in the mid-1960s. She noted later, "I had studied classical music but didn't get into folk music until I went to college. I didn't even like popular music when I was in high school. I didn't listen to the radio; the music I enjoyed was the kind I was playing."

MacGregor's efforts in pop music at the university started with folk and soon extended to folk-rock. She handled lead vocals for several campus bands and, after a while, branched out to doing keyboards work for several folk-rock aggregations. She liked those efforts, though she didn't think at the time of making music a full-time career. For a while, in fact, she took a step in the opposite direction by moving to Steamboat Springs, Colorado, in the summer of 1972. Mary didn't abandon all interest in the entertainment field, but taking up residence in a remotely located ranch house for four years ("It had no running water and an outhouse. It was fun for about a year.") kept her out of the mainstream of the music industry.

In the mid-1970s, MacGregor began to do an increasing amount of backing vocals on various commercials, traveling to cities like Minneapolis, Chicago, and Nashville for assignments. A turning point during those years was the work she did on a religious album called *He Lived the Good Life.* She was one of many artists who contributed to the LP, but her voice was one of the more distinctive elements in the collection. The recognition led to the chance to do some supporting vocals on a Peter Yarrow tour. Her work with him included doing backing tracks for his LP *Love Songs.*

Impressed with MacGregor's ability, Yarrow helped make arrangements for a series of recording sessions in Muscle Shoals, Alabama. She began taping material for her first solo album in the spring of 1976. The collection eventually was placed with Ariola America, the U.S. affiliate of the Ariola Record Company of West Germany. In 1977, Mary's single "Torn Between Two Lovers," written by Yarrow and Barry Beckett, was released, slowly picking up airplay until suddenly it was being featured on both top-40 and country stations all over the United States. Before the year was over, the single rose to the number-one position on the country, pop, and easy listening charts. It earned a gold- and platinum-record award (over 1.7 million copies sold) and pulled the album of the same title to hit status. In the trade magazine surveys for 1977, MacGregor was named Top New Female Artist by *Billboard, Cash Box,* and *Record World.*

Some polls placed Mary on the top country vocalist list. However, she told an interviewer, "I'm not really a country singer. The first album wasn't all country. The second album we did in Los Angeles rather than Alabama and we were in a totally different environment. A lot depends on where you go and the type of musicians you play with. I guess contemporary is a good word to describe my music, but it's hard to label it because I play rock 'n' roll, ballads. . . ."

During 1977 MacGregor was a guest on many TV programs, both variety and talk shows, and performed in clubs and other venues across the United States. She continued to be well received in 1978, mostly as an opening act, though her second album, a weaker effort, wasn't the blockbuster of her 1977 release.

During 1978, she was asked to contribute to the soundtrack for a new movie that would star Bill Murray of NBC-TV's *Saturday Night Live* fame. The result was the up-tempo song "Good Friend" that MacGregor performed for the background music of the film *Meatballs.* ("The song originally was a ballad, but I spiced it up with some doo-wops like you hear in

songs from the 1950s.") The soundtrack LP was issued by RSO Records in mid-1979.

During 1979, in between personal appearances, Mary worked on the material for her third album intended for release at year end.

MACK, WARNER: *Singer, guitarist, songwriter. Born Nashville, Tennessee, April 2, 1938.*

Like many Tennessee-born musicians, Warner Mack made his way to success in Nashville after a long swing southward. Born in the country-music capital in the 1930s, he was raised in Mississippi, where he learned guitar and listened to country-music programs on the radio.

When he finished high school, Warner performed for a time in local clubs, and before long had the chance to become a regular on the KWKH *Louisiana Hayride.* As the 1950s went by, he made personal appearances in many parts of the region and also was featured on Red Foley's *Ozark Jamboree.* Kapp Records signed him up and turned out many of his records, which appeared on the national charts in the late 1950s and early 1960s. These were included in best-selling Kapp LPs, *Warner Mack's Golden Country Hits, Volume I* (1961) and *Volume 2* (1963), *Best of Warner Mack,* and *Everybody's Favorites* (1966).

Warner's original name is MacPherson. Unlike many artists, he did not change it purposely to a stage name. However, when he began recording, the person preparing the label copy mistook Warner's nickname for his actual surname, hence Mack. Once the records came out this way, Warner decided to keep his new designation.

Mack's following mounted rapidly throughout the states in the early 1960s, resulting in a bid to join the *Grand Ole Opry.* Warner moved to Nashville and also changed record labels, joining the Decca roster. Though he had done well before, he soon achieved major star status in the mid-1960s with a series of hits. In 1965, he had three top-10 hits, one of which, "The Bridge Washed Out," was number one in the nation for many weeks. The other two were "Sittin' on a Rock" and a song he coauthored, "Sitting in an All Night Cafe." Warner followed up in 1966 with such top-10 hits as "Talkin' to the Wall" and "It Takes a Lot of Money"; in 1967, with "Driftin' Apart," "The Country Touch," "The Bridge Washed Out," and, with his sister, Dearn, "Songs We Sing in Church and Home." In 1968, he had the hit "I'm Gonna Move On," and, in 1969, "Leave My Dreams Alone" and "Don't Wake Me, I'm Dreaming."

In the mid-1960s, Warner had chart hits of two more of his own compositions, "Is It Wrong" and "Surely." These were added to such earlier writings as "Then a Tear Fell," "Last Night," "Yes, There's a Reason," "My Love for You," "If You See Me Cry," "Wake Up Crying," "Memory Mountain," "The Least Little Thing," "This Little Hurt," "I'll Be Alright in the Morning," and "Blue Mood."

Among his albums on Decca (later MCA) Records were: *The Bridge Washed Out* (1965); *Touch* (1966); *Songs We Sang* (1967); *I'll Still Be Missing You, Love Hungry, You Make Me Feel Like a Man* (c. 1970).

His affiliation with MCA ended in the mid-1970s. Still without a major recording contract by the end of the decade, Mack continued to be active as an in-person performer.

MACON, UNCLE DAVE: *Singer, banjoist, songwriter, band leader (Fruit Jar Drinkers, Dixie Sacred Singers). Born Smart Station, Cannon County, Tennessee, October 7, 1870; died Readyville, Tennessee, March 22, 1952.*

If the old saying "when they made him, they broke the mold" applies to anyone, it certainly is Uncle Dave Macon, one of the most flamboyant and endearing individuals in the history of folk and country music. The first "name" artist on the *Grand Ole Opry*, Uncle Dave delighted audiences for decades, yet didn't turn "professional" until he was forty-eight and didn't achieve stardom until he was close to sixty. Although he died in 1952, stories about his career continued to be told years afterward and reissues of some of his recordings were still coming out in the 1970s.

Macon was born and spent his early years on a Tennessee farm, but while he was a boy his family bought a hotel in Nashville frequented by show people. From some of the lodgers, he learned the basic techniques involved in playing the five-string banjo. As he grew older, he mastered the instrument, adding innovations of his own until he became one of the most influential banjo players of all time. He also kept on the watch for interesting songs to add to his repertoire and, in time, became almost a walking repository of what is now considered traditional folk and country music.

Still, he came close to being a complete unknown. During Macon's early years, he often entertained friends and relatives or performed at local functions, but only as a sideline and until he was almost fifty, never for pay. He worked as a hired hand on local farms for some years, then bought his own farm near Readyville, Tennessee. As the decades went by, although he often took center stage at square dances or other events, it seemed that farming would be his main occupation until the end of his days.

A chance event in 1916, material in the John Edwards Memorial Foundation at UCLA indicates, changed all that. It occurred when another farmer asked him to play for a party and Dave, who was "busy and tired," tried to put him off by saying he'd only do it if he was paid fifteen dollars. However, "to his surprise, the farmer accepted. At the party, among the many guests, was a talent scout for Loew's Theaters and he was impressed by Uncle Dave, so he offered to book his 'new find' at a leading theater in Birmingham, Alabama, for several hundred dollars per week."

Uncle Dave's freewheeling style, his driving banjo playing, sometimes done to the accompaniment of clog dance steps, high kicks, and other eye-catching action, "wowed 'em" not only in Birmingham but soon in cities and towns all over the South. While never completely divorcing himself from the rural home he loved so much, Dave increasingly found himself on the road for longer and longer periods of time. With the onset of the 1920s and the rise of radio and recordings, the stage was set for his move to prominence.

While his best-known recordings came out after he was an *Opry* member, he began cutting sides some years earlier. Ralph Rinzler, in liner notes prepared for a Decca commemorative album released in 1966 (in honor of his posthumous election to the Country Music Hall of Fame), stated, "In 1923, Uncle Dave was playing his banjo in Melton's Barber Shop in Nashville when a young fiddler named Sid Harkreader happened to walk in with his fiddle case under his arm. Shortly after that they were playing at Loew's Theater in Nashville for a three-week run. They went on to travel the circuit of Loew's Theaters throughout the South as part of a five-act vaudeville show going as far west as Dallas, Texas.

"The following year, Mr. Ed Holt of the Harley-Holt Furniture Company, sent Uncle Dave and Sid to Chattanooga to play at a furniture convention. They went on to Knoxville for another such gathering. There, a Mr. C. C. Rutherford of Sterchi Brothers Furniture Company offered to pay their expenses if they would go to New York and record for the Aeolian Company. They accepted the offer and 14 sides featuring Uncle Dave, with assistance from Sid on some songs, were issued from these sessions which took place in the summer of 1924."

Apparently the results were satisfactory because Macon returned to New York in April 1925 and April 1926, turning out many more songs each time. In the latter instance, he brought along guitarist Sam McGee who with his brother Kirk also became a featured *Opry* act later on. Among the songs recorded in 1926 were "Whoop 'Em Up Cindy," "Way Down the Old Plank Road," "The Death of John Henry," and "Late Last Night When My Willie Came Home."

In 1926, knowing that Macon not only was a superlative performer but also was increasingly well known to country fans, George Hay and the *Opry* made him a cast regular. Hay recalled in his book *A Story of the Grand Ole Opry* (issued in 1945): "During the first two or three months of the

year 1926 we acquired about 25 people on the *Opry*. When Uncle Dave came on, we moved him back so that he would have plenty of room to kick when he played. He has always been an actor who thought the microphone was just a nuisance. It took a long time to 'hitch' him to it."

Within a short time Uncle Dave was the *Opry* headliner. He worked both as a soloist and with various bands, one named the Fruit Jar Drinkers. Deeply religious and a regular bible reader (and sometime preacher), he often sang hymns and gospels. For those efforts he had a group called the Dixie Sacred Singers. From the mid-1920s until the late 1940s, he continued to command a wide following of *Opry* listeners and country concert-goers who often sang the praises of the artist variously nicknamed "The Dixie Dewdrop," "King of the Banjo Players," and "King of the Hillbillies."

He continued to record steadily throughout the late 1920s. The pace slowed somewhat in the 1930s because of the Depression, but Macon made a number of recordings in that decade. During those sessions, he was accompanied at various times by the McGee Brothers, "Fiddlin' Sid" Harkreader, fiddler Jasper Aaron "Mazy" Todd, and, beginning in the 1930s by his son Dorris. The recordings were made in either New York or Chicago and were issued on Brunswick or Vocalion labels.

Rinzler writes of those late 1920s sessions that, "surely the most interesting from a musical standpoint were those held May 7–11, 1927, in New York City. Those not only produced some of the finest recorded performances of Uncle Dave's career (including 'Tom and Jerry,' 'Tell Her to Come Back Home,' 'Sleepy Lou,' and 'Shall We Gather at the River'), but they provide us with some of the best examples of string band ensemble playing ever recorded. Uncle Dave seemed to revel in the sound of the reedy, yet excellent, fiddling of Mazy Todd and Kirk McGee. He crows and hollers with joy when Sam momentarily abandons his guitar bass line to beat out a clog rhythm on the top of his then new Martin. The ensemble singing is unique on the secular songs: Uncle Dave sticks to the melody, Kirk departs from singing unison and moves to tenor at the end of each line, and Sam barks out his own distinctive bass line which includes a winning combination of unison and bass harmony notes. Uncle Dave weaves his banjo syncopations and double-time back-up rhythms around the extraordinary subtle fiddle lead of Mazy Todd, while shouting exuberantly above the din his verses, square dance calls or just an expression of joy: 'Shout if you are happy! Kill yo'self.'

"A total of 50 songs (both sacred and secular) were made during that four-day period. The sessions preserved 'Rock About My Saro Jane,' 'Sail Away Ladies,' and 'Jordan is a Hard Road to Travel,' and through these memorable performances, these songs reached the (1960s) folk song revival where they underwent considerable arranging . . . almost succumbing in the process. 'Sail Away Ladies' even made a rock and roll record."

Another notable session took place in Chicago on July 25-26, 1927, with Sam McGee using an unusual banjo-guitar. In those sessions, notes Rinzler, " 'From Earth to Heaven,' 'Buddy Won't You Roll Down the Line,' 'I'm the Child to Fight' were recorded as five- and six-string banjo duets, probably the only examples of this instrumental combination recorded in country music."

Many of Uncle Dave's most popular songs were those he had either written himself or discovered in his travels. These included "All In, Down and Out Blues," "The Dixie Bee Line," "From Earth to Heaven," "Cumberland Mountain Deer Race," "They're After Me," "Rock About My Sara Jane," "Ain't It a Shame to Keep Your Honey Out in the Rain," "When the Train Comes Along," and his special banjo solos, dubbed "Uncle Dave's Beloved Solos."

Macon still was at the top of Opry's fans' lists in the early 1940s, though new young artists were beginning to take over the limelight. Thus he was featured in the 1940 Republic Pictures movie Grand Ole Opry. The film also focused on his son Dorris and such others as emcee Hay, Roy Acuff, and Little Rachel.

By the late 1940s, while still welcomed warmly by Opry crowds, he no longer ranked as a reigning superstar. Still he could get onlookers cheering and applauding such well-known numbers as "Two-In-One Chewin' Gum," "11-Cent Cotton, 40 Cent Meat," "Give Me the Gal with the Red Dress On," "Bully of the Town," "Rabbit in the Pea Patch," and his many other classics.

He was still basking in Opry listeners' applause three weeks before his death in 1952. Fourteen years later, in October 1966, he was voted into the Country Music Hall of Fame at the same time as his longtime friend and associate, George Hay. His bronze plaque on the Hall of Fame wall in Nashville reads, in part, "The Dixie Dewdrop . . . was a man whose delightful sense of humor and sterling character endeared him to millions. A professional performer on the Grand Ole Opry for 26 years, he was a 'minstrel of the countryside' prior to that. He was a country man who loved humanity and enjoyed helping others. A proficient banjoist, he was a singer of old-time ballads and was, during his time, the most popular country music artist in America."

In the 1960s and 1970s, occasional reissues of some of his recordings were released. In some of the folk collections of RCA Victor (for whom he did some sessions in the 1930s), some of the tracks were of his material. In the 1970s, three albums of his recordings were available from small companies, two on the RBF label and one on County.

MADDOX, ROSE: *Singer, guitarist. Born Boaz, Alabama, December 15, 1926.*

The family group is a recurring feature in the history of folk and country & western music. One of the most popular acts of post–World War II decades was the Maddox Brothers and Rose. The team comprised the four Maddox brothers, Cal, Henry, Fred, and Don and their sister,

Rose. In time, Rose went her own way to gain recognition as one of the top female vocalists of the 1960s.

The Maddox family grew up in the heartland of country music, Alabama. Their mother, in particular, encouraged their interest in music. Her strong influence was reflected for many years in the selection of songs and the engagements the Maddoxes played. However, the Depression weighed heavily on the family in the early 1930s. Finally, it seemed wise to leave Alabama. Mrs. Maddox bundled her family, then ranging in age from seven to sixteen, into a freight car for the long journey to central California. Once settled in the Bakersfield area, the Maddox children helped repair family finances by performing at local events. Their act became more polished as the 1930s progressed and, by the end of the decade, they were well regarded by country & western fans in many parts of the state.

In the early 1950s, the Maddox Brothers and Rose graduated from local appearances in California to regular cast status on the *Louisiana Hayride* in Shreveport. The combination of Cal on guitar and harmonica, Henry on mandolin, Fred on stand-up bass, Don in comic roles, and Rose as lead voice resulted in many song stylings that had audiences asking for more. As their popularity grew from *Hayride* network exposure, the Maddox Brothers and Rose became one of the most popular groups for one-nighters in the business. In addition to personal appearances, they also performed on most major country & western network shows, including the *Grand Ole Opry*.

The Brothers and Rose turned out many best-selling records for Columbia, King, and Capitol Records during the 1950s and early 1960s. These included such successes as "Philadelphia Lawyer," "Whoa, Sailor," "Tall Man," and the famous "Tramp on the Street." "Tramp on the Street" was one of many sacred and gospel-type recordings featuring a combination of western beat and country material. Their other standards of this kind included "Gathering Flowers for the Master's Bouquet" and "Will There Be Any Stars in My Crown?" Their LP credits included *I'll Write Your Name* on King and *Maddox Brothers and Rose* (1962) on Wrangler.

In the late 1950s, the Maddoxes again moved their base of operations to California. Their appearances ranged from station KTRB in Modesto to *Town Hall Party* in Compton. At the start of the 1960s, however, the group disbanded and Rose decided to go out on her own as a single act.

She soon had many notable recordings to her credit on Capitol Records, including the LPs *One Rose* (1960), *Bluegrass* (1962), and *Along With You* (1963). Her 1963 recording of "Sing a Little Song of Heartaches" was second only to Skeeter Davis' for most record sales by a female vocalist. She also teamed with Buck Owens on "We're the Talk of the Town," a recording that was third highest bestseller in the duet and vocal group category for the year. The result was selection in the *Cash Box* poll as the top country female artist of 1963. Similar awards were given her in Europe and New Zealand.

The year 1964 saw continued success for Rose. She again teamed with Buck Owens on such hits as "Loose Talk" and "Mental Cruelty." At year's end, she and Buck won the top duet award in national disc jockey polls. Also during 1964, Harmony Records issued the LP *Best of Rose Maddox*.

After the mid-1960s, Rose's success as a recording artist tapered off though she remained active as a performer for the rest of the decade, throughout the 1970s, and into the 1980s. After leaving Capitol, she recorded some material for Carthay Records and at the end of the 1960s was on the UNI label. In the early and late 1970s she had releases out on Starday Records, including the early 1970s album *Rose*.

MAGGARD, CLEDUS: *Singer, songwriter, actor, producer. Born September 21, mid-1930s.*

In electronics, the term feedback loop indicates a closed circuit where signals coming from a transmitter of some kind are fed back, in part, to amplify or enhance the next group of signals. In the same way, the growing interest in Citizen's Band (C.B.) radios in the mid-1970s spawned entry of new producers of the equipment along with more C.B. commercials and, in time, C.B.-related songs. Not unexpectedly, the new breed of "C.B. troubadours," like C. W. McCall and Cledus Maggard, sprang from the advertising community's popularizing of the devices.

For Maggard, country-music success was an unexpected turn for someone who had spent years in such fields as Shakespearean drama, musical comedy, and dramatic directing. But he adjusted easily to his new role and showed himself capable of treating other subjects of interest to country fans besides C.B.

Under his real name, Jay Huguely, he fell in love with show business at an early age and was taking part in school events during his elementary and high school years. Although he had a good voice and enjoyed singing, he didn't think of trying for a career as a vocalist. If he used his vocal talents, it was performing various roles in musical comedy. In his early years in the entertainment fields, he did some radio work, including comedy sketches. Later he expanded his efforts to include TV and stage work, mostly on a local or regional level, from the late 1950s to 1974.

During those years, he played almost every kind of role from Harold Hill, the band instrument con-man of *The Music Man*, to Shakespeare's Hamlet. His credits mounted up to over 450 plays in which he acted. When he wasn't doing that, he worked at such related tasks as directing, teaching Shakespeare and acting, and, for a while, running his own theater. His directing efforts involved some 380 plays.

Still, none of that brought lasting financial stability. In 1974, he got a job with Leslie Advertising in Greenville, South Carolina, working on commercials. He wore most of the hats—writing the material, helping perform it, and also supervising production. When the C.B. craze started taking hold in 1975, agency head Bill Leslie asked Jay to study the phenomenon with a view toward doing some commercials on it. As Huguely boned up on C.B. jargon, ideas for a novelty recording began to come to him. Though not exactly sure what he'd do with it, he went into a studio and recorded it. Friends' comments were so favorable, he recut it and had 2,000 copies pressed. The record became a local hit and, when word of it got to Mercury Records, that label offered to buy the masters and take over distribution.

Huguely, meanwhile, had decided to use the pseudonym Cledus Maggard. As he said in 1976, "About twenty years ago I worked at a radio station and performed skits on the air with other people. One of the continuing characters was Cledus Maggard, who was a guy who would give reports on local traffic conditions. When 'The White Knight' was going to be released, I thought Jay Huguely didn't sound right for a person doing that kind of record. And Cledus Maggard popped into mind."

It didn't take long for the single to appear on the playlists of stations across the United States. It moved rapidly up both country and pop charts, reaching number one on the country lists in mid-February 1976. It earned Jay a gold record and also another one for his debut Mercury LP, of which it was the title track. Before the year was out, Jay was on the country charts with two more singles, both co-written with his record producer, Jerry Kennedy, "Kentucky Moonrunner" in early summer and "Virgil" and the "$300 Vacation" later in 1976. During the next few years, he placed several other releases on the charts, including "The Farmer" in the summer of 1978.

MAINER, J. E.: *Banjoist, fiddler, band leader. Born Weaversville, North Carolina, July 20, 1898; died Concord, North Carolina, June 12, 1971.*

Though Jimmie Rodgers was called the "Father of Country Music," his stylings derived from a country-music tradition that had been strong for a long time before him. People like Gid Tanner, Eck Robertson, and J. E. Mainer and his band had been well known to southern and rural audiences years before Rodgers; Mainer, indeed, continued to perform and lead his own band right up to the time of his death in 1971.

Mainer summed up many of the details of his life in a letter to John Edwards, founder of the Edwards Foundation, some of which was reprinted with permission in the 1969 edition of *The Encyclopedia of Folk, Country, & Western Music,* and parts of which are presented in the quotations below.

Mainer wrote that he was born in a one-room log house in Buncombe County in the Blue Ridge mountains of North Carolina. "Started to play a five-string banjo when I were nine years old going to square dances. Me and my brother-in-law, he played the fiddle, he played left-handed. I stayed around home until I were fifteen years old then I left home and went to work in a cotton mill at Noceville [Knoxville], Tennessee. Worked there for seven years then I come to Concord, N.C. [which remained his home the rest of his life]: . . . Got me a job in the cotton mill here. In 1923 Wade come to Concord. I still had my banjo with me and Wade began to learn to play it. He were seventeen years old and he got to where he could play it pretty good by me showing him how to play it. Then I thought I would get me a fiddle, so I sold some seed and sent the money to the seed company and they sent me a little old tin fiddle. But I got to where I could play 'John Henry' it then I went and got me a good fiddle then we would play two hours ever' night. In about one year we could play most anything we wanted to. Then we met John Love who played a guitar. We got to going to fiddle conventions and we met Claud Moris [Claude Morris] in Old Port, N.C., who played guitar and we all four of us sure did love to play. Then we got to winning about all of the prizes wherever we went. Then the Crazy Water Crystals Co. heard about us and sent for me to come to their office in Charlotte, N.C. and they gave us a job playing for them, advertising for them. We worked over WBT Charlotte for four years when they sent us to WWL, New Orleans, Louisiana. We stayed there for a while then when they sent for us to come back to Charlotte, then they sent us to Raleigh, N.C.—WPTF—there for four years. In this time, John Love had married and had a baby then I nicknamed him Daddy John Love and I had nicknamed Claude Morris,

Zeke, and the boys is still carrying their nicknames today."

During those years, the band was called the Crazy Mountaineers after the sponsor. During the time J. E. and Wade, his brother, were together the band was called the Mainer Mountaineers, a name J. E. returned to after his years with the Crazy Water Crystal Company were over. Among the early recorded successes of the group were "Maple on the Hill," "Take Me in the Life Boat," and "Drunkard's Hic-Ups." During the heyday of the Crazy Mountaineers, Wade Mainer had his own group, though Wade and J. E. joined forces again later and made a number of recordings.

Continuing J. E.'s note to John Edwards, "We made records for the Victor Recording Co. [starting in the 1920s]. We made some records that were on top for about 4 years, then I left them [went to] Raleigh, N.C., and I got me another bunch and went back to Charlotte on another radio station, WSOC. I had Leonard Stokes and George Morris, Zeke's brother, and my banjo player but the first ones we made were in 1935 in Atlanta, Georgia. We made records for them ever' 6 months for 5 years. [Some of those were reissued in a number of RCA/Camden collections of early mountain music in the 1960s and 1970s.] I got married here in Concord the same year I come here. We had 6 children—2 girls and 4 boys. 2 of the boys and 2 girls were guitar players. Their names were Carolin, and the other were Mary. My old'st boys were J. E. Jr. and Glenn Mainer.

"I took them and went to Johnson City, Tennessee, in 1939. Went to work over radio station WSIS and we went to recording records for the King Recording Co. Worked for them for two years."

The pace slowed down for J. E. and his band after the start of the 1950s, but he remained active, sallying forth from his home in Concord to play at folk and country festivals while also working radio and TV whenever possible. In the post–World War II decades, Mainer and his group made recordings for the folk music archive of the Library of Congress. In the 1960s and at the start of the 1970s, he made a series of recordings of classic hill-country tunes for Rural Rhythm.

In the 1960s and up to Mainer's death, the group often was invited to take part in bluegrass festivals. At the time J. E. died of an apparent heart attack at his home in Concord on June 12, 1971, the group was getting ready to leave for such an event in Culpepper, Virginia. The makeup of the Mainer Mountaineers at the time was Mainer on fiddle, Bill Beaton on guitar, Morris Herbert on banjo, Earl Cheek on bass, and, on that time-honored but almost extinct instrument, the washboard, Jerry Cheek.

MANDRELL, BARBARA: *Singer, guitarist, steel guitarist, banjoist, saxophone player, accordionist, bass guitarist, band leader (the Do-Rites). Born Houston, Texas, December 25, 1948.*

At a very early age, Barbara showed that she had musical talent and, what may be even more remarkable, that she had the desire to pursue that talent, to work at it, to stay with it and turn it into a career. In that goal, she always had the strong support of her parents, who both were musically inclined (father Irby was a singer and guitarist and mother Mary a music teacher and pianist), and she, in turn, helped encourage other children in the family to follow similar paths.

When she was five years old, she gave the first indication of her ambition by asking her mother to teach her to play the twenty-four-bars accordion; thus she learned to read music before she could read English. She recalled for Douglas A. Green of *Pickin'* magazine (September 1978) that she made her public debut at five in a Houston, Texas, church. "I went to church with my parents, and dragged the accordion on up to perform, nobody knowing how I'd react. I only knew one song called, believe it or not, 'Guitar Boogie,' and I played it through. Everybody seemed to love it and gave me a lot of applause and eventually asked for an encore. The trouble was, I only knew one

song—so I played it again! If I'd known more tunes I might have played all night."

Soon after that, the Mandrells moved from Texas to Oceanside, California, where her father bought a music store. Some years later, Barbara added skills on a very different instrument to her repertoire. One of her father's acquaintances was steel guitar player Norman Hamlet, and eleven-year-old Barbara decided to take lessons on the instrument from him. She told Green, "There wasn't a better teacher in the world. I started off on a little Fender eight-string, but I had pedals even then. This was the era that Bud Isaacs and Ralph Mooney were revolutionizing the use of the steel guitar with all the pedal work and that's of course what I wanted to learn. Still, Norm made sure I knew all the western swing things like 'Boot Heel Drag,' giving me a good historical foundation as well as the latest licks. I spent countless hours with Norm."

Her pedal steel ability soon paid dividends. After she'd been studying for half a year, her father took her with him to a music trade show in Chicago, Illinois, where she was hired to demonstrate steel guitar work as part of the Standel Amplifiers display. By then, she also knew how to play saxophone and, after country star Joe Maphis heard her steel guitar work in Chicago, Mandrell got the chance to join his show in Las Vegas for a while playing pedal steel and sax.

Back in California, Joe helped her become a regular cast member (still at age eleven) of the local Southern California TV program *Town Hall Party*. When she was twelve, Mandrell made her network TV debut on ABC's *Five Star Jubilee*, telecast from Springfield, Missouri. All this attention inspired Irby Mandrell to form a family group comprising Barbara, himself, his wife, and two young men on guitar and drums. The drummer, then working his way through college, was named Ken Dudney. When Barbara was fourteen, she and Ken dated for a while, but they broke up for several years when she was in her mid-teens. Later, though, they reconciled and married in 1967, a union (graced by then with two children) considered one of the happiest in the country field as of the early 1980s.

Remembering the days of the Mandrell Family band, Barbara told Jack Hurst of the *Chicago Tribune (Chicago Tribune Magazine,* April 22, 1979), "We had a tight group, good music, and we'd incorporate Beatle tunes and old stuff like 'Up a Lazy River' and the 'Beverly Hillbillies' theme. I'd play sax, banjo, steel. [Inspired by the folk boom of the early 1960s, she learned banjo in her mid-teens, helped at one point by top banjoist Dale Sledd of the Osborne Brothers band]. We worked Camp Pendleton; we worked San Diego for the Navy; the El Toro [California] airbase. . . . There was lots of work to be had."

Mandrell kept trying out new instruments, among them the guitar and bass guitar. She told Green she was only a fair guitarist, no better "than the average Joe on the street—a few chords is all. I learned enough to play a boogie with the Mandrells' guitar player, you know, two of us playing the same guitar. . . . I love the bass and I always have. I can play it, but I don't really get down. I'm not the bass player my sister Louise is."

After marrying Ken Dudney, Barbara gave up professional music for a while in favor of staying home. But when Ken became an Air Force pilot and was sent overseas soon after the nuptials, she went to stay with her parents, a step fated to change her life around. The Mandrells moved to Nashville because Irby had decided to leave music and go into the contracting business with a brother who lived in the country-music capital. One Friday night in 1968 Barbara suggested Irby take her to watch the *Grand Ole Opry* because neither she nor he ever had seen a live *Opry* show.

Irby told Hurst, "We went, and halfway through the show she turned to me and said, 'Daddy, if you've got any faith in me, I'd like to try to get on the other side of the microphone again. I wasn't cut out to be in the audience.' "

It was her instrumental aptitude that gave her the initial boost. She got the chance to play with the Curly Chalker Trio at the Printer's Alley in Nashville. She was featured on steel but also did some vocals, and word got back to Columbia producer Billy Sherrill that he would be wise to visit the show. This resulted in her first recording contract, signed on March 1, 1969. Although traditional country always has been her first love, she has enjoyed other music formats as well, particularly rhythm & blues, to the point that some of her records became hits with black audiences. Her R&B efforts went back to the start of her recording career. She told Jack Hurst *(Chicago Tribune,* January 3, 1979), "My first record was an Otis Redding song. I've also done Joe Tex's 'Show Me' and Aretha Franklin's 'Do Right Woman, Do Right Man.' I've always dabbled in all areas of music."

However, the majority of Mandrell's record releases were unmistakably country and brought enough favorable response from fans and industry peers for her to be asked to become a regular *Grand Ole Opry* cast member in 1972, an association still maintained in the early 1980s. Among her chartmakers during her five-year stay with Columbia were "After Closing Time," a top-10 duet in late 1970 (with David Houston—all Mandrell–Houston recordings were on Columbia's Epic label); "Show Me" in 1972; "Give a Little, Take a Little" in 1973; "I Love You, I Love You" (with Houston), "Ten Commandments of Love" (with Houston), "This Time I Almost Made It," all 1974. Her albums of those years included *Treat Him Right* and, with David Houston, *A Perfect Match.*

In 1975, Barbara left Columbia for ABC/Dot, a switch that seemed to give her career new momentum. Her first single on the new label, "Standing Room Only," made the charts in late 1975 and entered the top 10 in early 1976. As the year progressed, she had such other chartmakers as "That's What Friends Are For" and "Love Is Thin Ice." She followed with even more popular songs, such as "Woman to Woman" and "Married but Not to Each Other," that went to number two on country charts and rose high on R&B lists as well. In late 1977 she had the top-10 hit

"Hold Me" and more successes the following year, such as "Tonight," in the top five during the summer.

Those increasingly impressive credits had won some notice from the country-music industry. In October 1978, for instance, she was one of the five finalists for the Country Music Association's coveted Female Vocalist of the Year Award, but, as had occurred twice before, she was an also-ran. But the groundwork had been laid and her move from star to superstar got under way almost as the echoes from the 1978 awards died away. In November 1978, Barbara had her first number-one single, "Sleeping Single in a Double Bed," on country charts in that position three weeks in a row and a major pop hit besides. In early 1979, she soon had a second number-one hit, "(If Loving You Is Wrong) I Don't Want to Be Right," which rose even higher on pop lists than "Sleeping Single." Also a major hit for her (by now ABC had been acquired by MCA Records) was "Fooled by a Feeling."

Her popularity indeed was soaring, and she kept up a hectic schedule of concert work and TV appearances. Among Mandrell's 1979 TV credits were cohosting the Academy of Country Music Awards in May, a special with Charo and Priscilla Mitchell, and appearances on Dick Clark's American Bandstand and the ShaNaNa's syndicated rock show. Among her other TV appearances of the mid- and late-1970s were guest spots on the Merv Griffin show, the Mike Douglas show, ABC's Wide World of Sports (with the Harlem Globetrotters), CBS's Third Annual Collegiate Cheerleading Championships, cohost of some segments of the Mike Douglas show, NBC's 77th Birthday Salute to Bob Hope, NBC's Elvis Presley Remembered—Nashville to Hollywood, The Rockford Files, and cohost of Home Box Office's Nashville Country Pop Festival.

In 1979, Mandrell not only cohosted the Academy of Country Music show but also was named the organization's Female Vocalist of the Year. This was echoed throughout the year when she won the same category in voting by the readers of Music City News and Radio & Records and by members of the Country Music Association. In 1979, both Cash Box and the American Music Awards voted "Sleeping Single in a Double Bed" Single of the Year. With continued recording and performing achievements in the early 1980s, Barbara added more trophies to her collection, including the 1980 Entertainer of the Year Award from the Country Music Association and the 1981 Entertainer of the Year Award from the Academy of Country Music. In the 1981 poll of the Music City News, she came out first for both Musician of the Year and Female Artist of the Year.

Mandrell's singles hits of the early 1980s included "Years," "Crackers" and "The Best of Strangers" in 1980, and "Love Is Fair/Sometimes, Somewhere/Somehow" and "Wish You Were Here" in 1981. Her charted albums during 1979-80 included Moods, The Best of Barbara Mandrell and Just for the Record, which was still on the lists in 1981. As of 1982, all of the albums Barbara recorded for ABC/Dot-MCA were still in print. They included This Is Barbara Mandrell (her debut LP), Midnight Angel, Lovers, Friends and Strangers, Ups and Downs of Love, Love Is Fair, and the three noted above. In 1982, MCA issued the LP Barbara Mandrell Live.

During the 1980-81 season, Barbara inaugurated her own TV show on NBC, an hour-long Saturday night program titled Barbara Mandrell and the Mandrell Sisters. Joining with her on the variety format were younger sisters Irlene and Louise. Although the show's ratings hardly were overwhelming, the program was one of the better music offerings on the air and was renewed for the 1981–82 season. Both her TV and personal appearance work continued to be an extended family affair in the early 1980s, with father Irby acting as manager and Ken Dudney serving as financial manager. (When not on the road, the Dudneys usually called home, where they resided with children Matt and Jamie, a large house fronting on Old Hickory Lake near Gallatin, Tennessee. However, they also could escape to a condominium in Aspen, Colorado, or another lakeside home in Dadeville, Alabama.)

One of the ironies of Mandrell's career was the fact that many of her hits were "cheatin' songs," though she herself favored the traditional idea of marriage. She told Hurst, "I think of myself as an actress. I try to make people believe what I'm singing. I'm a very sentimental, emotional person, and maybe a little of that comes out in my voice. For the few moments I'm singing "If Loving You Is Wrong, I Don't Wanta Be Right,' I really want to be with this married man that I have no right to. And if I'm singing 'I love you and the kids, and home is great,' then I live that too."

MANDRELL, LOUISE: *Singer, bass player, fiddler. Born Corpus Christi, Texas, July 13, 1954.*

Born into a family where musical skill was encouraged, Louise Mandrell naturally progressed from learning several instruments in her childhood to move on to begin a professional career in her teens. Though she hadn't made as much of a mark on the country field as her sister Barbara at the start of the 1980s, she had done well enough to suggest that that might change in later years.

Louise, who spent her first years in Texas, was in the early years of high school when older sister Barbara already was taking steps toward country-music stardom. In 1969, when Louise was fifteen, she joined Barbara's backing group, the Do-Rites, as bass player. After a while, she also got the chance to do some solo fiddle playing in the show. From 1969 through the early 1970s, Louise traveled an average of 100,000 miles a year or more with the Barbara Mandrell Show, performing throughout the United States and Canada at fairs, club dates, country concerts, and on TV.

After several years with Barbara, Louise accepted a job with the troupe headed by *Grand Ole Opry* star Stu Phillips. With Stu, she increased her role in the program. Besides playing backup for the main part of the show, she got the opportunity to do some solo numbers before introducing Stu to the audience. She toured widely with the show on the country-music circuit and she also was featured on Phillips' syndicated TV show during her stay with the group in the 1970s.

From Phillips, she moved to a new affiliation, this time with the Merle Haggard Show. Her role with Haggard was similar to the previous work with Phillips. She worked both as a backing musician and backing singer and featured female vocalist. During her stay with Haggard, Mandrell contributed to a number of his 1970s recordings.

By the latter half of the decade, Louise felt she was ready to make a name for herself as a solo artist. Her goals included organizing her own show and lining up a recording contract with a major label. By the late 1970s, she had accomplished both those objectives. She was signed by Epic Records, part of the Columbia Records organization, which also had her husband (whom she married during the 1970s), R. C. Bannon, on its roster. Among the places she headlined during the last years of the 1970s were the Kentucky State Fair, Michigan State Fair, Alabama State Fair, Southeastern Fair, many county fairs, concert halls, and major country nightclubs throughout the United States.

In the late 1970s, Mandrell had several singles on lower-chart levels, including "Put It on Me" in the fall of 1978 and "Everlasting Love" in early 1979. In terms of record success, she made more headway with a series of duets with husband R. C. Bannon. One of those, "Reunited," went to number thirteen on the national country lists. Another, "We Love Each Other," was in the top 50 in late 1979. In early 1980, Louise joined husband Bannon in a shift from Epic to RCA Records.

MAPHIS, JOE AND ROSE LEE: *Singing and instrumental duo, songwriters. Joe, born Suffolk, Virginia, May 12, 1921; Rose Lee, born Baltimore, Maryland, December 29, 1922.*

One of the most talented and popular husband and wife teams in country music, Joe and Rose Lee Maphis, at one time or another, were cast members of almost every major "barn dance" program in the heyday of that format. In addition, in more than three decades of show business work, they guested on almost every other country show from the *Grand Ole Opry* to *Hee Haw*. Over the years, Joe maintained his reputation as one of "the fastest guitarists alive," both as a featured performer and a session musican backing many well-known country stars.

The meeting place for Joe and Rose Lee was the *Old Dominion Barn Dance* on station WRVA in Richmond, Virginia. Before their paths crossed there in 1948, both had been professional artists while still in their teens. Otis W. "Joe" Maphis, born and raised near Harpers Ferry, Virginia, learned to play fiddle from his father and entertained at local square dances by the time he was ten. At sixteen, he was featured on station WBRA in Richmond. Besides fiddle, he also learned to play guitar, mandolin, and bass. Rose Lee started singing and playing guitar before she reached high school age. At fifteen, she had her own program on a Hagerstown, Maryland, station, billed as "Rose of the Mountains."

For a number of years in the 1940s, Joe was featured on many of the top shows emanating from the Midwest, including the *Boone County Jamboree, Midwestern Hayride,* and Chicago's *National Barn Dance.* Soon after he and Rose Lee met and married, they left Virginia and moved cross country to California. There they appeared on Cliffie Stone's Los Angeles *Hometown Jamboree* TV show for several years and later in the 1950s were featured on the *Hollywood Barn Dance* and the *Town Hall Party* telecast from Compton, California. Besides his duets with Rose Lee, Joe often teamed with Merle Travis on many songs.

Joe and his wife signed with Capitol Records in the 1950s, but also did considerable session work backing other performers. Some of those with whom they worked were Merle Travis, Ricky Nelson, Stuart Hamblen, and Tex Ritter. Among the many songs recorded by Joe and Rose Lee, which included some originals, were "Twin Banjo Special," "Katy Warren Breakdown," "Your Old Love Letters," "Flying Fingers," "Randy Lynn Rag," "Guitar Rock and Roll," "Tuning Up for the Blues" and "Honky Tonk Down Town." Joe also provided the sound track for such TV shows as *FBI Story* and *Thunder Road.*

From the 1950s through the 1970s, the Maphis show maintained a busy touring schedule. Their personal appearances over those three decades took them to all fifty states as well as France, Germany, Spain, the Philippines, Okinawa, Taiwan, and Vietnam. Over the years, they headlined at almost every country-music club in the United States and Canada and at almost every major state and county fair. Even in the late 1970s, they typically covered an average of 100,000 miles a year traveling to live dates. During the 1960s, Joe and Rose Lee left California to make Nashville their home.

They recorded a number of albums over the years either as a duo or with Joe in the spotlight. Among them were the Capitol LPs *Fire on the Strings* and *Joe Maphis* (June 1964). In the mid-1960s, they signed with Starday, which issued a series of albums including *Joe and Rose Lee Maphis* (November 1964), *King of the Strings* (mid-1960s), *Golden Gospel Guitar* (mid-1960s), and *Fastest Guitar Goes to the Jimmy Dean Show.* LPs of their material issued at the end of the 1960s and in the early 1970s included *Gospel Guitar* and *Volume 2* on Word Records and *Guitaration Gap* on Chart Records.

During the 1970s, Joe and Rose Lee took part in several of the annual Fan Fair Reunion Shows in Nashville, sponsored by the Country Music Association to focus on veteran artists. They were represented on the live album of the 1975 event, produced by CMA's own Foundation Records, with the track "Hot Time in Nashville Tonight."

MARSHALL TUCKER BAND: *Vocal and instrumental group from Spartanburg, South Carolina. Tommy Caldwell, born Spartanburg, November 9, 1950, died Spartanburg, April 28, 1980; Toy Caldwell, born Spartanburg, November 13; George McCorkle; Paul Riddle; Jerry Eubanks; Doug Gray, born Spartanburg, circa 1948. Tommy Caldwell replaced by Franklin Wilkie, 1980.*

After the Allman Brothers Band lost momentum in the mid-1970s following the untimely death of Duane Allman, a number of groups vied for the title of number-one Southern country-rock band. A major contender was the Marshall Tucker Band from Spartanburg, South Carolina, which seemed fitting since that talented six-person group had first drawn attention to itself in the early 1970s as the opening act for an Allman tour. Ironically, the Tucker band's position was threatened in 1980 by the death of one of its founders, bassist-vocalist Tommy Caldwell.

While the Tucker band was generally classified with the Allmans, the two groups actually were far from carbon copies. The Allmans strongly stressed blues elements in their music, whereas Marshall Tucker demonstrated much more diverse influences. In fact, the members themselves had a hard time finding a consensus about their main style, with lead guitarist (and major songwriter) Toy Caldwell stating they played "progressive country," his brother bass guitarist Tommy Caldwell and drummer Paul Riddle considering country-jazz the best description, lead singer Doug Gray favoring "bluesy rock 'n' roll," and rhythm guitarist George Mc-Corkle opting for "an American rock 'n' roll band which plays traditional American music." Anyone familiar with the band's material knows there is validity to all those definitions. In fact, it is perhaps the way the band melded so many diverse influences into its repertoire that made it popular with audiences throughout the United States and overseas as well. As Doug Gray told an interviewer in 1977, "Sure we're popular in parts of the South, but we're really big in places like New York and New Jersey. And our western market is really coming on strong. People tend to think southern bands have most of their appeal in the South, but that isn't necessarily true." The group proved this on many of its concert tours of the 1970s when it drew massive crowds in all parts of the country from Seattle to Miami. In late 1978, the band made its debut at New York's Madison Square Garden before an equally large and enthusiastic audience.

All of the band members grew up in Spartanburg, South Carolina, where most of them were as interested in blues and rock as country music. In fact, at one point in the late 1960s, some of the founding members were in a group called the Toy Factory that played mainly soul music. Some of that early experience is carried over in the blues and jazz elements in many of the group's arrangements.

As might be expected in a small town environment (Spartanburg has a population of about 45,000), the original members of the group knew each other from childhood and some had been in bands together during high school. The military call interrupted the musical activities of some of the men, but when they were discharged at the start of the 1970s, they soon were involved in the local rock and pop scene. In 1971, the Caldwell brothers joined with their four friends to form what was to become Marshall Tucker, and at the beginning of the 1980s, the same six artists were still together.

The name Marshall Tucker is mysteriously missing from the roster of the founding members. The name is a fictitious one. When the men were rehearsing in an old warehouse one of them found an old key wih the name Marshall Tucker on it. They promptly adopted it as their band designation.

The group began to play locally at first, then gained dates in neighboring states as their reputation spread. One of the bands they worked with was Wet Willie, whose members brought word to the executives of Capricorn Records in Georgia that Marshall Tucker was a group with promise. The band auditioned for the label and, in May 1972, was signed.

The band's debut LP, *The Marshall Tucker Band*, was issued in 1973, a year that saw the band begin to expand its reputation well beyond South Carolina on tour with the Allmans. The exposure didn't make the first album a smash success at the time, but it encouraged Capricorn and band members to look toward future progress. In 1974, the group provided two new albums, *A New Life* and *Where We All Belong*, and supported them with a back-breaking schedule of tours that kept them on the road most of the year. During the mid-1970s, the band typically gave 250–300 concerts a year, a schedule it cut back on once its reputation had been established. The intensive touring plus the quality of the original songs by band members began to pay dividends during 1974–1975 as each succeeding album rose a little higher on the charts and maintained steady sales patterns. By the end of 1975, the group had its first gold-record awards, finally going over the top with its debut LP on August 14, 1975, and later gaining one for *Where We All Belong* on November 7, 1975.

The gap between release and gold-record levels began to narrow. The band's fourth LP, *Searchin' for a Rainbow*, was issued in 1975 and earned a gold record on February 4, 1976. Meanwhile, other artists in country and pop were recording songs by some of the band members. During 1976, for instance, Waylon Jennings gained a top-5 hit with Toy Caldwell's "Can't You See." Other performers who recorded material by the Caldwells and other Marshall Tucker members were Kitty Wells, Hank Williams, Jr., and Gary Stewart. By 1977, *Searchin' for a Rainbow* became the band's first platinum album.

The group continued its series of hit LPs with *Long Hard Ride* in 1976 and *Carolina Dreams* in 1977. The latter also went platinum. *Carolina Dreams* was the most consistently well-written album to that point, demonstrating that all the members were becoming increasingly proficient as writers. Toy Caldwell remained the main contributor with the excellent songs "Fly like an Eagle" (which became a massive hit for Steve Miller), "Heard It in a Love Song," "Desert Skies," and "Tell It to the Devil." Tommy Caldwell provided a western-style number, "Never Trust a Stranger," and co-wrote the R&B-flavored "I Should Have Never Started Lovin' You" with George McCorkle and Doug Gray. McCorkle and Jerry Eubanks penned "Life in a Song."

Up to then, the band had almost exclusively succeeded as album artists, with none of its singles making top-chart levels. That changed with "Heard It in a Love Song," however, one of the better-selling singles of 1977. In 1978, the group expanded its LP achievements when its seventh LP on Capricorn, *Together Forever*, made the national charts and later was certified gold, making a full sweep—all seven

LPs up to then had earned the coveted award.

In 1978, the group's contract with Capricorn ran out. They decided to move to Warner Bros. Records, which for a number of years had distributed Marshall Tucker releases for Capricorn. The debut on the new label, *Running like the Wind,* came out in March 1979 and in short order was moving up the national hit lists.

In early 1980, the band's future seemed in jeopardy when Tommy Caldwell died from injuries in an auto accident in Spartanburg in April. There were thoughts of disbanding, but the group decided it would be more fitting for Tommy's memory to keep going. To take Tommy's place on bass, Franklin Wilkie, a long-time friend of the group members, was recruited.

Wilkie had played in a group called the Rants with Toy Caldwell and George McCorkle during 1964–66, leaving the group to enter college, where he worked with a band called Puzzle (1966–68). He then spent several years with the Air Force before returning to Spartanburg in the early 1970s. There he played for a time with Toy, Doug Gray, and Jerry Eubanks in Toy Factory, a group that later evolved into Marshall Tucker. When Tommy returned from the Marines to take over on bass, Wilkie moved to Atlanta to do studio work, then joined Garfeel Ruff, with whom he worked for six years.

By mid-1980, the reorganized band was touring again. Among its concert offerings were songs from its second Warner Bros. album and tenth overall called, simply, *Tenth.* In April 1981, Warner Brothers released the band's eleventh album, *Dedicated.* As the title indicates, it was dedicated to the memory of Tommy Caldwell. In the fall of 1981 the retrospective album *Best of Marshall Tucker* was on the pop charts.

MARTIN, GRADY: *Fiddler, guitarist, vibraphonist, band leader (the Slewfoot Five). Born near Chappel Hill, Tennessee, January 17, 1929.*

One of the multitalented musicians who helped make the "Nashville Sound" famous in the post–World War II decades, Grady Martin backed a virtual pantheon of artists from all facets of country and pop music in addition to making his own contributions as a soloist and band leader. Along the way, he pioneered or was among the outstanding exponents of such instrumental innovations as fuzztone, gut-string fills, straight-neck dobro, Echoplex, and double-neck guitar.

Born on a farm near Chappel Hill, Tennessee, Martin spent his boyhood years taking in the sights and sounds of rural life. When he was old enough, he helped in the chores and, after his father brought home a battery-operated Zenith radio, spent some of his leisure time listening to country music on the radio. On weekends, like countless Tennessee families, the Martins listened to the *Grand Ole Opry.* After hearing the great guitar playing on some of those programs, Martin recalled, "Right then I decided I didn't want to milk any more cows."

He began to seek ways of learning music himself, concentrating on the fiddle, though he started picking up some guitar chords as well. He began to frequent the country shows that, in those years, used to travel from town to town playing early evening dates at local school houses, observing the various fiddlers and practicing some of their techniques at home. In his teens, he played with local groups and sometimes asked to sit in with visiting bands.

"One night when I was fifteen, Big Jeff Bess heard me play fiddle and he went to my parents and asked them to let him take me to Nashville to play on the radio. Mom didn't want to let me, but Dad said I might as well go since I wasn't gonna be happy on the farm."

In Nashville, Grady steadily built up a reputation as a sideman and before long he was sought out for both group and session work. As a member of the Bailes Brothers band, he debuted on the *Opry* in 1946 and remained a regular performer on the show for many years, moving from the Bailes Brothers to backing groups for people like Curley Fox and Texas Ruby. By the time he was on the *Opry* a few years,

he had become as well known for his guitar work as for his fiddling.

Over the years from the late 1940s to the early 1980s, he worked as a session musician on hundreds of recordings. The first major success he contributed to began in a session in the converted garage studio of Owen Bradley, with Red Foley as featured artist. The effort produced Foley's best-selling single, "Chattanooga Shoe-Shine Boy." Among other milestones for Grady was his vibraphone work on Floyd Cramer's first massive hit of 1960–61, "Last Date." Martin also is credited with the first performance of the electric guitar technique known as fuzztone in his work on the Marty Robbins single "Don't Worry." Among others whom Martin backed over the years were Hank Williams, Henry Mancini, Bing Crosby, Johnny Cash, Kris Kristofferson, and Larry Gatlin, to name just a few.

During the 1960s and 1970s, Martin often headed his own band, the Slewfoot Five, on TV, live shows and a number of albums. In the mid- and late-1970s, his efforts included leading the TV band on the Nashville based T. Tommy Cutler show. During that period he also was active as a producer for Monument Records and made a number of recordings for the label as well. Among the acts he worked with on the production side was Brush Arbor, one of the best "progressive" country bands of the 1970s.

Martin often worked with Willie Nelson, and in the late 1970s and early 1980s he was a regular in the "Willie Nelson Family," touring worldwide with Willie's troupe and backing Nelson on most of his hit records of the period.

MBULU, LETTA: *Singer. Born Orlando Township, South Africa, circa 1944.*

There were hints of the richness of black South African music in a few of the songs that trickled to U.S. performers in the 1940s and 1950s. The full depth and beauty of the tradition, however, was not apparent until talented refugees from the racially-torn nation arrived on U.S. shores. Through widespread concert appearances of people like Miriam Makeba and Letta

Mbulu and the inclusion of South African songs in concerts of folksingers like Odetta and Harry Belafonte, new dimensions in folk music were offered to audiences across the United States and in many other parts of the world.

Letta Mbulu, like Makeba a member of the Xhosa tribe, was born in Orlando Township near Johannesburg and grew up in the black ghetto of Soweto. She demonstrated marked vocal talents at an early age and before long she was singing with the Union of South Africa Artists. While still in her teens, she joined a group called the African Jazz and Variety Troupe, an organization whose alumni included Miriam Makeba, Hugh Masekela, and a gifted writer/singer/arranger named Caiphus Semenya, whom Mbulu was to marry.

In her late teens, Letta was awarded a major part in a musical called *King Kong.* The show won acclaim from critics and audiences in London and later was well received in the United States. During the U.S. tour in 1964, Letta renewed acquaintances with Miriam Makeba, by then established in America as a major folk artist, who arranged for her to have an engagement at the Village Vanguard in New York. That three-week series suggested that as a performer Mbulu could claim equal rank with Makeba.

After such overseas triumphs, it was doubly disillusioning for the *King Kong* troupe to return to the mounting racial pressures of South Africa. On more than one occasion, Letta and her associates had humiliating experiences that they realized could easily have led to imprisonment or death. She told an interviewer in the 1970s, "We were constantly harassed by police patrols and no policeman would swallow the story that those expensive looking clarinets and saxophones were the property of the passengers and not the haul of a burglary. Sometimes arrested musicians had to prove their innocence by putting on a show in the police station. They literally had to blow their way to freedom."

All of that finally convinced many cast members, including the Semenyas and their young son Muntu, to seek a better life in the United States. In 1967 they established a new home in America, though Letta noted she always returned to Africa regularly to renew her roots. "I try to go 'home' every other year or so to see what is going on in music. To me, all of Africa is home. I don't go to South Africa where I was born. However, I go everywhere else, but just around the borders of South Africa. I have not been able to go because I have too many problems there. Or rather, they make problems for me."

Many of Mbulu's musical peers were well aware of her excellent voice and unusual repertoire of songs. For four years she toured throughout the United States and the world with Harry Belafonte. During those shows she sang a mixture of traditional African music and stylings of modern tunes running the gamut from ballads, blues, and soul to jazz. Her jazz attainments were recognized by Cannonball Adderley, with whom she worked for several years in the early 1970s. By the mid-1970s, Mbulu was esteemed as a major performer in many countries of the world; as an example, in 1973 she won first prize as Best Performer at the Onda Nueva World Music Festival in Caracas, Venezuela.

MCAULIFFE, LEON: *Singer, guitarist, band leader, songwriter. Born Houston, Texas, January 3, 1917.*

An integral part of the Texas Playboys legend almost from the beginning, Leon McAuliffe fittingly became front man for the new Playboys revival in the mid-1970s. It was McAuliffe, of course, whose steel guitar playing was a central element of Bob Wills' group from 1935 to 1942 and whose name was immortalized every time Wills would shout, "Take it away, Leon," for the next steel guitar break.

McAuliffe, like Wills, was a native Texan, born and raised in Houston. When he was fourteen years old, he was given a seven-dollar Stella guitar for a Christmas present and in a short time he was a proficient player. Actually he started to learn under the guidance of an instructor, but he quit when he mastered new material faster than his teacher could provide him with additional music. He became enamored of the steel guitar and, though he could play other instruments as time went by, it remained his forte throughout his career.

In 1932, he got a summer job on the staff of station KPRC in Houston. In 1933, he became a member of a station group called the *Swift Jewel Cowboys*. Meanwhile, Bob Wills and W. Lee "Pappy" O'Daniel had inaugurated the *Light Crust Doughboys* program on a Ft. Worth station. McAuliffe recalls, "The band was being reorganized in 1933 and O'Daniel liked the sound of the steel guitar but couldn't find anyone he liked in Ft. Worth. He contacted me and I went up and auditioned and got hired." Leon stayed with the Doughboys for close to two years while Wills was off on his own with the new band that became known as the Texas Playboys.

"After a while, Bob began to make changes, dropping some people and adding new ones—and new instruments. In 1935, for instance, he added a small piano and drums. His bass player, Kermit Whelan, could play steel guitar a little, but not full time. When he left in early 1935, Bob sent for me to play the steel guitar full time and I joined in March 1935." McAuliffe moved to Tulsa, Oklahoma, with the band, which became his home for many years. He played a major role in the band's rise to prominence not only with country fans, but for others who responded to their "western swing" stylings.

One of Leon's first contributions was his instrumental composition "Steel Guitar Rag," which became a staple of the Playboys' repertoire and remained so in the new phase of the mid- and late-1970s. He also coauthored another song that became a country & western classic, "San Antonio Rose." "When that song became a major hit for us in the early 1940s, it really established us as a nationally known band. Actually the song started as an instrumental, then we came back with it with lyrics in 1940–41."

Leon's career with the Playboys was interrupted by World War II. "My time with him ended in December 1942. Up to then we'd recorded several times a year and made ten western movies. When World War II came along, everybody began to get draft notices or left to take a defense job. Both Bob and I went into the service, but he didn't stay in very long. Actually he shouldn't have gone in in the first place because he was thirty-eight years old when he entered."

McAuliffe joined the Navy and became a flight instructor before leaving in 1946. After he got out, he continued his flying, buying his own plane that he often used to travel to various performing dates. He didn't ignore his music while in uniform, though, serving as a band member for many engagements with the Glenn Miller dance band led by Tex Beneke.

By the time Leon left the Navy, Wills had moved his operation to California. Leon opted to stay in Tulsa. "I didn't go back to him when I got out of the Navy. I started my own band [called the Western Swing Band]. I happened to appear on a couple of shows he was on, but that was the extent of our involvement until we got together for *The Last Time* album in 1973." Leon did well with his new group, though. The band won a wide following in the late 1940s and the early 1950s with their own radio shows on station KVOO and KRMG in Tulsa. McAuliffe then became owner and operator of his own facility, the Cimarron Ballroom in Tulsa, and changed the band's name to the Cimarron Boys. Under that designation, besides playing in their home club, they also traveled extensively during the late 1950s and much of the 1960s, performing throughout the United States and in European venues as well. During that period, McAuliffe also had his own TV show originating from Tulsa.

In the 1960s, the band was featured on many TV and radio shows, including the *Grand Ole Opry*, *Lawrence Welk*, *Jubilee U.S.A.*, *Country America Show*, *Town Hall Party*, and the *Buddy Deane Show*. From 1956 into the mid-1960s, the Cimmaron Boys were voted one of the top three country & western bands in major trade magazine polls.

Despite all that, Leon notes he and his band had to work extremely hard to make ends meet during those years. "Young people began to go for Bill Haley and then Elvis came along. It was rough to keep going. We had to travel longer and play more nights, but it was the only way to survive. Our schedule got rougher and rougher and the only way we could make it was with the airplane. Typically five of us took the plane from one date to the next and three drove.

"We had a complete show—not just one singer. Everybody in the band was a vocalist. Some could do comedy. We had little acts and comic bits we used. We could sustain a two-hour show easily with the kind of talent we had."

McAuliffe recorded many numbers with his various bands from the late 1940s into the mid-1960s. Most of these were written by others. "I've written some songs that are good, but not many. I can't manufacture 'em, they have to come to me. I wrote 'Steel Guitar Rag' and the bridge to 'San Antonio Rose'—the trumpeter wrote the words—but Bob has total credit. But I'm happy to trade that for 'Take it Away, Leon' any time. I wrote "Panhandle Rag," which was a hit for my band in 1948 and that's the last song I've written."

With his Western Swing Band, he had forty records for Columbia from the late 1940s to mid-fifties. During 1957–59, his Cimmaron Boys' releases came out on Dot Records and from the mid-1950s to mid-1960s, his recordings were issued by various labels including ABC-Paramount, Starday, Cimmaron, and Capitol. His LPs of these years included *Take Off* on Dot, *Cozy Inn* on ABC-Paramount, *Mister Western Swing* on Starday, *Swingin' Western Strings* on Cimmaron, and *Dancinest Band Around* on Capitol. Capitol, with whom he signed a long-term contract in the early 1960s, was his recording home for that decade and, as it happened, was the label for which he turned out the new Original Texas Playboy LPs in the mid- and late-1970s.

Steadily declining interest in western swing influenced Leon to break up his group and go into retirement by the late 1960s. He was living in Missouri doing some occasional session work when the call came from Bob Wills to do a retrospective album in 1973. "The Texas Playboys are back together because Bob wanted us to do a final album. He picked eight people to do it, all of whom had been in the band over its thirty or forty years of existence."

Wills suffered a stroke before the new album was finished, but Leon and the other seven hand-picked musicians completed it, and the album came out under the title *For the Last Time* in 1975. The response to the album was so good that Capitol asked McAuliffe and Leon Rausch to keep things going even after Wills' death. The result was a series of new LPs beginning with the March 1977 release *The Late Bob Wills Original Texas Playboys Today*.

Harking back to the Wills inspired album, Leon stresses, "Because the old man wanted us to do it, we agreed to do it. I credit Asleep at the Wheel [a new band that stressed western swing in its repertoire] with being a key in the Playboys resurgence. Like everything turned out right. Waylon and Willie started singing 'Bob Wills Is Still the King' and all of a sudden all these kids who'd been ignoring their parents' comments on what had been done musically in the past said, 'Hey, it's not too bad.'

"As for the new Playboys, musically we're doing the same thing we've done forty years ago. We still play the same style and if we play a new tune we adapt it to our style. But it's not a full-scale revival for most of us. We may play some key places if Capitol wants us to, but outside of Leon Rausch, who makes his living playing music, the rest of us go other ways. Some are retired, some have businesses, some have jobs, and one teaches school. We hold 'em down. We don't want to work too much and we're very dedicated to preserving the Bob Wills sound."

That sound, McAuliffe agreed in 1979, included his ringing steel guitar work and the memories it evoked of the famous Bob Wills "holler." "When Wills started his holler, I don't know, 'cause he was doin' it the first time I knew. Bob would play fiddle up to the time Tommy [Duncan] was to sing and he'd say 'Come in Tommy.' When we recorded 'Steel Guitar Rag,' before we cut it he said, 'You hit a chord and let me talk.' That's what I did—I hit a slide chord and he said, 'Lookout! Here comes Leon. Take it away, boy, take it away!'"

Based on interview with Irwin Stambler, 1979.

MCCALL, C. W.: *Singer, songwriter. Born Audubon, Iowa, November 15.*

Though the wild excitement of the Citizen's Band (C.B.) radio craze in the mid-1970s simmered down by the start of the 1980s, those handy communications items still were installed in millions of trucks and passenger cars. And, when either C.B. users or members of the public at large thought about C.B., C. W. McCall and his famous record "Convoy" almost always came to mind. But though "10–4" became another nickname for McCall, he had achieved notice as a country artist before "Convoy" and kept turning out successful singles on other topic years afterward.

Music was part of his natural environment as a child in Iowa, though classical and pop were stressed more than country in his home. Both his parents were musicians and, during the 1920s, took their small son along with them when they traveled the silent movie circuit playing the theater scores that accompanied those films. (McCall's original name was Bill Fries—pronounced Freez.) McCall was interested in learning more about music as he grew older and, in fact, enrolled as a music major at the University of Iowa, with a concentration in the classics and reed instruments.

However, before long he became bored with the intricacies of classical theory and arranging and dropped out. For a while he worked as a roving reporter, then eventually moved into advertising. He proved adept at the latter pursuit and became an important member of the staff of the Bozell Jacobs Agency, based in their midwest office. Even as his career in the music field expanded in the mid-1970s, he continued to devote much of his time to the ad field, still serving as creative director of Bozell Jacobs in the late 1970s.

He continued to have an interest in music and watched for opportunities to further that side of his creative nature. In 1974, he scored his first major breakthrough by signing with MGM Records.

Soon after, his single "Old Home Fill-Er-Up and Keep on a-Truckin' Cafe" was on the charts (summer 1974). This was the forerunner of an even more successful trucking number called "Wolf Creek Pass," which he co-wrote with L. C. Davies. The twosome collaborated on just about all the McCall hits, with C. W. using his real name, Bill Fries, on the writing credits most of the time. The single "Wolf Creek Pass" became a top-10 hit in early 1975 and the album of the same title also moved high on country charts.

In the fall of 1975, McCall was back on the charts again with the single "Black Bear Road," which moved to number one in the country charts late in the year. The album of that title did equally well, reaching number one at the end of 1975 and remaining in that lofty spot into 1976. The single "Convoy" burst on the scene even as "Black Bear Road" dominated the album charts. At the end of 1975 that C.B. anthem rose to number one on the country charts and also swept to upper levels of national pop lists. It passed the levels required for a Record Industry Association of America gold-record award in mid-December and McCall was given his plaque on December 19, 1975.

Soon after, he was busy with a new record label, Polydor. In the spring and early summer, he rewarded that label with a top-10 album, *Wilderness,* and a top-10 single, "There Won't Be No Country Music (There Won't Be No Rock 'n' Roll.)" Later in the year he had another chart hit, "Crispy Critters." Among the recognition given him by year end was selection as *Cash Box* magazine's Top Male Vocalist, Albums. In 1977, though the hot pace he had set cooled down a bit in the early part of the year, by November he was back in the top brackets with another major singles hit, "Roses for Mama."

At the start of the 1980s, McCall had a number of albums in print on MGM and Polydor. The MGM LPs were *Wolf Creek Pass* and *Black Bear Road.* The Polydor selections were *Rubber Duck, Roses for Mama* and *C. W. McCall's Greatest Hits.*

MCCLAIN, CHARLY: *Singer. Born Memphis, Tennessee, March 26, circa 1956.*

Though she has a masculine first name, there's nothing macho about Charly Mc-Clain. Indeed, with her flashing smile, dark brown eyes, flowing brown hair, and well-proportioned five-foot-one-inch figure, she was among the more eye-pleasing additions to country music's new wave of promising young singers in the late 1970s.

The middle child of three in a Memphis, Tennessee, electrician's family (she has a younger sister and older brother), she became interested in country music at an early age. After watching the first Country Music Association Awards TV show in the late 1960s, she reputedly told her family she expected to win the Female Vocalist Award in 1981. As she grew up, she began to take steps to make that prediction come true—or at least achieve a close approximation. Still, she could just as well have become an electrician, since she aided her father on his rounds at times and learned the basics of the craft.

It was because her father became seriously ill, McClain told Dolly Carlisle of *Country Music* magazine (April 1979), that she took a major step toward a singing career. "He was in the hospital for over a year with tuberculosis. During that time the children couldn't see him and our only means of communications was through taped messages. In the beginning we sent him talking tapes, but eventually they turned musical. Shortly afterwards, my brother and I formed a band and kept right on singing."

The two McClains helped assemble a band that worked at local functions in the early 1970s. But the group broke up when several members received draft notices. Charly then successfully auditioned for the Memphis-based *Mid-South Jamboree* program and became a cast member for a while until the show was phased out. In the mid-1970s, she added to her experience by joining the O. B. McClinton show, with whom she toured many places in the United States.

All of those jobs helped improve her stage presence and polish her performing style. They also increased her friends and contacts in the music field. Among the people McClain came to know were members of the Memphis band Shylo. She was watching them perform at the Mid-South Fair in Memphis in 1977 when she was asked to sing a few numbers with the group.

She told Dolly Carlisle, "They just called me up on stage." Soon after, she got a call from Larry Rogers, Shylo producer, to make a demo tape. "Larry took the tape to Billy Sherrill. I got a contract with Epic a few weeks later. It sounds like I had an easy way of it, but I had pushed tapes for years on Nashville's Music Row with no success. . . . It really hasn't been easy. There were a lot of promises made that never came through."

However, once Charly's voice became available on commercial records, it was easy for many country fans to become enamored of her singing style. Her debut LP on Epic, *Here's Charly McClain*, spawned her first chart single, "Lay Down." She did even better with the material recorded for her second album, *Let Me Be Your Baby*, issued in late 1978. First the track "Let Me Be Your Baby" reached upper-chart levels and, in November 1978, a second track, "That's What You Do to Me," made the country top 10.

Through much of 1978 she toured on her own, but by the end of the year, things were rolling along well enough for her to assemble her own traveling band, Bluff City. It was a psychological breakthrough, she admitted to Carlisle. "[Before] it was depressing to appear in a city never knowing what the circumstances were going to be or if the band that was to accompany me was going to be good. I was very tired. My new band has made all the difference in road work. Now I feel very proud of our act. It's polished, professional and I feel good."

She had reason to feel even better about her musical efforts over the next few years, particularly in the early 1980s when her popularity reached new heights. She finished the 1970s with additional recording credits, including the 1979 charted single "When a Love Ain't Right" and a duet with Johnny Rodriguez, "I Hate the Way I Love It," but started off the 1980s in even better style with the early 1980 bestseller, "Men." Later in the year she had such audience favorites as "Let's Put Our Love in

Motion" and "Women Get Lonely." In early 1981, she had what was to prove her most successful release to that point, the single "Who's Cheatin' Who," which reached number one on country charts in February. Before the year was over, she had other top-10 hits such as "Surround Me With Love" and "Sleepin' with the Radio On."

McCLINTON, DELBERT: *Singer, harmonica player, guitarist, songwriter. Born Lubbock, Texas, November, 4, 1940.*

He was known for years among fans of country blues and rhythm & blues as the "King of the White Texas Bluesmen." His style was respected and sometimes copied by many famous artists, from the Beatles to Waylon Jennings. His original songs were covered by many performers, in fields ranging from rock and R&B to country, providing major hits for some artists in the 1970s. Despite that, until the start of the 1980s he was virtually unknown to most of the music public outside Texas. Fortunately, the long overdue discovery of his great creative abilities finally came after decades of dues paying. As Jack McDonough headlined in *Billboard* (January 17, 1981): "20-Year Triumph: McClinton Charts."

The long road to that recognition began in Lubbock, Texas, where Delbert was born and lived until his family moved to Ft. Worth, Texas, when he was eleven. Considering his later affinity for the blues, he didn't emerge from the typical background of early poverty or broken family. He recalled having had a happy childhood and traced his interest in music and songwriting as something that just evolved naturally. "I started singing while I helped wash the dishes. It's one of those things you do, then someone starts paying you to do it." After a while he found himself making up some songs on his own, a task that came easily because of a habit of talking to himself. In his teens, he got his first guitar, a used Kay he bought for about $3.50, and soon was playing for friends and classmates at his Ft. Worth high school.

He quickly expanded his efforts outside

school. He told Suzan Crane of *Hit Parader*, "I was playing clubs probably when I was sixteen . . . no, before that . . . fifteen." He also was moving in and out of a series of bands—the Mellow Fellows, the Losers, the Bright Side, the Acme Music Company. Finally he formed one called the Straitjackets, which became the house band at a blues club south of Ft. Worth called Jack's Place.

He told Crane, "The blues was real popular in the Texas area. People like Howlin' Wolf and Jimmy Reed, Bobby Bland and Junior Parker, and Sonny Boy Williamson. Being the house band out there, and that being the club they usually came to, we backed 'em up. We also liked it, so we already knew all the songs.

"One night we were playing a song called 'Fanny Mae' by Buster Brown. We were backing him up and Jimmy Reed in the same night, and I had just bought me a harmonica because they were two of the best, ya know, and I was ready to learn. Well, we were sittin' in the dressing room before the show—I didn't drink at the time—but they were both passing a quart of Old Grand-Dad, and I was sittin' in the middle helping 'em drink it—I never did see the show!"

That might have been the starting point for McClinton's later "two fisted he-man" image. But it didn't keep him from pursuing his romance with the harmonica. He picked up tips from the greatest blues harp players he could find and added touches of his own that made him a premiere exponent of that instrumental style. He included some blues harp licks on his first record, a cover of Sonny Boy Williamson's "Wake Up Baby" on the Le Cam label. He used the pseudonym Mac Linton on the disc, which was the first by a white singer ever played on the Ft. Worth black station KNOK. Over the years, many of his other recordings found play-time on black stations.

In 1962, his harmonica backing helped bring rock artist Bruce Channel a chart hit single, "Hey Baby." Delbert was asked to tour with Channel, a job that took him all over the United States and, among other places, to England. British musicians quickly took note of McClinton's harmonica skills.

He recalled for Suzan Crane, "From the first night I was there, somebody in every band had a harmonica [and] come down to the dressing room and wanted to learn something. And this went on every night. . . . Well, one night we worked with the Beatles. They were the opening act for the Bruce Channel show and the only thing I knew about them was this girl had said 'I want you to hear this band; they're the hottest band in the North of England,' and they were. They had on these nice-looking lightweight black leather suits and whichever one I taught to play something on harp, I asked him where he got the suit, and I went into London the next day and got me a coat."

Later, when Delbert was back in Texas, he heard the results of his tutelage. It took the form of the harmonica work on the Beatles "Love Me Do."

In 1964, McClinton formed a group called the Ron-Dels that had some success with Texas fans. The group recorded some songs for three different labels, two of which were local hits, "Crying Over You" and "If You Really Want Me to I'll Go." The last named, written by Delbert, was covered by a number of artists and Waylon Jennings' version made the national country charts.

For the balance of the 1960s, McClinton continued to play the blues clubs, beer joints, and honky tonks in and around Texas without gaining much attention beyond his home borders. In 1970, though, a woman he was involved with, recently divorced and with settlement money in her purse, provided the incentive for a move to Los Angeles. The romance failed to last, which inspired some of McClinton's 1970s songs, but once in California he teamed with a friend named Glen Clark to make some recordings for the now long-defunct Clean Records. The team of Delbert and Glen had two album releases on Clean during the early 1970s that, he said, "not enough people know about yet." Discouraged at the state of the music industry in California ("We weren't speaking their language and they weren't speaking ours"), he returned to Texas in the summer of 1974 to try to put the pieces of his career together again.

He soon was receiving grateful applause from crowds at his old honky tonk haunts and negotiating a new record deal with ABC. The first of the new solo LPs, featuring all original songs, *Victim of Life's Circumstances,* was released in the spring of 1975. This was followed by *Genuine Cowhide* in 1976 and *Love Rustler* in 1977. The latter showcased McClinton's varied musical tastes, ranging from the R&B-tinged "Under Suspicion" to a southern rock version of Laura Lee's "Long as I Got You." Most of the tracks, including the excellent "Some People," were written by Delbert.

The ABC releases impressed many critics, but didn't have much impact on fans, R&B, country, or otherwise. In fact, it looked as though McClinton might achieve whatever success that would come to him from his writing rather than performing efforts. Artists had been including some of his material in albums and some singles right along; in 1978, Emmylou Harris had a number one country hit with his "Two More Bottles of Wine." At the end of the decade, the late John Belushi and Dan Ayckroyd included his composition "B Movie Boxcar Blues" in their hit *Blues Brothers* LP. Belushi and Ayckroyd, like many of McClinton's entertainment industry peers, were long-time fans of his, and when Delbert played the Lone Star Cafe in New York in the late 1970s, they went onstage to join his act. They were soon followed by such other luminaries as Jimmy Buffett, Leon Redbone, and Joe Ely.

In 1978, McClinton contracted for new albums with Capricorn Records. This resulted in two excellent collections, *Second Wind* (recorded with the Muscle Shoals Rhythm Section in Alabama), issued in 1978, and *Keeper of the Flame,* released in 1979. Unfortunately, Capricorn had gotten into financial difficulties and its demise dimmed the prospects for the new albums. In addition, the company's collapse also washed out negotiations McClinton was involved in for doing the soundtrack for the film *Middle Age Crazy.*

It was just another setback to join a long

list of frustrations. McClinton always had a reputation for artistic integrity, but while he had high standards that didn't mean he enjoyed living a relatively hand-to-mouth existence (and he had a wife and two sons to support). He told a reporter he was proud of his work, but wanted something more. "When you're in this business, you want to make money. You need a national hit . . . that's how you make money."

He was beginning to think such a hit was just wishful thinking. However, he kept on hoping. In 1980 he signed with the newly established Muscle Shoals Sound Records. His first album under the new agreement was *The Jealous Kind*, released in October 1980 and distributed by Capitol Records. Strangely, it was his first LP without a single original song by him. He explained, "This time I just didn't have any songs I considered high energy enough." The album quickly made the charts, as did the single from it, "Giving It Up for Your Love." Both recordings showed up on both country and pop lists and the single made the top 10 on pop charts in early 1981.

One reason he finally had such a breakthrough, he told Pete Oppel of the *Dallas Morning News* (March 24, 1981), was the support the record company had provided. "Because all the other record companies I've been with have folded . . . these companies never put any money into the albums. If you've got something to sell, you've got to put money into it to make people aware of it. I can name you three record companies right off the bat that didn't do that. But this one [Capitol Records] is and it's making quite a noticeable difference."

Looking back, he said, "Actually I'm proud of all the records I've made, so that, in itself, is successful. Of course, I wanted them to sell, but the fact that they haven't doesn't mean they're not good records."

By mid-1981, McClinton was in Muscle Shoals putting the finishing touches on a new album. This one included some of his own songs, such as "I Wanna Thank You Baby" and "Sandy Beaches," the latter the first single from the album. The LP was released by Capitol in November 1981, titled *Plain from the Heart*.

One reason he was always glad to have songs from many writers in his repertoire, McClinton said, was that he was never a prolific writer. This was due to "my pride in my music. I work hard to perfect my songs. I've taken as long as two years to finish one simply because it needed a line and I don't want to pad. I know when it can be better and if it can be better I want it to be. I want people to hear my songs, but I want them to hear their honesty."

McCLINTON, O. B.: *Singer, guitarist, songwriter. Born Senatobia, Mississippi, April 25, 1942.*

In the early 1970s, O. B. McClinton wrote a song called "The Other One," which referred to a case of mistaken identity: when he performed in country shows and clubs, people thought he was Charley Pride. It wasn't that his traditionally oriented country style was a carbon copy of Charley's, simply that they had the same skin color. But as the 1970s went by, if O. B. didn't achieve the same massive success as Charley, he did gain a strong following that admired him for his own approach to music and for the many excellent original songs that were part of his repertoire.

Obie Burnett McClinton became interested in music at an early age in his home state of Mississippi. He recalled to La-Wayne Satterfield of the *Music City News* (October 1973) that he often day-dreamed about show business as a boy growing up on his father's (Reverend G. A. McClinton) farm. "This wasn't hard to do if you're a kid of ten or eleven and put to doing a chore you don't want to do—hoeing crops, rounding up livestock, and 'following' a mule—and especially if your dad's farm is a big, 700-acre place, a most unusually sizable thing for a black man to own in Mississippi, and you are next to the youngest of seven (three boys and four girls) with plenty of secret places in which to hide."

Then and during his teenage years, his interest in singing grew stronger. One of his favorite artists was Hank Williams, much of whose style wore off, with the result that later on people sometimes told him, "Why, you sound just like Hank Williams."

He was still doing chores on the farm at

seventeen when he decided to run off and make his mark in entertainment. He wanted to go to San Francisco, but he only had a small amount of money and when he got to Memphis the sight of a guitar in a store window so enthralled him that he bought it with his travel money. He returned home, finished high school, and spent a lot of his spare time experimenting on the guitar.

Upon graduating, he returned to Memphis and earned a living at a variety of odd jobs. Still unsure of how to proceed, he applied to college and gained a choir scholarship from Rust College in Holly Springs, Mississippi. He spent four years there, singing in the A Cappella Choir, and was was graduated in 1966. He moved to Memphis once more, this time getting a DJ job with station WDIA, but that was cut short in December 1966 when, to avoid being drafted into the Army, O. B. enlisted in the Air Force. He spent four years in the service, stationed at various Air Force bases from Lakeland and Amarillo in Texas to Shaw in South Carolina. While in uniform, he polished his skills as a singer, winning a number of talent shows, and also began to turn out promising original songs. Most of his writing emphasis then was on R&B material, which got him a writing contract from Fame Publishing Co. in Muscle Shoals, Alabama.

After his discharge at the start of the 1970s, O. B.'s activities centered for a while in Muscle Shoals. His songs were reaping big rewards for many R&B artists. Among his credits were "Baby, You Got My Mind Messed Up" and "A Man Needs a Woman," recorded by James Carr; "You Can't Miss What You Can't Measure," a hit for Clarence Carter; and "Keep Your Arms Around Me," released by the great Otis Redding.

O. B. had made some relatively unsuccessful efforts to work as an R&B singer. He loved country but was doubtful a black could succeed in the field. However, Charley Pride's breakthrough plus the way people responded to O. B.'s Hank Williams phrasing gave him confidence he might do it.

He told Satterfield, "I was in Muscle Shoals and staying at the Holiday Inn writing a tune for Willie Hightower called 'The Back Road to Town,' and I learned I was staying next door to Al Bell." Bell, a top Stax Records executive, had been an acquaintance when both were Memphis DJs in 1966. McClinton sought him out and played some of his country tapes without telling Bell who was doing it.

"After listening to them for a while, Al asked, 'Who is he? Is he signed?' When I wouldn't tell, Al kept after me until I admitted it was me. He told me I was joking and the only way I could convince him that was really me singing on them tapes was to sing along with the tapes. He put me under contract on January 12, 1971." O. B. was assigned to the Stax country label, Enterprise.

After several releases received regional attention, O. B. made the national country charts with the single "Don't Let the Green Grass Fool You." O. B. not only sang but produced the record. During the 1970s, McClinton produced other artists' material as well. As the 1970s went by, He turned out a steady series of singles and albums, including his debut LP, *Country McClinton,* in 1972 and *Live at Randy's Rodeo* in 1973. Among his mid-1970s chart singles were "Yours and Mine" in early 1975, "Hello, This Is Anna" in mid-1978, and "Natural Love" in late 1978. The last two were on Epic Records, to which O. B. switched after Stax Records went out of business in the mid-1970s. In the early 1980s, he had some releases on Sunbird Records, including the single "Not Exactly Free," on the charts in the fall of 1980.

McCOY, CHARLIE: *Singer, harmonica player, guitarist, trumpeter. Born Oak Hill, West Virginia, March 28, 1941.*

Throughout the 1970s, an almost foregone conclusion was that when the votes were counted for Country Music Association Award nominees, Charlie McCoy would be one of the five finalists. To the general public, he was mainly known as one of the most-talented harmonica players in country music, but to his industry peers, he had long been recognized as one of the most versatile, multiskilled instrumentalists in the business.

Charlie, who was born in West Virginia

and spent some of his early years in Miami, Florida, began playing the mouth harp at the age of eight. Though that was his first love, as he grew up, he proved adept at a wide range of other instruments as well. He also handled some occasional singing chores during his high school years when he played with a variety of groups, from dance bands to country organizations. Unlike many Nashville session musicians who usually were essentially self-taught, at one point in his development Charlie studied music theory, music arrangement, conducting, and even took some singing lessons.

During the late 1950s and early 1960s, Charlie worked the rock circuit as well as country for a while. One Saturday night, when he was performing on a country show called the Old South Jamboree, he impressed a visiting artist named Mel Tillis. Tillis suggested that McCoy would do well to settle in Nashville, Tennessee, where he could find plenty of work as a session musician while trying to make his way as a soloist. Tillis' introduction to his agent, Jim Denny, brought the desired results. Starting in the 1960s, McCoy was working regularly in tour backup bands for stars of the *Grand Ole Opry.*

In 1961, he got a recording contract as a vocalist and over the next few years cut nine singles that made the country top 40. However, he was never quite able to break through to the top levels as a singer and his main source of income continued to be as a band member or session musician.

Initially, most of his session work resulted from assignments from Jim Denny's music publishing firm. Before long, his name was ranked with the best instrumentalists in Nashville and requests for such work came from a wide range of recording studios and organizations. During the 1960s, he backed many of the best-known names in show business, including Ann Margret, Elvis Presley, Bob Dylan, Joan Baez, Ringo Starr, Tom T. Hall, and many others. Some of his instrumental exploits became legendary. Rock artist and producer Al Kooper claimed that one of the most unusual incidents took place during one of Dylan's *Blonde on Blonde* sessions in

the mid-1960s. Because Dylan disliked overdubs, in one part of the arrangement McCoy played trumpet with his right hand while handling the bass guitar with his left "without missing a beat."

McCoy continued to do some of his own recordings in the late 1960s and early 1970s without making much headway on the charts. He also worked as a producer both for his own work and for some other artists, a practice he continued in the 1970s. In 1972, when McCoy seemed permanently destined for a low profile role throughout his musical career, an unexpected break changed things around. A disc jockey in Florida came across McCoy's harmonica rendition (on a four-year-old album) of a song called "Today I Started Loving You Again." The DJ started playing it and other stations followed suit. Released as a single, the track became a top-10 hit in early 1972; later in the year he hit again with the Hank Williams song "I'm So Lonesome I Could Cry."

McCoy followed up with a series of albums and singles on Monument Records that included such titles as *My Boy McCoy, Silver Wings,* and a harmonica version single of the old fiddle classic, "Orange Blossom Special." His charted singles in the mid-1970s included "Release Me," on the lists in late 1973 and early 1974; "Boogie Woogie" (with Barefoot Jerry) in the summer of 1974; and "Fair and Tender Ladies" in the fall of 1978. Among his chart albums in the mid-1970s were *Harpin' the Blues* in 1976, the 1978 retrospective LP, *Charlie McCoy's Greatest Hits,* and in mid-1979, *Appalachian Fever.*

During the 1970s, not only was he nominated as CMA Instrumentalist of the Year several times, he won the award twice. He was also similarly honored in annual roundups by major music trade magazines, including selection by *Cash Box* as its top country instrumentalist for both singles and albums in 1976.

In the 1970s, besides his recording and songwriting efforts, Charlie still backed many other artists. In addition, in 1977 he took over as music director of the syndicated *Hee Haw* country TV show, a post he still held at the start of the 1980s.

MCDANIEL, MEL: *Singer, guitarist, trumpeter, songwriter, band leader. Born Checota, Oklahoma, September 6.*

Even though pop musicians usually have to wait a while before their talents are recognized, the typical country or blues artist usually has to wait even longer. In Mel McDaniel's case the experience of waiting was manifest in his many songs that dealt with the joys and problems of everyday living.

Mel was born in Checota, but grew up in the towns of Okmulgee and Tulsa, Oklahoma. He showed a youthful interest in music when he took up the trumpet in the fourth grade and then started to learn guitar soon after. In his teens he played in local bands and, by the time his high school years were through, was working as a musician in Tulsa clubs. He managed to record several singles for some local labels, and then decided to try his luck in other locales, first in Ohio, then in Nashville, in the late 1960s.

His primary goal in Music City was to succeed as a songwriter. He worked in a gas station to earn a living while he tried to gain the attention of music publishers and performers. That didn't work out, so his next move was to far-off Alaska, where he became a favored country performer in Anchorage. Still, he knew stardom required being based in the lower forty-eight, and he jumped at the chance to return to Nashville in 1973, where he became a fixture for nine months playing at the Holiday Inn.

The quality of his deep voice for bringing out the shadings in country songs soon brought other work recording demonstration records for songwriters and publishers. He also formed an association with record producer Johnny MacRae, who finally got him the much sought-after contract with a major label, Capitol, in 1976. One of his first recordings for that firm made the country singles charts in May 1976 and Mel was on his way. Later in the year, he placed still another single on the charts, "I Thank God She Isn't Mine." This was followed by still more chart singles in 1977, "All the Sweet" early in the year and "Gentle to Your Senses (Easy on

Your Mind)," a top-20 chartmaker in August.

Thus Mel had four hit singles to his credit in just over a year without being represented with an album. That was rectified in late summer of 1977 with his LP debut, *Gentle on Your Senses,* which not only made the country hit lists but spawned two more chart songs, "Soul of a Honky Tonk Woman" and "God Made Love." McDaniel added to his growing following with in-person appearances across the country and on TV backed by his band, called A Little More Country. His achievements were recognized by members of the California-based Academy of Country Music, nominated him for Most Promising Male Vocalist of 1977.

In July 1978, his second Capitol album, *Mello,* was released. The first single from the album, "Border Town Woman," was on the charts during the summer of 1978. In 1979, Mel had such charted singles as "Love Lies" and "Lovin' Starts Where Friendship Ends." In late 1980, his single "Countryfied" showed up on the lists and rose into the top 20 in early 1981. Later in the year he had such charted singles as "Louisiana Saturday Night," "Right in the Palm of Your Hand," and "Preaching Up a Storm."

MCDONALD, COUNTRY JOE: *Singer, guitarist, harmonica player, songwriter, band leader (the Fish). Born El Monte, California, January 1, 1942.*

Country Joe McDonald didn't grow up in the country nor did he specialize in country music. He was essentially a member of the urban folk movement of the 1960s and, as such, identified with the many protest songs of the period. This identification tended to mask the fact that he was first and foremost an entertainer, and a good one, whose repertoire included songs of all kinds covering a wide range of topics.

He was born and raised in the Los Angeles suburb of El Monte which at the time had a strong following for country music, providing a sizable audience for the Los Angeles-area country radio and TV programs. During Joe's preteen years he did listen to a lot of those programs, but by the time he entered high school in the mid-1950s, rock 'n' roll was all the rage. Like most of his peer groups, Joe was a fan of early rockabilly stars like Elvis, Jerry Lee Lewis, and Bill Haley.

In high school, Joe became involved in teenage bands and, to a limited extent, school politics. He formed a rock group called the Nomads that performed at local parties and school events, with Joe handling lead vocals plus some still tentative instrumental work on guitar and harmonica. When a friend of his ran for student body president at El Monte High School, Joe wrote his campaign song, aided in the effort by other band members. The song, called "I Seen a Rocket," was composed "while we all were high on cigarettes and black coffee." It was, he noted wryly, "my first political act."

Ironically, considering his future course as a major antiwar activist, McDonald's first step after leaving high school was to sign up for a four-year hitch in the U.S. Navy. During those Navy years, though, his musical tastes gradually shifted from rock to the folk music that swept the United States for a time in the late 1950s and early 1960s. Before he received his discharge, he had added a number of traditional folk songs to his repertoire.

From the Navy, McDonald went back to the L.A. area and spent a year at Los Angeles City College. Affected by the growing restlessness among people of his generation, caused in part by the civil rights movement and growing opposition to involvement in the Vietnam War, he became discouraged about the LACC environment. His views about political conditions at home had started to alter and, while still at LACC, he had written a number of protest songs. He always stressed that he believed in basing one's views on the conditions that existed at the time. "The most revolutionary thing you can do in this country is change your mind."

Changing his mind about where he wanted to live, McDonald left Los Angeles and moved north to Berkeley, where he soon was performing in some of the small folk clubs and coffee houses in the bay area. He soon met and formed a strong friendship with guitarist Barry Melton, who, in 1965, joined him in forming Country Joe and the Fish with such other performers as David Cohen and "Chicken" Hirsh. In a short time, the group was a familiar presence at various festivals and political gatherings and also often was featured at a coffee house called the Jabberwock. The group soon developed a trademark routine, which began with the "Fish cheer," where the audience was asked to spell out either the band name or another four-letter word, followed by the band's rendition of the Country Joe composition "I Feel Like I'm Fixin' to Die Rag." The song, which became an anthem of the antiwar movement, first appeared in recorded form on an extended play version of a music magazine called Rag Baby in 1965. The magazine, one of the first notable underground publications, was published by Joe and Ed Denson, a one time editor of Sing Out! magazine who became Joe's manager.

In late 1966, Denson got the band its first record contract with New York-based Vanguard Records, and their debut LP, Electric Music for the Mind and Body, came out in April 1967. The album contained some songs that appealed to some of the radical adherents of the political movements of those times, but many that were more general in tone. In fact, though McDonald was against the Vietnam War, in many ways he was a moderate in philosophy. He often performed at the love-ins of the "flower children" of those years, sometimes passing up radical political gatherings to do so. In an effort at "cross-pollenization," he usually appeared at love-in concerts with all kinds of political buttons pinned to an old Army shirt and at mass demonstrations with the band's amplifiers covered with daisies.

His debut LP did reasonably well, thanks to word of mouth promotions, and the song "Not So Sweet Lorraine" became a favorite with fans both in the United States and in Europe. The band's first European tour in December 1967 demonstrated they were a hit with overseas rock fans. In the summer of 1968, McDonald demonstrated anew his nonviolent stand. Though he was supposed to lead the Fish at the Yippie Festival of Life in Chicago during the Democratic convention, he withdrew the Fish at the last moment. As he said at the Chicago conspiracy trial, "The vibrations were so incredibly vicious that I thought it was impossible to avoid violence on the part of the police. . . . there was a possibility that people would follow us to the Festival and be clubbed and maced and tear gassed. . . . I had no choice."

His second LP, which contained "I Feel Like I'm Fixin' to Die Rag," came out in early 1968 and his third, *Together*, in October 1968. Album number two included one of his best-known compositions, "Janis," a moving song about the great Joplin that, as Norma Whittaker pointed out, "turned out to be a tragically prophetic song."

Joe's interest in experimentation was emphasized in his fourth LP, *Here We Go Again*, released in May 1969. Joining him and original Fish members Cohen, Melton, and Hirsh were such varied contributors as members of the Count Basie Band, musicians from the Oakland Symphony, David Getz and Peter Albin of Big Brother and the Holding Company, and Jack Casady from Jefferson Airplane. Some rock critics complained he had retreated from his hard rock posture of previous years to more restrained stylings. His reply was "There is absolutely no reason why electronic music cannot draw on every musical tradition."

The year 1969 was a busy one for McDonald and the Fish. In the summer they were cheered by the half million attendees at the now legendary Woodstock concert. In midyear, Vanguard released *The Greatest Hits of Country Joe & the Fish* and, after a highly successful European tour in the fall, it issued *C.J. Fish*, a live compilation from that tour. In Europe, Joe completed an assignment to write and perform the music for a Danish film based on the Henry Miller novel *Quiet Days in Clichy*.

Joe was beginning to find his band association restrictive. In November 1969, he began to work on his debut solo LP on Vanguard, *Thinking of Woody Guthrie*. The collection suggested he was becoming more interested in his early folk and country roots. After the *Woody* LP, issued in January 1970, he started thinking about a new collection of country-flavored material. During 1970, he went to Nashville to record that material, released under the title *Tonight I'm Singing Just for You*. He continued to add to his solo catalogue throughout the early 1970s with a series of albums that caused one reviewer to write, "To an ever greater extent, he is the closest thing to the Woody Guthrie of the 1970s." His third solo LP was *Hold on—It's Coming;* his fourth, released in late 1971, was based on the Robert W. Service World War I book of poems, *Rhymes of a Red Cross Man;* and his fifth, issued in early 1972, was *Live, Incredible*. Also released in late 1971 was a retrospective album of his band years, *Life and Times of Country Joe & the Fish*.

By then, Joe had essentially turned his back on rock in favor of being a folk music troubadour. The road was a tough one to travel in a period long past folk music's halcyon days. McDonald found himself playing to small audiences in minor halls with a sprinkling of college dates as well. One of his political causes at the time was women's equality. During 1973, for example, he toured with a band called the All Stars whose four members included three women, his song sets typically including several numbers condemning sexism.

In early 1975, he ended his long association with Vanguard, which often had been marked by stormy arguments about musical directions between Joe and that label's executives. His credits on the label comprised sixteen albums, both solo and with the Fish. Later that year he signed with Oakland, California-based Fantasy Records, which issued his first LP on the label, *Paradise with an Ocean View*, and first single, "Breakfast for Two," in late 1975. Joe was still on the label in the late 1970s; in early 1978, Fantasy issued a new LP of his titled *Rock and Roll Music from the Planet Earth*, which featured, significantly, the track "Bring Back the Sixties, Man."

Joe admitted that one of the things hampering his career in the 1970s was his image problem as a "protest music" artist. Since such songs had become somewhat passé with new generations of fans in that decade, that label tended to keep people away from his concerts. As he told an interviewer in the mid-1970s, he felt that it was a bum rap. "People who know my music know that not much of it is protest stuff. Out of a catalogue of about two hundred and fifty songs, I have about ten songs that you could call protest songs. The rest are all kinds of songs."

The image pursued him in private life as well. Many people sought him out to talk about politics rather than music. "I get tired of people bugging me about politics. And they get mad when I don't want to talk about politics. I wish people were more concerned about the music I'm doing now and less about asking me political questions."

Of course, if Joe avoided politics as such, that didn't mean he wasn't involved in causes. During the 1970s, for instance, he worked for conservationist causes such as the Greenpeace Foundation. In connection with those activities, he wrote the song "Save the Whales" in the mid-1970s. He also spoke out for veterans' rights and performed at a Washington, D.C., rally in the spring of 1982 against federal cutbacks in veterans' health care programs.

MCDOWELL, RONNIE: *Singer, guitarist, songwriter, band leader (the Nashville Road). Born Portland, Tennessee, circa 1951.*

As a boy in the 1950s and 1960s, Ronnie McDowell was an ardent fan of Elvis Presley and, as a Tennessean, was heavily influenced by country music. In the end, both facets came together to make him one of the most promising new faces of the late 1970s.

His home town of Portland, Tennessee, which proclaimed itself "Strawberry Capital of the World," essentially was a rural village. Growing up in that farming area, Ronnie roamed the countryside picking berries, swimming, and doing farm chores. He liked music and tried his hand at learning to play the guitar, but didn't think of it as a possible career.

After he left school, he enlisted in the Navy. While stationed in the Pacific, he made his debut as a public performer when he sang at a show attended by Filipinos in Subic Bay. From then on, he entertained whenever he got the chance and, after getting his discharge at the end of the 1960s, decided show business was the place for him. Soon after leaving the service, he formed his band, the Nashville Road, in 1969. The group didn't become overnight national favorites, but found work in a succession of small clubs on the country-music circuit.

For most of the 1970s that was his pattern. McDowell made demonstration records, sometimes of his own compositions, in an effort to gain a recording contract with a major label, but without any breakthroughs. The turning point came the day that Elvis died. On first hearing the news the afternoon of August 16, 1977, he thought it was just a rumor or publicity stunt. But later, while heading home in his car, radio newscasts verified the great artist, indeed, had passed away. As he told an interviewer, he was deeply affected and began to work out a song in Elvis' memory. "The first words just came to me as I drove along and I just started writing the song in my head."

After completing the song, assisted by co-writer L. Morgan, he made a tape that soon led to production of a single. Within a week, it was being distributed all over the United States on the Scorpion label. Called "The King Is Gone," it proved to be an effective tribute to the legendary performer. The single rose to top country chart levels in the early fall of 1977 and Ronnie was asked to appear on many network TV shows, including Dick Clark's *American Bandstand*. Later Clark asked Ronnie to sing the soundtrack on a TV movie about Elvis' life that eventually was shown on ABC-TV in early 1979. Ronnie's soundtrack vocals bore an amazingly close resemblance to those of the late entertainer, though in other recordings McDowell demonstrated he could sing in a style that was his own.

McDowell was quick to prove he was more than a one-song artist. At the end of 1977, he had a new single on the charts, "I Love You, I Love You, I Love You," which remained on the lists into 1978. He added more charted discs on Scorpion later in the year, including, in the fall, "This Is a Holdup." Meanwhile, he was rapidly adding to his concert credits with appearances with his band in major country nightclubs and state and county fair engagements all over the United States and Canada. In 1979, his schedule included a cross-country tour with Conway Twitty and the Bellamy Brothers plus a set given before 82,000 people at the Silverdome in Pontiac, Michigan, which was taped for a CBS-TV special.

He began 1979 with a single of his own composition, "He's a Cowboy from Texas," on the charts. Soon after, he announced he had left Scorpion to sign with Columbia Records' Epic label. One of his goals in his new record affiliation, he told a reporter, was to establish his own identity again. "I'm very grateful for the Elvis thing. It's really done a lot for me, but now I just want to be myself. We're working on a new album here [in Nashville] tonight, and on it, I don't sound like Elvis at all."

His output for Epic got off on the right foot with a hit single of another original song, "World's Most Perfect Woman," in the early summer of 1979. His Epic debut album, *Rockin' You Easy, Lovin' You Slow,* came out in midsummer and proved a promising initial collection. In early 1980, he had another single in top-chart brackets, "Never Seen a Mountain," co-written with Buddy Killen who had produced his 1979 Epic LP. Soon after, his single "Lovin' and Livin'" (co-written with Buddy Killen) was in upper-chart positions and in the fall "Gone" made the top 40. In early 1981 his single "Wandering Eyes" made the lists, reaching the top 10 in February. He closed out 1981 with another charted single on Epic, "Watchin' Girls Go By."

McENTIRE, REBA: *Singer, songwriter. Born Chockie, Oklahoma, March 28, 1954.*

"My Mama—they used to say she coulda been as big as Patsy Cline if she'd had any breaks, but she was teachin' school by the time she was sixteen or seventeen. So she didn't have much of a chance. My father was a world champion steer roper. He rodeoed an awful lot, so

Mama, she taught us how to sing three-part harmony. That was a way she had to pass the time away with us kids. There was my sister Alice, and my brother, Pake, and my little sister Susie. . . . We've always lived right here in southeastern Oklahoma. It's a real small town, little bitty nothin' but people's houses. Daddy owns a 7,000 acre ranch—but we weren't no wealthy West Texas people or nothin.' It's mostly rocky, mountain country, but enough to run a few steers on."

That's the way Reba McEntire described her home region and early upbringing to Jack Hurst of the *Chicago Tribune* (June 14, 1979). The singing lessons she received from her mother often took place on the road when the family traveled from town to town with their father on the rodeo circuit. The first time Reba performed for a wider audience than her family, she recalled, was in the first grade Christmas program in Oklahoma, when she sang "Away in a Manger."

Throughout grade and high school, she continued to add to her performing credits, initially for amateur functions and later on for pay. While she was in the ninth grade, she was part of a country band led by one of her teachers. At other times she was part of an act with her brother and sisters. She told Hurst, "In high school we'd play over at Ardmore in them old clubs. For thirteen dollars apiece, we'd sing from nine 'til three o'clock in the morning."

As might be expected, Reba learned to ride a horse at an early age and later showed promise as a rodeo performer. In her teens, she did some rodeo riding, though many of her visits to various rodeos involved vocalizing. Still, after graduating from high school, she thought she might follow her mother into the teaching profession, enrolling in Southeastern Oklahoma State University as an elementary education major. She was a student there when the rodeo connection changed her career plans.

In 1974, McEntire got the chance to sing the national anthem at the National Rodeo Finals in Oklahoma City. She told Hurst, "At one of the performances a friend of mine who owns a dance place there called me over and said, 'Reba, I'd like you to meet this red-headed guy here: Red Steagall.' Well, about the next month—I was back in school down at Southeastern State at Durant, Oklahoma—Mama got a call from Red. He said, 'Do you think you could get Reba down here to cut a demonstration tape?' Pake had already decided he'd rather rodeo and Susie wasn't even out of high school. So I was the guinea pig."

In time, the demo tapes got Reba's singing activities rolling. During 1975, she was signed by Mercury Records, whose producers and recording engineers were greatly impressed by the range and power of the voice of the lithe five foot six inch-tall girl. For some of her initial recordings, producer Jerry Kennedy reported, he had to use two "limiters"—devices employed to prevent the sound input from causing distortions in the electronic signals—to capture her vocal quality. In most cases, not even one is needed for an artist's voice.

By 1976, McEntire's early singles were starting to show up on lower-chart levels, an example being "I Don't Want to Be a One Night Stand," in the 80s range in May. In 1977, Mercury issued her debut album, *Reba McEntire*, and, soon after, the respect she already had generated among her musical peers was indicated by a chance to debut on the *Grand Ole Opry*.

She had several more modest hits in late 1977 and early 1978, then teamed with Jacky Ward for a series of duets. The first single released by them was "Three Sheets in the Wind/I'd Really Love to See You Tonight," which reached the top 20 in July 1978. Late in 1978, Reba had a solo hit with her single "Last Night, Ev'ry Night." In early 1979, she had another single in upper-chart levels, "Runaway Heart." In August 1979, her second LP, *Out of a Dream*, was issued by Mercury. Included in the LP was a duet with Jacky Ward titled "That Makes Two of Us," which was issued as a single during the summer. At the end of 1979 McEntire's single of "Sweet Dreams" was a chart hit.

In the early 1980s, Reba's name showed up regularly on the bestseller lists. In 1980, her charted Mercury singles included "(I

Still Long to Hold You) Now and Then," "(You Lift Me) Up to Heaven," and "I Can See Forever in Your Eyes." In 1981, her successes included "I Don't Think Love Ought to Be That Way" and "Today All Over Again."

Rodeoing continued to be a major interest of McEntire's life. In 1976 she married a member of the Professional Rodeo Cowboy Association, Charlie Battles, whom she helped run a cattle-ranching operation in their Oklahoma home when they weren't away on their respective tour circuits. "Charlie's always backed me," she told Hurst. "He rodeos, and he knows how hard it is to go off by yourself and have to put up in a hotel. It's rough, but it's worth it. I always thought that if I didn't do it, my talent'd be taken away from me. And the money's good. It's got its bad days, but it pays more than waitin' tables.

"What do I want out of it? Oh, I don't know. I don't wanta do it the rest of my life, to get big and then go downhill just straggling along. I'd like to get popular enough to win a few awards, maybe be the best in the business for a while. Then if somebody came along and took my place, that'd be fine. I'd step aside and let some other person have a turn."

MCEUEN, JOHN: *Singer, banjoist, fiddler, guitarist, mandolinist. Born Long Beach, California, December 19, 1945.*

In the 1960s and 1970s, it wasn't uncommon for a member of a well-known pop band to also carve out a successful solo career as an adjunct to group activities. So it was with John McEuen, long-time mainstay of the Nitty Gritty Dirt Band who, when not touring or recording with that folk-country rock group, often was appearing by himself anywhere from small clubs and college auditoriums to places like Los Angeles' Universal Amphitheatre (where he opened for the rock band Heart in the summer of 1977).

McEuen was born and raised in Long Beach, California, and learned a range of stringed instruments in his youth. During his teens, he was influenced both by the rise of rock, as personified by Elvis and Jerry Lee Lewis, and the folk music boom of the late 1950s and early 1960s. Having some impact on his interest in making music a career was his older brother, William, who was a disc jockey for a while, then went on to become a respected producer of R&B and rock artists before moving into management. Bill handled several promising rock bands in the mid-1960s before shifting his primary emphasis to a Long Beach-based, folk-oriented rock group that several of John McEuen's school acquaintances started and that John soon joined. That group, originally called the Illegitimate Jug Band (because it played jug music without a jug player), became the Nitty Gritty Dirt Band.

Under Bill McEuen's direction, the group became an important factor in the pop field with a long string of chart hits after the success of the 1967 single on Liberty Records (later United Artists). John McEuen played on that recording and still was an integral part of band dynamics at the start of the 1980s (by which time the group had shortened its name to he Dirt Band). (See Nitty Gritty Dirt Band entry.)

During the 1970s, his instrumental skills were recognized by many of his peers in the country and country-rock field. As a result, he had the chance to support many major names when he could fit it into his schedule. Among those with whom he recorded during those years were Carter Family immortal Mother Maybelle (John and the Dirt Band paid tribute to the Carters in the 1972 LP *Will the Circle Be Unbroken*) and the great Merle Travis. He also played banjo on Michael Murphey's *Carolina in the Pines* and supported the Marshall Tucker Band on the LP *Long Hard Ride*.

In 1974, John began to do a limited number of solo concerts, mostly in smaller venues. As he told a reporter, "I want to play at sort of out-of-the-way places where I know I'll find people I like."

Although he played all kinds of instruments in those shows, he tended to stress banjo. He told David McCumber of the El Paso *Herald Post* (July 13, 1977) that a prime reason why he inaugurated solo work was that "I want to see the banjo become accepted for what it is—a versatile

instrument that can be an integral part of a piece of music. I don't want people to say, 'Oh, there's that corny country banjo' when I play. I want it to be right there. I like doing things that I just can't do when I'm doing a show with the band. I can play some of the old things on the banjo, some of the classical things, pick up the guitar or mandolin and do a song when I feel like it."

In a typical show, he might start with some bluegrass banjo, switch to some wild fiddle tunes, then slow the pace to perform a piece by Bach or some harpsichord music on banjo or one of the other instruments he can play. A highlight of his act in the late 1970s was a seriocomic arrangement of "Dueling Banjos" with a tape-recorded sequence to provide the second five-string. Putting his cowboy hat on the tape player, he would turn it on and the player alternately would issue humorous challenges to McEuen's banjo talents, then provide a mechanical alter ego for swirling dual banjo passages.

McEuen restricted his solo efforts to a dozen or two a year and devoted most of his other musical attention to Dirt Band chores. Home for John and the group in the 1970s was Idaho Springs, Colorado, where most of their recordings were made in their own studio. In 1977, he went with the Dirt Band on an extensive tour of the Soviet Union under State Department auspices. He told McCumber, "It was great to give the people something they really wanted, bypassing the government—something almost illegal for them. It was a great experience."

After he got back to the United States, he was off again on some solo engagements. The reason, he stressed, was that "I want to make my mark, you know. I want to hit a few licks that nobody else has."

McGARRIGLE, KATE AND ANNA: *Vocal duo, songwriters. Born Montreal, Quebec, Canada, early 1940s.*

An amazing number of music critics, both in the United States and in other countries, included the debut 1976 album of the McGarrigle sisters, *Kate and Anna McGarrigle*, in their ten-best albums of the year. This unabashed folk collection was bracketed with such unlikely list-fellows as the Rolling Stones *Black and Blue,* Bob Seeger's *Night Moves,* Rod Stewart's *A Night on the Town,* and Stevie Wonder's *Songs in the Key of Life.*

John Rockwell of *The New York Times* declared that "this folkish debut disk was the most charming, purely beautiful and sentimentally moving record of 1976." In England, *Melody Maker* enthused that "their astonishing debut signals a vote for virtually old-fashioned musical virtues in a year when musicianship and integrity were increasingly disregarded . . . qualities stressed by the use of such 'rustic' instrumentation as button accordions, fiddles, and banjos." The album itself displayed the many influences on which the McGarrigle's drew, from the folk music of their native French Canada (reflected in "Complainte pour Ste. Catherine") to blues, country, American folk song, and even Bahamian material ("Traveling on for Jesus").

Overnight the McGarrigles' names were placed on a level with such other Canadian folk artists as Gordon Lightfoot, Joni Mitchell (at least the folk-flavored Joni Mitchell of the 1960s), and Ian and Sylvia. Yet it was not the sudden rush to fame that it appeared to be. In fact, the McGarrigles had been active in folk music well before people like Lightfoot and Mitchell gained international attention, although the sisters didn't enter the limelight themselves until roughly a decade after those stars.

The McGarrigles grew up in a devoutly religious home where certain secular forms of music also were admired. There were a number of folk instruments in their home which they were encouraged to play and they also received classical music training. Their early schooling was in a convent school in the French Canadian village of St. Sauveur-des-Monts, Quebec, and they later went on to study at the university level.

As teenagers, the McGarrigle children were impressed with the folk music boom taking place in the United States in the mid- and late-1950s, with Pete Seeger and

the Weavers particular favorites. The girls formed their own singing group to perform folk songs that were popular at the time and also began experimenting with original compositions of their own. The first alignment came about in 1958, a trio comprising Kate, Anna, and a third sister, Jane. After a while, Jane left and her place was taken by Michele Forest. In the 1960s, Kate and Anna helped assemble a folk quartet called the Mountain City Four, whose other members were Peter Weldon and Jack Nissenson. None of those groups made the McGarrigles household names, either in Canada or in the United States, though they did gain experience performing in coffee houses, college halls, and occasional folk festivals. At times in the 1960s, both Kate and Anna went separate ways, sometimes doing solo singing work, at others concentrating on school or writing.

Although not much forward progress seemed to be occurring in terms of commercial success, the sisters were building up associations and contacts that were to play a role in their 1970s activities. In 1971, Kate made a number of appearances, including one at the Philadelphia Folk Festival, with singer and cello player Rosa Baran, that won some attention from folk enthusiasts. After that, Kate went back to doing occasional solo concerts over the next few years. During 1974 and 1975, Anna helped revive their duet efforts from time to time. Meanwhile, other things were happening both personally and creatively. The sisters' songwriting collaboration was resulting in material that was finding its way to other artists in the pop and folk fields. Besides that, the sisters were providing harmony backing vocals for Kate's husband, Loudon Wainwright III, the kind of work that often paves the way for future recording contracts.

A major milestone was Linda Ronstadt's selection of one of their songs for a new album she was preparing for Capitol. The song, "Heart like a Wheel," helped Linda accelerate toward stardom. Both the song and the album of that title rose to number one on U.S. pop charts. Even as that was going on, more long-time friends or admirers were recording other McGarrigle songs. Among them was Maria Muldaur, who included "Work Song" and "Cool River" in her new solo LPs on Warner Bros.

All of that wasn't lost on the Warner executives. The McGarrigles were signed in 1975 and went into the studios to work on their debut LP. That album, issued in January 1976, still ranks as one of the best folk releases of the mid-1970s. Unfortunately, it wasn't commercially successful, partly because Kate was pregnant when it came out, which prevented the sisters from touring in support of it. Later in the year, after the baby was born, they were able to organize a tour of England in which they sang such numbers as "Foolish You," "Kiss and Say Goodbye," their version of "Heart like a Wheel," "Blues in D," "Talk to Me of Mendocino," "Go Leave," "Complainte pour Ste. Catherine," and "Travelling on for Jesus." The tour made them well known there, though they remained in relative obscurity in the United States.

The sisters worked on their second album in late 1976 and early 1977. Called *Dancer with Bruised Knees*, it was released in February 1977. Perhaps because of the novelty of a folk record making top-10 lists it won more attention from fans, but it received less acclaim from reviewers. It did represent a good addition to the sisters' repertoire, however. In October 1978, the McGarrigles' third LP, *Pronto Monto*, was released, an album that included seven new songs by the sisters and several by such other writers as Galt MacDermot, Dana Lanken, and Charlie Singleton.

MCGEE BROTHERS: *Singers, instrumentalists. Both born Franklin, Tennessee; Sam McGee, May 1, 1894; Kirk McGee, November 4, 1899. Sam McGee died Franklin, Tennessee, August 21, 1975.*

At the Fourth Annual Country Music Fan Fair Reunion Show in Nashville, Tennessee, on June 14, 1975, one of the acts that awoke fond memories in many old-time fans was the Fruit Jar Drinkers. The group harked back to the very early days of the *Grand Ole Opry* and two of its four members, Sam and Kirk McGee (the oth-

ers were guitarist Hubert Gregory and Golden Stewart on bass), were closely linked with the work of the first great *Opry* star, Uncle Dave Macon. In their own right, guitarist Sam and fiddler Kirk represented some of the finest instrumental ability ever to grace the country field.

Like many country artists, they were born and raised on a family farm, in this case near Franklin, Tennessee. In fact, they continued to work on that farm throughout their lives, despite the demands of performing careers, and it was there that Sam died soon after the 1975 Fan Fair appearance. Their father was an accomplished fiddler and they were exposed to music almost from the time they were born. As soon as they could hold banjos, they were working with their father at local gatherings, though later they were to choose other instruments.

In their teens they played banjos at dances for as little as ten cents apiece. As Jon Pankake wrote in *Sing Out!* (November 1964, p. 47), they expanded their string abilities at this time to include the effects of Negro syncopated music. The boys had the chance to observe this style when the family moved for a short period of time to the central Tennessee town of Perry. As Sam told Pankake, the Negro rhythms "would just ring in my head."

A turning point in the brothers' lives came in 1923, when they heard Uncle Dave Macon perform in the first professional show they had ever seen. They were so enthusiastic about his flamboyant singing and playing that they determined to try to join his troupe. After persevering, they finally gained his approval in 1924 and accompanied him on the first of many tours on the country-music circuit. When Uncle Dave joined the *Opry* in 1926, the McGees were part of his first band on the radio show. Among the other names Macon called his group, the Fruit Jar Drinkers gained the most renown. (There is a certain amount of confusion here because for a time there was another group on the *Opry* also called Fruit Jar Drinkers.)

The career of the McGee Brothers, whose traditional style of playing made folk experts as well as country enthusiasts lay claim to them, flourished for many decades, both in concert with the career of Uncle Dave and on a solo level. Over the years, when they were making recordings with Macon they usually made some as a separate act, sometimes with Uncle Dave acting as their backing musician rather than the other way around.

The first recording session of Sam Mc-Gee with Macon took place in New York from April 14 to 17, 1926. Among the songs they placed on vinyl were such favorite numbers as "Whoop 'Em Up Cindy," "Way Down the Old Plank Road," "The Death of John Henry," and "Late Last Night When My Willie Came Home."

During May 7-11, 1927, both Sam and Kirk worked with Macon and another legendary performer, fiddler Mazy Todd, in what Ralph Rinzler describes "as some of the best examples of string band ensemble playing ever recorded. Uncle Dave seems to revel in the reedy, yet elegant fiddling of Mazy Todd and Kirk McGee. He crows and hollers with joy when Sam momentarily abandons his guitar bass line to beat out a clog-rhythm on the top of his then new Martin. The ensemble singing is unique on the secular songs. Uncle Dave sticks to the melody, Kirk departs from unison and moves to tenor at the end of each line, and Sam barks out his own distinctive bass line which includes a winning combination of unison and bass harmony notes."

During those sessions, the McGee Brothers and Todd recorded three songs, one with Uncle Dave playing supporting banjo. Kirk and Sam's own output in those 1927 sessions also included nine duets.

One of the more notable late 1920s sessions took place in Chicago on July 25-26, 1928. For those recordings, Sam used a very unusual instrument called a banjo-guitar he had picked up in the mid-1920s in Birmingham, Alabama. Discussing the sessions in liner notes for the 1966 Decca *Uncle Dave Macon* memorial album, Ralph Rinzler writes, " 'From Earth to Heaven,' 'Buddy Won't You Roll Down the Line,' and 'I'm the Child to Fight,' among others, were recorded as five- and six-string banjo

duets . . . probably the only examples of this instrumental combination recorded in country music. Sam also recorded 'Easy Rider' and 'Chevrolet Car' as solos on the six-string banjo."

The McGees, who often had solo spots on the *Opry* from the late 1920s on, in 1930 formed a new alignment called the Dixie-liners in which they joined forces with fiddler Arthur Smith. The act became one of the most popular on the *Opry* in the 1930s and made the team a favorite with country fans when it played local venues and country fairs throughout the South. Smith left in the late 1930s, but later rejoined the McGees for several appearances in the mid-1960s, including a 1965 appearance at the Newport Folk Festival in Rhode Island that won a standing ovation.

The McGees for a time teamed up with a comedy act called "Sara and Sally" at the end of the 1930s and in the early 1940s. After that, they became a featured part of Bill Monroe's show, performing with the Blue Grass Boys and also doing their own separate segment. They traveled throughout the United States with the Father of Bluegrass, typically finishing each Monroe stage appearance with a twenty-minute old-time country-music songfest.

In the 1950s, the McGees worked primarily as a separate brother act, as headliners on the country-music circuit. They remained *Opry* standbys, mainly as members of the Fruit Jar Drinkers. As the folk movement gathered momentum in the late 1950s, interest in the McGees arose among younger elements of the pop audience. The brothers were asked to appear in folk festivals around the nation and to play before audiences on many college campuses. That pattern continued into the mid-1960s, when rock once more pushed folk music to a subsidiary role.

The McGees, though, had remained charter members of the country field and held forth on many *Opry* programs as they had been doing for decades. In the 1970s, the brothers were still active in country music, but on a much less hectic level than in times past. Their musical ability, as audiences at the 1975 Fan Fair discovered, remained exceptional despite their advanced years. Unfortunately, their long association was ended when Sam was killed while working on his farm at the age of eighty-one.

Though the McGees made many recordings during their long career, little or nothing was available in the 1960s and 1970s other than individual tracks on "old time country" retrospective albums. The folk boom resulted in some releases, such as the 1965 Folkways LP, *McGee Brothers and Arthur Smith*, but those too were discontinued by the 1970s.

McGHEE, BROWNIE: *Singer, guitarist, songwriter. Born Knoxville, Tennessee, November 30, 1914.*

One of the great folk and blues artists, Brownie McGhee is inextricably linked with his long-time partner, Sonny Terry. But Brownie and Sonny both had long careers in music before joining forces, and, even over the decades of their close collaboration, they stressed the importance of each having his identity.

Brownie's early years were spent on the family farm near Kingsport, Tennessee, in a musical environment. His father, George, was an excellent singer-guitarist who often teamed with Brownie's uncle, John Evans, a fiddler, to play for local parties and dances. Even when George gave up the farm for a time to earn a living in various mill towns in eastern Tennessee, he often found time to join Evans for performing dates.

When young Walter (Brownie's given name) was four, he was stricken with polio, from which he recovered though he has walked with a limp ever since. His illness ruled out working long hours on farm chores in his youth (something his younger brother, Granville "Sticks" McGhee, later a professional guitarist, couldn't escape). Later on that left more time for Brownie to indulge his interest in music.

Even as a small child, he loved to listen to his father, uncle, and friends play blues and gospel music. When he accompanied them occasionally to performances, he got the chance to learn some of the basics of playing stringed instruments. His father

taught him some of the skills involved in playing guitar and, before he was eight, he also had his own banjo to practice on, a home-made gift from Uncle John. He started picking out music on the piano as well.

The family settled in Lenoir City, Tennessee, for several years, where Brownie completed elementary school. His musical endeavors included playing the organ in Solomon Temple Baptist Church and singing in the choir at the Sanctified Baptist Church.

Next stop for the McGhees was Marysville, Tennessee, where Brownie started high school. After finishing his freshman year, he spent the summer performing at resorts in the Smoky Mountains. In 1928, when he was fourteen, he decided to drop out of school and earn whatever he could as a singer and guitarist. For the rest of his teens, he drifted across Tennessee, working in medicine and minstrel shows and, for a while, with the Hagg Carnival.

In the early 1930s, his family needed his help back on the Kingsport farm. For several years he stayed home, pitching in on farm work, though he still found time to sing with a gospel quartet, the Golden Voices. He grew restless of rural life and, when he got the chance to head to Knoxville in the mid-1930s, he did so and formed a number of small bands that worked local events. But things got tight in the city in the late 1930s and Brownie went back to the hustler's life of playing for coins on street corners. He started in Asheville, North Carolina, then made his way to Winston-Salem, where he formed a team with harmonica player Jordan Webb. Word reached them that things were good for itinerant musicians in Burlington and Durham. While playing in those towns, Brownie became friends with such skilled performers as Blind Boy Fuller, Sonny Terry, then playing harp with Fuller, and Bull City Red. More important, they impressed Okeh Records talent scout J. B. Long with their ability, and Long offered to pay the duo's way to Chicago to make some recordings.

McGhee's first single was "Me and My Dog," which was pressed as the reverse

Barbara Mandrell

Country Joe McDonald

Roger Miller

Anne Murray

Bill Monroe

Maria Muldaur

The Marshall Tucker Band

side to Blind Boy Fuller's "Bus Rider Blues." He and Webb also made a number of other recordings in those initial sessions.

The Okeh schedule for June 1940 called for Blind Boy Fuller to make a number of recordings. Fuller went to Chicago, but a kidney infection, which eventually caused his death, kept him from going into the studios. Long then turned to Brownie and suggested he write a song in praise of Fuller that he also would record. McGhee complied and cut the song, "The Death of Blind Boy Fuller," using Fuller's own steel-bodied guitar. The artist's name on the record, instead of McGhee, was listed as Blind Boy Fuller No. 2. That was one of many pseudonyms under which Brownie was to record during his career. Some of the others were Spider Sam, Big Tom Collins, Henry Johnson, Tennessee Gable, and Blind Boy Williams.

After Blind Boy Fuller died, Long decided Sonny Terry and Brownie would be a good combination. They debuted in the early 1940s at a blues concert at the Riverside Stadium in Washington, D.C., where they shared the bill with Leadbelly. They didn't decide to make it a permanent team right away. However, after they recorded "Workingman's Blues" together in 1942, they agreed to make it a regular alignment.

The two moved to the New York area in the mid-1940s and soon became one of the most popular acts on the folk and blues circuit. Besides working with Leadbelly and other famous blues musicians, they often appeared with people like Pete Seeger, Woody Guthrie, and the Weavers. From that time throughout the 1950s, 1960s, and 1970s, the twosome appeared in countless coffee houses, clubs, and folk festivals across the United States and the world. In the 1960s and 1970s, they performed on dozens of major network TV shows and were practically institutions at the annual Newport Folk Festival. During the 1960s, they also made several national tours working with Harry Belafonte.

Not that they were anywhere near inseparable. Although they cut dozens of albums together, each sometimes made solo recordings under various nom de plumes.

Brownie also worked as a member of several Broadway shows, including a role in Tennessee Williams' *Cat on a Hot Tin Roof* and Langston Hughes' *Simply Heavenly.*

McGhee and Terry, together and separately, recorded for a dizzying array of labels over the years. Their work appeared, among others, on such labels as Folkways, Savoy, Alert, Decca, Jade, King, Verve, Bluesville, Main, and Prestige. Among their releases were *Blues, Traditional Blues, Blues and Folksongs* (1958); *On the Road with Burris* (1959); *Brownie's Blues, Blues and Folk* (1960); *Blues Around My Head* (1960); *At the Second Fret* (1963); *Blues Is My Companion* (1961); *Back Country Blues, Terry and McGhee, Just a Closer Walk with Thee, Blues and Shouts, At Sugar Hill* (1962); *Down Home Blues* (1963); *Work, Play, Faith, Fun* (1960); *At the Bunkhouse, Home Town Blues* (1965); and *Guitar Highway* (1966). In the 1970s, the duo recorded for Fantasy Records, Their LPs available on the label at the start of the 1980s included *Back in New Orleans* and *Midnight Special.* Other LPs still in print at the start of the 1980s were: *Brownie McGhee and Sonny Terry Sing, Brownie McGhee Sings the Blues, Preachin' the Blues;* on Folkways Records, *Live At the 2nd Fret* and *The Best of Brownie McGhee and Sonny Terry* Prestige.

Brownie discussed his philosophy of music and the blues with Michael Brooks for *Guitar Player* magazine (October 1973). He told Brooks, "My definition of the blues is 'truth.' Man being true to himself and being true to his listeners when he's performing or singing any song that the people consider the blues. Blues is words which have been hooked onto black people so long—but you don't have to be lonely to sing the blues. Just be honest with yourself as you tell your stories of the past and present, with a smile on your face. I'm not ashamed of my past, and that's why I say blues is truth, because I tell it like it is. I don't mess it up at all. Blues is my life, my living, my joy, my everything. And I can live with it."

He argued against arbitrary typecasting of blues artists. "A man could come from Mississippi and hang out around Texas for a while and he'd get marked 'Texas blues.'

I'm from Tennessee so automatically I can't play slide guitar, according to those people, because I've got to come from Mississippi to play slide. They mark people. I'm marked as a blues singer, a folk singer.

"Personally I mark myself as an entertainer and I don't care whether it's blues, folk, gospel, spiritual, jazz or what. I tell stories, and I'm an entertainer. I don't go out and tell people I'm a blues singer, because I could be wrong to them."

McGUINN, ROGER: *Singer, guitarist, songwriter, band leader (the Byrds). Born Chicago, Illinois, July 13, 1942.*

When folk music began to pale as a commercial force in the face of the British-spearheaded rock resurgence, artists like Bob Dylan and the Byrds held onto the attention of at least part of the pop audience by blending elements of folk with rock. The man who was the driving force behind the Byrds and kept that group as an important contributor to the music scene for almost a decade was Roger McGuinn. At the end of the 1970s, he was part of a new alignment of one-time Byrds stars called McGuinn, Clark and Hillman.

McGuinn was born to parents with an active interest in writing and public relations, who gave him the name James. He changed his name to Roger in 1968 as part of his conversion to a religious movement. During his early years, he was constantly on the move because his parents' activities required them to travel widely. For instance, at one point he accompanied them around the country during a publicity tour for their best-selling book, *Parents Can Win.*

Like many of high school age, Roger was enormously impressed with the rise of Elvis Presley in the mid-1950s. He hadn't really thought much about playing an instrument before that, but Elvis' music caused him to ask his parents to give him a guitar for his fourteenth birthday. However, though his first inclination was toward rock, he soon switched allegiance to folk music. As he recalled, "One of my high school teachers knew Bob Gibson [the folk music performer] and had him play for the class. I'd heard folksingers before, the Weavers and such, but I was really impressed by Gibson. I began to listen to folk music and some of the traditional blues people."

Roger not only taught himself guitar, but started to learn five-string banjo at the Old Town Music School in Chicago, in the late 1950s. "I had to quit because the lessons cost ten bucks apiece—I was still in school. I finally tried playing in a small club and one of the Limelighters heard me. He offered me a job backing them which I turned down until I graduated from high school. There was about a ten-minute lag between my graduating from high school and becoming a professional musician. I got a telegram from the Limelighters and they hired me to work at the Ash Grove [in Los Angeles] as an accompanist."

After close to two months with them, McGuinn moved to San Francisco, where he did some solo work in local folk clubs. The Chad Mitchell Trio was looking for a replacement and Roger got the chance to audition for them in New York, which led to an association that lasted for two and a half years. As a Trio member, he played in almost every major U.S. city as well as some overseas locales and recorded several albums.

He left the Trio in the early 1960s and served as lead guitarist for a folk segment of Bobby Darin's cabaret act for a time. In 1963, he settled in as a session musician-arranger and occasional songwriter for the New York folk music scene, often taking part in programs in Greenwich Village folk clubs. Among the artists he either worked or became friends with were Bob Dylan, Judy Collins, and a duo known as Tom and Jerry. He helped prepare some material and also accompanied the latter twosome, who are better known as Simon and Garfunkel. "I worked with Judy Collins on her third album. It was my first chance to really stretch out and try to do something. . . . She chose the material and we worked together to arrange things. I never toured with her though."

In mid-1964, McGuinn got the call to come to Los Angeles to take part in a new group being assembled there, the band soon to take shape as the Byrds. Although McGuinn wasn't the original catalyst for the group, he soon became it's central figure. He chose the name, for example, and his lead guitar work helped provide the ringing sound that was to be the group's trademark. (For more details, see the Byrds entry.) The group included three other folk music alumni, Gene Clark, David Crosby, and Chris Hillman, plus rock drummer Michael Clarke.

The Byrds signed with Columbia Records in September 1964 and started working on their initial recordings. One of the first results was the group's version of Dylan's "Mr. Tambourine Man," released in March 1965 and a top-10 hit around the world a few months later. The group solidified its rapidly rising status in the rock field with its debut LP, *The Byrds,* which came out in August 1965 and in a short period of time earned the group a gold-record award. Although only an indifferent in-person act for much of its early phase, the group kept turning out inspired new recordings that kept it in the forefront of the folk-rock movement from 1965 through 1967.

Ironically, even though McGuinn held the band together through numerous personnel changes from the mid-1960s and early 1970s and inspired steady improvement in its stage presence during the latter part of Byrds history, the band's recording success waned. The group continued to have an impact on developments in pop music even if its prestige with the mass audience slipped. For instance, in some tracks of *The Notorious Byrd Brothers* and particularly the 1968 LP *Sweetheart of the Rodeo,* the Byrds pioneered the country-rock field and were a forerunner of such late 1960s–early 1970s bands as the Flying Burritos, Poco, and the Eagles. During the last four years of the Byrds existence, McGuinn had honed their musicianship to where they could play rings around the organization of the early years and expanded their repertoire to all manner of rock stylings, but they never did regain their one-time prominence.

During 1972, McGuinn finally closed down the Byrds as a continuing organiza-

tion. He had become increasingly interested in solo work in the early 1970s, and for a number of years in the middle of the decade he concentrated on that aspect of his career. He turned out a number of LPs that are among some of his best work, though they never achieved mass audience acceptance. These releases include *Roger McGuinn, Peace on You, Roger McGuinn and Band, Cardiff Rose,* and *Thunderbyrd.* He toured widely in support of them during the mid-1970s, mostly playing medium-size halls or smaller clubs.

Toward the end of that phase in 1976–77, Roger became part of the Bob Dylan Rolling Thunder Revue, which was one of the major concert attractions of the time. Among those who shared the stage with him and Dylan were such major artists as Joan Baez, Joni Mitchell, and Mick Ronson. Interest in the series ran high and McGuinn's guitar work often won rousing ovations from tens of thousands of people who crowded into large stadiums to catch the show.

In 1978, McGuinn and two other original Byrds, Gene Clark and Chris Hillman, decided to form a new band called McGuinn, Clark and Hillman. By year end they were in the Criteria Studios in Miami working on their debut LP on Capitol Records. This time, Roger told a reporter, the personality clashes that brought major problems in the mid-1960s were past.

"We have a lot of the old rapport and memories. We've taken what we've learned and applied it. But we've all grown up and it's easier to work together. We're more accommodating. Patience is the key word."

The trio also hoped to develop a sound different from the Byrds. "The track on one of Gene's songs that might have come out 1960ish and Byrdsish sounds more like Steely Dan or the Average White Band. That gets me off."

The debut LP, *McGuinn, Clark and Hillman,* when it came out in February 1979, reflected the change in emphasis to some extent, though the group would not be mistaken for a heavy metal rock group. In early 1979 concerts, however, audiences tended to cheer loudest for the old Byrds replays, which indicated that McGuinn and company had an uphill fight to make a new way for themselves. On the other hand, the LP remained on pop hit charts for months proving there still was an audience interested in what they might offer. By 1980, though, Clark had decided to stop touring, and the second LP was attributed to McGuinn and Hillman *with* Gene Clark (who provided only two songs for the collection).

McLEAN, DON: *Singer, guitarist, banjoist, songwriter. Born New Rochelle, New York, October 2, 1945.*

The runaway bestseller of 1972 was Don McLean's "American Pie," which reached the number-one spot on the national U.S. charts as a single and as the title song of an album. Had there been separate folk charts, it would have reached the top there as well, since the song was an amalgam of folk and rock, a nine-minute-long summation of much of the currents of the 1960s decade. The starting point was the death of rock star Buddy Holly in 1959 ("I was a lonely teenage bouncin' buck/With a pink carnation and a pickup truck/But I knew I was out of luck/The day the music died"), presented as a symbol of the sorrows and occasional joys of the next ten years (the lines "I can't remember if I cried/When I read about his widowed bride," for instance, probably are a reference to President Kennedy's death).

"American Pie" proved a mixed blessing for McLean. It catapulted him to national prominence. But it also set a pinnacle so high that he couldn't seem to reach it again in later years. He turned out some interesting work, mainly in a folk vein, but wherever he went "American Pie" tended to overshadow his new offerings, at least until the early 1980s.

McLean, whose ancestors in the United States date back to colonial days, was born and raised in the New York suburb of New Rochelle, where he attended elementary and high school. His idol was Buddy Holly. "He was the person that made me learn the guitar. I loved the way he played and thought for a while that I might die playing rock 'n' roll, but by the time I was

eighteen [in 1963], I was deeply into folk music."

In high school he tended to be a loner, looking askance at schoolmates who "were afraid to strike out on their own and do what they really felt like doing." This attitude affected his approach to music. For a time as a teenager he played in school groups, but decided to restrict himself to solo work at fifteen because "I didn't like the problems of working with other musicians" or "being saddled with a lot of equipment."

He completed his precollege studies at Iona Prep School, a Catholic institution connected with Iona College in New Rochelle, and enrolled at Villanova University. He only stayed six months, the urge to make his way as a musician becoming too strong to deny. He began playing in coffee houses and small clubs in such upstate New York cities as Elmira and Binghamton, then moved on to work larger cities, performing in New York nightspots like the Bitter End and Gaslight and other clubs in Philadelphia, Baltimore, and several Canadian cities. During his travels, he became friends with such folk luminaries as Lee Hays, Josh White, Brownie McGhee, and Sonny Terry.

For a time, several years after leaving Villanova, he took night courses at Iona College, concentrating on philosophy and theology. "I took all kinds of stuff I knew I would never be exposed to again because I planned to be in music for the rest of my life. I knew I was going to make a living at music for the simple reason that I couldn't stand to wear a suit or do a day job."

In the mid-1960s, while continuing to play folk clubs all over the Northeast and Midwest, often hitchhiking from one town to the next, he found renewed interest in rock caused by the emergence of the Beatles. In addition, "I became a Stones freak for a time and I also dig James Brown [soul artist]—his band is fine."

In 1966, he began performing summers at the Cafe Lena in Saratoga Springs, New York, a folk art center run by Lena Spencer. The association proved particularly valuable two years later when the New York State Council of the Arts asked Lena to recommend someone to give free concerts in a special program. He recalled, "It was the summer of 1968 and I was broke. Lena got me a job with the state, figuring I'd make a good bureaucrat. I had to play in fifty river communities (billed as the Hudson River Troubadour), three times a day for a month or more while the state paid me $200 a week. Man, they got their money's worth. I sang about forty songs a day, sometimes sixty. That's cheaper than the juke box."

Those efforts, plus Don's activities on behalf of restoring the Hudson's ecology, brought him in contact with Pete Seeger. Seeger contacted him to join in the 1969 cruise of the sloop "Clearwater," a voyage from South Bristol, Maine, to New York City, undertaken by a group of folk singers to enlist public support against industrial pollution of the rivers. The project resulted in a National Educational Television special, "The Sloop at Nyack." Besides performing on that show, Don also edited a book about the voyage, published as *Songs and Sketches of the First Clearwater Crew*. Seeger, meanwhile, had become one of McLean's major enthusiasts, calling Don "the finest singer and songwriter I have met since Bob Dylan." Following the Clearwater activity, Don became a familiar figure at many folk concerts, appearing with people like Arlo Guthrie, Janis Ian, Lee Hays, and Seeger.

But he was finding favor with the broad spectrum of pop artists as well. At the start of the 1970s, he shared bills with Blood, Sweat & Tears, Laura Nyro, Dionne Warwick, and the Nitty Gritty Dirt Band. He had built up a repertoire of original songs besides continuing to try his hand at prose and poetry. He also was interested in films, working in 1971 with Bob Elfstrum, who helped prepare the Academy Award-nominated *Other Voices*, a movie in which twenty-five of Don's original songs were used.

But while many well-known entertainers thought highly of Don's growing body of songs, he was consistently frustrated in his efforts to place it with a record company. He approached twenty-seven different firms with tapes of what was to be his de-

but LP, *Tapestry*, and was turned down by all of them. Finally a small firm called Mediarts put it out in 1970 with very little fanfare and very little notice from the public.

McLean toured the country in support of *Tapestry*, singing in clubs and coffee houses from coast to coast. The tour didn't help sales much, but during his travels he began slowly assembling *American Pie*. He finished it in early 1971. By then United Artists was interested in him and gave him the go-ahead to work on a new album. The song debuted long before the LP came out, being presented on station WPLJ-FM in New York the day Bill Graham closed his rock theater Fillmore East.

The single and album came out late in 1971 and both were on the charts by year end. In February 1972, both reached number one; McClean was the rage of pop music all over the world. Soon the attention given his work caused a second song from *American Pie*, one about Vincent Van Gogh ("Vincent") to become an international hit. (Later, when the Van Gogh Museum opened in Amsterdam, the song was played at the inaugural ceremonies and still is played at the entrance area.)

McLean soon became unhappy about the whirlwind success of *American Pie*. It had, he believed, caused people to overlook the messages in such other compositions as "Three Flights Up," "And I Love You So," and "Tapestry." He also felt most people had missed what he considered the song's main theme "which isn't nostalgia, but that commercialism is the death of inspiration. If only one person can relate to it on that level, I'll be satisfied."

Much of his bitterness colored his next album, *Don McLean*, reflected in the strident tone of songs like "The Pride Parade" and "Narcissisma." The LP did provide him with another hit single, though, the fast moving "Dreidel." Some of that song's words were far from optimistic: "My world is a constant confusion/My mind is prepared to attack/My past a persuasive illusion/I'm watchin' the future—it's black."

For close to a year, McLean's state of

mind prevented him from writing any new material. He also sharply curtailed his concert work. However, a friend from Cafe Lena days, Frank Wakefield, helped restore McLean's interest in music. The result was an album called *Playin' Favorites*, which contained no originals but various folk, country, and bluegrass songs that appealed to Wakefield and McLean. Well-received tours of Europe and Australia added to Don's rebound, and he finally set to work on his next LP, *Homeless Brother* (the title sings the praises of the American hobo), which came out in 1974. The album was dedicated to folk music luminary Lee Hays, whom Pete Seeger had introduced to Don some years before. Hays and McLean had collaborated in adapting and arranging the traditional song "Babylon" for Don's *American Pie* album.

But though Don was writing again, he had lost the attention of much of his audience. His record sales declined and his association with UA came to an end. For two years little was heard from him; then in 1976, he signed with Clive Davis' new label, Arista. Late in the year he appeared in clubs across the United States in his first concerts since 1974. Among his material were two new songs, "Echo" and "Color TV Blues," which were included in his first Arista release, *Prime Time*, in 1977. Don toured in support of the album that year, but it was not a collection up to his earlier standards. He obviously continued to bear some of the scars from his earlier brush with being atop the musical pedestal and at one concert was so angered at the way record industry people talked to each other during his performance that he angrily suggested it was a waste of time playing for them. Emphasizing that point, he did not return for an encore, thus leaving out the awaited presentation of his gem—and personal bane—"American Pie."

After his career languished in the closing years of the 1970s, McLean scored a comeback in the early 1980s with a new association with Millennium Records. His debut LP on the new label, *Chain Lightning* (distributed by RCA Records), provided the hit single "Crying," which reached upper levels on both pop and country charts

in 1981. In his concert tour supporting the album he demonstrated new confidence and maturity, projecting a gracious and caring image to his audiences.

When his second Millennium LP, *Believers*, came out in October 1981, it was dedicated to the memory of Lee Hays, who had died earlier in the year. His first single from the album was "Castles in the Air," which had been the opening song on Don's first album release in 1970, *Tapestry*, for which Hays had written the liner notes. Appropriately, the 1981 single became McLean's second singles hit in his revitalized career.

MCMICHEN, CLAYTON "PAPPY": *Singer, fiddler, songwriter, comedian, band leader. Born Allatoona, Georgia, January 26, 1900; died Battletown; Kentucky, January 4, 1970.*

Serious students of country music history know of the importance of "Pappy" McMichen to the field's development, but few modern fans have ever heard his name. In his heyday, though, not only was he one of the finest fiddlers in the United States but also an influence on the careers of many pivotal artists. In fact, Bob Shelton suggested, in a brief biography of McMichen for a Newport Folk Festival program, that if Jimmie Rodgers is known as the "Father of Country Music," McMichen should be called "The Uncle of Country Music." Among the reasons for that label were McMichen's pioneering work on radio before the *Grand Ole Opry* was in existence and the fact that he helped arrange the 1927 audition that a then-unknown Jimmie Rodgers had with Ralph Peer—the first step to stardom for the legendary "Singing Brakeman."

McMichen was born and raised in rural Georgia. The usual pattern of country music get-togethers, square dances, church socials, and the like brought an early interest in singing and performing. The fiddle was the main instrument for those affairs, which Clayton could play quite well by the time he was high school age—he already had a reputation as one of the top fiddlers in the region.

After World War I, McMichen began

to perform with local groups in various parts of Georgia. In the early 1920s, he was featured on one of the pioneer country shows, on station WSB in Atlanta, long before the *Grand Ole Opry* was born. By the mid-1920s, he had settled in Atlanta and played with many of the top artists then in the city, including Gid Tanner and another great fiddler and long-time friend of Clayton's, Blind Riley Puckett. When Tanner formed his band, which gained fame as the Skillet Lickers, soon after Tanner made his first recordings in 1924 with Puckett, McMichen became a key member. The band used two fiddlers, Puckett and McMichen, after the latter joined. McMichen remained with the Skillet Lickers until 1931 as a featured performer, and his fiddling a highlight of many of the band's recordings of such songs as "Sally Goodin'," "Wreck of the Old 97," and "Down Yonder." Later generations still were awed by his technique when some of the 1920s recordings were reissued on traditional folk music LPs in the post–World War II era.

For a long time, in fact, Pappy was the recognized fiddling champion of the United States. He fiddled his way to victory for the first time in 1926 and won the title repeatedly after that. He walked off with his last championship in 1952.

After leaving Tanner, McMichen formed his own groups in the 1930s and, between bands, played with other popular country bands of the period. By the end of the 1940s, he had moved to Louisville, Kentucky. Besides continuing his career as a country artist, he also had his own Dixieland jazz band. Called the Georgia Wildcats, the band was featured on radio and TV in Louisville in the late 1940s and the first part of the 1950s.

McMichen retired in 1954. However, a decade later the organizers of the 1964 Newport, Rhode Island, Folk Festival sought him out and convinced him to take part in the show. His playing that summer was warmly received by the relatively youthful audience. His performance was recorded by Vanguard Records and released as part of the album *Traditional Music at Newport, 1964, Part 2*.

McNEELY, HARRY: *Singer, banjoist, guitarist (six- and twelve-string, dobro), harmonica player. Born Lafayette, Indiana, January 3, 1948.*

A versatile and highly accomplished instrumentalist, Larry McNeely has had a small but avid following among folk and country fans ever since he performed on a number of national TV shows in the late 1960s and early 1970s. Even if his exposure as a soloist has been limited, he still could fill small folk clubs across the United States in the 1970s and retained major stature among other artists as a first-rank session musician.

Considering the fact that he is acknowledged to be one of the finest banjo players extant, it's ironic that he failed with the instrument when he first took it up. By the time he became interested in the banjo at fifteen, he had been strumming guitar since he was twelve in his home state of Indiana. Since guitar seemed to come fairly easy, he assumed the same would hold true for banjo, but after about four months he had to put the five-string instrument aside. At sixteen, though, he made another effort and soon had the rafters ringing with exuberant folk and bluegrass melodies. His proficiency was demonstrated soon after, when, at age seventeen, he entered the International Five-String Banjo Contest at West Grove, Pennsylvania, and carried off first prize.

Of course he didn't restrict himself to regular banjo and guitar. By his late teens he also could play such variations as the twelve-string guitar and the dobro. He also mastered the harmonica and over the years has demonstrated outstanding skill with the mouth harp as well.

At seventeen, Larry had long decided that he would make music his life's work. To further that goal he moved from Lafayette to Knoxville, Tennessee, where he became lead banjoist for a group called the Pinnacle Mountain Boys. A year and a half later, in 1967, he appeared on the *Grand Ole Opry*, where his banjo artistry impressed both the audience and his fellow artists. One of the greatest of performers, Roy Acuff, quickly sought Larry's talent for his Smoky Mountain Boys.

Others in the country field had become acquainted with McNeely's potential by then. In 1966, Larry went to Chicago to play at the National Association of Music Merchants convention. Among the other musicians present was Glen Campbell, and the two had the chance to chat a little. In the fall of 1967, they met again at the annual Country Music Association convention and began to develop a rapport. Campbell admired McNeely both as an individual and a musician and, when he was lining up talent for his late 1960s CBS-TV show, he suggested Larry move to California. Once there, Larry found plenty to keep him busy. He had his pick of session work and often was featured instrumentalist on Campbell's shows. In the early 1970s, besides working with Glen, Larry appeared on such other TV programs as *The Return of the Smothers Brothers*, the *Merv Griffin* show, and the *Andy Griffith Show*. Campbell's *Goodtime Hour* was featured on CBS during the 1970–71 and 1971–72 seasons, and McNeely was a regular on the show throughout.

In the early 1970s, he recorded instrumentals for a number of films, including the soundtrack for the highly acclaimed movie of the William Faulkner comic novel, *The Reivers*, which starred Steve McQueen. NcNeely also provided soundtrack work for the Glen Campbell vehicle, *Norwood*. Up to that time, Larry was known more for his instrumental ability than vocal talents, but he showed he was a reasonably good singer in his soundtrack contributions for the ABC-TV movie *Alias Smith and Jones.*

After Larry's move to Southern California, he became a member of the backing band for Glen Campbell concert appearances. That work took him away from home many times in the 1970s as he accompanied Glen to all parts of the United States and a number of foreign nations. Fortunately for McNeely, Campbell's schedule wasn't as hectic as most Nashville-based country artists, which left a reasonable amount of time for McNeely to do a certain number of headline shows on his own. Some of those were in relatively small nightclubs, but he also played

before sizable audiences in appearances at colleges across the country.

In 1970, McNeely signed a recording contract with Capitol Records, which released his debut on that label, *Glen Campbell Presents Larry McNeely*, in January 1971. The album featured both his singing and instrumental talents on such songs as "MacArthur Park," "If You Got to Go," "Alexander Freedom," and "Shuckin' the Corn" (a free-wheeling banjo tune). In preparation for the next album, which was planned to use only his original compositions, he established his own publishing company, The Great Stoned Hiway Music Company, Inc.

MELANIE: *Singer, guitarist, songwriter. Born Astoria, Queens, New York, February 3, 1947.*

Though she often appeared with rock groups or in rock venues, there was never any doubt that most of the music Melanie sang, much of it original material, was in the folk tradition. She often was able to give it a modern twist that allowed her to vie for the attention of the mass audience even in the late 1960s and early 1970s, when folk music had retreated to a minority status.

Melanie, who was born in New York's borough of Queens, was the daughter of Fred and Polly Safka, her father of Ukrainian extraction, her mother of Italian. The family was musically oriented, particularly her mother. As she recalled, "My mother sang. She used to sing in clubs and she always sang interesting music, the kind of songs Billie Holliday sang. She always taught me as a little girl to sing songs she sang. Although I was too young to always understand the words, I knew the words meant something to mother and that inspired me."

While attending a variety of schools in New York, including William H. Carr Jr. High School in Bayside, Safka taught herself to play guitar along the way and, by the time the family had settled in Long Branch, New Jersey, already was interested in pursuing a music career. During her early teens, the folk music boom was in full swing and Melanie was attracted to the work of people like Pete Seeger, Woody

Guthrie and, later, Bob Dylan. At sixteen, while she was attending high school in Long Branch, she began singing in local clubs on Monday nights and going into New York on weekends to sing in folk clubs and coffee houses.

She also became interested in acting and attended the American Academy of Dramatic Arts in New York City after graduating from Red Bank High School in the mid-1960s. For a while during that period, Safka also studied ceramics at Penland School of Crafts in Penland, North Carolina.

Although she was doing some work as a performer and had been writing original songs for some time, Melanie's move into the recording field came as an accident, she told one reporter. While at the Academy, she went to audition for an acting role in an office building on Broadway and the doorman accidentally sent her to a music company. Noting her guitar, people at the company auditioned her and were impressed enough to sign her to a contract. It was a double find for her—while there she met Peter Schekeryk, who later became her husband.

The alignment helped bring her a recording contract with Columbia Records in 1967 and release of her first single in the fall of the year, "Beautiful People," backed with "God's Only Daughter." However, though she stayed with Columbia into 1967, not too much happened until she left to go with Buddah Records the following year. Her composition "What Have They Done to My Song, Ma," issued late in 1969, became a major hit. In 1970 she made the singles charts with "Lay Down" and "Peace Will Come" as well as the album charts with her Buddah LP, Candles in the Rain. (Candles was her third album, having been preceded by Melanie and Born to Be.) Her next albums on Buddah came out in rapid-fire fashion—Leftover Wine in mid summer 1970 and The Good Book in early 1971. The latter, though on the pop charts, didn't sell quite as well as Candles in the Rain.

Melanie was beginning to feel restless with her association and in 1971 decided to change direction in several ways. She and her husband set up their own label, Neighborhood Records, just about the same time that Melanie chose to cut back on touring in favor of raising a family. Earlier in the year she had been honored with an invitation to play at the opening of the United Nations General Assembly. This led to her being named the official spokeswoman for UNICEF. As she said, "They liked me and they asked me to do a tour for them."

One of her first efforts for Neighborhood was her song "Brand New Key," a frothy pop song that was released in the fall of 1971 and rose to number one in the United States in January. Also doing well was her first Neighborhood LP, Gather Me, which rose to top-chart levels and earned a gold record, as had "Brand New Key." Her newfound popularity wasn't lost on Buddah, which struck paydirt with material Melanie had recorded while still under contract to them. The single of the "Nickel Song" was a hit the first half of 1972, and so were the albums Garden in the City and Four Sides of Melanie. On Neighborhood, Melanie had such other chartmakers in 1972 as the album Stoneground Words and the singles "Ring the Living Bell" and "Together Alone."

The phenomenal public appetite for songs like "Brand New Key" and "Nickel Song" wasn't matched by critical approval. She was scolded in print, as she put it, for being "an ingenue, a sicky sweet person singing sicky sweet songs." The fact that she had written songs with considerably more depth over the years was forgotten. Melanie was thin-skinned about the subject and that, coupled with her desire to raise a family, caused her to drop out of the limelight for several years while two children were born.

In 1975, she came out of that temporary retirement to record a new album for Atlantic Records that was released with the title Photograph. The original material she provided was more complex in lyric structure than her previous work. It won accolades from the critical establishment, including a paean from John Rockwell of

The New York Times, who wrote that Melanie was "singing adult songs for adult people." He called the album one of the top-10 LPs of the year. However, the public thought otherwise and the album fell far short of her earlier efforts in the market place.

Not too much was heard from her for a while after that, though some of her recordings continued to sell years after their original release. As of early 1978, she had recorded nineteen albums and sold over 22 million records worldwide.

She returned to the recording wars in 1978 with a new release on Midsong International Records called *Phonogenic, Not Just Another Pretty Face*. The album contained four new original compositions, including "Runnin' After Love," "Spunky," and "Bon Appetit." The remaining ten songs were by other writers, including perhaps the most effective tracks of the album, her version of Jesse Winchester's "Yankee Man" and of Carole Bayer Sager's "Runnin' After Love."

MILLER, JODY: *Singer, ukulele player. Born Phoenix, Arizona, November 29, 1941.*

Neither in her speaking or singing voice does Jody Miller have the "twang" usually expected of a country artist. But she can use her voice to capture the essence of any type of song, whether it be pop, folk, or country, as she proved during a diverse career that covered all three areas.

The lack of a rural inflection can be traced to the fact that her early years were spent in the relatively cosmopolitan locale of Phoenix, Arizona. Country music, though, was a favorite of her fiddle-playing father, and she and her three sisters often vocalized to his playing. In Jody's teens, the family resided in Blanchard, Oklahoma, where she went to high school. By then Jody was strongly attracted to a singing career and, with two friends, formed a trio called the Melodies that performed at school shows and local gatherings.

Jody took off for Southern California after finishing high school to try to break into the music business. Unfortunately the try was cut short by an auto accident in which she suffered a broken neck. She went back to Oklahoma to recuperate. After she fought off the effects of the mishap, she returned to the performing field locally. The folk boom was in full swing in the early 1960s and, accompanying herself on the ukulele, she became a familiar figure as a folk artist in clubs and coffee houses in the Sooner state. While appearing at the Jester Coffee House near the University of Oklahoma at Norman, Miller was heard by the Limeliters, who urged her to go back to California and try again.

She told an interviewer, "The chance came when I had a two-week vacation. I went to Hollywood and went to see Dale Robertson of Capitol Records and asked for professional help." He thought she had promise and helped get her an engagement at one of the major folk and pop clubs, Doug Weston's Troubadour. Soon after, she had her first major recording contract with Capitol.

The first release, in 1964, was "He Walks like a Man." The single became a West Coast regional hit. "Unfortunately," Jody noted, "no one heard it in the East." The next year, though, she recorded "Queen of the House," a riposte to Roger Miller's hit "King of the Road." The single reached high levels on both country and pop charts. Adding to her luster in 1965 was an appearance at the San Remo Music Festival in Italy, where she won awards in both English and non-English-speaking categories. Her debut album came out in 1965, titled *Jody Miller*, and did reasonably well, as did the 1966 followup, *Great Hits of Buck Owens*. In early 1966, when Grammy Award votes were tabulated, she received one of those coveted trophies for "Queen of the House."

Miller's career slowed down soon after, partly because she had a marriage to consider after 1965. In the late 1960s, she and her husband, Monty Brooks, retired to their Oklahoma ranch, where Jody concentrated on raising her daughter, Robin. For a number of years little was heard of Jody, but at the end of the 1960s she began to do some concert work once more. "When I began performing again, all of a sudden I really enjoyed it. The audiences were overwhelming me with their response. They seemed to enjoy my singing. Suddenly I thought, 'I have got to have some record action to go with this.' "

It took only a short while for her to get a new contract, this time with Epic Records in 1970. With Billy Sherrill handling production, she soon had completed her first album for Epic. Titled *Look at Mine,* it was released in February 1971 and met good response from the buying public. Later in 1971, her single "He's So Fine" rose to upper-chart levels in both pop and country markets. (The record was nominated for a Grammy Award.) The album of that title was issued in October 1971 and was followed in September 1972 by the LP *There's a Party Goin' On.* Throughout the 1970s she had singles releases that showed up on country charts, including "House of the Rising Sun" in late 1973 and early 1974 and "(I Wanna) Love My Life Away" in 1978. Some of her other releases of the 1970s were "Baby, I'm Yours," "When the New Wears Off Our Love," and "Soft Lights and Sexy Music." Her Epic LPs of the mid- and late-1970s included *Good News, House of the Rising Sun,* and *Country Girl.*

MILLER, ROGER: *Singer, guitarist, banjoist, pianist, drummer, songwriter. Born Fort Worth, Texas, January 2, 1936.*

A free soul, as unpredictable in his way as the content of his many country standards, Roger Miller burst on the country and national audience in the mid-1960s to become one of the best-known singers and songwriters of the decade. He remained a popular figure in the music field in the 1970s, though without repeating his creative achievements of earlier years.

He was born Roger Dean Miller in Texas, but spent most of his youth in the small town of Erick, Oklahoma. He told an interviewer, "My father died when I was a year old. There were three little boys—I was the youngest—and my mother couldn't support us so she was going to put us in an orphanage. My father had three brothers and one lived in Arkansas, one in Oklahoma, and one in California. Each came

and took a boy home and raised him. I went to Oklahoma."

His uncle and aunt were poor and Erick was hardly a metropolis. "Erick is so small that the city limits signs are back to back. Its population is 1,500, including rakes and tractors. The school I went to [a one-room school] had thirty-seven students, me and thirty-six Indians. One time we had a school dance and it rained for thirty-six straight days. During recess we used to play cowboys and Indians and things got pretty wild from my standpoint."

Roger's sense of humor served him well, for life was something less than affluent. As a boy he helped his uncle on his farm. "I hated it all, but I hated most of all on Saturdays cleaning out the chicken house. A lot of people who grew up on a farm will know why I said 'Lord, give me a guitar and let me get out of here and make something of the world.' "

He pinned his hopes on country music partly because that was the kind of music he heard all around him and partly because he admired to country performer Sheb Wooley, who was an in-law of the Miller family. A friend later recalled Roger's uncle stating that "when the boy grows up he wants to be just like Sheb."

Once he'd made up his mind on his future career, young Roger spent many of his Saturday hours picking cotton to earn money to buy a guitar. It was one of the proudest days of his life when he finally could purchase a second-hand instrument. His schooling ended after the eighth grade, after which, hauling his guitar along, he wandered around Texas and Oklahoma for much of his teens working at an assortment of jobs. He worked as a ranch hand, herding cattle and dehorning them, among other things. He also spent some of his time riding Brahma bulls in rodeos. During those years, he not only learned many basic guitar chords, but picked up experience on banjo and piano as well.

Ordinarily you wouldn't think of entry into the Army as a fortunate turn, but for Roger it proved just that. When he joined up during the Korean War, it finally got him away from the back country and out into the world in general. It became a learning experience far better than his brief period in grade school. He noted, "When I got into the Army, I finally met some guys who really knew something about the guitar and they taught me and I learned what I could."

Part of his hitch was spent in Korea, his destination after basic training, where at first he drove a jeep. But his ability as a singer and musician got him into Special Services, where he became part of a country music band entertaining troops. Some of the songs he played were his own and the applause they received made him feel better about his chance for making it in music later on. Not only did he play guitar in that band, but also drums and fiddle.

He also thought some of the contacts he made would help. "When I was stationed in South Carolina, I met this sergeant who said he had a brother in the business, Jethro of Homer and Jethro. This sergeant could play the bass as well as Jethro could play the mandolin and we used to sit in the barracks and play. He was the one who really convinced me to go to Nashville after I got out of the Army. [Otherwise] I was probably going back to Oklahoma and work in a gas station."

The sergeant did arrange an audition for him at RCA after Roger got his discharge. "I just walked in and said to Chet Atkins, 'I want to audition, I'm a songwriter' and he said, 'Well, where's your guitar?' I said, 'I don't have one' and he said 'You can use mine.' So there's Chet Atkins and I'm using his guitar and I sang in one key and played in another. It was a disaster."

Discouraged, he thought of doing something else for a time. One job he attempted was fire-fighter in Amarillo, Texas. He slept through the alarm of the second fire of his career and was fired after two months. He returned to Nashville determined to break into the music field this time. He first got a job as a bellhop at the Andrew Jackson Hotel, then spent his free time hanging around studios, meeting people in the music industry, trying out for jobs. Slowly he got work, as a musician playing fiddle with Minnie Pearl and handling drums in Faron Young's backing group.

While all that was going on, he kept putting together new songs. Since he couldn't write music, he had to play or sing the song to someone else who would put it on paper. He made the rounds of music publishers and artists and finally began to attract some attention. After he joined the Ray Price show, Ray recorded one of his tunes, "Invitation to the Blues," and it made the charts. The song also was covered by Patti Page.

That success helped bring a full-time songwriting contract from the Faron Young organization. In the late 1950s and early 1960s, more and more artists recorded his material, examples being Ernest Tubbs' version of "Half a Mind" and Jim Reeves' recording of "Billy Bayou." Other hits Roger wrote for others included "You Don't Want My Love," "Hey, Little Star," "Lock, Stock and Teardrops," and "In the Summertime."

Roger wasn't satisfied with that. He longed to succeed as a performer too. "I had come to Nashville to be a singer, but I was unorthodox I guess. I'd sing songs for people and they'd say that would be good for someone else. I'd say what about me and they'd say, we'll get to you later . . . and it was quite a bit later when they got to me."

However, Roger finally did get a shot at recording for a major label when RCA took him on in the early 1960s. This led to his first top-10 hit, in 1961, "When Two Worlds Collide," co-written with country star Bill Anderson. On most of his later hits, though, he wrote both words and music himself.

After that breakthrough, however, he couldn't buy a hit for the next two years. Disheartened, he moved to Hollywood to enroll in a dramatic acting course. He had started the course when his singing career suddenly caught fire. He had signed with Smash Records, and his releases on the label caught the ear of DJs around the United States In 1964 he scored a top-10 country hit with "Chug-a-Lug" and a number-one success with "Dang Me." Both records also became favorites with pop fans. But 1964 was only a prologue to his sensational achievements of the next year. He turned out four bestsellers, one following on the heels of the other: "King of the Road," "Engine, Engine No. 9," "Kansas City Star," and "One Dyin' and a-Buryin'." Oddly, while all were top-10 country hits, none reached number one, whereas on pop charts, all reached the highest spot earning Roger four gold-record awards. "King of the Road," of course, has been his trademark song; by the 1970s, it had been recorded over 300 times by various artists and Miller's own single sold 2.5 million copies. During 1966, one of his songs, "In the Summertime," provided Andy Williams with a hit single that sold over 2 million copies.

This association inspired Andy to feature Roger on one of his NBC-TV programs in late 1965. Viewer reaction was so favorable that NBC asked Roger to host his own half-hour special, which was presented on January 19, 1966. That effort did well enough for Miller to do a fall weekly variety show that debuted on September 12, 1966. The ratings weren't healthy enough, however, and the show was canceled.

In the mid-1960s, Roger also appeared on many other variety shows, both pop and country, and was a favorite with live audiences. He performed in major venues from one end of the United States to the other. His engagement at Harrah's in Lake Tahoe brought out so many fans that additional performances had to be added.

Roger's output of 1964–65 won him an amazing total of eleven Grammy Awards. His 1964 trophies were for Best C&W Single ("Dang Me"); Best C&W Album (*Dang Me/Chug-a-Lug*); Best C&W Vocal Performance ("Dang Me"); Best C&W Song (writer's award, "Dang Me"); Best New C&W Artist of 1964. His 1965 awards were Best Contemporary (rock 'n' roll) Single ("King of the Road"); Best Contemporary Vocal Performance, Male ("King of the Road"); Best C&W Single ("King of the Road"); Best C&W Album (*The Return of Roger Miller*); Best C&W Vocal Performance, Male ("King of the Road"); Best C&W Song (writer's award, "King of the Road").

The two albums mentioned in the awards both rose to top-chart levels and won gold-record awards. Also earning gold-record awards in the mid-1960s were *Roger Miller/Golden Hits* and *Roger Miller, the Third Time Around*. His other 1960s LPs on Smash included *Words & Music* (1/67), *Walkin' in the Sunshine* (7/67); *Waterhole No. 3* (12/67), and *Roger Miller* (10/69). His other album credits in the 1960s included such RCA Camden releases as *Roger Miller* (12/64) and *One and Only Roger Miller* (9/65); *Amazing Roger Miller* on Nashville; and *Madcap Sensation* on Starday.

In the 1970s, Miller recorded for various labels, signing with Columbia Records for a while, among others. He started off the decade with an LP on Smash, *Roger Miller 1970*, and also had a collection on Columbia that year, *34 All-Time Great Sing-Along Selections* (12/70). His later Columbia releases included the album *Roger Miller Supersongs*, which spawned the single "I Love a Rodeo." Some of his other albums were *Country Side* on Starday and, on Mercury, *Best of Roger Miller* and *Trip in the Country*.

Although Roger continued to perform sporadically in the 1970s and occasionally was featured on network TV programs (including several appearances as a presenter on Grammy Award shows), he was much less in evidence than in the previous decade. He continued to write songs, some of which provided charted singles for other artists, and some that he placed on the charts himself. However, his own releases rarely made it past mid-chart levels. Among his charted singles in the decade were "Rings for Sale" on Mercury in 1972 and "I Believe in Sunshine" (late 1973-early 1974) and "Our Love" (1975) on Columbia. In the early 1980s, he gained a new recording alignment with Elektra Records; one result was the top-40 single "Everyone Gets Crazy Now and Then" in the fall of 1981.

His songwriting technique remained essentially the same even if it didn't bring the creative rewards of earlier times. "I write a line at a time, really. A line comes to me and then I sit down and sing it and then I write the next line and then I have two lines and I sing them. Then I do a third line and sing all three; then come up with the fourth. It's a line at a time, it's go back and come to it, it's like hitting a brick wall and each time you hit it, it gives a little. You find you've gotten the wall to give enough until you've written a whole song."

MILSAP, RONNIE: *Singer, guitarist, pianist, songwriter. Born Robbinsville, North Carolina, January 16, 1944.*

By the end of the 1970s, Ronnie Milsap had won nearly every country-music award for which he was eligible. This might not seem so unusual, except that he only was involved with country music since 1973. Additionally, he became a top country star performing the music in an essentially traditional way, ignoring the progressive approach of people like Willie Nelson and Waylon Jennings despite his earlier grounding in classical music and rock 'n' roll. His emphasis has mainly been on slow to medium tempo country ballads that, while sometimes having more sophistication in music and lyrics than country songs of the past, and delivered in a vocal style with a little less of the characteristic "twang" of older artists, differed from typical country offerings of the 1940s to early 1960s only in degree.

It reflected the fact that, though his musical training took a different direction, his initial exposure as a small child had been to radio programs that featured what might be called "roots" country music. As he said when he signed as a country artist with RCA in early 1973, leaving what had been a promising career as a rock performer, "All I heard the first six years of my life was country music and it's hard to get away from your roots."

Those early years brought the boy more than his share of misfortunes, partly inherited. His father was a third-generation epileptic. Ronnie was not epileptic, but he was born blind. A previous child of his parents had been stillborn. Ronnie's mother had trouble dealing with those tragedies and left the family while Ronnie still was a baby, leaving him to be raised by his father's parents.

Until the age of five, Ronnie did not know he was blind. His grandparents never mentioned it, and his playmates didn't treat him like he was different. But at the age of five, he went to the North Carolina State School for the Blind at Raleigh rather than the local public school. Being so young and far from home scared him, but in the long run proved a boon to his career, for it was there that he was first exposed to musical instruments.

It soon became apparent that he was a prodigy. At the age of seven, he could play the violin like a professional; he mastered the piano at eight and the guitar at twelve. In his teens he picked up some woodwind and percussion instruments and demonstrated skill with them as well. His first training was in the classics, and even when he became a country star he still liked to play classical music for his own enjoyment. "My favorite composers are Mozart and Bach," he said. "I like Mozart's melodies and since I am a methodical minded Capricorn, Bach's complicated techniques appeal to me."

However, rock 'n' roll was his passion in his teens. While in high school he formed a rock group with three other blind musicians. They called themselves the Apparitions and performed at local clubs and dances.

While he loved music, young Milsap wasn't positive he could support himself as a musician. Thus he entered Young Harris Junior College in Atlanta, Georgia, as a prelaw major. The first day of school, his two sighted roommates told him they didn't want to room with him because they didn't know how to act around a blind person. But when they all went down to the freshman orientation meeting held in a room with a piano, and Ronnie was seated by them on the piano bench, he couldn't resist the temptation to play. When the students heard him play his wild rock 'n' roll, he became the center of attention and the most popular student in the room. His roommates never again suggested he move out.

Ronnie completed two years at the junior college and was offered a full scholarship at Emory University Law School. But Ronnie had been performing steadily during his years at Young-Harris, and this eventually encouraged him to try to make a living playing music. He had become known for his instrumental abilities to performers and recording studio executives in Atlanta and was getting jobs as a backing artist at sessions and as a sideman for people like J.J. Cale. By the end of the 1960s, he had formed his own group, which became the house band at T.J.'s Club in Memphis, Tennessee, in 1969. In the late 1960s and early 1970s, Milsap and his group had recording agreements with several labels—Scepter, Chips Records, and Warner Brothers Records. Their output included the R&B hit "Never Had It So Good" and several other rock 'n' roll singles that had some chart action.

But Ronnie felt his career wasn't bringing him the satisfaction it should. His interest in country music had been rekindled when, in 1973, he picked up stakes and moved with his wife to Nashville. In April 1973, he signed with RCA Records country-music division and was soon in the studios working on his debut recordings. It didn't take long for him to make his presence felt in his new field. His first RCA single, "I Hate You," made the charts. At year end, his single "The Girl That Waits on Tables" was on the lists rising toward the top 10 in early 1974. He followed with such other 1974 top-10 bestsellers as "Pure Love," "Please Don't Tell Me How the Story Ends," and, at year end, "(I'd Be) a Legend in My Time," which went on to become a number-one hit in early 1974. Also on the charts from late 1973 and for much of 1974 was his album *Where the Heart Is.*

All of this translated into immediate recognition by his music industry peers as a major new talent. In the Country Music Association's voting for 1974, Milsap was named Male Vocalist of the Year. In Grammy polling, he was named winner of the Best Country Vocal Performance, Male, for 1974 for his single "Please Don't Tell Me How the Story Ends."

He continued to show his rapport with country fans in 1975 with such top-10 singles (besides "Legend in My Time") as "Too Late to Worry, Too Blue to Cry," "Daydreams About Night Things," and

"She Even Woke Me Up to Say Goodbye." He also had the best-selling LPs *Night Things* and *Legend in My Time.* The latter won the CMA award for Best Album of the Year. Nor did he slow down during the next two years. His 1976 successes included the top-10 single "What Goes on when the Sun Goes Down" and what has become one of his trademark songs, "(I'm a) Stand by My Woman Man" (number one for several weeks in August and September) plus the hit LP *20-20 Vision.* For much of 1977, his LPs *Ronnie Milsap Live* and *It Was Almost Like a Song* were on the charts (the latter remained on country lists more than a year and also was a pop chart hit), and his singles output included "It Was Almost like a Song," number one during the summer.

The honors he won for his 1976–77 work included being named CMA Male Vocalist of the Year both years and the 1976 Best Country Vocal Performance, Male, Grammy for "(I'm a) Stand by My Woman Man." He won two other CMA categories in 1977, making him the major winner of that year. Those were the most coveted honors of all, Entertainer of the Year and the Best Album of the Year for *Ronnie Milsap Live.*

Ronnie's 1978 hits included "Only One Love in My Life," number one most of July, and the bestseller "Let's Take the Long Way Around the World." His album *Only One Love in My Life* was on upper-chart levels throughout the summer and still on the lists in 1979. The LP won the CMA Best Album of the Year award for 1978. Ronnie closed out the decade with still more hits. His 1979 best-selling singles included "Nobody Likes Sad Songs," "Back on My Mind Again/Santa Barbara," and "In No Time at All" and the album *Images.*

By the end of the 1970s, Milsap had become one of the most popular artists in country music, headlining concerts throughout the United States and the world. Many of his recordings increasingly crossed over to pop charts and also often were on hit lists in other countries. In 1976, Ronnie became a regular cast member of the *Grand Ole Opry* and was still part of that revered institution in the early 1980s.

He began the 1980s with the hit single "Why Don't You Spend the Night," vying for number-one spot in March 1980. He followed with such other bestsellers as "Cowboys and Clowns" (which was issued on the Elektra Records label as part of the soundtrack from the movie *Bronco Billy*) and the number-one "My Heart/Silent Night (After the Fight)." At year end, *Billboard* magazine named him the Number One Country Music Single Artist of 1980. Also on the charts in 1980 was a new RCA album, *Milsap Magic*. In December his LP *Ronnie Milsap's Greatest Hits* was on the charts, eventually moving to number one in January 1981. The single "Smokey Mountain Rain" was in the top 10 as 1980 drew to a close, remaining on the lists into 1981. His best-selling singles of 1981 included "Am I Losing You" and "I Wouldn't Have Missed It for the World."

Thus despite his handicap and with only a few years' experience in the field, Ronnie Milsap truly had become a legend in his time. Once asked whether blindness, rather than being a hindrance, had helped him become a success, he had replied, "It gains immediate attention, but acceptance is another story. You've got to work for that, son." He did agree that he probably could pick up sensations and gain an understanding of individuals better in some ways than sighted people. "Your ears become your eyes. . . . I try to look inside people."

MITCHELL, JONI: *Singer, guitarist, pianist, songwriter, artist. Born Fort McLeod, Alberta, Canada, November 7, 1943.*

During her concert tour of early 1974, Joni Mitchell changed one of the verses to her classic folk composition "Both Sides Now" to run "But now old friends are acting strange/They shake their heads, they say I've changed. . . . And I have!" Indeed, at the time Mitchell was shedding her image of a shy, soft-spoken folk artist to a dynamic rock performer. Afterward, she continued to change, moving more and more toward the jazz idiom until, by the end of the 1970s, her music ranked among

the more interesting experiments in avant garde jazz. Whatever genre she worked in, she made important and lasting contributions. Even as jazz enthusiasts welcomed her to their ranks, folk performers still covered some of her earlier writings and aspiring rock performers often drew musical insight from some of her up-tempo recordings.

Joni was born Roberta Joan Anderson in Ft. McLeod, but grew up in Saskatoon, Saskatchewan, daughter of a schoolteacher mother and a former RCAF officer turned grocery store manager father. She found an early interest in art and, without benefit of lessons, became a fairly capable painter. In her late teens, she enrolled at the Alberta College of Art in Calgary with the thought of making a career in commercial art. She took along a baritone ukulele just for the fun of it and, after learning a few chords, started singing some folk songs during leisure moments. Friends urged her to go further with her musical talent, and she responded by finding work at a local coffee house called the Depression. Music became more and more engrossing while her interest in commercial art faded. The same wasn't true for painting, which remained a major love. Later on she created many excellent original pieces of art for use on her album covers.

She then began to go outside her local area to perform. On a train trip to take part in the Mariposa Folk Festival in Ontario, Canada, she wrote her first song, "Day After Day." Once in eastern Canada, she became enthusiastic about the folk scene and decided to stay. At nineteen she lived in Toronto, wrote more folk-style songs, and began to build a reputation with folk fans and other young performers in the city. She also met and married Chuck Mitchell, combining her married name with a modification of her middle one to create her stage name. It was as Joni Mitchell that she began to perform in coffee houses in Detroit after she moved there with her husband in mid-1966. They divorced soon after, but Joni Mitchell she remained. Meanwhile, the impact of her performance and the quality of her original material continued to improve.

As a Detroit critic enthused in 1967, "She is a beautiful woman. Her voice and her acoustic guitar are free, pure instruments in themselves; there is additional beauty in the way she uses them to convey such a full range of emotions. But if she knew only three chords, her performance would be justified by her songs alone. As a songwriter, she plays Yang to Bob Dylan's Yin, equaling him in richness and profusion of imagery and surpassing him in conciseness and direction."

Soon after that, Joni packed her belongings and moved to New York. There she quickly made important contacts with such people as record-company executive David Geffen, who advised her on record-industry operations (she signed with Reprise in 1967); Elliott Robert, who became her manager; and David Crosby, who encouraged her musical efforts. Word of her talents spread among her musical peers and soon people like Judy Collins, Buffy Sainte-Marie, Tom Rush, and Dave Van Ronk were including some of her songs in their acts and also telling audiences of her strengths as a performer. Before long her debut album on Reprise, *Song to a Seagull,* was released (in March 1968), and during 1968–69 she had her first song hit, "Both Sides Now." Mitchell's single did reasonably well, but the major success was for Judy Collins' version, which won a gold-record award. In the Grammy Awards voting for 1968, the award for Best Folk Recording went to Collins for her single of "Both Sides Now."

By 1968, Joni had moved to a home in Laurel Canyon above Los Angeles, where she still spent much of her time when not on the road throughout the 1970s. Besides that, after she became an acknowledged star, she also built a retreat for herself near Vancouver, British Columbia.

During the years she recorded for Reprise, she continued to be identified with folk music or, to some extent, with the soft rock field. Among the new standard numbers she wrote or had recorded success with during that period were "The Circle Game," "The Same Situation," and "Ladies of the Canyon."

Mitchell's second album on Reprise, *Clouds* (which featured her self-portrait on the cover), came out in May 1969 and was a chart hit. During the year, Joni was a guest several times on Johnny Cash's network TV show, singing "Both Sides Now" on one occasion. It was just one of many TV appearances she made in the late 1960s and early 1970s. Her third Reprise LP, *Ladies of the Canyon,* issued in April 1970, achieved gold-record status during 1970. One of its tracks was called "Woodstock." The song was in praise of the Woodstock nation, but also had the first intimation of some of the new directions Joni's writing would take in the 1970s.

She closed out her album efforts on Reprise on a high-water mark with *Blue,* released in June 1971, certainly one of the best albums of 1971 and arguably one of the best LPs of the decade. She wrote all ten songs on it, many of which underscored her ability to work several themes into a single song. An example is "All I Want," which begins, "Alive, alive, I wanted to get up and jive/I want to wreck my stockings in some juke box dive," but ends in her suggesting that those are only daydreams to supplement the more restrained yearning for love. The quality level remained high in every song, whether slow or fast, and such tracks as "My Old Man," "Little Green," "This Flight Tonight," "Carey," "River," and "The Last Time I Saw Richard" remain favorites of her long-time adherents.

Her move away from pure folk stylings was abundantly evident in *Blue,* though there still was a strong folk feeling to the overall collection. Some of the songs in that collection she had written on the piano, which she had only begun to play during preparation of *Ladies of the Canyon.* After completing *Blue,* she realized she was feeling increasingly uncomfortable about the inroads her career was making on her private life. She decided to take time out to reevaluate things and for the next year and a half stayed away from concerts, spending time in travel and visiting with friends.

However, she didn't give up writing and recording. She moved from Reprise to the newly formed Asylum Records, whose president at the time was David Geffen. (Asylum later was merged with Elektra.) Her first LP on that label was *For the Roses*, issued in November 1972. Backing her on the album was rock and jazz artist Tom Scott, who helped put together the "band sound" stressed in the collection. One of the tracks, the country-flavored "You Turn Me On, I'm a Radio," became a hit single, Joni's biggest to that point, and the album itself was on the national charts from late 1972 through most of 1973, earning Joni another gold-record award.

Although Mitchell was stressing more rock and jazz in her music by the time her next LP, *Court and Spark*, came out in January 1974, her appeal was not diminished. She held on to most of her earlier fans and added a lot of new ones. Proof was the success, both critically and commercially, of the LP that also spawned three hit singles, "Raised on Robbery," "Help Me," and "Free Man in Paris."

In early 1974, Joni went on her first major tour in a long while, accompanied by Tom Scott and the L.A. Express. Her new rock image was met by shrieks of joy, thunderous applause, and dancing in the aisles wherever the show played. Unlike earlier tours, when people like Jackson Browne opened for her, Scott and his band began with a hard-driving electric set. The results of that combination were captured, in part, in the double live album, *Miles of Aisles*, issued in November 1974. Her updated treatment of an earlier favorite, "Big Yellow Taxi," brought her another chart-making single.

She diverged from rock to avant garde jazz the next time out with the November 1975 LP, *The Hissing of Summer Lawns*. The lyrics, as often held true in the 1970s, were richly poetic and multilayered, accompanied by complex, usually minor key melodies. Discussing the material in the liner notes, she wrote, cryptically, "The whole unfolded like a mystery. It is not my intention to unravel that mystery for anyone, but rather to offer some additional clues."

Jazz continued to preoccupy Mitchell to a greater and greater extent as the late 1970s went by. Bassist Jaco Pastorius of Weather Report fame was one of those

who contributed to her *Hejira* album, which came out in November 1976. He was joined in session work on the next effort, *Don Juan's Reckless Daughter* (issued by Asylum/Elektra in December 1977) by such artists as Wayne Shorter, John Guerin, Chaka Khan, and Airto. The LP earned a gold record in 1978, as had all her previous albums except her first one.

Her next project particularly excited her since it was to be a joint effort with jazz great Charlie Mingus. Mingus, however, died in December 1978, before the project could be completed. When the LP was issued in June 1979, it was dedicated to Mingus and included some impressive paintings of him by Joni on the cover. (It was titled simply *Joni Mitchell/Mingus*). She toured in mid-1979 in support of the album and some of her performances were recorded live. That material provided the basis for her next LP (the two-record set), *Shadows and Light*, issued in September 1980. During 1981 Mitchell began work on another album (given the working title #9) for release in 1982.

MIZE, BILLY: *Singer, guitarist, songwriter, emcee. Born Kansas City, Kansas, April 29, 1932.*

When Billy Mize got started in country music, he intended it to be a hobby. Instead it ended up being his main vocation. Although he only broke through on the national level on occasion, he remained one of the most popular performers of country fans in the western United States throughout his career.

He was born in Kansas, but by the time he was of school age, his family, lovers of country music, had moved to California's San Joaquin Valley. Later the Mizes resided in the Riverside area. Both places had a fair amount of country activity, and Billy enjoyed listening to country music on radio from his early years on.

As he told *Music City News* (August 1975), "I got into playing country music when my father, who had been in the furniture business for years, brought home a steel guitar and said if I'd learn how to play it, he'd give it to me. I was 15 or 16 and still going to school when some school kids who liked country music and I formed a little band in Riverside, California. We played around on the weekends for the kids and in beer joints until I moved to Bakersfield my last year of high school. My influence in country music was mainly Bob Wills. I knew every song that Tommy Duncan had sung.

"The reason that I'm in country music, and in music is because I'm a fan of it. . . . I didn't really know that you could make a career of it. It appeared to me that the only ones who were making money out of country music were acts at ballrooms like Ernest Tubb, Gene Autry, and Bob Wills. So I didn't know that there was any other way than being a big star that you could make a living at this. I just did it because I wanted to hear the songs again. When we got the first little group together to go out and play we just wanted to hear the songs. That's how it started for me."

During those years, Billy was better known in school for his athletic ability. He was a starter on both baseball and football teams in high school.

The move to Bakersfield proved a turning point, since country music was much more respected in that area. He had his own band when he was nineteen, which played at the Harry Mack Inn. Billy played steel guitar and also sang with a musician named Bill Woods. "Bill Woods later got a radio show, a noon broadcast that lasted fifteen minutes on station KAFY and I got to appear on that. Later on, I got a disc jockey show while working clubs at night. Then TV came along with the *Cousin Herb Trading Post Show* in 1953. It started off with Bill Woods, Cousin Herb, and myself. In Bakersfield that was the date [September 26, 1953] of the first television show that went on in the area. So we were the first local TV personalities."

From then on, except for two years, Mize was a regular on that show until the mid-1960s. In 1966, he took over as host of the show for a while. But during those years he continued to do a lot of other things, including nightclub work, recording, and also going down to Los Angeles for TV work. He debuted on L.A. television in 1955 on the *Hank Penny Show* and remained a regular for some time. For several years he somehow managed to find time to do seven TV shows a week on L.A. stations and also get to Bakersfield for Monday through Friday appearances. In addition to his TV workload, he often performed in nightclubs six or seven nights a week.

All of that made him a familiar figure to West Coast fans but didn't give him much opportunity to cultivate audiences outside the area. In the late 1960s, Billy did expand his scope somewhat by performing in shows with national exposure. In 1966–67, for instance, he was host of the nationally syndicated *Gene Autry Show*, and he also began turning out his own *Billy Mize Show*, syndicated out of Bakersfield. His TV activities continued in one form or another in the 1970s. In the mid-1970s, he appeared in a show called *RFD Hollywood*, a series that was shot on location in Colorado and Utah. It was a country-music series that used the backdrop of various resort areas to try to increase viewer interest.

Mize began his major recording efforts in the 1950s when he signed with Decca Records. His output included several singles of his own compositions, such as "Who Will Buy the Wine," "I Saw Her First," "It Could Happen," and "Solid Sender." He also turned out his versions of songs by other country writers. From Decca, he proceeded to do some recordings on the Challenge and Liberty labels in the late 1950s and early 1960s before signing with Columbia Records. He remained with Columbia until 1970, when he signed with United Artists. His debut on that label was the album *You're Alright with Me.* (In 1969, Imperial Records, part of Liberty, released some of his previously recorded songs in the LP *This Time and Place.*) He had a number of charted singles on UA in the early 1970s, such as "Beer Drinkin' Honky Tonk Blues" in 1970 and "Take It Easy" in 1972.

After four years with UA, Billy signed with Mega Records in 1974. His mid-1970s singles releases on Mega included "Linda's Love Stop," "It's a Feeling Called Love," and "She Was Born to Love Me."

Throughout the 1960s and 1970s, in addition to his other work, Billy did a lot of session work, including steel and rhythm guitar on a great many of Merle Haggard's releases.

MONROE, BILL: *Singer, guitarist, mandolinist, fiddler, songwriter, band leader (the Blue Grass Boys). Born Rosine, Kentucky, September 13, 1911.*

"It's got a hard drive to it. It's Scotch bagpipes and old time fiddlin'. It's Methodist and Holiness and Baptist. It's blues and jazz and it has a high lonesome sound. It's plain music that tells a good story. It's played from my heart to your heart, and it will touch you."

That's how Bill Monroe describes bluegrass, "a music that I set out to have as my own. I never wanted to be known for copying any man. . . ." Although the elements that went into bluegrass were there before, in fact can be discerned in folk music going well back into the country's history, it was Monroe who blended them in a new way, particularly in his method of having the fiddle, mandolin, and banjo carry the lead in a format sometimes called "country music in overdrive." With his brother Charlie he spread the word of this new musical product of the border regions of the old South far and wide in the second half of the 1920s and early 1930s until he became known as the "Father of Bluegrass."

Monroe's love of country music, particularly country fiddling and mandolin playing, goes back to his earliest years growing up in the hills of Kentucky. Both his mother, Melissa, and uncle, Pen Vandiver, were excellent country fiddlers and Vandiver also was a fine mandolinist. As soon as he was old enough to handle a stringed instrument they helped start him on a path that was to lead to mastery of not only fiddle and mandolin but guitar as well. After a while, he could play guitar well enough that his uncle took him along as a backing musician while the older man set the pace at local dances. Later on Bill was to commemorate his uncle in the song "Uncle Pen."

Monroe was intensely curious about all kinds of music. Not only did he pay close attention to the traditional music he heard all around him as he grew up, he also recalled taking the opportunity of listening to the blues and gospel songs favored by local black artists. All of those influences found their way into the songs he was to write and the arrangements he made of both traditional and modern country material.

His older brother, Charlie, also was a fine instrumentalist, and another brother, Birch, played fiddle. The three brothers sometimes played together in local groups and, as time went on, became eager to form their own band. In the mid-1920s, the Monroe Brothers began to pick up a following in Kentucky and expanded their reputation with the advent of radio. They made their first broadcasts in 1927 and added more credits on various stations over the next decade. Their unique style of playing, dubbed "bluegrass" initially because of the connection with their home state, eventually made them favorites with country crowds over a steadily growing area. Gradually, from the end of the 1920s and into the early 1930s, audiences at country fairs and at local country shows in many parts of the Midwest and the South began to get enthused over Charlie's "houn' dog guitar" and Bill's "potato-bug mandolin."

Many of the favorites of Monroe Brothers' fans of those years were assembled in a 1960s Camden LP. Among the songs included in the album, *Early Bluegrass Music by the Monroe Brothers,* were "New River Train," "No Home, No Place to Pillow My Head," "The Great Speckled Bird," "Once I Had a Darling Mother," "On the Banks of the Ohio," "Rosa Lee McFall," "Bringin' in the Georgia Mail," "Weeping Willow Tree," "Just a Song of Old Kentucky," "Don't Forget Me," and "Mother's Not Dead, She's Only Sleeping."

Many of those songs were bluegrass versions of traditional songs, some traceable back to Elizabethan times. But Bill Monroe was also adding new compositions of his own. In 1930, he achieved his first big hit with one of them, an instrumental called "Kentucky Waltz." Among his other compositions of those years that helped bring both bluegrass music and the Monroe Brothers' band to the top ranks of country bands active in the 1930s were "Get Up John," "Blue Grass Ramble," and "Memories of You."

In 1938, the Monroe Brothers decided to go separate ways. Charlie started a band named the Kentucky Pardners while Bill organized the first of dozens of Blue Grass Boys alignments. Though Charlie's group did reasonably well for over a decade, it was Bill's band that almost immediately gained widespread public attention. In 1939 they were invited to join the cast of the *Grand Ole Opry*. Monroe became a fixture on the show and was still on its roster four decades later.

Almost immediately the Blue Grass Boys became a training ground for other skilled artists. Among the early members of the troupe were Sam and Kirk McGee, who closed the group's road show with a twenty-minute old-time country & western songfest, and two young sidemen named Lester Flatt and Earl Scruggs, who were to go out on their own later in the 1940s to challenge the master for bluegrass leadership. Among other folk and country & western luminaries to be part of the Blue Grass Boys at some point in their careers were Clyde Moody, Howdy Forrester, Don Reno, Red Smiley, Jimmy Martin, Carter Stanley, Vassar Clements, Chubby Wise, Cedric Rainwater, Stringbean, and Byron Berline.

In the 1940s, Bill began to write lyrics as well as melodies. In many cases, he added words to existing songs—one of which brought Eddy Arnold a top-10 hit in 1951 with his release of "Kentucky Waltz." Among other Monroe originals that were recorded by both Bill and a number of other artists over the years were "Blue Moon of Kentucky," "I Hear a Sweet Voice Calling," "Along About Daybreak," "Cheyenne," "Memories of Mother and Dad," "Gotta Travel On," "On the Kentucky Shores," and "Scotland." One of the first songs recorded by Elvis Presley in the early stages of his career was "Blue Moon of Kentucky."

During the mid-1940s, Monroe recorded for Columbia Records, in 1949 leaving to sign with Decca. Like many of Monroe's affiliations, the alignment proved a lasting one. He continued to record year after year for Decca and then on MCA, the label with which Decca merged. At the start of the 1980s, he remained on MCA's list with dozens of albums to his credit. Among his LPs on Decca were *Knee Deep* (8/58); *I Saw the Light* (10/58); *Mr. Bluegrass* (7/61); *All Time Favorites* (7/62); *Bluegrass Ramble, Bluegrass Special* (8/63); *Meet You in Church* (8/64); *Bluegrass Instrumentals* (1965); *High Lonesome Sound* (8/66); *Bluegrass Time* (8/67); *Voice from on High* (6/69); *Kentucky Bluegrass* (1970); and *Country Music Hall of Fame* (8/71). Some of his releases on other labels during the 1960s and early 1970s were *Bill Monroe and His Bluegrass Boys* (4/61, Harvard); *Father of Bluegrass Music* (10/62, Camden); *Songs with the Bluegrass Boys* (4/64, Vocalion); *Best of Bill Monroe* (7/64, Harvard); *Original Bluegrass Sound* (6/65, Harvard); *Bluegrass Style* (late 1960s, Vocalion); *16 All-Time Bluegrass Hits* (8/70, Columbia).

Over the years Monroe spent much of each year on the road. He gradually became a favorite with folk fans and during the folk music boom of the late 1950s and early 1960s, he often was featured on major folk concert tours and network TV shows. He and the Bluegrass Boys appeared at many major folk festivals during those years and later in the 1960s including a number of sets at the Newport Folk Festival. He remained a favorite of younger fans all through the 1970s and into the early 1980s, when his itinerary included many stops on college campuses across the United States. His reputation also spread far beyond U.S. borders—in the 1960s and 1970s he was enthusiastically welcomed on several tours of Europe, Canada, and many Pacific nations, including Japan.

In 1970, the Country Music Association membership acknowledged his great contributions by electing him to the Country Music Hall of Fame in Nashville. By then Bill didn't have very far to go to visit his memorabilia in the Hall of Fame since he long since had become a resident of Tennessee, spending his time off the road handling chores on a 288-acre farm in Sumner County.

During the 1970s, bluegrass adherents were cheered by the establishment of an annual bluegrass festival with Monroe as the host in Bean Blossom, Indiana. MCA Records recorded some of the festivals, resulting in two live albums during the 1970s, the two-record *Bean Blossom* set in the mid-1970s and the single disc *Bean Blossom '79*. In the early 1980s, Monroe still was turning out new solo LPs on MCA, such as the 1981 *Master of Bluegrass*.

As of 1982, MCA maintained an extensive catalogue of Monroe's recordings. Besides the three albums mentioned above, still in print in 1982 were *Greatest Hits, Mr. Bluegrass, Bluegrass Ramble, Bluegrass Special, Bluegrass Instrumentals, The High Lonesome Sound of Bill Monroe, Bluegrass Time, Bill and Charlie Monroe, A Voice from on High, Kentucky Bluegrass, Country Music Hall of Fame, I'll Meet You in Church Sunday Morning, Father and Son* (with James Monroe), *Together Again* (with James Monroe), *Road of Life, Uncle Pen, I Saw the Light, The Weary Traveler, Bill Monroe Sings Bluegrass Body and Soul, Bluegrass Memories, Best of Bill Monroe, Bluegrass Style,* and *Bill Monroe Sings Country Songs.*

MONROE, CHARLIE; *Singer, guitarist, songwriter, band leader (Kentucky Pardners). Born Rosine, Kentucky, June 4, 1903; died Reidsville, North Carolina, September 27, 1975.*

While Bill Monroe is justly honored as the "Father of Bluegrass Music," his older brother, Charlie, also had a hand in the development of the style. In the 1920s, in fact, it was Bill and Charlie's Monroe Brothers band, forerunner of Bill's Blue Grass Boys, that first excited country-music audiences with their new fast-paced blend of blues and traditional hill-country music.

Growing up in a rural area of Kentucky, Charlie and the other members of his family were part of a culture where music played an important role both as a leisure-time activity and, in the form of religious songs, an integral facet of churchgoing. Charlie, as did his younger brothers Birch

and Bill, learned to sing many hymns through the old "shaped note" hymnals. Many members of their family were adept at various instruments, used for informal get-togethers and dances, and all the Monroe children started learning to play one or more of them early in life. In Charlie's case he took up guitar (as did his sister Bertha) while Birch practiced the fiddle and Bill eventually settled on mandolin, although reluctantly, since he liked guitar more. He was forced into it by his older siblings, who wanted a mandolin sound to blend with their contributions to the family band.

As they grew up, all of the children performed separately or in various combinations at local functions. In the mid-1920s, Charlie, Birch, and Bill formed a loose alliance that led to their debut on a local radio station in 1927. Still, music seemed more a hobby than a way of making a living, and in the late 1920s, Charlie and Birch left Kentucky to find work in midwest factories. They first worked in the Detroit area, then moved on to jobs in oil refineries in Hammond and Whiting, on the East Chicago, Indiana, border. In 1929, Bill came north to join them. He found a position in the barrel house at the Sinclair refinery, where he remained on the payroll the next five years.

Once together again, the brothers resumed their musical association and picked up whatever work they could find in small clubs or, more usually, playing at local dances and house parties. In 1932, while the three Monroes and a friend, Tom Moore, were at a square dance in Hammond, Indiana, they were observed taking part in the dancing by a man named Tom Owens, who had a group that was part of the *WLS Barn Dance* tour. He approached the boys to join his troupe and they agreed; thus their first big break came as dancers, not musicians.

They remained with the *Barn Dance* tour for two years, primarily as dancers, but with opportunities to play their instruments as well. The relationship helped open some doors for them as musicians and they got the chance to work on station WAE in Hammond and later WJKS in

Gary, Indiana. By 1934, Bill and Charlie were thinking seriously of trying for full-time careers in music. The die finally was cast when Charlie was asked by officials of Texas Crystals, a patent medicine, to go on a show sponsored by them on a Shenandoah, Iowa, station. Charlie asked his brothers to join him, but Birch had the chance for a new job in an oil refinery and demurred.

The Monroe Brothers, Charlie and Bill, were so well received in Iowa they were offered a spot on a larger station in Omaha. After that, Texas Crystals sponsored a move to Columbia, South Carolina, and later in 1935 to a daily program on WBT in Charlotte, North Carolina. The response to the brothers' music by listeners and audiences at their live performance dates helped increase their self-confidence and desire to reach still wider numbers of people.

That confidence was shaken a bit in 1936 when Texas Crystals dropped them, but almost immediately they were hired by the larger Crazy Water Crystal Company. The latter not only sponsored their daily program on WBT, but saw that they were featured on the Saturday night WBT *Crazy Barn Dance*. During those years, Charlie and Bill also were heard by audiences of station WFBC in Greenville, South Carolina, and WPTF in Raleigh, North Carolina.

Talent scouts from RCA became interested in them in the mid-1930s and, after several attempts, managed to get the Monroes into the studio in Charlotte to record a series of songs in February 1936 issued on the company's Bluebird Label. Public response was good enough that they recorded another series in a later session before the brothers went separate ways.

During that period, though Bill provided many excellent original songs, Charlie maintained his role as leader and Bill was restricted to a mainly secondary slot. Bill grew restless at that arrangement and in 1938 the two parted company. Bill organized a band called the Kentuckians soon after, which later changed its name to the Blue Grass Boys, while Charlie organized his Kentucky Pardners.

Charlie remained active with his band throughout the 1940s and he retained a sizable following over those years. Bill, desiring to make a complete break with the past, left RCA for Decca at the end of the 1930s, but Charlie remained on the RCA roster. He made many recordings for RCA, many of which remain important contributions to bluegrass history, but his achievements were overshadowed by the immense success of his brother.

In 1952, tired of the touring grind, Charlie broke up his band and went back home to spend his remaining years on his Kentucky ranch. (See also Monroe, Bill.)

MONTANA, PATSY: *Singer, songwriter. Born Hot Springs, Arkansas, October 30, 1914.*

In the 1930s and 1940s, the *WLS Barn Dance* was probably the best-known country & western show in most of the country outside the South. One of the major attractions of the show was a dynamic western artist named Patsy Montana. Her stage name and her nickname of "The Yodeling Cowgirl" have a western ring to them, but her origins were a lot closer to the heartland of the *Grand Ole Opry* than to the Chicago-based *Barn Dance*.

As she told *Music City News* (August 1975, p. 20), "I grew up with 10 boys and no sisters around Hope and Hot Springs, Arkansas. [Her original name was Rubye Blevins.] My first exposure to country music would have been the old Jimmie Rodgers records and later on Gene Autry. I don't really remember a girl singer that I tried to follow. The only singer I remember in my early days out in California was Kate Smith."

Patsy attended both elementary and high school in Arkansas, graduating from Hope High School in the early 1930s. From there she went on to enroll in the University of Western Louisiana. She already had been enthusiastic about singing in her teens and by the time she went to college was spending more and more time perfecting her guitar playing and adding to her repertoire of country & western songs. Before long she cut short her educational efforts in favor of a show business career.

Recalling those early days, she noted, "I

got my name from Monty Montana, who was the world's champion yodeler. I started to work with two other girls in a trio and the name automatically became the Montana Cowgirls. My real name is Rubye and one of the girls was named Ruthie. The names conflicted when they were announced over the air. At the time we were working with Stuart Hamblen and he named me, being more Irish than the others, Patsy, while we were on the air.

"I appeared in a couple of western movies with Gene Autry and did several appearances in what they called 'shorts' in those days. Coming back from California to go to the World's Fair in Chicago, I stopped to visit my folks in Hope, Arkansas. My mother, who listened to WLS, told me to say hello to some of the acts she heard on the radio if I got the chance."

One result of following that advice was a meeting with a group called the Prairie Ramblers. The members asked her to join and she accepted, a move that resulted in Chicago becoming home for many years thereafter. The Ramblers, whose members claimed they all were born in log cabins in Kentucky, comprised Chuck Hurt, Tex Atchison, Jack Taylor, and Salty Holmes. Patsy and the Ramblers graced stages all over the United States and in several other nations from 1934 through 1948. During that time, they were featured in almost every county fair in the country. Starting in 1935, Montana and the group were regulars on the *National Barn Dance*, for which Patsy remained a headliner into the 1950s. In 1934 she married Paul Rose, and, after a while, she found time to start raising a family. (Rose, an entertainment industry executive, managed an act called "Mac and Bob," and was also his wife's manager for many years.)

Montana began her long recording career in 1933, with such songs as "I Love My Daddy Too" and "When the Flowers of Montana Are Blooming." Her voice was heard on many different labels from then until the start of the 1960s, including Surf, Columbia, RCA Victor, Vocalion, and Decca. As of the mid-1970s, she estimated she had been represented by over 200 singles as well as dozens of albums. Some of her single releases of the 1930s were "The Wheel of the Wagon Is Broken," "I'm an Old Cowhand," "There's a Ranch in the Sky," "Singing in the Saddle," "A Cowboy Honeymoon," and "Montana." In later decades she turned out such songs as "Old Nevada Moon," "My Million Dollar Smile," "I Only Want a Buddy, Not a Sweetheart," "If I Could Only Learn to Yodel," "Little Sweetheart of the Ozarks," "Deep in the Heart of Texas," "Good Night Soldier," and "Leaning on the Old Top Rail." Most of her albums were collector's items by the 1960s, but in the mid-1960s Starday released some of her recordings in the LP *Sweetheart*.

Patsy wrote many original songs during her long career. Among her compositions were "My Baby's Lullaby," "Me and My Cowboy Sweetheart," "The Buckaroo," "Cowboy Rhythm," "I'm a Little Cowboy Girl," "The Moon Hangs Low," "My Poncho Pony," "A Cowboy Gal," and "I've Found My Cowboy Sweetheart."

In the late 1940s and during the 1950s, Montana kept a busy schedule on the concert circuit and on TV. During 1946–47 she had her own radio program on ABC called *Wake Up and Smile*. She also brought her family into the act for a while. As she recalled for *Music City News*, "At one time, my daughters and I were the only mother and daughters team around. Judy was about five and Beverly was about eight. We traveled as the Patsy Montana Trio."

In 1959, there were reports that she had retired briefly to sell real estate in Manhattan Beach, California, which Patsy later denied. Although her stage work was much more limited in the 1960s and 1970s, she still performed steadily. In the 1970s, she began to find growing interest about her among college-age fans and she did a number of shows on college campuses, where, besides western numbers, she sang such classic country songs as "Wabash Cannonball" and "Great Speckled Bird." She also took part in a number of the 1970s Nashville summer Fan Fair Reunions along with many other veteran country artists.

Comparing her years of intensive touring with the modern era, she said, "When we first started traveling on the road, we didn't have conveniences like hair dryers and air conditioning. I guess you don't miss something you never had. I just wonder how many miles I have slept cramped in a car with my head on the neck of that bass fiddle. I sometimes wonder if some of these younger artists could do what we did. You have to have endurance to be in this business. I feel sorry for these kids who go directly to the top, because they only have one way left to go and that's down."

MONTGOMERY, MELBA: *Singer, songwriter. Born Iron City, Tennessee, October 14, 1938.*

Anyone given the opportunity to perform with country artists the likes of Roy Acuff and George Jones has to have above-average ability. So it was with brown-haired silken-voiced Melba Montgomery, whose vocalizing with those legendary performers made her one of the most highly regarded country stylists of the 1960s.

Melba came to her interest in music as a matter of course, growing up in a farm family in rural sections of Tennessee and Alabama. She sang in school events during her early years and began to consider making music a career as she grew older. She started to enter amateur contests, making her first major breakthrough in 1958 when she took part in the Pet Milk competition held in Studio C at Nashville's WSM, then and now the home station of the *Grand Ole Opry.* Her victory there set the stage for the chance to become a member of Roy Acuff's Smoky Mountain Gang. For four years, from 1958 to 1962, she was a cast member and performed before audiences the length and breadth of the United States.

In the early 1960s, Montgomery cut a number of solo sides for a small record company, which had little impact on the national public. But veteran music industry executive Pappy Daily, then head of United Artists' country & western division, liked her style and added her to the UA label in 1962. She turned out a number of singles, some of her own original com-

positions, that did well enough for the company to release her debut LP, *Melba Montgomery,* in April 1964. This was followed by the album *Down Home* in October 1964 and *Being Lonely* in January 1965.

Pappy also started teaming her with George Jones for a series of duets almost as soon as she joined UA. One of their first efforts was a single of Melba's composition "We Must Have Been Out of Our Minds," which became one of the year's top country hits, making the top 10 in the charts. Another Jones-Montgomery hit of the mid-1960s was "Don't Keep Me Lonely Too Long," a song that has been covered by fifteen other artists over the years since then.

In 1965, Daily left UA to set up his own record firm, Musicor, and both Jones and Montgomery were among the artists who went with him. One of their chart hits on the new label was the 1967 "Party Pickin'."

Besides working with Jones, Melba also recorded duets with another Daily protégé, Gene Pitney. Their most successful collaboration was on the Dallas Frazier song "Baby, Ain't That Fine." An album of their work, *Being Together,* was released on Musicor in August 1966. Montgomery's solo debut on Musicor was "Hallelujah Road," released in August 1966, followed by another LP, titled *Country Girl.* She also was one of the artists included in the mid-1960s Starday album, *Queens of Country Music.* Among her singles hits of the late 1960s were such songs as "Where Do We Go from Here" and "Eloy Crossing." In 1969, she signed with Capitol Records, which released her debut single on the label, "As Far as My Forgetting's Got," during the year and other singles and albums during the next few years. Capitol teamed her with Charlie Louvin in 1970, and their duet album, *Somethin' to Brag About,* was issued in February 1971.

Melba's career slowed down in the early 1970s and from the end of 1971 well into 1973 she essentially concentrated on maintaining a household for her husband, musician Jack Solomon, and writing new songs. During 1973, she signed with Elektra Records and started making new discs under the watchful eye of producer Pete

Drake. One of those songs, co-written by Montgomery and her husband, "Wrap Your Arms Around Me," made the charts in the fall of 1973. In May 1974, she reached a new milestone when her single "No Charge" rose to number two on the charts for her first big hit of the 1970s. She followed with more mid-1970s chart singles on Elektra (though none exceeded her success with "No Charge"), including "Your Pretty Roses Came Too Late" in 1974; "Don't Let the Good Times Fool You" and "Searchin'" in 1975; and "Love Was the Wind" in 1976.

In the late 1970s, Melba recorded for United Artists, including the 1977 chart single "Never Ending Love Affair." At the start of the 1980s she was on KARI Records and had the single "The Star" on the lists in late 1980.

MORGAN, GEORGE: *Singer, guitarist, songwriter. Born Waverly, Tennessee, June 28, 1925; died Nashville, Tennessee, July 7, 1975.*

A country music "traditionalist," George Morgan never felt at home in the progressive country era of the 1970s. But a host of country fans and fellow performers looked fondly on his many years of stardom and his compositions like "Candy Kisses," which promised to become all-time country standards.

George spent his first two years in Waverly, Tennessee, but a tragic accident to his father that took place two weeks before his birth drastically affected family fortunes. Jack Morgan, who had a small farm and earned additional money by cutting cross-ties for the railroad, was walking across a stretch of railroad, track while hunting groundhogs when his boot laces caught in a switchtrack. As luck would have it, a train was coming and, lacking a knife to cut the knotted lace, he had to fall back and break his leg to avoid being run over. The train cut off his leg.

As Morgan told Dixie Deen of *Music City News* (March 1967), "That put an end to his farming and cutting cross-ties days and when I was about two years old, after my brother Bill was born, my daddy had to move to Ohio to get work. . . . He got a job hauling coal with a horse and wagon."

By the time George was three, his father was able to send for the family. "He got a job with the Seiberling Rubber Company [in Barberton, Ohio] and he got a wooden leg around that time. I can remember times during the Depression that he would come home, take off that wooden leg, and the blood would be seeping out of that old stump stocking. These are not pleasant things," he told Deen, "but it is pleasant in my mind to know how much dad loved us to go through all this. I mean, he would work around the clock sometimes just to feed us."

Music, George recalled, was always one of the family's pleasures. "Every Saturday night, mom and dad both being from Tennessee, would tune in to the *Grand Ole Opry*. That was in the days of D. Ford Bailey, way before Roy Acuff and Minnie Pearl. I grew up listening to country music and my love for it was instilled because to my folks it was something from 'down home.'"

George went through grade school and entered high school in Barberton but dropped out in the eleventh grade to go to work. He agreed it wasn't the smartest move. "It wasn't because I had to go to work. We weren't all that poor and dad could have provided for me until I got through high school, but like so many foolish kids, I wanted to go to work." The job he took was in a Barberton restaurant, the first of a variety of occupations he essayed on the way to his music career.

During the mid-1940s, he interrupted his civilian chores to enlist in the Army. However, after three months he received an honorable discharge on medical grounds. After that, he put in time at a range of jobs, including working in a rubber plant, surveying in Oklahoma, and working in several restaurants in Ohio.

He had been playing guitar for some time and slowly was becoming more interested in the possibilities of the music field. In 1947, "we got a little band together and started working for peanuts, and sometimes not even for that."

When a small radio station opened in Wooster, Ohio, Morgan and his band auditioned for it and were hired. "There was no money in it. Our little country band opened up the station every morning for a couple of months, then the other guys in the band couldn't see any future in this and they all quit. I stayed on with my guitar."

While he was doing that, he came up with the song that was to prove his good luck charm, "Candy Kisses." He recalled for *Music City News*, "I was on the way to the station one morning and I was thinking about a girl and it occurred to me that my kisses meant less to her than the candy kisses my mother used to bring home had meant to me when I was a kid."

Meanwhile, he was finding favor with station audiences and his time slot was improved from an early morning one to a 5:00 P.M. period. He also began to have increased exposure on local shows and performed on station WAKR in nearby Akron. One of his disc jockey friends in Akron gave him his next move up by letting him know of an audition for one of the top country stations in the region, Wheeling, West Virginia's WWVA. George went there, auditioned, and was hired. It was, he noted, "my first big money in radio when they paid me $40 a week. I worked there for a while and then, I don't know why, I got discouraged and decided to quit radio."

Fortunately, station manager Paul Myers loved "Candy Kisses" and persuaded Morgan to make a demonstration record of it, which he sent to RCA Victor's Nashville offices. Bob Ross of RCA happened to play the record for WSM executives just when they were looking for new talent. They soon picked up the phone and asked Morgan to come to Nashville for an audition. Ironically, RCA didn't sign him. Even as he was arriving in Nashville, Columbia artists & repertoire executive Art Satherly was back in Wheeling trying to find him. Satherly hurried back to Nashville, sought out Morgan, and soon had him signed to a recording contract.

Things swiftly fell into line for George in 1948. He joined *Opry* station WSM and soon found "Candy Kisses" a major hit. He had to share honors with several cover records; including his release, there were

four top-10 versions of his song in 1948–49, though his was the number-one hit. (The others were by Cowboy Copas, Eddie Kirk, and Red Foley.) In 1949, he had four more top-10 hits: "Crybaby Heart," "Please Don't Let Me Love You," "Rainbow in My Heart," and "Room Full of Roses." He didn't have that volume of top-10 singles throughout the 1950s, though he did place many songs on lower-chart levels over the decade. His top-ranked singles of the period included "Almost" in 1952, a top-10 hit of his composition "I'm in Love Again" in 1959, and, in 1960, the top-10 single "You're the Only Good Thing."

After being a featured *Opry* star for the first part of the 1950s, Morgan left in 1956 to star on his own show on WLAC–TV in Nashville. He rejoined the *Opry* as a regular in 1959 and was still a show member in the 1970s. During the 1960s and 1970s, his TV credits included appearances on shows hosted by Bobby Lord, Porter Wagoner, the Wilburn Brothers, on *Hee Haw,* and on *Country Music Hall.* His personal appearances took him all over the United States and Canada and to audiences in Europe as well.

Among the other songs he recorded over the years were "Slipping Around," "You Loved Me Just Enough to Hurt Me," "You're Not Home Yet," "I'm Not Afraid," "A Picture That's New," "No Man Should Hurt as Bad as I Do," "You're the Only Star in My Blue Heaven," "Cheap Affair," "Cry of the Lamb," "Ever So Often," "Wheel of Hurt," "Lonesome Record," "Jesus Savior Pilot Me," "Little Pioneer," "Mansion Over the Hilltop," "No One Knows It Better than Me," "Oh Gentle Shepherd," "Shot in the Dark," "Walking Shoes," and "Whither Thou Goest."

His Columbia albums included *Candy Kisses, Morgan, By George, Greatest Country & Western Hits, Slipping Around, Tender Loving Care, Red Roses for a Blue Lady, George Morgan* (issued 3/64); *George Morgan and Marion Worth* (issued 9/64).

The early impact of rock on the country field played a part in a decline in his recording volume in the early 1960s. This finally resulted in a closing out of his association with Columbia in 1966, ending an eighteen-year relationship. He moved over to Starday Records, and his debut LP on the label, *Candy Kisses*, came out in early 1967. This was followed soon after by the album *Hits by Candelight*. Later releases on Starday included *The Best of George Morgan* and *The Real George Morgan*. He also was represented on the Nashville label in the early 1970s with *Room Full of Roses*.

During the 1970s, George recorded new material for a series of labels, including Step and MCA Records. During the last years of his career, he was on the Four Star label and was the master of ceremonies for that company's show during the summer of 1975 Fan Fair festivities in Nashville.

On May 26, 1975, Morgan suffered a heart attack while installing an antenna on the roof of his Nashville home. He recovered and resumed his music activities, but then found out he needed open heart surgery and entered Baptist Hospital in Nashville in early July for the operation. Unfortunately, complications arising from the surgery brought his illustrious career to a close—he died on July 7. Only a short time before going into the hospital he had made his last appearance on the *Opry*. It had been a joyous affair at a time when no one expected the tragedy of later weeks. His *Opry* friends had given him a cake in honor of his fifty-first birthday and George had proudly introduced his daughter, Lorrie, for her *Opry* singing debut.

MORRISON, BOB: *Singer, guitarist, songwriter. Born Biloxi, Mississippi, 1943.*

The album *Friends of Mine*, released in 1971, showcased a promising country artist named Bob Morrison. The LP since has become a collector's item. It didn't have much success, despite its quality, but Morrison went on to solidify a reputation as one of the finest writers of country material during the 1970s.

Bob was born and raised in Mississippi, where, where, when he was fifteen, he taught himself to play guitar and occasionally performed at local events. He was also proficient in sports, starring on his high school baseball, basketball, and track teams and later as a varsity performer at Mississippi State University. He also was a

good student, regularly making the Dean's and President's lists, graduating from MSU with a degree in nuclear engineering and later adding some credits at Howard University.

But he was to become increasingly interested in music. In his freshman year in college he was a band sideman and afterward formed his own quartet to play for campus affairs and at parties and clubs in nearby towns. In 1963, he got a job in a Biloxi folk club as a solo vocal and guitar act. By the mid-1960s he had decided to forgo engineering in favor of seeking his fortune in the entertainment field.

In the second half of the 1960s, he tried his hand at many aspects of music besides performing. He began to write original songs in earnest and also worked as an arranger and record producer. During those years, he joined with some friends to start his own publishing company. He also became acquainted with French singing star Charles Aznavour, who helped arrange for Morrison to translate some of the lyrics of Aznavour's French hits into English.

Morrison already had made some inroads with country artists as a songwriter when he signed with Capitol Records at the start of the 1970s. His debut album, *Friends of Mine*, issued in March 1971, featured Bob singing such original compositions as "Tell the Riverboat Captain," "She's Gonna Be a Friend of Mine," "Song for Wendy," "Sweet Sounds of September," and "If You'd Like to Be a Lady."

Bob made some recording efforts after that, but most of the time he concentrated on placing his songs with others. It was rare when more than a few months went by in the 1970s without one of the songs written or co-written by Morrison being recorded by a country singer. Among those who made the charts with Morrison tunes were Jim Munday with "The River's Too Wide" at the start of 1974; Dottie West with "Rollin' in Your Sweet Sunshine" (summer 1975); Freddy Weller with "Stone Crazy" (fall 1975); Mel McDaniel with "Have a Dream on Me" (early summer 1976) and "Soul of a Honky Tonk Woman" (winter 1977); Ray Price with

"Born to Love Me" (winter 1977); Charly McClain with "That's What You Do to Me" (top 10, December 1978); and the Kendalls with "You'd Make an Angel Wanna Cheat" (top 5, January–February 1980).

The Kendalls' hit (co-written by Bob with B. and J. Zerface) was the start of a particularly successful year for Morrison. A few months after it, "Are You on the Road to Lovin' Me Again" (co-written with D. Hult) was at the top of the charts in the form of a Debby Boone single. Other best-sellers were "Let's Put Our Love in Motion" (co-written with J. MacRae and L. Rogers), recorded by Charly McClain, and "Making Plans" (co-written with J. Russell), a top-10 hit for Porter Wagoner and Dolly Parton. As a result of that activity, Morrison was one of the five finalists for the 1980 Songwriter's Achievement Award of the Nashville Songwriters Association International. Bob had still more songs on the charts in 1981, including Mel Tillis' top-10 single of "One Night Fever" (co-written with J. MacRae).

MOSBY, JOHNNY AND JONIE: *Vocal and instrumental duo. Johnny born Ft. Smith, Arkansas, April 26; Jonie born Van Nuys, California, August 10.*

In country music, male-female vocal duets long have been a favorite with audiences. Few of the successful duos have been married to each other; a major exception is the team of Johnny and Jonie Mosby, who joined forces in the 1950s and were still going strong over two decades later.

Both of the Mosbys spent most of their early years in Southern California. Johnny was born in Arkansas, but his family moved to Los Angeles when he was quite young. Although he and Jonie enjoyed the pop music that dominated the music scene in L.A. while they grew up, they felt more comfortable with country sounds. Johnny assembled his own country bands during the 1950s and was well known to local country fans long before he crossed Jonie's path.

In early 1958, word was passed around the Los Angeles area that Johnny was looking for a female vocalist for his group. Jonie auditioned for the spot and demonstrated a strong, vibrant voice that won Johnny's attention. She got the job and soon was joining Johnny in bandstand duets. Later in 1958, the duo took their collaboration one step further by signing a marriage contract as well.

Soon after, in 1959, they finished recording their initial single, "Just Before Dawn." The record made the national country charts and the Mosbys were on their way. They followed with a series of chart singles in the first half of the 1960s, including "I'd Fight the World," "Don't Call Me from a Honky Tonk," and "Keep Those Cards and Letters Coming In." The trade magazine *Cash Box* took note of their growing national reputation when it named them the Most Promising Vocal Group in 1962.

In the early 1960s, the team was one of the most popular local country acts. For five years, they hosted their own two-hour show called *Country Music Time* on a local Los Angeles TV station. Jonie was featured on a similarly named daytime thirty-minute daily program. They also opened their own country nightclub, called "The Bander," in Ventura (about forty miles north of Los Angeles), which they operated for six years before selling it at the end of the 1960s to devote full time to their performing activities.

During the mid-1960s, they were represented on the Columbia and Starday labels. Starday issued the LP *New Sweethearts* and Columbia released the album *Johnny and Jonie Mosby* in March 1965. At the end of the decade, they signed a new recording contract with Capitol Records. One of their first efforts was the single "Make a Left, Then a Right," which rose to upper country-chart levels. They followed with two more chart singles in 1969, "Just Hold My Hand" and "Hold Me, Thrill Me, Kiss Me." The latter provided the title song for their debut Capitol LP, released in September 1969. Their achievements during that year brought them an award from the West Coast-based Academy of Country & Western Music as the Best Singing Group.

The Mosbys' decision to concentrate on

their entertaining career resulted in a move with their three daughters to Nashville during 1969. It also marked a wider touring effort for the pair and their band. Johnny noted in 1969 that living on the West Coast with three young children tended to limit personal appearances to that area. Jonie added, "It's hard to pull up roots and try to put them down again, but it's also much less complicated to work out of Nashville than it is from the coast." The result was a steady series of concerts by the Mosbys throughout the United States in 1969 and into the 1970s. During the early 1970s, Capitol released a number of new LPs that included *I'll Never Be Free, My Happiness, Oh, Love of Mine*, and *Mr. & Mrs. Country Music*.

MULDAUR, MARIA: *Singer, fiddler, guitarist. Born New York, New York, September 2, 1942.*

Over a lengthy and noteworthy career, Maria Muldaur has proved herself one of the most versatile and talented vocalists in popular music. She originally made her mark as a folk artist and played an important part in the folk movement of the 1960s, but, as she also demonstrated, she could handle almost any style of music with skill and freshness, ranging from ballads to jazz, blues/R&B, and rock 'n' roll.

Born and raised in New York's Greenwich Village, Maria didn't have to go far to hear the music she enjoyed. The Village was a hotbed of jazz activity during her childhood years and the core of the burgeoning folk boom in her teens. She described her early years as a "non-stop hootennany" replete with "bluegrass, folk, blues, guitar, and Italian accordion players. It was like a miniature folk festival every Sunday afternoon."

Although she enjoyed listening to blues and R&B artists and joined her peer group in admiring the early wave of rock 'n' rollers, folk music remained her main love as she moved into her late teens. Many of the leading folk artists of the time, such as the Seegers and the New Lost City Ramblers, made a practice of seeking out little-known but highly talented rural artists. One group founded to arrange for city appearances of such musicians was the Friends of Old Time Music. Maria, then a recent high school graduate, attended the first such concert, which featured the legendary Doc Watson and his North Carolina associates. She was inspired by Doc's vocals and striking guitar work, and by the fiddle playing of Doc's father-in-law, Gaither Carlton.

By that time Muldaur had already decided to try her lot as a performer and had started collecting folk songs for her repertoire. Like many urban folk aficionados, she decided the best way to become attuned to the authentic folk sound was to spend time with people who, in essence, lived it. So not long after the concert she made her way to Watson's home town, where she spent some time with the Watson family. Besides learning many of the songs Doc and his friends and neighbors knew, she took pointers from Gaither Carlton on country fiddling.

She returned to the Village, where she was a familiar figure at many of the informal get-togethers of young folk artists who had flocked to New York from all over the United States. She got the chance to sing and play the fiddle at some of the small clubs and coffee houses and also picked up change from working the party circuit. Muldaur arrived at her first major performing milestone in late 1963 when she was twenty-one. Blues luminary Victoria Spivey assembled a group to make a jug band record for her label; called the Even Dozen Jug Band, its members included, besides Maria, such people as John Sebastian and Steve Katz. Sebastian, soon after, was to go on to national fame with his folk-rock group Lovin' Spoonful while Katz later was a key figure in such major rock bands as the Blues Project and Blood, Sweat & Tears. The only LP of the Even Dozen Jug Band was released under the Elektra Records banner in January 1964.

Jug bands were a big thing in the folk field at the time. Among others vying for attention were Dave Van Ronk's Ragtime Jug Stompers and the Jim Kweskin Jug Band. The groups often crossed paths, sometimes sharing the same bill. This resulted in the meeting of Maria and a member of Kweskin's group named Geoff Muldaur, then living in Cambrige, Massachusetts. After the Even Dozen group broke up, Maria went to join Geoff, and, soon after, the two were married. Their relationship became an artistic partnership as well; when an opening came up in Kweskin's band, Maria was added to the roster.

For the rest of the decade, the Muldaurs remained members of that assemblage, helping Kweskin record a series of albums, mostly on Vanguard, but some on Reprise, including *Jug Band Music* (4/65), *Relax Your Mind* (3/66), *See Reverse Side* (2/67)—all on Vanguard—and *Garden of Joy* (11/67) on Reprise. The group toured throughout the United States and to a number of foreign countries and also played many major festivals, including a number of appearances at the Newport Folk Festival.

At the start of the 1970s, after Kweskin disbanded his group, the Muldaurs moved from Cambridge to Woodstock, New York. There they worked on a new act featuring just the two of them. This effort won them a new contract from Reprise and resulted in two LPs, *Pottery Pie* and *Sweet Potatoes.*

However, personal problems were beginning to crop up which finally resulted in their separating. After spending some time considering her next direction, Maria decided the time had come to try for a solo career. In 1973, she signed a solo agreement with Warner Brothers, the parent company for the Reprise label. Her debut solo LP, *Maria Muldaur,* was issued in the early summer of 1974 and Maria set out on a cross-country tour in support of it. The initial single release, a novelty number by David Nichtern called "Midnight at the Oasis," caught fire and moved high on the charts. By the time Muldaur finished her tour in June 1974, she had a gold-record award for the single plus a second one for the album. Although the emphasis was away from folk towards R&B, rock, and jazz influences, a folk flavor remained in that LP as on the succeeding ones, *Waitress in a Donut Shop,* issued in 1975, and the 1976 release *Sweet Harmony.*

After the last of those albums came out,

Maria decided a change of scenery was in order and relocated in Marin County above San Francisco. Once there she assembled a new band and made regular swings up and down the coast, besides playing extended engagements in clubs in the bay area. She also appeared with such diverse groups as the rock-oriented Jerry Garcia Band and the jazz-based Benny Carter Orchestra. On several occasions she was a featured performer at jazz festivals in various parts of the country.

In 1978, after a two-year hiatus, Muldaur was represented by a new LP, *Southern Winds,* with stylings ranging from soft folk ballad to driving R&B. She continued to explore different vocal shadings in her June 1979 release, her fifth solo LP, *Open Your Eyes.* Describing the evolution of her vocal approach in the 1970s, she told a biographer from Warner Brothers Records, "My depth of expression is growing; my voice is more relaxed and it's getting heavier as I get older. It's like I've had a flute all these years, a little delicate flute. But I started wanting to express other things. I thought somehow I'm gonna find a corner in my voice to convey more than just a crooning lullabye. Now I find there's a saxophone in there."

MULLICAN, MOON: *Singer, organist, pianist, songwriter. Born Polk County, near Corrigan, Texas, March 27, 1909; died Beaumont, Texas, January 1, 1967.*

Aubrey "Moon" Mullican's family assumed that he would someday succeed to the management of his father's rich eighty-seven acre farm. But when Moon was eight, his father bought a pump-organ that was to change Moon's future. Within a few years, he had worked out a two-finger right-hand style of playing that was to provide the grounds for his claim to the title "King of the Hillbilly Piano Players."

Moon's skill in organ playing continued to improve. He played for his church when he was in his teens, and after a while, he branched out into playing piano for local dances. In Lufkin, Texas, in the late 1920s, he took home his first paycheck for a musical performance and decided to make music his occupation.

He moved to Houston, where he began accompanying local folk artists and eventually formed his own band, which played at clubs and on radio in many places in Louisiana and Texas during the 1930s. For a time, he was featured on station KPBX in Beaumont, Texas. During the decade, he also made the first of many records on such labels as Coral, Decca, and King. In 1939, he went to Hollywood for a role in the film *Village Barn Dance*. Audiences in California clubs were as impressed with his personal appearances as those in the Southwest.

In the 1940s, Mullican returned home to Texas. Part of the time, he owned his own nightclubs in Beaumont and Port Arthur. In the mid- and late-1940s, he began to move into the big time with his records of some of his own songs. In 1947, he had a number-one bestseller in "New Jole Blon," on the King label. The song placed second as Best Hillbilly Record of 1947 in polls conducted by *Cash Box* and the Juke Box Operators association. The following year, he had the third-ranked song in those polls, as well as a gold-record-seller in his composition "Sweeter than the Flowers." Moon hit the top-10 bracket on the charts with another King Records success in 1950, "Good Night Irene," and topped it that same year with the number-one "I'll Sail My Ship Alone." He had a third major hit in 1950 with "Mona Lisa." Then, in 1951, another Mullican composition (co-authored with W. C. Redbird) closed out his cycle of hits, "Cherokee Boogie."

For the rest of the 1950s and early 1960s, Mullican was active with tours that took him into all the states and overseas as well. He was featured on his own program on KECK, Odessa, Texas, and guested on such shows as *Grand Ole Opry*, ABC-TV's *Jubilee U.S.A.*, and the *Big D Jamboree*. Some of his other recordings of these and earlier years were "Columbus Stockade Blues," "Sugar Beet," "Jole Blon's Sister," "Early Morning Blues," "The Leaves Mustn't Fall," "Well Oh Well," "Sweeter than the Flowers No. 2," "Moon's Rock," "Pipeliner's Blues," "Jambalaya," "Every Which-Away," and "Moon's Tune."

Moon's long and illustrious career ended in 1967 when he was stricken with a fatal heart attack in Beaumont.

MURPHEY, MICHAEL: *Singer, guitarist, songwriter. Born Dallas, Texas, early 1940s.*

Most artists in the 1960s and 1970s strongly resented being typecast musically. The best way to prevent that, of course, is to demonstrate capability in different stylings, something Michael Murphey certainly did in his writing and performing efforts, at times turning out mainstream rock, at others country or folk-rock, and at still others, country. Thus he kept his career options open, though he also tended to keep possible fans off balance.

Murphey came by his country leanings naturally. Born and raised in Texas, he heard a mixture of country, rock, and pop throughout his formative years. A precocious child, he taught himself to play a plastic ukulele at six and began writing stories and poems at seven. His poetic bent later showed up in some classic songs, such as "Geronimo's Cadillac" from his debut solo LP on A&M in 1971 and the gold-record hit "Wildfire" in 1975.

Michael was performing a blend of folk, country, and rock during his early years in high school and had appeared in many small clubs and coffee houses in the Southwest by the time he got his diploma. By that time he had headed a band that was very successful with Dallas fans and on local TV and had gained other honors as well, including placing some of his poems in a national poetry anthology. He had an offer to appear on a national TV series in his late teens, but declined in favor of concentrating on in-person singing dates.

When he was twenty, he moved to Southern California, where he enrolled at the University of California at Los Angeles, taking courses in writing and poetry. Six months after he arrived in Los Angeles he had a songwriting contract with Sparrow Music and also was a regular at Randy Sparks' (of New Christy Minstrels fame) folk night-club, Ledbetter's, in West Los Angeles. Those activities brought a widening circle of friendships with other promising but still unknown artists, people the likes of Jackson Browne, Don Henley, and Glenn Frey (later founding members of the Eagles), Linda Ronstadt, and Jerry Jeff Walker.

At one point in the mid-1960s, it seemed that Murphey might beat all of them into the national spotlight. He organized a band called the Lewis and Clark Expedition that won a lot of attention in local showcase performances in Los Angeles. The group's debut LP, *I Feel Good, I Feel Bad,* made the national charts. He recalled, "It was an exciting time, one of incredible experimentation and cross-pollination of musical styles." But somehow things fell apart, partly because of management problems and partly due to personality clashes. Discouraged, for a time Michael withdrew from the industry treadmill to a remote haunt in the San Gabriel Mountains east of L.A. He wrote songs but mailed them in to his publishers, avoiding personal appearances.

In the late 1960s, he decided to go back to Texas, settling in Austin, where he took part in the movement that laid the groundwork for much of the progressive country trend in the 1970s. He assembled a new band that combined folk, country, and even some jazz, with rock elements. The group gained a local following and proved to be a springboard to his solo career. After record producer Bob Johnston heard Murphey perform in the Austin area, he offered Michael studio time, which resulted in an album that aroused the interest of a number of major record firms.

After considering various offers, Murphey chose A&M, which released his album label debut, *Geronimo's Cadillac,* in 1971 and followed it with *Cosmic Cowboy Souvenir* in 1971. *Geronimo's Cadillac* was called "brilliant" by the *Times* of London and brought an accolade from *Rolling Stone* magazine that called Murphey "the best new songwriter in the country" (though by then he'd been turning out originals for a long time, many of which had been included in other performers' albums). *Cowboy Souvenir* became a cult favorite, but never a major hit.

A somewhat disgruntled Murphey left A&M and a while later signed with Epic.

He gave vent to some of his feelings when he took the stage at his first CBS sales convention and railed against industry overcontrol in "Nobody's Gonna Tell Me How to Play My Music." The song was included in his debut release on Epic in early 1974, *Michael Murphey.* In late 1974, he moved his family from Texas to Colorado, where he worked on material for his second Epic collection. Among the songs he recorded there at Caribou Ranch were "Wildfire" and "Carolina in the Pines," which became major singles hits in 1975 along with the album that contained them, *Blue Sky, Night Thunder.* In support of those releases, Murphey embarked on a highly successful cross country tour of the United States in 1975.

He continued to probe new musical and lyrical themes in succeeding albums with increasing emphasis on folk and country-styled material. He placed a number of songs on the singles charts in the second half of the 1970s, though none had the impact of "Wildfire." They included such songs as the rocker "Renegade" and country-oriented "Mansion on the Hill" from the late 1975 LP *Swans Against the Sun* and "Cherokee Fiddle" from the 1976 album release, *Flowing Free Forever.* His seventh solo album, *Lone Wolf,* came out at the start of 1978 and his eighth, *Peaks, Valleys, Honky Tonks and Alleys* in early 1978. The last named was one of the most heavily country-oriented albums in his career, having only a few dashes of rock on some tracks. The album included live updates of "Cosmic Cowboy" and "Geronimo's Cadillac," a fine rework of a 1972 song, "Backslider's Wine," and a new country-rock original (co-written with Gary Nunn) titled "Years Behind Bars."

MURRAY, ANNE: *Singer, ukulele player. Born Springhill, Nova Scotia, Canada, June 20, 1945.*

For someone who had to be persuaded to take her first job as a performer, Anne Murray had come far indeed by the early 1980s. After a career that had its ups and downs in the 1970s, she came back strongly the latter part of the decade to become firmly established as one of the reigning stars of both pop and country music. Yet she had come close to making high school teaching her life profession.

The daughter of a rural physician, she grew up with five brothers in the coal mining town of Springhill, Nova Scotia. Although brought up in a middle class home, Anne still was exposed to some of the rougher aspects of life. She told columnist Joan Sutton in 1978, "Living in a small town, that's pretty damned basic. Especially a coal mining town where every day these men flirt with death. Coal miners are pretty solid stock. They've had so many disasters in that town and they just bounce back. I've never seen anything like it. I'm sure that's got to have been an influence on me. Although I was never directly involved, all my friends' fathers were miners and there's a certain mentality, a certain very basic straight-ahead outlook on life."

Growing up in Springhill, Anne was exposed to country music, which was popular in Canada's rural areas, though she never thought of herself as a country singer until her career got under way. Her musical interests in high school tended more towards pop and folk. Still, it wasn't until she was half way through college at the University of New Brunswick that she made her first halting move toward show business, auditioning for a job on the CBC-TV summer show *Sing Along Jubilee* in 1964.

William Langstroth, later to become her husband, was cohost and associate producer of the show at the time. He recalled for *Billboard* magazine (October 20, 1979), that Murray was one of eighty-five applying for work. "We auditioned the chorus first and I remember she sat on a stool accompanying herself on a baritone ukulele, and led the others in 'Mary Don't You Weep,' which was a hot folk song of the sixties.

"After we were done there were only two of them left, Anne and another girl. But we couldn't hire her because we had all the altos we needed. I told her to keep in touch."

But she stuck in the mind of both Langstroth and his associate Brian Ahern. Two years later Langstroth wired and cabled the university trying to find her. When he did, she wasn't interested; she had decided she would take her B.A. and teach physical education in high school. "She gave me a lot of lip," Langstroth said. "I told her she should try again. She said, 'No way. I'm not coming to your stupid auditions.' But I kept talking and she showed up and we hired her." (She was on the show for four seasons).

Even then, Anne was dubious about his and Ahern's suggestions that she devote full time to music. Ahern in particular was anxious to groom her for recording work. As she told Bob Allen for an article in *Country Music* (July/August 1979), "I remember when I was still teaching [at a high school on Prince Edward Island], Brian Ahern sent me special delivery letters telling me to come on up to Toronto where he was learning to be a record producer. I thought he was crazy! In fact, when I did finally get there, I remember going down to the hock shop to get two of his guitars out of hock. That's how badly off he was. That was in the fall of '68."

Ahern persevered and got Murray the chance to record her first album, *What About Me*, on Arc Records, a small Canadian label. That, in turn, led to a recording contract with Capitol Records of Canada. One of the songs she recorded was "Snowbird." The single was released in the United States and became a major hit on both country and pop charts in 1970, as did her debut album on U.S. Capitol of the same title (issued in August 1970). The single earned her a gold record.

Capitol, which was based in Hollywood, California, brought her to the West Coast to try to give her the star treatment. Once in the United States, she guested on a number of TV shows, including many appearances on Glen Campbell's series. She also went out on intensive concert tours and recorded more material for Capitol. But it was something less than a halcyon time. For one thing, Anne felt ill at ease. She told a *Billboard* reporter (October 20, 1979), "I was plucked out of Springhill, Nova Scotia, and dropped on a Hollywood sound stage. I felt like Dorothy in Oz. Exactly like Dorothy, come to think of it. All I wanted to do was go home."

To add to her problems, there was a long relatively dry spell between major hits. She told Sutton, "The worst time was between 'Snowbird' and 'Danny's Song'—two and a half years waiting for that second song—that was really awful. Playing those dingy, terrible clubs all across the United States, for weeks and weeks and nobody cared. NOBODY! It was like beating your head against a stone wall. I learned nothing. It was a waste of time as far as I'm concerned. I gained nothing. I didn't make any money. I didn't do anything. A lot of people say you have to pay your dues and all that, but I don't think it was character building—I don't think it was anything but just rotten."

Murray did have a number of charted releases in the early 1970s, but for a long time none came close to the success of "Snowbird," a situation that causes industry people to begin to think of an artist as a one-hit phenomenon. Those interim singles were "Sing High—Sing Low" in 1970; "Talk It Over in the Morning," "A Stranger in My Place," and "Put Your Hand in the Hand" in 1971; and "Cotton Jenny" in 1972. Capitol also released a number of LPs over this period: *Anne Murray* (2/71); *Talk It Over in the Morning* (9/71); *Anne Murray/Glen Campbell* (11/71); *Annie* (4/72).

The turn around came after Capitol issued Anne's single of the Kenny Loggins composition "Danny's Song" in 1973. The song made both pop and country upper-chart levels as did the LP of that title issued in April 1973. Other singles on both pop and country charts in 1973 were "What About Me," "Send a Little Love My Way," and "Love Song." "Love Song" was on the lists from late 1973 into early 1974 and the album of that title, issued by Capitol in February 1974 also did well. The year 1974 provided some singles that only made pop lists—"You Won't See Me," "Just One Look," and "Day Tripper." But it also provided Anne with two major country chart hits, "He Thinks I Don't Care," which rose to number one, and "Son of a Rotten Gambler," which

made the country top five. Anne also had two more LPs released in 1974, *Country* (8/74) and *Highly Prized Possession* (11/74).

Things seemed to be going well for Anne as 1975 began. Early in the year she was awarded the Grammy for Best Country Vocal Performance Female for the *Love Song* album. Murray's position as a concert attraction and desired TV guest artist had never been stronger. Once more she felt something was missing from her life. She told Bob Allen, "There were times when I just couldn't go on. It happened to me twice. The year after 'Snowbird' [1971] I didn't know what I was doing. It was a matter of stopping and saying, 'Look, I don't *have* to do anything.' Then again in 1975 I just said, 'Look, I just don't see any point to any of this.'"

What she felt was wrong was the lack of a meaningful private life. In 1975, she decided to give up the entertainment grind for a while and regain control over her personal activities. In June 1975 she married William Langstroth. Both of them wanted a family and a few months later Anne was carrying their first child. The baby, a boy named William Stewart Langstroth, Jr., was born in August 1976. (A few years later, the Langstroths added a girl, Dawn Joann, born April 20, 1979.)

During Murray's absence from the music field in the mid-1970s, Capitol continued to release new recordings. Among them were the singles "Sunday Sunrise," "The Call," and "Uproar" in 1975; "Things" and "Golden Oldie" in 1976; and "Sunday School to Broadway" in 1977. LPs issued in the mid-1970s included *Together* (10/75) and *Keeping in Touch* (9/76). Most of those releases made the charts, but none was a massive success.

In 1978, after being out of the spotlight for several years, Anne decided to begin work as a singer again, but on her own terms. She intended to live and raise her family in Toronto (with occasional sojourns in her beloved Nova Scotia), record in Toronto studios, and only accept concert or TV engagements that suited her schedule. It was a matter, she told Bob Allen, of getting her priorities straight. "Someone can call me now and tell me there's a million dollar deal in Vegas and I'll say, well, what does this mean? Does that mean I have to work for six weeks? Does it mean I'll have to live in a hotel for six weeks? Because if it does, I'm not gonna do it.

"People wring their hands and tear out their hair at my attitude. But dammit, I just want it to be right y'know. I want it to be comfortable for me and my family, because they're the most important people. Nothing else is important anymore."

In late 1977, she went into the studios with producer Jim Ed Norman (her longtime association with Brian Ahern had ended amicably some time before) to work on a new LP. The result was the album *Let's Keep It That Way*, issued by Capitol in January 1978. From that came her first sizable pop hit single since 1974, a remake of the old Everly Brothers hit, "Walk Right Back." Her second single from the album, "You Needed Me," was a top-5 hit in both country and pop categories and was certified gold by the R.I.A.A. on November 1, 1978, for her second gold single. The album also was a bestseller with both pop and country fans, certified gold in October 1978 and reaching platinum in 1979.

Murray's 1978 efforts showed, as she said, "My career really took off." She earned three Grammy nominations for 1978 in the categories of Best Pop Vocal Performer, Female; Record of the Year; and Best Country Vocal Performance, Female. Her chart hits of 1979 were the singles "I Just Fall in Love Again," "Shadows in the Moonlight," and "Broken-Hearted Me" (number one on country charts in December) and the best-selling LP *New Kind of Feeling* (February 1979), which won a gold record by year end. She also turned out an excellent children's album in 1979, *Hippo in My Tub* (issued by Capitol in Canada and Sesame Street Records in the United States). She also served as 1979 Chairperson of the Canada Save the Children Fund and was honored by her country for adopting three foster children as part of her contribution to the program.

Anne started off the 1980s with another single on the charts, "Daydream Believer." As the year 1980 went by, she added such other top ranked singles as "Lucky Me," "I'm Happy Just to Dance with You," and "Could I Have This Dance," the latter number one on country charts in November 1980. During the year her charted albums included *I'll Always Love You, A Country Collection,* and *Anne Murray's Greatest Hits.* The last named was still in the top five in early 1981, by which time it had gone well past platinum-record levels, accounting for a worldwide sales total of over 3 million copies. In the early summer of 1981, her next LP, *Where Do You Go When You Dream* (April 1981) was on country lists. Among her charted singles of the year was the top-10 "It's All I Can Do."

During the late 1970s and early 1980s, while Murray's concert and TV work accounted for fewer days per year, it still represented more than a token effort. Her in-person appearances ranged from Las Vegas to Los Angeles' Greek Theater and New York's Carnegie Hall. Her radio credits included appearances on the *Grand Ole Opry* and her TV work included two guest spots on *Saturday Night Live;* host of *Solid Gold;* cohost of the *Mike Douglas* show for a week; *The Muppet Show;* Johnny Carson's *The Tonight Show;* and the *Merv Griffin* show; as well as a number of major specials with other major artists.

Murray's awards totals continued to mount in the early 1980s. In the Grammy competition, she won the nod for 1980 Best Country Vocal Performance, Female, for "Could I Have This Dance." She was top winner in the Canadian Juno Awards (Canada's equivalent of the Grammy) for 1980, winning in four categories. (That brought her career total of Juno trophies to sixteen). The Toronto *Sun* quipped that maybe the award should be renamed the "Annies."

N

NAYLOR, JERRY: *Singer, guitarist, disc jockey, TV emcee. Born Erath County, Texas, March 6, 1939.*

For Jerry Naylor, interest in the entertainment field started early. From the first time he heard sounds coming from a radio as a small boy, his one desire was to become a part of the music field. In a career that was still flourishing decades later, he took part in almost every aspect of the industry, from disc jockey to performer and TV host.

Jerry was born and raised on a small farm near the town of Chalk Mountain, Texas. His family encouraged his love for music: he took his first music lessons in San Angelo, Texas, when he was seven, and later studied piano and steel guitar. By the time he was twelve, in the early 1950s, he was good enough to join a country & western band that had a program on a San Angelo radio station. The following year, after winning a talent contest, he gained a recording contract with a local label. He formed his own band to make those initial recordings and then began heading the group in engagements in and around his home area. Throughout his teens, Jerry kept active in the music field every chance he got, his credits including appearances on such prestigious country shows as the *Big D Jamboree* in Dallas and the *Louisiana Hayride* in Shreveport.

Not only was he kept busy with his appearances, he was a jack of all trades on San Angelo station KPEP, where, besides doing a disc jockey show, he handled such chores as engineer and advertising sales representative. After receiving his high school diploma, he enrolled in Elkin Electronics Institute in Dallas over the summer to obtain his first-class radio and TV engineering license.

In 1957, the eighteen-year-old joined the special service branch of the Army. This led to European tours with Gary Crosby and the opportunity to do a radio show from Armed Forces Radio Service in Stuttgart, Germany. In 1958 he returned to Texas, where he got a job on the staff of radio station KINT in El Paso. His radio work over by nightfall, he took singing jobs just across the border at La Fiesta Night Club in Juarez.

In late 1959, Jerry's activities took him to Albuquerque, New Mexico, where he became friends with an excellent young guitarist named Glen Campbell. The two decided to raise their stakes and move on to Hollywood to try for better things in the music industry. For Jerry, the change in locale didn't result in any recording breakthroughs, but he did get a disc jockey job at station KRLA in Los Angeles. Meanwhile, an opportunity arose for Jerry to take the late Buddy Holly's place as lead singer of the Crickets. Jerry accepted and made several worldwide tours with the group in the first half of the 1960s and also made two movies with them before leaving at the end of 1964.

During 1965, Jerry was featured on the nationally televised (ABC-TV) *Shindig* rock show. He also signed his first contract with a major recording firm that year and turned out several albums and a number of singles in the mid-1960s. One of his efforts during those years was to sing the male lead in what was called the world's first "country opera," the score of which was released on Capitol's Tower Record label.

During the last half of the 1960s, Naylor appeared on many major TV shows both in the United States and England. His U.S. guest spots included the *Mike Douglas* show, *The Ed Sullivan Show,* and Dick Clark's *American Bandstand.* His English credits included *Juke Box Jury, Thank Your Lucky Stars, Palladium Show, Oh Boy,* and *Ready, Steady, Go.* At the end of the 1960s, Jerry was host of the nationally syndicated country show *Music City, U.S.A.*

In the 1970s, Jerry continued his diverse

activities in TV and as part of country package shows. He also had recording agreements with several labels in the 1970s that resulted in a number of national country chart singles in the next half decade. These included: "Is This All There Is to a Honky-Tonk" (Melodyland, 1975); "The Bad Part of Me," "The Last Time You Loved Me (Hitsville, 1976); "If You Don't Want to Love Her," "Rave On/Lady, Would You Like to Dance" (MCA, 1978); "But for Love," "She Wears It Well" (Warner Bros., 1979); "Don't Touch Me," duet with Kelli Warren (Jeremiah, 1979); "Cheating Eyes" (Oak, 1980).

NEAR, HOLLY: *Singer, songwriter, actress. Born Ukiah, California, June 6, 1949.*

Possessing an excellent voice and fine songwriting skills, Holly Near might well have become a fixture on U.S. hit charts had she opted to sing rock or been born a little earlier. In the tradition of the folk song protest movement of the 1960s, she reached maturity in the 1970s when the folk genre had been relegated to a minority position in music. Nonetheless, Near had the courage of her convictions and refused to change her folk style or writing approach for the sake of financial success.

Born in Ukiah in northern California, she spent her early years on a farm in Potter Valley just outside town. When she was ten, her family moved back into Ukiah. Her family enjoyed music and exposed Holly to folk music, country & western, Broadway musicals, and some of the popular music of the 1950s.

Holly enjoyed singing at a very early age and made her public debut in her home area at seven. From then on, she took part in many entertainment activities in the Ukiah region, including plays and musical events at school and in local playhouses. By the time she was in her teens, Holly sought and won assignments in a number of films and TV programs. At the end of the decade, she headed east to audition for the cast of the rock musical *Hair* and won one of the leads in the Broadway production.

She had already become politically active, having taken part in protests against the Vietnam War. In the early 1970s, she was the featured performer in Jane Fonda's controversial "Free the Army" show that toured Vietnam.

Near was making a name for herself on the folk music circuit (folk clubs and college campus concerts) in the early 1970s. Throughout the 1970s she was a featured performer in folk festivals all over the United States, including most of the major ones, and recordings of some of her sets often could be heard on stations that featured folk material.

She might have signed with a major record company, but Near decided she would have to give up too much control over her material if she went that route. Instead, she set up her own label in Ukiah, Redwood Records. Her debut LP, *Hang in There*, was recorded in 1973, and in 1974 she completed work on a live album. Working with her on both of these, providing vocal and instrumental backup, was Jeff Langley, a friend from Ukiah. He also helped record her third Redwood LP, *You Can Know All I Am*, issued in 1976. Her fourth LP, *Imagine My Surprise*, came out in 1979, and in 1980 she began work on her fifth album. Most of the songs in these, lyrics and music, were written by Holly.

Although her exposure to the music public was limited, she still managed to have considerable impact. As of the end of 1979, sales of her four albums totaled 155,-000, a very respectable figure for a label that depended essentially on word of mouth advertising. In 1979, the National Association of Independent Record Distributors named *Imagine My Surprise* best album of the year. *BAM Magazine* also named the LP the best album of the year by an independent label.

Holly toured steadily during the 1970s, albeit restricted mainly to small venues. Often the concerts were intended to tie in with some of the causes Near believed in. Thus her March 1979 set at the Fox Venice Theater in the Los Angeles area followed the benefit premiere of the labor-struggle film *With Babies and Banners*. She told the audience she wanted to put her energies into "community organizing, not Bahama vacations." Similarly, a year later she returned to Los Angeles (soon after having completed a forty-city national tour) to perform in a benefit concert for WAVAW (Women Against Violence Against Women). One of WAVAW's successful campaigns was to stop Warner Communications from using violent images of men and women on the record jackets of its various labels.

NEELY, SAM: *Singer, guitarist, songwriter. Born Cuero, Texas, 1948.*

Sam Neely's background and lineage had strong country & western roots. However, like many from his region who came to adulthood in the 1960s, his musical scope extended into the pop and rock fields. This proved a problem for Sam, because his songs and recordings tended to "straddle the borderline between pop and country," making them difficult for both fans and disc jockeys to classify. Thus he continued for a number of years to do fairly well in both fields without making a major breakthrough in either.

Sam was born and spent his first eight years in Cuero, a town near San Antonio, Texas. When he was eight, his family moved to Corpus Christi, which became his permanent home for almost all his youth and adult life, except for a short stay in Southern California. As he grew up, he followed such varied musical genres as rock, blues, country, and Tex–Mex. In high school he played in school groups and local bands. In the mid-1960s, he cut some records for a local label, one of which, "Cry, Cry, Cry," was well regarded by pop fans in his home area, and which was turned over to a New York company for wider distribution. Unfortunately, the company was too small to do much with it and the song suffered the fate of the majority of record releases in the United States.

Neely continued to pick up work as a musician in Corpus Christi and vicinity and kept writing new material. He had a local following, which helped bring him support from a transplanted Corpus Christi native named Rudy Duran, who lived in Hollywood at the time. In the early 1970s, Duran auditioned some of Neely's material for Capitol Records, which led to a recording contract. For a time, Neely moved to Los Angeles to work up a series of recordings for the label, including the album *Long Road to Texas*. His early releases won some critical approval, but limited fan response. Then the 1972 single "Loving You Just Crossed My Mind" reached the rarefied heights of the national top 20. Building on that, an album of the same title also achieved chart status for a while, as did such follow-up singles as "Rosalie" and "Blue Times," the latter the theme from the movie *Bonnie's Kids.*

Though Neely had shown promise, he hadn't become a national favorite, which led to a parting of the ways with Capitol. Sam also was homesick for Texas. He went back to Corpus Christi, where he settled down with his wife and son, going back to his pre-Hollywood routine of playing in local clubs and doing some songwriting when he had the time.

He didn't want to leave Texas, but he still had hopes of emulating artists like Jerry Jeff Walker and Asleep at the Wheel, who maintained national ranking while remaining in the Lone Star State. He got another chance to extend his audience when A&M signed him. His debut album on the label, *Down Home,* came out in 1975. His initial single release of that year, "Sadie Takes a Lover," didn't win much attention, but the second A&M single release, "You Can Have Her," made the top 10 on easy listening charts, top 30s on national pop charts, and top 40s on country lists. His country ratings disappointed him, since country DJs had seemed to like the song. "It wasn't a country record, exactly, but it had some country flavor and got a lot of good country airplay."

Things seemed bright for him, but once more problems arose to slow things down. This time it was that all too frequent bugaboo of entertainers, legal and contractual arguments with management people. Sam had to give up recording for a while and, by the time everything was straightened out, a lot of the momentum from his mid-1970s chart achievements had cooled. He signed with another record company, Elektra/Asylum, and recorded some new songs in early 1977. The first single, "Sail Away," was issued in July 1977, but made little headway.

NELSON, RICK: *Singer, guitarist, songwriter, band leader (the Stone Canyon Band). Born Teaneck, New Jersey, May 8, 1940.*

A youthful idol on TV and records in the 1950s and early 1960s, Rick Nelson had to work out new career directions when his parents' long-running *Ozzie and Harriet Show* finally was phased out in the mid-1960s. The choice he made in 1967 (when he debuted in a station KOBS country-music show at the Shrine Auditorium in Los Angeles) was to perform country material. It was no easy task to overcome the opposition of country purists to what they regarded as johnny-come-latelies from the pop field, but at the start of the 1980s, Rick could point to some successes and a growing amount of respect over the years for his abilities.

His show business career began as a child actor on the Nelson family program. He did not move into singing and recording until he was sixteen. His first record was the Fats Domino tune "I'm Walkin'," which Rick cut as a means of impressing a girl he wanted to date. The song turned out to be a smash hit, selling over a million copies in two weeks on Imperial. From 1957 through 1963, he remained one of the top stars in rock, placing a string of singles (and albums) on the charts while rolling up overall sales of an estimated 35 million records. His top-10 successes included "A Teenager's Romance," "Be-Bop Baby," "Stood Up," "Believe What You Say," "Poor Little Fool" (a number-one hit), "I Got a Feeling," "Lonesome Town," "Never Be Anyone Else but You," "It's Late," "Just a Little Too Much," "Sweeter than You," "Hello Mary Lou," and "Travelin' Man." The last named, a top-10 hit in 1961, was written by Rick and sold over 5 million copies worldwide.

Some of those songs, such as "Hello Mary Lou" and "Poor Little Fool," had a country flavor, reflecting Rick's early interest in that music form. As he told an interviewer in the mid-1960s, "I've liked country music for as long as I can remember. I've always been a big fan of guys like Johnny Cash and Jim Reeves. Most of my early records were at least part country."

In 1963, Nelson signed with Decca and for a while turned out a series of LPs that featured material more in the vein of Frank Sinatra or Johnny Mathis. The albums included such titles as *For You* and *Every Thought of You* in 1964; *Spotlight on Rick* and *Best Always* in 1965; *Love and Kisses* and *Bright Lights* in 1966. None did particularly well, nor was Rick himself enthralled with that change in image. He also felt certain, even if his audience didn't notice it, that he was maturing as a musician and singer. He worked hard to improve his skills and his peers generally agreed he had made progress.

He told Shaun Considine of *The New York Times* (January 23, 1972), "Sure, in the beginning I used to fake it on the guitar. I was too scared to play, and anyhow, no one could hear you with everyone screaming. But in time I learned to play and enjoy it. Also I had guys like Joe Osborne in my band and later Glen Campbell and James Burton on guitar [Burton later backed Elvis Presley]. We had some fantastic musicians' musicians at that time. . . ."

The idea of combining his love for country music with a need for a break with his past musical efforts finally bore fruit in 1967 when Nelson assembled his first country band and turned out the LP *Country Fever*. Before 1967 was over, he had his first mild country hit, "You Just Can't Quit," which reached number one in Los Angeles and several other major cities. Nelson gained favorable reviews for a series of concerts across the United States in which he was backed by a band that included Burton on guitar, Junior Nichols on drums, Lynn Russell on bass, Bob Warford on banjo, Clarence White on rhythm guitar, and Glenn D. Hardin on piano. Rick concluded he had found his musical niche and, from that time on, he never looked back.

In 1968, his second country release, *Another Side of Rick*, came out and was followed in 1969 by the live album *In Concert* and his third studio country LP, *Rudy the Fifth*. The latter LP spawned the chart-making single "She Belongs to Me." That song was written by Bob Dylan, and its success seemed an appropriate tribute to an artist whose work had greatly influenced Nelson's new style.

Rick had started to work with the first Stone Canyon Band lineup. The band members then were Allen Kemp, Randy Meisner (later a founding member of the Eagles), Pat Shanahan, and Tom Brumley. When he and the band started working together, he told Considine, "We improvised and experimented and listened to other people's work, people like Randy Newman and Tim Hardin. Then one day I heard *Nashville Skyline*, by Bob Dylan, and I knew where I wanted to go. I listened to that album for days. The songs were so simple, yet cryptic at times. I wanted to sing songs like that and, if possible, also write like that. So for a year and a half that's all I did. We'd rehearse during the day and I'd write at night." The new group debuted in the L.A. Troubadour in October 1969, heralding a new milestone in Nelson's country career.

In the early 1970s, Nelson and the Stone Canyon Band became increasingly popular on the college concert circuit. The group also did well performing in small clubs around the United States and Canada. Meanwhile, Rick was also appearing in rock revival concerts and occasionally acting on TV, including appearances in an episode of *Owen Marshall, Counselor at Law* and on a Sid and Marty Krofft variety special called "Fol-de-rol."

One of the rock nostalgia appearances at New York's Madison Square Garden in October 1971 laid the groundwork for Rick's most notable success in the early 1970s. He wanted to sing some of his new material, but the audience continued to scream for old pop songs. The frustration this aroused in him later gained expression in a song titled "Garden Party." In 1972, the single of the song gained Nelson his first top-10 hit in close to a decade and also provided the title number for a hit album on MCA Records. Looking back, he said, "I really didn't want to do the show. I'm not into that whole rock 'n' roll revival concept, but I had never played Madison

Square Garden and the idea of playing there before 22,000 people sounded interesting." His experience was translated into lyric lines that went: "When I got to the Garden Party/They all knew my name/ But no one recognized me/I didn't look the same."

People waited for a follow-up hit to the song, but the 1970s continued to go by with little progress toward that goal. Rick did place some singles on the charts during the rest of the decade, such as "One Night Stand" on MCA Records (which had absorbed Decca) in 1974 and "Dream Lover" on Epic in 1979, but none rose very high on the lists. Partly this was due to disheartening legal problems, including a drawn-out struggle between Nelson and Decca/MCA to void a twenty-year pact. Once that was out of the way, Rick signed with Epic Records, but once again met with frustration. He worked on a new album with legendary rock artist Al Kooper as producer, but when the material was completed, Epic refused to release it. Rick returned to the studios and produced a new collection himself called *Intakes*, which was not well received after its release in 1977.

The Epic arrangement ended soon after and in late 1979 Rick signed with Capitol Records. This resulted in the album *Playing to Win*, issued in early 1981. It was a distinct improvement over the Epic material. Though not a massive seller, it did well enough for Capitol to give the go ahead for Nelson to work on a new LP for release in 1982.

Meanwhile, as Rick had been doing over the years since founding his Stone Canyon Band, he kept up a busy in-person schedule in the early 1980s appearing at state and county fairs, on college campuses and in nightclubs on the folk and country circuit. The result was a healthy income and a considerable following even without appearances in the major venues of the largest U.S. cities.

NELSON, TRACY: *Singer, songwriter. Born Madison, Wisconsin, December 27, 1947.*

At times during her career it seemed as though Tracy Nelson was better known for having the same last name as Willie Nelson or for a supposed performing resemblance to Janis Joplin than for her vocal work. Her peers in the pop and country field valued her abilities highly, as indicated by the artists who wanted her to contribute to some of their recordings. By the start of the 1980s, though, she had a growing following in the country field that promised important things to come.

Born and raised in Madison, Wisconsin, her early interests had little to do with the country-music mainstream. As she told Jay Milner of the *Rocky Mountain Musical News,* "I started out as a folkie—spent a good deal of my time singing 'Silver Dagger'— and then I became a blues fanatic."

Helping to kindle her interest in blues and blues rock when she was in her teens were rock performers like Boz Scaggs and Steve Miller, both of whom attended the University of Wisconsin in the 1960s. She told Milner, "Steve and Boz played the Chi Psi house when I was in high school in Madison. I used to go hear them a lot. They'd left by the time I got to college, but they came back occasionally. . . . Anyhow, by the time I got out of high school the activist stuff had died out and there wasn't much going on, musically, there."

After a while, Tracy, who had become convinced she had the vocal ability to make a career out of music, left the Midwest for the San Francisco area. She found the going rough for a female artist, despite the prominence of Janis Joplin and Grace Slick in the West Coast rock sound. Most rock groups she contacted didn't even want to give a woman an audition because they feared possible problems that might result from adding a woman to an all-male band.

Nelson got some jobs, then decided the best route to go was to put together her own band. "There were so many people out there making so much money playing what I thought was substandard music and I said to myself, 'If they can do it, I can do it.'" She assembled her first band partly by recruiting the rhythm section from Doug Sahm, of Texas folk and blues-rock fame. "Doug's band was breaking up and I got his drummer, piano player, and bass player. Of course, they were all

Texans. . . ." Thus the band, called Mother Earth, had a strong Texas flavor and resulted in the misconception that Tracy herself came from the Texas music scene.

The band made some demo tapes showcasing Nelson's impressive vocal skills and, in short order, had a recording contract. They made a number of albums in the late 1960s and early 1970s that brought them a cult following and predictions that Tracy and the group would reach superstar status. Many critics tended to bracket Nelson with Janis Joplin in the sense that she was seen as an heir to Joplin's rock eminence. However, it was an inaccurate comparison and one that never sat well with Tracy.

She told Milner in 1977, "It interests me that people, after all this time are still doing it. Comparing us. The broad had staying power. But it used to just make me angry. I respected Janis for what she could do to an audience. That was her talent. Singing was not her talent. It made me grit my teeth. I did not like her singing. Hers is a perfectly valid art. . . . But when people compare me to her as a singer, and say I'm almost as good as Janis Joplin. . . . I'm a better singer than she could have ever been."

Nelson and her band signed with Mercury, which issued the debut album, *Mother Earth,* in 1968. The band set out on a cross-country tour of the United States that had the unexpected outcome of starting Tracy on the path toward country-music involvement.

The tour, as it happened, ended up in Nashville. A friend, guitarist Harvey Mandell, suggested she consider doing some recordings at the local Bradley's Barn studios. "We just did it for the hell of it," she recalled. As she got into the project, she began working with backing musicians like Pete Drake and fiddler Johnny Gimble. The product of that union was the album titled *Mother Earth Country* (also listed as *Tracy Nelson Country*), issued by Mercury in November 1969.

Tracy enjoyed that experience as well as the musical friends she made so much that she moved from California to Nashville in 1970. She made a number of additional albums with Mother Earth in the early 1970s that stressed rock elements, such as *Make a Joyful Noise* and *Satisfied* on Mercury and *Bring Me Home* on Reprise.

By the mid-1970s, Nelson had lost most of her interest in rock and was spending more time singing country material. When Atlantic Records started a country-music department during those years, they signed Tracy and released several albums that started to win her some attention from country fans. Helping to solidify her reputation as a rising young artist was the success of a duet single with Willie Nelson, "After the Fire Is Gone."

"The record did well everywhere," she told Milner. "It astounded me that country people accepted it. It really established me in my neighborhood in Tennessee. I live out in the sticks, outside of Nashville, and there are really old country people who just didn't have any use for me until I'd made a record with Willie. Then I was OK."

In the late 1970s, Tracy recorded a number of country albums for MCA Records and also toured many country venues all over the United States with her band. She sometimes worked on projects with other country stars, including a contribution to the 1979 Amazing Rhythm Aces album, singing the role of Elaine in Amazing Rhythm Aces' Russell Smith's story song, "Rodrigo, Rita and Elaine."

NELSON, WILLIE: *Singer, guitarist, songwriter, actor. Born Fort Worth, Texas, April 30, 1933.*

In the mid-1970s, Willie Nelson's name impinged on the consciousness of millions of people the world over. Starting with *Red-Headed Stranger,* his albums regularly brought millions of dollars into the coffers of his record company and his singles rose high on pop as well as country charts. By the end of the decade, he was acknowledged to be a superstar, not just of country music but in every facet of popular music. To those who knew him during his almost two decades of relative obscurity, when he played a steady succession of beer halls and honky tonks, to the countless singers who scored bestsellers with his composi-

tions (his great song "Night Life" sold an estimated 30 million records for dozens of other artists), the only question was why it took so long.

Part of it was his personality—essentially shy and self-effacing, he preferred to avoid the glare of publicity; part was the inability of the country-music establishment of the 1950s and 1960s to understand the groundbreaking features of his material, grittier and more probing than much of the country music fare of those years. As time went by, however, he shed his self-consciousness and demonstrated a quiet strength in his abilities—and the music world also came to admire the progressive country approach of such "outlaws" as Willie, Waylon Jennings, and their like.

Willie's character was a natural extension of his upbringing. Though born in Fort Worth, he was raised during his formative years by his grandparents in the rural central Texas town of Abbott, from whence came the nickname Abbott Willie. He grew up loving the remoteness and peace of farm life and, like many farm boys, learned to play the guitar (both of his grandparents played) and took part in after-work sings with his friends. Many of the songs he sang were those he heard on radio from the *Louisiana Hayride* or *Grand Ole Opry.*

After leaving high school, Nelson spent a short time in the Air Force, then settled in Waco, Texas, at the start of the 1950s after getting married. He enrolled in Baylor University on a part-time basis with the thought of an eventual career in farming, but dropped out after two years. During that time he helped earn tuition money and money to support his family (which had grown to include a daughter, Lana) by a variety of jobs, including selling vacuum cleaners, encyclopedias, and Bibles. He gave that up when he found a job as a disc jockey on a San Antonio, Texas, radio station. A platter spinner for the next seven years on stations in Texas, Oregon, and California, he got restless and began to perform as a country artist whenever he could find dates on week nights or weekends. During that period he started to write songs of his own, such as "Family Bible" and "Night Life."

At the start of the 1960s, he moved to Nashville to try to make his mark on the larger country-music market. His main goal was to follow up on his songwriting skills; he didn't think of himself as a possible headline performer. One of the first to take note of his skills was Hank Cochran, who heard some of Willie's material in a set at Tootsie's Bar ("where," Cochran recalled, "those of us who were aspiring songwriters used to hang out"). He helped Willie get a writing contract with Pamper Music. Ray Price was a part owner of Pamper at the time, and, after Willie and Ray became acquainted, Ray took Willie on as bass guitarist in Price's band.

While Willie worked as a sideman, his songs began to speak for him. Beginning in 1961, his reputation in the industry soared as a steady succession of his compositions made the hit lists. One of his first major credits was Patsy Cline's top-10 hit of "Crazy," followed in a short time by two other country hits for other artists. One of those was Ralph Emery's version of "Hello Fool" (co-written by Willie and Jim Coleman) and Faron Young's single of "Hello Walls." In 1962, Young collaborated with Willie on another bestseller, "Three Days." In 1961, Willie wrote another classic, "Funny How Time Slips Away," which provided Patsy Cline with a top-10 hit in the early 1960s.

Like many songwriters, Nelson made demonstration records of his material to try and get others to record the songs. Sometimes such recordings cause record executives to decide the writer is the best one to make the record, but Willie's half-whispering style on demos didn't impress them. It was partly due to his psychological outlook, he decided later. He told Al Reinert for a 1978 New York Times Magazine article (March 26, 1978), "You know, I always thought I could sing pretty good. And I guess it kinda bothered me that nobody else thought so. I guess I was into a lot of negative thinking back then. I did a lot of bad things, got in fights with people, got divorced. All that stuff. My head was just pointed the wrong way, you know. Then I started to do a lot of reading. I got into [Kahlil] Gibran [author of The Prophet], got really into Edgar Cayce and his son,

Hugh Cayce—books that had real positive attitudes.

"I was like a drunk that quit drinking. I kinda developed this real positive attitude toward my own life, got into my own life." But it took all of the 1960s before that happened.

Despite industry reservations about Willie's lifestyle and vocal skills, he didn't lack for recording opportunities. He was signed by Liberty Records even as he performed with Ray Price. The result was several chart-making singles, including two top-10 singles in 1962, the number-one ranked record of his composition "Touch Me," and a hit duet with Shirley Collie, "Willingly." For a time that success caused a flurry of personal appearances outside the small-club circuit, including a number of weeks in Las Vegas.

In late 1964, he was made a regular cast member of the Grand Ole Opry. He also left Liberty for RCA Records that year, remaining on the RCA roster into the early 1970s. As part of the growing Nelson legend, that part of his career is generally described in terms of abject failure, but in fact he had some moderate successes as a recording artist then. He placed a number of singles on the country charts, including "The Party's Over" and "Blackjack Country" in 1967 and "Little Things" in 1968. Some of his RCA albums also had reasonable sales, as well. Among his RCA LPs were Country Willie, His Own Songs (11/65), Favorites (6/66), Willie Nelson Concert (12/66), Make Way for Willie Nelson (5/67), The Party's Over (11/67), Both Sides Now (5/70), Laying My Burdens Down (12/70), Columbus Stockade Blues (12/70), Willie Nelson and Family (5/71), Yesterday's Wine (9/71), Words Don't Fit the Picture (3/72), and The Willie Way (8/72).

None of those efforts, however, did much toward gaining Nelson widespread recognition as a performer. He did have a following, but mainly among frequenters of small country bars and nightclubs where Willie could let down his hair and sing what he pleased how he pleased. In those years, he told Reinert, he just couldn't match his record efforts with his live act. "I'd get nervous. I just didn't feel comfortable in that kinda situation. You'd walk into the studio and they'd put six guys behind you who'd never seen your music before, and it's impossible to get the feel of it in a three-hour session. That was true for me, at least." So while he got comfortable royalties from discs of his songs made by others (among those who'd recorded his material by the early 1970s, besides almost every country star, were Frank Sinatra, Roy Orbison, Stevie Wonder, Al Green, Bing Crosby, Perry Como, Lawrence Welk, Aretha Franklin, Eydie Gorme, Timi Yuro, and dozens more), his career as an entertainer lagged.

To try to focus his thoughts and perhaps make a new start, he moved back to Texas from Nashville in 1972. The change did indeed effect a rebirth. In particular, he detected a latent interest in country music among younger fans. "I found that interest there and I also knew that they didn't have any place to go to listen to country music. . . . Their hair was too long to get into some of those places without getting into trouble . . . but I knew there was an audience there. . . . So I went down to the [rock-oriented] Armadillo World Headquarters and told them I wanted to play for their audiences and see if what I was thinking was right."

Willie laid the groundwork for his surge to stardom. During those years, he added to the impetus by opening his own club in Austin and, in the mid-1970s, organizing the annual rock-concert-style country festival Fourth of July picnics in Dripping Springs, Texas.

Willie, whose contract with RCA expired in 1971, next signed with Atlantic, just starting a new country section. He made three albums for that label, *Shotgun Willie*, *Trouble Maker*, and *Phases and Stages*, the last named, issued in early 1974, an unusual—for the country field—concept album describing the breakup of a marriage, one side from the woman's point of view, the other from the man's. The LPs did moderately well, but Atlantic disbanded the division in 1974 and Willie moved on to Columbia Records. In a crucial step, Columbia agreed to give Willie total creative control over his material. He produced his recordings and then gave them to Columbia for distribution. (After the success of his first LP, he formed his own Lone Star label under a distribution agreement with CBS.)

The results were quick in coming. During the summer of 1975, Willie had his first top-10 single in years, "Blue Eyes Cryin' in the Rain." That success was dwarfed by the tremendous response, at home and abroad, to his debut Columbia LP, *Red-Headed Stranger*. This also was a concept album using songs by Willie and others to paint a picture of love and death in the days of "the old west." The LP reached number one on country lists in the fall of 1975 and even made the pop top 40. In concerts supporting the album, Willie found he could draw enthusiastic capacity crowds to medium-size halls and even large auditoriums, including many young fans, instead of the smaller clubs he appeared in before. Backing him on the tour was a band that included many sidemen who had been with him for decades. Its typical makeup in the mid-1970s was his sister Bobbie Nelson on piano, Jody Payne on guitar, Chris Ethridge on bass, Mickey Raphael on harmonica, and drummers Paul English and Rex Ludwig.

Red-Header Stranger eventually went platinum, but even before it did, he was represented on another smash LP, *Wanted: The Outlaws*. Combining the talents of Willie, Waylon Jennings, Jessi Colter, and Tompall Glaser, the LP (a reissue by RCA of earlier recordings) was number one on country charts for many weeks in 1976 and a top-10 pop hit. The cross-country tour of the Outlaws backing the album remains one of the memorable live series in modern pop history. As a soloist, Willie continued to add to his laurels in 1976 with six top-10 singles: "Uncloudy Day," "I'd Have to Be Crazy," "Remember Me," "If You've Got the Money, I've Got the Time," and "Good-Hearted Woman," the last named a number-one hit. Willie also had a chart-making new Columbia LP in 1976, *Troublemaker*.

Nelson continued to consolidate his position as a superstar in succeeding years, turning out a stream of new material that sold millions of records demonstrating rare creativity and insight. And his concerts now vied with those of the most popular rock acts, drawing huge crowds to places like the Los Angeles Forum and New York's Madison Square Garden.

In 1977, Willie's tribute to the late Lefty Frizzell, *To Lefty from Willie*, was a best-seller, as were the singles "I Love You a Thousand Ways" and "Railroad Lady." In early 1978, he joined with Waylon Jennings for the LP *Waylon and Willie*, number one on country charts for weeks and arguably the finest country LP of the year. Several months after that came out, a new LP reflecting his interest in the pop music standards of earlier decades, *Stardust*, appeared and became a country and pop hit. It spawned such top-10 country singles as "Georgia on My Mind," "Stardust" (the Hoagy Carmichael classic), and "Blue Skies" (by Irving Berlin).

At the end of 1978, the LP *Willie and Family* was released and quickly took its place in upper country and pop chart brackets, where it remained well into 1979. (The "family" included notable musicians such as Johnny Gimble on fiddle and Grady Martin on guitar.) In early 1979, he teamed with Leon Russell for a series of memorable concerts that provided the basis for a midsummer live double LP, *One for the Road*. Later in the year, two more of his releases showed up on the album charts, *Willie Nelson Sings Kristofferson* and *Pretty Paper*. (In late 1979 and early 1980, Kristofferson toured a number of cities with Willie's show.) In August 1978, Willie also issued an LP of some of his early recordings, *Face of a Fighter*, on his own Lone Star Records label. All ten songs in the collection, originally recorded by Nelson in 1961, had never been recorded by other artists.

With his increasingly hectic schedule, Willie still found time to take a major supporting role (to Robert Redford and Jane Fonda) during 1979 in the movie *Electric Horseman*. His contributions included several vocals in the film score that took up one side of the soundtrack LP issued in 1980, including a new version of "Mamas Don't Let Your Babies Grow Up to Be Cowboys," which had been a singles hit in 1978 for Willie and Waylon.

In late 1979, Willie began work on another movie, *Honeysuckle Rose*, in which he costarred with Amy Irving and Dyan Cannon. When it was released by Warner Brothers in 1980, it was warmly received by almost all major critics, with considerable praise for Willie's acting contributions. The soundtrack album, issued by Columbia in the summer, was over platinum record levels by late fall. During the year, Willie had many other recording successes to add to an already astounding list. Early in 1980 his version of Kristofferson's "Help Me Make It Through the Night" was in the top ten and in February his single "My Heroes Have Always Been Cowboys" rose to number one on country charts. The following month his new version of his long-time hit composition "Night Life" (recorded with Danny Davis and the Nashville Brass) was in top-chart brackets followed a few months later with the hit single "Midnight Rider," and, with Danny Davis, the top-10 "Funny How Time Slips Away." A little later in the year he had the bestseller "Faded Love" (with Ray Price), and a song he wrote for *Honeysuckle Rose*, "On the Road Again," was number one (September). Also on the charts was an RCA release of an old Nelson recording on that label, "Crazy Arms," and another Columbia single, "Family Bible." Along with many of his previously released LPs still on the charts in 1980, he added such new hits as *Danny Davis with Willie Nelson and the Nashville Brass* and *San Antonio Rose*, the latter a duet album with Ray Price that helped revitalize Ray's career.

Willie began 1981 where he left off the previous year, with still more hits. Early in the year he made top-chart levels with a duet with Ray Price, "Don't You Ever Get Tired (of Hurting Me)" and the solo of his composition "Angel Flying Too Close to the Ground." He maintained an almost nonstop touring schedule in the early 1980s that took him across the United States several times and to many overseas venues as well, and he was featured on all manner of TV shows, from the PBS *Austin City Limits* program to many network and syndicated shows. The hectic pace caught up with him when he fell prey to physical problems during a tour stop in Hawaii in mid-1981, but after resting up for several months he was back to his normal routine by year end. By then, he had such other 1981 top-10 singles as "Somewhere Over the Rainbow," "Mountain Dew," and "Heartaches of a Fool." Also high on both pop and country charts in late 1981 was his new Columbia release, *Willie Nelson's Greatest Hits and Some That Will Be.*

Meanwhile, from the mid-1970s on, more and more honors began to come Nelson's way. In the 1975 Grammy voting, he received the Best Country Vocal Performance, Male, award for the single "Blue Eyes Cryin' in the Rain," and in 1978 got the same award for "Georgia on My Mind" plus, with Waylon, for Best Country Vocal Performance, Duo or Group, for "Mamas Don't Let Your Babies Grow Up to Be Cowboys." In the Country Music Association voting for 1976, *Wanted: The Outlaws* was named album of the year and "Good Hearted Woman" single of the year. In 1978, *Waylon and Willie* was one of the five final nominees for album of the year as was *One for the Road* in 1979. Willie also was one of the five finalists for Male Vocalist of the Year in 1976, 1978, and 1979 and for Entertainer of the Year in 1976 and 1979. In 1979, he won that most prestigious CMA award, Entertainer of the Year. He added still another Grammy to his collection in early 1981 for "On the Road Again," voted the Best Country Song of 1980. The following year he was one of the finalists for the Grammy for Best Country Vocal Performance, Male, for his recording of the old movie standard "Somewhere Over the Rainbow."

Discussing his feelings about American music in general and southern music in particular, Nelson was typically outspoken to interviewers in the late 1970s. Replying to Joe Bageant for an article for the *Rocky Mountain Musical Express,* he opposed musical categorizing. "Well, there really is no good reason to label music at all unless it helps to get the attention it deserves. I look at it all as just being American music, sound or whatever and, if you like it, you like it. It don't need a name to be enjoyable.

"Good music can be made anywhere as long as there are good people who enjoy making it, and recorded anywhere so long as there is a good studio. But . . . there is something about the South which produces an awful lot of good music of all kinds . . . not just country. For one thing, there is so much more of it in general, and the people will go a long way out of their way to enjoy it. It's a strong point of pride with many of us and it gets kept alive."

To Bageant's description of the "ingredient" that makes Willie's style so distinctive as "honky soul," he replied, "Yeah, I know what you mean. What we are is a bunch of niggers really. White niggers playin' what comes natural for other white niggers to listen to!"

NESMITH, MIKE: *Singer, guitarist, songwriter, band leader (First National Band, Second National Band). Born Houston, Texas, December 30, 1942.*

As a writer and musician, Mike Nesmith made a number of contributions to the folk and country fields. Some of his songs became hits for other artists over the years and several of his country-flavored solo rock albums are still among some of the underrated gems in pop music of the 1970s. For all that, he remained best known for his part in *The Monkees* TV show of the mid 1960s, a part of his career about which he always had decidedly mixed feelings.

His first musical love was the blues, a by-product of his early environment. He was born in Houston, but spent most of his youth in Farmer's Branch, just outside Dallas, where his family had inherited some property that turned out to be in the black ghetto. Recalling those years to Todd Everett *(Phonograph Record,* December 1970), he said, "Most of my friends were black, my first girl friend was black. I'm surprised that I didn't marry a black girl. I was married by a black preacher.

"Music didn't really mean anything to me until I was twenty. It was just something I'd hear in the back of a bar while I was shooting illegal pool. The kind of music I was exposed to? Well I remember when B.B. King had something like six hits in a row. They were hits to me because they were what got played a lot on the juke boxes. People like Ray Sharpe, Jimmy Reed. . . . Hell, they lived right there."

During high school, Mike did play a little saxophone, but he didn't begin to take a serious interest in music until he finished a two-year Air Force hitch in 1962. Inspired by the early 1960s folk boom, he took up guitar and, after about a year he was proficient enough to start playing rhythm guitar with local groups. He soon became an itinerant musician, working with bands around the country and doing some session work, including some backing assignments at Stax-Volt Records in Memphis. His travels eventually took him to Los Angeles in search of musical advancement, where he continued to perform in small folk clubs. In the fall of 1965, he heard about auditions for a new TV show and tried out in October. Considering that his competition included people like Steve Stills, he didn't expect much to happen, but to his surprise he was offered the job. His career with the Monkees was underway.

Selected to join him were David Jones, Peter Tork, and Mickey Dolenz, chosen mainly for their appearance and potential acting ability rather than their musical talent. Nesmith was upset when Monkees recordings initially were made by session musicians and falsely presented as being done by the TV foursome. Angered, Mike finally organized a revolt that changed the situation. However, the damage had been done—even after the Monkees did their own recordings, many people still were sure they were faked. The TV show debuted in September 1966 and remained on the air for three years. The group made fifty-six episodes in all of the half-hour show.

The group also gained a series of gold records for such albums as *Monkees Headquarters*, *Pisces, Aquarius, Capricorn and Jones Ltd.*, and *The Birds, the Bees and the Monkees*. The quartet also had many chart hit singles, including such Nesmith compositions as "Circle Sky" and "Tapioca Tundra." Tork left in 1967, but the other three continued to do the program and also extended concert tours. Program ratings

began to dwindle in 1969 and the Monkees disbanded by midyear.

Nesmith wasn't particularly sad about the breakup. Although the situation had been lucrative he hadn't held on to much of the money and, in addition, felt it had been creatively stifling. He wanted to concentrate on improving his image as a writer and musician and to do that assembled a new group in November 1969 and got a recording contract from RCA. Called the First National Band, its members were Red Rhodes, steel guitar and slide dobro; John Ware, drums and keyboards; and John London (legal name, John Carl Kuehne), guitar. Symbolizing the strong country roots of the group was Rhodes (born East Alton, Illinois, December 30, 1930), who had headed the house band at the famed Los Angeles Palomino Club for nine years and who was voted best steel guitarist for 1967 and 1968 in the Academy of Country Western & Music poll.

Things started off well. The debut LP, *Magnetic South*, issued in May 1970, made the charts as did a single from the LP, Nesmith's song "Joanne." A second album, *Loose Salute*, came out in late 1970 and also won considerable critical praise. That album spawned a charted single, the top 40 "Silver Moon."

Before Mike's third solo effort came along, the band was reorganized. Now called the Second National Band, its members included Rhodes, Johnny Meeks on bass guitar, and Jack Rinelli on drums. That group worked on the next LP, *Nevada Fighter*, issued in May 1971. The change in lineup, according to Nesmith, related to the ambitious plan he had for a series of concept albums that emphasized elements of folk and country & western music along with rock.

As he described the plan in the early 1970s, "The idea is to do a trilogy based on one of this country's original musical art forms, the music of the West and Southwest. My goal is to have three groups of three albums each—nine albums in all—providing insight into different consciousnesses at different periods of time. The first three albums were intended to present music from the consciousness of the old West, the second three on present day themes, and the third more futuristic.

"Musically, then, the First National Band arrangements were very simple and less complicated than later work. It was not only less sophisticated, but more sparse within the boundaries of music. The first three albums have some unusual effects on them, but these were achieved on the instruments themselves without special electronic manipulation. The second series is planned to use techniques used by today's groups, but not going overboard. The third series may just be an extension of the second or it may be much more advanced. For the Third National Band, almost anything may go, but there is one limitation. I don't intend to do anything in the studio that we can't reproduce on stage. If it can't be performed, there's no need to record it. There's very little truth in just being a recording act, from my standpoint." *

The first LP in the second grouping came out in late 1971, *Tantamount to Reason, Volume 1.* This was followed by a second album in early 1972 and *And the Hits Just Keep on Comin'* in August 1972. However, the response to the series was less enthusiastic than RCA hoped for, with the result that Nesmith never was able to complete the overall project.

In the mid- and late-1970s, Nesmith concentrated on songwriting. Several of his compositions provided chart-making singles for various country performers during those years. By the end of the decade, he was involved in the production of video films, one of which, *Michael Nesmith in Elephant Parts,* won the Grammy Award for Video of the Year (1981).

---

* Quotes from early 1970s interview with Irwin Stambler.

NEW CHRISTY MINSTRELS: *Vocal and instrumental group.*

What's in a name? Several million dollars, if the name happens to be New Christy Minstrels. This was the evaluation of the marketplace on the title associated

with one of the most exciting folk sounds of the 1960s. As is often the case with groups, the personnel of the Minstrels changed many times during its existence, but the general style remained what was expected by the group's fans throughout the world.

The founder of the group was a young San Francisco-based folk artist named Randy Sparks (born Leavenworth, Kansas, July 29, 1933). Sparks had lined up a number of other singers and instrumentalists in 1961 to supply an up-to-date version of the famed Christy Minstrels of the 1800s. Headed by Edwin "Pops" Christy, the original group had become legendary. In the years before the Civil War, Christy had led one of the most imitated minstrel troupes in the United States, credited with introducing many of Stephen Foster's greatest songs.

The New Christy Minstrels differed widely from the older organization. They performed old-time folk songs, but with up-to-date arrangements. They did not perform in blackface, and from the start included several female performers. In addition, many of their hit songs were original compositions by Sparks or other members of the troupe. Among the national hits turned out by the group in the early 1960s were "Green, Green," "Today," "Saturday Night," and "Liza Lee."

In 1962 and 1963, the group was featured in personal appearance tours across the United States and on many major network TV shows, and was represented on national hit charts with singles and LPs on the Columbia label. By 1964, the New Christy Minstrels was one of the best-known folk groups in the nation. During the summer, the group was featured on its own summer replacement TV show. That same year, the Minstrels performed on the White House steps at the invitation of President Lyndon Johnson.

During 1963 and 1964, Randy Sparks had withdrawn as an active performer to concentrate on managing the business affairs of the Minstrels. In 1964, he sold his interest in the group to the management firm of George Greif and Sid Garris for the not insignificant sum of $2,500,000.

Under the new management team, the group continued as a major attraction for several years. In early 1965, the New Christy Minstrels were the toast of Europe during their first overseas tour. The tour took them to England, Holland, and Scandinavia, and they capped the climax with a performance at the San Remo Festival in Italy. They gained top honors at the Festival with their renditions of "Si Piangi, Se Ridi (If You Cry, You Laugh)" and "Le Colline Sono in Flore (The Hills Are Full of Flowers)." Both songs were released on records shortly thereafter and made the top rungs of the Italian hit charts.

The sales count of New Christy Minstrels LPs through 1969 exceeded 11 million. Among the album titles were *Cowboys and Indians, Lands of Giants, Today, Presenting the New Christy Minstrels, New Christy Minstrels in Person, Tall Tales, Ramblin', Merry Christmas, Wandering Minstrels, Chim Chim Cheree, All Star Hootenanny, Greatest Hits, In Italy . . . In Italian,* and *New Kick.*

At the start of 1967, the personnel of the Minstrels were as follows: Dave Ellingson, born Ladysmith, Wisconsin; Peter Moore, born Chicago, Illinois, July 27, 1944; Michael McGinnis, born near Peoria, Illinois; Mark Holly, born St. Petersburg, Florida; Terry Benson (Williams), born Hollwyood, California, June 6, 1947; Kenny Rogers, born Texas; Monica Kirby, born Detroit, Michigan, 1946; Sue Pack, born Hollywood, California, 1946; and Mike Settle, born Tulsa, Oklahoma, March 20, 1941.

Settle, who previously sang with the Cumberland Three on tour with Shelley Berman (including a Carnegie Hall concert), was musical director of the group in the mid-1960s. After performing in coffee houses in Oklahoma, he had returned to a feature spot at New York's Bitter End. Before he joined the Minstrels, several of his original compositions were recorded by major folk groups, including The Limeliters, Peter, Paul and Mary, and the Brothers Four.

By the 1970s, none of the original members were still with the group. The name stayed the same, but the roster was usually in flux. After the mid-1960s, the group did little new work, though it was still in existence in the early 1980s.

NEW GRASS REVIVAL: *Vocal and instrumental group. Original personnel 1972: Courtney Johnson, born Barren County, Kentucky, December 20, 1939; Sam Bush, born Bowling Green, Kentucky, April 15, 1952; Curtis Burch, born Montgomery, Alabama, January 24, 1945; Ebo Walker. Walker left 1973, replaced first by Butch Robbins, then by John Cowan, born Evansville, Indiana, August 24, 1952.*

The blend of old-time bluegrass with more modern influences that sparked the revival of the music form in the 1970s sometimes was given the descriptive term "newgrass." Like many such terms, it tended to be used indiscriminately and was applied to a variety of groups with vastly different styles. However, one band that adopted it as its name went on to epitomize the best of modern bluegrass.

As charter member Sam Bush of the New Grass Revival told Ronni Lundy of *Bluegrass Unlimited* magazine (November 1978), "When we first started playing our music professionally, making our livings doing it, . . . what we could do best [was] straight bluegrass. As we've gone on, we've learned to play other things, other instruments, other kinds of music. Hopefully our music has evolved into another kind of music that everybody will know comes from bluegrass, but is not straight bluegrass."

Appropriately, Bush and another founding member, Courtney Johnson, were born and raised in Bill Monroe's home state of Kentucky, the birthplace of bluegrass. Sam was exposed to country and bluegrass at an early age thanks to his father's record collection, and later, influenced by the Flatt & Scruggs' TV show, saved his money to buy a mandolin when he was eleven. His interest in bluegrass, though, really blossomed when he and a musician friend named Wayne Stewart attended the 1965 Roanoke Bluegrass Festival. During the 1960s, Sam also took up fiddling and was good enough to place fifth at the national fiddle contest in Weister, Idaho, on his first try. After that he came in first three years in a row.

He, Stewart, and Alan Munde formed a group that brought Sam's record debut on the album *Poor Richard's Almanac*. When Munde left the group, Courtney Johnson took over on banjo. Johnson, who grew up in western Kentucky, started his musical efforts on the guitar when he was seven. He told Ronni Lundy, "I was influenced by country then a lot, because my dad was into it and played that. I heard a lot of frailing type banjo, too, when I was growing up because we always went to dances. But I never really got into banjo until I was 25 years old. My brother traded for one and I just started fooling with it—learned how to play it. I just quit playing guitar then. My first influence, what I learned to play, was Ralph Stanley type."

Courtney was a friend of both Munde and Bush before they joined forces and was a natural to replace the former when he went his own way. In 1970, Bush and Johnson moved to a new band, the Bluegrass Alliance, whose other members included Lonnie Peerce on fiddle and Ebo Walker on bass. In 1971, that group was performing in Savannah, Georgia, when the members met guitarist and dobro player Curtis Burch.

Burch, born and raised in Brunswick, Georgia, was exposed to bluegrass from his early years; his father liked it and sang bluegrass accompanying himself on guitar. Curtis learned some guitar chords in his early years, but wasn't impelled too much toward a musical career until he heard his first live bluegrass band perform, Jim and Jesse and the Virginia Boys. Almost as soon as they opened the show, he recalled, "I came out of my seat ten feet high and I thought, 'That's where it's at.' " He played for his own enjoyment and with friends but wasn't making much progress in earning a living in music until he joined the Bluegrass Alliance in November 1971.

In 1972, Peerce and the other four members parted company and the latter took the new title of New Grass Revival. That lineup played at bluegrass festivals and on the folk club and college concert circuit for a while, but in 1973 faced a crisis of sorts when Ebo Walker left. He was replaced for a time by Butch Robbins, but Robbins,

a skilled banjoist, chafed at having to concentrate on bass. After he departed, the group talked to several possible replacements, one of whom recommended they contact John Cowan.

Cowan, unlike the others, had no deep bluegrass roots. In fact, his early love was rock, particularly the Beatles. He started out playing trumpet, later played bass fiddle in the school orchestra, and, at thirteen learned electric guitar. He played with various teenage rock bands during his high school years in Evansville, Indiana, and later worked with country-rock groups.

When Cowan auditioned, the others liked not only his bass technique but his fine singing voice, which he had employed initially in his church choir. As Bush told Lundy, they decided John's musical background could add a new element to the bluegrass fusion the band was seeking. "John has a different direction that he brought in with us. It was the kind of direction I think we were all looking for. We all liked to listen to the Allman Brothers and people who had really hot bass players and we'd go, 'God, if we just had somebody that could do stuff like that and give us some other things to do.' "

After Cowan joined in 1973, a good amalgam was reached. He quickly learned much of the basics of bluegrass from the others and before long was as devoted a bluegrass fan as they were. The new roster proved to be well suited to the evolving bluegrass environment of the 1970s. Playing in festivals across the country and in clubs and concert halls all over the United States in the mid-1970s, the group stamped itself as one of the most talented of the modern bluegrass movement.

Not only did the band develop its own style of progressive bluegrass, but demonstrated the ability to play everything from traditional bluegrass on out. Thus in the summer of 1977, they won plaudits for both their own sets and for complementing such diverse performers as John Hartford and Byron Berline at the Telluride, Colorado, festival and Norman Blake and Dan Crary at a festival in Winfield, Kansas. Some of the New Grass Revival offerings became classics in their own right to the point that other bands copied such New Grass favorites as "Great Balls of Fire."

In the mid-1970s, the band began its recording career with the LP *New Grass Revival*, issued initially on the Starday-King label and later reissued on Gusto Records. The band's recording efforts really made headway after it signed with Flying Fish Records. The first LP to come out was *Fly Through the Country*. This was followed in the late 1970s by *When the Storm Is Over, Too Late to Turn Back Now*, and, in 1979, *Barren County*.

As the 1970s came to an end and the 1980s began, the New Grass Revival was well established as a major bluegrass institution. The band's commitments included occasional appearances on TV and radio and a touring schedule that kept it on the road forty-two weeks a year.

In 1980, the group teamed with Leon Russell for a wide-ranging concert tour that covered sixty-one dates in the United States and other shows in Australia and New Zealand. In their format, the New Grass Revival opened with its own set, then backed Leon for a rousing second half of the program. The series worked so well that another group of concerts was undertaken in 1981. During one stop in the 1980 schedule, on May 15th at the Perkins Palace in Pasadena, California, both audio and video tapes were made. The video material was intended for the home TV market; the audio recordings were used to prepare the 1981 album (issued on Russell's Paradise Records label, distributed by Warner Brothers) *Leon Russell and the New Grass Revival, the Live Album.*

NEW LOST CITY RAMBLERS: *Vocal and instrumental group. Original personnel, 1958: Mike Seeger, born New York, New York, 1933; John Cohen, born New York, New York, 1932; Tom Paley, born New York, New York, March 19, 1928. Paley replaced in 1962 by Tracy Schwarz, born New York, New York, 1932.*

A group that typified and was one of the bellwethers of the folk boom of the late 1950s and early 1960s was the New Lost City Ramblers. Appropriately, the driving force behind its formation was Pete

Seeger's younger brother, Mike. Like many of the folk groups of the period, it was formed by young musicians from northeast urban areas who became enthralled with the early traditional music associated with the South in general and hill-country regions of the South and Southeast in particular.

Mike Seeger, taking a cue from his brother Pete's folk music activities, developed an early interest. In his teens, he began studying the techniques used by rural artists playing instruments such as the fiddle, banjo, guitar, and autoharp by listening to records in the Library of Congress Archive of Folk Song. During the mid-1950s, he went into the back country with recording equipment to gain first-hand experience with the music. His field work led to the discovery and presentation to American folk audiences of many fine blues and folk performers.

At the time, many other young urban-bred folk enthusiasts were similarly tracking down traditional artists and material. Among them was mathematician Tom Paley and free-lance photographer John Cohen, who knew Seeger from folk-music sessions in New York. Their common interests led them to form a trio in the summer of 1958 devoted to preserving and extending the traditions of rural folk music. They took their group name from an early folk/country band called the Lost City Ramblers.

Cohen's leaning toward folk music had been influenced by his older brother, Mike, who played with a group called the Shantyboys just after World War II. John already could play several stringed instruments and had a repertoire of many folk songs when he entered Yale in 1952. He continued his folk song activities during his college years and, after graduation, often sang in New York coffee houses when not off on rural collecting tours. One of the many artists he discovered on those journeys was Roscoe Holcomb, who became the subject of an excellent documentary film prepared by Cohen. Called *The High Lonesome Sound*, it was released in 1964 and is now recognized as a classic of its genre.

Willie Nelson

Holly Near

Willie Nelson

New Lost City Ramblers (mid-1960s): l. to r., Mike Seeger, Mike Cohen, Tracy Schwarz

New Grass Revival

Paley, also a New Yorker born and bred, initially was steered toward the classics by his mother, who taught classical piano. His family moved to Hollywood for a while in the 1940s and he attended high school there. However, they returned to New York in time for him to get his high school diploma from the Bronx High School of Science in 1945. Though he loved science, he also began to develop an ear for folk music, listening to radio programs and records, and was inspired to learn banjo and guitar. During his years at the City College of New York, from which he received his B.S. in 1950, and later at Yale where he earned a master's in mathematics in 1952 and a doctorate in the late 1950s, playing and singing songs were a form of relaxation. For a long time he tried to follow dual careers as a mathematics teacher and musician, keeping the routine going even after joining the New Lost City Ramblers. (Eventually he had to make a choice—and mathematics won.)

In a short while the trio was performing in folk venues in New York and other eastern cities with good audience response. Before 1958 was over, the Ramblers' first album, The New Lost City Ramblers, came out on Folkways Records, establishing the future style of the group. As Mike Seeger wrote in the liner notes, "The songs . . . were recorded by commercial companies and the Library of Congress in the southeastern mountains between 1925 and 1935, and show the first attempt of the hill musicians to 'make a hit' with old traditional songs that had been in the mountains since pioneer days." The selections originally had been played and recorded by groups like the Fruit Jar Drinkers, Gid Tanner's Skillet Lickers, and the North Carolina Ramblers.

The New Lost City Ramblers' popularity soared as the folk boom took hold. They were invited to the first Newport Folk Festival in 1959 and performed at a number of later ones during the 1960s. Their Newport performances were included in the Vanguard Records Festival albums, including Newport Folk Festival, 1959, Newport Folk Festival, 1960, and Country Music and Bluegrass at Newport, 1963. Besides Newport, the trio appeared at many other folk festivals around the United States and became very popular on the coffee house, folk club, and college campus circuit of the early and mid-1960s.

Their albums became favorites with folk fans at the same time. Folkways issued Songs of the Depression in February 1960, followed by New Lost City Ramblers, Volume II, in December 1960, Volume III in July 1961, Volume IV in 1962, and Volume V in 1963. By the time Volume V appeared, Tom Paley had departed (in August 1962) to concentrate on teaching mathematics. His place was taken by New Yorker Tracy Schwarz. Tracy first became interested in country music by listening to New York radio programs of that kind of material in the 1940s. At the age of ten he started playing guitar and, in his teens, also mastered fiddle and banjo. When he went to college in Washington, D.C., in the late 1950s, he played in bluegrass and country-style bands.

After Tracy joined, he took part in a series of new albums. These included, on Folkways, American Moonshine and Prohibition Songs (3/63), Gone to the Country (3/64), Instrumentals (11/64); on Disc, Old Timey Music (12/64); and on Verve Folkways, Rural Delivery No. 1 (8/65) and Remembrances of Things to Come (2/67). In 1964, Aravel Records issued an album of material by the original trio titled Tom Paley, Mike Seeger and John Cohen Sing Songs of the New Lost City Ramblers. That same year, a collection of 125 songs from the group's repertoire, edited by Cohen and Seeger, was issued by Oak Publications, titled The New Lost City Ramblers Song Book.

In the 1970s, the group no longer was active. However, most of its Folkways material remained in that record firm's catalogue at the start of the 1980s. The selection, besides the five Volumes, included American Moonshine and Prohibition Songs, Depression Songs, Modern Times, "New" New Lost City Ramblers, On the Great Divide, and Remembrances of Things to Come.

NEW RIDERS OF THE PURPLE SAGE: Vocal and instrumental group. Original members, 1969: Jerry Garcia, born San Francisco, California, August 1, 1942; John Collins Dawson IV. Group expanded during year to include

David Nelson; Mickey Hart, born New York, New York; Phil Lesh, born Berkeley, California, March 15, 1940. Lesh replaced by Dave Torbert in 1970; Garcia replaced in fall 1971; by Buddy Cage, born Canada; Hart replaced in early 1971 by Spencer Dryden, born New York, New York, April 7, 1943; Torbert replaced by Skip Battin in 1974.

Several top-ranked San Francisco Bay area bands at the end of the 1960s spun off from older, more established groups to create a different type of sound. Thus some members of the Jefferson Airplane formed Hot Tuna to play blues and blues-rock material rather than acid rock and several members of the Grateful Dead spawned New Riders of the Purple Sage, which specialized in a combination of country and country-rock-styled material plus some forays into the West Coast rock sound.

The embryo stage of New Riders in 1969 took the form of a twosome made up of the Grateful Dead's best-known musician, Jerry Garcia, and songwriter, lead vocalist, and acoustic guitarist John Collins Dawson IV. Garcia, considered one of rock's finest guitarists, concentrated on playing pedal steel guitar, an instrument he had just begun to learn at the end of the 1960s. For a time Garcia and Dawson played in coffee houses and small clubs around the bay area as a twosome. After a while they added other members until the group was a quintet by the end of 1969. The others were country and rock electric guitarist David Nelson and two more Grateful Dead musicians, Mickey Hart on drums and Phil Lesh on bass. As was the case with Hot Tuna in its early stages, the members from the parent band played with the alternate group when it didn't conflict with their other dates. In a number of concerts throughout the early 1970s, the New Riders served as an opening act for the Grateful Dead. In 1970, for instance, the New Riders performed a well received set as part of the trans-Canadian Festival Express series, which showcased such major artists as Janis Joplin, The Band, and the Canadian folk music stars Ian and Sylvia.

By then Dave Torbert had taken over on bass from Phil Lesh. In the spring of 1971, the next change occurred when one-time Jefferson Airplane drummer Spencer Dryden replaced Mickey Hart on drums. The last Grateful Dead mainstay to remain with the New Riders was Jerry Garcia, but as 1971 went by, renewed interest in the Dead made it increasingly difficult for him to find time to work with his beloved musical progeny. When it became evident the New Riders would have to find a new pedal steel player to develop an independent existence, the members turned to Buddy Cage, whom they originally met during the trans-Canada Festival Express when he was working with Ian and Sylvia. Reached in Toronto, where he had been backing Anne Murray, he agreed to move to California and join the group. With his arrival in the fall of 1971, the band lineup was stabilized for the next few years.

By the time Cage agreed to join, the New Riders of the Purple Sage had completed its debut LP for Columbia. The album, New Riders of the Purple Sage, was released in September 1971. By year end, though, Cage was handling pedal steel and working with the band on a notable radio broadcast with the Grateful Dead in late December on New York station WNEW-FM. In 1972, the lineup of Dawson (also known as "Marmaduke"), Nelson, Cage, Dryden, and Torbert embarked on their first European tour in early summer and were greeted with marked enthusiasm. Later, after release of the second LP, Powerglide, in June 1972, the group took off on an extensive U.S. tour that brought them to dozens of major cities in all parts of the country. In November 1972, the band's third album, Gypsy Cowboy, was released.

The band continued intensive live engagements through most of 1973 and made several TV appearances, including a segment of ABC's In Concert show telecast in May. In between concert dates, the group went into the studio with Nashville producer Norbert Putnam and completed album number four, The Adventures of Panama Red, released in September 1973. Among the session artists on the album were folk singer Buffy Sainte-Marie, the Memphis Horns, and Donna Godchaux, who joined the Grateful Dead as a vocalist. The highlight of the year was four standing-room-only concerts in November at New York's Academy of Music.

The next band change occurred early in 1974, when Torbert left. His place was taken by former Byrds bass guitarist Skip Battin. However, the band's first live album, *Home, Home on the Road,* featured Torbert's bass work from the 1973 show. It was issued by Columbia in April 1974. During mid-1974, though, Battin contributed to sessions for the band's next collection. Called *Brujo,* that LP was issued in October 1974.

NEW SEEKERS, THE: *Vocal and instrumental group. Eve Graham, born Perth, Scotland, April 19, 1943; Lyn Paul, born Manchester, England, February 16, 1949; Peter Doyle, born Melbourne, Australia, July 28, 1949; Marty Kristian, born Leipzig, Germany, May 27, 1947; Paul Layton, born Beaconsfield, England, August 4, 1947.*

Heir to an honored name in the pop folk movement, the New Seekers, if anything, gained wider attention than the original aggregation. By diluting the folk emphasis of their predecessors, the group achieved considerably more commercial success. For a time in the mid-1970s, the New Seekers were among the most popular groups in England and Europe. Their eminence was relatively short lived, however; by the late 1970s the group had disbanded.

The driving force in the organization of the New Seekers was one of the original Seekers, guitarist Keith Potger (born Colombo, Ceylon, March 2, 1941). (Other original Seekers were Athol Guy, Judith Durham, and Bruce Woodley, all from Australia.) Potger, who performed with the new band until it began to develop a following of its own, worked with the original Seekers' manager, David Joseph, to assemble the unit, later sharing managing chores with Joseph. He noted, "We wanted to have a group able to dance, sing individually and in harmony and do comedy sketches. A prime aim was to avoid having a lead singer, as had been the case with the Seekers' Judith Durham."

After holding auditions and other talent searches, Potger and Joseph chose a quintet comprising Eve Graham on vocals and guitar, Lyn Paul on vocals, Peter Doyle on vocals, guitar, and drums, Marty Kristian on vocals, banjo, guitar, and harmonica, and Paul Layton on vocals, bass, piano, and guitar. This roster was finalized in June 1969.

All five members had considerable performing experience. Eve Graham sang with a number of groups in the early and mid-1960s, including one called the Nocturnes, and was vocalist with Cyril Stapleton's orchestra when she decided to join the New Seekers. A friend of hers from Nocturne days was Lyn Paul (real name Lynda Susan Belcher), who debuted as an entertainer at fourteen in 1963 at the Wythenshawe Labor Club. She appeared in a number of TV shows in England in the 1960s, including a part in the serial *Coronation Street.* After touring Europe with a teenage trio in the mid-1960s, she joined the Nocturnes in 1966. Paul Layton, the third member of the group's English contingent, started as a child actor, appearing in *Becket* with Richard Burton. Later he made his TV debut at thirteen in a series called *Dixon of Dock Green* and had many TV and film roles in the 1960s before an interest in songwriting changed his career direction late in the decade. He wrote several originals for the New Seekers, such as "Sweet Louise," all used as B sides on singles releases.

Kristian and Doyle both grew up in Australia, though Marty was born in Leipzig (original name Mark Vanags) to Latvian parents. He was taken to Australia at an early age and made his TV debut as a child on that country's *Go* program. Although he worked as a singer and actor throughout his teens, he entered the University of Melbourne as an architecture major. But he returned to his first love and in 1969 headed for London as a cruise ship entertainer, intending to audition for a role in *Hair.* Instead he tried out for the New Seekers and got the job.

Doyle sang and danced on Australian TV as a preteenager. He made his debut as a cabaret performer at fourteen. In 1968 he joined a group called the Virgil Brothers with whom he traveled to England, a move that brought him eventually into the New Seekers fold.

When the group began rehearsing in mid-1969, the original Seekers still were doing well with record buyers. In 1969, the Seekers had two top-10 albums, *Best of the Seekers* and *The Four and Only Seekers*. But gradually, finally convinced that the original quartet was permanently out of action, fans began to accept the new quintet. First in England, then by means of concerts in Australia and Germany, the New Seekers started to gain momentum. Their English appearances included a performance before the Queen at a Royal Command Performance, well-received dates at London's Talk of the Town, and a series of sold-out shows at the Palladium and Royal Albert Hall.

Soon after their formation, the group signed with Philips Records, which turned out such early LPs as *The New Seekers* and *Keith Potger and the New Seekers*. Neither of those were issued in the United States. (A number of other LPs in the early 1970s were for overseas release only, including *New Colours*, *The New Seekers Live at the Royal Albert Hall*, and *The New Seekers NOW!*) After gaining a strong position in England and Europe in the late 1960s and early 1970, Potger and Joseph turned the group's attention to the United States. Besides a number of concerts, the group was featured on *The Ed Sullivan Show*. The group began 1971 with an appearance on the *Andy Williams Show* and later completed major tours of the United States and Japan.

In the fall of 1970, the group had its first major U.S. singles hit (released on the Elektra label) with a cover version of Melanie's "What Have They Done to My Song Ma?" In 1971 they followed with the charted single "Beautiful People," which was the title track of their debut U.S. LP, also a success both in the United States and Europe. Their other chart hits of 1971 included "Nickel Song" and, on English lists, "Never Ending Song of Love." In late 1971, they came out with probably their best-known single, derived from a Coca Cola commercial jingle, "I'd Like to Teach the World to Sing (In Perfect Harmony)." The song entered the U.S. top 10 in January 1972. It was the title track for their

second Elektra album, which also rose to top-chart levels, as did the third Elektra LP, *Circles*, later in 1972. Also on the singles charts in 1972 were "Beg, Steal or Borrow" and "Dance, Dance, Dance."

In 1973, the group switched to MGM/Verve for U.S. distribution and debuted on that label with the single "Come Softly to Me" and the album of the same title. That was followed by a retrospective LP, *History of the New Seekers*. Later, the group returned to top-chart levels with a single of tunes from The Who's *Tommy*: "Pinball Wizard" and "See Me, Feel Me." In late summer 1973, the album *Pinball Wizards* rose to top chart-levels in the United States.

The group turned out a number of new releases in the mid-1970s, none of which had the impact of the early 1970s successes. Faced with declining public interest, the group finally broke up.

NEWBURY, MICKEY: *Singer, guitarist, songwriter. Born Houston, Texas, May 19, 1940.*

In recent decades, the rule of thumb is that a songwriter who can perform his or her songs has the best chance of succeeding in both areas. Many a singing star of modern times made it to the top by using original material even with only average vocal or instrumental skills. Mickey Newbury was a superb songwriter and had an above-average voice, yet he never could gain large-scale hits with his own recordings. However, his songs often were the vehicles for massive hits for many country and pop stars.

Newbury's compositions appealed to a broad range of people, he told Doug McClelland in the early 1970s, because he brought to them a diverse set of influences. "When I was growing up in Houston, there was a transient population that, over a six-year period, increased from half-a-million to about one-and-a-half-million. These people brought in all kinds of music. A lot of them moved in from the country because a living couldn't be made at farming. My family was country; their music was country music.

"Country music was all I heard as a kid. But that began to change when I was in high school [in the mid-1950s]. I'd listen to what was then called 'race' stations. Black music could only be heard on those stations. Black people were a minority and their music was considered minority music. Unfortunately, country had the same status.

"But I liked the music I heard then. There was a lot of jazz happening too. I grew up in a Mexican neighborhood, so I also had that kind of influence, though I don't really count that as part of my music."

During his teens, Mickey was enthusiastic about writing poetry. In his late teens, he got the chance to read some of his poems in local coffee houses in and around Houston. Most of the artists frequenting those places sang folk songs accompanying themselves on guitar. Mickey soon started combining melodies with his poetry. By the late 1950s, he was a pretty good guitarist and also was beginning to streamline his poetic beat to provide true lyrics. Still, for a while he was more interested in playing music than concentrating on commercially viable songs. He noted, "I didn't really start working on writing until I was about twenty-four."

For a while, he gave up both writing and performing when he joined the Air Force. After about seven months, he was stationed at a place that had a piano in the recreation room, where fellow soldiers often congregated. After a while, Newbury decided to join in on guitar. "I generally would borrow a guitar from a guy who had one—when you're making the kind of money they pay in the Air Force, you can't afford to buy one." For the rest of his stay in the service, he not only went back to his musical activities, but increased his efforts.

After his discharge, he began to try harder for a career in the field, moving to Nashville in the process. It took a lot of hard work and banging on doors, but it began to pay off in the mid- and late-1960s as an increasing number of performers began recording his compositions. One of his first successes was his composition "Funny Familiar Forgotten Feelings," which provided a top-10 country hit for Don Gibson and a pop hit for Tom Jones. The song that

really made the music industry take notice was "Just Dropped In (To See What Condition My Condition Was In)," a best seller for Kenny Rogers and the First Edition. The song brought the group its first gold-record single in 1968, but it was a number Mickey had been trying to place for four years. He soon had many other credits in the late 1960s and early 1970s, such as "Sweet Memories," a chart hit single in the pop field for Andy Williams and in country for Don Gibson and Dottie West, and "She Even Woke Me Up to Say Goodbye," covered by dozens of artists over the years.

Meanwhile, Newbury was building up experience as a performer, appearing in many locales in the late 1960s and throughout the 1970s. Besides stage work, he was a featured guest on many syndicated and network TV shows. He recorded some albums for several labels, which all flopped, before he signed with Elektra. In the late 1960s and early 1970s, he recorded a half dozen albums for that label, including *Mickey Newbury*, *I Came to Hear the Music*, *Lovers*, *Frisco Mabel Joy*, *Heaven Help the Child*, and *Live at Montezuma Hall/Looks Like Rain*. None of the Elektra releases was a smash hit, though they sold better than his earlier attempts. The *Live at Montezuma Hall/Looks like Rain* release paired a live concert set with a reissue of his second album, which had become a collector's item after being out of print for several years.

Besides Elektra, several record companies offered Newbury albums during the 1970s. RCA issued several LPs, including the March 1972 release, *Mickey Newbury Sings His Own Songs*. ABC's catalogue listed the albums *His Eye Is on the Sparrow* and *Rusty Tracks*. During the decade Mickey had a minor singles hit with his version of his "American Trilogy." The material later provided Elvis Presley with a bestseller. Major artists continued to record old and new songs by Mickey throughout the decade and into the 1980s. For her gold-record album *Diamonds and Rust*, Joan Baez selected three of his compositions, "Frisco Mabel Joy," "33rd of August," and "Angelline." The first two of those also were recorded by Waylon Jennings. Other performers who recorded Newbury songs were Willie Nelson, Ray Charles, and Jerry Lee Lewis.

In August 1981, a new solo album by Mickey, *After All These Years,* was issued by Mercury/Polygram, incorporating songs that spanned almost his entire writing career. The earliest was "Just as Long as That Someone Is You," written in 1959, and one of the latest a new narrative trilogy titled "The Sailor."

Reflecting on the fact that his output over the years appealed to artists from virtually every segment of popular music, he said, "In my writing, I always tried to show that, just because country people spoke ungrammatically, that didn't mean they couldn't have philosophical thoughts. I always wanted to sing to my audience rather than down to them. . . . I just believed it was easier to influence people through their hearts rather than intellectually."

NEWMAN, JIMMY C.: *Singer, guitarist, songwriter. Born Big Mamou, Louisiana, August 27, 1927.*

Given the nickname "Mr. Alligator Man" in the 1960s for one of his hit songs of that decade, Jimmy Newman ranked with Doug Kershaw as one of the prime interpreters of Cajun music in the country field. In such routines as "Bayou Talk and Big Mamou," he always could captivate audiences with his singing and story telling in the Cajun accents of his home region of Louisiana. But over his several decades as a featured artist, he proved himself just as comfortable with country songs of all kinds.

As a boy of half-French origin, Jimmy grew up in the midst of Cajun culture and picked up many of its popular songs both at home and from local get-togethers. He learned to play guitar well by his mid-teens and was soon performing for friends and small gatherings. In his preteen years, he also gained pleasure from going to see western films; as a result, his first idol was Gene Autry, whose songs he often sang. In the 1960s, he also cited Jim Reeves, Tom

T. Hall, and Glen Campbell as among his favorites.

When he was nineteen, in 1946, having decided on making music a career, he made his first move by singing with a band in Big Mamou, Lousiana. For several years he polished his act, heading his own band in small clubs and theaters in the South and Southwest.

He then got the chance to host his own show on KPLC Radio and TV in Lake Charles, Louisiana. He already had perfected the wailing Cajun signature, the electrifying "aieeee" call that prefaced many of his songs. That feature coupled with his strong voice soon won the attention of local audiences and paved the way for his advance to a major radio and TV show, the *Louisiana Hayride* in Shreveport. That kind of exposure not only helped make him a well-known performer beyond Louisiana borders, it also brought him a recording contract with Dot Records. In 1954, he gained national attention with the hit single of a song co-written with J. Miller, "Cry, Cry, Darling." He followed with other chartmakers, such as "Seasons of My Heart," "Blue Darling," and "Daydreaming." In 1956, he was asked to join the cast of the *Grand Ole Opry,* and the next year he had his best-selling record up to that time, still one of his most-remembered songs, "Falling Star."

During the late 1950s, besides appearing regularly on the *Opry,* he performed throughout the United States, a pattern that still held true through the 1960s and 1970s. He switched to MGM at the end of the 1950s and had such top-level chart hits as "You're Making a Fool Out of Me" in 1958, "Grin and Bear It" in 1959, and "A Lovely Work of Art" in 1960. In the mid-1960s, he left MGM for Decca and soon had a new series of singles on national country charts. Among them were such Bayou-flavored songs as "Alligator Man," "Big Mamou and Bayou Talk," and "Louisiana Saturday Night." Other songs that became staple items in his repertoire during the 1960s were "D.J. for a Day," "Blue Lonely Winter," "Bring Your Heart Back Home," "Angel on Leave," "City of the Angels," and "Back in Circulation." He added two more top-10 singles to his credits in the mid-1960s: "Artificial Rose" in 1965 and "Back Pocket Money" in 1966.

Jimmy's album output in the 1950s included such Dot collections as *Crossroads, Fallen Star,* and *Cry, Cry Darling,* some of which were reissued in the 1960s. On MGM he had such releases as *Songs of Jimmy Newman* in 1962 and *Folk Songs of the Bayou* in 1963. His LP output for Decca included *Artificial Rose* in 1966, *World of Music* in 1967, *The Newman Way* in 1968, and *Country Time* at the start of the 1970s.

During the 1970s, Newman's recording career slowed down and his name didn't appear on hit charts very often. (Among the labels he recorded for in the 1970s were Shannon and Plantations.) However, he retained a strong following among country fans for his concerts and radio-TV work. He was a guest on many network or syndicated shows during those years and was still a major cast member of the *Grand Ole Opry,* often hosting as well as singing on one of the show's segments, a pattern continuing into the 1980s.

NEWTON, JUICE: *Singer, guitarist, songwriter, band leader (Silver Spur). Born Virginia Beach, Virginia, February 18, 1952.*

"This isn't the way I planned it," Juice Newton told Dennis Hunt *(Los Angeles Times,* April 8, 1981) after achieving her first hit single after over a decade of performing. "It's a hard lesson when life doesn't go according to your dreams. When I started I was very young. This business seemed so glamorous. It had a mystique, an excitement. I thought I'd go in and be a hit before too long. After a while I saw I was wrong. I saw it was going to be a long hard grind.

"That's a drag, but that's the way it had to be. You can't let yourself wallow in disappointment. If you let yourself fall into that, there are demons in the night that'll get you. That's not fun."

Although not yet thirty when she said that, she was indeed a veteran of the music wars. Newton's initial exposure to the public came in her mid-teens as a folksinger in Virginia Beach coffee houses. Brought up in that town, the youngest of

three children of a Navy family (her father was a career Navy man), she had first become serious about music at thirteen when she got her first guitar and taught herself to play it. Though rock was dominant, folk music still had a strong impact in her area and, influenced by the music of people like Tom Paxton, Donovan, Dylan, and Joan Baez, Newton chose that musical direction.

In her mid-teens in the late 1960s, Juice was singing in local coffee houses whenever she could get the opportunity. (Her original name was Judy Kay Newton, but friends and family nicknamed her Juice at an early age. In the early 1970s, she had her first name legally changed to Juice). As she told Eliot Tiegel for an article in *People* (July 20, 1981), she was hardly an instant crowd pleaser. "I sounded horrendously bad and nobody wanted to sing with me."

After finishing high school, Juice headed for Los Altos Hills, California, to attend Foothill College. At first she kept up her folksinging efforts, then formed a folk-rock group called Dixie Peach with boyfriend Otha Young, still her love interest and music associate in the early 1980s. Actually, everyone who heard them and the band that evolved over the next few years, called Silver Spur (organized by Young), considered the group and Juice as part of the country-rock movement.

Newton recalled for Bill E. Burk of the *Memphis Press-Scimitar* (May 22, 1981), "I came to California and everybody said, 'Oh, you're a country singer.' I think they thought because of my accent and because they were never really exposed to folk music that that's what country music was. It didn't bother me. I liked that. If they needed to have a label, that was fine. . . . It took me by surprise, but as I started to listen to more country music, I realized there was a similarity there [between folk and country]. What made me happy about that was that it all came naturally—that's what came out of my mouth. All by itself."

In the mid-1970s, Juice and Otha moved from the San Francisco Bay area to Los Angeles in quest of a recording contract. Within six months, Juice Newton and Silver Spur were on the RCA Records roster.

The first result was the 1975 folk/country-rock LP *Juice Newton & Silver Spur*, followed a year later by *After the Dust Settles*. Neither album created much of a stir (though the single "Love Is a Word" did make lower country chart levels) and the group left RCA, signing with Capitol Records in 1977. Their debut album on Capitol, a much more country-oriented collection, was *Come to Me*, which featured Juice's version of "Good Luck Baby Jane," a song given to her by Bob Seger.

Again not much happened with the LP. In 1978, Juice and Otha disbanded Silver Spur (the name was revived when Young formed a new backing group when Newton's career picked up a few years later). For a while she worked as a backing vocalist, contributing to Bob Welch's album *French Kiss*. During 1978, Juice recorded material for a solo album on Capitol. Called *Well Kept Secret*, it gained some notice with overseas audiences, suggesting that better things might be in store.

Her second solo album on Capitol, the 1979 *Take Heart*, showcased Newton for the first time as an unabashed country artist. She stressed, "I'd been progressing in that direction at somewhat a steady pace. I now consider myself a country/pop singer. My accent is on country and my voice has a certain country flavor." The album wasn't a bestseller, but it did provide some singles that did better with country fans than earlier releases. In early 1980, "Sunshine" made the country top 40 and "You Fill My Life" was on the lists a number of months later in the year.

Then came the real turning point. In February 1981, Capitol issued her third solo LP (and fourth Capitol album overall), *Juice*. The single first issued was her version of "Angel of the Morning," originally a hit for Merrilee Rush in 1968. It appeared on country charts in short order and kept on rising until it reached number one in the spring. It also became a major pop hit. This was followed by still another hit single from the album, "Queen of Hearts," which earned her a gold record from the R.I.A.A., as had "Angel of the Morning." The third single from the album, "The Sweetest Thing," written by

Otha Young, also became a bestseller. One of the LP numbers, "River of Love," further underlined Juice's abilities—it was co-written by her and Young. The album itself rose high on both pop and country charts, reaching platinum-record levels by early 1982.

She told Dennis Hunt she intended to remain true to country music in the future. "I don't want to lose that country audience. . . . They've supported me all along." In addition, she said, she felt the country audience "is more willing to listen to a woman's point of view. They accept women easier. So it's more comfortable for a woman to have a career in country than in pop or rock.

"Maybe people in country, or men in the country scene, feel less threatened by women. In country, women can be emotional and feminine. In pop and rock you have to be more like the men to compete with them. I feel safer in the country scene. It's easier to be myself, easier to be a woman."

NEWTON, WOOD: *Singer, guitarist, songwriter. Born Hampton, Arkansas.*

One of the promising new singer-songwriters in the country field at the start of the 1980s, Wood Newton made his initial contacts in the music business through his skill as a photographer. Although he was highly regarded in that creative pursuit, he decided there was more chance to eat regularly by succeeding as a writer and performer.

Wood was born and raised in the small town of Hampton, Arkansas, where his father ran a hardware store. As he noted, "Where I'm from in South Arkansas is kind of like Louisiana and Mississippi. Flat, delta-type land—it's what you might call the deep South. A lot of my songs have that kind of southern feeling, but while I'm from that environment, I've also traveled some overseas, spent time in New York City, and I did graduate from the University of Arkansas."

Newton first took up guitar as a senior in high school, when his main influences were some of the rockabilly artists of the mid- and late-1950s and the folk and folk-rock offerings of people like Bob Dylan and Joan Baez. He played with friends and groups in high school and college, though he didn't really consider music as a possible career at the time.

As an occasional Nashville resident in the late 1960s and early 1970s, Newton was writing some original material, but it didn't seem to match the trends in the country field at the time. He had become reinterested in country music because of his enthusiasm for the Byrds' late 1960s LP, *Sweetheart of the Rodeo,* and some of Johnny Cash's efforts of those years. He still was restless and not sure of what craft to follow in the early 1970s, when his wanderings took him to Europe and North Africa in 1971. "My first taste of 'stardom' was in Marrakesh. Nobody had any tapes with them, but I had a guitar and could do songs by Crosby, Stills & Nash and Neil Young."

He spent more and more time in Nashville as the 1970s progressed, but mainly as a photographer. Wood became a staff photographer of the underground country-music magazine *Hank* and also shot magazine covers of Marshall Chapman, Jack Clement, and Charlie Daniels. Daniels liked his work enough to suggest he become official photographer of the annual country rock event, the Volunteer Jam.

Increasingly interested in writing music rather than concentrating on photographs of other musicians, Newton decided to make Nashville home, in the fall of 1976. He got a writing contract in October with the DebDave/Briar Patch Publishing Company from the demo records he had been cutting off and on since the mid-1970s. His new tapes in the late 1970s finally won him the chance to record for Elektra/Asylum Records. The debut single, "Last Exit for Love," produced by Even Stevens (who also co-wrote the song with D. Tyler), came out in late 1978 and made mid-chart levels in December. Encouraged by that, Elektra gave the go-ahead for Newton's debut LP, which was issued in March 1979.

NEWTON-JOHN, OLIVIA: *Singer, actress, songwriter. Born Cambridge, England, September 26, 1947.*

There was some grumbling among country music die-hards when Olivia Newton-John was named Country Music Female Vocalist of the Year for 1974. It didn't seem right, they suggested, for an artist from overseas who had primarily been known in England as a pop ballad and rock vocalist to suddenly gain such honors in her initial foray into the U.S. market. But most country-music people brushed that aside, noting that the U.S. audience had, in effect, validated Newton-John's credentials by buying her recordings in large numbers. Had she wanted to debate the matter, Olivia could have pointed out that the roots of country music lay in the centuries-old folk music of the British Isles and many a U.S. country star was descended from immigrants from her father's home region, Wales.

It was, in fact, folk music that first interested Olivia as a girl growing up in Australia. She was born in Cambridge, England, but her father, a college professor, had moved the family to Australia when Olivia was five to take an administrative post at a university. (Intellectual pursuits bulked large in Newton-John's family. Her grandfather was Nobel laureate Max Born.) When Olivia was in her late teens, she began to move away from folk toward the pop idiom.

Victory in a talent contest in Australia gained her a trip to England in the late 1960s, where her professional singing career began to accelerate rapidly. In the early 1970s she became one of the more successful young pop artists in Britain. As her reputation grew there, she naturally started thinking about the more affluent U.S. market, an idea matched by growing interest in her by American record firms. MCA Records offered a contract, and Newton-John began working on her initial recordings for the label in 1973. One of the first results was the single "Let Me Be There." The song proved acceptable to both pop and country listeners. Country fans liked it enough to move it onto the charts in late summer. The single moved steadily higher until it made the country top 10 by years end and remained there into 1974.

Olivia proved it was no fluke with an

even greater country hit, "If You Love Me (Let Me Know)," which became number one on country lists in the spring of 1974. With the pop volume added in, that effort earned a gold-record award, as did its predecessor. She showed her versatility by earning another gold record in the fall of 1974, this time for a pop single, "I Honestly Love You." Meanwhile, Newton-John also stormed the country album charts during 1974 with the gold record Let Me Be There in the spring and If You Love Me, on the charts in summer and still on them in early 1975.

With that kind of success, it's not surprising Olivia gained four Country Music Association Awards nominations for 1974, including Entertainer of the Year, Album of the Year, Single of the Year, and Female Vocalist of the Year. She came in number one in the last-named category.

She continued to be an almost perennial resident on the country charts throughout the 1970s. In 1975, her singles hits included "Have You Never Been Mellow," "Please Mr. Please," and "Something Better to Do," and her album Have You Never Been Mellow made the top 10. In 1976, she came up with the number-one country chart hit "Come on Over" in May and the top-10 single "Don't Stop Believin' " in late summer. In late 1975 and early 1976 she placed the LP Clearly Love on upper-chart levels and soon after had the top-5 album Come on Over. Still going strong in 1977, she turned out the top-10 album Making a Good Thing Better, whose title track also rose high on the singles charts.

In 1978, Olivia stressed rock rather than country, starring opposite John Travolta in the film Grease and having a featured part in the gold-record soundtrack album (issued by RSO Records). Her hit singles "You're the One That I Love," "Summer Nights," and "Hopelessly Devoted to You" were also issued by RSO. The first of those was certified platinum by the R.I.A.A.; the other two earned gold records. On the surface, it might have seemed she was turning strongly away from the country field, particularly when her next MCA solo album, Totally Hot, was issued in late 1978. However, a closer look at the album's contents showed that, de-

spite its title, it still had several country-oriented numbers, such as "Dancin' Round and Round" and "Borrowed Time," the latter an original composition by Newton-John.

Her next album effort was a collaboration with the major rock band the Electric Light Orchestra, titled Xanadu. That 1979 release offered music from a mediocre movie of the same name; the film did poorly, but the LP was a bestseller, reaching platinum-record levels and spawning the gold-record single "Magic." Olivia's first solo album of the 1980s, Physical, was released by MCA Records in the fall of 1981 and was in the top pop chart brackets soon after. Several of the songs from the album were spotlighted by Newton-John in her late-1981 TV special.

NILES, JOHN JACOB: Singer, instrumentalist (dulcimer, lute, piano), songwriter, folklorist, folk music collector. Born Louisville, Kentucky, April 28, 1892; died near Lexington, Kentucky, May 1, 1980.

The multitalented John Jacob Niles was a major force in preserving traditional folk music for close to six decades. In concert, his high-pitched, falsetto sounding style of singing took a little getting used to, but once that barrier was crossed, folk purists could delight in renditions of many of the finest folk songs to evolve during the long history of the genre. Niles, however, probably contributed more in other ways to preserving the folk song heritage than as a performer. Besides keeping alive the tradition of homebuilt musical instruments, he was an avid collector of songs and related material, compiling one of the largest folk music collections in the world.

John was born into a family with deep roots in the tradition of folk and classical music. His father, a farmer and skilled carpenter, was one of the best-known folksingers in the region as well as one of the best square-dance callers. His mother played the organ in church and also was an excellent classical pianist. From his father John learned to play several stringed instruments, and he was given a basic grounding in piano by his mother.

When still in public school, he was given a store-bought three-stringed dulcimer by his father, who told the boy he expected him to make his own instruments in the future. John learned to play that dulcimer, but when he was about twelve replaced it with one he made himself. From then on, he always made his own stringed instruments, including many interesting variations of three- to eight-stringed dulcimers and a number of lutes.

Niles began his folk music collection in high school, devising his own system of musical notation. At fifteen, he started a notebook of songs from his home region. According to Ray Lawless (Folksingers and Folksongs in America, p. 176), Niles' first paid performance took place about this time "when he accompanied a group of Chatauqua performers in a Saturday afternoon show."

John was graduated from DuPont Manuall High School in 1909 and took a job as a surveyor. His work took him through the mountains of the Kentucky region and gave him the chance to continue his folk music collecting. By 1910 he had an impressive collection of songs and began to perform for local churches and other groups.

His budding career as a folk artist was interrupted by World War I. He enlisted in the U.S. Army Air Corps and went to France in 1918, where he almost lost his life in a plane crash. He was partly paralyzed; it took some seven years before he could walk completely normally once more. Instead of returning home, he took his discharge and attended the University of Lyon and the Schola Cantorum in Paris, improving his background in classical music. In 1919, Niles returned to the United States and continued his studies at the Cincinnati Conservatory of Music. He also soon resumed his spare-time activity of giving folk song concerts.

After two years at the Conservatory, he moved to New York. He supported his folk music work with a variety of jobs, including that of emcee at the Silver Slipper Club, grooming horses for Ziegfield Follies extravaganzas, and working as a rose gardener. During the early 1920s, he gave folk concerts at major universities. At Princeton, John met Marion Kerby. The two developed a folk song program and toured widely in the United States as well as in most of the countries of Europe.

For several years during this period, Niles also worked as a chauffeur for photographer Doris Ulmann. He drove her throughout the Southwest, collecting folk material while she photographed various localities. In the late 1920s, the first collections of Niles' material was published. These books, based on his World War I experience, were Singing Soldiers (1927) and Songs My Mother Never Taught Me (1929). During the 1929–30 period, he also wrote a number of short stories for Scribner's magazine. In 1929, another Niles collection was called Seven Kentucky Mountain Songs.

In the 1930s, his reputation continued to grow as he turned out more books, arranged and composed new folk material, and gave upwards of fifty concerts a year. His published song collections of the decade included Songs of the Hill Folk (1936) and Ballads, Carols and Tragic Legends from the Southern Appalachian Mountains (1937). In 1939, he made one of his first major albums for RCA Victor, Early American Ballads.

In 1940, troubled by Hitler's excesses, he began an oratorio called "Lamentations." The piece was finally completed ten years later and given its initial performance March 14, 1951 at Indiana State Teachers College, Terre Haute. The work in its final form expressed opposition to all forms of authoritarian rule, including, as it did, what John called "a prayer to deliver the world from the curse of communism." Other long works by Niles are "Rhapsody for the Merry Month of May" and "Mary the Rose."

His recordings of the 1940s included Early American Carols and Folk Songs (1940) and American Folk Lore (1941). The latter was reissued on RCA's Camden label, with minor changes, in 1954. His concerts, which won critical acclaim for the choice of songs and Niles' sensitive dulcimer playing, continued to draw capacity audiences in the 1940s and 1950s. Particularly noteworthy was the 1946 midnight concert at New York's Town Hall in which an appreciative gathering heard him sing such favorites as "Black Is the Color of My True Love's Hair" (sung to a melody written by him), "The Seven Joys of Mary," "The Rovin' Gambler," and "I Wonder as I Wander" (for which he wrote the music).

His output of recordings and collections continued through the 1950s and 1960s. In 1957, RCA Camden issued the LP *John Jacob Niles: 50th Anniversary Album*. Niles also issued several albums on his own label, Boone-Tolliver, including *American Folk Songs* and *Ballads*. He was featured on a number of Tradition LPs, including *I Wonder as I Wander* (1957); *Ballads* (two LPs); and *An Evening with John Jacob Niles* (1960).

Other collections of Niles' material issued after World War II included *The Anglo-American Study Book* (1945); *Shape-Note Study Book* (1950); and the massive *Ballad Book of John Jacob Niles*. Among other well-known original Niles' compositions and arrangements presented in these books are such songs as "Sweet Little Jesus Boy," "The Cherry Tree," "Froggy Went a'Courtin'," "Down in Yon Forest," and "You Got to Cross That Lonesome Valley."

In the 1960s, despite his advanced years, Niles remained active as a performer, appearing on many a concert hall and college stage in the eastern United States. In 1965, RCA issued the LP *John Jacob Files: Folk Balladeer*, and in 1967 Tradition Records presented *The Best of John Jacob Niles*.

In the 1970s, Niles, who always kept close to his roots in Kentucky, spent most of his time at his Boot Hill Farm near Lexington. One of his last major projects was the *Niles-Merton Song Cycles*, published in 1972. In this work, he provided music accompaniment to poems of the Trappist monk Thomas Merton. At the start of the 1980s, his albums still in print included *The Best of John Jacob Niles* on Tradition and, on Folkways Records (including another of his best-known renditions, "I'm So Glad Trouble Don't Last Forever"), *John Jacob Niles Sings Folk Songs.*"

His long career came to a close in May 1980 when he died at Boot Hill Farm.

NIXON, NICK: *Singer, guitarist, songwriter. Born St. Louis, Missouri, March 20.*

It's not unusual for a country artist to work at other jobs while waiting for the big break to come, but usually those jobs are appropriately earthy—farming, truck driving, even working on the railroad. But white-collar sidelines are uncommon. Somehow the title "the singing optician" doesn't have quite the flair of, say, "the singing brakeman," which is perhaps why Nick Nixon doesn't bill himself that way.

Nixon grew up in a close-knit family in Missouri, where there was no lack of country-music programming to be found on radio or TV. Nixon enjoyed country tunes from his early years and sometimes sang some of them as well as other kinds of songs just for the fun of it. He recalled, "I always liked performing. I used to entertain my brothers and sisters at home, although I never thought of singing at all. My only goal was to play the guitar. I got one when I was eleven, but two years later it was stolen, so I forgot the whole thing for five years. My singing started because I needed a part-time job."

Nick got a job as an optician after finishing school and considered that would be his main role in life. However, he had friends who worked in local clubs, and one night one of them asked him to come up on stage. "I did 'Swinging Doors' and when people applauded, that was all I needed." Nixon decided working as a musician was a pleasant way to earn some extra money. He assembled a band called the Country Souls that began to play in clubs in and around St. Louis. The band's sound proved professional enough for it to find other jobs on occasion in towns or cities in Kansas, Illinois, and Arkansas during the mid-1970s.

The more Nixon performed, the more he became interested in expanding his musical efforts and cutting back on optical chores. He cut some demonstration tapes for perusal by record executives, which finally resulted in a contract with Mercury. The alignment produced a series of singles that made the country charts during the mid-1970s, mostly on lower levels, but at least signaling that better things might lie ahead. One of his first singles to receive attention was "A Habit I Can't Break," on country lists in the fall of 1974. This was followed by such other mid-1970s chartmakers as "I'm Too Used to Loving You,"

"She's Just an Old Love Turned Memory," "Rocking in Rosalee's Boat," and "Love Songs and Romance Magazines." The latter made the top 50 during the summer of 1977. In the fall of 1977, another single, "I'll Get Over You," moved into the upper half of the hit lists. Meanwhile, Mercury issued his debut LP in June 1977, *Nick Nixon*. His 1978 charted singles on Mercury included "She's Lying Next to Me," on the lists in late summer and early fall.

During the mid-1970s, Nixon's potential was recognized by many country stars for whom he co-wrote new material, such as "The Teddy Bear Song," recorded by Barbara Fairchild, and other numbers cut by Dick Curless, the Wilburn Brothers, and Roy Rogers.

NORMA JEAN: *Singer, guitarist. Born near Wellston, Oklahoma, January 30, 1938.*

Over the years, Porter Wagoner helped bring a number of very talented female vocalists to the attention of national audiences via his TV show and yearly tours. Among those who went on to stardom as individual performers after singing with his band for a number of years were Dolly Parton and Norma Jean.

Norma was born and spent her earliest years in rural Wellston, Oklahoma, where the primary musical fare was country & western. Showing a natural aptitude for singing, little Norma Jean Beasler charmed friends and family with several country songs before she could read and write. When she was five, the family moved to Oklahoma City, where she attended public school, a relocation that brought her in close contact with an aunt who was a skilled guitarist. The aunt began teaching the instrument to Norma, who picked it up rapidly. Before she was in her teens, she was good enough to play at local square dances.

When she was thirteen, she auditioned for radio station KLPR in Oklahoma City and gained her own three-times-a-week show. As her reputation increased in the area, she began to get the chance to share bills at fairs and other venues with people like Leon McAuliffe and Billy Gray. All of this helped to bring an invitation to join the *Ozark Jubilee* in Springfield, Missouri, in 1958. When she started working on that program she dropped her last name and became just Norma Jean.

Norma had her eye on Nashville and in 1960 made the break to Music City. She met Porter Wagoner during a personal appearance, and he was impressed enough to ask her to become the female singer on his syndicated TV show. Since Porter was a regular on the *Opry* show, this also opened the door for her to gain exposure on the quintessence of all country programs.

Norma's work on the *Opry* rapidly expanded her popularity with country fans and fellow *Opry* artists, two of whom, Marty Robbins and Marvin Rainwater, helped get her a recording contract from Columbia. She made a number of recordings for that label in the early 1960s, none of which created much of a stir, though some releases made lower-chart levels.

Things changed when she switched to RCA Victor in 1963. Before the year was out she had a major singles hit, "Let's Go All the Way." For many years after that, her name rarely was absent from the country charts for very long. In 1964 she turned out a top-10 hit, "Go Cat Go" and followed with another in 1965, "I Wouldn't Buy a Used Car from Him." She also had top chartmakers in the mid-1960s with such songs as "Put Your Arms Around Her," "Then Go Home to Her" and, in 1966, a top-10 duet with Bobby Bare, "Game of Triangles." Among her other singles of those years were "Lonesome #1," "I'm a Walking Advertisement," "You're Driving Me Out of My Mind," "The Shirt," "Please Don't Hurt Me," "Pursuing Happiness," "Conscience," "Keep an Eye on Me," and "Don't Let the Doorknob Hit You." By 1965, Norma Jean had taken her place as a major solo performer and became a regular cast member of the *Opry* in that capacity, an honor she still retained in the 1970s.

From the mid-1960s through the mid-1970s, she had dozens of albums to her credit, almost all issued by RCA. Her debut LP on the label came out in December 1964 and was titled *Norma Jean*. It was followed by such others as *Pretty Miss* (1/66), *Country's Favorite* (a rare non-RCA release issued by Harmony in February 1966), *Don't Hurt Me* (7/66), *Tribute to Kitty Wells* (12/66), *Norma Jean Sings Porter Wagoner* (12/66), *Jackson Ain't Big Town* (9/67), *Heaven's a Prayer Away* (2/68), *Let's Go All the Way* (reissue, late 1960s), *Best of Norma Jean* (12/69), *Another Man* (6/70), *It's Time* (12/70), *Norma Jean* (7/71), *It Wasn't God* (RCA Camden, 9/71), *Hank Cochran Songs* (10/71), *Thank You for Loving Me* (6/72), *I Guess That Comes from Being Poor* (8/72).

NYRO, LAURA: *Singer, pianist, songwriter. Born the Bronx, New York, fall 1947.*

A shy, soft-spoken, highly capable artist, Laura Nyro had an almost across-the-board impact on pop music of the late 1960s and early 1970s with original songs that combined often poetic lyrics with musical elements ranging from urban folk (somewhat in the Dylan tradition) to jazz and soul. The appeal her songs had to artists of all kinds of genres could be seen from the names of those who recorded some of them; a partial list includes Peter, Paul & Mary, Three Dog Night, Fifth Dimension, Blood, Sweat and Tears, Mongo Santamaria, Frank Sinatra, Barbra Streisand, Linda Ronstadt, and Aretha Franklin.

Music was a part of her life from her earliest years, on College Avenue in the Bronx. Her father was a jazz trumpeter and spent many hours practicing at home. Young Laura was intrigued by his playing and by other music she heard on the radio and on records. When she was eight, she wrote her first songs. Her commitment to music continued into her teens when she entered the High School of Music and Art in Manhattan, where her teachers felt she had considerable creative potential.

As Nyro moved into her teens, she continued to experiment with songwriting and with drugs, perhaps a little before her time. She considers one of her LSD trips a turning point in her life, when she gained confidence in her ability to succeed. Later she stopped using LSD. Her musical interests at the time ranged from Bob Dylan to jazz great John Coltrane. She began singing in local clubs in her late teens and impressed more than a few people in the music field with her promise. When she was

eighteen, she went cross-country to San Francisco, where she performed at the hungry i nightclub (long a proving ground for new folk stars) for two months.

Back in New York, Nyro signed with Verve/Folkways Records, which released her first album, *More than a New Discovery,* in 1966. Rights to the LP later were purchased by her primary record label, Columbia, which reissued it in January 1973 under the title *The First Songs.* By 1967, so many people in the pop and folk music audience were interested in her that she was asked to take part in the Monterey Pop Festival. It proved to be a disaster. Her kind of low key, often introspective music seemed out of place against the high-powered acid-rock offerings of people like Jimi Hendrix and Janice Joplin. She was hooted off the stage.

However, it proved only a temporary setback. People in other segments of music began to appreciate the subtleties of Nyro's work, the expert craftsmanship that made many of her songs adaptable to different musical arrangements. Six months after Monterey, her songs started to show up on the hit lists. The first major indication of this was the rise of the Fifth Dimension's version of "Stoned Soul Picnic" to number one in early 1968. Later that same group had major hits with Laura's "Wedding Bell Blues" and "Sweet Blindness." By the time "Stoned Soul Picnic" moved to the top of the charts, Laura had completed her first album for Columbia, with whom she had signed in 1968. Called *Eli and the Thirteenth Confession,* it was issued in March 1968 and contained a group of songs that revolved around the central theme of a young girl's path from childhood to maturity. An example of its content was the song "Emmie," whose lyrics include the lines "Emily/You're the natural snow/the unstudied sea . . . and I swear you were born a weaver's love/Born for the loom's desire." In another song, "Confessions," she wrote, "Love is surely gospel."

That album wasn't an immediate smash, but by word of mouth its excellence was relayed among fans and eventually it was on the charts for many months. Her next album, one of her best, *New York Tenda-berry*, came out in August 1969 and almost immediately was on the charts. It included such fine tracks as "Save the Country" and "Time and Love." It was followed by *Christmas and the Beads of Sweat*, released in November 1970, and her only album of non-Nyro material, recorded with the soul/R&B group Labelle, *Gonna Take a Miracle*, which came out in November 1971.

During the late 1960s–early 1970s period, other artists continued to do well with covers of Nyro's songs. In late 1969, Three Dog Night won a gold record for their recording of "Eli's Coming." In 1970, the Fifth Dimension had a million-seller in "Wedding Bell Blues" as did Blood, Sweat & Tears with "And When I Die." In 1971, Barbra Streisand scored a major success with Laura's "Stoney End."

After *Gonna Take a Miracle*, though Laura made some concert appearances, nothing new took shape in the recording studios. Finally, in 1972, she retired completely from the music field and for a long time nothing much was heard from her. She got married, severed all ties with industry people, and moved to a small town in Connecticut. Later, discussing the reasons for that sudden and complete break, she told Michael Watts of England's *Melody Maker* magazine, "It just got to the point where people who met you had preconceived notions. And your phone rings twenty times a day. It's really nice to get away to a place where you can say 'Now wait a minute' and throw the phone out the window. I think it's good to get away

from this horrible business when you begin to feel like a commodity. There are many other things in life."

For some three years Nyro remained in artistic seclusion, but eventually she got the incentive to take up writing and performing again. For one, she felt a new maturity in her approach to the art, for another, her marriage ended in divorce after three years. In late 1975, she pleased Columbia executives by agreeing to go into the studios and work on a new LP. That collection, *Smile*, was issued in February 1976 and proved to be a coherent, well-written, and well-sung group of songs that matched many of her finest efforts of the past. Although most were new songs, including "Midnight Blue," which provided a chart hit for other artists, another major track was "I Am the Blues," a song she had performed in 1971 on a British TV special. In support of the album, Laura made a coast-to-coast tour of the United States in early summer, showing that she was at the peak of her form as an entertainer.

That four-month tour with a full band provided the material for the live album *Season of Lights*, stressing versions of older songs. In June 1978, over two years after *Smile*, she was represented on Columbia by an album of newly recorded songs. Her tour for that album in mid-1978 included engagements at the Roxy in Los Angeles, Old Waldorf in San Francisco, New York's Bottom Line, and a final concert on a Saturday night in Manhattan's Central Park before a massive and responsive crowd.

OAK RIDGE BOYS: *Vocal quartet with band backup (the Oak Ridge Band). Quartet personnel as of early 1980s: Duane Allen, born Taylor-town, Texas, April 29, 1943; William Lee Golden, born Brewton, Alabama, January 12, 1939; Richard Sterban, born Camden, New Jersey, April 24, 1943; Joe Bonsall, born Philadelphia, Pennsylvania, May 18, 1948.*

When the Oak Ridge Boys began to achieve national recognition in the country-music field in the late 1970s, they had already won four Grammy Awards and fifteen Dove Awards (the gospel-music equivalent of the Grammy). They already had headlined a Las Vegas show and opened for such top acts as Roy Clark and Johnny Cash, had won awards in England and Sweden, and had toured the Soviet Union. By the mid-1970s, charter member Bill Golden noted, "We had reached the height of gospel success. We'd gone about as far as we could go." So the group turned to the secular field and soon eclipsed its gospel popularity.

Actually, by then no one in the group had been around when it first started. That had been during the World War II years. In the 1940s, a country quartet called the Country Cut-Ups formed in Knoxville, Tennessee, consisting of four singers and a piano accompanist, that often performed at the atomic energy research center in nearby Oak Ridge for workers not permitted to leave the facility for security reasons. After a while, the group became known as the Oak Ridge Quartet. Their most popular numbers proved to be gospel songs, so they gradually built their entire repertoire around southern-style gospel music.

After the war, the original group disbanded, but soon another foursome, based in Nashville, took over the name. From then until the current group stabilized in the mid-1970s, there were many changes in personnel over the decades. In all, including band members, about thirty performers have taken part in Oak Ridge efforts. Of the current group, the singer with longest tenure is Bill Golden, who joined in 1964. He grew up in Brewton, Alabama, where he graduated from East Brewton High School in the 1950s. His first public performance came at age seven when he played guitar and sang with his sister on Brewton radio station WEBJ. Before joining the Oak Ridge group he was involved with his family farm and worked in a pulp mill.

Lead singer Duane Allen got the chance to join the group in 1966. Born and raised in Texas, he completed high school there and went on to earn a bachelor's degree in music from East Texas State University. His first public performance came at four when he sang in church with his family. For a while he sang baritone with the Southernaires Quartet in Paris, Texas, and also was a disc jockey for a time. A guitar

player for many years before joining the Oaks, he was the only member of the quartet to play an instrument on stage as of the early 1980s. When the group moved into the secular field, he was the acknowledged leader.

New Jersey born and raised Richard Sterban became a quartet member in 1972. Like Allen, he had studied music in college, in his case Trenton State College. His first public performance came at seven when he sang a soprano solo in church. In later years, after his voice changed to a deep bass, he sang with such groups as the Keystone Quartet in Bristol, Pennsylvania, and the Stamps Quartet (which backed Elvis Presley) before joining the Oaks. Although strictly a singer with the quartet, he learned to play a number of instruments, including the trumpet, baritone horn, E-flat tuba, and sousaphone.

Last of the current Oaks, tenor Joe Bonsall, joined in 1973. He made his performing debut at the age of six on the Horn & Hardart amateur TV program in his native city of Philadelphia. While attending Frankford High School, he was a regular dancer on Dick Clark's *American Bandstand* TV program. His credits prior to joining the Oaks included singing with the local Faith Four group. His instrumental training was on the piano.

The Oak Ridge Quartet was already well known among gospel admirers before Golden and Allen joined in the mid-1960s, but its reputation was enhanced still further afterwards. In the voting for the 1970 Grammies, the group won the award for Best Gospel or Other Religious Recording for the single "Talk About the Good Times" on the Heart Warming label. After Sterban and Bonsall joined, the quartet won that award three times more, in 1974 for "The Baptism of Jesse Taylor" (Columbia Records); in 1976 for "Where the Soul Never Dies" (Columbia); and in 1977 for "Just a Little Talk with Jesus" (album track, Rockland Records).

By the time the group picked up its fourth gospel Grammy, it already was moving in new directions, something that caused some bitterness in the gospel field. For instance, one gospel record executive told *People* magazine (May 28, 1979), "We're serious about Christian ideals and morals. The Oaks made it quite clear that religion was not their concern." *People* writer Dolly Carlisle, in the same article, quoted Allen's rejoinder suggesting that the record executive was being hypocritical. He told her that gospel acts on-stage might come on "as the ministry, but backstage they look for who's going to pay the check. I feel less hypocritcal about it now."

Joe Bonsall told Carlisle that even before the group broke away from the gospel field, it was being looked at askance. "We were always the subject of gossip. We were the first to wear long hair and beards, and when we added a rock drummer we were talked about for months. At one time, our only goal was to make gospel as prestigious as any other kind of music. The gospel establishment wouldn't let us do it, so we took our business elsewhere."

The group made its first attempt at crossing over into country and popular music in 1974, when they signed with Columbia Records. Their Columbia secular recordings sold poorly; they actually sold fewer albums than when they worked the gospel circuit. (In gospel, for instance, they typically sold $5,000 worth of records at one concert; on the gospel circuit the singers pitch their own records at their concerts.) For a while things became desperate. The group's income shrank from an annual gross of $250,000 to a fraction of that. Then Johnny Cash came to the rescue, offering them a loan and hiring them as opening act for one of his Las Vegas concerts. Another helpful step came in the form of session work backing Paul Simon on what was to become a best-selling single, "Slip Slidin' Away."

Perhaps the most important move came when Jim Halsey, Inc., took over as manager of the group. He helped them assemble a country-music package and booked them as headliners at the Las Vegas Landmark Hotel in August 1975. In 1976 they opened with Roy Clark at the Frontier Hotel in Vegas and two weeks later left to tour the Soviet Union, performing in Riga, Moscow, and Leningrad.

All that was promising, but coming into 1977, the group remained better known for its gospel work than as a country or pop organization. In addition, the group had no major label affiliation. This was remedied in May 1977 when the Oaks signed with ABC Records. (Later, when ABC was acquired by MCA Records, the group remained on the new label roster.) This time success came almost immediately. Their debut LP, *Y'All Come Back Saloon,* spawned two number-one country singles on the way to becoming a chart hit itself: "Y'All Come Back Saloon" and a remake of the Bob Morrison tune "You're the One." They were guests on major TV variety shows, where their philosophy of "keep it happy, keep it exciting" stood them in good stead, for they were always interesting to watch as well as to listen to. They were named Top New Vocal Group of the Year for Singles in *Record World's* 1977 Country Music Awards competition, won *Billboard's* 1977 Breakthrough Award, and were named Best Vocal Group of 1977 by the Academy of Country Music.

The Oaks amplified these successes in 1978. Their second album, *Room Service,* was a bestseller, providing the hit singles "Crying Again" and "I'll Be True to You." They won a veritable cornucopia of awards for their work. All three major music trades lauded them: *Billboard* named them Number One Country Group; *Record World* called them the top Country Vocal Group— Singles and Albums; and *Cash Box* gave them the Singles Award for country vocal groups. In the Country Music Association voting for 1978, the quartet was named Vocal Group of the Year and the Oak Ridge Band the Instrumental Group of the Year. (The band, which then comprised four musicians, expanded to six at the start of the 1980s: lead guitarist Skip Mitchell, born Philadelphia, Pennsylvania; bass guitarist Don Breland, born House, Mississippi; keyboards, Garland Craft, born Kinston, North Carolina; drummer Fred Satterfield, born Los Angeles, California; rhythm & lead guitarist Pete Cummings, born Hendersonville, Tennessee; keyboards/rhythm guitarist Ron Fairchild, born Hendersonville, Tennessee.)

The group started off 1979 with another

smash hit, the single "Come on In." Later they added such other bestsellers as "Sail Away" and "Dream On" (on MCA) and a Columbia release of older material, "Rhythm Guitar." Their MCA LP *The Oak Ridge Boys Have Arrived* was on the charts most of the year after being released in March 1979. The group's awards for the year included the Country Vocal Group Singles Award from *Record World*; the Singles and Albums Award in that category from *Cash Box*; Best Vocal Group and Best Album honors from the Academy of Country Music; and nomination for Country Group or Duo of the Year in the American Music Award. The group also was among the finalists in the *Music City News* Fan Awards for Vocal Group of the Year, Band of the Year, Single of the Year, and Album of the Year.

The Oaks began the 1980s in similar style. The year 1980 brought such singles hits as "Heart of Mine" and the number one hits "Leaving Louisiana in Broad Daylight" and "Trying to Love Two Women." Also on the charts much of the year was the LP *Together*, released in February 1980. The year 1981 provided such hits as "Beautiful You," the number-one "Fancy Free," and the blockbuster single "Elvira," number one on country charts and a major pop hit as well. At the Grammy Awards TV program in February 1982, the Oaks performed the song, which also won the Grammy for Best Country Performance by a Duo or Group with Vocal.

During the late 1970s and early 1980s, the Oaks became a major headline attraction on country and pop circuits at home and overseas. Typically the group was on tour 200 to 250 days a year. In the spring of 1979, the tandem tour of the Oaks and Kenny Rogers set the record as the largest-grossing structured tour in the history of country music. The Oaks appearances during those years included capacity concerts at places like New York's Carnegie Hall and London's Royal Albert Hall as well as many other major venues around the world. The group also was a featured act at the International Jazz Festival in Montreaux, Switzerland. The Oaks TV appearances included *The Tonight Show, Don*

Kircshner Rock Concert, The Dukes of Hazzard, Hee Haw, Mike Douglas, Merv Griffin, Dinah!, The Midnight Special, "Lucy Comes to Nashville" (special with Lucille Ball), and many others. The quartet also took part one year in R.M. Macy's Thanksgiving Day Parade in New York.

OCHS, PHIL: *Singer, guitarist, songwriter. Born El Paso, Texas, December 19, 1940; died Far Rockaway, New York, April 9, 1976.*

Tremendously talented and passionately devoted to human rights, Phil Ochs gained a national reputation in the 1960s as one of the foremost exponents of politically related folk music. An activist for civil rights and against U.S. involvement in the Vietnam War, he often sang his sharply effective original songs on those subjects while taking part in marches or rallies favoring the causes he espoused. (He could and did write less controversial material, though he tends to be remembered mainly for his protest writings.) Perhaps, however, he cared too much. After considerable achievements during the 1960s, he seemed creatively exhausted in the 1970s when he took his own life at the age of thirty-six.

From a middle-class family, he was born in Texas, but for most of his youth his family lived in either New York or Ohio. His initial introduction to music emphasized the classics. He learned to play the clarinet and saxophone during his high school years and was good enough to make the college orchestra later on. His brother, Michael Ochs, recalls that though the first wave of rock 'n' roll came along while Phil was in his teens, it didn't have much impact on him, though it did on Mike. Nor was Phil into folk music at that time. Mike notes, "After classics, he was into country for a while, then into black music—rhythm & blues. The first time we agreed was on [Elvis] Presley. When the Kingston Trio surfaced in San Francisco, that had an effect on him and later [in college] Jim Glover turned him onto The Weavers and [Woody] Guthrie."

Before Phil went to college, he attended Staunton Military Academy in Virginia, where his classmates included notables like Barry Goldwater, Jr. The choice, Mike

Ochs states, was Phil's. "Basically our parents gave him the choice of a private or public [preparatory] school. He probably decided to go there because of the way the movies portrayed military schools and an identification with John Wayne."

From Staunton, Phil enrolled in Ohio State University in the late 1950s. His roommate, Jim Glover, was a folk music aficionado who played guitar and banjo. Besides impressing the pleasures of the genre on Phil, Glover also taught him to play guitar. Phil later won his first guitar from Jim as the result of a bet on the Kennedy-Nixon election. While still at Ohio State, he wrote his first song, "Ballad of the Cuban Invasion," which took a pro-Castro stance.

Phil had matriculated at Ohio State as a journalism major. He was in line to become editor of the school publication *The Lantern* when school authorities rejected him because they felt his views were too "left wing." Mike states, "He quit because of that with only one quarter to go to graduate. He decided to become a full-time singer and in the summer of 1961 played in Farragher's Bar in Cleveland as an opening act for a number of performers, including the Smothers Brothers, Judy Henske, and Bob Gibson. He learned basically from all the artists who came through and in the fall headed for New York's Greenwich Village."

It was a golden time for folk music in that locale. There were many small folk clubs in and around the Village and a now legendary group of young artists on hand, people like Bob Dylan, Joan Baez, and Judy Collins. Like them, Phil got his start by singing in the many basket-type clubs in the area, where whatever pay performers got resulted from passing a basket around the audience. "His first major gig," recalls Mike, "was in a place called the Third Side."

The contacts he was making began to pay off in opportunities for new exposure to the public. "His biggest break back then," says Mike, "came from appearing at the Newport Folk Festival in 1963 and 1964. [He was invited back again in 1966 and 1967]."

Those appearances helped focus attention on him from both fans and record executives. Actually, he already had been given the chance to audition for Vanguard for an album planned to present a number of promising new folksingers, called *New Folks*. He was signed by Elektra soon after. While his tracks for *New Folks* were recorded before his Elektra debut LP came out in early 1964 (titled *All the News That's Fit to Sing*), the two albums were released at about the same time. On the Elektra disc, Phil wrote all but one song. It was a promising first effort, but not as good as his next release on Elektra, *I Ain't a'Marchin' Anymore*. Issued in 1965, it included such songs as the title number and "Draft Dodger Rag," major expressions of antiwar sentiment, the pro-civil rights composition "Here's to the State of Mississippi," and another of his best-known numbers, "Heat of the Summer."

His third Elektra LP, *Phil Ochs in Concert*, was on the pop charts in 1966. Among its contents was "There but for Fortune," a song that provided Joan Baez with a hit single and that was covered by many other artists, including Peter, Paul & Mary, who called it one of the strongest songs they'd recorded. Also on the album was the love song "Changes," a song recorded by many artists over the years.

During the mid-1960s, Ochs kept up a busy performing schedule, including many free appearances at civil rights and antiwar events. He was a regular on the folk festival circuit, appearing at such concerts as the 1965 New York Festival, 1965 Canadian Mariposa Festival, 1966 Berkeley, California, Folk Festival, and 1966 Beaulieu Folk Festival in England. One of his concerts included a 1966 appearance at New York's Carnegie Hall, where the material for his *Live in Concert* LP was taped.

In the summer of 1967, Phil switched from Elektra to AM Records. His label debut, *Pleasures of the Harbor*, came out in late 1967. Besides songs like "Crucifixion," which philosophizes on assassination (reflecting great sadness over President Kennedy's death), the album included a number of more light-hearted numbers, such as "The Party," "Miranda," and

"Small Circle of Friends," which provided Ochs with one of his rare singles successes. Over the years, the album sold over 200,000 copies, the best sales total of any of Phil's LPs.

His next effort was the 1968 album *Tape from California,* whose title track is a rare rock-style type rendition by Phil. An excellent collection including such protest tracks as "The War Is Over" and "When in Rome," it also has a more bitter, less optimistic tone than in Ochs' previous collections. In his next A&M LP, *Rehearsals for Retirement,* issued in 1969, that tone is struck to an even greater degree. Both in title and content it suggested the end of an era, which, for Ochs, was indeed the case. It was reflected in his next album, the early 1970s LP *Greatest Hits,* which proved to be Phil's weakest effort yet. It was to be the next to last album recorded in his lifetime. The last album, *Gunfighter at Carnegie Hall,* came out in Canada in 1974 and wasn't released in the United States. The only other album of his recordings to come out in the 1970s was the 1976 posthumous two-record set *Chords of Fame,* issued shortly after his suicide and containing material from both his Elektra and A&M catalogue.

As to what caused Phil to take his life, outwardly it could be considered an outgrowth of his increasingly heavy drinking. Mike Ochs believes that the drinking was a symptom of underlying problems. "He was never a drug user. In the 1960s he drank on and off, but he was more a social drinker than anything else. As things began to go wrong for him he drank a lot more. But he was never an alcoholic as much as he drank.

"The problem was that he found he had writer's block and couldn't complete his songs anymore. He stopped writing them in the early 1970s. Then he decided he wanted to see the world and so he did. He visited Africa, South America, and Australia. In Australia he recorded one single and one in Africa. Basically, since he couldn't write songs he began looking for other things to justify his existence. He felt he had been a shaper of society and couldn't figure out how to keep doing that

He dabbled in other kinds of writing, doing some articles for the *Los Angeles Free Press."*

He spent a lot of his time in New York in the mid-1970s, where his activities included organizing two major benefit concerts. One of those was a celebration of the end of the Vietnam War, held in Central Park and featuring such artists as Paul Simon, George Harrison (of the Beatles), Joan Baez, and Harry Belafonte. The second was a concert to raise money for Chilean refugees, a concert, Mike Ochs remarks, "which brought Dylan out of political retirement."

After spending some time in California, in 1975 Phil went back to New York to live. He already had been subject to increasing fits of depression marked by manic drinking binges. He had refused to seek psychiatric help and, in early 1976, his feelings of hopelessness overwhelmed him and he killed himself.

Several months after his death, a memorial concert in his honor was held in New York featuring many luminaries of folk music's golden era, including Pete Seeger, Odetta, Tim Hardin, Ramblin' Jack Elliott, Melanie, Bob Gibson, Dave Van Ronk, and Eric Andersen. The show was taped for TV by the Public Broadcasting System and is still shown at times on various PBS stations.

One of the first biographies to be published was Marc Eliot's *Death of a Rebel,* issued by Archer Books through Doubleday. Mike Ochs hopes one day to present what he hopes will be a definitive drama about his brother's life. As of 1981, "I'm still working on it. I've been approached by a lot of people but the plans are just not right yet."

Based partly on a 1981 interview with Michael Ochs by Irwin Stambler.

O'DELL, KENNY: *Singer, guitarist, songwriter. Born Oklahoma, early 1940s.*

Although Kenny O'Dell has had some hit recordings of his own, he has gained most of his country music credits by behind-the-scenes work as a music publishing executive and, most important of all, a superb songwriter. His most cited achievement in the 1970s was the song "Behind Closed Doors," which brought Charlie Rich nationwide acclaim. Many more of O'Dell's writings found their way to the number-one spot on country-music charts in the 1970s, earning Kenny the heartfelt thanks of such artists as Loretta Lynn, Tanya Tucker, and Billie Jo Spears.

Kenny, though born in Oklahoma, later moved to California with his family. He had an early interest in music and wrote his first songs when he was thirteen. However, as he told a staff member of the Country Music Association newsletter *Country Music Close Up* (July 1976), "I really started putting songs together when I was about fifteen." He kept on writing new material and performing with teenage friends until he graduated from Santa Maria High School. Brashly, he then began his own record company. "I called the label Mar-Kay Records after my mom and dad, Marion and Kenneth." He pressed 600 copies of a song called "Old Time Love." "We got some airplay in Southern California, but I didn't know too much about the record business back then."

In the early 1960s, Kenny made some demonstration tapes that he tried unsuccessfully to place with established record companies. For a time he did some work with rock star Duane Eddy and decided to earn his living as a performer, forming a show group called Boys and Dolls. "We worked clubs, lounges, and cow towns in Nevada, Alaska, Hawaii and the Pacific Northwest for about 4½ years," he recalled for the CMA. He was persistent all the while, constantly working up new compositions and sending demonstration tapes to publishers and record executives.

Finally, in mid-1967 he broke through with his composition "Beautiful People." "I pitched the song to a few groups and finally a guy in Las Vegas heard it and started a label called Vegas Records and released it. When the record started making some noise, Vegas Records became affiliated with White Whale Records [then riding high on the successes of the rock group The Turtles] and 'Beautiful People' started to climb the charts. Bobby Vee put out a cover version and both records were racing each other up the charts and into the top 40." Later, Kenny also made the album charts with his debut LP on White Whale, also titled *Beautiful People*. Success sometimes breeds success, and, almost simultaneously, another O'Dell original, recorded by the Rose Garden on Atco Records, received heavy airplay and also entered the top 40.

With increasing interest among country artists in Kenny's offerings, he moved to Nashville. He settled there in 1969 after accepting a bid to become head of Bobby Goldsboro's music publishing operation. Like most talented music people, he dabbled in other parts of the field, recording a number of singles for Epic and Kapp Records in the late 1960s and early 1970s while also providing a steady flow of new song candidates to various artists.

Two people who were particularly enthusiastic about O'Dell's output were producer Billy Sherrill and singer-pianist Charlie Rich. In late 1972, Charlie made his first giant step toward establishing his credentials as a country superstar—after over a decade of near misses—with his version of O'Dell's "Take It on Home." The record became a top-10 hit in early 1973. Later in the year, things got even better when Charlie's single of "Behind Closed Doors" became a runaway national smash, moving to top levels of both country and pop charts. At the CMA Awards voting in the fall, the number was voted "Song of the Year," the top songwriter award; and also won the Best Single and Album Awards for Rich. Several months later, when the Grammy Awards took place, the song won nominations in five separate categories.

Discussing the song for CMA, O'Dell noted, "My wife really inspired the song. It's a feeling that could relate not only to us, but to other people. It's just a simple, straight-ahead lyric, something everyone can relate to—the special things between a man and woman behind closed doors."

After the Charlie Rich successes, other performers made the charts with a series of O'Dell songs. In late 1973, for instance, Anthony Armstrong Jones' recording of

Kenny's "I've Got Mine" was in the top 50. In mid-1975, his composition "Lizzie and the Rainman" made number one on the United States country singles charts in Tanya Tucker's interpretation. In May 1976, another number-one record accrued to his collection, this time gained by Billie Jo Spears with her single of "What I've Got in Mind." In late 1977, she had another top-level single with O'Dell's "Too Much Is Not Enough."

While that was going on, though, Kenny's own performing career was taking off, this time on Capricorn Records. Among his chart hits of the mid-1970s were "Soulful Woman" in early 1975; "Classified" and "Honky Tonk Ways" in mid-1975; a top-10 hit, "Let's Shake Hands and Come Out Lovin'" in September 1978; and a top-20 chartmaker late in that year, "As Long as I Can Wake Up in Your Arms."

O'KEEFE, DANNY: *Singer, guitarist, songwriter. Born state of Washington.*

"Dreams, my songs are made out of dreams. Dreams are where metaphors come to life. Anything that has meaning has metaphor. I'm trying to investigate that more thoroughly through hypnosis and other ways. Getting conscious during dreams would be ideal."

As his words to a biographer indicate, Danny O'Keefe is not a typical country-music songwriter. He is, in fact, an idealist who often submerged his musical potential in his quest for a better environment for mankind and the animal kingdom. But when he focused on music, he demonstrated the ability to write on many levels, turning out fine country compositions like "Good Time Charlie's Got the Blues."

O'Keefe grew up in the state of Washington, where he attended high school and college. Like his peer group he was influenced by the Beatles and the British invasion, the West Coast sound, and other facets of the rock movement. But he also found, over the years, that he could immerse himself in all manner of music, from folk and country to Latin.

He sang in small clubs in the Northwest during the late 1960s and early 1970s, by which time he already had assembled a body of original work. Eventually Danny felt he was ready to try for a recording career, and his efforts won him a contract from Cotillion Records that put him with producer Arif Mardin to work on his first album. That collection, titled *Danny O'Keefe,* came out in 1970. It included "Good Time Charlie" as well as a number of other excellent songs, but little happened with it. It was not until two years later that a single of the song attracted the attention of disc jockeys. The song became a major hit of 1972, rising to the top of the country charts and also moving high on the pop lists. Over the years since then, it has been covered by many artists.

That surge in popularity brought increased interest in O'Keefe from Atlantic Records. He was asked to make new recordings for the label, resulting in *Breezy Stories,* also produced by Arif Mardin, which came out in 1973, and a third and final LP for the label, produced by John Boyland and titled *So Long Harry Truman,* issued in 1975. Neither of those albums was a conspicuous success, despite many fine elements and the backing of artists like the Eagles and Linda Ronstadt on some tracks, but many of O'Keefe's songs from the LP impressed other performers. Among them were "Magdalena," recorded by Leo Sayer, "Angel (Spread Your Wings)," featured by Judy Collins, and "Quits," which was done by B. W. Stevenson, Chris Hillman, and Gary Stewart, among others. Stewart's single made it into upper country chart levels in late 1977.

Even as *So Long Harry Truman* was coming off the presses, Danny was turning his energies to the plight of the whales. In 1975, he joined many pop and folk artists, including Jackson Browne, John Sebastian, Odetta, John David Souther, Warren Zevon, and Eric Andersen, in the first Japan Celebrates the Whale Benefit in Tokyo. During the mid-1970s, he followed that up by taking a two-year leave from recording and performing, during which time he became a certified diver in order to study whales in their natural habitat and spent many months working with cetologists on information-gathering projects. Among other things, his group worked to devise a system that would permit piping music underwater in tones to which the mammals would respond and even sing along with. He recorded some of the material for future album use. Whales were not the only issue that stirred him up. Among his other studies was one involving the Nez Perce Indian tribe, which also inspired him to write an extensive musical series not yet recorded as of the early 1980s.

In late 1976, O'Keefe ended a two-year absence from recordings by signing a new contract with Warner Bros. His first LP on the label, *American Roulette*, was issued in April 1977. It had some good moments, but for the most part it fell short of his earlier efforts. His next collection, *The Global Blues*, which he coproduced himself with Jay Lewis, saw a return to form. The album, which contained a variety of stylings, from several fine country numbers to rock to Latin-flavored material, with some touches of jazz and folk in places, tended to fall in the same pattern as most of his work. Partly because he didn't do much in the way of personal appearances and partly because the record company seemed to provide less than total promotion, the album never came close to making the hit charts. Its original songs, though, in many cases had the quality to eventually provide hits for Danny's many admirers in the entertainment field.

ORBISON, ROY: *Singer, guitarist, songwriter. Born Vernon, Texas, April 23, 1936.*

Next to Elvis, the country-bred artist considered the most influential in the worldwide rise of rock 'n' roll was Roy Orbison, a man whom the Beatles felt privileged to tour with in 1963. Despite his tremendous achievements, by the time Elvis introduced Roy to the audience at the "Great One's" last Las Vegas show in 1977 as "the greatest singer in the world" it had been over a dozen years since his last major hit. A major reason for Orbison's decline had been a series of tragedies in the mid- and late-1960s that might have shattered weaker people completely. But Roy survived while cover versions of some of

his earlier songs brought chart hits for 1970s artists (including a number-one hit on country charts for Linda Ronstadt's version of his "Blue Bayou"). From time to time, he made comeback attempts as a performer, including a hit duet effort with Emmy Lou Harris in the early 1980s.

As might be expected of a boy growing up in Texas, his early influences were almost all country and gospel based. His father started teaching him how to play guitar when the boy was six and he was well versed in the instrument by the time he reached his teens. While attending high school, he was leader of his own country group, the Wink Westerners, and had his own radio show on station KVWC, Vernon, Texas. When he was sixteen, Roy represented Texas at the International Lions Convention in Chicago, singing and accompanying himself on guitar.

From high school he entered North Texas State University, where he met another young artist with show business ambitions, Pat Boone. Boone encouraged him to keep up with his music to which Roy responded by organizing a new band that soon backed him on a 1955 TV show presented on a Midland, Texas, station. His TV work and engagements at various venues with his group brought him in contact with many of the new rock-oriented country artists, including Jerry Lee Lewis, Elvis, and Johnny Cash. It was Cash who proved the main catalyst, suggesting that Orbison make a demo tape of some of his material and take it to Sam Phillips, head of Sun Records in Memphis. That move determined Roy's main musical direction from then on, pushing him into the rockabilly fold even though his main interests tended toward mainstream country.

As he told an interviewer, "I sent Phillips 'Oooby Dooby' because that was the kind of material Sun was releasing at the time. But I was really more interested in ballads. I hadn't felt comfortable doing rhythm & blues or rock. I got into it [rock] by accident. We were working a dance one New Year's Eve and someone asked for 'Shake, Rattle and Roll.' I planned to do it at midnight, but started too soon so we had to keep doing it over and over. By the time midnight came, I was used to it and began to incorporate some rock numbers into our list of songs."

Actually, he almost struck out with Sun. After Phillips heard over the phone that Roy was recommended by Cash, the record executive snapped "Johnny Cash doesn't run my business" and hung up. But he eventually heard the tape and the resultant single became a major hit of 1956.

After touring all over the United States with such artists as Cash, Jerry Lee Lewis, and Carl Perkins, Roy responded to an invitation from Wesley Rose of Acuff–Rose to become a staff writer and departed from Sun in 1957. One of his first efforts was "Claudette," named after his wife, which was recorded by the Everly Brothers and rose to number one. Jerry Lee Lewis also made the charts with Roy's "Down the Line" and Buddy Holly used some of Orbison's material in his repertoire.

Rose, who had also taken over as Roy's personal manager, arranged for a new recording contract with Fred Foster's Monument Records in 1959. Orbison's second release on the label, "Only the Lonely," became a smash success, selling over two million copies and earning Roy a gold record. This was followed by a stream of bestsellers, most of them originals by Roy, a few from other writers. Among his top-10 singles of the early 1960s were "Running Scared" and "Cryin' " (backed with "Candy Man") in 1961; "Dream Baby" (1962); "In Dreams," "Mean Woman Blues" backed with "Blue Bayou" in 1963; and "It's Over" and "Oh, Pretty Woman" in 1964. The last named was one of the most successful singles of the 1960s, selling over 7 million copies worldwide. In all, Orbison placed twenty-seven straight records on the charts the first part of the 1960s.

He became a major international star in 1963, contracting to tour Britain with a rock group that at the time had much slimmer credentials than he did, the Beatles. It brought a close rapport between all of them and it also involved an accidental event that reshaped Roy's image. During his plane trip to England, he forgot his regular glasses in his seat and so had to wear his prescription sunglasses. Everyone liked the effect, so from then on his combination of dark hair, dark glasses, and black suits became a personal trademark. After headlining with the Beatles, he returned to Europe in the mid-1960s for other tours with top groups, including several concert series with the Rolling Stones. He established a rapport with European fans that remained strong for decades. In the 1970s, when he was only vaguely remembered by many U.S. fans, he could always play before capacity houses overseas.

In 1965, after half a decade of unparalled success with Monument, he switched to MGM Records. His reasons were that "MGM offered access to motion pictures and television as well as records. It also provided financial security and that meant I would have all the time I needed to create." Soon after joining MGM, he made his first film, *Fastest Guitar Alive.* He also scored a mild hit with "Ride Away," but the sales fell far short of blockbusters like "Pretty Woman."

Still, he had had dry spells before and there seemed no reason why he wouldn't be making top-chart levels again in due time. At that point, fate struck a devastating blow. His wife, Claudette, was killed as a result of a motorcycle accident. Stunned and disorganized, he sought escape in an ever more intensive concert schedule. As he told Bob Hilburn of the *Los Angeles Times,* "All I was doing was surviving. I was trying to work my way out of the turmoil. It takes time to get back on your feet. I just wasn't up to the demands of recording.

"I've got nothing against a performer who only sings, but it really puts a strain on someone who writes the songs, arranges them and also sings. That's what I had been used to doing. For a while, I just couldn't put it together."

In 1967, it seemed as though Orbison had ridden out the storm. He began to find it easier to write again. Plans for new recordings began to take shape. Then tragedy hit with redoubled force. A fire at his Nashville home killed two of his three children. After weeks of grief, he gave up writing in favor of the old concert grind palliative.

Although he remained under contract to MGM, not much had happened from a recording standpoint even when he was in the mood to work, mainly because the company was going through continuous upheavals in executive personnel. When Mike Curb took over at the start of the 1970s, one of his first moves was to get Roy, whom he admired greatly, back in the studios. This resulted in some early 1970s album releases and a few singles, but Roy's long absence from the record field in the United States seemed to have dissipated interest in him at home.

Still popular elsewhere, however, Roy brought his live act to other parts of the world and was rarely in evidence in the United States for much of the 1970s. He did appear in concert with Johnny Cash in 1973 and made a few other special engagements, but that was about it. As he noted, "I tended to fulfill commitments around the world, then come home and rest." He didn't lack for engagements. He made many tours of Europe and Australia from the start of the 1970s to the end of the decade. Typical of his schedule was the period in 1974 when he worked foreign venues seven months straight with only nine days off, including dates in Crete and Taiwan.

Late in the decade, though, he and his work started to resurface at home. Linda Ronstadt scored a striking success with his "Blue Bayou" and his "Pretty Woman" became the theme for a series of TV commercials. Orbison tried a brief tour of California venues in 1977: the results were positive. Almost all the shows were sold out and were critically acclaimed, and his stature with fellow artists was indicated by the appearance in the audience at his Los Angeles date of the Eagles, Jefferson Starship, the Tubes, and Boz Scaggs.

To try to add new impetus, he signed a recording contract with a new label, Elektra, during 1978. (He had done some recordings for Mercury in the mid-1970s

after leaving MGM, but without any notable results. He did have some recording achievements during the decade, though, earning a gold record in Australia for a single release in 1974, and demonstrating his popularity with English fans when a reissue of some of his earlier material, the LP *The Very Best of Roy Orbison*, rose to number one in 1976.) His debut on Elektra, *Laminar Flow*, came out in May 1979 containing three new songs by him, two ballads, and a fast-paced rocker called "Movin'." To support the album he embarked on one of his most intensive U.S. tours in a decade.

Unfortunately, the album didn't catch fire with country or pop fans, though concert-goers enjoyed his tour performances, which included opening a number of shows for the Eagles. In 1980 things took a turn for the better when his duet single with Emmylou Harris (issued on Warner Brothers), "That Loving You Feeling Again," became a country hit. The recording won the Grammy Award for Best Country Vocal Performance by a Duo or Group for 1980. In 1981, his song "Crying" (co-written with J. Melson) gained a top-10 hit for Don McLean.

Among his album releases over the years were such Monument collections as *Greatest Hits* (10/62), *In Dreams* (3/64), *Early Orbison* and *More Greatest Hits* ('64–'65), *Orbisongs* (12/65), and *Very Best of Roy Orbison* (8/66). His 1960s MGM LPs included *There Is Only One* (10/65), *Orbison Way* (2/66), *Classic Orbison* (8/66), and *Sings Don Gibson* (1/67). In the early 1970s, MGM released such LPs as *Great Songs, Roy Orbison Sings Hank Williams, Roy Orbison Sings*, and *All Time Greatest Hits* (10/72). Some of his earliest recordings also were reissued during that period on the Sun label under the title *Original Sound*.

OSBORNE BROTHERS: *Vocal and instrumental brother act. Bob Osborne, born Hyden, Kentucky, December 7, 1931; Sonny Osborne, born Hyden, Kentucky, October 29, 1937.*

Strong-willed individuals, the Osborne brothers went their own way over the years, often blazing new trails in bluegrass music, frequently to the dismay of the traditionalists. One of their heresies was to play the music with any sort of band makeup that suited their own tastes. If they felt like adding drums, for instance, they did so even if old-time bands didn't use the instrument. In the early 1960s, they also raised the hackles of many purists by using electric instruments in their stylings, an approach taken up by many bluegrass and country bands as the decade went by.

The brothers were weaned on bluegrass music growing up in Kentucky. The Osborne boys had learned to pick out country music on the five-string banjo, Sonny's favorite, and the mandolin, Bob's preferred instrument, by the time they were high school age. When younger brother Sonny was only sixteen, he and Bob made their radio debut on station WROL, Knoxville, Tennessee, with Bob singing high lead (tenor) and Sonny handling the baritone vocals.

The brothers left WROL for WJR, Detroit, in 1954 and received increasing attention during guest appearances in country shows around the Midwest. In October 1956, they became featured regulars on the *WWVA Jamboree* in Wheeling, West Virginia. That same year they signed their first major recording contract with MGM Records. In 1959, they expanded to a trio by adding Benny Birchfield (born Isaban, West Virginia, June 6, 1937), who played lead guitar and five-string banjo and also handled lead vocals.

The advent of the folk music boom in the late 1950s had focused new attention on bluegrass music, and artists such as Bill Monroe and Flatt & Scruggs became headliners at folk music concerts and festivals. The Osbornes created a considerable stir on the steadily expanding college folk music circuit with a memorable appearance at Antioch College, Ohio, in early 1959. After that, they became a major act in the college field, touring all over the United States in 1959 and throughout the 1960s.

The Osbornes varied their formats, sometimes working just as a duo, sometimes with Birchfield as a trio, other times adding a number of other instruments. This still held true during the 1970s, when the Osbornes played a part in the revival of bluegrass in that decade. The music had seemed to reach a peak with fans by the mid-1960s, then suffered a decline that lasted into the early 1970s. A resurgence began at that point with a slow but steady rise in bluegrass festivals, concerts, and clubs as the decade progressed. By the end of the 1970s, there were strong bluegrass movements all over the United States and in other countries and the Osbornes were much sought after for concert dates and appearances at annual festivals, including Bill Monroe's Bean Blossom event.

During the 1960s, the Osbornes were featured at several Newport Folk Festivals in Rhode Island. Discussing their importance in program notes for the 1964 Festival, Ralph Rinzler wrote, "[The Osbornes] made a strong impression on bluegrass music for several reasons: They developed a distinctive style of ultra-modern trio harmony singing the two harmony parts sometimes following the melody in parallel motion until reaching a final cadence when each part would move up successively to exchange notes (i.e., baritone to lead, lead to tenor and tenor to high baritone or else, on occasion, up a third at a time). The instrumental techniques (Sonny's banjo, Bob's mandolin) were original in sound and approach as was their material. This pair of young Kentuckians has always maintained its own distinctive niche in bluegrass. Their sound is immediately recognizable, strongly individualistic."

The Osbornes and Birchfield were featured as guests a number of times on the *Grand Ole Opry* starting in 1959. In 1964, they became regular cast members and still appeared regularly on the show during the 1970s and into the 1980s. During the 1960s and 1970s, they performed on many major TV shows and played country and folk clubs, festivals, fairs, etc., in all fifty states. They also made several tours of foreign countries. Among the songs associated with them over the years were numbers like "Each Season Changes You," "Banjo Boys," "Lovey Told Me Goodby," "Fair and Tender Ladies," "Ruby, Are You Mad," "Take This Hammer," "Once More," "Mule Skinner Blues," "Don't Even Look at Me," and a

Odetta

The Oak Ridge Boys: l. to r., Joe Bonsall, Duane Allen, Bill Golden, Richard Sterban

Buck Owens

Roy Orbison

Phil Ochs

number of Boudleaux and Felice Bryant songs, including one that became the Osbornes theme, "Rocky Top."

The Osbornes turned out a number of albums during their seven years on MGM, an association that came to a close in 1963 when they moved to Decca. Among the MGM LPs were *Bluegrass Music* (4/62), *Bluegrass Instrumentals* (12/62), *Cuttin' Grass* (11/63), *Osborne Brothers and Red Allen*, and, in the late 1960s, *Osborne Brothers*. Their Decca albums included *Voices in Bluegrass* (8/65), *Up This Hill and Down* (8/66), *Modern Sounds* (8/67), *Up to Date & Down to Earth* (9/69), *Ru-Be-eeee, Osborne Brothers*, and *Country Roads* (last three, early 1970s).

In the mid-1970s, the Osbornes had a number of recordings on the MCA label, including a definitive two-record set, *The Best of the Osborne Brothers*. One of their MCA singles that made lower-chart levels was the 1976 release "Don't Let Smokey Mountain Smoke Get in Your Eyes." In the late 1970s, they recorded for the CMH label. In late 1977, they completed a two-disc set of Boudleaux and Felice Bryant songs titled, *The Osborne Brothers: From Rocky Top to Muddy Bottom*. Besides their theme song, the LPs included such numbers as "Hey Joe," "All I Have to Do Is Dream," "Love Hurts," and "Take Me as I Am (Or Let Me Go.)"

During the 1970s, the Osbornes were nominated for best band in the Country Music Association Awards competition on a number of occasions. Besides his performing activities, Sonny also found time in the late 1970s to write a column on banjo techniques and news of the bluegrass field for the *Banjo Newsletter*. In 1980, their CMH single "I Can Hear Kentucky Callin' Me" was on the charts.

OSMOND, MARIE: *Singer. Born Ogden, Utah, 1959.*

Although mostly known in the mid- and late-1970s as a pop and rock performer, the only woman in the Osmond family started her career with country material. In fact, her debut single was one of the best-selling country singles in 1973. While she joined brother Donny and other members of the large Osmond clan (the men in the brood total eight) in singing everything from sophisticated ballads to all-out rock in concerts and on the late 1970s Osmond TV show, she always included a country song in her repertoire now and then, some of which made the country hit lists.

Like all but one of the nine children, Marie was born in Ogden, Utah. (The exception is the youngest, Jimmy, who was born in Canoga Park, California.) The year she was born, the Osmond saga got under way when four of the boys started singing in church and rehearsing barber shop ballads. By the mid-1960s, the brothers had progressed to featured performers on the *Andy Williams Show*, later expanding to include brother Donny. So by the time Marie reached her teens, the Osmonds already were internationally known artists.

Her parents didn't want her to start in show business too young, though she demonstrated a good voice at an early age and curiosity about the entertainment field. Only when she was fourteen did the time seem propitious for her to pursue a singing career. She sang duets with brother Donny a few times during Las Vegas shows at the start of the 1970s, but it wasn't until a few years later that she really began to concentrate on performing.

She discussed plans for a recording effort with her brothers and family friend Mike Curb, previously president of MGM when the Osmonds became top disc stars on that label. The idea of starting out with country material arose from those sessions, including a suggestion from Curb that Sonny James produce the tracks. Marie signed with MGM early in 1973 and then flew to Nashville with her mother to start work with Sonny on the new project. A number of possible songs had been assembled, including one that had been a hit many years before called "Paper Roses." Marie admitted, "I'd never heard the song before they played it for me."

The single of the song was the first disc of Osmond's released and it became a massive hit, riding not only to the top of the country charts but to pop charts around the world. The debut album that contained it also was a chart hit.

She told an interviewer in early 1974,

"My voice isn't really a typical country twangy kind of voice, and I'm not strictly a country singer either, although my heart is now in country more than ever because everyone has been just so fantastic with me. I've really come to love country music and enjoy it. And I listen to a lot of country in order to keep up with what's going on."

In 1974, Osmond continued to stress country material, returning to Nashville to prepare a new album with Sonny James that was issued later in the year. She always had a certain amount of country content in albums she turned out after that, though increasingly the main elements were from other genres. In the mid-1970s, Marie teamed up with brother Donny as both a singing and recording team. In mid-1975, they made country charts with their version of "Make the World Go Away," issued on the Kolob label. In 1977, they included some country songs on their network *Donny and Marie* Show on ABC, a pattern that continued with the followup *Osmond Family* program.

OVERSTREET, TOMMY: *Singer, guitarist, band leader (the Nashville Express). Born Oklahoma City, Oklahoma, September 10, 1936.*

Increasingly in the 1960s and 1970s, the new stars in country music had urban rather than country roots. An example was Tommy Overstreet, who remarked in 1979, "I'm not a country boy. I was raised in a big city, but I feel more comfortable with country music, personally. I find it a more relaxed form of entertainment and performing. And I respect the loyalty of the audiences."

Of course, Overstreet came from a section of the United States where country music long had been a favorite of both urban and rural audiences. In addition, his blend of both influences matched the leanings of the many city-dwellers who looked back fondly on farm and ranch roots.

Tommy was born in Oklamoma City, but his father, an insurance seller, settled the family in Houston, Texas, where Tommy grew up. The boy had some interest in music that finally started to flower when his parents gave him a twelve-dollar

guitar when he was fourteen. As he told LaWayne Satterfield of *Music City News* (July, 1971), "My parents brought me the guitar and encouraged me to develop my playing ability. They sent me to a guitar teacher and I took two lessons before returning home and informing my mother that I knew more than the teacher."

Also an influence on his eventual decision to go into show business was a cousin named Gene Austin. Austin, one of the most successful pop singers of the 1920s (whose "My Blue Heaven" remains an all-time bestseller), gave him advice on and insight into the field. "He taught me the business," Tommy noted.

However, it was a much younger artist, a high school friend in Houston named Tommy Sands, who played the first key role in Overstreet's career. "Tommy . . . had a show on KTHT radio in Houston called *Kitchen Canteen*. The show was live and so he recommended me for the job. I stayed on the show for 13 weeks before leaving to play summer stock. The show was a musical production, *Hit the Road*. . . . It was one of the most successful plays in Houston."

Sands went on to become a successful pop vocalist working out of Los Angeles, but Overstreet remained in Texas. He stayed in Houston to finish high school after his folks moved to Abilene. When Tommy joined them, he attended the University of Texas in Abilene and also expanded his radio credits by working on a local radio-TV station as a host, singer, and set designer on a Wednesday night live music show.

Taking Gene Austin's advice that he go further afield to try for bigger things, he moved to Nashville in 1967. He auditioned for local industry executives and landed a contract with the then independent Dot Records in 1967. To supplement his income, besides recording and picking up work in local clubs he also managed several other Dot artists.

He wasn't an instant success, but his career moved ahead steadily at the end of the 1960s. He started to place singles releases on the national country charts, such as "Watching the Trains Go By," "Rocking a Memory," "Games People Play" (a version of the Joe South song that did reasonably well in the charts, considering the success of Freddy Weller's release of the same tune), and his first sizable success, "If You're Looking for a Fool." The latter was on the charts for fourteen weeks and, while it didn't make the top 10, it did well enough for Tommy to drop all other activities to concentrate on his singing and recording work. In the summer of 1971, this paid off with the single "Gwen, Congratulations," which rose to number one, the first of five number-one songs Tommy was to have from 1971 to 1979. Among his other massive hits were "(Jeannie Marie) You're a Lady" in 1974; "That's When My Woman Begins" in 1975; "Don't Go Country Girl on Me" in 1977; and "Heaven Is My Woman's Love."

Overstreet had one or more songs on the charts every year in the 1970s, such as "Ann (Don't Go Runnin')" in 1972 and "I'll Never Break These Chains" in 1974, both on Dot. After Dot merged into ABC to become ABC/Dot, Tommy remained one of the label's major stars, starting with such top-10 hits in 1975 as "I'm a Believer" and "From Woman to Woman" and continuing with such chartmakers as "Here Comes That Girl Again" in 1976; "This Time I'm in It for the Love" and "Don't Go City Girl on Me" in 1977; and "Better Me" and "Fadin' in, Fadin' Out" in 1977. At the end of 1977, Overstreet announced a new contract with Elektra/Asylum Records.

During the 1970s, Tommy toured throughout the United States and overseas with his band, the Nashville Express. The group's engagements weren't limited to country venues, however. As he noted, "With our stylings, I can fit into a Vegas situation or a concert situation or a club situation." His appearances included guest slots on many TV and radio shows, from the *Grand Ole Opry* to *The Tonight Show*. His engagements outside the United States included some visits to Canada and several tours of Europe. His popularity was particularly high in Germany in the 1970s, where he was ranked third favorite country artist after Johnny Cash and Don Wil-

liams. Even in places he didn't tour during the decade his recordings made him a favorite. In such places as New Zealand, Australia, and South Africa, he achieved number-one hits with no personal appearances. That popularity earned him the appelation "Mr. Country Ambassador" from some adherents. One of his number-one successes in Germany was a release of "Heaven Is My Woman's Love" sung in German.

He also was a favorite of audiences on the county fair and rodeo circuit. One result of that was his selection by the International Rodeo Association (in January 1979) as Entertainer of the Year.

His debut LPs on Dot at the start of the 1970s were the albums *Tommy Overstreet* and *This Is Tommy Overstreet.* Through 1977, he recorded fifteen other albums for Dot and ABC/DOT, for an overall total of seventeen. In early 1979, his debut on Elektra/Asylum, *I'll Never Let You Down*, was released. The album indicated Overstreet's diverse musical interests, with such songs as Neil Diamond's soft-rock song "Forever in Blue Jeans," progressive country numbers by Randy Goodrum ("You Needed Me") and Bob Millsap ("I'm Not Dead, Maria"), and others with more traditional country flavor. The single of the LP's title song was on the charts in the summer. At year end, his single "Fadin' Renegade" was on the lists, remaining on them into 1980. His charted singles in 1980, beside that, included "Sue" and "Me and the Boys in the Band."

OWENS, BONNIE: *Singer, guitarist, songwriter. Born Blanchard, Oklahoma, October 1, 1933.*

The career of Bonnie Owens Haggard paralleled the rise of Bakersfield, California, to the reputation of number-two country music center in the United States after Nashville. Not only was she a major performer in her own right, but both in private life and as an artist her activities merged with those of some of the pivotal members of the Bakersfield country movement. At one time or another she was the wife of Buck Owens and Merle Haggard, and her son, Buddy Alan, also became a successful country performer.

Recalling her early years for Dixie Deen of *Music City News* (January 1968), she stated, "I was born in Blanchard, a few miles south of Oklahoma City. I came from a pretty big family, six sisters and two brothers and we lived way out in the country." The closest neighbor, whose family included a little boy she liked, was a half mile away. "In the evenings I'd get outside and try to sing loud enough for him to hear me!

"During those times jobs were pretty hard to find and Dad worked for the WPA and I can remember dad going up to the little boy's father's dairy to milk for half a gallon of milk a day. Mother made all our clothes and I remember the first thrill I ever got was when I got a store bought dress for Christmas." At one point, to help family finances, Bonnie and all the others went to pick cotton.

The family then moved to Arizona, where things eased a bit. She told Deen, "Daddy saw to it that we all got a good education. Everyone finished school except me. . . . I was in my junior year when I decided I wanted to get married."

By then Bonnie already had made a few tentative steps toward performing. In her early years, she had a problem with stuttering but, like Mel Tillis, found she could overcome it when she sang. "I always was able to sing a song all the way through and I was proud of that. Once in a while we'd go to movies and Roy Rogers was very popular. My ambition was to star in a movie with Roy or Jimmie Wakely.

"When I was in the 8th grade in Arizona [in the mid-1940s] we had school assemblies and one day I got up enough nerve to get up and sing a song, just to show I could do it." In her teens, she began to consider the possibilities of a career in music and, in time, got a job as a singer and yodeler on the *Buck and Britt Show*, broadcast over station KTYL in Mesa, Arizona. From that, she and Buck Owens, to whom she was married by then, joined a band called Mac's Skillet Lickers, with whom they toured many western towns and cities.

In the mid-1950s, Owens made her way to Bakersfield, California. "I got my first big professional job there. Cousin Herb Hensen was starting a TV show and needed a girl singer. I was working another job too, at the time. I was a car hop. This was in 1956 and I stayed on that show (*Cousin Herb Hensen's Trading Post*) until it went off the air 10 years later." During some of those years, her mother moved to Bakersfield to help take care of Bonnie's two sons, Mike and Buddy, since her marriage to Buck had ended and her father had died. With that assistance, Bonnie was able to tour widely and work on improving her career outlook. In the early 1960s, she gained a recording contract from Marvel Records, which resulted in her first single release, "Dear John Letter."

Meanwhile, she was meeting new people in the field, including a promising young Bakersfield artist and writer named Merle Haggard. The two started working together and developed demo tapes that helped bring an alignment with the Tally Records label of Fuzzy Owens (no relation to Bonnie). The result was a hit single called "Just Between the Two of Us" in 1964 that helped focus both fan and industry attention on them.

In 1964, they were signed to a new recording contract, this time with a major label, Capitol. Their joint debut LP on Capitol, also titled *Just Between the Two of Us*, came out in 1966 and made a strong showing on the charts. It contained songs written by both Merle and Bonnie. From then on until she decided to take things easier in the 1970s, Owens was an integral part of the Merle Haggard Show, one of the most successful concert operations on the country circuit. She and Merle also made many appearances with Buck Owens as part of his show operation. Both in duets with Merle and as a soloist, she was featured in almost every major city in the United States and also performed on many major radio and TV programs, including, of course, the *Grand Ole Opry*.

Bonnie and Merle were voted the Best Vocal Duo for both 1965 and 1966 by the Academy of Country & Western Music. Owens also was selected as Top Female

Vocalist by the Academy for 1965. The two repeated as Best Vocal Duo in 1967 and were among the finalists in several later competitions. In 1965, the duo became a twosome in private as well as in public by exchanging marriage vows.

Most of Bonnie's recordings were in conjunction with Merle. She handled both lead and backing vocals on many of his LPs of the 1960s and 1970s. She also had a number of solo albums, though, and, in fact, her Capitol solo debut, *Bonnie Owens*, came out in October 1965, ahead of her first duet with Merle. That LP was issued simultaneously with Merle's solo debut LP on the label. Her other solo LPs included *All of Me* (1967) and *Mother's Favorite Hymns* (early 1970s).

During the 1970s, Bonnie's marriage to Merle fell apart and before the decade was over they were divorced. Although the event was trying for both of them, by the end of the decade the emotional wounds had healed sufficiently for Owens to resume work on a professional level with Haggard's performing troupe.

OWENS, BUCK: *Singer, guitarist, songwriter, band leader (the Buckaroos), TV show host. Born Sherman, Texas, August 12, 1929.*

"It's hard to get started in this business," Buck Owens once told an interviewer, "but it's simple. You've got to be at the right place at the right time with the right product. I just did what everybody else did. I'd pick and sing for everybody I could, wherever I could, anytime I could. I'd keep learning, keep doing it, get all my ducks set up in a row. Then, when opportunity knocks, you're ready." Buck might also have used the word persistence as a key factor, because he was going on thirty when opportunity finally knocked with a vengeance, but he was ready and responded with a series of successes that made him one of the country superstars of the 1960s and 1970s.

He was born and spent his early years in Sherman, Texas, son of sharecropper parents. If the family didn't have much in the way of material comforts, there was closeness and love of music in the childhood of Alvis Edgar Owens, Jr. He recalled, "As

long as I can remember, we always had a piano around the house and mama would sit and play the old hymns and we'd sing with her. She taught me most of 'em."

Like many families in the Southwest in the early 1930s, the Owenses were affected by the prolonged drought that led to the Dust Bowl era of the Depression years. Survival required trying to seek the family fortunes outside Texas. The promised land was California. Says Buck, "It was like *The Grapes of Wrath*, except that we didn't make it to California. We were all packed into a little car, five adults and five kids, with the mattress on top. We ended up in Arizona because the trailer broke down and we just couldn't go any farther."

The place that became home was Mesa, Arizona, where Buck got his first musical instrument, a mandolin his parents gave him on his thirteenth birthday. That year, to help out, Buck dropped out of school to go to work harvesting crops and hauling produce. "I was big enough and willing enough to do a man's work and I got a man's pay."

Meanwhile Owens was extending his musical abilities, teaching himself guitar and other instruments as well. "I was working all sorts of jobs, but I was also trying to learn to be a performer from anybody who would take the time to teach me." It paid off; he had his first radio show on a Mesa station when he was sixteen. One of the people who worked with him on radio and in a band called Mac's Skillet Lickers was a singer whom he married when he was seventeen, Bonnie Owens. When Buck was only eighteen, the Owenses had their first child.

Buck still had to keep busy at other tasks to support his family. One of his jobs involved hauling produce between Arizona and California's San Joaquin Valley. He was impressed with the region and also the fact that he had two uncles living in Bakersfield who were musicians and told him there was work in the area. Finally he decided to move his family there. He was twenty.

There were plenty of small country-music clubs in and around Bakersfield and, as his uncles said, jobs for good sidemen were available. Owens began playing with club bands, his main concern "trying to become a good guitarist." He did, indeed, impress the music fraternity with his skills in the early 1950s and, before long, he was earning session money backing many major country names. He often traveled down to Los Angeles to play guitar on recordings of such people as Tennessee Ernie Ford, Sonny James, and Tommy Sands.

At the time, he noted, he was satisfied with that niche. He didn't think of himself as a singer. He had a steady job in the house band at the Blackboard Club in Bakersfield. "I just wanted to be a picker and the boss told me to fill in for the singer who was gone that night. It was either sing or lose my job . . . so I sang." The crowd liked it, so he kept on singing. After a while, the band he was with left the club and, in fact, wanted to leave country music for different stylings. Buck remained true to country, going his own way to take Ferlin Husky's place as a member of Tommy Collins' band. His reputation grew, though his private life was troubled; by the mid-1950s his marriage to Bonnie ended in divorce. (She later married Merle Haggard.)

In the mid-1950s, the onset of rock and R&B had started cutting into country-music opportunities. Buck had to scramble to find enough engagements to keep going even as word of his ability was circulating around the country-music field. Finally he got a recording contract from Capitol Records on March 1, 1957. He cut some sides, providing a number of original songs for the sessions. Still, the first singles to come out hardly were blockbusters.

"It was 1958. I'd done some recording, worked several years at the Blackboard with Bill Woods, but I just didn't seem to be gettin' anywhere. So I left, went to Seattle because I had a chance to get on a station as a DJ, and I was there a year and a half. I'd already decided to give it up when 'Under Your Spell' caught on."

Now that the door had opened, Owens was quick to move on through. He went back to Bakersfield and commuted regularly between there and Los Angeles, working on new material. He scored two major hits in 1960s, "Excuse Me (I Think I've Got a Heartache")—a song he co-wrote with Harlan Howard—and "Above and Beyond." During 1960, he also met Don Rich, a talented musician who later became lead guitarist of Buck's band, the Buckaroos, founded in 1962. In 1961, Buck collaborated with Harlan Howard again on the top-10 hits "Foolin' Around" and "Under the Influence of Love." He also teamed up with Rose Maddox in a series of duets that produced two more top-10 hits, "Loose Talk" and "Mental Cruelty." They were named top vocal team of the year in disc jockey polls.

Buck had a relatively lean year in 1962 with only one top-10 hit, "Kickin' Our Hearts Around," but it was only a temporary lull. In 1963 he had a banner year with hits like the number-one ranked "Love's Gonna Live Here" (written by him), "You're for Me," and "Act Naturally." The last named made the pop top 40 as well as country lists and was covered by no less a group than the Beatles. From 1963 on, Owens became one of the leaders of the 1960s in the country field. He placed twenty-six straight singles in the number-one position of one or another of the country charts and also had a dozen number-one albums.

Helping Owens achieve this was Jack MacFadden, who became his manager and close associate from the early 1960s on. "I met Jack when he was managing Judy Lynn," Buck told *Music City News* (October 1969). "We had talked about his managing me, but it was five months later before I hired him. I was a bit skeptical at first because Jack had had so many jobs of one kind or another, but it just goes to prove one thing. Whenever a person finds the job he is suited for, he will do a good job . . . and Jack has certainly done that for me. He is so very good with the financial end of the business."

There was plenty to keep Jack busy as the 1960s progressed. Concert business was good all across the United States and Canada and TV credits mounted as Owens was featured on programs ranging from country variety to Ed Sullivan. All the while, Buck kept hitting the top of the national country charts with new Capitol releases. In 1964, his output included best-selling singles of his compositions "I Don't Care," "My Heart Skips a Beat," and "Together Again." Also at the top of the charts in 1965 were the singles "Gonna Have Love," "Buckaroo," "Only You," "Before You Go," and "I've Got a Tiger by the Tail." The last named, which he co-wrote with Harlan Howard, remains the one most often associated with him.

In 1966, he worked with Don Rich on the number-one single "Think of Me" and, with Rich and Nat Stuckey, co-wrote another classic, "Waitin' on Your Welfare Line." He also wrote his third number-one single of 1966, "Open Up Your Heart." In 1967, he wrote or co-wrote such winners as "Sam's Place," "Where Does the Good Times Go," and "Your Tender Loving Care." He was voted Top Country Male Artist for 1967 by *Billboard* magazine. By then he had other honors, as well. The Academy of Country & Western Music Awards in 1965 voted him Top Male Vocalist and Best Band Leader. During the next several years he again was named Best Band Leader, with the Buckaroos voted Best Band. In the first four Country Music Association polls, Buck Owens and the Buckaroos were selected as Instrumental Group or Band of the Year.

Buck finished the 1960s with still more charted singles. In 1968, he made the top 10 with "How Long Will My Baby Be Gone" and in 1969 achieved a country hit with his version of Paul Simon's "Bridge Over Troubled Water."

By the end of the 1960s, Owens also had begun building a considerable investment empire. He bought radio stations in California and Arizona, had a booking agency with MacFadden (OMAC), owned a cattle ranch in Paso Robles, California, run by his father, had his own song publishing house, Bluebook Music, as well as other business interests. By then one of his two sons from his first marriage, Buddy Alan, was on the way to making a name for himself as a vocalist. (He and his second wife, Phyllis, had three children, Jack, Johnny, and Terry.)

In the late 1960s, Buck's live engagements included two tours of Europe, a re-gion that also welcomed him back a number of times in the 1970s. One of his fondest memories was a performance given at the White House in 1968 by special invitation from President Lyndon Johnson. He also had his own syndicated TV show in the last years of the 1960s, but the major television opportunity came from another quarter in 1969. He was asked to take part in a summer show project that was to evolve into the extremely popular *Hee Haw* program. It actually began as a special, but after a while CBS-TV decided to expand it into a summer replacement show.

"To say that I was apprehensive isn't exactly right. I was afraid for the first one; then I was afraid for six. But when we found that we were to go for the summer I wasn't sure how I felt. Then as we got into it a little more I felt we would make it.

"What *Hee Haw* is is just a country *Laugh-In* with a *Beverly Hillbillies* motif. It's a spoof of what life is like for a lot of hillbillies. But you notice we're careful to present the music dead serious, just like we've always done."

To everone's surprise, *Hee Haw*, hosted by Buck and Roy Clark, went to number one on the national ratings. As a result, CBS ordered more segments for a regular version of the show that was first shown the next winter. As a prime-time program, it still was a hit, but CBS decided after a while the corn-pone humor didn't fit its hoped-for image. The show was canceled, but the *Hee Haw* organization refused to give up. It was revived as a syndication program and soon was doing as well or better with that approach than previously. In 1979, *Hee Haw* celebrated its first decade and seemed set to go on indefinitely. At the start of the 1980s, it was telecast regularly on over 200 stations all over the United States and Canada. During its tenure, Buck, Roy and other cast regulars welcomed just about every major country artist as *Hee Haw* guests at one time or another. As if working on *Hee Haw* wasn't enough of a task, Owens also hosted his own syndicated program, *Buck Owens Ranch Show*, which was syndicated in seventy markets as of 1980.

Nor did he neglect his recording career in the 1970s. He started out with such top-10 or top-20 hits the first part of the 1970s as "I Wouldn't Live in New York City (If They Gave Me the Whole Dang Town)" in late 1970, "I'll Still Be Waiting for You" and "Looking Back to See" (duet with Susan Raye) in 1972, "Big Game Hunter" (written by Owens) and "On the Cover of the Music City News" (Owens' version of Shel Silverstein's "On the Cover of the Rolling Stone") in 1974, and "Great Expectations" (written by Owens) and "Love Is Strange" (duet with Susan Raye) in 1975. Also on the charts in late 1975 was Buck's single of Jimmy Driftwood's "Battle of New Orleans."

In 1977, Buck's long association with Capitol came to an end and he signed with a new label, Warner Bros. After he left, Capitol leased his best early hits to Trip Records, which issued the definitive *16 Early Hits* album set. He started off relatively slowly on Warners with such moderate chart-making singles as "Nights Are Forever Without You" in early 1977 and "Do You Wanna Make Love" in early 1979. During the summer of 1979, though, he was once more in the top 10 with his duet with Emmylou Harris, "Play Together Again, Again" (co-written by him with C. Stewart and J. Abbott). At year end, he had another original, "Let Jesse Rob the Train," which moved to upper levels in early 1980. Later in the year his single of his composition "Love Is a Warm Cowboy" was a chart hit.

Over the years, Buck turned out dozens of albums, most of them on Capitol. Among his Capitol releases were *Buck Owens* (3/61), *Buck Owens Sings Harlan Howard* (8/61), *You're for Me* (10/62), *On the Band Stand* (6/63), *The Best of Buck Owens, Volume I* (6/64) (Volumes 2 and 3 came out later in the 1960s and Volume 4 in 1970), *Buck Owens Sings Tommy Collins* (11/63), *Together Again* and *My Heart Skips a Beat* (10/64), *I've Got a Tiger by the Tail* (5/65), *The Insrumental Hits of Buck Owens and His Buckaroos* (8/65), *Christmas Hits with Buck Owens and His Buckaroos* (late 1965), *Roll Out the Carpet* (3/66), *Dust on Mother's Bible* (6/66), *Carnegie Hall Concert* (9/66),

Most Wanted Band (5/67), *In Japan* (6/67), *Open Up Your Heart* (12/67), *It Takes People like You to Make People like Me* (1/68), *Buck Owens in London* (7/69), *Close-up: Buck Owens* (7/69), and *Tall Dark Stranger* (12/69). Other Capitol LPs of the late 1960s and early 1970s were *A Night on the Town, Sweet Rosie Jones, Meanwhile Back at the Ranch, Christmas Shopping, We're Gonna Get Together, The Great White Horse* (with Susan Raye), *I've Got You on My Mind Again, Anywhere U.S.A., Big in Vegas, Bakersfield Brass, Boot Hill, Bridge Over Troubled Water, Deluxe 3-Pack, Ruby, Rompin' and Stompin', The Kansas City Song, Under Your Spell Again, I Wouldn't Live in New York City, We're Gonna Get Together* (with Susan Raye), *Live at the White House,* and *Too Old to Cut the Mustard* (with Buddy Alan). During the 1960s and early 1970s, some of Buck's recordings also were released on the Starday and Hilltop label, the former including *Buck Owens* (1962), *Fabulous Sound, Country Hitmakers No. 1,* and *Sweethearts in Heaven,* and, on Hilltop, *If You Ain't Lovin'* and *You're for Me.* His debut album on Warner Bros. came out in the summer of 1976, titled *Buck 'Em.*

Besides his busy schedule of music industry activities, Owens also found time to help out charitable causes. One of his fund-raising operations for some years was the Buck Owens pro-celebrity invitational tennis and golf tournament. In 1977, he organized the Buck Owens Rodeo, which drew top cowboys from all over the United States to compete in Bakersfield each spring with proceeds going for such things as the Kern Community Cancer Center.

Looking back over his eventful career, Buck suggested that his success was due to a combination of planning and audience rapport. "There are singers and there are showmen. I know I'm no great singer, but I am a showman enough that I can communicate with the audience."

OZARK MOUNTAIN DAREDEVILS: *Vocal and instrumental group. Original personnel, 1971-1972: John Dillon, born Arkansas; Steve Cash, born Springfield, Missouri; Larry Lee, born Springfield, Missouri; Mike "Supe" Granda, born St. Louis, Missouri. Additions in*

mid-1970s: Buddy Brayfield; Randle Chowning; Steve Canaday, born Springfield, Missouri. Chowning replaced in early 1976 by Rune Walle, born Norway. Jerry Mills added May 1976. Ruell Chapman added mid-1976, born Springfield, Missouri. Roster reduced to Dillon, Cash, Lee, and Granda in 1978.

It wouldn't hurt to have a scorecard in following the fortunes of the Ozark Mountain Daredevils. This Springfield, Missouri-based band, with a repertoire ranging from bluegrass to straight-ahead rock, had a lineup that sometimes seemed as changeable as the weather. Although it often appeared to add and subtract members like a human erector set, some things remained constant. One was its core of four musicians—John Dillon (vocals, guitars, mandolin, fiddle, percussion); Steve Cash (vocals, harmonica); Larry Lee (vocals, drums, guitars, piano, synthesizer, percussion); and Mike "Supe" Granda (vocals, bass, guitars, mandolin, percussion)—and the other was a constant devotion to the members' home area of Missouri and Arkansas.

Of the three charter members, two, Larry Lee and Steve Cash, were born and raised in Springfield. Larry completed high school there and followed with two years in Southwest Missouri State University before enlisting in the Navy in 1965. After taking training as a postal clerk at Bainbridge, Maryland, he was stationed in Puerto Rico, where he formed a band called Trilogy that performed at base functions. He also began writing songs during that period. After his discharge, he worked with a band called Granny's Bathwater before joining the Daredevils in 1971.

Cash, whose interests included playing baseball and writing poetry and short stories while growing up in the Springfield area, eventually opted for music and songwriting. He worked in a number of small local groups, often with friends who later joined or sat in with the Daredevils, before his acquaintance with Lee and Dillon sparked formation of that group.

Dillon grew up on a farm in Stuttgart, Arkansas, where his mother, who played country songs on the harmonica, nurtured his interest in that music as well as in delta blues. She bought him a guitar and encouraged him to learn to play it. As he grew older, he also became aware of the country-rock movement, sometimes listening to bands like Ronnie Hawkins and the Hawks (which included Levon Helm of later Band fame) at local clubs. In 1965, he enrolled in Drury College in Springfield, Missouri, majoring in philosophy and theater.

He recalled, "Two years into school, music took over. I started writing songs and experimenting to find out what I could do musically. After I got out of school, I headed to Nashville with lots of songs under my belt, was signed by a management company and promptly got turned off to the music business. I was floundering around, got ripped off by my manager, headed back to Springfield with the intention of getting lost."

However, while working as a session rhythm guitarist, he met Steve Cash and Larry Lee. "We were a bunch of wayward writers looking for somebody to play with." They formed a group that also included John's wife for a time, which initially was called the Emergency Band, since its first performance was before some patients in a psychiatric ward. Various versions of the band evolved under such names as Buffalo Chips, Burlap Socks, and Family Tree before it became the Ozark Mountain Daredevils. They gained a manager, Steve Plesser, who sent a demo tape to producer Glyn Johns. Johns, in turn, brought them to the attention of A&M Records, which signed them and sent them to London to record their debut album. That effort, *Ozark Mountain Daredevils*, was issued in 1973.

By then Granda also was part of the band, having been in and out of it at times in its formative years. He notes, "I was born in St. Louis, went to college at Southwest Missouri State and have never lived outside Missouri." He too learned to play guitar in his youth and sang with a number of local bands before joining the Daredevils.

After Granda, the musician with the longest association with the group was Steve Canaday, who joined officially in 1975 and stayed several years, but who had worked with it in various ways for some time before. Canaday's father brought him a set of drums when he was a boy, he recalled. "Elvis was my hero, both my parents sang at church and my mother was one of four sisters who used to sing on the radio. I joined my first rock band in high school in 1958 and then I was a drummer and singer with several different bands. For a time I tried my hand at various kinds of jobs, but ended up back in Springfield where we opened what we hoped would be a music club called The New Bijou Theatre."

The club was a gathering spot for the future Daredevils. Larry Lee was a bartender and Cash, Granda, and Dillon first played as a group there. That phase ended when the club burned down after five months. Canaday, though, helped the boys make their initial demos and later worked in their management after they went with A&M. "I was so impressed with how good they were, four fine writers and there were good musical things happening."

Those things included growing popularity with both country and rock fans in the mid-1970s and the release of several singles that did well on the charts such as "Jackie Blue," co-written by Lee and Cash, "You Know like I Know," written by Lee, and "If You Want to Get to Heaven," co-written by Cash. The group continued to turn out new LPs, including *It'll Shine When It Shines* in 1974 and *The Car Over the Lake Album* in 1975. There were some new names on some of those recordings, including Buddy Brayfield (keyboards, oboe, vocals) and Randle Chowning (vocals, guitars). During that period, not only did the band tour throughout the United States, it also found a warm welcome in Europe with concerts in England, the Scandinavian countries, and on the Continent.

The overseas swing also proved helpful when Chowning left while the group was getting ready to do its next album. His replacement turned out to be Norwegian-born Rune Walle (vocals, guitars, banjo), whose group the Flying Norwegians had opened for some of the Daredevils' European concerts. Walle took part in the sessions that helped complete the 1976 LP

Men from Earth, whose content ranges from country-oriented numbers like "The Red Plum" to fast country rockers like "Breakaway" and "Noah" to pop ballads such as "You Know like I Know" and "It's How You Think."

During 1976, the band expanded to eight members. Besides Cash, Dillon, Lee, Granda, Canaday, and Walle, the others were Jerry Mills, who joined in May 1976, and Ruell Chapman. Mills' background included working as a DJ at KFML-FM in Denver and band or session work with the Nitty Gritty Dirt Band, Michael Murphey, and Mason Williams. Chapman, born in Springfield around 1953, "played my first gig at the Carousel Lounge in Springfield when I was nine years old. It was a country/western & soul band made up of real young kids." In later years, this keyboardist-vocalist played with local groups and was a top session musician in Springfield when the Daredevils asked him to join them for their 1976 Canadian tour.

Most of the 1976 roster took part in preparing the band's 1977 album, *Don't Look Down.* Besides their Daredevils' work, Steve Cash and John Dillon also played on *White Mansions,* the 1977 concept album on the Civil War that Paul Kennerley recorded on A&M.

The band's popularity seemed to slip somewhat at the end of the 1970s, which caused some readjustments in personnel, but the core of Cash, Dillon, Lee, and Granda remained intact. The group was represented on its first live album in 1978 when A&M issued the two-record set *It's Alive.* The album featured the band's best-known songs, including "Jackie Blue" and such new material as Steve Cash's "Commercial Success" and John Dillon's version of "Satisfied Mind."

At the end of the 1970s, the band signed a recording contract with Columbia Records. Actually, the group almost had been signed by the label when it was just getting started. At the time, Steve Canaday, on a trip to New York to visit relatives, had taken a demo tape of the band and managed to get it to Columbia executive John Hammond, Sr., who had liked it enough to send a representative to Missouri. However, as Larry Lee recalled in 1979, the emissary backed off when he found the group represented itself. "We hadn't a manager, an agent, a lawyer . . . nothing. He told us he wasn't prepared to talk business like that with the musicians themselves. And so he went back to New York."

In 1980, the label had no qualms about signing the group, though. The band's debut on Columbia, titled *The Ozark Mountain Daredevils,* was issued in March 1980. A few months later, while the band was getting ready to do a second album for the label, Columbia issued Larry Lee's debut solo LP.

P

PAGE, PATTI: *Singer. Born Claremore, Oklahoma, November 8, 1927.*

Primarily a pop singer, Patti Page also had an impact on country music in the years after World War II, an influence that grew as the years went by. In the late 1940s and in the 1950s, she enhanced country music's standing through a number of cross-over hits of country-style songs on pop charts. She was returning to her roots: her first blockbuster hit had been a country song.

Patti was one of a family of eight girls and three boys whose home state of Oklahoma was then, as now, a stronghold of country & western music. She was born in Claremore, but her family moved to Tulsa a few years later. She demonstrated singing talent at an early age and already was performing in school events by the time she finished elementary school. During high school, she continued those activities, singing and acting in school shows and community theater.

While in her teens, she auditioned for a singing job at a local station. The program director called her in for an interview, but it turned out he wanted a staff artist, not a singer. Luckily, Patti had studied art in high school. She decided a job's a job and went to work at the drawing board.

Her first break came when the station's regular singer quit. On the spot this time, Patti got the job. Soon she was given her own afternoon show. One October day, a band leader named Jack Rael was in Tulsa for a band date. He turned on his hotel radio and heard Page sing. Excitedly he

called the station to find out who it was. On finding that she was a local girl, he immediately contacted her and offered to become her manager.

Rael gave up his band to further Patti's career. First he got her a job with a big band. Then he gained an audition with the major Chicago network radio show, *The Breakfast Club.* Although still in her teens, she impressed show talent scouts with her poise and ability and was soon heard five times a week on the program. Before long she also had a record contract with Chicago-based Mercury Records.

She began to appear in major nightclubs in the Chicago area, and offers began to come in from other cities. Her credits expanded to include guest spots on other radio programs and she also was featured on an increasing number of TV variety shows. Patti could sing every type of song, but thanks to her Oklahoma unbringing, she had a way with numbers having a country & western flavor. She scored mild successes with singles like "Sentimental Music," "Detour," and "Money Marbles and Chalk" in the late 1940s and at the start of the 1950s.

Page did not use an arranger, preferring to work out her own stylings using a pitch pipe. One song that got the pitch-pipe treatment was Pee Wee King's "Tennessee Waltz." She and Rael liked the song, though they really didn't consider it a top-hit possibility. They decided to use it as the "B" side on a single, backing a song they thought had more potential. The "B" side, however, turned out to be her biggest hit. It rose to the top of the pop lists and also made top 10 on country charts, eventually selling over 3 million copies. (It didn't get a gold record because the gold record awards didn't start until 1958.) She followed with other bestsellers of the 1950s, including "How Much Is That Doggie in the Window?"

Patti was a guest star on most major TV variety programs in the 1950s and 1960s, including *The Ed Sullivan Show,* several times, *The Tonight Show,* and others. For several years she had her own major network show, beginning in 1955. During the 1950s and throughout the 1960s she remained a favorite on the supper club circuit, performing all over the United States and in a number of other nations as well. Although rock music dominated the pop field from the mid-1950s on, Page still occasionally placed a release on the charts, including her best-seller of 1963, "Say Wonderful Things."

She turned out dozens of albums from the late 1940s into the 1970s, most on her original label, Mercury, or on Columbia Records, which she joined in 1963. Her Mercury LPs included *Tennessee Waltz, Waltz Queen,* and *Let's Get Away from It All,* all issued in the 1950s, and, in the 1960s, *Golden Hits* (4/60), *Country Hits* (7/61), *Patti Page* (5/62), *Golden Hits of the Boys* (9/62), *On Stage* (4/63), *Golden Hits, Volume 2* (6/63), *Singing Rage* (10/63), *Blue Dream Street* (7/64), *Nearness of You* (11/64), *Y'all Come* (5/65). Her Columbia releases included *Say Wonderful Things* (10/63), *Love After Midnight* (4/64), *Hush Sweet Charlotte* (6/65), *America's Favorite Hymns* (7/66), *Greatest Hits* (9/66), *Today My Way* (12/67), and *Honey Come Back* (5/70).

The last-named LP, which featured her versions of popular country songs, was typical of much of her new output in the 1970s. Some of Page's other 1970s albums were *I'd Rather Be Sorry* on Mercury and, on Harmony Records, *Stand By Your Man* and *Green, Green Grass of Home.*

In the mid-1970s, Patti recorded a number of country-style songs that were issued on Columbia's Epic label. Several of these made the country lists, including "You're Gonna Hurt Me (One More Time)" and "Someone Came to See Me."

PARSONS, GRAM: *Singer, guitarist, songwriter, band leader. Born Winterhaven, Florida, November 5, 1946; died Joshua Tree, California, September 19, 1973.*

Immensely talented and dedicated, but haunted by personal demons that cut his life distressingly short, Gram Parsons never achieved the stardom that seemed his creative due. He did leave a legacy of original songs and influence on others that went a long way toward ultimately reaching his objective of uniting all segments of the pop music audience under the country/rock banner. As he outlined it at one point in the late 1960s, "We want the rock fans at the Whisky and the truck drivers at the Palomino to get together and talk to each other and understand each other."

Had he lived, he might have accomplished much of that and become a worldwide superstar. His musical heirs, however, including the Eagles and Emmylou Harris, contributed to bringing some of Parsons' dreams to pass.

Parsons was born in Winterhaven in the mid-1940s and grew up in the South, enamored, as he finished elementary school and moved into high school, of country, gospel, blues, and rockabilly. He showed talent as a musician at an early age, beginning piano lessons when he was only three. When he was thirteen, he decided to learn guitar "because Elvis played one." He had already become a Presley fan even when Elvis still was appearing as a country artist. "I can remember when Elvis first came down to town as second billing with Jimmie Dickens on the *Grand Ole Opry* Show. He was only about eighteen then, and they had it in the local high school gym and everybody came."

It didn't take Gram long to become proficient enough as a guitarist to be a key performer in a teen band called the Pacers. "We played Everly Brothers and attempted Ray Charles. That lasted for six months. At fourteen, I joined a band called the Legends—for six months—this time playing Everly Brothers and Chuck Berry. We worked all through Florida, did lots of club and TV work. This was about 1960–61."

He continued to play with various bands in his home region during the early 1960s. A good enough student to get accepted at Harvard University in 1965, he attended classes there briefly. "Acid was the major reason I dropped out—I had taken so much of it. Remember, I was interested in psychedelic trips, so I checked into them on my own and dropped out of Harvard."

He never had dropped out of music, so he formed a new band in Cambridge called the International Submarine Band. He moved the group to New York for a time in hopes of making it into the musical big time, then shifted again to Los Angeles. He did manage to record an LP for Lee Hazelwood's LHI label there, called Safe at Home, but that proved a commercial flop and the final alignment of the Submarine Band (which he reorganized several times) broke up. The LP demonstrated Parsons' continued love for both country and rock, with songs from such diverse sources as Merle Haggard, Waylon Jennings, Bob Dylan, and the Rolling Stones.

His next move was to the Byrds in 1968, where he had a kinship with another country-oriented member, Chris Hillman. The two helped persuade leader Roger McGuinn to go to Nashville to make a country-rock LP. The result was Sweetheart of the Rodeo, a compilation that included Byrds versions of songs by Haggard, the Louvin Brothers, Dylan, and two Parsons originals. One of the latter, "Hickory Wind," is a haunting country song that was presented with great impact by Emmylou Harris in her 1979 album Blue Kentucky Girl. The lyrics express some of the disparate rural and city influences tugging at Parsons: "It's a hard way to find out that trouble is real/In a faraway city with a faraway feel/But it makes me feel better/Each time it begins/Calling me home, hickory wind."

In 1969, Hillman and Parsons left the Byrds to form their own band, the landmark country-rock group called the Flying Burrito Brothers (see separate entry). The band's first LP, The Gilded Palace of Sin, whose features included the Parsons-Hill-man song "Sin City," came out on A&M that year and won strong critical praise, as did the band's concerts. Bob Dylan, among other major rock stars, called the group a favorite of his. Despite the band's great promise, it was a few years ahead of its time. The idea of combining country and rock was still anathema to most rock and country fans.

Still, things might have gone better if Gram hadn't been injured in a motorcycle accident in early 1970. After he recovered, he returned to the Burritos for a short time, but his musical ideas had changed somewhat during his recuperation, and he left to concentrate on solo work. His initial efforts came to naught in 1970, so he went to France for a while partly at the behest of Rolling Stones members, who esteemed his work. There were some discussions of a solo LP for him on their label, but again nothing happened.

Going back to Los Angeles, Parsons spent much of 1972 writing new material primarily in the country vein. This time he had record company interest, which led to release of his debut solo LP on Warner Brothers. Called Gram Parsons, it was heavily country-oriented, both in his original material and the other selections he sang. The album was flawed but showed promise. Warners approved a followup that was to come out in 1973 under the title Grievous Angel. Today, the LP is considered a major contribution to the melding of country and rock into a dynamic new music form, but it had little impact when it came out because by then Parsons was dead.

His death resulted from the problem he long had fought with varying degrees of success—drugs. On September 19, 1973, he was found unconscious on the floor of his room at Joshua Tree Inn. He was rushed to the Yucca Valley High Desert Hospital, but died soon after arrival. A strange incident took place in ensuing days. Still unknown individuals stole his coffin from the airport where it was awaiting transport back to his home and burned it near the Joshua Tree Monument.

Many who respected his ability mourned his passing, including close friend Emmylou Harris, who had done backing vocals on his solo albums and toured with his band briefly in his last months. She told a reporter later on, "Gram was a real pioneer. He cut straight through the middle with no compromises. He was never afraid to write from the heart, and perhaps that's why he was never really accepted. It's like the light was too strong and bright and people just had to turn away. They couldn't look at the light because it was all too painful. It could rip you up. Not many people can take music that real.

"If there's one thing in my life I really want to do it's get Gram's music out in the open where it should be. A lot of people who would've appreciated him never got to hear him. . . . I feel like I've glided in at a time when people are beginning to listen to country music. But what I'm trying to get them to realize is that they should look a little behind me to all that was going on before with Gram and the Burritos."

True to her word, Emmylou has had one or more Parsons' compositions on almost every solo album she has done. Thus on more than one occasion Parsons' name has appeared under songs ranked high on both pop and country charts in the mid and late-1970s.

PARTON, DOLLY: *Singer, guitarist, banjoist, actress, songwriter. Born Locust Ridge, Sevier County, Tennessee, January 19, 1946.*

Dolly Parton is a determined and knowing person. In the mid-1970s, then an acknowledged country star, she felt her career could go further. When she took steps to broaden her public following through some changes in musical direction and a wide-ranging public relations campaign orchestrated by a Los Angeles publicity firm, fans and country-music associates alike expressed alarm. She would destroy her career, they suggested, perhaps become a laughingstock by exposing herself to the comic barbs of interviewers like Johnny Carson. They reckoned without her inner strength and knowledge of her capabilities.

In part, some observers confused Parton's stage image with the actual person. The trademark large, fluffy blonde wig (she quipped to a Las Vegas audience in early 1981, "You'd be amazed how expensive it is to make a wig look this cheap"), well-developed chest, and Mae West-like figure suggested to some she was a dumb blonde. Those who met her knew otherwise: she was softspoken, attractive in a dignified way, and exuded both self-confidence and intelligence.

Those characteristics were evident in an interview with Robert Hilburn of the *Los Angeles Times* (Calendar Section, February 15, 1981, p. 66) when she recalled her important debut on Carson's *The Tonight Show* a few years earlier. "I didn't fear going on the [Carson] show because I work best one-to-one. I was a fan of Johnny Carson and I wanted people to notice me. I didn't care if it was for the right reasons or the wrong reasons at first. I felt I had a gift as a writer. I may not be a great singer, but my voice is different. I'm secure in those areas.

"If I could get their [viewers] attention long enough, I felt they would see beneath the boobs and find the heart, and that they would see beneath the wig and find the brains. I think one big part of whatever appeal I possess is the fact that I look totally one way and that I am totally another. I look artificial, but I'm not."

Dolly always claimed that her optimistic outlook went back to her earliest years as a child growing up in rural Tennessee in the foothills of the Smoky Mountains. She was the fourth of a dozen children born to Lee and Avie Lee Parton. "I was born with a happy nature and a happy heart," she remarked. "I was born with the gift of understanding people and loving them and I've never been unhappy. I've always seen the light at the end of the tunnel."

Although she recalls her childhood with affection, it was anything but an affluent one. Her father hadn't been able to scratch enough income from the soil to support his growing family (which lived in a two-room shack with an upstairs attic) and had to do construction work to try to make ends meet. The children had few toys and their clothes mostly were hand-me-downs or made from bits and pieces of material. There are hints in some of Parton's later songs based on her early years, such as

"Coat of Many Colors," that despite the warm family environment, the taunts of outsiders could cause pain.

Dolly started to sing almost as soon as she could talk. Before she could read or write, she would make up songs and ask her mother to write them down. When she was seven she began trying to learn guitar after making her first one from an old mandolin and two bass guitar strings. When she was eight an uncle gave her her first real guitar, a small Martin.

Even then she was thinking about a future in music. As she stated once about making music, "It's all I've ever known." She told Hilburn, "I knew I wanted to be a singer from the time when I was 7 or 8 and learned my first chord on the guitar. I also wanted to be a star—the biggest in the world. I wanted pretty clothes and attention and to live in a big house and buy things for Mama and Daddy. Of course, I didn't have any better sense in those days.

"But as I got older, I didn't lose track of those dreams. I just thought, 'Well, why can't I do all that?' The secret was to take one step at a time. That's what I've done. I'm not saying everything has been wonderful. I've had bad times, but I've always tried to maintain a good outlook. I've had heartaches and disappointments, but never so great that it blocked my vision of the future."

As she grew into young womanhood, music remained her passion. She sang almost all the time, while she washed the dishes, hoed corn in the fields, or attended church. "I was brought up in the Church of God," she said later. "It's a very free church. If anybody wanted to get up and sing or shout out an emotion, they would do it. There was a freedom there, so I came to know what freedom is, so I could know God and come to know freedom within myself."

Dolly didn't forsake a basic education. She completed elementary and high school. But at the age of eighteen, the day after she graduated from high school, she headed to Nashville, intent on pursuing her long-held dream. At first, she went to stay with the family of her uncle, Bill Owens. Owens had contacts with the music field and also was skilled at songwriting. He and Parton began to write some original songs, one of which, "Put It Off Until Tomorrow," finally was placed with country artist Bill Phillips and became a top-10 hit in 1966.

Almost as soon as Dolly reached Nashville, she met Carl Dean, an asphalt-paving contractor, whom she married two years later. She said in 1976, "My husband is a very home-based person. . . . He's good for me because he's so different in nature from me. We've been together twelve years, married for ten, and we've never had an argument. There's nobody else like him and I know in my heart that there will never be another person for me."

Since arriving in Nashville, Parton had been doggedly working to get a hearing for her singing ability and songwriting talents. The success of the Bill Phillips single helped open more doors, and in late 1966 she signed a recording contract with Monument Records. Before long she had her first releases out on the label, including her debut album, *Hello, I'm Dolly*, in July 1967. Company president Fred Foster wrote in the liner notes, "Sometimes you just know . . . sometimes. And that makes up for all the times you had to guess. . . ." Monument soon issued a second LP, *As Long as I Love*. The company released a number of singles by Dolly, two of which, "Dumb Blonde" and "Something Fishy," were chart hits in 1967.

Unfortunately for Monument, the firm didn't have long to savor the promise of its new-found artist. In 1967, major country-artist Porter Wagoner was in need of a female vocalist to replace Norma Jean, who was leaving his show. Dolly's releases on Monument attracted his attention and one day he called her on the phone to ask if she'd join his troupe. The opportunity was too good to pass up. At the time, Porter was one of the most successful performers and band leaders. Beginning in the summer of 1967, Dolly began to appear in Wagoner's tour dates and on his syndicated TV show. Wagoner was on RCA Records and that label hastened to sign up his new vocalist. Over a decade and a half later, Dolly still was a mainstay of RCA's recording roster.

It didn't take long for Dolly to make her mark on RCA both as a duet partner with Wagoner and as a solo performer. Her 1968 output included the hit duet singles "Holding on to Nothing" and "The Last Thing on My Mind" and the solo best-seller "Just Because I'm a Woman." Also on country charts for many weeks was the LP with Wagoner, *Just Between Me and You*. In 1969, she and Porter collaborated on the hit singles "Yours Love" and "Always Always" and hit album *Just the Two of Us*. During those years and in 1970, Parton had enough other solo and duet singles on the charts, including the 1970 number-one hit single "Mule Skinner Blues," for RCA to issue the first *Best of Dolly Parton* LP in late 1970.

During the first half of the 1970s, Dolly continued to add new entries to her list of classic recordings, and her intensive schedule of in-person dates impressed growing numbers of country fans with her finely tuned emotional control of her remarkable soprano voice. As her reputation continued to grow, she became restless at remaining under the aegis of the Wagoner show. In 1973 she left the show in favor of concentrating on her solo career, though Wagoner continued to produce her records until 1976. Among her singles successes of that period, mostly of her own compositions, were "Coat of Many Colors" in 1971; "Touch Your Woman" and "Washday Blues" in 1972; "Travelin' Man" in 1973; one of her trademark compositions, "Jolene," in 1973-74; "Please Don't Stop Loving Me" (duet, co-written with Wagoner) and "Love Is like a Butterfly" in 1974; "The Seeker" and "We Used To" in 1975; "Hey Lucky Lady," "All I Can Do," and "Is Forever Longer than Always" (duet with Wagoner) in 1976. Her duet hits with Wagoner also included "Daddy Was an Oldtime Preacher Man" and "If Teardrops Were Pennies and Heartaches Were Gold."

From the late 1960s through 1976, RCA issued one or more of Parton's albums each year, most of which made the charts. Among them were *Blue Ridge Mountain Bow* (1969); *Fairest of Them All, Real Live, Best of Dolly Parton* (1970); *Golden Streets of Glory, Joshua, Coat of Many Colors* (1971); *Touch Your Woman, My Favorite Songwriter, Porter Wagoner, The Right Combination/Burning the Midnight Oil* (with Wagoner) (1972); *Bubbling Over* (1973); *Jolene, Love Is like a Butterfly* (1975); *The Bargain Store, Best of Dolly Parton, Say Forever You'll Be Mine* (with Wagoner), *In Concert* (with Charley Pride, Ronnie Milsap, Jerry Reed, and Chet Atkins), *Dolly* (1975); and *All I Can Do* (1976). RCA also released some of her recordings on its Camden label, including *Just the Way I Am* and *Mine*. Also in print on Monument, besides the LPs noted earlier, was *In the Beginning*. Powerpak Records issued the LP *Release Me*.

By the mid-1970s, Dolly seemingly had accomplished all any country artist could desire. Her position as a soloist had been enhanced by the success of her new touring arrangements with her Traveling Family Band, composed mostly of her brothers, sisters, uncles, and cousins. She certainly didn't lack recognition from her peers. In 1968 she and Porter Wagoner had been voted Vocal Group of the Year by the Country Music Association, an honor they again won in 1971. In 1970, she was one of the final nominees in the Grammy competition for Best Country Vocal Performance, Female, for "Mule Skinner Blues." Increasingly in the 1970s she was ranked among the top ten female country soloists. In both 1975 and 1976, the CMA voted her Female Vocalist of the Year. All the major trade magazines—*Billboard, Record World,* and *Cash Box*—voted her the top female vocalist, country, of 1975.

But she was certain she still could scale new heights. In 1976, she decided to make the break, ending her recording association with Porter Wagoner, organizing a new backing band, and starting work on a new album aimed at having a more contemporary country sound than her previous work. Besides raising eyebrows in the country-music community in general, it brought a bitter reaction from Wagoner, triggering a lawsuit that engendered acrimony between the two artists for many years.

As it turned out, Dolly knew what she was doing. Her career did indeed developed from that of a country superstar to a reigning pop star and, at the start of the 1980s, a film star as well. The first step in this progression was the album *New Harvest . . . First Gathering*, released at the start of 1977 and soon on country charts. For a good part of the year it remained in the top 10, indicating that Dolly's country fans had not deserted her. Equally important, it made some inroads with the pop audience too. Late in the year, RCA issued another album that carried her star still higher, called *Here You Come Again*. The album was in the top 10 in country before 1977 was over and was still on the lists over a year later. Its title song became a major hit on both country and pop lists, showing up in late 1977 and staying on them into 1978. During 1978, she had such other singles hits as "Heartbreaker" and "Baby I'm Burning/I Really Got the Feeling." The album *Heartbreaker* was issued in late summer of 1978 and proved another bestseller. Dolly rounded out the decade with such other successes as the singles "You're the Only One" and "Sweet Summer Lovin'/ Great Balls of Fire" and the album *Great Balls of Fire*. In October 1979, she signed a multimillion-dollar agreement with the Riviera Hotel in Las Vegas calling for six weeks of appearances per year from 1980 through 1982. Discussions also began for Parton's first featured movie role in the film *9 to 5*, costarring Jane Fonda and Lily Tomlin. By then, she had won the highest honor the Country Music Association could bestow, Entertainer of the Year, presented to her at the 1978 CMA awards telecast.

The movie industry took note of her new acting career by arranging for her first appearance as a presenter on the 1980 Academy Awards telecast on ABC-TV, April 14, 1980. The month before, RCA issued a new album, *Dolly Dolly Dolly*, which featured the single release "Starting Over Again." Both releases did well on country charts as did another 1980 single, "Old Flames Can't Hold a Candle to You." In Feburary 1980, it was announced that after she completed work on *9 to 5* at 20th Century Fox, she would costar with Burt Reynolds in Universal Pictures' movie version of the stage play *The Best Little Whorehouse in Texas*. All of this didn't hurt her record sales; by early 1980 *Here You Come Again* had earned her her first platinum record and *Heartbreaker* had passed gold-record levels.

In November 1980, RCA issued her album *9 to 5 and Other Odd Jobs*, which featured as its title track the song Dolly wrote for her debut movie. The film was released in December 1980 and won glowing reviews, including enthusiastic approval of Parton's acting efforts by critics from most major U.S. publications. In March 1981, her single "9 to 5" brought her still another number-one ranked country disc. At the 11th Annual American Guild of Variety Artists awards telecast in May, she was voted the Entertainer of the Year and Female Country Star of the Year (She previously had been named Country Star of the Year by AGVA in 1978 and 1979.) By then she had made her debut at the Riviera in Las Vegas in a show which, though cut short by laryngitis, had been universally evaluated as a triumph, with several reviewers describing her work as "dazzling."

At the Grammy Awards in February 1982, Dolly was nominated in two categories for "9 to 5," Best Country Vocal Performance, Female, and Best Country Song (songwriting award), and won the Grammies in both cases. Unfortunately, she couldn't accept them in person because she had to enter a hospital in Los Angeles for surgery. (The operation caused a major reshuffling of her schedules for the year). Significantly, though she didn't win, she was one of five finalists in two noncountry categories, Song of the Year (for "9 to 5") and Best Album of Original Score Written for a Motion Picture or TV Special (co-written with Charles Fox. Soundtrack album, *9 to 5*, issued by 20th Century Fox Records).

PARTON, STELLA: *Singer, guitarist, songwriter. Born Sevier County, Tennessee, May 4, 1949.*

Musical talent often tends to run in families, as is the case with the Parton family. Stella Parton, following in her sister Dolly's footsteps, has become the second and perhaps not the last Parton to gain fame in country music.

Stella was the sixth of the twelve children born to Lee and Avie Lee Parton. The family lived on a farm, and their main form of entertainment was going to church. Stella's grandfather was the preacher of their church, the Pentecostal Church of God. He also doubled as a music teacher. As a child, Stella naturally took to music, and when she was nine years old she performed on a weekly television show in Knoxville, Tennessee.

Before Stella graduated from high school, she was married. At high school graduation she was pregnant and soon afterward gave birth to her son, Timmy. The marriage later ended in divorce.

For a few years, she performed around the Southeast and Texas. She recorded a few albums for small Nashville labels, such as Royal American and Music City. She had her own gospel group, the Stella Parton Singers, which worked the gospel music circuit. For years she was her own manager and booking agent. Despite the fact that her sister Dolly was gaining success in the country-music field, Stella was determined to make it on her own. When some club owners used Dolly's name to draw crowds for her, Stella began to include in her contract a clause forbidding this exploitation of Dolly's name.

In 1973, Stella met Bob Dean, a Nashville drummer and trumpet player. With his help, she formed her own record label, Soul, Country and Blues Records. In 1975, the new label released two of Stella's recordings, "Ode to Olivia" and "I Want to Hold You in My Dreams Tonight." Parton wrote the former song in response to the Academy of Country Entertainers who attacked Olivia Newton-John for not being "country" enough after she had been named Top Female Vocalist by the Country Music Association. She wrote the song because she felt that since Olivia had had a number of large country hits, she was indeed a country performer, and she felt that no one had the right to say what was country and what was not. The song became a substantial country hit.

"I Want to Hold You in My Dreams Tonight" was also written by Stella. She helped finance the recording of the song; she placed the recording session herself and also got somebody to release and distribute it. The song reached number seven on the *Billboard* country charts, and the album from which it came reached the number-twenty spot. The song also did well in England.

In late 1976, Stella signed with Elektra/Asylum records, and Jim Malloy became her producer. Her first album for that label, *Country Sweet,* provided her with three country hits, "I'm Not That Good at Goodbye," "Danger of a Stranger," which reached number twelve, and "Standard Lie Number One," which reached the number-fourteen position. "Danger of a Stranger" went as high as number thirty-five in England, where there are no separate country charts and her song was competing with those of top rock groups. Because of her success in England, Stella made a promotion tour there in December 1977.

Parton's second Elektra LP, *Stella Parton,* met with similar success. Her single "Four Little Letters" appeared on the country hit lists, and a second single, "Undercover Lovers," made it into the country top 40. The album also included two songs she had written herself, "Fade My Blues Away" and "Lie to Linda" (co-written by Billy Smith), and a gospel song, "Down to Earth," on which her mother, father, son, and seven of her brothers and sisters, as well as several other people, sing.

In the late 1970s, Stella appeared in a movie, *Cloud Dancer,* starring David Carradine, Jennifer O'Neil, and Joseph Bottoms. In it she played herself and sang *The Star-Spangled Banner* to some 30,000 people at the start of the movie. Early in 1978, she was named Most Promising International Artist at England's Wembley Festival. She was also one of the five finalists for the Academy of Country Music's Most Promising New Female Vocalist award.　　A.S.

PAUL, LES: *Singer, guitarist, songwriter, band leader, inventor. Born Waukesha, Wisconsin, June 9, 1915.*

When Les Paul made country-music history in the late 1970s through his memorable duets with Chet Atkins, many observers thought it was his initial exposure to the field. Les, after all, had become famous in the 1940s and 1950s for his superlative jazz and pop music output. In truth, he had actually been a major figure in the country field in his early years, and his pioneering work in electronic sound had helped revolutionize all phases of music from folk through rock after World War II.

Les showed an early musical flair as a child growing up in Wisconsin. (His original name was Lester William Polsfuss.) When he was nine, he took up both piano and harmonica. In those early years, he also demonstrated his inventive bent by experimenting with player piano rolls to make added sounds, building his own electric recorder with a wind-up motor and even considering the possibility during the 1920s of using radio components to amplify a guitar.

In the late 1920s he played in local speakeasies, Optimist and Lions clubs, and other local events under the pseudonym of Red Hot Red, the Wizard of Waukesha. During those years he made his radio debut on station WRJN in Racine, Wisconsin, and WHAD at Marquette University in Milwaukee; in 1928, he joined a cowboy band that worked station WLS in Chicago and also toured from Canada to Louisiana.

In the early 1930s, Paul became a local country star under the name "Rhubarb Red." But he also was becoming enamored of jazz and played under his own name with many major jazz artists in the Chicago area. He was making a princely sum for those days—$600 a week—as a country artist, with credits including a hit record for Montgomery Ward titled "Just Because." For a time he gave that up to play jazz piano for eight dollars a week. He formed his first trio then, but it got such poor response that in 1934 he resumed the Rhubarb Red phase on a variety of Chicago stations (WJJD, WIND, WBBM, and WLS, the home of the *National Barn Dance*) with joyous response from the audience.

He kept up his jazz work, though, and by the late 1930s the Les Paul Trio had become a feature on the Fred Waring network shows on NBC. His specialty by then wasn't piano but the electric guitar that he'd worked on for years to perfect. Les' credits of the time included doing the first TV broadcast with an orchestra in a show telecast by NBC in New York. In 1939, Les took the trio back to Chicago, where he served as musical director with stations WJJD and WIND and played with the Ben Bernie band on CBS. Still experimenting, in 1941 he built the first solid-body guitar, now a staple of pickers in rock, country, and even folk, with a pickup on it.

During the 1940s, Paul moved to Hollywood, where he and his trio became one of the best-known pop acts in the nation. Things were going well in 1948, the year his first multiple recording, "Lover," was released, when an auto accident disabled him for two years. His right elbow never returned to normal, but he came back to team up with Mary Ford (for many years his wife) for one of the superstar combinations of the 1950s. Their hit records were legion, including such songs as "Tennessee Waltz," "Little Rock Getaway," "Mockin' Bird Hill," "How High the Moon," "The World's Waiting for the Sunrise," "Tiger Rag," and "Vaya con Dios." Some of those songs continue to turn up on country charts. In 1976, for instance, Freddy Fender had a hit with "Vaya con Dios."

Les continued to contribute new ideas to the recording art, such as a multiple-track recorder with one-inch-wide tape for eight tracks, called Sel Sync; flat response for both record and tape; and other innovations. In 1964, tired of the touring grind, Les decided to put his musical activities aside in favor of working on even more new ideas. His activities were hampered, though, when a friend accidentally broke his eardrum with a playful slap, an injury that required three operations. In 1967, Les and Gibson Guitar Co. announced production of a new line of guitars named after Paul. That family of instruments continues to be one of the most used by professional musicians.

After his long layoff, Les started to do some in-person appearances in 1974. That led to a suggestion that he team up with Chet Atkins, whose reputation as a guitarist matched Paul's. The two began recording tracks for a debut album in 1976, and, when the album appeared in 1977, called *Chester and Lester*, there was no doubt that it represented consummate instrumental artistry. Their performance provided new sound dimensions for the various country-based songs in the collection. The album won a Grammy Award, presented on the nationally telecast show in early 1978, which also featured a selection performed by the duo. In 1978, a second LP by Chester and Lester was released by RCA.

PAXTON, TOM: *Singer, guitarist, songwriter. Born Chicago, Illinois, October 31, 1937.*

In some ways, Tom Paxton may have seemed an anachronism in the 1970s, a throwback to the folk scene of the 1960s. He still wrote material in that vein and was not interested in trying to make it in the rock field by slanting his material or performing style that way. Nonetheless, in his quiet way, Paxton continued to have an impact on at least some members of the post–folk boom generation. Besides that, many of his compositions had become classics in their own right and, over the years, artists of many different musical persuasions turned out their own versions of songs like "Bottle of Wine," "Morning Again," "Mr. Blue," and "The Last Thing on My Mind."

Tom spent many of his formative years in Oklahoma, a state laying claim to folk song legend Woody Guthrie, so it might be said he came by his love for that kind of music naturally. However, Paxton spent his first decade on the South Side of Chicago and was far more interested in athletics than music. His family moved to the small town of Bristol, Oklahoma, in 1948, but soon after they arrived his father died.

It was young Tom's first harsh exposure to the realities of life, though his mother managed to keep the family going in reasonable shape despite the loss.

In high school he spent more time in the drama department than music, though he started to learn guitar after an aunt gave him one when he was sixteen. He could play the instrument well by the time he entered the University of Oklahoma as a drama major, though he never was to come close to being a superior guitarist. After hearing a folk album by Ed McCurdy at a campus party, he began to work up his own repertoire of folk songs and later debuted as a folk performer in a campus variety show.

Still, he kept his eye on the stage, moving into summer stock after being graduated from college in 1959. He wasn't bad in that field, as indicated by the starring role he gained in *The Spoilers*. But his interest in music was increasing, so, after spending a six-month hitch in the Army, he decided to head for New York in 1960.

He arrived to find the Greenwich Village folk scene as active and interesting as he'd heard it would be. It was a heady time to be on hand, with such brash newcomers as Bob Dylan, Joan Baez, Phil Ochs, and dozens of others performing whenever and wherever they could and getting together at other times to compare material and talk about the music field. Looking back in 1977, he noted "The Village coffee houses were the dearest of blessings to a beginning performer, a place to be terrible and to learn from being terrible."

Paxton took advantage of it, working the small venues, often for no pay, with any money coming from passing the hat. His efforts impressed many of his peers and in a short time he felt confident enough of his abilities to audition for a replacement spot in the Chad Mitchell Trio. Milt Okun, the group's director, at first gave Tom the nod, then changed his mind. It was a bitter blow, but Okun kept in touch with Paxton, whose original songs—particularly one called "The Marvelous Toy"—had impressed him. He suggested to Tom that his forte was writing more than performing.

For a while, Paxton stressed entertaining

alone, working the U.S. coffee house circuit during 1961–62, usually accompanied by folksinger Gil Robbins. Starting in 1962, however, he turned out a growing list of new, often topical compositions. The quality of his work impressed many fellow artists, some of whom began incorporating Paxton songs in their repertoire. One such was The Weavers, who gave their version of his "Rambling Boy" in their 1963 Carnegie Hall concert.

Many of his songs of the first half of the 1960s were of the protest variety. He never gave up commenting on the shortcomings of society—his 1977 LP on Vanguard, *New Songs from the Briarpatch* examined such topics as capital punishment ("Bring Back the Chair"), the Nixon era ("Talking Watergate"), and the death of Chile's President Salvador Allende ("White Bones of Allende"). However, his approach to writing such material changed with time.

As he told Lorraine Alterman of *GO* (August 9, 1968), he thought the typical protest song missed the mark. "The main problem with the so-called protest songs is that the writers—and I include myself of a few years back—believed that it was enough to say what they felt was the truth. It was not important to say it well. That changed, at least for me. You must say what you think with the same skill that you would write a hit song with.

"There is a technique to the way I write, and that's relaxation. I'm learning how to sit down with a blank piece of paper and relax. For example, with the song 'Morning Again' I sat down with a blank piece of paper and nothing in my head but the phrase 'morning again.' The best hitters in baseball have all their concentration on hitting; they are relaxed."

As his catalogue of new material expanded, Tom was ready for an assault on the recording side of things. In 1964, Elektra signed him. (He had recorded some material earlier and an album of his stylings had come out on the small Gaslight Club label.) His debut LP on Elektra was issued in December 1964, and, if it wasn't a top-10 hit, it served to introduce him to a growing number of adherents around the country. Although the folk

movement was beginning to wane under the onslaught of the British rock invasion, it still was strong, particularly on college campuses, and Paxton was regarded as one of the finest artists in the field.

His stature already was on the rise in Europe when he visited England with his wife, Midge, in 1965 for a series of concerts. The English audiences took him to their hearts, and he was still attracting relatively large crowds for shows over there when only a minute segment of the U.S. music audience was aware of him in the late 1960s and throughout the 1970s. In the mid-1960s, though, he was active on the U.S. college and small-club scene and, before that period was over, he had appeared in those venues in all the states.

He continued to turn out a series of finely honed albums on Elektra as the 1960s went by, many new collector's items. Among them were *Ain't That News*, issued in December 1965, *Outward Bound* (11/66), *Morning Again*, *Things I Notice Now*, and a two-record set, *The Compleat Tom Paxton*. Among the songs that appeared in those releases were "The Man Who Built the Bridges," "What Did You Learn in School Today," "Brand New Baby," "The Willing Conscript," "Victoria Dines Alone," "Talking Vietnam," "Potluck Blues" (one of the most famous antiwar songs of the 1960s), "A Thousand Years" (a strong condemnation of neonazism), "What a Friend We Have in Hoover," and "Georgia on the Freeways."

In the early 1970s, he moved from Elektra to the Reprise label and turned out three albums, including *How Come the Sun* and *Peace Will Come*.

As the folk audience seemed to dwindle at home, Paxton spent more and more time abroad, where he remained a highly regarded troubadour. In the mid-1970s, he and his family settled down in England for a number of years. He enjoyed living there, but the lure of home eventually proved too strong and in early 1977 he and his family came back and settled in East Hampton on New York's Long Island.

As he said, "I've seen a good deal of the planet in the last seven or eight years and spent the better part of three or four of them living in England. I loved it, but it feels good to be back home again. In the last year," he noted in mid-1977, "I have been seriously rediscovering my own country. Everywhere I go, I meet people who remember the old songs and welcome the new ones." The first of the latter were presented on his debut LP on the Vanguard label, *New Songs from the Briarpatch*, issued in July 1977. The following year Vanguard issued another Paxton album, *Heroes*.

PAYCHECK, JOHNNY: *Singer, guitarist, songwriter. Born southern Ohio, May 31, 1941.*

In 1978, Johnny Paycheck's blockbuster single hit, "Take This Job and Shove It," certainly struck home to anyone who worked for wages. In a way, it symbolized much of Paycheck's career in previous years. Flirting with possible superstar status several times during the preceding decade and a half, Johnny seemed intent on destroying his chances through personal excesses that perhaps reflected deep-seated self-doubts about his goals and abilities.

Paycheck, who grew up in a rural area of southern Ohio, was attracted to country music from his boyhood, when he listened to country broadcasts. By his midteens, he had learned to play guitar and already was starting to write original songs, a talent that initially helped him stand out from the crowd of young country-music aspirants in the 1960s.

After playing in local clubs in Ohio, he began to expand his foothold in the field by working as a sideman with many country luminaries. In the late 1950s and early 1960s, he played bass guitar in the bands of Porter Wagoner, Faron Young, George Jones, and Ray Price. Meanwhile he was continuing to write new songs, which finally began to be picked up by an increasing number of country performers. More than a few charted tunes of the early 1960s bore the "written by J. Paycheck" legend. On some releases, Johnny's voice could be heard singing harmony. In fact, throughout the 1960s, he was asked to handle backing vocals for major artists whether or not he provided the song, because of the strong quality of his voice. Among those who em-

ployed his vocals to effect were Roger Miller, Ray Price, Faron Young, George Jones, Sheb Wooley, and Webb Pierce.

Despite that, no one tried to feature Paycheck until a record company artists & repertoire executive named Aubrey Mayhew happened to hear a demonstration recording Johnny made of one of his new songs. After Johnny's representative played it for Aubrey during the Country Music Association convention in November 1964, Mayhew sought Paycheck out and asked him to sign a management contract. A month later, Johnny's initial single was released, an original composition titled "Don't Start Countin' on Me." The record rose to upper country chart levels in early 1965 and was followed by an even more successful single, "The Girl They Talk About."

After that release began to pick up momentum, Mayhew arranged for Paycheck to join the package show headlined by George Jones and the Jones Boys. This time, instead of a backing musician, Paycheck was a featured performer. Between mid-1965 and mid-1966, that association brought Paycheck into live shows in all fifty states plus a twenty-day tour of Europe. Paycheck also worked two *Jimmy Dean Television Shows* with Jones and appeared on a number of other network programs as well. In October 1965, he turned out a third single, "A-11," that rose to the top 20.

Encouraged by Johnny's 1965 success, Mayhew and Paycheck set up their own record label the following year called Little Darlin' Records. One of his early releases on that label, "The Lovin' Machine," became a top-10 hit in 1966. However, even as major success seemed on the horizon, Paycheck was beginning to show signs of strain. Before the 1960s were over, incidents involving drugs and alcohol had resulted in his leaving the Jones show under a cloud during a Los Angeles engagement.

For a time, Paycheck's name was anathema to record company executives, and important engagements often were hard to come by. Epic Records' producer Billy Sherrill finally agreed to sign Johnny if he would reform. The two went into the studios in Nashville in the early 1970s, and, before long, Johnny had a new string of recordings riding high on the charts. Among those were "Song and Dance Man," a top-10 hit in early 1974, and "My Part of Forever," high on the lists in May. He continued to have releases on the charts the next few years, such as "I Don't Love Her Anymore" and "All American Man" (co-written with G. Adams) in 1975 and "Gone at Last" in early 1976, but things were beginning to turn sour again. Among other things, Johnny ran through all his earnings from his earlier efforts and was bankrupt financially and, to a considerable extent, emotionally.

However, he showed staying power. After hitting bottom for a time, he shook off his problems and persuaded Billy Sherrill he was ready for a sustained new effort. Once more they returned to the studios and, in a short time, Johnny was making greater inroads in the country market than ever before. In late summer his single of a song co-written with Sherrill, "11 Months and 29 days," made the top 10 and was followed in mid-1977 with the top-10 hit "I'm the Only Hell (Mama Ever Raised)." He bettered both those offerings with "Slide Off Your Satin Sheets," which made it to number one.

Then at the end of 1977, he achieved his greatest success with his single of David Allan Coe's composition "Take This Job and Shove It," which reached number one in the United States in early 1978. The song not only dominated the country roster for a time, it also rose high on national pop charts. Later in 1978, he had another top-10 single, "Me and the IRS," and at year's end, his single "Friend, Lover, Wife" (co-written with Billy Sherrill) was well inside the top 10.

During 1978, Paycheck became one of the most sought-after artists for live concerts and major TV shows. His TV appearances included The Midnight Special, Mike Douglas, Merv Griffin, and the Gong Show. Besides playing many of the traditional country spots, he also was featured in such pop- or rock-oriented locales as New York's Bottom Line, The Boarding House in San Francisco, and the Roxy in Los Angeles.

Paycheck was one of the five finalists for the 1978 Grammy in the Best Vocal Performance, Male, category. He didn't win at that time, but he sang "Take This Job" on the nationally televised 1979 Grammy Awards TV program. Even as he did that, he had new recordings moving rapidly up country charts, one being a duet with George Jones of Chuck Berry's old hit, "Maybellene." At the same time, two of his Epic albums were on the hit lists, Armed and Crazy and Johnny Paycheck's Greatest Hits, Volume II.

The 1980s began auspiciously for Johnny with the single "Drinkin' and Drivin' " moving toward the top 20. Later on, he had such 1980 charted singles as "Fifteen Beers," "When You're Ugly like Us" (duet with George Jones), and "In Memory of a Memory" (co-written by Johnny and R. Pate). In early 1981, he and George Jones had the top-20 single "You Better Move On," and a few months later he teamed with Merle Haggard for the chart single "I Can't Hold Myself in Line."

PEARL, MINNIE: Comedienne, singer. Born Centerville, Tennessee, October 25, 1912.

"Howdeee!" For decade after decade that high-pitched greeting meant only one thing to country fans—Cousin Minnie Pearl was about to convulse them with laughter. For years she was recognized as the "Queen of Country Comedy," and in the early 1980s she still reigned as the comedy star of the Grand Ole Opry. But she proved during her long and eventful career that her humor, "down home" though it might be in tone, was truly universal, equally laugh-provoking with urban as well as rural fans all over the world.

When she was born in Centerville, Tennessee, her parents gave her the name of Sarah Ophelia Colley. Although her home state long has been the hub of the country-music world, her upbringing certainly wasn't that of a farm girl. She was exposed to and enjoyed the classics, both literary and musical, and didn't pay too much attention to the country-music programs beginning to find their way onto southern radio stations. She told an interviewer, "Though my father used always to listen to the *Opry*, I didn't know too much about the singers until I began appearing on it. But once I started listening to them, I began to love the music. I've loved it ever since."

Actually, in her teens the pursuits that appealed most to young Sarah were teaching and the dramatic stage. Thus when she enrolled in fashionable Ward-Belmont College in Nashville in the late 1920s, she majored in stage technique. The art form that interested her most was dancing, at which she demonstrated considerable talent.

After completing college, Colley went on to teach dancing for two years. In 1934, she joined the Wayne P. Sewall Producing Company of Atlanta as a dramatic coach. For the next five years she toured throughout the southern states directing amateur plays, usually presented in local schools. During her travels, her natural flair for comedy began to assert itself as an accidental byproduct of her work.

Sarah recalled how that occurred for Bob Hilburn of the *Los Angeles Times*. "Minnie Pearl was born during the Depression. I had a job traveling from town to small town in the South putting on plays for church and civic groups. It was a big thing at the time. There were hundreds of people doing that kind of work.

"To help publicize the show in each town, I would appear before the Lion's Club and other groups. In return for them letting me announce my show, I'd do a couple of minutes entertainment for them. I'd do an interpretation of a country girl, Minnie Pearl."

As she went from town to town, she mentally stored more material based on insights and impressions gained along the way. It was to provide the basis for extended routines later on. Some of the material went back to her home-town memories. For instance, as a child Sarah recalled walking three miles along the railroad tracks to a switching station called Grinder's Switch. Using that as her

"home" instead of Centerville, she realized, had much more comic effect.

It actually was a tragic event that paved the way for making Minnie Pearl Colley's constant alter ego. After her father died in the late 1930s, she had to return to Centerville to take care of her mother. At first her main interest was teaching dramatics to local children. When she was asked to entertain at a local bankers' convention she revived Minnie Pearl. It went over so well that someone suggested it might go well on the *Grand Ole Opry*. She auditioned for *Opry* officials in Nashville and got mixed reactions. Everyone agreed it was funny, but some worried the audience might consider it a put-down of rural life. A compromise was reached. She was given a chance to perform, but well after the major artists had been on, at 11:05 on Saturday night. She was paid ten dollars for the effort. The fears quickly proved groundless: the audience loved her and fan mail began to arrive.

In 1940 Sarah was asked to become an *Opry* cast regular. Forty years later she remained one of the brightest stars in the *Opry* diadem. Her homespun humor and unique costume were as much a part of the American tradition by the 1960s and 1970s as Charlie Chaplin's tramp outfit.

Discussing Minnie, the well-educated Colley said, "Minnie Pearl is uncomplicated. She's apple pie and clothes dried in the sun and the smell of fresh bread baking. I don't think people think of her so much as a show business act as a friend. When I'm on stage, I'm just plain Minnie Pearl wearing my battered old straw hat and battered shoes. The price tag on my hat seems to be symbolic of all human frailty. There's old Minnie Pearl standing on stage in her best dress, telling everyone how proud she is to be there and she's forgotten to take the $1.98 price tag off her hat."

From the 1940s to the 1980s, she played in theaters, on concert stages, and at county and state fairs across the United States and Canada. On several occasions she toured a number of overseas countries. Colley was featured again and again on major variety and talk shows on all three networks and major syndicated series, ranging from *The Today Show* and *Tonight* to *Dinah!* and *Hee Haw*. Over the years she was just as likely to turn up on a pop music program as a country one, with equally ecstatic response from theater crowds and TV viewers. In 1957, her national reputation was recognized by Ralph Edwards, who selected her as the subject for one of his most popular NBC-TV *This Is Your Life* segments. Other honors came Sarah's way over the decades, including selection as Nashville's "Woman of the Year" in 1965 and nomination for the Country Music Hall of Fame in 1968. Although she didn't receive the required number of votes for election at that time, her name was resubmitted by CMA members regularly until the total was achieved in 1975.

In 1967, Colley's outside interests included a new food franchise organization called "Minnie Pearl's Chicken System, Inc." Unfortunately, though it flourished for a few years, in the end competition from the other chicken franchise outlets was too much.

Colley's recording efforts over the years were not as widespread, naturally, as those of singers and instrumentalists. Still, she was represented by a number of LPs on various labels. Among her albums were several on RCA, including *Monologue* and *How to Catch a Man*. She had one on Everest Records titled *Minnie Pearl*, and Nashville Records issued *Lookin' for a Feller*. Some of her best offerings came out on Starday in the 1960s, including the albums, *Cousin Minnie Pearl, America's Beloved,* and *Country Music Story.* One of her Starday singles, "Giddyup—Go Answer" made it into the country top 10 in 1966.

In 1975, a bronze plaque in her honor was placed in the Country Music Hall of Fame in Nashville. The tribute read, in part, "Humor is the least recorded, but certainly one of the most important aspects of live country music. No one exemplified the values of pure country comedy more than Minnie Pearl. . . . Her trademarks, the dime store hat and shrill 'How-dee! I'm just so proud to be here,'

made her the first country humorist to be known and loved worldwide."

PEDERSEN, HERB: *Singer, banjoist, songwriter. Born Berkeley, California, April 27, 1944.*

One of the most highly regarded banjo players in the 1960s and 1970s, Herb Pedersen performed with many of the best-known artists in folk, country, and rock. His name can be found on best-selling albums of many of those artists, including work as banjoist or backing vocalist on many of Linda Ronstadt's classic collections. In addition to that, he was a member of several major groups and also has turned out several solo albums.

Born and raised in Berkeley, California, he became interested in folk music during his high school years and began playing bluegrass music in 1962. His skills on banjo matured rapidly; by the mid-1960s his name already was becoming known in the music field. During those years he lived part of the time in Nashville, Tennessee. Recalling those times, he wrote, "I played with Vern and Ray from 1964–67. They recorded for Starday Records. For a time in 1967, I took the place of Earl Scruggs with the Flatt & Scruggs group. I also did several record dates for RCA in Nashville that year."

In 1967, he joined one of the best-known bluegrass groups (after Flatt & Scruggs), the Dillards. He remained a member of that group from then through 1971 and helped record such albums as *Copperfields* and *Wheat Straw Suite*. He also toured widely with the band and performed in major cities all over the United States and in a number of other countries. ("I have toured," he noted, "from Australia to Egypt.")

By the early 1970s, home for Pedersen was Los Angeles, where he soon was established as one of the top session musicians. He began recording in support of Linda Ronstadt in 1971 and contributed to many of her later albums, including the 1975 release *Prisoner in Disguise* and 1976 *Hasten Down the Wind*. Besides his work with Ronstadt, he recorded with Buck

Owens, Emmylou Harris, Kris Kristofferson, Rita Coolidge, Johnny Rivers, Eric Andersen, Earl Scruggs Revue, John Denver, and many others.

During the mid-1970s, Herb signed a recording contract with Columbia Records, which issued two solo albums of his, one in 1976 and the second in 1977. At the end of the 1970s, his efforts included touring with John Denver and acting as producer for the Dillards' 1979 LP release.

Over the years, he wrote a number of songs that were recorded by, among others, John Denver, Johnny Rivers, the Seldom Scene, and the Tony Rice Quintet. In late 1979, he wrote, "I've had a tune selected that I wrote to be included on the UNICEF 'Year of the Child' album to be released soon."

PEER, RALPH SYLVESTER: *Music publisher, record company executive, producer. Born Kansas City, Missouri, May 22, 1892; died Hollywood, California, January 19, 1960.*

He wasn't a singer, a picker, or a songwriter, but Ralph Peer had an immense effect on the development of country music. As a music industry executive, initially for other firms and later for his own publishing complex, he discovered many of the pivotal figures in modern country music. In particular, he contributed greatly to the genre by discovering Jimmie Rodgers and the Carter Family and helping to shape and promote their careers. In addition, his field recordings of many rural artists in the 1920s and 1930s helped in the preservation of an important part of the nation's folk heritage.

He was born in Kansas City, Missouri, the son of Abram Peer, a phonograph dealer. The exposure to many kinds of music in his father's shop stimulated Ralph's interest in the music industry. When he graduated from high school, he enrolled in Northwestern University, but after two years left to work in the recording field.

From 1911 to 1919 he was employed by the Columbia Phonograph Company of Kansas City, working up to assistant manager. He then accepted an offer from General Pittsburgh Corp., where he served as production director until 1927. His move east also resulted in a position as recording director of Okeh Records starting in 1920. A major pioneer in what then were called "race" records, he cut historic sessions with Mamie Smith and other blues artists.

In 1926, Okeh was absorbed by American Recording Company, which later became Columbia Records, Inc. At this point, Peer switched his recording activities to the Victor Talking Machine Company. For Victor, he covered the South, sometimes conducting recording activities in a sound truck or in hotel public rooms. He made a point of seeking performers of rural and mountain music, an idiom for which he coined the word "hillbilly." Many of the artists who responded to some of his newspaper ads came to him from the medicine and tent show circuit. He discovered many now-legendary names in country and folk music during the many auditions he held, but the most famous results occurred during a series held in Bristol, a city on the border of Tennessee and Virginia, the first week in August 1927.

During that week, he made the first recordings of two soon-to-be-famous acts, Jimmie Rodgers and the Original Carter Family. (He came close to missing Rodgers, whose backing band, the Tenneva Ramblers, left him and persuaded Peer to record them as a separate act.) He paid Rodgers twenty dollars for two sides, a lullaby titled "Sleep, Baby Sleep" and a ballad, "Soldier's Sweetheart."

Although the going rate then was ten dollars a side plus some kind of royalty arrangement, the Carters claimed they received a bigger payment for their debut recordings (which resulted in their debut single, "Wandering Boy" backed with "Poor Orphan Child"). Mother Maybelle Carter told Bill Williams in an interview taped for the Country Music Foundation Library, "I know we made six records and we got fifty dollars a side making them, and we got our royalty of about one-and-a-half percent—hardly one and a half percent."

As indications of audience interest appeared after the debut singles came out, Peer arranged for further sessions at Victor's main studios in New Jersey, beginning with one for Rodgers in November 1927 and for the Carters in May 1928. Those sessions provided some of their first big hits and also spurred Peer to form a new publishing firm. With Victor participating, he formed Southern Music Publishing Company in 1928. Forming a keystone for the growth of the firm were Jimmie Rodgers' compositions, which were still providing income for the company over fifty years later, though by that time they accounted for only a small fraction of Peer-Southern International's multimillion dollar a year business. Victor stayed in the operation until 1932, after which Peer became president and sole owner. He and his organization popularized and promoted country music, one of the first major concerns to concentrate on the field. After his death, his successors continued to expand and diversify Peer-Southern's activities in the entertainment area.

Many of the early songs published by the company became classics in both folk and country. Examples included "Roll Along Kentucky Moon" and "I'm Thinking Tonight of My Blue Eyes" (1929); "Mule Skinner Blues" (1931); and "Wabash Cannonball" (1933). Over the decades that followed, thousands of other major titles were added, including such standards as Jimmie Davis' "You Are My Sunshine" in 1942.

Never becoming complacent, Peer always sought new avenues to widen the scope of his operation. He is credited with setting up the first European offices for country music. By the late 1950s, he had opened offices in England, France, Australia, Mexico, South Africa, Japan, and the Central and South American countries. His Southern Music was an ASCAP affiliate from its inception. In 1940, he formed Peer International, one of the first major members of the BMI organization. By the start of the 1980s, Peer International still had the largest publisher catalogue affiliated with BMI.

As his music business flourished, Peer managed to find time for many other interests. He became an authority on international copyright law and set many industry guideposts in the field of performance rights. He also gained recognition in the horticultural field, receiving the Veitch Gold Medal from the Royal Horticultural Society of London, England, for his research on the camellia plant. In the years after World War II, he also showed an increasing interest in science, resulting in the collection of an impressive library of science books, with particular emphasis on nuclear subjects.

After his death in California in 1960, his widow, Monique Hildborg Thera Alexandra (whom he married in 1940), carried on the Peer tradition of extending the worldwide horizons of country music. Her support contributed to the growth of the Country Music Association as a strong industry organization devoted to achieving greater recognition for the country-music field as a whole. She also was instrumental in having former CMA board chairman Roy Horton assigned to help promote international interest in country music, a program that in time brought sizable followings for country artists and music in many parts of the world during the 1970s.

Thus, it came as no surprise when Peer's son, Ralph Peer, Jr., decided to follow in his father's footsteps. Peer, Jr. has served efficiently in several offices for CMA and in the interests of country music generally both here and abroad. He is already regarded as a worthy successor to his parents' legacy, and he is expected to maintain and expand their broad horizons in the industry.

PERKINS, CARL: *Singer, songwriter, guitarist, band leader. Born Jackson, Tennessee, April 9, 1932.*

Born the same year as his long-time close friend, Johnny Cash, Carl Perkins' career tended to parallel that of Cash's over the years. Both musicians started as country performers, picked up on rock, and became nationally known in that field in the mid-1950s and then moved back into the country market again in the 1960s and 1970s. Both also fought hard battles against drugs and other dangerous habits and won out. But in terms of level of artistic success, there's no doubt that Cash had a considerable edge.

Perkins' contributions to both progressive country and country-rock, however, should not be downplayed—they were considerable. His first and perhaps biggest accomplishment was his recording of his composition "Blue Suede Shoes" at Sam Phillips Sun Studios in Memphis in late 1955. He was part of the wave of young country-bred artists who helped propel rock to its dominant status with material recorded by Sun, a group that included Jerry Lee Lewis, Cash, Elvis Presley, and Roy Orbison. In early 1956, Carl's single of "Blue Suede Shoes" topped all three charts—pop, country, and R&B.

Preparations were made for him to receive his gold record for the song on the *Perry Como* show. Perkins left a concert in Norfolk, Virginia, toward the end of March 1956, to drive to New York for the event. Early the next morning, he was almost killed in an accident outside of Wilmington, Delaware. He stayed in bed for a year recuperating, during which time Elvis Presley's hit version of "Blue Suede Shoes" eclipsed Carl's. Presley sent a note to Carl after his Ed Sullivan debut suggesting that Perkins might have been the superstar if the accident hadn't occurred.

Although Carl had some minor rock hits in the late 1950s, such as "Your True Love" on Sun and "Pink Pedal Pushers" and "Pointed Toe Shoes" on Columbia, his career languished after the accident. At one point in 1963, he had about decided to quit show buisiness when his wife persuaded him to take an offer to tour England with Chuck Berry. While there, the Beatles gave a party in his honor and later demonstrated their esteem for him by recording three of his compositions, "Match Box," "Honey Don't," and "Everybody's Trying to Be My Baby."

Still, back home for a while, Carl's mental state went from bad to worse. Then, in the mid-1960s, as did Johnny Cash, Carl got his thinking straightened out and began to rebuild his life and career. In 1965, a bid from Cash for Perkins to join him for a two-day concert appearance in the South

led to a decade of association. "We got there and John had me come up and do a couple of songs. That two-day tour lasted ten years. That's how long I played with John." During Cash's network TV show from 1969–1971, Perkins not only did backing work but generally had a solo spot during each show.

The TV exposure brought a new recording contract from Columbia that led to several LPs, including *Greatest Hits* and *On Top* on 1969 and *Boppin' the Blues* in 1970. Concentrating on the country field, Carl had several songs on the charts in the early 1970s, such as "Me Without You" in 1971 and "Cotton Top" and "High on Love" in 1972.

In 1976, Carl left the Cash tour to organize a new band of his own featuring his sons, Stan on drums and Greg on bass guitar. They were still part of the tour group when Perkins' debut album on a new label, Jet Records, came out in the fall of 1978. Called *Ol' Blue Suede's Back*, it included country-rock versions of several Perkins songs, including the title track, plus such other familiar early rock numbers as "Maybellene," "Whole Lotta Shakin'," "Rock Around the Clock," and the Arthur Crudup Song that started Elvis on the road to superstardom, "That's All Right, Mama." He remained active and was still performing, in both concerts and clubs, to warm notices in 1981–82

PETER, PAUL & MARY: *Vocal and instrumental group, songwriters. Peter Yarrow, born New York, New York, May 31, 1938; Noel Paul Stookey, born Baltimore, Maryland, November 30, 1937; Mary Ellin Travers, born Louisville, Kentucky, November 7, 1937.*

In the mid-1960s, when revived rock 'n' roll ended the short-lived dominance of folk music, only a handful of the most talented performers managed to retain a hold on a large following. Peter, Paul & Mary, who came together in Greenwich Village at the start of the 1960s during the folk music ferment, remained headliners when folk music was no longer the vogue without moving markedly from their folk roots. Even more unusual, after the trio had been apart for a decade, they demonstrated that they still had major drawing power with their reunion concert tour of seventeen major U.S. cities in 1978.

Paul Stookey's early history seemed to make him an unlikely candidate for the Village scene. He was an early fan of rock 'n' roll as a teenager growing up in Baltimore. Later, he used his skills with electric guitar to work in a rock band, which helped pay his tuition at Michigan State University. He added to his earnings by working as an emcee in local clubs.

After receiving his degree, he moved to Pennsylvania with his family and worked at a number of odd jobs before deciding he wanted to try his hand as an entertainer again. After moving to New York, he went through months of near starvation trying to find show business jobs. It got to the point that he took a position in a chemical company to keep going while he sought work as a stand-up comic in his spare time. His persistence paid off, though, and he began to make a name for himself as a comic in Greenwich Village clubs by the end of 1960.

Mary Travers' family originally came from Louisville, Kentucky, but moved to New York when she was still a small child. She became interested in folk music, and, while still in elementary school, took lessons in the genre from teachers like Charity Bailey. In high school, in the early 1950s, she followed that interest still further, singing with various teenage folk groups. During those years, as a member of a group called the Songswappers, she made two appearances at Carnegie Hall.

Still, for a time it looked as though she too might have to find other routes to a professional entertaining career. One of her first efforts after finishing school was to get a job in the chorus of a Broadway show. Unfortunately, it flopped and she worked at various literary and advertising jobs during the day while trying to increase contacts in the music field nights and weekends. Among the people she became acquainted with were Stookey and a one-time music teacher and folksinger named Milt Okun. In the early 1960s, Okun was turning his attention away from working as an entertainer himself in favor

of handling management and production of the new flood of young talent he could see around him in New York.

Okun took an interest in Mary and Paul and encouraged them to form a team, which they started doing in 1961. He felt the act would work better if it expanded to a trio, which helped open the door for Peter Yarrow.

Yarrow, born and raised in New York, learned to play violin and guitar in his youth and was adept at both instruments by the time he enrolled at Cornell University in upstate New York. His major was psychology, but he enjoyed music and played in school functions and in local clubs. After getting his degree, he considered making psychology his career, but when he returned to New York, he couldn't avoid the lure of the folk music boom. He began working with various folk groups and attracted the attention of local folk fans. In May 1960, he was chosen as a cast member for a CBS special, "Folk Sound, U.S.A." That exposure, in turn, gained him a spot in the 1960 Newport Folk Festival, which reaffirmed his decision to make folk music his main occupation.

His reputation had increased still more by the time he joined forces with Paul and Mary in 1961. With Okun providing advice and assistance, things moved forward rapidly. The trio made their performing debut in New York in 1962 and in a matter of months were ranked among the most promising newcomers on the Manhattan folk scene. They also signed a recording contract with Warner Brothers, which was still their recording firm at the end of the 1970s. By May 1962, their debut LP was out; titled *Peter, Paul & Mary*, it proved one of the top debut releases of the year. Before 1962 was over, the trio had its first hit singles, "Lemon Tree" and "If I Had a Hammer."

If 1962 was successful, 1963 proved better. Their second LP, *Peter, Paul & Mary—Moving*, issued in March 1963, was a chart hit as was their next album, *Peter, Paul & Mary—In the Wind*, released in December 1963. The group had four major singles hits that year: "Puff (the Magic Dragon)," written by Yarrow; "Stew Ball"; and two Dylan songs, "Blowin' in the Wind" and "Don't Think Twice It's Alright." Their version of "Blowin' in the Wind" won the Grammy Award for the Best Folk Music Record of the year. By the end of 1963, Peter, Paul & Mary were one of the most sought-after acts in music and were featured on major TV shows and in concerts all over the United States and Canada. The group also headlined many major folk festivals (and even some rock festivals) through most of the 1960s, including a number of appearances at the Newport Folk Festival. During those years, some of the songs in their repertoire were written by one or more of them (sometimes all three, sometimes in collaboration with Okun), including such tunes as "On a Desert Island," "A-Soulin'," "Talking Candy Bar Blues," "Early in the Morning," and "It's Raining."

As the 1960s went by, the group kept adding to its credits both as stage attractions and recording artists. In 1964, they had the hit single "Go Tell It on the Mountain." In 1965, their album releases included *Peter, Paul and Mary in Concert*, issued in March, *A Song Will Rise*, released in May, and, in December, *See What Tomorrow Brings*. That year, they helped bring a very talented Canadian songwriter to the United States' attention with their single of Gordon Lightfoot's "Early Morning Rain." Later in the decade they were to do a similar favor for another then unknown troubadour with their gold-record version of John Denver's "Leavin' on a Jet Plane."

Their seventh LP release on Warner's was *Peter, Paul and Mary Album*, issued in October 1966. That year they were represented on singles charts with "The Cruel War." One of their best collections came out the following year with *Album 1700*, released in September 1967. They also had two singles that made national charts in 1967, "I Dig Rock 'n' Roll Music" and "Great Mandella." They followed with an album a year the next three years: *Late Again*, issued August 1968; *Peter, Paul and Mommy*, issued May 1969; and *The Best of Peter, Paul and Mary, Ten Years Together*, issued May 1970. They placed two more singles on hit lists in 1969, "Too Much of Nothing" and "Day Is Done."

By then the group was on the way to closing out that phase of its history. Part of the reason for the breakup was the natural desire of artists to strike out in new creative directions. But perhaps having the greater impact was a court case involving Yarrow in which he was charged with having illicit relations with a minor.

Stardom's pressures were partly to blame. Other members also could feel that impact. Paul Stookey, for instance, had become aware of a loss of contact with his family and decided that a return to a closer involvement with Christianity might help. That experience in 1968, he said, opened his eyes. "After the discovery that I needed God in my life, it became obvious that I had allowed a great distance to develop between me and my family, but since my body moves about two years after my mind, it wasn't until 1970 that I spoke about retiring."

Paul moved his family to several rural areas, eventually settling in Maine in 1973. As of 1982, his family included a seventeen-year-old daughter, Elizabeth, and twin daughters Anna and Kate, ten. His activities after leaving the trio included writing three albums on biblical parables and work on recording/animation projects in his own studio in Maine.

He also wrote a song in honor of Peter's marriage to Marybeth McCarthy, a niece of Senator Eugene McCarthy, titled "Wedding Song (There Is Love)." Yarrow eventually settled in Malibu, California, where, as of 1982, his children were a eleven-year-old daughter, Elizabeth, and a son, Christopher, nine. Throughout the 1970s, he remained active in the folk movement, appearing on folk shows on local California stations and taking part in various concerts and festivals. He also was a political activist in humanist causes and supported projects important to what he felt was the well-being of his home community.

Mary also continued to be active in various ways as the 1970s went by. At times she had her own music and interview program on Radio Pacifica in Los Angeles (KPFK). She also performed in many college concerts, did some nightclub work, and was featured on occasion with symphony orchestras, including those of Denver and Baltimore. Besides that, she lectured in colleges on the subject of "Society and Its Effect on Music." She also devoted much of her time to raising her two daughters, Erika (twenty-two in 1982) and Alicia (sixteen in 1982).

Reflecting on the way their lives had developed for a biographical article in connection with their 1978 recombination, Mary said, "We are the children of Pete Seeger. We came from the folk tradition in a contemporary form where there was a concern that idealism be a part of your music and the music a part of your life. If Paul explores it vis-à-vis a political activist position, it is all the same. It's a concern, wanting your music not to be schizophrenic. So the music becomes an extension of your caring and your soul—there's no schism between what you can do on stage and who you are. What we're trying for is a kind of health—and that's what we were always trying for."

The trio's decision to get together once more resulted in the September 1978 album *Reunion*. The songs included Dylan's "Forever Young," Margie Adams' "The Unicorn Song," Billy Joel's "Summer Highland Falls," and two new numbers cowritten by Yarrow with Barry Mann and Cynthia Weil, "Sweet Survivor" and "Like the First Time."

PHILIPS, STU: *Singer, guitarist, songwriter. Born Calgary, Alberta, Canada, January 19, 1933.*

By and large, musically speaking there really has been no border between the United States and Canada. Almost all the major American pop music forms found favor with large numbers of Canadians, which, to some extent, provided a proving ground for home-grown talent. In folk and country & western, for its relatively small population Canada has provided a sizable number of excellent artists, including Gordon Lightfoot, Hank Snow, and Stu Philips.

Stu grew up in the plains area of Canada. His home town was Calgary, though he spent some of his early years on a farm

near that city. His interest in country music began at an early age. As a child he tuned a crystal radio set to catch the sometimes static-plagued radio waves from far-off Nashville so he could listen to *Grand Ole Opry* broadcasts. As he grew older, the family radio took a turn for the better, but in both cases he was thrilled to hear the stylings of artists like Roy Acuff and Flatt & Scruggs in the early days and, as the years went by, Hank Williams, Chet Atkins, and George Jones.

From listening to both the *Opry* and local programs of C&W material, Stu taught himself to play guitar before he was in his teens. When he was thirteen, his guitar work impressed a friend's guitar teacher so much that he suggested that Stu enter a guitar contest. With his own version of Gene Autry's theme "Back in the Saddle Again," young Stu came in first and received a $200 prize.

During his teens, Stu spent more and more time polishing his playing and singing abilities. He assembled his own country band and played at local events. He also sought part-time jobs in the radio field and, after finishing school, continued to seek work in the field. From the late 1940s to the early 1950s, his radio credits, at one time or another, included working as announcer, producer, engineer, and disc jockey. After serving what amounted to an extensive apprenticeship, he began to gain an array of credits as a radio personality. For a while he did an early morning live country show called *Stu at Breakfast*. Later he hosted a folk-country radio show and also hosted such programs as an all-Saturday live event called *Town & Country* and a Friday show called *Cowtown Jamboree*.

His career continued to flourish throughout the 1950s from his radio and TV efforts and from work with a country-music show that appeared at fairs, rodeos, and in concert halls throughout Canada. At rodeos, Philips, who had learned to ride as a boy, led the opening parade astride his horse in the tradition of Autry and Roy Rogers. During the late 1950s and early 1960s his activities included a Canadian Broadcast System radio show called *Travelin' Balladeer* and a fifteen-minute network program, *The Outrider*. In the early 1960s he moved up to the leading role in the major Saturday night CBC program *Red River Jamboree*. He remained with the program for four and a half years before deciding to try to make his mark in the main arena of C&W in the United States. By then he already was a major recording artist in his homeland with many chart hits, including the single "Squaws Along the Yukon" and the LP *Echoes of the Canadian Foothills*.

As the mid-1960s approached, Philips was one of the biggest attractions on the Canadian country-music circuit and was also beginning to gain attention from U.S. record companies. Capitol Records was one of the first to issue some of his material, including *Stu Philips Feels like Singin'*, released in August 1965. During that period, Stu was beginning to guest on the *Grand Ole Opry*, and his career picked up even more when he signed with RCA Records, which released his debut LP, *Singin'*, in October 1966 and followed up with *Stu Philips* in April 1967. Producer for both of those efforts was Chet Atkins. By then Stu had moved his residence to Nashville, which put him in good position to realize his youthful dream of being a regular on the *Grand Ole Opry*. That goal finally came to pass on June 1, 1967.

In the late 1960s, Philips placed a number of singles on country charts, including such western-oriented songs as "The Great El Tigre" and "Bracers." Although he had been writing songs for some years, none of his own material provided him with chart success through the 1960s. The closest to doing that was his song "Rangeland," which became the theme for a western movie.

In the 1970s, Stu continued to be featured on the *Grand Ole Opry* and as the star of his own live show. In the mid-1970s he recorded on London Records, switching to the Paragon label later in the decade.

PIERCE, WEBB: *Singer, guitarist, songwriter. Born near West Monroe, Louisiana, August 8, 1926.*

The name Webb Pierce strikes a responsive chord with Louisianans. Like former governor Jimmie Davis, he is considered as great a state asset as its industry or natural resources.

Born and raised in Louisiana, Webb achieved national fame in country music in his home state before moving on to the *Grand Ole Opry*. Brought up in a rural area, Webb could play excellent guitar in his teens. As he won notice for performing in local events, he gained his first radio job on station KMLB in Monroe. Encouraged by his reception, he moved on to Shreveport in the late 1940s to try to gain a wider audience. However, for a while he made little progress and had to earn his living as a salesperson for Sears, Roebuck. He continued to pick up performing jobs in his spare time and finally won the attention of Horace Logan, program director of station KWKH in Shreveport, sponsor of the new *Louisiana Hayride* show.

Pierce joined the cast, and before long was one of the featured performers. In the early 1950s, his band included many performers who went on to greatness on their own, including Faron Young, Goldie Hill, Jimmy Day, Tommy Hill, and Floyd Cramer. He began to achieve a wider reputation with his first records on the Four Star label. Some of the songs that made the charts were his own compositions.

In 1952, after signing with Decca, Pierce's name began to appear on the top rungs of the hit charts. He scored with two top-10 recordings of his own compositions, "That Heart Belongs to Me" and "Wondering," and had a number-one-ranked record in "Back Street Affair." In 1953, he co-wrote the hit "Last Waltz" with M. Freeman, had such other hits as "I'll Go on Alone," "I'm Walking the Dog," and "That's Me Without You," and two number-one-ranked hits, "It's Been So Long" and "There Stands the Glass." In 1952–53 he received the first of many awards, *Ranch and Farm* magazine's citation as Number-One Folk Singer and the Juke Box Operators award as Number-One Singer of 1953.

Along with his close friend Red Sovine, Webb moved to Nashville as an *Opry* regular. The hits continued to pour forth in 1954, such as the number-one-ranked "Slowly" (written with T. Hill), number-

Willie Nelson and Dolly Parton, Country Music Association Awards, 1979

Johnny Paycheck

Peter, Paul & Mary (mid-1960s)

Carl Perkins

Minnie Pearl

Elvis Presley (early 1960s)

Elvis Presley

Elvis Presley's gold Cadillac (with some of his gold record awards installed in interior panels) on display at the Country Music Hall of Fame. Prior to being placed there, it was stored for a number of years in Grelun Landon's garage in Thousand Oaks, California

Charley Pride and RCA Records symbol, "Nipper"

John Prine

one-ranked "More and More," and top-10 "Even Tho" (written with W. Jones and C. Peeples), "Sparkling Brown Eyes," and "You're Not Mine Anymore" (written with the Wilburn Brothers). In 1955, Webb had three number-one songs, "In the Jailhouse Now," "Love, Love, Love," and "I Don't Care," the last co-written with Cindy Walker. In 1956, he teamed with Red Sovine in two hit duets, "Why, Baby, Why" and "Little Rosa." He also hit with "Any Old Time" and "Teenage Boogie," both original compositions. In the late 1950s, he had such top-10 hits as "Bye Bye Love," "Holiday for Love" (coauthored with Wayne Walker and A. R. Peddy), "Honky Tonk Song," "I'm Tired" (1957); "Falling Back to You," "Tupelo County Jail" (written with Mel Tillis) (1958); and "A Thousand Miles Ago" (written with Mel Tillis) (1959).

By the start of the 1960s, Pierce had toured throughout the United States and Canada and guest-starred on such other network shows as Red Foley's *Jubilee U.S.A.* His successes of the 1960s included "Fallen Angel," "No Love Have I" (1960), "Let Forgiveness In," "Walking the Streets," "How Do You Talk to a Baby" (written with Wayne Walker), "Sweet Lips" (written with Wayne Walker and Davy Tubb) (1961); "All My Love," "Take Time," "Crazy Wild Desire" (written with Mel Tillis) (1962); "Sands of Gold" (written with Cliff Parman and Hal Eddy), "Those Wonderful Years" (written with Don Schroeder) (1963); and "Memory Number One" (1964). He hit the charts again in 1968 with the single "Luziana."

Through the mid-1960s, Pierce had compiled one of the best album sales totals of any popular music performer. His LPs on Decca included *Webb Pierce; Wondering Boy; Webb!* and *Just Imagination* (1958); *Bound for the Kingdom, Webb Pierce* (1959); *Webb with a Beat, Walking the Streets* (1960); *Golden Favorites, Fallen Angel* (1961); *Hideaway Heart, Cross Country* (1962); *I've Got a New Heartache, Bow Thy Head* (1963); *Sands of Gold, Webb Pierce Story* (two LP records) (1964); *Memory Number One, Country Music Time* (1965); *Sweet Memories, Webb Pierce Choice*

(1966); *Where'd Ya Stay* (1967); *Merry-Go-Round World, Road Show* (late 1960s-early 1970s).

Pierce remained on Decca and its successor, MCA records, into the mid-1970s. By 1977, he had moved to the Plantation Records roster.

PILLOW, RAY: *Singer, guitarist, songwriter. Born Lynchburg, Virginia, July 4, circa 1940.*

A major name in country music in the late 1960s, Ray Pillow had to endure a series of relatively disappointing years the following decade. At the end of the 1970s, however, it appeared as though his career might, in effect, be "born again."

Pillow was born and raised in Virginia. He had a fine voice, which he employed for both pop music and country songs while attending high school and during his early college years in Virginia. However, he still wasn't certain about his lifetime vocation when he enlisted in the Navy for a four-year hitch in the late 1950s before completing his college work. Those service years seemed to hone his interest in music—country in particular, though he didn't go all out in that direction until earning his degree in the early 1960s.

One of his first attempts, after graduation, was to go to Nashville to compete in the National Pet Milk Talent Contest. It proved a losing effort and he returned home, a bit downcast but not pessimistic. He continued to develop his vocal skills and also spent some time writing original material. Before long he was getting work in local clubs in his home state and doing some TV and radio work. He found a manager, Joe Taylor, who soon was playing some of Ray's demonstration tapes for major record company executives. This led to a contract with Capitol in 1964.

Meanwhile Ray was gaining more and more exposure from in-person work and TV assignments. He was signed to appear on TV and radio shows sponsored by Martha White Flour and also tour with Martha White road shows. His performances impressed other industry people and he soon was among the guests on such programs as the *Porter Wagoner Show, Wil-*

burn Brothers Show, Bobby Lord Show, American Swing-Around, and NBC's Swingin' Country. As his name and voice became familiar to the country-music public, his singles began to appear on national hit lists. Among his chartmakers of the period were "Left Out," "Take Your Hands Off My Heart," and "Thank You Ma'am."

His first album, Presenting Ray Pillow, was issued by Capitol in December 1965. It was the forerunner to one of his biggest years ever. In 1966, he was teamed by Capitol with female star Jean Shepard and the result was a top-10 hit, "I'll Take the Dog." They also collaborated on a hit album of that title and another singles hit, "Mr. Do-It-Yourself." During 1966, Pillow was asked to become a cast regular on the Grand Ole Opry. He was a featured artist on that show in July 1967 when his next solo album, Even When It's Bad, was released. Industry surveys underscored his status at the time; polls run by Billboard and Cash Box magazines recognized him as "Most Promising Male Artist of 1966."

Ray remained a popular member of the Opry throughout the 1970s, though he wasn't able to develop much momentum as far as new recordings were concerned. He tried a variety of different record company associations during the decade, which resulted in some songs that made lower-chart levels, but wasn't able to add any new top-10 hits to his catalogue. At the end of the 1970s, though, several developments made the outlook seem more optimistic; as he said in 1979, "I have a whole new burst of energy and enthusiasm." One of those was an important acting role in a film called The Disc Jockey, released in mid-1979. (He had some earlier film credits, including a mid-1960s film, Country Boy.) He played the part of a top music star named Jerry Drake. He also signed a new recording contract in 1978 with MCA Records. His first singles releases included several songs he co-wrote with Larry McFadden, his first efforts at songwriting in many years.

In the early 1980s, Pillow still was a regular on the Grand Ole Opry, as he had been for many years. In 1981 First Generation Records announced that an album of Ray's vocals would be part of the nine-volume Stars of the Grand Ole Opry series.

PLACE, MARY KAY: Singer, songwriter, scriptwriter, actress. Born Tulsa, Oklahoma.

One of the most dynamic newcomers to the country-music scene in the mid-1970s, attractive, talented Mary Kay Place could well have become a major favorite before the decade was out were it not for her multifaceted abilities. Not only was she a fine singer, she also was an excellent actress and a skilled writer of stories and scripts, capabilities that brought a rush of assignments from the movie and TV fields.

She was exposed to both urban and country influences in her early years. She grew up in Tulsa, but spent summers with her grandparents in Rule and Port Arthur, Texas. Looking back, she noted, "It was two different worlds. In Tulsa, I wore oxford-cloth button down shirts and Villager madras skirts. Real Ivy League. But when I went to see grandma in Rule, it was pure country—a total change from my city existence in the way I dressed, the people I met, the things I did. So I had exposure to more than one kind of life."

While growing up in Oklahoma, Mary Kay enjoyed singing both pop and country songs for her own enjoyment and sometimes in school and local events. She also was active in school dramatics as she progressed through elementary and high school in Tulsa and then on to the University of Tulsa. After graduating from the university, she made her way to Hollywood to seek a career in some area of entertainment. Initially, she earned a living by doing first secretarial, then production work for a local TV station, then on such network series as the Tim Conway and David Steinberg shows.

Meanwhile, Place kept looking for ways to move to the other side of the lights. Her first breakthrough, of sorts, was the part of Fleegle the Dog on a children's TV show. Later she gained the attention of the All in the Family staff and received an assignment on that landmark show. She made her TV singing debut on it; she and a friend named Patty Weaver performed a humorous song she wrote called "If Communism Comes Knocking at Your Door, Don't Answer It." As the mid-1970s went by, she was kept busy with a steadily increasing amount of acting work, including roles on such TV shows as M*A*S*H and The Mary Tyler Moore Show and featured assignments in the films Bound for Glory (a movie biography of Woody Guthrie) and New York, New York.

When Norman Lear began the preliminary stages of preparation for Mary Hartman, Mary Hartman, Mary Kay auditioned and quickly received one of the plums on the series, the continuing part of Loretta Haggers. In that character, her role was that of an aspiring country singer with only average ability. From that series, Place went on to other parts in Lear efforts, first in the Fernwood Tonight series, then the successor, Forever Fernwood. In 1977, she signed an exclusive contract with ABC to appear in a number of movies for television.

Meanwhile, she remained very active on the writing front. During the mid- and late-1970s, Place wrote original scripts for many TV programs, including M*A*S*H, The Mary Tyler Moore Show, Paper Moon, Maude, Phyllis, and The Paul Sand Show. Besides that, she kept on adding to her backlog of country originals.

On her approach to writing music, Mary Kay commented, "When I'm writing songs, I don't think 'country.' If a song is in your body, it should come out, and it should come out as whatever it is—country or otherwise. I like singing some rock 'n' roll and I like bluesy stuff, emotional music that tugs at you. That's the thing about country songs, too. They always have an emotional base to them—even a song like 'A Boy Named Sue.' I like music that grabs you. Compulsive music. I like material that says 'I've been there,' and I like material that has a hook of some kind so you want to repeat it. And if I can only have one of those two things in a song, the first one is more important."

In 1976, Mary Kay finally got around to showing the country audience what she could do as singer and writer. Her debut Columbia album, Tonite! At the Capri Lounge, was released and was nominated one of five finalists for the Grammy Award for best country album of 1976. Her efforts also gained a nod from the trade magazine Record World, which named her the Top New Female Country & Western Singer of 1977. That year proved a winner for her in other ways—she won an Emmy for best supporting actress in a TV comedy series.

In late 1977, Place's second album was released on Columbia. Called Aimin' to Please, it contained her versions of such country tunes as the old Ira Louvin/Melba Montgomery hit "Something to Brag About" (Willie Nelson sang the part originally done by Ira Louvin) and Shel Silverstein's "Painting Her Fingernails." The collection included three new songs by Mary Kay, "Marlboro Man," "Dolly's Dive," and "Cattle Kate."

POINTER SISTERS, THE: Vocal group, all born Oakland, California. Ruth, born circa 1946; Anita, circa 1948; Bonnie, circa 1953; June, circa 1954.

At first glance, the Pointer Sisters might not be thought of as country artists; they are associated in most peoples' minds with jazz, pop, or R&B stylings. But the sisters made their mark in country as well, both as singers and as songwriters, a fact borne out by their nominations in country categories in both Grammy and Country Music Association competition in the mid-1970s.

The women, along with their two older brothers, began their musical careers as members of the choir of the West Oakland Church of God, where both their parents, Reverends Elton and Sarah Elizabeth Pointer, were ministers. As Ruth Pointer, oldest of the sisters, noted in biographical data for Planet Records in 1978, "Our parents naturally, as ministers, wanted to protect us from the bad lives people had led in the blues and jazz worlds. We weren't allowed to go to the movies or hear music other than gospel and TV soundtracks. [Later, as the women made their way successfully in the music world, their parents came around to being firm supporters.] In the beginning we had no one to imitate. We'd never heard of the Andrews Sisters or nostalgia. We started 'scatting' stuff." The situation, precluding any preconceived notions, later made all kinds of music seem interesting to them, including country. "We're a very country family," Ruth remarked.

The changing world helped make the elder Pointers relax their restrictions as the girls came of age. The three older sisters became enthusiastic about the idea of a singing career and sought work in the field while earning money in clerical jobs. Their initial attempts in 1969 met with no success, but a friendship with producer David Robinson finally led to session work as backup singers for Cold Blood's album *Sisyphus*. This was followed by more assignments, first with the Elvin Bishop group and then with artists like Dave Mason (who took them along on a European tour) and Taj Mahal. Finally they got their initial record contract in the early 1970s with Atlantic, which classified them as straight R&B singers. Two singles were released, which, according to the Pointers, "were heard only in our living room."

Then Robinson got them signed to ABC/Blue Thumb Records in 1973. That May, they made a sensational debut at Doug Weston's Troubadour in Los Angeles (by then, younger sister June had joined to make it a quartet), which led to appearances on major TV shows, including *Helen Reddy, The Tonight Show,* and *The Midnight Special.* In September, the sisters also were featured at the Monterey Jazz Festival. Their debut album on ABC, *The Pointer Sisters,* which included Willie Dixon's old Chicago blues song "Wang Wang Doodle," Allan Toussaint's "Yes We Can Can," and originals by the Sisters, "Sugar" and "Jada," found favor with national audiences and was certified gold by the R.I.A.A. on February 7, 1974.

Their second album continued the momentum, receiving a gold-record award on July 25, 1974, only a short while after its release. The sister's country inclinations were emphasized during 1974 by the original song "Fairytale." At the early 1975 Grammy Awards program of the National Academy of Recording Arts and Sciences,

the Pointers won the Grammy for 1974 Best Country Vocal Performance by a Duo or Group for the album track of "Fairytale." Anita and Bonnie, who penned the song, also were nominated for the songwriter's award, Best Country Song of 1974. The following year, the Pointers had another country-flavored song on the charts, "Live Your Life Before You Die." The song was one of the nominees for the 1975 Grammy Award for Best Country Vocal Performance by a Duo or Group at the early 1976 awards program. The Sisters, of course, continued to find favor for other types of songs, such as the pop hit "How Long (Betcha Got a Chick on the Side)," a song from their 1976 album, *Steppin',* which was their fourth release on ABC/Blue Thumb, having been preceded by *Live at the Opera House.*

Meanwhile, despite audience approval, the Sisters were unhappy. As June recalled, "We didn't read contracts in those days and we lived on the road and came home broke. But we enjoyed singing so much we just kept on." They also chafed at the typecasting of their record firm, which wanted to stress nostalgic songs with swing era feel, such as "Salt Peanuts" and "That's a Plenty" (which served as the title track for another ABC/Blue Thumb LP). "We weren't growing as singers. We didn't really know what our voices could do," June declared.

The girls were represented on two more ABC albums in the mid-1970s, *The Best of the Pointer Sisters* and, in 1977, *Having a Party.*

After the last album, which completed their contract agreement with ABC, the group broke up for a while. In 1978, though, three of the sisters, Ruth, June, and Anita, returned to action, joining a new label, Planet Records, which issued their debut LP, *Energy,* in November. The album was on the charts into 1979, for part of which it was joined by their second Planet LP (distributed by Elektra Records), *Priority.* During 1979, the trio had two major singles hits, "Fire" and "Happiness." *Energy* earned them their third gold-record album (the second was for the ABC album titled *That's a Plenty).* The single "Fire" from *Energy* also brought their first R.I.A.A. certified gold single. In 1980, their next Planet album, *Special Things*, on the charts the last third of 1980 and into 1981, spawned their second gold single, "He's So Shy."

(Meanwhile, Bonnie had launched her solo career, signing with Motown Records. Her debut LP, *Bonnie Pointer*, was issued in late 1979 and was on the charts soon after, staying on them well into 1980. The album was the source of two 1980 hit singles for her, "Heaven Must Have Sent You" and "I Can't Help Myself.")

In mid-1981, Planet released the fourth album by Ruth, June, and Anita on the label, *Black and White*. In September, the album was certified gold. Earlier that month the single "Slow Hand" from the album also was certified gold. In late September 1981, the second single from *Black and White*, "What a Surprise," was released and soon was on the charts. It was an auspicious month for the girls in other ways: at the conclusion of *Billboard* magazine's Talent Forum in New York's Savoy Hotel, the trio was named R&B Group of the Year.

POSEY, SANDY: *Singer, songwriter. Born Jasper, Alabama, June 18, mid-1940s.*

A reticent person by nature, Sandy Posey tended to say little about her innermost feelings or private life. As she stated in one of her relatively rare interviews, she preferred to let her recordings and concert appearances, in effect, speak for themselves. "I say what I want to say in my songs and I relate my feelings in the style I sing. I don't look at success by how big a recording is, but in terms of how many people benefit from what I sing."

For a time, it worked out well, and the talented vocalist gained recognition as one of the most promising new country artists of the 1960s. But her tendency to keep to herself also may have caused some gaps in her performing activity that delayed her reaching the heights long predicted for her.

Raised in the South—her birthplace was Jasper, Alabama, and most of her growing-up years were spent in West Memphis, Arkansas—she naturally had a strong af-

finity for country music and gospel songs as a child. She recalled first becoming interested in singing at five. It was obvious by the time Sandy was in her teens that she had a fine voice, though for a time she didn't think of singing as an important career option.

After graduating from high school, Posey moved to Memphis, Tennessee, in the early 1960s, where her first work was as a receptionist at the American Recording Studio. The people she worked with became aware of her vocal ability and, when a background vocalist failed to show up for a session, Sandy was given the chance to fill in. She did so well that she began to receive regular assignments as a backing singer, handling a wide range of stylings, from pop to country.

Her activities included doing demonstration tapes for songwriters. After she had been working as a backing vocalist for two years, Posey did a demo of a song called "Born a Woman." The tape not only sold the song, it also got her a recording contract. Her single of the song on MGM made the pop charts in 1966. She quickly followed with a series of releases that made either pop or country charts or both. Among them were "Single Girl" and "I Take It Back." MGM also issued a series of albums of her work, including *Sandy Posey* (issued 12/66), *Single Girl* (9/67), *Sandy Posey* (9/67), and *Best of Sandy Posey* (12/67).

The outlook was good, but in 1968, Sandy announced she was leaving the music business to get married and to try to decide what she wanted to do with her life. During that time away from the field, she reidentified with the Christian faith, a step she later said gave new meaning and direction to her life and music.

By the start of the 1970s, she had made the decision to start recording again. This time she joined Columbia Records and began working with producer Billy Sherrill. She now wanted to place most of her emphasis on country stylings rather than pop. Before long she had a major country hit, "Bringing Him Home Safely to Me." Later on, working with Richard Perry, she had another top-rated release with her version of a Presley hit, "Don't." She also increased her output of original songs, some of which were recorded by other artists.

Posey's career slowed down again in the mid-1970s for a while. She left Columbia and, by 1977, had a new affiliation with Warner Bros. Records. Her first sessions were directed by Chips Moman, who had produced her first hit, "Born a Woman." This time it resulted in a chart-hit single, "Born to Be with You." In late 1978, another release, a combination of two pop classics, "Love, Love, Love" and "Chapel of Love," made the country charts' top 20.

PRESLEY, ELVIS ARON: *Singer, guitarist, actor. Born Tupelo, Mississippi, January 8, 1935; died Memphis, Tennessee, August 16, 1977.*

When Elvis Presley died at the age of forty-two, the news shocked the world. Two days after he was found dead, his embalmed body was displayed in a casket in the foyer of his Graceland mansion in Memphis, Tennessee, and thousands of fans filed by to get a last glimpse of the revered rock star. So many people lined up to see the body in spite of the sweltering Memphis heat that dozens fainted from heat exhaustion while waiting to catch one last glimpse of their idol.

Five years after his death, other performers were still doing big business as Elvis impersonators. New books and magazine articles continued to keep alive the controversy about Presley's life and early death. All of this served as proof of Presley's lasting influence on the American rock scene and demonstrated that he was, even after his death, the one and only "King of Rock 'n' Roll, and a superstar to country fans as well.

The man who was later to hold such a special place in the hearts of millions of Americans as well as people all over the world came from a poor family in Mississippi. He was actually one of twin boys born to Vernon and Gladys Presley, but his brother died at birth. Music was a part of Elvis' life from the very beginning, and he often sang with his parents at camp meetings and church conventions even before he was old enough to go to school.

At the age of thirteen, Presley moved to Memphis, Tennessee, with his parents and soon was being asked to sing at local dances, church gatherings, and high school programs. He worked at odd jobs while in high school, and his first job upon graduation was as a thirty-five-dollar-a-week truck driver. In 1953, he decided to cut a record, just to find out how he sounded, paying four dollars to Sun Records' recording studio. When Sam Phillips, the owner of Sun Records, heard Elvis' voice, he felt that he had the potential for commercial success and asked him to come back and do some more cuts.

From those first Sun recording sessions in 1954, Elvis' career took off to a flying start. He soon won a job with the *Louisiana Hayride,* which in turn brought him to the attention of Colonel Tom Parker, who became his manager and remained in that capacity until Elvis' death. Parker proved to be a brilliant manager and publicist and was able to get Presley a great deal of concert dates when Presley was just starting out. (In his early performing phase on the country circuit Elvis was billed as "The Hillbilly Cat.")

In 1955, Elvis had his first top-10 hits on Sun with "Baby, Let's Play House" and the number-one-ranked "Mystery Train." Parker booked him to perform at the annual country & western Disk Jockeys Association meeting that year. Attending that meeting was Steve Sholes, then head of RCA Victor's Specialties Division, who was so impressed with Presley's performance that he bought out his recording contract with the financially troubled Sun Records for $35,000, one of the most lucrative gambles of all time, and, in retrospect, comparable to the purchase of Manhattan from the Indians for twenty-four dollars and some trinkets.

Throughout the rest of the 1950s, Elvis laid firm hold to the title of rock 'n' roll's "King." His first assault as an indelible influence on the American psyche came in 1956, when he made six appearances on Tommy and Jimmy Dorsey's Saturday night TV show. He sang his new release, "Heartbreak Hotel," and the song soon became number one on the popular as well as country & western charts. Those six performances made Elvis a top hit with young viewers especially, who reacted enthusiastically to his sexy low voice and physical appearance. Soon the young singer was signed to appear on other television shows, including his famous performances on *The Ed Sullivan Show*, in which he was filmed from the waist up so that viewers would not see the suggestive way he moved his hips.

No matter how rich and famous Elvis became, he seemed to retain his image as a nice country boy. And it is interesting to recall that he started out in country music and returned to country music when he made his "comeback" in the 1970s. In between, however, he followed the trend toward a more solid rock sound. He was most successful, though, when he let his country roots color his rockabilly music.

In 1956, Elvis signed a seven-year, one-picture-a-year contract with producer Hal Wallis. In the meantime, he continued to place recordings at the top of the music charts. His list of hits included "Hound Dog," "Love Me Tender," "Teddy Bear," "Jailhouse Rock," "All Shook Up," "Hard Headed Woman," "Don't Be Cruel," and "Wear My Ring Around Your Neck."

In 1958, Presley left show business for a two-year stint in the U.S. Army. When he returned to the business in 1960, he concentrated on making movies rather than on making personal or television appearances. Nevertheless, he continued to top the music charts with million-selling singles and albums. His number-one-ranked singles in the early 1960s included "It's Now or Never," "Are You Lonesome Tonight," "Can't Help Falling in Love," and "Return to Sender."

Presley made movies for Hal Wallis throughout the 1960s. Most of his films received only lukewarm receptions from movie critics, but nearly all of his films were well-attended and well-liked by masses of filmgoers. This was true of his early films, such as *Love Me Tender* (his first film), *Loving You, King Creole, Jailhouse Rock, It Happened at the World's Fair*, and *Roustabout*, and still applied to some of his efforts of the late 1960s, which included *Stay Away, Joe, Live a Little, Love a Little, Speedway*, and *Charro*.

Although Presley's popularity never really waned, as the 1960s were drawing to a close many of Elvis' long-time fans were showing signs of disenchantment with his low profile, while most of the younger generation that had grown up in the second half of the 1960s followed new idols. To combat this trend, Colonel Parker decided it was time for new directions. Parker and Elvis planned in-person engagements, a TV special, and a search for new songs to allow Elvis to return to the best-seller lists.

Considering what Elvis had to lose if he failed to live up to the image of his youthful successes, he was taking an enormous risk by actively returning to the popular music scene. But the result was triumphant, one of the most sensational comebacks in recent musical history. His first show at the International Hotel in Las Vegas in 1969 was a resounding success with both critics and audiences. Elvis packed the large main room of the hotel every night and pleased the management by agreeing to return several more times in the early 1970s. During the year, NBC-TV also released his first TV special, again an unqualified hit. He followed his Las Vegas concert with more successful concerts, including one in the huge Houston Astrodome, one in Madison Square Garden, and another in the 18,000-seat Los Angeles Forum.

Presley also returned to the national hit lists. His record rebirth can actually be traced to his 1968 recording of two Jerry Reed songs, "Guitar Man" and "U.S. Male." Both songs had an unmistakable Memphis/Nashville sound rather than a Hollywood beat. Elvis continued with this trend and started placing many singles on the popular hit charts. His 1969 output included "In the Ghetto," "Don't Cry Daddy," and "Suspicious Minds." In 1970 his chart singles included "The Wonder of You/Mama Liked the Roses" and "You Don't Have to Say You Love Me." In 1971 he hit with "I Really Don't Want to Know/There Goes My Everything," "Where Did She Go, Lord/Rags to

Riches," "Life/Only Believe" and "I'm Leavin'"; his 1972 hits were "Until It's Time for You to Go," "Separate Ways" and "It's a Matter of Time/Burning Love"; in 1973 he scored with "Steamroller Blues/Fool" and "Raised on Rock/For Ole Times' Sake." Other hits in subsequent years included "Kentucky Rain," "Moody Blue," "Way Down," and "(I'm So) Hurt."

Over the years of his active career, Elvis also turned out dozens of albums, most of which made pop and/or country charts. A sampling of those is: *Blue Suede Shoes, Elvis* (mid-1950s); *Golden Records, Volume 1, King Creole* (1958); *A Date with Elvis, For LP Fans Only* (1959); *Golden Records, Volume 2, Elvis Is Back* (1960); *Somethin' for Everybody, His Hand in Mine* (1961); *Pot Luck* (1962); *Girls, Girls, Girls, At the World's Fair, Golden Records, Volume 3* (1963); *Roustabout* (1964); *Elvis for Everyone* (1965); *Spinout* (1966); *How Great Thou Art* (1967); *Elvis Back in Memphis, From Memphis to Vegas* (late 1960s); *Almost in Love, At the International Hotel, Las Vegas, Let's Be Friends, Elvis in Memphis, Worldwide 50 Gold Award Hits, Volume 1* (1970); *Elvis Country, Love Letters, That's the Way It Is, Worldwide 50 Gold Award Hits, Volume 2, You'll Never Walk Alone* (1971); *Elvis as Recorded Live at Madison Square Garden, Elvis Sings Burning Love,* and *Hits from His Movies, He Touched Me* (1972); *Aloha from Hawaii Via Satellite, Raised on Rock/For Ol' Times Sake* (1973); *Elvis: A Legendary Performer, Volume 1, Elvis Recorded Live on Stage in Memphis* (1974); *Elvis Today* (1975); and *A Legendary Performer, Volume 2, The Sun Sessions* (1976).

Presley's untimely death saddened millions of his fans and also sparked a controversial investigation into its cause. Although his personal physician, Dr. George C. Nichopoulos, reported that a heart attack had caused Presley's death, the doctor was later accused of prescribing an abnormally high number of drug prescriptions for his famous patient. People close to Presley also spoke of his long-time addiction to amphetamines, barbiturates, and other drugs, which had grown worse since his divorce from his wife, Priscilla Ann Beaulieu Presley, in 1972. (They had been married for five years and had one daughter, Lisa.) No one could explain, however, why people who knew of Presley's problems allowed them to continue. Others close to Elvis spoke of his "death wish" and remarked that he had died at the age of forty-two, exactly the same age at which his mother had died while Elvis was in the Army. Some people said that Elvis had been so close to his mother that he had never been the same since her death.

His passing not only deeply affected millions of people the world over, it spawned a veritable flood of books and record releases to take advantage of those emotions. For a time it seemed as though anyone who had even a passing acquaintance with the star rushed into print with some sort of memoir. (However, most of his closest friends and advisers made little or no comment about his private life.) Among the books issued in the years immediately following his death (mostly issued in paperback) were *The Life and Death of Elvis Presley,* issued by Harrison House, and *My Life with Elvis,* by Becky Yancey with Cliff Linedecker, St. Martin's Press, both in 1977; *The Boy Who Dared to Rock: The Definitive Elvis,* by Paul Lichter, Dolphin Books, 1978; *Elvis in Concert,* by John Reggero, Dell Publications, 1979; *The Truth About Elvis,* by Jess Stearn with Larry Geller, Jove Books, *Elvis: The Final Years,* by Jerry Hopkins, St. Martin's Press, both 1980; and *Elvis,* by Albert Harry Goldman, A Kevin Eggers Book, 1982.

When Elvis died, he had a new album, *Moody Blue,* moving up the pop charts (as well as the charted single "Way Down"). As soon as word got out about the music public's tragic loss in mid-August 1977, there was a literal rush on record stores by fans who snapped up all his available records in print. RCA was soon releasing previous packages as well as new combinations of previously recorded material (assembled by RCA Records' Joan Deany) and still, for over a year after Elvis' death, record stores had trouble keeping any of his recordings in stock. Among the LPs that joined *Moody Blue* on pop or country charts or both by the fall of 1977 were *Legendary Performer, Volume 1; Elvis' Golden*

Records, Volume 1; Welcome to My World; and World Wide 50 Gold Awards, Volume 1. During 1978, his chart LPs included Legendary Performer, Volume II and Elvis Sings for Children and Grownups Too. The latter still was on country charts in 1979, a year in which there were such other best-selling LPs on those lists as Legendary Performer, Volume III; Our Memories of Elvis; and Elvis: a Canadian Tribute. In 1980, his chart hit LPs included Our Memories of Elvis, Volume II and Elvis Aron Presley. In early 1981, RCA released the LP Guitar Man, whose selections, RCA announced, had been re-engineered to reduce background sounds. The title track provided another number-one singles hit for Elvis when it reached that position on country charts in March 1981.

There seems little doubt that Elvis' memory will remain green among legions of fans for future times as has been the case with other great country or country/pop stars, such as Jimmie Rodgers and Hank Williams. Among memorials to his name already in existence by the early 1980s was a chapel erected on the second anniversary of his death by the Elvis Presley Memorial Foundation in his birthplace, Tupelo, Mississippi and his gold Cadillac displayed at the Country Music Foundation in Nashville, Tennessee.

Undoubtedly, analysis of the rock idol who had "everything"—talent, looks, money, and fame—yet who ended up a reclusive and lonely man behind the walls of his Graceland mansion will continue for many years to come. More importantly, however, present and future generations will continue to enjoy the recorded (and videotaped) musical legacy he left the world. Any serious Presley fan or scholar should acquire the Journal of Country Music, vol. IX, no. 2, published by the Country Music Foundation, 4 Music Square East, Nashville, TN 37203, for an excellent guideline to most of the books printed to date. —A.S.

PRICE, KENNY: Singer, instrumentalist (drums, guitar, banjo, bass fiddle). Born near Florence, Kentucky, May 27, 1931.

In 1966–67, a new name began to appear on national country-music hit charts. However, Kenny Price was not unfamiliar to audiences of the Midwestern Hayride; he had been a program favorite for well over a decade by then.

Born on a farm in northern Kentucky, Kenny fell in love with country music at an early age. When he was five, his family bought him a guitar from the Sears, Roebuck catalog. Kenny slowly learned to play and was skillful enough, in later years, to become a member of the school band. His good voice enabled him to sing at local events during his teens.

His goal, however, was not in music. He expected to follow his family tradition and become a farmer. When the Korean War came along, though, he entered the service and often entertained his friends with guitar playing and singing, which led to their urging him to try out for the Horace Heidt USO show. He won the assignment and racked up considerable performing hours before he was discharged.

Back home again, he decided to see if he could progress in the entertainment field. In 1954 Price auditioned for Cincinnati's WLW, and thus started a relationship that continued strong into the late 1960s. He became a regular on the Midwestern Hayride, his popularity attested to by a steadily increasing volume of fan mail.

A fellow cast member was Bobby Bobo, who founded his own record firm, Boone Records. Kenny joined a roster that included many well-known country & western performers. In 1966, he rewarded Bobo with a top-10 version of a Ray Pennington composition, "Walking on New Grass." He proved this was no fluke in 1967 with another top-10 hit, "Happy Tracks," also by Pennington. He had three other songs on the 1967 charts as well, including "Pretty Girl, Pretty Clothes, Pretty Sad." In 1968, his output included the best-selling single "My Goal for Today."

For much of the 1970s, Price was affiliated with RCA Records. His RCA chart singles included "California Women" in 1973; "Turn on Your Light (and Let It Shine)," "Que Pasa," and "Let's Truck Together" (written by Kenny) in 1974; "Easy Look" in 1975; and "Too Big a Price to

Pay" in 1976. By 1977 he had left RCA and was on the small MRC label. In the early 1980s, he recorded for Dimension Records, which issued such singles as the 1980 chart-maker "She's Leavin' (and I'm Almost Gone)."

PRICE, RAY NOBLE: *Singer, guitarist, songwriter. Born Perryville, Texas, January 12, 1926.*

If you had looked at the top levels of the country hit charts in early 1979, you would have observed a song titled "Feet," recorded by Ray Price. It was the same Ray Price whose name often could be found in the top-10 singles lists in 1952—and many other times in the intervening years. Few people in any area of country—or pop—music could match his consistency in maintaining a strong hold on a large segment of his audience for so many years. Changing with the times, demonstrating the ability to sing all kinds of songs, from folk music and traditional country to progressive country and sophisticated ballads, Price certainly ranks as one of the superstars of the modern country field.

Although his career reached its zenith when he lived in Tennessee, his roots were in Texas, where he spent his formative years. Ray was born in the small town of Perryville in rural Cherokee County in eastern Texas. He did plenty of farm chores as a youngster and also learned about horses and farm animals first hand, an interest he retained all his life. By the time he reached high school age, his family had moved to Dallas. He already had shown interest and talent in music by then. While still in grade school he started singing and performed in public at church festivals and other local events. By the time he finished high school, he had added to that experience and also became proficient on the guitar.

He enrolled at North Texas Agricultural College in Abilene as a veterinary major, but his education was interrupted by World War II. He joined the Marines for what was to become a four-year tour of duty, including service in the Pacific Theater of operations. After receiving his discharge in 1946, Price returned to Abilene to resume his schooling. Once back on campus, he varied the routine of studies with a growing number of appearances as a country performer in local clubs. In 1948, "The Cherokee Cowboy" made his radio debut on station KRBC (Abilene) *Hillbilly Circus.*

Still pursuing his degree with thoughts of making his livelihood as a rancher or farmer, Ray didn't at first think of music as more than a pleasant sideline. However, his performing career continued to move ahead in 1948 and 1949. When he was given the chance to join the cast of the prestigious *Big D Jamboree* broadcast over Dallas station KRLD, the matter was settled. His efforts during 1949 and 1950 began to make his name known to a steadily expanding number of fans. Parts of the program were broadcast nationally on the CBS network, with similar results as far as Ray was concerned. With that kind of exposure, a recording contract was in order; Price was signed to a regional label called Bullet. He made a number of singles for the label that made some inroads on several regional markets.

By 1952, he was ready to move up into the major leagues of country music. He signed with Columbia Records and before long had his first top-10 singles, "Talk to Your Heart" and "Don't Let the Stars Get in Your Eyes." During that year, he achieved the dream of all aspiring country artists, and joined the cast of the *Grand Ole Opry.* It made sense to relocate to Nashville, and Tennessee became his home state for several years before he returned to Texas.

Ray placed some songs on the charts in 1953, but didn't dent the top 10. However, he was back with a flourish in 1954 with three major hits: "Release Me," "I'll Be There," and "If You Don't Someone Else Will." Again he slacked off a bit in 1955, but had a banner year in 1956. His 1956 top-10 singles included "I've Got a New Heartache," "Wasted Words," and his first number-one national hit, "Crazy Arms." He sang that song to cheering audiences all over the United States that year, and it remained a key element of his stage show for decades afterward.

For the rest of the 1950s, Price's name rarely was absent from singles charts (he had a number of charted albums as well). In 1957, he scored with the top-10 "My Shoes Keep Walking Back to You"; in 1958 he had the top-10 "Curtain in the Window" and his second number-one hit, "City Lights"; in 1959 he closed out the decade with still another number-one success, "Same Old Me," plus the top-10 hits "That's What It's Like to Be Lonesome," "Heartaches by the Number," and "Under Your Spell Again." His name often was at or near the top of major polls during those years; for 1959, almost all the major music trade magazines named him Favorite Male Vocalist in the country & western category as well as honoring "Heartaches by the Numbers" as Best Record of the Year.

Some of the songs in Ray's repertoire by the early 1960s were original compositions, including such numbers as "Give Me More, More of Your Kisses," "I'm Tired," and the 1961 hit "Soft Rain." Although it was a new decade, with some changes in the kind of music favored by many listeners, Ray's career continued to prosper. In 1961, he made top-chart levels with "One More Time" and "I Wish I Could Fall in Love Today." In 1961, besides "Soft Rain," he made top-10 ranks with "Heart Over Mind." Some of his other major singles of the 1960s included "Walk Me to the Door" and "Make the World Go Away" in 1963; "Please Talk to My Heart" and "Burning Memories" in 1964; "The Other Woman" in 1965; "A Way to Survive" and "Don't You Ever Get Tired of Hurting Me" in 1966; and a remake of the old folk classic "Danny Boy" in 1967.

Many of his recordings of the 1960s featured lush orchestral backing, which caused some criticism from country traditionalists. Price told an interviewer in 1967, "Strings are essential to my type of song. Most of my songs are ballads and the strings provide the soul for the ballad. There have been some who objected to the big violin sections that I use on the records, but it's mainly people who have made up their minds before really listening to the record. When they do listen, they usually like it." For a typical concert of the 1960s, Ray often took along a backing group that included as many as eight to ten violins, an unusual touch for a country artist. For his records, though, he sometimes employed as many as three dozen violinists.

As the 1970s drew nigh, the progressive country movement was having a strong impact on the field. Just as the onslaught of rockabilly in the 1950s and the British rock invasion in the 1960s didn't seem to tarnish Price's image, neither did the new trend. In fact, Ray seemed to recognize the quality of some of the new songs being written by newcomers like Kris Kristofferson. In mid-1970, he recorded Kristofferson's "For the Good Times," which soon became one of the most important events in Ray's career. The single rose to the top of both country and pop charts in the United States and also became one of the runaway international hits of the year. It rapidly went over the million mark and was to sell in multiples of that as the 1970s progressed. Price's album of that title, issued in September 1970, also was a tremendous success and was still on country charts over two years later. In late 1970 and early 1971, Price had another worldwide bestseller with Kristofferson's "For the Good Times" (the album came out in January 1971), adding another series of gold records (United States plus a number of foreign ones) to his collection. He couldn't keep that sensational pace up indefinitely, but he still had a respectable batting average over the next few years, placing such songs as "That's What Leaving's About/Lonesomest Lonesome" (1972) and "Storms of Troubled Times" (1974) on upper-chart levels.

In the mid-1970s, Ray ended his long association with Columbia and moved to ABC/Dot. (Later he was briefly affiliated with Myrrh Records.) Even as he made that move, though, he was entering semiretirement. He still made some recordings, but he wanted to get away from the grind of TV shows and far-flung touring to concentrate on his long-time love of animal husbandry. He passed up concert engagements and remained on his large horse ranch near Dallas, Texas, raising and selling horses.

Many people were hardly aware he had given up much of his music activity, since he still kept placing singles on the hit lists. Among those were "Roses and Love Songs" in early 1975 and "Farthest Thing from My Mind" in mid-1975, both on ABC/Dot. Columbia also released one of his singles, "If You Ever Change Your Mind," in late summer of 1975, and the song moved to the upper-chart reaches. In 1976, his ABC/Dot single "To Make a Long Story Short/We're Getting There" made the top 40. In late 1977, a Columbia release, "Born to Love Me" made the top 20.

At the end of 1978, Price decided to return to full-time status, signing a new contract with Monument Records. Guesting on *The Tonight Show* in early 1979 (in earlier years, he had been a frequent visitor on the show, as he had been on many other nationally telecast talk and variety shows during the 1960s and 1970s), Ray told Johnny Carson that he had enjoyed his nearly five-year absence from the spotlight, but he had begun to miss the excitement of the entertainment field. His fans appeared to welcome him back, keeping his debut single on Monument, "Feet," on the charts for over three months.

Ray had several more singles on Monument in 1979 that made the charts, such as "There's Always Me" and "Misty Morning Rain," but they didn't reach uppermost levels and he found himself without a label. He decided to seek the help of Willie Nelson, who once had been a sideman in Price's Cherokee Cowboys backing band. (Other alumni of that group include Roger Miller, Johnny Paycheck, and Johnny Bush.) He recalled, "I was having trouble getting a contract, so I went to Willie and said, 'Since you're doing albums with other people, how about doing one with me?'"

The result was the duet album *San Antonio Rose*, issued by Columbia in June 1980 and on the album charts soon after. Willie and Ray sang some of the songs from the album at Willie's annual Fourth of July picnic in Texas and won roaring approval from the large crowd. By fall the LP was at number three on the charts and was still in the top 40 in early 1981. The LP provided Ray and Willie with two hit singles, "Faded Love" in the fall of 1980 and "Don't You Ever Get Tired (Of Hurting Me)" in early 1981. In 1981, the twosome was among the final nominees in Academy of Country Music Awards voting for duet of the year and album of the year as well as finalists in *Music City News* polling for duet of the year.

In February 1981, Price signed a new recording contract with Dimension Records. During the year his charted singles on the label included "Getting Over You Again," "It Don't Hurt Me Half as Bad," and "Diamonds in the Stars." In early 1981, Columbia Records issued an album of some of his recordings on that label titled *A Tribute to Willie and Kris*. He also became involved in a talent scout project called Ray Price's Country Starsearch 1981, which called for him to appear at the finals in all fifty states as well as star in a TV presentation of the winners.

PRIDE, CHARLEY: *Singer, guitarist, band leader (the Pridesmen). Born Sledge, Mississippi, March 18, 1938.*

Charley Pride is to country music as Jackie Robinson is to baseball. As Robinson did in sports, Pride broke the color barrier in a field where, on the prestige level, one had to be white to succeed. (Actually, Ray Charles had done well before Charley came along with country & western ballads, but Charles basically was a blues or pop type performer, whereas Pride was an all-out country artist.) Like Robinson, Pride was not just an adequate performer, he was a superstar, a fact recognized by the trade magazine *Cash Box*, which named Charley in 1980 the top male country artist of the decade (1970s).

Pride became interested in country & western music as a child in rural Mississippi. His choice was an unusual one for a black child in a region where the whites were country-music fans and most blacks preferred blues music. Of course, any kind of music was an escape from the drudgery of work in the cotton fields, the main occupation of his parents and Charley and his ten brothers and sisters as soon as each was old enough to contribute his or her meager earnings to the family coffers. He recalled that he was paid three dollars per hundred pounds of cotton picked from his childhood until he left home at seventeen.

He was the only one in his family who had any leaning toward music, blues or otherwise, spending his free time listening to country-music shows on the radio and singing the songs he heard for his own pleasure. One of his particular favorites from the late 1940s was Hank Williams. When Charley was fourteen, he got enough money together to buy a guitar and worked out his own method of playing from listening to various picking styles.

Although he could play pretty well by his late teens, he didn't consider music a likely career at the time. Strong and well built, he had natural athletic ability. Inspired by Jackie Robinson's breakthrough in professional baseball, Pride decided to try to make it in that field. His ability won him a place with the Memphis Red Sox of the Negro American League in the late 1950s and in time, after two years of military service, he moved up to a regular minor league assignment with the Helena, Montana, team. In 1960, he sang between innings of a ball game in Helena and won an ovation. He decided he wanted to sing more, and his landlady helped him get a job singing in a local country spot.

Pride still concentrated on baseball, spurred on by a brief tryout with the major league California Angels in 1961 as an outfield and pitching prospect. He had made Montana his home, working as a smelter for Anaconda Mining in the off season and finding nightclub work from time to time in local clubs. It was while singing in one of those spots in late 1963 that he was heard by country star Red Sovine. Red liked Charley's stylings and sought him out to offer him a recording audition. Pride held back for a time. A member of the New York Mets farm organization, he still had dreams of a successful big league career. Finally he decided it was worth taking Sovine up on his offer, and went to Nashville to audition for Chet Atkins. In 1964, Atkins agreed with Sovine that Pride had considerable promise and signed Charley to a contract with RCA Victor.

Pride cut his first record, "Snakes Crawl at Night," in August 1965, but it wasn't released until January 1966. In a short time it was a top-chart song, staying on the list for many weeks. Later in the year, he had another hit with "Just Between You and Me." In November 1966, his debut LP came out, Country Charley Pride, an album that made national country lists in 1967 and eventually earned him his first gold-record award.

After his sensational debut year in 1966, the doors began to open. In January 1967, he made his first appearance on the Grand Ole Opry, far from his last. Over the years, he often returned to the Opry stage, first at Ryman Auditorium and later at Opryland as a guest on the Opry or on dozens of other shows recorded or taped (for TV) from there. On a number of occasions he was featured on the Country Music Association award telecasts as a performer, presenter, or award recipient.

He continued to add to his laurels the balance of the 1960s. In the nominating process for Grammy Awards for 1966, Pride was one of five finalists for Best Country & Western Vocal Performance, Male, for his single "Just Between You and Me." He had two hit singles in 1967 with "Does My Ring Hurt Your Finger" and "I Know One." In 1968, he had such best-selling singles as "The Day the World Stood Still" and "The Best Part's Over" and a top-rated album, The Country Way (issued January 1968) that later won another gold-record award. (It was his third release after Pride of Country Music, which came out in July 1967. Other 1968 albums were Make Mine Country and Songs of Pride . . . Charley That Is.

Although country fans who came to his concerts for the first time in the late 1960s were surprised at his color—on records Charley didn't sound particularly "black"—they quickly accepted him as one of their own country stars. Year after year he added to his popularity as an in-person artist, headlining shows in places like the Playroom and Domino in Atlanta, Randy's Rodeo in San Antonio, Texas, and Panther Hall in Fort Worth, Texas. The last named provided the tapes for his first live album, *Charley Pride in Person at Panther Hall*, recorded in 1968 and issued in February 1969. The LP eventually went gold, as did his other two LPs released in 1969, *The Sensational Charley Pride* (7/69) and *The Best of Charley Pride* (12/69). The latter moved to number one on U.S. country charts in early 1970.

Nor did Pride's momentum slow coming into the 1970s. With his band, the Pridesmen, and a show featuring both established and new artists, he regularly played to capacity audiences in all major country music venues at home and abroad. His face and voice regularly graced major TV music shows, both network and syndicated. And he continued to turn out albums that provided that rare combination of creative entertainment and commercial appeal. Of the nine albums issued from 1970 through 1972, six won gold-record awards and almost all appeared not only on country charts but pop lists as well. The gold-record offerings were *Just Plain Charley* (1970), *Charley Pride 10th Album* (8/70), *From Me to You* (3/71), *Did You Think to Pray* (6/71), *Charley Pride Sings Heart Songs* (12/71), and *The Best of Charley Pride, Volume 2* (4/72). (The others were *Christmas in My Home Town*, 1970; *I'm Just Me*, 8/71; *A Sunshiny Day with Charley Pride*, 11/72; plus one Camden Records release, *Incomparable Charley Pride*, 11/72.)

Many of those efforts won nominations and awards in major competitions. Pride won two Grammies for 1971, one for Best Sacred Performance for the LP *Did You Think to Pray* and one for Best Gospel Performance for the single "Let Me Live." In 1972, he won a third Grammy for Best Country Vocal Performance, Male, for the album *Charley Pride Sings Heart Songs*. In addition, the CMA in the early 1970s voted him the group's most prestigious award, Entertainer of the Year, and also named him Best Male Country Vocalist of the Year. The Music Operators of America also named him Entertainer of the Year. Besides all that, he often was named the top male vocalist for country singles and/or albums by major music industry trade publications.

Through the rest of the 1970s, Charley continued to add to his already extensive plaudits. Each year his stage show played to in the neighborhood of a million fans. And his album and singles releases almost without exception made the charts, usually, in the case of albums, reaching the top 10, and the singles more often than not going as high as first, second, or third position.

His singles successes for the period included "Amazing Love," number one in late 1973 and still in the top 10 in early 1974; "We Could," in the top 10 in early summer 1974; "Then Who Am I?" number one in February 1975; "I Ain't All Sad," in the top 10 in the summer of 1975; "Hope You're Feelin' Me (Like I'm Feelin' You)," number one in October 1975; "The Happiness of Having You," number three in February 1976; "My Eyes Can Only See as Far as You," top 10 in May 1976; "A Whole Lotta Things to Sing About," top 10 early fall 1976; "I'll Be Leavin' Alone," number one in July 1977; "More to Me," number one in November 1977; "When I Stop Leavin' I'll Be Gone," number three in August 1978; and "Burgers & Fries," number one in December 1978 and still on the charts in early 1979. His 1979 hit singles included "You're My Jamaica", "Where Do I Put Her Memory," and, at year end, "Missin' You," which rose to number two on the charts in January 1980.

His charted LPs of the mid- and late-1970s included *Songs of Love by Charley Pride* (early 1973); *Sweet Country* (6/73); *Amazing Love* (issued early 1974); *Country Feelin'* (mid-1974); *Pride of America* (late 1974); *Charley* (summer 1975); *The Happiness of Having You* (late 1975); *Sunday Morning with Charley Pride* (early summer 1976); *She's Just an Old Love Turned Memory* (spring 1977); *I'm Just Me* (summer 1977); *Someone Loves You Honey* (early 1978); *Burgers & Fries/When I Stop Leavin' I'll Be Gone* (October 1979); and *You're My Jamaica* (mid-1979).

Charley started the 1980s in fine style with a tribute to Hank Williams, "I Got a Lot of Hank in Me." Released in early 1980, it rose to number one on U.S. country lists in May. Discussing the project earlier, he had noted "All the material in the album, except for one cut, will be Hank Williams' songs. The exception is the title song which I had especially written." He pointed out that it was a Williams' song, "Lovesick Blues," that he was singing back in Helena that helped draw the attention of Red Sovine (and Red Foley).

"The whole country music business owes a lot to Hank Williams—he more or less invented the word 'crossover' when you apply it to country music. My album is a way of giving back what I've taken from the man, his talent and his music."

In his years of prominence, Charley himself had been a factor in other artists' careers. Touring with him had proven valuable for a number of performers, both new or experienced and looking for more recognition. Among those he helped to become stars in their own right were Gary Stewart, Dave and Sugar, Johnny Russell, Johnny Duncan, and Ronnie Milsap.

Charley's single of "Honky Tonk Blues" from the Hank Williams album reached number one on country charts in April 1980. During the summer his version of Hank's "You Win Again" was a top chart hit. Later in the year he had such other bestsellers as "Dallas Cowboys" and "You Almost Slipped My Mind." In early 1981, he had the singles success "Roll on Mississippi" and, in the fall, had another blockbuster with "Never Been So Loved," number one in October.

During the 1970s, Pride settled with his family in Dallas, Texas. In general, he was treated with respect by the community, but there still were incidents that unfortunately demonstrated that prejudice remained alive and sick in some individuals. Friends of his, knowing he was an avid golfer, proposed him for membership in the all-white Dallas Royal Oaks Country Club. After the vote was taken, he got a letter from the club informing him his ap-plication had been rejected because of vetoes from at least four persons. Pride remarked, "They gave me no reason, but the only one I can think of is that I'm black . . . . I'm not concerned—there are plenty of places I can play golf."

PRINE, JOHN: *Singer, guitarist, songwriter. Born Maywood, Illinois, 1946.*

To paraphrase Dylan, with whom John Prine has sometimes been compared, "The times they have a-changed." Had Prine come along at the start of the 1960s and Bob's timetable instead had been that of John's, it might well be Prine who would now be hailed as a giant of the times and Dylan who was still fighting for recognition. Prine, in other words, stands squarely in the folk and folk/country-rock art form where Dylan held forth in his formative years. Unlike Dylan, though, Prine started out playing rock music, but he's given little evidence of wanting to move over to the more popular style since then, as Dylan did in the mid-1960s.

Prine, in fact, continued to live in a modest neighborhood in the Chicago area and to keep in touch with the working-class roots of his developing years even after gaining a measure of acclaim in the 1970s. He grew up in Maywood, Illinois, a blue-collar suburb of Chicago, where he was born in 1946. His father was a steelworker and president of the Maywood United Steelworkers Local. John's heritage goes back to Kentucky, where his parents came from and his grandparents spent most of their lives.

John's sensitive songwriting about grassroots American life obviously relates directly to his background. He saw other aspects of working-class life after he was graduated from high school when he worked as a postal employee and spent two years in the Army in the 1960s. John's brother, Dave, taught him guitar, and he had an interest in rock and country music in his teens.

At the start of the 1970s, he began to apply himself to writing songs and performing some of them in Chicago bars and clubs, urged on, as he recalled, by a desire to get away from the vicissitudes of tramping city streets in the wind, cold, and rain as a mail carrier. His performing debut came in 1970 at the Fifth Peg, where he sang "Sam Stone," "Paradise," and "Hello in There." Soon after, he began to appear regularly at another club, the Earl of Old Town.

Almost overnight, Prine was discovered. As he recalled, "It was rough to take. I felt like Lana Turner for the first couple of years, everything happened to me so fast. Sitting in a folk bar in Chicago just because I don't want to walk in the snow and deliver mail. And that was it; no sights or goals. Then in walk Paul Anka, Kris Kristofferson, and Samantha Eggar and it might as well have been Donald Duck and Mickey Mouse, it made as much sense. Next thing I know I'm on a plane to New York City. I'm in the Village and Kristofferson asked me to get up on stage and I sing three songs and the house comes down and Jerry Wexler asks me to sign his shoe and all this [excitement] happens and my father dies and I get a record out and I'm in Los Angeles, running around the country and people are calling me the next Bob Dylan and it was really just fuckin' goofy."

But the predictions of overnight stardom proved a trifle optimistic. There was nothing wrong with his output—the four albums he recorded on Atlantic from 1970 through 1974 (Diamonds in the Rough, Sweet Revenge, John Prine, Common Sense) represent some of the high points of American folk music in the 1970s, including as they do such compositions as "Sam Stone," "Hello in There," "Far from Me," "Six O'Clock News," "Yes I Guess They Oughta Name a Drink After You," "Granpa Was a Carpenter," and "Christmas in Prison." But folk music in those years was a minority art form, and while the albums sold reasonably well they didn't storm top-chart levels. Prine became accustomed to a slow, steady upward struggle over the years. As he noted, the mental strain at the beginning was such that "I'm surprised I'm in one piece; there's a thin line between Billboard and Bellevue."

For a while, after his fifth album on Atlantic, the retrospective Prime Prine, came

out in 1975, it looked as though Prine was backing off somewhat. He did do some shows, but for a long period no new records appeared. Meanwhile, he had, in effect, moved sideways, switching from Atlantic to another part of the Warner Communications conglomerate, Elektra/Asylum Records. This move made practical sense since Atlantic's product, for the most part, leaned toward up-tempo rock and soul while Elektra's roster had such names as Linda Ronstadt, Jackson Browne, and Judy Collins.

In midsummer 1978, John's first Elektra album, was issued, Bruised Orange, and proved to be a gem. The title song, in fact, is reminiscent of Kristofferson in his salad days but with lyrics that are more cerebral. ("For a heart wrapped in anger/Grows weak and grows bitter/You become your own prisoner/As you watch yourself sit there/Wrapped up in a trap/Of your very own/Chain of sorrow.") There were some hints of rock in the folk-country ballad co-written with Phil Spector, "If You Don't Want My Love," but the other tracks, such as "Fish and Whistle," "That's the Way That the World Goes Round," and "Crooked Piece of Time," remained in the folk-country domain. While hardly setting any sales records, the LP, with Elektra/Asylum's support, did gain the national charts for a number of months, a step forward compared to earlier releases. Prine's following was small but growing, as indicated by the capacity crowds at the clubs he played during his concert tour in support of the LP. Bruised Orange won plaudits from critics across the United States, and Time magazine cited it as one of the ten best albums of 1978.

John's second LP on Elektra, Pink Cadillac, was recorded at Sam Phillips Studios in Memphis and had a stronger rock 'n' roll flavor than previous collections. After it was issued in August 1979, New York Times reviewer Robert Palmer exclaimed that the LP "embodied the most authentic honky-tonk ambience in a new record in at least twenty years." Prine's third Elektra LP, Storm Windows, covered a spectrum from high-voltage rock ("Shop Talk," "Just Wanna Be with You") to ballads ("Storm

Windows," "One Red Rose") to country-flavored numbers like "It's Happening to You."

However, despite the generally excellent creative content of those albums and continued critical praise, Prine still could not find a mass following, with the result that his contract with Elektra was allowed to expire in 1981.

PROFFITT, FRANK: *Singer, guitarist, banjoist, songwriter, instrument maker. Born Laurel Bloomery, Tennessee, 1913; died Vilas, North Carolina, November 24, 1965.*

Except to folk music experts, the name Frank Proffitt doesn't mean much these days. However, the song he belatedly received credit for writing, "Tom Dooley," is an acknowledged folk classic. In addition to that, Proffitt was an important link in the chain that has preserved many traditional hill-country songs for today's and future generations.

The Proffitt family moved to the Cracker Neck sections of the eastern Tennessee mountains from Wilkes County, North Carolina, just after the Civil War. When Frank was a boy, his family moved to Reese, North Carolina, a few miles below the Tennessee border. There his father, Wiley Proffitt, earned a living as a farmer, cooper, and tinker.

Young Frank grew up in an atmosphere of what is now called folk music, where songs that were the forerunners of modern country music and today's "traditional" folk music provided one of the few forms of relaxation. His father, his Aunt Nancy Prather, and his Uncle Noah often sang old songs of the hills. Frank's father also made banjos and passed some of his skills along to his son. As Proffitt told the collecting team of Anne and Frank Warner (*Sing Out!* October–November 1963, p. 7):

"As a boy I recall going along with Dad to the woods to get the lumber for banjo-making. He selected a tree by its appearance and sounding . . . hitting a tree with a hammer or ax broadsided to tell by the sound if it's straight grained. . . . When the strings were put on and the pegs turned and musical notes began to fill the cabin, I

looked on my father as the greatest man on earth for creating such a wonderful thing out of a piece of wood, a greasy skin, and some strings."

Young Frank managed to finish sixth grade in the rural school before he had to devote all his hours to the farm. He continued his deep interest in music and spent most of his few free hours singing or listening to songs. As he grew older, he took more and more part in local gatherings, trading songs with others from the region and playing the banjo. In 1922, still a young boy, he had gotten his first store-bought instrument when he gathered enough premiums from selling goods of the Lee Manufacturing Company to trade them for a guitar.

He also was learning how to make his own instruments from his father and later in life became an expert at the craft. In fact, as time went by, he became as noted in the region for his instrument making as for his performing skills. He was particularly admired by the folklorists, who eventually sought him out for his ability in playing the fretless banjo he built for himself.

In 1932, he married Bessie Hicks, daughter of another musical family in the area, and moved to his own farm in Pork Britches Valley. The years passed much as they had before. The Proffitts raised a family of their own and farmed, and Frank played and sang whenever he could. A turning point occurred in 1938 when the Warners met Frank's in-laws while passing through the hill country seeking folk material. Nathan Hicks, in turn, introduced them to Frank. In the next few years, the Warners returned to record 120 of Frank's folk songs. One of those was a ballad about a tragedy involving the local people, Tom Dula and Laurie Foster. Other songs bore such titles as "Dan Doo" and "Moonshine."

The Warners, who performed as well, included "Tom Dooley" in their repertoire for decades, always mentioning its origins in Proffitt's home in the Tennessee–North Carolina hills. They maintained contact with Frank in the years after World War

II, sometimes visiting him to compare notes or collect new material. Then the Kingston Trio came out with a single of "Tom Dooley," a song they believed was traditional and thus in the public domain. At first nobody connected it with Proffitt, but that changed after a story about him came out in *The Carolina Farmer* in 1960. The revelation inspired a groundswell of support for Frank among folk music people that eventually led to a lawsuit that established Proffitt's rights to authorship.

One result of the furor was an invitation for him to appear at the University of Chicago's First Folk Festival. His work proved one of the Festival highlights and other invitations poured in. Although Frank was uncomfortable being away from home for extended periods of time, he did travel to New York for some concerts and also appeared at the Country Dance Society's Folk Music Camp near Cape Cod, Massachusetts, in the early 1960s. He continued to do some live performances in the mid-1960s, including taking part in the traditional music portions of the Newport Folk Festival in Rhode Island in 1964 and 1965. His material was included in some of the Vanguard Records LPs of the Festival.

Interest naturally arose in making new recordings for commerical release, and Sandy Paton took recording equipment to Proffitt's home to make tapes for Folkways Records. His first album, *Frank Proffitt*, came out at the start of the 1960s. His second LP, on Folk Legacy, titled *Trifling Woman*, came out in 1962.

Although his name had become famous in many parts of the world besides the United States, Frank spent most of his time on his beloved tobacco farm in North Carolina. In late 1965, after driving his wife 115 miles to a hospital in Charlotte for a needed foot operation, he returned home in seeming good health. He finished his dinner, lay down on his bed, and died in his sleep on November 24. In 1966, folk artists dedicated a number of concerts to his memory.

By the start of the 1980s, he still had two albums in print, the original Folkways release and a Folk Legacy LP titled *Reese,*

North Carolina, which contained Proffitt's version of "Tom Dooley."

PROPHET, RONNIE: *Singer, pianist, guitarist, songwriter. Born near Montreal, Canada, December 26, 1937.*

Although country music is primarily identified in many peoples' minds with the U.S. South and Southwest, it always has been a favorite in most rural areas, not only in the United States but in Canada. Canada over the years has always had many locally known country artists, some of whom, like Hank Snow, Stu Phillips, and Ronnie Prophet, went on to become favorites of American audiences as well.

Prophet grew up on a farm about seventy miles from Montreal and, like most farm children, started helping with the chores at an early age. He told an interviewer that he used to milk cows morning and night. Country music was the favorite of his family, particularly since a close relation, Ronnie's cousin Orval Prophet, was a well-known country performer in Canada. Listening to his cousin sing traditional country music on the radio made Ronnie daydream about following suit when he got older.

Like many of the exponents of the Nashville sound in the United States, Ronnie taught himself to play some instruments. (He stated in the mid-1970s that he never learned to read a note of music.) When he was twelve, he bought a cheap guitar and slowly, over a period of several years, figured out how to play it adequately if not uniquely. He also taught himself enough piano to be able to start handling keyboards at local barn dances when he was in his early teens. He had a pleasant voice and also a knack for comedy that he developed to provide a change of pace once he got into show business on a regular basis.

Entertainment proved more of an attraction than high school. As he became more involved in putting together his own groups (including at one time a kazoo band) for engagements at local dances and small clubs, he finally gave up school altogether.

Slowly, Prophet began to build a reputation in Canada as a country artist. He was just about coming into his own when the rock revolution came along in the mid- and late-1950s to drastically limit the opportunities for new country singers to gain large-scale engagements or contracts with major record labels.

Ronnie, however, had persistence and was still active in the country field in the 1960s when country music began to recover from the rock-caused depression and in the 1970s when country found an upsurge of interest both in the United States and Canada. One place where Prophet found a good reception was Nevada, where he became a regular visitor, appearing on bills with such stars as Danny Thomas. By then he had taken up permanent residence in Nashville, where he became a local celebrity as a featured artist at the Carousel Club.

In the 1970s, his career finally began to shift into high gear. He became a familiar figure to Canadian TV viewers as star of his own show on the CBC network, telecast from Toronto. He also was a guest performer not only on most nationally televised U.S. country shows but on such other showcases as the *Merv Griffin* show and Johnny Carson's *The Tonight Show.*

During the mid-1970s, Prophet signed a recording contract with RCA Records and achieved a number of chart singles for the label.

PRUETT, JEANNE: *Singer, guitarist, writer. Born Alabama, January 30.*

With southern and country music roots going back for generations, it's not surprising that Jeanne Pruett became one of the most respected female country stars of the 1970s. When she was a girl, her father recalled, Jeanne was "the best front porch tenor in these parts," though it was her ability as a writer, not a singer, that helped open the doors in Nashville.

"These parts" were in rural Alabama, where Jeanne and her nine brothers and sisters grew up. Her parents were country fans and young Jeanne could recall hearing the *Grand Ole Opry* on Saturday nights

from her earliest years. The typical musical get-togethers provided her with the initial opportunity to polish her performing skills. When the nights were warm and humid in the summer, she spent many hours on the front porch, she noted, "pickin' and singin' country."

As she grew up, Jeanne demonstrated her vocal talents in school events and at local functions, and she began to consider a career in music. In time that caused her to make her way to Nashville, where she landed a job as a writer with Marty Robbins Enterprises in the mid-1960s. She remained on the staff of that organization for seven years, turning out songs that were recorded by many important country artists, including Nat Stuckey, Bill Phillips, and Conway Twitty.

Pruett also sought chances to further her performing career, doing session work and gaining experience on the nightclub and fair circuit. Eventually, the demonstration tapes she made to help induce other artists to record some of her compositions caught the attention of Decca Records executives and brought a recording contract. Starting in the early 1970s, her name began to appear on country bestseller lists with regularity. Among her charted singles of that period were "Hold on to My Unchanging Love," "I've Forgotten More," and, in the spring of 1972, "Love Me," an original composition.

By 1973, Decca had been absorbed into MCA, and one of Pruett's initial contributions to the new designation was the top-10 (in May) single "Satin Sheets." When that rose to upper-chart levels, Jeanne already had been a featured guest on almost all the nationally syndicated TV shows produced in Nashville. She also had become an international favorite, a position aided by several headline tours of Europe. In 1973, her star status was further recognized when she became a regular cast member of the *Grand Ole Opry,* an affiliation still going strong in the 1980s. By then, she had left Robbins Enterprises to become an exclusive writer for Moss Rose Publications.

As the 1970s progressed, Jeanne continued to expand her list of hit recordings. In early 1974, she made upper-chart levels with "You Don't Need to Move a Mountain." In 1975, she placed "Just like Your Daddy" on the charts early in the year, had "Honey on His Hands" on bestseller lists for several months during the summer, and had another top-20 release in the fall, her composition "A Poor Man's Woman."

Late in the decade she left MCA and signed with a new label, IBC Records. She began the 1980s on IBC with the top-10 hit "Back to Back," a song she co-wrote with J. McBee. Later, in what was to prove a banner year for her, she had success with the singles "Temporarily Yours" and "It's Too Late." Her IBC album, *Encore!* issued in late 1979, was on album charts for many months starting in early 1980. In early 1981, Pruett had another single on the charts, "Sad Ole Shade of Gray," on Paid Records.

PURE PRAIRIE LEAGUE: *Vocal and instrumental group, originally from Ohio. Original members, 1970: Craig Fuller, born Ohio; George Powell, born Salem, North Carolina; John David Call, born Waverly, Ohio; Jim Caughlin; Jimmy Lanham. In 1972, lineup included Fuller; Powell; Call; Billy Hinds, born Covington, Kentucky, September 17, 1946; Michael Connor, born Covington, Kentucky, December 7, 1949; Michael Reilly, born Fort Thomas, Kentucky. In the mid-1970s, Fuller replaced by Larry Goshorn, born Cincinnati, Ohio; Call replaced by Timmy Goshorn, born Cincinnati, Ohio. In August 1977, Goshorn brothers and Powell left. Vince Gill, born Oklahoma City, Oklahoma, April 1957, added in September 1978. Patrick Bolin, born Los Angeles, California, circa 1952, added in January 1979. Bolin replaced in 1980 by Jeff Wilson, born Los Angeles, California.*

The album symbol of Pure Prairie League (the name comes from the title of a women's temperance group in an old film that starred Errol Flynn) was a diminutive Norman Rockwellish cowboy called Luke, a fictional figure that somehow outlasted all the original band members. However, despite many changes during the 1970s,

the band somehow maintained a thread of continuity from one alignment to the next and remained one of the more popular country-rock bands into the 1980s.

The two founding members were songwriter and rhythm guitarist George Powell and lead singer–guitarist Craig Fuller. Both grew up in Ohio (though Powell was born in North Carolina), as did a third original musician, guitarist John David Call, who was raised in Waverly and attended Ohio University as an engineering student and Ohio State University as a music major before joining Pure Prairie League. The other sidemen in the first band were Jim Caughlin and Jimmy Lanham. It was that group that worked on the original album *Pure Prairie League*, issued on RCA in March 1972.

As drummer Billy Hinds, who in 1979 had the most seniority, recalled, "The band originally started in Columbus, Ohio, and then ventured to Cincinnati where it played in a club called Billy's. I was working in another band at the same club and we got acquainted. I worked with them for a few months, then left. While I was gone, the others did the first album and first tour. After that, they asked me to come back and I helped record the group's second LP, *Bustin' Out* [issued in October 1972]."

When Hinds joined, he suggested that they might be interested in some of the people he'd worked with before, which soon resulted in pianist–keyboardist Michael Connor and bass guitarist Michael Reilly joining up. Connor noted in 1979, "Michael [Reilly], myself, and Billy had played a lot together before that. I remember Michael and I were in England at the time when we got a call from Billy to come back."

At first, only Connor was added. States Billy, "The three of us worked together well, so I tried to get them into the project. [By then, in 1972, the group had shrunk to a core of Hinds, Fuller, and Powell.] But we already had a bass player for the recording sessions so Connor became a member and when we were ready to tour Reilly came aboard." The band's background prior to that was a blend of western country, some blues, and varied rock; Reilly, who was raised in Kentucky, expanded the influences to include bluegrass. The strong bluegrass influence is noticeable in many of his lead vocal efforts over the years.

Still, for a while it looked as though the newcomers might have joined a sinking ship. *Bustin' Out* didn't make much of an initial impact and RCA dropped the group. In late 1973, though, a strange thing happened. The song "Amy" from the first album began to get steadily increasing airplay, thanks to the song's discovery by a number of disc jockeys. That brought enough requests for a single to cause RCA to turn one out, which promptly made national charts. The sequence of events caused the record company to re-issue *Bustin' Out,* which also spawned another highly regarded single, George Powell's composition "Leave My Heart Alone."

The contract termination and other problems caused a hiatus of some eighteen months, during which no new recordings were made and another major reorganization took place. "One thing that hit us," says Hinds, "was the loss of Craig Fuller. He got into trouble on a draft evasion thing and left. He was replaced by Larry Goshorn." Goshorn, who took over on lead guitar and also contributed vocal and writing skills, was raised in Cincinnati, where he had been playing guitar in local rock bands since high school. He always had been an admirer of the Everly Brothers, whom he ranked as a prime influence on his performing and writing style.

The belated success of the 1972 releases had renewed RCA's interest in the band and led to a new contract in 1974. The result of that was the April 1975 album *Two-Lane Highway,* the first on which Reilly and Goshorn performed. The LP and its title track both made national charts, indicating that, at last, Pure Prairie League had established a foothold with the public at large. In support of the new recordings, the revamped band spent over 200 days on the road, playing major cities all over the United States. It was a pace the group kept

up for the next few years, even though another long-time mainstay, John David Call, left, to be replaced by Larry Goshorn's brother, Timmy.

During that period, the group turned out a series of albums, most of which provided a single or two that showed up on the charts. These included "If the Shoe Fits," "Dance," and the group's first live album release, a two-record set titled *Live! Takin' the Stage* that came out in 1978. Also a 1978 release (in April) was another studio album, *Just Fly.*

By the time the last two albums were issued, Pure Prairie League had gone through still another drastic reshuffle. In August 1977, the last remaining founding member, Powell, departed, along with the Goshorns. "The Goshorns decided they could do better as a solo act, the Goshorn Brothers," Hinds says. "They sort of always wanted to do that," adds Connor. "They have a younger brother who's also a musician, so the three of them decided to try a new group."

As to Powell's reason for leaving, Hinds notes, "George had a little girl and decided he wanted to be a father and husband and give up the tour grind to stay home. He got a farm in Williamsburg, Ohio, where he decided to concentrate on writing songs and doing demos."

After that, with home now in the Los Angeles area, Reilly, Hinds, and Connor set about to recruit new members. After auditioning a great many candidates, the first choice in September 1978 was multi-talented Vince Gill, whose talents included vocals, songwriting, and such instruments as guitar, banjo, fiddle, dobro, and mandolin. Born and raised in Oklahoma City, he had a strong grounding in folk and country music as a boy and later played in a Kentucky-based bluegrass band called Boone Creek and traveled for close to three years with the Byron Berline group.

In February 1979, a fifth musician was added in the person of Los Angeles–born singer-songwriter-musician Patrick Bolin. Bolin provided such instrumental capabilities as saxophone and flute and an outlook more oriented toward mainstream rock.

He also had been a member for a while of a Los Angeles bar band "who played Steely Dan type stuff."

The new alignment completed the eighth Pure Prairie League LP in early 1979, *Can't Hold Back*. Even before the RCA LP came out in late May 1979, the band was trying out some of its new songs before audiences across the country. The response seemed to be highly favorable whether the group headlined on college campuses or opened for such country rock groups as the Charlie Daniels Band and Marshall Tucker Band in larger venues. The impact of the newest members was obvious in the new release, *Can't Hold Back*, which included Bolin's composition "Goodbye, So Long" and such Gill originals as "Can't Hold Back," "I Can't Believe," "Misery Train," "I'm Going Away," and "Jelene."

By the start of 1980, the group had left RCA and signed with Casablanca Records. In January 1980, Bolin was replaced by singer-guitarist Jeff Wilson, who helped record the band's debut LP on Casablanca, *Firin' Up*, issued in 1980. His contributions included co-writing two songs on the album, "Too Many Heartaches in Paradise" and "Let Me Love You Tonight." The latter song provided a top-10 single, the band's first top-10 hit since "Amy." In April 1981, Casablanca released Pure Prairie League's second album, *Something in the Night*. Band members for the LP were Reilly, Hinds, Connor, Gill, and Wilson.

"The important thing," declares Connor, "is that though we keep expanding our musical directions, it still falls into a recognizable pattern. Even though we've had changes in personnel and in musical emphasis, Pure Prairie League still sounds like Pure Prairie League."

Based partly on 1979 interview of Billy Hinds and Michael Connor by Irwin Stambler.

R

RABBITT, EDDIE: *Singer, songwriter. Born Brooklyn, New York, November 27, 1944.*

Although country music is now popular all over the United States and in many foreign countries, the majority of country artists have been, and still are, from the southern regions of the nation. One notable exception is Eddie Rabbitt. He was born in Brooklyn, New York, to Irish immigrant parents. His family later moved to East Orange, New Jersey, where Eddie spent the remainder of his youth. He learned the love of music from his father, Thomas, who later was to play fiddle on Eddie's "Song of Ireland" in the album, *Variations*. He learned to play guitar from his scoutmaster, Tony Schwickrath, who performed as a local country artist under the name Bob Randall. Eddie had only mastered two chords when Schwickrath moved out of town, but with those two chords and his voice he was able to win a talent contest at Kenettewapeck Summer Camp.

Eddie was now on his way to realizing the dream he had held since the age of five, to become a country-music singer. While still in high school, he won another talent contest, which enabled him to broadcast live from a Paterson, New Jersey bar, one hour out of a regular Saturday night radio show. One night in 1964, when Rabbitt was celebrating his graduation from night school (he had dropped out of high school) in a New Jersey bar, the bar's piano player quit and Eddie convinced the owner to hire him. Following this stint, Rabbitt was able to find work in New Jersey and in some New York bars for twenty-five dollars a night. The area proved to be quite a hotbed of country-music activity, but Eddie finally decided that to succeed in the field he would have to head south. So he went to Nashville, hoping to become a star.

Eddie had beginner's luck. The first song he wrote in Nashville, "Working My Way Up to the Bottom," was recorded by Roy Drusky, providing him with a hit. His luck did not continue, however, and in the next several months he was unable to sell any songs or to interest anyone in his singing. He started hanging out with such then-unknown talents as Kris Kristofferson, Billy Swan, and Larry Gatlin.

Eventually, Rabbitt's career picked up, and he was signed as a staff writer for the music publishers Hill and Range at a mere $37.50 a week. Many songs of his were recorded, some by major artists, but only a couple were hits.

At last Eddie won a recording contract on the basis of a song he wrote, "Kentucky Rain," but he found himself faced with a strange problem. Elvis Presley had heard the song and wanted to record it. Eddie had to decide between recording the song himself or letting Elvis have it. He decided to let Elvis record the song, hoping in that way to make some money and to bring some much-needed attention to himself. The song provided Elvis with his fiftieth gold record. The producer on Eddie's would-be recording contract, however, tore up the contract when he heard that the song had been given to Presley. Rabbitt recalls that the producer said, "If you're not interested enough in your own career to save your best song for yourself, then why should I care about your career? So let's just forget about the whole thing."

Nevertheless, Eddie's success continued to accelerate. In 1973 Ronnie Milsap recorded Eddie's composition "Pure Love," and it became a number-one hit. In 1974 Rabbitt signed a contract with Elektra Records and was at last able to sing his songs himself. His first single, "You Get to Me," reached number twenty-two nationally. Since then, he has scored with one hit after another.

Rabbitt had a major hit single with "Forgive and Forget," which led to his first album, *Eddie Rabbitt*. His second album, *Rocky Mountain Music* (1976), contained

three hits, "Drinking My Baby Off My Mind," "Two Dollars in the Jukebox," and the title song, "Rocky Mountain Music," which also crossed over to the pop charts. (Most of the songs were co-written by Eddie and Even Stevens. The two still were writing most of Rabbitt's hits in the early 1980s, usually with a third collaborator, D. Malloy.) In 1977 Eddie scored hit singles with "I Can't Help Myself" and "We Can't Go on Living like This" from his album *Rabbitt*. His 1978-released LP, *Variations*, provided him with three hit singles, "Hearts on Fire," the smash hit "You Don't Love Me Anymore," and "I Just Want to Love You." In 1979, he had a number-one-ranked hit, "Every Which Way but Loose," from the Clint Eastwood movie of the same name. At year end, his single "Pour Me Another Tequilla" was in the top 10, where it remained into early the following year. In 1980, he had another number-one hit from a movie, "Driving My Life Away," from the motion picture *Roadie*.

His number-one hit single "Gone Too Far" reached that pinnacle in May 1980. Late in the year his single "I Love a Rainy Night" showed up on the charts, rising to the top of the lists in early 1981. In the fall of 1981 Rabbitt had still another number-one hit single, "Step by Step" (October 1981), and "Someone Could Lose a Heart Tonight" began moving toward the top levels as the year drew to a close. His 1979 LP release *Loveline* was on the charts into 1980. Also on the charts that year were his albums *Horizon* and the *Best of Eddie Rabbitt*. Both earned gold records and were still in upper-chart positions in 1981.

In addition to Eddie's proven songwriting skills, his good looks make him a favorite with women fans. His voice has a pleading tone that adds distinction to his pleasant tenor voice. His songs often deal with traditional country themes, but his style is relaxed, a soft pop sound with jazz and country undertones. By the beginning of the 1980s, it became clear that not only had country fans adopted this Yankee as one of their favorite performers, but that he was catching on in the wider pop music market. He served as guest host on the late-night television variety show, *The Midnight Special,* and also had his own highly acclaimed television special.

Rabbitt claims, however, that he has not deliberately courted the pop market. As he told Tom Chester of *The Knoxville Journal,* "When you get out of the thing you do naturally, you lose it. We' ve had a lot of crossover things that have been getting good pop play. But I just do what I do, and it happens it does span more than the country market. . . . Country music is getting wider. People are getting into it and there's more acceptance of it. Since [President] Carter, people can be more proud of it. It seems like, though, country music is always five, six, or seven years behind the rock 'n' roll thing. Country is in the evolution stage of rock 'n' roll of seven years ago. But the pop scene is up against the wall as far as a new direction. Pop is stopped. It's been through the heavy metal and those scenes. Country music has moved up behind it. And the music is starting to flow into each other."—A.S.

RABBITT, JIMMY: *Singer, songwriter, musician, disc jockey. Born Holdenville, Oklahoma.*

The term "outlaw" has been used to denote a nonconforming, outwardly tough musician, usually from the state of Texas. Jimmy Rabbitt was born in Oklahoma, but he spent most of his youth in Texas, and in all other respects fits in with the general picture of a modern-day outlaw.

Jimmy did not at first seem particularly rebellious. After being graduated from high school, Eddie Payne (Rabbitt's original name; he legally changed his name to Jimmy Rabbitt during his radio career) joined the Marines for six months and then joined the reserves. After his stint with the Marines, he enrolled at American University in Washington, D.C., where he studied radio and television. He worked on the campus radio station for a while, but he got thrown off, allegedly because he played some Little Richard records, which were considered somewhat risqué at the time. Rabbitt's rebelliousness was beginning to emerge.

While in Washington, Rabbitt also kept up with his other main interest, singing and performing. He played with popular folk, hootenanny-style groups as well as with louder, rockabilly-type ones. During this time, he also managed to put out his first single, for a small record company, Colt .45 Records.

Rabbitt's first single did not gain too much attention so he decided to return to Texas to attend Tyler Junior College for two years. To support himself, he also sold shoes and played music at fraternity parties and in bars. During that time, he cut several singles that received local airplay and were picked up by larger labels. One day he went to a radio station to make a commercial for the shoe store for which he was working. One of the announcers at the station had quit and Rabbitt was hired on the spot for the position. He has been employed as a disc jockey almost consistently since then.

Jimmy worked briefly for stations in Corpus Christi and Port Arthur. He then was hired at KLIF in Dallas, where he became the city's top-rated disc jockey for more than five years. In his spare time, he continued to play music in various bands. At one point, in the mid-1960s, he formed a group called Positively 13 O'Clock, which recorded a song entitled "Psychotic Reaction." However, the national hit of the song was made by another group, named Count Five.

Eventually, Rabbitt was fired from KLIF, as happens very frequently with disc jockeys, and he began doing promotional work for Abnak Records, which handled the Five Americans and Jon & Robin and the In-Crowd. From the latter group came two of Rabbitt's current group members, Bobby Rambo (guitarist) and Rex Ludwick (drummer).

Jimmy moved to San Diego, where he worked on a radio station for about six months until he was hired by KRLA in Los Angeles in 1968. Since that time, he has worked for eleven different radio stations in the Los Angeles area. As he said, "I've been fired from more stations than most guys ever work for. I've quit from my share too." Despite all his job changes, he became known as one of the nation's top disc jockeys and was one of the handful of radio personalities to be named on *Esquire* magazine's "Heavy 100 of Rock 'n' Roll." He is credited with coining the term "progressive country" in a column he wrote for "The Bob Hamilton Report," a radio tip sheet.

As always, Rabbitt's dedication to music did not limit itself to playing other people's music. He continued to perform as well as to write songs. In 1970, he signed with a record company owned by the Smothers Brothers; he cut an album, but the company folded and the album was never released. In 1974, he cut an album for Atlantic Records' new country label, but that label also folded and again his hopes for a released LP were dashed.

Nevertheless, he persevered. He had tried to put together his Renegade band on various occasions and finally did so in 1975, when he assembled the musicians to play at the county-music Palomino Club in North Hollywood, California. Two shows sold out for that appearance and 300 people had to be turned away. When Ricky Nelson canceled the next weekend, because of the death of his father, Rabbitt took his place and again sold out both shows on both nights.

Among the people in the audience for one of the shows was Waylon Jennings, an old friend of Jimmy's from back in Texas. Jennings liked what he heard and agreed to produce an album for him on Capitol Records. The result was *Jimmy Rabbitt and Renegade.* This long-hoped-for first album did not produce any major chart hits. However, Jimmy Rabbitt and Renegade remain a major attraction at clubs in the Los Angeles area.—A.S.

RANDOLPH, HOMER LOUIS "BOOTS," JR: *Saxophonist, trombonist, ukulele player. Born Paducah, Kentucky, June 3, circa 1927.*

One of the staples of Boots Randolph's stage routine was to suddenly tell the audience "You're listening to the world's greatest hillbilly saxophone player" . . . pause for reaction . . . "Would you believe the world's ONLY hillbilly saxophonist." It's a bit of an exaggeration, because Randolph is a sophisticated instrumentalist who can play everything from jazz to classics on his

sax, but there's no doubt about his ability to make country songs sound like they belonged naturally to his kind of instrument.

Randolph was born in Paducah, Kentucky, into a family that enjoyed playing music. As soon as Boots was old enough to learn an instrument, he was entrusted with a ukulele and became part of the family band, which comprised his father on fiddle, mother on guitar, sister Dorothy on bass, and older brothers Earl and Bob on banjo and mandolin. Initially the group played amateur talent contests, but as the Depression times of the mid-1930s increased the urgency of finding ways to make ends meet, the group took any engagements available, including clubs, auditoriums, and run-down theaters.

Randolph recalled, "It was pretty standard for us to come home from those talent contests with the old car loaded down with cans of corn and peas and boxes of macaroni, bacon, and bread. We didn't have much money—but boy, did we eat."

By that time, the family had moved to Cadiz, Kentucky, where Boots attended elementary school. The year before Boots was ready for high school, his father presented him with a trombone. "My dad picked it up in a trade. Would you believe he swapped a .38 caliber pistol for the trombone? Well he did. I learned the slide by ear. My first tunes were 'Tuxedo Junction' and 'Sweet Sue.' "

Boots played in the school band both in elementary school and at Central High School in Evansville, Indiana, where his family moved when the United States entered World War II. In his junior year, he switched to the saxophone because "It seems like a sax was easier to play while marching in the school band than a trombone." After his father bought him a tenor saxophone, he and brother Bob organized a six-person group (sometimes expanded to eight) that played at local Army bases.

In 1945, when Randolph was eighteen, he was drafted into the Army and took basic training at Camp Lee, Virginia, later joining the Army band based at Camp Kilmer, New Jersey. "Our band would stand on the pier and serenade the boys coming home or shipping out."

After his discharge he went home and tried to pick up where he had left off. However, he got married and, finding music jobs scarce in Evansville in 1948, got a job in a factory for a while. "I got this job at the American Fork and Hoe Company. They put me to work driving wedges into hammer heads. I hit my fingers and thumbs more often than I did the wedges. After four weeks I decided to quit. I reasoned that if I ever hoped to play the sax again I'd need my fingers and thumbs and that if I stayed with those wedges I wouldn't have any left."

Randolph managed to find enough work as a sideman with various midwest combos to keep going. In 1954 he found steady employment at a night spot in Decatur, Illinois, where he remained for four years. He and an associate, James Rich, had written a tune called "Yakety Sax" at the time and they sent a tape of the country-oriented number to Chet Atkins, musical director at RCA Records' Nashville offices. The tape brought results. Atkins brought Boots to Nashville to do session work with major artists in both the pop and country fields and also signed him to a recording contract. Among those he supported were Al Hirt, Homer & Jethro, Perry Como, Roy Orbison, Teresa Brewer, Burl Ives, Eddy Arnold, Pete Fountain, and Elvis Presley.

However, his RCA recordings didn't have much impact on the public. After several years on the label, Boots left RCA and signed a new agreement with Monument Records. In a short time, his *Yakety Sax* album became a sensation with country fans. It was on the hit lists a good part of 1961, eventually passing gold-record levels in sales. From then on, Randolph became a familar face on country shows throughout the 1960s, 1970s, and into the 1980s. He often was spotlighted on the *Grand Ole Opry* and appeared in almost every major country-music program. Besides TV and countless in-person headline appearances, he was in a number of series with country-music themes.

Meanwhile, Monument continued to turn out a succession of albums and singles in the 1960s and 1970s, most of which sold solidly, if not sensationally, with a number of them showing up on country charts. Among the singles were "Yakety Sax," "Windy and Warm," "Hey Mr. Sax Man," "Yodelin' Sax," "Miss You," "I Really Don't Want to Know," and "Baby, Go to Sleep." The album releases include such 1960s offerings as *Yakety Sax*, *More Yakety Sax*, *The Fantastic Boots Randolph*, *Sax-Sational*, and *Boots with Strings*. Among the 1970s LPs were *Hit Boots 1970*, *Boots with Brass*, *Homer Louis Randolph* (issued 9/71); *Yakety Sax* (a two-record retrospective on Camden label); and *World of Boots Randolph* (9/72).

RAUSCH, LEON: *Singer, guitarist, band leader. Born Springfield, Missouri, October 2, 1927.*

When many people think of Leon Rausch, they primarily associate him with Bob Wills and the Texas Playboys. He did, of course, perform with that band, and in its later stages Wills still thought enough of him to select him as one of the eight musicians to re-record some of the old Playboys' favorites just before Bob's death. Rausch was well known to southwest country & western fans in his own right, however, as a band leader and recording artist for many years outside the Playboys organization.

Leon wasn't a Texan by birth, though Texas later became a second home. He grew up in Missouri in a family where performing country & western music was treasured. He learned to play several instruments in his childhood, and when he was eleven began to perform at local dances with his father, from whom he already had learned many country songs. As he recalls, those events often were very informal. "In those days we played wherever we could. People were happy to accommodate us because it was the only form of entertainment we had. If someone had a good layout in a house, we could roll the rug out. We played places that were pretty small where we played in one room and people watched or danced in the other. We made our money by passing the hat around."

Rausch continued those performances into his teens, when he joined the U.S.

Navy during World War II. After spending three years in the service, he got his discharge and headed home, intent on a career in country & western music. He worked in and around Springfield for a number of years before moving to Tulsa, Oklahoma, in 1955, which then was an active musical area.

"I started with Bob Wills in 1958," Rausch states. "I took Tommy Duncan's brother's place as singer in the band. At the time the Playboys were on a swing from California and they picked me up on the way back. I stayed with them until 1961. While I was with Bob he went to horns again and back to fiddles. We had eleven people in the band my second year with them.

"We did real well in Vegas. We played the Showboat in 1959 for the first time and the band sold really well. So finally the boys from downtown came and gave us a little more money to play the Golden Nugget four weeks in a row. In 1960, we decided we could move there and travel in and out of there a month at a time. During that time period, Tommy Duncan came back and they did an album on Liberty called *Together Again*. But there were personal problems in the band that caused difficulties. Part of it was Bob's disappointment that we didn't do better. We sold reasonably well but couldn't recapture the old glories. We did three albums together during 1960–61."

After leaving Bob Wills' group, Leon joined the group headed by Wills' brother, Johnnie Lee Wills, and stayed with that band until 1964. Soon after, Rausch organized his own band, which took the name the New Texas Playboys. He made Fort Worth, Texas, headquarters for the group and managed to line up enough engagements to make it a viable operation the rest of the 1960s. In 1967, the New Texas Playboys signed with Longhorn Records and had some success with singles like "I'm So Glad Mom Can't See Me Now" and "Painted Angels."

In the 1970s, most of Rausch's own efforts were with smaller groups. From the mid-1970s to early 1980s, he had a trio that played clubs, campuses, and concert halls in Texas and surrounding states. Leon got some mileage out of solo releases on the regional Derrick label in the mid-1970s. One of those singles, "She's the Trip I've Been On," made the national country charts during August and September 1976. He still had releases on that label at the end of the decade, such as "Palimony," on country charts from late 1979 into early 1980.

By then Leon also was featured vocalist in the newest incarnation of Bob Wills' band, the Original Texas Playboys. That project grew out of a decision made by Wills in the early 1970s, when he already was in ill health, to hand-pick a band made up of the best of all Playboys band members still active to record one more album. In 1973, Wills asked Rausch to join as bassist and vocalist. Wills suffered a stroke before the sessions were finished, but the revitalized band completed the work, the multirecord set, *For the Last Time*.

Several guest appearances by Rausch and the Playboys in late 1975 and early 1976, one with Asleep at the Wheel at Nashville's Exit-In club in October and another on the Public Broadcasting System syndicated *Austin City Limits*, helped increase the group's new audience. This led to a contract from Capitol Records, whose inital album was *The Late Bob Wills' Original Texas Playboys Today*, issued in March 1977. Later, more albums were prepared with Rausch continuing as lead singer, including *Live and Kickin'*, issued in early 1978, and an early 1979 LP.

Those albums and related concerts brought together two famous Leons in the Playboys at the same time, Rausch and McAuliffe. As Rausch noted with a smile, having McAuliffe's first name, at least professionally, had caused some problems. "Bein' as my name's Leon, too, I always have to explain to people when they say 'Hey, ain't you the "Take it away Leon" guy?' that Bob always used to say that to McAuliffe. Actually, Leon is my middle name—my full name is Edgar Leon Rausch."

Based on an interview with Irwin Stambler ir 1979.

RAVEN, EDDY: *Singer, guitarist, songwriter. Born Lafayette, Louisiana, August 19, early 1940s.*

To many people Louisiana's prime musical identification is with Dixieland jazz. But country fans know that's only part of the state's contribution to American music. t's the homeland of Cajun music, the clasic country songs of Jimmie Davis, and such early rock greats as Jerry Lee Lewis. All of those elements had an impact on another Louisiana son, Eddy Raven, who was grounded in country and Cajun lore by his father, switched to rock, then returned to become a major contributor to modern country music in the 1960s, 1970s, and 1980s.

His father, an enthusiastic country fan, was only too happy to find Eddy musically inclined at an early age and had visions of the boy someday reaching a national audience from the *Opry* stage. For a time things seemed headed that way. Eddy had his first guitar at seven and could play many classic country songs on it before he was in his teens. But it was the 1950s, an exciting new music form called rock was coming to the fore, and, despite his father's objections, that came to be his prime interest for an extended period.

The Raven family was on the move for much of Eddy's teen years, as his father's work took him to other parts of the South. When Eddy was fourteen, he was living in Georgia, playing in local bands and already thinking about writing original material. That year, Eddy gained his own fifteen-minute radio show on station WHAB and also cut some sides on the small Cosmo label, one of which became a local hit. However, that phase of his career was cut short when the family moved back to Lafayette.

Eddy, determined to keep active in the music field, got a job at a local studio. Successful songwriter and performer Bobby Charles (whose credits included "See You Later Alligator" and "Walking to New Orleans") lived in the vicinity and came by the studio looking for new material. He and Eddy met, and the occasion induced Raven to write the song "Big Boys Cry." After considering it, Charles recorded it,

and the single received considerable airplay locally.

During those years, Raven was swept up in the rock revolution. He admired the work of Elvis, the Everly Brothers, and Buddy Holly and sought the chance to perform with local rock groups. Later he stressed that one factor that made him go that route was that "the girls liked it. But I was never as rock as the other rockers. My roots were country." Still, he was primarily a rock musician for about a decade, performing with various bands along the Gulf Coast from the late 1950s through the mid-1960s. Some of the material he played was in the blues-rock vein; he was a sideman with Johnny and Edgar Winter for a while, before the Texans went on to national fame in the late 1960s.

At the end of the 1960s, Eddy was out of rock and spending much of his time in Louisiana seeking to make his way in the country field. It was slow going at first. Eddy wrote more songs and made a number of recordings on local labels, but made little progress toward finding a wider audience. Long-time country star Jimmy C. Newman, however, was impressed with a country-flavored Cajun album of Raven's and offered to give him some Nashville introductions. In July 1970, Raven met Jimmy in Music City and, soon after, Newman's sponsorship resulted in Raven's signing a writing contract with Acuff–Rose Publishing. During the early 1970s, Eddy brought a series of excellent songs from Louisiana to Nashville. One of these, "Country Green," proved to be a top-5 hit single for Don Gibson. More successes followed: Jeannie C. Riley made the charts with her version of Eddy's "Good Morning Country Rain" and Gibson gained another top-5 disc with "Touch the Morning."

Having won his spurs as a writer, Eddy moved to Nashville to pursue his performing career. One of his first engagements was at the King of the Road Motor Inn, where he started as a lounge act and quickly became a headliner in the main room. With that kind of showcase, he soon had his first major label recording contract, with ABC/Dot. During the mid-1970s, he had a number of singles on country charts,

including some of his original compositions as well as songs by other writers.
Among them were "Last of the Sunshine
Cowboys" (1974); "Ain't She Something
Else," "Good News, Bad News," and
"You're My Rainy Day Woman" (all
1975); and "Free to Be" and "The Curse of
a Woman" (1976). His in-person activities,
of course, expanded far beyond Nashville.
He traveled to most of the regular stops on
the country-music circuit and also was featured several times at the Landmark Hotel
in Las Vegas. He also appeared on most
major country TV and radio shows, including the most prestigious one, the
Grand Ole Opry.

His increased performing schedule
didn't seem to interfere too much with his
writing efforts. In the mid- and late-1970s,
a steady series of recordings of new Raven
songs appeared by such artists as Lefty
Frizzell, Roy Clark, Roy Orbison, Jerry
Reed, Moe Bandy, Carl Smith, Connie
Smith, Randy Corner, and Roy Acuff.
Acuff savored one of his first top-level
chart hits in some time with Eddy's "Back
in the Country." Both Randy Corner and
Connie Smith gained top-10 hits, Randy
with "Sometimes I Talk in My Sleep" and
Connie with "I Don't Want to Talk It Over
Anymore" and "The Latest Shade of
Blue." A particular honor for Raven was
the selection of "Back in the Country" as
the theme song for the 1975 ABC-TV spe-
cial, *The Grand Ole Opry at 50.*

In the late 1970s, Eddy recorded briefly
for Monument Records, one result being
the charted single of his composition
"You're a Dancer" in 1978. He then moved
to Dimension Records, which led to a series of charted singles in 1979 and the
early 1980s such as "Sweet Mother Texas"
(co-written with S.D. Shafer); "Dealin'
with the Devil" (Raven and Shafer),
"You've Got Those Eyes" (co-written with
D. Powelson), "Another Texas Song" (Raven), all 1980; and "Peace of Mind"
(Raven), early 1981. During 1981, Eddy left
Dimension and signed a new agreement
with Elektra Records. His debut single,
written by him, "Who Do You Know in
California," was in the top 30 soon after its
release in late 1981.

RAYE, SUSAN: *Singer. Born Eugene, Oregon, October 8, 1944.*

The TV show *Hee Haw,* as the name implies, strongly stresses "barnyard" humor.
But it has also featured many of today's
brightest established country-music stars
and provided a showcase for promising
new talent. One who made a name for
herself in the show's early days was Susan
Raye, a protégé of the show's cohost, Buck
Owens.

Born in Eugene and raised in the small
town of Forest Grove, near Portland, Oregon, Susan had no early desire to become
a singer. It was her mother who prompted
Susan to audition as a country singer at a
local radio station. Raye, then seventeen,
won the audition and became a regular on
the station for a year. Besides doing a live
country show in the morning, she served
as an afternoon disc jockey.

Her singing improved steadily, as did
her standing with local country fans. Eventually, in the mid-1960s she became a
regular on a Portland TV show called *Hoedown.* It was during one of those club dates
in 1965 that Jack McFadden, Buck Owens'
manager, heard her perform and brought
word back to Owens' Bakersfield, California, headquarters. Owens arranged for
plane tickets to Bakersfield and, after listening to Susan sing, agreed she had potential. A few months later, Raye was
added to the cast of an Owens' tour of
Washington and Oregon.

When the tour ended, Susan went back
home to continue her TV and nightclub
work, until, in 1968, she decided to return
to Bakersfield and sing with the Owens
organization. "I really started to care about
today's country music and for improving
my own performance, and Bakersfield
seemed the best place to start," she said.

Her devotion paid off. The following
year she received a contract from Capitol
Records, which released her debut single,
"Maybe If I Close My Eyes," in September
1969. The single made the country charts,
the first of many to do so throughout the
first half of the 1970s. Besides solo work,
she also recorded a number of duets with
Buck, which led to her album debut in
April 1970. Later in the year she scored a

major singles hit with "One Night Stand," the title song for her solo debut on Capitol in August 1970. By then Raye had a featured spot on *Hee Haw* and also was in demand for personal appearances around the United States.

From 1970 through 1975, Raye kept adding to her list of chart singles, which included the top-10 songs "Stop the World and Let Me Off" in 1974, "Whatcha Gonna Do with a Dog like That" in 1975, and a number of top-10 or top-20 duet singles with Buck, such as the 1975 hit "Love Is Strange." During those years, Capitol turned out a steady stream of her LPs, including *One Night Stand, Bill Jones, Pitty, Pitty Patter, Happy Heart, Wheel of Fortune, My Heart Has a Mind of Its Own,* and *Whatcha Gonna Do with a Dog like That?*

REED, JERRY: *Singer, guitarist, songwriter, actor. Born Atlanta, Georgia, March 20, 1937.*

Patience, talent, a sense of humor—all those combined to make Jerry Reed one of country music's brightest stars of the 1970s, after an apprenticeship that lasted over two decades. Proud of his role as a family man, he made it to the top without the excesses that plagued the careers of many other artists. As he told writer Red O'Donnell, "I'm so normal it's sickening—really square. I've never been part of the drug or heavy booze scene. I get high on music. And I want to have a clear head when I write or perform that music."

Reed's love for music went back to his early years growing up in Atlanta, Georgia, working in the cotton mills. Like many other country musicians, music offered a way out of a working-class environment. He played guitar in grade school and began to appear at small clubs in and around Atlanta with country bands in his early teens.

When he was sixteen, a policeman friend extolled his guitar skills to Atlanta publisher-producer Bill Lowery, noting that Jerry also wrote promising songs. The result was a management contract. In 1955, Lowery obtained a writing and recording contract for Jerry with Capitol Records. The recording side didn't make any breakthroughs, but there was rising interest in

his songs in the late 1950s and early 1960s. Among those who recorded some of them were Brenda Lee and Elvis Presley. One of Reed's numbers that Elvis put on vinyl in the 1960s was "Guitar Man."

Jerry moved to Nashville after a stint in the service to pursue his songwriting, supplementing his income with session work. In fact, during the first half of the 1960s, he gained a reputation as one of Nashville's best backing guitarists and was offered more assignments than he could handle. Besides playing behind most of country and pop music's top names, he often accompanied major artists on concert tours.

Still hoping to move into the spotlight himself, he finally found encouragement in 1965. Another guitar wizard, Chet Atkins, RCA Nashville's artists & repertoire executive, signed Jerry with the company. Looking back, Reed told an interviewer from the Lexington (Kentucky) *Herald,* "I couldn't get a hit to save my life, and I'd been there [Nashville] three years. Then Chet Atkins began recording me for RCA records and we haven't been off the charts since. Chet just said, 'You're doing it wrong, Mr. Reed; let's try it this way,' and damned if he wasn't right."

The first result was the album *The Unbelievable Guitar and Voice of Jerry Reed.* Although it wasn't a smash hit after its release in 1967, RCA officials were satisfied with it. Their confidence was rewarded with the late 1960s LPs *Nashville Underground, Alabama Wild Man, Better Things in Life,* and *Jerry Reed Explores Guitar Country* (November 1969). Reed's following among fans increased, as did respect from his entertainment industry peers. Soon considered one of country and pop music's top writers, from 1956 to 1970 he won four BMI country awards (for "Misery Loves Company," "Remembering," "A Thing Called Love," and "U.S. Male") and two BMI pop awards (for "That's All You Gotta Do" and "Guitar Man"). Jerry appeared as a guest on two major TV programs, *Johnny Cash* and *The Glen Campbell Goodtime Hour* 1969 summer replacement show, as his performing career also advanced.

In 1970 everything finally came together to bring Reed national acclaim. He had three chart hit albums: *Cookin'*, issued in March, *Me and Jerry*, a duet with Chet Atkins issued in midyear, and *Georgia Sunshine*, released in September. It was also the year he turned out one of his best-known singles, a song about a man who might be called the Paul Bunyan of the bayous, "Amos Moses." This song provided him with his first number-one country hit and also went high on the pop charts. For his year's work, he gleaned such honors as his first Grammy for Best Instrumental Performance *(Me and Jerry)* and a nomination for Best Country Male Performance and a BMI award, both for "Amos Moses." The Country Music Association in 1970 named him Instrumentalist of the Year.

Reed became a regular on *The Glen Campbell Goodtime Hour* on CBS-TV for the 1970–71 season, returning for the 1971–72 season. During the summer of 1971, he toured the United States with Campbell. Jerry's album releases in 1971 included the smash hit *When You're Hot, You're Hot*, issued in May, whose title song, "I'm Movin' On", became one of the year's best-selling singles (Harmony, 6/71), and *Ko-ko Joe* (10/71). Those efforts won him a second Grammy, Best Country Male Performance for "When You're Hot, You're Hot," and a second straight selection by the CMA as Instrumentalist of the Year. In the CMA competition, he also was among the finalists in six other categories, including Male Vocalist and Entertainer of the Year. On March 29, 1971, Reed was awarded a gold record from the R.I.A.A. for the single "Amos Moses."

Jerry's 1972 RCA LPs included *Smell the Flowers* (4/72), *Me and Chet*, with Atkins (6/72), *Best of Jerry Reed* (8/72), *Jerry Reed* (10/72), and, on Camden, *Oh What a Woman* (11/72). During the year he was part of the concert series called "Festival of Music," sharing top billing with Chet Atkins, Floyd Cramer, and Boots Randolph. He continued to add to his list of BMI songwriting awards, receiving honors for such early 1970s country efforts as "Georgia Sunshine," "Amos Moses,"

"Talk About the Good Times," "When You're Hot, You're Hot," "A Thing Called Love," and "Ko-ko Joe." He also was given BMI pop awards for "A Thing Called Love," and "Amos Moses." His charted singles in 1972 included "Alabama Wild Man," "Another Puff," and "Smell the Flowers."

During the summer of 1973, he was featured on the NBC-TV show *Music Country, U.S.A.* following the release of his chart-hit album *Lord Mr. Ford*. He also appeared on *Hee Haw* and won BMI country awards for "Alabama Wild Man" and "You Took All the Ramblin' Out of Me." In 1974, his TV credits included appearances on *Southern Sportsman, Hee Haw, Dinah!, Merv Griffin,* and Johnny Carson's *The Tonight Show,* and once again on *Music Country, U.S.A.* Jerry, who had left BMI for ASCAP, received ASCAP awards in 1974 for being artist and producer of the recordings "A Good Woman's Love" and "Uptown Poker Club."

A new career phase opened for Reed in 1974 when he joined the cast of Burt Reynolds' movie, *W.W. and the Dixie Dance Kings.* More than a few movie critics took favorable notice of his work in the film. In 1976, he worked with Reynolds again on the movie *Gator,* and the following year on the new Reynolds opus, *Smokey and the Bandit.* The film surprised the critics by becoming one of the unexpected hits of the cinema year. In 1978, Jerry started work on another movie project, this time a comedy starring Dom DeLuise. That film, titled *Hot Stuff,* was released during the summer of 1979. In 1980, he was part of the cast of *Smokey and the Bandit II.*

During the mid- and late-1970s, Jerry usually placed several singles on the charts each year, a situation that continued in the early 1980s. His charted RCA releases in 1980 were "Sugar Foot Rag," "Age/Workin' at the Carwash Blues," and "Texas Bound and Flying"; in early 1981, the single "Caffeine, Nicotine and Benzedrine (and Wish Me Luck)" was on lower-chart rungs. His charted albums in the early 1980s included *Jerry Reed Gets into Jim Croce* and *Texas Bound and Flying.*

REEVES, DEL: *Singer, guitarist, songwriter, disc jockey, actor, TV show host. Born Sparta, North Carolina, July 14, 1933.*

Dubbed by some music commentators the "Dean Martin of country music" for his relaxed and easy stage manner, Del Reeves, like Martin, consistently retained the respect of a sizable audience during a long, eventful career. As a writer, performer, and TV personality, he had a strong impact on the country field from the 1950s into the 1980s.

Born and raised in North Carolina, Del was influenced by country music almost from the cradle. By the time he was in his teens he was performing many country & western songs in school shows and local functions. In the 1950s, he moved to California to further his musical career. Working in many local country-music events, he began to gain recognition for his abilities as a master of ceremonies, and by the late 1950s had his own TV show in the Southern California area. For four years, into the early 1960s, Del emceed the show and became acquainted with many of the most talented artists in the country field. With his wife, Ellen, he composed many songs that were recorded by such artists as Roy Drusky, Carl Smith, Rose Maddox, and Sheb Wooley.

His first recording contract with a major label came in the late 1950s when he joined Decca. In 1961, he gained his first top-10 hit when his single "Be Quiet Mind" became one of the year's most popular country releases. A few years later, he moved to United Artists and turned out two of the top country & western records of 1965, "The Belles of Southern Bell" and "Girl on the Billboard." The latter rose to number one and held that position for many weeks. During this period, Reeves turned out several hits that just missed top-10 status, such as "One Bum Town" and "Blame It on My Do Wrong." In 1966, he made the top 10 again with the single "Women Do Funny Things to Me."

In that year, Reeves' status in the country field led to an invitation from the *Grand Ole Opry* to come to Nashville as a regular performer. He remained there as part of the honored *Opry* tradition into the 1980s.

Beside appearing at the *Opry*, Del continued to tour widely, reaching audiences in all fifty states before the 1960s were over and performing in a number of foreign cities as well.

Through the late 1970s, Del remained a stalwart of United Artists' country efforts. His mid-1960s album releases included his debut on the label in October 1965, *Del Reeves, Doodle-Oo-Doo-Doo* (1/66), *Del Reeves Sings Jim Reeves* (3/66), *Special Delivery* (7/66), *Gettin' Any Feed* (10/66), *Struttin' My Stuff* (5/67), and *Six of One* (10/67). Some of his recordings were repackaged by Pickwick Records on the LP *Mr. Country Music*. His albums of the late 1960s and early 1970s on UA included *Best of Del Reeves, Volumes 1 and 2, Del Reeves Album, Big Daddy*, and *Friends and Neighbors*. Sun Records included tracks by him on such LPs as *Country Concert Live!, Out in the Country*, and *Great Country Songs*. In 1972, Liberty issued an LP titled *Superpak*.

In the late 1960s and early 1970s, Reeves extended his list of major song hits to include "Landmark Tavern," "Philadelphia Phillies," "A Dozen Pair of Boots," and "The Best Is Yet to Come." He also had a modest hit in 1970 with "Right Back to Lovin' You." In the mid-1970s, the recording phase of his career slowed down. His singles hits were modest ones for the most part, showing up on the lower levels of the charts, as was the case with "Prayer from a Mobile Home" in 1974, "Puttin' in Overtime at Home" and "You Comb Her Hair" in 1975, and "I Ain't Got Nobody" in 1976. Things picked up, though, when he teamed up with another UA artist, Billy Jo Spears, for a series of singles successes that included "On the Rebound" and "Teardrops Will Kiss the Morning Dew" in 1976. In 1978, Del had a solo single on the charts, "Dig Down Deep." In the spring of 1980 his single "Take Me to Your Heart" on Koala Records was on lower-chart levels.

Del's talents brought him stardom in other fields as well. During the 1960s his film credits included appearances in *Gold Guitar, Forty Acre Feud, Cottonpickin', Chickenpickers*, and *Second Fiddle to a Steel Guitar*.

His entertaining activities continued to

prosper in the 1970s. Featured on major network and syndicated TV shows as a guest throughout the decade, he starred in a syndicated weekly variety show called *The Del Reeves Country Carnival* in the late 1970s.

REEVES, JIM: *Singer, guitarist, songwriter. Born Panola County, Texas, August 20, 1924; died July 31, 1964.*

The bronze plaque in the Hall of Fame in Nashville reads: "The velvet style of Gentleman Jim Reeves was an international influence. His rich voice brought millions of new fans to country music from every corner of the world. Although the crash of his private airplane in 1964 took his life . . . posterity will keep his name alive . . . because they will remember him as one of country music's most important performers." The last sentences have proved prophetic; well over a decade after Reeves' untimely passing, releases of previously unissued recordings, and reissues of earlier hits kept his name on the charts into the 1980s.

Born in rural Texas, James Reeves was more interested in sports than music as a boy. He was a first-string pitcher at the University of Texas in his sophomore year when he was drafted by the St. Louis Cardinals. Practicing on the Cardinals' farm team, he injured his leg sliding into second base. The leg did not heal properly and his doctors told him to forget baseball. He turned to entertainment as his only other skill.

Although he enjoyed playing the guitar and singing, Reeves did not think of a career as a musician right away. He had a good speaking voice and a knowledge of country music and used it to start working as an announcer. By the early 1950s he was a staff regular at station KWKH in Shreveport, home of the *Louisiana Hayride* country program. He performed occasionally in local clubs in his spare time and cut some records on the Abbott label. One of these, "Mexican Joe," caught on with the public. Jim, quite unexpectedly, found himself with a top-10 country hit.

Shortly afterward, he became a part of the *Hayride* cast. His stock went up some

more when he scored a second top-10 success when his duet with Ginny Wright on Fabor Records, "I Love You," made the national charts in 1954. Also a chart hit that year was his single "Bimbo." Those accomplishments brought a contract offer from RCA Victor and a relationship that lasted for the rest of his career. "Yonder Comes a Sucker," his own composition, and his initial success for RCA, was a top-10 hit in 1955.

By the end of the 1950s, Reeves was a Nashville resident and a regular on the *Grand Ole Opry*. His first worldwide tour, accompanying a USO group to play for troops in Europe in 1954, preceded a string of four more tours for American troops throughout the world. In 1957, he was given his own daily show on ABC-TV, and was featured, during the late 1950s, on such programs as *The Ed Sullivan Show, The Steve Allen Show*, Dick Clark's *American Bandstand*, and *The Jimmy Dean Show*, among others. Jim continued this pattern in the early 1960s, traveling to all fifty states and throughout the world. In 1962, he received tumultuous welcomes from crowds throughout Africa and Europe, where he was immensely popular. In Norway alone he earned more than sixteen gold, silver, diamond, and platinum records through the late 1960s.

In his recording career in the United States, Reeves had scored more top-10 hits as of the early 1970s than any other country artist except Eddy Arnold and Webb Pierce. From 1955 to the end of the 1960s, he had one or more top-10 singles every year. Backing him on these efforts, from 1955 to the end of his life, was his band, the Blue Boys. His 1950s top-10 singles hits included "According to My Heart" and "My Lips Are Sealed" in 1956; his own composition, "Am I Losing You," and "Four Walls" in 1957; "Anna Marie," "Blue Boy," and number-one-ranked "Billy Bayou" in 1958; and his all-time bestseller, "He'll Have to Go" (a number-one hit), and "Home" in 1959.

Reeves continued with four top hits in 1960: "I Know One," "I Missed Me," "I'm Getting Better," and a reissue of "Am I Losing You." He turned out ten more top-

10 hits between the start of 1961 and mid-1964: "The Blizzard" (1961); "Adios Amigo," "What I Feel in My Heart," "I'm Gonna Change Everything," "Losing Your Love" (1962); "Guilty," "Is This Me?" (1963); number-one-ranked "I Guess I'm Crazy," "Love Is No Excuse" (with Dottie West), and "Welcome to My World" (1964).

Naturally, Reeves was represented by many LPs in his lifetime, a number of which reached gold-record status. His initial LP was *Bimbo,* issued in 1955. This was followed by such albums on RCA/Camden as *Jim Reeves* (12/57), *Girls I Have Known* (8/58), *Warn the Heart* (9/59), *He'll Have to Go* (4/60), *According to My Heart* (6/60), *Intimate Side of Jim Reeves* (8/60), *To Your Heart* (11/61), *Tall Tales* (4/61), *Country Side* (4/62), *Touch of Velvet* (6/62), *We Thank Thee* (8/62), *Gentleman Jim* (3/63), *Good 'n' Country* (Camden, 12/63), *International Jim Reeves* (9/63), *Kimberley Jim* (4/64), and *Moonlight and Roses* (7/64).

In July 1964, returning home to Nashville from an engagement, Reeves was killed when his plane crashed during a thunderstorm. His voice was not stilled, however—under the direction of his widow, Mary, previously unreleased recordings enlarged her husband's legend. In the mid- and late-1960s, Jim was represented on the singles charts by many more bestsellers, a number of which reached number one on country charts. Among those were "I Won't Forget You," "Is It Really Over," and "This Is It," the last two ranked number one in 1965; number-one "Distant Drums" and "Snow Flake" in 1966; number-one "I Won't Come in While He's There" in 1967; and, in 1968, "That's When I See the Blue (In Your Pretty Brown Eyes)" and "I Heard a Heart Break Tonight."

His posthumously released albums included such gold-record successes as *Distant Drums* (1966) and *Touch of Sadness* (1968). Other LPs included *Best of Jim Reeves* (8/64), *Have I Told You Lately* (Camden, 12/64), *Jim Reeves Way* (3/65), *Best, Volume 2* (2/66), *Yours Sincerely* (12/66), *Blue Side of Lonesome* (6/67), *My Cathedral* (12/67), *Best, Volume 3* (8/69), *Writes You a*

Record (3/71), *Something Special* (8/71), *God Be with You, Young & Country* (11/71), *Jim Reeves* (two discs, Camden, 6/72), *My Friend* (3/72), *Missing You* (11/72). In the early 1980s, a major best-selling album, *Don't Let Me Cross Over,* was released.

In the 1970s, Reeves' name continued to appear on country lists. Among his singles hits for the decade were "The Writing's on the Wall" and "Missing You" in 1972; "I'd Fight the World" (1974); "You Belong to Me" (1975); and "It's Nothing to Me," "Little Ole Dime" (1977).

As the decade came to a close, still another Reeves single, "Don't Let Me Cross Over," was moving up the charts, making it to the top 20 in early 1980. In January 1980, a second hit single made the charts, "Oh, How I Miss You Tonight," which rose into the national top 10 in mid-month. This was followed later in the year with electronically achieved "duet" singles with current performer Deborah Allen, which resulted in the hit "Take Me in Your Arms and Hold Me." Late in the year, his solo single "There's Always Me" rose to upper-chart levels, and the song served as the title cut for an album that was on the charts in late 1980 and early 1981.

REYNOLDS, MALVINA: *Singer, guitarist, songwriter. Born Berkeley, California, 1900; died circa late 1970s.*

In early 1964, an unusual song made its way to the top of the popular hit charts. The melody was not particularly new, nor was the message—except in musical form. The lyrics to "Little Boxes" were an ironic comment on conformity, focusing on the stifling lack of individuality in the typical suburban housing tract.

The song was a typical folk song composed after World War II. Malvina Reynolds had been long known in folk music circles for her contributions to this art, but the unsyrupy sentiments of "Little Boxes" brought her to the attention of a national audience. It was not the first nor the last of the many protest songs she wrote. Later compositions won the affections of a succeeding generation of folk fans who, when she was in her late sixties and early seventies, dubbed her "The Singing Grandmother." The term, as Reynolds noted in 1970, was a misnomer. She had a daughter, but no grandchildren. However, she pointed out, it represented a term of respect from young people who needed someone older to look up to. "I came along looking like their mothers and grandmothers and I understand. I know what's bugging them. I have sympathy. My friends ask me how I can be so tolerant of the kids. Maybe it's because they're other people's kids."

Born and raised in California, Malvina completed work on a doctorate in literature at the University of California at Berkeley, intent on pursuing an academic career. Interested in folk music and folk traditions for quite some time, she wrote her doctoral thesis on a medieval folk tale. By the end of the 1930s, though she enjoyed teaching, she felt that her creative interests were still unfulfilled.

An old 78-rpm record of John Jacob Niles singing "Cherry Tree Carol" inspired her to sing and write traditional folk songs. Slowly, word of her talents began to spread, until some of her songs were added to the repertoire of the Almanac Singers. In the years that followed, many folksingers, including such notables as Woody Guthrie and Pete Seeger, often sang her compositions.

By the time the folk movement occupied the world spotlight at the end of the 1950s, Reynolds was recognized as one of the most important writers in the modern folk vein. She also found an increasing number of places to perform her material, appearing at a growing number of festivals. The pattern continued in the 1960s, when her credits included sets at such major events as the Newport Folk Festival and the Berkeley Folk Festival.

Reynold's song output in the 1950s included "Magic Penny" (1955); "Bury Me in My Overalls" (1956); "Bring Flowers," "Let Us Come In," "Little Land," "Nobody," "Pied Piper," "We Don't Need the Men" (1958); "Don't Talk to Me of Love," "Faucets Are Dripping," "Oh, Doctor," "Patchwork of Dreams," "Somewhere Between," "The Little Mermaid," "The Mira-

cle," "There'll Come a Time," "We Hate to See Them Go," and "Where Is the Little Street?" (1959). Two of her best-known songs of those years were collaborations. In 1957, she provided the words to Woody Guthrie's music for "Sally, Don't You Grieve," and, with Alan Green, wrote "Turn Around," which for years was used in Eastman Kodak commercials.

Malvina's 1960s copyrights included "From Way Up Here," written with Pete Seeger (1962), and such others as "Alone," "Dialectic," "Let It Be," "Sausalito Fire," "The Desert" (1960); "Quiet," "Rand Hymn," "Temptation," "The Emperor's Nightingale," "This World," "Upside Down" (1961); "Andorra," "I Wish You Were Here," "Little Boxes," and "You Can't Make a Turtle Come Out" (1962). In 1963, she turned out a song that became a favorite with singers like Bob Dylan and Joan Baez, "What Have They Done to the Rain," an antinuclear message number. As the 1960s went by she took part in antiwar and pro-civil rights concerts and demonstrations and wrote many songs of protest about these subjects as well as about pollution and discrimination against women. She was still steadily churning out new songs at the end of the 1960s, such as the 1969 composition "Daddy's in the Jail."

Many of her early songs are included in the Oak Publications songbook *Little Boxes and Other Handmade Songs by Malvina Reynolds* (1963). Malvina also recorded a number of her own folk song treatments. Folkways issued one of her LPs, *Malvina Reynolds*, in January 1960 and released another album of the same title in April 1967. Also released in April 1967 was a Columbia Records LP, *Malvina Reynolds Sings the Truth*. During the summer of 1970, Century City Records issued an album in which Reynolds' singing was backed by such groups as the Byrds and the Sunshine Company. The producer of the LP was an old friend, Alex Hassilev, previously of the Limeliters folk trio, which had included many of Malvina's songs in their act. Later in the 1970s, *Malvina Reynolds* was released on the Cassandra label.

Commenting on the choice between academics and music, Reynold's declared, "I'd much rather be a songwriter than a college professor. I think like a songwriter. I guess that means I think in songs. I like to say in my songwriting what other people are thinking and feeling—say what's in their minds and hearts."

RICE, BOBBY G.: *Singer, guitarist, songwriter, band leader. Born Wisconsin, July 11.*

Though Bobby G. Rice grew up in Wisconsin, far above the Mason-Dixon line, he was to become one of the better-known country artists of the 1970s. Born into a family of country musicians, it was only natural for him to make his public debut singing a country song when he was three. In the early 1950s, his father opened a country dance hall called the Circle D Ballroom, where, in time, Bobby and other people from the area played in the house band. Later Bobby and some school friends assembled a group that not only played there, but also found work playing in country nightspots and for various functions in other parts of Wisconsin and the surrounding states.

Eventually, Rice went his own way, working as a sideman with various country groups. For a while, during the 1960s, he played rock 'n' roll. By the end of the decade, though, he once more was concentrating on country music, both as a songwriter and leader of his own band.

This time his efforts began to pay off more handsomely; Bobby landed a recording contract and turned out a number of singles that were regional or national hits on smaller labels. Among those releases of the late 1960s and early 1970s were "Sugar Shack," "Hey Baby," "Lover Please," "Mountain of Love," and "Suspicion." Some of these tunes were included in his 1972 album on Royal American Records, *Hit After Hit*. In 1972, he signed with Metromedia Records. He made upper-chart levels with the single "You Lay So Easy on My Mind" in early 1973. Later in the year he made the national lists with "You Gave Me You."

By 1975 Rice had switched to GRT Records and had the hit single "Write Me a Letter" early in the year. In the summer, he had a second hit with "Freda Comes, Freda Goes" and in the fall scored modestly with a third single, "I May Never Be Your Lover (But I'll Always Be Your Friend)." In the summer of 1976, he made middle-chart levels with "You Are My Special Angel" and, a year later, showed up on lower levels with "Just One Kiss Magdalena." In 1978, now recording for Republic Records, he had two charted singles, "Whisper It to Me" in the summer and "The Softest Touch in Town," on the lists for a number of months at year end. At the end of 1979, Bobby had another release on the charts, "You Make It So Easy" on the Sunset label, which carried over into 1980. His charted singles in the early 1980s were "The Man Who Takes You Home" in 1980 and "Livin' Together (Lovin' Apart)" in 1981, both on Sunbird Records.

RICE, TONY: *Guitarist, songwriter. Born Los Angeles, California.*

A spur to the bluegrass revival of the 1970s was the arrival on center stage of many young, extremely talented exponents of the style. An important member of that group was Tony Rice, one of the finest flatpicking bluegrass guitarists.

Tony, born in Los Angeles, moved cross-country at an early age to Virginia, close to the center of bluegrass activity.

During the 1960s, he was influenced by many bluegrass musicians, both the old-timers and such newcomers as the Dillards and the White brothers, Clarence and Rowland. Clarence had particular impact on Rice's early work. After playing with various local groups during his high school years, Tony went on to achieve initial notice in the 1970s as a member of J. D. Crowe and the New South.

As the 1970s went by, Rice continued to be active in the bluegrass movement both as a touring artist and session musician. In 1975, he met David Grisman during one of those session jobs and the two became close friends. In the late 1970s, when Grisman assembled the David Grisman Quintet, Tony became a band member. Besides touring widely with the band, Rice took part in recording the Quintet's mid-1970s debut album, independently produced by Grisman. In 1979, he was represented on the group's first LP on the Horizon label, entitled *Hot Dawg*.

The Grisman material was a hard-to-classify blend of musical genres, embracing elements of classics, bluegrass, and jazz. In addition to taking part in that project, Rice maintained his bluegrass credentials with a series of solo LPs in the second half of the 1970s. During the mid-1970s, he completed three albums, one each for the King Bluegrass, Rebel, and Rounder labels. In 1979, he had two more LPs released, one by Rounder and the other by Kaleidoscope Records.

RICH, CHARLIE: *Singer, pianist, songwriter. Born Colt, Arkansas, December 14, 1932.*

The struggle for success in the music world is so brutal that among many industry people it breeds indifference to the fate of other aspirants. So it is a great tribute to Charlie Rich that his belated rise to stardom in 1973 was almost universally welcomed by those in his field. His renown was finally achieved primarily as a country-music performer, but his talent was such that he could easily have made it in rock 'n' roll, blues, or jazz.

As a child growing up on a small cotton plantation near Colt, Arkansas, Charlie was exposed to many types of music. He heard white gospel music at the Baptist church he and his parents faithfully attended; he heard blues from the black field hands who worked on the plantation; and he heard country on the radio listening to the *Grand Ole Opry*. Piano was the instrument he studied as a child, and, enamored of Stan Kenton and devoted to jazz, he played the tenor saxophone in his high school band.

After one year at the University of Arkansas, he joined the Air Force during the Korean War. In Enid, Oklahoma, where he was stationed, Charlie was playing in a jazz band and performing with a small combo in town when he married his high school sweetheart, Margaret Ann, the group's vocalist.

Rich tried farming for a year after his discharge for added financial security (his wife was soon to have their third child) before he returned to his music, with the encouragement of his wife.

During this time, Charlie became a regular performer in Memphis piano bars, while he and Margaret Ann wrote songs, sometimes together, sometimes individually. Margaret Ann, without telling Charlie, brought a tape of the songs to Bill Justis, artists and repertoire executive for Sun Records of Memphis. Justis listened to the songs; he liked them but he felt that they weren't commericial enough. He signed Rich as a session musician and told him to keep writing songs.

Charlie started out at Sun by backing performers such as Johnny Cash and Roy Orbison. He also wrote songs recorded by a number of other aritsts, including "The Ways of a Woman in Love," "Break Up," "I'll Make It All Up to You," and "I Just Thought You'd Like to Know." At the end of the 1950s, Sun started issuing some of Rich's own recordings. The third release included the song "Lonely Weekends," which was on the national charts from mid-March 1960 into August. Unfortunately, none of his followup records caught on, in large part because of a lack of sufficient support from Sun Records.

Rich switched to RCA Records and had a minor hit, "Big Boss Man." A few years later he switched labels again, to Mercury Records, and had a smash rock hit, "Mohair Sam," in 1965, but once again he failed to produce any followup hits. Again he returned to a life of engagements in small bars and clubs, mostly in the Midwest. His fall from the heights of success hit him very hard, and he reputedly turned to pills and liquor to try to boost his confidence. He moved to Hi Records in the mid-1960s without any noticeable improvement in outlook and finally joined Epic, a subsidiary of Columbia Records, in 1968.

Charlie's move to Epic proved to be the turning point in his career. He was teamed with producer Billy Sherrill, a partnership that proved to be dynamic. Sherrill believed in Rich's talent and worked hard to win him the attention he deserved. Some of their earliest collaborations under the Epic label became regional hits but none made the upper levels of the charts. Those that made the lower rungs on the hit charts included the album *Big Boss Man* and the singles "July 12, 1939," "Nice 'n' Easy," and "Life's Little Ups and Downs" in 1970; the single "A Woman Left Lonely" in 1971; and the single "A Part of Your Life" in 1972. "Life's Little Ups and Downs," one of Charlie's favorites, is one of a number of songs written by his wife, Margaret Ann. For the most part, however, Rich's early years with Epic were disappointing and frustrating.

Finally, in 1972, Charlie achieved the breakthrough he needed. He recorded "I Take It on Home," written by Kenny O'Dell, and the song entered the country-music top 20. This song and another O'Dell composition that Charlie recorded, "Behind Closed Doors," impressed Bill Williams, a public relations executive who had just joined the Epic Nashville office. Williams gave Rich a great deal of publicity and arranged for him to make numerous personal appearances. His efforts paid off and "Behind Closed Doors" climbed to the number-one position on the country charts in 1973. The song also crossed over to the pop charts and sold over a million copies, earning a gold record and becoming one of the major hits of that year.

Rich's followup song, "The Most Beautiful Girl," did even better, selling more than 2 million copies to achieve platinum status. In 1973, he received many awards, including a Grammy as Best Country Male Vocalist and the Country Music Association's awards for Male Vocalist of the Year, Single of the Year, and Album of the Year for *Behind Closed Doors*. After nearly twenty years in the business, Charlie had finally achieved the success many people had felt he deserved all along. Some of his earlier recordings were released by RCA in 1973 in an album called *Tomorrow Night*, which did very well, ensuring that Rich's earlier output would not be forgotten.

The year 1974 was also extremely suc-

cessful for Charlie Rich. That year, "the Silver Fox," as Rich came to be called because of his prematurely gray hair, was honored as Entertainer of the Year by the Country Music Association, probably the most coveted award in country music.

His hit singles from 1974 were "There Won't Be Anymore," "I Don't See Me in Your Eyes Anymore," "A Very Special Love Song," and "I Love My Friend" (number one in October). His 1975 successes on Epic were "My Elusive Dreams," "Everytime You Touch Me," and "All Over Me." In 1976, his charted hits were "Road Song" and "Since I Fell for You," and in 1977, his Epic releases included the number-one hit (in August), "Rollin' with the Flow." In 1978, he had a charted single on United Artists label, "I Still Believe in Love," and, on Epic, the top-10 "Beautiful Woman" and the number-one duet (with Janie Fricke) of his composition "On My Knees" in September.

Charlie closed out the 1970s with his name often appearing on country charts with both new and old releases. His 1979 charted singles, for instance, were "The Fool Strikes Again," "Life Goes On," and "I Lost My Head" on UA, "Spanish Eyes" on Epic, and "I Wake You Up When I Get Home" on Elektra. He had, by then, severed his relationship with Epic and signed with Elektra. In 1980, his hit list singles were "You're Gonna Love Yourself in the Morning" on UA, "Even a Fool Would Let Go" on Epic, and "A Man Doesn't Know What a Woman Goes Through" on Elektra.

Charlie Rich's voice remains one of the most distinctive and easily identifiable voices in all of country music. His performing style is a successful combination of all the musical influences in his life: gospel, blues, rock, country, and jazz. Perhaps, as his wife, Margaret Ann, suggested, the fact that he was so difficult to typecast was one reason success eluded him for so long. Nevertheless, the blending of all those musical elements with Charlie's deep, expressive voice has led to the formation of a sound sure to prove of major importance in the progression of country music in the years to come and sure to maintain Rich as a talent of legendary proportions.—A.S.

RICH, DON: *Singer, guitarist, songwriter. Born Olympia, Washington, August 15, 1941; died 1974.*

Recognized as one of the best lead guitarists in country music, Don Rich played an important role in the rise of superstar Buck Owens, performing as lead musician of Buck's backing band, the Buckaroos. In fact, more than once Owens referred to him as "my right arm." Not only did Don meld the Buckaroos into one of the nation's most highly regarded country bands, he also achieved a number of hits of his own as a solo performer or in collaboration with Buck's son, Buddy Alan.

Rich was born and raised in Washington and recalled making his first efforts at playing guitar and singing when he was only three and a half. He progressed rapidly—in fact, at five he was already singing on local radio. When he was six, he took his first violin lessons and before long was fiddling with dance bands and playing violin on local radio shows. He continued to develop his skills and performing credits in his teens and, at fifteen, handled lead guitar for country artist Ted Mitchell.

In 1958, when he was seventeen, he met Buck Owens, who had moved to Washington state during the early phase of his career. Don worked with Owens at dances and on a TV show in the Tacoma area until the success of some of Owens' Capitol recordings caused Buck to return to California. Don stayed on in his home region, completing high school and enrolling in college as a music major with the objective of becoming a teacher.

However, by the end of 1959, Don decided he preferred a career as a musician. In January 1960, he headed south to join Buck on a full-time basis. By then, he could play enough different instruments to qualify as a one-man band, had he decided to do so. After a few years in which Don essentially organized pick-up bands to back Buck in various towns, they decided

to form a permanent band that was given the name the Buckaroos. From the early 1960s on, Rich and the band backed Owens on hundreds of singles and dozens of albums, many of them top-10 successes. The band was also on the road as part of the Buck Owens Show several hundred days every year. Later, starting in 1969, Rich and the Buckaroos joined Buck on the *Hee Haw* TV show.

Besides backing Owens, Rich and the Buckaroos made a number of albums of their own from the mid-1960s to the 1970s. The band's debut LP, *The Buckaroos*, came out on Capitol in February 1966. It was followed by *The Buckaroos Strike Again!* (December 1967). Some of the group's other releases were *Rompin' and Stompin'* and *The Buckaroos Play the Hits*. The latter, issued in April 1971, was the first all-instrumental album by the band. On it, Don Rich played a variety of instruments—electric guitar, acoustic rhythm guitar, high third guitar, dobro, gut string guitar, and fiddle. The other band members at the time were Jerry Wiggins (born Clinton, Oklahoma) on drums and percussion; Doyle Singer (born Danville, Arkansas) on bass guitar; and Jim Shaw on piano, organ, bass, harmonica, and synthesizer. Rich also had a solo LP in the early 1970s titled *That Fiddlin' Man* and recorded several songs with Buddy Alan that did well on the charts, including "Cowboy Convention," a top-20 single in 1970.

Don's career came to an end when he was killed in an auto accident in 1974.

RIDDLE, ALMEDA: *Singer, fiddler, pianist. Born Heber Springs, Arkansas, November 21, 1893.*

One of the artists who became legendary with folk purists as a result of the research into the American folk heritage by the father-and-son team of Professor John Lomax and his son Alan was Almeda Riddle. It was Alan Lomax in particular who preserved some of her finest traditional renditions in several extensive folk music collections he prepared after World War II. Apart from that, the Arkansas balladeer's album work was relatively sparse, but always provided important contributions to folklore annals.

Almeda grew up in rural Arkansas and still resided there at the end of the 1970s, known to folk adherents as Granny Riddle. In her youth, the old folk ballads derived from the music of Elizabethan times—and earlier—in the United Kingdom and Ireland still were sung at family gatherings in many parts of the South, Southwest, and border states. From her father and other relations and friends, Riddle learned many folk songs that she preserved and sang throughout her life. Her father, who was a fine musician, also helped her learn to play both fiddle and piano.

In her home area her ability was well known, but hardly anyone outside the region took much notice. However, in the years after World War I, there was increasing interest in searching out and preserving the old songs, secular and religious, that were in danger of dying out with the advent of advanced methods of communication and the rising tide of popular music.

Throughout the 1930s and 1940s, Alan Lomax worked steadily with his father to find previously unknown folk balladeers and bring their talents to wider notice. One of John Lomax's most famous discoveries, of course, was the art of Leadbelly. Equally important was Alan Lomax's work in preserving Almeda Riddle's trove of songs (and her performing style), which he pursued in the years after the elder Lomax's death in 1948.

During the 1950s, Alan went to Arkansas to tape some of Riddle's material for the Library of Congress archives. Later, in wide-ranging efforts for commerical folk companies, he included more of her material. In some cases, folk scholars excitedly discovered that her renditions were rare modern-day equivalents of ballads collected in the nineteenth century by the first great American folklorist, Professor Francis J. Child of Harvard. Some of these tracks were included in the twelve-volume set on Prestige/International Records called *Southern Journey* and others in Lomax's seven-record set for Atlantic called the *Southern Folk Heritage Series.*

With the broad interest in folk music in the United States in the late 1950s and early 1960s, eager young folk enthusiasts sought Riddle out either to listen to her sing at home or to try to include her in various festivals. She took part in some of them during the decade. She also agreed to make her first solo album for Vanguard in the early 1960s. Titled *Almeda Riddle,* it was issued by Vanguard in February 1965. On the album, she sings without instrumental backing.

After that, though she continued to be alert and active, there was a long hiatus before another album appeared. Finally, in the early 1970s, Rounder Records made a new collection titled *Songs and Ballads from the Ozarks.* Some years later, in early 1979, Almeda's third solo album was issued by Rounder, *More Songs and Ballads from the Ozarks.*

RITCHIE, JEAN: *Singer, dulcimer player, guitarist, songwriter, author, folk music collector. Born Viper, Kentucky, December 8, 1922.*

In her 1955 book, *Singing Family of the Cumberlands* (Oak Publications, 1963), Jean Ritchie described how the folk music heritage had been handed down from parents to children in her family in an unbroken line going back to colonial times. In telling the story of her roots and upbringing, she also described a way of life common to many other families in the hill-country culture whose original members were in the first wave of emigration from England, Scotland, Wales, and Ireland. The book, in effect, constituted a sort of roadmap to the development of the traditional folk music that was the core both of the folk revival of post–World War II years and the parallel rise in the popularity of country music.

Ritchie, the youngest of fourteen children of a musically active family, was born in the tiny hamlet of Viper in Crockett County, deep in the Cumberland Mountains of Kentucky. The county was named after a direct ancestor of Jean's who had been among the first settlers of the region in the 1700s. Jean's father, Balis Ritchie, had taught school in the nearby town of Dwarf before marrying her mother, Abigail Hall, of Viper, when she was fifteen.

Although their house looked more like a dormitory, Ritchie recalled it as a lively and happy place to be. All the children lent a hand, tending the cornfield in summer as soon as they were old enough. When work was done, all looked forward to evenings of fun with friends and relations, singing and playing the banjo, guitar, dulcimer, and fiddle.

Singing was an integral part of life in the Cumberlands. The people sang as they worked in the fields, joined with their neighbors in sings at socials and other events, and sang hymns and gospel songs lustily in church on Sundays. Many of the songs were traditional folk songs handed down and modified by generations of settlers from the British Isles. In the case of the Ritchies, some of the songs the family sang had been brought from England by James Ritchie, Jean's great-great-great grandfather, in 1768. Among those traced back to James and his son, Crockett Ritchie, were "Nottamun Town" (Nottingham, England), "Lord Bateman," "Old Sally Buck," and "Killy Kranky."

Other songs that Jean and her brothers and sisters sang included such traditional ones as "Fair Ellender," "Hush Little Baby," "Twilight A-Stealing," "Shady Grove," "Somebody," "I'm Goin' to Boston," "I've Been a Foreign Lander," "Maria," and "Old Tyler." Their repertoire made the Ritchie family one of the best-known singing clans in the region. During Jean's childhood, folk music collectors used to come to the Ritchie house to note down some of those numbers.

Jean's singing and collecting continued steadily as she went through elementary school, the new high school of Viper, and, after that, college. Despite the family's limited resources, quite a few of the children managed to get to college. She entered the University of Kentucky in Lexington in the early 1940s and completed work for her B.A. in the mid-1940s. She won the Founder's Day Award, impressing both classmates and instructors with her knowledge of folklore and traditional music, as well as her skill as an instrumentalist. Ritchie's work on the dulcimer was particularly striking and, later on, she awakened considerable interest in the mountain dulcimer from her concerts and festival appearances in the 1950s and 1960s.

In the years immediately after graduation, she began to make a name for herself in the folk field with a series of concerts in eastern and southeastern states. She also applied for and won a Fulbright Scholarship to do folk song research in Great Britain.

Back home in the 1950s, Ritchie quickly became an integral part of the folk music boom. She performed in folk clubs and concert halls, festivals, and college campuses all over the United States, sometimes sharing the bill with other well-known folk artists. Besides singing traditional material, she also wrote original songs or variations of older ones, including "A Tree in the Valley-O," "The Cuckoo She's a Pretty Bird," "Let the Sun Shine Down on Me," and "What'll I Do with the Baby-O." She also compiled several books of folk songs—*The Swapping Song Book, From Fair to Fair,* and *Folk Songs of the Southern Appalachians.*

During the 1960s, Jean was a familiar figure at the major folk festivals in the United States and at some in other countries. She appeared several times at the events at the University of Chicago, University of California at Berkeley, and at traditional gatherings in the South and Southeast. She was very active in the Newport Folk Festival, both on stage and off, and performed at the Newport series in 1963, 1964, 1965, 1966, and 1967. Some of her performances were included in the Vanguard Records Festival coverage. When the Newport event was reorganized in 1963, she became a member of the Board of Directors, and later became a member of the Newport Folk Festival Foundation when her term as director terminated.

Ritchie was represented by a number of albums from the late 1950s to the late

1970s. One of her earlier efforts, originally released in 1959 but still in the Folkways Records active catalogue in the early 1980s, was called *A Folk Concert*, featuring Jean, Oscar Brand, and David Sear. Her early 1960s output included *Jean Ritchie* on Elektra Records, *Best of Jean Ritchie* (2/61) on Prestige Records, and, on Folkways, *Ritchie Family of Kentucky, Child Ballads in America* (two records, 4/61), and *Precious Memories* (5/62). Verve/Forecast issued the LP *Jean Ritchie with Doc Watson Live at Folk City* (5/66).

Although the mass audience interest in folk music had subsided by the 1970s, there still was a sizable number of devotees, and Jean remained active as a performer in college concerts and the small folk club circuit. She recorded several albums for Sire Records, including the January 1970 release *Clear Waters Remembered* and the 1977 LP *None but One*, which surprised many folk fans with its underlying rock format in several numbers.

RITTER, TEX: *Singer, guitarist, songwriter, actor, author. Born Nederland, Texas, January 12, 1906; died Nashville, Tennessee, January 2, 1974.*

The epitome of a man of the West, Tex Ritter achieved many firsts in his long career in entertainment. His credits as performer and writer covered almost every major phase of western lore from cowboy songs to a pioneering radio program, *The Lone Ranger*. Appropriately, he was one of the first five individuals voted into the new Country Music Hall of Fame in 1964, a year when he also was serving as president of the Country Radio Association (a post he also held in 1965).

Ritter was a true son of pioneer heritage. Born Maurice Woodward Ritter on a farm and ranch in Nederland, Panola County, Texas, he began to learn the basics of roping and riding from his earliest years. The land, settled by his great-grandfather in 1830, was a 400-acre homestead his forebears claimed when it still was part of Mexico. The youngest of six children born to James Everett and Elizabeth Matthews Ritter, Tex grew up in an atmosphere much like that recreated in countless western movies, with cattle roundups and ranch hands spinning tall stories or singing songs in their leisure time in the bunkhouse.

From an early age, he demonstrated a promising singing voice. However, when he graduated from high school in 1922 (with honors), he wasn't thinking about a show business career. Instead, he enrolled as a law major at the University of Texas. While there Tex impressed his classmates and instructors with his knowledge of Texas folklore and eventually worked out a combined singing and lecturing program.

Invitations to give his show, called *The Texas Cowboy and His Songs*, caused Ritter to wander farther and farther afield from the university. When one tour took him to Chicago, he settled there for a while and enrolled at Northwestern University to continue his law studies. He sang on local stations, where audience acceptance made him think of trying for bigger things in radio and theater. He left Chicago for New York in 1930.

One of the first things he did after arriving was to join the New York Theatre Guild. In 1931, this led to his appearing in the Broadway play *Green Grow the Lilacs*, a play by Lynn Riggs that gave graphic insight into the ranch country of Ritter's youth and provided the basis for the blockbusting Rodgers and Hammerstein musical *Oklahoma!*

Tex wanted to add to his radio credits, but many New York programmers doubted that eastern audiences would take to his strong Texas drawl. He persisted, and once he was on the air, the flood of favorable mail proved his point. Tex rapidly became an important factor in both regional and national radio fields. As a writer and performer, he played a key role in the original *Lone Ranger* series. During the 1930s, he performed on such major radio shows as *Death Valley Days, Tex Ritter's Camp Fire*, and *Cowboy Tom's Round-Up*. In 1933, he embarked on a recording career, signing with Columbia Records and turning out the first of hundreds of singles and albums.

With his background, Ritter was a natural for the burgeoning western film industry. In the mid-1930s, this prompted a move from New York to Hollywood. He first signed with Grand National Films in 1936 and completed his first movie, *Song of the Gringo,* the same year. In the years that followed, he made many more westerns, mostly from the mid-1930s through the mid-1950s, taking part in about eighty films in all. He worked for such studios as Monogram, Columbia, and Universal. When not making films, he toured the country coast-to-coast with his own company, playing to enthusiastic audiences at theaters, rodeos, and state fairs. Tex's personal magnetism continued to attract audiences all through his life, though he cut back sharply on in-person work by the second half of the 1960s.

In the 1950s and 1960s, he also was featured on many major TV shows, both general variety and country & western. After the western movie field slowed down with the advent of TV, Ritter left California for a new home in Nashville, where he soon was a regular on the *Grand Ole Opry.*

In the early 1970s, Ritter continued to be active in country-music industry affairs. He narrated the Country Music Association album *Thank You, Mr. President* and also presented it to then-president Richard Nixon. In 1971, Ritter was given the Founding President's award by the CMA and in 1971 headed the CMA United Nations overseas tour. In October 1973, Tex delivered a speech in tribute to members of the Hall of Fame at the Country Music Association Anniversary Banquet.

Ritter was Capitol Records' first country artist when he signed with that company in 1942. His association with the label extended over three decades, into the 1970s. His early work for Capitol included such albums as *Children's Songs and Stories by Tex Ritter, Cowboy Favorites by Tex Ritter, Tex Ritter and the Dinning Sisters,* and *Sunday School for Children.* Among his many singles releases (a number of which featured original songs by him) were "Someone," "There's a Gold Star in Her Window," "There's a New Moon Over My Shoulder," "Jealous Heart," "You Two-Timed Me One Time Too Often," "One Little

Tear Drop Too Often," "Have I Told You Lately That I Love You," "Rye Whiskey," "Boll Weevil," "Dallas Darlin'," "Deck of Cards," "Fort Worth Jail," "You Are My Sunshine," "Bad Brahma Bull," "I've Got Five Dollars, and It's Saturday Night," "Pledge of Allegiance," "The Fiery Bear," and "Blood on the Saddle."

Tex placed several dozen singles on country hit charts over the years, including a number of songs that reached the top 10. His first major success came in 1948 with his top-10 single of Al Dexter's "Rock and Rye Rag." In 1952, he had a major pop hit with his single "High Noon," the title song from the Gary Cooper film classic of the same name, that stayed in the top 10 on pop charts for months. In 1961, he scored a top-10 hit with "I Dreamed of a Hillbilly Heaven," a song he co-wrote with Eddie Dean and Hal Sothern. In 1967, he once more graced upper-chart levels with "Just Beyond the Moon."

His Capitol albums included *Songs* (4/58), *Blood on the Saddle* (2/60), *Border Affair* (12/63), *Friendly Voice* (11/65), *Hillbilly Heaven* (12/65), *Best of Tex Ritter* (11/66), *Just Beyond the Moon* (9/67), *Sweet Land of Liberty* (6/67), *Green Green Valley* (late 1960s); *Supercountrylegendary* (early 1970s), and the three-record set, *The Legendary Tex Ritter* (11/73). He also was represented on Pickwick with *Tex Ritter Sings His Hits* (11/67) and *My Kinda Songs* (two discs, early 1970s) and on Hilltop with *Love You Big as Texas.*

During the second half of 1973, Tex completed a new single, a recitative written by Gordon Sinclair of Canada titled "The Americans (A Canadian's Opinion)," which was released by Capitol in early January 1974, a few days after Ritter's death. On January 2, 1974, he suffered a heart attack while visiting a friend. He was rushed to Baptist Hospital after first aid was administered, but could not be revived, and died at 7 P.M.

The bronze plaque in his honor at the Hall of Fame sums up his contributions: "One of America's most illustrious and versatile stars of radio, television, records, motion pictures, and Broadway stage. Untiring pioneer and champion of the country music industry, his devotion to his God, his family, and his country is a continuing inspiration to his countless friends throughout the world."

His album titles still in the active catalogue of Capitol Records at the end of the 1970s were *An American Legend, The Best of Tex Ritter, Blood on the Saddle,* and *Hillbilly Heaven.*

ROBBINS, HARGUS "PIG": *Pianist, keyboard musician, composer. Born Spring City, Tennessee.*

The session musicians, who play the instruments to back the singer or singers on a recording, are often extremely important to the sound of a particular record, but they seldom achieve star status. Hargus "Pig" Robbins, however, is one session musician who gained enough fame to become a soloist in his own right.

Hargus learned to play piano at the Tennessee School for the Blind in Nashville, which was where he went to school. He wanted to play country music but his instructors didn't teach country songs, so he taught himself to play in the country style he heard on the radio and on records. At age fifteen, he stopped the lessons and began to develop his own style.

After he graduated from high school, Hargus played in Nashville clubs and at parties. When he played piano for a friend's demo record, his playing attracted more attention than his friend's singing. Soon he decided to join the Musicians Union and become a session musician. A couple of years later he had already become one of the top keyboard session musicians in Nashville.

Robbins first attracted a great deal of attention when he played piano on George Jones' hit single "White Lightnin'" in 1960. Since that time, he has backed up countless major country-music singers. He has also played piano for many rock musicians. He backed Bob Dylan on his album *Blonde on Blonde,* and he has backed Simon and Garfunkel, among others. In the 1950s he recorded his own rock 'n' roll album,

for which he also did the vocal, under the name of Mel Robbins, but the LP failed to become a hit.

By the late 1970s, Hargus' musicianship had been honored through the receipt of some top awards. In 1976 he was named the Country Music Association's Instrumentalist of the Year. In 1977 he was accorded a similar honor by the Academy of Country Music. He was also voted Most Valuable Player by the Nashville chapter of the Recording Arts and Sciences in 1977. That year the NARAS Nashville chapter also named him Super Picker of the Year. In 1978, "Pig," as he is sometimes called, won a Grammy Award for Country Instrumentalist of the Year.

The honors he had been receiving enabled Robbins to embark on a solo recording career. In 1977 he signed with Elektra/Asylum Records. His first album was entitled *Country Instrumentalist of the Year.* He produced the album himself, and he was accompanied by some of the finest Nashville musicians.

Hargus' second album was *Pig in a Poke.* Once again, he produced the LP himself and arranged all the songs. Again he was backed by some of the finest Nashville session musicians. The album featured a lot of old standard songs as well as an original composition, "Roamin' Round." He performed at the Wembley Country Music Festival in England in March 1978. In 1981, Hargus was again one of the five finalists for the CMA Instrumentalist of the Year award.—A.S.

ROBBINS, MARTY: *Singer, guitarist, pianist, songwriter. Born Glendale, Arizona, September 26, 1925.*

One of the great names in modern country & western music, Marty Robbins seemed to epitomize the strengths and virtues of the legendary cowboy. Brought up in cowboy country, he became one of the most beloved interpreters of cowboy ballads and updated, country-flavored pop variants. Survival against often sizable odds was his trademark, both as a performer and an individual. In the highly competitive modern C&W field, he remained a top-ranked writer and singer from the 1950s into the 1980s. In his personal life, he disregarded the dangers of high speed racing, continuing to compete despite several near fatal accidents; he also bounced back from a massive heart attack, keeping strong and active for many years thereafter.

Robbins' saga began in a rural area of Arizona in the small town of Glendale, where he was born and spent his first twelve years. One of a family of nine children (seven brothers and one sister), he recalls the lonesome atmosphere of the desert region his family called home, and the warm family life that centered around his father and grandfather. His father played the harmonica, one of the earliest musical influences on Marty, and his grandfather, who had worked as a traveling medicine man, was a teller of tales and singer of cowboy songs.

"His name was 'Texas' Bob Heckle. He had two little books of poetry he would sell. I used to sing him church songs and he would tell me stories. A lot of the songs I've written, with the exception of 'El Paso,' were brought about because of stories he told me. Like 'Big Iron' I wrote because he was a Texas Ranger. At least he told me he was."

Western movies were also an influence on young Marty. Gene Autry was a particular idol and Marty sometimes worked mornings picking cotton at a field ten miles away from home to earn enough to see the latest Autry film. He recalled sitting in the first row, "Close enough so I could have gotten sand in the eyes from the horses and powder burns from the guns. . . . I wanted to be the cowboy singer, simply because Autry was my favorite singer. No one else inspired me."

In 1937, the family moved to Phoenix, where Marty later attended high school. When he was nineteen, he signed up for a three-year hitch in the Navy, his first opportunity to see the world beyond Arizona. While he was stationed in the Pacific, he learned to play the guitar and, before long, was using it as an aid in writing his own songs. After he was discharged, toward the end of the 1940s, he went back home with some thoughts about a performing career. When a friend who had a local band gave him the chance to work with the group on occasion, Robbins snapped at it. As he gained experience, he began to seek more opportunities to do solo work, which led to more club dates in and around Phoenix. In between engagements, he sometimes earned money by working on construction projects.

While driving a brick truck one day, he listened to a local country show on radio station KPHO. He sought out the program director, told him he thought he could do better than the cowboy singer, and won a place on the program. KPHO-TV provided an opportunity for Marty to fill in for a nonshowing guest, which eventually led to hosting his own show, *Western Caravan*. Little Jimmy Dickens guested on the show one day and was so impressed by Robbins' ability that when he got to California, he suggested that his label, Columbia, look into the matter. A company official went to Phoenix, agreed with Dickens, and soon Robbins was a Columbia recording artist.

His first release on the label was "Love Me or Leave Me Alone." Neither this nor his second single was a blockbuster, but things changed sharply with the next release, "I'll Go It Alone," a top-10 hit, as was another original composition, "I Couldn't Keep from Crying." Soon after that, Fred Rose of Acuff–Rose Music Publishing flew to Phoenix to sign Marty as a writer. With that kind of interest and a growing list of credits for appearances in major western cities, it didn't take long before the *Grand Ole Opry* also beckoned. Within six months after *Opry* manager Harry Stone had arranged for Marty's initial guest appearance, Robbins was asked to become a regular (the year was 1953). He moved to Nashville, where, besides appearing on the Saturday night main *Opry* program, he did an early morning show on station WSM. Over a quarter of a century later, Robbins still was a mainstay on the *Opry*.

Things slowed a bit for Marty in 1954, when he failed to dent the country top 10, but in 1955 he was back again with the hit "That's All Right." In 1956, he achieved his first number-one-ranked song with "Singing the Blues," the beginning of a long string of such top hits. In fact, two of his three top-10 hits of 1957 made the up-permost rung—"Knee Deep in the Blues," "The Story of My Life," and "White Sport Coat." The latter, written by Marty, was a major hit in the pop field as well as coun-try and made Robbins a national celebrity. His status continued for the remainder of the decade; he turned out such hits as his composition "She Was Only Seventeen" in 1958, "Stairway of Love" in 1958, and one of his all-time favorite compositions in 1959, "El Paso."

At the start of the 1960s, he had another major hit, "Big Iron," followed in later years with "Don't Worry (Like All the Other Times)," and "It's Your World," both in 1961; "Devil Woman" in 1962; number-one-ranked "Beggin' to You" in 1963; "One of These Days" and "The Cowboy in the Continental Suit" in 1964, all written by him. He also gained top-10 status for other writers' songs with such singles as "Ruby Ann" (number one) in 1962, "Ribbon of Darkness" (number one) in 1965, "The Shoe Goes on the Other Foot Tonight" in 1966, and "Tonight, Car-men" in 1967. During the 1960s, he received several awards, including a Grammy in 1960 for "El Paso," also named the Best Country & Western Recording. It was the first Grammy presented for a country song.

At the end of the 1960s, Robbins suf-fered a massive heart attack that shocked and worried his legions of fans. Tens of thousands of cards and letters of encour-agement poured into the hospital where he underwent surgery and to his home, where he was recuperating. By the start of the 1970s, though, he was back in full swing, giving little indication of any undue con-cern or letup. Within a short time he had another major country hit with his com-position "My Woman, My Woman, My Wife." The song earned him a second Grammy, this time for the Best Country Song of 1970.

Another love of Marty's that worried

friends, family, and fans for many years was his infatuation with fast cars. During the 1960s, he started to indulge a long-time desire by racing stock cars on dirt tracks. He proved to be a cool and capable driver and, continuing even after his heart seizure, he progressed from local events to the big time, the National Association NASCAR Grand National Division, where he could compete against people like Richard Petty and Cale Yarbrough. In 1972, he did so well in one of his first efforts on major NASCAR tracks that he was named Rookie of the Southern 500. In July 1974, the racing fraternity held a Marty Robbins Night in honor of his con-tributions to the sport. However, the next year, three hair-raising crashes caused him to heed the pleas of close associates and concentrate on music. In one of those races, at Charlotte, North Carolina, he de-liberately hit a concrete wall at over 145 mph to avoid slamming broadside into an-other driver's stalled car.

Over the decades as a recording artist, Robbins turned out over sixty albums. The first to earn him a gold record was *Gunfigh-ter Ballads and Trail Songs*, issued by Co-lumbia in September 1959, which included the song "El Paso." Other releases on the label included such LPs as *Singing the Blues* (1956, reissued on Harvard 9/69); *The Song of Robbins* (1957); *Song of the Islands* (2/58); *Marty's Greatest Hits* (1958); *Marty Robbins* (12/58); *More Gunfighter Ballads and Trail Songs* (9/60); *More Greatest Hits* (6/61); *Just a Little Sentimental* (10/61); *Portrait of Marty* (10/62); *Devil Woman* (11/62); *Hawaii's Calling Me* (8/63); *Return of the Gunfighters* (11/63); *Island Woman* (1964); *R.F.D.* (10/64); *Turn the Lights Down Low* (3/65); *What God Has Done* (3/66); *The Drifter* (9/66); *My Kind of Country* (5/67); *Tonight, Carmen* (9/67); *It's a Sin* (8/69); *Marty's Country* (11/69); *My Woman, My Woman, My Wife* (6/70); *Marty Robbins' Greatest Hits, Volume III* (6/71); *Marty Robbins Today* (9/71); *The World of Marty Robbins* (12/71); *Marty Robbins's All Time Greatest Hits* (9/72); and *Bound for Old Mexico* (11/72). Other Columbia titles are *I've Got a Woman's Love, Streets of Laredo, Marty Rob-bins Favorites, The Story of My Life, Saddle*

Tramp, The Bend in the River, Heart of Marty Robbins, From the Heart, Have I Told You Lately That I Love You, El Paso City, Adios Amigo, Alamo, Best of the Gold '50s, Vol. I, Best of the Gold '50s, Vol. II, Best of the Gold '60s, Marty After Midnight, By the Time I Get to Phoenix, Christmas with Marty Robbins, Country Hymns, Country Love, Vol. II and Vol. III, Country's Greatest Hits, Greatest C&W Hits, No Sign of Loneliness, 20 Years of Number One Hits, World of Country Giants, World's Favorite Hymns.

Marty also was represented by several albums on the MCA label. These included This Much a Man, Marty Robbins, and Good and Country.

Over the years his in-person appearances took him to all corners of the United States and Canada and made him a favorite with overseas audiences as well. During the 1970s, he made regular tours of England, Australia, and Japan as well as occasional swings through many other countries. Although his concerts numbered in the hundreds at some points in his career, by the end of the 1970s, he limited them to a still sizable average of eighty a year. His TV appearances could fill several pages as well. Beside guesting on many network shows, including, in the late 1970s, Dean Martin's Music Country and The Midnight Special, he had his own TV series for a number of years. In the occasional TV versions of the Grand Ole Opry (which remained primarily a radio show), he was always prominently featured. In addition, he took part in ten movies over the years, including a singing cowboy role in the film Guns of a Stranger.

As of the late 1970s, Robbin's achievements were among the more monumental ones of modern country music. By then he had written over 500 songs, won over twenty-five BMI awards for songwriting excellence, had a top-10 record all but one year since 1959, had one or more chart records for nineteen straight years, and been on Billboard magazine charts 73 percent of the time over almost two decades. He also had been voted into the Nashville Songwriters Association Hall of Fame, with the CMA Hall of Fame election certain sometime in the future.

Robbins' singles hits in the early and mid-1970s included "Jolie Girl" in 1970; "Love Me/Crawlin' on My Knees" in 1973; "El Paso City" and "Among My Souvenirs" in 1976; and "I Don't Know Why, I Just Do" in 1977.

Marty finished the decade with one of his better years as a singles artist, having four releases in top-chart positions at various times: "Please Don't Play a Love Song," "Buenos Dias Argentina," "All Around Cowboy" and "Touch Me with Magic." In the early 1980s, he still did reasonably well, though the uppermost levels seemed to elude him. In 1980, his charted singles included "She's Made of Faith" and "An Occasional Rose"; in early 1981, "Completely Out of Love" was in the top 50. "She's Made of Faith" and "Completely Out of Love" were Robbins compositions. In the early 1980s, he continued to be a featured artist on the Grand Ole Opry.

ROBERTSON, DON: *Singer, instrumentalist (piano, organ, trumpet, trombone, tenor horn), arranger, composer, conductor. Born Peking, China, December 5, 1922.*

Few songwriters in the country & western field could claim as many successes as Donald Irwin Robertson. The greatest artists of the last forty years beat a path to his door for compositions for new song hits. His background as a skilled musician led to the development of several piano styles, including creation of the country style of piano, later popularized by Floyd Cramer, and an adaptation of the bluegrass banjo pickin' sound for the keyboard.

Don was introduced to music at the age of four by his mother, a talented amateur pianist and poet. The family was then living in China, where Don's father was head of the Department of Medicine at Peking Union Medical College. When Don was five, the family moved to Boston, then Chicago, where Dr. Robertson served as a professor at the University of Chicago. Young Don continued his piano lessons and began composing at seven. His first bent was classical music, particularly since his father often listened to symphonies in the evenings. Don also enjoyed singing hymns during these years in his church choir.

When Don was nine, the family began spending summer vacations at Birchwood Beach in Michigan, near the home of the Carl Sandburg family. The families became close friends and Robertson learned many folk and western ballads at Sandburg's knee as well as receiving instruction in guitar chording.

Don's interest in music continued when he entered high school. In order to join the school band, he learned several brass instruments. Meanwhile, he began to play piano with local dance bands, becoming a professional musician at fourteen.

He also pursued his interest in writing poetry, prose, and short stories. This later provided a foundation for his lyric writing. His father hoped Robertson would follow in his footsteps, and Don did take a premed course at the University of Chicago. However, he finally resolved the conflict in favor of music and dropped out of college in his fourth year. Soon after, he was working as a music arranger at station WGN in Chicago.

In 1945 Robertson moved to Los Angeles, playing in nightclubs and augmenting his living by making demonstration records of new songs for publishers and songwriters. This eventually led to a job as a demonstration pianist with Capitol Records. Don had written many kinds of music up to this time, including symphonic and jazz compositions. Now he began to concentrate on folk and country material, reflecting the earlier influence of Carl Sandburg.

After writing dozens of songs, some in collaboration and after many months of turndowns from singers and publishers, Don finally clicked with Hill and Range in 1953. The firm placed three of his songs with Rosemary Clooney, Eddy Arnold, and Frankie Laine, and one, "I Let Her Go," was a mild hit. In 1954, however, Don's career moved into high gear when Eddy Arnold scored a major hit with "I Really Don't Want to Know." The song became a country standard, providing Robertson with a BMI Award, a total of more than one hundred fifty versions by different re-

cording artists, and sales of more than 5 million through 1969. Hank Snow also had a hit in 1954 with Don's "I Don't Hurt Anymore," which stayed on the charts for half a year.

Don had a smash of successes for the balance of the 1950s. His successes included "You're Free to Go" (Carl Smith); "Condemned Without Trial" (Eddy Arnold); "Unfaithful" (Hank Snow); "Go Back You Fool" (Faron Young); "Hummingbird" (Les Paul with Mary Ford); "Born to Be with You" (the Chordettes); "I'm Counting on You" (Elvis Presley, Kitty Wells); and "Please Help Me, I'm Falling" (Hank Locklin). The latter, which gained Robertson an ASCAP Award, sold more than two million records.

In 1956, Don scored a major hit with his own recording of "The Happy Whistler," which reached Number 9 on the pop charts. Throughout his career Don provided piano or other instrumental backing for many top artists and groups, including Nat Cole, Elvis Presley, Waylon Jennings, Jessi Colter, Ann Margret, Al Martino, Ray Price, and Charley Pride. During these years he wrote twelve songs especially for Elvis Presley, including "Anything That's a Part of You," "There's Always Me," "Marguerita," "They Remind Me Too Much of You," "Love Me Tonight," "No More," and "I'm Yours."

During the 1960s, Robertson continued to turn out hit compositions. These included "I Love You More and More Each Day" (Al Martino); "Does He Mean That Much to You" (Eddy Arnold); "Ninety Miles an Hour," "I Stepped Over the Line," "The Queen of Draw Poker Town" (Hank Snow); "Wallpaper Roses" (Jerry Wallace); "Go Away" (Nancy Wilson); "Ringo" (Lorne Greene); "Longing to Hold You Again" (Skeeter Davis); "Outskirts of Town," "Watching My World Fall Apart" (the Browns).

RCA Victor issued an LP on which Don played a dozen of his hits, titled *Heart on My Sleeve*. In 1966 he signed a new contract with Victor for recordings under the supervision of A&R producer Chet Atkins.

When the Country Music Hall of Fame was opened in 1967, Robertson's name was one of those proudly displayed in the "Walkway of Stars."

Visitors to Disneyland in California, Disney World in Florida and Tokyo Disneyland, can hear Don (in his disguise as Gomer the computerized bear) featured at the piano playing his own composition, "Pianjo", in the opening number of the Country Bear Jamboree.

In 1972 Don was inducted into the Nashville Songwriters Association's Hall of Fame.

Some of Don's collaborators (usually just on the lyrics) over the years have been: Hal Blair, Howard Barnes, Jack Rollins, Lou Herscher, John Crutchfield, Sheb Wooley, Harold Spina and Jack Clement. As this book goes to press, Don is collaborating with Billy Swan, John Crutchfield, Sheb Wooley, Irene Robertson and Gene and Charlene Dobbins, and is playing on occasional recording sessions and TV and concert performances.

ROBERTSON, ECK: *Fiddler. Born Amarillo, Texas, November 20, 1887.*

There must be something invigorating about old-time fiddle playing—so many of these performers lived such long and full lives. A. C. "Eck" Robertson, considered one of the most skilled of the old-time fiddlers, began his career in the 1890s and was still going strong in the 1960s.

Robertson, raised in rural west Texas, learned the fiddle at an early age. Working at many odd jobs as a boy, he played for local socials in his spare time. Eck, along with his brothers, used to walk hundreds of miles to listen and pick up pointers from top-flight fiddlers visiting the region.

By the turn of the century, he was already well regarded as a fiddle player by people in the west Texas region. In the first two decades after 1900, Eck moved around Texas playing in fiddle contests or providing background music for early movies. One of his innovations was to appear in full western costume. Some folklorists credit him with pioneering the wearing of western garb by country & western artists.

Civil War veterans conventions also provided Robertson with employment. At the 1922 meeting in Virginia, he met fiddler Henry Gilliland, and the two decided to go to New York to try to make records. They managed to get a tryout with Victor, which released some of their numbers after they returned home. Their rendition of "Sally Goodin'," in particular, has long been considered one of the all-time-great fiddle performances.

Eck's routine changed little through the 1920s. Although Victor wanted to make more Robertson disks, they didn't know where to find him. Finally, in 1930, Ralph Peer located him and a session was held for Eck and his family. This might have launched a major recording career for Robertson, but the Depression intervened.

In the mid-1930s, Eck was featured on a Dallas radio station. He was little known outside Texas, but he was in demand for local events in his home state throughout the 1930s and 1940s. He continued to be a major figure at fiddling contests throughout the Southwest and won prizes in many of them. In the 1950s, interest in Robertson revived nationally with the new folk music trend. The 1951 *Folkways Anthology* focused attention on Eck through inclusion of his "Brilliancy Medley." At about the time the record was released, Eck was going strong in still another Texas fiddling contest. In 1962, he traveled to Idaho for a contest and won first prize in the old-time fiddler's category.

Eck's virtuosity was emphasized by John Cohen of the New Lost City Ramblers in *Sing Out!* (April–May 1964, p. 57): "On the record of 'Sally Goodin',' one can hear more than a dozen variations on the simple theme. There are syncopated passages, single-string, double-string harmonies, blues notes, drone notes, short rapid grace notes which sound more like piping, and themes played entirely high up on the fingerboard as well as those in the first position."

ROBESON, PAUL: *Singer, actor, born Princeton, New Jersey, April 9, 1898; died Philadelphia, Pennsylvania, January 23, 1976.*

Despite his important contributions to

American arts, Paul Robeson for many years almost became a nonperson. Condemned in his homeland for his political beliefs during the McCarthy era, he was blacklisted as a performer and his recordings were withdrawn from record stores. It was not until his waning years that his reputation was restored and he again received acclaim for his many achievements. Typical of the witchhunts of the 1950s, he was condemned for being a "left-wing activist" although he stated publicly he had never been a communist. There were many who tried to quell his influence, but there is no doubt of his artistic abilities and of his impact on many aspects of twentieth-century culture, including folk music.

Born and raised in relatively comfortable circumstances in New Jersey, Paul was the son of a highly regarded Presbyterian minister who had escaped slavery. The father-son relationship was always supportive and loving. As Robeson said in later years, "When people talk about my voice, I wish they could have heard my father preach."

After graduating from Somerville, New Jersey, High School in 1915, Paul (full name Paul Leroy Bustill Robeson) passed the scholarship examinations for Rutgers University and became the third black man to be accepted. At Rutgers, he continued to achieve good grades while also starring on the football team, where he was an All-American end in 1917 and 1918. After gaining his B.A. degree in 1919, he went on to enroll in Columbia Law School the following year.

While at Columbia, he began to show a flair for acting. As an amateur, he had a major role in *Simon the Cyrenian* at the Harlem YMCA in New York. In 1921, the play moved to the Lafayette Theatre, where Robeson made his professional debut in the same role. He received his law degree from Columbia in 1923, but law no longer seemed as appealing as the theater. When the opportunity came to join the Provincetown Playhouse for the summer of 1923, he took it. His performances in the lead roles in Eugene O'Neill's *The Em-*

peror Jones. and in *All God's Chillun Got Wings* made a strong impression on critics. In 1924, he starred in the New York production of the O'Neill play.

Although Paul had an excellent voice, for which he took some classical training, he didn't sing professionally until 1925. Early that year, he and close friend Larry Brown, a talented pianist/composer, organized a concert act that featured Negro spirituals and folk songs. It was an almost immediate success. In April 1925, the act won standing ovations from a packed house in a New York concert hall. For the rest of the year and into 1926, the concert was presented to enthusiastic audiences across the United States and in England and Europe. In 1926, Robeson signed a recording contract with a major company and was to prove a top-selling artist on records. From 1926 through the early 1940s, he recorded more than 300 numbers, ranging from operatic arias to folk and pop songs.

In October 1926, he was on Broadway playing the lead role in *Black Boy*. The play was short-lived, but his acting was as fine as ever. During that period, the musical *Show Boat* was drawing capacity crowds in its initial run, but while Robeson is almost always identified with it, he did not perform the role of Joe in the original cast. He first made his mark, particularly for his show-stopping treatment of "Old Man River," in the London version of 1928. It was not until 1930 that he performed in *Show Boat,* in New York at the Casino. That year he also first appeared in his most acclaimed acting role, as Othello in Shakespeare's classic. It was a part he took up again to great effect from 1943 to 1945.

During the 1930s, he continued as one of the major concert artists in the world, performing a wide variety of songs on stages throughout the United States and in many other countries. His repertoire included lyrics in most of the world's major tongues; a talented linguist, he mastered some twenty languages in his lifetime.

He also made an impact on the burgeoning film industry in the early 1930s with the recreation of his lead role in *Emperor*

Eddie Rabbit

Jim Reeves

Charlie Rich

Hargus "Pig" Robbins

The Original Jimmie Rodgers,
"The Singing Brakeman"

Tex Ritter

Kenny Rogers & Dottie West

Jones for United Artists. In 1936, he sang "Old Man River" for the cameras as Joe in the Universal film of *Show Boat*. In all he made eleven films, his last efforts being *Tales of Manhattan* and *Native Land* in 1942.

Robeson's singles and albums sold reasonably well in the 1930s and early 1940s, some occasionally becoming bestsellers. His greatest success as a recording artist came in 1939, when his disc of *Ballad for Americans* was one of the year's most popular releases.

By then, he had become increasingly active in fighting for black rights. He credited his first trip to Russia in 1934 with his growing awareness of racial problems. Because he found no apparent racial bias in the Soviet Union, he became an open admirer of their system and, in fact, sent his son, Paul, then nine, to school there in 1936 to avoid racial prejudice. With the onset of World War II, his friendship with the Russian system actually stood him in good stead, but all that changed when the Cold War erupted in the second half of the 1940s.

The first tremors of the coming political storm occurred in 1946, when Robeson was called before a commission of the California state legislature. Questioned about his political affiliations, he stated he was not a communist party member. When the same questions were put to him a few years later by the House Un-American Activities Committee, he refused to answer on grounds of principle, and his long ordeal began. Pressure began to build on concert agencies and record companies to no longer feature his work. When he tried to appear at the Peekskill Music Festival in New York in 1949, riots broke out against his performing. Although he would have been welcomed by European fans, from 1950 through 1958 the U.S. State Department refused to issue him a passport. Still the object of inquiries by the U.S. Congress, when he was asked by a committee member in 1956 why he didn't move to Russia, Robeson replied, "Because my father was a slave and my people died to build this country, and I am going to stay here until I have a part of it just like you."

Despite that statement, when the climate changed in the late 1950s and the U.S. Supreme Court restored his passport, Robeson went into a sort of voluntary exile for some years. Before moving to England, though, he gave a farewell concert at New York's Carnegie Hall in 1958, his first performance there in eleven years. The concert was recorded and released in several volumes. Later, a repackage of Volume 1 was available in the late 1970s on Vanguard Records under the title *The Essential Paul Robeson*. After a short tour of the U.S. West Coast, Robeson left for Europe. On April 6, 1958, he was in Russia, where there was a massive birthday celebration in his honor.

He returned to the United States in 1963, which remained his home for the rest of his life. However, his health was failing and by the early 1970s, he lived in complete retirement. He remained a hero of the black civil rights movement, his stature increasing with each passing year. On April 15, 1973, a seventy-fifth birthday salute was given him at Carnegie Hall, attended by celebrities from stage, screen, and the civil rights movement. Among those paying tribute was the widow of Dr. Martin Luther King, Jr., Coretta King.

Meanwhile, releases continued of some of his earlier recordings. In 1972, RCA Victor issued *Songs of My People*. Vanguard included three of his LPs in its catalogue, *Paul Robeson at Carnegie Hall, Paul Robeson Recital,* and *Ballad for Americans/Carnegie Hall Concert, Volume 2*. Also available in the 1970s were *Spirituals and Popular Favorites* on Columbia Records and *Songs for Free Men* on Odyssey Records.

Robeson died in Philadelphia in early 1976, but honors continued to come his way posthumously, including the belated placement of a plaque with his name on it in the Walk of Stars on Hollywood Boulevard.

ROBISON, CARSON J.: *Singer, band leader, songwriter. Born Oswego, Kansas, August 4, 1890; died Pleasant Valley, New York, March 24, 1957.*

One of the most familiar voices on New

York radio for many years belonged to Carson Robison. He helped build up a strong following for country & western music in the East, and his many pioneering efforts in the field made him a figure of national importance as well.

Robison was exposed to country and folk music from his early years in his home state of Kansas. He sang at local gatherings on many occasions during elementary and high school in the Oswego area. Carson moved to Kansas City in 1920 and was one of the first country & western singers ever to have his voice sent out on the radio.

Carson built up a strong reputation in the Midwest, which served as a basis for his next move, to New York in 1924. In the big city, he soon began his recording career for RCA Victor, initially as a whistler. Throughout the 1920s and early 1930s, he performed on radio and also was featured in vaudeville tours in the East and Midwest. Many of the audience favorites by then were songs he had written himself. In 1932, Robison formed his first group, the Buckaroos. The group accompanied him on radio shows, and during the 1930s toured England with him.

During the 1940s and 1950s, Robison made his base of operations Pleasant Valley, New York. He eventually named his group of those years the Pleasant Valley Boys. Many of his recordings made the hit brackets during the 1930s and 1940s. Probably his biggest success was his MGM top-10 1948 recording of his own composition "Life Gets Tee-Jus, Don't It?" The song provided hit records for many other artists in the decades that followed. Another Robison comic staple of the 1940s and 1950s was "I'm Going Back to Whur I Come From." He also was responsible for a western classic, "Carry Me Back to the Lone Prairie."

Some of Carson's other compositions are "Barnacle Bill the Sailor," "My Blue Ridge Mountain Home," "Left My Gal in the Mountains," "1942 Turkey in the Straw," "Home Sweet Home on the Prairie," "There's a Bridle Hangin' on the Wall," "The Charms of the City Ain't for Me," "Goin' Back to Texas," "Little Green Valley," "New River Train," "Wreck of the Number Nine," and "Settin' by the Fire."

Robison died on his beloved farm in Pleasant Valley, New York, in early 1957. He had remained active in music up to a short time before his death.

RODGERS, JIMMIE (C.): *Singer, guitarist, songwriter. Born Meridian, Mississippi, September 8, 1897; died New York, New York, May 26, 1933.*

Generations of country-music fans and performers have looked back in awe at a figure they knew only from pictures or from records. The most revered name in country-music history, an acknowledged founding father of modern country & western patterns, Jimmie Rodgers achieved all this in just a few brief years in the national spotlight.

Rodgers was born and raised in rural Mississippi, where country music was a part of his environment, as was the country blues of the Negro field hands. Singing was one of the few pleasures that relieved the long hours of work for black and white alike (although Jimmie gave little thought to a music career).

In his teens, he worked briefly as a cowboy, but soon left wrangling for his first job on the railroad. Railroading, he felt, would be his life's work. For close to a decade, he worked on the roads as a brakeman, sometimes entertaining his fellow workers with popular country songs and sometimes with songs of his own on the guitar he had learned to play in his youth. His own compositions were a strangely moving blend of traditional country music, railroad songs, and country blues.

Jimmie might have remained a brakeman were it not for his failing health. He had contracted tuberculosis, and, by 1923–24, he no longer was fit for the rugged demands of railroading.

By then he was a family man with a wife and daughter to support. He had wooed Carrie Cecil Williamson, daughter of the Reverend J. T. Williamson, a Meridian minister, years before and won her hand on April 7, 1920. Their only surviving child, Carrie Anita, was born the following year. Jimmie's wife remained with him through rough periods and happy ones, helped nurse him in his battle with TB, and, after his death, played a role in preserving his contributions to country music and helping others continue the tradition he had started.

Rodgers decided to see if he could earn money as a performer. While Carrie worked as a clerk in a Meridian store, Jimmie toured as a blackface banjo player in a medicine show. Later he joined a tent show, where he performed in whiteface and managed to get enough money together to buy out the owners. Just when the outlook looked brighter, disaster struck. In 1925 the tent and equipment were wiped out by a tornado. Jimmie turned to railroading again and almost killed himself doing it. Then a friend came to the rescue by finding him a job as a city detective in Asheville, North Carolina. The higher elevation of the town brought an improvement in his condition, and, by 1927, his wife and daughter joined him there.

Rodgers soon became bored with a detective's life. He formed a new act with three stringed-instrument artists; their first job was a free show in May 1927 on radio station WWNC for the Asheville Chamber of Commerce. The group, the Jimmie Rodgers Entertainers, slowly increased its appearances, and he talked the members into joining him on a summer tour north to Baltimore. After reading newspaper ads in July announcing that Victor Recording Company would hold field auditions in Bristol on the Tennessee–Virginia border in August, he changed the band's schedule.

He holed up in a cheap hotel across State Street from the hotel where Victor representative Ralph Peer was staying. His band, though, apparently bore a grudge against him and, unknown to him, went to Peer and asked that he record them separately under the name Tenneva Ramblers. When Jimmie went to see Peer, on August 4, 1927, * Peer didn't intend to record him, but Rodgers managed to persuade him to change his mind. Peer agreed, but only for one solo single. Jimmie cut two songs, "Sleep Baby Sleep" and "The Soldier's Sweetheart" and left with a payment of twenty-dollars from Victor.

The Bristol session over, Jimmie and Carrie drove their old car to Washington, D.C., where Carrie worked as a waitress in a tearoom and Jimmie picked up whatever work he could find as a performer. His first single, he found out, was finding some acceptance, and he and Carrie pooled their meager resources so Jimmie could go to New York and see if Peer would let him make more records. Peer was willing, and, in November 1927, Rodgers recorded two more songs in Victor's Camden, New Jersey, studios: "Away Out on the Mountain" and a song tentatively called "T for Texas," replete with Jimmie's fanciest yodels. Issued as "Blue Yodel Number 1," the first of many "blue yodel" discs Rodgers was to make, it started slowly after its release, then really took off. By early 1928 it was a major hit and Jimmie was asked to return for more recordings.

In 1928, his output included "Blue Yodel Number 2" ("My Loving Girl Lucille"); "Blue Yodel Number 3" ("Evening Sun Yodel"); "Memphis Yodel"; "My Little Old Home Down in New Orleans"; and "Ben Dewberry's Final Ride." Almost every one of them exceeded a million copies sold a short time after issue. The story went that farmers all across the United States would go to the general store and order "A loaf of bread, a pound of butter, and the new Jimmie Rodgers record." But his appeal wasn't rural only. He could appeal to all people, as was proven by the crowds that flocked to see him after Gene Austin added him to his show at the Earle Theater in Washington, D.C.

For the rest of his life, Jimmie Rodgers was one of the country's performing roy-

---

* August 4 is the date given by RCA archivists: the date of August 1 also is given in the same report.

alty. He toured the South and Southwest, where crowds fought to hear him, touch his clothes, or just get a brief glimpse of his frail form. His records continued to be avidly snapped up by his fans for the few years of life left to him. By early 1933, he had rolled up sales of almost 20 million records.

Beside releases noted above, his output included such hits as "Treasure Untold," "Lullaby Yodel," "The Sailor's Plea" (1928); "Hobo Bill's Last Ride," "Yodeling Cowboy Blues," "Mississippi River Blues," "The Land of My Boyhood Dreams," "That's Why I'm Blue," "Jimmie's Texas Blues," "Any Old Time" (1929); "The Mystery of Number Five," "Those Gambler's Blues," "I'm Lonesome Too," "For the Sake of Days Gone By" (1930); "Let Me Be Your Side Track," "My Good Gal's Gone Blues," "T.B. Blues," "The Wonderful City" (with the Carter Family), "When the Cactus Is in Bloom" (1931); "Gambling Barroom Blues," "Roll Along Kentucky Moon," "No Hard Times," "Down the Road to Home" (1932); "Somewhere Down Below the Dixon Line," "Mississippi Delta Blues," "Cowhand's Last Ride," and "Old Love Letters" (1933).

Among his other singles between 1927 and 1933 were "Mule Skinner Blues," "T for Texas," "Travelin' Blues," "One Rose That's Left in My Heart," "The Brakeman's Blues," "Daddy and Home," "My Time Ain't Long," and "Prairie Lullaby."

In addition to his personal appearances, Jimmie sang on several radio programs. He also made a movie short for Columbia pictures.

The money rolled in and Rodgers enjoyed spending it. He bought expensive cars and established a lavish home for himself and his family in Kerrville, Texas. He also was always willing to give funds to friends in need—or who said they were in need. That he always seemed to spend his income as fast as it came in wasn't too surprising. He knew his meteoric career had a time limit on it from the beginning. His health, always precarious, deteriorated badly in the winter of 1932–33, and he had to sell the remote Kerrville property and settle in San Antonio, Texas, where medical help was closer.

The bills kept piling up, and, feeling better in the spring of 1933, he was determined to try to complete another recording session up north. Accompanied by a trained nurse, he traveled to Galveston in a private train compartment, then embarked on a luxury cruise on the S.S. Mohawk to New York. Once there, he negotiated a lucrative new contract with Victor and began to make new recordings on May 17. But the improvement in health had proved deceptive. It soon was apparent he was in no shape to work.

Bob Gilmore, an assistant to Ralph Peer, recalled, "Jimmie was very ill . . . he had a nurse with him and a big Cadillac arranged so that he could lie down and rest. . . . In the recording studio he was propped up so that he could sing with the least expenditure of energy . . . and sometimes he would stop, in order to catch his breath."

Instead of the twenty-four songs he and Peer intended to make, he cut the list to twelve, completing the last group on May 24. He longed to return home, but was in no condition to travel. He spent his last days in New York's Taft Hotel, where he died on May 26, 1933. In all, between August 4, 1927 and May 24, 1933, he recorded 113 songs, all of which still were available on RCA long-playing records in the 1970s.

Artists still were making the hit charts with some of his compositions in the 1980s, as dozens of top performers had done over all the decades since his death. His influence spread from contemporaries like Gene Autry and Ernest Tubb to such others as Merle Haggard, Elvis Presley, and Charley Pride. Over the years, many songs were written in his memory, beginning with Bradley Kincaid's 1934 offerings, "The Death of Jimmie Rodgers" and "Jimmie Rodgers' Life," and continuing with Ernest Tubb's tributes in 1936, "The Last Thought of Jimmie Rodgers" and "The Passing of Jimmie Rodgers" on up to Elton Britt's country chartmaker of 1967–68, "The Jimmie Rodgers Blues," a biography of Rodgers made by combining the titles of most of his songs. He was the first member elected to the Country Music Hall of Fame, on November 3, 1961.

Countless musicians, from Ernest Tubb to artists of the 1970s, used guitar techniques developed by Rodgers. His methods were described as follows in *Golden Guitars, The Story of Country Music* (by Irwin Stambler and Grelun Landon, N.Y., Four Winds Press, 1971):

> Rodgers' guitar phrasing often started with tuning the strings a half tone lower than is done conventionally. He then placed a capo next to the top fret, bringing it to tune and giving it a brighter voice because the strings were then tensed over metal rather than the ivory bridge. He played the bass strings with a straight pick on the neck of the guitar, above the acoustic hole, to accomplish a distinctive instrument-voice blend. In pickups between choruses, or on sustained notes, he used to pick the same bass notes just above the bridge and below the acoustic hole to lead into the following vocal note.
>
> These pickup runs and tight neck playing, along with some flicking finger strums across all the strings for accents, helped show the guitar's potential as a lead instrument. (The accepted practice of the day, used by such popular stars as Bradley Kincaid, was to apply the guitar in the background to chord along behind the mandolin, violin or other dominant front sounds.)
>
> Rodgers also ended his songs by having the guitar play a bass sign-off signature. About the same time, Sara and Maybelle Carter of the Carter Family trio used bass runs to maintain the rhythm, an innovation for group playing.
>
> Rodgers used 'dirty blues' figures, but in the lower register, a technique often used by today's rock groups as well as old time boogie-woogie pi-

anists. These figures, with the sub-themes, were the basis for riffs used in the swing bands and were often converted for use as the melody line in popular big band songs of the 1930s and 1940s.

In the decades after Rodgers' death, RCA continued to reissue his recordings in various combinations. In the long-playing record era following World War II, the company always had a number of Rodgers' LPs in its active catalogue. That list, as of the early 1980s, included the albums *Legendary Performer, Best of the Legendary Jimmie Rodgers, Country Music Hall of Fame: Jimmie Rodgers, Jimmie the Kid, My Rough and Rowdy Ways, My Time Ain't Long, Train Whistle Blues, This Is Jimmie Rodgers, Short but Brilliant Life of Jimmie Rodgers,* and *Never No Mo' Blues.*

RODGERS, JIMMIE (F.): *Singer, guitarist, songwriter, emcee. Born Camas, Washington, September 18, 1933.*

During the late 1950s, few ballad singers could buck the driving heat of rock 'n' roll that dominated the hit charts. An exception was a young man from the state of Washington with an illustrious name, Jimmie Rodgers. Not only did he gain much airtime for his recordings in the folk vein, he also became a national teenage idol as great, in those years, as the most strident rock performer.

James Frederick Rodgers' march to musical success began in his childhood in Camas, Washington, where his piano-teacher mother started giving him lessons at an early age. When he enrolled as a music major at Clark College in Vancouver, Washington, he was thinking more of a career as a music instructor. His plans were interrupted by the Korean War, which resulted in Jimmie's enlistment in the Air Force for four years.

Rodgers ended up in Seoul, Korea, where he bought an old guitar for a few dollars to help pass the time. Eventually he formed a group called The Rhythm Kings, which performed at bases in the Far East and later in the United States. While stationed outside Nashville, Tennessee, Jimmie gained his first job as a solo singer at the Unique Club in that city.

After his discharge, he returned to Camas and joined a small band that worked in nightclubs in the Portland area. After a while, he decided to leave and try to make his way on his own, specializing in folk-type songs. He could not get bookings for many months, but finally was signed to appear at the Fort Cafe in Vancouver, Washington. Audience reaction was so favorable that he was held over for seventeen weeks.

During this period, a fellow performer, Chuck Miller, caught the act and urged Jimmie to try for a New York recording audition. Rodgers gained a hearing from Roulette Record executives there. They particularly liked "Honeycomb," a song that he learned at the Unique Club, and had him tape it for them. Jimmie went back to Camas, but in a short time Roulette called him back to make a commercial version of the song. "Honeycomb" shot to the top of the charts soon after its release, becoming one of the major hits of 1957. Jimmie followed with two more million-sellers that year, "Are You Really Mine" and "Kisses Sweeter than Wine." He was now nationally known and was asked to appear on many network television shows, including Dick Clark's *American Bandstand*, *The Ed Sullivan Show*, *Dinah Shore*, and *Perry Como*.

In 1958, Rodgers added two more top-10 hits to his credit, "Oh-Oh, I'm Falling in Love Again" and "Secretly." In the next few years, he scored with such other songs as "Bimbombey," "Woman from Liberia," and "I'm Goin' Home." Jimmie's success in 1958 resulted in his own TV show on NBC network. In 1959, his life was reviewed on NBC's *This Is Your Life*. During these years, Jimmie toured extensively throughout the United States and overseas, appearing in concerts and nightclubs in almost every major city in America.

As Jimmie's success grew, he moved his family (he married his childhood sweetheart, Colleen McClatchey, in 1957) to Granada Hills, California, at the far end of the San Fernando Valley, near Hollywood. In 1960 he made his first movie for 20th Century–Fox, *The Little Shepherd of Kingdom Come*. His second for Fox, *Back Door to Hell*, was released in 1964.

Rodgers switched to Dot Records in 1962, as both performer and artists & repertoire executive for folk music. His efforts for Dot included such songs as "Rainbow at Midnight," "Face in the Crowd," and "No One Will Ever Know." In the mid-1960s he starred in a new syndicated TV show, the *Folk Song World of Jimmie Rodgers*.

Over the decade 1957 to 1967, Jimmie's total of 30 million record sales included many hit LPs as well as singles. His LP output for Roulette included *Jimmie Rodgers; His Golden Year; Twilight on the Trail; When the Spirit Moves You; Folk Song World, Folk Songs; Best of Folk Tunes* (1961); and *15 Million Seller* (1962). For Dot, Rodgers provided such titles as *No One Will Ever Know* (1962); *Folk Concert, My Favorite Hymns, Honeycomb* (1963); *World I Used to Know, 12 Great Hits* (1964); and *Deep Purple* (1965). Rodgers was also represented in 1964 on the Hamilton label with *6 Favorite Hymns/Ballads of Jimmie Rodgers*.

In late 1967, Jimmie signed for a new movie, *To Catch a Robber by the Toe*. Before he could go to Europe to work on the film, his career was interrupted by a controversial mishap. In the early morning hours of December 2, 1967, Rodgers was found unconscious in his car near a freeway off-ramp close to his San Fernando Valley residence.

He apparently had been hit on the head by a blunt instrument, assumed to have been wielded by a robber. Later, it was revealed that he had been forced to the side of the road by an off-duty police officer for what was claimed to have been erratic driving. When Rodgers got out of his car to discuss the matter, the police claimed he accidentally fell and hit his head. Rodgers, whose memory of events was unclear after his head injury, disputed the Los Angeles Police Department version of the affair in a damage suit later filed against the city.

It was some time, though, before Rodgers was in condition to tell his side of the story. For many weeks, he remained in critical condition. After several operations, he was able to leave the hospital in mid-1968 and resume some of his entertainment activities. However, whether due to the hiatus caused by those injuries or the downturn in folk music interest belatedly catching up with him, he was unable to recapture his earlier audience rapport. Although he made several attempts at a comeback over the next decade, none proved successful.

RODRIGUEZ, JOHN RAUL DAVIS "JOHNNY": *Singer, guitarist. Born Sabinal, Texas, December 10, 1952.*

The enormous crossover success of Freddy Fender in 1975 made many people see him as the first Mexican-American country superstar. In actual fact, he followed in the footsteps of a young performer named Johnny Rodriguez, who erupted on the country scene a few years earlier and remains one of the major luminaries of the field.

Rodriguez, like Fender, was born into a poor Texas family. He was the youngest of nine children living in a four-room shanty in Sabinal, a town ninety miles from the Mexican border. He hardly remembers his father, who died of cancer when Johnny was three, yet his memories of growing up in the rural town are surprisingly pleasant. As he told Bill Williams and Bob Kirsch of *Billboard*, "I know what struggling is. But I was always around music while I was growing up and I decided to sing country because that's what I am. My older brother, who has passed away, was a rodeo man and he'd sing a lot of country songs, often in Spanish. That's where I came up with the idea of doing some of my songs in English and half in Spanish."

He told Jerry Bailey of the *Country Music Beat* that his original opportunity came while he was a teenager jailed for goat-rustling. His jailhouse singing enthralled a Texas Ranger who brought him to the attention of a promotor named Happy Shahan. Shahan, in turn, hired Johnny to perform in cowboy garb at the tourist attraction he ran called Alamo Village.

Shahan, who took over as the youngster's manager, brought country star Tom T. Hall to hear him. Hall said he'd call on Rodriguez if an opening came up in his band.

Johnny waited a bit, then made his way to Nashville. "I had about eight dollars with me," he told Bailey, "I had this old guitar wrapped in a cellophane bag. I must have looked like a weirdo in downtown Nashville. I figured everybody saw me walking around and said 'Well, there's another squirrel.' I was too, boy. I was right in the middle of it all."

However, Hall, when contacted, agreed to pick him up. "Tom T came by and picked me up in a black Cadillac he had back then. I never will forget it. I couldn't think anything but 'Wow!' So the next week I went to work for him playing lead guitar. Then I started fronting the band and eventually recorded 'Pass Me By.'"

The recording was Rodriguez's first single on Mercury Records, and it surprised even him by racing up the country charts to the number-four position. The next release, "You Always Come Back to Hurting Me," did even better, reaching the number-one position. His debut LP, *Introducing Johnny Rodriguez*, also was a hit, making the country top 10 soon after its release in 1972 and going to number one on all three major charts—*Billboard*, *Cash Box*, and *Record World*. Johnny showed that his success was no fluke with more recordings that verified his position as one of the most effective of the new country singers. His followup album was a top-10 hit in 1973 as was the next one, titled *My Third Album*, in the first half of 1974. The latter spawned the top-10 country hit single "Something."

During 1974, Rodriguez made his debut as a TV actor. He played a bit part in an *Adam-12* show that was shown on network TV in the fall. Encouraged by his performance, he agreed to accept a part in the western movie *Rio Diablo*.

His emphasis, however, remained on his country efforts both as a concert artist and recording star. Mercury released a *Greatest Hits* album in mid-1976 that rose to top-chart levels, as did his 1977 LP, *Practice Makes Perfect*. In 1978 he was represented in the top 20 by the album *Love Me with All Your Heart*. Among his chart singles in the late 1970s were "I Wonder if I Said Goodbye," number one in September 1976, "If Practice Makes Perfect," a top-20 hit in June 1977, and such fall chartmakers as "Eres Tu" and "Love Put a Song in My Heart."

In 1979, Johnny left Mercury and signed with Epic Records. His debut album on Epic, produced by Billy Sherrill, was titled *Rodriguez*. His first single on his new label was "Down on the Rio Grande." Late that year, his single "What'll I Tell Virginia" came out and made upper-charts levels. Also on the lists in late 1979 and early 1980 was a duet single with Charly McClain, "I Hate the Way I Love It." Other charted singles by Rodriguez in the early 1980s were "North of the Border" in the fall of 1980 and "I Want You Tonight" in early summer 1981.

ROGERS, DAVID: *Singer, guitarist, songwriter. Born Atlanta, Georgia, March 27, circa 1939.*

His father wanted him to become a doctor, advice David Rogers later offered, unsuccessfully, to his own teenage son, but David had other ideas. For a long time it appeared he had made the wrong choice, but persistence paid off, and, in the 1970s, David Rogers finally earned his spurs as an important country artist.

He was born and raised in Atlanta, where country music was dominant. He started learning guitar before he was in his teens and was playing in local functions during his early high school years. His father, however, disapproved. Later on, he told Carol Offen of *Country Music* magazine (December 1973), when he had his own big tour bus, "I liked to park the bus in front of his house once in a while. Y'know, it's got my name all over the thing."

Rogers began playing country nightclubs in Atlanta and the vicinity when he was sixteen, supplementing his relatively meager income with day jobs such as selling pots and pans door to door and, for a period, working as a structural draftsman.

The Longhorn Club, where he was popular with both the fans and management, was his favorite. The owner, who was to become Rogers' manager, was Kathleen Jackson. She had been running a grocery, when she was persuaded by the aspiring young musician who delivered her bread, Pete Drake, to open a club. After the Longhorn opened, Pete Drake played there, and he and Rogers became friends.

Rogers performed at the Longhorn off and on until it closed in the early 1960s. After that, Jackson asked him to appear at her new club, The Egyptian Ballroom. After some extended engagements, he decided he needed to widen his audience and concentrated on lining up dates in other towns and gaining a recording contract. Jackson decided to work with him in his endeavors, helping him prepare some demo tapes that were brought to Pete Drake, by then a fixture in Nashville, in the mid-1960s. Drake thought David had potential, but recommended that more extensive demos be made in Nashville with new material. Rogers told Offen, "The session come off real good and Kathleen Jackson paid for it, 'cause I didn't have the money."

The material, which stressed Rogers' soft ballad style, was submitted to local Columbia executive Frank Jones by Drake. Jones liked the treatment well enough to send the tapes to the home office in New York. The result was a long-term recording contract for Rogers from Columbia.

David moved his family to the Nashville area and settled in Donelson, Tennessee, soon after he began his initial sessions for Columbia. By the end of the 1960s, his name began to show up on the national country charts as fans around the United States started to take note of his talents. He backed his record releases with extended touring, but still, as the 1970s began, he ranked as a supporting artist on most bills rather than a headliner. That tended to be the case during his six-year association with Columbia, though he placed a fair amount of singles on hit lists, including some that made the top 10. His early 1970s chartmakers on the label included such songs as "I Wake Up in Heaven" in 1970 and "Goodbye" in 1972.

The latter title proved appropriate because in mid-1973, Rogers left Columbia to join the newly established (and relatively short-lived) country-music operation at Atlantic Records. Almost immediately things took a turn for the better for him. His singles "Just Thank Me" and "It'll Be Her" moved to the top levels of the charts, as did the album titled *Just Thank Me.* He now had the opportunity to headline major venues around the country; his intensive concert work kept him and his band on the road an average of 100,000 miles and 200 to 250 days each year the rest of the 1970s.

Rogers placed several more singles on the charts on Atlantic, such as the early 1974 "Loving You Has Changed My Life," before that company abruptly shut down its country operations. David experienced a certain amount of dislocation before he signed with a new label and set about to repair the damage.

His new recording company home was Republic, which hardly ranked among the largest operations in the field. But with Rogers' ability and his already sizable following, he soon was posting new chart hit releases. In late summer of 1976, he was represented by the single "Whispers and Grins" and in mid-1977 reached mid-chart levels with "I Love What My Woman Does to Me." During the summer of 1978, "Let's Try to Remember," a song Rogers wrote with D. Pfrimmer, was on the country lists for several months. In the spring of 1979, he had one of his top singles hits of the decade with "Darlin'." In early 1980, his Republic single "You're Amazing" was on upper-chart levels.

ROGERS, GAMBLE: *Singer, guitarist, songwriter, humorist, author. Born Winter Park, Florida, January 31, 1937.*

"You can never blame a man for bein' human unless he makes a habit of it"—"An expert ain't nothin' but an ordinary man away from home"—"The Lord gives me grace, but the devil gives me style."

Gamble Rogers usually set audiences roaring with laughter with his short, witty sayings and extended, rambling stories. In fact, he has been compared with Will

Rogers as a story teller on the one hand and, on the other, to Doc Watson as a fine guitarist. That he was not an acknowledged superstar at the start of the 1980s seemed mainly due to the vagaries of the entertainment industry that limited his exposure. Those who saw him on stage or in the many programs he appeared in on the U.S. National Public Television network in the 1970s had no doubt that he was one of the most underrated artists of the decade.

Tall tales, down-home humor, and country music came as naturally to him as breathing. Born in Florida but raised in Georgia, Gamble was surrounded by those influences from his early years. He told Paul Hendrickson of *Rolling Stone* (May 23, 1974), "I found out I could tell a story when I was still a little kid visiting my kin up in North Georgia. My cousins and I'd be running wild in the mountains all day, hunting snakes and digging frogs and when we'd come in for supper, I'd start telling stories. That's all I do now. They usually have a basis in fact. I just dress them up in a mock-heroic, florid, baroque style and rave on like a Bible-belt preacher."

Rogers also had a talent for singing that he developed over the years along with his skills as an instrumentalist. He liked country music and folk music, but also recalled being strongly impressed by his first glimpse of a then unknown artist named Elvis Presley. He often tells that anecdote as part of his stage act, in which he also uses his guitar to demonstrate how folk and gospel music gave birth to rock.

"Back about 1954, I went to see the *Grand Ole Opry.* At the end of the show, out skittered this strange young man wearing an After Six tangerine-colored jacket, a lemon-colored tux shirt with ruffles, pistol-legged sharkskin pants, black and white saddle oxfords, his hair done up in a coiffure that cosmetic scientology has long since dismissed as belonging to the era of the decadent duck's ass. When he was done, those of us who weren't too dumbfounded rushed back stage.

" 'Who is that?' we all asked. 'Why, he's the Hillbilly Cat.' 'But what's his name?' 'Why Elvis, Elvis Presley.' "

After wandering across country at one point with his brother, working at odd jobs, including selling Bibles door to door, and even, during one phase, trying his hand at writing a novel, Gamble finally decided to devote his energy to a show business career. In the late 1950s, he headed for New York.

He arrived in the midst of the folk boom and made friends with a number of young folk artists who had flocked to Manhattan from all over the country. Eventually, in the 1960s, he became a member of a folk group called the Serendipity Singers, which achieved a modest reputation in the music field for some years. With that group he toured widely doing concert work and also gained a number of TV and recording credits.

In 1968, Rogers went out on his own as a solo artist. It was the beginning of a long, hard struggle that kept him on the road almost constantly over the next decade, playing small folk clubs and college campuses, moving in and out of old hotels and low-cost motels as he painfully built a following. It took six years before he scored his first important breakthrough. He took part in the 1974 Philadelphia Folk Festival, which was taped for the Public Broadcasting System. PBS issued the material as a series of TV programs, also presented on Canadian stations, not only spotlighting Gamble's set but also using his dynamic instrumental tribute to Doc Watson, "Deep Gap Salute," as the theme for all the shows.

The response of both critics and viewers to Rogers' work was strongly positive. This encouraged PBS to feature him in a show of his own, *Gamble Rogers—Live at the Exit In*, taped in Nashville. As the 1970s went by, he was featured increasingly on PBS and on major folk festivals, including annual appearances at the Philadelphia Folk Festival; Winnipeg, Canada, Festival; Florida Folk Festival; and Mariposa (Toronto, Canada) Folk Festival. In the late 1970s, he taped a thirteen-week series as a guest commentator on National Public Radio's top-rated *All Things Considered* program. Again, listener approval was impressive and he was asked to return for another full

season, with his commentary as a weekly feature on the show.

(Rogers demonstrated his talent as a playwright with PBS as well. He wrote an hour script for the National Public Radio *Earplay* drama series titled "Good Causes, the Confessions of a Troubadour.")

At the end of the 1970s, he finally got the chance to make his solo album debut, something that had eluded him for years. Issued on Mountain Railroad Records, *Gamble Rogers* featured material ranging from comic sketches like "Habersham County Mephistopheles" (which contains the line "The Lord gives me grace, the devil gives me style") through several of his "Southern gothic art songs" to country, folk, and rock songs like Billy Joe Shaver's "Honky Tonk Heroes" and his own "Black Label Blues" and "Deep Gap Salute."

Meanwhile, in increasingly well-attended in-person appearances, Gamble continued to create audience awareness of his various alter egos, with particular emphasis on "the deputy sheriff of DeKalb County, Georgia," whom he knew personally. "He swaggered up . . . and said, 'Boy, don't you be talking spiteful and nasty to me like some of them hippy-dippy punks that come through here every day from Macon, drivin' them Volkswagen buses with sleepin' bags and chemical commodes in the bed of 'em like they was some kinda mobile orgy. I was writin' out a ticket for one of them long-haired fruits when he leaned out the window and said 'Baaaby, gimme five cheeseburgers and a Coke.' I pulled him outta that thing and chucked his ass through an *Impeach Earl Warren* sign.' "

ROGERS, KENNY: *Singer, guitarist, songwriter. Born Houston, Texas, August 21, 1937.*

Certainly the phenomenon of country music, and pop music too, in the late 1970s and early 1980s was Kenny Rogers. With the huge success of his 1977 single "Lucille," after twenty years of performing Kenny was on the way to bonafide superstardom. Some country purists looked on this development with less than all-out enthusiasm; though as a born and bred Texan, Kenny came from authentic country-music territory. His route to country music was by way of jazz, rock, and pop, a background that helped him record a single like "Lady," which made number one on pop, country, and soul charts in 1980. Despite the nay-sayers, though, country fans had no qualms about supporting him and his achievements, and in return, he played a major role in sustaining the country-music boom that got under way in the 1970s.

Rogers made it to the top from suitably humble beginnings. The fourth of eight children born to Edward and Lucille Rogers, he grew up in Houston under somewhat difficult circumstances. His parents were loving, but his father, a carpenter and shipyard worker (who also played the fiddle), had a hard time making ends meet in the Depression years and, worse still, was an alcoholic. As a child, Kenny spent a number of years with his family in a federal housing project and several rented houses.

His brother Randy told Sue Reilly and Kent Demaret of *People* magazine (December 1, 1980), "I think we felt a little bit like outsiders. We'd go to church in an old pickup truck and stoop down low in the seats because we didn't want anybody to see us. I think all that boosts Kenny in thinking, 'I just don't want to go back. There's nothing wrong with it, but I don't want to go back.'"

Kenny sang in the church choir and in a glee club as a boy and also started to learn to play instruments, including the piano. Recalling his guitar progress, his mother told *People*, "Kenny never had a guitar lesson, he just picked it up. On the weekends he was at one of the music stores, daylight until dark. He must have drove those people crazy, playing all the guitars they had down there. Oh gee, him and Mickey Gilley [another neighborhood boy at the time] used to come over to the house and Kenny would hammer on the guitar and Mickey on the piano. I thought they were going to run me out of the house."

In high school, Kenny formed his own rockabilly group, the Scholars, to play at dances and local events. He signed a re-

cording contract while still in high school with Carlton Records and had a local hit with the 1958 single "That Crazy Feeling" (backed with "We'll Always Have Each Other"). His second single, "For You Alone," backed with "I've Got a Lot to Learn," was also issued in 1958. Carlton issued an LP, *One Dozen Goldies,* in 1959, the last solo release Rogers was to have for some years.

He briefly enrolled at the University of Houston, but dropped out in favor of playing bass and singing with a jazz group, the Bobby Doyle Trio. He toured nationally with the combo, and they had an album released on Columbia in 1962. He left them to work with the Kirby Stone Four, and in 1966 moved to Los Angeles and joined the New Christy Minstrels. He had a brief fling on Mercury Records in 1966, which resulted in one single release ("Here's That Rainy Day," flip side "Take Life in Stride") and several unissued recordings: "He Will Break Your Heart," "Please Send Me Someone to Love," "If You Don't Share Your Love," and "Rubber Soul."

In 1967, Rogers and Mike Settle, another Minstrel, decided to try their hand at rock music. They formed the group the First Edition with two other singers. The group later became a fivesome after a switch in personnel in which two of the original members, including founder Settle, left the group. The First Edition was a highly successful combo. It offered an alternative to the heavy metal, psychedelic sound popular in the latter half of the 1960s. In fact the group often sang country songs and fit in well in their frequent appearances on Johnny Cash's television show. Their hits included "Just Dropped in to See What Condition My Condition Was In," "Ruby, Don't Take Your Love to Town," "Something's Burning," "Reuben James," and "Heed the Call." They eventually came to be known as Kenny Rogers and the First Edition, as Kenny's voice seemed to be the most readily identifiable voice in the group. In 1971 the group hosted its own syndicated television variety show, *Rollin' on the River* which was soon picked up by many United States and Canadian stations.

As the years passed, however, group members began to get bored with their act and also to wane in popularity. In 1975, Rogers decided to part from the First Edition and to try his luck on his own as a solo country artist. Although he signed a contract with United Artists (the name later was changed to Liberty) and had singles out on the label in 1975, at first the response was only nominal. Adding to his problems, his marriage of twelve years to Margo Gladys Anderson was winding up with considerable bitterness on both sides. (This was his third marriage.) He had close to two dry years as a performer; money was tight and he played small Las Vegas lounges and appeared on TV commercials selling quick and easy music lessons. He credits the love and support of his girl friend and later fourth wife, Marianne Gordon (whom he met while guesting on the *Hee Haw* TV show on which she was a regular) with seeing him through those lean days.

Even when things were slow, he was confident the picture would brighten. He told Peter J. Boyer of the Associated Press, "I never had any doubt in my mind. I never felt I had a good voice, but I always knew that I had a very commercial voice. When I got this band together, I predicted that within one year I'd have a top-10 record. I always knew that with the right piece of material, I could pop with a record any given day."

Sure enough, in 1977, Kenny's recording of "Lucille" became a giant hit, soaring to the top of the country and pop charts. The song sold over 4 million copies. Kenny followed with another hit, "Sweet Music Man," which he wrote himself. The song has already become a standard and has been recorded by a number of other artists, both pop and country.

One day, Rogers ran into singer Dottie West in a Nashville recording studio. On the spur of the moment, they recorded a song she was working on as a duet. "Every Time Two Fools Collide" became a top country hit in early 1978. Later in 1978, the duo had a hit with "Anyone Who Isn't Me Tonight." At the Country Music Association's awards in 1978, Kenny and Dottie were named the Top Vocal Duo of the Year.

Kenny continued to turn out his own solo hits. "The Gambler" became a number-one-ranked single in late 1978 and early 1979. In 1979 he had hits with "While She Waits" and "Coward of the County." (In fact, after "The Gambler" made the top 10, every single he released through the fall of 1981 also entered that charmed circle.) He had become one of the top performers in both pop and country fields and one of the most recognizable and well-liked celebrities in the United States.

During the late 1970s, Rogers complemented his recording efforts with intensive touring as well as many appearances on TV, including periods of hosting *The Tonight Show*. In 1980, he averaged 200 concerts a year, typically selling out major venues and often setting new attendance records. In 1981, with his position as a superstar well established and demands of TV movies increasing, he cut back to 100 or so appearances. Backing him on his live shows, as of the early 1980s, was a band (called Bloodline) led by drummer Bobby Daniels and including Eugene Golden on keyboards and vocals; Steve Glassmeyer on keyboards, flute, soprano sax, and vocals; Edgar Struble on keyboards and vocals; Randy Dorman and Rich Harper on guitars; and Chuck Jacobs on bass guitar.

Describing one of his concerts in Fort Worth, Texas, Roger Kaye of the Fort Worth *Star Telegram* wrote (1/12/81), "[Rogers] has the knack for making a large arena show seem like a much more intimate experience than it is, and that's due to his casual approach. Rogers talks to a crowd of 14,000 in the same way he might address a gathering of 14 or less. He makes it seem like it's all among friends."

In 1980, Kenny appeared in his first made for TV movie, *Kenny Rogers as the Gambler*. Telecast on the CBS network, it achieved the highest rating of any TV movie shown over the previous two years. Rogers also starred in three variety specials on the same network, "A Very Special Kenny Rogers," "Kenny Rogers and the American Cowboy," and "Kenny Rogers' America." In the fall of 1981, he was featured in his second TV movie, *Coward of the County*. Also in print in the early 1980s was a book he co-wrote with music publicist Len Epand, published by Harper & Row, *Making It with Music*.

Rogers didn't slight the recording field in the early 1980s. The song that became the title of his second TV movie, "Coward of the County," was number one on singles charts in January 1980. In the spring, a new duet pairing, with singer/songwriter Kim Carnes, provided the bestselling single "Don't Fall in Love with a Dreamer." During the summer, he hit with "Love the World Away" and, in November, had "Lady" in number-one position on country charts. "Lady," written and produced by Lionel Ritchie of the Commodores vocal group, became his biggest seller to date, chalking up over 1.5 million copies sold by mid-1981. His albums had done equally well from the late 1970s into the early 1980s, with releases like *The Gambler* (1978) and *Kenny* (1979) reaching number one on country charts for many weeks and remaining on the lists into the 1980s, to be joined by such others as *Gideon* (whose songs all were written by Kim Carnes and her husband Dave Ellingson), *Kenny Rogers Greatest Hits*, and *Share Your Love*. The *Greatest Hits*, LP, issued in 1980, by the fall of 1981 had sold over 14 million copies. *Share Your Love*, released in the summer of 1981, had sales of over 2 million copies two months afterward. As of that time, Rogers' manager, Ken Kragen, estimated he had sold more than $200 million worth of records in three years.

A list of Rogers' record releases from his First Edition days to late 1981, compiled by Todd Everett, is as follows. His singles were, on Reprise, with the First Edition, "I Found a Reason" b/w "Ticket to Nowhere" (1967); "Just Dropped In" b/w "Shadow in the Corner of Your Mind," "Dream On" b/w "Only Me," "Look Around, It's Only Me" b/w "Charlie the Fer de Lance" (1968); "But You Know I Love You" b/w "Home Made Lies,"

"Ruby (Don't Take Your Love to Town)" b/w "Girl Get a Hold of Yourself," "Reuben James" b/w "Sunshine" (1969); "Something's Burning" b/w "Momma's Waiting," "Tell It All Brother" b/w "Just Remember You're My Sunshine," "Heed the Call" b/w "Stranger in My Place" (1970); "Someone Who Cares" b/w "Mission of San Nohero," "Take My Hand," "Where Does Rosie Go" b/w "What Am I Gonna Do?" (1971); and "School Teacher" b/w "Trigger Happy Kid" (1972). On the Jolly Roger label, Kenny and the First Edition were represented by the singles "Lady Play Your Symphony" b/w "There's an Old Man in Our Town," "(Do You Remember) The First Time" b/w "Indian Joe," "Today I Started Loving You Again" b/w "She Thinks I Still Care" (1972); "Lena Lookie" b/w "Gallop County Train," "What's She Gonna Do" b/w "Something About Your Song," and "Makin' Music for Money" b/w "Stranger in My Place" (1973). On United Artists, Rogers' singles were "Love Lifted Me" b/w "Home-Made Love," "A Home Made Love" b/w "There's an Old Man in Our Town" (1975); "While the Feeling's Good" b/w "I Would Like to See You Again," "Laura (What's He Got That I Ain't Got)" b/w "I Wasn't Man Enough" (1976); "Lucille" b/w "Til I Get It Right," "Daytime Friends" b/w "We Don't Make Love Anymore," "Sweet Music Man" b/w "Lyin' Again" (1977); "Every Time Two Fools Collide" b/w "We Love Each Other" (with Dottie West), "Love or Something like It" b/w "Starting Again," "Anyone Who Isn't Me Tonight" b/w "You and Me" (with Dottie West); "The Gambler" b/w "Momma's Waiting" (1978); "She Believes in Me" b/w "Morganna Jones," "All I Ever Need Is You" b/w "Won't You Play Another Somebody Done Somebody Wrong Song" (with Dottie West), "Til I Can Make It on My Own" b/w "Midnight Flyer" (with Dottie West), "You Decorated My Life" b/w "One Man's Woman," "Coward of the County" b/w "I Want to Make You Smile" (1979); "Don't Fall In Love with a Dreamer" b/w "Going Home to the Rock—Gideon Tanner" (with Kim Carnes), and "Love the World Away Saying Goodbye" b/w "Requiem—Going

Home to the Rock" (1980). On Liberty Records, Kenny turned out "Lady" b/w "Sweet Music Man," "Lady" (Spanish version) b/w "Sweet Music Man" (1980); and "What Are We Doing in Love" b/w "Choosin' Means Losin'" (with Dottie West) (1981).

Album releases were, on Reprise, *First Edition* and *First Edition's Second* (1968); *First Edition '69, Ruby Don't Take Your Love to Town* (1969); *Something's Burning, Tell It All Brother* (1970); *Fools* (movie soundtrack), *Kenny Rogers and the First Edition's Greatest Hits, Transitions* (1971); and *The Ballad of Calico* (two records) (1972). Albums on Jolly Rogers were *Back Roads, Monumental* (1972); and *Rollin'* (1973). United Artists solo albums were *Love Lifted Me* (1976); *Kenny Rogers/Lucille, Daytime Friends, Ten Years of Gold* (1977); *Every Time Two Fools Collide* (with Dottie West), *Love or Something like It* (title track written by Rogers with Steve Glassmeyer), *Convoy* (movie soundtrack), *The Gambler* (1978); *Kenny Rogers and Dottie West—Classics, Kenny* (1979); and *Gideon* (1980). On Liberty, he had the LPs *Kenny Rogers Greatest Hits* (1980); *Share Your Love* (1981); the duet "What Are We Doing in Love" on Dottie West's LP *Wild West,* and *Kenny Rogers' Christmas* (1981). Rogers also contributed the track "Love the World Away" included in the Elektra LP of the original *Urban Cowboy* soundtrack. Warner Brothers Special Products issued a two-record TV package, *Kenny Rogers and the First Edition*, released on the Lakeshore Music label.—I.S./A.S.

ROGERS, ROY: *Singer, guitarist, actor. Born Cincinnati, Ohio, November 5, 1912.*

The "King of the Cowboys" almost became the "King of the Bootmakers." Roy's father was a skilled shoemaker, and for a time Roy worked in a shoe factory. Luckily for movie audiences the world over, a cross-country trip in a beat-up jalopy helped launch Rogers (whose real name was Leonard Slye) on his fabled Hollywood career.

After seven years in Cincinnati, the family moved to a farm near Portsmouth, Ohio, where Roy learned to ride his first horse, a black mare that once raced at the county fair. Another favorite pasttime of Roy's was the movies; on Saturday afternoons, he would go to see Buck Jones and Tom Mix films at the local cinema.

When he was a teenager, his family moved back to Cincinnati because of low finances. There Rogers met a man who owned a thoroughbred horse farm. He took a liking to Roy and gave him the chance to perfect his horsemanship. Around this time, Roy's family drove out to California to visit his newly married sister. When they returned to Portsmouth, Roy's dream was to return to California to work in the movies.

He bought a guitar and soon learned to play. In the late 1920s, he knew enough cowboy songs to sing and double as square-dance caller at local dances. In 1930, hearing that a distant relative was going to California, Rogers hitched a ride. His first jobs in Los Angeles were picking peaches and driving a sand and gravel truck. Roy became a favorite with his co-workers, entertaining them with his singing and guitar playing in the barracks at night. The excellent response made him think more seriously about a career as a musician.

He first joined a group of five other musicians called the Rocky Mountaineers. It was enjoyable, but not profitable, so he organized his own group, the International Cowboys. Still the results were not impressive. He broke up this group and soon joined a new one with two other young performers, Tim Spencer and Bob Nolan. They called their act the Sons of the Pioneers. Local audiences liked them, and before long they were making a respectable profit. They soon managed to gain a record date. When one of their first recordings became a major hit, the men were on their road to stardom.

The Sons of the Pioneers played more and more engagements in major western cities. They also were signed for a series of radio sketches. Roy branched out on his own in small singing roles in cowboy pictures. Hearing that Republic Studios was looking for a new cowboy lead, Roy applied for an audition. He was turned down, but sneaked in with a group of extras and got a hearing anyway.

The timing proved right. Gene Autry (whom the Sons of the Pioneers had backed in some films) had a falling out with the studio and walked out. Republic chief Herbert J. Yates promptly signed Rogers for the lead in the 1938 western *Under Western Skies*. From then on, Roy starred in one western after another, often accompanied in the singing segments by the Sons of the Pioneers. From that 1938 beginning through the 1951 movie *Spoilers of the Plains*, he made eighty-eight westerns in all, earning the title of "King of the Cowboys." His horse, Trigger, became as well known as the Lone Ranger's horse, Silver.

His leading lady for many of the 1940s films was Dale Evans. After Roy's first wife died in 1946, he married Dale. Rogers recalled for Bob Thomas of the Associated Press in January 1975, "That was 27 years ago and people said, 'We'll give 'em a year.'" Republic's Yates was so sure the public wouldn't accept Dale as Roy's girlfriend after the marriage that he dropped her from the series. Rogers told Thomas, "The studio got a jillion letters of protest and Yates had to put Dale back in the pictures."

After TV almost wiped out the movie western, Rogers and Evans started their own TV series, performing in 101 episodes through the late 1950s. In addition, the duo kept up busy recording sessions and traveled widely for in-person appearances in theaters and at rodeos and state and county fairs.

But the pressures of such a heavy schedule apparently caught up with Roy in 1958, when he developed a heart condition. The first signs appeared, he told Thomas, in 1975 when "I was hunting deer at 9,000 feet in Utah. I had just shot and cleaned one and the two fellows I was with put it on a carrier with a bicycle wheel to take it down the mountain. I had gone about 150 feet and my arms started hurting. I couldn't get air, but I thought it was the altitude."

After he returned home, though, those sensations continued. Finally going into a clinic for an examination, he found he had angina pectoris. For the next year, he had to sharply limit his activities. However, he stuck to the required regimen and rebuilt his health to the point that he could resume some, if not all, of his entertainment work in the 1960s. He still was in good shape in the mid-1970s, telling Thomas, "Now I can ride my motorcycle and do almost everything, except a rough-and-tumble fight in a film." At the start of the 1980s, Rogers and Evans still were making a limited number of concert appearances each year. They also made occasional TV appearances, such as cohosting one of the NBC-TV *Nashville Palace* programs in the fall of 1981.

In the mid-1960s, Roy, Dale, and their family (which included children by previous marriages and a number of adopted children) settled in Apple Valley in California's Mojave Desert. One of the things they did there was to open the Roy Rogers Museum, whose exhibits include, beside career memorabilia, Roy's stuffed horse, Trigger. (Average annual tourist volume through the museum from the late 1960s through the start of the 1980s was about 100,000 people.)

Roy's other activities of the 1970s included providing his name for a string of fast-food restaurants and, in 1974-75, taping introductions for a syndicated TV series of old westerns, *Roy Rogers Presents the Great Movie Cowboys.*

His record releases included the 1974 single "Hoppy, Gene and Me" and later in the 1970s, on Capitol Records, the LP *The Country Side of Roy Rogers* and the charted single "Money Can't Buy Love."

During the heyday of his career in the 1940s and 1950s, most of his material was released through RCA Victor. His Victor albums included *Roy Rogers' Souvenir Album, Roy Rogers' Roundup, Skip to My Lou and Other Square Dances* (with Spade Cooley), and *Roy Rogers and Dale Evans.* Some of Roy's single recordings were "You Can't Break My Heart," "Don't Blame It All on Me," "Rock Me to Sleep in My Saddle," "My Chickashay Gal," "Hawaiian Cowboy," "Dusty," "Home on the Range," "Old Fashioned Cowboy," "Stampede," "Smiles Are Made Out of Sunshine," "Frosty the Snow Man," "I'm a-Rollin'," and "Yellow Bonnets and Polka Dot Shoes." (See also Evans, Dale: Sons of the Pioneers)

RONSTADT, LINDA: *Singer, songwriter, Born Tucson, Arizona, July 15, 1946.*

By the age of thirty-four Linda Ronstadt had already become something of a "grand old lady" in the country-rock musical genre. Although still young and highly attractive, she had been performing for over a dozen years and had been a pioneer, paving the way for other female country and rock singers and greatly popularizing the country-rock sound.

Linda grew up in Tucson, Arizona, where her preteen idols were Hank Williams and Elvis Presley. She liked rock music but also listened to country and Mexican music. After a year at the University of Arizona, Linda left for California to pursue a career as a singer.

With two friends, Bob Kimmel and Ken Edwards, Linda formed a group called the Stone Poneys. They made three albums for Capitol and had a rock hit in 1967 with "Different Drum." However, the group broke up in 1968 and Ronstadt started off in her own direction.

Her first album, *Hand Sown, Home Grown*, evidenced a shift from the soft-rock sound of the Stone Poneys to a stronger country emphasis. The album was a good one, featuring such songs as "Silver Threads and Golden Needles," which was to become a favorite with audiences through the late 1970s, and country standards like John D. Loudermilk's "Break My Mind" and Ivy J. Bryant's "The Only Mama That'll Walk the Line." However, she had no chart hits from the album. Her second solo LP, *Silk Purse*, continued in the country vein. The album was on the pop charts for a few months, and a single cut from the album, entitled "Long, Long Time," became a top-30 hit and won Ronstadt her first Grammy nomination.

For her third album, *Linda Ronstadt*, Linda assembled a new band, which included Glenn Frey and Don Henley. They later went on to form their own band, the Eagles, a popular and influential country-rock group. In 1973, Ronstadt signed with Asylum records and released the album *Don't Cry Now.* This LP was met by critical as well as popular success. Linda stepped up her touring schedule, and she was on her way to reaching a wide audience of rock, pop, and country fans.

The turning point in Linda's career came in 1974, when she signed Peter Asher as her manager as well as her record producer. Their first collaboration was the album *Heart like a Wheel*, which became number one on the pop charts and soon achieved platinum status. (Ironically, this album came out on her old label, Capitol, rather than her new one, Asylum. She still owed Capitol an album under her previous contract and she and Asher decided to get it out of the way.) Her single "You're No Good," a remake of an old rock standard, became a number-one hit, as did "When Will I Be Loved," also from the *Heart like a Wheel* album. Her version of Hank Williams' "I Can't Help It if I'm Still in Love with You," from the same LP, won her the Grammy Award for Best Female Country Vocal in 1975. In addition, "Don't Cry Now" returned to the charts to become Linda's second gold record.

Ronstadt's second album produced by Peter Asher was *Prisoner in Disguise,* released on Asylum in 1975. This LP was a bit more rock-oriented than some of her previous albums. The big hit single was "Heat Wave," a remake of a soul hit from the early 1960s. But as always Linda also included more traditional country cuts, such as Dolly Parton's "I Will Always Love You" and Neil Young's country-flavored "Love Is a Rose," which became a hit on the country charts. *Prisoner in Disguise* achieved gold-record status almost immediately after its release and turned platinum soon afterward.

The year 1976 proved to be a continuation of Linda's previously successful years. She released a new album, *Hasten Down the Wind,* which included, for the first time, two songs that she had written herself, "Lo Siento Mi Vida" (co-written with bassist and former Stone Poney member Kenny Edwards and also with Linda's father) and

"Try Me Again" (co-written with musician Andrew Gold). Other album cuts were "That'll Be the Day," an old Buddy Holly song, which added fuel to the growing Buddy Holly revival craze, and her version of Willie Nelson's "Crazy." Both became pop as well as country hits. The album achieved platinum status, and it won for Linda a Grammy Award for Best Female Pop Vocal Performance. That year, the Playboy Poll named her the Top Female Singer in both pop and country categories.

Ronstadt's next album, *Simple Dreams*, was released in August 1977. It contained five major hits, three of which were top country chart hits. These were "Blue Bayou," which won a Grammy Award for Best Single, "Poor Poor Pitiful Me," and "I Never Will Marry," recorded together with Dolly Parton. Two other cuts were smash rock hits, "Tumbling Dice" and "It's So Easy." Linda was named once again as Top Female Singer in both pop and country divisions in the Playboy Poll. *Simple Dreams* sold 3.5 million copies in less than a year in the United States alone. Ronstadt continued to receive a great deal of media attention, and she appeared on the covers of *Time, Rolling Stone,* and *People* magazines, as well as many others.

September 1978 saw the release of Linda's next album, *Living in the U.S.A.* The title song, a Chuck Berry rock song, made the upper echelons of the country and rock charts. In 1980, she had another hit album with *Mad Love* and another number-one-ranked single with "Hurt So Bad."

From these statistics, one may easily deduce that Linda Ronstadt is a superstar. She had her first hit at the age of twenty-one and, although she had a few years without a major hit, she was rarely far from the top of the hit lists. Her voice has a natural quality, although the voice is operatic and nearly flawless. That natural quality reflects her personality. She seems to be a person without pretenses, which, along with her lovely voice, has endeared her to her fans. This charm has always helped her career, for even in her dry years her fans were always fiercely loyal to her. Girls and women could identify with her giggling stage manner and her songs about failed romance. Men found her pretty and sexy, but not threatening. She often went on stage without shoes, because she didn't like to wear them; on the cover of *Silk Purse* she posed along with some pigs because, as she said in one television interview, she thought pigs were nice.

Ronstadt also carried her honesty into the songs she chose to record. As she told Robert Hilburn of the *Los Angeles Times* in December 1974, "Though the melody has to match up with what I can do, the lyrics are the main thing. I look for something that feels like it is about me. Just like a songwriter will write a song that is about some feeling he just went through, I can't really sing a song that doesn't express my feelings in some way." This attitude, perhaps more than anything else, accounts for her numerous appearances at the top of the hit charts.

In addition, Linda was able to become one of the first artists to cross over with her songs with any regularity. Country fans could accept her country-rock songs because she had always leaned toward country even when singing rock and soul songs. All her albums included some traditional country or rockabilly songs. She always seemed, no matter what she sang or how popular she became, to be basically a "down-home" type of person. Ronstadt's ability to cross over paved the way for other performers to do the same, notably Dolly Parton, Tanya Tucker, and Emmylou Harris.

Ronstadt was also something of a pioneer as a woman rock singer. When she started out, there were very few woman rock stars. There were women country singers, but they tended to fit into a narrow mold, appearing to be ultrafeminine and singing songs that identified them mainly as wives and mothers. Linda was one of the women who helped break ground so that today it is not uncommon to hear women in both rock and country singing about anything and everything.— A.S.

ROSE, TIM: *Singer, guitarist, songwriter. Born Washington, D.C., September 23, 1940.*

Tim Rose never quite made it to stardom, though he came agonizingly close a number of times. A gifted songwriter and effective if low-key performer, he seemed destined for great success when he first appeared on the New York pop scene in the early 1960s, but somehow there always seemed to be a piece of the puzzle missing. Nonetheless, he turned out an excellent body of work over the years and had an influence on both folk and rock.

Born and raised in the Washington, D.C., area, Rose played in a number of local bands in his teens, winning his high school's highest musical award. At the University of Virginia he majored in history and psychology, earning money for college by working in one of Lester Lanin's society dance orchestras. After a year and a half of college he decided that neither school nor old-style pop music was exciting enough and enlisted in the Air Force. While stationed in the Midwest, Tim formed a rock group with other fliers called the Abstracts, which was considered one of the best in the Air Force in 1962.

After receiving his discharge, Tim moved to New York. In a short time he had organized a folk trio called the Big 3, whose other members were Cass Elliott, later to become famous with the Mamas and the Papas, and James Hendricks (who went on to write a number of songs that became hits for Johnny Rivers). The group had great potential, but was a bit before its time. It featured folk material, but with the then unusual approach of employing some electric guitar plus drums.

Rose said later, "I remember the big names in the business throwing hands to heads at the thought of mixing folk with rock. But a couple of months later, folk-rock became an accepted musical form. That proved one thing to me. In this business you've got to go ahead and do what you want to do."

But the Big 3 had other problems. Rose told a reporter, "I was 'fired' from the group when Cass and Jimmy decided they didn't want to work with me anymore. They had gotten married—and had been married for months—and they didn't even tell me. That's how close we were."

After performing briefly with an obscure group called the Thorns, Tim decided to make his way as a solo act only, come what may. He worked when he could, wrote new material, and made the rounds of recording companies in the mid-1960s, for the most part meeting only frustration. It was an outlook he expressed incisively in the lyrics to his song "Goin' Down Hollywood": "Soon I met reality/It hit me in the face/No one cared to hear my songs/Was dreamin' all a waste?/First I had to sell my car/Just to buy a meal/My lady found another man/This whole thing sounds unreal/But it's all goin' down in Hollywood."

He didn't lack for near misses, though, as he told Richard Trubo (*Los Angeles Times Calendar*, July 16, 1972): "I had a chance to join the Rolling Stones, but I was extremely anti-group at the time and turned it down. I also refused an opportunity to join the Christy Minstrels. I was considering an offer George Harrison made to produce an album of mine and put a group around me, but the label I was with then [Columbia], nixed the idea before it got off the ground."

However, Tim's signing with Columbia in 1967 was a promising step forward. The debut disc, *Tim Rose*, came out in early 1968 and contained such songs as "Hey Joe (You Shot Your Woman Down)," "Morning Dew," "Come Away, Melinda," "Where Was I?," and "I Got Loneliness." Rose's version of "Hey Joe" was adopted by Jimi Hendrix for a chart hit single. "Morning Dew" has been covered by many artists over the years. The album and Rose's debut single on CBS Records in England, "I Guess It's Over," found a wider audience in that country than either the LP or the U.S. initial single, "Long-Haired Boy," achieved. During 1968, Rose was well received in such places as London's Royal Albert Hall, Yugoslavia, and the international pop music festival, Musica '68, held on Majorca.

A second album by Rose came out on Columbia in 1969, but it fared relatively poorly with the U.S. public. In 1970, Tim moved to Capitol, which released the album *Love, A Kind of Hate Story*, in January

1971. It was a release that had some good cuts but, as Rose himself agreed later, suffered from a lack of consistency and from overproduction. He remedied many of those defects in his fourth solo LP, *Tim Rose,* which came out on Playboy Records in 1972. The release provided an excellent showcase for Rose's composing and performing skills and received considerable critical praise as well as much more airplay than previous efforts. Overall, though, perhaps because he was the first artist on the new Playboy label, it never received enough sustained promotional support to expand Rose's essentially cult following to a broader public audience.

ROUSE BROTHERS: *Vocal and instrumental group, songwriting team. Ervin Rouse, Gordon Rouse, Earl Rouse, all born North Carolina.*

The Rouse Brothers separately and as a team played thousands of dates in country nightclubs from New York to Miami in a career that stretched from the 1930s to the 1970s. However, other than the people who saw their act, most country fans knew little about them because of their lack of recording success. Almost everyone was aware of their classic original fiddle tune, "Orange Blossom Special," though most thought it was a traditional song.

The boys were members of a large family, containing fifteen children all told, born and raised in rural North Carolina. Country music was an integral part of life, and quite a few of the Rouses learned one or more instruments and played in local groups. Ervin, Gordon, and Earl had the greatest persistence, and as the 1930s progressed managed to move from their home-town region to major cities on the East Coast.

Even before the brothers sallied forth from North Carolina, they were working up original material. One of their ideas for improving their position in the music field was to sell some of the songs to major publishers. It was rough going, as Ervin told Everett Corbin of *Music City News* (October 1969), "We walked all over New York and were turned down by all the music publishers. We were told that 'your music will never amount to anything.' We

were discouraged and encouraged to 'stay out of the music business.' "

However, the Rouses had their musical skills to fall back on. If they couldn't sell their songs, they still could try to find work as performers, and eventually they began to get enough jobs to keep them going. In time they were able to do well enough to find bookings in such important clubs as New York's Village Barn and Miami's Royal Palm (where they shared one bill with Sophie Tucker).

It was while traveling from a New York engagement to another in Miami, Ervin told Corbin, that "Orange Blossom Special" was born. "We wrote it on the same day [in 1936] the Orange Blossom Special passenger train was christened at Miami. We were riding with our manager, Lloyd Smith, from Miami to New York and he challenged us to write a song about the train. "We took the challenge and it was completed by the time we got to Orlando." The tune, he noted, was co-written by him and Gordon and was intended to be a combined "fiddling, singing, talking" song.

The Rouses copyrighted the song and initially sold the publishing rights to a New York firm whose copyrights later were acquired by Leeds Music. However, they didn't get the chance to record it for several years. In 1939, they finally signed with RCA's Bluebird label and recorded an album of country songs, including a number of other original compositions. During the early 1940s, the Rouses also made some recordings for ABC Records' country label, Melatone, but neither their RCA or Melatone efforts found a wide public response.

Meanwhile, though, "Orange Blossom Special" had a life of its own. More and more country artists included it in their repertoire and more and more recordings by major performers were released over the decades. A number of versions made the charts. In 1965, a single by Johnny Cash rose to top 10 in the U.S. country lists and showed up on pop charts as well.

The Rouses continued to remain relatively anonymous, though they kept writing songs—particularly Ervin—and performing. Some of Ervin's other material was recorded by major artists. In 1945, he wrote "Sweeter than the Flowers," which provided chart hits for both Roy Acuff and Moon Mullican later in that decade. Mullican's release was a top-10 hit in 1948.

During one of Johnny Cash's network TV programs in 1969, he paid homage to the Rouses by having them perform "Orange Blossom Special" on the show. The brothers came up to Nashville for the program from their home in Miami, where they had been living for close to two decades. All were still working at the time, Earl handling vocals, guitar, and fiddle, Gordon vocals and fiddle, and Ervin vocals and fiddle.

ROWAN, PETER: *Singer, guitarist, saxophonist, songwriter, band leader (Earth Opera, Old and in the Way, Muleskinners). Born Wayland, Massachusetts.*

An important figure in pop music from the mid-1960s on, Peter Rowan left his imprint on many musical genres, from traditional bluegrass to rock 'n' roll. Whether as a sideman in other artists' groups or, more often, as leader of his own band, his musicianship and original contributions were of the highest calibre.

Born and raised in Massachusetts, Peter learned to play guitar in his early teens and played with a country rock group during high school. He continued to play at Colgate University until he left the school two years later to work as a sideman with groups playing small-time bars and clubs.

In the mid-1960s, he decided he needed to widen his horizons. He moved to Nashville, where he impressed Bill Monroe with his guitar and vocal talents and became a member of the Blue Grass Boys. In late 1967, eager to go out on his own, he left that band and returned to the Boston area. The result was Earth Opera, a rock band that blended country, blues, and some jazz elements into a rock format. Earth Opera's makeup during 1967 was Rowan on lead vocals, guitar, saxophone (and a main songwriter), multitalented instrumentalist David Grisman handling saxophone and some stringed instruments, John Nagy on bass, Bill Stevenson on keyboards, and Paul Dillon on drums. The band had some

success, having regional hits with the singles (on Elektra) "The Red Sox Are Winning," "Time and Again," "Dreamless," and "When You Were Full of Wonder," and winning good concert reviews. However, it was unable to achieve the massive exposure needed for rock stardom and disbanded by the end of 1968.

While with Bill Monroe, Rowan had become friends with violinist Richard Greene. In the late 1960s, Greene joined a new folk-rock band called SeaTrain. The group was looking for additional members, and, in late 1969, Greene phoned Rowan from California (Peter was still in the Boston area) and asked him to join. Rowan agreed, and later helped record SeaTrain's debut LP on Capitol Records, *SeaTrain*, issued in early 1971. He also worked on the second album, *Marblehead Messenger*. In 1972, though, the band reorganized and Rowan was one of those who departed.

In the mid-1970s, he returned to his earlier love, bluegrass. One of the bands he assembled was called Old and in the Way. Its members included old friend David Grisman, plus John Kahn on string bass and such luminaries as Grateful Dead guitarist Jerry Garcia and country fiddle virtuoso Vassar Clements. The group remained intact for a relatively short time, though it did make some recordings, including the live 1973 LP, *Old and in the Way*, issued by Rounder Records. Two of the band's best offerings were written by Rowan—"Midnight Moonlight" and "Panama Red."

Another bluegrass band Peter helped form in the 1970s was called Muleskinner. He was joined not only by David Grisman but by Richard Greene. That band gave a number of notable concerts in folk clubs, bluegrass festivals, and other venues around the United States.

At the end of the decade, Rowan moved away from bluegrass to write songs with a southwest United States flavor. These compositions dealt with cowboys, Indians, and Mexican-Americans. They provided the main input for a new LP, titled *Peter Rowan*, issued by Flying Fish Records in mid-1979. His band members on that collection included Richard Greene, fiddler Tex Logan, and the great Tex–Mex accordionist Flaco Jimenez, who had previously toured and recorded with Ry Cooder.

RUSH, TOM: *Singer, guitarist, pianist, songwriter. Born Portsmouth, New Hampshire, February 8, 1941.*

For a while in the first half of the 1960s the name Tom Rush brought the image of a major force in current music trends to the minds of a sizable segment of the American music audience. However, with the resurgence of rock 'n' roll exported by the Beatles and the British invasion of the mid-1960s, Rush, like most of the other folk luminaries, moved into the wings. Tom has continued to turn out finely crafted, sensitive records since then, but their delights have been sampled by a select few of the general public still faithful to the folk idiom. Still, to those individuals, Rush remained a major name, and his concerts at various folk centers always were eagerly awaited. And, as a look at the albums of contemporary artists like Jackson Browne and others in the California folk-rock movement indicate, Rush's abilities as a songwriter continued to be recognized by artists with mass followings.

Considering that folk music is now deemed relatively genteel in music circles, it's odd to think that his family members were not very enthusiastic about their son's choice of calling. When he was growing up in Concord, New Hampshire, where his father taught mathematics at St. Paul's School, Tom's initial exposure to music took the form of classical piano lessons. Ivy League education was very much a family tradition; Rush was sent to Groton School, in Groton, Massachusetts, in the eighth grade.

He recalled, "It was straight out of Dickens. They had a black mark system and depending on the nature of the offense, you could be given up to six black marks. Each was worth an hour's time doing something. Sometimes it was copying out of the Bible, sometimes it was walking in circles. Every now and then they would have you do something constructive, like

sweep up the woodworking shop or model for an art class."

In retrospect, the most important event during his high school years was when he received his first guitar during his junior year at Groton. "I never did take lessons on the guitar, which is probably why I enjoyed it so much. I got a little band together and we played before the Saturday night movies and for parties and things. We were doing Gene Vincent imitations and Carl Perkins imitations, you know, old time rock 'n' roll. Subsequently, I became interested in folkier type of music. When I went to Harvard, I found that Cambridge was the hotbed of folk."

At the time he was accepted there, in the 1950s, the folk boom was in full swing, inspiring such then-unknowns as Joan Baez to sing in local coffee houses. Rush also followed that path, working one or two nights a week for small amounts of money, sometimes passing the hat.

His popularity encouraged him to begin his recording career. "I made a record on a little fly-by-night label. It wasn't quite a vanity record. Somebody was paying me to make it. It was really a small scale operation. The guy was distributing it to stores out of the trunk of his car. Then a friend of mine, Paul Rothschild, got a job as A&R man for Prestige Records and signed up most of the Cambridge folk scene, except for a few artists who went with Vanguard Records."

Tom made some albums for Prestige in the early 1960s, then dropped out of school for a while in the middle of his junior year to see if he could earn a living as a singer. "Most of the time I was staying around Boston working two nights a week. I was only taking home $10 a night, but somehow I managed. I ate a lot of liver."

Having proved he could support himself, albeit marginally, he went back to Harvard and got his degree. "I didn't really intend to be a professional singer, but I graduated with a degree in English Lit, which doesn't really prepare you for anything." He continued to work as a Boston folksinger for a while, his reputation slowly growing not only locally but in other folk centers. After Rothschild moved to Elektra and worked out a new contract with Rush, Tom became a fixture on the New York folk scene and took up residence for a while in a Manhattan apartment. His concertizing took him far afield in the mid-1960s, including appearances on campuses and in concert halls and clubs throughout the United States, as well as three tours of England.

His Elektra albums rank among the more notable folk releases of the mid- and late-1960s. His debut on Elektra, *Tom Rush*, was released in March 1964 and was followed by several more. Commenting on his LP *The Circle Game*, with a title track by the soon-to-be-discovered folk composer Joni Mitchell, the *New York Free Press* (March 28, 1968) critic typified many reviewers in writing, "[the album] screams for recognition. . . . Tom Rush is a musician who projects sensitivity. He can handle the dangerous emotions of love and tears as few have ever been able to bare themselves with their voice and response."

Although Rush retained a faithful following, the sales of his recordings by the end of the 1960s paled compared to the reigning rock and soul royalty. There was still enough demand for his output, though, for Columbia to welcome the chance to add him to its roster in late 1969. His debut release on the label, *Tom Rush*, was on record racks in 1970. In 1971, his second Columbia LP, *Wrong End of the Rainbow*, was issued, followed in May 1972 by *Merrimack County* and, during the summer of 1974, by *Ladies Love Outlaws*.

In the 1970s, Tom moved back to New Hampshire, where he took up residence on a 400-acre farm. An environmentalist, he spent some of his time at home in the mid-1970s building a windmill electrical generation system. He also indulged in such other hobbies as sculpting and hang gliding.

Into the 1980s, he continued to turn out new songs while sometimes reworking arrangements for earlier ones. Although he could hardly sell out large rock venues, as might have been possible during the early 1960s, he commanded respectable attention in college auditoriums and folk clubs whenever he chose to tour. His show usually included such favorite original compositions as "No Regrets," "Rockport Sunday," and "Wrong End of the Rainbow" as well as a sprinkling of songs by other writers, often promising newcomers whose careers Rush enjoyed aiding.

RUSSELL, JOHNNY: *Singer, guitarist, songwriter. Born Sunflower County, Mississippi, January 23, early 1930s.*

Although John Bright Russell already was showing promise as a performer before he was in his teens, it took almost two decades before he gained public recognition for that side of his personality. In between, though, he made his mark as a songwriter with material that was welcomed not only by many country artists, but by such pop stars as the Beatles.

Russell spent the first eleven years of his life in Sunflower County, Mississippi, in the heart of country-music country. His family moved to California when he was twelve, and in his teens he became active as a professional entertainer, playing for school events as well as appearing in club dates and on local TV shows.

During the mid-1950s, he was spending an increasing amount of his spare time writing original songs. He managed to get tapes of some of them to Chet Atkins in Nashville, who thought enough of one of them, "In a Mansion Stands My Love," to include it in a Jim Reeves recording session. That event persuaded Johnny to move to Nashville for a while in 1958. The song was issued as the "B" side of a Jim Reeves single. The "A" side, "He'll Have to Go," became a number-one country hit in 1959. Russell's song was overshadowed by the latter, but he still was in the happy position of receiving royalties from a gold-record single.

Because rock was causing a depression in the country field at the time, Atkins had to forgo signing Johnny to a recording contract, though he indicated he would like to if Johnny could wait. Russell opted to try other avenues which led to two abortive recording and publishing alignments.

When those didn't work out, he moved back to California in the early 1960s.

As it happened, it was a good move. Soon after he returned, he got a message from Buck Owens that he was interested in a song Russell had been trying to place for two years. "Act Naturally" became a top-10 hit for Buck in 1963. Later, the song found an even wider audience when it was recorded by the Beatles. Meanwhile, Russell continued his songwriting, but spent much of his time throughout the 1960s running a music publishing company. He didn't abandon performing, making whatever in-person appearances he could fit in between his other activities. During that time, California remained his main base, though he sometimes lived in Nashville for extended periods of time. Among those who recorded his songs in the 1960s were Burl Ives, Patti Page, Loretta Lynn, the Wilburn Brothers, and Del Reeves.

At the start of the 1970s, the long-delayed contract between RCA and Russell finally materialized. Before long, his name was showing up in the top levels of country charts with such singles successes as "Mr. and Mrs. Untrue," "What a Price," "Mr. Fiddle Man," and "Rain Falling on Me," a track record of four hits out of his five initial releases on RCA. He added such others in the early and mid-1970s as "Rednecks, White Socks and Blue Ribbon Beer," "Catfish John," and "The Baptism of Jesse Taylor." His in-person work picked up strongly in the first half of the 1970s with engagements taking him on the road fifteen to twenty days each month. He also was featured on major TV shows, including *Dean Martin's Country Music, Dinah Shore, Music Country, U.S.A.,* and *Pop Goes the Country.* He also was asked to perform at major industry events, including the Country Music Association Awards Banquet.

His chart successes of the mid- and late-1970s included "That's How My Baby Builds a Fire," on country charts in early 1975, "Hello I Love You," a top-10 hit on RCA in mid-1975; "Our Marriage Was a Failure" in late 1975; and "This Man and Woman Thing" in 1976. In 1977, Russell decided it was time to move on and signed

a new recording contract with Mercury Records. His charted singles on that label included "Ain't No Way to Make a Bad Love Grow" in 1979, "We're Back in Love Again" in 1980, and "Song of the South" in late 1980, early 1981.

In the late 1970s, Russell became increasingly interested in acting. He played a bit part on the TV show *J.D. and the Salt Flat Kid* and in 1978 was negotiating for larger roles in future TV productions. Meanwhile, he kept up his singing efforts, including regular appearances at Las Vegas hotels.

RUSSELL, LEON: *Singer, pianist, trumpeter, guitarist, songwriter. Born Lawton, Oklahoma, April 2, 1942*

Some people were surprised when Leon Russell, rock superstar, began turning out country-oriented albums in the 1970s, starting with *Hank Wilson's Back, Vol. 1* in late 1973. They shouldn't have been, considering Leon's exposure to folk and country material in his Oklahoma childhood and his early association with pioneers of the rockabilly era.

Still, his first training wasn't in a pop or country format, but in classical music. His father, a clerk for the Texas Company, and his mother both played the piano and started him on the instrument when he was three. He continued those studies until he entered high school. "I didn't really have the hands for classical stuff," he said, "and my teachers discouraged me from making up my own music."

He turned to the trumpet with the goal of becoming a pop musician, formed a band (he had to lie about his age—fourteen—to get a job in a Texas nightclub), and performed in many concerts and dances in Oklahoma during 1956-57. These performances included sessions with Jerry Lee Lewis and a group called Ronnie Hawkins and the Hawks. Looking for broader horizons, in 1958 teenaged Leon moved to Los Angeles, where "I'd borrow a friend's ID to get a job, then I'd return the card and work until I was stopped by the police for being underage and out after curfew."

By the early 1960s, his talents on piano,

trumpet, and a variety of other instruments earned him a glowing reputation in the music industry. He became one of the most sought-after session musicians in Los Angeles. One of the first producers to seek him out was Phil Spector, who employed Leon's talents on the 1963 LP *Ronnie and the Ronettes.* During the mid-1960s, Russell was particularly active with Gary Lewis & the Playboys, contributing his ability in the form of sideman, arranger, and, sometimes, songwriter on fourteen albums of Gary's. Among his other credits of those years was work on Herb Alpert's 1965 success, *Whipped Cream and Other Delights,* handling piano on the Byrds classic 1965 single "Mr. Tambourine Man," and doing similar session work for Frank Sinatra, Ike and Tina Turner, the Righteous Brothers, Paul Revere and the Raiders, and others.

One of his early solo efforts was the 1965 single on Dot Records, "Everybody's Talking 'Bout the Young," which didn't make much headway. He made a single, released in 1966, for A&M Records, which Leon says he would just as soon forget about.

In 1967, Russell dropped much of his outside work to concentrate on building his own studio. He still did some work with friends, including Delaney & Bonnie, performing with them on many dates in the late 1960s and early 1970s, including the network TV show *Shindig,* and backing them on a number of their recordings.

But Leon was eager to strike out on his own in the late 1960s, and, as one step toward that end, he teamed up with another young musician, Marc Benno. Calling themselves Asylum Choir, they made some tapes that earned them a contract from Smash Records in 1968, which led to the release of their debut LP in 1969, *Asylum Choir.* The LP got good reviews, but commercially was not successful. Meanwhile, through Delaney & Bonnie, Leon had become acquainted with blues/rock singer Joe Cocker and his manager Denny Cordell. Cordell asked Russell to work on Cocker's second LP and, impressed with Russell's skills, took him back to England to work up material for a solo LP. The collaboration resulted in the formation of a new label by the two, called Shelter Records, to handle Russell's product. The first album, originally titled *Can a Blue Man Sing the Whites,* later changed to *Leon Russell,* came out in early 1970 and, while it didn't challenge for top spots, remained on the hit lists a respectable number of months. As the year went by, Russell bolstered his growing reputation by touring with Joe Cocker in the famous *Mad Dogs and Englishmen* series.

Russell's activities continued at a frantic pace in 1970-71 with session work on LPs by the Rolling Stones, Glen Campbell, Rita Coolidge, Delaney & Bonnie, and Dave Mason. He also took part in the landmark Concert for Bangladesh in New York's Madison Square Garden. His visibility contributed to the enormous success of his next release on Shelter, *Leon Russell and the Shelter People,* which was a bestseller for many months in 1971 and for much of 1972, earning him his first gold record.

Similar fortune awaited successive releases, such as *Carney* (which spawned his major hit "Tight Rope"), issued in 1972, and the three-record 1973 release *Leon Live* (featuring material made at the several concerts in which Leon played before tens of thousands of fans).

By the end of 1973, when *Hank Wilson's Back* came out, Russell was acknowledged as one of the brightest stars in pop music. This LP was a change of pace; it contained his treatment of such folk and country standards as "Battle of New Orleans," "Am I That Easy to Forget," "She Thinks I Still Care," and "Rollin' in My Sweet Baby's Arms." It was a fine offering, but it puzzled reviewers and fans alike and gained only a fair response from record buyers. One cut, however, "Rollin' in My Sweet Baby's Arms," rose high on country lists, indicating to Leon that he could find a following in the genre.

In 1974, Leon moved in still another direction musically with the LP *Stop All That Jazz,* which met with only lukewarm response. The same year, he backed a singer named Mary McCreary on her LP *Jezebel,* on Shelter. It was a harbinger of things to come—two years later she married him. In 1975, Russell proved he still had drawing power with the pop audience by turning out the gold-record LP *Will o' the Wisp*. At the time, Leon's relationship to Shelter Records was tenuous and he soon left to form a new company, Paradise Records, with distribution arranged through Warner Brothers Records.

His first release on the new label, appropriately, was a duet with Mary Russell in celebration of their marriage, called *The Wedding Album*. In 1977, the duo followed up with *Make Love to the Music* and, in 1979, Leon backed Mary on her solo collection *Heart of Fire*. From 1975 through 1977, he did some session work in addition to his work with Mary, but didn't complete any solo releases. He finally broke that silence with *Americana* in 1978, an album that was one of the weakest he'd done in his career.

Increasingly from the mid-1970s on, Russell had been including country-oriented material in his recordings. In 1979, he stressed that side of his musical interests more than ever, and it seemed to act as a catalyst in restoring his standing in pop music in general. In late 1978 and early 1979, he teamed up with a long-time friend, country giant Willie Nelson, for a series of concerts that since have become almost legendary with music buffs. In 1979, a two-record set taken from those appearances was issued on Columbia, titled *One for the Road*, presenting superb versions of all kinds of songs, from pop standards of the 1940s and 1950s to classic country and folk tunes. The album was nominated by the Country Music Association for Best Album of the Year and deservedly took top honors. During the same period, a new collection of Leon's came out on Paradise, titled *Life and Love*, that was as consistently strong in music and performance as *Americana* had been weak. The album presented both sides of Leon—several fine country and country rock tracks and a number of blues rockers that harked back to his work of the early 1970s. By the end of 1979, Russell could point to a banner year that included receiving a gold-record award for *One for the Road* and the rise of the single "Heartbreak

Hotel" to number one on country charts.

For much of the late 1970s, Leon devoted most of his time developing his own videotaping facility, called Paradise Video (used by such people as former Eagle band member Randy Meisner and James Taylor). In early 1980, he formed a new musical alliance with the progressive bluegrass group, New Grass Revival. From then through 1981, they performed a series of concerts across the United States and in Australia and New Zealand that rank with the best those artists have presented. In May 1980, one of those shows was taped by Paradise Records and some of the renditions (including bluegrass numbers; such Russell originals as "Stranger in a Strange Land," "One More Love Song," "Pilgrim Land," "Georgia Blues," and "Prince of Peace"; and versions of songs by the Beatles, Rolling Stones, and Hank Williams) were issued on the February 1981 LP, *Leon Russell and the New Grass Revival, the Live Album*. While it was a good album, it fell short of capturing the raw energy and chilling impact of the actual concerts.

RYLES, JOHN WESLEY: *Singer, guitarist. Born Bastrop, Louisiana, December 2, 1950.*

For John Wesley Ryles, the second time around indeed proved to be the best. A nationally known country artist at seventeen in 1968, his career had soured by the 1970s and for the first half of the decade he was rarely heard of. But he returned to action in 1976 and this time secured his reputation as an important influence in country music.

Ryles was born in Louisiana, though he spent most of his early years in Texas. He recalled, "I have always wanted to be a musician. I came from humble beginnings and when I was very young we didn't have electricity at our home—no radio, television—nothing. The only thing we had to entertain ourselves was singing. In the summertime it was too hot to sit in the house, so we'd sit out on the front porch and sing for two or three hours in the evening."

That's a familiar theme in both folk and

country histories, as was the next step, formation of a family group as a way out of poverty. The Ryles Family singers got started on a local radio show, and rose a notch higher in 1958 when they moved to Fort Worth, Texas, where they joined the cast of the "Cowtown Hoedown" at the Majestic Theater. Later on, the Ryles clan went to nearby Dallas to join the *Big D Jamboree,* a nationally broadcast and telecast show in the 1950s and 1960s.

In the early 1960s, as a twelve-year-old, he got a job as a tenor banjo player on one of the incarnations of the Lightcrust Doughboys. The name had remained a fixture in Dallas for decades, though original founder Bob Wills had had no connection with it since the 1930s. John's instrumental and backing vocal work was good enough to allow him to become a member of club bands in the Dallas area during the next few years.

When he was sixteen, he decided the time was ripe for an effort at a solo career. He got his father to move the family to Nashville, where he earned a living engineering in studios, doing club band work, and making demonstration records for other artists. He also made some tapes of his own, which the Hubert Long Agency, with whom he'd signed, passed around the industry.

As he told *Country Scene* magazine in February 1978, "I had done a few demos with Moss Rose [a music publishing company] in Nashville and was working at a little club in western Tennessee when Audie Ashworth came down and asked me if I wanted a recording contract with Columbia Records." Ryles came across a song called "Kay" that he liked, and his producer, George Ritchie, agreed to include it in the session. Released as a single, "Kay" became one of the major country hits of 1968, not only reaching the country top 10 but placing in the national pop chart top 50.

However, it wasn't a harbinger of success. The next efforts were not overly impressive either as songs or chart hits. A management change resulted in Ryles being dropped from the label, ironically dur-

ing the time that the song "I've Just Been Wasting My Time" was moving up the hit lists to become his second top-10 hit. At nineteen, a thoroughly discouraged young performer moved to Missouri, where he did some club work while trying to make up his mind whether to stay in music or find some other way of making a living.

Ryles continued to appear in small country clubs for several years as part of the large array of journeymen musicians who earn precarious livings from playing other people's hits for sometimes unappreciative audiences. He was working on one such engagement when an old acquaintance, Johnny Morris, came by and suggested they cut some new recordings. Ryles was dubious at first: "My confidence was at a low ebb." But the lure of a return to the higher levels of the field was still strong. Morris and Ryles went to Muscle Shoals, Alabama, and recorded some songs that were released on a local label, Music Mill Records. One of those, "Tell It Like It Is," made the charts for several weeks in 1976, and another song, "When a Man Loves a Woman," also received some airplay. He followed with an even more impressive disc, "Reconsider Me," which made the top 20 and led to a national distribution arrangement with ABC–Dot Records.

At first, John Wesley had twinges of déjà vu. His debut single for ABC, "Fool," made the lower end of the charts at ninety-seven, moved to ninety-nine, and then disappeared after just two weeks. But it was picked up again four months later, particularly by disc jockeys in Houston, where it moved to number one. This was soon echoed by acceptance in other cities, and Ryles had his first major success in eight years. Also making a dent on the album lists in the summer of 1977 was his ABC debut LP, *John Wesley Ryles.* The follow up single, "Once in a Lifetime Thing," indicated that this time Ryles had staying power by moving to number four on country charts in October 1977.

Ryles' second album on ABC, *Shine on Me,* also did well, as did the title track, which added another candidate for a future Greatest Hits album. The album also included one of the relatively few originals written by Ryles, "Next Time," but, he declared, certainly not the last of his writing efforts.

After MCA acquired ABC in the late 1970s, Ryles' recordings came out on that label. His chart-making singles on MCA included "You Are Always on My Mind" in 1979; "Perfect Strangers" and "Cheater's Trap" in 1980; and "Somewhere to Come When It Rains" in 1981.

S

SAHM, DOUGLAS: *Singer, guitarist, songwriter, band leader. Born San Antonio, Texas, November 6, circa 1942.*

During the 1960s and 1970s, Doug Sahm flirted with stardom but never quite made it. Despite that, he had a strong influence on trends in both country and rock domains as an early progenitor of country-flavored rock and as a close friend and associate of many of the Austin-based progressive country artists of the late 1960s and 1970s.

His initial grounding was in country. When he was a child growing up in Texas in the late 1940s, he told Robert Hilburn of the *Los Angeles Times* (June 16, 1974), "I started playing the steel guitar when I was about six. I wore a little cowboy suit and played for some of the bands that came to town. I had lots of offers to go to Nashville and the *Grand Ole Opry*, but my mother was pretty insistent about me staying in school."

As he grew older, like a typical child of the 1950s, his interests expanded to include rock and blues. "It was a great musical trip in Texas in those days. I lived halfway between a blues club and a country-music club, so I had Bobby Blue Bland on one side of me and Hank Williams on the other. You can't beat that."

Doug kept improving his guitar style and playing with local bands. In his teens, he began to cut some records on local labels and had some regional hits before the end of the 1950s. He was continuing to make progress in the rock field in the early 1960s when the British invasion, spearheaded by the Beatles and Rolling Stones, began to dominate the U.S. market. Figuring that if you can't beat 'em, join 'em, in 1965 he organized a group he called the Sir Douglas Quintet in an effort to camouflage its American origins. The group soon had a single on the national charts, "She's About a Mover," which was included on the group's debut LP on the Tribe label that was issued in August 1966. (In the 1970s, the song was available on the Tribe LP *Best of the Sir Douglas Quintet.*) The excellent musical blend the Quintet offered was taken note of by many leading figures in rock, from Bob Dylan to the Beach Boys and Rolling Stones. The Quintet toured with the last two bands as well as a number of other well-known groups in the mid- and late-1960s. However, despite the band's great promise, it never quite broke through to stardom.

In the late 1960s, Sahm moved his headquarters to the San Francisco bay area. He began recording for Smash Records, the first album being *Honkey Blues*. Now living in Big Sur, he wrote songs like "Mendocino" and "Dynamic Woman." The first of those was the title song for his group's second Smash LP, one that remains an underground favorite. Later Smash issued a third album, *Together After Five.* However, though Doug turned out some excellent original material and the band received considerable praise from its musical peers, it never made much of a dent in the charts in the late 1960s and early 1970s and finally disbanded in 1972.

Sahm gained a new contract that year from Atlantic and went to New York to record an album on which he was joined by Bob Dylan. The album, *Doug Sahm and Band,* which contained both all-out rock and country-based material, had some high spots, but overall proved a disappointment. Sahm completed a second album for Atlantic *(Texas Tornado)*, which also didn't fare too well with the public. At that point, Doug moved back to Texas and became part of the Austin progressive country/country-rock scene, along with such others as Willie Nelson and Jerry Jeff Walker.

In 1974, he was asked to work on some new material by the one-time Creedence Clearwater Revival drummer Doug Clifford. After completing a single called "Groover's Paradise," Clifford and Sahm worked out a deal with Warner Brothers for a new album effort.

Other Sahm albums issued in the 1970s included *Rough Edges* on Mercury, *Texas Rock for Country Rollers* on Dot and, on Philip, *1 + 1 + 1 = 4* and *The Return of Doug Saldana*. The last named contained songs reflecting the Tex–Mex and related music Sahm had been exposed to while growing up in San Antonio.

SAINTE-MARIE, BUFFY: *Singer, songwriter, guitarist, actress. Born on Indian reserve, Saskatchewan, Canada, February 20, 1941.*

For most of her career, Buffy Sainte-Marie was classified as a fighter for Indian rights and a charter member of the antiwar protest movement of the 1960s. In fact, her composition "Universal Soldier" was almost an anthem for the protestors of the Vietnam War. But, as she often pointed out, that was only one side of her musicianship, albeit one for which she never apologized. She told a reporter from *Life* (December 10, 1965, pp. 53–54), "I have written hundreds of songs and only a half dozen are of protest. I believe in leaving politics to the experts, only sometimes the experts don't know what's going on."

And, in fact, Sainte-Marie's writings contained many sensitive songs about love and life in general, including her late 1960s offering "Until It's Time for You to Go," which gained record successes for a number of artists. Still, her protest image worked against her for a long time, pushing her into the background on the U.S. music scene while she kept her performing career alive by finding work outside the United States.

Although she seemed a bit uncertain of her heritage in the 1960s, later on Buffy ascertained that she was born in Canada of Cree Indian extraction. When she was a few months old, however, she was adopted by a couple from Maine who were part Micmac Indian. Most of her growing up years, however, were spent in Wakefield, Massachusetts, where she attended high school and also taught herself to play guitar. With a view toward a teaching career, she entered the University of Massachusetts, from which she received a degree with honors in Oriental Philosophy and Education in the early 1960s.

However, folk music proved too strong an attraction, particularly after a guest appearance at a hootenanny at the Gaslight Cafe in Greenwich Village brought a management offer from Herb Gart. Under his aegis she soon was working the East Coast coffee house circuit, often appearing there and in folk concerts with many of the stars of the folk boom.

A bout with bronchial pneumonia in 1963 incapacitated Buffy for six months, having an adverse impact on her voice and almost ending her performing career for a time. She also had to fight off an addiction to codeine that resulted from the illness, which she described in her song "Codeine." In 1963 she also wrote "The Universal Soldier," which appeared the following year in her debut album for Vanguard Records, *It's My Way*. Her career by then was on a strong upswing, with concert offers from across the United States and Canada and opportunities to appear on major radio and TV shows. She continued to turn out new albums on Vanguard, including *Many a Mile* (released in April 1965), *Little Wheel Spin,* (8/66), *Fire, Fleet, Candlelight* (8/67), *Illuminations* (9/69), and *She Used to Wanna Be a Ballerina*.

Other Vanguard releases of the 1960s and 1970s were *I'm Gonna Be a Country Girl Again, Moonshot, Quiet Places, Native North American Child (An Odyssey)*, and *Best of Buffy Sainte-Marie, Volumes 1 and 2*.

A number of Sainte-Marie's songs continued to deal with the Indians' plight. Among those were "Native North American Child," "My Country 'Tis of Thy People You're Dying," and "Now That the Buffalo's Gone." Sometimes she punctuated her performances with a demonstration of the native Indian mouth-bow, an instrument she learned to play from another Cree Indian folk artist of the period, Patrick Sky.

By the late 1960s, her career was in decline in the United States. A steady series of tours throughout Europe and countries of the Far East (Japan, Australia, New Zealand) made her a favorite of those audiences. In the United States Buffy's appearances became increasingly rare in the late 1960s and much of the 1970s, a situation intensified by her decision to take up residence on a hilltop in Hawaii in 1967, her home into the late 1970s. Her hopes of returning to the top in the United States were never completely abandoned. She switched record labels from Vanguard to MCA in the early 1970s, and, when that didn't bring any rewards, signed with ABC Records in September 1975. That affiliation also proved disappointing, leading to one of her weakest LPs, *Sweet America*.

In the mid-1970s, Sainte-Marie continued to be featured in Canadian concerts and TV specials and also became a regular member of the cast of the American *Sesame Street* children's TV program, in which she contributed not only as a performer but as a writer of special material, including a number of children's songs. (In the children's field, she already had written and illustrated a book.) In early 1978 she introduced viewers to her year-old son, Dakota Starblanket Wolfchild, born of her marriage to Dakota Sioux artist and TV producer Sheldon Peters Wolfchild.

In 1978, Buffy decided to take her recording activities back into her own hands. She bought back rights to the last four LPs she'd made on Vanguard, MCA, and ABC, noting that they had received little exposure when they first were released. Her plans were to reissue those on her own record label, for which she recorded a completely new album in 1978.

Looking back on the ups and downs of her career in early 1978, she told Jennifer Sedor of the *Los Angeles Times* (March 31), "It only takes a feather to tip the scale in this business, but it took me a while to realize my fall was also a matter of politics rather than mass listener turn-off. But I've accepted myself as an alternative performer in America. My time will come again. Meanwhile I'm doing other things. I travel, I write, I'm rich, I buy the clothes I want, and if I'm not a tremendous success here, at least I have the respect of the industry and success abroad." That success, among other things, included a command performance for Queen Elizabeth in the mid-1970s.

SCRUGGS, EARL: *Banjoist, guitarist, songwriter, band leader (Foggy Mountain Boys, Earl Scruggs Revue). Born Cleveland County, North Carolina, January 6, 1924.*

When the giants of modern country music are remembered, Earl Scruggs' name will be one of the first to come to mind. Apart from his many contributions as a songwriter and recording artist, his innovations in the art of the banjo created a revolution that affected the use of the instrument not only in country but in every facet of pop music. In fact, in a later—and controversial—phase of his career, Earl experimented with new blends of traditional and current styles, using an electrified banjo as part of his country, folk, and rock-oriented Earl Scruggs Revue.

Although he upset many country and folk purists with his innovations, he succeeded in attracting many new fans to the intricacies and delights of what has become known as the Scruggs Picking Style. The approach, based on the use of three fingers in the five-string banjo picking pattern, modifies the sound of the instrument with the Scruggs Tuner. The tuner allows the banjo player to achieve unusual warping of the strings for all kinds of distorted effects. These innovations, combined with Scruggs' intricate lead runs and background fills, caused Al Rudis of the *Chicago Sun-Times* to make the apt statement, "What Segovia is to the guitar, Earl Scruggs is to the five-string banjo."

Born and raised in North Carolina near the town of Selby, Earl first started teaching himself banjo at the early age of four and could play simple tunes on the instrument at the age of five. At ten he had already invented the three-finger picking style that was to become his trademark. Before long, he was a local celebrity, playing with a band on a local radio station when he was fifteen. To help himself financially, he worked at a textile mill for a while in his teens, but that demanding job only reinforced his desire to make his career in music. By the time he left Bolling Springs High School in 1942, his skills as a banjoist (he also learned to play excellent guitar by then) had matured to the point that band jobs were becoming available well outside his home section.

At one point, he worked for a time with the Morris Brothers (whose early recordings have sometimes been reissued on old-time folk music collections) on a Spartanburg, South Carolina, radio station. He retained fond memories of that period, and, in the 1970s, had the Morris Brothers take part in a Public Broadcasting System program titled "Earl Scruggs Family and Friends." (Also on the program were other famous names in country, folk, and rock, including Bob Dylan, Joan Baez, Roger McGuinn and the Byrds, and Doc and Merle Watson).

Scruggs' first major milestone came in 1944, when he won the attention of Bill Monroe, the "Father of Bluegrass Music." Earl became a member of one of the most famous of Monroe's Blue Grass Boys lineups, a band whose other members included a dynamically talented young guitarist named Lester Flatt. Earl and Lester remained members of the Monroe troupe until 1948, apearing regularly with Bill on the *Grand Ole Opry* radio show and touring all over the country with his stage act.

But Flatt and Scruggs became restless working for someone else. In 1948, they left to form their own band, the group that was to become the legendary Foggy Mountain Boys. With the help of Flatt's friend Mac Wiseman, they gained a spot on the *Farm and Fun Time* program on station WCYB, Bristol, Virginia, the first of a series of stations they played all over the South and border states in the early 1950s. The exposure catapulted them to headlin-

ers of the *Opry* in 1953, where they remained featured *Opry* stars until the act broke up after over two decades of notable accomplishments.

Almost as soon as Flatt & Scruggs was formed, they gained a recording contract with Mercury that lasted until 1951. They switched to Columbia, the Flatt & Scruggs label throughout the rest of their career, turning out dozens of albums and singles, many of which not only made uppermost levels of country charts but often appeared on national pop lists too. During the 1950s and 1960s, when Flatt & Scruggs toured many foreign countries in addition to their regular 200 or more U.S. concerts, their recordings sometimes showed up on overseas hit lists as well.

Many of Flatt & Scruggs' most famous songs were written or co-written by Earl. His compositions included "Flint Hill Special," named for his home community in North Carolina, "Randy Lynn Rag," in honor of his oldest son, later lead singer of the Earl Scruggs Revue, "Earl's Breakdown," "Foggy Mountain Breakdown" (the song that provided the name for the Flatt & Scruggs band), "Foggy Mountain Special," "Foggy Mountain Chimes," "Rocky Mountain Rock," and perhaps his most successful commercial effort, "The Ballad of Jed Clampett," the theme for the *Beverly Hillbillies* TV program. The Flatt & Scruggs single of that song was number one on both country and pop charts for a number of weeks in 1962. Among the songs that Scruggs co-wrote with various other writers were "Shuckin' the Corn," "Crying My Heart Out Over You," "Someone You Have Forgotten," "I Won't Be Hanging Around," and "Building on Sand."

In its over twenty years of existence, the Flatt & Scruggs team remained one of the most popular in the United States, much of the time having its own syndicated TV show aired all over the nation. Both separately and as part of the act, Flatt and Scruggs won all kinds of honors, including Grammy Awards.

However, even as early as 1960, internal strains were beginning to develop that eventually led to Flatt & Scruggs' breakup in 1969. Flatt loved the traditional, mainly acoustical approach to country and bluegrass, while Earl, influenced by his growing brood of talented young sons, was becoming restless with long-established ways. He traced some of his desire for a new direction to when, rehearsing for a TV show in 1960, he jammed with blues saxophonist King Curtis, who also was a guest on the program. "I saw where the banjo was more versatile than just straight bluegrass, and it sounded so good to me until I just couldn't get it off my mind."

As the 1960s went by, Earl wanted to work some amplified, sometimes rock-based material into the Flatt & Scruggs repertoire, but met with resistance from his partner. Finally the two split up and Scruggs started working up a new act in 1969 with his two sons, Randy and Gary. Randy, who started learning guitar before he was in his teens, had played on every record his father had made since Randy was thirteen. He took over on lead guitar in the new Revue and handled much of the arranging and a considerable amount of the songwriting in collaboration with older brother Gary.

Gary came to show business a little later than other family members. Although he also learned several instruments as a boy (his Revue chores, besides lead vocals, include electric bass, harmonica, and guitar), for a time he seemed headed toward another career. He enrolled in and graduated from Vanderbilt University in Nashville as a philosophy major, though with music as a minor. Before making the Revue his primary interest, he teamed with Randy to do two albums on the Vanguard label, *All the Way Home* and the *Scruggs Brothers*.

By the start of the 1970s, Earl and his family-based act were playing a variety of venues from small folk clubs to college auditoriums around the United States. For a time in the mid-1970s, the other band sidemen were Jody Maphis on drums and Jack Lee on piano. By 1978, it had become an all-family affair, with Randy's brother-in-law Taylor Rhodes (born Nashville) taking over from Maphis on drums (and also handling some rhythm guitar) and Steve Scruggs doing the keyboard work. Steve,

youngest of Earl's boys (born 1958), had taken over on keyboards a few years earlier. Also multitalented, he could play a half dozen other instruments.

The Revue signed with Earl's long-time label, Columbia, and turned out one or more LPs every year for most of the 1970s. Another of the group's efforts was composing and performing the soundtrack for the movie *Where the Lilies Bloom;* Columbia released the soundtrack album in 1974. (In previous movie assignments, Earl Scruggs had played his "Foggy Mountain Breakdown" as the main background music for *Bonnie and Clyde*.) In 1975, the Revue joined with Earl in celebrating his twenty-fifth anniversary as a Columbia recording artist. That effort included a "super session," where support was provided by thirty-nine first-rank pop music stars, including Johnny Cash, Loggins and Messina, Alvin Lee, Dan Fogelberg, Tracy Nelson, Billy Joel, Michael Murphey, Leonard Cohen, and Buffy Sainte-Marie. The *Earl Scruggs Revue Anniversary Album Volume I* was issued in 1975 and *Volume II* in 1976.

Other 1970s albums by the Revue include *Family Portrait*, issued in 1976; *Live from Austin City Limits*, released in 1977; *Strike Anywhere*, issued in 1977; and *Bold & New*, issued in 1978. The latter was the first Revue LP produced by Chips Moman (Ron Bledsoe produced the earlier ones), who also coauthored with keyboardist Bobby Emmons one of the *Bold & New* songs, "The Cabin." Five of the songs in that album were co-written by Gary and Randy Scruggs ("Take the Time," "Someone like You," "Louisiana Lady," "Found Myself a New Love," and "Our Love Is Home Grown"), who also had provided originals for many of the previous collections. The singles issued on Columbia in the mid- and late-1970s included "If I'd Only Come and Gone" in 1973; "Where the Lilies Bloom" in 1974; "Travelin' Prayer" in 1974; "Tall Texas Woman" in 1976; and "The Cabin" in 1978.

Earl Scruggs stated that he was happy with the way his career had gone since Flatt & Scruggs broke up. His new alignment gave him the freedom to have a drummer in the band, considered a heresy in traditional bluegrass groups. He felt that the heavier beat employed in typical Revue arrangements made even the more traditional numbers the band played sound better. "I remember back in the old days, when groups didn't even carry a bass fiddle," he told James Carrier of the Associated Press (January 2, 1976). "But the guitar player would take the deepest guitar that put out the fullest, deepest, bassiest sound for his vocal. And also they would stomp their feet quite a lot to add a beat to the group. So I thought that a good drummer and a set of drums would make a much better sound than a group of people pickin' and stompin' their feet against the floor.

"I didn't know how it would work, but it sounded too good not to try it. I just needed something to stimulate my feelings. I was getting bored and unhappy doing the same things for over 20 years.

"I feel I'm pickin' a better banjo now than I ever did. I feel I'm playing music with a much more exciting [flair] than I would be if I was playing back [with Flatt] because I wasn't mentally into it. There I just got to where I was not playing too good. I just got tired of playing the old routine.

"I just don't think you can stay with the same songs all your life without going along with the times. You've got to keep working on your material, doing them different ways or you just get out of the ball game, that's all."

(*See also* FLATT, LESTER.)

SEALS AND CROFTS: *Vocal and instrumental duo. Jim Seals, born Sidney, Texas, circa 1940; Dash Crofts, born Cisco, Texas, circa 1940.*

Both born and raised in small southeastern Texas towns, both involved in music from an early age, Jim Seals and Dash Crofts had enough in common to bring them together and to keep them making music together for over two decades. Their association brought them through various musical stages at various times, from rock to jazz and back to rock. Later they added another unifying factor to their relationship: both of them converted to the Baha'i faith, a change that affected not only their lives but their music as well.

Listening to their music, one might think folk and rock music were their major influences, but country music and the classics were the early influences on Seals and Crofts. Jim Seals had been exposed to country music since his infancy; his grandfather had his own country-music group that frequently got together for local hoedowns. One of his earliest memories is of when he was four; the fiddle player from his grandfather's group came to Seals' house. When little Jimmy heard him play, he became so excited that his grandfather ordered him a fiddle from the Sears catalogue. When the fiddle finally arrived, however, Jimmy became frustrated that he couldn't master it immediately and put it under the bed, where it gathered dust for a year. Then one night he had a dream that he could play. When he got up, he took out his fiddle and found that he could play a little bit. By the time he was nine, he played the instrument so well that he won the Texas state fiddle championship. By this time he had also started picking out chords on his father's guitar.

Growing up in Texas, Dash Crofts could not avoid hearing country music, but it was in the classics that he first got his training. He started picking out tunes on the household piano when he was five. His mother recognized his talent and encouraged him to study the classics, which she loved. Dash studied diligently on the piano until he was nine, when he decided he would rather devote his spare time to playing ball. Several years later his interest in music revived, this time the result of listening to late-night broadcasts of rhythm & blues from a Memphis radio station. He decided to concentrate on mastering the drums instead of the piano.

By the time Crofts met Seals in the local junior high school, Jim had amassed many hours' experience playing with country-music bands. He also had learned a new instrument, the tenor saxophone. The time was the mid-1950s and the popularity of rock 'n' roll music was on the rise, so the two merged forces as part of a high school rock band.

Out of high school, Seals and Crofts moved to California in 1958. There they became the nucleus of a rock group called the Champs. The group turned out one of the all-time rock successes, "Tequila," which sold an estimated 6 million copies on the Challenge Records label and was one of the top-10 hits of 1958. For the next seven years the Champs headlined many shows all over the world, though its star had set by the time it broke up in 1965.

After this, Crofts went back to Texas, while Seals remained in California writing music and doing odd recording sessions. A year later, he began playing sax and rhythm guitar with guitarist Louie Shelton and bass player Joseph Bogan. The group needed a drummer, so Jim called Dash in Texas, and within a few days the group was complete. In the year that followed the four musicians met Marcia Day, who was to become their manager, and they all took up residence in a three-story grey house, known as "Marcia's Place," located on Hollywood Boulevard in Los Angeles.

Day had a profound influence on the lives of all four of the men. She introduced them to the Baha'i faith, which most of them adopted, and she also introduced them to her five daughters. Three of the daughters joined with the men to form a group called the Dawnbreakers. In the two years the group remained together, Dash, Louie, and Joe, married Billie Lee Day, Donnie Day, and Lana Day respectively. Not long afterward, Seals married Ruby Jean Anderson, another resident of Marcia's Place.

The Dawnbreakers did not stay together as a group very long, in part because of their religious conversion. They decided to take time to study the Baha'i Sacred Writing and to pray and meditate. During this time, Jim and Dash began to experiment with new vocal harmonies. Dash found a new challenge in learning to play the mandolin and Jim virtually abandoned the saxophone for the guitar. As a result, the duo started developing musical forms very different from their previous efforts. In addition, Louie Shelton began to pursue his interest in production (he had produced

Seals and Crofts since their first Warner Brothers album, *Year of Sunday*, released in November 1971), and Joe Bogan mastered the technology of record engineering.

The duo of Seals and Crofts made their first professional appearance in 1969 at a small club in Riverside, California, filling in for the headlining act, which had taken ill. The next two years were lean and difficult, although their first two albums for the TA label, *Seals and Crofts* and *Down Home*, won some critical notice. Nevertheless, they continued to perform at various nightclubs and attracted a faithful underground following.

Soon it became clear that Seals and Crofts were headed for success. Their first Warner Records release, *Year of Sunday*, appeared on the hit charts at the end of 1971. *Summer Breeze*, issued in August 1972, did even better, reaching the number-seven position nationally in December and achieving a gold-record award in early 1973. The album and the single of the same name continued to sell enough copies to qualify for platinum status. Their next album, *Diamond Girl*, was greeted with critical acclaim and also went gold and then platinum.

Seals and Crofts consistently turned out hit singles and albums in the next few years. Their LP *Unborn Child*, released in February 1974, achieved gold status. "I'll Play for You" went gold as did their album and title single, *Get Closer*, released in April 1976. The LP *Seals and Crofts Greatest Hits*, released in October 1975, rose to the top of the hit charts and soon sold enough copies to gain a third platinum album for Seals and Crofts. In 1977 they released their first soundtrack album, for the movie *One on One*. They also scored an animated film for Hanna-Barbera, which was produced by the newly-formed Day Five Productions.

After their religious conversion, many of Seals and Crofts' songs reflected their religious beliefs, often expressing a feeling or an inspiration gained from studying the Baha'i sacred texts. Their music changed because of their new-found faith, becoming much softer, more folk than rock-oriented. Their new sound, however, is rather difficult to classify, for it reflects the diverse elements of their musical background, a new blend of jazz, country, rock, folk, and, at times, classical music as well.

The immense commercial success of Seals and Crofts enabled them to move from Marcia's Place on Hollywood Boulevard to their own community in the Los Angeles suburb of San Fernando, where they not only live but also produce and record their albums.

In concert, Seals and Crofts do not try to preach or to impose their faith on the crowds. Their live performances often feature bluegrass and country-style solos on the mandolin, fiddle, and guitar by Dash and Jim as well as their usual fare. On the road, they have been prone to playing pranks like one they did in Boston, when they made home-made UFOs out of plastic cleaning bags, drinking straws and birthday candles. When the lit candles were placed in the straw framework, the bags filled with hot air and began to float. The "UFOs" caused an uproar around Boston that night; many people called radio stations and the police. As Crofts told Shel Kagan of *Circus Magazine*, "They called out the Air Force, and one lady said on a radio talk show that she saw the windows on the things and little people inside. We've got the clippings to prove it, too."—A.S.

SEATRAIN: *Vocal and instrumental group. Andy Kulberg, born Buffalo, New York; Richard Greene, born Beverly Hills, California, circa 1945; Peter Rowan, born Wayland, Massachusetts; Lloyd Baskin, born New York, New York; Larry Atamuniak, born Toronto, Canada, circa 1946; Jim Roberts, born Buffalo, New York. Group makeup in 1973: Kulberg; Baskin; Peter Walsh, born Chicago, Illinois; Bill Elliott, born Cambridge, Massachusetts; Julio Coronado, born Arizona, circa 1940.*

SeaTrain was only in existence for less than half a decade, but in that period it won high esteem for its often innovative blends of folk, country, and rock. Its work had an impact on the creative efforts of both new and established artists in all those fields during the 1970s. Years later,

many people who never heard the band in action kept copies of the group's relatively meager output among their cherished possessions.

The original driving force behind the band was Andy Kulberg, who learned a wide range of instruments, including flute, piano (which he played in elementary school), guitar, and string bass. After attending Boston University and the Boston Conservatory of Music, he enrolled at New York University to continue some of his music studies. While there, he became a charter member in a landmark blues-rock band of the 1960s, the Blues Project. In its latter stages, the band moved from New York to Marin County, California where it finally expired.

After that, Kulberg sought to form a new band that would carry out his concept of combining elements of the classics, folk music, and rock. In conjunction with former Blues Project drummer Roy Blumenfeld, he started trying out various combinations of musicians in 1968, which finally shook down into the first recognizable SeaTrain roster in late 1969. One of those he sought was the fine violin player Richard Greene (see separate entry), whose experience as a country/bluegrass instrumentalist brought a new musical dimension to the band. Greene brought Peter Rowan's (see separate entry) name to Kulberg's attention, and Andy added the Massachusetts-born musician and vocalist to the group. Rowan, who met Greene while playing guitar and bass guitar with Bill Monroe's Blue Grass Boys, earlier had performed with a Buddy Holly rockabilly-type band in his high school years and had attended Colgate University for two years before deciding to work at music full time. Among his activities after leaving Bill Monroe was formation of a Boston-based rock band called Earth Opera. After that disbanded, he joined SeaTrain.

The band still was in its early phase when it played one of its first engagements in Boston. Joining them for that session was vocalist-keyboardist Lloyd Baskin, born in New York, and raised in New Jersey. Baskin had played piano in his high school years before studying design at Syracuse University. After five years, he turned back to music with a band called the All Night Workers from upstate New York that had a local hit record with "All Your Eggs in One Basket." In 1968, he moved to Boston to work on some original recordings and perform in the local cast of *Hair* before he first discovered SeaTrain. He didn't join right away, but when SeaTrain returned to play at the Tea Party in May 1970, Lloyd reintroduced himself and was hired. Not long afterward, the fifth member of the quintet that was to make the group's debut album was added. The band needed a drummer, and SeaTrain's manager was interested in Larry Atamuniak, a Toronto native, then a member of Ronnie Hawkins' backing group. Atamuniak was contacted by phone in late spring, met the band in Toronto in June, and agreed to take over the drum seat.

The new roster soon was gaining attention from music observers around the United States. After a performance in Washington in July 1970, the *Washington Star* critic wrote, "These five young men have formed what could be in time one of the finest musical aggregations anyone may be listening to for a long while."

Playing an important role in some of those decisions was an artist who was part of SeaTrain, though not a musician. Jim Roberts, a childhood friend of Kulberg's from Buffalo, was to be the band's lyricist-in-residence. Besides contributing lyrics to Kulberg and other writers, he also had poetry published in a number of literary journals.

After honing its musical style, SeaTrain concentrated on gaining a record contract. That soon was forthcoming from Capitol, which agreed to the idea of the band's working on its first album in England. That album was released in early 1971 in conjunction with a U.S. tour in support. Called *SeaTrain*, it reminded many people of some of the early work of The Band. The album made the pop charts soon after its release and remained there through much of the summer. A single from the album, "13 Questions," made hit lists in

early spring and stayed on them for over three months. Both on record and in person, the band emphasized its diverse roots with offerings ranging from Greene's spirited rendition of the classic fiddle tune "Sally Goodin'" to folk/country-rock to hard-driving rock.

In late 1971, the band's second Capitol LP, *Marblehead Messenger*, was released and also made the charts for a number of months. The outlook seemed propitious, but internal strains were besetting the band. Richard Greene, for instance, wanted to get back to solo work and finally left in 1972. Other departures caused other changes. By the time the group finally got to work on a new album, only Kulberg and Baskin remained from the 1971 lineup. Taking Rowan's chair was Chicago-born Peter Walsh. He played in a number of local bands before moving to California to join first a band headed by Barry Goldberg, then Pacific Gas and Electric. After earning a precarious living as a street musician, he accepted an invitation from SeaTrain.

The 1972 band gained a two keyboards capability with the addition of Bill Elliott. Besides piano, which he started playing at six, Elliott also had become proficient in clarinet, bass, and accordion. His route to SeaTrain included working with Peter Rowan's younger brothers, Chris and Loren, in the Boston area and later backing comedian-singer Martin Mull. Mull and Elliott collaborated on music and lyrics for several portions of the National Educational Television program *The Great American Dream-Machine*. For a time in the early 1970s, he moved to Vermont to concentrate on songwriting and composing, but a call from SeaTrain in mid-1972 caused a return to the music wars.

Taking over on drums was Julio Coronado from Arizona. His credits included entering the Navy School of Music in 1960 followed by a stint at Northwestern University. After playing with all kinds of local groups, he joined the Ed Shestel Quartet in 1966, which won the Best Band award at the Indiana Collegiate Jazz Festival. Later he played with the Tex Beneke-

Glenn Miller Band and the Bill Rinehart Dixieland Jazz Band before Peter Walsh's recommendation brought the SeaTrain assignment in 1972.

The group moved from Capitol to Warner Brothers Records in 1972 and worked on a new LP that was issued in early 1973. Called *Watch*, it was less satisfying than the previous collections, though it still had many worthwhile elements. The band also had an album release on A&M Records titled *SeaTrain*. The group stayed together for a while, doing a series of concerts in various parts of the United States, but by 1974 it had disbanded permanently.

SEBASTIAN, JOHN B.: *Singer, harmonica player, guitarist, pianist, arranger, band leader (Lovin' Spoonful). Born New York, New York, March 17, 1944.*

Best known for his rock 'n' roll efforts, John Sebastian nonetheless had strong folk roots; much of his music over the years contained both folk and, to some extent, country elements. Reflecting that influence, in fact, was the name of his extremely successful rock group of the mid-1960s, the Lovin' Spoonful, which was derived from one of the songs of legendary folk-blues artist Mississippi John Hurt.

Sebastian, the son of harmonica virtuoso John Sebastian, Sr., was born and raised in New York City's Greenwich Village. His parents saw to it that he took classical piano lessons as a child; in addition, he played the harmonica in emulation of his father. As his interest in the growing folk music movement of the late 1950s and early 1960s grew, he added guitar playing skills as well.

In his mid-teens, John began to frequent some of the folk clubs and coffee houses in the Village, where he often got the chance to join other aspiring young performers or, on occasion, to do some solo turns. One of his first formal associations in the early 1960s was with a group called the Even Dozen Jug Band, which made one album—on which John performed—before breaking up. In 1962, he teamed up with three others—Zalman Yanovsky, Cass Elliot, and Denny Doherty—in a group called the Mugwumps. That folk quartet stayed together only a short time, but the individual members were all heard from again. Elliot and Doherty later became half of the Mamas and Papas, and recalled some of the history of both their group and the Mugwumps in the song "Creque Alley." Yanovsky eventually became a charter member of the Lovin' Spoonful.

After graduating from high school, for a time Sebastian went to Marblehead, Massachusetts, where he worked as a sailmaker. At the start, he wasn't quite sure what he wanted to do, but finally decided to return home and enter New York University. He spent a short time in college, then dropped out to try to follow music full time. His particular focus at the time was on blues, so he headed south to try to meet some of the famous old time blues musicians and collect songs of that genre. One of his first contacts was Lightnin' Hopkins, with whom he spent much of 1964 studying Hopkins' musical style and meeting other blues artists. One of those artists was Mississippi John Hurt, who taught Sebastian many of his favorite songs, including one that contained the line "I love my baby by the lovin' spoonful."

In 1965, back in New York, John organized a band whose members included Yanovsky on lead guitar, Steve Boone on piano and bass guitar, and Joe Butler on drums. After an acclaimed engagement at New York's Nite Owl Cafe, the band became a favorite of New York pop fans, and, after Kama Sutra Records signed them, soon extended their sway coast to coast. The band's repertoire covered just about all musical bases: jug band, folk, country, gospel, ragtime, blues, and pop ballads, all with an underlay of rock 'n' roll. Sebastian sang lead on a succession of hits, most of which were original compositions, including "Do You Believe in Magic" (a massive hit in late summer of 1965), "Younger Girl," "Nashville Cats," "Summer in the City" (number one in the United States in the summer of 1966), "Daydream," "You Didn't Have to Be So Nice," and "Did You Ever Have to Make Up Your Mind." Sebastian demonstrated his arranging skills in many innovative numbers, such as "Groovin'," "Big Noise from Speonk," "Jugband Music," "Lovin' You," "Your Eyes," "Lonely," and "Bes' Friends."

Sebastian managed to sandwich in work on two film scores during those years, *You're a Big Boy Now* and, for Woody Allen, *What's Up, Tiger Lily*. The Lovin' Spoonful provided soundtrack music in both cases. Besides those activities, the band toured widely, headlining rock shows across the country and also guesting on many network TV programs.

Their productivity came to a sudden halt in 1967, when members of the band were picked up on drug possession charges. However, there were other pressures causing members to lose interest in the operation. The band might have kept going, but the enforced layoff caused by the legal entanglement led to some soul searching that precluded such a step.

John stated later, "It wasn't fun anymore. The band for about two years was really groovy. I guess what made it groovy was the chemistry of the people in the group. But after about two years, it began to get really muddied.

"We could have gone on cranking it along for a few more years and started to collect the enormous sums we were just beginning to get. Of course, breaking up wouldn't have been the best thing from a businessman's point of view. Lots of people were really brought down, but they were concerned with money rather than the music."

Having made up his mind, Sebastian moved on to new projects, beginning with work on music for a Broadway play, *Jimmy Shine*, starring a then relatively unknown actor named Dustin Hoffman. The show didn't do much, but it helped give John confidence he could do well on his own.

At the end of the 1960s, Sebastian settled in Los Angeles and started a relatively low-key approach to life in which he did a lot of composing and arranging with a certain amount of personal solo appearances mixed in. His music continued to stress folk content combined with a certain amount of pop-rock flavor. He began to

make his mark as a festival artist, first with a set at Big Sur, California, then with a gripping performance at the now legendary Woodstock, New York, event. His contributions to that show were featured both on the live album and the successful film.

Although his Woodstock effort is considered a highlight of his career, he wasn't even an original invitee. A close associate recalled, "Ironically, he wasn't even supposed to be in the festival. He happened to be there and they needed another act so he filled in. As a result, he was featured on the record and in the movie and made a small fortune." (The reports were that he ended up with something like $150,000 in royalties.)

That incident helped get things going for him as a solo artist in the early 1970s. He gave several hundred concerts during those years and appeared at more festivals, including a show-stopping appearance at Britain's Isle of Wight show in mid-1971, where a crowd of some 200,000 urged him on for two hours with several standing ovations.

His recording work the first half of the 1970s was for Warner Brothers, which released his debut solo LP on the Reprise label in 1970 under the title *Cheapo, Cheapo Productions Presents the Real John Sebastian*. The LP provided a charted single, "She's a Lady." This was followed by such other albums as *John Sebastian*, *The Four of Us*, and *Real Live*. Also extant in those years was an MGM release, *John Sebastian Live*. Sebastian also wrote the theme song for the TV show *Welcome Back, Kotter*, and both the single of *Welcome Back* and the Reprise album of that title made the pop charts, though the LP was well below the creative levels of other Sebastian recordings.

In the mid-and late-1970s, Sebastian was less active as an in-person artist and concentrated more on writing material for films and TV. An example was his score for a 1979 animated TV feature called *Romie 0 and Julie 8*.

SEEGER, MIKE: *Singer, guitarist, banjoist, pianist, folk music collector, writer. Born New York, New York, 1933.*

The name Seeger almost has become a synonym for the folk music movement in the United States since the 1930s. What seems to be a dynasty was founded by musicologist and folklorist Dr. Charles Seeger, Sr. His interest in folk music was passed along to his seven children by two wives. His first family of three included the great Pete Seeger. Of the four children by his second wife, Mike, Peggy, and Penny Seeger all had an impact, in varying degrees, on the folk music field.

Michael, called Mike, the eldest of the four offspring of Charles Seeger's marriage to Ruth Crawford, spent many of his early years in Washington, D.C., where his parents were assisting the Lomaxes in compiling the Archive of Folk Song of the Library of Congress. Thus young Mike was exposed to a wide range of folk information and met the many accomplished folk artists who visited the Seeger household. His half-brother was another good source of information.

By the time Mike began high school he was pretty well indoctrinated. For a while, he learned the Spanish guitar, but when he was eighteen he switched to the banjo and the guitar, more conventionally used in folk music. One of his deep interests was the traditional hill-country music that laid the foundation for the more urban folk song genre of the post–World War II years. In the early 1950s, he began to travel through the rural parts of the United States, seeking out old-time performers and collecting traditional folk songs. Although only in his twenties, he contributed greatly to folk research, making tapes of many important songs and bringing many "lost" artists, such as Dock Boggs, to the attention of current audiences.

By the mid-1950s, Seeger was performing at many coffee houses and festivals in the United States. In 1958, he joined forces with two other artists, John Cohen and Tom Paley, to form the New Lost City Ramblers, which became the premier old-timey group of the late 1950s–early 1960s folk boom. The Ramblers sang many of the songs discovered by its members on collecting tours and also added to their repertoire from older records, material in the Archive of Folk Music, and other sources.

Among the many songs that won sustained applause from audiences throughout the United States and abroad were "Oh Babe It Ain't No Lie," "The Girl I Left Behind," "Lady of Carlisle," "Red Rocking Chair," "Battleship of Maine," "Hopalong Peter," "The Cannonball," "Old Bell Cow," "East Virginia Blues," "Freight Train," "Fly Around My Pretty Little Miss," "The Girl on the Greenbriar Shore," "Tom Dooley," "Whoop 'Em Up Cindy," and "Arkansas Traveler." These and many other songs were included in their book, The New Lost City Ramblers, issued by Oak Publications in 1964.

Both during and after his association with the New Lost City Ramblers (which disbanded in the mid-1960s), Mike Seeger continued to make solo recordings and find time for other music-related activities. He provided liner notes for folk song albums, went off on collecting tours, and provided articles on folk music for various folk music magazines and journals. His solo LPs of the 1960s included, on Folkways, Mike Seeger (issued March 1963) and Tipple, Loom and Rail (7/66) and, on Vanguard, Hello Stranger (7/64). His efforts in the 1980s continued pretty much as they had been in the 1960s, though with much less public attention in that rock-dominated decade.

At the end of the 1970s, several of his albums were in the current Folkways catalogue—his 1966 release, Tipple, Loom and Rail plus American Folk Songs and Old Time Country Music.

(See also New Lost City Ramblers: Seeger, Peggy: Seeger, Pete).

SEEGER, PEGGY: *Singer, guitarist, banjoist, songwriter. Born New York, New York, June 17, 1935.*

Another member of America's first family of folk music, Margaret "Peggy" Seeger (MacColl) was the second of four children of musicologist Charles Seeger's second marriage (to Ruth Crawford). The half sister of Pete Seeger and full sister of Mike Seeger, her contributions to the folk music revival in all parts of the world surprised no one.

Peggy heard all kinds of folk songs from her earliest years, since her father was continuously collecting and listening to tapes and records not only from the United States but many other nations. As the children grew up, they became more interested in performing the music than in the analytical pursuits of their academically oriented parents. Peggy recalled that the family was not a singing family in the sense of the Ritchie Family, but "we always heard songs and we chose our own favorites."

The many talented folk artists who paid housecalls inspired her to learn a number of instruments, including guitar and banjo. Her half-brother Pete, of course, was making a name for himself as a stellar folk artist and he and folk music friends often visited the Seeger house in Washington, D.C., and New York, where Peggy advanced through elementary and high school. Her interest in folk music continued to grow while she attended Radcliffe College in the early 1950s. After leaving Radcliffe, she went to Europe in 1955, traveling through Holland, Belgium, France, and Italy, singing and collecting songs.

In 1956, the opportunity to perform a role in the English production of *Dark of the Moon* played a major role in the course of her life. Alan Lomax, son and co-worker of Dr. John Lomax, curator of the Archive of Folk Song of the Library of Congress helped her get the part. (The Lomaxes were long-time friends of the Seeger family.) Once in England, Seeger soon joined a folk song quartet that included Scottish folk expert and song-writer Ewan MacColl. Two years later, she married him and settled in England, which remained home for the MacColls into the 1980s.

Before they married, she returned to the United States in 1957 to perform at concerts, festivals, and clubs in many parts of the country. She was particularly well received at the Gate of Horn in Chicago, where she remained for a six-week engagement. That summer she followed a familiar new-left pattern of the post-World War II era, taking part in the World Youth Festival in Moscow. She journeyed from Russia to Red China, then back through Russia to England to meet Ewan MacColl. After their marriage, both continued to be familiar figures on the folk scene, separately or together, in Europe and the United States

By the late 1950s, Seeger already had made a number of recordings. She continued to turn out LPs on various labels during the 1960s and 1970s as a solo performer or with other artists, including her husband. In the 1970s all of her releases were performed with Ewan. Her 1960s albums included one called *Three Sisters*, with her two younger sisters, Penny and Barbara on International Records, one with Tom Paley on Elektra issued in May 1965, and, with Ewan, *Classic Ballads* on Tradition and *Bothy Ballads* on Folkways. Her 1960s solo albums included *Best of Peggy Seeger* (Prestige, April 1961) and a ten-inch disc on Folkways, *Songs of Courting and Complaint.*

Throughout the 1970s, Peggy and Ewan remained active on the folk music concert circuit, mainly in England and on the Continent, though they occasionally performed in folk clubs and colleges across the United States. Many of the songs in their repertoire were originals by MacColl, plus some written or adapted by Seeger. One of Ewan's compositions that had been part of their repertoire as well as other folk artists' for much of the 1960s suddenly gained mass audience attention in 1972, when Roberta Flack's version of "The First Time Ever I Saw Your Face" became a million-seller and later won MacColl a Grammy Award.

By the start of the 1980s, Peggy and Ewan were represented by two albums recorded during the 1970s, *Folkways Record of Contemporary Song* and, on Rounder Record, *At the Present Moment.* (See also Seeger, Mike; Seeger, Pete.)

SEEGER, PETE: *Singer, guitarist, banjoist, songwriter, musicologist, author. Born New York, New York, May 3, 1919.*

By the beginning of the 1980s, Pete Seeger was considered an institution in

American folk and pop music, a father figure whose contributions as an artist and writer were highly valued by people of all ages in and out of the music field. His concerts were reviewed, almost always favorably, on entertainment section pages.

Such widespread popularity, however, had not always followed his career. During the 1950s, the soft-spoken Seeger appeared on the front pages, accused of subversion by Congressional committees and called unpatriotic by more than a few United States dignitaries. He was not without his defenders, though, who fought staunchly for his right to free speech and maintained his reputation as a giant in the annals of twentieth-century music history in America and the world.

In none of their rhetoric could anti-Seeger people damn him as a recent immigrant to American shores. Indeed, the Seeger lineage could be traced back to early colonial times. Over the years, several members of the family made important contributions to many facets of American life. His father, Dr. Charles Seeger, had been recognized as one of the world's foremost musicologists as well as an important classical conductor before Pete was born; he continued his research in ethnomusicology into the 1970s. His mother, Constance de Clyver Edison, was a violinist and teacher.

Young Peter R. Seeger went to private schools in Nyack, New York, and in Connecticut before entering Harvard College. Up to the time he was sixteen, Pete had little interest in folk music, but a trip with his father to a folk festival in Asheville, North Carolina, changed his mind. As he later recalled, "In 1935 I was 16 years old, playing tenor banjo in the school jazz band. I was uninterested in studying the classical music which my parents taught at Juilliard. That summer I visited a square dance festival in Asheville, North Carolina, and fell in love with the old-fashioned five string banjo, rippling out a rhythm to one fascinating song after another. I liked the melodies, time tested by generations of singers. Above all I liked the words.

"Compared to the trivialities of most popular songs, the words of those songs had all the meat of human life in them. They sang of heroes, outlaws, murderers, fools. They weren't afraid of being tragic instead of just sentimental. They weren't afraid of being scandalous instead of giggly or cute. Above all, they seemed frank, straightforward, honest. By comparison, it seemed to me that too many art songs were concerned with being elegant and too many pop songs were concerned with being clever. So in 1935 I tried learning some of this music."

In spite of his musical direction, he entered Harvard in 1936 as a sociology student. But in 1938, he abruptly left school to ride the rails or hitchhike all over the United States with the objective of developing his skills as a painter while also collecting songs. In doing this, Seeger made the acquaintance of such other performers as Leadbelly, Woody Guthrie, and Earl Robinson. He also drew closer to his father's friend, Dr. John Lomax, Curator of the Archive of Folk Song at the Library of Congress in Washington. By 1939–40, Pete was an archive assistant and also went on field trips with the Lomaxes.

In 1940, he was instrumental in founding one of the best-known groups in U.S. folk music history (in association with Woody Guthrie, by then a close friend), the Almanac Singers. It was a loosely knit framework that encompassed the efforts of Seeger, Guthrie, and many other important folk singers of the period. Guthrie's son Arlo noted that the Almanacs were "anybody who happened by." Pete toured the country for many months with Woody. Seeger, Guthrie, and the others, often sang at labor and migrant meetings and composed prounion and antifascist songs. A good part of their repertoire, though, came from traditional folk music. Although the Almanacs were only in existence a few years, they made a number of albums, including *Dear Mr. President, Talking Union, Sod Buster Ballads,* and *Deep Sea Shanties.*

The event that caused the dissolution of the Almanacs was America's entry into World War II. In 1942, Seeger was drafted and spent more than three years in the Army, mainly entertaining troops throughout the Pacific.

After his discharge in December 1945, Seeger helped start a form of songwriters' union called People's Songs, Inc. At its pinnacle, the union had 3,000 members, including such luminaries as Sonny Terry, Tom Glazer, Alan Lomax, and Guthrie. Part of the activities included hootenannies, which were forerunners of the more ambitious hoots of the late 1950s and early 1960s. Seeger's projects included a movie short, *And Hear My Banjo Play*, in 1946 and a Los Angeles revival of the folk musical *Dark of the Moon*.

In the late 1940s, Seeger joined another folk music stalwart, Lee Hays (with whom he co-wrote a number of folk music standards over the years, including "If I Had a Hammer"), to create a now legendary group called The Weavers. The initial foursome in 1948 was Seeger, Hays, Fred Hellerman, and Ronnie Gilbert. "We couldn't earn a dollar. The Weavers was about to break up when we were offered a job at a shoddy nightclub. In six months, we found ourselves with a recording contract, a best-selling record [the single 'Good Night Irene'], managers, agents, publicity men and the whole thing." In 1949 and the early 1950s, The Weavers turned out hit after hit, including "Tzena, Tzena," "On Top of Old Smokey," "Kisses Sweeter than Wine," "So Long, It's Been Good to Know You," and "Wimoweh." After that landmark appearance at the Village Vanguard in late 1949, The Weavers took the country by storm, performing in major concert venues all over the United States (including several appearances at Carnegie Hall in New York) and guesting on major TV shows. Through 1952, when the onslaughts of the McCarthy era forced the group to disband for a time, The Weavers' record sales totalled many millions.

Before reuniting the Weavers in 1955, Seeger forged a solo career in concerts all over the world. His efforts included a series of six concerts at Columbia University in 1954–55, on "American Folk Music and Its Origins." But the storm clouds were rapidly forming on the horizon, and for a long time Seeger kept his career going in the face of monumental adversity, including widespread blacklisting on U.S. TV and concert circuits.

His legal troubles with the U.S. government began in 1955, when he took the Fifth Amendment in refusing to answer questions on "subversive" affiliations and actions put to him by the House Committee on Un-American Activities. He was later indicted on ten counts of contempt of Congress, charges that did not come to trial for five years. When the case came up, he was found guilty on some charges and sentenced to a year in prison. (However, as a result of appeals, he only spent four days in jail.) All the charges finally were dismissed by the U.S. Court of Appeals on May 18, 1962.

From the time of the HUAC hearings until the late 1960s, the blacklist kept him off TV. However, he was hardly inactive. He worked with The Weavers from 1955 to 1957 and then went on to help revive the Newport Folk Festival at the end of the 1950s. During this time, he was contributing to *Sing Out!* magazine and also working on new songs and records. (His writings, over the years, besides his regular column in *Sing Out!*, included a number of books on various aspects of music. His *How to Play the Five String Banjo*, first issued in 1948, was selling close to 20,000 copies a year at the end of the 1970s. Some of his other books were *Henscratches and Flyspecks: Or How to Read Melodies from Songbooks in 12 Confusing Lessons* and *The Incompleat Folksinger*.)

From the mid-1950s on, his recordings continued to pour out for decades on a variety of labels, including Columbia, Vanguard, Folkways, Decca, and, in the late 1970s, Warner Bros. Among his 1950s and 1960s LPs were a six-record set on Folkways titled *Folk Ballads*, issued between 12/57 and 7/61; *At Carnegie Hall* (Folkways, 7/58); *Champlain Valley Songbag* (Folkways, 2/60); *Pete Seeger's Gazette* (Folkways 3/59, 1/62); *Rainbow Design* (Folkways, 7/60); *Sing Out* (Folkways, 8/61); *Story Songs* (Columbia, 10/61); *At the Village Gate* (two records, Folkways, 5/62); *Indian Summer* (soundtrack, Folkways, 2/61); *Bitter and Sweet* (Columbia, 1/63); *Broadside* Vol. 1 & 2 (Broadside, 11/63); *We Shall Overcome* (Columbia, 1/64); *Live Hootenanny* (Aravel, 2/64); *At the Village Gate* (Disc, 11/64); *Live Concert* (Aravel, 11/64); *Folk Songs*, (Capitol, 12/64); *I Can See a New Day* (Columbia 1/65); *Songs of Struggle and Protest* (Folkways, 1/65); *Broadside* (Folkways, 1/65); *Freight Train* (Capitol, 12/64); *Strangers and Cousins* (Columbia, 6/65); *In Concert* (Verve/Forecast, 8/65); *On Campus* (Verve/Forecast 9/65); *Pete Seeger* (Arc Folkways, 1/66); *Little Boxes* (Verve/Forecast, 2/66); *Live at the Village Gate* (Verve/Forecast, 1/66); *God Bless the Grass* (Columbia, 3/66); *Dangerous Songs?* (Columbia, 8/66); *Waist Deep in the Big Muddy* (Columbia, 8/67); *Greatest Hits* (Columbia, 12/67); *John Henry & Other Folk Favorites* (Harmony, 8/69); and *Young vs. Old* (Columbia, ten/69). Among his other recordings of those years were the LPs on Folkways: *American Industrial Ballads, Darling Corey* (ten-inch record), *Frontier Ballads* (two records, ten inch); *Goofing Off Suite* (ten inch), *Love Songs for Friends and Foes, Sampler* (ten inch), *Talking Union, With Voice Together We Sing*; on Stinson, *Concert*; and with sister Peggy and brother Mike, a two-record set on Prestige, *The Seegers*, issued August 1965.

During the 1960s, many of Pete's songs were played by other musicians in fields ranging from folk and country to rock. The Kingston Trio had a hit with his "Where Have All the Flowers Gone" in the early 1960s, and in the mid-1960s the song "Turn! Turn! Turn! " (with lyrics derived from the Bible) was a gold-record rock hit for the Byrds.

As might be expected, Pete was in the forefront of the anti-Vietnam War outcry. Along with young folksingers like Phil Ochs and Joan Baez, he took part in many concerts opposing U.S. involvement in the conflict. It was an attitude that enhanced his popularity on college campuses, where he was a favored performer for decades. (As he said at one time, "When The Weavers were blacklisted out of existence, I began touring colleges and have been ever since.")

In late 1967, he made his first appearance on TV in more than a decade when the Smothers Brothers invited him to perform on their show. They had to fight a strong effort by CBS executives to continue the ban. After the show, Pete returned to be featured on two more Smothers Brothers segments. On one of those, he sang the song "Waist-Deep in the Big Muddy," whose rejection by network censors from his first Smothers' show appearance had created a national furor. In the 1970s, he was hardly a familiar face to TV viewers, but the blacklist faded away and he did turn up from time to time, primarily on public television.

At the end of the 1960s, Seeger helped organize a campaign to restore the ecology of the Hudson River. He and other folksingers cruised the river in the sloop "Clearwater," giving concerts to publicize their concern. Among those he enlisted for the voyage was a young folksinger named Don McLean, whose career was helped immeasurably by the exposure. The National Educational Television special, telecast at the start of the 1970s, titled *The Sloop at Nyack*, was one result of the concert series. Prior to that, Seeger had his own show on public TV, called *Rainbow Quest*, in 1968 and 1969. He also hosted a number of programs dealing with folk music topics as the 1970s went by. One of his appearances on public TV in the late 1970s was in a joint concert from the Wolftrap performing center (near Washington, D.C.) with Woody Guthrie's son, Arlo. (Pete and Arlo often toured together, including a highly successful series of concerts across the United States in 1981.)

Pete's recordings continued to come out on various labels throughout the 1970s. His early 1970s albums included *Pete Seeger Sings and Answers Questions* (two records, Broadside, 2/70) and *Rainbow Race* (Columbia, 8/71). He kept up a rigorous concert schedule that included a number of appearances over the years for charitable causes and U.N. appeals. No longer a pariah on the regular concert circuit, he played many venues, large and small, all over the United States including a number of appearances at New York's Lincoln Center. His album releases in the late 1970s were on Warner Brothers and included *Pete Seeger and Arlo Guthrie in Concert*. By 1981, he had left Warner Brothers, but the preceding LP and one solo album, *Circles and Seasons* (released in July 1979), remained in the company's catalogue.

SEEKERS, THE: *Vocal group. Athol Guy, born Melbourne, Australia, January 5, 1940; Judith Durham, born Melbourne, July 7, 1943; Bruce Woodley, born Melbourne, July 25, 1942; Keith Potger, born Colombo, Ceylon, March 2, 1941.*

One of the fresh sounds to grace the folk music field of the mid-1960s came from Australia by way of Liverpool, England. It took the form of the Seekers, a personable foursome consisting of three natives of Melbourne and a fourth individual, Keith Potger, who was born on the island of Ceylon in the Indian Ocean. (He has few memories of his exotic birthplace; his family moved to Australia when he was six.)

All four attended school in Melbourne, but did not meet until they began their working careers. Athol and Bruce discovered a joint interest in music when they became acquainted in the advertising agency where they both worked. Later they met Judith, who was a secretary for a Melbourne firm, and Keith, who produced radio shows.

They combined forces to sing folk music, ranging from songs from Australia and England to Negro spirituals and Woody Guthrie compositions. By spring of 1964, they had made several appearances in local coffee houses. Their style met with quick success with Melbourne folk fans and led to a number of spots on TV shows in the city. Later in 1964, they decided they were ready to try for a wider audience and left for England.

English producers were equally impressed with the new group. The result was an appearance on the top British TV show, *Sunday Night at the Palladium*, three weeks after they reached London. Their performance made them one of the most discussed new groups in England. They were signed by E. M. I., the major English recording company and main stockholder in Capitol Records in the United States.

One of their first singles, "I'll Never Find Another You," released in December 1964, became the number-one song in England in March 1965. Capitol released it in the United States, backed with the spiritual "Open Up Them Pearly Gates," and it became a major pop hit in the States as well. American audiences also took to the first LP released by Capitol, *The New Seekers*. Soon after, the Seekers turned out another hit, "A World of Our Own." The LP of the same title included such songs as "Leavin' of Liverpool," "Just a Closer Walk with Thee," "Allentown Jail," "Four Strong Winds," "This Land Is Your Land," and such Bob Dylan songs as "Don't Think Twice, It's All Right" and "The Times They Are A-Changin'."

During the rest of the 1960s the group made several worldwide tours, appearing in both the United States and Australia. In 1967, they scored with another hit, the title song from the movie *Georgy Girl*. The reverse side of the record was "When the Stars Begin to Fall." Capitol also released an LP of theirs titled *Georgy Girl*. By the end of the decade, the group disbanded. Their LP *Best of the Seekers* could still be found in the Capitol catalogue at the end of the 1970s.

SEELY, JEANNIE: *Singer, songwriter, music industry executive. Born Titusville, Pennsylvania, July 6, 1940.*

An intelligent, animated performer, Jeannie Seely ranked as one of country music's finest female artists of the 1960s and 1970s. Her list of blockbuster hits is not extensive, but that may partly be due to her insistence on doing material in which she believed and in her own style, a combination that for a time was somewhat more progressive than many members of the audience were prepared to accept.

Born and raised in a small Pennsylvania town (population about 350), Jeannie started her own weekly regional radio show. Eventually she added many other radio credits, including hosting a show that was broadcast over the U.S. Armed Forces Radio for two years.

Her career really started to move forward after she moved to the Nashville area in the 1960s. She performed duet work with three major artists, Porter Wagoner,

Ernest Tubb, and Jack Greene, but the biggest contributor to her career was writer/performer Hank Cochran, who provided her with a series of songs. He also became her husband.

Discussing the events that first got things rolling, Seely told Geoff Lane of *Music City News*, "It all happened after I moved [to Nashville]. Norma Jean wanted to spend more time with her daughter; the child was going to school and Norma was missing so much of her childhood years. I was rooming with Porter's [Wagoner's] secretary and it just happened to all fall into place. Porter hired me to take Norma's place on the road. I did some touring when I lived in California [before moving to Tennessee], but not really on a professional basis. On the Ernest Tubb TV show, I worked as a single, but a lot of times when they booked Ernest, they wanted a girl on the show. So I traveled with Ernest quite a bit, but not full time."

Her name really became known to country fans in 1966, when Monument Records issued her single of Hank Cochran's "Don't Touch Me." The song made the national country top 10 and later won her the Grammy Award for Best Country & Western Vocal Performance, Female, for 1966. The following year she had another top-10 singles hit with "A Wanderin' Man," and, in 1968, her three chart-making singles included the top-10 success "Welcome Home to Nothing."

In 1969, Seely switched record companies, signing with MCA Records. The move brought about a third duet alignment, this time with Jack Greene. One of their first joint efforts was the single "I Wish I Didn't Have to Miss You." It rose to number one in the United States and paved the way for a vocal collaboration still going strong a decade later. Jeannie and Jack and his band, the Jolly Greene Giants, became the central performers in one of the most popular touring shows of the 1970s, as well as a featured assemblage on the *Grand Ole Opry*, which had signed Jeannie as a regular cast member back in 1967.

Looking back on the show's origins, Seely told Geoff Lane, "It was my idea for Jack and I to form the show. I've had people ask me why I didn't want a group of my own. I don't like to be alone and traveling alone was really getting to me. It was like one airport, one cab, one motel, one backstage dressing room after another, always by myself. I got to where I'd get so depressed I was not enjoying what I was doing. Forming a band of your own is a great responsibility and mostly, when the girls do it, they've got a husband who can travel with them and kind of share that responsibility. I wouldn't have that because Hank [Cochran] cannot travel with me and take care of his career. As a writer, he needs to be in Nashville a lot of the time handling the business end of things. [Jeannie, it should be noted, also has taken a hand in various aspects of the music business. Among her assets are a knowledge of music publishing, commercial law, economics, banking, and finance]. We travel about as much as any troupe out of Nashville. In fact, last year we traveled 175,000 miles, and that was by bus, not flying miles."

During the 1970s, Jeannie's name showed up on upper-chart levels quite a few times. Among her hits were "Tell Me Again" in late 1970 and early 1971, "Can I Sleep in Your Arms Tonight Mister" in the fall of 1973, "Lucky Ladies" in early 1974, and "I Miss You" in the spring and summer of 1974. Most of her hit releases were written or co-written by Hank Cochran.

In the second half of the 1960s and in the 1970s, Seely also completed a number of albums, including such LPs on Monument as *Jeannie Seely* (issued 11/66) and *Thanks, Hank* (7/67) and, on MCA, *Please Be My New Love.*

SESSIONS, RONNIE: *Singer, guitarist, songwriter, band leader (Ambush). Born Henrietta, Oklahoma, December 7, 1948.*

Since most country artists do much of their performing work in nightclubs, it's not surprising that some of them adopt honky-tonkin' as a way of life. In Ronnie Sessions' case, it came close to destroying a career that seemed bright at the start of the 1970s but in severe jeopardy a few years later. Fortunately, marriage and children helped him to restore his upward momentum by the end of the decade.

Born in Oklahoma but raised in Bakersfield, California, Ronnie's talent as a singer was evidenced at an early age; he was already charming audiences at the age of seven. At eight he turned professional and made his first recordings when he was nine. At ten, he was appearing in major venues, including the Golden Nugget in Las Vegas.

Before finishing his schooling he recorded a number of sides for Gene Autry's Los Angeles-based Republic Records (none of which came close to making the national charts). After graduation he decided the best way to further his career was to move to Nashville, which he did in 1971, to audition for several record labels. He was signed by MGM. One of the singles he recorded for his new company was Hoyt Axton's "Never Been to Spain." Released in midsummer 1972, the record began to pick up airplay and, by fall, was in the upper levels of the country charts. Sessions soon was guesting on major country TV programs and radio shows and gracing the stages of major country clubs across the United States.

However, he wasn't able to match the success of that single with his followup releases on MGM. He already had begun to make a reputation for himself as a "highliver," and the increasing frustration of recording flops accelerated that trend. Critics began to write him off as a one-shot artist.

After his contract with MGM ran out, Ronnie gained a new affiliation with MCA Records. At first the change seemed to have only a minor impact. He recorded some singles that made the charts, but only the lower levels, examples being "Makin' Love," which got into the seventies in late fall of 1975, and "Support Your Local Honky Tonks" (advice Session's continued to take), which hovered around eighty in April 1976. But Ronnie and producer Chip Young persevered and, finally, in 1977, things took a turn for the better with such singles as "Me and Millie" and, in particular, "Wiggle Wiggle," his first re-

lease to make top-chart levels since 1972.

By late 1977, Sessions also had decided to straighten his lifestyle. He began to make plans for a new band in hopes of returning the luster to his in-person efforts. As he recalled to Kelly Delaney of *Country Music* magazine (January/February 1979), "Almost a year ago I decided it was time to reach out and go for it. I mean it still ain't no room full o' roses yet. But at least things are better than they were last winter. That was one of the roughest times I've ever been through. I'd just put the band together, but we didn't have any money comin' in because most of the time we were rehearsin' and the few gigs we did have got cancelled because of the bad weather."

To cut costs, he invited the four band members (the group was named Ambush) to move into his home. By then, his family circle included a wife and baby daughter. "We had to practice. We didn't have the money to do anything else. You might say I was not only raisin' a baby, but a band too. . . . Maybe that slack period was actually a blessing in disguise. All those months of practicin' really helped us get tight, not only musically, but as friends too."

It paid off in an increasingly warm reception from reviewers and fans as well when Sessions' new manager began to line up a growing number of engagements. By the end of 1978, Sessions and Ambush had as much work offered as they could fit into a busy schedule. Equally important, Ronnie had a new hit single, "Juliet and Romeo," on the charts in the fall that stayed in the upper brackets into early winter.

Sessions told Kelly Delaney that he thought the most rewarding part of his career was yet to come. "You know, some years ago my producer at the time told me I might oughtta consider giving up bein' a singer and take a day gig. I thought about it too. But I've been an entertainer since I was seven years old. I really don't know how to do anything else, so I decided to hang in there. I've still got a long ways to go, but I'm mighty glad I didn't take that advice."

SHAVER, BILLY JOE: *Singer, songwriter. Born Corsicana, Texas, 1941.*

One of the most original of the new breed of country songwriter that came to the fore starting in the late 1960s and early 1970s, Billy Joe Shaver established a reputation in the industry for his wild exploits as well as his creative talents. As he said about the former, "Sad to say, most of the stories you hear about me are true and then some. It use'ta be that no matter what I did, I jumped in all the way, with both feet in the trough. I always used to seem to be in the wrong place at the right time."

Billy Joe experienced a lot of hardships and saw much of the rougher side of life long before he decided to try for a place in the country music field. In fact, his troubles started before he was born; his parents separated before his birth in Corsicana, Texas, at the start of the 1940s and his mother placed him and his young sister in the care of their grandmother. (He told a Columbia Records interviewer in 1981, "My mother was actually a honky tonk girl, though she's a good Christian lady now and she prays for me a lot. She worked in honky tonks in Waco and Dallas.")

His grandmother had little money, but she cared for the children and encouraged her grandson's interest in music as he got a little older. "She would take me down to the grocery store down the road from us and every time she'd get a little behind on her credit she'd ask the woman if she would extend it. And [the woman] would say she would if she'd get that little boy to sing! They used to put me up on an old cracker barrel or somethin' and I'd sing my heart out." Most of the songs the boy picked up from listening to the radio, adding some lyrics of his own in some cases.

But as Billy Joe approached high school age, there wasn't much leeway for the luxury of continuing his education. He had to drop out of school after the eighth grade and go to work on farms run by several uncles. "I'd stay with one and then go on to another one and stay with him a while. I got passed around quite a bit."

Later on, he branched out to work at a variety of other jobs to increase his income. Among the occupations he tried in his teens and early twenties were bronc busting and bullriding, gas station attendant, a hitch in the U.S. Navy, and sawmill work. The last named proved very costly; as a result of a sawmill accident, he lost parts of four fingers on his right hand. He also sold cars for a time, "but I wasn't very good at it."

He was still interested in music, and, as time went on, he began to make an effort to move in that direction. Starting in the late 1960s, he made periodic trips from Texas to Nashville, making the trip either by hitchhiking or driving his old pick-up truck, to seek auditions from music publishers or artists & repertoire executives. Again and again the results were nil, but he persisted. Finally, he made his way to Bobby Bare's small publishing office. "At first Bobby told me he wasn't looking for any new writers, so I hung my head and started to walk out. Man, I must have looked pathetic, because he said, 'Aw, wait a minute! Where's your tapes?' I told him I didn't have any tapes, that my songs were all in my head. But he let me stay anyway and play him one song. Before I was through, he was drawing up the papers to sign me. I'll always admire Bobby for havin' such good taste."

At the beginning, Bare paid Shaver a small advance while the latter worked up new material and Bobby worked on getting word of Shaver's abilities around Nashville. The advance hardly allowed lavish living; to make ends meet, Billy Joe slept in Bare's office. But things soon began to change as a growing number of country artists recognized the promise of Billy Joe's compositions. One of the first to use this material, besides Bare, was Kris Kristofferson, who included Shaver's composition "Good Christian Soldier" in his 1971 *Silver Tongued Devil* LP. Another artist quick to recognize Shaver's potential was Tom T. Hall, who used Shaver's composition "Old Five and Dimers like Me" as a single as well as the title song for an ablum. In 1973, Waylon Jennings based an entire album, *Honky Tonk Heroes,* on Shaver material. As the 1970s went by, many other country stars recorded Billy Joe's songs, including Elvis Presley ("You Ask Me To"); Johnny Cash ("Old Chunk of Coal," "Jesus Was Our Savior," "Cotton Was Our King"); Bobby Bare and Johnny Rodriguez ("I Couldn't Be Me Without You"); the Allman Brothers Band ("Sweet Mama"); and such others as Jerry Jeff Walker, Tennessee Ernie Ford, and the Sons of the Pioneers. Billy Joe included some of those in his own performing repertoire, as well as such others as "Ain't No God in Mexico" and "I've Been to Georgia on a Fast Train."

Shaver began to record some of his own vocal renditions in the early 1970s, starting with some tracks made for MGM that were coproduced by Bobby Bare and Willie Nelson. Kris Kristofferson urged his own label of the time, Monument Records, to sign Billy Joe; the result was the 1973 LP *Old Five and Dimers like Me*, produced by Kris. The LP still ranks as one of the best country-music collections of the 1970s. In the mid-1970s, Shaver moved to Capricorn, completing two albums, *When I Get My Wings* and *Gypsy Boy*.

Unfortunately, Billy Joe's recording career was set adrift for a time when the Capricorn label went out of business. However, other performers continued to come to him for new material or turned out new versions of previous compositions, so he didn't have to worry about camping out in a publishing office again.

In late 1980, he signed a new recording contract with Columbia Records. His debut album on the label, *I'm Just an Old Chunk of Coal . . . But I'm Gonna Be a Diamond Someday*, was released in April 1981.

SHEPARD, JEAN: *Singer, bass player. Born Pauls Valley, Oklahoma, November 21, 1933.*

In the early part of Jean Shepard's career, some onlookers at her concerts found it hard to keep from laughing at the sight of the diminutive (five feet one inch) blue-eyed blonde dwarfed by a huge bass fiddle. However, their smiles turned to cheers as she demonstrated both prowess as a musician and a strong, vibrant voice that belied her small stature. She was, in fact, a

giant among female country singers who went on to become an admired regular cast member of the *Grand Ole Opry* for many years.

In the small town of Pauls Valley, Oklahoma, Jean's birthplace, children were almost weaned on country & western music. Jean loved the music, and after her family moved to Visalia, California, near Bakersfield, the western capital of country music, she joined an all-girl country band called the Melody Ranch Girls when she was fifteen. The group played dances and other events in and around Visalia. It continued to function for several years and, just before graduation, got the chance to make a recording for Capitol Records.

Unfortunately, the record sank without a trace. However, Jean kept on singing. In the early 1950s, Hank Thompson heard her while touring through that part of California. At the time he was with Capitol Records, and he passed the word about her talent to company executive Ken Nelson. In a short time, Nelson had added her to the Capitol roster. Her first single came out soon after, "Crying Steel Guitar Waltz."

Capitol executives teamed her with one of their top male prospects, Ferlin Husky, and the two began turning out duets and touring together. That alignment lasted two years and resulted in Shepard's first major hit, "Dear John Letter," a number-one success in 1953. Recalling those times in 1971, she said, "Back then, when I started recording, country music was really big. In 1952, Ferlin and I did a show in Toronto—some 30,000 people came to the concert! Later country and western music faded a bit, but taste in music goes in cycles, like tastes in fashion. Country music is popular again, bigger than ever, but even if it loses some of its commercial appeal, it will always be around."

One of the odd circumstances of those days, as she recounted in 1974 to Carol Offen of *Country Music* magazine, was the need for her to become, briefly, the ward of Ferlin Husky. When "Dear John" hit, it was logical for her to tour nationwide with him, but since she was still under twenty-one, she couldn't legally leave the state on her own. To get around this, it was decided to make Husky her legal guardian. Jean told Carol with a laugh, "Imagine having Ferlin Husky as your guardian!"

After working with Husky, Shepard began to concentrate on her solo career. It took a little while for her recordings to catch on, but after several chart-makers that didn't go much beyond middle levels of the top 40 or 50, she clicked in 1955 with two top-10 hits, "Beautiful Lies" and "Satisfied Mind." Those were the last top-level successes she was to have for a long while, though she continued to record steadily and was warmly welcomed by fans at country shows around the United States.

Meanwhile, she had been asked to join the cast of Red Foley's highly regarded show, sent to many other stations from station KWTO, Missouri. After two years there, her ability won her entrée to the most coveted spot of all, regular cast member of the Grand Ole Opry. She joined the Opry in 1956 and was still on the show's roster at the start of the 1980s. It was the setting for some great joys and wrenching sorrows. After a few years with the program, Shepard married another luminary of the period, Hawkshaw Hawkins. In early 1963, they were parents of a fifteen-month-old boy and Shepard was in her eighth month of pregnancy with a second child when Hawkins went to an ill-fated benefit concert with Patsy Cline and Cowboy Copas. On the way back from the show, all were killed in a private airplane crash.

Although long since happily remarried to musician and road manager Benny Birchfield by the time she talked to Carol Offen, she admitted, "It's funny, but I still feel a little strange around this time every year." (The interview date was March 7, two days after the anniversary of the crash.) Nashville still was home for her as it had been since she joined the Opry. In the 1970s and early 1980s, Jean and her family lived in Hendersonville, Tennessee, near neighbors of Johnny and June Cash.

From the mid-1950s until the early 1970s, she recorded a large number of albums for Capitol. During that time, the company issued one or more of her LPs

every year. Among that output were Songs of a Love Affair, Lonesome Love, This Is Jean Shepard (issued November 1959), Got You on My Mind (4/61), Heartaches and Tears (3/62), Jean Shepard (11/63), Lighthearted and Blue (12/64), It's a Man Every Time (12/65), Many Happy Hangovers (7/66), I'll Take the Dog (12/66), Heart, We Did All We Could (3/67), Yours Forever (9/67), and in the late 1960s and 1970s—Best By Request, Woman's Hand, Here and Now, Just as Soon, and Just like Walkin' in the Sunshine. Some of her material also was released on the Hilltop label, including the albums Under Your Spell Again and Hello Old Broken Heart.

Jean became a favorite with Opry fans instantly and her stock rose even higher in the mid-1960s with a series of top-10 hits. The first of those was the 1964 single "Second Fiddle (to an Old Guitar)." In 1966, she added two more top-10 successes, one a duet with Ray Pillow, "I'll Take the Dog," the other a solo single, "If Teardrops Were Silver."

In 1967, she had the top-10 hit single, "Yours Forever." In the early 1970s, her Capitol chart hits included "Another Lonely Night," on top-chart levels in late 1970 and early 1971, "Then He Touched Me" in 1971, which received a Grammy nomination, and, in 1972, "Just like Walkin' with Sunshine."

However, as she told Offen, she was starting to feel that Capitol was beginning to take her for granted, and, after twenty-one years on the label, asked for and got her release from her contract with the firm. She then signed with United Artists, for whom she recorded such mid-1970s chart singles as "Come on Phone" in 1974, "I'm a Believer (in a Whole Lot of Lovin')" in 1975, and, in 1976, "Another Neon Night," "Mercy," and "Ain't Love Grand."

Throughout the 1960s and 1970s, Shepard maintained a breakneck touring schedule for much of the year. Besides appearing on a wide range of network and syndicated country shows during those decades, she also kept up an annual tour schedule involving over 150,000 miles of travel and 200 days on the road.

She remarked to Offen that, even though she had been performing for many years, she was still flexible enough to try out new techniques. For instance, "I used a hand mike the other night. You see I never use one. And I don't move around much on stage. Basically, I just stand there, throw my head back and sing. But everybody's using a hand mike these days and my husband's been after me to try it. I didn't think he thought I'd be game enough to do it though. Boy, you shoulda seen how all the guys in the band looked at me. They were so shocked. . . .

"I'm proud of the fact that I can still hold my own with all the new girls coming into the business. I enjoy competition. Most of the new vocalists are a good ten years younger than I am, y'know. Even though I didn't win a Grammy, what's most important to me is that I'm still in the running."

SHEPPARD, T. G.: *Singer, guitarist, songwriter. Born Humboldt, Tennessee, July 20, 1944.*

Like many country artists, T. G. Sheppard (real name, Bill Browder) had to wait quite a few years before he became known to a sizable number of country fans. However, he was able to stick with it during many lean years of performing by earning a living in other phases of the business. He wasn't the first and certainly won't be the last entertainer to make his way from behind-the-scenes promotion work to the glare of personal stardom.

His saga began in the town of Humboldt, Tennessee, where he was born and spent his early years. There was always music to be heard in his house—his mother was a gospel pianist and music teacher—and T. G. enjoyed gospel and country songs from his childhood on. He started to learn guitar before he was high school age and already was seeking opportunities to perform in his teens.

When he was sixteen in 1960, he moved to Jackson, Tennessee, where he was a sideman in several local country bands for a year. After that he packed up and headed to a larger locale, Memphis, where he joined the band headed by Travis Womack as a guitarist and backing vocalist.

During those years, in addition to band work, Sheppard also added to his income by working as a recording session musician. Some demo tapes that he had made eventually brought him a recording contract from Atlantic Records. He made a number of singles for Atlantic, released under the pseudonym Brian Stacy, one of which, "High School Days" made upperchart levels.

However, since his career as an entertainer wasn't making any phenomenal progress, it made sense to find a job in another segment of the business. This move, in the early 1960s, took the form of a position as promotion and advertising manager with Hot-Line Distributors in Memphis. He did well enough there to move, in time, to RCA Records as its southern region promotion executive. After some years with RCA, he decided to form his own independent company in Memphis, Umbrella Promotion, later called Unbrella Productions. He opened offices for his firm in a building that also housed the Onyx recording studios. After listening to the constant sound of recording sessions, he longed to get closer to the creative side of the field again. Before long he was doing some record producing of his own and singing professionally once more.

His involvement in the business side of music finally led to a contract for him with Melodyland Records. The song that helped bring that about was one brought to him during the summer of 1973 by a young writer named Bobby David, titled "Devil in the Bottle." Sheppard was enthusiastic about the song and, at first, tried to place it with some established country singers. However, no one accepted it, so he finally recorded it himself. The single came out in the fall of 1974 and soon made lower-chart levels. Helped by Sheppard's promotion efforts, it rose steadily higher until, in February 1975, it nestled in the number-one spot on U.S. country charts.

While in Memphis he became friendly with Elvis Presley. Elvis, delighted with T.G.'s success, gave him a new touring bus. He flew T.G. to Dallas in his private plane and simply handed him the keys to the bus once the plane touched down.

Analyzing its success, he told Bill Littleton of *Music City News* (February 1976), "Being in the promotion business probably had more to do with me having a hit the first time out with 'Devil in the Bottle' than anything else, except that 'Devil' was a hit quality song to begin with.

T.G. also proved successful in acquiring the services of Jack D. Johnson, who became his manager. Johnson had previously served in the same capacity for Ronnie Milsap and Charley Pride during the critical years of their professional lives.

"I knew what to expect and how to go about getting what I wanted—it wasn't like walkin' into the business cold and startin' from scratch. I feel sorry for kids who find themselves with hits without knowing enough about the business to keep the ball rolling."

T. G. certainly knew how to do that. He emphasized it with another major singles hit during the summer of 1975. The song, "Tryin' to Beat the Mornin' Home," which he co-wrote with R. Williams and E. Kahanek, made it to number one at the end of June. In the fall, he had another top-10 hit with the single "Another Woman" and in early 1976, scored still another bestseller with "Motels and Memories."

By then, Sheppard was well on the way to becoming a concert favorite on the country circuit. From 1975 on, he maintained a heavy touring schedule that took him to all parts of the United States and Canada. He also was featured on major country broadcasts, including several appearances on the *Grand Ole Opry*.

During 1976, he changed labels, achieving a top-level hit with his version of Neil Diamond's "Solitary Man" in the summer. Later in the 1970s, he moved over to Warner/Curb Records, for whom he continued his series of chart-making singles and albums. He had a top-10 hit on Warner's in the summer of 1978 with "When Can We Do This Again" and matched that in the fall and winter with "Daylight," in the top 10 in November 1978. Among his charted singles in 1979 were "Happy Together," "Last Cheater's Waltz," and the top-10 hit "You Feel Good All Over." He started the 1980s in similar

fashion with another number-one hit, "I'll Be Coming Back for More," and followed with such major successes as "Smooth Sailin'" in early summer and "Do You Wanna Go to Heaven?," number-one ranked in October 1980 on Warner/Curb. In 1981 he had such bestsellers as "I Feel like Loving You Again" and "I Loved 'Em Every One." His charted LPs on Warner/Curb included *3/4 Lonely* in 1979-80 and *Smooth Sailin'*, on the lists from late 1980 into 1981.

Though he enjoyed his status as a top country artist, he also admitted he had to try to cope with the changes it caused in his private life. He told Littleton, "The . . . 15 years [I was] involved in promotion, I would get up at eight or nine a.m. and go to work and be home at five or six p.m. And I would have Saturdays and Sundays off. Usually at night I would be out entertaining disc jockeys or have a client in town; we [he and his family] never really got to talk that much. But now, even being away from home so much, when I do get home we have so much to talk about, to get caught up on. When we find ourselves drifting apart, we sit down and talk. And we try to say, 'Well, now, why are we drifting apart? What's happening right now to make us do this? We usually pinpoint it and correct it right there.

"My wife and I are trying to stay close even though I am on the road. When I am out, I try to call home at least twice a day. I have a little boy . . . and the most important thing is keeping in contact with him."

SHERRILL, BILLY: *Pianist, saxophonist, songwriter, record producer, record industry executive. Born Phil Campbell, Alabama, circa 1938.*

Few people in the country music field have had the impact of Billy Sherrill. As a writer, as a selector of songs for specific artists, and as one of the most successful record producers in recent country music, Billy has been one of the most prolific starmakers in the industry. Among those who could credit much of the basis for their rise to prominence to Sherrill's contributions are superstars like David Houston, Charlie Rich, Johnny Duncan, and Johnny

Paycheck. Legions of others could thank Sherrill for helping them achieve some of their most notable successes.

Music was a staple item in Billy's early life in Alabama—but not pop or even country. Gospels and hymns were the stylings stressed in his family, since his father was a traveling evangelist. When Billy became old enough to learn to play the piano he was pressed into service to help out at his parents' prayer meetings. After a while, though, his tastes changed and he switched from piano to saxophone and was soon working with bands that played honky-tonks all over the southern states.

Among the places Sherrill and his band worked in the late 1950s and early 1960s was the Jinmachi Club in Fort Campbell, Kentucky. The prayer-meeting atmosphere he was accustomed to was a thing of the past. The first night his group took the stage there, an altercation broke out and one man was killed.

After a while, he got tired of the life on the road and moved to Nashville to work in some of the other phases of the business. In addition to writing original material, he got a job working for the Nashville recording studios of Sam Phillips. Phillips had founded Sun Records in Memphis, whose alumni included such greats as Elvis Presley, Johnny Cash, and Jerry Lee Lewis. With Phillips' organization, Sherrill learned the ropes of recording and producing and before long his work attracted attention from other record operations. In the mid-1960s, he joined Epic Records and started an association that was to last for the rest of the 1960s and into the 1980s.

He was soon working with the relatively few country artists then on the Epic label. One of them was a promising newcomer from Louisiana named David Houston. Among the songs Billy suggested Houston record was one Billy had written with a friend named Glenn Sutton (who was still co-writing songs with him at the start of the 1980s) called "Almost Persuaded." The number was recorded as the "B" side of an upcoming Houston single. The "B" side, though, turned out to be the winner, capturing a steadily growing number of airplays in 1966 and becoming one of the

major country hits of the year. It made Houston a star and began a string of successes for Sherrill still going strong fourteen years later.

As the 1960s went by, Sherrill added more and more names to the artists whose production chores he handled. Among them was Barbara Mandrell, who made many noteworthy duets with David Houston, Andy Griffith, Charlie Walker, and, in the late 1960s, an artist whose career never had achieved the luster expected, Charlie Rich. For a number of years, although Sherrill and Rich kept striving for new, striking recordings, the stature of the Arkansas singer-pianist-songwriter remained relatively constant. Rich sometimes got discouraged, but Sherrill remained confident. Finally, in the early 1970s, Rich's fortunes started to take a turn for the better. Then Sherrill found Charlie a song titled "Behind Closed Doors" that became one of the major hits of 1974. The song reached number one on country charts and rose to top levels of the pop charts. The same thing happened to the Behind Closed Doors album Sherrill produced and the followup LP, Very Special Love Song. The title song from the latter album, written by Sherrill and Norro Wilson, was a top-10 hit in May 1974.

Even as Sherrill was helping to rejuvenate Charlie's career, he was working with a new young singer named Tanya Tucker. With the material he chose and his production expertise, Tanya soon was considered one of the top-10 female country singers even as Rich held similar honors among male artists.

As the mid- and late-1970s went by, it was rare that a song written or co-written by Sherrill was absent from the hit charts. In 1976, for instance, Johnny Paycheck clicked with "11 Months and 29 Days," co-written by Sherrill and Paycheck. Soon after, Tammy Wynette had a hit with "You and Me," in a top-chart position in September 1976 and co-written by Billy and G. Richey. Other top-10 or top-20 chartmakers in the late 1970s were "Southern California," recorded by Tammy Wynette and George Jones and written by Sherrill, Richey, and R. Bowling (on the charts in the summer of 1977); "Baby, I

Love You So," on the charts at the same time, recorded by Joe Stampley and written by Sherrill and Norro Wilson; "One of a Kind," top 10 for Tammy Wynette in November 1977, co-written by Sherrill and S. Davis; "Beautiful Woman," by Sherrill, S. Davis, and N. Wilson, a hit for Charlie Rich in mid-1978; "Hello Mexico," top 10 for Johnny Duncan in September 1978 (by Sherrill, S. Davis, and Glenn Sutton); "Friend, Lover, Wife," top 10 for Paycheck in December 1978, by Sherrill and Paycheck; "Please Don't Play a Love Song," top 10 for Marty Robbins in late 1978, by Sherrill and S. Davis.

Among the well over a hundred other songs Sherrill arranged, wrote, or co-wrote over the years were "After Closing Time," "Already It's Heaven," "Another Lonely Song," "Baby's Come Home," "Brown Sugar," "Crying Steel Guitar," "The Day That Love Walked In," "Faith," "Gonna Go Down," "Good Lovin' Makes It Right," "Honey Let Me Be," "I Left Your Bags at the Honky Tonk," "I Wish I Had a Mommy like You," "Jamaica Blue," "Lighter Shade of Blue," "One More Chance," "Rock and Roll Teenager," "Rules of the Game," "Stand By Your Man," "Tia Maria," "Sugar Lips," "There's a Song on the Jukebox," "Tipsy," "The Ways to Love a Man," "Wonders of the Wine," and "Your Elusive Dreams."

In the mid-1970s, the artists produced by Billy included, (besides Charlie Rich, George Jones, Tammy Wynette, and Johnny Paycheck), Barbara Fairchild, the late Bob Luman, Brenda Smith, Jody Miller, Troy Seals, and Steve Davis. Others he produced over the years included Freddy Weller, Gene Austin, Avant-Garde, Stan Hitchcock, Lois Johnson, Debbie Lori Kaye, Kris Kristofferson, Jim & Jesse McReynolds, Nashville Strings, Patti Page, Jimmy Payne, Peaches & Herb, the Poppies, Sandy Posey, Pozo Seco, Vivian Reed, Shel Silverstein, Jerry Vale, Bobby Vinton, Charlie Walker, Chuck Woolery, Otis Williams, Merle Kilgore, Nancy Ames, the Staple Singers, Ted Taylor, Goldberg Blues Band, Glenn Sutton, and Vicky Fletcher.

In the mid-1970s, Sherrill ranked as one of the most respected producers and innovators in the country field. His title at CBS Records by then was Vice President, Artists & Repertoire, Nashville office.

SIEBEL, PAUL: *Singer, guitarist, fiddler, songwriter. Born Attica, New York, early 1940s.*

A sensitive songwriter, a fine balladeer in the folk-country-blues tradition of Dylan, Kristofferson, and even the early king of country music, Jimmie Rodgers, Paul Siebel had a lot going for him, except timing. He came along just after the folk boom of the late 1950s and early 1960s had peaked and so never got the attention his talents seemed to deserve.

Though he loved the work of country greats like Rodgers, Hank Williams, and Hank Snow and wrote a number of songs on country & western topics ("Pinto Pony," "Nashville Again"), his roots were in the North. He was born and raised on a farm in Attica, a town in upstate New York not far from Buffalo. His first exposure to music took the form of classical violin lessons when he was still a small child. As a teenager, he became interested in folk and country music and learned to play the guitar, singing traditional folk songs, tunes of Woody Guthrie, and songs made famous by Jimmie Rodgers and Hank Williams.

Siebel started to perform in small clubs and coffee houses in Buffalo when he was drafted; he spent two years in the armed forces. After his discharge, he headed for New York in 1963, where he worked in a baby carriage factory in Brooklyn and became a part of the Greenwich Village folk scene nights and weekends. Part of the time, he added to his income by singing in Village "basket houses," so called because the basket was passed around for contributions from the audience.

In 1966, Paul began to supplement his country and folk repertoire with original compositions. Among the songs that he penned in the mid-1960s were "Louise," the sympathetic story of a truck-stop prostitute, "The Ballad of Honest Sam," a satirical look at politicians, and perhaps his best-known piece, "Any Day Woman." The lyrics of the latter demonstrate his understanding of the human condition ("If you don't love her/Better let her go/You'll never feel her/You're bound to let it show/Love's so hard to take/When you have to fake/Everything in return").

Songs like that helped make him a favorite with Boston folk fanciers in the mid- and late-1960s. Though he achieved a considerable reputation locally, his name remained unfamiliar outside the East. As the 1960s drew to a close, he became part of the movement among many folk/country and rock artists to Woodstock, New York, joining such well-established artists as Dylan and The Band in residence there.

Still, as the 1970s began Siebel remained obscure, partly because he had never been given a contract by a major record firm. It looked as though this would at last be remedied when Elektra signed him. His debut LP on the label, *Woodsmoke and Oranges,* won strong approval from all sides in 1970. *Rolling Stone* magazine called it a milestone event in country/rock/pop. The effort illustrated the force and flexibility of his vocal style and his story-telling talents in tracks such as "Nashville Again" and "She Made Me Lose My Blues," in which he displayed yodeling skills that would have made Jimmie Rodgers proud.

He followed up with another highly satisfying collection in his second album, *Jackknife Gypsy.* The title song showed that Siebel could handle the folk-rock idiom well when he wanted to, while other tracks extended over a range of folk and country stylings, such as the western-oriented "Pinto Pony" and "Legend of the Captain's Daughter," which included fiddle backing by Doug Kershaw in the Cajun-flavored number. The album included such other excellent originals as "Prayer Song," "Jasper and the Miner," and "Hillbilly Child."

More encomiums resulted, such as this glowing tribute by Ellen Sander in *Saturday Review* (January 30, 1971): "His writing is precise, tight and full of images that appear in a phrase, develop into flesh and feeling and flash through changes that live throughout the song. . . . After Siebel finishes his musical novelette, one is left with a dramatic impression of a brief lifetime having passed, its every aspect explored,

the net result established, played and gone."

Despite many deserved tributes of that nature, Siebel did not break through to the mass audience, partly because of his own reluctance to endure the grind of continuous concertizing. He noted in 1971, "If I go on tour and make $40,000 a year and live in motels, what will I have after it's over?" That he could do well touring was indicated when he opened one show for The Band in California and won a standing ovation from the crowd. However, Siebel drew back from heavy touring in the mid- and late-1970s. He continued to make appearances at folk clubs in various parts of the country, but this low profile kept his name from wider prominence despite his high standing with other artists.

During the 1970s, many of his songs were performed by singers from diverse parts of the pop spectrum. Bonnie Raitt, for instance, recorded a number of Siebel's compositions (as did Linda Ronstadt) and often spotlighted "Any Day Woman" in her concerts.

SILVERSTEIN, SHEL: *Singer, songwriter, poet, cartoonist. Born Chicago, Illinois, 1932.*

Looking something like a cross between Mr. Clean and a character from the Arabian Nights, Shel Silverstein is an unlikely candidate for country-music fame. Adding to the confusion are his many vocations—poet, author, and, prominently, cartoonist. Yet when he turned his attention to music, whether pop, folk, or country, he proved to be as deft as in his other activities.

He demonstrated an excellent talent as a humorist and artist in his youth and, when he went into the U.S. Army, soon became a staff artist for the service's *Stars and Stripes* magazine. Back in civilian life in the mid-1950s, he rapidly built up a reputation as a cartoonist, contributing to the pages of the first issues of *Playboy,* an association that lasted into the 1970s. His cartoons appeared in dozens of other publications from the early 1950s into the 1970s. One of his best-known series appeared in *Time* magazine starting in 1967, with the running title "Now Here's My Plan."

Creatively restless, he always was looking for other fields to conquer. When the folk boom came along, Silverstein took an active part as a singer and writer. In 1961, he completed an album called *Inside Folk Song* whose contents included a song still often played by folk artists, "The Unicorn Song." During the 1960s he turned out varied material, ranging from comic country songs like the Johnny Cash hit "A Boy Named Sue" to love ballads and satiric material. Some of his efforts were included in his Cadet LP, *Shel Silverstein*, released in August 1967.

He also was represented on book lists in the 1960s with such offerings as a collection of some of his cartoons, *Grab My Box*, and an illustrated children's book, *Uncle Shelby's ABC*. He was starting to lose interest in his artwork, though. As he told Chris Van Ness of the L.A. *Free Press* in 1972, "The drawing got painful. It just got to be no fun. When the thing you do best stops being fun, it just puts you through such terrible changes. I don't miss it; since it's no fun. I don't miss it. But you start thinking about what you are and who you are and you really have to look at yourself as a person rather than an artist."

Luckily he found the energy to try again. The result was the 1972 children's book classic, *The Giving Tree*, and other books as well. His 1960s and 1970s output, besides the titles noted above, included *Lafcadio, the Lion Who Shot Back, Uncle Shelby's Zoo, Don't Bump the Glump*, and *Where the Sidewalk Ends*.

At the start of the 1970s, Shel helped propel a previously unknown bar band called Dr. Hook and the Medicine Show to national attention. It proved an excellent association, since the country-rock-oriented Dr. Hook's members were as zany in their own way as Silverstein.

Recalling the way the relationship came about, Dr. Hook vocalist Dennis Locorriere said, "We were playing this bar in New Jersey and one time we gave a guy who said he had contacts a demo tape of two of our songs and one of Bob Dylan's. He met an acquaintance in an elevator in New York and told him, 'I've got this group in New Jersey who are too crazy for me' and gave him the tape. The other guy was mu-

sic director of the movie *Who Is Harry Kellerman, and Why Is He Saying All Those Terrible Things About Me?* He liked us and fought to have us record the soundtrack. Shel was signed to do the score so that's how we got together." * (Silverstein previously had scored the film *Ned Kelly*.) One result was the fine soundtrack song "The Last Morning."

After that Silverstein provided all the songs for the group's early albums on Columbia. Those included such chartmakers as "Sylvia's Mother" and the 1973 smash, "Cover of the Rolling Stone." A takeoff on the song by Buck Owens with the title changed to "Cover of the Music City News" was a country chart hit as well. One of Shel's best songs for Dr. Hook was "Sing Me a Rainbow."

After Dr. Hook was well launched, Silverstein turned his sights on other efforts to a great extent, though he still turned out material with band members from time to time. As Ray Sawyer of Dr. Hook said in 1979, "For us, Shel will always be there." Locorriere added, "We write with him now when we see him, 'cause he travels a lot. Shel's the kind of guy who'll go to the bathroom saying 'I'll see you in a moment' and you won't see him until five years later." *

During the 1970s, Silverstein continued to turn out solo albums from time to time, including *Freaker's Ball* on Columbia in 1972 and another LP in 1978. Many of his compositions were comic or satiric, as evidenced by such titles from *Freaker's Ball* as "Sarah Stout Won't Take the Garbage Out" and "Don't Give a Dose to the One You Love Most" (the latter a song used in several anti-VD campaigns).

All the while, though, he continued to turn out somewhat more conventional songs that found favor with country artists and audiences. Examples are "Queen of the Silver Dollar," the first big hit for Dave and Sugar in late 1975–early 1976, "The Winner," a top-20 success for Bobby Bare in the early summer of 1976, and the late summer 1976 hit for Dr. Hook, "A Couple

* *From an interview with Irwin Stambler.*

671

More Years" (co-written with Dennis Locorriere).

His association with Bobby Bare in the mid- and late-1970s was as close as his early years with Dr. Hook. The two collaborated on what was claimed to be "the first concept album in modern country music," the two-record 1975 release, *Bobby Bare Sings Lullabies, Legends and Lies*. Among the Silverstein compositions Bare placed on the singles charts were "Sylvia's Mother" (1972); "Daddy," "What If," and "Marie Laveau" (both 1974); "Alimony" (1975); "The Winner," "Put a Little Lovin' on Me" (1976); and "Redneck Hippie Romance" (1977).

At the start of the 1980s, Shel was still pursuing his mixture of creative efforts. One of his projects was a new children's book, *A Light in the Attic*, issued by Harper & Row in the fall of 1981.

SIMON, PAUL: *Singer, guitarist, songwriter, actor, record producer. Born Queens, New York, October 13, 1941.*

The team of Simon & Garfunkel indisputably was one of the premiere acts of the 1960s. Despite the fact that the duo's songs primarily were in what might be called a contemporary folk vein with any rock touches essentially secondary, the team vied with the best of the rock bands for mass audience attention and respect. Thus it was not surprising that there were many cries of alarm when the team broke up soon after its wondrously fine song and album, *Bridge Over Troubled Waters*, came out. Fortunately, both Simon and Garfunkel proved as capable of sustaining individual careers as working in harness.

There were some harsh words said when the split occurred, particularly by Simon, who claimed in a *Rolling Stone* interview that one reason he hastened the event was the feeling that he was the main creative force in the partnership. Another contributing factor, though, was Garfunkel's increasing desire to further his acting activities. But perhaps the primary reason was simply that the two had been together too long, having formed their initial association when both were teenagers in Long Island. As Tom and Jerry, they had their first taste of success in 1956–57 with the rock hit "Hey Schoolgirl." After an interval, they came back in the 1960s to place hit after hit on U.S. and international pop lists and were bestowed with the accompanying popularity that kept them on the move for much of each year playing sold-out concerts all over the United States and the world.

It's not surprising that all the pressures involved finally caused a coolness between the two friends. By 1973, though, with his solo career well established, Simon could take a more well rounded view of the matter. He told Robert Hilburn of the *Los Angeles Times* (May 27, 1973, Calendar section), "Some people thought it was unnecessary to say some of those things. But that's how I felt. I do think there is no question that I was angry when I said that, but I don't think I exaggerated too much.

"What I didn't do that I should have done was to say how good Artie is. I said what I thought he didn't do, but I didn't say, for instance, 'Here's a guy who had one of the finest voices in popular music, who has a very intelligent mind, who was enthusiastic about his work . . . and who offered very useful ideas.' I didn't emphasize his legitimate strengths.

"I wasn't feeling very friendly toward him [then]. The anger was a reflection of the tensions we had gone through during the making of *Bridge*. We both said this is ridiculous. If it is this hard to make an album, this should be the last album. It was very tense."

That album, of course, and the single from it, were the main stories of the 1970 Grammy Awards, but soon after, the word came out that the duo was going separate ways. There was both anticipation and worries as Paul prepared his solo debut on Columbia. But fears quickly were put to rest when *Paul Simon* came out in February 1972. The album was one of the year's finest, with Paul reaffirming his skill as one of the great lyricists and melodists of his era. The LP easily earned a gold record and provided several singles hits, including the top-10 "Me and Julio Down by the Schoolyard." His next album, *There Goes Rhymin' Simon* (released in spring 1973) proved even better, providing a series of memorable songs that included "Kodachrome," "American Tune," the gospel-rock "She Loves Me like a Rock," "Was a Sunny Day," and the unusual "Take Me to the Mardi Gras," which blended Dixieland and reggae.

The themes in the album ranged from a relaxed evaluation of memory's tricks when it comes to romance ("Kodachrome") to a solemn assessment of the United States in the early 1960s ("American Tune"). His lyrics, as always, verged on the poetic: "If you took all the girls I knew/When I was single/And brought them all together/For one night/I know they'd never match/My sweet imagination/Everything looks worse/In black and white" (from "Kodachrome"), or "We came on the ship/They call the Mayflower/We come on the ship that sailed the moon/We come in the age's most uncertain hour/And sing an American tune" (from "American Tune").

In the spring of 1973, Paul made his first concert tour of the United States since his rift with Garfunkel. He felt he couldn't fill huge auditoriums on his own, so he stuck to smaller venues of 3,000 to 5,000 seats or less. It was a case of too much humility. Tickets for the concerts were snapped up almost as soon as they went on sale and there probably were enough disappointed fans to fill any hall Simon & Garfunkel had played in years past. One of the products of the tour was a live album, *Live Rhymin'*, that was a bestseller in line with his first two efforts.

Because of Paul's perfectionist attitude about his work, there was a close to two-year wait before Simon fans could buy a new studio LP. When it arrived in the fall of 1975, it proved another gem. Called *Still Crazy After All These Years*, it offered a letter-perfect collection of Simon songs, including such hits as the title track and the equally potent "Fifty Ways to Lose a Lover." The LP earned a gold record on November 17, 1975, on the way to platinum levels.

At the Grammy Awards in early 1976, that effort gained Simon two Grammies, one for Album of the Year and the other

for Best Pop Vocal Performance, Male. In accepting one of them in person, Paul joked about the fact that the main reason he won was the absence of new releases from Stevie Wonder, saying "I want to thank Stevie Wonder for not having a new album out this year."

With those two victories, he could point to a total of nine Grammies won over his career, the others going back to his days with Garfunkel. Of that total, five were for various aspects of *Bridge Over Troubled Water* (1970), one for Record of the Year in 1968 (*Mrs. Robinson*), and another in 1968 for the same release, for Best Vocal Performance, Male Duo.

In the late 1970s, disputes arose between Simon and Columbia Records that caused a long delay in the next phase of his career. After a long legal wrangle, Simon ended his association with Columbia and, in 1979, signed a new agreement with Warner Brothers. In the interim, Columbia had issued a retrospective album of his solo work in the 1970s, *Greatest Hits, Etc.*

In 1980, Paul's first album on Warner Brothers, *One Trick Pony*, was released and had earned a gold record award by year end. It remained on the charts into 1981. In the summer of 1981, Simon was reunited with Art Garfunkel and the two gave a memorable free concert before an estimated half million people in New York's Central Park.

As Simon had noted earlier to Robert Hilburn, he sometimes was plagued with self doubts about his ability to create viable new material. "I'm neurotically driven. It has always been that way. What happens is I finish one thing and start to take a vacation. I lay off for a while and then I get panicky. . . . I say to myself, 'Oh my God, I'm not doing anything. I can't write anymore. It's over.' All that kind of thing. . . . Then I laugh and tell myself, 'Don't be silly. This is exactly what happens every time you finish an album. So, of course, you write again.'

"And so I continue to take it easy for a while. I don't write for a while longer and then I say, 'Hey, this is no kidding. You're really not writing now.' And somewhere along the line, I really believe I'm not going to write again and I get panicky and start to write. I don't want to think that I peaked in my twenties. There is so much more time ahead."

SKY, PATRICK: *Singer, guitarist, banjoist, harmonica player, mouth-bow player, songwriter, author. Born Liveoak Gardens, Georgia, October 2, 1940.*

Though not too well known by the end of the 1970s, and represented by only a handful of recordings from the mid-1960s to the start of the 1980s, Patrick Sky had an important influence on folk music. Many of his songs became staple items in the folk music repertoire of other artists and his knowledge of folk music and willingness to impart it to others played a role in the success of artists like Buffy Sainte-Marie.

Patrick "Pat" Sky was born in Georgia but spent most of his youth in the La-Fouche Swamp region of Louisiana, where some of his ancestry, Cree Indian, originated. He was exposed to folk and country & western influences from his earliest years, playing the banjo, guitar, and harmonica before he was in his teens. Many of the songs in his concerts of the 1960s and 1970s were traditional songs his grandmother had taught him as a child.

After performing in his home area for a few years, Pat went on to college, spent some years in the Army, and then, after leaving the service, decided to concentrate on music. In the early 1960s, he began to sing in small clubs and coffee houses in various parts of the country. In time, he moved on to New York, the center of folk music activity in the 1960s.

There he soon won over the Greenwich Village folk fans and also became friends with many of the promising folk artists thronging the Village and other parts of the city. As his popularity increased, so did the interest of recording firms, resulting in a contract from Vanguard in late 1964. His Vanguard debut, *Patrick Sky*, came out in the summer of 1965 and won immediate critical acclaim. *HiFi/Stereo Review* called the LP "very good" and the performance "infectious." Among the songs included were "Everytime," "Hangin'

Round," "Come With Me," "Love," and "Many a Mile."

The last of these was one of a number of original Sky songs on the album. It also was a song on the way to becoming a classic in the modern folk idiom. His friend Buffy Sainte-Marie used it as the title song for one of her albums. She also included it and other Sky compositions in her concerts, appearances that also featured her use of the mouth-bow. Sky had begun using that primitive Indian instrument in his act, having recreated its design and use from his knowledge of his Cree Indian heritage. He, in turn, coached Buffy in mouth-bow technique. Among his other original songs that have been and are being used by other folk artists are "Separation Blues," "Hangin' Round," "Nectar of God," and "Love Will Endure."

Sky's second album on Vanguard, *Harvest of Gentle Clang*, came out in September 1965. Though an interesting album, it didn't have much of an impact on the increasingly rock-oriented audience. Pat left Vanguard and made two albums on the MGM label in the late 1960s. His last 1960s release came out on Verve/Forecast Records in August 1969.

Although he was active in music in the 1970s, Pat's concentration on traditional music sharply limited his potential audience. He gave occasional folk concerts, made a few recordings, and spent part of his time building Irish uilleann pipes (which he also played expertly). In 1972, he released the album *Songs That Made America Famous* on his own label, Rainbow Collection. He did that, he said, because the lyrics (which satirized many aspects of American life) were too outspoken and vulgar for a major label to accept them. Later in the 1970s, he completed an album of traditional folk music issued on the Leviathan label titled *Two Steps Forward—One Step Back*.

SMITH, ARTHUR: *Singer, guitarist, band leader, songwriter, producer of package music shows, music publisher, business executive. Born Clinton, South Carolina, April 1, 1921.*

You might not think of the name Arthur Smith in connection with the 1973 movie hit *Deliverance* or its theme song, "Duelin' Banjos." In fact, the name escaped the people who incorporated the song into the project, but "Duelin' Banjos" didn't escape Smith's notice. Though it took two years of legal action, he proved that he and musician Don Reno had written the song and the court awarded him not only equitable royalties but the right to the award that named the tune Best Country Music Song of 1973. Of course, it wasn't the first time in a long and generally extremely successful career that Smith had fought for his rights and won. Over the years, with great energy and an iron will, he had carved out a niche for himself as performer, songwriter, and entertainment industry giant who, by the end of the 1970s had been one of the United States' largest producers of syndicated radio shows for many years.

Born in Clinton, South Carolina, his family moved to Kershaw when he was four. His father was a loom fixer in a textile mill, but his sparetime interest was in music. Smith recalled, "My father ran the town band and we always had a room full of instruments. I used to play trumpet when the band played in Kershaw on Sundays."

When only in eighth grade Arthur started a country band with two brothers, Ralph and Sonny, who after two years recorded some sides for a major record firm. Arthur, ever the spark plug, had opted for a music career after his high school graduation in the late 1930s, even though he was an A student (president and class valedictorian) with scholarship offers from Wofford College, the Citadel, and an appointment to the U.S. Naval Academy. Dixieland jazz was then his heart's calling and he didn't want to miss the chance to have a fifteen minute program on station WSPA in Spartanburg, South Carolina.

The group he assembled with his brothers, the Crackerjacks, found the going rough. "We nearly starved to death playing Dixieland," Smith noted. Still, it took World War II to end the program. His brothers joined the services and Arthur moved on, for a time, to a solo job on WBT in Charlotte. Arthur entered the Navy in 1944, serving with the Navy Band

and working in the Personnel Bureau in Washington. He made those years pay off musically thanks to his continued effort at songwriting. His composition "Guitar Boogie," which he recorded on MGM Records, became a major hit, the biggest of his recording career. It eventually sold over 3 million copies. The resulting royalties, helped him to "get going financially. Business has always intrigued me. I started out investing here and there in real estate and stocks and one thing led to another."

After the war, Arthur plunged into the music field, moving in several directions. Besides reorganizing his own act, he began to recruit others and soon was putting together variety shows for station WBT radio and WBT-TV in Charlotte, North Carolina. It was a logical step from there to packaging shows for live engagements throughout the South and for presentations on other radio and TV stations. Those shows, which rapidly became among the most popular grass roots music packages of the 1950s, blended traditional and popular country-artists and material. Gospel and hymn singing was an integral part of the format, reflecting Arthur Smith's deep religious grounding. In 1947, he started teaching Bible classes and was still somehow finding time for that in his busy schedule decades later when his enterprises spread far beyond the music field.

Over the years, the format of the Arthur Smith Shows remained flexible, attracting all types of noted individuals. During the 1950s and 1960s, for instance, people from outside the country-music field who were guests included Richard Nixon, the Rev. Billy Graham, actor E. G. Marshall, and the sophisticated piano team of Ferrante and Teicher. Of course, almost every well-known country artist was presented, a situation which still held true into the 1970s when some of the stars included Johnny Cash, Charlie McCoy, Jimmy Dean, and Red Sovine, to name just a few. A feature of the 1970s was a segment called Bluegrass Corner, where the spotlight fell at one time or another on performers like the Osborne Brothers, Earl Scruggs, and Bill Monroe.

Not a few of the songs played on Smith's shows from time to time were his own. Among his credits were such numbers as "Banjo Buster," "I Saw a Man," "Feudin' Banjos" (of which more later), and "Shadow of the Cross." Writing religious songs always was a major interest of Smith and, of the more than 200 songs he had written or co-written by the 1970s, over a quarter were hymns or gospels. His religious writings brought many awards from church organizations over the decades.

Smith, an accomplished instrumentalist on both guitar and mandolin, continued to be active as performer and recording artist in the 1950s and 1960s. His 1960s record releases included *Arthur Smith and the Crossroads Quartet* in 1962 on Starday, *Arthur Smith* on Hamilton (1964), and a number of recordings prepared in his own studios in Charlotte, including the single "Jet Set" in the mid-1960s issued on the Dot label. In the gospel field, the Crossroads Quartet, organized by Smith soon after his Navy hitch, ranked as one of the best. The group's recording efforts as of the late 1960s included three albums of favorite old hymns.

The name Crackerjacks was assumed by Smith's main secular group on his show, though it no longer was a Dixieland band. Among main members of the group were brother Ralph, instrumentalists Tommy Faile (added in 1950) and Wayne "Skeeter" Hass (added in 1953), and five-string banjo ace Carl "Happy" Hunt. Faile and Ralph Smith joined forces to do comedy sketches under such names as "The Radio Twins," "Brother Ralph and Cousin Fudd," and "The Counselors of the Airways."

Though his own show remained his prime concern, Arthur Smith and his organization produced many other major shows over the years. Among them were *Johnny Cash*, the *James Brown Show*, *Flatt & Scruggs*, and George Beverly Shea's *Hymntime*.

Smith's empire as of the late 1970s, besides the *Arthur Smith* television show, included the Arthur Smith Studio, where activities embraced production of records, radio shows, and commercials, a music publishing firm, Clay Music Co., and various other investments. Among his holdings were shares of Mutual Hardware Insurance Co., operating in nine southeastern states, of which he was a director and investment board member. At one stage of his career, he started the Arthur Smith Inns Corporation and a chain of supermarkets, though by the late 1970s he had sold those interests. The TV show's popularity had grown slowly but steadily over the years; by the mid-1970s it was being shown in 31 cities across the United States.

Shortly after the film *Deliverance* was released, Smith entered a legal action against Warner Brothers over the song "Duelin' Banjos." The number, he claimed, was actually a composition he and another musician, Don Reno, had devised in 1955. In that composition, called "Feudin' Banjos," Smith had played tenor banjo and Reno five-string banjo. "The whole idea was two banjos feuding." After a two-year battle, Smith won, the settlement awarding him close to $200,000, half of all future royalties from the *Deliverance* arrangement, and undisputed royalties for him and his publisher, Combine Music Corporation, on all future recordings of the song. Perhaps most rewarding for him was the conveyance of the 1973 award naming "Duelin' Banjos" Best Country Music Song of the Year.

SMITH, CAL: *Singer, guitarist, band leader. Born Sabbiaw, Oklahoma, April 7, 1932.*

There might have been some confusion among casual country fans in the 1970s about whether Cal Smith was a misspelling of long-time star Carl Smith's name. But there was no doubt in the devoted country fan's mind that these were two individuals, alike in the fact that both were keystones of country music, but certainly different in style and approach. Cal Smith's deep-pitched voice wouldn't be mistaken for Carl's higher register nor did Cal have the writing ability of Carl.

In fact, Cal realized relatively early in his career that he was an interpreter rather than originator. He told Sharon Rowlett of the *Rocky Mountain Musical Express* for a May 1978 article, "You know, a while back my wife was putting together pictures and clippings we've accumulated on the road.

She ran across some papers and started reading. It was songs I'd started writing a long time ago. They were bad. I mean they were awful. I told her to throw them in the fireplace, but she said, 'No, papa, I want to keep them!' I found out I wasn't a songwriter so I just quit writing."

But he never gave up singing and playing country music, an obsession all his life. He told Rowlett that he had received support from his parents. "They knew I was going after music 'cause I've been crazy about music ever since I could walk. Momma and Daddy always supported me any way I wanted to go. The way they looked at it, they'd rather I be playing in a beer joint than out on the streets getting in trouble. 'Course I was a hot-headed little devil and I was into fights about half the time, but there I was less likely to be getting into jail. When I started in the music business, my folks was right with me."

Smith could play reasonably competent guitar before he was high school age and already had many hours as a working musician under his belt before he was out of his teens. His professional debut took place when he was fifteen, he told Rowlett, "in a little place called 'The Remember Me Cafe.' They served dinners. Actually, all it was was a beer joint, but they had a little old place off to one side where they served dinners. Most of the people around there worked in the vineyards and they'd be too tired to cook supper so they'd come down there at night and guzzle beer. When they got through eating, a boy named Jim Rice and me played music. [Their pay was $1.50 a night plus food.] Since we got $1.50, I had to make it up by eating."

That initial pay was symbolic of what was to be Smith's lot for many years. Throughout the 1950s, he worked as often as he could in music, but rarely could get enough income to support himself. To make ends meet, he worked at a wide variety of jobs including truck driver and steel mill worker. His first wife wanted him to give up music in favor of a steady living. "She gave me a choice of her or my music. I'm still playing my music." However, his second marriage in the late 1950s was going strong two decades later.

Cal also had some jobs as a disc jockey during the 1950s and spent a while in the U.S. armed forces. But no matter where he was, he kept singing and pickin' and, finally, things began to turn in his favor. Cal was performing in a group in the San Jose, California, area with a musician named Bill Drake, who had a brother, Jack, in Ernest Tubb's Texas Troubadours. When Tubb played San Jose, Cal got to meet Jack and Ernest, which led to his auditioning for the group. Soon Smith was touring the United States as a permanent member of that famous band. The Troubadours appeared not only on network radio and TV shows, but on the stage of the *Grand Ole Opry* in Nashville.

In the mid-1960s, he got the chance to sign with Kapp Records, which turned out such albums of his as *All the World, Goin' to Cal's Place* (issued in October 1967) and *The Best of Cal Smith*. He began to receive some attention from country fans in the late 1960s, though not enough to make him a household name. The Smith that often dominated the top-chart levels during those years was the one called Carl. By the start of the 1970s, he was represented on the Decca label, on which he had such releases as the 1972 charted single, "For My Baby."

Cal's long pursuit of artistic recognition finally paid off in the early 1970s after Decca merged with MCA Records. He turned out several promising releases before really hitting paydirt with a song called "Country Bumpkin" in 1974. The song (written by Don Wayne) rose to number one on country charts and, when it came time for Country Music Awards earned a nomination for Single of the Year, Song of the Year, and, in the Album of the Year category, the LP of that title (also a bestseller) was included in the finalists. The LP honors went to Charlie Rich, but the other two awards were for Cal and Don Wayne.

For the next few years, Smith's name often showed up on country charts, often in the top levels. In early 1975, he had the top-10 single "It's Time to Pay the Fiddler." In June 1975, he again had a top-10 hit with "She Talked a Lot About Texas" and finished out the year with the hit single "Jason's Farm." In early 1976, he had the single "Thunderstorms" on the charts and in 1977 made the lists with "Helen" and "Throwin' Memories on the Fire." His charted MCA singles the last part of the decade included "Bits and Pieces of My Life" in 1978 and, in 1979, "The Rise and Fall of the Roman Empire." However, his MCA material no longer made upper-chart levels and, in the early 1980s, he and the label parted company.

SMITH, CARL: *Singer, guitarist. Born Maynardsville, Tennessee, March 15, 1927.*

One of the most successful country & western performers of the 1950s and 1960s, Carl Smith got his start cutting grass. At least, it was through the proceeds from this activity that young Carl was able to pay for his guitar lessons in his home town of Maynardsville. By the time he was thirteen, he felt he was ready to try his hand in an amateur talent contest; the crowd obviously felt the same way. It was then that Carl decided he wanted to become a country & western performer.

A few years later, he got his first big chance in Knoxville. One of the regular performers on station WROL needed a replacement and Carl subbed for him. His work was good enough to win him a regular job on the station. After an interruption of eighteen months in the armed services, he got his discharge and returned to WROL in the late 1940s. For a while he decided to expand his horizons by appearing on other stations, including one in Augusta, Georgia, and another in Asheville, North Carolina.

In the end, though, WROL remained his good luck charm. He returned there to work with Mollie O'Day and Archie Campbell. Audience acceptance was strong, and Carl's reputation increased to the point of winning him a bid to join the *Grand Ole Opry*. His debut came in 1950, and within a short time he was one of the most popular personalities.

Along with the *Opry* job came a contract with Columbia Records. One of his first discs, "Let's Live a Little," was one of the major hits of 1951. For the next decade, it was a rare week when a Carl Smith record

was not high on the charts. He added two more hits in 1951, "If Teardrops Were Pennies" and "Mr. Moon." His 1952 output included four major hits: the number-one-rated "Just Don't Stand There," "Are You Teasing Me," "It's a Lovely, Lovely World," and "Our Honeymoon." The following year, Carl gained number-one chart position for a second time with "Hey Joe." Other 1953 hits were "Satisfaction Guaranteed," "This Orchid Means Goodbye," and "Trademark." In 1954, Smith had best-sellers in "Love" and "Loose Talk." The latter was number one on the hit charts for more than thirty weeks. It won Carl *Billboard's* Triple Crown award and *Down Beat* magazine's Best New Western Band of the Year award. Other major hits included "Kisses Don't Lie" and "There She Goes" (1955); "Why Why" (1957); "Your Name Is Beautiful" (1958); "Ten Thousand Drums" (1959); and "Foggy River" (1960).

Through the 1960s, Carl was featured in person and on TV and radio around the world. His tours took him to all states of the United States, all of Canada's provinces, and throughout Europe and the Far East. His TV guest spots included the *Porter Wagoner Show*, *Wilburn Brothers Show*, and the *Philip Morris Country Music Show*. In the mid-1960s, his weekly TV show—Carl Smith's *Country Music Hall*—was telecast coast-to-coast in Canada. During this period, he also appeared in two movies, *The Badge of Marshal Brennan* and *Buffalo Guns*.

In the 1960s, Smith and his talented wife, country songwriter Goldie Hill, resided with their three children on a large ranch near Nashville. As of the early 1980s Carl still called Nashville home.

Smith's album output in the 1950s and early 1960s included *Great Country and Western Hits; Easy to Please; Sunday Down South; Let's Live; Smith's the Name; Carl Smith's Touch;* and *Kentucky Derby*. Throughout the 1960s, he regularly turned out one or more LPs a year on Columbia, such as *Greatest Hits* (2/63); *Tall, Tall Gentleman* (12/63); *There Stands Glass* (6/64); *I Want to Live and Love* (3/65); *Kisses Don't Lie* (11/65); *Man with a Plan* (7/66); *Gentleman Sings* (3/67); *Carl Smith Sings His Favorites* (9/67);

and *Greatest Hits, Volume 2* (7/69). Carl also had several LPs on Harmony label in the 1960s, including *Best of Carl Smith* (10/64) and *Satisfaction Guaranteed* (6/67). Carl regularly placed singles releases on the charts all during the 1960s, though his percentage of top-10 successes didn't approach his 1950s output. In 1967, for instance, he had five singles on the charts, but none in the top 10. He finished up the decade in reasonably good style, making top-chart levels in 1968 with a remake of his 1960 hit, "Foggy River," and had two top-10 hits in 1969, "Faded Love and Winter Roses" and "Good Deal Lucille."

At the start of the 1970s, Carl wound up his twentieth year on Columbia Records, an event celebrated by release of the two-record *Anniversary Album*, issued in August 1970. Other Columbia LPs of the early 1970s included *I Love You Because* (3/70); *Carl Smith with Tunesmiths* (10/70); *Bluegrass* (5/71); *Don't Say You're Mine* (5/72); and *If This Is Goodbye*. He also was represented on the Harmony label with *Knee Deep in the Blues* (6/71). Among Carl's charted singles on Columbia in the early 1970s was "If This Is Goodbye" in the fall of 1972. It had a symbolic title, since Carl's long association with the label was coming to an end. He signed with Hickory Records and placed a number of singles on the charts, mostly on lower rungs, such as "The Way I Lose My Mind" in 1975 and "If You Don't, Somebody Else Will" in 1976.

Though his recording status waned in the 1970s, Carl remained a popular figure on the country-music concert circuit and also continued to be active as a radio and TV performer.

SMITH, CONNIE: *Singer, guitarist. Born Elkhart, Indiana, August 14, 1941.*

From a large family and on her way to having a large one of her own (she eventually had four, two boys and two girls), Connie Smith gave in to the urging of friends in early 1963 and entered a country-music talent contest. That event changed her career from homemaker to entertainer. She eventually became one of country music's foremost female vocalists.

Connie's hometown was Elkhart, In-diana, where she was one of fourteen children. Her interest in country music went back to her early years. She recalled, "I was bashful as a kid, but I remember clear back when I was five years old I'd say, 'Someday I'm gonna sing on the *Grand Ole Opry.*' Of course, I said it with a laugh, because I didn't want anyone to know just how much I wanted to."

Later on, an accident gave her inspiration to take another step toward her eventual performing role (though she didn't envision such a future at the time). While Connie was mowing the lawn as her contribution to family chores, the blades uprooted a rock and sent it back against her leg like a shot. She suffered injuries so severe, there even was fear she might lose her limb. During the long weeks in the hospital, she began to learn to play guitar to pass the time. As she grew older, she combined her guitar and vocal talents to take part in local shows and even gain some TV exposure.

Still, the idea of succeeding in music seemed only a dream to her. After she got married and settled down to raise a family in a midwestern town, show business seemed even more unattainable. But her feelings about it changed after some friends persuaded her to enter a talent contest at a park called Frontier Ranch near Columbus, Ohio. Smith won the contest, and among those who had seen the show was country star Bill Anderson, who came over to congratulate her.

About six months later, she went to one of his performances and went backstage to renew acquaintances. He invited her to come to Nashville to sing on his show and, when she did, provided her with the music to his composition "Walk on Backwards." That, in turn, led to his asking her to help with some demonstration tapes he was making in May 1964. Connie returned home and, soon after, got a call from Bill, who was on tour in Minneapolis. He had played the tapes for top agent Hubert Long, who had then gotten Chet Atkins to listen to them. The result was an arrangement whereby Anderson provided some new songs and Atkins arranged for RCA to sign Smith to a recording contract. The first single, "Once a Day," was released by RCA in August 1964. After a slow start, it began to move and by November was number one on country charts, where it stayed an amazing two and a half months. When the year was over, *Billboard* named her "Most Promising Country Female Singer of 1964," an honor she won in 1965 as well.

During 1965, she added three more top-10 hits to her credits, "I Can't Remember," "If I Talk to Him," and "Then and Then Only." Her status was improving so rapidly that on June 13, 1965, she was asked to become a cast regular on the *Grand Ole Opry*. In 1966, she kept right on rolling with such top-10 hits as "Ain't Had No Lovin' " and "Nobody but a Fool" and in 1967 made top-chart levels with "I'll Come a-Runnin'." In 1968, she had the top-10 hits "Runaway Little Tears" and "Baby's Back Again" plus such hit albums as *Soul of Country Music* and *I Love Charley Brown*. At the end of 1968, *Billboard* ranked her third-best female vocalist of the year behind Loretta Lynn and Lynn Anderson.

During the mid- and late-1960s, Smith starred on almost every major country TV show and many general variety programs, including *The Jimmy Dean Show, American Swing Around, Singin' Country, Ralph Emery, Bobby Lord Show*, and *Lawrence Welk*. In concert tours, she was featured on bills having such stars as Loretta Lynn, George Jones, Bill Anderson, George Morgan, Rex Allen, Jimmy Dean, and Sonny James. She appeared in several country films, including *Road to Nashville, Las Vegas Hillbillies*, and *Second Fiddle to a Steel Guitar*.

Her debut album on RCA, *Connie Smith*, came out in May 1965. This was rapidly followed by a series of releases including *Cute'n'Country* (12/65), *Connie Smith Goes to Nashville* (5/66), *Born to Sing* (11/66), *In the Country* (Camden, 4/67), *Connie Smith Sings Bill Anderson* (7/67), *Downtown* (3/67), *Best of Connie Smith* (11/67), *Soul of Country Music* (2/68), and *I Love Charley Brown* (mid-1968). Demonstrating her religious feelings, she recorded several albums of that kind, including *Great Sacred Songs*. She was active in some of the Reverend Billy

Graham's efforts, taking part in his programs at Expo '72.

Connie remained on the RCA Records roster into the early 1970s. Her singles hits included two top-10 discs in 1972, "Just What I Am" and "If It Ain't Love (Let's Leave It Alone)." Her early 1970s albums on RCA were *I Never Once Stopped Loving You* (10/70), *Where Is My Castle* (3/71), *Just One Time* (8/71), *Come Along and Walk with Me* (12/71), *City Lights, Country Favorites* (Camden, 4/72), *Ain't We Havin' Us a Good Time* (6/72), and *If It Ain't Love* (8/72).

In 1973, Smith departed RCA and signed a new contract with Columbia Records. Late in the year she had her first single hit on the new label, "Ain't Love a Good Thing," which entered the top 10 in early 1974. Later in the year, she had another chartmaker in "Dallas." She had many more charted singles on Columbia in the mid-1970s, including "Why Don't You Love Me" (top 15 in summer 1975), "The Song We Fell in Love To" (fall 1975), and, in 1976, "(Til) I Kissed You," "So Sad (To Watch Good Love Go Bad)," and "I Don't Wanna Talk It Over Anymore."

By 1977, Smith was recording for Monument records, turning out such charted singles as "I Just Wanna Be Your Everything" in 1977 and "Smooth Sailin' " in 1978. Monument issued her album *New Horizons* in early 1978.

At the start of the 1980s' she was still a regular cast member of the *Grand Ole Opry*.

SMITH, MARGO: *Singer, songwriter. Born Dayton, Ohio, April 9, 1942.*

Historically, the typical country singer, male and female, naturally came from a farm family or rural environment. Recently, indicative of the increasing urban tilt of the field, important artists have come from different settings, including a number of performers who started out as school teachers, examples being Donna Fargo and Margo Smith.

Margo, who grew up in Ohio, became interested in folk and country music early in life. After earning her teaching credentials, Betty Lou Smith, as she was known to her pupils, sometimes used folk and country songs to add interest to some of her classes. Some of the songs were original compositions. In a short time, she was finding outlets for her talents before adult audiences, sometimes singing at PTA meetings, other times at local gatherings. As time went on, she became well known for her musical ability in many parts of Ohio.

After a while, Smith took heed of friends' suggestions and gave up teaching in favor of a singing and songwriting career. Her work on local stations and in country concerts gained the attention of music publishers and record companies. Her persistence with demonstration tapes and auditions finally paid off in 1975 when she signed a recording contract with 20th Century-Fox Records.

Even more exciting was the success that met her very first disc. An original composition called "There I Said It" picked up momentum during the early summer and rose to number five on the national country charts in June. In the fall, she had another single, "Paper Lion," also an original, in upper-chart positions. Things seemed to be falling in place nicely. An increasing number of live engagements as an opening act for many of the best-known artists in the country field provoked predictions that she would soon become a headliner herself.

At this point, Margo had a moment of panic when she found out that 20th Century had decided to phase out its country division. However, by then she had enough of a reputation to command attention from other labels. In early 1976, she signed with Warner Brothers, then beginning to build up its country division, and was assigned to Norro Wilson as producer. This proved to be an even better alignment than her previous arrangement. In short order she had three top-10 singles, including "Save Your Kisses for Me," in the top-10 in August 1976, followed by "Take Your Breath Away" and "Love's Explosion." Her single "Don't Break the Heart That Loves You" did even better, rising to number one and staying there for several weeks.

As the late 1970s went by, Smith stead-ily added to a list of impressive credentials. She shared bills with a Who's Who of country music, including Tammy Wynette, Charley Price, Charlie Rich, Tom T. Hall, Don Williams, the Statler Brothers, Faron Young, Conway Twitty, Sonny James, and Ronnie Milsap. Among the network or syndicated TV shows on which she was featured were *That Nashville Music, Pop Goes the Country, Hee Haw, Music Hall America,* and the *Chuck Barris Rah Rah Show.* Perhaps most rewarding for her personally was the opportunity to appear a number of times on the *Grand Ole Opry* radio program.

In the late 1970s, Smith's albums and singles on Warner Bros. continued to do well with country fans and more than a few of her recordings promised to take their place among the best releases of the decade. Among her charted singles of those years were "My Weakness" (co-written by Margo and Norro Wilson), in the top 20 in midsummer 1977; "It Only Hurts for a Little While," in the top 30 in July 1978; "Little Things Mean a Lot," which reached second or third position in various charts in November 1978; and "If I Give My Heart to You," in upper-chart levels in early summer of 1979. Other well-received 1979 singles were "Still a Woman" and "Baby My Baby." Her 1980 charted singles included "The Shuffle Song" and "He Gives Me Diamonds, You Give Me Chills." In early 1981, she had a best-selling duet single, "Cup of Tea," recorded with Rex Allen, Jr.

SMITH, SAMMI: *Singer, songwriter. Born Orange, California, August 5, 1943.*

For a long time, Sammi Smith was known, unfairly, as a one-hit artist. The enormous success of her version of Kris Kristofferson's "Help Me Make It Through the Night" in 1971 propelled her into the spotlight so suddenly it seemed to obscure all that had gone before and much that came after. A combination of circumstances, personal and contractual, pushed her into the background for much of the 1970s until she began to be rediscovered at decade's end.

Sammi, whose father was a serviceman, was born in California, but moved constantly thereafter with her family in a disjointed childhood spread over Oklahoma, Texas, Arizona, and Colorado. She was, in fact, still a child when she moved into show business. "I don't know how I got started, but I was working at a club called Someplace Else [in Oklahoma City] six nights a week when I was eleven. When I first started I was singing rock 'n' roll; then I worked with big bands, doing pop material. I kind of drifted into country, but I like to mix it up. I wouldn't want to stick to just one thing."

Smith continued to sing in local bars and clubs during the mid-1960s, but there were stretches of time when she was on the sidelines. "I went to see a promoter about getting some work. He was doing a Johnny Cash show in Oklahoma City and somebody told Marshall Grant, Johnny's bass player, I was a singer and we got a tape and a few days later he called me and said he thought he could get me on a label, which he did."

The label was Columbia and resulted in her moving to Nashville in 1967. Sammi remained on the label until the start of the 1970s with limited success—only three minor hits. However, she met a janitor at the Columbia studio who was to prove an important friend—Kris Kristofferson. Later she became the first female vocalist with Waylon Jennings' band, touring with him for a year. Waylon suggested that RCA sign her when the Columbia contract ran out, but to no avail. She signed, instead, with a small Nashville label, Mega Records. Her first single release, "He's Everywhere," didn't do badly, reaching the country top 30, but it was the next single that really took off. She'd made demo tapes of a number of Kristofferson songs, all of which became major hits, but only one of which she recorded. The song, of course, was "Help Me Make It Through the Night," which reached number one on country charts and the top 10 on national pop charts in 1971. In early 1972, the song earned Smith a Grammy as Best Female Country Vocalist for 1971.

One of Sammi's problems was that, despite the song's smash success, Mega remained an independent. This minimized the promotional and distribution backing for her followup songs. One might think her years with Mega after 1971 were ones of failure. Actually, she recorded seven albums, in all, for the label and from 1972 to 1976 placed sixteen other singles on country charts. These included "Today I Started Loving You Again" which reached number nine, "Then You Walk In," which rose to ten, and such others as "I've Got to Have You" (thirteen), "The Rainbow in Daddy's Eyes" (sixteen), "Long Black Veil" (twenty-six), and "For the Kids" (twenty-seven).

Mega went downhill financially, going out of business in 1976. That, plus Smith's desire to spend time with her family (as of 1978, she had four children of her own and had adopted twin Apache children) slowed down her career, despite the fact that her country-music peers had great regard for her talent. Kristofferson, for instance, commented, "She's blessed . . . with a voice that's somehow tough and tender and touchingly honest with the same sadness that haunted the songs of Edith Piaf. . . . She's one helluva writer, with a gift for lyrics and melody that makes a body want to smile. . . . And she sure ain't hard to look at."

Smith's writing ability was evinced with three songs on her first hit Mega album, including "When Michael Calls," B side of "Help Me Make It Through the Night." Many artists recorded her compositions during the 1970s, including such songs as "Cedartown, Georgia," a chart hit for Waylon Jennings and "Sand-Covered Angels," a hit for Conway Twitty.

She became a close friend of Waylon Jennings and Willie Nelson, moving to a home near Dallas in 1973 as a result of her interest in the Austin, Texas, progressive country movement. In the mid-1970s, she moved from there to Globe, Arizona, where she became involved in programs to help the Indians on the San Carlos Apache Reservation (she is part Kiowa–Apache). This led to the organization of a country-music benefit show to help build a new school on the reservation and aid Apache education in general. Among those who donated their services for the first show, April 29 and 30, 1978, were Johnny Cash, Mickey Newbury, Johnny Rodriguez, and Steve Young.

After Mega folded, meanwhile, Sammi signed a new contract with Elektra. Her first album was released in 1976, the second one, *Mixed Emotions*, in 1977, and the third, *New Winds/All Quadrants*, in May 1978. Her husky, sultry voice showed to good advantage in all, and her career began to pick up momentum. Her debut single, "As Long as There's a Sunday" made the country top-50 and she followed with such other chart hits as "Loving Arms," "I Can't Stop Loving You," "Days That End in Y." The 1978 success, which had such other fine tracks as "Norma Jean" (about Marilyn Monroe), "I Ain't Got No Time to Rock No Babies," "Lookin' for Lovin'," and "It's Too Late," was the most interesting since her 1971 blockbuster.

Unfortunately, her arrangement with Elektra didn't work out as hoped for and she left the label. In 1980, she reappeared on the Sound Factory Label and had the single "I Just Want to Be with You" on the charts in late 1980 and early 1981 and "Cheatin's a Two Way Street" later in 1981.

SNOW, HANK: *Singer, guitarist, harmonica player, songwriter. Born Liverpool, Nova Scotia, Canada, May 9, 1914.*

For a country with only about a fifth the population of the United States and relatively far removed from the country-music heartland, Canada has contributed a surprisingly high percentage of performers to the field. Among them is one of the all-time modern country greats, Hank Snow, whose successes as recording artist and songwriter placed him in the top 10 on the U.S. country roster after World War II.

Snow's original interest in the music was stirred by a love of western movies. Tom Mix in particular was a favorite, though Mix, of course, was not a singer. As he recalled, "America . . . always I just loved the sound. I would go to any movie when I lived in Canada if it showed anything of America. Texas was always big on my

mind." Later on, when Hank began to write C&W songs, the state still bulked large in his consciousness. "I wrote a lot of songs about Texas, you know. I'd read about these places, seen them in the movies."

Part of the youngster's infatuation with the relatively far-off glamour of the U.S. was based on a need to escape from an unhappy home life. "I was the victim of a broken home at the age of eight and inherited a very cruel stepfather." His stepfather, he claimed, often beat him and threw him out of the house. "I really didn't have any childhood. When you don't know where you are going to sleep for the night . . . or find food . . . you can't think with the mind of a child. You have to think with the mind of a man."

When other boys were getting ready for high school, Hank was earning a living at sea. To escape his stepfather's ire, he ran away, getting a job as a cabin boy. Off and on for much of his teens he worked at sea. "It was a bad situation, but a great education. It teaches you the hard realities of life." He had learned to play the harmonica and his shipmates welcomed the relief from boredom that Hank's playing provided.

In between voyages, Snow worked a variety of jobs, including selling newspapers, Fuller brushes, and being a stevedore. His earnings from a two-week job unloading salt from a freighter provided the money to buy his first guitar for $5.95. About that time he first heard recordings of the great Jimmie Rodgers, and he was soon spending his spare time trying to work out some of Rodgers' songs on the guitar. Still in his early teens, he began to perform in local bars or even in the streets, sometimes for a few dollars, often for no formal pay. "When I started unprofessionally in the entertainment field at about fifteen," he recalled, "I was encouraged by people who thought I had a bright future. That changed the whole picture for me."

After a while, he concentrated more and more on his performing work, gradually building up a following in the Halifax area. One of his first breakthroughs was the chance to have his own show on station

Pete Seeger

Paul Simon

Warner Bros./Charles Porter

Pete Seeger

Hank Snow (mid-1960s)

Paul Siebel

Good Ol' Boys: Joe Stampley
(left) and Moe Bandy

The Statler Brothers

Ray Stevens

Gary Stewart

The Stoneman Family (mid-1960s) with the late Ernest V. "Pop" Stoneman seated, center, with his autoharp

Earl Scruggs Revue

CHNS in Halifax. He called himself Hank, the Singing Ranger, the name he was known by for well over a decade.

He still had his heart set on eventually cracking the U.S. market, acknowledging that it wouldn't be an overnight thing. He realized that he needed an affiliation with a major record company and managed to get an audition with RCA's Canadian branch in the autumn of 1936. He traveled from Halifax to Montreal with only enough money for round trip train fare, food, and a hotel. To conserve his funds, he walked five miles between studio and hotel. "They said they would audition me the next day and asked if I had my material prepared. I didn't know anything about having material prepared . . . but I said yes. I went back to the hotel and wrote two songs that night."

His audition went reasonably well and, in October 1936, he signed with RCA Victor, a relationship that was to last for nearly half a century. That alignment plus increased touring made him a featured artist throughout Canada over the next few years, but he remained virtually unknown in the United States. However, he was meeting many American artists in his travels, including a Texan who shared his love for Jimmie Rodgers, the now legendary Ernest Tubb. It was Tubb who arranged for Snow's U.S. debut in Dallas in 1944 and also urged others in the country to take note of the Canadian's talents. During the mid-1940s, Hank finally had the pleasure of seeing one of his recordings make inroads into the U.S. market, a single titled "Brand New Heart." However, almost until the end of the decade, though Hank performed increasingly in the United States, he remained primarily a Canadian artist, and RCA released his records only in that country.

In 1949, RCA finally changed the pattern, and the response among American fans was sufficient to make the company try releasing still more Snow discs in the United States. His 1949 singles, including the modest hit "Marriage Vows," still came out with the name Hank, the Singing Ranger. In 1950, he switched to his full

name and soon had two smash hits, "Golden Rocket" and "I'm Movin' On," both written by Hank and both number-one successes on U.S. charts. By the time those were released, Hank already was a regular cast member of the *Grand Ole Opry*, which he had joined in January 1950. It was Ernest Tubb who had persuaded the *Opry* to add Hank and decades later, both Ernest and Hank continued to host major segments of the *Opry* Saturday night radio (and sometimes TV) program.

After 1950, Hank made the Nashville area home (at the start of the 1980s, he lived in nearby Madison, Tennessee) and became a U.S. citizen. He continued to grow in stature as a performer and individual, adding to his laurels almost every year from the 1950s through the 1970s with hit recordings, noteworthy concert tours, and a growing string of country music accolades.

In 1951, for instance, he placed four songs in the country top 10: "Bluebird Island," "Music Makin' Mama from Memphis," "Unwanted Sign on Your Heart," and "Rhumba Boogie." The latter reached number one on country charts and also was a hit in the pop field. His esteem with the U.S. country public was demonstrated when he suffered severe injuries in an auto accident. He received 22,000 get well cards. Hank recovered and went on to turn out such 1950s and 1960s hits as "Fool Such as I," "Girl Who Invented Kissing," "I Went to Your Wedding," "Lady's Man" (1952); "Honeymoon in a Rocket Ship," "Spanish Fire Ball," "When Mexican Joe Met Jole Blon" (1953); "I Don't Hurt Anymore" (number one), "Let Me Go Lover" (1954); "Cryin', Prayin', Waitin', Hopin'," "Mainliner," "Yellow Roses" (1955); "Conscience, I'm Guilty," "Stolen Moments," "These Hands" (1956); "Tangled Mind" (1957); "Chasin' a Rainbow," "The Last Ride" (1959); "Miller's Cave" (1960); "Beggar to a King" (1961); "I've Been Everywhere" (number one, 1962); "Ninety Miles an Hour," "The Man Who Robbed the Bank at Santa Fe" (1963); "The Wishing Well" (1965); "I've Cried a Mile" (1966); "Down at the Pawn Shop"

(1967); "The Late and Great Love of My Life" (1968); and "The Name of the Game Was Love" (1969).

Over the decades, Snow's album output was among the most prolific of any country artist. By the start of the 1980s, he had more than 100 LPs to his credit and still turned out one, two, or more new ones each year. Among the RCA titles from the late 1950s into the 1970s were *Country Classics, Country Guitar, Jamboree, Just Keep a-Movin', Sacred Songs* (1958); *When Tragedy Struck* (1959); *Songs of Jimmie Rodgers* (1960); *Souvenirs* (1961); *Sings with the Carters* (1962); *I've Been Everywhere, Railroad Man* (1963); *Songs of Tragedy* (1964); *Favorite Hits* (1965); *Spanish Fire Ball, Christmas with Hank Snow* (1967); *Hits Covered, I Went to Your Wedding* (1969); *In Memory of Jimmie Rodgers, Cure for the Blues* (1970); *Tracks and Trains, Award Winners* (1971).

He also had a number of albums issued on RCA's Camden label over the years, including *Hank the Singing Ranger* (1960); *Southern Cannonball* (1961); *One and Only Hank Snow* (1962); *Last Ride* (1963); *Old and Great Songs* (1964); *I Went to Your Wedding* (1969); *Memories Are Made of This* (1970); *Wreck of the Old 97* (1971); and *Lonesome Whistle, Legend of Old Doc Brown* (1972).

One of the pleasantest memories for Snow went back to late 1953, when he went to Meridian, Mississippi, to dedicate a memorial to that town's famous son, Jimmie Rodgers. Over the years he almost never missed the annual celebration to Rodgers held there. In late 1954, he became the first guitarist to record duets with "Mr. Guitar," Chet Atkins. That same year, Hank's "I Don't Hurt Anymore" was named the best country record of the year in a *Cash Box* magazine poll, and in 1955, the poll indicated it was the most programmed record of the year. Almost a decade later, in 1963, another Snow classic, "I'm Movin' On," was voted the all-time favorite country music record by the nation's disc jockeys in a *Billboard* survey. This resulted in the magazine presenting Hank with its Award of Achievement.

Over the years, his contract with RCA was renewed steadily until an arrangement finally was concluded extending through the year 1987. That agreement provided still another milestone for an illustrious career, permitting completion of a fifty-year affiliation between Hank and the label, the longest running association between an artist and a record company.

SONS OF THE PIONEERS: *Vocal and instrumental group. Founding members, early 1930s:* Leonard Slye (Roy Rogers), *born Cincinnati, Ohio, November 5, 1912;* Bob Nolan, *born New Brunswick, Canada, April 1, 1908, died Los Angeles, California, June 16, 1980;* Tim Spencer, *born Webb City, Missouri, July 7, 1908, died Apple Valley, California, April 26, 1976;* Karl Farr *(added 1934–35), born Rochelle, Texas, April 25, 1909, died West Springfield, Massachusetts, September 20, 1961;* Hugh Farr *(added 1934–35), born Llano, Texas, December 6, 1903, died Casper, Wyoming, March 17, 1980;* Lloyd Perryman, *born Ruth, Arkansas, January 29, 1917, died Colorado Springs, Colorado, May 31, 1977;* Pat Brady *(added 1937), born Toledo, Ohio.*

Even today, when anyone thinks of vocal groups in western music, one name stands out above all others: the Sons of the Pioneers. With different combinations of performers, the group has remained active from its inception in the early 1930s to the present day, though in its "golden years," roughly from the mid-1930s to the end of the 1940s, its makeup remained essentially stable, including for most of that period, Bob Nolan, Tim Spencer, the Farr brothers, Hugh and Karl, Lloyd Perryman, and Pat Brady. During those years, such songs as Bob Nolan's "Cool Water" and "Tumbling Tumbleweeds" and Tim Spencer's "Room Full of Roses" brought the group fame across the United States and in many other countries as well.

Appropriately for a group that brings to mind boots and saddles and the cowboy life of times past, one of the original members was a young, banjo-playing and singing performer named Leonard Slye, who went on to fame as Roy Rogers in western movies, where he gained the title "King of the Cowboys." Recalling the early days to Terry Atkinson of the *Los Angeles Times*

(Calendar section, August 21, 1977), Rogers said the first step came in 1931 in Los Angeles, California, when, as a member of an all-instrumental group called the Rocky Mountaineers, he persuaded the others that having a singing group would boost audience interest. In response to an ad he placed in a local paper, Bob Nolan came on to form a duet with Roy. Nolan had been born in Canada to American parents and had moved first to Tucson and then Los Angeles. At the time, Nolan was working as a lifeguard on Venice Beach in Los Angeles.

Later, the group expanded to a trio with the addition of one of Nolan's Venice friends, Bill "Slumber" Nichols. Then, Rogers told Atkinson, "Bob decided to quit and went to caddy at the Bel-Air Country Club. So we put another ad in the paper and Tim Spencer answered." Recalling his route to that point in a letter to Grelun Landon (January 11, 1967), Spencer wrote, "I left Missouri and moved into New Mexico in 1915. Father and Mother homesteaded 360 acres of land there. Later the Spencer family moved to Oklahoma and then on to California in 1930. There I met Roy Rogers and Bob Nolan, which formed the nucleus of the Sons of the Pioneers."

Rogers continued, "Tim, Slumber and I worked together for a while. But eventually I joined the Texas Outlaws. Slumber hitched up with another group and Tim went back to work for Safeway."

Roy, however, remained confident that a western trio had a lot of potential and he soon began rehearsing a new one with some of his former associates. "Spencer, Nolan and I got a room in a little boarding house on Carlton Way just off Bronson [in Hollywood] and we rehearsed until our voices gave out." When they felt they were ready, they brought their act to the attention of the Texas Outlaws group and soon joined to become a part of the Outlaws' radio program on Los Angeles station KFWB from 1934 to 1936. The boys first called themselves the Pioneer Trio, Rogers noted, but an announcer accidentally introduced them as the Sons of the Pioneers and they were called that from then on.

During those years, more personnel were added to the group. During 1934-35 instrumentalists Karl and Hugh Farr joined up, and, in 1936, tenor Lloyd Perryman was a new recruit. The group struck out on its own as members of the *Hollywood Barn Dance* on KHJ, and also started nibbling at the movie field individually and collectively. Some members contributed songs to western films and played roles in Columbia "B" westerns.

By the time Roy Rogers left to work as a featured performer in westerns for Republic Pictures, the Sons had become a six-member group consisting of Nolan, Spencer, Perryman, the Farrs, and singer-comedian Pat Brady, who joined in 1937. (Prior to Brady's addition, Rogers had been cast as the comic in many of the group's routines.) Though no longer officially a member, Roy never forgot the group, seeing to it that they sang and acted in many of his movies. (Brady, of course, was one of Roy's regular sidekicks and comedy contributors in movies and later in Rogers' long-running TV series.) However, that didn't take place right away. The Sons were obligated to work for Columbia Pictures as singers in westerns starring Charles Starrett from 1936 to 1940. In 1940, they signed with Republic and appeared in many films with Roy under a contract that ran until 1949.

From the late 1930s on, the Sons of the Pioneers established its own identity as a live performance group and as major recording artists. Nolan and Spencer were the main creative forces, each providing hundreds of original songs either for the group's repertoire or for use by others in western films or recording sessions. Nolan provided many memorable songs during the group's heyday, but, of course, is most often remembered for "Cool Water" and "Tumbling Tumbleweeds." The latter actually was first written as "Tumbling Leaves" from some of Nolan's sensations while looking at falling leaves one autumn day from his West Los Angeles apartment. Spencer's most successful offerings came somewhat later than Nolan's. He wrote Landon, "In 1946 I wrote the song entitled, Cigareets, Whuskey and Wild, Wild

Women' which sold in excess of one million records. In 1949 I wrote the song entitled, 'Room Full of Roses,' which sold over a million recordings. I have written more than 250 western songs for motion pictures starring the Sons of the Pioneers and Roy Rogers."

The Sons' early recordings included work on Decca and Columbia labels. The main share of their output, though, came during a long-term alignment with RCA Victor that lasted until the late 1960s. Their Decca output included "Cool Water" and "There's a New Moon Over My Shoulder" and, on Columbia, "Open Range Ahead" and "The Devil's Great Grandson." Their contract with Columbia expired in 1939 and in 1940 they signed with RCA Victor. During the 1940s, they had many hit singles (and some best-selling albums) on Victor, including "Cool Water," "Tumbling Tumbleweeds," "Timber Trails," "Blue Shadows on the Trail," "Blue Prairie," "Pecos Bill," "Carry Me Back to the Lone Prairie," "Home on the Range," "Have I Told You Lately That I Love You," "Lie Low Little Doggies," "Cigareets, Whuskey," and "Room Full of Roses."

Besides appearing in an estimated 100 films from the late 1930s to the early 1950s, films that starred not only Roy Rogers but others like John Wayne, Bing Crosby, and Randolph Scott, the group kept up an active touring schedule that took it to rodeos, fairs, theaters, and night clubs across the United States. Their travels also took them to Canada and many other countries. In 1951, they were featured in a western concert at New York's Carnegie Hall.

By the early 1950s, though, some of the momentum began to go out of the group as it started to lose its primary writers. Bob Nolan stepped down from concert work in 1949. Roy Rogers said, "He's always been a loner. That's what made him retire in 1949 from touring. He just got tired of traveling." (However, Nolan continued to record with the group until 1957.) Tim Spencer wrote Landon, "I resigned from the Sons of the Pioneers as a singing member in 1952 and took over the management

of the group through 1954. I then started a religious publishing company by the name of Manna Music. Since 1954, and to this date [1967], Manna Music has grown into a major publishing house. Our composition entitled 'How Great Thou Art' has in the past ten years, sold over one million copies of sheet music."

In the early 1950s, one of the new members of the group was Ken Curtis. His place was taken by Kentucky-born Dale Warren in 1952; Warren still was the lead singer of the group in the late 1970s.

With the departure of Spencer and Nolan, the amount of new material provided from within the group declined sharply. The Sons continued to maintain a sizable performing schedule, though, and had considerable TV guest appearance credits in the 1950s and 1960s and, to a lesser extent, in the 1970s. Among their 1960s TV credits were Johnny Carson's *The Tonight Show, Joey Bishop, Steve Allen, Merv Griffin* and the *Kraft Music Hall.* Beside keeping up its concerts at rodeos and fairs from the mid-1950s through the early 1980s, the group had several overseas tours to such places as Japan, Australia, and Europe.

RCA continued to release new albums of the group's recordings (including some reissues) to the end of the 1960s. These included *Wagons West* (RCA Camden Records, 4/58); *Cool Water* (5/60); *Room Full of Roses* (7/60); *Lure of the West* (6/61); *Tumbleweed Trail* (4/62); *Good Old Country Music* (Camden, 12/62); *Our Man Out West* (2/63); *Cowboy Hymns* (5/63); *Trail Dust* (12/63); *Country Fare* (7/64); *Down Country Trails* (12/64); *Best of the Sons of the Pioneers* (2/66); *Songs of Bob Nolan* (7/66); and *Campfire Favorites* (4/67). Other label releases in the 1960s included *Tumbleweed Trails* (Vocalion, 5/64) and *Best of the Sons of the Pioneers* (Harmony, 7/64).

For a time, in the late 1960s, the Sons was a quartet composed of Perryman, Warren, Roy Lanham (guitarist, born Kentucky), and Billy Armstrong (fiddle). In the 1970s, Pat Brady returned to join Warren, Lanham, Perryman, and tenor Rusty Richards (born Orange County, California), for several years. At other times, the roster included Billy Liebert and Rome Johnson. When the Hollywood Chamber of Commerce decided to install a new star in the Walk of Fame honoring the Sons on September 24, 1976, the group members were Perryman, Warren, Richards, Lanham, and Liebert. Perryman remained active with the group up to shortly before his death in May 1977. His place was taken by Rome Johnson.

The group first was nominated for the Country Music Hall of Fame in the late 1960s, but did not receive enough votes from CMA members to be welcomed into that assemblage until 1980, the year that two of its earliest members, Nolan and Hugh Farr, died.

SORRELS, ROSALIE: *Singer, songwriter, author. Born Idaho, 1933.*

A folk artist in the traditional sense, Rosalie Sorrels collected authentic stories and songs of the people and wrote original material that satisfied her own creative needs, rather than bending to the tides of commercialization. Although she received added exposure during the brief folk music boom a decade or so after World War II, she went her own way, keeping a low profile while delighting folk circuit audiences from time to time with her anecdotes and finely crafted vocal offerings.

Sorrels gained particular attention as an exponent of folk music of Idaho and Utah, her home area. As a girl growing up in the small towns and rural areas of those states, most of the songs she gathered in her youth and young womanhood "are very personal things," states her notes for one of her Folkways albums of the early 1960s. "Until recently, I never sang them much for anyone but myself or people who were very close to me, like my husband or children. I sing more when I am working, or when I am alone. I have been singing most of my life. My family all love music, and I just naturally like to sing. I remember my grandfather singing songs like 'The Ship That Never Returned' or 'Ella Speed,' while he separated the milk. . . . I used to stay with them every summer on their farm in Twin Falls, Idaho.

"My father always sang, and had picked up two or three instruments . . . learning to play them by ear. The music I've been exposed to was a conglomeration of opera, jazz, popular, western, and folk styles, but folk songs seem to be the most satisfying to me. One of the songs I learned within my own family was 'The House Carpenter.' My father's mother, who was originally from Canada, had it among some other songs and poems she kept in an old scrapbook.

"In singing the songs, and swapping them with others—people who also sing for their own enjoyment—I began to discover many songs that were learned in the oral tradition. Songs from childhood and the neighborhood kids, or older brothers and sisters—songs that were passed along from one to another by ear, or written in old song books or scrapbooks like my grandmother's.

"The more songs I learned, the more interested I became in their backgrounds. I began to try to find out where the songs were from. I've never had so much fun in my life as I've had tracking down songs and the people who sing them—people like Dick and Jean Person who live in Cascade, Idaho. Dick is a fish and game warden in that area. I learned 'Brigham Young,' 'The Death of Kathy Fiscus,' 'I'll Give You My Story,' 'Empty Cot in the Bunkhouse,' 'Wreck of the Old Number Nine,' and 'The Philadelphia Lawyer' from them."

Rosalie was aided in her efforts by husband Jim Sorrels, whom she married in the 1950. Sorrels, who played guitar, enjoyed singing and playing music with Rosalie and also contributed new songs himself, some collected while he was working as a telephone lineman for Mountain States Telephone Company in Idaho. The Sorrels jointly went on folk song collecting expeditions in the 1950s and 1960s and at one point taught classes in folk guitar at the University of Utah.

Sorrels' reputation as a folksinger began to reach folk adherents well beyond the U.S. mountain states and eventually led to her first recordings for Folkways Records. One of her first Folkways LPs was the 1961 *Folk Songs of Idaho and Utah*. The album helped spark interest in her work and led to increased concerts in folk clubs and on the college circuit. However, Rosalie never believed in allowing the commercial side of the music field to interfere with her private life and, as a result, both her concerts and new recordings occurred at relatively infrequent intervals.

As the 1960s went by, in addition to her repertoire of traditional folk music, Sorrels' added some fine creations of her own. (Besides writing songs, she also was a poet.) She also liked to interpret some of the compositions of another mountain states folk artist, U. Utah Phillips, featuring several of his union and train songs in her Folk-Legacy LP, *If I Could Be the Rain* (issued 6/67). Mitch Greenhill provided instrumental backup on that album. Though Rosalie always remained faithful to her basic musical principles, she was not inflexible and, over the years, added material with some jazz or country-rock flavor. Those changes seemed to add depth and interest to her overall concerts, which remained favorites with a small but constant group of fans throughout the 1970s.

During the 1970s, the pattern was not much different from the previous decade. Sorrels gave folk music concerts in many parts of the United States and other countries, but at a relatively leisurely pace, and recorded a new album every now and then. From the end of the 1960s to the start of the 1980s, the LPs were issued on a variety of labels. Those released in the early part of that period included *Travelin' Lady* on Sire Records and in the mid- and late-1970s, *Always a Lady* and *Moments of Happiness* on Philo Records.

SOUTHER, J. D.: *Singer, guitarist, drummer, saxophonist, pianist, songwriter. Born Detroit, Michigan, November 2, 1945.*

Although he was a part of the Southern California folk and country-rock explosion of the late 1960s to early 1970s that made stars of Jackson Browne, Linda Ronstadt, and the Eagles, J. D. Souther took somewhat longer than his friends and associates to reach that status. He made important contributions as songwriter, session musician, and sometime musical adviser to the success of the others. Finally, after several

starts as soloist and band member, he achieved a growing number of hits under his own name late in the 1970s and seemed marked for even greater things in the 1980s.

Born in Detroit, John David Souther moved to Texas with his family at an early age and grew up in the city of Amarillo. He showed musical talent as a boy and, in his teens, learned to play a wide variety of instruments, from guitars and piano to drums. His early musical interests were diverse, ranging from the classics through jazz and bebop to country and rockabilly. Among his early favorites were Buddy Holly, Ray Charles, and Hank Williams. His schooling covered many aspects of music, from musical history to theory, harmony, and composition.

During the mid-1960s, Souther made the Los Angeles area his home, where he sought to further his career as a songwriter and musician. He had worked with a number of local pop bands when his path crossed that of a recent arrival from the Midwest, Glenn Frey, in the late 1960s. Frey began dating a girl whose sister was Souther's girl friend, bringing Frey and Souther in contact. Finding common musical ties, they soon formed a duo called Longbranch Pennywhistle. At first things seemed to look promising for them. They gained a record contract from Amos Records, which issued a debut album of their work. The duo made some progress in the pop club scene. Still far from flush economically, Frey and Souther shared a sixty-dollar-a-month apartment in Los Angeles' Echo Park district with another struggling artist, Jackson Browne.

In 1970, the duo sought to get out of their contract with Amos and the resultant legal entanglements sidelined them. Unable to work, they finally decided to go separate ways. Frey moved on to become part of Linda Ronstadt's backing band, which evolved into the Eagles in 1971, while Souther began to perform as a soloist. In 1971, he signed with Asylum Records, which brought out his debut LP, *John David Souther*, in the summer of 1972, the same year Asylum released the first Eagles' album.

Unlike the Eagles' debut, Souther's album was not a chart hit, though it demonstrated his considerable skills as singer and songwriter to good advantage. While Souther was trying to make his mind up about his next step as an entertainer, his friends were eager to use his material in their own endeavors. Souther collaborated with Eagles' members on several songs in that band's second LP, *Desperado*. Both Linda Ronstadt and Jackson Browne generally included one or more Souther songs in their albums. When the Eagles began work in early 1974 on what was to become their first massive hit album, *On the Border*, the first two songs they recorded were collaborations with Souther, "The Best of My Love" and "You Never Cry like a Lover." The title song of Linda Ronstadt's *Prisoner in Disguise* LP was a song by Souther.

In late 1973, rather than continue on as a solo performer, Souther decided to join with two veteran artists, former Byrds and Flying Burritos member Chris Hillman and Buffalo Springfield/Poco alumnus Richie Furay, in a new band. The debut LP of that band, the *Souther Hillman Furay Band*, came out on Elektra/Asylum in the summer of 1974. Initially, it seemed that the threesome was on the threshold of impressive new success. The group was warmly received in an extensive tour of the United States in the summer and fall of 1974 and the LP stayed on upper pop chart levels during that time, earning the band a gold record award from the R.I.A.A on September 23, 1974. (The Eagles' "Desperado" was awarded a gold record the same day.)

Encouraged, the band went back to the studios to work on the next LP in late 1974 and early 1975. That album, *Trouble in Paradise*, came out in the spring of 1975. Unfortunately, the title proved quite appropriate. There already was discontent among SHF members about musical directions, and, when Furay was injured and incapacitated, the group broke up, with Souther once more seeking a solo role.

With Elektra/Asylum supporting his plans, he started work on his second solo LP, with Peter Asher as producer, in the fall of 1975. That LP, *Black Rose*, came out during 1976, showcasing a new group of Souther songs, which, however, seemed more pretentious than his previous work. In his concert tour in support of the album, in fact, there was greater audience response to his performance of some of the latter, such as "Faithless Love," "Don't Cry Now," "Run like a Thief," and "Silver Blue." The disparity probably was the major reason the new album did not do particularly well.

For the next few years, though Souther's material continued to show up on new releases by many artists and Souther himself did considerable session work and some concerts with major folk-rock artists, his own entertainment career essentially was in limbo.

Then he signed with a new label, Columbia Records. His first LP on that label, *You're Only Lonely*, came out in mid-1979, and this time all the elements for success seemed in place. Backed by a tight-sounding band, he offered an interesting array of numbers, ranging in style from fast-paced folk-rockers to country-tinged ballads. The concerts he gave in places like New York's Bottom Line to the Los Angeles Roxy, with stops at important venues in between, were among the most effective of his career. The new album remained on the pop charts from soon after its release to the first part of 1980. The title song became a singles hit on both the pop and country charts.

SOVINE, RED: *Singer, guitarist, songwriter, band leader. Born Charleston, West Virginia, July 17, 1918; died April 14, 1980.*

Esteemed for his acting almost as much as his singing, Red Sovine's deep baritone voice was used to good effect for straightforward country vocals as well as dramatic vignettes delivered against an instrumental backdrop. Although he could sing anything from up-tempo songs to plaintive ballads as well as anybody in the country field in the post–World War II decades, it was his recitations that eventually gained him a unique niche in the country pantheon.

Woodrow Wilson "Red" Sovine was born and raised in Charleston, West Virginia, where he already was an accomplished guitarist and vocalist while in his teens in the 1930s. At seventeen, he became a member of a group called Jim Pike and the Carolina Tar Heels and performed with them regularly on the Friday night *Old Farm Hour Show* at radio station WCHS. An opportunity arose for them to move up to the prestigious WWVA station in Wheeling, where the group was featured on the famous Saturday night *WWVA Jamboree.*

In 1947, Sovine formed his own band, the Echo Valley Boys. They appeared for a time on WWVA, then moved to Shreveport, Louisiana, to join the cast of the KWKH *Louisiana Hayride,* whose star at the time was Hank Williams. When Hank left for the *Grand Ole Opry* on June 3, 1949, KWKH executives tabbed Red as the logical successor. Besides gaining the top spot on the *Hayride,* Red and his band fell heir to a fifteen-minute daily program of Hank's called the *Johnny Fair Syrup Show.*

While no one could completely fill the shoes of a giant like Williams, Red won the regard of *Hayride* fans in his own right. He remained a favorite of Louisiana fans into 1954 and won the approval of his musical peers. Among fellow *Hayride* cast members was singer-songwriter Webb Pierce, who became a close friend of Sovine's. The two often sang duets together and also co-wrote many songs. In 1954, both Webb and Red were given invitations to join the *Grand Ole Opry* and both accepted. Sovine settled in Nashville in the mid-1950s and remained a resident of Music City the rest of his life.

Both performers did well as *Opry* artists and rising recording stars in the mid-1950s. In 1956, they blended their vocal and instrumental talents on two major hit singles, "Why, Baby, Why" and "Little Rosa." The two turned out a number of other charted singles and original songs together in the late 1950s. In the 1960s, though, they tended to go separate ways.

Red continued to be a top-ranked country star in the 1960s and 1970s, turning out many singles and albums on a variety of labels. His biggest number of hits in those two decades was on Starday Records, though he had releases that made hit lists

on such other labels as Decca and Chart. His biggest singles success in the 1960s was the Starday release "Giddyup Go," which rose to number one in the United States during 1965. His Starday albums of the 1960s included his label debut, *Red Sovine,* issued in October 1961, *Country Ballads of the '60s* (12/62), *Little Rosa, Giddyup Go* (1965), *Town & Country Action, Nashville Sound, I Didn't Jump the Fence, Phantom 309,* and *That's Truckdrivin'.* His Decca LPs included the late 1950s release *Red Sovine and Music Time,* reissued in May 1966. Other 1960s albums included *Giddyup Go* and *Dear John Letter* on Nashville Records, *Fine* on Somerset Records, and *Farewell, So Long,* issued by Metro (part of MGM Records) in August 1967.

Among his original compositions of the 1950s and 1960s were such offerings as "Don't Be the One," "Missing You," "Long Night," "Class of '49," "I Didn't Jump the Fence," "Too Much," and "I Think I Can Sleep Tonight." Pre-1970s chartmakers included, besides songs noted earlier, "You Used to Be My Baby," "Don't Drop It," "Don't Be the One," "I Hope You Don't Care," "I'm Glad You Found a Place for Me," "The Intoxicated Rat," "How Do You Think I Feel," "My New Love Affair," "I'm the Man," and "Best Years of Your Life."

By the end of the 1960s, Sovine's extensive in-person tours had taken him to all fifty states, many parts of Canada, and Europe. He was a familiar face to fans on the state and country fair and rodeo circuits, a situation that still held through much of the 1970s. He always kept his eye open for newcomers during his travels and helped alert Nashville to more than a few fine performers. His most notable discovery came in the early 1960s when he heard a ballplayer turned singer perform in a Montana club. He helped the artist get a record company audition, the opening phase of the career of Country Charley Pride.

Things slowed a bit for Red in the early 1970s, but in the mid-1970s, he found a new series of hits. In late summer of 1975, he made lower-chart levels with his emotionally charged single on Chart, "Daddy's Girl." Early the following year, he dipped into his earlier repertoire for a repeat singles hit with "Phantom 309" on the Starday label. In the summer, he surged all the way to the top with another recitative offering, "Teddy Bear." Co-written by Red with D. Royal, B. Burnette, and T. Hill, that Starday single reached number one in the United States in late July 1976. A month later, his album of the same title also moved into the number-one spot, capping one of Sovine's most notable years of his career. His achievements won him a number of awards, including a special category set up for him by *Cash Box* magazine in its annual poll—"Top Recitation Performer."

He was still active and well regarded by country fans when he was felled by a fatal heart attack in 1980.

SPEARS, BILLY: *Singer, fiddler, band leader (Billy Spears Band, Swingshift). Born Hartshorne, Oklahoma, October 26, 1930.*

In the fall of 1979, a remarkable event happened—Billy Spears embarked on a tour of the plains and mountain states with a new band, Swingshift. That might not sound very unusual, but a year earlier Billy had been paralyzed in a freak accident and there had been doubt about his walking normally again, much less being able to handle the intricate fingering that made his reputation as a first-rate fiddle player. But in the fall of 1979, he was on stage once more and, if his playing was a bit rusty at times, he still was doing quite well.

It was an important turn of events for Spears. Although music always had been, in effect, in his blood, for a long time it was a sideline. Then, at an age when most men start thinking about pension benefits, he gambled on earning his living as a musician.

As a boy growing up in Oklahoma, he had almost accepted folk and country & western music as a way of life. Family members and friends often got together to sing and play such music; in his household, in particular, fiddle playing was a family tradition. By the time Billy was thirteen, he had taken up the instrument and in a short time could match skills with some of the best fiddlers in the area. Still,

he didn't start performing professionally until he was in his early twenties at the start of the 1950s (after a tour of duty in the armed forces). He worked with many of the best in the country field, including Ferlin Husky, Jean Shepard, and T. Texas Tyler. He was a member of Tyler's Western Band in 1953, which toured all over the United States and Canada.

Soon after working with Tyler, Spears decided to give up touring in favor of a more settled family life. He got a job as a baker and eventually worked himself up to the position of food service director at the University of Kansas in Lawrence. He remained in the food field for twenty years, many of them at the university, and played fiddle mainly for his own enjoyment or to entertain friends and family. But everyone kept telling him he was too good to hide his talents from the public. Finally, in 1974, he heeded those suggestions and quit his job a few years short of eligibility for retirement benefits.

It took a certain amount of spadework, but by the mid-1970s, the switch seemed to be working out well. With his Billy Spears Band, he toured college campuses, country-music clubs, and occasional festivals from Kansas to the Rocky Mountain states and slowly built a reputation as an important exponent of bluegrass and western swing music. Although after four years of road work in mid-1978 the group was still considered a regional organization. Billy's prowess on fiddle had become known to fans from California to Washington and, to a lesser extent, in the eastern United States. With the growing boom in both bluegrass and western swing, it seemed only a matter of time until Spears could get a major record alignment that might bring national acclaim.

All that seemed academic after Billy took an ill-fated dive into the old swimming hole near his boyhood home in Oklahoma on August 3, 1978. Dares from fellow musicians at a get-together compelled him to jump in, and he hit a submerged log that paralyzed him from the neck down. He was taken first to a hospital in Muskogee, then transferred to the Veterans' Administration facility in Kansas

City. After months of recuperation, feeling started to come back to various parts of his body. Meanwhile his friend and band manager, Dwight Haldeman, organized several benefits that helped raise funds to pay Billy's expenses until he could get back on his feet.

By the summer of 1979, Spears had amazed his doctors with his recovery and by late summer he was eagerly getting ready to perform regularly once more. In the fall, the new band association won standing ovations from audiences in Colorado and the outlook looked promising. Besides Billy, Swingshift's roster included two-time national banjo champion Lynn Morris; Jimmy Ray on guitar and vocals; Bob Case on pedal steel guitar (the last two holdovers from the old Billy Spears Band); Pat Rossiter on mandolin, dobro, guitar, banjo, and vocals; Pete Wyman on bass; and Bill Brennan on drums.

SPEARS, BILLIE JO: *Singer, songwriter, band leader. Born Beaumont, Texas, January 14, 1937.*

Country music gets down to the joys and pressures of everyday life for the most part, sometimes with a rural setting, more often in recent times with urban connotations. So it was that Billie Jo Spears struck fire with many young women in the 1960s with her first major hit, "Mr. Walker, It's All Over," a song about a girl who quits a secretarial job to escape the attentions of an overeager boss.

The situation was familiar to Billie Jo, who worked for a while as a secretary with the Beaumont Bag and Burlap Company in her home town. Of course, she felt that the job was only a way station on the road to a music career, which she'd first pursued when she was thirteen, when she got a job in a local spot. She had to give it up because of her youth. Later, she resigned her secretary's job not so much because of harassment but to pick up her career goal as a singer at Yvonne's Night Club.

A talent scout named John Rhodes heard Spears sing and recognized her potential. She went to Nashville at his behest to sign with United Artists (she later took up residence in nearby Hendersonville,

Tennessee) and turned out a number of recordings for the label during the mid-1960s. One of those was the chart success called "The Stepchildren," the name she gave to her backup band.

In 1963, she switched labels to Capitol. Her output for that label in the late 1960s and early 1970s included such albums as *With Love, Country Girl,* and *Just Singin'* and singles releases including "Marty Gray," "True Love," "I Stayed Long Enough," and "Come on Home." During those years she already was finding rapport with audiences across the United States and Canada. In early 1970, she was part of the Capitol "Country Caravan," which brought the delights of that home-grown music to such faraway places as Sweden, Holland, England, Norway, and Ireland. She also did a number of USO shows in West Germany. Throughout the 1970s, she appeared on many TV shows, including several appearances on the long-running *Hee Haw* series.

Billie Jo had a number of songs on the charts during her stay with Capitol, but few of them progressed very far up the ladder. Overall, her career seemed to be slowing down, which prompted a move back to her original affiliation with United Artists in the mid-1970s. The switch seemed to provide new momentum and her name achieved new luster with country fans in the second half of the decade. Examples of her chart hits included "Silver Wing and Golden Rings," on the lists in late 1975 and early 1976, "What I've Got in Mind," a top-5 hit in May 1976, "Misty Blue," a top-10 success that August, and "Too Much Is Not Enough" on the charts in September of 1978.

Another facet of Spears' career in the latter 1970s was her recording work with another country star, Del Reeves. Their output included such chart singles as "On the Rebound" and "Teardrops Will Kiss the Morning Dew."

Billie Jo's association with United Artists continued to be fruitful at the end of the 1970s and the start of the 1980s. She had an excellent year in 1979 with five singles appearing on upper-chart levels: " '57 Chevrolet," "Livin' Our Love Together," "I Will Survive," "Yesterday," and "Love

Ain't Gonna Wait for Us." At the end of the year she had another single, "Rainy Days and Stormy Nights", which moved up the lists to number twenty-one in early January 1980. A few months later she had the single "Standing Tall" in the top 15. In the summer, she placed "Natural Attraction" in upper-chart positions and in early 1981 had the chart hit "Your Good Girl's Gonna Go Bad."

STAFFORD, JIM: *Singer, guitarist, banjoist, keyboards player, comedian, songwriter, actor. Born Eloise, Florida, January 16, 1944.*

Novelty songs always have had an important place in America's pop music idiom and, in the mid-1970s, Jim Stafford seemed to have almost a monopoly on the field. Taken by his wildly funny lyrics, the public sometimes overlooked his ability as a musician and his serious side as singer and actor.

As he noted, both sides of the coin were important in the environment in which he grew up. "You had to have a sense of humor to live in Eloise, Florida. It was built around a citrus plant. My people are country musicians from Tennessee. They just picked banjos, guitars, and fiddles . . . and when they came down here as migrant workers, they picked oranges, limes, and lemons." His father managed to avoid the picker's fate by going into the dry cleaning business.

The musical influence showed up in Jim (full name James Wayne Stafford) who started fooling around with the guitar early in life and could play well enough to perform at local events in his teens. When he started going to high school he had some thoughts of becoming a commercial artist or going into the ministry, but both those ideas paled for him when he became active in a rock group at fourteen.

He switched to the country field at twenty-one and moved to Nashville to try out on the *Opry* and develop a career as writer or soloist. He spent two years in Music City without making major progress, then moved to Atlanta where circumstances caused Stafford to combine his comic talent with music. "I was playing go-go clubs with a drummer friend. I'd play the bass pedals on the organ and the guitar at the same time and I'd talk out of necessity. I couldn't ad lib my own name at first. Then the drummer quit and I was beside myself." He worked long hours in his spare time to develop a routine. This led to his writing novelty songs, since he felt his voice wasn't good enough for other kinds of material. An early effort was sparked by a go-go girl named Karen and came out as "I Ain't Sharin' Sharon."

The song didn't ring any bells, but his new act started to. In time it brought opportunities to perform in major venues around the United States in the late 1960s and early 1970s. Among the places he played were major Miami Beach hotels, the Cellar Door in Washington, D.C., Mr. Kelly's in Chicago, and the Bitter End in New York.

During that period he continued to write new material and, when the opportunity arose, tried to use it to further his writing or recording career. In 1973, Jim took one of his pieces, a song titled "Swamp Witch," to a high school friend, Kent LaVoie, who had become a recording success under the name Lobo. LaVoie was impressed with the song and so was his record producer, Phil Gernhard, who played a tape of it for MGM head Mike Curb. Curb was even more excited then Gernhard. He noted, "It had a special quality all its own. Jim Stafford reminded me of no one else around. He was no carbon copy, but an original artist."

Stafford was signed to MGM and soon had his debut LP, *Jim Stafford,* completed. The collection proved to be one of the happenings of 1974, spawning a series of hit singles that kept Stafford's name on the singles charts well into 1975. The first to earn a gold record was "Spiders and Snakes," which won the award from the R.I.A.A. on March 6, 1974. The other three were "Swamp Witch," "My Girl Bill," and "Wildwood Weed." Stafford was voted Top New Vocalist of 1974 by *Record World* and was ranked fourth as Top Male Vocalist behind Elton John, Stevie Wonder, and John Denver. Stafford's second album on

MGM, *Not Just Another Pretty Foot*, was issued during 1975 and provided two more charted singles, "Your Bulldog Drinks Champagne" and "I Got Stoned and I Missed It."

During the mid-1970s, Stafford savored his new-won fame by appearing before all types of audiences, ranging from college crowds, state fairs, pop concerts, and a number of engagements in major hotels in Las Vegas, Reno, and Lake Tahoe. Among the artists he worked with on various bills were Charlie Rich, Tina Turner, and Olivia Newton-John. He was a guest on many network and syndicated TV shows in the mid- and late-1970s, including *Dinah! Merv Griffin, Sha Na Na, The Jim Nabors Show, Midnight Special, Rock Concert, Opryland USA, The Captain and Tenille,* and *Dick Clark's 25th Anniversary Special.* He also was cohost on several programs of the *Mike Douglas* show and, during the summer of 1975, was host of his own replacement variety show.

In the late 1970s, Stafford made his TV acting debut, playing the role of Sandy Duncan's husband in the "Lost and Found" episode of ABC-TV's sitcom series *The Love Boat.* During 1978–79, his TV activities including working with ABC on a possible future situation comedy and taping an hour-long special for syndication titled *Jim Stafford's Grand Central.* Making it easier for him to work on these projects was his move during the 1970s into a large house in the Hollywood hills. At the start of the 1980s, he was one of the cohosts of the TV program *Those Amazing Animals,* telecast on the ABC-TV network.

His musical projects in the late 1970s included writing and performing three songs for the score of the Disneyland animated film *The Fox and the Hound* (released 1981) and a return, after a hiatus, to album work. The album, slated for 1979 release, was prepared under the aegis of Mike Curb, who signed Jim for his Warner/Curb Records operation.

Commenting on his approach to crafting comedic songs, he said, "You have to construct it so people will stay with it and like it. It's like writing a little book. Humorous songs . . . well, they're so much harder to write. It's like telling a joke. You can't tell it blatantly. You do that—and you can do it once—and then it's all over."

STAFFORD, TERRY: *Singer, guitarist, songwriter, band leader. Born Hollis, Oklahoma, 1941.*

Quiet and self-effacing offstage, Terry Stafford found it difficult to gain the publicity needed to make headway in the highly competitive modern music business. But he did have persistence, and his talents as a writer and entertainer eventually had an impact on the country and pop fields.

Born and raised in Hollis, Terry's early musical awareness was kindled by country music, though when he began to perform locally in his teens, the rockabilly hits of the day were the highlights of his repertoire. "I was influenced by the same country music that Buddy Holly, Elvis Presley, and Roy Orbison grew up around."

In 1961, a year after high school graduation, he headed to Southern California to seek his fortune as a rock artist. He made the rounds of publishing and recording firms, passing out tapes of his work as performer and songwriter. It took a lot of time and effort, but he finally made some headway, signing with a small label, Crusader. In 1964, he had a national hit with his single "Suspicion."

However, he wasn't able to maintain that pace and, in time, returned to the country field both as writer and musician. After a while, he began to place songs with major artists and hit paydirt when Buck Owens made upper-chart levels with "Big in Vegas."

He had his own band at the start of the 1970s and was able to find a certain amount of work on the country circuit. He kept in touch with music executive John Fisher, who had headed Crusader Records when Stafford recorded for that label. Fisher believed in Terry's potential and brought him to the attention of Atlantic Records when that normally R&B house decided to start a country-music division in the early 1970s. It soon seemed like a good arrangement for all parties as Terry began placing singles on the country charts. In 1973, he hit with his version of the pop hit, "Say, Has Anybody Seen My Sweet Gypsy Rose?" He went into 1974 with a top-30-placed original composition, "Amarillo by Morning" and in early summer was on the charts again with "Captured." He also completed an album that included a country version of his old hit, "Suspicion."

Just when things seemed going well, Atlantic abruptly decided to close its country section. Said Terry ruefully, "I had been looking for that label for a long time, someone who would take an interest in me and in promoting me. When they quit, I really felt bad about it, but that's how it goes."

For a while, in the mid-1970s, he made some recordings for Melodyland, Motown Record's new country label. In 1977, he was on the roster of a small label, Casino. While waiting for a hoped-for new surge of record successes, he continued to work the country circuit with his band.

STAMPLEY, JOE: *Singer, pianist, songwriter. Born Springhill, Louisiana, June 6, 1943.*

With an unusual consistency in song selection and performance, Joe Stampley established himself as one of the giants of country music in the 1970s. It was rare that any of his singles or albums failed to reach upper-chart levels, even rarer when any release failed to catch the public fancy at all. If there's a country-music heaven, it would have to bring a smile to the face of Hank Williams, who, appropriately, gave Stampley some of the first words of advice and encouragement when Joe was a small boy.

Stampley, born in Springhill, Louisiana, in June 1943, says, "I'm a wild and crazy Gemini. Except for seven years when I lived in Baytown, Texas, as a boy, Springhill's always been my home. It's in northern Louisiana near the Texas border and only about a mile from Arkansas. It's not Cajun country. They eat grits down south and we eat cornbread and taters up north."

His family loved country music and so did he, particularly the music of Hank Williams. "Got so I knew every song he

recorded. I met him when I was about seven at a radio station in Baytown. It really was a thrill. I told him how much I liked his singing and that I tried to imitate him. He said, 'Just be yourself and act like yourself and later on it might pay off for you.' "

Taking the advice to heart, Joe kept on singing country songs as he moved toward his teens and also started working on some originals of his own. The piano was his instrument. "I musta been about eight years old when I started learning the piano, playing Hank Williams's songs mostly at the time. I never played the guitar. I can play a few chords, but nothing that amounts to anything. I can play the ukulele, though."

By the time Joe was in his midteens, he showed enough promise as a writer to attract the attention of Merle Kilgore, a disc jockey on a Springhill station. He was impressed enough by the fifteen-year-old Stampley's talents to collaborate on some songs with the boy. "Merle got me a record contract with Imperial Records in 1957–58. The record bombed, but it sold 500 copies in my little home town and I thought that was pretty good."

Undaunted, Joe kept preparing new material and keeping his eye open for opportunities. He had become increasingly involved in rock music during those years. "I got off onto rock when I was in high school and was a big fan of Little Richard, Elvis, Jerry Lee, a lot of R&B groups like the Miracles, and particularly the Impalas. The Impalas had a record called 'I Ran All the Way' that really knocked me out."

In 1961, Stampley made contact with Chicago-based Chess Records, which issued another single of his. Once more the recording sank almost without a trace. For a good part of the early and mid-1960s, Joe was involved with a rock group called the Uniques that played the southern raunch 'n' roll circuit for a number of years. The group played in bars, clubs, and occasionally at college dances throughout the South and succeeded in building up a certain amount of following. The band was signed by Shreveport-based Paula Records in the mid-1960s and for a while it looked as though fate might smile more brightly than in the past on Joe. A single of a song he co-wrote with Kilgore called "Not Too Long Ago" became a regional hit in 1966 and sold a half million copies. ("We also made regional charts with 'All These Things'; later on it was a big country hit for me on ABC/Dot in the 1970s".) However, the followup releases did poorly and Joe's performing career marked time at the end of the 1960s.

But when Joe returned to his first love, country, in the 1970s, everything finally came together for him. "The way that came about was that I started writing country songs about 1970 and began sending demos of them to Al Gallico [of Algee Music in Nashville]. He said 'You should be recording your own country stuff' and arranged for a contract with Paramount Records. [Gallico soon became Joe's manager.] The first country song I put out was 'Qounette McGraw from Smackover Arkansas'."

By the time the next one was ready, Paramount had been bought by ABC/Dot. "My first real breakthrough came in 1972 when I did a single called 'If You Touch Me (You've Gotta Love Me).' [The song reached number one on country charts in September 1972.] Ever since then my releases have consistently been in or around the top ten and I've had a total of six number-one songs."

He had three other number-one singles during his stay with ABC/Dot, the other three being "Soul Song," "I'm Still Loving You," number one in early 1974, and "All These Things," number one in the summer of 1976. Among his other chart hits on ABC/Dot were his composition "How Lucky Can One Man Be," a chart hit in early summer of 1974, "Penny," a top-10 hit in early 1975, "Unchained Melody," on the lists in mid-1975, "Cry like a Baby," a chartmaker in the fall of that year, and "The Night Time and My Baby," a top-20 hit in September 1976. Stampley also turned out a series of LPs that made the country lists during the first half of the 1970s. ABC issued his *Greatest Hits, Volume 1* in June 1975 and it moved into the top 20 soon after.

In 1975, Stampley switched to Epic Records, losing no momentum. His initial single release, produced by Norro Wilson, "Roll on Big Mama," became a number-one hit. His third single on Epic, "Billy Get Me a Woman" (after *Big Woman*) was also a major hit, in the top 10 in November 1975. His last 1975 single was "She's Helping Me Get Over You," which was followed in early 1976 by another top-10 single, "Whisky Talkin'," in the summer. His other singles produced by Wilson included, in 1976, "Was It Worth It" and "There She Goes Again"; and, in 1977, the top-10 hits "Baby I Love You So" and "Everyday I Have to Cry Some."

In 1978, Stampley's work for Epic enrolled a new producer, the equally accomplished Billy Sherrill. The first result of the new association was the early 1978 singles success "Red Wine and Blue Memories." This was followed by the top-10 September 1978 offering "If You Got Ten Minutes (Let's Fall in Love)," a Stampley original composition. In early 1979, the team made it three out of three with the top-5 single "Do You Ever Fool Around?"

Later in the year, he had two other top-selling releases, "Put Your Clothes Back On" and "I Don't Lie." In January 1980, his duet with Moe Bandy, "Holding the Bag," made the top 10. Other 1980 chart hits Stampley and Bandy collaborated on were "Tell Ole I Ain't Here" and "Just Good Ol' Boys." Stampley's solo hit singles in 1980 included his own composition "There's Another Woman," "After Hours," and "Haven't I Loved You Somewhere Before." His early 1981 successes included the solo "I'm Gonna Love You Back to Loving Me Again" and the Bandy duet, "Hey Joe (Hey Moe)," the latter from the album of the same title, issued in 1981.

After release of Joe's debut LP on Epic in 1975, every album through early 1979 made the charts. His second LP on the label, *Billy Get Me a Woman,* issued in late 1975, was still in the top 30 in early 1976. The next release, "The Sheik of Chicago," in early summer of the year, made midchart levels and the next one, "All These Things," rose to the top 5 in September 1976. His fifth album on Epic, *Saturday*

Night Dance, showed up on hit lists in the summer of 1977 as did *Red Wind and Memories* later in the year. In late 1979, Epic issued its first *Greatest Hits* LP, which moved up the lists at year end. In the fall of 1979, Stampley teamed up with Moe Bandy for another hit album, *Just Good Ol' Boys.*

Looking back on the 1970s, Stampley said in late 1979, "I've played in every state in the union and such other places as Bermuda, England, Sweden, Holland, and Canada. I've sold a lot of records. I haven't had a million seller, but I've had a number sell over 200,000 copies which is good in the country field. I had one called 'Soul Song' that crossed over into the top 30 on pop charts and sold about a half million. Songs like 'Roll on Big Mama' and 'You Ever Fool Around' sold over a quarter million each. I had about seventeen albums released on Epic and ABC during the decade.

"One of my greatest thrills was playing the *Grand Ole Opry* back when it was in the Ryman Auditorium and thinking about all the great artists who played on that stage. Overall I played the Opry six or seven times in the 1970s. And, of course, it's also a good feeling to know my name is on the sidewalk of the Country Music Hall of Fame in Nashville."

Based on an interview with Irwin Stambler, late 1979.

STARLAND VOCAL BAND: *Vocal and instrumental group. Bill Danoff, born Springfield, Massachusetts, May 6, 1946; Taffy Danoff, born Washington, D.C., October 25, 1944; Jon Carroll, born Washington, D.C., March 1, 1957; Margot Kunkel, born Honolulu, Hawaii, September 7, 1947.*

The Starland Vocal Band moved into the national spotlight during 1976–77 with the song "Afternoon Delight," a major success on the pop charts for the group and a country hit in another performer's version. The song was the handiwork of group mainstays Bill and Taffy Danoff, who earlier had played important roles in the rise of John Denver by co-writing with John his first smash hit, "Country Roads."

The Danoffs, who met and married as a result of their musical interests, both were born and raised on the East Coast. In their teens they were influenced by both the folk boom of the late 1950s and early 1960s and the folk and country-rock genre of the mid-1960s. By the late 1960s, Bill and Taffy were active in the folk and folk-rock concert and club circuit in the Washington, D.C., area where they lived and met many other young aspirants in the field, including John Denver.

It was their relationship with Denver that eventually had a pivotal effect on all their careers. At the time, the Danoffs were performing under the name Fat City and spending much of their spare time writing songs. Denver liked their material and, in fact, used one of their compositions, "I Guess He'd Rather Be in Colorado," in his act at the start of the 1970s. The song struck a chord often present in Denver material, the longing to leave rather drab urban surroundings for a more blissful existence in rural contentment.

During 1970, Denver's touring work brought him to Washington, D.C., where he spent some time one evening at the Cellar Door nightspot with the Danoffs. They asked John over to their home, where, after a minor car accident in which Denver broke a thumb, the Danoffs showed John a song called "Country Roads" they'd been trying to complete for a month. He pitched in and by the time the sun came up, the task was through.

The song was recorded for Denver's next album, *Poems, Prayers and Promises,* as was "I Guess He'd Rather Be in Colorado." The Danoffs provided backing vocals on the songs under the name Fat City. "Country Roads" was released as a single in early 1971 and made mid-pop chart levels in March and eventually rose to number one, earning Denver his first gold record on August 18. It also helped bring the LP a second gold record, on September 15, 1971, honors in which the Danoffs shared. "Country Roads" since has become a standard, recorded and re-recorded by dozens of artists.

That success helped the Danoffs gain a record contract from RCA in the mid-

1970s, which resulted in their LP *Aces.* Later, they organized a foursome, adding Washington area performers Jon Carrol (born and raised there) and Margot Kunkel (born in Hawaii, but a Washington resident by the time the group was assembled). The new group soon signed with John Denver's label, Windsong (distributed by RCA) and began work on its debut album during 1975. That album, *Starland Vocal Band,* came out in January 1976. Two singles were taken from the LP, "California Day" and "Afternoon Delight." The latter, written by Bill Danoff, became a runaway hit in 1976, rising to the top of the hit lists and eventually selling over 3 million copies, well over platinum-record levels. A cover record by Johnny Carver made it to the country-music top-10 in September 1976.

During the year, Starland Vocal Band toured throughout the United States and also was featured on many major network and syndicated TV shows. When the Grammy Awards neared for the year 1976, the group and its music was nominated in several categories. On the Award show, telecast from Hollywood, California, in February 1977, the foursome sang "Afternoon Delight." After the various envelopes were opened, it was disclosed that the Starland Vocal Band had won the Grammies for "Best New Artists of the Year" and "Best Arrangement for Voices."

In 1977, a second LP came out on Windsong, *Rear View Mirror,* followed in 1978 by the album *Late Night Radio.*

STARR, KENNY: *Singer, guitarist, band leader. Born Topeka, Kansas, September 21, 1953.*

Pursuing a career in music was an idea that seemed to come to Kenny Starr almost with his ABCs. He was singing in public before he was in elementary school and had his first band before he was ten. Despite that head start, however, it still was a long hard road before he finally gained national attention in 1976.

Born in Topeka, his family soon moved to Burlingame, Kansas, where his father worked in the coal and construction industries. It was there that Kenny's interest in pop music was kindled almost as soon as he learned to talk. When he was five, he made his public debut at the local Veterans of Foreign Wars meeting house, the first of a series of VFW performances. When he was nine, he went a step further, organizing his first band, the Rocking Rebels, which played in local clubs. During 1963, he formed another group, Kenny and the Imperials, that toured the area and brought him an income of ten to fifteen dollars a performance.

When he reached his teens, his main preoccupation was with pop and rock material. However, when he was sixteen, he became interested in country music and soon had a new band called Kenny Starr and the Country Showmen, which found good audience response in local country nightspots.

Giving him encouragement was an Air Force retiree named Bob Hampton, who also wrote country songs. Just after Kenny graduated from high school, Hampton entered him in a talent contest sponsored by radio station KFDI in Wichita, Kansas. Kenny sent in a demonstration recording of the Ray Price hit "I Won't Mention It Again." In time, Kenny was selected as one of the finalists and, after he performed in the KFDI show, was named the winner.

Concert promoter Hap Peebles was on hand to hear the seventeen-year-old and liked what he heard. He arranged for Kenny to have a spot on a concert in Wichita featuring Conway Twitty and Loretta Lynn. When Starr finished his number, Lynn and her husband congratulated him and offered to help him if he came to Nashville. He was only too happy to comply and, once there, became a regular cast member with the Loretta Lynn Show, touring throughout the United States and Canada and to a number of other countries throughout the 1970s.

Before long, he was signed to a contract by Lynn's record company, MCA. He recorded several singles in the early and mid-1970s, some of which, like "That's a Whole Lotta Lovin'" (on hit lists in the spring of 1973) made lower-chart levels. However, by mid-1975, not much more had happened and MCA thought about dropping him from the label. When this was taken up with people in Lynn's office, it was pointed out to MCA that Kenny had not been given the chance to record new material for some time. It was agreed to give him another opportunity. Starr went into the studio in Nashville and recorded several numbers, including a Sterling Whipple composition called "Blind Man in the Bleachers."

The latter was issued as a single in late 1975 and soon entered the charts on lower levels. Unlike earlier releases, this one kept going steadily upward until, at the start of 1976, it reached number one on U.S. country lists. Suddenly Kenny was a star, at least for the moment. The song ranked as one of the biggest successes of 1976 and won many honors and awards both for Starr and Sterling Whipple.

Kenny placed several more songs on the charts in the later 1970s, such as "Slow Drivin'" in the summer of 1978, but none approached the levels reached by "Blind Man in the Bleachers."

STATLER BROTHERS, THE: *Vocal quartet. Don S. Reid, born Staunton, Virginia, June 5, 1945; Harold W. Reid, born Augusta County, Virginia, August 21, 1939; Philip E. Balsey, born Augusta County, Virginia, August 8, 1939; Lew C. De Witt, born Roanoke County, Virginia, March 8, 1939.*

Despite the name Statler Brothers, only two of the members of this vocal quartet are brothers and none of them is named Statler. Statler is actually the name of a regional brand of tissues. When the group was about to go to work touring with Johnny Cash, they were trying to think of a new name for themselves. Harold Reid saw a box of Statler Tissues across the room and said, "How about Statler? That's as good as anything." As group member Don Reid said, "We could just as easily be known as the Kleenex Brothers."

No matter what they might have called themselves, the foursome probably would have succeeded, for the group features a great deal of vocal talent as well as the considerable writing skills of the Reid brothers and Lew C. De Witt.

All four of the "Brothers" grew up in rural Virginia. They first sang together in 1955 in Lynhurst Methodist Church in Staunton. They disbanded three years later, but then regrouped in 1960, calling themselves the Kingmen, singing primarily gospel music at local churches, banquets, and on local television shows. However, they all kept their day jobs.

In 1963 the quartet met Johnny Cash at a show in Roanoke, Virginia. Harold Reid persuaded the show's promoter to let him talk to Cash and he told him about the group. Cash asked them if they could get to nearby Berryville on Sunday. At Berryville Cash asked them to open the show for him, even though he had never heard them. After the show Cash told the group he liked them, so when they went home Harold persisted in calling the country superstar until Cash finally asked them to go on the road with him. Now officially renamed the Statler Brothers, the foursome toured with Cash for eight years. This exposure enabled them to win a recording contract with Columbia Records.

The Statler Brothers had their first national hit in 1966 with "Flowers on the Wall," which was written by De Witt. The single reached the top 10 on the country charts and the number-one spot on the national pop charts. The song also won two Grammy Awards for the group.

The quartet's affiliation with Johnny Cash continued. When Cash had his own television variety show in the late 1960s and early 1970s, the Statlers became a regular feature, often singing traditional gospel songs as well as their own material. In 1970 they ended their contract with Columbia Records and signed with Mercury Records.

The decade of the 1970s was phenomenally successful for the Statler Brothers. They had numerous top-10 country singles. Among them were "Bed of Roses," on the charts in late 1970 and early 1971; "Do You Remember These?" and "The Class of '57" in 1972 (the latter won them a Grammy Award); "I'll Go to My Grave Loving You" and "I Was There" in 1975; "Some I Wrote" in 1977; and "The Official Historian of Shirley-Jean Burrell" in 1978. Other mid-1970s hits were "Whatever

Happened to Randolph Scott" and "Do You Know You Are My Sunshine." In 1979 they made the top 10 with such singles as "Nothing as Original as You" and "How to Be a Country Star." Also in top chart positions during 1979 were "Who Am I to Say" and "Here We Are Again."

Many of their songs were written by Don and Harold Reid. The songs were unusual in that they often featured comedic touches, twists, and puns, while simultaneously dealing with poignant themes such as the dashed hopes of youth ("The Class of '57") and eternal devotion to one's mate ("I'll Go to My Grave Loving You," "Thank God I've Got You"). In 1978 the Statlers had a hit single with "Who Am I to Say," which was written by Harold's sixteen-year-old daughter, Kim.

The Statler Brothers' vocal style carried over from their gospel days, with traditional four-part arrangements. Don usually acted as emcee; Harold sang bass; Lew sang baritone, and Phil Balsey took the tenor role. In addition to their popular country recordings, the quartet continued to perform and record gospel music. In 1975 they recorded two gospel albums, *Holy Bible—Old Testament* and *Holy Bible— New Testament*. They had spent seven years researching this project and wrote fifteen of the twenty-two songs on the album.

For years the Statler Brothers were unrivaled as the top vocal group in country music. They won the Country Music Association Award for Top Vocal Group for an unprecedented seven years in a row. They yielded the title to the Oak Ridge Boys in 1978, only to come back and win this honor again in 1979. Their album *The Best of the Statler Brothers* remained on the country top 40 for over four years, the first LP in the history of *Record World* magazine to achieve that. The album was certified gold in July 1977, went platinum in June 1978, and, by early 1980, approached sales of 2 million, the double platinum level. Other of their best-selling LPs were *The Country America Loves* and *Short Stories*, both released in 1977.

In 1980, the group celebrated its tenth anniversary on Mercury Records. It started the year in good shape with the LP *The*

Statler Bros. Xmas Card (issued in 1979) moving up the charts and, on the singles charts, "(I'll Even Love You) Better than I Did Then" moving toward top positions. Also on the hit lists for a while in early 1980 was a holdover from 1979, Don Reid's composition "Nothing as Original as You." Early in the year, the LP *The Best of the Statler Brothers Rides Again, Volume II*, came out and quickly showed up on the charts to be joined in the summer by the *10th Anniversary* LP. The track "Charlotte's Web" from that album, issued as a single, made the top 10 in September 1980.

As of the Mercury anniversary date, it was announced, the group had released twenty albums and twenty-nine singles on the label, sold more than 10 million records, and been named Top Vocal Group in the *Music City News* Cover Awards (voted on by publication readers) every year from 1971 through 1980. Other statistics for the decade included: over 1,500 concerts performed before over 7 million people; distance traveled close to a million miles; 188 songs recorded, of which group members wrote 125. On July 4, 1980, the group also welcomed 60–70,000 people to its eleventh annual Happy Birthday U.S.A. concert in Staunton, Virginia, a day-long charity fund-raising event. The crowd at the first free concert had been about 6,000. (In 1981, the group gave its twelfth annual performance.) During the year, the Statlers played themselves in Burt Reynolds' *Smokey and the Bandit 2*, in which their song "Charlotte's Web" was part of the score. Their contributions included singing their 1970s number-one singles hit, "Do You Know You Are My Sunshine."

The group continued to add to its laurels in 1981, placing such singles as "Don't Forget Yourself" and "In the Garden" on bestseller lists.—I.S./A.S.

STEAGALL, RED: *Singer, guitarist, songwriter, music publisher. Born Gainesville, Texas, December 22.*

Over the years, Red Steagall tried his hand at many things—rodeo riding, selling agricultural and chemical products, raising cattle. He did well at all of them, but in the end he went back to his first love, country music, and became a major figure in the field as a writer and performer.

As befits a man who could write songs like "Lone Star Beer and Bob Wills Music," Red spent a good part of his teen years at local Texas corrals trying his skills as a bronc buster and bull rider. Already an accomplished guitar player, when he went to West Texas State University, he formed a country band that played clubs in and around the school to help pay his tuition. Some of his income was also used to take care of rodeo entry fees, where he proved one of the better bull riders.

After Steagall obtained his degree in agriculture, he got a job as a sales representative with an agrochemical company and traveled throughout the Southwest and mountain states in that capacity for most of the first half of the 1960s. After a while, he began to pick up occasional singing engagements at some of the towns he visited on his selling trips. He became particularly popular in the skiing resorts of Colorado and Utah.

In the mid-1960s, he got an offer he couldn't refuse. United Artists Music in Hollywood asked him to sign on as a record promotion executive. Being able to work full time in music and also spend time getting acquainted with disc jockeys around the country seemed more attractive to Red, who was increasingly enthusiastic about a music career. He was writing original music by then, and one of his songs was picked up by the great Ray Charles and turned into a rhythm & blues singles hit. With that credit under his belt, he left UA and started a new operation, establishing his own music publishing company and also acting as a West Coast representative for several Nashville publishers.

His songs began to find their way into more and more recording sessions of country artists. In 1968, this resulted in Red Saunders reaching high chart levels with his single of Steagall's "Beer Drinking Music." Soon after, Del Reeves had similar success with "Keep on Keepin'." Steagall, who had signed a recording contract with Dot Records, had some single action of his own with "Walk All Over Georgia" and

"A Dozen Pair of Boots." Red closed out his Dot affiliation for a while with another singles hit, "Alabama Woman."

In the 1970s, Red moved his operation back to Nashville and signed a new recording agreement with Capitol Records. The result was another succession of chart singles and albums during the first part of the decade. Among his chart-making singles of that phase were "Party Dolls and Wine," "Somewhere My Love, "True Love," "The Fiddle Man," "I Gave Up Good Morning Darling," and "Finer Things in Life."

During the mid-1970s, Red headlined on major TV programs and in first-ranked clubs across the United States and Canada. Among his TV credits were appearances on the *Grand Ole Opry,* regular cast status on NBC's *Music Country, U.S.A.,* guest spots on the *Porter Wagoner Show, Hank Thompson Show, Wilburn Brothers Show,* and *Hee Haw.* In 1975, he played a role in the movie *Sing a Country Song.* His club appearances included a number of dates at Southern California's number-one country nightclub, the Palomino, similar action at the Western Place in Dallas, Panther Hall in Fort Worth, Stagecoach Inn in Stamford, Texas, the Brandin' Iron in San Bernardino, California, Knott's Berry Farm in Buena Park, California, and dozens of other venues of that order.

In the mid-1970s, Steagall returned to the label he'd first gained attention on, Dot, which by then was a part of the ABC Records organization. One of his early releases on ABC/Dot became a classic of the 1970s. Called "Lone Star Beer and Bob Wills Music," the single rose to top chart levels in the early spring of 1976. Along with the new interest in western swing generated by groups like Asleep at the Wheel and Commander Cody, the song sparked a revival of the old Wills band that led to several new album releases under the direction of Leon McAuliffe. Later in 1976, Steagall had another chart hit with his song "Truck Drivin' Man." In mid-1977, he was on the charts again with the single "Freckles Brown." By the end of the decade, Red had left ABC/Dot and signed with Elektra. That resulted in such 1980 charted singles as "3 Chord Country Song" (co-written by Red and D. Steagell), "Dim the Lights and Pour the Wine," and "Hard Hat Days and Honky Tonk Nights."

With the income from his recordings and songs, Red could indulge his other love, agriculture. During the 1970s, he spent most of his leisure time on his large farm in Lebanon, Texas.

STEVENS, EVEN: *Singer, guitarist, songwriter. Born Lewiston, Ohio, late 1940s.*

Anyone who read the fine print in the chart listings of Eddie Rabbitt's increasingly successful records in the 1970s often would have noted the name E. Stevens. The same name, together with Rabbitt's or, later on, Shel Silverstein's, often cropped up in song credits for releases of other artists, indicating Stevens was no journeyman writer. And, with occasional solo releases in the mid- and late-1970s, Even Stevens also demonstrated that he had the talent to move from behind the scenes into the spotlight sometime in the future.

Stevens, who grew up in the Cincinnati area, got his early musical grounding in church-related songs. His father was a minister who also enjoyed gospel singing and trained his children to do likewise. As Stevens grew up, he listened and enjoyed secular music as well, though he continued to play gospel music with his family in his teens. By then, he had learned guitar, which he used to accompany those sessions.

After he finished high school, he enlisted in the Coast Guard and was sent to San Francisco. "It was while I was there that I started writing songs," he recalled. "At the time I mainly was doing it for my own enjoyment." But he also found time to entertain his friends and play some folk clubs in the Bay area.

After finishing his stint, he moved back to Cincinnati in 1970, where he kept writing new songs while working as a disc jockey. One day he got a phone call from an uncle who was a musician living in Nashville. "He heard that I was playing in clubs and writing songs, so he sent word that if I wanted to come down and see if my songs were any good, he would put me up for a couple weeks. I wasn't writing country music at all in those days."

Stevens (not his real name) told Vernell Hackett of *Music City News*, "He was a big help to me because he was able to get me studio time, so I cut some sessions on songs I wanted to pitch to artists and he kinda helped me get the general feel of the music industry."

After a while, Stevens began to get more into the country vein with his material, though it was slow going for a while. In 1971, he met another young aspiring writer named Eddie Rabbitt at a party. Rabbitt had written a song Elvis Presley recorded and also was eager to make his way as a performer. The two found common ground and soon became roommates as they worked on a steadily growing supply of new songs. Many of those proved to be bedrock for Rabbitt's career in the mid-1970s, providing him with a series of releases that reached higher and higher chart levels as the 1970s went by.

Among the early Rabbitt/Stevens compositions that found their way onto Rabbitt discs and tapes were "If I Put Them All Together I'd Have You," "The Days That End in Y," "We Can't Go on Living like This," and "Hearts of Fire." In late 1975, Rabbitt had a top-10 hit with their collaboration "I Should Have Married You" and added to the top-10 successes in 1976 with the release "Rocky Mountain Music/Do You Right Tonight." In 1977, the two could point to such Rabbitt charted singles as "I Can't Help Myself" and "We Can't go on Like This." In December 1978, Rabbitt scored one his biggest hits ever with the single "I Just Want to Love You," number one on U.S. country charts. (It involved a third co-writer, D. Malloy.)

By then there often were charted songs co-written by Stevens and Shel Silverstein of Dr. Hook–Bobby Bare fame. As was the case with Rabbitt, Stevens told Dale Anderson of the Buffalo, N.Y., *News* in November 1977, the collaboration with Silverstein resulted from a chance meeting. The two met while Silverstein was walking down a Nashville street. "He was on his way to the airport, but he decided to stay a couple more weeks. We wrote about 30 songs together. We'd write 5 or 6 songs a day sometimes, but it comes out to one out of 30 that's any good, that's a special song."

The work with Silverstein added to a catalogue of Stevens' work that already was impressive in sheer numbers. As of the early 1980s, his work with Rabbitt alone totaled over 400 songs. The general nature of his music, he told Anderson, was a blend of country, rock, folk, and "Ohio" music "with a little gospel flavor thrown in for good measure." And, in fact, like many writers, he worked with anyone who might have an idea that hit his fancy; thus he and Dan Tyler co-wrote a late 1970s song recorded by Stella Parton, "Four Little Letters." He, Tyler, and Rabbitt combined forces at times, an example being "Hearts on Fire." Stella Parton had a hit in 1977 with the Stevens-Silverstein composition "The Danger of a Stranger"; George Jones made the charts with "If I Put Them All Together I'd Have You"; and Sammi Smith, among dozens of others, released a number of singles bearing Stevens' and his co-writers' names.

Although Stevens seemed to be more interested in writing than performing, he had shown ability as a singer over the years and agreed to sign with Elektra in 1974. One of the first positive results of that was the 1975 single "Let the Little Boy Dream," which made the top 40. There was a gap of a few years before his debut LP came out, but it finally appeared in the fall of 1977. Called *Thorn on the Rose*, it included some Silverstein-Stevens tunes ("Too Many Nights Alone," "I'm from Outer Space") and some Rabbitt ones, such as "Delta Queen." One of the first singles from the LP was a duet with Sherry Grooms called "The King of Country Music Meets the Queen of Rock 'n' Roll." Also contributing to the almost autobiographical nature of the album was a gospel number, "A Piece of the Rock," in which Stevens' father and sister aided in the vocals.

Musing over the choice between increas-ing his meager recorded output or concen-trating on writing, he told Hackett, "I'm not sure I want to perform and do exten-sive concert tours, but I do know I'd like to continue to record my own material."

On the other hand, as he said to Ander-son, "I've been a barber, a Morse code op-erator and a pottery maker, but writing—it's the best life in the world. There's no hours, no boss and you just get paid for playing. This may sound trite, but I just want to be able to make more records. I don't want to have to worry about success."

STEVENS, RAY: *Singer, pianist, songwriter, comedian, record producer. Born Clarksdale, Georgia, January 24, 1939.*

Combining an infectious sense of humor with fine musical skills, Ray Stevens cre-ated a unique niche for himself, first in the pop and rock field, then in country & western. Oddly, he was first known as a pop star though he made Nashville (the lodestone of country music) his home from the start of the 1960s. It was not until the 1970s that he was regarded as a full-fledged country star.

Ray was exposed to all forms of mu-sic in his Clarksdale, Georgia, home. He showed considerable promise in his early years as a classical pianist. In high school (Albany, Georgia), he formed his own R&B and blues band with school friends and played local clubs and dances. He also per-formed as a stand-up comedian between the group's sets. His musical favorites at the time were mainly R&B artists such as the Coasters, Drifters, and Midnighters. But as rockabilly artists like Elvis and Jerry Lee Lewis came to the fore, he turned his attention to that new format. Meanwhile, besides his band activity, teenage Ray also worked weekends as a disc jockey on a local station.

In 1956, the family moved to Atlanta, where Ray began taking some of his songs around to publishers. In 1957, he gained his first recording contract with a subsidi-ary of Capitol Records, an association that didn't turn out to be particularly produc-tive. Ray, though, intended to continue his education. He enrolled at Georgia State

University, majoring in classical piano and music theory, but also found time to perform with a small combo.

At the end of the 1950s, it looked as though his recording career might get into high gear when his single "Sergeant Preston of the Yukon" began moving up the charts in 1959. It sold well over 200,000 copies, then had to be withdrawn because of a lawsuit brought by a syndicate that owned the radio program rights to the title.

Stevens got his B.A. degree from Georgia State, then moved to Nashville in 1961. In 1962, he was back on pop hit lists again, this time with a composition that could well vie for a place in the Guinness Book of Records for title length: "Jeremiah Peabody's Polyunsaturated Quick Dissolving Fast Acting Pleasant Tasting Green and Purple Pills." He followed this with a string of many hits, the best known of which probably is "Ahab the Arab," in which he played the parts of Ahab and his camel, Clyde. Other comic gems of those years were "Freddie Feelgood" and "Hairy the Ape."

Stevens didn't want to become typecast as only a novelty songwriter, so he shifted gears from recording to behind the scenes work in the mid-1960s. For a number of years he made his living primarily as an arranger and record producer. Among those artists he was associated with were Patti Page, Brook Benton, Brenda Lee, Charlie Rich, and Ronnie Dove. In early 1966, he felt he was in a position to resume his recording career on his own terms, and he signed a new pact with Monument. From the beginning, the idea was that he could record serious songs as well as comic or satiric ones. As he noted, "I had built up a comedy image that was hard to break, but the lull between records had let the image die down. This made it possible for me to do something serious."

He soon showed he was capable of serious writing in 1968 with "Unwind" and "Mr. Businessman." The latter pointed to the shortcomings of a society where people ignored "the laughter of the children" while blindly pursuing economic success ("Tuesday evening with your harlot/

And Wednesday it's your charlatan analyst . . ."). The widespread audience acceptance of the new material brought Ray the opportunity to perform in large auditoriums and concert halls around the United States. He also was featured on major talk shows, *The Ed Sullivan Show*, and many other network TV programs.

But his interest in humor was not abandoned, as evidenced by his massive 1969 hit, "Gitarzan," with lyrics that went, in part, "He's free as the breeze/He's always at ease/He lives in the jungle/And hangs by his knees/He swings through the trees/Without a trapeze/In his B.V.D.s." He followed that with another novelty hit, "Along Came Jones," then turned his hat around once more with the fine gold-record 1970 single, "Everything Is Beautiful." The album of the same title also was a chart hit during 1970-71, as was the novelty single "Bridget the Midget." "Everything Is Beautiful" marked his move to a new label, Barnaby, with whom he remained until the mid-1970s.

Stevens was getting additional recognition for some of those efforts from the recording industry. "Gitarzan" received a Grammy Awards nomination for best male vocal performance of 1969 and "Everything Is Beautiful" not only received a nomination in 1970 but won Ray a Grammy.

During the 1969-70 TV season, Ray's guest appearances on the *Andy Williams Show* were so successful that he got the chance to host the summer replacement series in 1970. Joining him in hosting the show were Lulu and Mama Cass. Later, Ray made a number of additional appearances on the 1970-71 version of Williams' variety program.

He placed many other singles on the charts during the early 1970s on both Monument and Barnaby labels. The Monument chartmakers included "Have a Little Talk with Myself" and "Sunday Mornin' Comin' Down"; Barnaby successes included "America, Communicate with Me," "Sunset Strip," "All My Trials," "A Mama and a Papa," and "Turn Your Radio On." Also on best-selling album lists in 1971 was the Barnaby LP *Greatest Hits.*

Signifying his closer ties with the country field in the early 1970s was the 1973 singles hit "Nashville." Ray also was featured on the NBC-TV show *Music Country, U.S.A.*, which began as a 1973 summer replacement and came back as a regular series in the spring of 1974. Throughout the 1970s, Stevens was a guest on many country-music network and syndicated shows and on a number of country-music TV specials.

In 1974, he placed the novelty single "The Streak" in the top 10 of both pop and country charts. The release became his top-selling single to that point, going well past platinum levels on the way to sales of over 4 million copies. In the summer of 1975, he had great success with a new version of the old Errol Garner song "Misty." By the time "Misty" was placing the Barnaby banner in the country top 10, Ray had left that label in favor of Warner Brothers. Before 1975 was over, Ray had his first Warners single on the charts, "Indian Love Call."

In 1976, Stevens' chart-making singles included "Young Love" early in the year, "You Are So Beautiful," in upper country chart levels in the summer, and "Honky Tonk Waltz," a chart hit in late summer-early fall. His debut album on Warner Brothers, *Just for the Record*, was issued in the spring of 1976. His second Warner's LP in 1977, titled *Feel the Music*, which he arranged and produced, includes samples of both his serious and comic sides. One of the latter was a countrified version of "In the Mood," released as a single under the alias the Henhouse Five Plus Two. The latter made inroads on both pop and country charts. Also on the charts in 1977 was the single "Dixie Hummingbird."

In April 1979, his third LP for Warner Brothers, *The Feeling's Not Right Again*, was issued. The album was the fourteenth LP of his career. Among original compositions included in the 1979 release were "Get Crazy with Me," "Daydream Romance," "Feel the Music," "Be Your Own Best Friend," and his tongue-in-cheek "I Need Your Help Barry Manilow," the last named a top-10 singles hit for Ray in early 1979.

During 1979, Stevens left Warner Brothers and signed with RCA. In the spring of 1980, his single of his composition "Shriner's Convention" was on upper-chart levels for the new label. The album of that title also was on the charts in the summer. His other charted singles on RCA in the early 1980s included "Night Games" in 1980 and "One More Last Chance" in 1981.

STEWART, GARY: *Singer, guitarist, songwriter, band leader. Born Kentucky, 1944.*

In private, Gary Stewart comes across as a soft-spoken, shy, introspective individual. That image isn't changed too much when he first comes onstage in his workaday-looking clothes and battered fedora, à la Hank Williams (whose songs he often sings). But once he starts singing and gets his guitar strings vibrating, he conveys a restless urgency that quickly establishes his authority with the audience and marks him as one of the major creative forces in modern country music.

Stewart's name generally is associated with his current home state of Florida, but his roots go back to Kentucky where he was born. His family, a large one ("I was one of eight or nine children—something like that"), was exposed to country music for the most part in the Blue Grass state. But when the clan moved to Florida, when he was twelve, the music heard on radios and records encompassed a much broader group of styles. As a result, in his teens, Gary became a rock musician for a time and toured with regional groups.

Tiring of the road, Gary relegated music to part-time status while he worked days at an aircraft factory near the Florida town of Okeechobee. He got a regular job singing and pickin' at a nightclub called the Wagon Wheel. His performances, which offered mostly well-known songs but included a few originals, caught the attention of Mel Tillis, who sometimes visited the Wagon Wheel when he returned to his home state from Nashville. Tillis suggested that Gary pursue his songwriting bent more diligently.

Acting on that advice, Stewart moved to Nashville and did get his writing operation under way. His output during that phase of his career included chart hits for Billy Walker ("When a Man Loves a Woman" and "She Goes Walkin' Through My Mind") and Jack Green ("There's a Whole Lot About a Woman a Man Don't Know") as well as songs recorded by people like Nat Stuckey, Jim Ed Brown, Peggy Little, Roy Rogers, Cal Smith, Roy Drusky, and Jimmy Dean.

Gary made some stabs at doing his own recordings, but his characteristic self-doubts tended to hold him back, though he did make some sides for two record companies. "But the recording was kinda accidental. I enjoyed going into the studio and cutting records, but I really didn't have my heart in it. I just wanted to make a go of it as a songwriter."

Part of the problem also was Stewart's longing for the calmer environment of Florida. Eventually, he decided to move back to Florida. "I got homesick. I just needed to sit around in the sun and take it easy, which I did." Before going back, he made a demo tape that underscored his ability to sing a range of material. "We did a bunch of Motown songs—rhythm and blues things—and made 'em into country songs." The tape caught the ear of Roy Dea, then a producer for Mercury Records. Dea initially called Gary in Florida to recruit him for Mercury, but moved to RCA before anything happened. So it was that Stewart signed with RCA in 1973.

Gary's talents as an excellent pianist as well as guitarist (he had done some session work in Nashville) kept his phone ringing. Nat Stuckey called him to join his backing group. From that work, Stewart moved over to Charley Pride's band, the Pridesmen. Pride gave him the opportunity to do some of his own songs before the main act began, which started attracting a following for Gary from country audiences.

The first single issued by RCA was Gary's composition "Drinkin' Thing." The song was pulled out of circulation in favor of another single, "Ramblin' Man," which did reasonably well, but nowhere near as well as the reissue of "Drinkin' Thing." That song and another 1974 release, "Out of Hand," moved to top country chart levels and marked Stewart as an important new country influence.

His first album, *Out of Hand*, was one of the best debut albums of 1975 and followed by an equally well-crafted collection, *Steppin' Out*, in 1976. Gary backed those releases with concerts throughout the United States with his own three- or four-piece group. His following grew steadily, though not explosively, as the 1970s went by. Critics almost universally acclaimed him as a first-rank artist.

Stewart's albums and singles consistently made the charts, examples being the LP *Your Place or Mine*, a top-20 chartmaker in 1977, and *Little Junior* in 1978. His chart singles included "Ten Years of This" in 1977 and "Single Again" in 1978. His charted singles in the early 1980s included "Cactus and a Rose" and "Are We Dreamin' the Same Dream/Roarin' " in 1980 and "Let's Forget That We're Married" (co-written with J. Lewis and S. Tackett) in 1981.

STEWART, JOHN: *Singer, guitarist, songwriter. Born San Diego, California, September 5, 1939.*

When the spotlight dimmed for folk music in the mid-1960s, many artists accepted the fact and adjusted to playing before small audiences and recording for specialty labels. One who rebelled against taking such a role was John Stewart, who went out as a soloist after the breakup of the Kingston Trio determined to develop broad interest in his material. For a decade, though he had a following on the folk circuit and turned out many excellent albums, it seemed a lost cause. But perseverance finally paid off with major success at the end of the 1970s.

Stewart, whose father was a racehorse trainer, was born in San Diego, California, and grew up in that state. As a teenager in the mid-1950s, he was influenced by Elvis and the other rock pioneers. After learning to play guitar, he formed his own rock band in high school called John Stewart and the Furies. The band played small clubs in the Southern California area and managed to record a single called "Rocking Anna" that came out on Vita Records.

After finishing high school, John entered Mount San Antonio Junior College in Walnut, California, leaning toward music, but not sure about whether he could make a living at it.

By then, the folk music boom was under way and John found his calling. He noted, "The lyrics were adventurous, you could play the song with a guitar and they were easy to sing." John not only worked up versions of traditional folk songs, he began to write new ones. In 1959, after attending a Kingston Trio concert, he managed to get backstage to talk to the group that was becoming one of the favorites of the mass audience of the late 1950s. The meeting led to the group's adopting some of his material for their repertoire. "They said, 'Sign right here.' It was that easy. They recorded 'Molly Dee' and 'Green Grasses.' Then their manager told me that Roulette Records wanted a folk group, so I formed one. We rehearsed on the airplane to New York."

The group named itself the Cumberland Three. During its two-year span, the trio recorded three albums, none of which made much impact on the market. Besides that, it found a respectable amount of concert work on the folk club coffee house circuit. Meanwhile, Stewart kept in close contact with the Kingston Trio, helping with arrangements and supplying new songs from time to time. When charter member Dave Guard got tired of the grind and decided to leave in 1961, Stewart was the natural choice to replace him.

The Trio was still riding high with concertgoers and record buyers then and the momentum continued after John joined. During his years with the group John was able to place a sizable number of awards in his collection, including gold records for the LPs *String Along* (1962) and *The Best of the Kingston Trio* (1964). He also contributed to a number of top-10 singles, such as "Greenback Dollar," "Where Have All the Flowers Gone," and "The Reverend Mr. Black."

By 1966, though, the glory years of the group were behind it. The resurgent rock movement of the mid-1960s drastically cut into the following for folk groups and it was finally decided to disband (though new incarnations sprang up in later years). John's last work with the Trio appeared in the 1967 Capitol release, *Farewell Album.* After that, he set his cap for a solo career. He told an interviewer he was happy for that development: "I was bored. It was a very formal group, so we were limited in what we could do."

The road to individual stardom proved a rougher one than he expected. In the mid- and late-1960s, he achieved better results as a songwriter than as a performer. A number of his compositions were chartmakers for other artists, including the Monkees with "Daydream Believer," the Lovin' Spoonful with "Never Going Back to Nashville," and several artists with "July You're a Woman." Stewart signed with the Trio's old label, Capitol, and completed such superb LPs as *California Bloodlines* in 1969 and *Willard* in the early 1970s; they received near unanimous critical acclaim, but were all but ignored by the public at large.

Stewart switched to Warner Brothers Records in the early 1970s and such LPs as *Lonesome Picker Rides Again* and *Sunstorm* were issued, again with disappointing results. John still received a warm welcome from folk diehards on college campuses and in small folk clubs across the country, but without commercial record breakthroughs. Still searching for the right combination, he signed with RCA, which issued several albums in the mid-1970s: *Wingless Angels, Cannons in the Rain,* and the 1974 live album, *Phoenix Concerts.* Once more the reaction was less than monumental.

As the late 1970s came into view, the outlook looked increasingly dismal for John. He had no recording contract and his income from concert work was marginal. As he played for small, admiring groups on the folk circuit, he pleaded with his listeners to help him by writing record companies he was approaching to give him another opportunity. Whether that resulted in a flood of letters is hard to say, but he finally did complete an agreement with RSO Records, then rising high on the disco hits of the Bee Gees.

His first album for RSO, *Fire in the Wind*, came out in 1978. Receiving more promotion than most of his previous solo albums, it didn't threaten any of the best-selling LPs of the year, but made a reasonably respectable showing with record buyers. Then came the 1979 LP *Bombs Away Dream Babies* (a title that came from Stewart's still close friend, Dave Guard), arguably one of his finest combinations of compositions and musical treatment since *California Bloodlines*. It must be admitted that there was more of a rock tone to the tracks than before, something that didn't escape the notice of folk music critics. However, the mixture proved to be what was needed to attract attention both from John's staunch folk supporters and new groups of fans.

The single "Gold" from the collection received airplay across the United States in the summer of 1979, a song that gave voice to John's longtime frustration with his lot in pop music ("There's people out there turnin' music into gold"). This single lived up to its name, reaching the top 5 nationally and helping make the album a chart success. The other songs issued as singles from the LP also did very well, "Midnight Wind" and "Lost Her in the Sun." Helping out were two backing artists who felt Stewart was a major talent too long ignored, Lindsey Buckingham and Stevie Nicks of Fleetwood Mac.

In early 1980, his third LP on RSO, *Dream Babies Go Hollywood*, came out. Among those supporting him this time were Phil Everly, Linda Ronstadt, and Nicolette Larson.

STEWART, REDD: *Guitarist, pianist, fiddler, songwriter. Born Ashland City, Tennessee, May 27, 1921.*

One of the closest relationships in country music over the years was that between band leader PeeWee King and his gifted sideman, Redd Stewart. Stewart for more than two decades provided the King aggregation with solid musical grounding in almost every instrument in the band. Equally important, Stewart teamed with King to write some of the most durable standards in country & western music.

Redd was born in Tennessee, but his family soon moved to Kentucky. He learned to play piano and guitar while still in grade school and appeared in his hometown Louisville area in the early 1930s. Louisville was a hotbed of country music activity during this period, numbering such rising young stars as PeeWee King and Gene Autry among its radio performers.

Redd played with small groups in town and then became a member of one called the Prairie Riders. Later, when PeeWee King formed his Golden West Cowboys, Redd was asked to join. Redd appeared on the *Grand Ole Opry* with PeeWee for a number of years. While on the *Opry* in 1946, Redd and Peewee collaborated on their first major song hit, the one that helped propel Kay Starr to national fame, "Bonaparte's Retreat."

In 1947, Redd moved with King to PeeWee's own radio show on WAVE radio in Louisville. The show was a weekly feature first on radio, then on WAVE-TV for a decade (1947–57). In 1948, Stewart and King collaborated on "Tennessee Waltz," which became one of the top songs of the year. Through the mid-1960s, more than 10 million records of the song, by various performers, were sold. (At the end of the 1970s, a new version by Lacy J. Dalton was a chart hit.) During the 1950s and 1960s, Redd toured the country many times with the King band. He and PeeWee King were featured on the 1964 Starday LP *PeeWee King and Redd Stewart*.

Redd also turned out some of his own recordings over the years, including the LP *Favorite Old Time Tunes*. His single records included "Homestead," "Bonaparte's Retreat," "I'm Getting Tired," "Thy Burdens Are Greater than Mine," "Gee But I Hate to See Me Go," "When You Are Waltzing with the One You Love," "Tennessee Waltz," and "Slow Poke."

STEWART, WYNN: *Singer, guitarist, band leader, songwriter. Born Morrisville, Missouri, June 7, 1934.*

A will-o'-the-wisp at times, Wynn Stewart had so much nervous energy that he often whisked from one entertainment project to the next while the previous one still seemed to be building up momentum. The result was that, while he accomplished a great deal in country music, concentration on writing and performing at certain times might have brought a much wider following. Nonetheless, he remained an important figure in the field for over four decades and was still placing songs on the hit charts at the end of the 1970s.

As a child in Missouri, he became interested in music almost as soon as he could talk. When he was only five, he made his first public appearance, singing a solo in church accompanied on piano by his Aunt Leota. As he grew older, he added more songs to his repertoire, both gospel hymns and some of the country songs he heard on *Grand Ole Opry* programs on Saturday nights. He also learned to accompany himself on guitar and was soon good enough to gain a regular spot on a country show over station KWTO in Springfield, Missouri.

That phase of his career was cut short when he was fourteen. His family moved to the Los Angeles, California, area. As soon as they were settled in, Wynn formed his own band and began to find work at local benefits and on radio. At fifteen, he was in the studios making a demonstration recording that eventually won him a recording contract in 1950 with Intro Records in Hollywood.

Not too much happened with that association, but Wynn kept working with local country groups, polishing his performing skills while also working on original songs in his spare time. In 1953, he took an important step forward by organizing a new band that included some of the best musicians in the area in the country field. The roster included Bobby Austin, George French, Roy Nichols, Jim Pierce, Helen Price, and, on steel guitar, the noted Ralph Mooney. A recording of one of his compositions, "Strollin'," won the attention of Capitol Records and brought a contract with that major firm in 1954. His debut single, "Waltz of the Angels," proved a chart hit and was followed by such other mid-1950s successes as "Keeper of the Keys," "Hold Back Tomorrow," and "You Took Her Off My Hands," among others.

In the late 1950s, Stewart moved to Las Vegas and switched from Capitol to Challenge Records, owned by a close friend named Joe Johnson. Before long Stewart had the first of a series of releases out on the Challenge subsidiary, Jackpot Records. One of the first of those was a song written by Harlan Howard, whose wife Jan was a Challenge artist, called "Above and Beyond." Wynn's release was a hit in the West, but a cover of the song by Buck Owens became a national top-10 hit in 1960. Jan Howard made a number of recordings with Stewart in the early 1960s, including "Wrong Company," "Yankee Go Home," and "We'll Never Love Again." During those years, Wynn was beginning to make a national reputation as well. In 1960, he had a top-10 national hit with the single of his composition "Wishful Thinking." He also provided Challenge with a number of other charted releases, such as "Playboy," "Big, Big Love," "Loversville," "Another Day, Another Dollar," "One More Memory," and "One Way to Go."

For a while, Stewart gave up touring to run his own nightclub, called the Nashville Nevada Club. Besides running the club and leading his band there, his Las Vegas activities the first part of the 1960s included serving as program director and DJ at the Vegas station KTOO and hosting his own TV show on the same station. Naturally, many people from the music business visited the city and often spent time at Wynn's club. One of those was Capitol Records producer Ken Nelson, who liked the kind of music Stewart and his band offered. A main reason for Stewart's departure from Capitol in the 1950s had been the inroads of rock 'n' roll, which caused a severe depression in the country recording field for a time. By the mid-1960s, country had come back strongly and Nelson felt that re-signing Stewart would be profitable for both parties. For his new affiliation, Wynn assembled a band called the Tourists, whose members were Jimmy Collins, Dave Allen,

Bobby Edrington, and Dennis Bromeck. He also gave up the club and moved his family to Hacienda Heights, California. He commented, "It's much more important for an artist to travel and meet new country music fans than to have the top country night club."

With his new band he began turning out a series of new recordings, including such mid-1960s singles as "Shamarie," "I Keep Forgetting," "Half of This, Half of That," "Rosalie," "Angels Don't Lie," "Does He Love You like I Do," and "Ole What's 'Er Name." His 1967 output included his most successful effort, the single "It's Such a Pretty World Today," which rose to number one on the country charts. In 1968, he had another big year with the top-10 hits "Something Pretty" and "Love's Gonna Happen to Me," both also title songs of Capitol albums. His album releases of 1968–69 included *Songs of Wynn Stewart, In Love,* and *Let the Whole World Sing It with Me.* In the early 1970s, he was represented by such albums on Capitol as *You Don't Care What Happens to Me, It's a Beautiful Day,* and *Baby, It's Yours.* His singles releases in 1970–71 included "It's a Beautiful Day" b/w "Prisoner on the Run," and "Heavenly" b/w "You're No Secret of Mine."

By the mid-1970s, things had slowed down for Wynn on Capitol and he changed labels once again, this time to the new Playboy Records country group. The affiliation brought renewed rapport with country fans, as reflected by such chartmakers as "Lonely Rain" in the summer of 1975 and the top-20 hit in September 1976, "After the Storm." At the end of the decade, he moved on once more to Win Records. One of the early results of that relationship was the early 1979 singles hit, "Eyes Big as Dallas."

STONE, CLIFFIE: *Singer, band leader, bass violist, songwriter, disc jockey, record industry executive. Born Burbank, California, March 1, 1917.*

Clifford Gilpin Snyder, better known as Cliffie Stone, never ventured too far from his native California, but he made an in-delible mark on the country-music field as a performer and entertainment field executive. He was particularly effective as a discoverer and manager of new talent, helping to forward the careers of such artists as Tennessee Ernie Ford, Molly Bee, Dallas Frazier, and many others.

His affinity for country music came naturally. His father, whose stage name was Herman the Hermit, was a successful comedian who played with many leading country stars in variety shows in California and elsewhere. (He later appeared on many of his son's TV shows.) Nonetheless, Cliffie's initial interest was in more pop-oriented material.

While attending Burbank High School in the 1930s, he was active in both music and acting events. He played trombone and bass fiddle, and performed for two seasons in comedies at the Pasadena Community Playhouse. The bass proved the most helpful later when he used it in a comedy routine he and Gene Austin put together for Ken Murray's Hollywood Blackouts.

In the mid-1930s, Stone played bass with such major dance bands of the period as Anson Weeks and Freddy Slack. After he started getting work as a country disc jockey in 1935, he swung away from the pop music of the period toward country & western. One of his first shows was the *Covered Wagon Jubilee* of KFVD. During the late 1930s and early 1940s he emceed the *Lucky Stars Show* on KFWB for seven years. In the 1940s, he also led the band and was featured comedian on the CBS network *Hollywood Barn Dance* radio program. For many of those years his early morning show, *Wake Up Ranch,* was one of the most popular in the area. He also was an associate of songwriter-performer Stuart Hamblen in many activities. As one of the most popular people on Los Angeles–area radio, he was so much in demand during the mid-1940s that from 1943 to 1947 he often was master of ceremonies for as many as twenty-five to twenty-eight western radio shows a week.

In 1946, Capitol Records signed Stone in the dual role of head of country & western music and recording artist. He formed a new band for the latter effort and soon was turning out a steady stream of singles for the label. Among his releases of the 1940s and 1950s were "My Pretty Girl," "Spanish Bells," "When My Blue Moon Turns to Gold Again," "Christmas Waltz," "Blues Stay Away from Me," "Bryant's Boogie," and "Blue Canadian Rockies." He turned out several dozen albums during his long affiliation with Capitol, with some of the later releases including *Party's on Me* (1958), *Cliffie Stone Sing Along* (1961), and *The Great Hank Williams* (1964).

During those years and on into the 1960s, Cliffie wrote a number of originals, some of which made the hit charts in versions by him or other artists, in collaboration with people like Merle Travis, Eddie Kirk, and Leon McAuliffe. Among those compositions were "No Vacancy," "Divorce Me C.O.D.," "So Round, So Firm, So Fully Packed," "Steel Guitar Rag," and "Sweet Temptations."

In 1947, he met a fellow announcer from a Pasadena station named Ernie Ford. He quickly recognized Tennessee Ernie's potential and became his manager for ten years. Ford was one of the major additions to the Capitol roster. (He also was instrumental in bringing other important artists on board, including Hank Thompson.) Ford also became a regular in the early stages of a new TV program Cliffie organized called *Hometown Jamboree*. That program became one of the most eagerly awaited Saturday night variety shows in the Southern California area, one of the highest rated programs throughout its ten-year run.

Many of the best new talents in country music came to the fore on the *Jamboree*, which also showcased many established artists as guests or regulars. Among those featured on it over the years, besides Tennessee Ernie, were Polly Bergen, Merle Travis, Wesley Tuttle, Molly Bee, Bucky Tibbs, Tommy Sands, Joanie O'Brien, Billy Strange, Jeanne Black, Speedy West, Jimmy Bryant, Gene O'Quin, Ferlin Husky, Dallas Frazier, Harold Hensley, Billy Armstrong, and Billy Liebert. Also a regular was Cliffie's father, Herman the Hermit.

While keeping that show going, Stone also had a hand in Tennessee Ernie's mushrooming success. He produced Ford's show on ABC radio, CBS radio, NBC daytime TV, and later the highly ranked night-time TV series sponsored by Ford Motor Co. He handled production chores for that show for four years until a minor illness forced him to step down.

In the 1960s, Cliffie cut back on his performing chores in favor of management activities. His operations included some artist management work, a booking agency, and a number of music publishing firms. One of these, Central Songs, he sold to Capitol Records in 1969; another one, Snyder Music Corp., remained under his aegis into the 1970s. During the 1960s and early 1970s, he also continued his record production work, handling assignments for such labels as Tower and UNI. At the end of the 1960s, he still did some recording work for Capitol, commuting by then from his twenty-acre ranch in outlying Saugus, California.

A considerable amount of his time in the 1960s and 1970s was devoted to industry affairs. He served on committees and in executive capacities for both the Country Music Association in Nashville and the California-based Academy of Country & Western Music. In the 1970s, he served a term as president of the latter organization. As of the late 1970s, his main concern in a professional sense was directing the affairs of ATV Music Company. He also promoted a number of bluegrass events in California in the late 1970s and at the start of the 1980s.

STONEMAN FAMILY: *Vocal and instrumental group founded by Ernest V. "Pop" Stoneman, born Monarat, Carroll County, Virginia, May 25, 1893; died Nashville, Tennessee, June 14, 1968.*

In the years after World War II, much of traditional country music had been obscured by newer commercial versions. One family that still preserved much of the flavor and content of the old-time ballads and dance tunes was the renowned Stoneman clan.

The man who built the modern Stoneman musical dynasty was talented, rugged Ernest "Pop" Stoneman. Born in a log cabin in rural Virginia, he grew up in a family whose roots were deep in American history. His great, great, great, great-grandfather had come to America as a cabin boy from England. (His mother's family, named Bowers, had originally emigrated from Germany.)

As in many rural homes, singing the old folk tunes and hymns, or variations of them, was a looked-for pleasure. Young Ernest enjoyed singing and performing from his early youth; he learned to play the harmonica and jew's-harp before he was ten and the banjo and autoharp by the time he was in his teens.

Continuing to improve his skills as he reached manhood, he played at local affairs but earned his keep in other ways. In the 1920s, the rise of the recording industry changed all this. Word of the collecting efforts of such record representatives as Frank Walker and Ralph Peer began to filter down to many rural artists.

As a result, Stoneman and Peer met and Pop's first record session was set up for the Okeh label. The session took place at the company's studios on September 24, 1924. (Later, Pop sometimes remembered the date, erroneously, as having been in 1925.) The songs were "The Sinking of the Titanic," "The Face That Never Returned," "Freckled Face Mary Jane," and "Me and My Wife." In 1926, Peer set up another session in which Stoneman and his group recorded "Sourwood Mountain." During those sessions, Pop added guitar playing to his talents.

During the balance of the 1920s, Pop toured widely, making personal appearances in many parts of the country. He also continued to turn out new recordings. He taught his wife to play fiddle and added other artists to his group, such as Uncle Eck Dunford. The Stonemans performed with many country-music greats from 1926 to 1931, including the Bailes Brothers, Riley Puckett, and Uncle Dave

Macon. Among their songs were such titles as "When the Springtime Comes Again," "Say, Darling, Say," "The Black Dog Blues," "New River Train," "Hallelujah Side," "Cumberland Gap," "Hang John Brown," and "Bile Them Cabbage Down." Some of the songs were variations on traditional ballads or original compositions of Pop's.

The Depression had its effect on all country music in the early 1930s. With record dates few and far between and engagements hard to find, the Stonemans settled outside Washington, D.C. Pop got a job in a naval gun factory and, with his wife, concentrated on raising a family (twenty-three children were born, of whom thirteen survived to adulthood), playing occasional night dates when work was available.

As the children grew up, they learned instruments themselves and joined with their parents in working up song stylings. At the end of World War II, the Stoneman Family began to receive an increasing number of invitations to perform at concerts in many parts of the East and South. Some of the children married and left, but throughout the 1950s and 1960s Pop could always count on half a dozen or more for performing dates. The growth of interest in traditional country music in these decades resulted in new opportunities for the group. They played on many college campuses and at a number of major folk festivals. In 1962, the Stoneman Family made their debut on the *Grand Ole Opry* and returned several more times in the years that followed.

For a time, the group was persuaded by their managers to move to Los Angeles, California, to take advantage of the still flourishing folk movement. The move took place in April 1964, and led to guest apparances on such shows as *Shindig*, *The Steve Allen Show*, "The Meredith Willson Special," *The Jimmy Dean Show*, and "The Danny Thomas Special." The Stonemans also were featured at the Monterey Folk Festival.

During these years, new chances to record came from many different labels. In

1957, the group turned out *Banjo Tunes and Songs* for Folkways. Starday issued the LP *Ernest Stoneman and the Stoneman Family* in 1962, and another Stoneman Family album in 1964. World Pacific issued the LP *Big Ball in Monterey* in 1964. In the mid-1960s, the Stonemans were signed by Columbia Records.

As the mid-1960s went by, the fadeout of the folk boom and the resurgence of rock caused the group to reevaluate its position. By late 1965, the Stonemans found they weren't doing well enough in music to pay their bills. Jack Clement, then their comanager, suggested that Nashville might be a better base, so the group moved there in January 1966. Things seemed to pick up. They got more bookings in venues ranging from big city nightclubs to county fairs and were signed to turn out their own TV show, *Those Stonemans*, for the 1967–68 season. And Pop Stoneman and four of his children were voted top vocal group for 1967 by the Country Music Association. Pop, however, fell ill in early 1968 and died in Nashville in June.

Some of the family decided to reorganize and keep the Family going in the music field. Five banded together for this, Roni, Pattie, Donna, Van, and Jim Stoneman. All could sing and, between them, could play almost every instrument usually employed by a traditional country band, including Roni on banjo, Pattie on autoharp, Donna on mandolin, Van on guitar and dobro, and Jim on bass fiddle. Some of them, of course, were adept on several instruments. The decision to continue performing, it was noted by the CMA when Pop Stoneman was one of the nominees for the Country Music Hall of Fame in 1981, made the Stonemans "the longest continuous act in Country Music."

Jack Clement signed the group to MGM Records soon after they re-formed, which led to such releases as the charted single "Tupelo County Jail" (the first single issued on the label) and the LPs *The Stonemans* in 1966, and *Stoneman's Country* in 1967. In August 1969, the Stonemans left MGM and signed with RCA Victor. That alignment led to such recordings as the

July 1970 LP *In All Honesty* and the LP *California Blues* (December 1971).

Later in the decade the group recorded for the CMH label.

STOVALL, VERN: *Singer, guitarist, songwriter. Born Altus, Oklahoma, October 3, 1928.*

More than one country & western star has graduated from the open range to the music field. Vern Stovall moved from a close association with cattle to the front ranks of the entertainment industry. He couldn't have been happier, since his "range" was the indoor one of a slaughterhouse.

Born in Altus, he was raised on farms in Oklahoma, first in El Rino, on the banks of the South Canadian River, then in Vian, near Muskogee, Oklahoma. Vern had a good voice as a child, and as soon as he was old enough, was a regular member of the church choir. In Vian, he also had many opportunities to sing at local gathering. During these years, he also mastered the art of guitar playing.

After graduating from high school in 1947, he moved to Sacramento, California, where he found a job in a slaughterhouse. He progressed from menial jobs to the respected one of butcher. All the while, though, his interest in music grew. Whenever he could get work, he sang and played guitar in local clubs. As word of his ability spread, he began to meet some of the top country & western performers who were based in California.

In 1958 he made the break, moving to Pomona in Southern California, where he joined the group headed by Fred Maddox of Maddox Brothers and Rose. Until 1961, he was a featured member of the band as vocalist and rhythm guitarist. During this time, he met songwriter-musician Bobby George. They decided to collaborate on songs. In 1961, the collaboration extended to a new band formed by Vern, which included such other artists as Phil Baugh and Freddy Rose. The band built up a considerable following in the Los Angeles area from 1961 to 1965.

Meanwhile, many of the Stovall–George compositions began to be picked up by recording artists. The list included "The Long Black Limousine," first recorded by Vern, then by many others, including Bobby Bare and George Hamilton IV; "Who'll Be the One," recorded by Ray Price; and "One More Memory," recorded by Wynn Stewart.

In the early 1960s, Vern gained two new, close friends in the persons of Claude and Janet McBride. Claude had his own small label and produced a number of Stovall sides, including "Country Guitar." The latter, in which Phil Baugh was featured with Vern, began to move nationwide. To gain wider distribution, Claude leased the record to Dewey Groom's Longhorn label. A second hit followed, "One Man Band."

Groom then signed Vern to a long-term contract, and Stovall moved to Longhorn's home city of Dallas. His first single for Longhorn was "Breaktime" backed with "Wreck of the Old 88." Soon after, Vern was teamed with Janet McBride in the hit recording "I'm Wild Bill Tonight." In 1967, Vern was represented on the charts with his own composition (co-written by Gene McCoslin) called, appropriately, "Dallas."

STRINGBEAN: *Singer, banjoist, comedian. Born Annville, Kentucky, June 17, 1915; died Nashville, Tennessee, November 11, 1973.*

One of country music's finest banjo players, Stringbean carried on the tradition of the *Grand Ole Opry*'s first star, Uncle Dave Macon, in fine style. His blend of intricate picking and down-home humor remained popular with audiences for decades after Uncle Dave's passing and only a tragic incident ended that rapport in 1973.

Stringbean, born David Akeman, was raised on a farm near Annville, Kentucky, and developed an interest in the banjo almost from the cradle. His father was an expert banjo-picker, and David and his four brothers and three sisters enjoyed listening to him play and often joined in sing-alongs. When he was fourteen, his dreams finally came true when his father gave him a banjo. He had, of course, picked up basics on his father's banjo, but with his own he was able to progress even faster. Before long he was good enough to

entertain at local dances, barn raisings, and other events.

At eighteen, by then a tall gangling six feet two inches tall, he started playing professionally in the Lexington, Kentucky, region. In two years' time he was working on station WLAP in Lexington. As the late 1930s went by, he continued to increase his reputation with fans and other country artists, touring or performing with Lew Childre, Bill Monroe, Ernest Tubb, Red Foley, and Uncle Dave Macon.

He gained a particularly close friendship with Uncle Dave, who taught him much of his own technique. In recognition of their close relationship, Uncle Dave willed his "godchild," whose nickname was "The Kentucky Wonder," one of his banjos upon his death in 1952. Beginning in 1942, Stringbean was a regular cast member on the *Opry* and remained a featured performer on both the radio and occasional TV versions of the show up to his death. A feature of his act was his comic costumes, usually consisting of a loud shirt that extended almost to his knees and pants that seemed to start where the shirt ended. As did fellow musician and comic Grandpa Jones, Stringbean used his banjo skills as a change of pace from his humorous sketches and routines. In the years after World War II, he not only starred on the *Opry*, but performed on Red Foley's ABC programs for a dozen years.

His considerable talent came through more on records, where he was a noted exponent of the old-time country banjo sound. He turned out many singles and albums on several labels from the 1940s into the 1970s. Among his best-known single releases of the 1950s and 1960s were "Run Little Rabbit Run," "I Wonder Where Wanda Went," "Short Life and Trouble," "Train Special 500," "Barnyard Banjo Picking," "Crazy Viet Nam War," "20¢ Cotton and 90¢ Meat," "Hey Old Man," "John Henry," "Big Ball in Nashville," and "Pretty Little Pink." His LPs on the Starday label included *Kentucky Wonder* (2/62), *Stringbean* (10/62), *Salute to Uncle Dave Macon* (5/63), *Old Time Banjo Picking and Singing,* and *Way Back in the Hills of Kentucky* (2/64). In the early 1970s he was represented on the Nugget label with the LP *Me and My Old Crow*.

When the *Hee Haw* TV program started on the CBS network in 1969, Stringbean was one of the original cast members. Besides taking part in many of the comedy sketches, he sometimes joined in banjo band numbers with Grandpa Jones, Roy Clark, Buck Owens, and other cast members.

In late 1973, his associates on the program were shocked to learn of the brutal killing of Stringbean and his wife, Estelle. They both were found shot to death in their home in the Nashville area. Apparently they had returned home after Stringbean's appearance on the *Opry* on November 11 to surprise a burglar, or burglars, who killed them and fled.

STUCKEY, NAT: *Singer, guitarist, songwriter. Born Cass County, Texas, December 17, 1938.*

In general terms, some of the major early milestones in Nat Stuckey's career could be compared to those of the late Jim Reeves. Both came from east Texas, both first won attention as disc jockeys on station KWKH in Shreveport, Louisiana, and as performers on the network country show *Louisiana Hayride*. However, the similarities stop there. Stuckey, very much his own man, made a conscious effort to insure that his vocal style differed from Reeves. As he said, "I always felt complimented when people told me I sounded like Jim Reeves, but that's also why I had to change my style." And, of course, Stuckey's career blossomed years after the fatal plane crash that claimed Reeves' life.

Stuckey, whose formal name is Nathan Wright Stuckey II, grew up in Cass County, where country & western was revered by most of his family and friends. "An uncle taught me most of what I know about playing the guitar and the rest I sort of picked up myself. I've never had any formal training. I had a semester of voice at Arlington State College where I took the two-year course leading to an associate degree in radio and television."

After completing the course, he natu-rally strove to get into the radio/TV industry, which led to his ultimately joining KWKH in the 1960s. His experience performing at small clubs and with local bands back home gave him an in to a spot on the *Louisiana Hayride*. In the mid-1960s, he gained a recording contract from Shreveport-based Paula Records, a relationship which quickly bore fruit for both parties.

For Paula, he soon proved both a regional and national success. During 1967 and 1968, Nat placed six singles on the charts, including one that made the national top 10. These included "Oh Woman" and "All My Tomorrows" in 1967 and "My Can Do Can't Keep Up with My Want To" in 1968. He also had a charted album for Paula in 1967, *Nat Stuckey Sings*. Some of his other Paula hits were "Leave This One Alone" and one of his compositions most covered by other artists, "Sweet Thing." Among his other often-recorded compositions of the 1960s and early 1970s were "Pop a Top," "Don't You Believe Her," "Waitin' in Your Welfare Line," "Adorable Woman," and "The First Day."

Stuckey took another page from Reeves' book in 1968 when he signed a new recording contract with RCA and moved to Nashville. He rewarded his new label with chart hits on his debut single, "Plastic Saddle" and "Joe and Mabel's 12th Street Bar and Grill." RCA, which had bought up some of his material from Paula, released his debut LP *Nat Stuckey Sings* in late 1968. This was followed by a string of album releases such as *Sunday Morning with Nat Stuckey and Connie Smith* (3/70); *Old Man Willis* (5/70); *Country Fever* (10/70); *She Wakes Me with a Kiss* (4/71); *Only a Woman like Me* (8/71); and *Forgive Me for Calling You Darling* at year end. During those years he placed a number of singles on the country lists, including "She Wakes Me Every Morning" in late 1970 and early 1971.

In the late 1960s and early 1970s he also became one of an increasing number of country artists who brought their talents to the attention of European audiences. His fourth tour to Europe in the fall of 1970 was made in company with Dottie West and Hank Snow.

In the mid-1970s, Nat switched to MCA Records and placed a sizable number of albums and singles on the charts for that organization. The singles included "The Way He's Treated You" in the summer of 1976; "That's All She Ever Said Except Goodbye" in the fall of 1976; "Buddy I Lied" in the summer of 1977; "I'm Going Home to Face the Music" in late 1977; and, in 1978, "The Days of Sand and Shovels."

SUN, JOE: *Singer, songwriter. Born Rochester, Minnesota, September 25, 1943.*

A record promotion executive, whose job involves going around to radio stations to get airplay for his company's records, obviously would have some excellent contacts if he wanted to try his hand at performing. The problem is that almost all promotion executives are salespeople, not singers. Joe Sun was an exception, so it's not too surprising that he became one of the more promising new recording artists of the 1970s.

Sun was born and raised in Rochester, Minnesota, which was, he noted "home of the mighty Mayo Clinic." It was hardly a hotbed of country music, and, in fact, Joe's main musical love as a teenager was rock 'n' roll. He had a way with words, so he broke into the music field as a disc jockey playing rock records on a Minneapolis station. Later he shifted his record spinning activities to Key West, Florida.

As time went on, he got restless with that routine and a little bored with rock music. He was trying to figure out what to do next when he came across one of Mickey Newbury's records in the promotion material record firms regularly send to DJ's. "One day I got a new Mickey Newbury record in and it blew me away. I didn't know a thing about Nashville or what they were doing," he told Laura Eipper of *The Tennessean* in 1979, "but I could understand the words and I knew they were doing something great."

In 1972, this prompted him to move to Nashville with a vague idea of trying to make his way in the country field, preferably in something more creative than a late-night DJ show. In ensuing months he worked at all kinds of jobs, all more or less related to writing or performing. Among other things, he drew cartoons for *The Tennessean*, wrote for a local entertainment magazine, and at times, when the pickings were slim, earned some income as a handyman in night clubs. He also wrote songs, developed his ability as a guitar player, and put together several bands. However, his guitar playing left something to be desired; his musical efforts didn't progress much. When the opportunity to work as a promotion executive for London and Hi Records came along, he took it. He proved to be a natural, particularly because of his DJ background, and over the next three years he gained a reputation as one of the best in the promotion field.

In the mid-1970s, a close friend named Bruce Fisher was managing a new label, Ovation, and approached Sun to come aboard as promotion executive. Fisher had just discovered a father and daughter team known as the Kendalls; after Joe heard some of their demo tapes, he agreed to make the shift. He told Eipper, "It was exciting. I knew they'd be a smash, but even I was surprised when they sold a million copies of 'Heaven's Just a Sin Away.'"

In a short time, both Sun and Fisher were part of one of the fastest growing independent labels in the country field. However, Joe still harbored dreams of getting away from behind-the-scenes work. Fisher apparently sensed that and one day queried Sun about his future plans. "I told him I really wanted to sing and he asked what was holding me up. I told him I didn't play guitar well enough and he asked me what that had to do with singing. So we went into the studio to cut three demos and we wound up with three masters, including 'Old Flames' and 'I Came on Business.' It was magical. I've never had a session quite like that."

The first of those, "Old Flames Can't Hold a Candle to You," was issued on Ovation in the summer of 1978. It received plenty of airplay and caught the fancy of country listeners. By late summer, it was well inside the national country top 15 on the way to sales of over 100,000 copies. Late in the year, Sun had another chart-maker in the single "High and Dry," which made the top 20 and was still on the lists into 1979. In the spring of 1979, his single "I Came on Business for the King/Blue Ribbon Blues," was in the upper-chart levels. (Sun co-wrote "I Came on Business" with J. Hemphill.) In late 1979 and early 1980, he had another chart-hit single, "Out of Your Mind." He followed with three more chart hits in 1980, "Shot gun Rider," "I'd Rather Go on Hurtin'," and "Bombed, Boozed and Busted." In early 1981, he had another single on upper-chart levels, "Ready for the Times to Get Better."

During 1979 and 1980, Sun played throughout the United States backed by his new band, Shotgun. He told *The Tennessean*, "I still call the jocks, because they're my friends, and in a way I still have a chance to do a little promotion when we're traveling to different towns. I miss it [record promotion], but I sure am glad to be off the phone eight damned hours a day."

SWAN, BILLY: *Singer, keyboards player, guitarist, songwriter. Born Cape Girardeau, Missouri, May 12, 1942.*

The year 1974 was a big one for Billy Swan. His single "I Can Help," his own composition, was one of the major hits of the year. Although suddenly everybody knew his name, he had hardly been a stranger to the music field; he hung on, often by the skin of his teeth, for a decade and a half before having at least a temporary fame. He called the kind of music he was writing and performing progressive rockabilly, indicating that his roots had been in the first wave of country-bred rock stars that came forward in the mid-1950s.

Swan, who was born and raised in the Mississippi River town of Cape Girardeau, recalled enjoying the films of Gene Autry and hearing the singing of Hank Williams on the radio. What really gripped him musically, however, was the onset of rock when he was in his early teens. As he told Robert Hilburn of the *Los Angeles Times*,

"Jerry Lee Lewis had the biggest impact on me. He was even bigger than Elvis to me. I dug that piano. 'Whole Lotta Shakin' Goin' On' and 'Great Balls of Fire' were the greatest things I ever heard. And there was Buddy Holly. I remember I used to get up in a tree and swing, singing 'Oh Boy' as loud as I could."

In high school he wrote a poem called "Lover Please," which lay around the house for a while. A year and a half later, he added music and played the completed song for some friends who were part of a local rock group. They liked it and added it to the repertoire they took along with them to Memphis, where they had a chance to record for a small label established by Bill Black, Elvis Presley's bassist and founder of the famous Bill Black Combo. The song was recorded as a "B" side of one of the band's singles, but nothing happened with it.

However, a record producer heard the recording and, some time later, suggested it be added to a session by R&B singer Clyde McPhatter. McPhatter's version took hold and became a national top-10 hit in 1962.

Meanwhile, Billy was still in Missouri performing with local groups. He decided the time was ripe to follow up the success of "Lover Please" by becoming a full-time professional songwriter. It turned out to be easier said than done.

Once in Memphis, he had to figure out a way to earn some money. He hadn't decided on anything yet when he paid a visit to Elvis Presley's mansion, even then a magnet for rock enthusiasts. He struck up a conversation with the gatekeeper, who turned out to be Elvis' uncle, Travis Smith. Smith's son had gotten married and left the Smith home, so Swan ended up being a boarder there. That, in turn, led to his spelling Travis at times as the Presley gatekeeper.

He told Hilburn, "I never knew Elvis very well, but every so often he'd rent a local theater or the skating rink or the fairgrounds and we'd all go with him. They'd start showing the movies around midnight. I remember seeing *Donovan's Reef* one night, but never any of Elvis' films."

Since he didn't seem to be making much progress on his career, Swan moved again, this time to Nashville. He kept writing new songs and picked up work as a sideman when he could. However, he made more progress in nonmusical chores. Among the jobs he had in the mid-1960s was working as a "roadie" for Mel Tillis and the Masters of Music Festival, a show that featured Chet Atkins, Boots Randolph, and Floyd Cramer.

He picked up work at local recording studios, sometimes as a gofer or messenger and, for a year and a half, as a "studio assistant" at Columbia, which essentially was euphemism for janitor. Just after handling the maintenance chores for the Bob Dylan session from which the *Blonde on Blonde* album evolved, Billy quit his job. His replacement was another famed janitorial alumnus, Kris Kristofferson.

Things took a turn for the better for Swan in the late 1960s. He began to work as a record producer for such Nashville executives as Monument Records' president Fred Foster and Bob Beckham, the head of the Combine Music publishing firm. The artist Swan was most closely associated with during that period was Tony Joe White. Billy produced three albums for White, which included the song that gave Tony Joe his biggest singles hit, "Polk Salad Annie".

Billy, who was also doing session work and some nightclub band work, helped out on Kris Kristofferson's first album on Monument. After the album was issued, Kris enlisted Swan's help in forming a tour band. A bass player was particularly needed, so Swan learned to play the instrument in a three-day period before Kristofferson's debut at the Los Angeles Troubadour. After working as a sideman for Kristofferson for a while Billy moved to other bands in the early 1970s, including Kinky Friedman and Billy Joe Shaver. (By the end of the decade he was touring in Kris' band again, something he still did at the start of the 1980s.)

He was still pressing for the opportunity to do his own recordings and finally got the go-ahead from Monument. His debut effort, recorded in 1973 and 1974, gave a good synopsis of his musical leanings. It included such country songs as "Wedding Bells" and "Ways of a Woman in Love," the old R&B-rock hit, "Shake, Rattle and Roll," Elvis' "Don't Be Cruel," and some originals, including "I Can Help." "Wedding Bells" was the first singles release in the spring of 1974. It turned up on some regional lists, but it was the next release, "I Can Help," later in the year, that paid off. The song, inspired by his wife, Marlu, stayed on national charts for weeks in the fall and brought Billy his first gold-record award from the Recording Industry Association of America on December 2, 1974. The album, also titled *I Can Help,* was on both country and pop charts in late 1974 and early 1975.

Billy's career slowed down again during 1976–77. He moved from ABC to A&M in 1978 and was represented on the charts in the summer with the single "Hello! Remember Me?" At the start of the 1980s he was recording for Epic Records, and his single "Do I Have to Draw a Picture" made country charts in the spring of 1981.

T

TAJ MAHAL: *Singer, guitarist, pianist, harmonica player, bassist, vibraphonist, mandolinist, dulcimer player, songwriter. Born New York, New York, May 17, 1942.*

From the mid-1960s to the early 1970s, if you wanted to find Taj Mahal, most of the time all you had to do was go down to the Ash Grove folk club on Melrose Avenue in Los Angeles. He was almost always there, teaching classes in mouth harp or folk blues during the day, watching folk and blues artists or taking part in occasional jams at night. He had a growing reputation among his peers for his musicianship and writing ability, but it took a while for it to expand to where he had more than a folk following. In time, though, he gained his due to some extent as an interpreter of American folk, rock, and blues material and as one of the first U.S. artists to concentrate a great deal of attention to African roots.

Taj was born in New York City in a section where many of the residents were of Jamaican origin. His father, a respected jazz arranger and pianist, was born of West Indian parents, though his school-teacher mother (who also sang gospel songs) was from South Carolina. His family moved to Springfield, Massachusetts, when he was young, where his first and only music instructor gave up after a week of trying to get the boy started on piano. "He'll never be a musician," that worthy said. It turned out that Taj was just a late bloomer. During high school years he began to learn a whole range of instruments on his own, including piano, guitar, and harmonica. Still, he didn't play any of them exceptionally well. So when he went to the University of Massachusetts in Amherst, he took his degree in animal husbandry.

Before he finished college, however, his skill as a singer and musician began to show marked improvement. In the early 1960s, he started winning some attention as a blues artist in local Boston-area coffee houses. After he finished college, he made his way to California, settling in Santa Monica and frequenting the Ash Grove, where he made friends with many aspiring young folk artists over the years.

He worked as a soloist whenever he could find gigs and sometimes teamed with other musicians in blues or rock bands. In the mid-1960s, one of the initially promising efforts was a group he formed with Ry Cooder called the Rising Sons. The band won a Columbia Records recording contract and started work on an album that was never completed. Cooder later said the reason was that too many other good blues-rock bands had come to the fore in the meantime.

Columbia executives, though, felt there might yet be a future for Taj on their label. Renewed public interest in blues and blues-rock late in the decade opened the door for him to do some solo work for the label. The first fruits of his labor, *Taj Mahal*, in early 1968, won mixed reviews but brought increased interest in him in places other than Southern California. This trend received a little more impetus with his next LP, *The Natch'l Blues*, which he supported with a series of concerts in clubs around the United States backed by a band that featured guitarist Jesse Ed Davis. Both album and show won praise from *Rolling Stone* magazine, which stated, in part, that Mahal "is one of the most enjoyable and entertaining performers around." His impact "was direct and immediate; he's one of the few people you can actually hear smiling."

One result was a rising level of sales for his next album, issued in November 1969, *Giant Step/De Old Folks at Home*. Along with his increased exposure Mahal was also becoming more active with black organizations fighting for increased civil rights. He gave benefit performances for a number of these groups and that also heightened a new interest in exploring roots music on an international level. In his early career phase, he won attention for his versions of country-blues songs like "Stealin'," "Statesboro Blues," and "Divin' Duck Blues." As the 1970s went by, he constantly probed other black-related music forms—African music, mainly West African, Caribbean forms from calypso to reggae, and various forms of jazz.

To further explore his international background he moved from California to Spain in the early 1970s, from there making some trips to Africa and also embarking on several tours of Europe that won him an enthusiastic following in many nations. He had several LPs on U.S. charts during those years, including the two-disc set *Real Thing* released in August 1971. During 1971, he returned to the United States for several activities, including appearances at folk festivals in Big Sur, California, and Washington, D.C., and work on material for the movies. In particular, his score for the movie *Sounder* was credited with achieving much of that film's overall effect on the audience. Besides providing the scoring, he also played the role of Ike. In another movie project, he provided the "Whistlin' Dixie" segment of the soundtrack for *Clay Pigeon.*

In 1972, his next two LPs on Columbia, *Happy Just to Be like I Am* and *Recyclin' the Blues and Other Related Stuff* were on U.S. album charts part of the year. Over the next few years, he was represented on Columbia by several more albums: *Oooh So Good 'n' Blues, Mo' Roots,* and *Music Keeps Me Together.* Experimentation continued to be the keynote throughout. As an example, he used the backing of an all-tuba group on the song "Happy Just to Be like I Am." At other times he employed various blues band arrangements, unusual percussion effects, and sometimes African instruments like the thumb piano.

In the mid-1970s, Mahal's association with Columbia ended and he began a new alignment with Warner Brothers. An early project there was to write the score for a film about prison injustices, *Brothers.* After that, Warner's issued his debut solo album on the label, *Music Fuh Ya' (Musica Para Tu).* The tracks, which presented material ranging in styles from blues to reggae/calypso, included such songs as "Sailin' into Walker's Cay," "Freight Train," "The Four Mills Brothers," "Baby You're My Destiny," "Curry," and "Truck Driver's Two Step."

His second Warner's album, *Evolution (The Most Recent)* was issued in January 1978. Typical of Taj's sometimes tongue-in-cheek approach to his craft was the name of the instrumental title track, *The Most Recent (Evolution) of Muthafusticus Modernisticus.* Other songs ranged from salsa to an occasional return to country blues, as in Mahal's original composition *Queen Bee.* Though not a commercial success, the LP was, like most of Mahal's albums, interesting and often challenging. In late 1977, one of his new credits was a feature spot on NBC-TV's late-night satirical show, *Saturday Night Live.* In 1981, Columbia issued the retrospective album, *The Best of Taj Mahal.*

TALLEY, JAMES: *Singer, guitarist, songwriter. Born Tulsa, Oklahoma, November 9, 1942.*

If laudatory press clippings were gold, James Talley would have been a millionaire by the end of the 1970s. Certainly, one of the finest writer-performers in the American folk-balladeer tradition, his down-to-earth offerings ranged over a wide form of stylings from folk and country to blues and western swing. He was deservedly compared to people like Woody Guthrie and Hank Williams. He even numbered among his fans President Carter and wife Rosalynn, who invited him to appear at the Inaugural Ball and personally greeted him after his performance. Unfortunately, his newfound prestige was not immediately convertible into mass public acceptance.

Born in Oklahoma to blue-collar parents, he and his family moved to the state of Washington when he was three so his father could find construction work. During those years, James' father gave his son some of his original musical delights, singing songs by Jimmie Rodgers, Woody Guthrie, and others of country and folk fame. Talley senior also admired western swing, an influence James Talley later was to pay tribute to in his composition "W. Lee O'Daniel and the Light Crust Doughboys" on his debut album.

The family moved southward again when James was eight, this time to Albuquerque, New Mexico, his home for the next sixteen years. He played trumpet in his junior high school band, then switched to guitar when he was fifteen. It was to be his main instrument from then on. The first song he worked out on the guitar was an old Leadbelly song about prison life called "I Got Stripes." His musical interests expanded to include not only Anglo folk and country material, but the musical influences of Albuquerque's Mexican-American population. Still, he wasn't thinking of making a career of music at the time. Instead, he got his B.A. and went on to graduate school at the University of New Mexico and, briefly, at the University of California at Los Angeles to get a Ph.D. in American studies, with emphasis on art in this country in the 1930s. It wasn't long before he became discouraged about the art scene. He enjoyed painting, but later noted, "Art at graduate school was just like [commercial] music. It's what's hip, what's in."

He was making some early attempts at writing when he met Pete Seeger, who was in Albuquerque for a concert. Seeger stressed that the best songs are "in your own back yard." Taking that to heart, Talley wrote a song called "Ramon Esteban" about a highway worker he met during summer employment. That was the first of a collection of songs about the New Mexico Chicano experience called "The Road to Torreon."

He finished the collection in Nashville, where he located in 1968 after driving up from Albuquerque in an old 1949 Willys panel truck. He had hopes of making his way as a songwriter and artist, but Music City doors didn't swing open readily. To make ends meet, he found work as a public welfare case worker, a job that introduced him to the hopes and difficulties of the poverty ridden. It gave him new insight into the blues and was to be reflected in the song "Bluesman" in his third album. (The song was a tribute to B. B. King, who made his first trip to the Nashville studios to play guitar on the "Bluesman" track.)

As the 1960s gave way to the 1970s, he made slow progress in his musical pursuits. He met some talented sidemen, such as Texas fiddler Johnny Gimble and dobro guitarist "Uncle Josh" Graves, who were to contribute fine backing work on his albums. He also began to find occasional engagements in small clubs and on some college campuses. His reputation grew by word of mouth among folk adherents to the point that in 1974 he was invited to take part in the Smithsonian Festival of American Folklife.

By then Talley, who had married and started to raise a family, earned his living with construction and carpentry jobs. He kept trying for a recording agreement and was finally signed by Atlantic, which was trying to start a country department, but with little result. Then James met a Nashville businessman who wanted to build a recording studio and bartered his carpentry work for studio time. This allowed him to make his first album, which was titled *Got No Bread, No Milk, No Money, But We*

Sure Got a Lot of Love. He borrowed $3,000 to press 1,000 copies, some of which he offered for sale at concerts and others of which he mailed to country stations and record executives. In time, this led to Capitol buying the master, which was reissued in June 1975.

The almost unanimous critical acclaim for the work raised hope that the next LP, *Tryin' like the Devil,* issued in February 1976, would start Talley on the road to stardom. Again the critical response was glowing. But the brutal honesty of the songs made it difficult for commercial outlets to back the album. As an example, one song, "Give My Love to Marie," told of a coal miner ill with black lung disease, the only result of twenty-five years of slaving underground. ("There's millions in the ground/But not a penny for me.") But there were indications that there was an audience out there. The track "Are They Gonna Make Us Outlaws Again" was issued as a single and made lower country-music chart levels.

Talley was finding strong critical support as well for his personal appearances. Most newspaper columnists highly praised his concert work. Indeed, the audiences at the small clubs he worked across the United States generally shared that enthusiasm. He also remained popular on the college circuit. However, without much support from radio stations, most people seemed unaware of his talents. Refusing to change or water down his material in favor of "commercial" success, James still felt he could find a large following if he could just get a fair hearing.

He told *People* magazine (July 11, 1977), "I want those mothers of mine on the radio, but it seems next to impossible for a James Talley song to break into an AM playlist. In this industry, executives just want to sell plastic—they may as well melt down records into ashtrays—and radio guys just want to sell ad time. So they program the Conways and Lorettas, the Tammys and Georges to keep listeners on until the next station break."

Talley's third LP, *Blackjack Choir,* was issued by Capitol in January 1977. The content continued to be as strong and diverse as the other two, but once more the response was disappointing. Again the critics cheered and the buyers stayed away in droves. Talley continued his concerts before a small but devoted following, but Capitol dropped him from the label.

TANNER, GID: *Fiddler, singer, bandleader. Born Thomas Bridge, near Monroe, Georgia, June 6, 1885; died Dacula, Georgia, May 13, 1960.*

One group a country & western fan of the 1920s and 1930s was sure to know was Gid Tanner and his Skillet Lickers. Tanner organized his band soon after becoming one of the first recorded artists in the country field, and before it disbanded in the 1930s, the group had made 565 records. Few of these are available today, but those that are stand the test of time surprisingly well. This is evident, for example, from Skillet Licker renditions of "Ida Red" and "On Tanner's Farm" on the RCA Victor LP *Smoky Mountain Ballads.*

Like many country greats, James Gideon Tanner was born on a farm, maintaining his chicken farm in Georgia right up to his death. Young Gid fell in love with local fiddle music almost as soon as he could do chores on his parents' farm. At fourteen, when an uncle died and left him a fiddle, he lost no time in learning how to play it. In his teens he was already making a reputation for himself playing at local dances and fairs. In the 1920s he began to branch out, taking part successfully in several of the famous fiddle contests of Fiddlin' John Carson.

Thus when a Columbia Records' talent scout moved through the area looking for artists to make the firm's first country records, Tanner was a name that he heard much about. He asked Gid to come to New York, and Gid took George Riley Puckett with him. The two made their first records on March 7, 1924. The recordings were well enough received that Tanner's name became known across the South. Soon after, he formed his Skillet Lickers. Puckett (born Alpharetta, Georgia, 1890; died College Park, Georgia, July 13, 1946) became lead singer of the band.

Through the late 1920s and the early 1930s, the group was one of the most popular in country music. From 1926 to 1929 it included, besides Tanner and Puckett, Clayton McMichen and Tanner's brother, Arthur. McMichen remained with Tanner until 1931. Various other musicians played with the band in the 1930s, including Tanner's son, Gordon, and Jimmie Tarleton. In the 1930s, the Skillet Lickers were featured on radio stations in many parts of the United States, including Covington, Kentucky; Cleveland, Ohio; Chicago; and Atlanta.

The top hit of the Skillet Lickers was "Down Yonder." Other hits included "The Wreck of the Southern Old 97" and "Sally Goodin'."

A typical arrangement of Tanner's group was described in *Who's Who in Country Music* * as follows: "[The band used] two fiddles, often doubling each other at the unison for lead, a back-up guitar and a banjo. All four members sang and Puckett usually took the lead." (See also McMichen, Clayton.)

TARLETON, JIMMIE: *Singer, guitarist, banjoist, harpist, songwriter. Born Chesterfield County, South Carolina, May 8, 1892; died circa 1979.*

An amazingly gifted musician, Jimmie Tarleton provided American folk and country music with a legend and some of the most famous songs in the folk-country repertoire. Those who heard him play never forgot it, even those who attended some of his performances in the mid-1960s, when he came out of a long, enforced retirement. Had Tarleton been born twenty years later, he might have become wealthy and famous in his lifetime. As it was, he settled for a flat fee of seventy-five dollars for his most famous compositions, "Columbus Stockade Blues" and "Birmingham Jail."

Johnny James Rimbert Tarleton was born on a farm near the Pedee River in Chesterfield County, South Carolina. His father played a homemade banjo and taught Jimmie to play when he was six (he

---

* *1965–66 edition, published by Thurston Moore, Colorado.*

was also studying the French harp). His mother sang many old hill-country ballads, including such songs as "Barney Mc-Coy," "Kitty Wells," "Lowe Bonnie," and "Wish I Was a Single Girl Again." Jimmie learned these and sang and recorded them later in life. By the time he was nine, he had also mastered the guitar. Jimmie enjoyed the evening family sing-alongs, and as he grew up, he performed at local dances, barn raisings, and other events.

By the time Jimmie was in his teens, he had decided to try to play professionally, moving north during the World War I decade and working at odd jobs while performing nights in bars and cafes in New York and nearby Hoboken. After several years of this, he headed west, working as a textile mill hand in Texas, Oklahoma, and Arkansas. In his spare time, he picked up whatever he could in the way of dates at local honky-tonks.

In the early 1920s, things were looking up a little for country performers, who were in demand for rural fairs and traveling medicine shows. The mid-1920s found him playing with groups in the Columbus, Georgia, region. In 1926, he teamed up with guitarist-singer Tom Darby. The record industry was beginning to find a market for country records and was looking for new artists. This opened the door to Tarleton and Darby, who gained a record date in Atlanta in April 1927. They were asked to come back several more times that year. On November 10, they recorded "Columbus Stockade Blues" and "Birmingham Jail," both written by Jimmie, who had composed the latter some years earlier after spending time in the jail for moonshining. The boys were offered a royalty agreement, but Darby talked Tarleton into settling for seventy-five dollars for both songs.

Tarleton continued to record for several labels over the next few years, including Columbia (1927–30), RCA Victor in 1932, and American Record Corp. in 1933. He recorded more than seventy-five songs, many of which were made into major hits by others. During the 1920s and early 1930s he toured the country with many major artists, including Gid Tanner and the Skillet Lickers, Arthur Smith, the Delmore Brothers, and Jimmie Rodgers.

Life was far from easy, though. In 1932, he was caught riding the rods home from a recording session in New York for RCA Victor. A short term in an Atlanta jail resulted in the song "Atlanta Prison Blues." In 1931, he had to work at odd jobs, including a short period as a mill hand in East Rockingham, North Carolina, where he worked with the Dixon Brothers. All three artists traded song material and instrumental techniques.

Since the Depression had ruined much of the country-music market, Tarleton retired from an active music career in 1935. For the next twenty years he worked at various jobs, finally ending up in Phoenix City, Alabama, in the mid-1960s. There he was discovered by folk music collectors who wanted to discuss some of his great early country recordings. One collector, Gene Earle, taped some of Tarleton's music in December, 1963 for a proposed LP. This, in turn, led to an invitation from the owner of the Ash Grove in Los Angeles. In August 1965, at his week's engagement in Los Angeles, Tarleton showed cheering audiences that he was still a superlative artist.

TAYLOR, CHIP: *Singer, guitarist, songwriter, record producer. Born Yonkers, New York, circa 1942.*

Chip Taylor's road to country-music status was, to say the least, rather unorthodox. He wasn't from the rural South or even from a farm. His parents didn't play high lonesome sounds on stringed instruments in the living room of their urban East Coast home. For a time it looked as though he might earn his keep as a golf pro rather than in music. Nevertheless, he became an important figure in the country scene in the 1970s.

Born and raised in Yonkers, New York, about forty miles north of New York City, the third son of Barbara and Elmer Voight, Taylor's first exposure to music was the general pop material of the 1940s and early 1950s. At the time, there was little country music available on New York area stations. But he discovered that far off stations like WWVA in Wheeling, West Virginia, sometimes came through during late-night hours, and he fell in love with the country sound. After a while, he could indulge his tastes more often when a country format was introduced on New York area station WJRZ.

In the mid-1950s, as a high school student, he played a lot of sports, but he also had a good singing voice and was collecting a repertoire of country and rockabilly material. He became a member of a country band called the Town and Country Brothers, performing such songs as Johnny Cash's "Big River" and a number of Elvis' hits.

At the University of Hartford in Connecticut, he did some singing and also was on the golf team. He retained his interest in country music, though he also followed rock 'n' roll, but between music in general and golf, the latter was his favored activity. It remained so after he enlisted in the Air Force reserve in 1963, to the point that when he finished his tour of duty he decided to try becoming a golf professional. That career came to an abrupt end in the mid-1960s because of a wrist injury.

Fortunately for Taylor, he had an alternative. He had started to write original songs and he was able to interest East Coast publishers and artists. His material covered the gamut from rock and soul to country, and by the late 1960s his credits started to mount up. From those years through the early 1970s, he had dozens of songs recorded by major artists in almost every phase of pop music. The list includes "Wild Thing," recorded by the Troggs, Jimi Hendrix, and Fancy; "I Can't Let Go," the Hollies; "Anyway That You Want Me," the Troggs, Evie Sands, the American Breed; "I Can Make It Without You," Pozo Seco Singers, Jackie DeShannon; "Welcome Home," Dusty Springfield, Walter Jackson; "I Can't Wait Until I See My Baby's Face," Baby Washington, Dionne Warwick; "Strange Song," Harry Belafonte, the Sandpipers; "Storybook Children," Billy Vera and Judy Clay; "Try (Just a Little Bit Harder)," Janis Joplin; "Angel of the Morning," Merrilee Rush, Connie Caton, and a number-one national

hit for Juice Newton in 1981; "Just a Little Bit Later on Down the Line," Bobby Bare; "He Sits at My Table," Willie Nelson; "If You Were Mine, Mary," Eddy Arnold, Jim Ed Brown; "The Long Walk Home," Floyd Cramer, Al Hirt; "Sweet Dream Woman," Waylon Jennings; "Son of a Rotten Gambler," Anne Murray, Al McCarther; "Clean Your Own Tables," Stoney Edwards, Johnny Cash.

Besides his writing activities, Taylor showed talent as a record producer. Among the artists he worked with in the 1960s and early 1970s were James Taylor, Evie Sands, Billy Vera and Judy Clay, Neil Diamond, and Al McCarther.

Chip still was interested in developing his performing capability and finally signed a contract with Warner Brothers in the early 1970s, which led to his debut LP in 1973, *Chip Taylor's Last Chance.* He placed a number of singles on the charts under that banner, including his compositions "Me as I Am" in early 1975 and "Early Sunday Morning," which was in the top 30 in mid-1975. Later that year, his album *This Side of the Big River* was on the national country lists.

In 1976, he signed with Columbia Records, which released his debut on the label, *Somebody Shoot Out the Jukebox* in September of that year. Accompanying him on the LP was his band of four years, Guest Train. After a brief stay with Columbia, Taylor moved on to a new recording association with Capitol, which issued *Chip Taylor's Saint Sebastian* in the late 1970s.

TAYLOR, JAMES: *Singer, guitarist, cellist, songwriter. Born Boston, Massachusetts, March 12, 1948.*

A child of the modern era, James Taylor initially expressed the feeling of alienation, the sense of restlessness that beset those who came of age during the years of the Vietnam War. Later, his music conveyed a more relaxed atmosphere combined with a desire to come to terms with life that typified his generation's attitudes once the agony of Vietnam was over. However, while finding favor with his peer group, he also appealed to listeners of all ages because of the strong country-folk elements in his writing.

When he attained the rank of superstar in the early 1970s, he was only in his early twenties. But in his brief lifetime to that point, he had packed in experiences ranging from exultation to degradation. In this sense, his background was similar in part to some of the black blues artists. Unlike them, his scars were self-inflicted.

Raised in a loving and affluent family, his early years were sheltered and—in what was probably a major element in the problems he and his brothers and sister encountered—few of his wishes were denied.

He was born in Boston's General Hospital, where his father, from an old, affluent southern family, was completing work on his medical degree. His mother, daughter of a Massachusetts fisherman and boat builder, had a good voice and was trained as a lyric soprano, but gave up the idea of a career in favor of raising a family. She allowed her children to start lessons on various instruments, but did not pressure them to continue when they resisted formal instruction.

As James grew up, he moved between two beautiful locales: a twenty-eight-room house near the campus of the University of North Carolina in Chapel Hill, where his father was a member of the medical faculty and eventually dean of the medical school, and a summer house near the white beaches of Martha's Vineyard off the coast of New England.

The family enjoyed music, and James heard both his father and mother singing at family get-togethers as he went through public school and on to the expensive Milton Academy near Boston. One of his close friends on Martha's Vineyard was a musically oriented boy named Danny Kortchmar (nee Kootch). When Taylor was fifteen, he and Danny won a local hootenanny contest with Danny playing harmonica and James guitar and both alternating on vocals. At the time, both were followers of folk music, though they soon turned their attention to rock.

James found his time at private school trying. He was not sure of his goals and missed his family and friends. At sixteen,

he felt he had to get away and left school for a term to return to North Carolina and join his older brother Alex in a rock band called the Fabulous Corsairs. He then returned to Milton, but at seventeen found himself becoming increasingly despondent. His despondency became suicidal and he signed himself into a mental institution, McLean Hospital in Belmont, Massachusetts.

He spent nine months there during 1965, managing to improve his emotional outlook, though he still had occasional stretches of despair. He completed work for a high school degree before leaving for New York, where he reestablished contact with Danny Kortchmar. Calling himself Danny Kootch, he was forming a new band called the Flying Machine. The group played a number of low-paying engagements in the New York area. Taylor, who played guitar and sang, also wrote a number of original compositions for the band, some of which—"Knocking Round the Zoo," "Night Owl," and "Rainy Day Man"—he included in his debut LP a year later.

Living in a small apartment, mostly on money from his parents, eighteen-year-old Taylor made his home a haven for many alienated people. After a while, he began to join some of them in experimenting with drugs, eventually getting hooked on heroin. He addressed the problem in his song "Fire and Rain" in such lines as "Won't you look down on me, Jesus/ You've got to help me make a stand/ You've just got to see me through another day."

Realizing he had escaped one trap just to fall into another, he decided to leave New York and try to kick the drug habit. He went to London in 1968 and rented studio time to make tapes of some of his material. He took them to the Apple Record Company and managed to get them auditioned by producer Peter Asher, originally of the Peter and Gordon vocal duet (and later producer of Linda Ronstadt's big hits of the 1970s). Asher liked them, as did Beatle Paul McCartney, and the debut LP *James Taylor* came out in midyear. The LP didn't sell well, though one of the tracks,

"Carolina on My Mind," a folk-flavored tune, later became a hit.

Taylor returned to the United States in December 1968 and spent another brief period in a mental hospital, Austin Riggs, in Stockbridge, Massachusetts. By mid-1969, he felt well enough to go back to work and he made a well-received appearance at Los Angeles' Troubadour in July. Peter Asher had become his manager and, with Apple in legal difficulties, he gained James a new contract with Warner Brothers. He produced Taylor's label debut, *Sweet Baby James*, which came out in the spring of 1970. With strong promotion help from Warners, this LP became a bestseller. It took a little while, but by November the LP was in the U.S. top 10; it stayed on the charts well into 1971, selling more than 2 million copies. It also brought the Apple album back to life, eventually bringing Taylor a gold-record award for that one as well. In late 1970, Taylor also had a number-one single hit with "Fire and Rain."

Now a national celebrity, Taylor performed to turn-away crowds in twenty-seven cities across the United States in March and April 1971. Joining him for the show were such fine musicians as Danny Kootch and the Jo Mama Band, drummer Russ Kunkel, bassist Lee Sklar, and singer-pianist Carole King. Besides adding to Taylor's reputation, the tour was instrumental in Carole King's emergence as a major folk-rock star in her own right.

In the spring of 1971, his second album on Warner Bros. came out, *Mud Slide Slim and the Blue Horizon*. A fine collection, it also was an over-a-million seller. Taylor's version of Carole King's song "You've Got a Friend," from the album, also was a major success, reaching number one in July. Meanwhile, a reissue of material from his early days with Kootch and the Flying Machine was a chart hit in early 1971.

Much of the original material in *Mud Slide Slim* described the emotional problems that went along with sudden success. Those new pressures caused self-doubts that started to be reflected in his work. His next LP, *One Man Dog*, though it was a top-10 hit in 1972 and spawned two chart singles, "Don't Let Me Be Lonely Tonight" and "Long Ago Far Away," was not up to the level of earlier collections. Nor was his next album, *Walking Man*, much of an improvement.

Fortunately, this phase soon went by, thanks mainly to a milestone in his private life, his relationship with singer-songwriter Carly Simon. When the two married in 1972, it was a major social highlight. More important, Taylor evidenced a new self-confidence and emotional maturity. In redoing many of his best-regarded numbers for Warner Bros.' *James Taylor's Greatest Hits*, he demonstrated new depth and shading in his vocal treatment of numbers like "Carolina on My Mind" and "Something in the Way She Moves." In 1975, a new album titled *Gorilla* proved to be his best work since the early 1970s both as a performer and writer. Meanwhile, he and his wife joined forces on entertaining new material, such as their duet on the 1974 hit single "Mockingbird" from her LP *Hotcakes.*

There also was obvious change in his stage presence. In the early part of his career, he often seemed shy and ill at ease on stage. From the mid-1970s on, he became a much more relaxed performer, able to achieve much closer rapport with audiences and projecting considerably more effective stylings.

Taylor's 1976 album, *In the Pocket*, on the charts during the summer and fall, proved to be his last release on Warner Bros. By 1977, he had moved to Columbia Records, which issued his debut on that label, *JT*, in midsummer. By August, the album was in the top 10 and later earned a gold record. A well-balanced album, one of its high spots was Taylor's version of the Jimmy Jones R&B hit "Handy Man," which provided him with a top-10 single. His second album release for Columbia, *Flag*, was issued in 1979, and his third, *Dad Loves His Work*, in the spring of 1981.

TAYLOR, KATE: *Singer, guitarist. Born Boston, Massachusetts, August 15, 1949.*

A member of the illustrious Taylor clan, Kate never had quite the musical dedication of brother James. But when she did try her hand at it, she demonstrated an intriguing performing style which, though there were some similarities to her three brothers' efforts, was distinctively her own. Her musical tastes were more wide-ranging than James', running the gamut from straight folk and country to rhythm & blues and soul rock.

Born in Boston, she spent most of her childhood in Chapel Hill, North Carolina, where her father, Dr. Isaac Taylor, was a member of the medical faculty of Duke University, of which he became dean in the 1960s. Some of the time, the Taylor children went to their mother Trudy's home area in Massachusetts. Kate declared at one point, "I'm proud of my split Yankee-Southern heritage."

The Taylor home life was warm and almost completely unstructured. Kate and her brothers (she was the only girl in the family) decided for themselves whether or not to take music lessons. All of them dabbled in learning such things as cello and guitar, but soon dropped the lessons. Kate later taught herself to play guitar. Her parents liked pop music, but of the 1940s and early 1950s variety. "They fell in love to the music of that day and sang their favorite songs to us children."

As Kate entered elementary school in the mid-1950s, Elvis and the first wave of the rock revolution came along. She was also influenced by the R&B music her brothers listened to on the radio. She recalled, "I used to sing along with people on the radio a lot. I liked Ray Charles, Elvis, Otis Redding, Aretha Franklin, Diana Ross. In junior high school [in the early 1960s] I got into the folk thing. I liked Dylan, Joan Baez."

Kate, as did her brothers, had emotional problems that led to their enrolling in a private high school, the Cambridge School, in Weston, Massachusetts, in the 1960s. They still found everyday life too difficult to deal with and all, at one time or another, voluntarily entered institutions for psychiatric help. In Kate's case, she went into the McLean Hospital in Belmont, Massachusetts, in 1967. She was advised to keep up her music as a form of therapy, which led to the organization of a pop group called Sister Kate's Soul Stew Kitchen. The stay proved a great help and she was able to leave in 1968, though she decided against completing her high school education.

As James' career in music began to move ahead, he sometimes took Kate with him on tour or during recording work. One such trip brought Kate to England, where James introduced her to Peter Asher, then working with Taylor on album material for the Beatles' Apple Records, later a top producer for U.S. labels whose clients included Linda Ronstadt. Kate sang some songs for Asher, who was impressed and told her he would help launch her career some day.

To her surprise, he didn't forget his promise. He later sent her a recording contract for an album on Cotillion Records. She recalled, "I had my first recording experience with Peter Asher in 1969–70. We recorded one album for Atlantic's Cotillion label. We put together a tour and it and the album were very well received."

The album touched all facets of her musical interest. The tracks included Kate's version of the Elton John–Bernie Taupin "Country Comfort" songs with John Hartford playing banjo in support of her vocals, a track of the folk-country tune "White Lightning," a fast-paced rocker, "Look at Granny Run, Run, Run," and a medley of brother James' "Lo and Behold" and the Byrds' "Jesus Is Just Alright."

Called *Sister Kate,* the LP was issued in March 1971 and still remains a gem of a collection. It did very well with the buying public as well, reaching upper-chart levels. The way seemed clear for Kate to become a major figure in the 1970s pop music scene. But though fans and critics waited expectantly for the next album, years went by and nothing happened.

Taylor said in 1977 that she hadn't intended to drop from sight. She had gone home for a few weeks' vacation after finishing her 1971 cross-country tour (climaxed with a July 4th weekend appearance at Central Park with the Beach Boys), but "one thing led to another." Other things kept sidetracking her, and, despite record company pleadings, she couldn't seem to get around to anything new in the music field. Instead, she did things that pleased her in her private life. As she told a Columbia Records biography writer in 1978, "It would take eight years for me to really tell what happened, moment by moment. I lived in a tipi during the warm months of the year and made various things with my hands out of the materials from my home. I met my husband, Charles Witham, and we fished, we revived the art of wampum-bead manufacturing from the hard-shell clam; and made a succession of sizes of tipis to fit our growing family." The last statement refers to the birth of their daughter, Elizabeth, in 1976.

However, not long after that, Taylor became interested in recording again and began working with her brother James at Atlantic Studios in New York. Among the early recordings, which James coproduced and also did backup vocals and guitar, were a song Kate co-wrote with Duane Giesemann called "Jason and Ida" and a song by musician Walter Robinson called "Harriet Tubman," written as part of a folk opera on the underground railway of slavery days.

For her new work, Kate signed with Columbia Records, which issued her debut single on the label in August 1977. Called "It's in His Kiss," a rock number, the single reached the middle-chart levels, indicating that Kate still had a considerable following. In May 1978, her album *Kate Taylor* was issued, a fine compilation with a high folk and folk-rock content.

TAYLOR, LIVINGSTON: *Singer, guitarist, songwriter. Born Weston, Massachusetts, 1951.*

Although all the members of the famous Taylor clan, whose musical scion was Livingston's older brother James, had elements of folk and country music in their styles, Livingston perhaps stressed those aspects the most. In fact, much of his original body of work was essentially in the folk vein, and he was considered a part of the Northeast folk fraternity when he started to make his mark as a performer in his late teens.

All the Taylor children, of course, found themselves straddling different cultures with their father, Dr. Isaac Taylor, a member of an old southern family and their mother, Trudy (a lyric soprano by training) from long-established New England roots. As the family shuttled between New England and Chapel Hill, North Carolina, where Dr. Taylor became dean of the medical school, Livingston and his brothers and sister were exposed to diverse musical influences, from country to blues and pop.

Emotional illness was a dark thread in their early years, perhaps triggered in part by drug experiences. In succession, James, then Livingston, and later Kate all entered McLean Hospital, a private sanitorium in the Boston area. Livingston began to experience acute depression while attending a private Quaker-run high school in Westtown, Pennsylvania, in the mid-1960s and, aware that James was completing treatment at McLean, followed him there in 1967. He was, he recalls, suicidal, but somehow kept pulling back from the brink, telling himself, "Liv, you're really on the deep end this time."

Music therapy was a part of the treatment, and he soon became engrossed in singing and playing guitar. After he left the hospital at the end of the 1960s, he settled in a secluded house in Weston and sallied forth to perform in small clubs and coffee houses.

He might have been happier if brother James hadn't hit it so big just about then. The national spotlight that glared on James' activities tended to make Livingston's efforts seem like an attempt to ride on his brother's coattails. Liv, on the other hand, already was embarked on his own musical odyssey when James became famous and probably would have made an impact on the music field under any circumstances.

As he told an interviewer in 1970, soon after he had signed his first record contract with Capricorn, "I don't want 'superstardom' or anything like that word implies. I want to develop and become known gradually, so that I can build something that will last for a lot of years. Something that gets better and better with every album. I don't write a whole lot of songs, because every one I write has to be as good as it can possibly be." To further those efforts, the then nineteen-year-old explained, he spent three to four hours a day in his Weston house when not on the road, writing new songs, improving his piano playing, and learning flute and banjo.

His music was different from other Taylor family members'. It was softer, with much less emphasis on rock rhythms. That difference perhaps worked against him at a time when rock was the overwhelming arbiter of pop music. He turned out a series of albums on Capricorn in the early 1970s that won him a following, but nowhere near as large a one as for James' blockbuster efforts. His debut LP on Capricorn came out in the summer of 1970. Called *Livingston Taylor*, it made lower-chart levels and provided two songs, "Carolina Day" and "Sit on Back," that made national pop singles charts in 1971. His next album, *Liv,* released in late 1971, had much greater impact, remaining on the charts well into 1972, though never achieving gold-record levels. The single "Get Out of Bed" also received good response in early 1972. In 1973, his third LP on Capricorn, *Over the Rainbow,* also showed up on pop charts for some months.

During those years, Taylor toured through much of the country, where his quiet, ingratiating manner made the slender, tall, blond artist many friends among folk and soft-rock fans. He enjoyed performing, though he felt somewhat dissatisfied with the way his career was going. Those feelings and other personal and record business considerations caused him to essentially retire from the recording field for almost all of the mid-1970s. But while he kept a low profile in that sense, he stayed on the concert circuit, working mostly small clubs and college venues, and kept experimenting with new approaches to songwriting.

He felt he was growing and improving himself creatively even without the exposure of nationally promoted albums and singles. As he noted when he finally returned to those endeavors in 1978, "I know what my audience wants and they're going to get it. Playing live is how you make a career. I've been playing to audiences for the last five years and the only way they can be exploited is with quality and good taste. There's no 'new and improved Livingston Taylor'—I've always been good. And, above all else, I'm an entertainer."

During the summer of 1978, Epic Records released Liv Taylor's first new album in five years. Called *3-Way Mirror,* it indicated he had moved more strongly into folk-rock than basic folk stylings, though many of the compositions could have been performed in the latter vein. Among his new songs were the relatively fast-paced "L.A. Serenade" and such others as "How Much Your Sweet Love Means to Me," "Train Off the Track," and "No Thank You Skycap," the latter featuring Maria Muldaur as a guest vocalist. During his touring efforts in support of the album, he got the chance to play before a number of very large audiences, since many of his late 1978 appearances were as opening act for Linda Ronstadt.

TAYLOR, TUT: *Dobro player, mandolinist, guitarist, banjoist, composer. Born Georgia, circa 1924.*

Tut Taylor has become famous for his flat picking style of dobro playing; in fact, he has long been considered the premier dobro player in Nashville and from the 1950s through the 1970s was one of the city's busiest session musicians, performing on countless country and country-rock recordings. However, as is often the case, his style was formed by accident, because he taught himself to play and didn't know that other people used fingerpicks to play the instrument.

Tut came from a musical family in a backwoods area of Georgia. Since times were hard when he was young, about all they had to entertain themselves with was music. Tut started picking up the banjo at the age of ten and the mandolin when he was twelve. When he was about fourteen he heard Oswald Kirby play the dobro and fell in love with the sound of the instrument. He didn't know what that instrument was, however, so he wrote to Roy Acuff at the *Grand Ole Opry.* Mildred Acuff wrote him back a postcard saying it was a dobro. Tut rushed out and bought one as soon as he could. Since he played the mandolin with a flat pick, he assumed the dobro was played the same way.

Tut's love of the dobro is evident in his statement to Douglas Green of *Guitar Player Magazine*: "I love the sound of all dobros. They're very much like women, all different. My wife and my dobro are my two favorite things."

Over the years, Taylor bought many dobros, and he became renowned as a dobro collector. However, since he gave the instruments to other dobro-lovers his own collection has diminished quite a bit. Another sideline of his is the running of the Tennessee Dulcimer Works, a company that manufactures guitars, banjos, dulcimers, and mandolins.

Tut is known as a creative as well as a skillful dobro player. He has backed such artists as John Hartford and Leon Russell and he has also recorded his own solo albums, two of which are *Friar Tut* and *Pickin' Flat*, recorded on his own King Tut label. (*Friar Tut* was picked up by Rounder Records and was in its catalogue as of the start of the 1980s. Also still in active catalogues at the time were *Dobrolic Plectoral Society* on Takoma Records and *The Old Post Office* on Flying Fish Records.) Tut is famous for playing unusual items on the dobro, songs that usually are not played on the instrument, such as fiddle tunes and songs like "Sweet Georgia Brown."—A.S.

TERRY, SONNY: *Singer, harmonica player, songwriter. Born Greenwood, Georgia, October 24, 1912.**

In the tradition of so many troubadours over the centuries, Sonny Terry provided visions of beauty and emotional satisfaction for millions of sighted people the world over, though he himself was afflicted with blindness. Like Doc Watson, Blind Blake, and Blind Lemon Jefferson, he ranks as one of the most important folk artists of the twentieth century. Unlike them, he was

---

*Date and place as given by Terry in 1976. Earlier biographies stated he was born near Durham, North Carolina, October 24, 1911.

not blind from birth, but lost his sight as the result of two childhood accidents.

Teddell Saunders "Sonny" Terry spent most of his youth in North Carolina. Born into a poor family, his father, Reuben, owned a small farm twenty miles north-northeast of Durham and scratched out a living with the assistance of all family members who could help with the chores.

In his leisure time, Reuben Terry loved to play the harmonica, and his young son soon wanted to emulate him. He recalled for Mark Schiffer of *Picking Up the Tempo* in 1976, "When I was a kid, 'bout four or five, my father used to play harmonica, you know. . . . He'd go to work in the daytime, you know, and he'd come back at night, you know, reach up and git his harp after he'd git through eatin' supper, play a tune. I'd watch him where he'd put it, you know. So when he'd have to go to work the next day, I'd git a chair up there and git it. And when he found out I was gittin' it, I'd 'ready found out how to play a tune on it, you know! So one night, he said, 'Boy, you been after my harp. It ain't lyin' like the way I put it. I didn't lay it like that.' I wouldn't tell no lie. I told 'Yeah, pa, I did have it.' And my mother told him, she took it for me then, she said, 'Well, he can play it now.'

"Dad said, 'Well, son, you been playin' my harp. I not gonna let you play my harp. I'm gonna buy you one.' Then one Friday night he went to town and bought me a harp. I was scared to tear his up, you know. I wanted to tear it up and see where da sound was comin' from . . . (chuckles). And so he come back and he seed my harp tore up, you know. I had it lyin' out on the floor. He said, 'See that, son. I payed a quarter for that thing the other day. You done tore it up. That dear little thing you tore up there gonna make a livin' for you one day when I'm dead and gone.' And he tol' the truth. I wish he 'as here to hear me say it."

Sonny continued to spend many hours improving his harp playing after that. Before long he was able to pick out any of the gospel and work songs he heard around him. While still a boy, he started to play his harmonica in local churches. As word of his talent spread, he was asked to perform in churches or in church concerts in other parts of the region.

The death of his father, caused by a transport truck accident, resulted in Sonny, by then completely blind, leaving home for good. As he wandered around the South adding secular songs to his repertoire—mainly blues and ballads—he earned money entertaining in small clubs or on street corners. By the early 1930s, his name was becoming known to other blues artists and to the growing number of folklorists interested in collecting blues songs. He performed with many now legendary artists in the 1930s, including, at time, his good friend Leadbelly.

The performer he became most closely associated with during the period was Blind Boy Fuller. Recalling their first meeting, he told Mark Schiffler, "He was playing one side of the street and I was playing the other." The two teamed up, their efforts resulting, among other things, in a trip to New York to take part in the 1938 "Spirituals to Swing" concert. They also made a number of records together in the late 1930s. In 1939, while playing in Durham, North Carolina, with Fuller, Sonny became acquainted with another guitarist named Brownie McGhee. They liked each other's style and, after Fuller's death in 1940 left Terry without a partner, he and McGhee began to work together.

However, it was an off and on association for some years and even when the two became almost inseparable on the concert circuit, they still found time to do solo recordings. Thus for extended periods during the 1940s, Terry toured with another guitarist named Alec Stewart and also performed widely with Pete Seeger. That exposure to folk audiences across the United States helped achieve a growing national reputation for him. During that decade, Terry made New York his home and continued to reside there through the 1970s while Brownie McGhee kept his home in California. McGhee also lived in New York in the 1940s, through a period of folk music ferment when they shared the stage often with people like Leadbelly, Josh White, Seeger, and Woody Guthrie. At one time in that decade, Brownie and Sonny combined with Seeger and Guthrie to form a group called the Streamline Singers.

Although Terry was recording with various artists and on many small labels in the 1930s and 1940s, it was not until 1949 that he made his first major album. Under the supervision of Jac Holzman, founder of Elektra Records, he recorded some of his best work in an LP titled *City Blues*. The album featured Sonny and Alec Stewart on such songs as "Little Annie," "Louise Blues," "Down in the Bottom Blues," "Baby, Baby Blues," "Custard Pie," "Kansas City," "Late One Saturday Evening," "Old Woman Blues," "Hard Luck Blues," and "Chain the Lock on My Door." In the decades that followed, Sonny was featured as a soloist on many other albums on various labels. In the 1950s, these included *Folk Blues* on Elektra, *Harmonica and Vocal Solos and Washboard Band* on Folkways, *Sonny Terry and His Mouth Harp* on Stinson, and *Mouth-Harp* on Riverside. His solo albums of the 1960s included *Sonny's Story* (1961) and *Sonny Is King* (1963) (both Bluesville), *Get Together* (Verve/Forecast, 9/65), and *Sonny Terry* (Archives of Folk Music, 1/66). His active albums of the 1970s included a re-issue of *Sonny Is King* (an album also featuring Lightnin' Hopkins) on Prestige Records.

A major event in the Terry-McGhee affiliation was their appearance on January 28, 1950, in a Leadbelly Memorial Concert at New York's Town Hall. Their set won such ecstatic applause that it influenced them to concentrate on joint efforts. From then on, they became major figures on the blues and folk circuit, playing before capacity crowds in concerts all over the United States, Canada, and many other nations. Their 1950s appearances included holdover engagements at such highly regarded clubs as the Ash Grove in Los Angeles and the hungry i in San Francisco. They became familiar figures at the many folk festivals that became prominent in the late 1950s and 1960s, including performances at several of the annual summer events in Newport, Rhode Island. The pattern continued throughout the 1960s and

1970s. At the end of the 1970s, the duo still was giving several hundred live concerts every year.

The record output of Terry and McGhee was extensive, including dozens of titles on many different labels. The first duet LP made by them on the Folkways label, *Brownie McGhee and Sonny Terry*, came out in 1958 and still was in the company's catalogue at the end of the 1970s. Another still available LP was their 1958 two-record set *Back to New Orleans*, which included two of Terry's best-known numbers, "Fox Hunt" and "Stranger Blues." By the end of the 1970s, besides a number of other albums on Folkways, the team's credits covered collections on such labels as Savoy, Fantasy, Verve, Bluesville, Sharp, and Prestige. In the mid-1970s, they recorded for A&M Records, one of their releases being the 1975 LP *Sonny and Brownie*. (See also McGhee, Brownie.)

THOMAS, B.J.: *Singer. Born Houston, Texas, August 7, 1942.*

Most observers considered B.J. Thomas essentially a pop singer and, indeed, he did make his first breakthroughs as a rock entertainer. But he was weaned, in essence, on country and gospel, and many of his greatest hits were derived from those genres. Not surprisingly, his songs often crossed over from pop to country or vice versa.

Thomas was born and raised in Houston, where family and friends knew him as Billy Joe. Later on, he used his first initials to avoid confusion with another rising star of the 1960s, Billy Joe Royal. From his early years, B.J. enjoyed singing both church and country music. One of his early country idols was Hank Williams. In his early teens he sang both in his church choir and high school choral group, but was becoming increasingly interested in the siren call of rock 'n' roll. When he was fifteen, in 1965, he joined a rock band called the Triumphs, which played initially for local parties and dances in the Houston area.

The band won a record contract with a local label and had some local hits, including one titled "Lazy Man." B.J. rapidly had become the focal point of the group, which changed its name to B.J. Thomas and the Triumphs. His ability won the attention of Scepter Records, for whom Thomas soon recorded an updated version of the Hank Williams country classic, "I'm So Lonesome I Could Cry." The record made the top 10 in the United States in 1966 and rose to number one in Australia. B.J. added two more top-20 chart hits before the year was over, "Billie and Sue" and another country-based release, "Tomorrow Never Comes." His achievements caused both *Cash Box* and *Billboard* magazines to name him Most Promising Vocalist of 1966.

After a relatively slow 1967, when he placed a number of songs on the charts, but none in the top 10 or 20, he roared back in 1968 with two gold-record singles, "The Eyes of a New York Woman" and "Hooked on a Feeling," the latter portraying some of his personal problems. By the late 1960s, he had become one of the most popular attractions on both the concert circuit and TV. He headlined in major venues across the United States ranging from the Copacabana in New York to San Francisco's Fairmont Hotel and major Vegas clubs. During one appearance in New York, he was involved in a stabbing incident in which one of his lungs was punctured. One of the results of that, it was claimed, was an increased dependence on drugs that eventually threatened to ruin his career.

But things seemed bright professionally at the start of the 1970s. At Dionne Warwick's suggestion, Burt Bacharach and Hal David chose B.J. to sing their song "Raindrops Keep Falling on My Head," the theme for the Paul Newman movie *Butch Cassidy and the Sundance Kid*. The movie was one of the most successful films of 1970 and the single proved B.J.'s greatest smash to date, selling over 3 million copies. The song won the Oscar for Best Song of the Year. B.J.'s album of the same title sold over a million copies to earn him his first album gold-record award in 1971. In late 1970, B.J. earned still another gold record for his single "I Can't Help Believing." Also a hit for him was the Bacharach/David song "Everybody's Out of

Town" and, in 1971, "No Love at All," "Mighty Clouds of Joy," and "Most of All," the last named the title song for a chart hit album. In early 1972, he turned out one of his trademark songs of later years, "Rock 'n' Roll Lullaby" and such other chart hits as "Happier than the Morning Sun" and "That's What Friends Are For."

But despite all his success and audience adulation, emotionally things weren't going that well for him. His restlessness perhaps was reflected in a move to a new label, Paramount, which seemed to coincide with a downturn in recording achievements. For most of 1973, for instance, he only had one chart single on the label, "Songs."

Thomas was, in the meantime, exhibiting almost suicidal tendencies, using more and more drugs, drinking too much, and generally doing everything to excess. He recalled, "The more hit records I had, the more miserable I became. I got a lot of reasons from my friends and shrinks but that was no answer. When I sat down to drink, I would drink too much; I was smoking three or four packs of cigarettes a day." Somehow he kept going for a while, though the day of reckoning was approaching as he neared physical and emotional exhaustion. It was something his fans might have found hard to understand, particularly when he returned to the forefront in 1974 with the massive pop and country hit, his version of Chips Moman's "Somebody Done Somebody Wrong Song."

His problems mounted as he got into contractual wrangles with his management. He became further depressed when Paramount Records was absorbed into ABC Records. For a year he gave up performing and recording activities while he worked to overcome his difficulties and put his life back in some sort of order. During that time, he turned to religion for succor and, like Jimmy Carter, became a born-again Christian.

As Thomas told an interviewer, "That experience really brought everything into focus. It set my priorities right—making records, my personal life, everything. For the first time in my life, I had ambition. When I started my career, I knew I could sing, but I had no ambition. I just cut records and when one made it, that was fine; and if it didn't, it made no difference. But I couldn't do it myself. . . ."

When he returned to action, he signed with a new label, MCA. His first LP, *B.J. Thomas*, spawned a major hit, "Don't Worry Baby." Simultaneously, Thomas was demonstrating renewed interest in religious music. In 1977, he recorded a gospel collection on Myrrh Records titled *Home Where I Belong*. That LP rose to number one on the gospel charts and was nominated for a Grammy Award. He continued that pattern the following year with a secular LP on MCA, produced by long-time friend Chips Moman, who co-wrote (with Mark James) the title song, "Everybody Loves a Rain Song," and another gospel album on Myrrh. The latter, titled *Happy Man*, which indicated Thomas' inner feelings at the end of the 1970s, brought him a Grammy Award for Best Inspirational Performance of 1978.

At the start of the 1980s, he became one of the first artists signed for MCA's new "contemporary Christian" label, Songbird. His debut album was titled *For the Best* and was followed by the LP *B.J. Thomas in Concert*. The latter contained both religious and secular songs, with his renditions of numbers like "Walkin' on a Cloud," "Raindrops Keep Fallin' on My Head," "Mighty Clouds of Joy," and "Nothing Could Be Better."

Thomas explained that he didn't see a dichotomy in the choice of material. "I'm not a Christian entertainer, I'm an entertainer who is a Christian. I definitely have the freedom to do any kind of music I want to do. But I sing contemporary Christian songs because they have a positive and uplifting message. And more importantly, especially when discussing secular markets, I felt that contemporary Christian music makes a positive statement while not always making a Christian statement.

"Some people are confused as to what a Christian song is. What it isn't is a negative statement, but a positive one. A line from a pop song such as 'I don't need you anymore, I've found somebody new' is a positive statement for a pop song, but a negative statement for contemporary Christian music."

THOMPSON, HANK: *Singer, guitarist, harmonica player, songwriter, band leader (Brazos Valley Boys). Born Waco, Texas, September 3, 1925.*

If anyone was heir to the mantle of Bob Wills in the post-World War II decades, it was Hank Thompson, whose big band sound played a prominent role in country & western music of the 1950s and 1960s. Thompson's stylings, though, were wider ranging, incorporating many of the new country sounds that came along from the late 1940s on thanks to such artists as Hank Williams and Elvis. Although Thompson and his Brazos Valley Boys could play Wills' style "Western swing," they were equally adept at honky-tonk music and "down home" country songs too.

As a boy growing up in Waco, Texas, in the early 1930s, Hank was influenced by everything from the then-popular Jimmie Rodgers 78s to the *Grand Ole Opry*. His first love instrumentally was the harmonica. Inspired by the growing number of western movies where the singing hero often strummed a guitar, he began to play that instrument as well. Gene Autry was a particular favorite.

In response to his request for a guitar, his parents finally bought a four-dollar model for him as a Christmas present. With that treasured instrument, Hank spent hours figuring out chord patterns and trying to emulate the guitar runs of some of the country & western stars of the day. This finally paid off in the early 1940s when he got a job performing in a Saturday morning youth program at a local theater that was broadcast on station WACO. A flour company liked him and sponsored him on a show called *Hank the Hired Hand*. After six months, and having gained his high school degree in January 1943, Hank enlisted in the U.S. Navy, where he remained for three years on a tour of duty that included extensive voyages throughout the South Pacific.

After his discharge, he attended Princeton University in New Jersey for a time, then decided he'd had enough of higher education. He went back to Waco to do a noon show on station KWTX. Response to his efforts was so good, he put together his own band, named the Brazos Valley Boys. They soon became a popular attraction in shows and dances all over central Texas. Hank had written a number of original songs by then, some while in the Navy, and in 1946 recorded two of them on the local Globe Records label. The two releases, "Whoa Sailor" and "Swing Wide Your Gate of Love," did well, and he began to gain a following in other parts of the country. A number of country artists also recorded another of his compositions, "A Lonely Heart Knows."

Tex Ritter was one of Thompson's most enthusiastic listeners. He arranged an introduction for Hank to Capitol Records officials, who signed him in 1948, the beginning of an association that lasted until 1966 (though Capitol kept releasing Hank's LPs several years after that) and encompassed dozens of major hit recordings. In his first year on Capitol, Thompson turned out two major successes, "Humpty Dumpty Heart," a top-10 single, and "Today." In 1949, he had two more top-10 hits, a remake of "Whoa Sailor" and a new composition, "Green Light."

In the early 1950s, Hank had a number of records that made the charts, but none that gained the highest levels. His fortunes changed in 1952 with the top-10 hit "Waiting in the Lobby of Your Heart," co-written with the long-time Brazos Valley Boys lead singer Billy Gray. The same year, he achieved his first number-one-ranked record with "Wild Side of Life." In 1953, he had the top-10 hits "Wake Up Irene" and "No Help Wanted." He followed with a banner year in 1954, when he placed five singles in the country top 10: "Breakin' the Blues" (co-written with Billy Gray and A. Blasingame), "Honky Tonk Girl" (co-written with C. Harding), "New Green Light" (by Hank), "We've Gone Too Far" (co-written with B. Gray), and "You Can't Have My Love" (co-written with Gray, Harding, and M. Roberts). The last-named record featured a duet between Billy Gray and a new vocalist soon to be a star in her own right, Wanda Jackson.

By the time those songs were being played on stations across the United States, Thompson had moved band headquarters from Texas to Lake Tenkiller in eastern Oklahoma. It was the same year (1953) that he and the band helped set attendance records at the Texas State Fair. The engagement became an annual event, and decades later Hank and his group still returned to headline there. During the 1950s and 1960s, the group performed at many other major fairs and rodeos across the nation and usually had extended appearances at Nevada hotels each year. The band also was featured on many TV shows over the years, including *The Jimmy Dean Show, The Tonight Show* with Johnny Carson, *American Swing Around*, NBC-TV's *Swingin' Country*, and the WGN *Barn Dance*. From the mid-1950s into the late 1970s, Hank often was on the road a good part of the year. In the mid-1960s, the band typically averaged 240 personal appearances annually, a pace that slowed somewhat in the 1970s. Those shows took Hank and the band to all fifty states, many major Canadian cities, and on a number of tours of the Far East and Europe.

On occasion, Thompson flew from one U.S. engagement to the next in his own plane. A licensed pilot, he had logged many flying hours by the late 1970s, when he owned a twin engine Cessna 310. It was sometimes his mode of transportation on hunting and fishing trips from his home in Sand Springs on the Keystone Reservoir in Oklahoma.

From the early 1950s to the early 1960s, Hank had one or more top-10 singles every year on Capitol except for 1957. Those included such originals as "Don't Take It Out on Me," and "Wildwood Flower" in 1955; "I'm Not Mad, Just Hurt" in 1956; "I've Run Out of Tomorrows" in 1959 (co-written with L. Compton and V. Mizi); and "A Six Pack to Go" (co-written with J. Lowe and D. Hart) in 1960. He also had top-10 hits by other writers: "Squaws Along the Yukon" in 1958 and "Oklahoma Hills" in 1961.

Hank was represented by many albums on Capitol from the late 1940s to late 1960s. Among his early and mid-1950s LPs were *Songs of the Brazos Valley, North of the Rio Grande, All Time Hits,* and *Hank.* In the late 1950s, releases included *Hank's Dance Ranch* (6/58), *Favorite Waltzes* (2/59), and *Breakin' In* (4/59). He led off the 1960s with the album *Most of All* (5/60) and followed with *This Broken Heart* (1/61), *Old Love Affair* (9/61), *At the Golden Nugget* (11/61), *No. 1* (7/62), *Cheyenne Days* (1/63), *Best* (5/63), *State Fair of Texas* (10/63), *Golden Hits* (5/66), *Luckiest Heartache* (4/66), and *Breakin' the Rules* (10/66). Although he left Capitol in 1966, there were still plenty of recordings left for a number of new releases, including *Best* (3/67), *Countrypolitan Sound* (4/67), *Gold Standard Collection* (5/67), and *Just an Old Flame* (10/67).

By the time Thompson signed with Warner Bros. in 1966, he had rolled up record sales on Capitol of over 30 million albums and had placed around 100 records on the hit charts. For most of his tenure with Capitol, the Brazos Valley Boys were ranked number-one country band in many important polls. The group held that position on both *Billboard* and *Cash Box* magazine lists thirteen consecutive years, from 1953 to 1966.

He still had pulling power in the mid-1960s even though country swing bands were generally losing favor. His first single on Warner Bros., for instance, made national charts, as did the LP of that title, *Where Is the Circus.* However, the new association didn't prove comfortable for the parties involved, and in 1968 he signed with ABC/Dot. This alignment still held firm over a decade later.

Thompson was on the ABC/Dot roster when he celebrated his twenty-fifth year as a recording artist in 1971. In honor of that landmark, ABC issued a two-record set, *Hank Thompson's 25th Anniversary Album.* Other releases on the label in the late 1960s and early 1970s included *Hank Thompson Sings the Gold Standards, (Hank Thompson) On Tap, in the Can, or in the Bottle, Smokey the Bar, Hank Thompson Salutes Oklahoma, Hank Thompson's Brazos Valley Boys, Next Time I Fall in Love (I Won't),* and *Cab*

Driver. His mid- and late-1970s LPs included *Hank Thompson's Greatest Hits, Volume 1, Kindly Keep It Country, A Six Pack to Go, Hank Thompson Sings the Hits of Nat King Cole, The Thompson Touch,* and *Doin' My Thing.*

While almost all his material came out on ABC or Capitol, some of his recordings were presented on releases (mostly reissues) on other labels. Among those were *Country Greats* on Paramount, *New Rovin' Gambler* on Pickwick, and *You Always Hurt the One You Love* on Hilltop.

Although Hank wasn't the dominant force in country music in the late 1970s that he'd been a decade or two earlier, he still commanded the respect of musical peers and a sizable number of country fans as well. Among other honors that came his way in the second half of the 1970s was his selection by *Country Music Magazine* as the reigning country "King of Swing."

By the end of 1970s, ABC had been absorbed by MCA, and Thompson's releases at the start of the 1980s appeared on that label. In early 1980, he had the chart-hit single "Tony's Tank-Up, Drive-In Cafe" on MCA and, in August, was represented by a new LP, *Take Me Back to Tulsa.* As of that release date, MCA estimated that Hank had achieved in his career, over 100 charted singles, including two dozen that had made *Billboard's* top 10.

THROCKMORTON, SONNY: *Singer, guitarist, songwriter. Born Carlsbad, New Mexico, April 2, 1940.*

Sonny Throckmorton's father was a minister who often gave him sermons inveighing against the sinfulness of nightclub life and suggested that Sonny avoid the music field because of the odds against success. By the time he was thirty-five, Throckmorton tended to agree with those predictions, but after attempting to find another profession, he made one more try—and hit pay dirt.

As might be expected for the son of a Pentecostal minister, Sonny's initial exposure to music was in the gospel vein. His father played guitar and a sister played piano. As a boy, Sonny joined with them in singing and playing religious songs during church services or functions.

Because his father moved from one location to another as part of his task of establishing and building new Pentecostal churches, Sonny spent time in a number of different towns in the Southwest and West as a child. When he was in his teens, the family lived in Texas, where he graduated from high school in Wichita Falls. From there he went on to Midwestern State University in that city, with thoughts of gaining a B.A. in English. A professor told him that he ought to consider almost any line of work other than writing. As Throckmorton told a Nashville reporter in 1979, "I don't think she meant songwriting. But she wasn't entirely wrong. If I had to sit down and write articles, I'd starve to death."

By then, his father had relocated to California, where he had set up a new church in San Francisco. Since Sonny had become interested in rock 'n' roll during his high school and college years, San Francisco, a mecca for rock clubs, seemed a logical move. It was hardly reassuring for Throckmorton senior to know that at a club in one part of town the sign outside read "Sonny Throckmorton appearing here tonight" while he was giving sermons about why parishioners shouldn't go to nightclubs on Saturday nights.

Still, despite the minister's qualms, the two managed to coexist. In the early 1960s, despite his college professor's forecast, Sonny was beginning to try writing original songs, though he used material by others, for the most part, in his act. In 1962, he moved to Los Angeles for a time, where he signed a recording contract with an independent label. That didn't turn out too well, so he went back to San Francisco. Not long after, he married wife Brenda, whom he met as a member of his father's congregation.

Although he persevered as an entertainer, progress still was slow. He decided, in 1964, to move to Nashville, since his musical interests had moved back toward country. Writing steadily by then, he found jobs with several Nashville publishing offices, and some of his songs began to spark interest among country performers.

Sonny's hopes rose in the 1960s when Bobby Lewis had a hit single of his "How Long Has It Been." Several other artists released singles of Sonny's songs, but while a few made lower-chart levels, most were failures.

Throckmorton had set a deadline for himself: if he hadn't succeeded in the music field by the time he was thirty-five, he'd quit. When he reached that age in 1975, he reluctantly bowed to what seemed like the inevitable and took his family (which, by then, included two daughters) back to Texas. He discovered, however, that outside of a few odd jobs he couldn't find a way to make a steady living. Thus, he recalled for Bob Millard of *Country Scene* magazine in April 1979, "I fished a lot and watched TV a lot and really just did a whole lot of nothing."

After six months, he was more than ready when Nashville friends began to call on him to return. The musical climate was changing and artists were becoming increasingly interested in some of his previous songs that still were circulating in Nashville. His old publishing firm, Tree International, also showed renewed interest, and Sonny went back to Nashville, happy to sign a new writing contract.

He set about preparing new material and, in a short time, between his previous catalogue and new products, he had the first of what was to soon become almost a flood of recordings by various artists. By mid-1977, singles of his material were showing up on low- and mid-chart levels. Then, late in the year, he really got hot with several blockbuster singles on the charts at the same time. From the fall of 1977 to the fall of 1978, over ninety cuts of his songs were issued; for all but a few weeks during that span, he had one or more songs on the charts, sometimes with as many as six or seven titles on at the same time.

In late 1977, he could point to a number-one hit, Dave & Sugar's version of "Knee Deep in Loving You." During the same period, Jerry Lee Lewis' single of "Middle Age Crazy" rose to number four on country charts. Johnny Duncan added

another number-one hit to Throckmorton's credits with the single "Thinking of a Rendezvous." Sonny had a near miss when Merle Haggard's single of "If We're Not Back in Love by Monday" (co-written with Glenn Martin) rose to number two on country lists. The single also made it to number thirty-four on pop charts. Millie Jackson's R&B styling of the same song rose to number three on R&B charts. In the summer of 1978, T. G. Sheppard had a top-10 hit with "When Can We Do This Again," co-written by Sonny and C. Putman. Other chart-makers in 1978 included Connie Smith's single of "Smooth Sailin' " (cowritten with C. Putman) and Tommy Overstreet's release of "Fadin In, Fadin' Out," co-written by Sonny and Bobby Braddock. Sonny's achievements in 1978 were recognized by his peers in early 1979, when the Nashville Songwriters Association voted him songwriter of the year for 1978, an honor given him again in 1980.

During 1978, Throckmorton got a new chance to demonstrate his singing talent. He signed with Mercury Records, which released his debut LP, *Last Cheater's Waltz,* in July 1978. The LP included some of his songs that had already been hits for others plus a number of completely new compositions. The disc demonstrated that Sonny was a capable, if not overpowering singer, with the ability to impart emotional shadings to many of his songs. The debut single from the album, "I Wish You Could've Turned My Head (And Left My Heart Alone)" came out in late 1978, followed in early 1979 by "Last Cheater's Waltz."

As his career flourished, he was glad to find his father's attitude had changed. He told AP reporter Joe Edwards in early 1979, "He's beginning to like it now. He was a totally devoted preacher and God's word was first. He wanted me to do something constructive with my life. He was trying to save souls and here I was in music. But he thinks it's neat I can make a living with a pencil."

The pencil continued to prove proficient as the 1970s gave way to the 1980s. In early 1979, a song co-written with D.

Cook, "I Had a Lovely Time," provided a hit for the Kendalls. In May, Jerry Lee Lewis made upper-chart levels with Sonny's "I Wish I Was Eighteen Again." At year end, Johnny Russell scored a mild hit with "Ain't No Way to Make a Bad Love Grow." In early 1980, Sonny hit another bonanza period with multiple songs on the charts: in March, Moe Bandy had a top-10 hit with "One of a Kind" (co-written with B. Fischer) at the same time that comedian George Burns' new version of "I Wish I Was Eighteen Again" was in the top 15. Also moving up the charts in the month were the singles "The Way I Am" (recorded by Merle Haggard) and "Temporarily Yours" (co-written with B. Fischer, recorded by Jeanne Pruett). In early 1981, T. G. Sheppard made number one on country singles charts with Sonny's "I Feel like Loving You Again" (co-written with B. Braddock).

Discussing his "overnight success" with Joe Edwards, Sonny alluded to the twelve years of trying and the countless songs written, rewritten, or discarded. The trick of becoming a good songwriter, he said, "is applying yourself and working hard. Maybe after you write 1,500 songs, people will say you can write."

This is his advice for hopeful writers: "Learn your craft, then be lucky. Keep yourself attuned to thought waves. Study people. A great way to learn about people you are writing about is to know what you yourself are."

THUNDERKLOUD, BILLY, AND THE CHIEFTONES: *Vocal and instrumental group. Billy Thunderkloud, Jack Wolf, Richard Grayowl, Barry Littlestar, all born British Columbia.*

Although Indians and Indian lore occasionally have found attention in country & western song (and even more so in folk music), only a handful of Indians have entered the field as performers. Some artists, among them Johnny Cash, lay claim to some Indian blood, but few have direct tribal roots. An exception is Billy Thunderkloud and the Chieftones, a group of four full-blooded Indians from the Canadian Northwest.

All of the members are from the Tsimshian Indian nation and grew up in northwest British Columbia. (The Tsimshians are well known for their artistic work, particularly the many striking totem poles carved by generations of tribal members.) The featured member of the group, Billy Thunderkloud, is a hereditary Gilksan chief.

While all four individuals had some musical leanings during their childhood years, none of them paid much attention to country music until they went off to take courses at an Indian residential school in Edmonton, Alberta, Canada. In fact, although they were members of the same Indian nation, it wasn't until Thunderkloud, Jack Wolf, Richard Grayowl, and Barry Littlestar moved to Edmonton that they became friends. There they came under the influence of school supervisor John Radcliffe, a devotee of English music-hall material as well as country music. The interaction between him and the four boys led to the development of their own country & western style.

When they decided to form their own group, Thunderkloud took over as a lead singer while also contributing skills as a guitarist, bassist, drummer, and dancer. Jack Wolf demonstrated ability as a lead guitarist and also an arranger, while Grayowl became the primary drummer and Littlestar bass guitarist. (All members can handle vocals and each can double on one or more additional instruments.)

Encouraged by the reception of their efforts by classmates, the group began to expand its appearances to local clubs in its home areas and, after a while, to engagements in other parts of Canada and the United States. In the mid-1970s, Thunderkloud and the Chieftones signed with 20th Century Fox Records and recorded a number of singles for the label. During the summer of 1975, one of those, "What Time of Day," made top-chart levels. Later in the year, the single "Pledging My Love" turned up on the charts. In 1976, the group switched to Polydor Records. One of its first charted releases on that label was its version of John Loudermilk's "Indian Na-

David Gahr

Sonny Terry and Brownie McGhee

The Original Texas Playboys (late 1970s), l. to r. foreground: Bob Kiser, Johnny Gimble, Jack Stidham; back row, l. to r.: Al Stricklin, Leon McAuliffe, Smokey Dacus, Keith Coleman, Tommy Allsup (producer, standing), Leon Rausch

Jimmie Tarleton (1920s)

Mel Tillis

Tompall & the Glaser Brothers: l. to r., Tompall, Jim, Chuck

Conway Twitty

Loretta Lynn and Conway Twitty

Ernest Tubb

Tanya Tucker

tion," which showed up on the lists in early summer of 1976. In the late summer, the group's release of the old pop standard "Try a Little Tenderness" made the country top 50.

TILLIS, MEL: *Singer, guitarist, songwriter, band leader, actor, music publisher. Born Pahokee, Florida, August 8, 1932.*

"One reason I'm here tonight is to d-d-dispel those rumors going around that Mel Tillis has quit st-st-stuttering. That's not true. I'm still stuttering and I'm making a pretty good living at it t-t-too!"

That typical audience greeting reflects the strength of an individual who can take a problem like a major speech defect and turn it into an asset by making maximum use of his natural-born talents. Certainly that is true of Mel Tillis, who has been a premier country-music songwriter for decades, bringing him the highest Country Music Association accolade in 1977, Entertainer of the Year.

As to why Tillis developed his trademark stutter, he once told a reporter, "When I was three in Pahokee, Florida, I caught malaria and stuttered ever since. Some people said it was an emotional problem and would go away. I felt embarrassed and sensitive about it as a youngster, but it didn't go away." As he grew up, he went to a number of university speech clinics to try to solve the problem. "I had been unable to meet people, was afraid to get up in front of an audience. I even had a fear of answering the telephone. But let me tell you, it's much better to face the problem head on." The clinics hadn't been able to eliminate the stammer, but Mel had learned to live with it.

Tillis had learned to play guitar while growing up in Florida, but hadn't decided on how he'd earn a living when he enlisted in the Air Force at the start of the 1950s. He got out in 1955, spent two semesters at the University of Florida before dropping out in 1956, then went home to work at all sorts of odd jobs, from truck driver to strawberry picker. As he told John T. Pugh from *Music City News* (May 1970), "It was then that I wrote a song entitled 'I'm Tired.' Webb Pierce recorded it, it was a

number-one hit and I got the hell out of that strawberry patch in a hurry."

It was part of a pattern of lucky breaks that paved the road to Nashville. He told Pugh, "I was having a hard time. I was down to my last couple of bucks when a singer in the Duke of Paducah band had to have an operation. I was asked to fill in. So I went on the road with them and made enough to live on for awhile. . . . And for the first couple of years, 1956 and 1957, this is pretty much how it went. My wife, Doris, and I would go down to our last few dollars but every time our prayers were answered and something would break for us so we could keep going."

At the time, despite his initial writing success, Mel wanted to emphasize a performing career. Although he stuttered in conversation, his voice came through loud and clear when he sang. "Singing is a kind of mechanical helper. With the various instruments playing along, the rhythm and everything moving, my voice just seems to flow with it . . . like following the bouncing rubber ball."

He actually cut his first record in 1956, his version of the folk classic "It Takes a Worried Man." But industry people suggested that he needed original material, either his own or from another writer, to succeed as a vocalist. Since a newcomer's access to professional material can be limited, he turned his attention to writing and penned an estimated 350 songs during his first six years. The Tillis touch caught the fancy of the country-music field, and a stream of new recordings of his material by a who's who of the industry issued forth from the late 1950s into the 1960s. In 1963, the trend reached its first peak with Bobby Bare's recording of "Detroit City," a top-10 hit in the country field and a strong entry on the pop side too. By the end of the decade it had become a classic, recorded 115 different times for a sales total of 4.5 million records. Among the many other chartmakers from Mel's pen in the 1960s was "Ruby, Don't Take Your Love to Town," which was recorded by many country artists but earned a gold record in the pop version by Kenny Rogers and the First Edition.

Mel, however, still had his sights set on performing success. He recorded a number of his songs for Columbia Records in the late 1950s and mid-1960s, but none was a massive hit, though a fair number made the charts. (His Columbia chartmakers included "The Violet and the Rose," "Walk on By," "Georgia Town Blues," and "Sawmill".) After his switch to Decca he made the charts with "How Come Your Dog Don't Bite Nobody But Me," co-written with Webb Pierce, plus several other releases that made lower-chart levels. He was still seeking at least a top-20 or top-30 success when he switched to Ric in the mid-1960s, then Kapp. He finally did achieve that initial breakthrough, not with one of his own songs but one provided by Harlan Howard, "Life Turned Her That Way." Later, he scored his biggest singles hit of the decade with "These Lonely Hands of Mine," written by Lamar Morris.

As the 1960s went by, things kept looking brighter for Tillis the entertainer. With his band, the Statesiders, he became one of the major attractions on the country music circuit, starring in clubs, auditoriums, and country fairs across the United States. It was a pattern that continued throughout the 1970s to even greater effect, since Mel began to frequent the upper levels of both singles and album charts with his many releases of the decade. (As of the late 1970s, the makeup of the Statesiders included the relatively unusual combination of the three fiddle players along with guitar, drum, and keyboards. Throughout the 1970s, Mel and the band averaged about 250 concerts a year.)

Starting in the late 1960s, Tillis became increasingly visible on national TV. Besides being featured on many *Grand Ole Opry* shows and specials telecast from *Opry* facilities in Nashville throughout the 1970s, he also appeared on such shows as *Tony Orlando and Dawn, AM America, Dinah!, Match Game, Merv Griffin, Hollywood Squares, The American Sportsman,* Johnny Carson's *The Tonight Show, Good Morning America, The Midnight Special,* as a regular cast member of *Glen Campbell's Goodtime Hour, Love American Style,* and the *Ian Tyson Show* in Canada. In the summer of 1977, he

also cohosted his own summer replacement on ABC titled *Mel and Susan Together.*

Mel extended his acting roles when he accepted movie parts. In the movie *W.W. & The Dixie Dance Kings,* released in the mid-1970s (starring Burt Renolds) he played a dual role—himself and a service station attendant. He also had a small part in the 1979 TV movie *Murder in Music City.*

A familiar face on the Country Music Association Awards Show from its inception in 1967, he performed on a number of the programs and also was nominated in one category or another on several occasions. In the 1975 awards, for instance, he and Sherry Bryce were nominated as best vocal duo. In 1977, of course, he was nominated and won in the voting for Entertainer of the Year.

In the late 1960s, Mel signed a recording contract with MGM Records, which released such albums as *Arms of a Fool/Commercial Affection, Mel Tillis at Houston Coliseum with the Statesiders, Living and Learning/Take My Hand* (with Sherry Bryce and the Statesiders), *One More Time, Very Best of Mel Tillis,* and *World to End.* Mel had a good share of singles on the charts under the MGM banner during the first half of the 1970s, either solo vocals or duets with Sherry Bryce. Among the duets were "Let's Go All the Way Tonight," "You Are the One," and "Mr. Wright and Mrs. Wrong," the first two in 1974 the other in 1975. Solo chart singles included "Woman in the Back of My Mind." (All those songs, it might be added, were handled by Sawgrass Music, the publishing firm Mel established in the late 1960s.) By 1976, Mel had moved again, this time to MCA. He made even greater inroads on the country hit lists than in the first part of the 1970s. In 1976, he had a number one hit on MCA with "Good Woman Blues" and did well with the single "Love Revival," a top-20 entry; in 1977, he had such hit songs as "Burning Memories" and "I Got the Hoss." In 1978, he placed "I Believe in You" in the top 5 in the summer and repeated the trick in the late fall with "Ain't No California," still on the charts in 1979. Other best-selling 1979 singles on MCA were "Send Me Down to Tucson/Charlie's Angel" and "Coca Cola Cowboy." His 1979 MCA charted LPs were *Mr. Entertainer, Are You Sincere,* and *I Believe in You.*

In 1979, Tillis left MCA for Elektra/ Asylum Records. His first single release for that label, "Me and Pepper," came out in October. His debut LP on Elektra/Asylum came out in May 1980, titled *Your Body Is an Outlaw.* The title track, issued as a single, quickly made upper-chart levels. His 1980 singles on Elektra included "Lying Time Again," on the charts early in the year; "Your Body Is an Outlaw," a summer hit, and "Steppin' Out" on upper-chart positions late in the year. (MCA also issued a new LP in early 1980, *M-M-Mel Live.)* At the end of 1980, Elektra released the single "Southern Rains," which rose to number one in February 1981. In the summer of 1981, Mel had another best-selling single for Elektra with "A Million Old Goodbyes."

TOMPALL AND THE GLASER BROTHERS: *Vocal and instrumental trio, all born in or near Spalding, Nebraska. Tompall Glaser, September 3, 1933; Charles "Chuck" Glaser, February 27, 1936; James "Jim" Glaser, December 16, 1937.*

The number of country-music superstars to come out of Nebraska is almost infinitesimal. But any state that can lay claim to the birthplace of such talents as the three Glaser brothers must be considered an important link in the progress of country music. Both as a group and as individuals, the Glasers left their mark on the field, not only as performers and writers but as discoverers and developers of other major artists.

The boys' love for music was inspired by their father Louis, a skilled guitarist who saw to it that his sons learned the instrument at early ages. The oldest, Tompall, gave his first performance at seven and later was joined by Chuck and Jim, when they were old enough, in an act that gained experience at PTA meetings, class picnics, and other local functions.

They loved country music from the start, though their father had some doubts

at one point, Jim Glaser told John Pugh of *Music City News* (December 1971). "At first our dad didn't want us in the business because there was no place in Nebraska to play country music except dives and honky-tonks. When we were singing country music, it wasn't the 'in' thing it is now, and we were looked down on, even out there. But we never considered quitting or changing. We just knew we had to get to Nashville."

The boys persisted in their efforts to make a music business career. In their teens in the mid-1940s, they had their own TV show in Holdredge, Nebraska. In the mid-1950s, hearing that an *Arthur Godfrey's Talent Scouts* unit was going to be in Omaha, the Glasers traveled the 180 miles from Holdredge to audition. They did so well they were presented on Godfrey's nationally televised show.

Still looking for a chance to break into the country field, in 1957 they managed to get past the door guardian at a Marty Robbins concert to meet him. This led to their first chance as professional recording artists on his label, Robbins Records. Their debut single, written by Chuck, was "Five Penny Nickel." The record was far from a blockbuster, but the experience encouraged the brothers to move to Nashville in January 1958.

Jim told John Pugh, "Growing up in the middle of Nebraska like we did, we were so far out, we never had a chance to see anybody, or learn from anyone, or be influenced by anyone or anything we ever saw. So we came [to Nashville] pretty primitive, I'm afraid. Not one of us even knew how to dress. And country music was still looked down upon—especially here. In fact, Nashville has probably been one of the last places in the country to accept country music. But we were in the country music colony, so we weren't aware of it. We loved the music community, and eventually grew up to love all of Nashville."

Once in Nashville, the brothers renewed their acquaintance with Robbins and got the chance to work with him. As Tompall recalled "He asked us to go out on the road as his back-up group, and we were with him for almost two years. But it became obvious we were going to have to act as a main act, or always be typed as a back-up group."

Being in Nashville brought exposure to major record firms, and, in 1959, the Glasers got a contract from Decca as Tompall and the Glaser Brothers. The Glasers also picked up much needed extra income by working as recording session musicians.

Their session credentials from those years are impressive. They backed Marty on his classic hit "El Paso" and also supported Claude King on his bestseller, "Commancheros." Besides working with Robbins, the band toured with some other well-known people, including Johnny Cash, with whom they appeared at New York's Carnegie Hall.

Hoping to make it big, they left Robbins, but at first the going was slow. "After we left Marty, we still didn't have any hit records," Jim recalled. "Then Johnny Cash called us for his back-up vocal group. We told him we didn't want that image, and he always presented us as talents in our own right, like he does with the Statler Brothers."

That association with Cash, which lasted for three years until the Glasers felt they really were ready to headline on their own, undoubtedly played an important part in gaining widespread audience acceptance. But also contributing was work with the *Grand Ole Opry*. The Glasers first were featured on the show in 1960. Then, in 1962, they were signed as regulars and still maintained that status with the show a decade afterward.

An indication that things were moving forward was the appearance of many of their recordings on national charts as the 1960s progressed. Among the chart-making singles on Decca written by one or more of the brothers were "She Loves the Love I Give Her," "A Girl Like You," and "Let Me Down Easy." Other Decca hits were "Teardrops 'Til Dawn," "Odds and End," and "Baby They're Playing Our Song." The vocal blend the trio used on most of those releases was the same one they generally employed whenever they appeared together in later years with Tompall handling lead, Jim tenor, and Chuck baritone.

In the mid-1960s, the Glasers became dissatisfied with their Decca Records association and switched to MGM in 1966. Before long, they had two new hit singles on the new label, "The Last Thing on My Mind" and "Gone, on the Other Hand." With the now legendary Jack Clement handling most of the production chores, they added many more chart hits during the late 1960s and early 1970s. Their debut MGM LP, *Tompall and the Glaser Brothers*, was issued in June 1967 and was followed by such other LPs as *Award Winners* and *Rings and Things*. During those years, the brothers topped many polls as the best vocal group in country music. From the mid-1960s into the early 1970s, they gained four designation from the *Music City News* on four occasions, in *Billboard* polls two times, *Cash Box* three times, and, in 1970, won the Best Vocal Group award in the Country Music Association voting.

They achieved equally important successes in other parts of the music industry. In the songwriting end, for instance, all the brothers wrote songs that put other artists' names on country charts. Jimmy Glaser's catalogue included such often covered songs as "Thanks a Lot for Trying Anyway" and "Sitting in an All Night Cafe." Tompall wrote "Stand Beside Me," a major hit for Jimmy Dean in the mid-60s, and, with Harlan Howard, penned "The Streets of Baltimore," a smash success for Bobby Bare in 1966. Another performer who scored with a Tompall composition was Jimmy Newman, who made top levels with "You're Making a Fool Out of Me."

The Glasers also became very active in music publishing, record production, and other aspects of the business side of music. Glaser Productions was set up to handle booking and artist guidance. By the end of the 1960s, the brothers also owned three music firms, Glascap (ASCAP), Glaser Publications (BMI), and Glace (SESAC). Most of their original songs were published under those banners, including "History Repeats Itself," "All Night Cafe," "Streets of Baltimore," "A Taxpayer's Letter," "Stand Beside Me," and "You Take the Future."

Some of the Glasers' efforts went into production. Chuck, in particular, signed with Decca in the mid-1960s and produced sessions of people like Jimmy Payne, Leon McAuliffe, Gordon Terry, and John Hartford. Hartford, in fact, was a Glaser discovery. When he came to the Glaser offices with his great song "Gentle on My Mind," it had been turned down by almost every major music firm in Nashville.

The brothers still were doing most of their performing work together in the early 1970s, though increasingly they were turning their gaze toward more individual work. Jimmy had signed with Monument Records for some solo recordings in the late 1960s and Tompall also had already started to do a lot of solo appearances by the end of the decade. The brothers still could make the hit charts as a group, as was indicated by such early 1970s hits as "Faded Love" and "California Girl and the Tennessee Square."

At the end of the 1960s, Chuck and Tompall also became increasingly committed to the progressive country movement spearheaded by people like Waylon Jennings and Willie Nelson. When they opened their own recording operation, Glaser Studios, in 1969, it became Nashville headquarters for many so-called country-music outlaws, including people like Jennings, Nelson, Steve Young, Kinky Friedman, Mickey Newbury, and many others, and continued as a progressive mecca well into the 1970s.

The pressure of this and other outside activities plus the individualistic outlook of the Glasers began to affect their performing work. Although they continued to be one of the most popular groups in country music at the start of the 1970s, their relationship became difficult. As Jim Glaser said in 1981, "We tried to be too involved. We had too much going on, running publishing companies and staying on the road all the time. Things got to be very hectic and the tension just mounted until it

peaked in 1973." Tompall added, "It was all personalities. Nobody would compromise."

Thus, although each had done some separate work prior to 1973, after their final falling-out over group activities, all three decided to go off on their own full time. They sold their publishing companies to Famous Music and got rid of most of their other joint enterprises. Tompall intended to concentrate on performing, though he did some production work, including coproducing Waylon Jennings' 1973 LP *Honky Tonk Heroes*. Jim also went in that direction, turning out solo recordings on MGM and MCA and touring widely throughout the United States and abroad, including several very successful tours of England. He placed a number of singles on the charts, including one co-written with Jimmy Payne, "Woman, Woman (Have You Got Cheatin' on Your Mind)," that made upper-chart levels. Chuck opted for behind-the-scenes work, continuing his production work with a number of artists, including Kinky Friedman and the Texas Jew Boys, a group he also managed. He also headed his own booking agency, called Nova.

Chuck's efforts came to an abrupt halt for a while after he suffered a massive stroke in 1975. It affected the left side of his body, and his doctors thought its effects might prevent him from ever singing or walking again. However, he refused to give up, and doggedly went through rehabilitation for several years to recover his lost faculties.

Meanwhile Tompall continued to work hard on the concert circuit and as a recording artist. During the mid-1970s his material was issued on MGM and ABC labels. He placed a number of singles on the charts, the most successful of which was "Put Another Log on the Fire," issued in the spring of 1975.

It was his work with progressive country friends Willie Nelson, Waylon Jennings, and Jessi Colter that brought him a lot of attention in the mid-1970s. Some of his stylings were included in the RCA 1975 collection, *Wanted: The Outlaws*, one of the biggest-selling albums in pop music history and the most successful album to that point in country music. The album won a gold record on March 30, 1976 and went on to exceed double-platinum levels later on, the first country LP ever to achieve that. In connection with the album, Tompall made several major tours with the others to venues all across the United States and Canada and in a number of overseas countries.

In 1978, Louis Glaser became very ill and his sons returned to Nebraska to be with him over Christmas. Chuck recalled in an interview for Elektra/Asylum Records in 1981, "It was the first time we three had been together longer than ten minutes in more than six years. We decided we didn't hate each other after all. We fooled around with some tunes [Chuck having regained use of his singing voice] and realized our musical tastes had come together again. When we got back to Nashville, I found a Tim Henderson song called 'Maria Consuela' and played it for Tompall. He called Jim and we decided to record it in our studio."

The single was released on Elektra/Asylum and made the charts. This was followed by more new Tompall and the Glaser Brothers singles, including the hit single "Lovin' Her Was Easier. . . ." In late 1981, the brothers had their first LP ready for release on Elektra/Asylum.

TRASK, DIANA: *Singer. Born Australia, June 23, 1940.*

"Strong-willed" is perhaps an understatement for describing Diana Trask. Few artists who have established excellent reputations in the pop music field would think about throwing it over completely to try for a full-time career as a country singer. And that refers to American-born entertainers. For someone who grew up half a world away to try to make it in a field she had no experience in before—and where there was sure to be little enthusiasm from the close-knit homegrown talent—normally would seem foolhardy. But Diana Trask not only persevered, she won her country-music peers over to the point that she was welcomed with open arms for her *Grand Ole Opry* debut in the late 1960s.

During her childhood and teen years in her native Australia, Diana never even heard of country music (though it must be noted that some Australians did follow that art form; a young man named John Edwards, for instance, working by mail correspondence, succeeded in building up one of the foremost collections of country material, which he later willed to a friend in America who placed it with the University of California at Los Angeles). Australians were familiar with pop and jazz, however. As Diana grew up, she became one of the better young jazz singers in Australia. Not surprisingly, she longed to go to the homeland of jazz.

But there was more opportunity in the pop field and Trask was just as capable of singing novelty tunes and ballads as any band vocalist of the period. Eventually, when she came to the United States, it was the pop field that brought her to the attention of the American public. In the first half of the 1960s she was featured on many major radio and TV programs. During one engagement, when she was singing on the *Don McNeil Breakfast Show* in the early 1960s, she met Tom Ewen, whom she married soon after. In later years, Tom took over as her manager. Despite Diana's brief attempt at retirement to begin raising a family, her popularity continued to rise in the U.S. pop field. Helping it along was a two-year sojourn as a featured vocalist on the *Sing Along with Mitch* TV show.

Still, rock was the dominant factor in pop music in the 1960s, so there was some incentive for Trask to evaluate the future direction of her career. The thought of what to do struck her when she accepted an invitation in the mid-1960s to attend a disc jockey convention in Nashville. She went to see the *Grand Ole Opry,* and, as she told Betty Hofen of *Music City News* (February 1970), "That is when my desire to sing country really began. I guess it was mostly because there, on the *Opry* stage, I saw human beings acting as human beings. And I liked it."

Imbued with the idea, she returned east and first tried to convince her agent and then her record company that she was serious. She decided she ought to leave her label, Columbia, because she wanted one "a little more country" (which is strange, in retrospect, since Columbia in the 1970s became one of the major forces in the country field). "The best I could get was an audition with a folk label and even though the folk label literally threw me out, the audition did convince my agent I could sing country."

Soon after, Diana and Tom decided to pack their bags and move to Nashville for an all-out effort. It took a lot of knocking on doors and phone calls, but she finally found a receptive audience in the form of executive Buddy Killen of Tree International. She signed with Tree, then went about learning her craft. She told *MCN*, "I had to study country music eight months before I did any recording. . . . I bought all the records of people I admired. Then, for months at a time, I just listened and listened to what they did."

The crash course worked and Diana demonstrated to the people at Tree that she could handle a country song with the best of them. A contract was arranged with Dot Records, which soon had her debut single, "Lock, Stock and Teardrops," ready for release. That record did reasonably well and succeeding releases in the late 1960s, such as her version of the country classic "I Fall to Pieces," did even better. Before 1969 was over, her status as an important new force on the country scene was underscored by her appearance on the *Grand Ole Opry*. As she told *Music City News*, "It was terrifying. I don't think I've ever been so scared of anything in my life. Even today I still get extremely nervous about it. But the *Opry* will always be one of my favorite places to perform."

She had the chance to do that several more times as her career moved steadily ahead in the first half of the 1970s. Her debut album *From the Heart* made country hit lists in early 1970 (it was issued in October 1969) as did several more of her succeeding LPs. Trask also had a string of singles that made country lists, such as "When I Get My Hands on You" in January 1974, "Lean It All on Me" in the spring of 1974, "Oh Boy" in early 1975, and "There Has to Be a Loser" in mid-1975.

TRAUM, HAPPY AND ARTIE: *Vocal and instrumental duo, songwriters, authors. Happy, born New York City, 1939; Artie, born New York City, 1943.*

In the annals of folk and rock music of the 1960s and 1970s, the names of Happy and Artie Traum recur frequently. As songwriters, band and session musicians, and commentators, they exerted a strong influence on developments in both fields. As performers, they themselves had the healthy respect of the unfortunately dwindling folk audience in the Beatles and post-Beatles era, and as teachers they provided the groundwork in elements of guitar playing for many young musicians who went on to make names for themselves in pop and rock genres.

Growing up in the New York area in the years when the likes of Pete Seeger and Woody Guthrie were sowing the seeds of a folk music renaissance, both Happy Traum and his younger brother Artie were inspired to learn folk guitar. Both brothers were particularly enthralled with traditional blues music and, desiring to sit at the feet of a master of the idiom, Happy sought out Brownie McGhee during the 1950s. Under McGhee's tutelage, he developed into an excellent blues artist and by the end of the 1950s, Traum was starting to build a reputation as one of the best young folk and blues instrumentalists on the East Coast.

In the late 1950s and early 1960s, Happy had the chance to meet and perform with a number of his idols, including Pete Seeger. He also was part of the youthful folk flowering that took place in Manhattan's Greenwich Village at the start of the 1960s. One of the groups he became involved with at the time, called the New World Singers, blended elements of the older and younger folk spheres. The association paved the way for his first recordings on an album titled *Broadside: Volume 1*. On that disc, Happy took part as a soloist and a member of the New World Singers. Other people who took part in that effort were Pete Seeger, Phil Ochs, and someone listed on the credits as "Blind Boy Grunt," a pseudonym for Bob Dylan.

Happy worked with the New World

Singers (whose personnel varied during its existence) for a number of years and toured throughout the United States with them. He also helped record material on Atlantic Records, including the January 1964 release *New World Singers.*

Happy already was writing extensively on music in the early 1960s. He had a regular column in the major folk music magazine *Sing Out!* on guitar-playing techniques. During the mid-1960s, he had several books on folk music and guitar playing released, including *Fingerpicking Styles for Blues Guitar* by Oak Publications and *The Blues Bag,* issued by Consolidated Music Publishers. Starting in the late 1960s and continuing into the 1970s, he took over as editor of *Sing Out!*

Artie followed his brother into the folk field in the 1960s, though he later devoted some of his time to the rock side of pop music. He picked up many of the blues techniques he used over the years from Happy, as well as from the many blues artists with whom he came in contact. During the mid-1960s, both Traums were sought-after session musicians for all kinds of formats, from folk to rock and blues. Among the people Artie backed during those years were Judy Roderick, Jean Ritchie, David Sanos, and John Sebastian's Lovin' Spoonful.

He started his recording career as a member of the True Endeavor Jug Band, a folk-blues group whose members included Danny Kalb, Sam Charters (writer of many books on blues and blues musicians), and Artie Rose. Their debut LP was issued by Prestige Records in March 1964. Artie then moved on to work with the Danny Kalb Quartet, a group beginning to stress blues-rock material that later became the famous Blues Project. Later in the 1960s, Artie performed with a series of rock and folk groups including the New York Public Library, the Children of Paradise, and Bear. He helped record the latter's album titled *Bear* that was released on the Verve/Forecast label. A number of the songs played by those groups were originals by Artie. At the end of the 1960s, Artie also wrote and recorded the score for the movie *Greetings.*

Artie also taught classes in guitar playing at times, and turned out a number of articles on his favorite subject, as did his brother. Later he collaborated with Happy on the instructional book *Rock Guitar,* published by Consolidated Music Publishers in the early 1970s.

In the late 1960s, the brothers began to work together as a duo more often. They were featured at the Newport Folk Festivals in 1968 and 1969 and also performed in such other events as the Fox Hollow Festival, Philadelphia Folk Festival, Woodstock Sound Festival, and at the Woodstock Playhouse. They continued to perform together in small clubs in the 1970s and added more festival appearances to their credits. In the latter part of 1970, they often could be seen on the educational television program *Free Time* and took part in a number of other public broadcast shows on folk and pop music as the decade went by.

At the start of the 1970s, they signed a record contract with Capitol Records, which released two of their LPs in the early 1970s, *Happy and Artie Traum* and *Double-Back.* Though excellent albums, neither found much buyer response, partly due to very limited promotion, partly to the rock dominated times, and they were out of print after a few years. Later in the decade, the brothers became affiliated with the folk-oriented Rounder Records organization. At the start of the 1980s, the Traums had three albums in Rounder's catalogue: *Mud Arcs, Music Among Friends; Hard Times in the Country;* and *Woodstock Mountain.*

TRENT, CHARLES W. "BUCK": *Singer, banjoist. Born Spartanburg, South Carolina, February 17, early 1930s.*

The banjo always has had an honored role in country music. In fact, at one point in the field's early history, the banjo was far more widely used by local musicians than the guitar. One of the first country stars, in fact, was the charter member of the *Grand Ole Opry,* banjo player extraordinaire Uncle Dave Macon. Following in that tradition are such first-rank banjo experts as Roy Clark and Buck Trent, both of whom often joined in banjo duets on the nationally syndicated *Hee Haw* show.

Clark, of course, is better known to the general public, but Trent was already highly regarded by country peers when Roy was still learning his instrument. Trent was born and raised in Spartanburg, South Carolina, where country music was as natural as hominy grits and black-eyed peas. Considering the environment, it was unusual that his mother started his music lessons on Hawaiian guitar when he was eight. However, after some sixty lessons, Buck switched to his life-long first love, the banjo.

Like his later associate Roy Clark, Buck was something of a banjo prodigy and was good enough to start playing professionally at the age of eleven on Spartanburg radio station WSPA. During those years, he also performed on another local station, WORD. In high school he worked with various local bands at school hops, square dances, and the like. When he was sixteen, TV already was taking hold and he got a job in a country show on WLOS-TV, Asheville, North Carolina, under the pseudonym of "Cousin Wilburn."

Wanting to expand his horizons, he moved to California at eighteen and soon was appearing regularly as a cast member of several shows that were popular with Southern California audiences during the first half of the 1950s. Among those that displayed his talents were the *Town Hall Party* and Cliffie Stone's *Hometown Jamboree*, both of which were proving grounds for many of the top names in country music after World War II.

Later in the 1950s, Buck settled in San Angelo, Texas, for a year as leader of a local band and then went on to Atlanta, Georgia, where he had his own program on WJBF-TV. In 1960, he made the jump to the most prestigious environment of all, the *Grand Ole Opry*, where he was a member of Bill Carlisle's group. Trent worked with Carlisle on several recordings released by Mercury Records. In 1962, he transferred to Porter Wagoner's syndicated TV show, where he often was given a solo spot for his banjo pyrotechnics. He re-mained a top sideman with Wagoner from 1962 through 1973.

The *Hee Haw* show, meanwhile, had achieved success on a nationally syndicated basis in the 1970s, and Trent began working with the show's cohost, Roy Clark. On January 2, 1974, the two shared joint billing at the Frontier Hotel in Las Vegas, Trent's first move toward recognition on the national level. During the mid-1970s, the Clark–Trent collaboration bore fruit in the form of a well-received album on ABC/Dot called *A Pair of Fives*. Trent remained on the ABC roster as the 1970s went by as well as a regular cast member of *Hee Haw*. By the late 1970s he was often headlining his own show at fairs and rodeos as well as regularly performing at major hotels in Las Vegas and Reno.

TRAVIS, MERLE: *Singer, banjoist, guitarist, fiddler, songwriter. Born Ebenezer, Kentucky, November 29, 1917.*

One of the more important songwriters as well as performers in country music for many years, Merle Travis was also an innovator in the field. He originated a method of guitar playing called "Travis-style" that has been adopted by countless performers since Merle started using it decades ago. In addition, he also is credited with an early version of the solid body guitar, a concept that became the basis for the electric guitars favored by all rock musicians as well as an increasing number of folk and country performers since the 1960s.

Born and raised in Kentucky, Merle Robert Travis knew the state's mining towns well and often wrote of the troubles and sorrows of digging coal, though he himself managed to stay out of the mines. He told Irby M. Maxwell in an interview for *Guitar Player* magazine (June 1969), "I was born in Southwest Kentucky in a little place called Ebenezer in Muhlenberg County. Once I made a record called 'Nine Pound Hammer' and there's a verse in it called 'It's a long way to Harlan, it's a long way to Hazard,' and when I tell them I am from the other side of the state why they say, 'Well, you've sung about Harlan and

Hazard,' and I would tell them, 'I've sung about heaven all my life, and nobody's ever accused me of being there.' "

Merle's father relaxed after work by playing the five-string banjo. Young Merle loved the music and tried to play the banjo himself. His father gave him an old one when he was six and Merle could play it fairly well in a few years. Several years later, his brother made him a homemade guitar. Merle's unusual way of playing the guitar, the famed Travis style, resulted from his applying banjo technique to the new instrument. He used his thumb as an accompaniment while the forefinger played the melody on the higher pitched strings. Merle told Maxwell, "I was about 12 when I started to learn some little old chords [on the guitar]. The first instrument I began to play with was a five-string banjo. I was always fascinated by string instruments and I learned to fiddle a little bit. Very little."

After finishing grade school, Merle quit formal education and earned money playing for square dances, fish fries, and "chitling rags." He improved his guitar playing by observing many Kentucky performers, including Mose Rager and Ike Everly, the latter the father of the Everly Brothers. "They used to play at parties and little get-togethers on Sunday afternoon or just anywhere that there were two guitars." Their style, he noted, was similar to what he uses. "A thumb pick, and one little ole finger. I seldom use anything but my thumb and index finger, but on some things I use three fingers. My usual is to thumb pick and no pick on my third finger of my right hand."

For a while in his teens, he worked for the Civilian Conservation Corps. As soon as he earned enough to buy a thirty-dollar Gretch guitar, he joined a friend hitchhiking around the country. They played on street corners and slept in train stations, parked cars, or on park benches. His wanderings eventually took him to Evansville, Indiana, in 1935, where he sang on a marathon broadcast on a local station. A group called the Tennessee Tomcats heard the broadcast and asked him to join them. For some months he toured the Midwest with them and was paid the princely sum of thirty-five cents a day. At times his path crossed that of fiddler and band leader Clayton McMichen. McMichen liked Merle's playing and one day sent Travis a telegram to join his band, the Georgia Wildcats. Travis joined in 1937 and toured widely with the group, playing fairs, local shows, and fiddling contests, where McMichen sometimes matched skills with fiddlers like Natchez the Indian and Curly Fox.

It was with the Georgia Wildcats that Travis debuted on radio station WLW in Cincinnati in the late 1930s. After a while, he had a featured spot on the show and progressed to more important roles on network radio programs. He played such well-known shows of the period as the *Plantation Party* and *National Barn Dance* and was a cast regular for a number of years on the *Boone County Jamboree*, which later became known as the *Midwestern Hayride*, on WLW. During his six years on that station, he shared bills with many of the most famous names in country music. For a time, he was part of a quartet (The Brown's Ferry Four) whose other members were Grandpa Jones and the Delmore Brothers, Alton and Rabon.

Travis' career was interrupted by World War II, when he enlisted in the Marines and spent several years as a leatherneck. After receiving his discharge, he settled in Southern California, where he worked with such performers as Cliffie Stone, Tex Ritter, and Wesley Tuttle. He was a cast regular for a number of years on Stone's *Hometown Jamboree* TV program and also appeared on many other country radio and TV programs originating in the Los Angeles area.

Merle, of course, had been writing original material for some time and now he had the chance to record some of it (as well as songs by other writers) on a major label, Capitol. He had good success with such singles as "No Vacancy," "Divorce Me C.O.D," "So Round, So Firm, So Fully Packed," and "Cincinnati Lou." His first Capitol album in 1947, *Folk Songs of the*

Hills, included his composition "Sixteen Tons." Not much happened with the number at the time, but some years later, Tennessie Ernie Ford recorded it and the song became one of the major hits of 1955 and went on to be one of the top-selling singles of all time. Other hit songs written by Merle are "Smoke, Smoke, Smoke That Cigarette," "Dark as a Dungeon," "Sweet Temptation," and "Old Mountain Dew."

It was during the late 1940s that Merle came up with his solid body guitar idea. He told Maxwell, "As far as I know, I had the first solid body that you play Spanish style. I got an idea when I heard a steel player playing and thought, with electric pickups, why have the hollow body. I bet a solid body would be good and the sustainability would be much better. I drew a picture on the back of a program sheet (the layout including having all the tuning pegs on one side) in a show we were doing over in Pasadena called Hometown Jamboree. . . . I asked a friend of mine, Paul Bigsby, if he could make it. He said, 'Sure, I'll build it.' I still have it." He recalled that a friend named Leo Fender saw him play it, asked if he could borrow it to build a similar instrument "and as far as I know that was the first Fender guitar."

During the 1950s, Travis was featured on both local and national TV shows telecast from the West Coast. He also headlined country concerts all over the United States. With the advent of the folk boom, he often was featured at major festivals both in the United States and other countries. His wide-ranging live appearances continued in the 1960s when he moved to Nashville, where he was a popular regular cast member of the Grand Ole Opry. During the 1960s and 1970s, he performed before audiences in every state in the union, every province of Canada, and in major nations throughout Europe and the Pacific Basin. He remained a Capitol Record recording artist from the mid-1940s to the late 1960s. His albums during his last decade with Capitol included Back Home (12/57), Walkin' the Strings, Travis! (3/62), Songs of the Coal Miners (9/63), and Best of Merle Travis (3/67). A collection of his record-

ings also came out on Pickwick Records in the mid-1960s, Our Man from Kentucky.

Travis continued to be active in the 1970s, though not on as hectic a schedule as previous years. He continued to appear on the Opry and guested on various country shows, both televised and concerts. He was nominated for the Country Music Hall of Fame several times during the decade and finally was voted onto that distinguished roster in October 1977.

TUBB, ERNEST: Singer, guitarist, composer, publisher. Born Crisp, Texas, February 9, 1914.

Ellis County, Texas, is about forty or fifty miles south of Dallas. It was picture-book cottonwoods ranch country when young Ernest Tubb stretched his growing frame and dreamt of becoming a cowboy movie star. A mail-order guitar and self-instruction book were still in his future at that point, although he did some singing with the string bands that played dances, mostly square dances, around the country.

At eighteen, in the Depression year of 1932, Tubb got a paying job in San Antonio as a soda jerk. By then he could play guitar, though not as well as he desired. Two years later, still in San Antonio, he talked himself into a singing and picking job at KONO and married Lois Elaine Cook. The year 1935 was a decisive one; he met Carrie, the gracious widow of Jimmie Rodgers. Ernest had never met Rodgers, but the Singing Brakeman's recordings had long ago convinced Tubb to give up his boyhood cowboy star notions. Jimmie became Ernest's ideal as the young Texan copied Rodgers' phrasing for a time and absorbed the already substantial Rodgers lore. Also in the hot summer of 1935, Ernest's first son, Justin, was born on August 20th.

By 1936, Carrie Rodgers and the Tubbs had become close friends. She not only gave Ernest the original Jimmie Rodgers guitar, but also obtained an RCA Victor recording contract for him. She arranged a theater personal appearance tour and acted as his manager for a short time. He recorded at the old Texas Hotel in San Antonio, making cuts of "The Passing of

Jimmie Rodgers" and "Jimmie Rodgers' Last Thoughts." These were released on RCA Victor's Bluebird label. Things were looking up, but life still consisted of the grind of one-night stands and spells of unemployment.

Sadness also was part of these years. A second son, Rodger Dale, was born and died in 1938. Tubb wrote "Our Baby's Book" in his memory; the song remained one of the most requested ones in his repertoire. In 1939, Violet Elaine, "Scooter Bill," was born.

The start of one of the industry's longest and most successful recording affiliations came in 1940 when Tubb was signed by Decca Records. In San Antonio, Texas, on April 4, he recorded two songs he had written, "Blue Eyed Elaine" and "I'll Get Along Somehow." They sold records, enough at any rate for a twenty-dollar-a-week job at KGKO in Fort Worth. This job, in turn, soon gave him the chance to become identified with a commercial sponsor.

He became known as "The Gold Chain Troubador," for the Gold Chain Flour Company, earning a full seventy-five dollars a week. But things were discouraging for Tubb and he seriously considered giving up his career for a defense job, where the pay was steady and certain. Things suddenly turned around when he decided to record a song he had been playing around with. It has become his all-time hit, a gold-record-seller, "Walking the Floor Over You." The song started opening doors, even those to Hollywood.

He made two western movies in 1942. Charles Starrett was the established star in both, and both can still be seen in those very late television showings under the original titles of Fighting Buckaroo and Ridin' West. Hollywood was not exactly shaken by this. But the effort did help gain him a guest appearance late in the year on the Grand Ole Opry. Opry audiences and executives were impressed with him. In 1943, he became a regular member and was still a fixture on the Opry as of 1981. The following year he appeared in another motion picture, Jamboree, and in 1947, in the film Hollywood Barn Dance. Along with better-paying personal appearances and thousands of miles of traveling each month, Tubb set a precedent by appearing at Carnegie Hall.

The money was easier and he started expanding business interests, working out a music firm arrangement with Jean and Julian Aberbach of Hill and Range Songs, Inc. He also founded the Ernest Tubb Record Shop in Nashville, later relocated to 417 Broadway near the original Opry. Another milestone was the arrangement with WSM for broadcasting the Midnight Jamboree, immediately following the Opry broadcast each Saturday night.

Although Ernest had three songs on the Billboard top-10 charts in 1948, it was a bittersweet year; he and Elaine were divorced. He continued having one hit after another in 1949, with a final count of seven songs on the top 10 and one a near miss. The latter was "My Tennessee Baby" dedicated to Olene Adams Carter, who soon married him. The others were "Blue Christmas," "Don't Rob Another Man's Castle," "Have You Ever Been Lonely," "I'm Bitin' My Fingernails and Thinking of You," "Slippin' Around," "Tennessee Border No. 2," and "Warm Red Wine."

Tubb and Red Foley recorded a duet in 1950, "Goodnight Irene," which gained the top honors for the year. Tubb continued his grueling round of appearances by airplane, car, train, and bus, covering more than 100,000 miles a year, playing concerts, honky-tonks, parks, everywhere he could be booked with his band, the Texas Troubadors. Daughters Erlene Dale and Olene Gayle were born in 1951 and 1952 before his first Korean and Japanese tour with Hank Snow.

Foul weather and exhaustion brought on a lingering illness that made him leave the Opry until November 1954. Three more children, Ernest Dale Tubb, Jr. (1956), Larry Dean (1958), and Karen Delene (1960), joined the Tubb home at a time when Tubb was successfully recuperating between his still hectic schedules of road trips. His traveling in the 1960s was in his own bus, outfitted for mileage comfort.

His recordings of "Thanks a Lot" in 1963, the duet with Loretta Lynn on "Mr. and Mrs. Used to Be" in 1964, and the millionth sale on "Walking the Floor Over You" in 1965, showed his continued popularity. This was acknowledged in 1965 by his election to the coveted Country Music Association's Hall of Fame.

Close to 200 single records were released by Tubb over the years to 1981, along with numerous albums. Other hits include "Rainbow at Midnight," "It's Been So Long, Darling," "You Nearly Lose Your Mind," "Women Make a Fool Out of Me," "Take Me Back and Try Me One More Time," "Tomorrow Never Comes," and "Thanks a Lot."

His 1960s LP credits include several on Vocalion label, such as *Texas Troubadours* (1960) and *Great Country* (12/69). His many Decca albums include such titles as *Ernest Tubb Favorites; Daddy of 'Em All; Importance of Being Ernest; Story of Ernest Tubb* (two LPs, 1959); *Record Shop* (1960s); *Golden Favorites, All Time Hits* (1961); *On Tour* (1962); *Just Call Me Lonesome, Family Bible* (1963); *Thanks a Lot* (8/64); *Country Dance Time, My Pick of the Hits* (both issued 8/65); *Mr. & Mrs. Used to Be* (9/65); *Hittin' the Road* (1/65); *Stand By Me* (6/66); *Hits Old and New* (11/66); and *Singin' Again* (8/67). His Decca album releases of the late 1960s and early 1970s included *Greatest Hits, Volume 2; One Sweet Hello;* and *Good Year for the Wine.*

While Ernest didn't have much impact on the hit charts in the 1970s, he continued to be very active and much revered and honored by performers old and new and by countless fans, particularly those who came to applaud his segment of the *Grand Ole Opry*, broadcast by then from the new *Opry* headquarters in Opryland. Throughout the 1970s and into the 1980s, he continued to host his *Midnight Jamboree* radio show broadcast live from the Ernest Tubb Record Shop Number 2 next door to Opryland. Throughout the decade and in the early 1980s, he kept up his hectic touring schedule, still averaging 200 working days as of 1981. Although nominally still on the Decca roster at the end of the 1970s, his output tapered off to zero on the label. By

the start of the 1980s, only three titles remained in the active album catalogue of MCA (which had absorbed Decca): *Ernest Tubb's Golden Favorites, Ernest Tubb's Greatest Hits,* and the two-record set *The Ernest Tubb Story.*

On February 9, 1979, coinciding with Tubb's sixty-fifth birthday, a tribute LP came out on Cachet Records titled *Ernest Tubb: The Legend and the Legacy.* Among the stars whose contributions were overdubbed on Tubb's renditions by producer Pete Drake (Tubb was not aware of this until the album was completed) were Willie Nelson, Waylon Jennings, Charlie Daniels, Loretta Lynn, Conway Twitty, Justin Tubb, Charlie Rich, Cal Smith, Merle Haggard, Johnny Paycheck, George Jones, Marty Robbins, the Wilburn Brothers, Vern Gosdin, Ferlin Husky, and many more. Also issued in early 1979 was a single from the album, "Waltz Across Texas," featuring Ernest, Willie Nelson, Charlie Daniels, and Charlie McCoy.

Fittingly, the LP rose to upper-chart levels and was one of the top-50 best-selling LP releases of the year.

TUBB, JUSTIN: *Singer, guitarist, songwriter. Born San Antonio, Texas, August 20, 1935.*

A great deal of entertainment magic seems to go with the name Tubb. It's a magic that carried over from one generation to the next as Justin Wayne Tubb proved a worthy heir to the mantle worn by his Country Music Hall of Fame father, Ernest.

Justin naturally was steeped in country-music lore from the cradle. He spent some of his boyhood years in San Antonio before attending Castle Heights Military School at Lebanon, Tennessee, 1944–48. During his high school years in San Antonio, Justin already showed his potential playing a mean guitar and singing at school events.

He enrolled at the University of Texas at Austin for the 1952–53 session. But the pull of country music was too great and he left for a disc jockey job at WHIN in Gallatin, Tennessee, during 1953–54. Besides spinning platters, he entertained his audience by singing; many of the songs in his repertoire were his own compositions. It didn't take long before he signed with Decca in 1953 and had a number of records receiving plays across the nation, including his own compositions "Ooh-La-La" and "The Story of My Life."

In 1954, Tubb joined with Goldie Hill on a top-10 hit, "Looking Back to See." He also turned out such records as "Something Called the Blues," "I'm Lookin' for a Date Tonight," "I Miss You," "Sure Fire Kisses," "Fickle Heart," and his own song, "Sufferin' Heart." By now his name was well known nationally and he was asked to become a *Grand Ole Opry* regular in 1955. He sang such new songs that year as "I Gotta Go Get My Baby," "Chuga-Chuga, Chica-Mauga," "My Heart's Not for You to Play With," "I'm Sorry I Stayed Away So Long," "All Alone," "Within Your Arms," "Who Will It Be?" and "Pepper Hot Baby." His 1956 output included his own "I'm Just a Fool Enough" and such other records as "You Nearly Lose Your Mind," "Lucky, Lucky Someone Else," and "It Takes a Lot of Heart."

Some of his other recordings of the 1950s included his own "I'm a Big Boy Now" and "The Life I Have to Live"; "Miss the Mississippi and You," "Desert Blues," "The Party Is Over," and "If You'll Be My Love" (1957); "Sugar Lips" and his own "Rock It Down to My House" and "Almost Lonely" (1958); and two of his compositions, "I Know You Do" and "Buster's Gang" (1959). Decca also issued an LP of Tubb's work in 1958 called *Country Boy in Love*.

Tubb left Decca in 1959 and signed with Starday for 1960–62. (He also turned out one release for Challenge during this period.) In 1962, he went with RCA Victor. During the 1960s, many top performers sang Justin's compositions, including his father, the Wilburn Brothers, Faron Young, Webb Pierce, Patsy Cline, Jim Reeves, Mac Wiseman, Skeeter Davis, Cowboy Copas, Red Sovine, Teresa Brewer, Ray Price, and Hank Snow. A number of these were top-10 hits, including Hawkshaw Hawkins' version of "Lonesome 7-7203," a number-one-rated hit of 1963; Faron Young–Margie Singleton with

"Keeping Up with the Joneses," and Jim Reeves–Dottie West with "Love Is No Excuse" in 1964.

Justin continued to turn out hit records of his own, such as "Take a Letter Miss Gray" in 1963 and "Dern Ya" in 1964. He also had great success with his LPs in the 1960s, including the 1962 Starday releases *Modern Country Music Sound of Justin Tubb* and *Justin Tubb, Star of the Grand Ole Opry*. In the mid-1960s, he was represented on RCA Victor with such albums as *Justin Tubb* (3/65), *Where You're Concerned* (9/65); *The Best of Justin Tubb* (1965); *Together and Alone* (8/66); and *That Style* (8/67). At the end of the decade he had some recordings come out on the Paramount label, including the album *Things I Still Remember*.

His personal appearances during the 1960s took him to almost all of the states and the Canadian provinces. He also toured Germany. His TV guest spots included the *National Barn Dance* and *WWVA Jamboree*.

From a recording standpoint, the 1970s weren't very rewarding for Tubb, whose traditional approach to the music, like that of his father's, suffered under the combined inroads of country-rock and progressive country. He complained during a backstage interview at the *Opry* in the late 1970s (during a nationally televised TV show) that the problem for traditional artists was getting any kind of coverage for record releases on country radio programs. He told the interviewer he was sure there was a large audience for the kind of music he believed in, but that without radio coverage there was no way for those people to know about new songs in that style.

Meanwhile, though recording opportunities were sparse in the 1970s and early 1980s, Justin didn't lack for work. He toured steadily, guested on many country TV shows and continued to be a fixture on the *Grand Ole Opry*.

TUCKER, TANYA: *Singer. Born Seminole, Texas, October 10, 1958.*

At the end of the 1970s, a blurring of the edges in country music gave rise to many hybrid forms that helped bring across-the-board pop interest to many country artists.

Still, country audiences, while fiercely loyal to favorite performers, tend to look askance at any changes in style, as Tanya Tucker found out in the late 1970s. However, with her vibrant voice and dynamic stage presence, it seemed reasonable to assume she might attract a broader following, as 1970s star Dolly Parton and Crystal Gayle had done.

Tucker was only in her twenties at the time, but she had been a country star for most of the decade, having achieved her first top-10 country single in her early teens. Her parents had encouraged her musical interests when she was a small child, the youngest of three children of construction worker Beau Tucker and his wife Juanita. After the family moved to Phoenix in 1967, the girl's attraction to country music was fostered by her father, who took her to concerts by such artists as Ernest Tubb, Mel Tillis, and Leroy Van Dyke.

By the time the family moved again, this time to St. George, Utah, Tanya's singing efforts made her parents decide that she could succeed in the entertainment field. When the film *Jeremiah Johnson* was being shot on location in Utah, Juanita Tucker took her daughter to audition for a major part. Tanya missed out on that, but did earn some money as a bit player.

Convinced of Tanya's abilities, the Tuckers later moved to Las Vegas, Nevada, hoping to make connections with entertainment industry executives. They had Tanya cut a demonstration tape that caught the ear of songwriter Dolores Fuller, who brought her to the attention of Billy Sherrill, artists & repertoire head of Columbia Epic Records in Nashville. Billy liked what he heard and signed Tucker for Epic. In March 1972, Tanya and her father went to Nashville for her first recording session, where she taped the song "Delta Dawn." Released as a single, it became one of the major country hits of the year, reaching the top 10 on the charts of all three major music industry trade magazines. The debut album, also titled *Delta Dawn,* became a country bestseller.

Another track from that album, "James-town Ferry," provided another singles hit, actually a double hit, since the reverse side, "Love's the Answer," also moved high on the charts. In 1973, Tanya, then only fourteen, proved her debut was no fluke by coming out with a well-crafted second album, *What's Your Mama's Name.* Not only did the album reach the top rungs of the charts, but the title song rose to number one on the national country lists. During 1973 and 1974, Tucker achieved a series of other hit singles on Columbia, including such number-one successes as "Blood Red and Going Down," "Would You Lay with Me (in a Field of Stone)," and "The Man Who Turned My Mother On."

Tanya and her advisers decided not to remain with Columbia and when her contract expired, in late 1974, she moved over to MCA. Her debut on that label proved that her popularity remained strong: *Tanya Tucker* rose into the country top 10 on most charts. Her 1975 singles hits included "San Antonio Stroll" and "Lizzie and the Rainman," the latter number one on U.S. country charts in July 1975. In early 1976, she made the charts with the album *Lovin' and Learnin'* and the single "You've Got Me to Hold Onto." Later in the year, Columbia released one of her previous recordings, "Here's Some Love," and it moved up to the top rungs. In 1977, she had a top-10 single, "It's a Cowboy Lovin' Night" and the hit album *Ridin' Rainbows.*

Through the mid-1970s, she was featured on almost every important network TV show, including the *Grand Ole Opry.* Her name generally appeared on lists of the best five or ten country female vocalists, including a number of nominations over the years in the Country Music Association awards. In 1974 and 1975, for instance, she was one of the five finalists for Female Vocalist of the Year.

In 1978, Tucker decided to move from conventional country toward the country fusion end of the spectrum. The change included assembling a new band with more rock flavor and moving back to Columbia for her new album, *TNT.* The debut of the "new" Tanya took place during a show at the *Grand Ole Opry* on November 1, 1978, with perhaps a predictable result. When she started singing a series of songs in country-rock fashion (including "Heartbreak Hotel," Buddy Holly's "Not Fade Away," and "Texas (When I Die)," some of the audience booed lustily. Still, by the time the set was over she apparently had won over most, if not all, of the audience.

Her manager, Steve Gold, said afterward, "She wasn't the pure-as-country little girl they'd come to know and love and some just couldn't take the reality of change. We won't change anything because of a handful of dissidents. They're probably the same kind of people who booed Bob Dylan when he stepped out and played that amplified guitar of his years ago."

TNT was one of the top-selling LPs of 1979 and Tucker also had the best-selling single "Texas (When I Die)." Her LP *Tear Me Apart* was on the country top 50 from late 1979 into early 1980. By the time her duet with close companion Glen Campbell ("Dream Lover," MCA) showed up on the singles charts in September 1980, it was apparent that Tanya was backtracking somewhat from her recent pop image. Later that fall, she had a hit with "Pecos Promenade," in the top 10 in November. The same month her new LP *Dreamlovers* was on country charts. In early 1981 she had a top-10 hit with the single "Can I See You Tonight" on MCA and later in the year reached upper-chart levels with "Lovin' What Your Lovin' Does to Me," a duet with Glen Campbell issued on his label, Capitol.

In early 1982 she was signed by Arista Records, including sessions in the Nashville studios produced by the rising hitmaker/producer, David Malloy.

TURNER, MARY LOU: *Singer, songwriter, band leader. Born Hazard, Kentucky, June 13.*

One of the delights of the *Bill Anderson Show* for much of the 1970s, Mary Lou Turner's singing verified once more Anderson's ability as a discoverer of above-average talent. But she found the role of

duet partner too confining and, in 1979, embarked on a solo career in hopes of becoming one of the major female country vocalists of the 1980s.

Born in Hazard, Kentucky and raised in Dayton, Ohio, where the musical influences were more pop and rock, Mary Lou nevertheless leaned toward country. Her father was a musician and a country-music advocate who passed that outlook on to his daughter. He encouraged her interest in singing and was only too happy to approve of her debuting in public as a child. She continued to add to her singing experience in her teens, which, in turn, served as a springboard for an audition for the *WWVA Jamboree* in Wheeling, West Virginia, a try-out arranged by her father.

Jamboree executives agreed that she was a fine entertainer, and she joined the show as a regular at the end of the 1960s. In the 1970s, when the program was syndicated to many other cities in the United States under the title *Jamboree U.S.A,* Turner was one of the featured performers.

In the early 1970s, Jan Howard, who had been Bill Anderson's regular duet partner for several years, decided to leave the *Bill Anderson Show*. When it became known that he was looking for a replacement, more than 200 prospective vocalists sent in demo tapes and asked for auditions. However, after Anderson watched one of Mary Lou's performances on the *Jamboree*, he decided she was the singer he was looking for.

She joined his troupe in 1973 and before long was making recordings with him on MCA Records that were showing up on top-chart levels. Among their top-10 singles records were "That's What Made Me Love You," in the top 10 in May 1976, and "Where Are You Going, Billy Boy," in the top 10 in the late summer of 1977. They also completed a series of LPs together, including the chart-making *Sometimes* in 1976 and *Billy Boy and Mary Lou* in 1977. In 1975, she also signed with MCA as a solo artist, but those recordings proved less successful than her duet work.

As a member of the Anderson Show, Turner toured several hundred days each year, a routine that took her to all the states of the union and a number of foreign countries. She also performed with Anderson on his syndicated TV show and on many other major country radio and TV programs, including the *Grand Ole Opry*. Despite all those commitments, she still considered herself a regular cast member of *Jamboree U.S.A*, and returned several times each year to sing on the show.

In early 1979, Mary Lou announced that she was terminating her association with the Anderson Show. As she told a reporter at the time, "I think a lot of people are reading a lot into the move, but the decision is mine and it has been made. I am concerned about my career. I have suffered a loss of identity since I left [the *Jamboree*] and now I have decided to have my own show and my own band."

The reason she felt restricted, she declared, was that the Anderson Show typically was booked for many package shows in which she rarely could sing more than one or two solo songs. That, she said, prevented her from developing an act of her own. "The last six years have been very educational in all respects, and I have learned what to do and what not to do. I don't want to offend anybody, but I know I must do my own thing now and that's why I will put my own band together. I will have a show equal to anything that comes out of Nashville because I will make it that way."

In early 1980, she took one step toward her new goals with the charted single "I Wanna Love You Tonight" on Churchill Records.

TWITTY, CONWAY: *Singer, guitarist, songwriter, band leader (the Twitty Birds). Born Helena, Arkansas, September 1, 1933.*

In country music, the golden touch is relatively rare compared to pop music. Many first-rank country artists whose recordings constantly appear at the top of the charts go years without reaching gold-record levels. But one performer who had the golden touch was Conway Twitty, who proved a major favorite first in rock 'n' roll and then in country, winning R.I.A.A.

gold-record citations on many occasions in both career phases.

Twitty was born and raised in country-music country. His real name was Harold Lloyd Jenkins, the son of a Mississippi River boat captain. As a child, Harold often accompanied his father on ferry trips. When he was five he started to teach himself guitar and often sang to his accompaniment while sitting in the boat's pilot house.

Jenkins was an early country bloomer and formed a band when he was ten, the Phillips County Ramblers. The group proved competent enough after a short time together to gain its own radio show on station KFFA in Helena. Although music continued to be an important part of Jenkins' life as he progressed into his teens, he considered going into the ministry while a high school student. He also was a star on his high school baseball team and was offered a contract from the Philadelphia Phillies when he graduated.

The time was the mid-1950s, and the military draft was still in effect. The U.S. Army called Harold to the colors, and he spent several years in uniform. While stationed in Japan, he formed a group called the Cimarrons that played in service clubs around that nation.

When he got out of the Army, he already was aware of the new sound coming to the fore, rock 'n' roll. Influenced by the music of people like Elvis and Jerry Lee Lewis, Jenkins joined the floodtide of young southern-based artists coming into the field. He decided Harold Jenkins lacked the flair needed for a pop career and picked a pseudonym, taking his first name from the town of Conway, Arkansas, and his last from Twitty, Texas. It didn't take long for his new name to catch on. With his rock band, which performed many original compositions by Conway, he stormed the top of the national charts in 1958 with the single of his composition "It's Only Make Believe." The song easily went past the million-copy mark for Twitty's initial gold-record breakthrough.

He kept up the pace during the late 1950s and early 1960s with a string of singles and albums on MGM Records that made the charts. He had another gold-record award hit in 1960 with "Lonely Blue Boy" and had many other releases that sold well over a half million copies each. With his group he toured widely, playing before capacity crowds in all fifty states as well as cities in Canada, Europe, and other foreign locales. He was featured on many major network TV showcases, including a number of appearances on Dick Clark's *American Bandstand* and *The Ed Sullivan Show.* Between 1958 and the mid-1960s, his rock releases sold over 16 million copies. During those years he also appeared in six movies, for three of which he supplied title songs and/or scores: *Platinum High, Sex Kittens Go to College,* and *College Confidential.*

By the mid-1960s, things were slowing down for Conway in the pop arena and he shifted back to his first love, country & western. He chose Oklahoma City, Oklahoma, as operations base and assembled his first country band, the Lonely Blue Boys. Several friends put him in touch with Decca record producer Owen Bradley, who signed him on the label and had him in the studio for his initial sessions in 1965. It was the start of a recording alignment still going strong a decade and a half later. Also on the label was an already established female country vocalist, Loretta Lynn, and not long after Conway joined Decca, discussions of possible duet efforts were under way.

Back in Oklahoma City, Conway and the Lonely Blue Boys were building a strong local following. When the first UHF-TV country station went on the air on June 1, 1966, the *Conway Twitty Show* was announced as a weekly feature. In a short time, the show, taped by KLPR-TV, was seen in other parts of the country in syndication. But it soon became apparent that for the kind of exposure Twitty needed, Oklahoma City was off the beaten path. By the late 1960s, Twitty had moved to the Nashville area and his name soon became known in the country field. His records began to play throughout the United States as he became a featured performer on the *Grand Ole Opry* and such

other major country TV shows of the period as *Johnny Cash* and *Hee Haw.*

In 1968, he made pop chart levels with "Next in Line" and "Image of Me." In 1969, he added two more major hits, "To See My Angel" and "I Love You More Today." He topped all those in 1970 with the blockbuster single "Hello Darlin'." The song not only rose to number one on country charts, it crossed over to pop lists, as indeed did many of his recordings of the 1970s. It ended up the sixth best-selling single in the country field for the year. Later in the decade it was requested by a team of U.S. astronauts and Russian cosmonauts circling the globe in a joint space mission. Also a top-10 hit in the 1970s was the single "That's When She Started to Stop Loving Me."

In 1971, he made the charts with such singles as "I Wonder What She'll Think About Me Leaving" and "What a Dream." But the year was equally impressive for his collaboration with Loretta Lynn. Their output included several top chart hits, including the eighth-best seller for the year, "After the Fire Is Gone." Their album *We Only Make Believe* was one of the fifty best-selling LPs for 1971. (Twitty had three solo LPs on that select list, *I Wonder What She'll Think, How Much More Can She Stand,* and *Fifteen Years Ago.*) At year's end, the Country Music Association voted Loretta and Conway the best country duo, an award they won the next three years in a row.

Both as a soloist and with Lynn, Conway's pace hardly slackened as the 1970s went by. In 1972, his hits included "She Needs Someone to Hold Her," "I Can't See Me Without You," "I Can't Stop Loving You/(Lost Her Love On) Our Last Date," and, with Loretta, "Lead Me On." All but the first were title songs on chart hit LPs. In 1973, Conway's releases started coming out under the MCA imprint (MCA owned Decca) and included such successes as "Baby's Gone," "Louisiana Man," "You've Never Been This Far Before," and, with Loretta, "Mississippi Woman." The last two were title songs on hit LPs.

In 1974, Conway scored with the single "I'm Not Through Loving You Yet" (co-written with L.E. White). The following year he had top-10 singles hits of his compositions "Linda on My Mind" and "Don't Cry Joni/Touch the Hand" and his duet with Lynn, "Feelins'." In 1976, his composition "After the Good Is Gone" provided him with a number-one country hit. Also in the top 5 or better that year were the duet "The Letter" (co-written by Conway and C. Haney) and "The Game That Daddies Play." In 1977, his original "I've Already Loved You in My Mind" rose to the top 10 and his duet with Loretta, "I Can't Love You Enough," was a number-one success. Late in the year he had another top-10 single with a remake of the Little David Wilkins song "Georgia Keeps Pulling on My Ring." In 1978, he and Loretta made top-chart levels with "From Seven Till Ten/You're the Reason My Kids Are Ugly"; his solo releases "Boogie Grass Band" and "Your Love Had Taken Me That High" made the top 5.

In the 1970s, Twitty changed the name of his backing group from Lonely Blue Boys to the Twitty Birds. As of 1978, band members were John Hughey on steel guitar, Gene Hughey on bass, Tommy "Pork Chop" Markham on drums, Al Harris on piano, Charlie Archer on guitar, and Jack Hicks on harmonica and banjo. Throughout the 1970s, Conway and his group averaged over 200 engagements a year.

By the end of the 1970s, Twitty's activities covered a spectrum of businesses and organizations. He owned several music publishing firms: Hello Darlin' Music, Neverbreak Music, and Twitty Bird Music (the latter co-owned with Tree International). In addition, he and Lynn jointly owned United Talent Agency, which in the late 1970s booked over $5 million in talent out of Nashville. In another direction, he also was part owner in the late 1970s of the Nashville Sounds baseball team, a member of the Southern League.

Besides the four CMA Awards credited to Conway and Loretta, he had many other awards as of 1978. These included twenty-two CMA nominations, a Grammy in 1971, four American Music Awards, six Academy of Country Music Awards, four-

teen *Music City News* Awards, thirteen *Billboard* Awards, and two Truckers' Awards.

As the 1970s ended and the 1980s began, there seemed no slackening in the popularity of Conway as a soloist or of the Twitty-Lynn duet team. In singles during 1979, Conway had three major solo hits, "Your Love Has Taken Me That High," "Don't Take It Away," and "I May Never Get to Heaven." He had two solo LPs on the charts much of the year, *Conway* and *Cross Winds,* and *The Very Best of Loretta Lynn and Conway Twitty* was on the charts from mid-1979 well into 1980. For much of that time, their LP *Diamond Dust* also was on the lists. In late December 1979, his single "Happy Birthday Darlin' " rose to number one.

In January 1980, Conway and Loretta had the top-10 single "You Know What Your Lovin' Does to Me/The Sadness of It All." A few months later, Conway had the top-10 single "I'd Love to Lay You Down" and in April placed the LP *Heart and Soul* in the country top-10 album list. In early summer, he and Loretta had the single "It's True Love" in upper-chart levels. In the latter part of the year, Twitty had the chart-hit single "A Bridge That Just Won't Burn" and the LP *Rest Your Love on Me.* The solo single "Rest Your Love On Me/I Am the Dream (You Are the Dream)" and duet "Love What Your Lovin' Does to Me" both came out early in 1981 and were in the top 10 in April.

TYLER, BONNIE: *Singer. Born Swansea, Wales, 1953.*

The British Isles have produced a fair number of singers who scored major successes with country material, including Olivia Newton-John (born in England, though she grew up in Australia), Tom Jones, and, in 1978, Bonnie Tyler. Unlike her compatriots, Tyler did not consciously select country-style songs. Her smash 1978 recording "It's a Heartache" took her by surprise when it moved to the top of the country charts.

She surprised interviewers as well, who found that her spoken accent had the lilt of Wales in it rather than the twang of Tennessee. As she said, "I guess it's because when I was a little girl I always loved singing and I liked so many American artists. I sang along with the recordings. Wilson Pickett, Tina Turner, Neil Sedaka, rhythm & blues singers in general were a really big influence on me. I picked a lot of phrasing up from American vocalists. I've got a really broad Welsh accent, but it doesn't sound like that on records. When people first heard 'It's a Heartache' they thought I came from Nashville."

Born and raised in Swansea, like many Welsh people Tyler loved music from her earliest years. She became imbued with the idea of succeeding as a pop singer, and by the late 1960s had her own band that played many of the clubs in her home section of Wales.

Bonnie's career was moving along satisfactorily when she ran into problems with her voice. "I began to have a lot of trouble with my throat at the start of the 1970s. It was the problem of nodules on my vocal chords that a lot of singers run into. It popped up in 1971 and 1974 and both times cleared up with a month's rest. But then it came back for a third time in 1976, and that time it lasted. It was frightening. You go to talk and sometimes the words don't come out. I went to the doctor and he said, 'You've really done it now.' He scraped the nodules off and I spent quite a time recuperating. But it didn't change my voice as much as some people think. My voice always has been husky, and this just made me a bit more husky." *

In fact, the quality of her voice after treatment seemed to have much more impact on listeners. The catalyst in her rapidly moving career was the songwriting team of Ronnie Scott and Steve Wolfe, who watched her act at the Town's Man Club in Wales and asked her to make some demonstration recordings of their material. One of the first results was a single for RCA called "Honeycomb," which fell flat. But another song, "Lost in France," issued on Chrysalis Records, became a major hit almost everywhere but in

---

* Based on an interview with Irwin Stambler in 1978.

the United States. Tyler followed up with another international hit that also missed fire in the States, "More than a Lover." That song and "Lost in France" were on her Chrysalis debut LP, *The World Starts Tonight*.

Chrysalis, however, didn't pick up their option and Tyler returned to RCA, who reaped the benefit of "It's a Heartache," a song that rose to number one on singles charts all over the world. Similar success met her 1978 RCA debut LP of the same title, which made the top 10 in the United States on both the pop and country charts.

TYLER, T. TEXAS: *Singer, guitarist, band leader, songwriter. Born Mena, Arkansas, circa 1916; died Springfield, Missouri, January 23, 1972.*

With his best-selling recitative single "Deck of Cards" in 1948, T. Texas Tyler helped set a pattern that still was carried on in the 1970s by country stars like Red Sovine and Jimmy Dean. His composition, which was about a soldier's pack of cards representing major points in the gospels, heralded a pattern in Tyler's later life as he became increasingly engrossed with religion.

Born in Arkansas and raised in Texas, Tyler learned to play the guitar before he was in his teens and at sixteen started to perform locally. During the 1930s, determined to further his musical career, he went east, gaining a spot on the *Major Bowes Amateur Hour* and also joining a radio show in Newport, Rhode Island. Late in the decade, he started moving westward. En route to Los Angeles he picked up experience with a variety of country & western groups, including the Ozark Ramblers, Dixie Melody Boys, and Oklahoma Melody Boys.

His career was interrupted by service in the U.S. Army during World War II, a period that provided material for several of his most successful songs. After receiving his discharge in 1946, Tyler returned to L.A. and settled in Hollywood, where he organized a band that was to become a major factor in the country & western field in the late 1940s and the 1950s. He also signed a recording contract with a small label, Four Star Records, whose producer and record executive, Don Pierce, was to play a major role in Tyler's rise to star status.

Tyler already was on the Four Star roster when Pierce bought a partial interest in the firm. Going on the road as a salesman, Pierce found that the only Four Star artist dealers were interested in was Tyler. Pierce took a closer look at the performer's potential and developed a close working relationship. One of the first results was two major hits in 1948, "Deck of Cards" and "Dad Gave My Dog Away," the latter co-written by Tyler. The two joined forces on a number of other hits in succeeding years, including "Remember Me," "Filipino Baby," "Divorce Me C.O.D.," and "Bummin' Around," the last named a top-10 hit in 1953.

In the late 1940s and early 1950s, T. Texas had his own show on Los Angeles TV called *Range Round Up*. In 1950, the magazine *Country Song Roundup* voted the program Best Country Music Show of the year. Tyler also made a number of western films, including *Horsemen of the Sierra* for Columbia Pictures in 1949. That same year, he was featured in a country & western concert held at New York's Carnegie Hall.

During the 1950s and 1960s, Tyler headlined shows in all parts of the United States and appeared on many radio and TV programs, including several guest spots on the *Grand Ole Opry*. During the 1950s, he signed with Pierce's new label, Starday. Among his singles were "Oklahoma

Hills," "Home in San Antone," "Honky Tonk Girl," "Beautiful Life," "The Old Country Church," "In the Sweet By and By," "Follow Through," and "Fairweather Baby." For much of the 1960s, most of Tyler's releases came out on the King Records label, though there also were releases on various others, including Starday, Pickwick, and Capitol.

One of his Starday albums was the 1964 *Sensational New Hits of T. Texas Tyler*, which provides an indication of his repertoire at the time. The album songs included "Dear Souvenirs" and "Crawdad Town" (both written by Tyler), "Texas Boogie Woogie," "Invitations," "My Talk About Leaving," "Just Like Dad," "Injun Joe," "Morning Glory," "It's a Long, Long Road Back Home," "Sunset Years of Life," and "Little Piece of Life."

Some of his other LPs extant in the 1960s were *T. Texas Tyler* (King, released 11/59); *Great Texas, T. Texas Tyler, T. Texas Tyler Sings Sacred Country Songs*, all on King; *Favorites*, Wrangler Records (7/62); *Hits of T. Texas Tyler*, Capitol (10/65); *Great Hits*, Pickwick.

Long known as a devout man, during the 1960s Tyler's interest in religion reached the point that he decided to give up performing in favor of the ministry. It was a career he seemed eminently suited for in view of his long-time reputation in the entertainment field as "the man with a million friends." In the early 1970s he contracted cancer and died in 1972 in Springfield, Missouri.

#

VAN RONK, DAVE: *Singer, guitarist, band leader, songwriter. Born Brooklyn, New York, June 30, 1936.*

One of the best blues singers of the urban folk movement of the 1950s and 1960s was Brooklyn-born David Van Ronk. His renditions of such songs as "Willie the Weeper," "Cocaine Blues," and "Bad

Dream Blues" marked him as one of the most original white performers in this basically black idiom. In the mid-1960s, though, he turned instead to traditional jazz and jug band work, claiming that it is musically dishonest for a performer to sing blues without living through the harsh conditions that gave rise to them.

His own upbringing was a relatively comfortable one. He attended public schools in Brooklyn and Queens, learned the guitar, and after high school, performed with jazz groups in New York. His first interest was New Orleans jazz. He was aware of the growing volume of folk music, but paid little attention to it until 1957, when he worked briefly with Odetta and gained new insight into the folk tradition.

He was particularly attracted to blues material and listened to recordings and performances of many artists, especially the renditions of Josh White. Soon he was singing folk music, including a heavy leavening of blues, at local New York spots. He also experimented with other styles of black music, including jug playing. In 1958, he and jug player Sam Charters made a jug band record for Lyrichord.

Van Ronk's reputation as a blues singer increased steadily. In the late 1950s, he signed with Folkways records and turned out two well-received LPs, one in 1959 and another in 1961. In 1962, he moved over to the Prestige label and turned out such LPs as *Inside* (1962), *Dave Van Ronk, Folksinger* (1963), and *In the Tradition* (1964). Though much of the material was in the jazz or blues vein, he also showed his ability to perform other kinds of songs with such numbers as "Lady Gay" and "Come All Ye Fair and Tender Ladies." The first two Prestige LPs also included such notable tracks as "Cocaine Blues," "Motherless Child," and Dave's version of Bob Dylan's "He Was a Friend of Mine."

In the mid-1960s, he began to concentrate more on jazz and jug band material than blues. His performance at the 1964 Newport Folk Festival was mainly jazz. He formed his own jug band, which featured Sam Charters, called the Ragtime Jug Stompers. In 1964, he signed with Mercury and turned out an LP titled *Ragtime Jug Stompers*. His second Mercury LP was turned out in August 1964 and called *Just Dave*. He continued to appear in concerts both in the United States and abroad, including the 1965 New York Folk Festival at Carnegie Hall. Van Ronk's performances included some of his own compositions, such as "Bad Dream Blues," "Bambee, If You Leave Me," "Pretty Mama," and "Frankie's Blues."

In the mid-1960s, several of Dave's albums came out on the Verve/Forecast label, such as *Dave Van Ronk* (8/65); *Gambler's Blues* (12/65); and *No Dirty Names* (12/66). In September 1967, Prestige reissued his early 1960s LP, *Folksinger*. At the end of the decade, he was on the Polydor label briefly; that company issued the LP *Van Ronk* in 1969.

From the mid-1960s into the 1980s, Dave continued to be one of the most respected folk artists, though with the field now having only a small percentage of the available audience, his exposure was limited. Throughout those years he maintained whatever performing schedule he could, appearing on college campuses and in small folk clubs in the United States and abroad. Under those circumstances, his output of new recordings was relatively meager in the 1970s. One new collection was the LP *Sunday Street*, issued by Philo Records in 1976. At the start of the 1980s he was represented by several other albums in the active catalogues of various companies, including *Dave Van Ronk* on Fantasy, a reissue of his first two Prestige LPs, *Inside Dave Van Ronk* and *Folksinger* (both originally recorded in 1962); *Black Mountain Blues* and *Dave Van Ronk Sings Earthy Ballads and Blues* on Folkways; and, on Prestige, his early 1960s LP *In the Tradition*.

VAN ZANDT, TOWNES: *Singer, guitarist, songwriter. Born Fort Worth, Texas, early 1940s.*

For a long time Townes Van Zandt was considered one of Texas' best kept secrets. During the late 1960s and early 1970s, this highly talented performer and songwriter was one of the most respected artists in Houston and vicinity, but it wasn't until the mid-1970s that his songs began to be recorded by major folk and country stars and his own recordings found a sizable audience outside the Lone Star state.

Although Townes was a native Texan, it

took him a long time to reestablish residence there. Before settling in Houston in the mid-1960s, he spent time in such places as Montana, Colorado, Illinois, and Minnesota. The reason, he told Bob Claypool of the *Houston Post* (June 1, 1977), was that "my father was in the oil business, that's why we traveled around so much. I got out of high school in Minnesota. I went to a private military school for two years, which I think has a lot to do with my sometime multifrantic behavior.

"Then I went to the University of Colorado for awhile, then finally dropped out of school and became a folk singer. College was, well, I sorta went off the deep end at the University of Colorado. I was apparently not stable enough to go there. I hit that place like a saddle bronc hits the arena—coming right out of military school and all. No way it could last, and it didn't.

"So I came here and started singing. Got into town about a year after the folk boom had died down, in like 1966, and the first place I played was a club on the Westheimer called The Jester. That was the first place I ever got real money for singing. This guy, who turned out to be Don Sanders, came up to me in there and said I also oughta try this place called Sand Mountain. So I went over there with him and we did a little short set. . . . There was this song I used to do called 'The Blues,' and I sang it that night. It was a talking blues about, you know, dropping out of the second grade to join the KKK and the guy said 'You got too much education.' Then I did another one called 'The Vietnamese Blues,' which had a chorus about 'leaving Vietnam to the Vietnamese.' "

Although Sand Mountain's operators were a little dubious at first, they finally asked Townes back, and he became a regular attraction there and at such other places as The Old Quarter and local coffee houses. Not only did local folk and country fans sing his praises, so did fellow musicians and writers. One of those impressed with his talent was Mickey Newbury, who suggested that Townes try for a recording contract. Van Zandt did that, but with a small regional label, Poppy Records. In the late 1960s and into the 1970s he turned out a series of albums (six in all, including *Townes Van Zandt*, released 12/69; *Delta Momma Blues*, 11/70; and *High, Low and In Between*) that received only limited distribution but have become cult classics. Among the original songs included on those discs were such powerful numbers as "Poncho and Lefty," "Tecumseh Valley," "Mr. Gold and Mr. Mud," and "To Live Is to Fly." In the mid-1970s, some of those were included in charted albums by major artists. "Poncho and Lefty," for example, was covered by both Emmylou Harris and Hoyt Axton in 1977 releases.

Part of the reason for Van Zandt's relatively slow progress in the music business was his individualism and the desire to keep a low profile. In the early 1970s, for instance, he spent the entire summer in an isolated spot in the Colorado mountains. He told Claypool, "I stay in the mountains until the weather runs me out and then I come back into the world in September." Finally, in 1976, his manager John Lomax convinced Van Zandt that he should put more emphasis on his career. In October 1976, Townes finally moved to Nashville (even there, he managed to find a place for himself and his wife, Cindy, in a mountain area fifteen miles from town) and signed a new recording contract with Tomato Records. The initial effort was planned to be a double live album based on tapes of performances at Houston's Old Quarter in 1973–74.

Meanwhile, Van Zandt's songs became known to a wider range of performers and an increasing number of new album releases in the late 1970s included versions of one or more Townes originals.

W

WAGONER, PORTER: *Singer, guitarist, songwriter, band leader (the Wagonmasters). Born West Plains, Missouri, August 12, 1930.*

American network TV executives looked down their noses at country music after World War II. But the viewing public thought differently, as indicated by the dozens of syndicated shows by top artists in country music that flourished throughout the 1960s and 1970s. Among the most popular of those was Porter Wagoner's, whose vocal talents and showmanship resulted in a program that was still finding favor long after most top-rated network shows were only memories. At the end of the 1970s, the program was fast coming up on the twenty-year mark with a weekly exposure of more than 100 stations having a total audience of over 45 million people.

It was an achievement that perhaps embodied the traits of level-headedness and persistence usually attributed to people from Porter's home state of Missouri. The show's content reflected Wagoner's lifelong love affair with country music, which began when he was a farm boy growing up near the small town of West Plains in Missouri. When Porter wasn't occupied with farm chores or schooling, he liked to listen to country programs on the radio. While still a preteenager, he learned to play guitar and often played and sang along with country songs broadcast over local stations.

In 1944, young Porter got a job as a clerk in a West Plains market to help out his family's limited finances. He often took his guitar along and, when business was slow, entertained customers and the store owner by singing and picking. After a while, the idea came to use the boy's talent as an advertising device. The market owner sponsored him on a fifteen-minute program on local radio. Both show and store prospered in the late 1940s and Wagoner's stylings came to the attention of E. E. "Si" Siman of radio station KWTO in

Springfield, Missouri. Siman signed Porter to perform on a weekly show on the station in the fall of 1951.

That proved to be the right place and the right time for the aspiring singer. The now legendary Red Foley was in the process of organizing his *Ozark Jamboree* for origination from Springfield. He added Wagoner to the cast and also spent some time schooling the young man in some of the finer points of interpreting country material. Before long the pupil had progressed so well that he became a featured artist on the *Jamboree*, which by then had achieved national TV coverage.

About the same time, RCA executive Steve Sholes signed Porter to a recording contract. Though Sholes stayed with Wagoner for almost four years, Porter's recordings struck no spark with country fans. That all changed in 1955 when Porter's single "Satisfied Mind" became a top-10 national hit. From then through 1982, it was a rare year when Porter's name didn't show up on the charts. After he made hit lists with "Eat, Drink and Be Merry" in late 1955 and "What Would You Do (If Jesus Came to Your House)" the following year, his reputation as one of the fastest rising newcomers in the field was solidified. His status was recognized in 1957 by the *Grand Ole Opry*, which invited him to join the regular cast.

In 1960, Porter signed to do his own syndicated show originating from Nashville, where he lived by then. In its first year of existence, the show was telecast on eighteen stations. By the late 1960s the number had grown to eighty-six and in the 1970s went over the 100 mark. Cast regulars over the years included many people who went on to individual stardom. This was particularly true of the female singers Wagoner recruited for the show. In the mid-1960s, he was joined by Norma Jean, who sang both solo numbers and duets with Porter. In the late 1960s, that role fell to another highly gifted artist, Dolly Parton. Between 1968 and 1975, Porter and Parton almost always were among the five finalists in CMA voting for Best Vocal Duo of the Year. Also a crowd pleaser on the TV program was Porter's band, the Wagonmasters.

The regulars as well as guest artists generally accompanied Wagoner on intensive in-person tours of the United States and Canada, which averaged 230 days on the road in the late 1960s and hardly less than that in the 1970s.

Porter kept adding new hits to his repertory every year in the 1960s, starting with "Your Old Love Letters" in 1960. That was joined by such other chart successes as "Cold Dark Waters Below" and "Misery Loves Company" in 1961; "I've Enjoyed as Much of This as I Can Stand" in 1963; "Sorrow on the Rocks" in 1964; "Green Green Grass of Home" in 1965; "Skid Row Joe" in 1966; "The Cold Hard Facts of Life" in 1967; and "Be Proud of Your Man" in 1968. In 1968, he also reached top-chart levels with two duets with Dolly Parton, "Holding on to Nothing" and "The Last Thing on My Mind." Through the end of 1968, he ranked among the top twenty singles artists of the post-World War II years, with thirteen top-10 singles and one number-one song ("Misery Loves Company)" to his credit.

Throughout his career, Porter also loved to sing gospel music. In the mid-1960s, he made a number of gospel recordings with the Blackwood Brothers that were among the best of that genre released in the decade. Those efforts brought him three Grammy Awards for religious albums from the National Academy of the Recording Arts and Sciences. In 1966, the award was for the Best Sacred Recording (*Grand Ole Gospel*), in 1967 for Best Gospel Performance (*More Grand Old Gospel*), and in 1969 for Best Gospel Performance (*In Gospel Country*).

From the mid-1950s through the end of the 1970s, Porter was represented by dozens of album releases on RCA, many of which made country charts. In the 1960s, five of his albums were top-10 hits. Among his releases were *Porter Wagoner* (3/62); *Duets with Skeeter Davis* (7/62); *Porter Wagoner Show* (5/63); *Satisfied Mind* (12/63); *Y'All Come* (12/63); *In Person* (7/64); *Blue Grass Story* (3/65); *Thin Man* (8/65); *Old Log Cabin for Sale* (4/65); *Grand Old Gospel* (2/66); *On the Road* (5/66); *Your Old Love Letters* (3/66); *Confessions* (10/66); *Best of Porter Wagoner* (10/66); *I'm Day Dreamin'* (Camden, 2/67); *Soul of a Convict* (3/67); *Cold Hard Facts* (6/67); *More Grand Gospel* (10/67); *Green Grass of Home* (Camden, 2/68); *Just Between You and Me* (2/68); *Feeling* (Camden, 7/69); *Always, Always* (with Dolly Parton, 9/69); *Me and My Boys* (9/69); *Skid Row Joe Down in the Alley; Howdy Neighbor* (Camden, 1970); *Best of Porter Wagoner, Volume 2* (7/70); *Down in the Alley* (12/70); *Porter Wayne and Dolly Rebecca* (with Parton, 5/70); *Once More* (with Parton); *Simple as I Am* (6/71); *Best of Porter Wagoner and Dolly Parton* (8/71); *Porter Wagoner Country* (Camden, 7/71); *You Gotta Have a License* (2/70); *Two of a Kind* (with Parton, 4/71); *Porter Wagoner Sings His Own Songs* (10/71); *Blue Moon of Kentucky* (11/71); *Right Combination/Burning the Midnight Oil* (with Parton, 3/72); *What Ain't to Be* (3/72); and *Ballads of Love* (8/72).

As the LP *Sings His Own* indicates, Porter made the charts with more than a few of his original writings, though he always was happy to use good material wherever he could find it. When he teamed with Dolly Parton, the alignment brought together two individuals who were first-rate writers as well as entertainers. Thus the 1975 top-10 duet single "Say Forever You'll Be Mine" was a Parton composition while their top-10 1976 single "Is Forever Longer than Always" was a Wagoner song (co-written with F. Dycus). Porter also had several solo hits with Dolly's compositions, an example being "Carolina Moonshine" in early 1975. Among other Wagoner singles that made the charts in the mid- and late-1970s were "George Leroy Chickashea" in early 1974; "Tore Down/Nothing Between" in late 1974; "I Haven't Learned a Thing" in late 1977; and "Ole Slew Foot/I'm Gonna Feed 'Em Now" the end of 1978.

Porter ended the 1970s and opened the 1980s with a minor hit on RCA, the single of his composition "Hold on Tight." In the summer, he had the single "Is It Only 'Cause You're Lonely" on lower-chart levels. In the fall, RCA began to release material that Porter and Parton had recorded in the years they had been a duet team. The first of these, the single "Making Plans," was a top-10 hit in late September and, at year end, their "If You Go, I'll Follow You" made upper levels. Also high on the album charts in the fall was the album *Porter and Dolly.*

Lawsuits followed Dolly's departure from Porter's organization in the latter part of the 1970s but were eventually resolved as each went their separate way.

WAITS, TOM: *Singer, pianist, songwriter. Born Southern California, December 7, 1949.*

Tom Waits' work contains elements of jazz, blues, R&B, rock—so one might consider him an odd candidate for a folk and country encyclopedia. But many folk fans claim him as one of their own because his blend of music and his multilayered lyrics provide vignettes of many aspects of modern life, in the folk tradition.

Waits himself seemed to be living the kind of Damon Runyonesque existence on the seamy underside of American culture he describes in many of his songs. In the late 1970s, when Waits' renown was building, he still resided in a run-down motel in a seedy section of Santa Monica Boulevard in Los Angeles and greeted callers in a room littered with empty beer cans and wine bottles and butt-filled ashtrays scattered over such oddities as an old stove, a slightly askew, aged card table, and an ancient-looking upright piano.

As he talked to his interviewer, he flicked ashes from his cigarette onto a pile of books near one elbow, appearing to reflect more kindly on the recent past than the apparently bright future ahead. (That year, 1978, his activities included providing Bette Midler with the song "I Never Talk to Strangers," included in her LP and his 1978 album, *Foreign Affairs,* which made the national charts; writing special songs for Diane Keaton; and providing three songs for the score of the Sylvester Stallone movie *Paradise Alley,* in which Waits

had a character part as well.) "I've got a lot of miles under my belt. Played a lot of dives and a lot of small clubs. I'm still playing beer joints—just played one called the Choo Choo Room. I still keep a low profile. I still keep one foot in the streets."

Tom indicated with a wave of his hand that it's the back alleys, the flophouses he's slept in (and where he still holes up at times on the road) that have stimulated his creativity and provided the themes for many of his best-known songs.

He compared most of his songs to miniature short stories. "I don't think I'd write stories for books or magazines. If I'd write a short story, I'd put it in an album. 'Potter's Field' (a song in the LP *Foreign Affairs)* is like a short story for me. Anything I write isn't valid for me unless I can perform it on stage or use it in an album."

California has always been home. "I grew up in East Whittier. My father, Jesse Frank Waits, was named after the James Brothers and he grew up in LaVerne, California." He remarked that, while he liked to show off a bit as a teenager, he never thought of going into show business at the time. "I used to take regular jobs. I never really looked at the world of entertainment as a thing I could parlay into money. You don't really find it; it finds you. I had a lot of different jobs before moving over. It takes a great deal of courage to get up on stage. It's really an unnatural act."

After dropping out of school and working at everything from driving delivery trucks to selling vacuum cleaners, Tom got a job as a doorman at a club in San Diego in the late 1960s. "I started working at the door taking tickets. I saw a variety of acts—string bands, country & western, comedians, miscellaneous performers. I liked it. I made eight bucks a night and lived next door." Almost without his knowing it, he became interested in music. One time while visiting his parents, he came across an old piano of his mother's in the garage and started to teach himself to play.

Soon Waits had a small repertoire. "I played a couple of Ray Charles songs. I used to do an Elvis Presley impersonation. I did some folk songs and I was also sort of toying with writing."

After a while, he felt confident enough to drive up to Los Angeles and try out on the amateur shows called "Hoot Nights" at the Troubadour nightclub. One of those visits in 1969 resulted in his acquiring a manager, a long-time associate by now, named Herb Cohen. The two met at the bar and Cohen suggested that they work together. With typical Waits' tongue-in-cheek recall, he noted, "We met and he asked to borrow a dollar. Actually, he told me he just needed it until his brother straightened out. . . . His brother is a hunchback."

The alliance worked out, but it took a lot of persistence and hard work on both sides. Once Cohen started getting engagements for Waits, he toured constantly, which he still did at the start of the 1980s. "I usually hit about fifty cities per tour. At one time I might have stayed in a joint for a while, but these days generally I do all one nighters so I can play in more cities."

As Tom's following slowly began to build in the early 1970s, he gained a recording contract from Asylum/Elektra. In 1971 his debut album, *Closing Time*, came out and was followed during the next few years by *Heart of Saturday Night* and *Night Hawk at the Diner*. Although Waits had started playing low-down bars, by the mid-1970s he was a major attraction on college campuses. He felt good about the fact that his audience wasn't restricted to academia, however. "I'm not limited to the college scene. It's not just young people that listen to me. I get letters from waitresses, truck drivers, fry cooks, people from all different walks of life."

The offbeat nature of much of his material caused some critics to refer to him as a musical evocation of the beat generation of the 1950s. In truth, his music, while it has some of the flavor of the beat movement, goes off in many other directions. He himself dislikes being so typecast. "I didn't even have a driver's license back in the fifties. I think some of the books written by beat writers represent an important event in the content of American literature. But I'm not nostalgic. I wouldn't want to live in the 1950s. I mean I've read a lot

of those cats. But y'know I'm not a throwback. I don't live in a vault. I try to stay abreast of current affairs."

Certainly by the latter half of the 1970s, Waits had proven his ability to stay abreast of the musical tastes of his growing audience. His 1977 LP *Small Change* and the 1978 *Foreign Affairs* were among the more interesting releases of those years and did well on the charts. In late 1978, he was represented by his sixth Elektra/Asylum LP, *Blue Valentine*. In the fall of 1980, his next LP, *On Heart Attack and Vine*, was on the national pop charts. In late 1981, some of his material was packaged for European release only, in an LP titled *Bounced Checks*.

His parents, he claimed, were well satisfied. "My dad teaches a language course in downtown L.A. now. He supports what I do. Thinks I'm a chip off the old block. He's proud of me." His mother had been a little dubious about his career direction in the past, he admitted, but things like the mid-1970s special on him on the Public Broadcasting System TV network had brought her around. "I was in *Vogue* magazine a while back. A little shot of me in a club in New York. It said I was 'up and coming.' My mother liked that."

Based on an interview with Irwin Stambler, late 1978.

WALDMAN, WENDY: *Singer, guitarist, songwriter. Born Los Angeles, California, 1951.*

With a pure, strong voice and a sure touch for the acoustic guitar, Wendy Waldman was one of the relatively few new hopefuls in the folk song tradition during the first part of the 1970s. Had she been born a decade earlier, she might have developed a mass following à la Joan Baez or Judy Collins. As it was, in the mid-1970s she shifted ground to rock and contemporary ballads for a time, though without abandoning the folk genre completely.

Wendy was born and raised in Los Angeles, the daughter of comfortable, middle-class parents. Her father earned a good living writing soundtrack music for motion pictures. She naturally was started on piano lessons at an early age and handled guitar and dulcimer effectively by her mid-teens. Her initial interest tended toward folk music and she began to perform in folk groups in and around Los Angeles in the late 1960s. Joining her in many of those endeavors was Peter Bernstein, son of composer Elmer Bernstein.

In the early 1970s, Waldman was often featured on folk music radio shows and festivals. By then she had a good supply of original compositions to go with the traditional folk songs or versions of songs by modern writers. Her talents were beginning to be appreciated not only by folk music fans but by artists in the Southern California folk and country-rock movement. One indication of this was the inclusion by Maria Muldaur of two of Wendy's songs ("Mad Mad Me" and "Vaudeville Man") on her first LP for Warner Brothers. Coincidentally, Muldaur's album came out almost simultaneously with Waldman's debut on the label, Love Has Got Me, in late 1973. It was a well-crafted album that displayed Wendy's interest in both folk and folk-rock formats.

The album didn't make Wendy an overnight star, though it did increase her stature beyond the relatively limited bounds of the early 1970s folk scene. She was active in other ways in 1973. She contributed backing vocals on Linda Ronstadt's debut album on the Asylum label, Don't Cry Now, which was issued in September 1973. She was asked back to work on Linda's Heart like a Wheel, the Capitol release in late 1974 that finally made Ronstadt a superstar. Earlier that year, Waldman's second LP came out on Warner Brothers, Gypsy Symphony, released in June 1974. Many of her compositions on her first two releases were covered by other artists, including "Gringo en Mexico" (on Maria Muldaur's 1974 album), "Mad Mad Me," and "Cold Back on Me."

Commenting on the wide range of subjects covered in her songs at the time, Wendy said, "I look at the world as a philosopher, a painter using the tools the world gives me. As many pictures and emotions as there are in the world, that's how many potential songs are out there. There's no immaculate conception in creativity. You'll listen to eighty different influences and they are going to infuse into your blood if you're open to them. That's the mark of originality—the amount of experience you're willing to possess."

In her third album, Wendy Waldman, released in March 1975, there seemed to be a partial return to her folk roots. The rock underlay was less noticeable in such tracks as "Secrets," "Sundown," and "Wild Bird." Her stock remained high with her peers in the mid-1970s even if her profile with the general public was lower than she might have desired. On her fourth Warner album, The Main Refrain, supporting work was provided on some tracks by such people as Ronstadt, Taj Mahal, Karla Bonoff, and Andrew Gold. Waldman not only sang a new selection of original songs, including "Soft and Low," "West Coast Blues," and "Living Is Good," she also did the arranging as she had done for some tracks on her debut release. The production chore was handled by old friend Peter Bernstein.

The gap between albums four and five was somewhat longer than for her previous efforts. In between, Wendy moved from Hollywood to Seattle, Washington, where she organized a new band with stronger rock direction. She also enlisted the services of Mike Filcher, who had produced the first hit albums of the rock group Heart, to work on her next collection. The result was Strange Company, released in May 1978, an album that marked her strongest departure yet from the folk arena. The album alienated many of her followers, who previously had accepted her modifications of her folk approach. Still, though different, it was a good release, containing songs with sensitive lyrics and haunting melody lines, indicating that Waldman, like Bob Dylan, could work effectively in many musical domains. The tradeoff probably worked to her advantage, bringing her talents to a somewhat wider spectrum of fans, as demonstrated by good concert attendance. However, it still wasn't enough to make her album work commercially successful.

WALKER, BILLY: *Singer, guitarist, songwriter. Born Ralls, Texas, January 14, 1929.*

In the little town of Ralls, Texas (population 1,779), ranching and country & western music vie for popularity. To home-town boy William Marvin Walker, music won out, though for a time he did work as a ranch hand.

Billy's interest in country & western came early; he learned to play the guitar while still in grade school in Ralls, listening to radio programs and country & western records. By the time he moved to New Mexico in 1942 he was an excellent, though amateur, performer. It was not long before he reached a height of six feet three inches and was nicknamed "The Tall Texan."

In 1944, he became a regular on station KICA in Clovis, New Mexico, remaining there until he finished high school. In the late 1940s he formed his own band and toured the Southwest until 1949, when he joined the cast of the *Big D Jamboree,* broadcast over a number of stations from KRLD in Dallas, Texas. From there he moved over to the *Ranch Time Show* on a Waco, Texas, station.

Later in the 1950s Walker joined the cast of the famed *Louisiana Hayride* on station KWKH in Shreveport. His potential already had been recognized by Columbia Records; his association with the label lasted for fifteen years, coming to an end in 1965. In the mid-1950s, he was making progress as a writer and entertainer, attested to by the major awards given him in 1954 by BMI and *Cash Box.*

In 1955, Billy, also known as "The Travelin' Texan," traveled again, this time to Red Foley's *Ozark Jamboree,* originating in Springfield, Missouri. He remained one of the stars of the show into 1960, when he was asked to become a regular member of the *Grand Ole Opry* cast in Nashville, where he was still a featured artist two decades later.

Billy turned out a series of chart-making singles (and some albums) in the late 1950s and early 1960s. It took a while, though, before he penetrated the uppermost levels. Finally, in 1962, he turned out a record, "Charlie's Shoes," that went all the way to number one on the national country lists. It was, as they say, only the beginning. From then until 1972, he continued to add to his top-10 credits on the various bestseller lists, achieving a total of twenty-six and an overall total of thirty-eight chart-making singles. From 1972 to the start of the 1980s, he added still more recordings to those totals.

Among his top-10 hits of the 1960s were "Willie the Weeper" (1962); "Circumstances" and "Cross the Brazos at Waco" (1964), "Matamoros" (1965); "A Million and One" (1966); "Del Rio," "Anything Your Heart Desires," and "Bear with Me a Little Longer" (1967); and "Ramona" and "Sundown Mary" (1968). The last five were on Monument Records, which Billy signed with in 1965.

Some of Walker's other well-known recordings of the 1950s and 1960s were "Forever," "Funny How Time Slips Away," "The Old French Quarter," "Blue Mountain Waltz," "Go Ahead and Make Me Cry," "Let Me Hear from You," "Let's Make Memories Tonight," "Pretend You Just Don't Know Me," "The Record," "Thank You for Calling," and "Whirlpool." Billy also wrote many songs, some of which were hits for other artists. These included "Anything Your Heart Desires," "Make Believe," " 'Til We Can Make It Come True," "What Makes Me Love You like I Do?," "It's Doggone Tough on Me," and "Pretend You Just Don't Know Me."

Walker's output included many LPs. His work for Columbia included *Hits* (7/61); *Greatest Hits* (3/63); *Anything Your Heart Desires* (4/64); *Thank You for Calling* (12/64); and *The Gun, the Gold and the Girl* (6/65). After going to Monument, he turned out such LPs as *Million and One* (11/66), *Billy Walker Way* (7/67), *Portrait* (7/69), and *Darling Days.* In the late 1960s and early 1970s, Columbia reissued some of his material in the LPs *Greatest Hits, Volume 2* (7/69) and *Goodnight* (7/69). Several of his albums also were issued on the Harmony label, such as *Anything Your Heart Desires* (4/64), *Big Hits* (4/67), *Charlie's Shoes*, and *There May Be No Tomorrow* (5/72).

His personal appearances in the 1950s and 1960s took him to all fifty states several times over and also to many nations overseas. His records in the mid-1960s were particularly popular in Germany. He guested on many nationally televised shows including *The Jimmy Dean Show* and Johnny Carson's *The Tonight Show*. His credits also included two movies, *Second Fiddle to a Steel Guitar* and *Red River Round-Up*. The pattern continued in the 1970s when he and his band, the Tennessee Walkers, were a popular attraction on the country nightclub and fair circuit. They also appeared on most of the major syndicated country TV shows produced in Nashville in the 1970s. During the decade, Billy also starred in his own syndicated TV program, *Country Music Carousel*.

His name continued to appear on the national charts on a succession of labels from the start of the 1970s on into the 1980s. He started off the period by leaving Monument for MGM Records in March 1970. By year end, he had a top-3 hit with the single "She Goes Walking Through My Mind." In 1972 he hit upper-chart levels for MGM with the single "Sing Me a Love Song for Baby." Among his other charted releases on the label was "How Far Our Love Goes" in early summer of 1974. By 1975, Walker was on the RCA Records roster and in June he had a top-10 hit with "Word Games." He provided such additional charted singles on the label as "If I'm Losing You" in the fall of 1975, "Don't Stop in My World" in early 1976, "(Here I Am) Alone Again" in the early summer of 1976, and "Love You All to Pieces" in late summer.

The following year, he showed up briefly on the MRC label, making the charts with a duet with Brenda Kaye Perry, "Ringgold Georgia." In 1978, his charted single "You're a Violin That Never Has Been Played" was on Scorpion Records. In early 1980, he had the single "You Turn My Love Light On" moving up the lists. The song, written by him, was recorded on

the Caprice label. In the fall of 1980, his duet single with Barbara Fairchild, "Love's Slipping Through Our Fingers," on Paid Records, was on lower-chart levels.

WALKER, JERRY JEFF: *Singer, guitarist, songwriter, band leader (Four-Man Deaf Cowboy Band, Lost Gonzo Band). Born Catskill Mountains, New York, March 16, 1942.*

For years Jerry Jeff Walker was known almost solely for writing the classic folk-flavored song "Mr. Bojangles." But in the mid-1970s, having completed the circuit from folk to rock to country, he gained new luster as one of the foremost writers and performers of the progressive country movement.

Although he became an exponent of the so-called Austin sound in the 1970s, he was a transplanted Texan. Born and raised in upstate New York in a family where music was almost a way of life, Jerry was exposed to a range of influences, since his grandparents were members of a square dance band and his mother and sister were part of an "Andrews Sisters-type trio." Still, though he sang a lot as a youngster, he also took up other pursuits. He was a starting forward on his high school basketball team, which won the New York championship, and he wanted to become an astronaut.

But he hadn't ignored singing and had also taken up the guitar. Always restless, at sixteen he quit high school to wander around the country for a while, including a stay in New Orleans, earning money by singing in bars and passing the hat. He returned home after a while to complete his high school education, graduating in 1959. By then he was an ardent fan of the folk movement and sang songs written by such people as Pete Seeger, Woody Guthrie, and the original Jimmie Rodgers.

At the start of the 1960s Walker was singing in small clubs and coffee houses in the East. But before long the wanderlust caught hold again and he was off to the far reaches of the United States, booked for appearances in coffee houses and on college campuses throughout the West and Southwest. On one of those tours in the mid-1960s, he met songwriter–musician Bob Bruno while working in Austin, Texas, a city that he fell in love with. The two formed a folk-rock band called Circus Maximus that they brought to New York and won a recording contract with Vanguard Records in 1967. Their debut album, *Circus Maximus*, was issued in December of that year. The band won a local reputation playing in New York area clubs for the next few years.

Walker had been writing original material for some time, including what was to become the famous "Mr. Bojangles," a song about an old street dancer Jerry Jeff had met one time in a New Orleans drunk tank. One day in the late 1960s, Jerry Jeff and folk artist David Bromberg visited New York station WBAI-FM in Greenwich Village and sang "Bojangles." The disc jockey, Bob Fass, taped it and played it many times thereafter. The exposure brought the song to the attention of other singers, which led to hit cover versions by Nilsson and the Nitty Gritty Dirt Band. It also helped convince Jerry Jeff to go out as a solo artist again. He signed with Atlantic Records, which released his version of the song. Ironically, it fell flat. It was not until he included a new version on a mid-1970s album that he had a hit of his own.

The Atlantic alignment proved nonproductive. Three LPs came out on the label (*Mr. Bojangles* and *Five Years Gone* in 1969 and *Being Free* in 1969), but little happened with them. Jerry Jeff had some well-received solo engagements in places like the Bitter End in Manhattan, then faded from view for a while, at least as far as the general public was concerned. He stayed for a while in Key West, Florida, then regrouped in the early 1970s, moving to Austin, where he bought some land in the hills near the town and built a house. He signed a new recording contract with MCA and recorded an album with some friends and a portable tape recorder that was released in 1973 as *Jerry Jeff Walker*. He called his band of those years the Four-Man Deaf Cowboy Band. With them he began to gain new attention from folk and country fans in 1973, making the charts with the single "L.A. Freeway" (a song

written by his friend Guy Clark) and the album *Viva Terlingua*, which was on national pop charts the end of 1973 and early in 1974.

Viva Terlingua was recorded in one of Walker's favorite spots of the mid-1970s, the ghost town of Luckenbach. It had been bought by a grizzled Texan named Hondo Crouch, who had become almost a second father to Jerry Jeff. Luckenbach, of course, later was made nationally famous in the hit song performed by Waylon Jennings.

On the album Jerry's voice was more grainy and "craggy" than the pure, pleasant voice of his earlier performing years. Typifying his hard driving life of the mid-1970s, the feeling and intensity he put into a song, particularly in personal appearances, overcame the limitations of range of the new voice and often seemed to impart more meaning to the material.

The peccadilloes that had produced those changes, of course, became part of his mystique. Audiences often came to his concerts in part to see if he showed up and in what condition. Legends aside, Jerry pointed out that he couldn't have achieved the output he did if he did everything reputed about him. As he told John Morthland of *Country Music* magazine, "I've broken in some journalists. Meaning they've exaggerated the point. Being loose when I'm performing is something I've always tried for. I think music should be performed and played as if we were not too uptight about it."

Walker also stressed that he got to almost all his concerts, because he owed it to fans and because he gets pleasure from entertaining. A favorite statement of his over the years was that he got many personal returns from the "pure joy of playing."

In the mid-1970s, Jerry Jeff continued to expand his following all over the country with a steady stream of new albums backed by a tight country-rock group called the Lost Gonzo Band. Those releases included his third MCA LP, *Collectibles*, recorded live in Austin and issued in 1974, followed by *Ridin' High, It's a Good Night for Singing* (on the charts in 1975), and *A Man Must Carry On*, a chartmaker in 1976. The last named was a live album recorded on the road in five U.S. cities. While Jerry Jeff was mixing it he heard that Crouch had died, and converted the album into a tribute to him, including a rendition of one of Hondo's poems. Talking about Crouch fondly, he reminisced to Morthland, "He just made magic. I never been anyplace he was where there wasn't magic."

After that album, the Lost Gonzo Band decided to try to make it on its own, though MCA did issue another album in 1978 of Walker and Gonzo Band material called *Contrary to Ordinary.*

By that time, Jacky Jack (as Walker was called by close friends), had moved on to another record company, Elektra/Asylum. His debut LP on that label, *Comfort and Crazy,* came out in November 1978. The title song was a Guy Clark composition and the album included a Jerry Jeff original, "Good Loving Grace." However, the Elektra association didn't work out as hoped for and, by 1981, Jerry Jeff was back with MCA, which released the album *Reunion* in May 1981. (Prior to that, MCA issued the 1980 retrospective LP, *The Best of Jerry Jeff Walker.*)

Talking about his work, he said, "You see these gray hairs? I been pickin' a long time, man, and I'm going to play the way I always played and there's going to be a little of something you just picked up on and there may be something here I sang ten years ago, but it's all going to be mixed in here. . . . It's a picture of life. I like to have people come up to me and say thank you for the night that you came into our room. Me and my wife were just kinda layin' around by the fire or something and your music, it felt like you were talkin' to us and we enjoyed it. That's great!"

WALLACE, JERRY: *Singer, guitarist, actor, songwriter. Born Missouri, December 15, 1933.*

A man of many talents, Jerry Wallace perhaps is familiar to more people for his acting ability than his notable achievements in country music. His credits include varied roles, often in character parts, in more than 200 TV shows during the 1960s and 1970s. But they also embrace many charted country releases, including some number-one singles.

Wallace, who grew up in Missouri, found an interest in country music as a boy, and one of his first efforts was to learn guitar. As he grew up, he also demonstrated potential in acting, including a penchant for mimicking well-known personalities. Later on, his skill at such impersonations provided a unique facet of his stage act. From the second half of the 1960s into the 1980s, he delighted audiences all over the world with a combination of country vocals and impersonations of thirty other singers.

He made his early mark in TV, both as an actor and a narrator, and continued to do that type of work whenever the occasion arose. Among the shows he contributed to over the years were the *Daniel Boone* series, *The Richard Boone Show* on NBC, *Hec Ramsey* and Rod Serling's *Night Gallery.* He also had featured parts in shows like *Goodbye Charlie, Flipper's New Adventures,* and *Johnny Reno.*

During the 1960s, he began to concentrate more attention on the country-music field with a series of recordings that made upper levels on the charts. Some of them, like "Primrose Lane" and Cindy Walker's "In the Misty Moonlight," were hits in both the country and pop domains. Another successful single of his early country-music phase was "Shutters and Boards."

In the mid-1960s, he recorded for Mercury Records, which issued the album *Jerry Wallace* in May 1966. In 1967, he had moved to Liberty Records and by the early 1970s he had switched to Decca. His work for Decca included several very successful singles, such as "To Get to You," in the top 15 in the spring of 1972, and "If You Leave Me Tonight I'll Cry," which rose to number one on U.S. country lists in September 1972. Decca issued a number of LPs of his material, including the early 1970s album *This Is Jerry Wallace.* (He had LPs out on several other labels in the late 1960s and early 1970s, including one on Sun titled *Primrose Lane.*)

Jerry remained with Decca until the mid-1970s, when a slowdown in record sales led to a parting of the ways. He still had a sizable following, though, as indicated by a series of singles that made the charts the latter part of the decade. Among those was a song he co-wrote with K. Young, "I Miss You Already," which was on upper-chart levels for BMA Records for several months in the late summer of 1977. In late 1978, now recording for 4-Star, he had a song in the country top 40, "I Wanna Go to Heaven." He rounded out the decade with a chartmaker called "You've Still Got Me" on still another label, Door Knob, the end of 1979, that was still on the lists in early 1980. Later in the year he placed the singles "Cling to Me" and "If I Could Set My Love to Music" on the hit lists.

WARD, JACKY: *Singer, guitarist, impressionist, disc jockey. Born Groveton, Texas, November 18, 1946.*

One of the more talented impressionists in country ranks, Jacky Ward made his mark primarily by being himself. His way with country songs made him one of the country audience's favored recording artists of the 1970s.

Ward, born in Groveton, Texas, ninety miles from Houston, grew up in a musically oriented family. "Ever since I've been able to think music," he said, "I've wanted to sing." He began singing when he was six years old and made his first appearance in public when he was eight, performing at a political rally in Texas. As he went through elementary and high school, he sought the stage spotlight any time he could, sometimes varying his singing with efforts at comedy or imitations of well-known artists. At fifteen, he already was on his way in the entertainment field, performing in bars and nightclubs in his home area.

In his late teens, Jacky did a hitch in the U.S. Army, where he earned the rank of sergeant. After that, he returned home determined to make his way in show business. For a while he earned part of his living working as a salesperson during the day while working as a disc jockey at night. As he noted, "Being a disc jockey gave me a good insight in the business. I thought if I could get my foot in the door, somethin' would happen."

His DJ work did, of course, bring con-tacts in the country-music field. He was able to find performing dates when he was finished with his stint at the station, and in time found the openings for attempts to place some of his demonstration tapes with record firms. His big break came when a friend helped finance his debut single, "Big Blue Diamonds," issued on Target Records. The song became a regional hit in Houston and with promotional efforts (including a distribution arrangement with a major record company) made the national bestseller lists. His debut album, also titled *Big Blue Diamonds*, came out on the Target label in 1972. In the next few years, he had success with a series of singles that included "Smokey Places," "Pretty Girl, Pretty Clothes, Pretty Sad," "Words," "Dream Weaver," and "You're the One I Sing My Love Song To."

From 1972 on, Ward began to establish himself as an in-person artist, playing clubs across the United States and making several appearances in the lush casinos of Las Vegas. In his act, besides singing his hit songs, he imitated such people as Elvis Presley, Ernest Tubb, Walter Brennan, Chill Wills, Gabby Hayes, John Wayne, Johnny Cash, and such R&B groups of the 1950s and 1960s as the Platters and the Diamonds. By the mid-1970s, his radio and TV credits included spots on many syndicated programs and on the *Grand Ole Opry*.

He became a mainstay on the Mercury Records roster in the mid-1970s; his releases for the label were regularly on the charts throughout the second half of the decade on into the 1980s. His 1970s hits included "Stealin' " and "Dance Her By Me (One More Time)" in 1975; "I Never Said It Would Be Easy" in 1976; "Why Not Tonight" and "Fools Fall in Love" in 1977; "I Want to Be in Love" and "Rhythm of the Rain" in 1978; "Wisdom of a Fool" in 1979.

During the late 1970s, Ward teamed up with Reba McEntire for several hit singles on Mercury Records, including "Three Sheets to the Wind/I'd Really Like to See You Tonight," in the national top 10 in mid-1978. In 1979 his chart-hit singles on

Mercury were "Rhythm of the Rain," "You're My Kind of Woman," and "Wisdom of a Fool." He began 1980 with the single "I'd Do Anything for You" on upper-chart levels and, as the year progressed, had such other chartmakers on Mercury as "Save Your Heart for Me" (in the top 20 in midsummer), and "That's the Way a Cowboy Rocks & Rolls," in the top 10 in November. In early 1981, he had another major hit with "Somethin' on the Radio."

WARNES, JENNIFER: *Singer, songwriter, actress. Born Orange County, California, circa 1947.*

Jennifer Warnes once said, "I find singing to be The Art. The magic of the voice. When you take everything out and just let the voice stand alone, there's nothing more beautiful. You see, the voice has no frets, like a guitar has. You cannot play the piano between the cracks. But the voice is like a violin, it can lilt and fall in between the notes—that's where you find the voice of human emotion—in the cry, the laugh, the moan and the sigh.

"One's sound is as particular as one's physique, as sensitive as one's nerve, as expressive as one's openness of heart. I figure the best way to become a great singer is to learn something about life, and this will all tell in the voice. Voices don't lie."

That analysis certainly seemed to hold true for Warnes. After a relatively untroubled initial phase as a performer, the vicissitudes of life caught up with her and almost destroyed her career. But she fought back and, with seeming new insight reflected in her singing style and musical direction, made considerably more impact on the musical public in her "second flowering."

Jennifer, who grew up in Southern California in a reasonably well-off middle-class family, first sang in public at the age of five. Her primary interest as she was growing up was in folk music, though she was aware of developments in rock and country fields as well. She also was interested in acting, parlaying that skill with a good voice into a role in a local company of the late 1960s rock musical, *Hair*.

She gained even wider exposure in the late 1960s as a regular cast member of the highly successful CBS-TV network variety show, *The Smothers Brothers Comedy Hour*. Known only as Jennifer, she acquitted herself well as a vocalist and as an occasional participant in some of the program's comic skits. She also got a recording contract from Warner Brothers, which released several LPs at the end of the 1960s and in the early 1970s, such as *See Me* (March 1970) and *Jennifer*. Although *The Smothers Brothers* show was caught in political cross-fire and canceled, her career seemed to be in reasonably good shape. She had a record contract and was finding work as a session vocalist and backup singer for people like Leonard Cohen.

In 1972, things began to unravel. Warnes was in Europe touring with Leonard Cohen when she accidentally heard that Warner Bros. had dropped her from its roster. She told Dennis Hunt of the *Los Angeles Times* (May 22, 1977), "I came home as soon as I heard. I didn't have much money. I couldn't afford to get my car fixed or pay my phone bill. My boyfriend and I had broken up. Little by little my world was crumbling."

At least Jennifer's romance seemed to straighten out for a while. But in 1974, the same boyfriend, who was working as a cab driver, was murdered during a robbery. The killer ran off with only $12.50 from his deed.

After that tragedy, she retired to an isolated cabin in the Carmel, California, area to think things out. She told Hunt, "I needed a radical change. I had grown weak and dependent in many respects and I felt it was time to find out whether I could be strong and stand on my own two feet and confront some of my fears. I was about 26 then. I covered a lot of ground inside myself that year. I stayed there until I got horribly bored. When I got bored I knew it was time to come back. So I moved back to L.A. and put a band together and started putting my career back together again."

She rehearsed the band and began considering the kinds of songs she wanted to use. Her emphasis now was away from basic folk music and toward country and folk-rock flavored material. This was reflected in her debut LP on a new label, Arista, titled *Jennifer Warnes*, that was released in early 1977. It included her versions of songs like the old Jim Reeves hit "He'll Have to Go," Boudleaux Bryant's country-rock "Love Hurts," new, contemporary folk-rock songs on the order of "The Right Time of the Night," and her own composition, "Daddy Don't Go." The album wasn't an overnight hit, but it made the charts in February and slowly picked up steam. Helping it along was public reaction to the single of "Right Time of the Night," which made the national top 10. She added a second hit from the LP with the single "I'm Dreaming."

After a cross-country tour in support of the album in the spring of 1977, Jennifer had a new-found popularity that far outstripped her earlier fame. She found plenty to keep her busy besides slowly working up material for a second album in the late 1970s. She worked with Linda Ronstadt doing backup vocals for Warren Zevon's Elektra LP *Excitable Boy*. She also did vocal work on the Jack Tempchin folk-rock ballad hit "Peaceful Easy Feeling" and sang the title song for the successful movie *Norma Rae*. She also did the vocal arrangements during 1978–79 for Leonard Cohen's new LP that was issued on Columbia in the fall of 1979. Besides singing backing vocals on a number of tracks, she did some highly effective duets with Cohen.

Warnes' second Arista LP, *Shot Through the Heart*, came out in mid-1979 and followed a course similar to the previous album. By year end it had spawned a hit single and had sold steadily, if not spectacularly, moving gradually higher on the charts. It did well enough on country charts in 1980 to end the year as one of the top fifty bestsellers in the field. At the start of 1980, her single "Don't Make Me Over" was on the country charts for a short time. In 1981, she sang one of Randy Newman's songs written for the soundtrack of the movie *Ragtime*. In November, Arista issued a new single by her titled "Could It Be Love?"

Her new career seemed to have a much more solid base than her Smothers Brothers years. As she said, "I'm not all that tough now. I've just matured. After what I've been through, I had to grow up."

WATERS, MUDDY: *Singer, guitarist, harmonica player, band leader, songwriter. Born Rolling Fork, Mississippi, April 4, 1915.*

One of the legendary figures of the post–World War II era, Muddy Waters had a dramatic influence on every phase of music except classical. As a performer, writer, and preserver of traditional black music, he contributed to developments in blues, R&B, folk, country, and rock. One of his most famous songs, "Rollin' Stone," inspired the name of the English rock group, a song by Bob Dylan, and the title of *Rolling Stone* magazine.

Muddy was heir to the great black delta blues tradition, though it took a number of years until he became seriously involved in the music. In the rural part of Mississippi where he grew up, poverty was the normal state of affairs and music—gospels and blues—a way of dealing with it. In his case, his mother died when little McKinley Morganfield (his real name) was three. His father, Ollie Morganfield, sent him to his grandmother's house in Clarksdale, Mississippi. At an early age, McKinley was working as a field hand in the Clarksdale area.

Clarksdale was a hotbed of blues singing and Muddy heard many great artists in his youth. He also listened to many blues renditions by local people, both while they worked and at evening socials and get-togethers. It was during those years that he later said he got what became his stage name. His grandmother, he said, "used to say I'd sneak out and play in the mud when I was little so she started calling me Muddy. The kids added Waters; it was a 'sling' [meaning slang] name and it just stuck."

There are some contradictions about when he started earning money in music and when he started to learn guitar. Though he always noted he used to sing at local get-togethers fairly early in life, his early biographies stated that he really didn't stress it or learn to play guitar until he was twenty-two. More recently he claims that he was playing harmonica at thirteen, earning fifty cents a night plus food, which later escalated to eighteen dollars a night working with several sidemen in the 1930s. He recalls starting to learn guitar at seventeen, rather than twenty-two, basing much of his "bottleneck" style on the playing of blues musicians like Eddie "Son" House and Robert Johnson.

By the start of the 1940s, word of this Mississippi farm hand's ability was starting to circulate among academic folk music collectors. As a result, collector Alan Lomax traveled to Mississippi to record some of Muddy's performances for the Library of Congress Archive of Folk Song. Initially, with associate John Work, Lomax recorded two numbers in 1940, "I Be's Troubled" and "Country Blues." Later, several more sides were recorded. Those tracks were available in the late 1970s on Testament Records Collectors Edition. In 1941, eager to break away from the drudgery of farm labor, Muddy joined the Silas Green tent show as an accompanist for blues singers. That work was short-lived, but it inspired Waters to look for new opportunities to make a career in music.

In 1943 he headed for Chicago, where he soon had a job in a paper mill. For the next few years, he held several other regular jobs while trying to make his way as a performer in the evenings. He met a number of other artists then working in the city, including Big Bill Broonzy, and his name began to be mentioned when recording executives were in the market for new blues recording artists. In 1946, Waters recorded three sides for Columbia, which, however, were never issued. In 1947, things finally fell into place when he signed with Chicago-based Aristocrat Records. He turned out two songs for his debut single, "Gypsy Woman" and "Little Anna Mae." Soon after, he provided the label with two big hits, "I Feel Like Going Home" and "I Can't Be Satisfied." For the balance of the 1940s, he slowly increased his stature in the industry with his own recordings and as a sideman for other artists.

After a short, unsuccessful fling with Columbia Records in the late 1940s, he returned to Aristocrat, which by then had been absorbed by Chess Records. Muddy formed his own band in 1950 and became one of the bread-and-butter artists of that label in the 1950s.

He rose to the ranks of featured attractions on the R&B circuit from 1950 on, playing all the major ghetto-area entertainment centers, including many appearances at Harlem's Apollo Theater. Meanwhile, he placed a steady series of songs on the R&B bestseller lists during the decade. In 1951, he had top-10 hits with "Louisiana Blues" and "Long Distance Call," following those with "She Moves Me" in 1952 and "Mad Love" in 1953. Nineteen fifty-four was a vintage year, in which he presented "Rollin' Stone" (also known as "Catfish Blues") and such R&B top-10 singles as "I'm Ready," "I'm Your Hoochie Coochie Man," and "Just Make Love to Me." In 1955, he made R&B hit lists with another Waters standard, "Mannish Boy," and later in the decade added such other noteworthy hits as "Close to You" and "Got My Mojo Workin'."

His career hit a new high in 1958 when he made a triumphal tour of England, where his concerts had a strong impact on many aspiring young British musicians who were to become the cutting edge for the British rock surge of the 1960s. The universality of his work was apparent in the way artists and audiences from such varied fields as folk, jazz, and rock all venerated his music. From the late 1950s to the start of the 1980s, he and his band were perennial favorites at major festivals all over the world. Among the major events to which he returned again and again were the Monterey Jazz Festival, Newport Folk Festival, and the Newport Jazz Festival, both in its Rhode Island home of the 1960s and its New York locale in the 1970s.

Over the decades, Muddy made many dozens of albums on a variety of labels. Interestingly, in the latter 1970s his albums were marketed by Columbia Records, finally bringing him success in an alignment that had only resulted in false starts early in his career. Among his releases on Chess were *Best of Muddy Waters* (issued 10/58), *Muddy Waters Sings Bill Broonzy* (1959), *Muddy Waters at Newport '60* (2/61), *Folk Singer* (5/64), *Real Blues* (4/66), *Brass & the Blues* (1/67), *More Real Blues* (4/67), *Bluesmen* (1967), *After the Rain* (on Cadet Records, 8/69), and *They Call Me Muddy Waters* (1971). The last named gained him a Grammy as the Best Ethnic or Traditional Recording (including blues) of 1971. He had both critical and chart success with his 1972 albums *Live at Mr. Kelly's* and *London Sessions. London Sessions* won him his second straight Grammy for Best Ethnic or Traditional Recording. Other Chess albums in Waters' catalogue as of the mid-1970s included *Sail On, Muddy Waters at Woodstock, Can't Get No Grindin', Electric Mud, Fathers and Sons,* and *McKinley Morganfield, a/k/a Muddy Waters.* He contributed several tracks to the 1973 Buddah album of the New York Newport Jazz Festival session called *The Blues: A Real Summit Meeting.*

Although Muddy was in his sixties the second half of the 1970s, his career seemed to generate new momentum rather than slow down. Throughout those years, he maintained a breakneck schedule that might have exhausted much younger artists. Keeping up a tour schedule of thirty-five to forty weeks a year, he traveled all over the United States and the world.

Nor did his recording work suffer. He signed with Columbia Records' Blue Sky label in the mid-1970s and started working on a series of new albums, with Johnny Winter of rock fame as producer, that explored new facets of the man and his music. The first LP, issued in 1977, was called *Hard Again* and showed Waters at the top of his form backed by a band consisting of Winter, James Cotten, Charles Calmese, and long-time Waters' sidemen "Pinetop" Perkins, Bob Margolin, and Willie "Big Eyes" Smith. That was followed in 1978 by the equally impressive *I'm Ready,* one of the year's best albums, in which his sessions reunited him with some of his 1950s sidemen, harmonica player Big Walter Horton and guitarist Jimmy Rogers. In 1979, material recorded during his 1977

and 1978 national tours was issued on the LP *Muddy "Mississippi" Waters Live.*

Many other highlights of Muddy's illustrious career took place in the 1970s. In 1971, he and his group were the subject of a documentary presented by the National Educational Television network. The hour-long program gave some insight into Muddy's skills and philosophy with the story of a typical live program (at a Chicago blues club), beginning with rehearsals and continuing through the set. An award-winning show, it was replayed again in 1972 and at intervals thereafter.

In November 1977, Waters was a guest of honor at the farewell concert of The Band folk-rock group in San Francisco. He shared the stage with such other legendary artists as Bob Dylan, Dr. John, and Van Morrison. His performance of "Mannish Boy" was an important part of the concert album, *The Last Waltz,* issued in 1978, and the Martin Scorcese-directed concert film of the same title, released some time later.

On August 9, 1978, he was one of the artists to perform at the annual White House staff picnic in Washington, D.C. During his forty-minute set, he and his group played such songs as "Hoochie Coochie Man," "I Got My Mojo Working," and "The Blues Had a Baby and They Called It Rock and Roll" to several ovations from the more than 700 guests. Commenting on Muddy's musical stature, President Jimmy Carter told the gathering, "As you know, Muddy Waters is one of the great performers of all time. He's won more awards than I could name. His music is well known around the world, comes from a good part of the country and represents accurately the background and history of the American people."

His honors during the 1970s included winning five Grammy Awards and election in 1973 by *Ebony* magazine readers to the Black Music Hall of Fame. His Grammies, in addition to the 1971 award previously mentioned, were all for Best Ethnic and Traditional Recording: he won in 1972 for the LP *The London Sessions;* 1975 for *The Muddy Waters Woodstock Album;* 1977 for the album *Hard Again;* and 1979 for the album *I'm Ready.* In 1980, Waters again won in that category for the album *Muddy "Mississippi" Waters Live.*

WATSON, DOC AND MERLE: *Father and son vocal and instrumental team. Doc born Deep Gap, North Carolina, March 2, 1923, Merle born North Carolina, February 8, 1949.*

Fads came and went—folk music was in, then it was out; the British invasion and acid rock prospered, then waned; progressive country came to the fore—through it all, Doc Watson blithely went his own way, playing his vast repertoire of songs traditional and new, folk and country, with skill and feeling. And, accompanied by his talented son Merle, he continued to be a favorite of a sizable number of fans, drawing capacity crowds to as many shows at the start of the 1980s as he had done when first discovered by music fans at the start of the 1960s.

At one point, many audiences cheered Doc as much for his magnificent spirit as for his performing work. Like Riley Puckett, one of Doc's boyhood heroes, he had the ability to charm and entertain people despite the great handicap of blindness. Later on, his achievements had so transcended his lack of sight that few paid much attention to it. The important thing was that Doc was perhaps the finest exponent of guitar flat-picking in the world. Besides that, he was a virtual walking encyclopedia of folk and country songs, from classic ballads to modern country, including, in the 1970s, such unlikely additions as Carl Perkins' rockabillly standard, "Blue Suede Shoes." Contributing to the warmth of a typical Watson concert was the fine second guitar work of Merle, likely one day to inherit his father's mantle, with particular emphasis on his excellent bottleneck slide guitar efforts.

For both Watsons and particularly for Doc in his childhood, music was a way of life. His father, a farmer, led the singing at the local Baptist church. In addition, General Dixon and Doc's mother, Annie, gathered the family around each evening for Bible reading and hymn singing. But young Arthel (his real name) didn't hear

gospel music only. As he told Ralph Rinzler (*Sing Out!*, February–March 1964), his mother sang the children to sleep with such songs as "Omie Wise," "House Carpenter," and "The FFV." From his grandparents he learned such folk songs as "Waggoner's Lad," "Uncloudy Day," "Talk About Suffering," and "Tom Dula."

The first instrument Doc learned to play was the harmonica. His father gave him one one Christmas and then handed the boy another new one each succeeding holiday. When he was six he heard a cousin play "Goodbye Little Bonnie Goodbye" on a five-string banjo and fell in love with the banjo sound. He didn't get his own until a few years later when his brother Arnold married and Arnold's new brother-in-law gave Doc a homemade instrument. Doc's father helped him learn to play it, then made him a better banjo out of hickory, maple, and catskin.

A few years later, when Doc was attending the Raleigh School for the Blind, he added the guitar to his attainments. His father provided the difference between Doc's savings and the amount needed to buy a guitar. Before long, Doc could play guitar well too and organized a duo with his older brother Linny, with Doc holding forth on lead guitar and lead vocals and Linny playing supporting guitar and singing tenor. The music they played came from a variety of sources—material friends and neighbors played, phonograph records, and the country-music programs that Doc loved to listen to. Among the artists whose material they sang were the Carter Family, Skillet Lickers, Monroe Brothers, and Delmore Brothers.

When Doc was seventeen, he earned enough money cutting wood to buy a new guitar from Sears, Roebuck. He used this to play "The Mule Skinner Blues" in his first stage appearance, at a fiddlers' convention in Boone, North Carolina. From then on, he played at other local functions when the chance arose. When he was eighteen, he joined a group that was sometimes heard over local radio stations. It was during one of those shows, when he was nineteen, that he got his nickname.

The announcer liked the name of Doc's friend Paul Greer, who played with Doc, but felt Arthel seemed too stuffy. While this was being discussed on the program, a women standing outside and listening to it on a loudspeaker shouted "call him Doc," and from then on Doc it was.

Those activities remained a low- or non-paying sideline for many years until, he told writer Chet Flippo, "In 1954 I met a man from Johnson City, Tennessee, whose name was Jack Williams. He came to my house that summer and when he heard me play the guitar, he said, 'Doc, let's start a little band. We'll get you an electric guitar and I'll teach you a few of the pop standards.' Jack and I worked together for eight years, sometimes with a five-piece band and sometimes four. We played in V.F.W. clubs and for lots of other organizations in eastern Tennessee and western North Carolina. The music we played was a combination of rock and roll, country and western, old pop standards and a few of the old square dance tunes."

As it turned out, it was old-time music that paved the way for Doc's step into the national spotlight. He kept on playing traditional music at home with friends, family, and particularly a musician named Clarence Ashley. Ashley taught Doc such songs as "The Cuckoo" and "Rising Sun Blues," better known as "House of the Rising Sun."

Ashley's reputation as a traditional artist lured some of the folk-music collectors from New York and vicinity to North Carolina. As Doc recalled, "Ralph [Rinzler] came to record Clarence Ashley [in 1960] and Clarence introduced him to me. After hearing me, Ralph persuaded me that I had something to offer in the way of entertainment. Ralph showed me the ropes and got me started on the road. If it hadn't been for his encouragement, I wouldn't have done it—no way." Some of the playing that kindled Rinzler's enthusiasm can be heard in the LP that resulted from his visit, the Folkways release *Old Time Music at Clarence Ashley's*.

The session led to an invitation for Ashley's group to come to New York for a Friends of Old Time Music concert at Town Hall in early 1961. Doc's solo spots in the concert attracted attention that finally brought the chance for him to appear at Gerde's Folk City in December 1962. He won well-deserved rounds of applause for such renditions as "The Storms Are on the Ocean" and "Willie Moore." In 1963, Doc really broke through with a thunderous ovation from 13,000 fans who listened to his set at the Newport, Rhode Island, Folk Festival and with a concert at Town Hall with Bill Monroe and the Blue Grass Boys.

In the mid-1960s, with folk followers across the United States eager to hear more of this newly discovered troubadour, Doc not only toured more and more widely, but also was represented by a growing catalogue of recordings. Folkways issued a series of albums, including one with Jean Ritchie called *Jean and Doc at Folk City*, as well as *Progressive Bluegrass* and *The Watson Family, Volumes I and II*. Joining Doc in the family albums were his mother, his brother Arnold, and Arnold's talented father-in-law, Gaither Carlton. Those discs included such songs as "The House Carpenter," "Bonaparte's Retreat," "Ground Hog," "Darling Corey," "The Train That Carried My Girl from Town," and "Every Day Dirt."

In 1964, Doc signed a contract with Vanguard Records that remained his main label throughout the 1960s. His debut on the label, *Doc Watson*, was issued in September 1964. The following year, he introduced a new individual to Watson fans when he added his then fifteen-year-old boy Merle on second guitar. The first collection featuring the father and son team was *Doc Watson & Son*, issued on Vanguard in June 1965. From then on Merle was almost always part of his father's concerts and record releases, with his playing gaining in purity and dexterity with the passing years. Though better known for his slide guitar work, when Merle wanted to he could handle the flat pick almost as adeptly as Doc.

As the 1960s went by, each year brought new LPs from Vanguard, including *Southbound* (8/66), *Home Again* (7/67), *Good Deal, Ballads from Deep Gap* (which featured a number of solos by Merle), and *Doc Wat-*

son on Stage. Doc also was represented in a number of collections on Vanguard of various artists, such as *Country Music & Bluegrass at Newport, Old Time Music at Newport,* and *Greatest Folksingers of the Sixties.* At the end of the 1960s and start of the 1970s, Doc had a number of releases on Poppy Records: *Then and Now, Two Days in November,* and *Elementary Doctor Watson.* Columbia also could point to his work on two albums, one titled *Strictly Instrumental* (with Flatt & Scruggs) and the other *Earl Scruggs, Family and Friends.*

For a time in the late 1960s and at the start of the 1970s, Doc and Merle were relatively submerged as a result of the fadeout of the folk music movement in favor of revitalized rock. However, they always were welcomed in concerts on college campuses and in small folk venues. Unlike other folk stars of the 1960s, they never were in danger of having to stop performing, though their audiences did shrink somewhat.

However, with the new surge of interest in mainstream and progressive country, they bounced back easily to featured status. Helping to highlight their importance were two Grammy Awards voted them in successive years, both for Best Ethnic or Traditional Recording. In 1973, they won for the Poppy album *Then and Now* and in 1974 for *Two Days in November.*

In the mid-1970s they signed a new recording contract with United Artists, which turned out one or more albums of their work the second half of the 1970s and into the 1980s. Among those releases were *Doc Watson/Memories, Lonesome Road, Look Away!* and *Live and Pickin'.* (During the 1970s, Vanguard also issued the album *Old Timey Concert.*)

Throughout the 1970s, Doc and Merle, supported by various-sized backing bands, had more concert offers than they could handle. Among the songs they played in various appearances in the mid- and late-1970s were such original Jimmie Rodgers tunes as "Mean Woman Blues," "T For Texas," "The Mississippi and You," and "I Recall a Gypsy Woman"; such old-time songs as "Little Maggie" and "The Cuckoo Bird"; a bluegrass number like "Salt Creek," Carl Perkins' "Blue Suede Shoes"; the old country standard "Rollin' in My Baby's Arms"; Mississippi John Hurt's "Spikedriver Blues"; Woody Guthrie's "Goin' Down the Road Feelin' Bad," and many others.

Merle spoke for both himself and his father when he told an interviewer in the late 1970s, "There are a lot of good musicians coming up, but they aren't going into the old-time music, or at least playing it really well. I think one problem is they just don't feel the music. The old traditional folk-type tunes are really a music of the people, and if you didn't grow up with it and don't know the feeling of what you're playing, it's hard to play it."

WATSON, GENE: *Singer, guitarist, songwriter. Born Palestine, Texas, October 11, 1943.*

For many years, Texas was best known in the folk, country, and western fields for its many practitioners of western music, including the likes of Tex Ritter and Bob Wills. Beginning in the 1960s, though, the state became the incubator for a bumper crop of fine country musicians, including Gene Watson.

Watson, who spent most of his early life in Lamar County near Paris, Texas, was a member of a family that had strong religious and musical ties. His father and brother both played guitar and encouraged Gene to take up the instrument at an early age. And all of them sang in the local church, where Gene had his first taste of performing before an audience. By the time Gene was thirteen, he had a feeling that music might become a career for him, and, indeed, he sang professionally in his area of Texas throughout his teens. When he was eighteen, he cut his first record for a small label. A few years later, he moved to the city of Houston where there were more opportunities for young musicians to try for the big time.

However, though Watson found engagements in clubs and country shows in the early 1960s, it wasn't enough to make a living. As a result, he had to get most of his income from the auto repair field. It was a pattern that lasted so long that there was a time it looked as though music would always be a sideline. As he recalled in the mid-1970s, "Not too long ago I was doing body work on cars all day and playing in clubs at night. That kind of schedule will kill you, but it's what I wanted to do. Just before I signed with Capitol, I had to make the decision whether to be content with just being a body man for the rest of my life or getting into the music business full time. I figured if I made it, that was fine. If I didn't at least I could say I tried. So I gave up my body work. But I didn't sell my tools."

Not that Gene didn't have some success during the 1960s and early 1970s. He cut some twenty records during those years, some on the Reeder label, owned by Ross Reeder, who remains as Gene's manager and producer and coproducer of his recordings. Some of them became regional hits, including such singles as "Bad Water," "I'm a Fool for Leaving" (which also made the national country charts), "John's Back in Town," and "Shadows on the Wall." Watson gained enough recognition to guest on the *Grand Ole Opry* at one point, but still couldn't concentrate on music as his sole profession. He remarked, "The records I made then had good material and excellent backing musicians, but the thing about a recording on a small label is lack of distribution and promotion. That's what held me back."

Watson's luck finally changed after Reeder brought him to Nashville to record a song that had been around a while, "Love in the Hot Afternoon." Released on the Reeder label initially, it started to do well enough for Capitol Records to agree to take over. The single became a national major hit in mid-1975, as did Gene's Capitol debut LP of the same title. Two more songs from the album were released as singles and made the top 10. "You Could Know as Much About a Stranger" and "Where Love Begins," the latter going up to number five in late December 1975. In May 1976, his second album, *Because You Believed in Me*, came out and made the top 10 in the charts in August, with the title song entering the top 20 in the summer. Later, the album provided another chart

single, "Her Body Couldn't Keep You Off My Mind."

His third album, *Paper Rosie*, came out in January 1977 and demonstrated that his hold on a growing country following remained strong. The title song got up to the number-three spot on national charts. Album number four, *Gene Watson's Beautiful Country*, came out in October 1977 and demonstrated a continuing growth in both content and quality. Two of the songs made the top 10 in single lists, "The Old Man and His Horn" and "I Don't Need a Thing at All." In mid-1978, Capitol issued Gene's first "hits" collection, *The Best of Gene Watson*, which included both his Capitol successes plus four of his earlier releases.

In 1979, Gene had two LPs on the charts, *Reflections* and *Should I Come Home*, the latter still on them in early 1980. His charted singles in 1979 included "One Sided Conversation," "Farewell Party," "Pick the Wildwood Flower," and "Should I Come Home (or Should I Go Crazy)?" The last named remained on the lists into 1980. Although his affiliation with Capitol was coming to an end—by 1981 he was on the MCA roster—Capitol still had a series of best-selling singles of Gene's in 1980: "Raisin' Cane in Texas," "Nothing Sure Looked Good on You," and "Bedroom Ballad." The LP *No One Will Ever Know* was on the charts in the fall of 1980. In early 1981 he had a single on Warner/Viva, "Any Way You Want Me," that showed up on country charts. His MCA debut single, "Between This Time and the Next," was in the top 10 in March 1981.

WEAVERS, THE: *Vocal and instrumental group. Original personnel (1948): Pete Seeger, born New York, New York, May 3, 1919; Lee Hays, born Little Rock, Arkansas, 1914, died upstate New York, August 26, 1981; Fred Hellerman, born New York, New York, May 13, 1927; Ronnie Gilbert. Seeger replaced by Erik Darling, born Baltimore, Maryland, September 25, 1933.*

A legendary group, one of the most broadly successful in recent folk-music history, The Weavers might have accomplished far more than they did if the Congressional investigators of the mid-1950s hadn't persecuted some of their members. The group proved that folk music could enthrall the mass audience years before the folk boom of the late 1950s came along, a development in which The Weavers also took part.

The group was formed in 1948 under the aegis of veteran folk singers and instrumentalists Lee Hays and Pete Seeger. Hays and Seeger had performed together in the early 1940s as part of a group called the Almanac Singers, another landmark folk organization whose members included at times such other luminaries as Woody Guthrie, Burl Ives, Millard Lampell, Bess and Butch Hawes, Cisco Houston, Josh White, and Earl Robinson. The onset of World War II caused disbandment, with Seeger entering the service for several years. After leaving the Army, Seeger did some solo work, then helped form The Weavers. It was Hays, though, who gave the group its name. He recalled that the group evolved from informal songfests in the basement of Pete Seeger's Greenwich Village home in 1949.

The group made its New York debut at the Village Vanguard in late 1949 and soon was one of the favorites of both pop and folk fans in the city and environs. With more engagements in nightclubs, concert halls, and college campuses and expanding exposure on radio and TV in the early 1950s, The Weavers quickly gained a national reputation. The group, which recorded on both Decca and Folkways during that period, placed a number of songs on the hit charts, including the traditional folk ballad "On Top of Old Smoky," Leadbelly's "Good Night Irene," and Woody Guthrie's "So Long, It's Been Good to Know You."

Looking back on those times for a *Sing Out!* interview in 1979, Lee Hays stated, "When we first went to audition for Decca Records, one of the Kapp brothers [then a Decca executive, later a founder of Kapp Records] came out and said, 'You have to decide whether you want to be good or commercial.'

"I told him when he came back that we decided we wanted to be good *and* commercial. Then what orchestra leader Gordon Jenkins did was to take our songs and package them with big orchestras and choruses, and immediately we had two enormous hits." (Those were "On Top of Old Smoky" and "Good Night Irene" in 1950.)

The McCarthy era, marked by political investigations into the background of many people in the entertainment field, had a major impact on the group's fortunes. It disbanded in 1952 partly due to the political climate and to some extent because of career goals of some members. It reassembled in 1955 with Seeger still a member. In 1957, though, he permanently stepped down as a full-time member, still working with them on occasion in later years. Hays, Gilbert, and Hellerman remained in the group throughout its history, but three different people took Seeger's spot at various times: Erik Darling, Frank Hamilton, and Bernie Krause. Darling, a singer, guitarist, banjoist, and songwriter, born in Maryland but raised in New York, spent the longest time of the three as a Weavers' member, working with them from 1958 to 1962, when he left to form a group called the Rooftop Singers, which had a major hit in 1963 with his song "Walk Right In."

Among The Weavers' record successes of the late 1950s and early 1960s were such songs as "Tzena, Tzena, Tzena," "Kisses Sweeter than Wine" (a Hellerman contribution), and "Wimoweh." Also in their repertoire was their version of the Hays-Seeger classic, "If I Had a Hammer." Their album releases in the late 1950s and 1960s included, on Decca, *Best of The Weavers* (7/59); *Folk Songs Around the World* (12/59); and *Weavers Gold* (7/62). Most of the group's releases during those years were on Vanguard Records, including *At Home* (8/58); *At Carnegie Hall* (1960); *At Carnegie Hall, Volume 2, April 1, 1960* (1960); *Traveling On* (1960); *Almanac* (4/62); *Reunion at Carnegie Hall* (12/63); *Reunion at Carnegie Hall, Part 2* (8/65); *Songbag* (10/67).

Although recordings by the group continued to be issued in later years, The Weavers officially disbanded after a farewell concert at Chicago's Orchestra Hall in December 1963. In November 1981, the four original Weavers, Seeger, Hellerman, Gilbert, and Hays, came together to celebrate the twenty-fifth anniversary of their famed concert at Carnegie Hall in New York. Lee Hays' health had been failing for some time, though, and in August 1981, he suffered a fatal heart attack in his upstate New York home.

In 1982, *Wasn't That a Time*, a movie of the events leading up to the concert and the concert itself, was released. The film was dedicated to Hays.

WEISBERG, TIM: *Flutist, songwriter, band leader. Born Hollywood, California, 1943.*

The flute and related instruments have a long and honored heritage in folk music history, but for most of the twentieth century, their main role has been in classical music. A number of musicians in recent times, prominent among them Tim Weisberg, have given the flute new status in genres ranging from folk to rock and jazz.

Tim was born and grew up in the film capital of Hollywood, but his family was only peripherally related to entertainment. His father had a strong interest in sports, having been a star athlete in his youth, and worked as a cinema technician. His mother worked as a statistician. Neither parent was a musician, but they encouraged any interests their son developed. His first instrumental effort was on the accordion when he was eleven. However, he soon turned his attention to swimming, a sport at which his father once had excelled.

In junior high school, he started to learn the flute. It wasn't an instrument he'd longed to play. When it was his turn to choose an instrument in music class, it was the only instrument left. He showed an aptitude and his music teacher helped further his skills. After a while, Tim was good enough to become a member of the Robin Hood Band, a marching and concert group sponsored by an insurance company. Among other young members were Tom Scott and Jim Gordon, later to become well known in the jazz and rock fields.

Tim still considered music mainly a hobby throughout most of his school years. He was on the swimming team in high school, as he was when he went to college at California State University at Northridge, where he also played on the water polo team. Although the school had a good music department, Tim's major was anthropology, in which he earned his B.A. in the mid-1960s. After that, he went on to earn a master's degree in educational psychology.

Until the mid-1960s, most of Weisberg's flute playing was of classical compositions. Although he was interested in rock 'n' roll, particularly since some of his friends were in rock bands, he could only play by rote. Cellist Fred Katz finally taught him how to improvise. With the opportunity to play more freely, Tim switched his emphasis from classics to various pop music forms.

He began to perform at fraternity parties and, as his confidence increased, in local bars, presenting flute versions of popular hits of the day. By the late 1960s, the die was cast; he devoted his efforts to achieving success in the pop field. His act was good enough for him to get jobs opening for major artists, ranging from folksingers like Buffy Sainte-Marie to rock performers like Frank Zappa. His material, appropriately, covered the gamut from folk-flavored numbers to jazz to hard driving rock.

His goal, naturally, was to gain a record contract with a major label, though it wasn't easy to find executives who could see a successful future for pop flute records. But Tim persisted and achieved his objective in 1971, signing with A&M. His debut on the label, *Another Time*, had a respectable enough reception from critics and fans to warrant follow ups. He turned out a second LP in 1972, a third in 1973, and an album entitled 4 in late 1974. By then the LPs were making the national charts, 4 staying on them from late 1974 through February 1975. Succeeding A&M albums, such as *Listen to the City*, issued in late 1975, and *Live at Last*, released in the fall of 1976, had similar long chart runs.

In late 1976, Weisberg moved from A&M to United Artists Records; his debut on the latter, *Tim Weisberg Band*, was on the charts in early 1977. His second on UA, *Rotations*, was issued in April 1978 and also was a chart hit for a while.

During 1978, he began a new series of recording sessions with folk and folk-rock performer Dan Fogelberg. Their strongly folk-flavored collaboration, *Twin Sons of Different Mothers*, came out on Fogelberg's label, Columbia, in the fall of 1978. An excellent album, it had the most impact of any of Tim's projects up to then, entering the national top 10 soon after release and staying there a number of weeks. The album earned him a gold-record award.

In 1978, Weisberg ended his relationship with UA and signed a new contract with MCA Records. The first result was the early 1979 release, *Night Rider*. His second MCA LP, *Party of One*, was issued in early 1980; his third, *Travelin' Light*, came out in August 1981.

WELLER, FREDDY: *Singer, guitarist, songwriter. Born Atlanta, Georgia, September 9, 1947.*

Even though the lines of demarcation have blurred considerably between all forms of pop music, typecasting in the public mind is still a problem, as Freddy Weller is well aware. Although most of his professional life has centered on country-music, many country fans still think of him as a refugee from the Paul Revere and the Raiders rock group.

As a child, Freddy was a fan of country-music shows on radio and TV in his native Atlanta. By the time he reached his early teens he had learned to pick country guitar to accompany his vocal efforts to the point that he tried his luck on a country-music show called *Georgia Jubilee* that was based in the Atlanta suburb of East Point. The show drew much of its personnel from a series of talent contests. Freddy first won a weekly contest, went on to triumph in the monthly show, and, though he lost in the quarterfinals, was still asked back to perform as a semiregular.

At the time, Atlanta not only remained a center of country activity, but was the hub of a growing country rock genre. Weller became friends with one of the prime exponents of that style, Joe South, as well as another rising star, Billy Joe Royal. Both worked in Freddy's behalf. South helped him get work as a studio musician for the

Bill Lowery organization and also encouraged his song-writing abilities. Some of those songs were recorded by other artists.

Royal was impressed with Freddy's guitar work and asked him to accompany him on a number of tours in the mid-1960s. When Royal took his own band along, Weller generally played rhythm guitar. If Billy Joe employed a house band, Freddy took over as lead guitarist and band leader for Billy.

In 1966, Royal played a package show with Paul Revere and the Raiders. Revere was impressed with Weller's playing and filed it away for future reference. When guitarist Jim Valley quit the group in 1967, Revere phoned Weller to take over. Freddy was reluctant at first, but finally gave in and caught up with the band on the road. For some concert series, fellow Atlantan Tommy Roe became part of the bill. Roe and Weller started collaborating on both rock and country songs, one result of which was the Tommy Roe rock hit "Dizzy."

Weller told both Revere and lead singer Mark Lindsay that he wanted to get back to doing some country material. Revere put him in contact with Columbia's New York office, which, in turn, suggested discussions with Nashville executives. The latter said they'd listen if he brought something in. Mark Lindsay agreed to produce some demonstration tapes, from which a Weller composition, "Home," was chosen as the main offering and a Joe South song, "Games People Play" as the "B" side. When Billy Sherrill listened to the tape in Nashville, though, he preferred the latter rendition, which provided the basis for a recording contract signed by Freddy in Februrary 1969.

By the time the single was released, Weller was on an overseas tour with the Raiders. He recalled, "We were touring in Europe when I heard it was a hit. [Mark Lindsay had called Columbia's Los Angeles office long distance to see how it was doing and was amazed to hear it had reached number one on country charts]. Suddenly I got this solo recognition—as a country artist. Some people got angry too. They thought 'What's this rock 'n' roller trying to do coming into our territory.'" Even a decade later, when Freddy had been turning out country recordings only, some country fans still recalled his rock roots.

In the early 1970s, Freddy decided to leave the rock band area completely to concentrate on his solo country work. He turned out several more country songs that did well on the charts, such as "Promised Land," proving that he wasn't a one-hit artist.

During the rest of the 1970s, he consistently had singles or albums on the country hit lists, both original compositions and interpretations of other writer's offerings. These included such Columbia singles as "Sexy Lady" in 1974, "Liquor, Love and Life" in 1976, "Merry-Go-Round" and "Nobody Cares but You" in 1977, "Bar Wars" in 1978, and "Go for the Night" (late 1979, early 1980). "A Million Old Goodbyes" was his first 1980 issued single to show up on the charts, and later in the year he had a second release on them, "Lost in Austin."

WELLS, KITTY: *Singer, guitarist, songwriter. Born Nashville, Tennessee, August 30, 1919.*

For longer than any other performer, Kitty Wells reigned as unofficial "Queen of Country Music." While she would have to add "emeritus" to the title from the 1970s on, she still ranked as one of the most respected performers in the country field even if her name only showed up occasionally on the hit charts in comparison to the many top-10 successes of the 1950s and 1960s. (From 1952 through 1969, she had twenty-five top-10 songs, almost twice the total of the nearest female country singer of those years.)

Wells, whose real name was Muriel Deason, grew up in Nashville, but had to go much further afield to establish a reputation as an up-and-coming country artist. She sang along with country music on the radio as a girl. By the time she was fifteen, she could play the guitar and began to perform at local dances in the Nashville area. A few years later, in 1936, she made her radio debut on station WSIX in Nashville. In 1938, she married Johnny Wright of

the Johnnie and Jack country duo. She was featured on their show and traveled widely with the troupe. She got her stage name of Kitty Wells courtesy of her husband. During this period, her voice reached country listeners via appearances on a great many radio stations, such as WCHS, Bluefield, West Virginia; WNOX, Knoxville, Tennessee; WPTF, Raleigh, North Carolina; and WEAS, Decatur, Georgia. At the time, the country field was dominated by male artists. Still, she might have become a nationally recognized star then except for the fact that she concentrated part of her time on raising a family.

As her children got a little older, Wells began to expand her singing efforts. In 1947, she was given a guest spot on the *Grand Ole Opry*. That same year, she, her husband, and co-worker Jack Anglin, plus their band, the Tennessee Mountain Boys, signed on as regular cast members of the *Louisiana Hayride*, broadcast from Shreveport. All of them gained an increasingly wider reputation across the United States from their work on the show from 1947 to 1952 and from a series of successful recordings, initially by Johnny and Jack, then by Kitty. Her breakthrough came in 1952 with her single "It Wasn't God Who Made Honky Tonk Angels." Issued on Decca, it was number one on U.S. country charts for many weeks, selling some 800,000 copies. During ensuing years, it sold at a slower pace, but steadily, until, by the 1970s, it had gone past the million-copy mark.

With Wells, her husband, and Jack Anglin all having top-10 hits to their credits, it wasn't long before the *Grand Ole Opry* came after them. During 1952, they agreed to join the premier country radio program and moved to Nashville, which was still Kitty and Johnny's home in the 1980s. In 1953, though she didn't have a blockbuster the equal of "Honky Tonk Angels," she still placed several singles on the charts, including a top-10 hit, "I'm Paying for That Back Street Affair."

She shifted into high gear in 1954-55 with such hits as "One by One" and "As Long as I Live," both duets with Red Foley, and "Making Believe" and "Lonely Side of Town." In 1956, she hit the top 10 with

"Searching Soul" and in 1957 scored with "I'll Always Be Your Fraulein" and "Repeating." She rounded out the decade with such national successes as "I Can't Stop Loving You" (1958) and "Amigo's Guitar" (co-written by Kitty and John Loudermilk) and "Mommy for a Day" (1959). Decca recognized her importance to the company by signing her to a lifetime contract in 1959, an agreement still in effect in the 1970s after Decca had become MCA Records.

She continued to hold sway at the top of the hit lists as the 1960s progressed, starting off with a big 1960 bestseller, "Left to Right." In 1961, she turned out another number-one hit, "Heartbreak U.S.A," and had a big year in 1962 with such top-10 singles as "Day into Night," "Unloved, Unwanted," "We Missed You," and "Will Your Lawyer Talk to God?" She missed the top 10 a few times in 1963, but came back in 1964 with "Password" and "The White Circle on My Finger" and made the top 10 in 1965 with "You Don't Hear." In 1967, she made upper-chart levels with the single "Love Makes the World Go Round." While she fell short of top-10 honors the last few years of the decade, she still was one of the most successful country recording artists, placing four singles on the bestseller lists in 1968 and several more in 1969. Some of her 1960 releases were duets with such artists as her husband, Johnny Wright, Webb Pierce, and Roy Drusky.

Among Wells' other best known songs were "Cheatin's a Sin," "I Don't Claim to Be an Angel," "God Put a Rainbow in the Cloud," and "How Far to Heaven?"

She also completed many albums for Decca during the 1950s and 1960s, many of which were high on the album charts. Among her LPs were Lonely Street (10/58), After Dark (7/59); Dust on the Bible (9/59); Kitty's Choice (5/60); Kitty Wells (mid-1950s); Seasons of My Heart (1960); Golden Favorites (4/61); Heartbreak U.S.A. (7/61); Queen of Country Music (4/62); Singing on Sunday (1963); Especially for You; Kitty Wells Story (two records, 10/63); Country Music Time (10/64); Burning Memories (4/65); Lonesome, Sad and Blue (8/65); Family Gospel Sing (11/65) Songs Made Famous by Jim Reeves (4/66); All the Way (8/66); Kitty Wells Show (1/67); Love Makes the World Go Round (6/67); Together Again, with Red Foley (9/67); Queen of Honky Tonk (12/67); on Vocalion Records, Kitty Wells (1/67) and Heart (8/69). Her album releases of the late 1960s and early 1970s included such Decca collections as Bouquet of Country Hits, Singing 'Em Country, Your Love Is the Way, They're Stepping All Over My Heart, and Pledging My Love.

Kitty's chartmakers in the late 1960s and early 1970s included "They're Stepping All Over My Heart," "Sincerely" (on the charts in the spring of 1972), and "Easily Persuaded," a hit in mid-1973. At the time the last named was released, MCA Records reported that during her years on the Decca/MCA roster she had turned out a total of 461 singles and forty-three albums.

From the mid-1950s through the end of the 1970s, Kitty's in-person appearances took her around the world several times. By the start of the 1980s, besides having performed in all fifty states, she also had traveled to all Canadian provinces, Germany, France, Italy, Holland, and England. In 1969, she and her husband began a syndicated TV show called The Kitty Wells/Johnny Wright Family Show, which remained a staple for viewers all over the United States and Canada for many years. Their son, Bobby Wright, joined them on the program and in the concert package they took to major cities and county and state fairs. Wells often was featured on other TV programs, including, in the 1950s and 1960s, The Ozark Jamboree, Jimmy Dean Show, Nightlife and Carl Smith's Country Music Hall. In the 1970s, she appeared on Johnny Carson's The Tonight Show and Hee Haw, among others. She also was one of the country artists featured in the film Second Fiddle to a Steel Guitar.

Over the years, Wells received many honors. From 1953 to 1968, various polls voted her the number-one female country singer. In 1954, Governor Frank Clement of Tennessee presented her with a citation as Outstanding Tennessee Citizen, and she was honored with various tributes from other states in later years. In 1976, she received the greatest honor of all for a country performer, election by her peers to the Country Music Hall of Fame in Nashville.

In addition to all her other activities, she also assembled several books, including *Favorite Songs and Recipes*, published in 1973.

WEST, DOTTIE: *Singer, guitarist, songwriter. Born McMinnville, Tennessee, October 11, 1932.*

Dottie West might be called the "Queen of Duets," because in her long and eventful career she recorded notable material with four different singing partners: Jim Reeves, Don Gibson, Jimmy Dean, and Kenny Rogers. Still, her career is even more remarkable for her solo work, both as a performer and a songwriter.

Looking back over her singing collaborations in June 1979, she told Mark Lundahl of the *San Bernardino* (California) *Sun,* "My first duet was with Jim Reeves. At that time he saw me as a new artist and songwriter and he wanted to help get my name around.

"I think the chemistry really worked for Don Gibson and me. But we only recorded one album because he didn't want to go on the road. He was too interested in just writing songs, so that teaming fell by the wayside. You can't just be recording and stay at home. Your fans want to see you."

And of her late 1970s pairing with Kenny Rogers, which brought her career to new heights, "Recording with Kenny has broadened my audience. He's kind of a unique crossover artist because he's gone from the pop field to country. Singing for his crowd is kind of like singing for the folks that Elvis drew. There are all ages and all types of people."

But those events and the many others that made her a country-music superstar were far from the mind of the little girl growing up as a member of a low-income farm family in Tennessee. The oldest of ten children, Dottie was burdened with her share of responsibilities: chopping cotton, working in sugar cane fields, and sometimes cooking for her huge family. But it wasn't all hard physical work. Her parents loved country music and saw to it that the

children were exposed to it as well as to the activities at the nearby Southern Baptist Church. As a child, Dottie began learning guitar from her father, Hollis March, who "could play anything with strings on it." She also began singing in the church choir.

A string of part-time jobs in her teens helped finance her music lessons and her future college education. Her dream came true at the start of the 1950s, when she enrolled at Tennessee Technological University in Cookeville as a music major. (In recognition of her achievements, in 1966 that school established the Dottie West Music Scholarship.)

During her first week on campus, she met a boy named Bill West, who shared her love for country music (though in her courses she explored all musical forms). His goal was to get an engineering degree, but he could play excellent steel guitar and was soon accompanying Dottie at school events. Before long, they decided to marry, an alliance that lasted through many years on the road and four children before ending in divorce in 1969.

Both Wests graduated, Bill with an electronics degree and Dottie as a music major. Bill quickly got a job with a Cleveland electronics company and they moved to Ohio. For five years he persevered at engineering while they supplemented their income by appearing as a country music team. One show they appeared on regularly was Gene Carroll's *Landmark Jamboree* TV show in Cleveland. In 1959, after Dottie gained a recording contract from Starday Records, the time was ripe for a move to Nashville.

Nothing dramatic happened right away, but it didn't take long for the Wests to become friends with many other struggling young artists, many of whom were to become top names in the future, such as Willie Nelson, Hank Cochran, and Roger Miller. It was from informal get-togethers with people like that, Dottie recalled, that she discovered her talent as a songwriter.

"It was through guitar-pulling sessions that I really became a writer," she told James Albrecht of *Country Style* magazine (July 1978). "When I first went to Nashville, Patsy Cline was my best friend. I had idolized her singing before that, and we became good friends. . . . She never wrote songs. But she really got me into going to what we called guitar pullings at the time. We'd sit with one guitar in the room and we'd pass the guitar around and everybody would sing the song they had written that day and try to knock each other out. So it really kept you on your toes and you wrote a lot of songs that way. I learned a lot from Willie Nelson, Hank Cochran, and Roger Miller."

The first complete song she came up with in those years was "Is This Me?" written in 1961. The song was recorded by Jim Reeves and became a hit for him. It also earned Dottie a BMI Writer's Award. That success coupled with Jim Reeves' recommendation of her singing potential to Chet Atkins led to a long-term contract with RCA Records in 1962. (Prior to the RCA alignment, Dottie had left Starday and worked briefly with Atlantic Records.) Soon after the RCA deal, the Wests were given a songwriting contract by Tree Publishing Company.

It took a little while for the momentum to build up, but in 1964, Dottie West moved from relative obscurity to country-music prominence. Helping to bring that about was the Wests' composition "Here Comes My Baby." Soon after the single came out, it was nestling in the country top 10 and was covered by pop artists like Perry Como. Since then over 100 artists in both country and pop have released their own versions of the song, an accepted perennial standard.

West made her initial mark as a duet artist, teaming with Jim Reeves on a top-10 version of Justin Tubb's "Love Is No Excuse." The promising pairing was brought to an abrupt end with Reeves' tragic death in a plane crash. It was an event that took much of the pleasure away from Dottie's selection as a regular cast member of the *Grand Ole Opry*, an association still firm at the end of the 1970s. "Here Comes My Baby" was nominated for a Grammy Award, the first of sixteen such nominations West was to attain through 1979. (It also was her only winner over that period,

bringing her the Award for Best Country Vocal Performance for 1964.)

Dottie followed with a string of charted songs, including such major hits as "Would You Hold It Against Me?" in 1966, "Paper Mansions" in 1967, "Rings of Gold" (number one as a single and as title song of an album) with Don Gibson in 1968, and "I Was Born a Country Girl" (written with Red Lane) in 1969. Other charted singles of those years were "Gettin' Married Has Made Us Strangers," "What's Come Over My Baby?" and, with son Dale, "Mommie Can I Still Call Him Daddy?"

In the mid- and late-1960s, West's personal appearances covered all fifty states, Canada, and Europe. Her guests spots on TV included *The Jimmy Dean Show,* Carl Smith's *Country Music Hall,* and a regular slot on the *Faron Young Show.* She also appeared in two movies, *Second Fiddle to a Steel Guitar* and *There's a Still on the Hill.* On July 10, 1965, her home town of McMinnville honored her with "Dottie West Day."

In 1970, West accepted an offer from the Coca-Cola Company to write a commercial based on her song "I'm a Country Girl," an alliance that was to prove more important than she might have predicted. The commercial featuring the song did so well that in 1972 the company offered her a lifetime contract to write advertising numbers. (As of the end of 1979, she had provided fifteen such commercials.) The first results of that agreement was a 1973 song, co-written with Coke commercial producer Billy Davis, called "Country Sunshine." From its advertising use, the song won Dottie a Clio Award for best commercial of the year, the first such honor ever given a country artist. Perhaps more important, her single of it became a hit, helping to restore her musical fortunes, which sagged a bit in the early 1970s, possibly due to the trauma of her breakup with Bill West. (In the mid-1970s, she married drummer Byron Metcalf, who, as Bill had been, was a member of her tour group.) "Country Sunshine" has become Dottie's theme song.

Her activities in the mid-1970s included repeated tours of Europe, which brought such accolades as being voted Top American Female Vocalist (country) in England in 1972 and 1973. In 1976, she also changed record companies, joining United Artists. The immediate result was the single "When It's Just You and Me," the biggest-selling single of West's career to that point, but the move led as well to her phenomenally successful work with Kenny Rogers.

She had known Rogers before signing with UA as a solo artist. As she told Janet Martineau of *The Saginaw News* (July 21, 1979), "I love to sing harmony and Kenny and I have been friends for a long time. He and Marianne [his wife] are just friendly, nice people, and they would come to our home to visit and spend the night when they were in Nashville."

So there already was a rapport when the two coincidentally were slated to have successive recording sessions for UA one night. "He came by my sessions and watched me record while he was waiting. Then he decided to come in and help me record a song called 'Every Time Two Fools Collide.' It was to have been a single for me and I had already cut the track—the music was in my key, so that's why Kenny hit some high notes in there he had never hit before."

The single turned out to be a hit. "We all felt the magic and the chemistry was right. And the company said, 'Hey, you guys have got to do an album.' " The result was an album titled *Every Time Two Fools Collide*, which moved to the top of the country charts and was a crossover into pop as well. As of late 1979, it had exceeded 550,000 copies sold, for a gold record award. In 1979, they followed with another LP called *Classics* that did even better (565,000 copies as of fall 1979), for a second gold-record success.

In November 1979, UA issued another album by Dottie titled *Special Delivery*, her thirty-third LP (including duets) to come out over two decades. Among those LPs were *Sensational Dottie West* on Starday (early 1960s), *I Fall to Pieces* on Nashville, and some tracks on the Starday LP *Queens of Country Music*. Her 1960s RCA releases included *Here Comes My Baby* (7/65), *Dottie West Sings* (2/66), *Suffer Time* (8/66), *With*

All My Heart (2/67), *Sacred Ballads* (8/67), *Sound of Music* (Camden, 9/67), *I'll Help You* (12/67), and *World of Music*. Among her 1970s LPs on RCA were *Country & West* (7/70), *Forever Yours* (with the Jordanaires, 11/70), *Legend in My Time* (3/71), *Careless Hands* (5/71), *Have You Heard* (11/71), and *I'm Only a Woman* (7/72).

The West–Rogers duet brought opportunities to perform in some of the largest concert halls in the United States and in other countries. Dottie also made her debut as a guest on Johnny Carson's *The Tonight Show* in the late 1970s and was featured on many other network and syndicated talk shows. In October 1979, the twosome won the Country Music Association award for Vocal Duo of the Year, an honor they also were given in 1978.

During 1979, Dottie and Kenny's LPs *Classics* and *Every Time Two Fools Collide* remained on the charts most of the year. They also had the singles hits "Anyone Who Isn't Me Tonight," "Til I Can Make It on My Own," and "All I Ever Need Is You." The whirlwind success of this duet work seemed to have had a depressing impact on her UA solo releases for a time. But after she changed producers (from Larry Butler to Brett Maher and Randy Goodrum) that situation improved. First fruits of that collaboration included the LP *Special Delivery* and the 1980 top-10 single "A Lesson in Leavin'." Other solo singles hits in 1980 and 1981 included "You Pick Me Up (and Put Me Down)," "Leavin's for Unbelievers," and "Are You Happy Baby?," which reached number one in 1981. Also on upper-chart levels in 1981 was her solo album *Wild West*.

During 1980, West's marriage to Byron Metcalf had broken up. She told *Country Style* writer Jim Albrecht (May 1981), "Byron was an alcoholic. And I had lived with this. But the harder our schedule became, the worse it was for him. And that really was the problem.

"This is the first time I've said this, but I don't think he'd mind because since then he talks about it. He went to the hospital and has not had a drink since. But it was too late for our relationship. . . ."

Her schedule, of course, was backbreaking. In 1980 she made personal appearances totaling 320 shows, according to her management firm, Kragen & Company, with no letup in 1981. Besides TV appearances with such artists as Kenny Rogers, Mel Tillis, Larry Gatlin, Eddie Rabbitt, and the Oak Ridge Boys, and hundreds of concerts, she also made most of the major talk shows and hosted her own cable-TV special.

WEST, HEDY: *Singer, banjoist. Born Cartersville, Georgia, April 6, 1938.*

A singer of many of the most traditional folk songs, Hedy West heard her first folk music in her mother's arms in the hill country of western Georgia. Her grandmother played the banjo and sang classic ballads or nonsense songs to the children, and her father, Don West, was one of the best known poets of the South. Other friends and relatives also came to the West home to sing and play, including her Uncle Gus, who was one of the most popular fiddlers of the region.

Hedy's parents wanted her to learn music and started her on piano lessons when she was only four. Her interest in music continued to increase as she got older, veering more and more toward the folk idiom. In high school, she taught herself to play the banjo, following her grandmother's example. Soon she was singing some of the old songs at local gatherings. Word of her ability spread beyond Cartersville and she was asked to appear at other folk-music events. In 1956, seventeen-year-old Hedy won hearty applause for her singing in a festival at Boone, North Carolina. Two years later, her reputation was further increased when she won first prize in a folk song contest in Nashville, Tennessee.

After this, her career began to move into high gear. She traveled north to play in coffee houses in Chicago and New York. This led to an invitation to appear in a hootenanny run by *Sing Out!* magazine at Carnegie Hall. Pete Seeger was impressed with her ability and asked her to join him in a two-week engagement at the Village Gate in New York.

Some of her renditions were then included in a Vanguard LP called *New Folks.* Soon after, she was featured on her own LP, *Hedy West.*

By the mid-1960s, West had sung at most major festivals in the United States and given recitals across the country. Audiences were enthralled with her performances of such songs as "Mister Froggie," "Single Girl," "The Wife of Usher's Well," "Lord Thomas and Fair Elender," "Little Old Man," "Cotton Mill Girl," "Pan of Biscuits," and "The Brown Girl."

In addition to singing, Hedy wrote words and music to classical material and composed her own songs. Her output included music to go with her father's poems, "Anger to the Land." The 1963 country hit by Bobby Bare, "500 Miles Away from Home," is credited to West, Bare, and Charlie Williams.

At the end of the 1960s Hedy moved to London and performed widely in Europe. At the end of the 1970s, only one album of her work was generally available in the United States, the excellent *Old Times and Hard Times* LP on the Folk-Legacy label.

WHIPPLE, STERLING: *Singer, guitarist, songwriter. Born Eugene, Oregon, 1948.*

Although originally considered a regional form of music, country & western expanded its audience over the decades until its fans and artists encompassed every corner of the United States and, indeed, much of the world. The Northwest made its contributions to the field's progress with such talents as Danny O'Keefe and Sterling Whipple, both of whom wrote songs that rose to number one on country charts in the 1970s.

Whipple grew up in the Columbia River section of Oregon in a middle-class family. His father was a public-interest lawyer, someone who preferred to take cases of the underprivileged, such as blacks and Indians, years before the ferment of the civil rights movement made such an effort fashionable. In college, Sterling's ambition was to follow his father into the law, although he had always had strong musical interests.

Sterling's parents encouraged his interest, buying him his first guitar when he was seven. He fooled around with it over the years and eventually could play reasonably well, though his bent by the time he reached his teens was toward rock rather than country. He played with some local groups during high school and later formed a rock band with some friends during his college years. A major in political science and psychology, he helped defray his college costs by performing; his group played in a union labor hall for $600 a week. They tended to play the chart hits of the day, but Whipple started adding some originals of his own to their repertoire.

He continued to work with the band after entering law school. But once he began taking legal courses, the idea of making law his lifetime work paled. He quit after a year. As he told an inverviewer, "A year after I left school, I was still having nightmares about going to classes and not being prepared."

Now music seemed his main occupation. He and his group put together some demo tapes in hopes of getting a recording contract. Country songwriter-performer Mickey Newbury came across them and was impressed with Whipple's writing. He suggested that Sterling could have a good future as a country writer if he moved to Nashville. Sterling, though, preferred to change the band's style to a pop or soft rock format so they could work as a lounge group while his wife, Linda, finished her last two years of college.

That worked for a while, but by the early summer of 1974, Whipple found himself essentially out of work. In June, he figured he might as well give Nashville a try. Soon after, he got a writing contract from Tree International Publishing, where his initial efforts included a collaboration with established writer Glen Martin. As time went on, Whipple branched off into doing both words and music himself. His name started showing up in the credits for chart-making singles. At the end of 1975, he hit the mark with a vengeance when Kenny Starr released a single of Whipple's "Blind Man in the Bleachers." The song rose to number one on the country lists

and established Sterling as a major new creative force in country music.

Inspiration for the song, he told an interviewer, began in church. "I was sitting in church one Sunday morning and the preacher told a true story about a football team in the Northeast. I took the basic elements of the story and dramatized them, then I put my own emotions and experiences into the song." The main theme of the song was about a blind man who couldn't see his son play football. For Whipple, the lyrics reflected sadness about the death of his father before Sterling achieved prominence in the music field. His father had worried about his son's choice of career and death had prevented him from seeing his success.

Before the 1970s were over, Whipple's name had appeared on the charts many more times, first as writer alone, then as writer and performer. In early 1976, Cal Smith made the charts with his "Thunderstorms" and later in the year still more well-known singers hit pay dirt with Whipple compositions. In early and midsummer, first Mac Davis, then Gary Stewart had top-20 hits with, respectively, "Forever Lovers" and "In Some Room Above the Street." During that time, Dickey Lee gained the top-40 with "Makin' Love Don't Always Make Love Grow." In mid-1977, Bobby Borchers made the top 10 with Sterling's "Cheap Perfume and Candlelight" and in the fall Tom Bresh placed "That Old Cold Shoulder" on the charts. In mid-1978, Tommy Overstreet made top-chart levels with "Better Me" and Kenny Starr placed "Slow Drivin' " on the lower rungs. In November 1978, Mel Tillis had a major hit, thanks to Sterling's "Ain't No California," in the top 10 many weeks and as high as number four for a time.

In 1978, Whipple signed a recording pact with Warner Brothers Records. His debut single rose to number twenty-three on the country lists. Late in the year he had another chart single, "Then You'll Remember," which reached number twenty-five in December.

Commenting on his new role, he said, "I

want to create a new outlet for the songs I write. My songs are not easy to learn and, in fact, many are too wordy for mainstream producers to record with their artists. Plus I am interested in exposing some of my songs myself because I think people . . . want to know what a songwriter is really feeling and thinking."

WHITE, JOSH, JR.: *Singer, guitarist, songwriter, actor. Born New York, New York, early 1940s.*

Even today, when folk music has been relegated to what seems like permanent minority status, the name Josh White rings a bell with many people who are more attuned to rock and pop. But there are two Josh Whites—Senior, who died in 1967, and Junior, still very much an active part of the folk scene in the 1980s. In performance, he reflected many of the virtues of his father and, in some ways, even exceeded him in vocal ability and creativity, particularly as compared to Josh Senior in his declining years. However, the younger White wasn't able to achieve the stardom he seemed capable of in an era dominated by other music forms.

The younger White, as might be expected, got his original inspiration from watching his illustrious father perform. In fact, when he was only four, in the 1940s, he was allowed to join his father on stage one night. His parents encouraged him, sending him to a children's acting school in New York for some years.

Even as he was taking those lessons, he was already gaining professional credits on Broadway. In 1949, he was a member of the cast of *How Long Till Summer?*, for which he received an award for Best Child Actor. Three years later he was back on Broadway again in *The Man* and followed that with a role in *Touchstone* in 1953. In 1957, he performed in an off-Broadway show, *Take a Giant Step*, and two years later he was on the Great White Way once more in *Only in America*. His appearance in *The Long Dream* in 1960 essentially culminated that phase of his career, though he did take some acting parts in other live shows from time to time.

During the 1950s and 1960s, White varied his acting work with singing engagements, sometimes working with his father. A frequent guest on TV shows over the years, from the 1950s through the 1970s he appeared on such national telecasts as *Mike Douglas, Joey Bishop, Donald O'Connor, Arthur Godfrey's Talent Scouts, The Today Show, Mike Wallace, Hootenanny, Barbara McNair, Della Reese Show,* and many more. From 1950 to 1963, he also spent a good part of his time acting on dramatic programs for TV, including roles on *Kraft Theater, Ship Ahoy, Studio One, Harlem Detective, Armstrong Circle Theater,* and *Ben Jarod.* In 1967, he wrote the music for the documentary, *The Freedom Train,* for junior and senior high school use, which was produced by Spoken Arts. His contributions to that film included acting and singing.

During the years after his father's death, Josh paid homage by presenting his concerts in the same fashion made famous by the elder artist. He almost always appeared alone, sitting on a straight-back chair, and accompanying himself on acoustic guitar. His program included a range of material, from traditional folk songs to musical theater numbers and some original compositions. In the mid-1970s concerts, for instance, his program included songs by such diverse writers as Mickey Newbury, Cole Porter ("Miss Otis Regrets"), Bobby Darin ("I've Been Down So Long"), and Gordon Lightfoot. Among the original songs he presented were numbers like "Think About Me, Think About You," a lighthearted song with a little rock 'n' roll flavoring.

During the 1960s and 1970s, White performed in clubs all over the United States including the Bitter End in New York City, Troubadour in Los Angeles, Playboy Club in Chicago, The Cellar Door in Washington, D.C., and Passim's in Boston. His New York appearances included programs at Madison Square Garden, Lincoln Center, and Town Hall. He also made several trips to Europe and, in addition to his live concerts, was a guest many times on Swedish TV and the BBC and Granada networks in England. He gave many of his concerts in those years on college campuses, averaging about 150 college appearances a year.

In the mid-1970s, he cut back on touring because he wanted to spend more time with his growing children in his upstate New York home. In 1978, Josh decided it was time to increase his activities once more. One move was a new recording contract with Vanguard that resulted in the mid-1978 release *Josh White, Jr.* A single from the LP, "Marco Polo," received considerable airplay on FM stations that summer. In support of the album, he also went on a five-week, eleven-country tour of Europe later in the year.

During 1978 and 1979, White appeared at major folk festivals in Philadelphia, Vancouver, Canada, and at the Bread and Roses Festival in San Francisco. His TV work included guesting an Irish Rovers' TV special in Canada that won a Canadian Emmy Award. He also was on stage once again at venues on the East and West Coasts.

WHITE, JOSH, SR.: *Singer, guitarist, songwriter. Born Greenville, South Carolina, February 11, 1908; died Manhasset, New York, September 5, 1969.*

A lighted cigarette placed behind one ear, one foot resting on a chair while he sang and played, Josh White personified the magic of folk music for decades. He had become such a trademark of the idiom by the 1930s that future audiences all over the world could visualize his stance while listening to that vibrant voice pour forth blues, ballads, gospel, and work songs from the hundreds of recordings he made during his long career. Even today, long after his death, those often matchless performances still remind millions of people of his importance to folk music in particular and every phase of popular music as well.

Like many black artists over the years, Joshua Daniel White's roots were in religious music. His father was a Baptist minister in South Carolina, and the gospels and hymns he often heard at the church meetings were a regular part of his life. Later he was to break from his religious

background, and from his home, where his parents had separated.

He moved into the "entertaining" field as an assistant to one of the blind Negro minstrels who made a precarious living singing on street corners and in small clubs, mostly in the South and Midwest. For ten years he served as the "eyes" of such artists as Blind Lemon Jefferson, Willie Johnson, John Henry Arnold, and Joel Taggart. It was a legendary circle, whose teachings helped lay the groundwork for the apprentice Josh's equally brilliant contributions to folk music history. Besides committing the many different songs each sang to his memory, Josh also blended elements of their different guitar styles to form his own unique instrumental technique. As a teenager, he already was beginning to gain a major reputation among his music peers, if not in the broad population.

In the late 1920s, his career was abruptly threatened when an accident caused paralysis in one hand. His voice was still as good as ever, though, and he managed to find enough work to survive. He gravitated to New York, where he was to become almost a fixture on the folk scene for the rest of his life. His initial breakthrough was gaining the role of Blind Lemon Jefferson in the play *John Henry,* starring Paul Robeson.

By then he already had signed with a major record company. For his first session, he recorded twenty-eight songs for Columbia in Chicago. Between the mid-1930s and the end of the 1960s, he recorded material released on dozens of albums for a wide range of companies, including Decca, Mercury, London, Columbia, Folkways, Stinson, Period, and ABC Paramount. He also recorded many songs for the Archive of American Folk Song of the Library of Congress. Most of the songs he sang were traditional folk music, including a wide variety of blues, spirituals, and work songs. Besides providing his own arrangements and interpretations of these folk songs, he contributed original material to some or occasionally wrote new songs of his own. Examples of material he wrote in whole or part are "The Gray Goose," "I Had a Woman," and "Ball and Chain Blues."

White's strength of character and determination to surmount adversity enabled him to overcome the injury to his arm. Over a five-year period from the late 1920s through the early 1930s he continued to exercise his arm and fingers day after day and year after year until he finally regained the ability to play guitar. Not only did he restore mobility to his hand, he toiled over his playing skills until he was once more a first-rate guitarist. By the mid-1930s, he was accompanying himself successfully on concert tours of college campuses and clubs around the country. As his fame grew, he expanded it still further with appearances on network radio, including sessions with a group called the Southernaires on NBC.

At the start of the 1940s, White's name was well known throughout the United States and in many other countries around the world. During 1941–42, he gave many programs with singer Libby Holman. He had a solo show at the Cafe Society Uptown club in New York that ran for three years in the 1940s, and was asked by President Franklin Delano Roosevelt to give a special concert at the White House. In 1941, he was asked to make a good-will tour of Mexico for the United States with the Golden Gate Quartet. At other times in the 1940s, he was featured at such other New York clubs as the Village Vanguard and Cafe Society Downtown. When he wasn't booked into New York venues, he was welcomed on the club and concert circuit in major cities all over the land. A guest on many radio shows, in 1944 he had his own fifteen-minute program on station WNEW in New York. In the mid-1940s, he also made a number of broadcasts for the Office of War Information.

The same pattern continued into the 1950s and 1960s. Josh was featured in clubs and folk festivals in the United States and overseas, where his repertoire often included such favorites as "Ballad of John Henry," "Jim Crow Train," and "Strange Fruit." He performed a number of times at the annual Newport Folk Festival over those decades. TV also showcased his talents at times: a guest on many network programs, he was particularly in demand for the folk-oriented shows of the late 1950s and early 1960s. Among his credits were several spots on the 1963–64 ABC-TV *Hootenanny* presentation.

Although Josh White recorded for many record labels, his longest association was with Elektra. Among his albums on that label were such late 1950s releases as *Josh at Midnight, Josh,* and *Chain Gang Songs* (issued in April 1959). His 1960s LPs on Elektra included *Spiritual and Blues* (2/61), *House I Live In* (7/61), *Empty Bed Blues* (2/62), *Live* (4/62), a two-record *Best of Josh White* set, and the *25th Anniversary Album.* The entire first side of the last named constituted a musical narrative prepared by Josh. Besides that, he presented many of his familiar renditions, including "Black Girl," "Free and Equal Blues," "Live the Life," "Sam Hill," "Where Were You Baby," "Delia's Gone," "Run, Momma, Run," and "You Don't Know My Mind."

His other releases included a number of albums on Mercury, such as *Josh White with Josh, Jr.,* and *Beverly* (3/62), *Beginnings, Volume 1* (5/63) and *Volume 2* (1/64). His Stinson LPs included *Josh White Sings* and *Josh White Sings the Blues.* A Period release teamed him with another famous blues musician—*Josh White and Bill Broonzy*—and Decca released the LP *Josh White* in April 1958. Other albums were *The Josh White Story, Volumes 1 and 2* and *Josh White Live* (4/62) on ABC Paramount; *Josh White Program* on London; and *Josh White* on Archive of Folk Music (issued 3/67). The songs presented on *The Josh White Story* included "Boll Weevil," "Frankie and Johnny," "House of the Rising Sun," "Hard Time Blues," "Good Morning Blues," "The Gray Goose," "Trouble in Mind," "Sometimes I Feel like a Motherless Child," "Red River," "I Has a Woman," "Strange Fruit," and "Two Little Fishes and Five Loaves of Bread." The London album included such numbers as "Call Me Darling," "Like a Natural Man," "The Lass with the Delicate Air," "Foggy,

Muddy Waters

Muddy Waters

Doc Watson

Vanguard/Dan Seeger

Jerry Jeff Walker

Bob Wills

Jesse Winchester

Dottie West

Hank Williams, Jr.

Tammy Wynette

Tammy Wynette and George Jones

Foggy Dew," "Waltzing Matilda," and "He Never Said a Mumbling Word."

White was in ill health the last few years of his life and died in a Manhasset hospital the afternoon of September 5, 1969 while undergoing heart surgery. After his death, the commemorative album *In Memoriam* was released on Tradition Records.

WHITMAN, SLIM: *Singer, guitarist, songwriter. Born Tampa, Florida, January 20, 1924.*

Examining the biographies of country-music stars, one can see in more than a few cases that sports' loss was music's gain. In the case of Slim Whitman, during his teenage and young adult years, he focused on baseball except during World War II, when he enlisted in the Navy and learned to play guitar from his shipmates. He had been a promising pitcher, with good hitting capability.

Otis Dewey Whitman, Jr., born and raised in Tampa, Florida, with four brothers and sisters, was a star pitcher on his high school baseball team. After his discharge from the Navy in 1945, he returned to baseball and signed a contract in 1946 with the Plant City Berries of the Orange Belt League. His pitching record the following year was a cool 11–1 and his hitting a hot .360. To bring in extra income, he turned to performing music in local clubs.

The exposure led to the chance to sing on station WDAE in Tampa in 1948. As his reputation grew with country fans, he expanded his efforts in the field. In 1949, he made a major step forward when he got a recording contract with RCA Victor through the recommendation of Col. Thomas A. Parker who, at that time, was managing the career of Eddy Arnold. One of his first songs for the label, "Casting My Lasso to the Sky," won some national attention. He began to get more impressive performing credits, including a 1949 appearance on a Mutual network show with The Light Crust Doughboys. Soon after, he moved to Shreveport to become a regular on the KWKH *Louisiana Hayride*. The show was broadcast over many other stations, helping to greatly increase his following among U.S. country fans.

Still, Slim's recordings on RCA didn't make much headway on the bestseller lists. In 1952, he signed with a West Coast independent, Imperial Records, a move that soon paid big dividends. His first year on the label, he achieved a top-10 hit with the single "Keep It a Secret," the first of many such successes in the 1950s and 1960s. In 1953, he had a top-10 hit with "North Wind" and in 1954 he had two, "Secret Love" and "Rose Marie." The last two, country versions of, respectively, a pop song and a musical comedy standard, were the beginning of a trend that lasted the rest of his career. Some other chart makers between the early 1950s and the mid-1960s were "Love Song of the Waterfall," "The Bandera Waltz," "Amateur in Love," "China Doll," and "Indian Love Call." In 1965, he had the top-10 single "More than Yesterday" and in 1968 equaled that with the single "Rainbows Are Back in Style."

Many of those recordings rose to upper-chart levels throughout Europe, as well as in Canada, Japan, Australia, Taiwan, and South Africa. This was underscored by strong audience response to his concerts in those areas in the 1960s and 1970s. In fact, in the 1970s, his popularity in some overseas nations probably exceeded that in his homeland. When Slim's chart-making releases in the United States were sparse, he still could make strong inroads on hit lists abroad. Thus, in a major English music poll, he was voted the number-one international star for four different years in the 1970s.

From the mid-1950s into the 1970s, Whitman made dozens of albums for Imperial Records and for successor labels (Imperial was acquired by Liberty, which later became part of United Artists.) Among these were the following (on Imperial unless otherwise noted): *Slim Whitman Favorites* (two discs, mid-1950s); *Slim Whitman Sings* (issued 11/58); *My Best to You* (10/59); *Million Record Hits; Just Call Me Lonesome; Once in a Lifetime; Annie Laurie; Forever; Slim Whitman; Songs of the Old Waterwheel; I'll Never Stop Loving You; Cool Water; Heart Songs & Love Songs; I'm a Lonely Wanderer; Yodeling; Irish Songs* (all early

1960s); *All Time Favorites* (4/64); *Country Songs/City Hits* (10/64); *God's Hand in Mine; Love Song of the Waterfall* (5/65); *Reminiscing* (11/65); *More than Yesterday* (4/66); *Birmingham Jail* (Camden Records, 6/66); *Unchain Your Heart* (Sun Records, 6/66); *Travelin' Man* (10/66); *Time for Love* (1/67); *15th Anniversary* (4/67); *Lonesome Heart* (Sun, 7/67); and *Memories* (1/68).

Late 1960s and early 1970s LPs included *Million Sellers* (Liberty Records); *Slim!* (Liberty); *Ramblin' Rose* (Sun); *Slim Whitman* (Sun, 12/69); *Great Country* (Sun); *Tomorrow Never Comes* (United Artists Records); *Guess Who* (UA); *It's a Sin to Tell a Lie* (UA); *Best of Slim Whitman* (UA, 1972); and *Superpak* (Liberty).

During the 1970s, Whitman had several charted singles on the UA label, including "It's All in the Game" in the spring of 1974. At the start of the 1980s, he had a new album out titled *All My Best*, which included his versions of such old standards as "Una Paloma Blanco," "Vaya con Dios," "Rose Marie," "Red River Valley," and "Have I Told You Lately That I Love You." That album was a "TV package," marketed by means of TV commercials rather than sold in record stores. The results were phenomenal; by the fall of 1980 *All My Best* had sold an amazing 2 million copies. That kind of impact didn't go unnoticed by U.S. record firm executives. When Slim came to give a performance at the Cleveland Richfield Coliseum, Steve Popovich, president of Cleveland International Records, met with him and started discussions leading to Whitman's signing with the firm. He arranged for distribution through Epic Records, and in the fall Slim's debut single on Epic/Cleveland was issued. In a short time, "When" was in upper-chart levels. Soon after, his initial Epic/Cleveland LP, *Songs I Love to Sing*, was on record store racks. In the spring of 1981, his single "I Remember You" was on the country charts and in August 1981, his second Epic/Cleveland LP, *Mr. Songman*, was issued.

At that time, Epic pointed out, Slim's credits included over fifty albums recorded on various labels with combined sales of more than 50 million worldwide. In the late 1970s, his overseas highlights included having a single of "Rose Marie" number one on British pop charts for eleven consecutive weeks, something even the Beatles had never accomplished; the same single at the start of the 1980s still held the Australian record for all-time best-selling 45 rpm disc. His career to then had provided over thirty top-50 singles and nineteen gold-record level releases.

As of 1982, Whitman and his wife, Jerry, lived in Middleberg, Florida. On the road for his many concerts worldwide, he was backed by a six-piece band fronted by his twenty-three-year-old son, Byron.

WILBURN, TEDDY AND DOYLE (WILBURN BROTHERS): *Vocal duo, guitarists, songwriters, music publishers. Both born Thayer, Missouri: Virgil Doyle, July 7, 1930; Thurman Theodore "Teddy," November 30, 1931.*

Many groups or duos in the music field go under the name of "brothers" without the slightest relationship. The Wilburns, though, are authentically titled. In fact, until 1951, the act was known as the Wilburn Family and included two older brothers, Leslie (born Thayer, Missouri, October 13, 1925) and Lester (born Thayer, Missouri, May 19, 1924). Also part of the Wilburn family group was Vinita Geraldine Wilburn, born Thayer, Missouri, June 5, 1927.

The Wilburns grew up in rural Missouri, where the boys were performers at very early ages. In 1938, they began by singing on street corners in Thayer. In a short time, they progressed to more professional performances, appearing in shows in many parts of Missouri, then extending their activities to neighboring states. Their audience rapport was excellent, and the older artists with whom they appeared soon spread the word that the Wilburns were rising stars.

In 1941, the Wilburn Family was asked to join the *Grand Ole Opry*. The boys quickly attracted a national following in the next few years. World War II interfered with their careers, but afterward, they once more starred on the *Opry*. In 1948, the group moved to Shreveport for a featured spot on the KWKH *Louisiana Hayride*. They remained until 1951, when the act was once more broken up, this time by the Korean War.

When the act resumed in 1953, it consisted of Teddy (Thurman Theodore) and Doyle (Virgil Doyle). They returned to the *Opry* and remained regular cast members. Through the mid-1950s, they toured the country and turned out many records that chalked up respectable sales. Their lists of credits during this period included first place in the *Arthur Godfrey's Talent Scouts* TV show. In 1956, they provided Decca Records with a top-10 hit, *Go Away with Me.* From then on, Wilburn Brothers songs were on the bestseller lists regularly. As their reputation increased, the brothers diversified into other parts of the music business. In the late 1950s, all four brothers helped form a new music publishing firm, Sure-Fire Music. The music turned out by the company included a number of songs written by the Wilburns. The brothers had three major hits in 1959, "A Woman's Intuition," "Somebody's Back in Town," and "Which One Is to Blame," the first two of which bore the Sure-Fire imprint.

The 1960s proved even more successful for the brothers than earlier decades. In 1962, they had one of the top hits in the country, "Trouble's Back in Town." The following year, they had many hits, including two in the top 10, "Roll Muddy River" and "Tell Her So." Their mid-1960s top-10 score included "It's Another World" (1965) and "Someone Before Me" (1966). Decca Records recognized their worth, signing them to a life contract in the mid-1960s.

Some of their other recordings during the 1950s and 1960s were "Knoxville Girl," "I Can't Keep Away from You," "Mister Love," "Look Around," "Deep Elem Blues," "Cry, Cry Darling," "Always Alone," "You Will Again," and "I'll Sail My Ship Alone." The brothers' songwriting activity included "That's When I Miss You," "I Know You Don't Love Me Anymore," "Need Someone," and "Much Too Often."

During the 1960s, the men toured all fifty states. They starred on Australian TV for thirty-nine weeks as part of the Roy Acuff *Open House* show. They were also featured on guest spots on *American Bandstand* and *Jamboree U.S.A.* They added to their business enterprises by establishing the Wil-Helm Talent Agency. The agency, formed in conjunction with country artist Smiley Wilson, became one of Nashville's top booking firms. By the mid-1960s, it represented such stars as Loretta Lynn, Jay Lee Webb, the Osborne Brothers, Harold Morrison, Jean Shepard, Martha Carson, Slim Whitman, and Charlie Louvin.

The Wilburn Brothers turned out many successful LPs during the 1950s and 1960s. These included *Carefree Moments* on Vocalion (1962) and several dozen albums on Decca. Among the latter were *Wilburn Brothers; Wilburn Brothers Sing Folk Songs; Big Heartbreak; Take Up the Cross; Side by Side* (1959); *Sing, Lovin' in God's Country* (1961); *City Limits* (1962); *Trouble Back in Town* (1963); *Never Alone* (1964); *Country Gold* (1965); and *Two for the Show* (1967).

The Brothers remained on Decca and its successor, MCA Records through the mid-1970s. At the start of the 1980s, they remained active on the concert circuit and still were *Grand Ole Opry* cast members.

WILLIAMS, DON: *Singer, guitarist, songwriter. Born Floydada, Texas, May 27, 1939.*

When Don Williams accepted his award for the Country Music Association's Male Vocalist of the Year in October 1978, he wore what he usually wears—faded blue jeans, denim jacket, and a worn-out hat that was designed for him when he appeared in the Burt Reynolds movie *W.W. and the Dixie Dancekings.* He was being honored for his music, which sounds as simple and relaxed as the way he dresses.

The son of a mechanic, Don's family traveled frequently when he was young. His mother taught him to play guitar at the age of twelve. He listened mostly to country music but also enjoyed listening to Elvis Presley, Chuck Berry, and other early rock figures. After awhile, his family settled in Corpus Christi, Texas, where Don went to high school.

After graduating from high school, Don spent two years in the Army. During this time he also met and married his wife, Joy. After he left the Army, he held odd jobs, such as driving a bread truck and working in the oil fields of Texas. He worked on music evenings with his friend Lofton Kline and they began singing at local bars. They called themselves the Strangers Two. In 1964 they met Susan Taylor when she was on the same bill with them at a college dance. She joined forces with Kline and Williams and they became known as the Pozo Seco Singers. They had a top-10 national hit in 1965 with their recording "Time." They had a few minor hits after that and eventually wound up playing in lounges and rowdy dance halls, which Williams grew to detest. The group disbanded in 1971.

His experience with that group was the major cause for his intense dislike of promotion campaigns that invaded his privacy and the basis of his newfound desire to maintain creative independence. He told Jim Jerome for a *Playboy* article (March, 1978), "It was real canned—the song order, what I said, how the others reacted. It just cut the heart out of it for me. I swore I'd never paint myself into that corner again."

After Pozo Seco disbanded, Williams decided to quit the music business and opened a furniture store with his father-in-law. But by the next year, he was longing to get back to making music. He went to Nashville, primarily to become a writer. He looked up some of the contacts he had made while he was a Pozo Seco singer and connected with Allen Reynolds of the Jack Clement organization, which included JMI Records and Jack Music Publishing. Don was hired by them to try to get other artists to record his songs and other songs from the publishing company's catalogue. Some of his compositions were recorded, but they were different enough for that time to cause many artists to think twice about recording them.

However, Williams believed strongly in his songs, and he decided to record them himself. With Allen Reynolds producing, he turned out *Don Williams, Volume One* on the JMI label. The album included the now-classic hits "Amanda" and "In the Shelter of Your Eyes," the latter on country charts in 1972. At that time, most Nashville songs featured elaborate instru-

mental backings; nevertheless, Williams' gentle, subdued music caught on. Williams and Reynolds teamed up again for *Don Williams, Volume Two.*

Soon afterward, JMI Records folded, and Don signed with ABC/Dot Records and began to produce his own recordings. His first ABC album was *Don Williams, Volume Three,* on hit lists in 1974, followed in 1975 by the top-10 hit LPs *You're My Best Friend* and *Don Williams' Greatest Hits.* In 1976 and 1977, he had more album releases on top-chart levels: *Harmony, Visions,* and *Country Boy,* the last named staying on into 1979. His LP *Expressions,* issued in 1978, was his last release on ABC/Dot before that organization was absorbed by MCA Records, which remained his label as of the early 1980s. From these albums came a long string of country hit singles, many of which made number one on U.S. charts. Those include "You're My Best Friend," "Some Broken Hearts Never End," "Till the Rivers All Run Dry," "Louisiana Saturday Night," "Say It Again," "I Wouldn't Want to Live if You Didn't Love Me," "Country Boy," "She Never Knew Me," "The Ties That Bind," "Rake and Ramblin' Man," and "Tulsa Time." "Tulsa Time" (written by Danny Flowers, guitarist of Don's backup band) was named single record of the year in 1979 by the Academy of Country Music.

Although Williams' records sold very well, for a time he seemed to be more of a star in Great Britain than in the United States. In 1975, he was named both Male Country Singer of the Year and Country Performer of the Year by the Country Music Association of Great Britain, and his LP *You're My Best Friend* was named Album of the Year. In 1976, six of his albums were in the top 20 on Great Britain's year-end charts; four of his albums were in the top 5. He attracted the admiration of English rock guitarist-singer Eric Clapton, and they later shared a concert bill in Nashville.

In July 1977, Williams scored a major concert triumph when he appeared at New York's Carnegie Hall and received three standing ovations from the crowd. To reproduce the sound from his albums as closely as possible on stage, Williams used only two musicians other than himself, Danny Flowers on harmonica and guitar and David Williamson on bass. After being nominated several times for the Country Music Association's Male Vocalist of the Year Award, he finally won that honor in October 1978.

Many of Williams' hits from the mid-1970s on were by other writers, particularly Bob McDill and Wayland Holyfield. However, Don always loved to write new songs of his own. Describing his writing style, Jennifer Bolch of the *Dallas Times Herald* (May 28, 1979) noted that Williams told her he usually wrote the music first, then added the lyrics. "The music comes first, typically a flowing, gentle hummable tune with its backbone hiding in the hypnotic rhythm. Then the lyrics. 'I just sit down and fool around with the guitar, and when I get something that seems to set a mood, the words start to come,' he explained."

Much has been written about Don's quiet lifestyle. He lives on a ranch outside Nashville with his wife and two sons and does much of the ranch work himself. He is a regular Sunday churchgoer; he doesn't drink or use drugs. He is basically a quiet, unassuming family man, who doesn't go out of his way to call attention to himself.

Don's music, however, has gained plenty of attention; his style has been described by critics as "restrained, unadorned, even dignified" and "so smooth and mellow it's almost conservative." Williams himself calls his music "intensely simple," but he says, "It's the hardest music I've ever made. It seems like it would be simple but it takes more time than anything I've ever done because I try and make every sound count!"

Many observers marveled at the fact that Williams managed to gain a massive following without engaging in large scale "hype" campaigns or going in for flashy costumes or headline-catching exploits. Asked about this by Linda Luoma for *Music City News* (June 1979, p. 13), he replied, "I really don't try to make any accounting for my success except to say that I try to do what I honestly believe in—and I've never done anything because I thought I was better than other people.

"Classically speaking, I don't think I've ever wanted to talk about the same things that other country artists want to talk about in their music. I try not to be taken in by whatever the going gimmick is. The main things I've always been concerned with in my music and my songwriting, more than anything else, are people's feelings for each other, rather than triangle situations or sittin' down in a bar to drink your blues away.

"To me, country music is not a form of music that deals with things that are extremely controversial or profane or anything else that would make it a radical, extremist form of music. My idea of country music is as a family form of entertainment. I just try to make country music the way I like to hear country music."

He told Jim Jerome, "As many people know me as an artist as I can really care about. It'd be a real compliment to my music—and to writers like Bob [McDill] and Wayland [Holyfield]—if we reached a broader market. I'd be a fool to be hard-nosed and unreasonable, if it's s'posed to happen. But you can get buried in promotion and manipulation out there. Greed does strange things to people. I never want to get so filthy stinkin' rich that I become a hermit who can't go out on the street."

At any rate, Don's approach continued to pay off with best-selling singles and LPs for his new MCA label. In 1979, besides "Tulsa Time," he had such best-selling chart singles as "Lay Down Beside Me" and "It Must Be Love." His LP *Expressions* stayed on the charts in 1979 and into 1980, as did the MCA *Best of Don Williams Volume II* release. In 1980, his singles hits included "I Believe in You," "Good Ole Boys like Me," "Love Me Over Again," and "It Must Be Love." He also had two new albums on upper-chart levels, *Portrait* (issued in late 1979) and *I Believe in You.* In the spring of 1981, he had another top-10 single, "Falling Again."—I.S./A.S.

WILLIAMS, HANK, JR.: *Singer, guitarist, banjoist, songwriter, band leader (the Cheatin'*

Hearts, The Bama Band). Born Shreveport, Louisiana, May 26, 1949.

Unlike many other sons of famous fathers, Hank Williams, Jr., was immensely talented. If his name hadn't already been famous, he undoubtedly would have made it so both as performer and writer. Having to compete with the towering legend of his father presented the almost insoluble challenge of coming to terms with the benefits and limitations of his position.

Hank Jr. was born in Shreveport, where his father, already an established star on the *Louisiana Hayride*, was readying himself for the next major step—to be a featured artist on the *Grand Ole Opry*. When the child was three months old, the family moved to Nashville, where Hank Jr. grew up and attended elementary and high school. He was only three years old when his father died.

Hank Jr. showed a flair for music at an early age; he began to play guitar before he was in his teens. He also was a fine athlete, playing on such varsity teams in high school as football, basketball, boxing, and swimming. By then, however, he already was beginning to follow in his father's footsteps, with increasing exposure to country-music audiences. By the time he was fourteen, he was accompanying his mother, Audrey Williams, with her Caravan of Stars show when school was out. Record companies were showing a marked interest in this promising performer with a trademark name, but Mrs. Williams took her time in agreeing to such an alignment for the boy.

Finally, in 1964, both she and Hank Jr. felt the time was right for such a move. They moved to California and signed him with MGM Records. While he started recording his debut material, he continued his high school work with a private tutor and also enrolled in a Hollywood professional school. As expected, the emergence of a new scion of the Williams family interpreting the classic songs of his father intrigued country fans. His debut album, *Hank Williams, Jr., Sings*, issued by MGM in May 1964, started selling briskly soon after its release. In a short time, he had his

first top-10 hit with his single of his father's "Long Gone Lonesome Blues," an impressive success for a fifteen-year-old. In December 1964, his next LP came out titled *Your Cheatin' Heart*. The title song became his theme song and the name of his four-man backing band. (Later he changed his backing band's name to The Bama Band.)

Young Hank's rapport with country audiences continued to grow throughout the mid-1960s. His albums and singles continued to do well and by the late 1960s, he was giving 200 or more live shows a year, often to record-breaking crowds. Among his credits for those years were appearances on such national TV shows as *The Ed Sullivan Show*, *The Tonight Show*, *Mike Douglas*, *Shindig*, *Kraft Music Hall*, and countless fairs, rodeos, and festivals. He also was featured in several MGM films, including the 1967 *A Time to Sing*.

His album releases in the mid-1960s included a concept album combining some of his performances with those of his father (issued 6/65); *Ballads of Hills and Plains* (11/65); *Blues Is My Name* (5/66); *Shadows* (8/66); *My Own Way* (6/67); and *Best of Hank Williams, Jr.* (12/67). He scored a second top-10 singles hit in 1966 with his father's "Standing in the Shadows." Although much of his repertoire was made up of Hank Sr.'s writings, Hank Jr. also wrote original material. He received BMI Songwriter Awards for some of them; one he was awarded at sixteen made him the youngest person ever to receive the honor.

In both large and small venues, he drew huge audiences. One of the most impressive occasions occurred on May 4, 1969, when he and Johnny Cash drew a capacity crowd at Cobo Hall in Detroit. The concert gross, reported as $83,000 for tickets and $100,000 when programs and album sales were added in, was the highest ever for a country concert to that point.

In his part of the show, supported by the Cheatin' Hearts, whose lead musician was Lamar Morris, and members of his father's Drifting Cowboys, he held the stage for over an hour to wild acclaim from the audience. His program, much of which was recorded and released in October 1969 in the MGM LP *Hank Williams, Jr., Live at Cobo Hall in Detroit*, included "Detroit City," a solo on the five-string banjo of "Foggy Mountain Breakdown," "Standing in the Shadows," "Jambalaya," "I'm So Lonesome I Could Cry," "You Win Again," "Games People Play," "She Thinks I Still Care," "Darling, You Know I Wouldn't Lie," "Your Cheatin' Heart," and "I Saw the Light."

In the late 1960s and early 1970s, Hank was represented on record racks by a veritable flood of LPs. They included the MGM releases *Sunday Morning, Greatest Hits, Volume I, Greatest Hits, Volume II, Roy Orbison Way, Removing the Shadow* (with L. Johnson), *Hank Williams, Jr., All for the Love of Sunshine, I've Got a Right to Cry, Sweet Dreams* (with the Curb Congregation), *Songs of Johnny Cash,* and *11 Roses.*

He didn't lack for singles hits in the first part of the 1970s. Among his charted releases were "So Sad (To Watch Good Love Go Bad)," a duet with Lois Johnson that made the top 10 in late 1970; "Send Me Some Lovin'," another duet with Johnson in the spring of 1972; "Pride's Not Hard to Swallow," on hit lists in the fall of 1972; "The Last Love Song," top 5 in early 1974; "Rainy Night in Georgia," top 10 in early summer 1974; and "The Same Old Story," a chartmaker in mid-1975.

During the early 1970s, Hank, only in his early twenties, reevaluated his goals in life, his relationship to his father and his generation. As he wrote in his autobiography, *Living Proof* (issued by G. P. Putnam's Sons in October 1979), "I'd been singing Daddy's songs almost every night for the past fifteen or sixteen years and I thought I knew everything there was to know about it. What I'd forgotten was that knowing is not the same as feeling. I knew my father, but I had let his soul slip away from me, and a lot of other people had found it. . . ."

He also commented, "They were polarized times, and the music was (and still is) the cutting edge of the times. If you listened to country music, you were a redneck asshole, and if you listened to rock and roll, you were a hippie freak. So what happened to the Allman Brothers in Ma-

con, Georgia, was of no concern to the pickers in Nashville, Tennessee, a couple of hundred miles up the road. But it was important to me, because those Georgia boys were trying to tell me something."

Determined to modernize his musical outlook, he moved from Nashville to the small town of Cullman, Alabama. He spent time talking to the musicians and studio operators in Muscle Shoals, where much of the new blends of country and rock were being brought to recorded life. The result of that was the album *Hank Williams, Jr., and Friends,* the friends including people like Charlie Daniels, Allman alumnus Chuck Leavell, and Toy Caldwell of the Marshall Tucker Band. The album was confusing to many of the long-time Williams' family adherents, though it has since become something of a progressive country classic.

Hank was sure he was on the right path, but his efforts were suddenly interrupted by a near fatal mishap. Taking a short vacation before returning to the music wars, he went hiking in the Rockies in Montana during August 1975. While making his way at 11,000 feet, a snowfield collapsed and catapulted him down the mountain some 500 feet. He hit a boulder and, though badly injured, survived. After being rescued by helicopter, he spent long periods in the hospital and at home convalescing.

After recuperating for a long period of time, Hank began to resume his career, though his backlog of recordings was such that his name rarely was absent from hit charts very long. Thus MGM had a singles hit in early summer 1975 with one of Hank Jr.'s original compositions, "Living Proof," even as Hank was on the move to a new label. (That song provided the title for his autobiography, on which he started working in the late 1970s.)

Mike Curb, who had been president of MGM for a number of years when Williams, Jr. was on that label, had set up his own company, Curb Records, and Hank Jr. went along. He turned out a number of charted singles for the Warner/Curb organization, including "One Night Stands," on hit lists in late 1977, and "I Fought the

Law" in late summer and early fall of 1978. He also completed two LPs for Warner/Curb, *One Night Stands* (issued 4/77) and *The New South* (10/77), both reissued on Elektra/Curb in August 1981.

In 1979, the record affiliation moved laterally when Hank joined several other Curb country artists on the Elektra roster. (Elektra and Warner's both are part of Warner Communications Co.) The first result of that was his spring 1979 album on Elektra/Curb, *Family Traditions*, which included several of Hank's new compositions based on some of the incidents in his life, such as "I Just Ain't Been Able," "Paying on Time," and "I've Got Rights." The title song from the album was nominated for a Grammy for Best Country Vocal Performance, Male, for 1979 and also brought Hank a BMI Writer's Award, the first he'd received since the 1974 BMI honor for "The Last Love Song."

Hank's career took a strong upward turn after his move to Elektra. He turned out a string of fine albums that ranked among the best progressive country collections of the early 1980s. These included *Whiskey Bent and Hell Bound* (10/79); *Habits Old and New* (7/80); *Rowdy* (1/81); and *The Pressure Is On* (8/81). From his Elektra LPs came such notable singles as "To Love Somebody," "Family Tradition," "Whiskey Bent and Hell Bound" (a number-one hit), and "Women I've Never Had"—all released in 1979; "Kaw-Liga" and "Old Habits" in 1980; and the number-one 1981 hits, "Texas Women," "Dixie on My Mind," and "My Rowdy Friends." When the last named (from *The Pressure Is On*) made number one in October 1981 it marked his twenty-fifth top-10 single and sixth number-one hit. He backed those releases with a series of impressive live appearances, backed by his tour group, The Bama Band, whose members as of 1981 were Cliff Pippin on drums, Joe Hamilton on bass, Eddie Long on steel guitar, Dixie Hatfield on keyboards, Lamar Morris on lead guitar, and Wayne Turner on rhythm guitar.

WILLIAMS, HANK, SR.: *Singer, guitarist, songwriter, band leader (The Drifting Cowboys).*

Born Georgiana, Alabama, September 17, 1923; died West Virginia, January 1, 1953.

In his short, troubled lifetime, Hank Williams inspired millions with his music, though he was unable to translate his talent to an inner happiness for himself. Along the way, the creative standards he set posed a challenge that only the best efforts of talented writers and performers could come close to matching. His impact on country music has been as great as another troubadour who died too young, the original Jimmie Rodgers.

Born in the small town of Georgiana, Alabama, a rural farming area, he was the son of a railroad engineer, and his mother played the organ for services and gospel sings at the local church. She began to teach young Hiram Hank Williams gospels and hymns as soon as he could talk, and, by the time he was six, he was one of the youngest members of the church choir. On his eighth birthday, he was given a guitar as a present. Although he didn't receive guitar lessons, he picked up whatever he could from experimenting and, whenever possible, watching others play. For a while, he learned several chords from trailing after an old black street musician named Tee-Tot.

The idea of earning a living in music came to him slowly. He had an intuitive feel for melody, but for a time music to the boy was mainly something one did in church, or performed for the fun of it with family or friends. But by the time he reached his teens, he was copying some of the songs he heard on radio or records and sitting in with local groups. When he was fourteen, he organized his own band and started looking for opportunities to play at local hoedowns and other events. When he could, he went to country-music shows by established artists passing through the area. Roy Acuff recalled later that Hank was like many of those small town aspirants who often could be found hovering on a street corner with a Sears, Roebuck-type guitar, hoping to be discovered. He remembered Hank in the late 1930s as a shy, skinny, nervous boy in his mid-teens.

But young Hank wasn't ready for a step up yet. He had years to spend in run-down dance halls and honky tonks in his home state before he was to achieve stardom, although he was not without home area accomplishments. Soon after he organized his first band the group auditioned for the manager of station WSFA in Montgomery, Alabama, and came out with a job. The group, which was the initial incarnation of his Drifting Cowboys, remained as regulars on WSFA for over a decade. The first musician who was to become a charter member of the Drifting Cowboys of Williams' glory years was steel guitarist Don Helms, who joined in 1943 in Alabama and remained with Hank almost all the time until Williams' death.

Still, Hank might never have become more than a regional performer if it hadn't been for his early marriage to Audrey Williams. Strong-willed and confident of Hank's talent, she became a combination booking agent, road manager, and drum beater for her husband. Although Hank and his band still played in seedy bars and at country fairs, she was instrumental in increasing the number of those dates and extending the locations to many other states besides Alabama. Both Audrey and Hank constantly began looking for contacts and opportunities to move up in the music world. Hank already was writing some of the original songs that were to make him famous, and one goal was to link up with a publisher and, hopefully, a recording company.

The place to go was Nashville, where, in 1946, the contact with Fred Rose, cofounder with Roy Acuff of the Acuff–Rose publishing house, was finally made. With Audrey urging the exceedingly tense Hank on, he sang five songs for Rose. The songs impressed Fred, but it was hard for him to associate the quality in them with the ill-at-ease country bumpkin sort of fellow who presented them.

Rose claimed throughout his life that he decided on a test, telling Hank to go into another room and "Write some kind of a song right here on the spot as proof!" Fifteen minutes later, according to Rose, Williams came back with "Mansion on the Hill," still a classic song that is often rerecorded not only by country but by pop

artists like John Denver and Michael Murphey. Williams was signed by Acuff–Rose and, in the next half a decade, became the firm's most important writer. Not only did the company publish Hank's material, Rose collaborated with Williams on some of his later efforts.

The next important step in establishing Williams' credentials was a record contract. In 1947, this fell into place when veteran music executive Frank Walker signed him for the newly established MGM Records label. In August 1948, Hank took another step forward when he became a regular on the KWKH *Louisiana Hayride* in Shreveport, for many years second only to the *Grand Ole Opry* for country variety show honors. It was during this period that his son Hank Williams, Jr., was born (in May 1949). Hank and the Drifting Cowboys began to make their mark rapidly. A short time after joining the *Hayride*, they had their first disc on country hit lists, "Move It on Over." People began to talk about some of the other remarkable new songs Hank was singing and officials of the *Grand Ole Opry* started to take notice. As more of Hank's singles showed up on country charts the first part of 1949, the *Opry* decided he should be asked to join. He accepted joyfully and moved his band and family to Nashville. (He made his *Opry* debut on June 11, 1949.) From then on, Williams dominated the country-music field with half a dozen or more hit records every year. By the early 1950s, his genius was becoming apparent to the pop music field in general, and renditions of some of his songs by pop artists were selling in the millions throughout the world.

His successes in 1949 included the number-one-rated "Love Sick Blues." Other top-10 songs that year included his compositions "Mind Your Own Business" and "You're Gonna Change," plus "My Bucket's Got a Hole in It," and "Wedding Bells." All four of his gold records for 1950 were his own songs, "I Just Don't Like This Kind of Livin'," "Long Gone Lonesome Blues," "Moaning the Blues," and "Why Don't You Love Me?" Both "Long Gone Lonesome Blues" and "Why Don't You Love Me?" reached number one on country charts. The same was true of his seven top-10 hits of 1951, "Baby, We're Really in Love," "Crazy Heart," "Dear John," "Hey, Good Lookin'," "Howlin' at the Moon," "I Can't Help It," and "Cold, Cold Heart." During the year, Tony Bennett's version of "Cold, Cold Heart" became a multimillion-selling hit, the first indication that Hank was more than "just" a country star.

Williams scored in 1952 with such songs as the number-one hit "I'll Never Get Out of This World Alive"—all too immediately prophetic; his all-time standard composition "Jambalaya," "Half as Much"; "Honky Tonk Blues"; and "Settin' the Woods on Fire." Although he died at the start of 1953, his records continued to dominate the singles charts that year with titles like "Kaw-Liga," "I Won't Be Home No More," "Weary Blues from Waitin'," and "Your Cheatin' Heart" (all written or co-written by him) and a number-one hit of a Rose-Heath song, "Take These Chains from My Heart." Besides the top-10 hits listed above, Hank recorded and/or wrote dozens of other songs of equal quality that made lower-chart levels or provided major hits in later years for other artists.

Even as his reputation as a writer and recording artist soared, Williams' life was unraveling. The seeds of destruction already had been sown before he made the big time. He had been drinking steadily as a teenager and was an alcoholic before he was out of his teens. As the years went by and the pressures mounted, he tried other crutches, working his way through various pills until, at the end, he was as much a drug addict as an alcoholic. The victim of many phobias, including fear of the dark, he also became increasingly jealous and suspicious of his wife and friends. His life with Audrey became a series of fights, recriminations, and reconciliations. Things finally reached a breaking point, however, and they separated and divorced in the early 1950s.

His inner turmoil spilled over into his performing work. Increasingly undependable, he would show up for concerts in a drugged state, often incoherent, and sometimes he would fail to show up at all. Buck

Moon, writing in the *Rocky Mountain Musical Express,* recounted talking to people who had seen such appearances in the latter stages of Williams' career. One said, "Up to a point, liquor and pills just made him sing better and better. Then, all of a sudden, he'd just cave in. Sometimes he'd get real mean. You never knew which way he was going to go."

Another stated, "Oh, I don't think he was so much a hateful guy inside. It was more like he would be burned . . . or burned out as they call it. Blind crazy drunk and nothin' mattered."

His relationship with the *Opry* naturally disintegrated. After several warnings, he was suspended, a move that his son and his legion of fans still consider uncalled for. It was an event Hank felt deeply, though whether his staying on the *Opry* would have materially changed his downhill slide is doubtful.

Williams continued to attempt to keep going. He made some sincere efforts at rehabilitation, but instead of going to medical or psychiatric experts, he consulted several people considered "quacks." Some of the treatments he was given probably contributed to the physical decline that resulted in his death.

In September 1952, he married again, this time to a nineteen-year-old named Billie Jean Jones, who later wrote a biography of him. The marriage took place on an auditorium stage and people paid fifty cents apiece to watch the ceremony. Before and after, Hank kept on performing wherever he could, though without his band. The Drifting Cowboys declined to go back on the road with Williams because of the growing problems in dealing with him the last half-year of his life. He was sleeping in the back seat of a Cadillac driving through West Virginia during a series of one-night stands when he died on New Year's Day of 1953.

As often happens, he was honored more in his passing than in his lifetime. To a great extent, the true measure of his greatness didn't begin to appear until after his death. Members of the Drifting Cowboys note that while they were doing all those memorable songs with Hank they had little awareness that something unusual was taking place. Hank himself probably didn't think of his achievements as anything representing that much of a departure from the general country field. One writer commented, "Hank Williams was never quite aware of the true measure of his contribution. His life, like those of his fellow country-music performers of his own time and of today, was that of an itinerant musician, traveling the tank towns with his band, returning to Nashville long enough to make a new recording and hitting the road again."

In six years, he managed to compress what would have been a lifelong achievement for others. He completed enough recordings for a sizable number of new releases after his death and his overall catalogue has been packaged and repackaged year after year since then. Some have been reworked with the addition of whole orchestras as background in some cases or in electronically achieved duets with son Hank, Jr., who hardly knew his father.

New LPs of his work were constantly coming out in the 1950s, 1960s, 1970s, and 1980s. Among the MGM LPs were *Honky Tonkin* (issued in the 1950s); *Lonesome Sound* (3/60); *Wait for the Light to Shine* (10/60); *Greatest Hits* (2/61); *Hank Williams' Spirit* (8/61); *On Stage* (3/62); *Greatest Hits, Vol. 2* (7/62); *Beyond the Sunset* (6/63); *Very Best* (11/63); *Greatest Hits, Vol. 3* (3/64); *Very Best, Vol. 2* (7/64); *Lost Highway* (10/64); *Hank Williams' Story* (four discs, 1964); *Kaw-Liga* (7/65); *Hank Williams* (Metro, 2/65); *Mr. & Mrs. Metro* (2/66); *Movin' On* (8/66); *Legend Lives Anew* (9/66); *Again, with Hank Williams, Jr.* (11/66); *More Hank Williams,* with strings (2/67); *Immortal Hank Williams* (Metro, 6/67); *I Won't Be Home No More* (9/67); *Essential Hank Williams* (9/69); *Life to Legend* (early 1970s); *24 Greatest Hits* (early 1970s). Others included *Unforgettable; Wanderin' Around; First, Last & Always; Hank Williams; Hank Williams, Vol. 2; I Saw the Light; I'm Blue Inside; Let Me Sing a Blue Song;* and *Hank Williams Lives Again.*

At the start of the 1980s, LPs of Hank's still in MGM's current catalogue included *Hank Williams Live at the Grand Ole Opry; Hank Williams Sr.'s Greatest Hits; Home in Heaven; I Saw the Light; 24 of Hank Williams' Greatest Hits; 24 Greatest Hits, Vol. 2;* and *Very Best of Hank Williams.*

In 1961, the newly established Country Music Hall of Fame dedicated the first bronze plaques of selectees. One of those was for Hank Williams, the other two, appropriately, for the original Jimmie Rodgers and Fred Rose. His plaque reads, in part, "Performing artist, songwriter . . . Hank Williams will live on in the memories of millions of Americans. The simple, beautiful melodies and straightforward, plaintive stories in his lyrics of life as he knew it will never die. His songs appealed not only to the country music field, but brought him great acclaim in the 'pop' music world as well."

Indeed, by the time that plaque was mounted, Hank already was legendary and became even more in succeeding years. Anyone who ever came in contact with him (and many who never met him) had favorite stories of his life and times, some true, most apocryphal. His songs flourished, not only in his own recordings, but in countless new versions by major artists. Almost every year, some well-known country, pop, or rock star completed an album of Hank's compositions. He also was blessed with a worthy heir in his namesake, Hank Williams, Jr., who became the premier interpreter of his father's material, though not before waging a fierce struggle to escape the blanket of his father's reputation and achieve success on his own terms.

Many tributes were paid to Hank on radio and TV, including a 1979 tribute to his memory that interspersed performances of some of his songs by various artists, including Hank, Jr., with episodes from his life. Hank, Sr.'s songs still could provide major hits for others in the 1980s, as shown by Charley Pride's top-10 single "Honky Tonk Blues" and best-selling LP *There's a Little Bit of Hank in Me.*

For the millions of people familiar only with Hank Williams' songs, it's hard to equate the insight, sensitivity, and, in some cases, exuberance with the tormented image of the man, particularly in his last years. Probably the variance is due to the fact that Hank was a very sick man at a time when few people recognized his addiction as a form of illness. In all likelihood, the true essence of the man comes through in his creative legacy.

(See also Drifting Cowboys; Hank Williams, Jr.)

WILLIAMS, PAUL: *Singer, guitarist, songwriter, actor. Born Omaha, Nebraska, September 19, 1940.*

Small in stature but a giant creatively is the best way to describe Paul Williams. As a performer and actor, he proved at home on concert stages or in movies and TV, equally adept as a singer-comedian or a dramatic actor. His original compositions provided hits either for himself or other artists in almost all categories of pop music from country and easy listening to rock.

Born in Omaha, Nebraska, Williams was one of three sons of an architect. His father's work required moving to projects in various parts of the country, so his sons rarely stayed in one place long in their youth. When Paul was thirteen, his father died in an automobile crash and Paul went to live with an aunt in Long Beach, California, where he remained for the next five years.

Paul, who wasn't too sure what he wanted to do in life, moved to Albuquerque, New Mexico, for a time in the early 1960s. There he earned a living in a title insurance office by day and at various sidelines nights and weekends, including constructing theater sets. His association with a theater group led to a chance to do some acting. His acting skills developed rapidly and, as his reputation grew, brought the opportunity to take a starring role on an Albuquerque children's TV show.

Perhaps gaining encouragement from his brother Mentor's progress as a musician with Los Angeles groups, Paul decided to try for bigger things. Turning down the TV job, he returned to Southern California, where he found some work doing TV commercials. Then came the chance to play a fourteen-year-old genius with dangerous proclivities in the 1964 film *The*

Loved One. He added to his movie credits with a bit part in *The Chase,* which starred Marlon Brando.

In the mid-1960s, Williams, who had tried his hand at writing all kinds of material in previous years, decided to concentrate on his songwriting skills. One of his first collaborations was with folksinger and songwriter Biff Rose. The two got a writing contract from A&M Records and soon had a song, "Fill Your Heart," on the "B" side of the Tiny Tim novelty hit, "Tiptoe Through the Tulips." About the same time, another Williams effort, co-written with Roger Nichols, provided Claudine Longet, Andy Williams' wife, with the song "It's Hard to Say Goodbye."

Paul, who had learned to play guitar, assembled a group called the Holy Mackerel in the late 1960s and managed to get a contract from Reprise Records. With Mentor Williams contributing as a singer and songwriter, the group made one LP, which sank without a trace in the commercial market. The group disbanded, but Reprise, impressed by Paul's promise, asked him to do a solo collection. That LP, called *Someday Man,* came out in March 1970, but did little better than his *Holy Mackerel* LP.

After that debacle, Paul decided to regroup and fall back on writing. With Roger Nichols, he wrote the song "Out in the Country," which provided Three Dog Night with a singles hit. One of Williams and Nichols' ventures after that was a sixty-second melody for a bank commercial. Since they liked what they came up with, they also completed the number. It proved a wise decision. Called "We've Only Just Begun," the song was recorded by the Carpenters and made the top 10 as a single and as the title track of a Carpenters 1971 album.

Meanwhile, Paul was off on another project. He composed the lyrics and also sang on a cantata composed by Michael Colombier called "Wings," released on A&M in the early 1970s. His association with A&M soon took the form of a new solo recording contract. This time his albums caught the public fancy and such album releases as *An Old Fashioned Love Song, Life Goes On, Here Comes Inspiration, A Little*

Bit of Love, and Ordinary Fools did well on the pop charts during the mid-1970s. Many of the songs on those albums were hits for Paul or other performers and a number of them made up the 1977 greatest hits LP, Classics, on A&M. By then Paul already was looking for a new record label; he signed with Columbia's Portrait Records, and his debut on that label, A Little on the Windy Side, was released in early 1979.

In the mid-1970s, Williams renewed his movie work with a vengeance. One of his multifaceted efforts was the 1974 film Phantom of the Paradise, for which, besides providing music, he played the starring role and coauthored the script. He received both Academy Award and Golden Globe nominations for his work. During the same period he also wrote the song "Nice to Be Around" for the movie Cinderella Liberty and the score for Bugsy Malone. From 1974 to 1976, Paul appeared in concert in all parts of the United States, was a guest or host on many network TV shows (including several stints of spelling Johnny Carson on The Tonight Show), and wrote and acted in a variety of TV projects. His TV credits included writing the script for the 1975 premiere episode of Baretta and writing and starring in a Hawaii Five-O episode.

During 1976, Paul busied himself with an important new venture, a rework of the classic film A Star Is Born starring Barbra Streisand and Kris Kristofferson. As musical supervisor, he wrote eight of its eleven songs, five with Ken Ascher, two with Rupert Holmes, and one with Barbra Streisand. The one with Barbra, the film's "Love Theme" (also called "Evergreen") became phenomenally successful. It rose to number one on the hit charts and earned Paul and Barbra the Grammy for Best Song of 1977. The same song also won them an Academy Award.

In the late 1970s, Williams kept up his breakneck pace, working on a variety of projects that normally would be enough to keep several people busy. He wrote the title song for a prospective TV series called Just Another Day, acted as musical supervisor for a series starring Barbi Benton called

Girls, Girls, Girls, collaborated with Ken Ascher on music for the CBS Musical of the Week, "Baby Needs Shoes", wrote title tunes for the films Agatha and The End, wrote the score and acted in the movie You Want It . . . You Got It, and did the score, with Ken Ascher, for The Muppet Movie. The last named, released in July 1979, was hailed by critics as one of the delights of the year. To wind up his busy decade, he spent much of 1979 on location in Toronto, Canada, acting in a celluloid vehicle called Sin Sniper.

WILLIAMS, TEX: *Singer, guitarist, banjoist, harmonica player, band leader, actor. Born Ramsey, Fayette County, Illinois, August 23, 1917.*

Although Nashville remains the unofficial capital of country & western music, there has long been a strong contingent of artists who called the West Coast home. One of those who played an important role in making that section an important part of the national country & western scene was Tex Williams, whose firsts included posting the first million-selling record for Hollywood-based Capitol Records and serving as first president of the Academy of Country and Western Music.

Although Sol Williams' nickname is Tex, he was born and raised in rural areas of southern Illinois. Considering that he was to become a movie cowboy, his bout with polio when he was only one or two years old was a major challenge. As he told Lee Rector of Music City News (August 1975), the illness "left me with a slight limp. I figured that there was no use in even thinking about making pictures."

But music didn't seem that unlikely, particularly since he was born into a family where playing instruments and singing were taken as a natural part of life. "How I got into the business of making music," he told Rector, "was after supper we got the banjos and fiddles and guitars out and played for a couple of hours. We listened to the Grand Ole Opry every night on an old Atwater-Kent radio."

Tex's skills were considerable when he was in his teens. At thirteen, he got his own program on station WJBL in Decatur, Illinois. "I was what you might call a one man band. I played a five string banjo and harmonica as I sang sad cowboy songs." When he was fourteen, he moved his act to station WDZ, Tuscola, Illinois, and played at many functions during his high school years.

However, it was more of a hobby than a job until Tex was out of high school. At nineteen, he went west to the state of Washington to join his brother. Once there, he got a job playing with a professional group called the Reno Racketeers. Two years later, he headed south to Los Angeles to seek more rewarding opportunities.

Once there he became acquainted with Tex Ritter and worked with that now legendary figure in a western called *Rollin' Home to Texas.* This was the first of many films in which he appeared from the late 1930s into the 1950s. His companions in some of them were Charles Starrett, Buster Crabbe, and Judy Canova. In the late 1940s and early 1950s, he was under contract to Universal International, taking part in twenty-four features until the inroads of TV caused the phasing out of westerns.

When he wasn't working on movies, Williams had plenty to do as a musician. One of his first efforts in that field was to join the Spade Cooley band as sideman and lead vocalist. At the first recording session with Cooley in 1943, Tex sang the vocal on "Shame on You," which was a major C&W hit of the mid-1940s. He remained with Cooley during the war years, then decided to go on his own in 1946, forming a twelve-piece band, the Western Caravan, and signing a recording contract with Capitol Records. In a short time, he established himself as one of the label's major artists. His initial release, "The Rose of the Alamo," sold over 250,000 copies. Several releases later, he topped that with his single of the Tex Ritter–Merle Travis song "Smoke, Smoke, Smoke." The song became a tremendous success in both country and pop fields, the first million-seller issued by Capitol. Some of Williams' other well-received singles of the period were "California Polka," "Texas in My Soul," and "Leaf of Love."

In the late 1940s and early 1950s, Tex played to capacity audiences in such places as the Aragon Ballroom in Chicago, Orpheum Theater in Los Angeles, and Oriental Theatre in Chicago. During those years, he also turned out a steady string of singles and albums on Capitol, working with such stars as Jo Stafford, Roberta Lee, Dinah Shore, and Tennessee Ernie Ford. In the 1950s, he also had his own local TV show on KRCA in Hollywood.

Williams and his band kept up a hectic schedule during those years. At one point, when he wasn't touring with his group the band was appearing five nights a week at the Riverside Rancho in the Southern California area or headlining the show at Tex's own club, the Tex Williams Village in Newhall. Throughout the 1950s up to the time the group was disbanded in 1965, it was often featured on major radio and TV programs, including the *Grand Ole Opry, Spike Jones Show, Jo Stafford Show, National Barn Dance, Swingin' Country* (NBC), *Gene Autry's Melody Ranch, The Jimmy Dean Show, Midwestern Hayride,* and *Porter Wagoner Show.* Tex also starred for a time on his own NBC network program, *Riverside Rancho.*

Tex stopped using a regular band, he told Rector, when he sold his club in 1965. "After that, I really had no use for a band. As a matter of fact, I couldn't maintain a band. When you have a band, you have to keep those guys working. It had reached a point where I really didn't care to work that much. You've got to work four or five nights a week to keep those kids up. They've all got families too."

Not that Williams gave up performing himself. He was still doing personal appearances over a decade later. "Now when I go to Las Vegas or Reno or somewhere in Nevada where you do four or maybe eight weeks, I take a local group that I've worked with."

During the 1960s, Tex recorded for several labels, including Decca and Boone. His Decca albums included the early 1950s *Tex Williams,* issued in December 1962. One of his singles on Decca, "Deck of Cards," was still in the catalogue in the 1970s. He was represented by several LPs on Liberty and Imperial in the mid-1960s, such as *Tex Williams Live at the Mint* (the Mint Club in Las Vegas) (1963) on Liberty and *Voice of Authority* on Imperial (June 1966). In January 1967, Sun Records issued an LP titled *Tex Williams*. In the late 1960s, he recorded material for Kentucky-based Boone Records, including two releases that remained on national charts for thirty weeks. Boone also released the LP *Two Sides of Tex Williams*.

Tex recorded a number of records in Nashville in the early 1970s, but by mid-decade was back in Los Angeles studios working for Granite Records. He was signed to that label by long-time friend Cliffie Stone, who had originally signed him for Capitol in 1946. His debut on Granite was an album issued in 1974 and four singles, including a remake of the Nat "King" Cole hit "Lazy Hazy Days of Summer," issued during 1974–75. Those releases did well enough for Cliffie and Tex to begin work on additional singles and a second album.

WILLS, BOB: *Fiddler, songwriter, band leader (the Texas Playboys). Born Hall County, Texas, March 6, 1905; died Fort Worth, Texas, May 13, 1975.*

Bob Wills' considerable contributions to country music were recognized by his election to the Country Music Hall of Fame in 1968. By then, he had mellowed a good deal or he might have objected to the honor. He certainly didn't take kindly to the gradual elimination of the shortening of the descriptive phrase "country & western" to just "country." He was, after all, the pioneer of "western swing." Beyond that innovation, he never liked being known as a rural artist; his conscious musical taste leaned strongly to jazz and blues. In truth, however, it was his marriage of those elements with the folk music traditions of his native Texas (black, Spanish, and white) that made him a major innovator in mid-twentieth century popular music.

He didn't have to look far for musical inspiration as a child. His father, John Wills, was an excellent country fiddler. During Bob's early years, though, the family was very poor and got by eking a living from agricultural field work and whatever John Wills could earn for his fiddle playing. When the family moved from Bob's natal area in East Texas to a new location 500 miles to the northwest, the then eight-year-old had to help out by picking cotton along with his father and other family members. The migrant camps the Wills clan stayed in en route (in a journey made in a covered wagon) was shared by other poor workers, black, white, and Mexican. Those weren't the pleasantest surroundings, but in retrospect, they proved important by exposing young Bob to black blues and other ethnic music.

Before Bob was ten, he already was introduced to a musical instrument, but not the fiddle. He started to learn to play the mandolin, encouraged by his father, who wanted Bob to be able to provide backup for John's fiddle playing. Wills later told the story of learning to play fiddle at ten because of a cousin's difficulties in learning a tune. Bob said he could learn it faster and he proved his point. After that, he borrowed his cousin's fiddle until he had worked up about half a dozen fiddle tunes.

According to Charles R. Townsend, professor of history at West Texas State University, in his late 1970s biography of Wills (*San Antonio Rose,* University of Illinois Press), Bob made his first solo appearance as a fiddler at ten. Townsend writes that the event took place in 1915 near the town of Turkey in west Texas. Bob had gone on ahead to await his father, who was to play for a dance on a local ranch. To silence the increasingly restless crowd when his father didn't show up on time, the boy finally picked up his dad's fiddle and played the tunes he knew. He did so well that even when Wills Sr. arrived, having been busy "frequenting the corn-liquor wagons," Bob continued to hold the spotlight until the dance was over.

As the years went by, Bob continued to increase his repertoire and performing skills, playing with his family part of the time and with various local bands during his teens. Although he sometimes worked at other jobs when he needed spare income, once he reached adulthood he had pretty well committed himself to a musical career.

Although he had always loved music, growing up in the "Bible Belt" he had sometimes had doubts about going down that path. In fact, for a time he considered giving up the entertainment field in favor of entering the ministry. Later on, that part of his life returned to cause misgivings about his chosen occupation. He once mused, "I see a big crowd dancing. Here I am up here making the music, and they're out there, and some of them might be drinking and all of this and that. I feel like I'm sinning, or causing other people to sin."

Wills had been a professional musician for a long time when he made the moves that were to start him on the route to stardom at the beginning of the 1930s. Renowned steel guitarist Leon McAuliffe recalled, "Bob Wills in about 1931 came to Fort Worth [Texas], just himself and a guitar player. He met a singer named Milton Brown and they went on radio KFJZ as the Wills Fiddle Band. They got their show sponsored by Aladdin Lamp Company. Called themselves the Aladdin Laddies. They were so popular they got themselves sponsored on a network of radio stations called the Texas Quality Network. That was WBAP, Fort Worth, and also WFAA, and KPRC in Houston, and WOI in San Antonio. The company sponsoring them was the Burris Mill and Elevator Company that manufactured Light Crust Flour. That's where the Light Crust Doughboys [see separate entry] came from."

Bob stayed with the Doughboys for a while, then moved on. According to McAuliffe, "Milton and Bob went separate ways. Bob went to Waco and called his band Bob Wills and the Playboys. In the summer of 1933, he moved to Oklahoma City for a short stay and then on to Tulsa in February 1934 where his band became the Texas Playboys. At that time it included Bob; Tommy Duncan; two brothers, June and Kermit Whelan; Bob's brother, Johnny Lee Wills; and a cousin

Em Lansford. When they'd been in Waco they had an announcer named Everett Stover who played trumpet. Stover quit his job and went with them to Oklahoma. Also they met a fella who had a department head position with Cities Service Oil in Waco, O. W. Mayo, who quit his job and joined them and became business manager.

"The band went on station KVOO in Tulsa. They all lived in the basement of the building. They'd been in Tulsa, played on KVOO every day for a couple months, then booked a job (at a ballroom) in another Oklahoma town. They had packed houses, so they made money for the first time. They were playing some original tunes. Bob hadn't written 'San Antonio Rose' yet, but there were things like 'She's Killin' Me,' 'Fan It,' and 'Take Me Back to Texas,' which later was called 'Take Me Back to Tulsa.' Also did some Stuart Hamblen tunes: 'My Mary,' 'Brown Eyed Texas Rose.'"

From then on, as Bob's reputation continued to grow in Tulsa and the Southwest, he gave a lot of thought to improving his band. For the almost ten years before World War II brought a close to that phase of the Playboys saga, he steadily expanded and refined the group. In the early years, noted McAuliffe, "Most of the guys were relatives, but not as good musicians as he wanted. Also as he wanted to add other instruments like more horns and drums." [Those instruments were anathema to the traditional country & western acts of the period, but Wills always had his own ideas. He once noted, 'I've loved horns since I was a little boy.']

"As Bob began to make changes, the first thing he added was the drums. Then his bass player Kermit Whelan left—Kermit had played steel guitar a little bit, but not full time—and he added me in March 1935. Smokey [drummer William Eschol 'Smokey' Dacus] had come on a few months earlier. Meantime he added a saxophone and decided on a piano. He'd had a couple of piano players. Tommy Duncan, when he wasn't singing, played piano some. He wanted a good piano player because he'd been signed by Columbia to record in September. He knew Al Strickland in Fort Worth and sent for him. Joe Ferguson didn't come in until January 1937. Joe won a singing contest in Tulsa so Bob let him do a guest shot on the show and hired him and had two singers. He put Joe to playin' tenor sax and that didn't work out too well. Bob and his cousin Em didn't get along too well, so Em left and Bob taught Joe to play bass.

"Eldon [Shamblin] joined in early 1937. The style of rhythm guitar he played and the chords he knew really was a boost to the band.

"Bob added trombones starting in 1935 with his first record session. He kept going from there with more brass instruments, and with other changes from time to time."

The second half of the 1930s and the early 1940s amounted to a golden era for the Playboys. Once his recordings began to come out on Columbia, Wills began to achieve a national reputation. By the early 1940s, he was becoming one of the best-selling record artists and his music was being broadcast to all parts of the United States on network radio. His cries of "Ah, ha! San Antone" and "Take it away, Leon" became national catchwords.

Bob's star was on the ascendant just before the United States entered World War II. McAuliffe stated, "The band reached a point in 1941–42 when we began to get more contracts. We had 'San Antonio Rose' for a hit. Originally it was an instrumental, but we came back with words in 1941–42. By the early 1940s, we had added four saxes, three trumpets and two trombones. We were playing a lot of pop tunes. By then Bob had kinda phased out most of the original band. While it was good, it was limited in what it could do and he wanted to play all kinds of music."

Through that period, the Playboys recorded regularly for Columbia and were featured in major venues throughout the West and Southwest. It also became part of the movie scene, performing in ten western films. But the war brought things to a halt. Recalled McAuliffe, "My time

with Bob ended in December 1942. World War II was here and everybody began to get draft notices or take defense jobs. Bob went into the service too. He didn't stay very long. He shouldn't have gone in the first place because he was thirty-eight years old when he went in."

In his years with Columbia, Wills recorded the songs that still are the ones primarily associated with his name. Besides "San Antonio Rose," he had such other major hits as "Steel Guitar Rag," "Faded Love" (co-written with his father), "Texas Playboy Rag," "Mexicali Rose," "Take Me Back to Tulsa," "New Worried Mind," and "Yellow Rose of Texas." His original compositions numbered in the hundreds. In addition to songs like "San Antonio Rose" and "Texas Playboy Rag," his credits include numbers like "Texas Two Step," "Wills Breakdown," "Lone Star Rag," and "Betty's Waltz."

A few more of his relatively successful Columbia singles are "Cotton Eye Joe," "Bob Wills Special," "Oozlin' Daddy Blues," "Ida Red," "Osage Stomp," "Oklahoma Rag," "Bob Wills Boogie," "Ten Tears," and "Steel Guitar Stomp."

While Bob was in the service, he had given what was left of his band and his radio show and dance schedule to his brother, Johnny Lee Wills. After his discharge he went to California to organize a new Playboys group. He remained in California well into the 1950s, changing his base of operations several times, including a stay in Sacramento. The band had some success, but the musical fabric of the country was changing and Wills wasn't able to return to the heights he had enjoyed in the early 1940s.

The group recorded for MGM Records in the 1950s, though never achieving hits of the "San Antonio Rose"–"Steel Guitar Rag" era. Among the singles issued on MGM were "Spanish Fandango," "Little Cowboy Lullaby," "Cotton Patch Blues," and "Blues for Dixie."

In the late 1950s, Wills decided to return to the scene of his early triumphs, his band makeup still changing either through attrition or his search for a better sound. It was during this period that Leon Rausch joined. He noted, "I started with him in 1958. I took Tommy Duncan's brother's place. He left him in California and he picked me up on the way back. I stayed with him until 1961. He went back to horns and back to fiddles. We had eleven people in the band the second I was with them.

"We showed real bad when we came to Tulsa in 1958. Bob couldn't figure out why he couldn't be king of the hill again. But it had been fifteen years and he'd hardly played Oklahoma for that time. But we did sell well in Vegas. We played the Showboat in 1959 for the first time and the band sold real well. So finally the boys from downtown came and gave him a little more money to play the Golden Nugget four weeks in a row. In 1960 we decided we could move there and book in and out of Vegas a month at a time.

"During that time, Tommy Duncan came back and they did an album on Liberty, *Together Again*. Personal problems were a difficulty. The album sold reasonably well, but couldn't recapture the old thing. All in all we did three albums in 1960–61."

The pattern remained essentially the same after Rausch left. Wills kept hoping for a new breakthrough, but it seemed an increasingly lost cause as rock 'n' roll dominated the music picture. Wills' albums continued to be available for most of the 1960s on either Liberty or Harmony labels, though his new output was meager. His Liberty titles included *Living Legend, Mr. Words and Mr. Music,* and *Bob Wills Sings and Plays*. On Harmony, he was represented by titles like *Bob Wills Special* and *Home in San Antone*. The decade was marked, though, by Wills' election to the Country Music Hall of Fame in 1968.

By the start of the 1970s, western swing seemed relegated to the pages of musical history books. Most of the veteran Playboys artists were playing part time, working at other jobs, or were in retirement. But a new generation of musicians began to rediscover the art form as the decade went by, typified by the essentially East

Coast, college-spawned band, Asleep at the Wheel. And artists like Merle Haggard continued to pay tribute to Wills in some of their new recordings.

Wills himself was confident that his music had lasting qualities and in 1973 conceived the idea of hand-picking a band of some of the best musicians who'd played in the Playboys over the years for a greatest hits collection. The result was the multidisc *For the Last Time* set that came out on United Artists in the mid-1970s. The band members were Smokey Dacus on drums, Al Stricklin on piano (Stricklin wrote a book called *My Years with Bob Wills,* published by Naylor Press in 1976), Leon McAuliffe on steel guitar, Leon Rausch on bass and vocals, Joe Ferguson on bass, Eldon Shamblin on electric guitar, and Keith Coleman and Johnny Gimble on fiddles (both first joined Wills in 1949).

Before the sessions were completed, Wills suffered a stroke and was confined to a rest home in Fort Worth, Texas. After a series of strokes, he died there in May 1975, aware, however, that interest in his music was reviving. After his death, Leon McAuliffe and Leon Rausch took over as coleaders of the re-formed band. With the approval of Bob's widow, Betty, the band began to do a series of stage and TV appearances. It also signed with Capitol for a new series of LPs, starting with *The Late Bob Wills' Original Texas Playboys,* issued in March 1977. (In August 1976, Capitol also released an LP based on tapes of earlier Bob Wills' radio broadcasts, *Bob Wills and His Texas Playboys in Concert.*) In January 1978, a second LP by the McAuliffe-Rausch aggregation appeared, *Live and Kickin'.* In the CMA voting for 1977 Instrumental Group of the Year, the Original Texas Playboys was named the winner.

At the start of the 1980s, besides the LPs just noted, many other Wills LPs were in the active catalogue of several companies. On Columbia was the title *Bob Wills Anthology and Remembering. . . .* MCA offered *Bob Wills and His Texas Playboys, Bob Wills in Person, Bob Wills Plays the Greatest String Band Hits, King of the Western Swing, Living Legend, The Best of Bob Wills and His Texas*

Playboys, and *Time Changes Everything*. Liberty had *Bob Wills Sings and Plays*, Epic provided *Fathers and Sons*, and RCA marketed *Western Swing Along*.

It seemed, as Waylon Jennings said in 1975, "It don't matter who's in Austin, Bob Wills is still the King."

McAuliffe and Rausch quotes based on 1979 interviews with Irwin Stambler.

WINCHESTER, JESSE: *Singer, pianist, drummer, songwriter. Born Bossier City near Shreveport, Louisiana, May 17, 1944.*

It's generally conceded that Jesse Winchester would have been a star, perhaps even a superstar, by the mid-1970s if he hadn't fled to Canada to express opposition to the Vietnam War. As it is, the series of finely crafted albums he turned out from 1969 through 1977 did reasonably well considering he wasn't able to tour in support of them in the United States until 1976, when President Carter pardoned war protesters. In the late 1970s, Jesse started touring U.S. cities and his new album sales rose perceptibly. Equally impressive were the number of country and pop artists who gained chart successes with some of Jesse's songs during the decade.

Jesse was born in Louisiana into a proud family tradition. (He originally was named James R. Winchester after his father, an Air Force Captain.) One of his forebears invented the famous Winchester firearm, Robert E. Lee was a blood relation and other family members were prominent in Memphis affairs from the city's earliest times. He was in direct line of descent from a cofounder of the city, and his grandfather gave the funeral oration at the burial of blues great W. C. Handy.

When Jesse's father returned from the war in the South Pacific, he came back a pacifist, and took up farming. Jesse noted that his father was "one of the original hippies in the late forties; he decided against joining the family law firm to take up farming instead and get closer to the land." Jesse grew up on the farm until he was twelve, when his father decided to move back to Memphis where he finally gained a law degree and practiced until he died in 1962. Jesse already had become immersed in pop music by then, finding particular empathy with the early R&B and rockabilly artists such as Elvis Presley, Carl Perkins, Chuck Berry, Bo Diddley, and Jerry Lee Lewis. In high school in Memphis, he played with various bands, first as a drummer, later as a piano player, in groups called the Midnighters and Church Keys.

He continued his interest in music as a sideline when he went back east to enter Williams College in Massachusetts, from which he received his B.A. in 1966. His major was German, and he spent some time traveling in Europe before he returned to Memphis to work as a pianist in local clubs. When his draft notice came in 1967, he had a hard choice to make. "It was a very hard decision and my mother didn't tell me what she thought at the time—she said I had to do what I felt was right. She later said she thought it was the right decision. The hardest part was hurting my grandfather who was the patriot of the family. He was my father's father and I was very close to him spiritually. He had a strong sense of honor and duty and his attitude could be summed up by the phrase, 'my country, may she always be right, but right or wrong, still my country.'"

Deciding he had to leave, Winchester moved to Montreal, where he answered a newspaper ad to become a member of a band called Les Astronauts. By the end of the 1960s, he had gone out on his own, playing piano in small clubs like the Back Door Cafe across from McGill University. In 1969, he opened a concert for The Band at Montreal's Place des Arts, and his performance, plus the original songs he was writing by then, so impressed The Band's Robbie Robertson that he became one of Jesse's most ardent proponents.

Robertson helped Jesse get a recording contract from Ampex and produced the first album, *Jesse Winchester*, issued in 1970. The album contained such striking numbers as "Yankee Lady," "Biloxi," and "Brand New Tennessee Waltz," the latter a bittersweet song about the travail of exile ("I've a sadness too sad to be true/So have all your passionate violins/Play a tune for the Tennessee Kid"). The album won critical praise in the United States, including praise from *Rolling Stone*, which called him the most promising new artist of 1970, but the album failed commercially without adequate promotion.

Some of the songs have done well for others, however. "Yankee Lady" was recorded by Tim Hardin and Melanie and "Brand New Tennessee Waltz" has appeared on many albums, including those of Joan Baez. The well-known manager Albert Grossman shared Robertson's continued faith in Jesse and signed him for his Bearsville label. The debut album on Bearsville in 1972, *Third Down, 110 to Go* (the title refers to Canadian football, where the field is 110 yards long rather than 100 as in the United States), fared almost exactly the same as the Ampex effort. It too provided songs for others: "Isn't That So" was recorded by Peter Yarrow and became an English chart hit for a British group. Undaunted, Winchester and Grossman kept on with new releases, such as *Learn to Love It* in 1974 and *Let the Rough Side Drag* (1976). Important tracks from the former include "Defying Gravity" and "Mississippi on My Mind," the latter giving country artist Stoney Edwards a top-level hit. The 1976 album had many delights, including the title track and "Blow on Chilly Wind."

Although Jesse could travel freely to and from the United States after 1976, he had decided Canada was his true home. He received Canadian citizenship in 1973, though he became increasingly active on the U.S. concert circuit. His debut tour of the States in early 1977, backed by a Canadian band he'd assembled the previous year called Midnight Bus (Martin Harris on bass, Bobby Cohen on lead guitar, Ron Dann on pedal steel, and Dave Lewis on drums), proved to stateside audiences that Winchester provided a highly entertaining, professionally polished show. The tour, which coincided with release of his new Bearsville LP *Nothing but a Breeze*, received coverage from *Newsweek, Time, People, Rolling Stone,* and an extended segment on the NBC network show *Weekend*. In 1978, however, the initial frenzy had died down, and his sixth album (fifth on Bearsville), *A Touch on the Rainy Side*, though as consistently rewarding, failed to make the U.S. charts as its immediate predecessor had done.

WISEMAN, MAC: *Singer, guitarist, songwriter, producer, disc jockey. Born Crimora, Virginia, May 23, 1925.*

In concert in the early 1980s, a big, heavyset man with a graying beard and (usually) smiling, round face, Malcolm B. "Mac" Wiseman looked like the archetypal veteran folk-country music star. It was a proper designation, for Wiseman is an important figure in country music in general and bluegrass in particular in a career that, in the early 1980s, was rapidly rounding out its fourth decade.

As Mac told Everett Corbin of *Music City News* (October 1973, p. 30), he was born into a family of modest means, but one where "we were always blessed with music, mostly country and mountain style.

"My daddy owned one of the first hand-wound phonographs in our little rural community and owned the first battery powered radio in our area. I recall that people came from several miles distance on Saturday night to listen to the *Opry* and the *WLS Barn Dance*, often staying until the wee hours of the morning or sometimes all night, then having breakfast and going home."

He told Corbin that he started to play the guitar when he was about twelve, "never thinking or dreaming it would lead to anything in the music world."

As Mac grew up, his interest in music intensified and he went on to study at the Shenandoah Conservatory of Music in Dayton, Virginia. After graduation, he began his entertainment industry career as a newscaster and disc jockey for radio station WSVA in Harrisburg, Virginia. While he held this job, he also found time to perform with local country bands. He found performing to his liking and joined Bill Monroe and the Blue Grass Boys for a short time, cutting several of the all-time great bluegrass duets with Monroe.

In 1947, he was host of the highly popular *Farm and Fun Time* program on WCYB, Bristol, Virginia. He had become friends with two young bluegrass artists in Monroe's Blue Grass Boys band, Earl Scruggs and Lester Flatt. When the latter decided to leave the band in 1948, they moved over to become regular performers on WCYB. With Wiseman, they formed the since legendary Foggy Mountain Boys, with whom Mac worked for several years, including featured spots on station WROL in Knoxville, Tennessee, in 1949 and on the WRVA *Old Dominion Barn Dance* in Richmond, Virginia.

In 1951, Mac decided to work as a solo artist. That year he starred on the *Louisiana Hayride* in Shreveport and was also offered a recording contract with Dot Records. He had a string of hit recordings, such as "Shackles and Chains," " 'Tis Sweet to Be Remembered," "Ballad of Davy Crockett," "Love Letters in the Sand," and "Jimmy Brown the Newsboy," which remained on the national charts for thirty-three weeks.

For a time, Mac devoted a lot of his time to working behind the scenes in the record industry. From 1957 to 1961 he served as artists & repertoire executive for Dot Records and he ran the company's country-music department. In 1961, he left Dot for Capitol Records as a performer and producer, though Dot continued to release albums by him after his departure. He returned to Dot in 1966 as a recording artist, but only for a short time, completing material for three albums, one of which featured old standards backed with heavy string orchestral arrangements and one that was folk-oriented. His album credits on Dot after those were completed included *Mac Wiseman* (issed 1/58); *12 Great Hits* (9/60); *Keep on the Sunnyside* (12/60); *Fireball Mail* (3/62); *This Is Mac Wiseman* (5/66); *Bluegrass* (10/66); and *Master at Work* (11/66). He also had material on the Hilltop label in the 1960s, such as the LP *Mac Wiseman*, and, on Hamilton Records, *Songs of the Dear Old Days* (11/66).

From the mid-1960s on, he was a frequent performer at the steadily growing number of bluegrass festivals that came into existence in the United States and in other countries. He was a featured artist at one of the first of the large bluegrass events, staged in 1965 by Carlton Haney. The attendance was small, but the festival was the forerunner of the future, when crowds of 100,000 were not unusual.

In 1969, Wiseman signed a new recording contract with RCA, which issued several of his albums in the early 1970s, including one he cut with old friend Lester Flatt. The debut LP on RCA was titled *Johnny's Cash and Charley's Pride* and came out in June 1970. RCA also released a single of the title track.

During the 1970s, though his career as a recording artist was relatively uneventful, Mac was in the forefront of the decade's bluegrass revival. While he continued to perform traditional bluegrass rather than the progressive formats of new artists, he achieved excellent rapport with college students, who admired his flowing vocal style and superb guitar playing. As he told Corbin in 1973, "A good fifty percent of my work now is on the college circuit, and some ninety to ninety-five percent of the requests are for the older, traditional songs.

"I think it is the unbelievable interest shown by these college students which is making bluegrass music so popular, and I think it is just on the threshold of what it is going to do. I base this on factual information on attendance at college concerts and the big bluegrass festivals."

One thing he also could point to: at least one of his early LPs, the 1956 Dot *'Tis Sweet to Be Remembered*, found strong new sales response in the 1970s thanks to his concert work.

In April 1973, Wiseman also brought the bluegrass message overseas as the only U.S. bluegrass artist invited to appear at England's prestigious Wembley Festival.—A.S.

WOOLEY, SHEB: *Singer, guitarist, songwriter, actor, comedian. Born Erick, Oklahoma, April 10, 1921.*

Diversification doesn't work for everyone, but it paid off for Sheb Wooley. In his long career, he achieved considerable success in a variety of entertainment field occupations, including those of country singer and comedian, songwriter of both pop and country hits, movie and TV actor, and music executive. Carrying diversification a step further, for many years he was as well known under his comic pseudonym of Ben Colder as under his own name.

Sheb, who grew up on a farm in Oklahoma, heard country music from his earliest years. He was a preteenager when he got his first musical instrument. He told an interviewer, "I persuaded my dad to swap a shotgun for a guitar. He showed me a few chords." Sheb took it from there and while he was in high school formed a band that played for local dances and was given a twice-a-week radio show on a local station.

After leaving high school, he worked for a time as a pipe welder in an oil field until he decided there had to be a better way to make a living. "One day I threw away my helmet and came to Nashville."

He told Audrey Winters of *Music City News,* "In Nashville [in the mid-1940s] I worked at WLAC radio and would guest frequently on [the WSM show] *Noontime Neighbors* and I cut a couple of records for Bullet Records." He stayed for a year in Music City, then moved to Fort Worth, Texas, where his musical career took a major step forward, starting with a show on station WBAP in 1946.

"I fell into a deal similar to the *Light Crust Doughboys* radio show, only this was a show sponsored by Calumet Baking Powder. The show was on twenty-five major radio stations. I emceed the show, wrote the commercials and created the Chief [the Indian chief the company featured on its product label]. We toured all the southwestern states and the show lasted three years."

At the end of the 1940s, Wooley headed west, settling in Los Angeles, where he sought to combine careers in movies and records. He achieved the latter goal, signing a recording contract with MGM Records, an association that lasted into the

1970s. To bolster his acting hopes he lined up a Hollywood agent and also spent three months as a student at the Jack Koslyn School of Acting. In 1949, he began work in movies and on TV while continuing to add to his experience as a singer and songwriter.

His first big film break occurred when he successfully auditioned for a part in the movie *Rocky Mountain,* a film in which he played the "heavy" while Errol Flynn and Patrice Wymore portrayed the hero and heroine parts. Throughout the 1950s and on into the 1960s, he had plenty of movie work, performing in such films as *Man Without a Star* with Kirk Douglas, *Little Big Horn* with John Ireland, and in such classics as *High Noon* (where Wooley played Ben Miller, the man seeking to gun down hero Gary Cooper) and *Giant.* All in all, Wooley appeared in over forty films.

His face became equally well known to TV viewers for parts in a number of western programs. His most famous role was that of Pete Nolan in the long-running network TV series *Rawhide,* which was on the air regularly for seven years in the late 1950s and early 1960s. Wooley was with the show for five years of its seven-year run.

Meanwhile, many of Sheb's compositions, not a few of them wildly funny, kept on embellishing the repertoires of country & western pop singers. In 1953, his parody of two hit songs, "When Mexican Joe Met Jolie Blon," provided a top-10 hit for Hank Snow. While on location for the movie *Giant,* he wrote a song called "Are You Satisfied" that sold a fair number of records when he recorded it for MGM, but provided a best-selling disc for Rusty Draper. In the late 1950s, Sheb wrote a new novelty song called "Purple People Eater" and this time his single was the blockbuster, eventually selling over 3 million copies in both the pop and country markets.

"After 'Purple People Eater,'" he told Winters, "every song I wrote would go pop, such as 'Sweet Chile' and 'Star of Love.' But in 1961 I wrote 'That's My Pa' [a number-one-ranked country hit on MGM in 1962] and this put me back into country music. Also it was my first MGM session in Nashville.

"Jim Vianneau, A&R man for MGM, farmed me out for a while to Jack Clements. This was when I recorded 'Almost Persuaded #2' [a top-10 single in 1966] and 'Son, Don't Go Near the Eskimos.' The pseudonym Ben Colder was originated then. We made an album of this type song and kept doing it regularly afterward."

The first Ben Colder LP came out in October 1963 and was followed later in the 1960s by such albums as *Big Ben Strikes Again* (1/67), *Wine, Women & Song* (9/67), *Have One On* (9/69), and, in the early 1970s, by *Best of Ben Colder*, *Wild Again*, and *Live & Loaded*. Under his own name, Wooley's LP output included *Very Best of Sheb Wooley* (5/65) and *It's a Big Land* (2/66). The Colder imprint appeared on a series of hit singles at the end of the 1960s, such as "Purple People Eater #2" in 1967, "Tie the Tiger Down" in 1968, "The Lincoln's Parked at Margie's Again," and "Carroll County Accident." Wooley closed out the 1960s with a best-selling cover version of "Harper Valley P.T.A.," which went over the 300,000 copy mark.

During the 1960s, the Wooley/Colder act delighted audiences all over the world. Sheb was featured on almost every major country TV program that came along during the decade and also had his own set a number of times on the *Grand Ole Opry*. His contributions were acknowledged by the Country Music Association, which voted him best comedian of 1968. In 1969, he was asked to join the cast of the new CBS network country show, *Hee Haw*, remaining a member of the cast of that highly popular program into the 1970s.

Although his recording activities slowed down in the 1970s, Wooley remained a concert attraction and still was maintaining a busy in-person performing schedule at night clubs and fairs in the early 1980s.

WRIGHT, BOBBY: *Singer, guitarist, bassist, trumpeter, drummer. Born Charleston, West Virginia, March 30, 1942.*

When you're the son of country stars Kitty Wells and Johnny Wright, it's natu-rally assumed you'll take to the field with alacrity if you have the talent. In Bobby Wright's case, he shunned his parents' field in favor of a successful TV acting career, but later returned to the fold to become an important addition to country music in the 1970s.

Bobby was born in Charleston, West Virginia, in 1942, where his parents were appearing on the *WWVA Jamboree*. When he was nine months old, they relocated to Nashville, where Bobby spent most of his early years, except for a five-year period from 1947 to 1952 in Louisiana, when his parents were featured on the *Louisiana Hayride* in Shreveport. In 1958, the Wrights were asked to become regular cast members of the *Grand Ole Opry* (where his father's team of Johnnie and Jack became a favorite of *Opry* crowds and his mother gained the title "Queen of Country Music"). Madison, Tennessee, then became home.

Although it wasn't his chief interest, Bobby wasn't uninvolved in music and was proud of his parents. He even made his recording debut at the age of eleven. However, as he told Everett Corbin of *Music City News* (September 1971), "I didn't pursue it because at the time I was more interested in basketball and football." He was interested in sports and drama in high school and, in fact, he met his wife-to-be, Brenda, during a dance following the basketball game between her high school, Donelson, and Madison High. By the time they were married in December 1962, Bobby was in Las Vegas filming an episode of the *McHale's Navy* TV series.

One of the entrées into the show was his guitar-playing ability, which he developed from his elementary school years. (He added skills on other instruments over the years, including bass, trumpet, and drums.) He recalled for Corbin that a family friend from *Opry* station WSM, Ott Devine, paved the way. "He told me Hollywood producer Peter Tewkesbury was looking for a young southern boy who plays the guitar." The audition, for which Wright traveled to California, was for an hour-long dramatic show called *It's a Man's World*. The project failed, but his tryout paid off in another direction. "Someone had the brainstorm to do a TV comedy and the producer of *McHale's Navy* saw my screen test and said I was perfect for the part of the radio operator."

Wright had returned to Tennessee, but in three months he was back on the coast working on his first *McHale's* episode. He remained a regular on the show for its lifetime, from 1962 into 1966. Now an established actor, he went on to other programs in the late 1960s, appearing on such shows as *Pistols and Petticoats* and *The Road West.*

At the end of the 1960s, Bobby decided it was time to head east. "I decided that I would come back to Nashville and try my luck in the music industry. I really didn't intend to pursue a music career until the TV series." Soon he was a member of the Kitty Wells–Johnnie Wright Family Show, touring throughout the United States on the country, state fair, and rodeo circuit. During 1970–71, he and his family taped the first fifty-two half-hour shows for a syndicated TV program and added more in later years. With Bobby's arrival, the family also began to add appearances in country nightclubs in large urban areas to their schedule as well as dates in Army service clubs. His sister Ruby, a vocalist and recording artist, was also part of the show.

Besides its U.S. dates, the Kitty Wells–Johnny Wright Show also found a strong following overseas. During the early 1970s Bobby was offered the opportunity to make debut appearances in Germany, where the show was booked at least once a year, and in England.

Wright signed with Decca Records at the start of the 1970s, which began to release a series of singles by him. The response built slowly, but his tenth release, "Here I Go Again," rose to upper-chart levels in mid-1971 and made the first ballot in the CMA voting for Song of the Year. His debut LP of the same name was released in October 1971.

WRIGHT, JOHNNY: *Singer, guitarist, fiddler, songwriter. Born Mount Juliet, Tennessee, May 13, 1914.*

One of the royal families of country music, the Johnny Wright clan provided country enthusiasts with many great moments for more than three decades. Johnny's wife, Kitty Wells, won the title "Queen of Country Music Singers" while Johnny starred as an individual performer and as half of the team of Johnnie and Jack.

The musical tradition in the Wright family went back several generations. Johnny's grandfather was a champion old-time fiddler in Tennessee, and his father was a gifted five-string banjoist. Thus he was exposed to many country-music performances during his youth in Mount Juliet and was tutored on several instruments.

He sometimes performed for school events during his public school days. After finishing school, he began to perform in the region. In 1936, he began his first radio engagement on station WSIX, Nashville. One of the members of his show was a talented young singer named Muriel Deason. Johnny decided she needed a new stage name and chose Kitty Wells from a popular song, "I'll Marry Kitty Wells." Two years later, they married.

The WSIX show was the beginning of a long career as a radio performer that included appearances on WCHS, Charleston, West Virginia; WHIS, Bluesfield, West Virginia; WNOX, Knoxville; WEAS, Decatur, Georgia; WPTF, Raleigh, North Carolina; and WAPI, Birmingham, Alabama. For most of these engagements, he starred with Jack Anglin, with whom he formed the team of Johnnie and Jack in 1938. With their supporting group, the Tennessee Mountain Boys, they toured widely in the next few years and the period after World War II.

In 1947, the Wrights and Jack Anglin joined the cast of the KWKH *Louisiana Hayride* in Shreveport. In 1951, Johnnie and Jack scored two major national hits, "Crying Heart Blues" and "Poison Love." The team was given the high sign in 1952 from the *Grand Ole Opry* and moved to Nashville. Johnnie and Jack had a big year in 1954 with such top-10 national hits as "Beware of It," "Goodnight, Sweetheart, Goodnight." and "I Get So Lonely." Two other top hits were "South of New Orleans" and "The Moon Is High and So Am I." Many of the audience favorites were songs written by Wright and Anglin. During their twenty-five-year association, they wrote more than 100 songs, many of which were bestsellers for other major artists. Their LP output included *Hits of Johnnie and Jack* on RCA Victor (1960) and *Johnnie and Jack* (1963) and *Sincerely* on Camden.

The team came to an end on March 8, 1963 when Jack was killed in a car crash near Madison, Tennessee. Johnny reorganized the Tennessee Mountain Boys, adding Kitty Wells and their daughter Ruby, and Bill Phillips. The new troupe was acclaimed on a cross-country tour, the forerunner of many appearances around the United States during the 1960s. In 1965, Johnny scored another top-10 hit with his recording of "Hello Viet Nam." The song provided the title for a successful LP. Johnny's credits in the 1960s included two other LPs, *Saturday Night* and *Country Music Special*. Besides appearing in all fifty states during this period, the Johnny Wright group also traveled to Canada, the Far East, and many parts of Europe.

Some of the other songs recorded by Wright over the years are "I Get So Lonely," "Sailor Man," "Leave Our Moon Alone," "Lonely Island Pearl," "That's the Way the Cookie Crumbles," "Sweetie Pie," "Humming Bird," "Baby, It's in the Making," "All the Time," "Pleasure Not a Habit in Mexico," "What Do You Know About Heartaches," "You Can't Divorce My Heart," "Banana Boat Song," "I Want to Be Loved," "I Love You Better than You Know," "Love, Love, Love," "Live and Let Live," "Keep the Flag Flying," "Nickels, Quarters and Dimes," "Dear John Letter," "I Don't Claim to Be an Angel," "You Can't Get the Country Out of a Boy," and "Three Ways of Knowing."

Johnny also appeared in a movie, *Second Fiddle to a Steel Guitar*. During the 1970s, he and his wife cohosted their own syndicated *Kitty Wells–Johnny Wright* TV show. (See also Wells, Kitty)

WYNETTE, TAMMY: *Singer, guitarist, accordionist, pianist, songwriter. Born near Tupelo, Mississippi, May 5, 1942.*

From a tar-paper shack in Mississippi to worldwide acclaim as top female vocalist in country music (a French critic called her The Edith Piaf of country America) describes the spectacular saga of Tammy Wynette. Overcoming many obstacles, she fought her way to stardom and set new standards for country singers in the 1960s and 1970s.

Tammy's vicissitudes began before she had any understanding of the world around her. She was only eight months old when her father, guitarist William Hollis Pugh, died. Her mother had to go to Birmingham, Alabama, to earn a living in an aircraft factory, leaving Tammy in the care of her grandparents (whom she lived with until she was thirteen). Her early years on her grandparents' farm in Mississippi, she recalled, were much like the life described in the song "Ode to Billy Joe." When she was old enough she picked and chopped cotton and baled hay along with the hired hands. The fact that her grandfather paid her the going pay rate, which served as her allowance, gave her a spirit of independence that served her well in later years.

After World War II, her mother returned to help bring her up. By that time, Tammy had had her first taste of music, singing Sacred Harp religious songs. (In this form of singing, notes were sung instead of words.) She also picked up some country songs as a child. "The first song I ever learned to sing," Tammy told Dixie Dern of *Music City News*, "was 'Sally Let Your Hands Hang Down' and I remember my grandfather, one of the greatest people in the world, used to get such a kick out of hearing me sing that. Then I learned a song that Kitty Wells and her daughter, Ruby, had out called 'How Far Is Heaven.' Mother asked me to learn that. . . . It was so close to home, you see, Daddy being dead."

She recalled singing "Sally" for company as a little girl. "My granddaddy would wink and say 'come here, Nellie Belle (he always called me Nellie Belle), come here and sing "Sally" for me.' Then they would all get such a kick to see me—I was just about five years old—play the piano and sing that song. My grandmother hated it! She didn't think it was a nice song at all."

As she grew older, she became interested in learning to play some of the instruments left her by her father. The collection included guitars, accordion, piano, mandolin, and bass fiddle. Her mother let Tammy take music lessons, but tried to persuade her daughter to use music only as a hobby. The lessons went on for five years, ending before Tammy was in her teens.

Wynette's youthful desire to become a performer was strong. In her teens, she loved to entertain. As she told Deen, "I remember in high school whenever the bell would ring for a fifteen- or twenty-minute recess . . . I might go for a Coke or doughnut, but then I always headed to the auditorium and the piano. That is where I spent all my extra time in school. A whole gang would come in and sit around and play and sing and that was every day, every single day I was in school. Every time there was a chapel program they always called me in to round up people to do it. They knew that was my interest."

However, just before finishing high school she traded her music dreams for marriage and settled in Tupelo, Mississippi, with her husband. After a few months, they returned to the rural environment, taking up residence near her grandparents' home, about fifty miles from Tupelo. After her first daughter was born, Tammy learned hairdressing. She worked for a time in a beauty shop in Tupelo and then switched to a job as a chiropractor's receptionist.

Her working career was interrupted by new additions to her family. She had a second daughter and was carrying a third when her marriage broke up.

Wynette moved to Birmingham, Alabama, and worked in a beauty shop until her next child was born. The baby girl was born prematurely and developed spinal meningitis soon after Tammy brought her home. She nursed the child, helped by her relations, until the baby was sufficiently on the way to recovery for her to go back to work to support her family and also attempt to pay off over $6,000 in bills incurred during her baby's illness. She

needed some way of augmenting her income. In the back of her mind she always had thought about doing something with her musical skills and now necessity forced her to. She persisted in seeking work as an entertainer and finally managed to get a performing role on the *Country Boy Eddie Show* on WBRC–TV in Birmingham.

She also sang in clubs in several southern cities, including Memphis, and began writing songs with Fred Lehner of station WYAM in Birmingham. Doors began to open for her in the music field, and, after she took part in a Porter Wagoner package show and he asked her to perform with the show in several local towns, she felt confident that she could earn a full-time living as an entertainer.

Her prime need was a recording contract, and she began to make the rounds of recording companies. Wynette traveled to Nashville and auditioned first for United Artists, then for Hickory and Kapp. Each visit resulted in a little more interest, but no contract. Her Kapp reception was so good she returned to Birmingham expecting a call or letter any day. But several months went by and nothing happened. She went up to Nashville again, partly to try other companies and partly to try to place some songs with Epic that a friend of hers had written with one of the label's major artists in mind.

Not much happened with the songs, but Epic executives were impressed with her potential, and the long-sought recording contract finally materialized. Soon after signing with Epic in 1966, Wynette recorded a single of Johnny Paycheck's composition "Apartment #9." The record became a big hit in 1967 and, when she followed with an even greater number, the top-10 hit "Your Good Girl's Gonna Go Bad," her position as one of the most promising newcomers was secure. Adding weight to that was the choice of another 1967 hit, "I Don't Wanna Play House," by members of the National Academy of the Recording Arts & Sciences as the Best C&W Solo Vocal Performance, Female, of 1967. She had still another top-10 hit in 1967 in a duet with David Houston, "Elusive Dreams."

Proving that 1967 was no one-time phenomenon, Tammy turned out equally impressive recordings during the closing years of the 1960s, including such country classics as "D-I-V-O-R-C-E" and "Take Me to Your World" in 1968 and "Stand By Your Man," a number-one hit in 1969. The last-named song earned her a second Grammy for Best Country Vocal Performance, Female, of 1969. By late 1969, she had enough legitimate successes for Epic to issue her *Greatest Hits, Volume 1* LP, which did so well with country fans that it was certified gold by the Recording Industry Association of America, the first album by a female country vocalist to do that.

During the late 1960s, Tammy became one of the most popular concert artists on the country-music circuit, playing before enthusiastic crowds throughout the United States. She also was a guest on major network TV programs and, in 1969, signed on as a regular cast member of the *Grand Ole Opry,* an affiliation still in effect at the start of the 1980s.

The 1970s proved to be as rewarding for Wynette in terms of record success as the late 1960s had been. Besides turning out her usual quota of solo hit singles, she teamed up with George Jones in the early 1970s for one of the top-ranked duets in the country field. The two became husband and wife in the early 1970s, a highly publicized merger that later turned into a highly publicized marital break-up. Among the hit singles Tammy achieved by herself or with George the first half of the 1970s were "The Wonders You Perform" in 1970; "The Cere-money" (with Jones) and "My Man" in 1972; "Another Lonely Song" (co-written with Billy Sherrill and N. Wilson) in 1974; and "I Still Believe in Fairy Tales" in 1975. Some of her other hit songs of the late 1960s and early 1970s were "I'll See Him Through," "Run, Woman, Run," "The Wonders You Perform," "We Sure Can Love Each Other," "Good Lovin'," and "Bedtime Story."

In the late 1960s and early 1970s, many honors and awards came Tammy's way. She was almost always one of the three finalists in the *Music City News* poll for Top Female Vocalist and came in first several times. She also regularly made the top five finalists in Country Music Association voting for Female Vocalist of the Year and three times won the award.

Her name continued to show up regularly on the top rungs of national country charts in the second half of the 1970s. Among her singles bestsellers were " 'Til I Can Make It on My Own" (early 1976), "Golden Ring" (number one in August 1976), "You and Me" (fall 1976), "Southern California" (with George Jones, summer 1977), "One of a Kind" (late 1977), and "Womanhood" (fall 1978).

Besides her achievements as a singles artist, Wynette also had an unusually good track record as an album artist. Most of her LPs made the country charts, with many of them entering the top 10. Her debut on Epic, *Tammy Wynette,* came out in June 1967. This was followed by such late 1960s albums as *Your Good Girl's Gonna Go Bad, D-I-V-O-R-C-E, Inspiration,* and the first volume of her *Greatest Hits.* At year end, she had three LPs on the country lists, *The World of Tammy Wynette, Tammy's Touch,* and *Greatest Hits.* In early 1970, she made the charts with the albums *First Songs of the First Lady* and *Ways to Love a Man* (issued 3/70). At year-end she had three LPs on the country lists, *The World of Tammy Wynette, Tammy's Touch,* and *Greatest Hits.* In 1971, her albums included *We Sure Can Love Each Other* (7/71) and *Greatest Hits, Volume 2* (10/71). Also issued during 1971 was a duet album with George Jones, *We Go Together,* which made upper-chart levels in early 1972. Also a chart hit in the spring of 1972 was Tammy's *Bedtime Story.* In the fall, she and George teamed up again for the top-10 album *Me and the First Lady.* Among Tammy's other chart-making LPs of the 1970s were *Another Lonely Song* (top 10, May 1974), *We're Gonna Hold On* (with George Jones, top 20, May 1974), *Woman to Woman* (late 1974-early 1975), *Til I Can Make It on My Own* (number three in May 1976), *Golden Ring* (with George Jones, top 10, fall 1976), *Let's Get Together* (top 20, early 1977), *Womanhood* (top 20, August 1978), and *Tammy Wynette's Greatest Hits, Volume IV* (top 10, late 1978).

During the 1970s, Wynette's stage appearances took her to many overseas nations in addition to her concerts all over the United States and Canada. Her popularity in Europe was particularly high; in 1976 she was named Number One Female Vocalist of Great Britain in an English poll. By the end of the 1970s, worldwide sales of her recordings approached the 20 million mark, and her total of number-one-ranked singles and albums was thirty-five.

In the fall of 1979, her autobiography (as told to Joan Dew), *Stand by Your Man*, was published by Simon and Schuster. During the year, her 1978 albums *Womanhood* and *Greatest Hits, Volume IV* were on the charts for long periods. Her 1979 release, *Just Tammy*, also made the lists. In 1980, she teamed up with George Jones once more.

The pain of their earlier relationship, she asserted, had faded into the background. She said, "George and I never lost respect for each other. Our marriage didn't work, but that was the only thing that didn't work for us. We've always worked well professionally." This seemed borne out by the success of their 1980 duet single, "Two Story House," that rose to number two on the charts in May 1980. A few months later, Tammy had a hit solo single with "He Was There (When I Needed You)." In the fall, Tammy and George had the single "A Pair of Old Sneakers" on the charts for a number of months. In the spring of 1981, she had a new album, *You Brought Me Back*, from which the single hit "Cowboys Don't Shoot Straight (Like They Used To)" was culled.

YOUNG, FARON: *Singer, guitarist, actor, songwriter, band leader (the Country Deputies), music publisher, trade paper publisher. Born Shreveport, Louisiana, February 25, 1932.*

One of Faron Young's hit records of the mid-1950's began "Live fast . . . ," a motto that could be used to describe several aspects of his life. One of those included an intense devotion to country music that made him a top star in his early twenties and one of the most diverse operators in the field a decade later.

Although city-born, Faron moved to the country as a child when his father bought a small dirt farm outside Shreveport. While still in public school he received his first guitar and spent many hours figuring out chords and fingering. When Faron entered Fair Park High School in Shreveport, he could sing many of the top country hits, providing his own guitar accompaniment. It wasn't long before he formed his own band and played at school affairs as well as local fairs and hoedowns.

At the start of 1950s, Faron entered Centenary College of Louisiana. For a while he tried to continue to combine studies with part-time musicianship. However, he had become well known in the region as an exciting performer and the offers of musical advancement were too tempting. He joined station KWKH and soon moved over to the cast of the *Louisiana Hayride*. Another rising star, Webb Pierce, also was on the *Hayride*. Pierce took Young on as a featured vocalist for tours over the entire southern region.

In 1951, Young was signed by Capitol Records. He quickly turned out two hit recordings, "Tattle Tale Tears" and "Have I Waited Too Long." In 1953, he became a regular cast member of the *Grand Ole Opry*. His meteoric rise was delayed by the Korean War: he entered the Army in the fall of 1952. No sooner did he finish basic training than he won an Army talent show on ABC–TV. Between 1952 and 1954, he toured the world entertaining troops and was starred on the Army's radio recruiting show.

Even before his discharge, Faron was making a dent in the national ratings. In 1953, he had a top-10 recording of his own composition "Goin' Steady" on Capitol. In 1954, he returned to Nashville to rejoin the *Opry*. He received a royal welcome from a rapidly growing number of fans and soon had another top-10 hit, "If You Ain't Lovin'." He hit his stride in 1955 with such national successes as "Go Back You Fool," "It's a Great Life," and "Live Fast, Love Hard and Die Young." He was voted "America's Number One Artist of 1955" by *Southern Farm and Ranch* magazine.

There were very few months in the years that followed when Young was not represented on the national hit charts. In 1956, he had top-10 hits in "I've Got Five Dollars and It's Saturday Night" and "Sweet Dreams." In 1957, he scored with "I Miss You Already." He rounded out the 1950s with such hits as "Alone with You" and "That's the Way I Feel" in 1958 and the number-one-ranked "Country Girl" in 1959. During the 1950s, besides touring widely, Faron made his acting debut in several movies, including the 1958 *Country Music Holiday* with Ferlin Husky and Zsa Zsa Gabor. He was also featured in *Daniel Boone* and *Hidden Guns.*

Faron began the 1960s with two top-10 hits he coauthored, "Face to the Wall" (with Bill Anderson) and "Your Old Used to Be" (with Hilda Yoimd). In 1961, he coauthored a hit—"Backtrack"—with Alex Zanetis. He also turned out another number-one-rated song, "Hidden Walls." He was represented in 1962 with "The Comeback" and "Three Days" (coauthor, Willie Nelson) and in early 1963 with "Down by the River."

In 1963, Faron switched labels from Capitol to Mercury. He continued to provide his new company with national hits, including "The Yellow Bandana" in 1963, "You'll Drive Me Back" in 1964, "Walk Tall" in 1965, "I Guess I Had Too Much to Dream Last Night" in 1967, "She Went a Little Farther" in 1968, and "I've Got Precious Memories" and "Wine Me Up" in 1969.

Young's output of LPs by the mid-1960s was well over the two dozen mark. The titles on Capitol included *Sweethearts or Strangers; This Is Faron Young* (1958); *Talk About Hits* (1959); *Best of Faron Young, Fan Club Favorites* (1961); *All Time Great Hits* (1963); and *Memory Lane* (1964). His Mercury LPs included *This is Faron; Faron*

Young Aims at the West (1963); *Songs for Country Folks, Dance Favorites* (1964); *Songs of Mountains and Valleys* (1965); *Faron Young's Greatest Hits* and *Faron Young Sings the Best of Jim Reeves* (1966); *Unmitigated Gall* (4/67); and *I've Got Precious Memories* (7/69).

During the 1960s, Young toured all the states and made several trips to Germany, France, Mexico, and England. By the mid-1960s, he had many other flourishing projects, including his own music publishing firm, Vanadore Music, and his own monthly paper, *Music City News.* Long an ardent auto racing driver and fan, he was also owner of Sulphur Dell auto track in Nashville. Among his souvenirs was a letter from President Johnson thanking Young for playing at a number of the President's speaking engagements during the 1964 campaign.

Faron started off the 1970s with the charted album *Wine Me Up* on Mercury. He continued to turn out a series of new LPs on the label during the first half of the decade, including *Occasional Wife/If I Ever Fall in Love, Step Aside, It's Four in the Morning,* and *This Little Girl of Mine.* His early 1970s singles output included such top-10 discs as "It's Four in the Morning" and "This Little Girl of Mine" in 1972 and "Some Kind of Woman" in 1974. "It's Four in the Morning" was voted Best Single of 1972 by the Country Music Association of Great Britain. In the mid-1970s, his charted singles included "Another You" and "Here I Am in Dallas" in 1975, "Feel Again" and "I'd Just Be Fool Enough" in 1976, and "Crutches" in 1977. Though he placed many singles on the charts in the first half of the decade, his recording career slowed down markedly as the 1970s went by, perhaps because of the pressures of his nonperforming activities. He left Mercury for MCA Records in the late 1970s and turned out some material for them, including the 1979 LP *Chapter Two,* but nothing that resembled his hits of earlier years. By the start of the 1980s that association ended.

Meanwhile, he retained a strong following for his concert work and remained a cast regular of the *Grand Ole Opry,* still featured on the show in the early 1980s.

He appeared on many country TV specials throughout the 1970s and into the 1980s, including the 1979 Hank Williams, Sr. memorial show. He continued to serve as publisher of the *Music City News*, still one of the country-music field's major trade papers and influences in the early 1980s.

YOUNG, JESSE COLIN: *Singer, guitarist, band leader, songwriter. Born New York, New York, circa 1942.*

Among the names that crop up in a rundown of the early 1960s folk ferment in New York are artists like Bob Dylan, Joan Baez, Pat Sky, Phil Ochs, John Sebastian—and Jesse Colin Young. Young, a fine singer and reasonably proficient guitarist, moved over to folk-rock just about the same time as Dylan. Although he never achieved the resounding success of the Minnesotan, his work had an impact on the genre that was still being felt at the beginning of the 1980s.

Jesse came from an Ivy League upper-middle-class family. As he stated in biographical information for Elektra Records in 1978, "My father and his brother both went to Harvard, and both taught there and then my uncle went on to become the dean of the graduate school at Yale and my father became an executive comptroller in business, so it was a real heartbreaker for my family for me to be thrown out of school [at fifteen, Young was discharged from the prestigious Phillips Andover Academy in Andover, Massachusetts for playing his electric guitar during study hour]. But it probably saved me from going to Harvard and getting locked into the corporate challenge."

As a child, he recalled loving some of his family's opera records of Caruso. In the early 1950s, he was attracted to Alan Freed's rock program on New York radio and the R&B show called *Jocko's Rocket Ship* on WWRL. At the age of eight he sang at a reunion of his father's Harvard class (1925). "The old man had taught me all the Harvard fight songs and there I was singing in front of hundreds of people, accompanied by an accordion player." He was to think of performing again not long after.

Although he'd been sent down from Phillips Andover, Jesse completed public high school and went on to enter Ohio State University (a school that spawned other folk artists, such as Phil Ochs). There was strong interest in folk music on campus and Jesse was captivated by the bluegrass sounds of Bill Monroe as well as roots blues as performed by people like T-Bone Walker. The next year, his love for folk and blues caused him to abruptly leave school and head east to join the growing group of young musicians playing that kind of material in and around major East Coast cities.

"A couple of years later I was sitting in this apartment on the lower East Side, sitting at Lightning Hopkins' knee and being allowed to play music with him, and being patted on the shoulder! Later I took Lightning to a motorcycle race. He was in his blue serge suit, wearing a big ring; he was King of the Blues and perfectly at ease in a place where there were no black people."

Jesse sang in small clubs and coffee houses on the Greenwich Village circuit, often earning money by passing the hat. In the early 1960s a musician named Bobby Scott, a sideman for Bobby Darin, became enthusiastic about Young's talents and paid for and produced his first album, *Soul of a City Boy*. The album was released by Capitol in 1964 and, while not a howling success, helped bring Jesse an engagement at the major Boston folk center, Club 47. That, in turn, led to other dates in folk clubs. However, Young, like Dylan, was already leaning toward blending rock into his material, which sometimes didn't sit well with folk listeners. Scott continued to support Jesse, producing another LP, *Young Blood*, which was issued by Mercury and which included the John Sebastian band for backing. (Soon after, Sebastian was on the way to stardom with a band called the Lovin' Spoonful.)

The experience encouraged Young to start his own band. He got together with another folk music artist, Jerry Corbitt, to form the Youngbloods. The idea took shape when Corbitt and Young crossed paths in Cambridge, Massachusetts. Soon after, they added Memphis-born (September 26, 1941) Joe Bauer on drums and hit the road. "The PA's weren't set up for the folk-rock sound and some people hated it, as it was not too quiet. We made a circuit of Toronto, Springfield, and Philadelphia and when we got to New York, Banana joined." The band had started in Cambridge, and that, oddly, was Banana's home-town (born circa 1946), though he joined in Manhattan. He brought considerable experience on electric guitar and keyboards to the new band.

The group rehearsed for much of 1966, occasionally playing club dates that helped bring notice from underground fans and publications. It also helped whet record company interest; several offered contracts before the year was out. The group finally settled on RCA and began recording initial material in late 1966. The debut album, titled *The Youngbloods,* was issued in February 1967. It attracted some attention mainly on the East Coast, and one song, "Grizzly Bear," became a regional hit in the East and Midwest. It was another track that eventually became the band's most famous, "Get Together" (written by Dino Valente), a plea for human cooperation that still is often played on rock stations and sometimes at folk festivals. (The album later was retitled *Get Together.*)

RCA released their second album, *Earth Music,* in November 1967. Before their next LP got under way, they had moved to San Francisco in 1968. In 1969, their last LP for RCA, *Elephant Mountain,* came out, just when they achieved their first gold record for "Get Together," recently issued as a single. That success prompted RCA to reissue the debut album under the name *Get Together.* RCA also issued a retrospective called *The Best of the Youngbloods.*

In 1970, the group's contract with RCA ended and, about the same time, Jerry Corbitt departed to try a solo career. The others went on for a time as a trio, setting up their own custom label, Raccoon, for their new work. They signed a distribution agreement with Warner Brothers, which issued four LPs of the band in the early 1970s: *Rock Festival, Ride the Wind, Good and Dusty,* and *High on a Ridge Top.* Raccoon also added other acts, producing and issuing several bluegrass and folk albums,

including those of singer-songwriters Michael Hurley and Jeffrey Cain.

However, Young was becoming restless with the band alignment, as indicated by his debut solo album on Warner Brothers, *Together,* which reached upper-chart levels in late 1972. By 1973, when he had similar response to his second solo effort, *Song for Juli,* the Youngbloods were no more.

Since then, Young has stressed his solo work, which reached a peak in his Warner Brothers phase with the 1974 album *Light Shine* and 1975 *Song Bird,* both works that effectively combined Young's diverse musical interest with tracks that varied from folk or blues-dominated rock to more hard driving material. The songs for the last named LP were composed by Jesse during a cross-country tour in which he opened for Crosby, Stills, Nash, and Young. His 1975 album for Warner Brothers, issued in 1976, was a live album titled *On the Road.* In 1977, his final Warner's collection came out, *Love on the Wing,* coproduced by him and Felix Pappalardi, an old friend who had produced the first two Youngbloods albums. (Charlie Daniels produced the third RCA disc.)

In 1978, a new stage in his career began with a move to Elektra/Asylum, which issued his debut on the label, *American Dreams,* in the fall. The album, which was somewhat uneven, included such unusual items as a disco-flavored song, "Slow and Easy," a remake of a Buddy Holly tune, "Rave On," and an ambitious "Suite," which Young states is autobiographical. "I really didn't start out to write a suite; it just started out as pieces and, as more of these pieces came together, it became a bigger picture. The suite, which has five sections, with other movements within them, encompasses elements of blues, rock 'n' roll, Jamaican music and all the American influences."

YOUNG, NEIL: *Singer, guitarist, songwriter. Born Toronto, Canada, November 12, 1945.*

A variety of influences shaped Neil Young's evolution into one of the foremost folk-rock writers and practitioners of the late 1960s and throughout the 1970s. His musical interests first were stirred by the broadcast recordings of the initial wave of rock stars from the United States. Later he briefly became a part of the folk movement before combining those forms into folk (and later country) rock formats.

Although born in Toronto, Neil spent much of his early years further west in Winnipeg. He became interested in rock music when Canadian radio began to broadcast the mid-1950s recordings of people like Bill Haley and Elvis Presley. In his teens, he began to make his first serious efforts to become a musician, first teaching himself to play an Arthur Godfrey-style ukulele and later progressing to acoustic guitar. In the early 1960s, he worked the coffee house circuit with various groups and then organized his own folk-rock band, Neil Young and the Squires, which became a local favorite in Winnipeg.

Looking for more career opportunities, he gave up band work and moved to Los Angeles in 1966, intending to concentrate on writing and solo vocalizing. But once there, he renewed acquaintances with Steve Stills and Richie Furay, whom he had met previously on the folk circuit. They persuaded him to join their new group, Buffalo Springfield. It was an excellent match—Neil's fine guitar work and his original song contributions played a key part in making the band one of the all-time great folk-rock combinations, even though it remained intact for less than two years. Among the classic Springfield songs provided by him were "On the Way Home," "Broken Arrow," "Expecting to Fly," "Mr. Soul," and "I Am a Child."

After the band broke up in 1968, Young again wanted to strike out as a solo performer, but was sidetracked to some extent by the arguments of Crosby, Stills, and Nash in favor of his joining their superstar assemblage. He accepted only because they claimed that it would be a loose alignment in which each member was free to pursue his individual music goals if he so desired. However, before he joined them in mid-1969, he already had completed work on his debut solo LP on Reprise Records, Neil Young, issued in January 1969, and moved on to a second

one. For that collection, he brought in a new backup band, a group called Crazy Horse he had first heard at the Whisky A-Go-Go on Los Angeles' Sunset Strip. The group originally contained Danny Whitten on guitar, Billy Talbot on bass guitar, and Ralph Molina on drums. He expanded it to a quartet for a time by adding producer-arranger-songwriter-instrumentalist Jack Nitzsche. The LP that resulted from the new association was Everybody Knows This Is Nowhere, issued in May 1969. The album became one of the major successes of 1969–70 and Neil's solo reputation was ensured.

Even as he began working with Crosby, Stills, Nash, and Young, he was thinking about his next solo effort. He only remained a regular member of that now legendary band into the early 1970s, but helped turn out two best-selling and still classic albums, Deja Vu (3/70) and Four Way Street (4/71), both issued on Atlantic Records.

In between those two, Reprise released his third solo effort, After the Gold Rush, arguably one of the all-time great folk-rock LPs. For this LP, Neil prepared such songs as "Southern Man," "Tell Me Why," "Only Love Can Break Your Heart," "Don't Let It Bring You Down," and "I Believe in You." The completed album was certainly rock 'n' roll, but with the subtle flavor of folk music and with lyrics tinged with poetry. After it was issued in August 1970, it was acclaimed by critics and record buyers alike with magazines like Time and Newsweek calling it a candidate for record of the year. It went on to go well past gold-record award levels (as did its predecessor).

Young's next solo LP didn't come out until February 1972, but it too was a blockbuster. Called Harvest, it contained such hit songs as "Old Man," "War Song," and, most notable of all, Neil's number-one rock standard, "Heart of Gold." The album provided him with a third gold record. In addition to his other projects, in the early 1970s, Neil wrote, directed, and took part in the film Journey Through the Past. The original soundtrack album came out in November 1972 and remained on the charts well into 1973, though the film itself never came out during that year. The LP easily went past gold-record levels. His next solo album, *Time Fades Away,* came out in October 1973 and won another gold record. However, as a whole it didn't measure up to the previous few albums and some critics wondered whether Neil might have written himself out.

As the decade went by, though, Young proved that those fears were groundless with a body of material that often matched his best work of the early 1970s. His LP *On the Beach* (7/74) was much better than *Time Fades Away* and his two 1975 releases, *Tonight's the Night* and *Zuma* (issued, respectively, in June and November), were among the year's best. Those LPs reflected considerably more despair and disillusionment than his earlier work. *Tonight's the Night,* for instance, was a concept album that explored his feelings about the deaths from drug overdoses of Crazy Horse's Danny Whitten and another friend from the Crosby, Stills, Nash, and Young band, Bruce Berry.

In the mid-1970s, he returned briefly for some recording and concert work with Steve Stills, which resulted in the September 1976 LP *Long May You Run.* After that, he only did solo work (usually working with Crazy Horse, by then a threesome of Talbot, Molina, and, on guitar and keyboards, Frank Sampedro) starting with the June 1977 album, *American Stars 'n Bars,* a gold-record winner. In October 1977, Reprise issued one of the best retrospective collections of a major pop artist to come out in the period, the three-record LP set *Decade.* In September 1978, another new solo LP, *Comes a Time,* was released. In support of his June 1979 LP, *Rust Never Sleeps,* Neil and Crazy Horse embarked on a coast-to-coast U.S. concert tour, his first in several years. The concerts were among the best of the late 1970s and the LP went gold, as did the release based on those concerts, *Live Rust,* in 1980.

YOUNG, STEVE: *Singer, guitarist, songwriter. Born southern United States, mid-1940s.*

It's difficult to say why a very talented artist, highly regarded by his musical peers and able to turn out above-average recordings, may languish for years with little public recognition. So it has been with Steve Young, of whom Waylon Jennings once said, "Steve Young is the second greatest country music singer—to George Jones, of course." While some of his compositions became hits for others, at the start of the 1980s he still was little known, though many expected that, like Willie Nelson, his time would come some day.

Born in the South, Young was influenced by a variety of artists in his youth, from rock 'n' roll greats like Elvis Presley to blues artists, folk artists, and progressive country performers like Jennings, Nelson, and Johnny Cash. In his teens, he already was playing guitar and seeking work in the music field. After leaving school he picked up experience by playing a succession of veteran's halls and honky-tonks around Alabama and Georgia. By the end of the 1960s, he had served a long apprenticeship on that circuit and already had accumulated a group of original songs.

Eventually, the trail led to Los Angeles, where Young made his initial contacts with the major music industry companies and managed to complete an album titled *Seven Bridges Road* that came out on Reprise Records in the early 1970s and later was available on Blue Canyon Records. Not much happened with the album, though it did bring him increasing attention from some hard-core followers of new trends in country music. Word about his ability spread among what was known as the outlaw segment of country, a term that embraced people like Jennings, Nelson, Jerry Jeff Walker, Tompall Glaser, and their associates. Many of them went to hear Steve perform if they got the chance and came away highly impressed. Some of those artists, along with other members of the country field, included a song or two by Steve in their album sessions. In 1973, in fact, Waylon Jennings used Steve's song "Lonesome, Orn'ry and Mean" as the title track of an album. His rendition of the number remains one of the best tracks in Jennings' career.

During the 1970s, Young moved to Nashville. He still mainly played small clubs and bars and still found a better reception for his songs from other performers than from the public. There were hopes that this might change when discussions began for a new recording contract with RCA. He finally signed in February 1976, and three months later his debut on the label, *Renegade Picker*, was released. The album contained an impressive group of original songs, strongly delivered by Young, and won deserved praise from many reviewers. But Steve got lost in the shuffle of a large company and did not get much promotional support. The same thing held true for a second LP, *No Place to Fall*, issued a year later.

Neither of his RCA albums made much headway in the marketplace, though both promised to become collectors' items in the future. By the late 1970s, that association ended and Young's career marked time for a while.

ACADEMY OF COUNTRY MUSIC

The Academy of Country Music (originally called the Academy of Country and Western Music) was founded in Los Angeles, California in 1964 in response to the needs of the industry and fans in the western and southwestern United States. The geographical distance from Nashville precluded active participation on a regular basis of many artists, songwriters, music publishers, and record companies with the acknowledged hub of country music in Nashville. From the outset, the Academy was oriented towards a broad service thrust, embracing considerations of fans as well as industry personnel rather than being strictly a trade organization as is the Nashville-based Country Music Association. While many CMA stalwarts, like Cliffie Stone, Johnny Bond and Bill Boyd, maintained a visible Nashville presence, they also devoted much time and effort on behalf of the Academy.

Initially regional in character, over the years the Academy has expanded its scope towards national impact. This is reflected in the shift of its awards show (first presented in 1965) from a local event to one that is telecast nationwide and to other countries as well. The Academy's program (on NBC-TV as of 1982) was produced by Dick Clark in the early 1980s and reflects a more "Hollywood" presentation, where media stars join country music artists for gala presentations, a format eschewed by the CMA telecast.

Providing continuity in Academy activities from its early years to the 1980s, has been executive secretary, Fran Boyd.

ACADEMY OF COUNTRY AND WESTERN MUSIC AWARDS *

1965

Man of the Year	Roger Miller
Top Male Vocalist	Buck Owens
Top Female Vocalist	Bonnie Owens
Best Vocal Group	Merle Haggard and Bonnie Owens
Best Band Leader	Buck Owens
Most Promising Male Vocalist	Merle Haggard
Most Promising Female Vocalist	Kaye Adams

* Awards are determined by vote of the Academy membership except for the Pioneer Award and the Jim Reeves Memorial Award, both of which are chosen by the Board of Directors. The Pioneer Award, created in 1968, is "for the recognition of outstanding and unprecedented achievement in the field of country music." It is not necessarily an annual award and has had more than one recipient in a year. The Jim Reeves Memorial Award, created in 1969, is "presented annually to an individual, not necessarily a performing artist, who had made substantial contributions towards furthering international acceptance of country music during the preceding calendar year."

1965 (cont.)

Best Songwriter	Roger Miller
Best TV Personality	Billy Mize
Best Radio Personality	Biff Collie
Best Producer/A&R Man	Ken Nelson
Best Music Publisher	Central Songs, Inc.
Best Nightclub	Palomino Club (Los Angeles)
Best Talent Management	Jack McFadden
Best Publication	Billboard

Sidemen:

Best Steel Guitar	Red Rhodes
Best Fiddle	Billy Armstrong
Best Lead Guitar	Phil Baugh
Best Bass	Bob Morris
Best Piano	Billy Liebert
Best Drums	Muddy Berry

1966

Man of the Year *	Dean Martin
Top Male Vocalist	Merle Haggard
Top Female Vocalist	Bonnie Guitar
Top Vocal Group	Bonnie Owens and Merle Haggard
Band Leader/Band	Buck Owens Buckaroos
Most Promising Male Vocalist	Billie Mize
Most Promising Female Vocalist	Cathy Taylor
Most Promising Vocal Group	Bob Morris and Faye Hardin
Best TV Personality	Billy Mize
Best Radio Personality (tie)	Biff Collie/Bob Kingsley
Best Producer/A&R Man	Ken Nelson
Best Music Publisher	Central Songs, Inc.
Best Country Nightclub	Palomino Club
Best Talent Management/Booking Agent	Jack McFadden
Song of the Year	"Apartment #9" (Bobby Austin/Fuzzy Owen/Johnny Paycheck)

Sidemen:

Lead Guitar	Jimmy Bryant
Steel Guitar (tie)	Tom Brumley/Ralph Mooney
Drums	Jerry Wiggins
Bass	Bob Morris
Fiddle	Billy Armstrong
Piano	Billy Liebert

1967

Man of the Year	Joey Bishop
Top Male Vocalist	Glen Campbell
Top Female Vocalist	Lynn Anderson
Top Vocal Group	Sons of the Pioneers
Top Duet	Merle Haggard/Bonnie Owens

* Award based on contributions to advancing country music.

Band Leader/Band	Bucky Owens Buckaroos
Most Promising Male Vocalist	Jerry Inman
Most Promising Female Vocalist	Bobbie Gentry
Best TV Personality	Billy Mize
Best Radio Personality	Bob Kingsley
Best Country Nightclub	Palomino Club
Song of the Year	"It's Such a Pretty World Today" (Dale Noe/Freeway Music)
Album of the Year *and* Single Record of the Year	*Gentle on My Mind* (Glen Campbell/A&R: Al DeLorey)

Sidemen:

Lead Guitar	Jimmy Bryant
Steel Guitar	Red Rhodes
Drums	Pee Wee Adams
Bass	Red Wooten
Fiddle	Billy Armstrong
Piano	Earl Ball

1968

Man of the Year	Tom Smothers
Directors' Award	Nudie
Pioneer Award	"Uncle Art" Satherly
Most Promising Female	Cheryl Poole
Most Promising Male	Ray Sanders
Top Female Vocalist	Cathie Taylor
Top Male Vocalist	Glen Campbell
Album of the Year	Glen Campbell and Bobbie Gentry
Single Record of the Year (Award to Artist)	"Little Green Apples"/Roger Miller
Song of the Year (Award to Composer)	"Witchita Lineman"/Jim Webb
Top Vocal Group	Johnny & Jonie Mosby
Band of the Year (Club)	Billy Mize's Tennesseans
Band of the Year (Touring)	Buckaroos
Radio Personality (Regional)	Tex Williams
Radio Personality (Los Angeles)	Larry Scott
TV Personality	Glen Campbell
Country Nightclub (Regional)	Golden Nugget
Country Nightclub (Metropolitan)	Palomino
Steel Guitar	Red Rhodes
Piano	Earl Ball
Lead Guitar	Jimmy Bryant
Fiddle	Billy Armstrong
Drums	Jerry Wiggins
Bass	Red Wooten

1969

Man of the Year	John Aylesworth - Frank Peppiatt
Pioneer Award	Bob Wills
Jim Reeves Memorial Award	Joe Allison
Man of the Decade	Marty Robbins
Specialty Instrument	John Hartford

1969 (cont.)

Rhythm Guitar	Jerry Inman
Comedy Act	Roy Clark
Most Promising Male Vocalist	Freddy Weller
Most Promising Female Vocalist	Donna Fargo
Top Female Vocalist	Tammy Wynette
Top Male Vocalist	Merle Haggard
Album of the Year	*Okie From Muskogee*
Single Record of the Year	"Okie From Muskogee"
Song of the Year	"Okie From Muskogee"
Top Vocal Group	Kimberlys
Band of the Year	Merle Haggard's Strangers
Disc Jockey	Dick Haynes
TV Personality	Johnny Cash
Nightclub	Palomino Club
Steel Guitar	Buddy Emmons
Piano	Floyd Cramer
Lead Guitar	Al Bruno
Fiddle	Billy Armstrong
Drums	Jerry Wiggins
Bass	Billy Graham

1970

Man of the Year	Hugh Cherry
Jim Reeves Memorial Award	Bill Boyd
Pioneer Award	Tex Ritter, Patsy Montana
Entertainer of the Year	Merle Haggard
Top Male Vocalist	Merle Haggard
Top Female Vocalist	Lynn Anderson
Album of the Year	*"For The Good Times"*
Single Record of the Year	For The Good Times
Song of the Year	For The Good Times
Top Vocal Group	Kimberlys
Most Promising Male Vocalist	Buddy Alan
Most Promising Female Vocalist	Sammi Smith
Country Nightclub	Palomino Club
TV Personality	Johnny Cash
News Publication	Billboard
Radio Station	KLAC, Los Angeles
Disc Jockey	Corky Mayberry, KBBQ
Comedy Act	Roy Clark
Band of the Year (Non-Touring)	The Tony Booth Band
Band of the Year (Touring)	The Strangers
Steel Guitar	J. D. Maness
Piano	Floyd Cramer
Lead Guitar	Al Bruno
Fiddle	Billy Armstrong
Drums	Archie Francis
Bass	Billy Graham & Doyle Holly

1971

Man of the Year	Walter Knott
Jim Reeves Memorial Award	Roy Rogers
Pioneer Award	Bob Nolan, Stuart Hamlin, Tex Williams

Entertainer of the Year	Freddie Hart
Top Male Vocalist	Freddie Hart
Top Female Vocalist	Loretta Lynn
Album of the Year	*Easy Lovin'*
Single Record of the Year	"Easy Lovin' "
	Freddie Hart
Song of the Year	"Easy Lovin' "
Top Vocal Group	Conway Twitty/Loretta Lynn
Most Promising Male Vocalist	Tony Booth
Most Promising Female Vocalist	Barbara Mandrell
Country Nightclub	Palomino Club
TV Personality	Glen Campbell
Radio Station	KLAC, Los Angeles, Ca.
Disc Jockey	Larry Scott (KLAC)
Comedy Act	Roy Clark
Band of the Year (Non-Touring)	Tony Booth Band
Band of the Year (Touring)	Strangers
Steel Guitar	J. D. Manness
Piano	Floyd Cramer
Lead Guitar	Al Bruno
Fiddle	Billy Armstrong
Drums	Jerry Wiggins
Bass	Larry Booth

1972

Man of the Year	Lawrence Welk
Jim Reeves Memorial Award	Thurston Moore
Pioneer Award	Cliffie Stone, Gene Autry
Entertainer of the Year	Roy Clark
Top Male Vocalist	Merle Haggard
Top Female Vocalist	Donna Fargo
Album of the Year	*Happiest Girl/USA*
Single Record of the Year	"Happiest Girl/USA"—Donna Fargo
Song of the Year	"Happiest Girl/USA"
Top Vocal Group	Statler Brothers
Most Promising Male Vocalist	Johnny Rodriquez
Most Promising Female Vocalist	Tanya Tucker
Country Nightclub	Palomino Club
TV Personality	Roy Clark
Radio Station	KLAC, Los Angeles, California
Disc Jockey	Larry Scott
Band of the Year (Non-Touring)	Tony Booth Band
Band of the Year (Touring)	Strangers
Steel Guitar	Buddy Emmons
Piano	Floyd Cramer
Lead Guitar	Al Bruno
Fiddle	Billy Armstrong
Drums	Jerry Wiggins
Bass	Larry Garner (Booth)

1973

Song of the Year	"Behind Closed Doors"/Kenny O'Dell
Entertainer of the Year	Roy Clark
Single of the Year	"Behind Closed Doors"/Charlie Rich

1973 (cont.)

Top Female Vocalist of the Year	Loretta Lynn
Top Male Vocalist of the Year	Charlie Rich
Album of the Year	*Behind Closed Doors*/Charlie Rich
Most Promising Female Vocalist	Olivia Newton-John
Most Promising Male Vocalist	Dorsey Burnette
Top Vocal Duet or Group of the Year	Brush Arbor
Country Nightclub	The Palomino
Band of the Year (Non-Touring)	Sound Company/Ronnie Truhett
Band of the Year (Touring)	Brush Arbor
Steel Guitar	Red Rhodes
Piano	Floyd Cramer
Lead Guitar	Al Bruno
Fiddle	Billy Armstrong
Drums	Jerry Wiggins
Bass	Larry Booth
Jim Reeves Memorial Award	Sam Oouvello
Pioneer Award	Hank Williams
Disc Jockey of the Year Award	Craig Scott, WJJD, Chicago
Radio Station of the Year	KLAC, Los Angeles

1974

Bass Guitar	Billy Graham
Drums	Jerry Wiggins
Fiddle	Billy Armstrong
Lead Guitar	Al Bruno
Piano	Floyd Cramer
Steel Guitar	J.D. Mannes
Country Disc Jockey of the Year	Larry Scott
Country Radio Station of the Year	KLAC
Band of the Year (Touring)	Strangers
Band of the Year (Non-Touring)	The Palomino Riders
Country Nightclub of the Year	Palomino Club
Most Promising Female Vocalist	Linda Ronstadt
Most Promising Male Vocalist	Mickey Gilley
Top Vocal Group of the Year	Loretta Lynn/Conway Twitty
Album of the Year	*Back Home Again*/John Denver
Male Vocalist of the Year	Merle Haggard
Female Vocalist of the Year	Loretta Lynn
Single of the Year	"Country Bumpkin"/Cal Smith
Entertainer of the Year	Mac Davis
Song of the Year	"Country Bumpkin"/Don Wayne
Jim Reeves Memorial Award	Merv Griffin
Pioneer Award	Merle Travis/Tennessee Ernie Ford/ Johnny Bond

1975

Bass	Billy Graham
Drums	Archie Francis
Fiddle	Billy Armstrong
Lead Guitar	Russ Hansen
Piano	Jerry Lee Lewis
Steel Guitar	J.D. Manness
Rhythm Guitar	Jerry Inman

Country Radio Station of the Year	KLAC, Los Angeles, Ca.
Country Disc Jockey of the Year	Billy Parker, KVOO, Tulsa, Oklahoma
Country Music Nightclub of the Year	Palomino
Band of the Year (Touring)	Strangers (Merle Haggard)
Band of the Year (Non-Touring)	Palomino Riders (Jerry Inman)
Most Promising Female Vocalist	Crystal Gayle
Most Promising Male Vocalist	Freddy Fender
Top Vocal Group	Conway Twitty/Loretta Lynn
Album of the Year	*Feelings* (Loretta Lynn/Conway Twitty)
Male Vocalist of the Year	Conway Twitty
Female Vocalist of the Year	Loretta Lynn
Single Record of the Year	"Rhinestone Cowboy" (Glen Campbell)
Entertainer of the Year	Loretta Lynn
Song of the Year	"Rhinestone Cowboy" (Glen Campbell)
Jim Reeves Memorial Award	Dinah Shore
Pioneer Award	Roy Rogers

1976

Bass	Curtis Stone
Fiddle	Billy Armstrong
Drums	Archie Francis
Lead Guitar	Danny Michaels
Piano	Hargus "Pig" Robbins
Steel Guitar	J.D. Maness
Rhythm Guitar	Jerry Inman
Radio Station	KLAC, Los Angeles
Disc Jockey	Charlie Douglas, WWL, New Orleans
Nightclub	Palomino
Band of the Year (Touring)	Red Rose Express
Band of the Year (Non-Touring)	Possum Holler
Most Promising Female Vocalist	Billy Jo Spears
Most Promising Male Vocalist	Moe Bandy
Top Vocal Group	Conway Twitty/Loretta Lynn
Album of the Year	*Gilley's Smoking*/Mickey Gilley
Male Vocalist of Year	Mickey Gilley
Female Vocalist of Year	Crystal Gayle
Single Record of the Year	"Bring It On Home"/Mickey Gilley
Entertainer of the Year	Mickey Gilley
Song of the Year	"Don't the Girls Get Prettier At Closing Time"/Mickey Gilley
Jim Reeves Memorial Award	Roy Clark
Pioneer Award	Owen Bradley

1977

Bass	Larry Booth
Drums	Archie Francis & George Manz
Fiddle	Billy Armstrong
Keyboard	Hargus "Pig" Robbins
Lead Guitar	Roy Clark
Steel Guitar	Buddy Emmons
Specialty Instrument	Charlie McCoy
Radio Station	KGBS, Los Angeles
Disc Jockey	Billy Parker

Country Nightclub	Palomino
Band of the Year (Touring)	Asleep At The Wheel & Sons Of Pioneers
Band of the Year (Non-Touring)	Palomino Riders
Top New Female Vocalist	Debby Boone
Top New Male Vocalist	Eddie Rabbitt
Top Vocal Group	Statler Brothers
Album of the Year	*Kenny Rogers*/Kenny Rogers
Top Male Vocalist	Kenny Rogers
Top Female Vocalist	Crystal Gayle
Single Record of the Year	"Lucille"/Kenny Rogers
Entertainer of the Year	Dolly Parton
Song of the Year	"Lucille"/Kenny Rogers
Career Achievement	Johnny Paycheck
Jim Reeves Memorial	Jim Halsey
Pioneer Award	Sons Of Pioneers

1978

Bass	Rod Culpepper
Drums	Archie Francis
Fiddle	Johnny Gimble
Keyboard	Jimmy Pruett
Lead Guitar	James Burton
Steel Guitar	Buddy Emmons
Specialty Instrument	Charlie McCoy
Radio Station	KVOO, Tulsa, Oklahoma
Disc Jockey	Billy Parker
Country Nightclub	Palomino
Band of the Year (Touring)	Original Texas Playboys
Band of the Year (Non-Touring)	Rebel Playboys
Top New Female Vocalist	Cristy Lane
Top New Male Vocalist	John Conlee
Top Vocal Group	Oak Ridge Boys
Album of the Year	*Ya'll Come Back Saloon*/Oak Ridge Boys
Top Male Vocalist	Kenny Rogers
Top Female Vocalist	Barbara Mandrell
Single Record of the Year	"Tulsa Time"/Don Williams
Entertainer of the Year	Kenny Rogers
Song of the Year	"You Needed Me"/Anne Murray
—Jim Reeves MemorialJoe Cates	Joe Cates
Pioneer Award	Eddie Dean

1979

Bass	Billy Graham
Fiddle	Johnny Gimble
Drums	Archie Francis
Guitar	Al Bruno
Keyboard	Hargus "Pig" Robbins
Steel Guitar	Buddy Emmons
Specialty Instrument	Charlie McCoy (Harmonia)
Band of the Year (Non-Touring)	Midnight Riders
Band of the Year (Touring)	Charlie Daniels Band
Radio Station of the Year	KFDI, Wichita, KS
Disc Jockey of the Year	King Edward IV, WSRC, Roanoke, VA

Country Nightclub of the Year	Gilley's, Pasadena, TX
Top New Female Vocalist	Lacy J. Dalton
Top New Male Vocalist	R.C. Bannon
Top Vocal Group	Moe Bandy/Joe Stampley
Album of the Year	*Straight Ahead* (Larry Gatlin)
Top Male Vocalist	Larry Gatlin
Top Female Vocalist	Crystal Gayle
Single Record of the Year	"All the Gold in California"/Larry Gatlin
Entertainer of the Year	Willie Nelson
Song of the Year	"It's a Cheatin' Situation"/Moe Bandy
Country Music Movie of the Year	*Electric Horseman*
Jim Reeves Memorial Award	Bill Ward (Metro Media)
Pioneer Award	Patti Page
Artist of the Decade	Loretta Lynn (1969-1979)

1980

Bass	Curtis Stone
Fiddle	Johnny Gimble
Drums	Archie Francis
Guitar	Al Bruno
Keyboard	Hargus "Pig" Robbins
Steel Guitar	Buddy Emmons/J.D. Maness
Specialty Instrument	Charlie McCoy (Harmonica)
Band of the Year (Touring)	Charlie Daniels Band
Band of the Year (Non-Touring)	Palomino Riders
Radio Station of the Year	KLAC, Los Angeles
Disc Jockey of the Year	Sammy Jackson
Nightclub of the Year	Palomino Club/Gilley's Club
Top New Female Vocalist	Terri Gibbs
Top New Male Vocalist	Johnny Lee
Top Vocal Group	Alabama
Top Vocal Duet	Moe Bandy/Joe Stampley
Album of the Year	*Urban Cowboy*/Soundtrack
Top Male Vocalist	George Jones
Top Female Vocalist	Dolly Parton
Single Record of the Year	"He Stopped Loving Her Today"/George Jones
Entertainer of the Year	Barbara Mandrell
Song of the Year	"He Stopped Loving Her Today"/George Jones
Country Music Movie of the Year	*Coal Miner's Daughter*
Jim Reeves Memorial Award	Ken Kragen
Pioneer Award	Ernest Tubb
Special Achievement	George Burns

1981

Bass	Joe Osborn/Curtis Stone
Fiddle	Johnny Gimble
Drums	Buddy Harmon
Guitar	James Burton
Keyboard	Hargus "Pig" Robbins
Steel Guitar	Buddy Emmons
Specialty Instrument	Charlie McCoy (Harmonica)

1981 (cont.)

Band of the Year (Touring)	Strangers (Merle Haggard)
Band of the Year (Non-Touring)	Desperado's (Johnny & Jonie Mosby)
Radio Station of the Year	WPLO/Atlanta, Georgia
Disc Jockey of the Year	Arch Yancey/KNUZ
Country Nightclub	Billy Bob's Texas
Top New Female Vocalist	Juice Newton
Top New Male Vocalist	Ricky Skaggs
Top Vocal Group	Alabama
Vocal Duet	David Frizzell & Shelly West
Album of the Year	*Feels So Right* (Alabama)
Top Male Vocalist	Merle Haggard
Top Female Vocalist	Barbara Mandrell
Single Record of the Year	"Elvira" (Oak Ridge Boys)
Entertainer of the Year	Alabama
Song of the Year	"You're The Reason God Made Oklahoma"/David Frizzell & Shelly West
Jim Reeves Memorial Award	Al Gallico
Pioneer Award	Leo Fender
Tex Ritter Award (Country Motion Picture)	*Any Which Way You Can*

COUNTRY MUSIC ASSOCIATION

The Country Music Association (CMA) was formed in 1958 in Nashville, Tennessee, by industry members primarily as a response to the overwhelming rock 'n' roll wave then sweeping the United States. It was a period when radio stations defected to rock in a swelling wave that threatened to throttle exposure of efforts by country performers, songwriters and disc jockeys in both recordings and personal appearances. To counteract this, CMA enlisted the energies and combined talents of industry people throughout the United States in programs to preserve and advance country music. CMA's efforts have played a major role in reviving recognition of the art form and elevating it to its present influential status in popular music at home and abroad.

CMA has emerged as the world's largest trade organization and, in 1982, opened its first overseas office in London, England. CMA initiated its own awards show in 1967 and has been a leader in the drives to stop record counterfeiting and piracy, assist country radio stations (grown from around 80 in 1961 to about 1500 in 1982) in all areas and, in 1982, was involved in supporting home taping legislation. Jo Walker-Mendor, now the Executive Director, has been active since CMA's inception in the development of the organization.

COUNTRY MUSIC ASSOCIATION AWARDS
Annual winners by categories

Category 1
ENTERTAINER OF THE YEAR

1967 Eddy Arnold
1968 Glen Campbell
1969 Johnny Cash
1970 Merle Haggard
1971 Charley Pride
1972 Loretta Lynn
1973 Roy Clark
1974 Charlie Rich
1975 John Denver
1976 Mel Tillis
1977 Ronnie Milsap
1978 Dolly Parton
1979 Willie Nelson
1980 Barbara Mandrell

Category 2
SINGLE OF THE YEAR

1967 "There Goes My Everything"—Jack Greene—Decca
1968 "Harper Valley PTA"—Jeannie C. Riley—Plantation
1969 "A Boy Named Sue"—Johnny Cash—Columbia
1970 "Okie From Muskogee"—Merle Haggard—Capitol
1971 "Help Me Make It Through The Night"—Sammi Smith—Mega
1972 "The Happiest Girl In The Whole U.S.A."—Donna Fargo—Dot
1973 "Behind Closed Doors"—Charlie Rich—Epic
1974 "Country Bumpkin"—Cal Smith—MCA
1975 "Before The Next Teardrop Falls"—Freddy Fender—ABC/Dot
1976 "Good Hearted Woman"—Waylon Jennings/Willie Nelson—RCA
1977 "Lucille"—Kenny Rogers—UA
1978 "Heaven's Just A Sin Away"—The Kendalls—Ovation
1979 "The Devil Went Down To Georgia"—Charlie Daniels Band—Epic
1980 "He Stopped Loving Her Today"—George Jones—Epic

Category 3
ALBUM OF THE YEAR

1967 *There Goes My Everything*—Jack Greene—Decca

1968 *Johnny Cash At Folsom Prison*—Johnny Cash—Columbia

1969 *Johnny Cash At San Quentin Prison*—Johnny Cash—Columbia

1970 *Okie From Muskogee*—Merle Haggard—Capitol

1971 *I Won't Mention It Again*—Ray Price—Columbia

1972 *Let Me Tell You About A Song*—Merle Haggard—Capitol

1973 *Behind Closed Doors*—Charlie Rich—Epic

1974 *A Very Special Love Song*—Charlie Rich—Epic

1975 *A Legend In My Time*—Ronnie Milsap—RCA

1976 *Wanted—The Outlaws*—Waylon Jenings, Willie Nelson, Tompall Gloser, Jessi Colter—RCA

1977 *Ronnie Milsap Live*—Ronnie Milsap—RCA

1978 *It Was Almost Like A Song*—Ronnie Milsap—RCA

1979 *The Gambler*—Kenny Rogers—UA

1980 *Coal Miner's Daughter* (original motion picture soundtrack)—MCA

Category 4
SONG OF THE YEAR

1967 "There Goes My Everything"—Dallas Frazier

1968 "Honey"—Bobby Russell

1969 "Carroll County Accident"—Bob Ferguson

1970 "Sunday Morning Coming Down"—Kris Kristofferson

1971 "Easy Loving"—Freddie Hart

1972 "Easy Loving"—Freddie Hart

1973 "Behind Closed Doors"—Kenny O'Dell

1974 "Country Bumpkin"—Don Wayne

1975 "Back Home Again"—John Denver

1976 "Rhinestone Cowboy"—Larry Weiss

1977 "Lucille"—Roger Bowling and Hal Bynum

1978 "Don't It Make My Brown Eyes Blue"—Richard Leigh

1979 "The Gambler"—Don Schlitz—Writers Night Music

1980 "He Stopped Loving Her Today"—Bobby Braddock/Curly Putman—Tree International

Category 5
FEMALE VOCALIST OF THE YEAR

1967 Loretta Lynn

1968 Tammy Wynette

1969 Tammy Wynette

1970 Tammy Wynette

1971 Lynn Anderson

1972 Loretta Lynn

1973 Loretta Lynn

1974 Olivia Newton-John

1975 Dolly Parton

1976 Dolly Parton

1977 Crystal Gayle

1978 Crystal Gayle

1979 Barbara Mandrell

1980 Emmylou Harris

Category 6
MALE VOCALIST OF THE YEAR

1967 Jack Greene

1968 Glen Campbell

1969 Johnny Cash

1970 Merle Haggard

1971 Charley Pride

1972 Charley Pride

1973 Charlie Rich

1974 Ronnie Milsap

1975 Waylon Jennings

1976 Ronnie Milsap

1977 Ronnie Milsap

1978 Don Williams

1979 Kenny Rogers

1980 George Jones

Category 7
VOCAL GROUP OF THE YEAR

1967 The Stoneman Family

1968 Porter Wagoner and Dolly Parton

1969 Johnny Cash and June Carter

1970 The Glaser Brothers

1971 The Osborne Brothers

1972 The Statler Brothers

1973 The Statler Brothers

1974 The Statler Brothers

1975 The Statler Brothers

1976 The Statler Brothers

1977 The Statler Brothers

1978 The Oak Ridge Boys

1979	The Statler Brothers
1980	The Statler Brothers

Category 8
VOCAL DUO OF THE YEAR
(added in 1970)

1970	Porter Wagoner and Dolly Parton
1971	Porter Wagoner and Dolly Parton
1972	Conway Twitty and Loretta Lynn
1973	Conway Twitty and Loretta Lynn
1974	Conway Twitty and Loretta Lynn
1975	Conway Twitty and Loretta Lynn
1976	Waylon Jennings and Willie Nelson
1977	Jim Ed Brown and Helen Cornelius
1978	Kenny Rogers and Dottie West
1979	Kenny Rogers and Dottie West
1980	Moe Bandy and Joe Stampley

Category 9
INSTRUMENTAL GROUP OR BAND OF THE YEAR

1967	The Buckaroos
1968	The Buckaroos
1969	Danny Davis and the Nashville Brass
1970	Danny Davis and the Nashville Brass
1971	Danny Davis and the Nashville Brass
1972	Danny Davis and the Nashville Brass
1973	Danny Davis and the Nashville Brass
1974	Danny Davis and the Nashville Brass
1975	Roy Clark and Buck Trent
1976	Roy Clark and Buck Trent
1977	The Original Texas Playboys
1978	The Oak Ridge Boys Band
1979	The Charlie Daniels Band
1980	The Charlie Daniels Band

Category 10
INSTRUMENTALIST OF THE YEAR

1967	Chet Atkins
1968	Chet Atkins
1969	Chet Atkins
1970	Jerry Reed
1971	Jerry Reed

1972	Charlie McCoy
1973	Charlie McCoy
1974	Don Rich
1975	Johnny Gimble
1976	Hargus "Pig" Robbins
1977	Roy Clark
1978	Roy Clark
1979	Charlie Daniels
1980	Roy Clark

Category 11
COMEDIAN OF THE YEAR
(discontinued in 1971)

1967	Don Bowman
1968	Ben Colder
1969	Archie Campbell
1970	Roy Clark

Category 12
HORIZON AWARD
(added 1981, requirements listed below)

The HORIZON AWARD is awarded to that artist, whether individual or a group of two or more, who has demonstrated, in the field of country music, the most significant creative growth and development in overall airplay and record sales activity, live performance professionalism, and critical media recognition during the eligibility period. No act shall be eligible for the HORIZON AWARD which has previously won that award or which has been a final ballot nominee for any other Country Music Association annual award as an individual or as a group 75% or more of whose members comprise the act.

Nominations for the HORIZON AWARD shall be made by the Board of Directors and officers of the Country Music Association, as they may from time to time determine, and shall be submitted to the membership of the Association upon the second round of the voting for the annual Country Music Association Awards pursuant to the rules and regulations governing the balloting on such annual awards. The HORIZON AWARD is an annual award.

TOP CMA AWARDS NOMINEES

(34) Loretta Lynn

Entertainer of the Year 1971, 1972 *, 1973, 1974, 1975

Female Vocalist of the Year 1967 *, 1968, 1969, 1970, 1971, 1972 *, 1973 *, 1974, 1975, 1977, 1980, 1981

Vocal Duo of the Year (with Conway Twitty) 1971, 1972 *, 1973 *, 1974 *, 1975 *, 1976, 1977, 1978, 1979, 1980, 1981

Song of the Year ("Coal Miner's Daughter") 1971

Single of the Year ("One's On The Way" MCA) 1972

Album of the Year (*Entertainer of the Year* MCA) 1973

Album of the Year (*Louisiana Woman-Mississippi Man* MCA) 1973

Single of the Year ("As Soon As I Hang Up The Phone" MCA) 1974

Album of the Year (*Feelin's* MCA) 1975

Album of the Year (*I Remember Patsy* MCA) 1977

(31) Merle Haggard

Entertainer of the Year 1967, 1968, 1969, 1970 *, 1971, 1972, 1973, 1977

Male Vocalist of the Year 1967, 1968, 1969, 1970 *, 1971, 1972, 1973, 1974

Single of the Year ("The Fugitive" Capitol) 1967

Album of the Year (*I'm A Lonesome Fugitive* Capitol) 1967

Album of the Year (*The Best Of Merle Haggard* Capitol) 1968

Album of the Year (*Same Train, Different Time* Capitol) 1969

Vocal Duo of the Year (with Bonnie Owens) 1970

Single of the Year ("Fightin' Side of Me" Capitol) 1970

Album of the Year (*Fightin' Side of Me* Capitol) 1970

Song of the Year ("Fightin' Side of Me") 1970

* Single of the Year ("Okie From Muskogee" Capitol) 1970

* Album of the Year (*Okie From Muskogee* Capitol) 1970

Song of the Year ("Okie From Muskogee") 1970

Album of the Year (*A Tribute To the Best Damn Fiddle Player in the World* Capitol) 1971

* Album of the Year (*Let Me Tell You About A Song* Capitol) 1972

Album of the Year (*If We Make It Thru December* Capitol) 1974

Song of the Year ("If We Make It Thru December") 1974

(26) Conway Twitty

Entertainer of the Year 1971, 1975

Male Vocalist of the Year 1970, 1971, 1972, 1973, 1975, 1976

Vocal Duo of the Year (with Loretta Lynn) 1971, 1972 *, 1973 *, 1974 *, 1975 *, 1976, 1977, 1978, 1979, 1980, 1981

Single of the Year ("Hello Darlin' " Decca) 1970

Album of the Year (*Hello Darlin'* Decca) 1970

Song of the Year ("Hello Darlin' ") 1970

Album of the Year (*Lead Me On* MCA) 1972

Album of the Year (*Louisiana Woman—Mississippi Man* MCA) 1973

Single of the Year ("As Soon As I Hang Up The Phone" MCA) 1974

Album of the Year (*Feelin's* MCA) 1975

(24) Dolly Parton

Entertainer of the Year 1976, 1977, 1978 *

Female Vocalist of the Year 1968, 1969, 1970, 1971, 1972, 1974, 1975 *, 1976 *, 1977, 1978

Vocal Group of the Year (with Porter Wagoner) 1968 *, 1969

Vocal Duo of the Year (with Porter Wagoner) 1970 *, 1971 *, 1972, 1973, 1974, 1975

Single of the Year ("Here You Come Again" RCA) 1978

Album of the Year (*Here You Come Again* RCA) 1978

Album of the Year (*Coat of Many Colors* RCA) 1972

(23) Tammy Wynette

Female Vocalist of the Year 1967, 1968 *, 1969 *, 1970 *, 1971, 1972, 1973, 1976

Vocal Group of the Year (with David Houston) 1967

Single of the Year ("D-I-V-O-R-C-E" Epic)
1968
Album of the Year (D-I-V-O-R-C-E Epic)
1968
Album of the Year (Stand By Your Man
Epic) 1969
Song of the Year ("Stand By Your Man")
1969
Vocal Duo of the Year (with George Jones)
1971, 1972, 1973, 1974, 1975, 1976, 1977,
1980, 1981
Song of the Year ("Till I Can Make It On
My Own") 1976

(22)   Roy Clark
Entertainer of the Year 1969, 1970, 1973 *,
1974
Comedian of the Year 1969, 1970 *
Instrumental Group of the Year (with Buck
Trent) 1975 *, 1976 *
Instrumentalist of the Year 1967, 1968,
1969, 1970, 1971, 1972, 1973, 1974, 1975,
1976, 1977 *, 1978 *, 1979, 1980 *

(21)   Chet Atkins
Instrumentalist of the Year 1967 *, 1968 *,
1969 *, 1970, 1971, 1972, 1973, 1974, 1975,
1976, 1977, 1978, 1979, 1980, 1981
Instrumental Group of the Year (with Jerry
Reed) 1972, 1973
Instrumental Group of the Year (with
Merle Travis) 1974
Instrumental Group of the Year (with Les
Paul) 1978, 1979
Instrumental Group of the Year (the Masters Three) 1967

(21)   Waylon Jennings
Entertainer of the Year 1975, 1976, 1977
Male Vocalist of the Year 1974, 1975 *,
1976, 1977
Vocal Duo of the Year (with Willie Nelson) 1976 *, 1977, 1978, 1979
Album of the Year (The Ramblin' Man
RCA) 1975
Song of the Year ("Rainy Day Woman"
RCA) 1975
* Single of the Year ("Good Hearted Woman" RCA) 1976
* Album of the Year (Wanted—The Outlaws
RCA) 1976
Single of the Year ("Luckenbach, Texas"
RCA) 1977
Album of the Year (Ol' Waylon RCA) 1977
Single of the Year ("Mammas Don't Let

Your Babies Grow Up To Be Cowboys"
RCA) 1978
Album of the Year (Waylon and Willie
RCA) 1978
Single of the Year ("Amanda" RCA) 1979
Vocal Duo of the Year (with Jessi Colter)
1981

(18)   Charley Pride
Entertainer of the Year 1968, 1969, 1970,
1971 *, 1972, 1973
Male Vocalist of the Year 1968, 1969, 1970,
1971 *, 1972 *
Single of the Year ("All I Have To Offer
You Is Me" RCA) 1969
Album of the Year (Charley Pride Live and in
Prison RCA) 1969
Single of the Year ("I'm So Afraid Of Losing You" RCA) 1970
Album of the Year (Just Plain Charley RCA)
1970
Single of the Year ("Kiss An Angel Good
Morning" RCA) 1972
Album of the Year (Charley Pride Sings
Heart Songs RCA) 1972
Album of the Year (There's a Little Bit of
Hank in Me RCA) 1980

(18)   Kenny Rogers
Entertainer of the Year 1977, 1978, 1979,
1980, 1981
Male Vocalist of the Year 1977, 1978,
1979 *, 1980, 1981
Vocal Duo of the Year (with Dottie West)
1978 *, 1979 *
* Single of the Year ("Lucille" UA) 1977
Album of the Year (Kenny Rogers UA) 1977
Single of the Year ("The Gambler" UA)
1979
* Album of the Year (The Gambler UA)
1979
Single of the Year ("Coward of the County"
UA) 1980
Album of the Year (Kenny UA) 1980

(17)   Johnny Cash
Entertainer of the Year 1968, 1969 *, 1970
Male Vocalist of the Year 1969 *, 1970
Vocal Group of the Year (with June Carter)
1967, 1968, 1969 *
Vocal Duo of the Year (with June Carter)
1970, 1971
Single of the Year ("Folsom Prison Blues"
CBS) 1968
* Album of the Year (Johnny Cash At Folsom
Prison CBS) 1969

Johnny Cash, (cont.)
* Single of the Year ("A Boy Named Sue" CBS) 1969
Single of the Year ("Daddy Sang Bass" CBS) 1969
* Album of the Year (*Johnny Cash At San Quentin* CBS) 1969
Album of the Year (*Hello I'm Johnny Cash* CBS) 1970

(17)   Willie Nelson
Entertainer of the Year 1976, 1979 *, 1980
Male Vocalist of the Year 1976, 1978, 1979, 1980, 1981
Vocal Duo of the Year (with Waylon Jennings) 1976 *, 1977, 1978, 1979
* Single of the Year ("Good Hearted Woman" RCA) 1976
* Album of the Year (*Wanted—The Outlaws* RCA) 1976
Album of the Year (*Waylon and Willie* RCA) 1978
Single of the Year ("Mammas Don't Let Your Babies Grow Up To Be Cowboys" RCA) 1978
Album of the Year (*One For the Road* CBS) 1979

(16)   Jerry Reed
Entertainer of the Year 1971, 1972
Male Vocalist of the Year 1971
Instrumentalist of the Year 1969, 1970 *, 1971 *, 1972, 1973, 1975, 1978
Instrumental Group of the Year (with Chet Atkins) 1972, 1973
Single of the Year ("Amos Moses" RCA) 1971
Single of the Year ("When You're Hot You're Hot" RCA) 1971
Album of the Year (*When You're Hot You're Hot* RCA) 1971
Song of the Year ("When You're Hot You're Hot") 1971

(15)   Glen Campbell
Entertainer of the Year 1968 *, 1969, 1970
Male Vocalist of the Year 1968 *, 1969
Vocal Group of the Year (with Bobbie Gentry) 1969
Album of the Year (*By the Time I Get To Phoenix* Capitol) 1968
Album of the Year (*Gentle On My Mind* Capitol) 1968
Single of the Year ("By The Time I Get To Phoenix" Capitol) 1968

Instrumentalist of the Year 1968
Single of the Year ("Galveston" Capitol) 1969
Album of the Year (*Wichita Lineman* Capitol) 1969
Single of the Year ("Rhinestone Cowboy" Capitol) 1975
Album of the Year (*Rhinestone Cowboy* Capitol) 1975
Single of the Year ("Southern Nights" Capitol) 1977

(15)   Ronnie Milsap
Entertainer of the Year 1975, 1976, 1977 *, 1978, 1981
Male Vocalist of the Year 1974 *, 1975, 1976, 1977 *, 1978
* Album of the Year (*A Legend In My Time* RCA) 1975
Album of the Year (*Night Things* RCA) 1976
* Album of the Year (*Ronnie Milsap Live* RCA) 1977
Single of the Year ("It Was Almost Like A Song" RCA) 1977
* Album of the Year (*It Was Almost Like A Song* RCA) 1978

(14)   George Jones
Vocal Duo of the Year (with Tammy Wynette) 1971, 1972, 1973, 1974, 1975, 1976, 1977, 1980, 1981
Single of the Year ("He Stopped Loving Her Today" Epic) 1980
Male Vocalist of the Year 1980 *, 1981
Entertainer of the Year 1981
Album of the Year (*I Am What I Am* Epic) 1981

(14)   The Statler Bros.
Entertainer of the Year 1979
Vocal Group of the Year 1967, 1971, 1972 *, 1973 *, 1974 *, 1975 *, 1976 *, 1977 *, 1978, 1979 *, 1980 *, 1981
Album of the Year (*The Originals* Mercury) 1979

(13)   Barbara Mandrell
Entertainer of the Year 1979, 1980 *, 1981
Female Vocalist of the Year 1976, 1977, 1978, 1979 *, 1980, 1981
Vocal Duo of the Year (with David Houston) 1973, 1974
Single of the Year ("If Lovin You Is Wrong I Don't Want To Be Right" MCA) 1979

Single of the Year ("I Was Country (When Country Wasn't Cool)" MCA) 1981

(11)   Danny Davis and The Nashville Brass
Instrumental Group of the Year 1969 *, 1970 *, 1971 *, 1972 *, 1973 *, 1974 *, 1975, 1976, 1977, 1978, 1979

(11)   Charlie Daniels Band
Instrumental Group of the Year 1976, 1978, 1979 *, 1980 *, 1981
Vocal Group of the Year 1979, 1980
* Single of the Year ("The Devil Went Down To Georgia" Epic) 1979
Entertainer of the Year 1980
Song of the Year ("In America")—Charles Hayward/William Joe DiGregorio/Charlie Daniels/John Thomas Crain/Fred Edwards/James Marshall—1980
Single of the Year ("In America" Epic) 1980

(10)   Floyd Cramer
Instrumentalist of the Year 1967, 1968, 1969, 1970, 1971, 1972, 1973, 1980, 1981
Instrumental Group of the Year (the Masters Three) 1967

(10)   Charlie McCoy
Instrumentalist of the Year 1972 *, 1973, 1974, 1975, 1976, 1977, 1978, 1979, 1980, 1981

(10)   Don Williams
Male Vocalist of the Year 1976, 1977, 1978 *, 1979, 1980, 1981
Album of the Year (*Country Boy* ABC) 1978
Single of the Year ("Good Ole Boys Like Me" MCA) 1980
Single of the Year ("I Believe in You" MCA) 1981
Album of the Year (*I Believe in You* MCA) 1981

(9)   Larry Gatlin, Larry Gatlin & the Gatlin Brothers Band
Male Vocalist of the Year 1977, 1978, 1979
Entertainer of the Year 1980
Vocal Group of the Year 1980, 1981
Instrumental Group of the Year 1980, 1981
Single of the Year ("All the Gold in California" Columbia) 1980

(8)   Asleep At The Wheel
Vocal Group of the Year 1975, 1976, 1977
Instrumental Group of the Year 1976, 1977, 1978, 1979, 1980

(8)   Porter Wagoner
Vocal Group of the Year (with Dolly Parton) 1968 *, 1969
Vocal Duo of the Year (with Dolly Parton) 1970 *, 1971 *, 1972, 1973, 1974, 1975

(7)   Alabama
Vocal Group of the Year 1980, 1981
Instrumental Group of the Year 1980, 1981
Entertainer of the Year 1981
Single of the Year ("Old Flame" RCA) 1981
Album of the Year (*Feels So Right* RCA) 1981

(7)   Lynn Anderson
Female Vocalist of the Year 1967, 1968, 1969, 1970, 1971 *
Single of the Year ("Rose Garden" CBS) 1971
Album of the Year (*Rose Garden* CBS) 1971

(7)   Crystal Gayle
Entertainer of the Year 1978, 1979
Female Vocalist of the Year 1976, 1977 *, 1978 *, 1979, 1980

(7)   Jack Greene
* Male Vocalist of the Year 1967
* Single of the Year ("There Goes My Everything" Decca) 1967
* Album of the Year (*There Goes My Everything* Decca) 1967
Vocal Duo of the Year (with Jeannie Seely) 1972, 1973, 1974, 1975

(7)   Emmylou Harris
Female Vocalist of the Year 1976, 1977, 1978, 1979, 1980 *, 1981
Album of the Year (*Roses in the Snow* Warner Bros.) 1980

(7)   Oak Ridge Boys
Vocal Group of the Year 1977, 1978 *, 1979, 1980, 1981
Entertainer of the Year 1981
Single of the Year ("Elvira" MCA) 1981

(7)   Po' Boys
Instrumental Group of the Year 1968, 1969, 1971, 1972, 1973, 1974, 1975

(7)   Charlie Rich
* Entertainer of the Year 1974
Male Vocalist of the Year 1973 *, 1974
* Single of the Year ("Behind Closed Doors" Epic) 1973
* Album of the Year (*Behind Closed Doors* Epic) 1973
Single of the Year ("The Most Beautiful Girl" Epic) 1974
* Album of the Year (*A Very Special Love Song* Epic) 1974

(7)   Wagon Masters
Instrumental Group of the Year 1967, 1968, 1969, 1970, 1971, 1972, 1973

(6)   Buckaroos
Instrumental Group of the Year 1967 *, 1968 *, 1969, 1970, 1971, 1974

(6)   Johnny Gimble
Instrumentalist of the Year 1975 *, 1976, 1977, 1978, 1980, 1981

(6)   Tom T. Hall
Entertainer of the Year 1973
Male Vocalist of the Year 1973
Song of the Year ("Harper Valley P.T.A.") 1968
Song of the Year ("I Remember The Year Clayton Delaney Died") 1971
Single of the Year ("Old Dogs, Children, and Watermelon Wine" Mercury) 1973
Album of the Year (*Tom T. Hall . . . The Storyteller* Mercury) 1973

(6)   Osborne Brothers
Vocal Group of the Year 1970, 1971 *, 1972, 1973, 1974, 1975

(6)   Stoneman Family
Vocal Group of the Year 1967 *, 1968, 1970
Instrumental Group of the Year 1968, 1969, 1970

(5)   Bill Anderson
Entertainer of the Year 1967
Vocal Group of the Year (with Jan Howard) 1968
Vocal Duo of the Year (with Jan Howard) 1970
Vocal Duo of the Year (with Mary Lou Turner) 1976, 1977

(5)   Eddy Arnold
Entertainer of the Year 1967 *, 1968
Male Vocalist of the Year 1967, 1968
Album of the Year (*Best of Eddy Arnold* RCA) 1967

(5)   Jim Ed Brown
Album of the Year (*I Don't Want To Have To Marry You* RCA) (with Helen Cornelius) 1977
Vocal Duo of the Year (with Helen Cornelius) 1977 *, 1978, 1979, 1980

(5)   Archie Campbell
Comedian of the Year 1967, 1968, 1969 *, 1970, 1971

(5)   June Carter
Vocal Group of the Year (with Johnny Cash) 1967, 1968, 1969 *
Vocal Duo of the Year (with Johnny Cash) 1970, 1971

(5)   Jessi Colter
Single of the Year ("I'm Not Lisa" Capitol) 1975
Song of the Year ("I'm Not Lisa") 1975
Female Vocalist of the Year 1975
* Album of the Year (*Wanted-The Outlaws* RCA) (with Waylon, Willie & Tompall) 1976
Vocal Duo of the Year (with Waylon Jennings) 1981

(5)   Helen Cornelius
Album of the Year (*I Don't Want To Have to Marry You* RCA) (with Jim Ed Brown) 1977
Vocal Duo of the Year (with Jim Ed Brown) 1977 *, 1978, 1979, 1980

(5)   Dave and Sugar
Vocal Group of the Year 1976, 1977, 1978, 1979
Single of the Year ("The Door Is Always Open" RCA) 1976

(5)   John Denver
* Entertainer of the Year 1975
Male Vocalist of the Year 1975
Single of the Year ("Thank God I'm A Country Boy" RCA) 1975
Album of the Year (*An Evening With John Denver* RCA) 1975

* Song of the Year ("Back Home Again")
1975

(5)   Donna Fargo
* Single of the Year ("The Happiest Girl In the Whole USA" Dot) 1972
Album of the Year (*The Happiest Girl . . .* Dot) 1972
Song of the Year ("The Happiest Girl . . ." Dot) 1972
Female Vocalist of the Year 1972, 1973

(5)   Janie Fricke
Female Vocalist of the Year 1978, 1979
Vocal Duo of the Year (with Johnny Duncan) 1978, 1979, 1980

(5)   Glaser Brothers
Vocal Group of the Year 1969, 1970 *, 1971, 1972, 1973

(5)   Freddie Hart
Single of the Year ("Easy Loving" Capitol) 1971
* Song of the Year ("Easy Loving") 1971
* Song of the Year ("Easy Loving") 1972
Male Vocalist of the Year 1972
Entertainer of the Year 1972

(5)   Sonny James
Entertainer of the Year 1967
Male Vocalist of the Year 1967, 1969
Album of the Year (*Best of Sonny James* Capitol) 1967
Album of the Year (*200 Years of Country Music* CBS) 1976

(5)   Anne Murray
Female Vocalist of the Year 1974, 1979, 1980, 1981
Single of the Year ("You Needed Me" Capitol) 1979

(5)   Mel Tillis
Song of the Year ("All The Time") 1967
Vocal Duo of the Year (with Sherry Bryce) 1975, 1976
Entertainer of the Year 1976 *, 1978

(5)   Dottie West
Female Vocalist of the Year 1967
Vocal Group of the Year (with Don Gibson) 1969
Vocal Duo of the Year (with Don Gibson) 1970

Vocal Duo of the Year (with Kenny Rogers) 1978 *, 1979 *

(4)   The Carter Family
Vocal Group of the Year 1970, 1971, 1972, 1973

(4)   Ben Colder
Comedian of the Year 1967, 1968 *, 1969, 1970

(4)   The Kendalls
* Single of the Year ("Heaven's Just A Sin Away" Ovation) 1978
Album of the Year (*Heaven's Just A Sin Away* Ovation) 1978
Vocal Group of the Year 1978, 1979

(4)   Olivia Newton-John
Entertainer of the Year 1974
Single of the Year ("If You Love Me Let Me Know" RCA) 1974
Album of the Year (*If You Love Me Let Me Know* MCA) 1974
* Female Vocalist of the Year 1974

(4)   Ray Price
Single of the Year ("Danny Boy" CBS) 1967
Album of the Year (*Danny Boy* CBS) 1967
* Album of the Year (*I Won't Mention It Again* CBS) 1971
Male Vocalist of the Year 1971

(4)   Curly Putman
Song of the Year ("My Elusive Dreams") 1967
Song of the Year ("D-I-V-O-R-C-E") 1968
Song of the Year ("He Stopped Loving Her Today") 1980*, 1981

(4)   Jeannie Seely
Vocal Duo of the Year (with Jack Greene) 1972, 1973, 1974, 1975

(4)   Billy Sherrill
Song of the Year ("My Elusive Dreams") 1967
Song of the Year ("Stand By Your Man") 1969
Song of the Year ("The Most Beautiful Girl in the World") 1974
Song of the Year ("Til I Can Make It On My Own") 1976

(4) Cal Smith
Single of the Year ("The Lord Knows I'm Drinking" Decca) 1973
* Single of the Year ("Country Bumpkin" MCA) 1974
Album of the Year (*Country Bumpkin* MCA) 1974
Male Vocalist of the Year 1974

(3) Moe Bandy
Vocal Duo of the Year (with Joe Stampley) 1980 *, 1981
Album of the Year (*Just Good Ol' Boys* Columbia) 1980

(3) Don Bowman
Comedian of the Year 1967 *, 1968, 1969

(3) Bobby Braddock
Song of the Year ("D-I-V-O-R-C-E") 1968
Song of the Year ("He Stopped Loving Her Today") 1980 *, 1981

(3) John Conlee
Male Vocalist of the Year 1979, 1980
Album of the Year (*Rose Colored Glasses* MCA) 1979

(3) Johnny Duncan
Vocal Duo of the Year (with Janie Fricke) 1978, 1979, 1980

(3) Freddy Fender
* Single of the Year ("Before The Next Teardrop Falls" ABC/Dot) 1975
Male Vocalist of the Year 1975
Album of the Year (*Before the Next Teardrop . . .* ABC/Dot) 1975

(3) Bobbie Gentry
Single of the Year ("Ode To Billie Joe" Capitol) 1967
Song of the Year ("Ode To Billie Joe") 1967
Vocal Group of the Year (with Glen Campbell) 1969

(3) Terri Gibbs
Female Vocalist of the Year 1981
Horizon Award 1981
Single of the Year ("Somebody's Knockin' " MCA) 1981

(3) David Houston
Vocal Group of the Year (with Tammy Wynette) 1967

Vocal Duo of the Year (with Barbara Mandrell) 1973, 1974

(3) Kris Kristofferson
* Song of the Year ("Sunday Morning Coming Down") 1970
Single of the Year ("Why Me" Monument) 1973
Song of the Year ("Why Me") 1973

(3) Bob McDill
Song of the Year ("The Door Is Always Open") 1976
Song of the Year ("Amanda") 1979
Song of the Year ("Good Ole Boys Like Me") 1980

(3) Oak Ridge Boys Band
* Instrumental Group of the Year 1978, 1980, 1981

(3) Johnny Paycheck
Male Vocalist of the Year 1972
Vocal Duo of the Year (with Jody Miller) 1972
Album of the Year (*Armed and Crazy* Epic) 1979

(3) Jeanne Pruett
Single of the Year ("Satin Sheets" MCA) 1973
Album of the Year (*Satin Sheets* MCA) 1973
Female Vocalist of the Year 1973

(3) Boots Randolph
Instrumentalist of the Year 1968, 1971
Instrumental Group of the Year (Masters Three) 1967

(3) Jeannie C. Riley
* Single of the Year ("Harper Valley P.T.A." Plantation) 1968
Female Vocalist of the Year 1968, 1969

(3) Hargus "Pig" Robbins
Instrumentalist of the Year 1976 *, 1977, 1981

(3) Marty Robbins
Single of the Year ("My Woman, My Woman, My Wife" CBS) 1970
Song of the Year ("My Woman, My Woman, My Wife" CBS) 1970
Male Vocalist of the Year 1970

(3) Connie Smith
Female Vocalist of the Year 1967, 1970, 1972

(3) Sammi Smith
* Single of the Year ("Help Me Make It Through The Night" Mega) 1971
Album of the Year (*Help Me Make It Through The Night* Mega) 1971
Female Vocalist of the Year 1971

(3) Joe Stampley
Vocal Duo of the Year (with Moe Bandy) 1980 *, 1981
Album of the Year (*Just Good Ol' Boys* Columbia) 1980

(3) Texas Troubadors
Instrumental Group of the Year 1967, 1968, 1969

(3) Tanya Tucker
Female Vocalist of the Year 1973, 1974, 1975

(2) Roger Bowling
* Song of the Year ("Lucille") 1977
Song of the Year ("Coward of the County") 1980

(2) Sherry Bryce
Vocal Duo of the Year (with Mel Tillis) 1975, 1976

(2) Roger F. Cook
Song of the Year ("Talking In Your Sleep") (with Bobby Ray Woods) 1979
Song of the Year ("I Believe in You") 1981

(2) Dallas Frazier
* Song of the Year ("There Goes My Everything") 1967
Song of the Year ("Elvira") 1981

(2) Don Gibson
Vocal Group of the Year (with Dottie West) 1969
Vocal Duo of the Year (with Dottie West) 1970

(2) Lloyd Green
Instrumentalist of the Year 1973, 1974

(2) Homer & Jethro
Comedian of the Year 1967, 1968

(2) Jan Howard
Vocal Group of the Year (with Bill Anderson) 1968
Vocal Duo of the Year (with Bill Anderson) 1970

(2) Archie Jordan
Song of the Year ("It Was Almost Like A Song") 1977, 1978

(2) Jordanaires
Vocal Group of the Year 1973, 1974

(2) Richard Leigh
Song of the Year ("I'll Get Over You") 1976
* Song of the Year ("Don't It Make My Brown Eyes Blue") 1978

(2) Minnie Pearl
Comedian of the Year 1967, 1968

(2) Chips Moman
Song of the Year ("Hey Won't You Play Another Somebody Done Somebody Wrong Song") 1973
Song of the Year ("Luckenbach, Texas") 1977

(2) Les Paul
Instrumental Group of the Year (with Chet Atkins) 1978

(2) Original Texas Playboys
* Instrumental Group of the Year 1977
Vocal Group of the Year 1978

(2) Buck Owens
Entertainer of the Year 1967
Male Vocalist of the Year 1967

(2) Ben Peters
Song of the Year ("Kiss An Angel Good Morning") 1972
Song of the Year ("Before The Next Teardrop Falls") 1975

(2) Don Rich
Instrumentalist of the Year 1969, 1974

(2) Linda Ronstadt
Female Vocalist of the Year 1975
Single of the Year ("Blue Bayou" Asylum) 1978

(2)   **Bobby Russell**
* Song of the Year ("Honey") 1968
Song of the Year ("Little Green Apples")
1968

(2)   **Junior Samples**
Comedian of the Year 1969, 1970

(2)   **Red Sovine**
Single of the Year ("Teddy Bear" Starday)
1976
Album of the Year (*Teddy Bear* Starday)
1976

(2)   **Kenny Starr**
Single of the Year ("The Blind Man In The
Bleachers" MCA) 1976
Album of the Year (*The Blind Man In The
Bleachers* MCA) 1976

(2)   **Ray Stevens**
Single of the Year ("The Streak" Barnaby)
1974
Song of the Year ("The Streak") 1974

(2)   **Merle Travis**
Instrumental Group of the Year (with Chet
Atkins) 1974
Instrumentalist of the Year 1970

(2)   **Buck Trent**
Instrumental Group of the Year (with Roy
Clark) 1975 *, 1976 *

(2)   **Mary Lou Turner**
Vocal Duo of the Year (with Bill Anderson) 1976, 1977

(2)   **Jerry Wallace**
Single of the Year ("To Get To You" 4-
Star) 1972
Male Vocalist of the Year 1972

(1)   **Amazing Rhythm Aces**
Vocal Group of the Year 1976

(1)   **Anita Kerr Singers**
Vocal Group of the Year 1967

(1)   **Bobby Bare and Family**
Vocal Group of the Year 1975

(1)   **Bellamy Brothers**
Vocal Group of the Year 1981

(1)   **Jack Blanchard**
Vocal Group of the Year (with Misty Morgan) 1970

(1)   **Gary Bond**
Song of the Year ("She's All I've Got")
1972

(1)   **Rory Bourke**
Song of the Year ("The Most Beautiful
Girl") 1974

(1)   **Box Car Willie**
Horizon Award 1981

(1)   **The Browns**
Vocal Group of the Year 1967

(1)   **Ed Bruce**
Song of the Year ("Mammas Don't Let
Your Babies Grow Up To Be Cowboys")
1978

(1)   **Patsy Bruce**
Song of the Year ("Mammas Don't Let
Your Babies Grow Up To Be Cowboys")
1978

(1)   **Brush Arbor**
Vocal Group of the Year 1974

(1)   **Milton Brown**
Song of the Year ("Every Which Way But
Loose") (with Stephen Dorff and Thomas
Garrett) 1979

(1)   **Jimmy Buffett**
Single of the Year ("Margaritaville" ABC)
1977

(1)   **Larry Butler**
Song of the Year ("Hey Won't You Play
Another Somebody Done Somebody
Wrong Song") 1975

(1)   **Hal Bynum**
* Song of the Year ("Lucille") 1977

(1)   **Rosanne Cash**
Horizon Award 1981

(1)   **Don Chapel**
Song of the Year ("When The Green Grass
Grows Over Me") 1969

(1)   **Jean Chapel**
Song of the Year ("To Get To You") 1972

(1)   **Cherokee Cowboys**
Instrumental Group of the Year 1967

(1)   **Coal Miner's Daughter**
Album of the Year (Original motion picture soundtrack MCA) 1980 *

(1)   **Hank Cochran**
Song of the Year ("It's Not Love But It's Not Bad") 1973

(1)   **David Allen Coe**
Song of the Year ("Take This Job And Shove It") 1978

(1)   **Charlie Daniels**
* Instrumentalist of the Year 1979

(1)   **Mac Davis**
Entertainer of the Year 1974

(1)   **Pete Drake**
Instrumentalist of the Year 1967

(1)   **Stephen Dorff**
Song of the Year ("Every Which Way But Loose") 1979 with Milton Brown and Thomas Garrett

(1)   **Eagles**
Vocal Group of the Year 1976, 1977

(1)   **Bobby Emmons**
Song of the Year ("Luckenbach, Texas") 1977

(1)   **Buddy Emmons**
Instrumentalist of the Year 1979

(1)   **Bob Ferguson**
* Song of the Year ("Carroll County Accident") 1969

(1)   **Kye Fleming**
Song of the Year ("I Was Country [When Country Wasn't Cool]") 1981

(1)   **David Frizzell**
Horizon Award (with Shelly West) 1981

(1)   **Thomas Garrett**
Song of the Year ("Every Which Way But Loose") (with Stephen Dorff and Milton Brown) 1979

(1)   **Four Guys**
Vocal Group of the Year 1975

(1)   **Gatlin Family and Friends**
Instrumental Group of the Year 1979

(1)   **Steve Gibb**
Song of the Year ("She Believes In Me") 1979

(1)   **J. Gillespie**
Song of the Year ("Heaven's Just A Sin Away") 1978

(1)   **Bobby Goldsboro**
Single of the Year ("Honey" UA) 1968

(1)   **Grandpa Jones**
Comedian of the Year 1970

(1)   **The Hager Brothers**
Vocal Group of the Year 1971

(1)   **Sam Hogin**
Song of the Year ("I Believe in You") 1981

(1)   **Debbie Hupp**
Song of the Year ("You Decorated My Life") 1980

(1)   **V. Keith**
Song of the Year ("Before The Next Teardrop Falls") 1975

(1)   **Wayne Kemp**
Song of the Year ("Yes Darling You Know I Wouldn't Lie") 1969

(1)   **Dickey Lee**
Song of the Year ("The Door Is Always Open") 1976

(1)   **Charlie Louvin**
Vocal Duo of the Year (with Melba Montgomery) 1971

(1)   **Gene MacLellan**
Song of the Year ("Put Your Hand In The Hand") 1971

(1) **Marshall Tucker Band**
Instrumental Group of the Year 1977

(1) **G. Martin**
Song of the Year ("It's Not Love But It's Not Bad") 1973

(1) **Masters Three**
Instrumental Group of the Year (with Atkins, Cramer, Randolph) 1967

(1) **C.W. McCall**
Single of the Year ("Convoy" MGM) 1976

(1) **Jody Miller**
Vocal Duo of the Year (with Johnny Paycheck) 1972

(1) **Melba Montgomery**
Vocal Duo of the Year (with Charlie Louvin) 1971

(1) **Jack Moran**
Song of the Year ("Skip A Rope") 1968

(1) **Dennis Morgan**
Song of the Year ("I Was Country [When Country Wasn't Cool]") 1981

(1) **Misty Morgan**
Vocal Group of the Year (with Jack Blanchard) 1970

(1) **Bob Morrison**
Song of the Year ("You Decorated My Life") 1980

(1) **Dale Noe**
Song of the Year ("It's Such A Pretty World Today") 1967

(1) **Kenny O'Dell**
* Song of the Year ("Behind Closed Doors") 1973

(1) **Bonnie Owens**
Vocal Duo of the Year (with Merle Haggard) 1970

(1) **Carl Perkins**
Song of the Year ("Daddy Sang Bass") 1969

(1) **George Richey**
Song of the Year ("Till I Can Make It On My Own") 1976

(1) **K. Robbins**
Song of the Year ("I'm A Stand By My Woman Man") 1977

(1) **Johnny Rodriguez**
Male Vocalist of the Year 1973

(1) **John Rostill**
Song of the Year ("If You Love Me Let Me Know") 1974

(1) **Leon Russell**
Album of the Year (*One For The Road* CBS) 1979 with Willie Nelson

(1) **Don Schlitz**
* Song of the Year ("The Gambler") 1979

(1) **Earl Scruggs Revue**
Instrumental Group of the Year 1975

(1) **Billy Joe Shaver**
Song of the Year ("I'm Just an Old Chunk of Coal") 1981

(1) **T.G. Sheppard**
Horizon Award 1981

(1) **B.J. Thomas**
Single of the Year ("Hey Won't You Play Another Somebody Done Somebody Wrong Song" ABC) 1975

(1) **Tompall Glaser**
* Album of the Year (*Wanted-The Outlaws* RCA) (with Waylon, Willie & Jessi) 1976

(1) **Allen Toussaint**
Song of the Year ("Southern Nights") 1977

(1) **Glen Douglas Tubb**
Song of the Year ("Skip A Rope") 1968

(1) **Twitty Birds**
Instrumental Group of the Year 1975

(1) **John Volinkaty**
Song of the Year ("Satin Sheets") 1973

(1) **Wayne Walker**
Song of the Year ("All The Time") 1967

(1) **Waylors**
Instrumental Group of the Year 1976

(1)   **Don Wayne**
* Song of the Year ("Country Bumpkin")
1974

(1)   **Larry Weiss**
* Song of the Year ("Rhinestone Cowboy")
1976

(1)   **Freddy Weller**
Single of the Year ("The Games People
Play" CBS) 1969

(1)   **Shelly West**
Horizon Award (with David Frizzell) 1981

(1)   **Billy Edd Wheeler**
Song of the Year ("Coward of the County")
1980

(1)   **Sterling Whipple**
Song of the Year ("The Blind Man in the
Bleachers") 1976

(1)   **Wilburn Brothers**
Vocal Group of the Year 1972

(1)   **The Don Williams Band**
Instrumental Group of the Year 1981

(1)   **Jerry Williams**
Song of the Year ("She's All I've Got")
1972

(1)   **Norro Wilson**
Song of the Year ("The Most Beautiful
Girl In The World") 1974

(1)   **Bobby R. Woods**
Song of the Year ("Talking In Your Sleep")
1979 with Roger Cook

(1)   **Faron Young**
Single of the Year ("Four In the Mornin' "
Mercury) 1972

THE COUNTRY MUSIC HALL OF FAME

The Country Music Hall of Fame elections are conducted under the auspices of the Country Music Association. Hall of Fame inductees are selected each year by an anonymous panel of 200 electors, each of whom has participated actively in the music business for at least fifteen years and has made a significant contribution to the industry. These electors vote by secret ballot and the results are tallied by a national accounting firm, Deloitte, Haskins & Sells. Winners are traditionally announced on the televised CMA Awards Show in October.

The Hall of Fame building is located in the Country Music Hall of Fame and Museum, which was opened in 1967, and is operated and maintained by the Country Music Foundation where each year more than 500,000 visitors enjoy its exhibits.

COUNTRY MUSIC HALL OF FAME MEMBERS *

(Hall of Fame is located in Nashville, Tennessee)

1961 *
(Original members in 1961 limited to deceased)
JIMMIE RODGERS, born Meridian, Mississippi, September 8, 1897; died New York, New York, May 26, 1933
FRED ROSE (publisher, songwriter, singer, pianist), born Evansville, Indiana, August 24, 1897; died Nashville, Tennessee, December 1, 1954
HIRAM KING "HANK" WILLIAMS (SR), born Mount Olive, Alabama, September 17, 1923; died January 1, 1953

1962
ROY CLAXTON ACUFF, born Maynardsville, Tennessee, September 15, 1903

1964
WOODWARD MAURICE "TEX" RITTER, born Panola County, Texas, January 12, 1906; died Nashville, Tennessee, January 2, 1974

1965
ERNEST DALE TUBB, born near Crisp, Texas, February 9, 1914

1966
RICHARD EDWARD "EDDY" ARNOLD, born near Henderson, Tennessee, May 15, 1918
JAMES RAE DENNY (manager, publisher, talent booker), born Buffalo Valley, Tennessee, February 28, 1911; died Nashville, Tennessee, August 27, 1963
GEORGE DEWEY HAY (The Solemn Old Judge, emcee, Grand Ole Opry), born Attica, Indiana, November 9, 1895; died Virginia Beach, Virginia, May 9, 1968
DAVID HARRISON "UNCLE DAVE" MACON, born Smart Station, Tennessee, October 7, 1870; died Readyville, Tennessee, March 22, 1952

* Year members elected

1967

CLYDE JULIAN "RED" FOLEY, born near Berea, Kentucky, June 17, 1910; died Ft. Wayne, Indiana, September 19, 1968
JOSEPH LEE "JOE" FRANK (promotion manager), born Limestone County, Alabama, April 15, 1900; died May 4, 1952
STEPHEN HENRY "STEVE" SHOLES (record company executive), born Washington, D.C., February 12, 1911; died Nashville, Tennessee, April 22, 1968

1968

JAMES ROBERT "BOB" WILLS, born Limestone County, Texas, March 6, 1905; died Ft. Worth, Texas, May 13, 1975

1969

ORVON GENE AUTRY, born near Tioga, Texas, September 29, 1907

1970

WILLIAM SMITH "BILL" MONROE, born near Rosine, Kentucky, September 13, 1911
THE CARTER FAMILY "original" Carter Family—Alvin Pleasant Delaney "A.P." Carter, born Maces Spring, Virginia, December 15, 1891; died Maces Spring, Viriginia, November 7, 1960
Sara Dougherty Carter Bayes, born Wise County, Virginia, July 21, 1899; died Lodi, California, January 8, 1979
Maybelle Addington "Mother Maybelle" Carter, born Nickelsville, Virginia, May 10, 1909; died October 23, 1978

1971

ARTHUR EDWARD "UNCLE ART" SATHERLEY (record industry executive), born Bristol, England, October 19, 1889

1972

JIMMIE HOUSTON DAVIS, born Beech Grove, near Quitman, Louisiana, September 11, 1902

1973

CHESTER BURTON "CHET" ATKINS, born Luttrell, Tennessee, June 20, 1924
PATSY CLINE (Virginia Patterson Hensley), born Winchester, Virginia, September 8, 1932; died Camden, Tennessee, March 5, 1963

1974

OWEN BRADLEY (pianist, band leader, record company Artists & Repertoire man), born Westmoreland, Tennessee, October 21, 1915
FRANK "PEE WEE" KING (Frank A. Kuczynski), born Abrams, Wisconsin, February 18, 19

1975

MINNIE PEARL (Sarah Ohelia Colley), born Centerville, Tennessee, October 25, 1912

1976

KITTY WELLS (Muriel Deason), born Nashville, Tennessee, August 30, 1919
PAUL COHEN (record company executive), born Chicago, Illinois, November 10, 1908; died April 1, 1970

1977

MERLE ROBERT TRAVIS, born Rosewood, Muhlenberg County, Kentucky, November 29, 1917

1978

LOUIS MARSHALL "GRANDPA" JONES, born Henderson County, Kentucky, October 20, 1913

1979

HUBERT LONG (manager, booking agent), born Poteet, Texas, December 3, 1923; died Nashville, Tennessee, September 7, 1972
CLARENCE EUGENE "HANK" SNOW, born Liverpool, Nova Scotia, May 9, 1914

1980

JOHN R. "JOHNNY" CASH, born Kingsland, Arkansas, February 26, 1932
CONNIE B. GAY (impresario, broadcaster, music industry executive), born Lizard Lick, North Carolina
SONS OF THE PIONEERS (Roy Rogers, Bob Nolan, Tim Spencer, Karl Farr, Hugh Farr, Lloyd Perryman)

1981

VERNON DALHART (Marion Try Slaughter), born Jefferson, Texas, April 6, 1883; died September 15, 1948
GRANT TURNER (radio announcer), born Baird, Texas, May 17

ADDENDUM

LYNN, LORETTA: *Singer, guitarist, band leader. Born Butcher Holler, Kentucky, April 14, 1935.*

From an unlikely place called Butcher Holler, Loretta Lynn went on to become the reigning queen not only of country music, but popular music as well. By the start of the 1980s, with the success of her autobiography and the movie based on that book, she was probably the most famous "Coal Miner's Daughter" in the world, a heady achievement for a girl from humble origins whose main goal as a teen-aged bride was to make a good home for her husband and growing family.

She grew up in a log cabin in the Kentucky mountains and was known to her friends and family as Loretta Webb. Her parents named her after the movie star Loretta Young. The actress' picture had been one of several clipped from fan magazines by Mrs. Webb to help brighten up the cabin walls. Comforts were few, Loretta Lynn recalled, but there was a lot of warmth and love during her childhood years, particularly in the close rapport she had with her coal miner father.

As Loretta grew toward her teen years, she helped with the household chores and got what education she could from a mountain grade school which she attended through eighth grade (which she took twice). She was still only thirteen when she met a boy named O.V. Lynn—usually called by one of two nicknames, "Mooney" or "Doolittle"—at a school social. He was attracted to her and they started dating. Within a month, he managed to get her father's approval for them to marry.

When they married, Mooney had a job with the Consolidated Coal Company, but before a year was past, he lost it. With other work scarce, Mooney and Loretta's brother Jay Lee (Junior) Webb decided to hitchhike cross country to look for jobs in Washington. After finding a position on a farm, Mooney sent travel money home to his 14-year-old wife, by then pregnant with their first child. Though Loretta went to join him in Custer, Washington, it was a wrenching experience to leave her home and, particularly, her beloved father. Later, as she noted in her autobiography, one of her greatest sorrows was to be far from her family when her father died.

For about four years, Loretta's occupation was taking care of their living quarters (three little rooms and an outhouse, and no running water) and ministering to a growing family. (She had four of their six children before she was 21.) She was good at housework, she stressed, as evidenced by her winning all the blue ribbons awarded for food canning one year at the Washington State Fair. Meanwhile her husband was the breadwinner, first as a farmworker, later in the logging field. When things slowed down in logging, Loretta had to do housecleaning work to augment the family income. Around the house Loretta sometimes sang to the children or just to keep her mind occupied. Taking note of that, her husband began to mull over the possibilities of turning her talents to economic use. On her eighteenth birthday, he bought her an inexpensive guitar and urged her to learn to play it.

Loretta managed to pick up the rudiments of guitar playing and Mooney kept trying to figure out ways of getting her career underway. Bolstered by a number of drinks one Saturday night, he took her to the local grange hall in Custer and convinced the country band playing there to let Loretta try out for the radio show they taped on Wednesdays. Though the band assumed they wouldn't show up, they appeared at the designated time and Loretta sang so well she was asked to become a member of the Saturday night show. In the late 1950s she formed her own band, with brother Jay Lee Webb on guitar to back her on dates at clubs in Custer and other towns in the Northwest.

Both Lynns now were excited about Loretta's prospects, blissfully unaware of the tremendous gap between where they were and what usually was required for success in the country music big time. As Loretta became more confident about her singing style, they looked for some way of breaking into the record field. They managed to get backing from a Vancouver businessman to make her first recording. Called "I'm a Honky Tonk Girl," it was pressed on the Zero record label. Mooney somehow found a way to get a list of country radio stations and soon was mailing off review copies of the 45 rpm disc to DJs across the country. Many of them, surprisingly, took the time to listen to it and quite a few began to play it, even though, as it turned out, there were no copies that fans could buy in the stores.

Loretta and Mooney were nothing if not resourceful. As soon as they heard the record was getting some airplay, they decided to do their own promotional tour. She later recalled to an interviewer after hearing it was on the charts, "We didn't even know what the charts was. But, by golly, me and Doolittle loaded up in that old car, and Shirley and Jay Lee Webb—my brother and his wife—kept all four kids, and we took out to hit ever' radio station that was country. Zero records gave us money to buy gas—but not food—and we went all the way across the country one way and come back another way, eatin' baloney and cheese and crackers and sleepin' in the car."

Hugh Cherry, long a major country disc jockey in Los Angeles, remembered when his station was a stop on that early 1960s trip. "I was working as a late night jock on KFOX in Long Beach, California. One evening the buzzer rang and a voice said, "Hello, I'm Loretta Lynn, and a disc jockey in Seattle, Washington said I should come to Los Angeles and see Hugh Cherry. I've got a record for you.' So I let her in and

she comes up very talkative and animated.

" 'I understand that if somebody wants to get a hillbilly record to break in California that you are the man to see. Well, I've got one right here—"Honky Tonk Girl". It's mine!'

"I put it on the turntable and the record was really good. . . . Loretta said she was going to Nashville to get the record played there and to be on the *Grand Ole Opry.* I said to her, 'But honey, don't you know that it sometimes takes three or four years to get on the *Opry?*' Loretta replied, 'I can't wait that long.'

"Well, a few months later I began to hear some rumblings out of Nashville about her. "Honky Tonk Girl" became a hit, and soon Loretta was on the Decca label. And sure enough she got on the *Grand Ole Opry* . . . a bit sooner than I expected."

By any yardstick, Loretta's rise qualifies as meteoric. Although an unknown in 1961 with only one single to her credit on an obscure label, in 1962 she was on the way to stardom. It was a year in which she got her first top-10 single from Decca, appropriately named "Success," and was asked to become a regular on the *Opry.* As she and her family settled in to their new Nashville surroundings, her name was becoming known to country fans the length and breadth of the United States. In fact, *Cashbox* magazine named her the Most Programmed Female Country Star for 1962.

She was beginning to experience the excitement and exhilaration of success as well as its pitfalls—resentment among some of her country music peers at her swift rise, the strain of constant touring along with the natural nervousness of a newcomer on the scene. At that point, she was greatly helped by a new-found close friend, established star Patsy Cline. As Loretta wrote in her autobiography, Patsy's warmth and understanding had an impact on her life almost as great as her father's. Thus Loretta reacted with a tremendous sense of loss to news of Patsy's untimely death in a plane crash in March 1963.

Loretta continued her career with steadily growing approval from fans and critics.

Througout the mid- and late 1960s she kept adding to the list of hit singles and albums to her credit, including a number of songs she wrote herself. In 1963, she had the top-10 single, "Before I'm Over You" and, in 1964, "Wine, Women and Song." In 1965 she had the top-10 singles "Blue Kentucky Girl," "Happy Birthday" and "The Home You're Tearing Down" and, in 1966, "Dear Uncle Sam," "You Ain't Woman Enough To Take My Man Away," and the number-one ranked "Don't Come Home a Drinkin'." The first two were written by her and the third co-written. "Don't Come Home a Drinkin'" stayed on the lists into 1967, when Loretta had another top-10 hit, "If You're Not Gone Too Long." In late 1967, *Billboard* magazine named her the Top Country Female Vocalist for that year. In 1968, she made the top 10 with the singles "Fist City" and "You've Just Stepped In (From Stepping Out on Me)."

She also established herself as a major album artist during those years, with most of her releases on Decca making the charts and many achieving top-10 status. *Loretta Lynn*, her debut LP on the label, came out in early 1964. Among the other albums that followed during the decade were: *Before I'm Over You* (1964); *Songs From My Heart, Blue Kentucky Girl* (1965); *I Like 'Em Country* (1966); *Don't Come Home a Drinkin', Singin' With Feelin'* (1967); *Fist City* (1968); and *Woman Of the World* (1969). Other albums released at the end of the 1960s and in the early 1970s were: *Wings Upon Your Horns, Coal Miner's Daughter, Hymns, I Wanna Be Free, Loretta Lynn Writes 'Em and Sings 'Em* and *We Only Make Believe*. The last named was a duet album with Conway Twitty, also a Decca Records (later MCA) superstar. The Lynn/Twitty duo became one of the most successful in country music history, achieving dozens of top-10 hit singles and albums during the 1970s and into the early 1980s. One of their early collaborations, "After the Fire Is Gone," won the 1971 Grammy Award for Best Country Vocal Performance by a Duo or Group.

From the mid-1960s on, Loretta accrued many nominations and awards in every poll covering the country music field. In the very first Country Music Association annual awards (1967) she was named Female Vocalist of the Year and in 1972 she won the highest award given by the CMA, Entertainer of the Year. She and Conway Twitty were nominated many times to the final five for CMA Vocal Duo of the Year and won the award several times. Loretta won the Academy of Country Music Female Vocalist of the Year award a number of times in the 1970s; Conway and Loretta were voted ACM top duo several times; and in 1975 Loretta was voted ACM Entertainer of the Year. (In fact, in the 1975 ACM awards Loretta won in three categories: Female Vocalist of the Year, Album of the Year for *Feelin's* with Conway, and Top Vocal Group with Conway.) All in all, as of the early 1980s Loretta has received more awards from the CMA and ACM than any other performer.

During the 1970s and early 1980s, Loretta's name could almost always be found on the country singles and album charts. In some cases, her recordings crossed over onto the pop charts. In 1970 she had one of the year's best selling singles with her rendition of "Coal Miner's Daughter." Later in the decade it served as the title for her autobiography and the movie based on the book. Loretta's best selling singles in the first half of the 1970s included "Here I Am Again" (1972); "They Don't Make 'Em Like My Daddy," "Trouble In Paradise" (1974); "Love Is the Foundation" (1973); and "Home" (1975). With Conway Twitty, she had such hits as "Mississippi Woman—Louisiana Man," "Before I Hang Up the Phone," and, in 1975, "Feelin's."

In the second half of the 1970s her chart makers included the MCA releases "When the Tingle Becomes a Chill," "Red, White and Blue" (1976); "Why Can't He Be You" (1977); "Spring Fever," "We've Come A Long Way Baby" (1978); and "I Can't Feel You Anymore," "I've Got a Picture of You on My Mind" (1979). With Conway Twitty her successes included "The Letter" (1976); "I Can't Love You Enough" (1977); "From Seven Til Ten/You're the Reason My Kids are Ugly" (1978); and "You

Know Just What I'd Do/The Sadness of it All" (1979).

Her charted albums during the 1970s included *Lead Me On* (with Twitty, 1972); *One's on the Way* (1972); *They Don't Make 'Em Like My Daddy, Country Partners* (with Twitty) (1974-75); *Back to the Country, Home, Feelin's* (with Twitty) (1975); *When the Tingle Becomes a Chill* (1976); *Unlimited Talent* (with Twitty, number one, 8/76); *I Remember Patsy, Dynamic Duo* (with Twitty) (1977); *Honky Tonk Heroes* (with Twitty, 1978); *Diamond Duet* (with Twitty), and *The Very Best of Loretta Lynn and Conway Twitty* (1979).

Throughout the 1970s Loretta kept up a whirlwind schedule of concerts and television appearances, sometimes performing with Conway Twitty. Her in-person shows totaled about 125 a year, involving 150,000 miles per year of travel in her specially outfitted bus. Her television credits included taking part in three regular season *Dean Martin* shows in 1973 and two of his summer series as well as guest spots on a *Frank Sinatra Special, Ed Sullivan, Kraft Music Hall, Dick Cavett, David Frost, Merv Griffin, Dinah Shore, The Mac Davis Show, The Flip Wilson Special—Travels with Flip,* the *50th Anniversary of the Grand Ole Opry,* the *Bill Cosby Special (Cos)* and Johnny Carson's *Tonight Show.* She was also spotlighted on the CBS documentary program *Magazine* and was twice co-host in the mid-1970s of the NBC-TV *Midnight Special* program. President Jimmy Carter invited her to perform on the CBS Pre-Inaugural Special.

One of her major projects in the mid-1970s was completing an autobiography spanning the period of her life from age 13 to 25, in collaboration with *The New York Times* correspondent George Vecsey. Released in hard cover by Henry Regnery Company, *Coal Miner's Daughter* became one of the top-10 selling books of 1976. Issued as a paperback by Warner Books in April 1977, it went past the 1.2 million sales mark during the summer. The movie rights were purchased by Universal Studios and by the fall of 1979, production neared completion starring Sissy Spacek as Loretta, Tommy Lee Jones as Mooney, and Beverly D'Angelo as Patsy Cline.

The movie *Coal Miner's Daughter* was previewed in the Kennedy Center, Washington D.C., in early 1980. It received excellent reviews there and soon had enthusiastic support from critics in other major cities. The film became one of the year's hits and the soundtrack album on MCA was in the country top 10 by April, where it stayed for months.

The movie naturally spawned still more interviews for Loretta on television and in newspapers and magazines. However, she continued with business as usual in the early 1980s, turning out new recordings and touring. Her chart singles included "Pregnant Again" (she never hesitated writing or singing about 'controversial' aspects of modern life, as indicated previously with releases like "The Pill"), "Naked In the Rain," "Cheatin' on a Cheater" (1980); and "Somebody Led Me Away" (1981). Her duet hits with Conway Twitty in the early 1980s included "It's True Love" (1980) and "Love What Your Lovin' Does to Me" (1981). Early 1980s charted LPs by Loretta included *Loretta* and *Lookin' Good.*

Her continued emphasis on personal appearances related to her philosophy about the dynamic between a performer and audiences. "If you're gonna record," she told an interviewer, "you gotta be out there with the people that buy your records. That's the way I feel about it." People who couldn't get tickets to her standing-room-only shows could still see her perform on television. Among the specials that featured her talents in the early 1980s was the spring 1982 show on NBC *Loretta Lynn—The Lady, The Legend.*

Based partly on a 1979 interview with Jack Hurst.

NASHVILLE SONGWRITERS ASSOCIATION, INTERNATIONAL
Awards and Presentations *

SONGWRITER OF THE YEAR

1967	Dallas Frazier	1975	Ben Peters
1968	Bobby Russell	1976	Bob McDill
1969	Merle Haggard	1977	Roger Bowling and Hal Bynum
1970	Kris Kristofferson	1978	Sonny Throckmorton
1971	Kris Kristofferson	1979	Sonny Throckmorton
1972	Tom T. Hall	1980	Bob Morrison
1973	Kris Kristofferson	1981	Kye Fleming and Dennis Morgan
1974	Don Wayne		

SONG OF THE YEAR

1978	"You Needed Me" Randy Goodrum	1980	"He Stopped Loving Her Today" Bobby Braddock and Curly Putman
1979	"She Believes In Me" Steve Gibb	1981	"You're the Reason God Made Oklahoma" Larry Collins and Sandy Pinkard

SONGWRITERS HALL OF FAME

Name	Year Inducted
Joe Allison	1978
Bill Anderson	1975
Gene Autry	1970
Carl Belew	1976
Johnny Bond	1970
Bobby Braddock	1981
Albert Brumley	1970
Boudleaux Bryant	1972
Felice Bryant	1972
Smiley Burnette	1971
Jenny Lou Carson	1971
A. P. Carter	1970
Wilf Carter	1971
Johnny Cash	1977

---

* NSAI is an organization based in Nashville, Tennessee, whose goal is "to advance, promote, foster, and benefit composers and authors of musical compositions," primarily in the country & western field. The Songwriter of the Year (established 1967) and Song of the Year (established 1978) awards are based on the vote of NSAI membership.

Those elected to the Hall of Fame are presented with a bronze sculpture called The Manny. Since 1977, the maximum number of songwriters that can be inducted annually is limited to four.

Jack Clement	1973
Zeke Clements	1971
Hank Cochran	1974
Ted Daffan	1970
Vernon Dalhart	1970
Jimmie Davis	1971
Alton Delmore	1971
Rabon Delmore	1971
Al Dexter	1971
Danny Dill	1975
The Reverend Thomas A. Dorsey	1979
Stephen Foster (Special Award)	1976
Dallas Frazier	1976
Lefty Frizzell	1972
Don Gibson	1973
Rex Griffin	1970
Woodie Guthrie	1977
Merle Haggard	1977
Tom T. Hall	1978
Stuart Hamblen	1970
Vaughn Horton	1971
Harlan Howard	1973
Bradley Kincaid	1971
Pee Wee King	1970
Kris Kristofferson	1977
Hudie "Leadbelly" Ledbetter	1980
John D. Loudermilk	1976
Charles Louvin	1979
Ira Louvin	1979
Vic McAlpin	1970
Elsie McWilliams	1979
Bob Miller	1970
Eddie Miller	1975
Roger Miller	1973
Bill Monroe	1971
Moon Mullican	1976
Ed Nelson, Jr.	1973
Steve Nelson	1973
Willie Nelson	1973
Mickey Newbury	1980
Bob Nolan	1971
Tex Owens	1971
Leon Payne	1970
Ben Peters	1980
Curly Putman	1976
Marty Robbins	1975
Jack Rhodes	1972
Tex Ritter	1971
Don Robertson	1972
Carson J. Robison	1971
Jimmie Rodgers	1970
Fred Rose	1970

Hank Snow	1978
Joe South	1979
Tim Spencer	1971
Ray Stevens	1980
Redd Stewart	1970
Gene Sullivan	1971
Mel Tillis	1976
Floyd Tillman	1970
Merle Travis	1970
Ernest Tubb	1970
Jimmy Wakely	1971
Cindy Walker	1970
Wayne Walker	1975
Wiley Walker	1971
Don Wayne	1978
Ray Whitley	1981
Marijohn Wilkin	1975
Hank Williams	1970
Bob Wills	1970
Scotty Wiseman	1971

SONGWRITERS HALL OF FAME

Inducted in 1970

Gene Autry
"Back in the Saddle Again" (C)
"Goodbye Little Darlin' Goodbye"
"Silver Haired Daddy of Mine"
"Be Honest with Me"
"Here Comes Santa Claus" (C)

Johnny Bond
"Tomorrow Never Comes"
"Cimmaron"
"I Wonder Where You Are Tonight"
"Ten Little Bottles"

Albert Brumley
"I'll Fly Away"
"I'll Meet You in the Morning"
"Turn Your Radio On"
"Jesus, Hold My Hand"

A. P. Carter
"Wildwood Flower"
"Wabash Cannon Ball"
"Will the Circle Be Unbroken"
"Keep on the Sunny Side"

Ted Daffan
"Born to Lose"
"No Letter Today"
"Worried Mind"
"Truck Driver's Blues"

Vernon Dalhart
"Prisoner's Song"
"Wreck of the Old 97"
"Death of Floyd Collins"

Rex Griffin
"Just Call Me Lonesome"
"The Last Letter"
"I Told You So"
"Won't You Ride in my Little Red Wagon"

Stuart Hamblen
"It Is No Secret (What God Can Do)"
"Texas Plains"
"My Mary"
"This Ole House"
"Remember Me, I'm the One Who Loves You"

Pee Wee King
"Tennessee Waltz" (C)
"Slowpoke" (C)
"Bonaparte's Retreat" (C)

Vic McAlpin
"To My Sorrow"
"Standing at the End of the World"
"God Walks These Hills With Me"
"Almost"
"What Locks the Door"

Bob Miller

"Rockin' Alone in an Old Rocking Chair"
"Seven Years With the Wrong Woman"
"Little Red Caboose Behind the Train"
"In the Blue Hills of Virginia"

Leon Payne

"I Love You Because"
"You've Still Got A Place in My Heart"
"Lost Highway"
"Empty Arms"
"Fools Rush In"

Jimmie Rodgers

" 'T' for Texas"
"Mother, The Queen of my Heart"
"Waitin' For A Train"
"Train Whistle Blues"

Fred Rose

"Red Hot Mama"
"Hang Your Head in Shame"
"Foggy River"
"Blue Eyes Crying in the Rain"
"Take These Chains From My Heart"

Redd Stewart

"Tennessee Waltz" (C)
"Slowpoke" (C)
"Bonaparte's Retreat" (C)

Floyd Tillman

"I Love You So Much It Hurts Me"''
"Slippin' Around"
"It Makes No Difference Now"

Merle Travis

"Nine Pound Hammer"
"Smoke, Smoke, Smoke"
"Sixteen Tons"
"I Am A Pilgrim"

Ernest Tubb

"Walkin' the Floor Over You"
"It's Been So Long Darlin' "
"Try Me One More Time"
"Soldier's Last Letter"

Cindy Walker

"Distant Drums"
"You Don't Know Me"
"In the Misty Moonlight"

Hank Williams

"Your Cheatin' Heart"
"Lovesick Blues"
"Cold, Cold Heart"
"Jambalaya"

Bob Wills

"Faded Love"
"Take Me Back to Tulsa"
"Maiden's Prayer"
"San Antonio Rose" (C)
"Texas Two Step"

Inducted in 1971

Smiley Burnette

"Ridin' Down the Canyon"
"Mama Don't Allow No Music"
"My Home Town"
"It's My Lazy Day"

Jenny Lou Carson

"Let Me Go, Lover"
"Jealous Love"
"Don't Rob Another Man's Castle"

Wilf Carter

"I'm Thinking Tonight of my Blue Eyes"
"The Fate of Old Strawberry Roan"

Zeke Clements

"Just A Little Lovin' (Will Go A Long Way)"
"Why Should I Cry"
"Smoke on the Water"

Jimmie Davis

"You Are My Sunshine"
"Nobody's Darlin' But Mine"

Delmore Brothers (Alton and Rabon)

"Blues Stay Away From Me"
"Brown's Ferry Blues"

Al Dexter

"Pistol-Packin' Mama"
"Down at the Roadside Inn"
"Wine, Women and Song"
"Rosalita"
"Too Late to Worry (Too Blue to Cry)"
"Guitar Polka"

Vaughn Horton
"Mockin' Bird Hill"
"Address Unknown"
"Teardrops in my Heart"

Bradley Kincaid
"Legend of Robin's Redbreast"

Bill Monroe
"Blue Moon Over Kentucky"
"Kentucky Waltz"
"Uncle Pen"

Bob Nolan
"Cool Water"
"Tumblin' Tumbleweeds"
"NE-HAH-NEE (Clear Water)"

Tex Owens
"Cattle Call"
"Give Me A Home on the Lone Prairie"

Tex Ritter
"Boll Weavil Song"
"Green Grow the Lilacs"
"Rye Whiskey"
"High, Wide and Handsome"

Carson J. Robison
"My Blue Ridge Mountain Home"
"Life Gets Teejus, Don't It"
"Wreck of the Number Nine"

Tim Spencer
"Room Full of Roses"
"Cigarettes, Whiskey, and Wild, Wild Women"
"Timber Trail"

Gene Sullivan
"Live and Let Live"
"I Might Have Known"

Jimmy Wakely
"Those Gone and Left Me Blues"
"Too Late"
"I'll Never Let You Go, Little Darling"
"You Can't Break the Chains of Love"

Wiley Walker
"When My Blue Moon Turns to Gold Again"

Scotty Wiseman
"Have I Told You Lately That I Love You"
"Remember Me"
"Mountain Dew"

Inducted in 1972

Boudleaux and Felice Bryant
"Rocky Top"
"Dream, Dream, Dream"
"Bye, Bye Love"
"Wake Up Little Susy"

Lefty Frizzell
"If You've Got the Money (I've Got the Time"
"Always Late"
"Mom and Dad Waltz"

Jack Rhodes
"Satisfied Mind"
"Conscience, I'm Guilty"
"Beautiful Lies"

Don Robertson
"Please Help Me, I'm Falling"
"I Really Don't Want to Know"
"I Don't Hurt Anymore"
"Does My Ring Hurt Your Finger"

Inducted in 1973

Jack Clement
"Just A Girl I Used to Know"
"I Know One"
"Just Between You and Me"
"Miller's Cave"
"Guess Things Happen That Way"

Don Gibson
"Oh, Lonesome Me"
"I'd Be A Legend In My Time"
"I Can't Stop Loving You"

Harlan Howard
"Heartaches by the Number"
"Pick Me Up on Your Way Down"
"The Chokin' Kind"
"She Called Me Baby"
"Busted"

Roger Miller
"King of the Road"
"Dang Me"
"When Two Worlds Collide"
"Husbands and Wives"
"Engine, Engine Number Nine"

Steve Nelson
and Ed Nelson, Jr.
"Bouquet of Roses"
"Frosty the Snowman"
"With This Ring I Thee Wed"

Willie Nelson
"Hello Walls"
"Funny How Time Slips Away"
"Crazy"
"Night Life"
"Healing Hands of Time"

Inducted in 1974

Hank Cochran
"Make the World Go Away"
"Don't Touch Me"
"Little-Bitty Tear"

Inducted in 1975

Bill Anderson
"City Lights"
"Still"
"Po' Folks"
"Tips of My Fingers"

Danny Dill
"Detroit City" (C)
"Partners"
"Let Me Talk to You"
"The Long Black Veil" (C)
"The Comeback"
"Sweet Lips"
"A Pain A Pill Can't Locate"
"So Wrong"
"Esther"
"Why Don'tcha Come Home"
"Old Courthouse"
"Who Rides With Billy"

Eddie Miller
"Release Me"
"There She Goes"
"Thanks A Lot"

Marty Robbins
"El Paso"
"White Sport Coat"
"You Gave Me A Mountain"
"My Woman, My Woman, My Wife"

Wayne Walker
"Burning Memories"
"All the Time"
"I've Got A New Heartache"
"Are You Sincere"

Marijohn Wilkin
"Waterloo"
"Long Black Veil" (C)
"One Day At A Time" (C)
"Scars in the Hands of Jesus"

Inducted in 1976

Carl Belew
"What's He Doing in My World"
"Am I That Easy to Forget"
"That's When I See the Blue"
"Lonely Street"
"Stop the World"

Dallas Frazier
"There Goes My Everything"
"All I Have to Offer You is Me" (C)
"Hickory Holler Tramp"
"Ain't Had No Loving"
"Alley Oop"
"Mohair Sam"

John D. Loudermilk
"Abilene" (C)
"Talk Back Trembling LIps"
"Waterloo"
"Bad News"
"Break My Mind"

Moon Mullican
"You Don't Have To Be A Baby To Cry"
"Sweeter Than the Flowers"
"Moon's Tune"
"I'll Sail My Ship Alone"
"Cherokee Boogie"
"I Was Sorta Wondering"
"Pipe Liner Blues"

Curly Putman
"Green, Green Grass of Home"
"Elusive Dreams" (C)
"Blood Red and Going Down"
"Set Me Free" (C)
"D-I-V-O-R-C-E" (C)

Mel Tillis

"Detroit City" (C)
"Ruby, Don't Take Your Love to Town"
"I Ain't Never" (C)
"Heart Over Mind"
"One More Time"
"Mental Revenge"
"Memory Maker"

Special Award—1976—Stephen Foster

Inducted in 1977

Johnny Cash

"I Walk the Line"
"Don't Take Your Guns to Town"
"Folsom Prison Blues"
"San Quentin"
"Understand Your Man"

Woodie Guthrie

"Oklahoma Hills"
"This Land is Your Land"
"So Long, It's Been Good to Know You"
"This Train is Bound For Glory"

Merle Haggard

"Okie From Muskogee"
"My Mother's Hungry Eyes"
"If We Make It Through December"
"Sing A Sad Song"
"Today I Started Loving You Again"

Kris Kristofferson

"For the Good Times"
"Help Me Make It Through The Night"
"Why Me"
"One Day At A Time" (C)

Inducted in 1978

Joe Allison

"Teen Aged Crush"
"He'll Have To Go"
"Live Fast, Love Hard, Die Young"
"I'm A Lover, Not A Fighter"
"It's A Great Life"
"Rock City Boogie"
"He'll Have To Stay"

Tom T. Hall

"I Washed My Face in the Morning Dew"
"Harper Valley PTA"
"Old Dogs, Children, and Watermelon Wine"
"I Love"
"Country Is"
"I Like Beer"

Hank Snow

"I'm Movin' On"
"Rhumba Boogie"
"Golden Rocket"
"Bluebird Island"
"Brand On My Heart"
"Music Makin' Mama From Memphis"

Don Wayne

"Saginaw Michigan"
"The Belles of Southern Bell"
"Country Bumpkin"

Inducted in 1979

The Reverend Thomas A. Dorsey

"Peace In the Valley"
"Take My Hand, Precious Lord"

The Louvin Brothers (Charles and Ira)

"Born Again"
"If I Could Only Win Your Love"
"Satan Lied to Me"
"When I Stop Dreaming"
"The Family Who Prays"
"Are You Teasing Me"

Elsie McWilliams

"For Jimmie Rogers"
"Sailor's Plea"
"My Old Pal"
"Mississippi Moon"
"I'm Lonely & Blue"

Joe South

"(I Never Promised You) a Rose Garden"
"Walk A Mile In My Shoes"
"Games People Play"
"No Man Is An Island"
"Down In the Boondocks"

Inducted in 1980

Hudie "Leadbelly" Ledbetter

"Good Night Irene"

Ben Peters
"Kiss An Angel Good Morning"
"That Was Before My Time"
"Daytime Friends and Nightime Lovers"

Ray Stevens
"Ahab The Arab"
"Mr. Businessman"
"Everything is Beautiful"
"The Streak"

Mickey Newbury
"She Even Woke Me Up to Say Goodbye"
"Sweet Memories"
"American Trilogy"
"San Francisco, Mabel Joy"

Inducted in 1981
Bobby Braddock
Ray Whitley

NATIONAL ACADEMY OF RECORDING ARTS & SCIENCES GRAMMY AWARDS *

The National Academy of Recording Arts & Sciences is a nonprofit organization composed of more than 4500 members nationwide representing the entire spectrum of creative people in the phonograph recording field. It was formed, in 1957, to advance the arts and science of recording, and to foster creative leadership for artistic, cultural, educational and technical progress in the recording field. The organization is also known as the 'Recording Academy' or by its initials, NARAS.

The Recording Academy is best known for its annual Grammy Awards which are given for outstanding artistic and/or technical achievements during each award's eligibility year to those deemed by their voting peers to be most worthy of the honor. The Grammy Awards are presented on nationwide television in late February or early March over CBS and reach over 55 million viewers throughout the world each year.

Best Folk Recording

1959 THE KINGSTON TRIO AT LARGE, The Kingston Trio

1960 SWING DAT HAMMER, Harry Belafonte

1961 BELAFONTE FOLK SINGERS AT HOME AND ABROAD, Belafonte Folk Singers

1962 IF I HAD A HAMMER, Peter, Paul and Mary

1963 BLOWIN' IN THE WIND, Peter, Paul and Mary

1964 WE'LL SING IN THE SUNSHINE, Gale Garnett

1965 AN EVENING WITH BELAFONTE/ MAKEBA, Harry Belafonte and Miriam Makeba

1966 BLUES IN THE STREET, Cortelia Clark

1967 GENTLE ON MY MIND, John Hartford

1968 BOTH SIDES NOW, Judy Collins

1969 CLOUDS, Joni Mitchell

Category discontinued after 1969

Best Country Song

1964 DANG ME, Roger Miller, composer

1965 KING OF THE ROAD, Roger Miller, composer

1966 ALMOST PERSUADED, Billy Sherrill, Glen Sutton, composers

1967 GENTLE ON MY MIND, John Hartford, composer

1968 LITTLE GREEN APPLES, Bobby Russell, composer

1969 A BOY NAMED SUE, Shel Silverstein, composer

1970 MY WOMAN, MY WOMAN, MY WIFE, Marty Robbins, composer

1971 HELP ME MAKE IT THROUGH THE NIGHT, Kris Kristofferson, Fred Foster, composers

1972 KISS AN ANGEL GOOD MORNIN', Ben Peters, composer

1973 BEHIND CLOSED DOORS, Kenny O'Dell, composer

1974 A VERY SPECIAL LOVE SONG, Norris Wilson & Billy Sherrill, composers

1975 (HEY WON'T YOU PLAY) ANOTHER SOMEBODY DONE SOMEBODY WRONG SONG, Chips Moman & Larry Butler, composers

* Folk, country and western awards or awards related to Encyclopedia entries only.

Best Country Song (cont.)

1976 BROKEN LADY, Larry Gatlin, composer
1977 DON'T IT MAKE MY BROWN EYES BLUE, Richard Leigh, composer
1978 THE GAMBLER, Don Schlitz, composer
1979 YOU DECORATED MY LIFE, Bob Morrison, Debbie Hupp, composers
1980 ON THE ROAD AGAIN, Willie Nelson, songwriter
1981 9 TO 5, Dolly Parton, songwriter.

Best Country Vocal Performance, Female

1964 HERE COMES MY BABY, Dottie West
1965 QUEEN OF THE HOUSE, Jody Miller
1966 DON'T TOUCH ME, Jeannie Seely
1967 I DON'T WANNA PLAY HOUSE, Tammy Wynette
1968 HARPER VALLEY P.T.A., Jeannie C. Riley
1969 STAND BY YOUR MAN, Tammy Wynette
1970 ROSE GARDEN, Lynn Anderson
1971 HELP ME MAKE IT THROUGH THE NIGHT, Sammi Smith
1972 HAPPIEST GIRL IN THE WHOLE USA, Donna Fargo
1973 LET ME BE THERE, Olivia Newton-John
1974 LOVE SONG, Anne Murray
1975 I CAN'T HELP IT (IF I'M STILL IN LOVE WITH YOU), Linda Rondstadt
1976 ELITE HOTEL, Emmylou Harris
1977 DON'T IT MAKE MY BROWN EYES BLUE, Crystal Gayle
1978 HERE YOU COME AGAIN, Dolly Parton
1979 BLUE KENTUCKY GIRL, Emmylou Harris
1980 COULD I HAVE THIS DANCE, Anne Murray
1981 9 TO 5, Dolly Parton

Best Country Vocal Performance, Male

1965 KING OF THE ROAD, Roger Miller
1966 ALMOST PERSUADED, David Houston
1967 GENTLE ON MY MIND, Glen Campbell
1968 FOLSOM PRISON BLUES, Johnny Cash
1969 A BOY NAMED SUE, Johnny Cash
1970 FOR THE GOOD TIMES, Ray Price
1971 WHEN YOU'RE HOT, YOU'RE HOT, Jerry Reed
1972 CHARLEY PRIDE SINGS HEART SONGS, Charley Pride
1973 BEHIND CLOSED DOORS, Charlie Rich
1974 PLEASE DON'T TELL ME HOW THE STORY ENDS, Ronnie Milsap
1975 BLUE EYES CRYING IN THE RAIN, Willie Nelson
1976 (I'M A) STAND BY MY WOMAN MAN, Ronnie Milsap
1977 LUCILLE, Kenny Rogers
1978 GEORGIA ON MY MIND, Willie Nelson
1979 THE GAMBLER, Kenny Rogers
1980 HE STOPPED LOVING HER TODAY, George Jones
1981 (THERE'S) NO GETTIN' OVER ME, Ronnie Milsap

Best Country Instrumental Performance

1968 FOGGY MOUNTAIN BREAKDOWN, Flatt and Scruggs
1969 THE NASHVILLE BRASS FEATURING DANNY DAVIS PLAY MORE NASHVILLE SOUNDS, Danny Davis and The Nashville Brass
1970 ME & JERRY, Chet Atkins and Jerry Reed
1971 SNOWBIRD, Chet Atkins
1972 CHARLIE McCOY/THE REAL McCOY, Charlie McCoy
1973 DUELING BANJOS, Eric Weissberg, Steve Mandell
1974 THE ATKINS-TRAVIS TRAVELING SHOW, Chet Atkins, Merle Travis
1975 THE ENTERTAINER, Chet Atkins
1976 CHESTER & LESTER, Chet Atkins & Les Paul
1977 COUNTRY INSTRUMENTALIST OF THE YEAR, Hargus "Pig" Robbins
1978 ONE O'CLOCK JUMP, Asleep At The Wheel
1979 BIG SANDY/LEATHER BRITCHES, Doc & Merle Watson

1980 ORANGE BLOSSOM SPECIAL/
HOEDOWN, Gilley's "Urban Cowboy"
Band
1981 COUNTRY—AFTER ALL THESE
YEARS, Chet Atkins

Best Country Vocal Performance By A Duo Or Group

1967 JACKSON, Johnny Cash, June Carter
1969 MACARTHUR PARK, Waylon
Jennings and the Kimberlys
1970 IF I WERE A CARPENTER, Johnny
Cash and June Carter
1971 AFTER THE FIRE IS GONE, Conway
Twitty and Loretta Lynn
1972 CLASS OF '57, The Statler Brothers
1973 FROM THE BOTTLE TO THE
BOTTOM, Kris Kristofferson, Rita
Coolidge
1974 FAIRYTALE, The Pointer Sisters
1975 LOVER PLEASE, Kris Kristofferson,
Rita Coolidge
1976 THE END IS NOT IN SIGHT (THE
COWBOY TUNE), Amazing Rhythm Aces
1977 HEAVEN'S JUST A SIN AWAY, The
Kendalls
1978 MAMMAS DON'T LET YOUR
BABIES GROW UP TO BE COWBOYS,
Waylon Jennings & Willie Nelson
1979 THE DEVIL WENT DOWN TO
GEORGIA, Charlie Daniels Band
1980 THAT LOVIN YOU FEELIN'
AGAIN, Roy Orbison & Emmylou Harris
1981 ELVIRA, Oak Ridge Boys

Best New Country and Western Artist °

1964 ROGER MILLER
1965 THE STATLER BROTHERS

Best Country and Western Album °

1964 DANG ME/CHUG-A-LUG, Roger
Miller, producer, John Kennedy
1965 THE RETURN OF ROGER MILLER,
Roger Miller

Best Country and Western Recording (Single) °

1958 TOM DOOLEY, The Kingston Trio

1959 THE BATTLE OF NEW ORLEANS,
Johnny Horton
1960 EL PASO, Marty Robbins
1961 BIG BAD JOHN, Jimmy Dean
1962 FUNNY WAY OF LAUGHIN', Burl
Ives
1963 DETROIT CITY, Bobby Bare
1964 DANG ME, Roger Miller; producer:
Jerry Kennedy
1965 KING OF THE ROAD, Roger Miller
1966 ALMOST PERSUADED, David
Houston
1967 GENTLE ON MY MIND, Glen
Campbell

° Categories discontinued, first two after
1965, third after 1967

Best Ethnic Or Traditional Recording

1970 GOOD FEELIN', T-Bone Walker
1971 THEY CALL ME MUDDY WATERS,
Muddy Waters
1972 THE LONDON MUDDY WATERS
SESSION, Muddy Walters
1973 THEN AND NOW, Doc Watson
1974 TWO DAYS IN NOVEMBER, Doc &
Merle Watson
1975 THE MUDDY WATERS
WOODSTOCK ALBUM, Muddy Waters
1976 MARK TWANG, John Hartford
1977 HARD AGAIN, Muddy Waters
1978 I'M READY, Muddy Waters
1979 MUDDY "MISSISSIPPI" WATERS
LIVE, Muddy Waters
1980 RARE BLUES, (Dr. Isaiah Ross,
Maxwell Street Jimmy, Big Joe Williams,
Son House, Rev. Robert Wilkins, Little
Brother Montgomery, Sunnyland Slim)
Norman Dayron, producer
1981 THERE MUST BE A BETTER
WORLD SOMEWHERE, B.B. King

Best Gospel or Other Religious Recording

1961 EVERYTIME I FEEL THE SPIRIT,
Mahalia Jackson
1962 GREAT SONGS OF LOVE AND
FAITH, Mahalia Jackson
1963 DOMINIQUE, Soeur Sourire; (The
Singing Nun)
1964 GREAT GOSPEL SONGS, Tennessee
Ernie Ford and the Jordanaires

Best Gospel or Other Religious Recording (cont.)

1965 SOUTHLAND FAVORITES, George Beverly Shea and the Anita Kerr Singers
1966 GRAND OLD GOSPEL, Porter Wagoner and the Blackwood Brothers
1967 MORE GRAND OLD GOSPEL, Porter Wagoner and the Blackwood Brothers
1968 THE HAPPY GOSPEL OF THE HAPPY GOODMANS, Happy Goodman Family
1969 IN GOSPEL COUNTRY, Porter Wagoner and the Blackwood Brothers
1970 TALK ABOUT THE GOOD TIMES, Oak Ridge Boys
1971 LET ME LIVE, Charley Pride
1972 L-O-V-E, Blackwood Brothers
1973 RELEASE ME (FROM MY SIN), Blackwood Brothers
1974 THE BAPTISM OF JESSE TAYLOR, Oak Ridge Boys
1975 NO SHORTAGE, Imperials
1976 WHERE THE SOUL NEVER DIES, Oak Ridge Boys
1977 SAIL ON, Imperials
1977 JUST A LITTLE TALK WITH JESUS, Oak Ridge Boys
1978 WHAT A FRIEND, Larry Hart
1978 REFRESHING, The Happy Goodman Family
1979 HEED THE CALL, Imperials
1979 LIFT UP THE NAME OF JESUS, The Blackwood Brothers
1980 WE COME TO WORSHIP, Blackwood Brothers
1980 THE LORD'S PRAYER, Reba Rambo, Dony McGuire, B.J. Thomas, Andrae Crouch, The Archers, Walter & Tremaine Hawkins, Cynthia Clawson

Best Traditional Gospel Performance

1981 THE MASTER V, J.D. Summer, James Blackwood, Hovie Lister, Rosie Rozell, Jake Hess

Best Contemporary Soul Gospel Performance

1981 DON'T GIVE UP, Andrae Crouch

Best Traditional Soul Gospel Performance

1981 THE LORD WILL MAKE A WAY, Al Green

Best Contemporary or Inspirational Gospel Performance

1981 PRIORITY, The Imperials

Best Inspirational Performance

1967 HOW GREAT THOU ART, Elvis Presley
1968 BEAUTIFUL ISLE SOMEWHERE, Jake Hess
1969 AIN'T THAT BEAUTIFUL SINGING, Jake Hess
1970 EVERYTHING IS BEAUTIFUL, Jake Hess
1971 DID YOU THINK TO PRAY, Charley Pride
1972 HE TOUCHED ME, Elvis Presley
1973 LET'S JUST PRAISE THE LORD, Bill Gaither Trio
1974 HOW GREAT THOU ART, Elvis Presley
1975 JESUS, WE JUST WANT TO THANK YOU, Bill Gaither Trio
1976 THE ASTONISHING, OUTRAGEOUS, AMAZING, INCREDIBLE, UNBELIEVABLE DIFFERENT WORLD OF GARY S. PAXTON, Gary S. Paxton
1977 HOME WHERE I BELONG, B. J. Thomas
1978 HAPPY MAN, B.J. Thomas
1979 YOU GAVE ME LOVE (WHEN NOBODY GAVE ME A PRAYER), B.J. Thomas
1980 WITH MY SONG I WILL PRAISE HIM, Debby Boone
1981 AMAZING GRACE, B.J. Thomas

Best Soul Gospel Performance

1968 THE SOUL OF ME, Dottie Rambo
1969 OH HAPPY DAY, Edwin Hawkins Singers
1970 EVERY MAN WANTS TO BE FREE, Edwin Hawkins Singers

1971 PUT YOUR HAND IN THE HAND OF THE MAN FROM GALILEE, Shirley Caesar
1972 AMAZING GRACE, Aretha Franklin
1973 LOVES ME LIKE A ROCK, Dixie Hummingbirds
1974 IN THE GHETTO, James Cleveland and the Southern California Community Choir
1975 TAKE ME BACK, Andrae Crouch and the Disciples
1976 HOW I GOT OVER, Mahalia Jackson
1977 WONDERFUL!, Edwin Hawkins & The Edwin Hawkins Singers (contemporary)
1977 JAMES CLEVELAND LIVE AT CARNEGIE HALL, James Cleveland (traditional)
1978 LIVE IN LONDON, Andrae Crouch & The Disciples (contemporary)
1978 LIVE AND DIRECT, Mighty Clouds of Joy (traditional)
1979 I'LL BE THINKING OF YOU, Andrae Crouch
1979 CHANGING TIMES, Mighty Clouds of Joy
1980 LORD, LET ME BE AN INSTRUMENT, James Cleveland & The Charles Fold Singers
1980 REJOICE, Shirley Caesar

Best Pop Vocal Performance—Female

1967 ODE TO BILLIE JOE, Bobbie Gentry (Best Contemporary Vocal Performance, Female)
1971 TAPESTRY, Carole King
1974 I HONESTLY LOVE YOU, Olivia Newton-John
1975 AT SEVENTEEN, Janis Ian
1976 HASTEN DOWN THE WIND, Linda Ronstadt
1978 YOU NEEDED ME, Anne Murray

Best Pop Vocal Performance—Male

1960 GEORGIA ON MY MIND, Ray Charles
1960 GENIUS OF RAY CHARLES, Ray Charles (Best Performance, Album)
1965 KING OF THE ROAD, Roger Miller (Best Contemporary Vocal Performance, Male)

1967 BY THE TIME I GET TO PHOENIX, Glen Campbell
1967 BY THE TIME I GET TO PHOENIX, Glen Campbell (Best Contemporary Vocal Performance, Male)
1968 LIGHT MY FIRE, Jose Feliciano
1970 EVERYTHING IS BEAUTIFUL, Ray Stevens
1971 YOU'VE GOT A FRIEND, James Taylor
1975 STILL CRAZY AFTER ALL THESE YEARS, Paul Simon
1977 HANDY MAN, James Taylor
1980 THIS IS IT, Kenny Loggins

Best Pop Vocal Performance, Duo Group or Chorus (Chorus previously separate category, 1959-69)

1962 IF I HAD A HAMMER, Peter, Paul and Mary
1963 BLOWIN' IN THE WIND, Peter, Paul and Mary
1965 FLOWERS ON THE WALL, Statler Brothers (Best Contemporary Vocal Group)
1968 MRS. ROBINSON, Simon & Garfunkel
1975 LYIN' EYES, Eagles

Best Performance By a Chorus

1960 SONG OF THE COWBOY, Norman Luboff Choir
1962 PRESENTING THE NEW CHRISTY MINSTRELS, The New Christy Minstrels

Best Instrumental Performance

1967 CHET ATKINS PICKS THE BEST, Chet Atkins

Best R&B Vocal Performance—Female

1971 BRIDGE OVER TROUBLED WATER, Aretha Franklin

Best R&B Vocal Performance, Male

1966 CRYING TIME, Ray Charles
1970 THE THRILL IS GONE, B.B. King
1975 LIVING FOR THE CITY, Ray Charles

Best R&B Recording °

1958 TEQUILA, The Champs
1960 LET THE GOOD TIMES ROLL, Ray Charles
1961 HIT THE ROAD JACK, Ray Charles
1962 I CAN'T STOP LOVING YOU, Ray Charles
1963 BUSTED, Ray Charles
1966 CRYING TIME, Ray Charles

° Category discontinued after 1967

Record of the Year

1968 MRS. ROBINSON, Simon & Garfunkel; producers, Paul Simon, Art Garfunkel, Roy Halee
1970 BRIDGE OVER TROUBLED WATER, Simon & Garfunkel; producers, Paul Simon, Art Garfunkel, Roy Halee
1971 IT'S TOO LATE, Carole King; producer, Lou Adler
1974 I HONESTLY LOVE YOU, Olivia Newton-John; producer, John Farrar
1977 HOTEL CALIFORNIA, Eagles; producer, Bill Szymczyk
1981 BETTE DAVIS EYES, Kim Carnes; producer, Val Garay

Album of the Year

1968 BY THE TIME I GET TO PHOENIX, Glen Campbell; producer, Al de Lory
1970 BRIDGE OVER TROUBLED WATER, Simon & Garfunkel; producers, Paul Simon, Art Garfunkel, Roy Halee
1971 TAPESTRY, Carole King; producer, Lou Adler
1972 THE CONCERT FOR BANGLA-DESH, George Harrison, Ravi Shankar, Bob Dylan, Leon Russell, Ringo Star, Billy Preston, Eric Clapton, Klaus Voormann; producer, George Harrison, Phil Spector
1975 STILL CRAZY AFTER ALL THESE YEARS, Paul Simon; producers, Paul Simon, Phil Ramone

Song of the Year

1959 THE BATTLE OF NEW ORLEANS, Jimmy Driftwood, composer

1968 LITTLE GREEN APPLES, Bobby Russell, composer
1969 GAMES PEOPLE PLAY, Joe South, composer
1970 BRIDGE OVER TROUBLED WATER, Paul Simon, composer
1971 YOU'VE GOT A FRIEND, Carole King, composer
1972 THE FIRST TIME EVER I SAW YOUR FACE, Ewan MacColl, composer
1977 (tie) LOVE THEME FROM A STAR IS BORN (EVERGREEN), Paul Williams and Barbra Streisand, composers; YOU LIGHT UP MY LIFE, Joe Brooks, composer
1979 WHAT A FOOL BELIEVES, Kenny Loggins and Michael McDonald, composers
1981 BETTE DAVIS EYES, Jackie DeShannon and Donna Weiss, songwriters

Best New Artist

1965 TOM JONES
1967 BOBBIE GENTRY
1968 JOSE FELICIANO
1969 CROSBY, STILLS & NASH
1976 STARLAND VOCAL BAND
1977 DEBBY BOONE

Best Recording for Children

1969 PETER, PAUL & MOMMY, Peter, Paul & Mary
1980 IN HARMONY/A SESAME STREET RECORD, The Doobie Brothers, James Taylor, Carly Simon, Bette Midler, Muppets, Al Jarreau, Linda Ronstadt, Wendy Waldman, Libby Titus & Dr. John, Livingston Taylor, George Benson & Pauline Wilson, Lucy Simon & the Simon/Taylor Family; producers, Lucy Simon, David Levine
1981 SESAME COUNTRY, The Muppets (creator, Jim Henson), Glen Campbell, Crystal Gayle, Loretta Lynn, Tanya Tucker; producer, Dennis Scott

Best Album of Original Score from a Motion Picture or TV Special

1968 THE GRADUATE, Paul Simon, Dave Grusin, composers

Best Arrangement Accompanying Vocalists

1967 ODE TO BILLY JOE, Bobbie Gentry; Jimmie Haskell, arranger
1970 BRIDGE OVER TROUBLED WATER, Simon & Garfunkel; Paul Simon, Art Garfunkel, Jimmie Haskell, Ernie Freeman and Larry Knechtel, arrangers
1974 DOWN TO YOU, Joni Mitchell; Joni Mitchell, Tom Scott, arrangers
1975 MISTY, Ray Stevens; Ray Stevens, arranger

Best Arrangement for Voices (Duo, Group or Chorus)

1976 AFTERNOON DELIGHT, Starland Vocal Band; Starland Vocal Band, arrangers
1977 NEW KID IN TOWN, Eagles; Eagles, arrangers

Best Album Notes

1968 JOHNNY CASH AT FOLSOM PRISON, Johnny Cash, annotator

1969 NASHVILLE SKYLINE, Bob Dylan; Johnny Cash, annotator
1972 TOM T. HALL'S GREATEST HITS, Tom T. Hall, annotator
1974 FOR THE LAST TIME, Bob Will & His Texas Playboys; Charles R. Townsend, annotator
1975 BLOOD ON THE TRACKS, Bob Dylan; Pete Hamill, annotator

Best Engineered Recording, Non-Classical

1959 BELAFONTE AT CARNEGIE HALL, Harry Belafonte; Robert Simpson, engineer
1968 WICHITA LINEMAN, Glen Campbell; Joe Polito, Hugh Davies, engineers
1970 BRIDGE OVER TROUBLED WATER, Simon & Garfunkel; Roy Halee, engineer
1975 BETWEEN THE LINES, Janis Ian; Brooks Arthur, Larry Alexander, Russ Payne, engineers

RECORDING INDUSTRY ASSOCIATION OF AMERICA *
(RIAA)
Gold and Platinum Recording Awards

Date Awarded	Company	Title	Artist
1958			
Aug. 11	RCA Victor	Hard Headed Woman (S)	Elvis Presley
1959			
Jan. 21	Capitol	Tom Dooley (S)	Kingston Trio
Feb. 20	Capitol	Hymns	Ernie Ford
1960			
Feb. 17	RCA Victor	Elvis	Elvis Presley
April 18	Capitol	Kingston Trio at Large	Kingston Trio
April 18	Capitol	Kingston Trio	Kingston Trio
Oct. 24	Capitol	Here We Go Again	Kingston Trio
Oct. 24	Capitol	From the hungry i	Kingston Trio
1961			
June 22	Capitol	Sold Out	Kingston Trio
Oct. 10	Capitol	Spirituals	Ernie Ford
Oct. 17	RCA Victor	Elvis' Golden Records	Elvis Presley
Oct. 16	RCA Victor	Belafonte at Carnegie Hall	Harry Belafonte
Dec. 14	Columbia	Big Bad John (S)	Jimmy Dean
Dec. 21	RCA Victor	Blue Hawaii	Elvis Presley

---

* Awards listed are only for folk, country & western categories or recordings associated with artists included in this book. (S) indicates a single record as opposed to an album. Certifications are based on totals of both record and tape sales.

RIAA requires a minimum of one million copies sold for gold record certification of a single. For a platinum award (the platinum award category was created in 1976), two million copies sold of a / single is required. For gold record album certification, prior to 1975 sales totaling $1 million was required; from 1975 on this was changed to 500,000 unit sales having a minimum dollar volume of $1 million based on 33-1/3 of the list price of each record or tape sold. A platinum album certification requires sales of at least one million copies based on 33-1/3 of the list price of each record or tape sold.

Date Awarded	Company	Title	Artist

1962

March 12	Capitol	*Star Carol*	Ernie Ford
March 22	Capitol	*Nearer the Cross*	Ernie Ford
March 30	RCA Victor	Can't Help Falling In Love (S)	Elvis Presley
June 27	Capitol	*String Along*	Kingston Trio
July 19	ABC-Paramount	I Can't Stop Loving You (S)	Ray Charles
July 19	ABC-Paramount	*Modern Sounds in Country & Western Music*	Ray Charles
Dec. 10	Warner Bros.	*Peter, Paul and Mary*	Peter, Paul and Mary

1963

March 12	RCA Victor	*Calypso*	Harry Belafonte
March 12	RCA Victor	*G. I. Blues*	Elvis Presley
Aug. 13	RCA Victor	*Elvis' Christmas Album*	Elvis Presley
Aug. 13	RCA Victor	*Girls, Girls, Girls*	Elvis Presley
Aug. 13	RCA Victor	*Belafonte Returns to Carnegie Hall*	Harry Belafonte
Aug. 13	RCA Victor	*Belafonte*	Harry Belafonte
Aug. 23	RCA Victor	*Jump-Up Calypso*	Harry Belafonte
Aug. 27	Warner Bros.	*Moving*	Peter, Paul and Mary
Nov. 13	Warner Bros.	*In the Wind*	Peter, Paul and Mary

1964

Sept. 4	Capitol	*The Best of the Kingston Trio*	Kingston Trio
Oct. 16	Columbia	*Ramblin'*	New Christy Minstrels
Oct. 30	Monument	Oh, Pretty Woman (S)	Roy Orbison
Nov. 2	Columbia	*Johnny Horton's Greatest Hits*	Johnny Horton

1965

Jan. 21.	Warner Bros.	*Peter, Paul and Mary in Concert*	Peter, Paul and Mary
Feb. 11	Columbia	*Ring of Fire*	Johnny Cash
May 19	Smash	King of the Road (S)	Roger Miller
Sept. 1	Smash	*Return of Roger Miller*	Roger Miller
Sept. 21	Columbia	*Gunfire Ballads & Trail Songs*	Marty Robbins

Date Awarded	Company	Title	Artist

1966

Date Awarded	Company	Title	Artist
Jan. 29	Vanguard	*Joan Baez*	Joan Baez
Jan. 29	Vanguard	*Joan Baez, Vol. 2*	Joan Baez
Jan. 29	Vanguard	*Joan Baez in Concert*	Joan Baez
Feb. 11	Smash	*Golden Hits*	Roger Miller
Feb. 14	Columbia	Sounds of Silence (S)	Simon & Garfunkel
March 24	Monument	*Roy Orbison's Greatest Hits*	Roy Orbison
May 12	RCA Victor	*My World*	Eddy Arnold
July 20	RCA Victor	*The Best of Jim Reeves*	Jim Reeves
Aug. 4	Smash	*Dang Me*	Roger Miller
Aug. 16	Mercury	*Think Ethnic*	Smothers Brothers
Nov. 1	RCA Victor	*Elvis Presley*	Elvis Presley
Nov. 1	RCA Victor	*Elvis' Golden Records, Vol. 2*	Elvis Presley
Nov. 1	RCA Victor	*Elvis' Golden Records, Vol. 3*	Elvis Presley
Dec. 20	Columbia	Battle of New Orleans (S)	Johnny Horton

1967

Date Awarded	Company	Title	Artist
Jan. 19	Epic	Mellow Yellow (S)	Donovan
Feb. 7	Monument	*Yakety Sax*	Boots Randolph
Feb. 22	Mercury	*The Two Sides of the Smothers Brothers*	Smothers Brothers
April 10	RCA Victor	*An Evening with Belafonte*	Harry Belafonte
July 6	Columbia	*Parsley, Sage, Rosemary & Thyme*	Simon & Garfunkel
July 14	Columbia	*I Walk the Line*	Johnny Cash
Aug. 14	Capitol	Georgy Girl (S)	The Seekers
Aug. 25	Columbia	*Sounds of Silence*	Simon & Garfunkel
Aug. 25	Columbia	*Blonde on Blonde*	Bob Dylan
Aug. 25	Columbia	*Highway 61*	Bob Dylan
Aug. 25	Columbia	*Bringing It All Back Home*	Bob Dylan
Sept. 11	Capitol	Ode to Billie Joe (S)	Bobbie Gentry
Oct. 9	Capitol	*Ode to Billie Joe*	Bobbie Gentry

1968

Date Awarded	Company	Title	Artist
Jan. 5	Columbia	*Jim Nabors Sings*	Jim Nabors
Jan. 5	Columbia	*Bob Dylan's Greatest Hits*	Bob Dylan
Feb. 16	RCA Victor	*How Great Thou Art*	Elvis Presley
Feb. 26	RCA Victor	*Distant Drums*	Jim Reeves
March 6	Capitol	*Best of buck Owens*	Buck Owens
March 13	Columbia	*The Byrds' Greatest Hits*	The Byrds
March 19	Columbia	*John Wesley Harding*	Bob Dylan
March 28	RCA	*The Best of Eddy Arnold*	Eddy Arnold

Date Awarded	Company	Title	Artist
April 4	United Artists	Honey (S)	Bobby Goldsboro
April 6	ABC	*Modern Sounds in Country & Western Music, Volume 2*	Ray Charles
April 6	ABC	*Greatest Hits*	Ray Charles
April 9	RCA	*Loving You*	Elvis Presley
April 18	Columbia	*Bookends*	Simon & Garfunkel
June 10	Columbia	Mrs. Robinson (S)	Simon & Garfunkel
August 16	ABC	*A Man and His Soul*	Ray Charles
August 26	Plantation	Harper Valley P.T.A. (S)	Jeannie C. Riley
October 4	RCA	*Feliciano*	Jose Feliciano
October 17	Capitol	*By the Time I Get to Phoenix*	Glen Campbell
October 17	Capitol	*Gentle on My Mind*	Glen Campbell
October 30	Columbia	*Johnny Cash at Folsom Prison*	Johnny Cash
November 1	Columbia	Little Green Apples (S)	O.C. Smith
November 18	Capitol	*Wichita Lineman*	Glen Campbell
November 20	Apple	Those Were the Days (S)	Mary Hopkin
November 27	United Artists	*Honey*	Bobby Goldsboro
December 20	Plantation	*Harper Valley P.T.A.*	Jeannie C. Riley

1969

Date Awarded	Company	Title	Artist
January 10	Capitol	*Hey Little One*	Glen Campbell
January 20	Elektra	*Wildflowers*	Judy Collins
January 22	Capitol	Wichita Lineman (S)	Glen Campbell
January 27	Warner Bros.	*Album 1700*	Peter, Paul and Mary
January 29	Capitol	*Gentry/Campbell*	Bobbie Gentry and Glen Campbell
February 18	Monument	*Boots with Strings*	Boots Randolph
February 24	Scepter	Hooked on a Feeling (S)	B.J. Thomas
March 4	Columbia	*Wednesday Morning 3 A.M.*	Simon & Garfunkel
April 9	RCA	*His Hand in Mine*	Elvis Presley
April 16	Capitol	*Galveston*	Glen Campbell

Date Awarded	Company	Title	Artist
April 22	Epic	*Donovan's Greatest Hits*	Donovan
May 7	Columbia	*Nashville Skyline*	Bob Dylan
May 7	Parrot	*Fever Zone*	Tom Jones
May 7	Parrot	*Help Yourself*	Tom Jones
June 4	Parrot	*This Is Tom Jones*	Tom Jones
June 11	MGM	*Hank Williams Greatest Hits*	Hank Williams, Sr.
June 11	MGM	*How the West Was Won*	Soundtrack
June 11	MGM	*Your Cheatin' Heart*	Hank Williams, Sr.
June 16	Monument	Gitarzan (S)	Ray Stevens
June 25	RCA	In the Ghetto (S)	Elvis Presley
July 3	Parrot	*Tom Jones Live!*	Tom Jones
July 22	RCA	*Elvis TV Special*	Elvis Presley
July 24	Columbia	*Johnny Cash's Greatest Hits*	Johnny Cash
August 12	Columbia	*Johnny Cash at San Quentin*	Johnny Cash
August 14	Columbia	A Boy Named Sue (S)	Johnny Cash
September 19	Capitol	*Glen Campbell—Live*	Glen Campbell
September 29	Reprise	*Alice's Restaurant*	Arlo Guthrie
September 29	Imperial	Put a Little Love in Your Heart (S)	Jackie De-Shannon
September 30	Atlantic	*Crosby, Stills & Nash*	Crosby, Stills & Nash
October 3	Parrot	*I'll Never Fall in Love Again*	Tom Jones
October 8	Elektra	*Who Knows Where the Time Goes*	Judy Collins
October 14	Capitol	Galveston (S)	Glen Campbell
October 27	Parrot	*Tom Jones—Live at Las Vegas*	Tom Jones
October 28	RCA	Suspicious Minds (S)	Elvis Presley
November 10	Columbia	Rudolph, the Red Nosed Reindeer (S)	Gene Autry
November 24	Parrot	*Green Green Grass*	Tom Jones
November 26	Capitol	*The Band*	The Band
December 12	RCA	*From Vegas to Memphis*	Elvis Presley
December 23	Scepter	Raindrops Keep Falling on My Head (S)	B.J. Thomas
December 24	Decca	*Buddy Holly Story*	Buddy Holly & the Crickets
December 30	Warner Bros.	Leaving on a Jet Plane (S)	Peter, Paul and Mary
December 30	Coral	That'll Be the Day (S)	Buddy Holly & the Crickets

1970

Date Awarded	Company	Title	Artist
January 19	Dunhill	*Easy Rider*	Soundtrack
January 19	RCA	*The Best of Charley Pride*	Charley Pride
January 21	RCA	Don't Cry Daddy (S)	Elvis Presley
January 28	RCA	*From Elvis in Memphis*	Elvis Presley

Date Awarded	Company	Title	Artist
January 29	Columbia	*Hello, I'm Johnny Cash*	Johnny Cash
January 29	Warner Bros.	*See What Tomorrow Brings*	Peter, Paul and Mary
February 9	RCA	*Alive Alive-O!*	Feliciano
February 9	Columbia	*Bridge Over Troubled Water*	Simon & Garfunkel
February 18	Parrot	Without Love (S)	Tom Jones
February 19	Capitol	*Try a Little Kindness*	Glen Campbell
February 27	Columbia	Bridge Over Troubled Water (S)	Simon & Garfunkel
March 20	RCA	*Feliciano/10 to 23*	Jose Feliciano
March 25	Atlantic	*Deja Vu*	Crosby, Stills, Nash & Young
April 1	Epic	*A Gift from a Flower to a Garden*	Donovan
April 13	Decca	*Don't Come Home a Drinkin' (with Lovin' on Your Mind)*	Loretta Lynn
April 16	Epic	*Tammy's Greatest Hits*	Tammy Wynette
April 24	Parrot	*Tom*	Tom Jones
April 30	Warner Bros.	*A Song Will Rise*	Peter, Paul and Mary
June 12	Columbia	Cecilia (S)	Simon & Garfunkel
June 22	Columbia	*Self Portrait*	Bob Dylan
June 26	Barnaby	Everything Is Beautiful (S)	Ray Stevens
July 22	Scepter	*Raindrops Keep Fallin' on My Head*	B. J. Thomas
August 14	RCA	The Wonder of You (S)	Elvis Presley
October 2	Capitol	*Okie from Muskogee*	Merle Haggard and the Strangers
October 16	Reprise	*Everybody Knows This Is Nowhere*	Neil Young with Crazy Horse
October 16	Warner Bros.	*Best of Peter, Paul and Mary (Ten) Years Together*	Peter, Paul and Mary
October 16	Warner Bros.	*Sweet Baby James*	James Taylor
October 19	Capitol	*Stage Fright*	The Band
November 2	Reprise	*After the Gold Rush*	Neil Young
November 16	Capitol	Snowbird (S)	Anne Murray
November 24	Atlantic	*Stephen Stills*	Stephen Stills
December 11	Columbia	*New Morning*	Bob Dylan
December 18	Columbia	*The Freewheelin' Bob Dylan*	Bob Dylan
December 21	Elektra	*In My Life*	Judy Collins
December 23	Reprise	*Ladies of the Canyon*	Joni Mitchell

1971

Date Awarded	Company	Title	Artist
January 15	Parrot	*I Who Have Nothing*	Tom Jones
February 3	Columbia	Rose Garden (S)	Lynn Anderson

Date Awarded	Company	Title	Artist
February 23	RCA	*On Stage February 1970*	Elvis Presley
February 23	RCA	*Charley Pride's 10th Album*	Charley Pride
February 23	RCA	*Just Plain Charley*	Charley Pride
February 23	RCA	*Charley Pride in Person*	Charley Pride
March 3	Columbia	*For the Good Times*	Ray Price
March 11	Capitol	*The Fightin' Side of Me*	Merle Haggard & the Strangers
March 25	Columbia	*Rose Garden*	Lynn Anderson
March 25	Parrot	She's a Lady (S)	Tom Jones
March 29	RCA	Amos Moses (S)	Jerry Reed
April 6	Elektra	*Whales & Nightingales*	Judy Collins
April 8	Atlantic	*If I Could Only Remember My Name*	David Crosby
April 12	Atlantic	*Four Way Street*	Crosby, Stills, Nash & Young
April 26	Mega	Help Me Make It Through the Night (S)	Sammi Smith
April 30	Warner Bros.	*Mud Slide Slim and the Blue Horizon*	James Taylor
June 7	Ode	*Tapestry*	Carole King
June 14	Warner/Reprise	*If You Could Read My Mind*	Gordon Lightfoot
July 21	Ode	It's Too Late (S)	Carole King
August 18	RCA	Take Me Home, Country Roads (S)	John Denver
August 26	Atlantic	*Stephen Stills 2*	Stephen Stills
August 26	Atlantic	*Songs for Beginners*	Graham Nash
September 13	Warner Bros.	You've Got a Friend (S)	James Taylor
September 15	RCA	*Poems, Prayers and Promises*	John Denver
October 22	Vanguard	The Night They Drove Old Dixie Down (S)	Joan Baez
November 15	Reprise	*Blue*	Joni Mitchell
November 29	Capitol	Easy Loving (S)	Freddie Hart
December 9	Ode	*Carole King Music*	Carole King
December 13	Buddah	*Candles in the Rain*	Melanie
December 16	Neighborhood	Brand New Key (S)	Melanie
December 23	Columbia	*The World of Johnny Cash*	Johnny Cash

1972

Date Awarded	Company	Title	Artist
January 3	United Artists	American Pie (S)	Don McLean
January 3	United Artists	*American Pie*	Don McLean
January 3	Columbia	*Bob Dylan's Greatest Hits, Volume 2*	Bob Dylan
January 5	RCA	*Aerie*	John Denver
January 12	Parrot	*She's a Lady*	Tom Jones
January 18	Decca	*Loretta Lynn's Greatest Hits*	Loretta Lynn
January 27	Elektra	I'd Like to Teach the World to Sing (S)	The New Seekers
January 31	Vanguard	*Blessed Are*	Joan Baez
January 31	Vanguard	*Any Day Now*	Joan Baez
February 3	Shelter	*Leon Russell & the Shelter People*	Leon Russell

Date Awarded	Company	Title	Artist
February 15	RCA	*Charley Pride Sings Heart Songs*	Charley Pride
February 18	Warner/Reprise	*Harvest*	Neil Young
March 1	Columbia	*Paul Simon*	Paul Simon
March 8	RCA	Kiss an Angel Good Mornin' (S)	Charley Pride
March 15	Atlantic	The Lion Sleeps Tonight (S)	Robert John
March 31	Parrot	*Tom Jones Live at Caesars Palace*	Tom Jones
April 21	Warner Bros.	Heart of Gold (S)	Neil Young
May 15	Capitol	*Glen Campbell's Greatest Hits*	Glen Campbell
May 15	Decca	*Hello Darlin'*	Conway Twitty
May 30	Atlantic	*Graham Nash & David Crosby*	Graham Nash & David Crosby
May 30	Atlantic	*Manassas*	Stephen Stills
June 13	Neighborhood	*Gather Me*	Melanie
July 6	Columbia	*Simon & Garfunkel's Greatest Hits*	Simon & Garfunkel
August 2	Columbia	Sylvia's Mother (S)	Dr. Hook & the Medicine Show
August 4	RCA	*Elvis as Recorded Live at Madison Square Garden*	Elvis Presley
August 23	Dot	The Happiest Girl in the Whole U.S.A. (S)	Donna Fargo
September 19	Shelter	*Carney*	Leon Russell
September 20	Columbia	Baby Don't Get Hooked on Me (S)	Mac Davis
October 19	RCA	*The Best of Charley Pride*	Charley Pride
October 23	Capitol	*Easy Loving*	Freddie Hart
October 27	RCA	Burning Love (S)	Elvis Presley
November 1	Ode	*Rhymes & Reasons*	Carole King
November 2	Capitol	*The Best of Merle Haggard*	Merle Haggard
November 2	Capitol	*Rock of Ages*	The Band
November 24	Decca	Garden Party (S)	Rick Nelson
December 14	Warner Bros.	*Summer Breeze*	Seals & Crofts
December 18	Warner Bros.	*One Man Dog*	James Taylor
December 22	Asylum	*For the Roses*	Joni Mitchell
December 30	RCA	*Rocky Mountain High*	John Denver

1973

Date Awarded	Company	Title	Artist
January 4	Dot	Funny Face (S)	Donna Fargo
January 29	Dot	*The Happiest Girl in the Whole U.S.A.*	Donna Fargo
February 2	Columbia	*Loggins & Messina*	Loggins & Messina
February 13	RCA	*World Wide 50 Gold Award Hits, Volume 1*	Elvis Presley
February 13	RCA	*Elvis—Aloha from Hawaii Via Satellite*	Elvis Presley
March 7	Columbia	Your Mama Don't Dance (S)	Loggins & Messina

Date Awarded	Company	Title	Artist
March 7	Warner Bros.	Dueling Banjos (S)	Eric Weissberg
March 7	Warner Bros.	*Dueling Banjos* Deliverance sound-track performed by	Eric Weissberg & Steve Mandel
March 7	Columbia	*Baby Don't Get Hooked on Me*	Mac Davis
March 27	Warner/Reprise	*Kenny Rogers & the First Edition Greatest Hits*	Kenny Rogers & the First Edition
April 2	Bell	The Night the Lights Went Out in Georgia (S)	Vicki Lawrence
April 4	Columbia	The Cover of the Rolling Stone (S)	Dr. Hook & the Medicine Show
May 11	Columbia	*Sittin' In*	Loggins & Messina
May 25	United Artists	*William E. McEuen Presents Will the Circle Be Unbroken*	Nitty Gritty Dirt Band
June 14	RCA	*The Sensational Charley Pride*	Charley Pride
June 14	RCA	*From Me To You*	Charley Pride
June 14	RCA	*The Country Way*	Charley Pride
June 15	Columbia	*There Goes Rhymin' Simon*	Paul Simon
June 25	Warner Bros.	*Diamond Girl*	Seals & Crofts
June 26	Ode	*Fantasy*	Carole King
June 26	Shelter	*Leon Live*	Leon Russell
June 28	RCA	*Elvis—That's the Way It Is*	Elvis Presley
July 24	ABC/Dunhill	Bad Bad Leroy Brown (S)	Jim Croce
August 27	RCA	*Farewell Andromeda*	John Denver
September 4	Epic	Behind Closed Doors (S)	Charlie Rich
October 9	Columbia	Love Me Like a Rock (S)	Paul Simon
October 24	Columbia	*Angel Clare*	Art Garfunkel
November 2	ABC	*Life and Times*	Jim Croce
November 8	Monument	Why Me (S)	Kris Kristofferson
November 9	Monument	*The Silver Tongued Devil and I*	Kris Kristofferson
November 26	ABC/Dunhill	*You Don't Mess Around with Jim*	Jim Croce
November 27	Epic	*Behind Closed Doors*	Charlie Rich
November 29	Monument	*Jesus Was a Capricorn*	Kris Kristofferson
December 6	ABC/Dunhill	*I Got a Name*	Jim Croce
December 7	Kolob	Paper Roses (S)	Marie Osmond
December 7	Columbia	*Full Sail*	Loggins & Messina
December 7	Warner/Reprise	*Time Fades Away*	Neil Young
December 10	Epic	The Most Beautiful Girl (S)	Charlie Rich

Date Awarded	Company	Title	Artist
September 19	Atlantic	*So Far*	Crosby, Stills, Nash & Young
September 20	MGM	I'm Leaving It (All) Up to You (S)	Donny & Marie Osmond
September 23	Asylum	*Desperado*	Eagles
September 23	Asylum	*The Souther-Hillman-Furay Band*	The Souther-Hillman-Furay Band
September 23	Columbia	*Stop and Smell the Roses*	Mac Davis
September 23	Reprise	*On the Beach*	Neil Young
October 9	MCA	I Honestly Love You (S)	Olivia Newton-John
October 14	MCA	*Let Me Be There*	Olivia Newton-John
October 16	Ode	*Wrap Around Joy*	Carole King
October 22	ABC	*Photographs and Memories, His Greatest Hits*	Jim Croce
October 23	RCA	*There Won't Be Anymore*	Charlie Rich
November 25	Columbia	*Mother Lode*	Loggins & Messina
November 27	Asylum	*Miles of Aisles*	Joni Mitchell
December 17	Elektra	*Verities and Balderdash*	Harry Chapin
December 18	Monument	*Me and Bobby McGee*	Kris Kristofferson
December 24	Asylum	*Late for the Sky*	Jackson Browne
December 31	Elektra	Cat's in the Cradle (S)	Harry Chapin

1975

Date Awarded	Company	Title	Artist
January 3	RCA	Back Home Again (S)	John Denver
January 8	RCA	*Elvis—A Legendary Performer, Volume 1*	Elvis Presley
January 9	RCA	*Did You Think to Pray*	Charley Pride
January 9	RCA	*(Country) Charley Pride*	Charley Pride
January 31	Capitol	*Heart Like a Wheel*	Linda Ronstadt
February 12	Columbia	*Blood on the Tracks*	Bob Dylan
February 19	RCA	*An Evening With John Denver*	John Denver
February 21	MGM	*I'm Leaving It All Up to You*	Marie & Donny Osmond
February 26	MCA	*Have You Never Been Mellow*	Olivia Newton-John
February 28	ABC/Dunhill	*Together for the First Time*	Bobby Bland and B.B. King

Date Awarded	Company	Title	Artist
March 5	MCA	Have You Never Been Mellow (S)	Olivia Newton-John
May 22	ABC/Dot	Before the Next Teardrop Falls (S)	Freddy Fender
May 23	ABC	(Hey Won't You Play) Another Somebody Done Somebody Wrong Song (S)	B.J. Thomas
June 26	RCA	Thank God I'm a Country Boy (S)	John Denver
June 30	Asylum	*One of These Nights*	Eagles
July 30	Kama Sutra	*Fire on the Mountain*	The Charlie Daniels Band
July 31	Epic	Wildfire (S)	Michael Murphey
August 14	Capricorn	*The Marshall Tucker Band*	The Marshall Tucker Band
August 25	Asylum	*Don't Cry Now*	Linda Ronstadt
August 29	ABC/Dot	*Before the Last Teardrop Falls*	Freddy Fender
September 5	Capitol	Rhinestone Cowboy (S)	Glen Campbell
September 11	Columbia	*Between the Lines*	Janis Lan
September 12	Warner Bros.	*Gorilla*	James Taylor
September 16	MCA	Please Mister Please (S)	Olivia Newton-John
September 18	ABC/Dot	Wasted Days and Wasted Nights (S)	Freddy Fender
September 19	RCA	*Windsong*	John Denver
September 29	MCA	*Clearly Love*	Olivia Newton-John
September 29	Warner Bros.	*I'll Play for You*	Seals & Crofts
October 8	Asylum	*Prisoner in Disguise*	Linda Ronstadt
October 8	Asylum	*For Everyman*	Jackson Browne
October 20	A&M	*Kris & Rita Full Moon*	Kris Kristofferson and Rita Coolidge
October 24	RCA	*Rocky Mountain Christmas*	John Denver
November 7	Capricorn	*Where We All Belong*	The Marshall Tucker Band
November 7	ABC Records/ Atlantic Tape	*Wind on the Water*	David Crosby and Graham Nash

Date Awarded	Company	Title	Artist
November 11	A&M	*Diamonds and Rust*	Joan Baez
November 17	Columbia	*Still Crazy After All These Years*	Paul Simon
November 17	Epic	*Blue Sky—Night Thunder*	Michael Murphey
November 18	RCA	I'm Sorry (S)	John Denver
November 19	Elektra	*Judith*	Judy Collins
December 4	Asylum	*The Hissing of Summer Lawns*	Joni Mitchell
December 5	Warner Bros.	*Seals & Crofts Greatest Hits*	Seals & Crofts
December 5	Columbia	*Breakaway*	Art Garfunkel
December 31	Capitol	*Rhinestone Cowboy*	Glen Campbell

1976

Date Awarded	Company	Title	Artist
January 14	Columbia	*Desire*	Bob Dylan
January 29	MGM	*Black Bear Road*	C.W. McCall
February 4	Capricorn	*Searchin' for a Rainbow*	The Marshall Tucker Band
February 24	Asylum	*Eagles—Their Greatest Hits 1971-1975*	Eagles
March 9	Shelter	*Will O' the Wisp*	Leon Russell
March 11	Columbia	*Red Headed Stranger*	Willie Nelson
March 11	Columbia	Fifty Ways to Leave Your Lover (S)	Paul Simon
March 16	RCA	*Bustin' Out*	Pure Prairie League
March 25	Ode	*Thoroughbred*	Carole King
March 30	RCA	*The Outlaws*	The Outlaws: Waylon Jennings; Willie Nelson; Jessi Colter; Tompall Glaser
April 27	MCA	*Come On Over*	Olivia Newton-John
April 29	MCA	*You've Never Been This Far Before/ Baby's Gone*	Conway Twitty
May 17	Capitol	Only Sixteen (S)	Dr. Hook
May 20	GRT/Casino	I.O.U. (S)	Jimmy Dean
May 21	Columbia	All the Love in the World	Mac Davis
July 15	Windsong	Afternoon Delight (S)	Starland Vocal Band
August 17	RCA	*Spirit*	John Denver
August 19	Columbia	*Native Sons*	Loggins & Messina
September 22	Columbia	*Hard Rain*	Bob Dylan

Date Awarded	Company	Title	Artist
October 19	ABC Records/ Atlantic Tape	*Whistling Down the Wire*	David Crosby and Graham Nash
October 19	Warner Bros.	*In the Pocket*	James Taylor
October 26	Warner/Reprise	*Summertime Dream*	Gordon Lightfoot
November 15	Asylum	*The Pretender*	Jackson Browne
November 16	Asylum	*Jackson Browne*	Jackson Browne
November 16	Gusto/Starday	Teddy Bear (S)	Red Sovine
December 1	Big Tree	*Nights Are Forever*	England Dan & John Ford Coley
December 8	MCA	*Don't Stop Believin'.*	Olivia Newton-John
December 8	Asylum	*Greatest Hits*	Linda Ronstadt
December 10	Capitol	*That Christmas Feeling*	Glen Campbell
December 13	Asylum	*Hotel California*	Eagles
December 22	Warner Bros.	*James Taylor's Greatest Hits*	James Taylor
December 23	Asylum	*Hejira*	Joni Mitchell
December 23	Columbia	*A Star Is Born*	Kris Kristofferson and Barbara Streisand
December 23	Polydor	*Donny and Marie Featuring Songs from Their TV Show*	Donny & Marie Osmond
December 29	Shelter	*The Best of Leon Russell*	Leon Russell

1976 Platinum Awards

Date Awarded	Company	Title	Artist
February 24	Asylum	*Eagles—Their Greatest Hits 1971-1975*	Eagles
March 4	Columbia	*Desire*	Bob Dylan
October 6	RCA	*Spirit*	John Denver
October 28	Asylum	*Hasten Down the Wind*	Linda Ronstadt
November 24	RCA	*The Outlaws*	The Outlaws: Waylon Jennings; Willie Nelson; Jessi Colter; Tompall Glaser
December 15	Asylum	*Hotel California*	Eagles

Date Awarded	Company	Title	Artist
		1977 (Gold)	
January 12	Warner/Reprise	*Long May You Run*	Stills & Young Band
February 10	Capitol/Ariola America	Torn Between Two Lovers (S)	Mary MacGregor
March 1	Polydor/MGM	*24 Greatest Hits*	Hank Williams, Sr.
March 10	Phonogram/Mercury	*The Best of the Statler Brothers*	The Statler Brothers
March 21	Elektra/Asylum	New Kid in Town (S)	Eagles
March 24	RCA	*Dreaming My Dreams*	Waylon Jennings
March 30	RCA	*John Denver's Greatest Hits, Volume 2*	John Denver
April 19	Warner/Reprise	*Gord's Gold*	Gordon Lightfoot
April 20	Capitol	Southern Nights (S)	Glen Campbell
May 10	Columbia	*The Best of Friends*	Loggins & Messina
May 12	Elektra/Asylum	Hotel California (S)	Eagles
June 2	Warner/Reprise	*Carolina Dreams*	The Marshall Tucker Band
June 14	RCA	*Ol' Waylon*	Waylon Jennings
June 20	ABC	*Changes in Latitudes, Changes in Attitudes*	Jimmy Buffett
June 22	United Artists	Lucille (S)	Kenny Rogers
June 28	Atlantic	*CSN*	Crosby, Stills & Nash
July 5	Columbia	*J.T.*	James Taylor
August 1	RCA	*Are You Ready for the Country*	Waylon Jennings
August 9	CBS/Epic	*Nether Lands*	Dan Fogelberg
August 10	United Artists/Imperial	*Travelin' Man* (S)	Rick Nelson
August 16	Warner Bros.	*A New Life*	The Marshall Tucker Band
August 18	A&M	*Anytime . . . Anywhere*	Rita Coolidge
August 30	A&M	(Your Love Has Lifted Me) Higher and Higher (S)	Rita Coolidge
September 6	A&M	*Ozark Mountain Daredevils*	Ozark Mountain Daredevils
September 8	GRT	The King Is Gone (S)	Ronnie McDowell

Date Awarded	Company	Title	Artist
September 12	RCA	Way Down (S)	Elvis Presley
September 12	RCA	*Pure Gold*	Elvis Presley
September 19	Elektra/Asylum	*Simple Dreams*	Linda Ronstadt
September 20	Columbia	*Celebrate Me Home*	Kenny Loggins
September 23	Capitol	*Simple Things*	Carole King
September 30	RCA	*Welcome to My World*	Elvis Presley
October 5	Capitol	*Southern Nights*	Glen Campbell
October 7	RCA	*From Elvis Presley Boulevard, Memphis, Tennessee*	Elvis Presley
October 11	Warner/Bearsville	*American Stars 'N Bars*	Neil Young
October 19	Warner Bros.	You Light Up My Life (S)	Debby Boone
October 21	MCA	*Greatest Hits*	Olivia Newton-John
October 25	RCA	*Elvis—A Legendary Performer, Volume 2*	Elvis Presley
October 25	Columbia	*The Johnny Cash Portrait/His Greatest Hits, Volume 2*	Johnny Cash
October 25	Warner Bros.	*You Light Up My Life*	Debby Boone
November 1	Arista	*You Light Up My Life*	Original Soundtrack
November 1	CBS/Epic	*Captured Angel*	Dan Fogelberg
November 4	RCA	*Elvis Sings the Wonderful World of Christmas*	Elvis Presley
November 14	United Artists	*We Must Believe in Magic*	Crystal Gayle
November 17	Columbia	*Greatest Hits, Etc.*	Paul Simon
December 1	RCA	*I Want to Live*	John Denver
December 1	RCA	*His Hand in Mine*	Elvis Presley
December 1	RCA	*Elvis Country*	Elvis Presley
December 15	United Artists	*Daytime Friends*	Kenny Rogers
December 16	MCA	*Viva Terlingua*	Jerry Jeff Walker
December 27	RCA	*Here You Come Again*	Dolly Parton
December 28	Elektra/Asylum	*Running On Empty*	Jackson Browne

1977 (Platinum)

Date Awarded	Company	Title	Artist
January 19	Elektra/Asylum	*Greatest Hits*	Linda Ronstadt
January 21	Columbia	*A Star Is Born*	Kris Kristofferson & Barbra Streisand
April 12	Elektra/Asylum	*The Pretender*	Jackson Browne
August 18	Atlantic	*CSN*	Crosby, Stills & Nash

Date Awarded	Company	Title	Artist
September 1	Columbia	*J.T.*	James Taylor
September 12	RCA	*Moody Blue*	Elvis Presley
October 7	RCA	*Ol' Waylon*	Waylon Jennings
October 12	Elektra/Asylum	*Simple Dreams*	Linda Ronstadt
October 14	RCA	*In Concert*	Elvis Presley
October 19	A&M	*Anytime . . . Anywhere*	Rita Coollidge
November 21	Warner Bros.	*James Taylor's Greatest Hits*	James Taylor
November 22	Warner Bros.	You Light Up My Life (S)	Debby Boone
December 1	RCA	*Elvis Sings the Wonderful World of Christmas*	Elvis Presley
December 13	Warner Bros.	*You Light Up My Life*	Debby Boone
December 14	ABC	*Changes in Latitudes, Changes in Attitudes*	Jimmy Buffett
December 15	MCA	*Greatest Hits*	Olivia Newton-John

1978 (Gold)

Date Awarded	Company	Title	Artist
January 12	Polydor	*New Season*	Marie & Donny Osmond
January 13	RCA	*Waylon Live*	Waylon Jennings
January 13	RCA	My Way (S)	Elvis Presley
January 23	Asylum	Blue Bayou (S)	Linda Ronstadt
February 1	RCA	Here You Come Again (S)	Dolly Parton
February 2	A&M	We're All Alone (S)	Rita Coolidge
February 3	RCA	*Waylon & Willie*	Waylon Jennings & Willie Nelson
February 10	RCA	*It Was Almost Like a Song*	Ronnie Milsap
February 13	Asylum	*Don Juan's Reckless Daughter*	Joni Mitchell
February 15	United Artists	*Ten Years of Gold*	Kenny Rogers
February 28	20th Century	Sometimes When We Touch (S)	Dan Hill
March 2	Columbia	*Watermark*	Art Garfunkel
March 17	20th Century	*Short Fuse*	Dan Hill
April 4	CBS/Ode	*Carole King . . . Her Greatest Hits*	Carole King
April 5	ABC	*Son of a Son of a Sailor*	Jimmy Buffett
April 12	Polydor/RSO	You're the One That I Want (S)	Olivia Newton-John & John Travolta

Date Awarded	Company	Title	Artist
April 25	Warner Bros.	*Endless Wire*	Gordon Lightfoot
May 2	Capricorn	*Together Forever*	The Marshall Tucker Band
May 5	Columbia	*The Sound in Your Mind*	Willie Nelson
June 7	Elektra	*Greatest Stories —Live*	Harry Chapin
June 12	RCA	*The Best of Dolly Parton*	Dolly Parton
June 16	RCA	It's a Heartache (S)	Bonnie Tyler
June 21	A&M	*Love Me Again*	Rita Coolidge
June 27	Columbia	*Street Legal*	Bob Dylan
June 27	RCA	*It's a Heartache*	Bonnie Tyler
July 20	Columbia	*Stardust*	Willie Nelson
July 27	Warner Bros./ Reprise	*Elite Hotel*	Emmylou Harris
August 16	RCA	*Heartbreaker*	Dolly Parton
August 31	MCA	Hopelessly Devoted to You (S)	Olivia Newton-John
August 31	Polydor/RSO	Summer Nights (S)	Olivia Newton-John/John Travolta & Cast
September 14	Columbia	*Nightwatch*	Kenny Loggins
September 15	United Artists	*When I Dream*	Crystal Gayle
September 15	United Artists	*Love or Something Like It*	Kenny Rogers
September 22	Asylum	*Living in the USA*	Linda Ronstadt
September 26	RCA	*I've Always Been Crazy*	Waylon Jennings
September 29	CBS/Epic/Full Moon	*Twin Sons of Different Mothers*	Dan Fogelberg & Tim Weisberg
October 12	Capitol	*Let's Keep It That Way*	Anne Murray
October 13	RCA	*Only One Love in My Life*	Ronnie Milsap
October 26	Capitol	You Needed Me (S)	Anne Murray
October 30	Capricorn	*Marshall Tucker Band's Greatest Hits*	The Marshall Tucker Band
November 6	Polydor	*Goin' Coconuts*	Marie & Donny Osmond
November 10	ABC	*You Had to be There*	Jimmy Buffett
November 13	Capitol	*A Retrospective*	Linda Ronstadt

Date Awarded	Company	Title	Artist
November 15	MCA	*Totally Hot*	Olivia Newton-John
November 21	Warner/Reprise	*Comes a Time*	Neil Young
November 30	United Artists	*The Gambler*	Kenny Rogers
December 14	Columbia	*Tanya Tucker's Greatest Hits*	Tanya Tucker
December 18	CBS/Epic	*Take This Job and Shove It*	Johnny Paycheck
December 18	RCA	*Elvis—A Legendary Performer, Volume 3*	Elvis Presley
December 19	Mercury	*Entertainers . . . On and Off the Record*	The Statler Brothers
December 26	Capitol	Sharing the Night Together (S)	Dr. Hook

1978 (Platinum)

Date Awarded	Company	Title	Artist
February 1	Columbia	*Greatest Hits, Etc.*	Paul Simon
February 15	United Artists	*We Must Believe in Magic*	Crystal Gayle
April 11	RCA	*Waylon and Willie*	Waylon Jennings and Willie Nelson
April 28	RCA	*Here You Come Again*	Dolly Parton
May 10	ABC	*Son of a Son of a Sailor*	Jimmy Buffett
May 12	RCA	*I Want to Live*	John Denver
May 23	Capricorn	*Carolina Dreams*	The Marshall Tucker Band
July 18	Polydor/RSO	You're the One That I Want (S)	Olivia Newton-John & John Travolta
July 20	United Artists	*Ten Years of Gold*	Kenny Rogers
August 25	Asylum	*Running on Empty*	Jackson Browne
September 22	Asylum	*Living in the USA*	Linda Ronstadt
October 13	Columbia	*Nightwatch*	Kenny Loggins
December 5	MCA	*Totally Hot*	Olivia Newton-John
December 12	CBS/Epic/Full Moon	*Twin Sons of Different Mothers*	Dan Fogelberg & Tim Weisberg
December 19	Capitol	*Let's Keep It That Way*	Anne Murray
December 26	Columbia	*Stardust*	Willie Nelson

Date Awarded	Company	Title	Artist

1979 (Gold)

Date Awarded	Company	Title	Artist
January 19	RCA	*John Denver*	John Denver
February 5	Capitol	*New Kind of Feeling*	Anne Murray
February 5	Elektra	Fire	The Pointer Sisters
February 12	MCA	A Little More Love (S)	Olivia Newton-John
February 13	Elektra	*Energy*	The Pointer Sisters
February 13	Columbia	*Willie & Family Live*	Willie Nelson
February 23	MCA	*TNT*	Tanya Tucker
February 27	Warner Bros.	*Nicolette Larson*	Nicolette Larson
April 12	MCA	*Legend*	Poco
May 15	Columbia	*Flag*	James Taylor
May 16	RCA	*Greatest Hits*	Waylon Jennings
June 28	Epic	*Million Mile Reflections*	The Charlie Daniels Band
July 2	United Artists	*Classics*	Kenny Rogers and Dottie West
August 2	Columbia	*One for the Road*	Willie Nelson and Leon Russell
August 6	United Artists	She Believes in Me (S)	Kenny Rogers
August 9	Reprise	*Decade*	Neil Young
August 21	Epic	The Devil Went Down to Georgia (S)	The Charlie Daniels Band
August 22	Capitol	When You're in Love with a Beautiful Woman (S)	Dr. Hook
August 28	Reprise	*Rust Never Sleeps*	Neil Young
September 11	Capitol	*Pleasure and Pain*	Dr. Hook
October 16	RCA	*Ronnie Milsap Live*	Ronnie Milsap
November 13	RCA	*Great Balls of Fire*	Dolly Parton
November 19	CBS	*Adventures of Panama Red*	New Riders of the Purple Sage
December 26	Columbia	*Slow Train Coming*	Bob Dylan
December 26	CBS	*Home Free*	Dan Fogelberg
December 27	MCA	*Volcano*	Jimmy Buffett

Date Awarded	Company	Title	Artist
		1979 (Platinum)	
February 27	United Artists	*The Gambler*	Kenny Rogers
August 16	Epic	*Million Mile Reflections*	The Charlie Daniels Band
September 7	RCA	*Greatest Hits*	Waylon Jennings
December 26	CBS	*Nether Lands*	Dan Fogelberg
January 10	CBS	*Miss the Mississippi*	Crystal Gayle
January 16	United Artists	*Kenny*	Kenny Rogers
February 1	RCA	*A Christmas Together*	John Denver & the Muppets
February 1	Asylum	*The Long Run*	Eagles
February 1	Asylum	Heartache Tonight (S)	Eagles
February 6	CBS	*Keep the Fire*	Kenny Loggins
February 7	Capitol	*I'll Always Love You*	Anne Murray
March 3	RCA	*What Goes Around*	Waylon Jennings
March 6	Columbia	*Willie Nelson Sings Kristofferson*	Willie Nelson
March 7	United Artists	Coward of the County (S)	Kenny Rogers
March 7	United Artists	*Classic Crystal*	Crystal Gayle
March 11	Warner Bros.	*Live Rust*	Neil Young & Crazy Horse
March 13	Epic	*Phoenix*	Dan Fogelberg
March 21	MCA	*Y'All Come Back Saloon*	The Oak Ridge Boys
May 12	Asylum	*Mad Love*	Linda Ronstadt
May 28	United Artists	*Gideon*	Kenny Rogers
June 6	Columbia	*Straight Ahead*	Larry Gatlin
July 3	Columbia	*Electric Horseman* (Original Motion Picture Soundtrack)	Various artists
July 10	Capitol	Sexy Eyes (S)	Dr. Hook
July 14	Asylum	*Urban Cowboy* (Original Motion Picture Soundtrack)	Various artists
July 15	MCA	Magic (S)	Olivia Newton-John
August 19	MCA	*Xanadu* (from Original Motion Picture Soundtrack	Olivia Newton-John & Electric Light Orchestra

Date Awarded	Company	Title	Artist
August 22	RCA	*Music Man*	Waylon Jennings
August 29	MCA	*The Oak Ridge Boys Have Arrived*	The Oak Ridge Boys
September 15	Asylum	*No Nukes*	Jackson Browne, Graham Nash, other artists
September 29	Epic	*Full Moon*	The Charlie Daniels Band
October 7	MCA	*The Best of Don Williams, Volume 2*	Don Williams
October 14	Warner Bros.	*One Trick Pony*	Paul Simon
October 15	Columbia	*Music From the Original Soundtrack, Honeysuckle Rose*	Willie Nelson & Family
October 24	Elektra	*Horizon*	Eddie Rabbitt
October 24	Elektra	*The Best of Eddie Rabbitt*	Eddie Rabbit
October 24	Warner Bros.	*Sweet Forgiveness*	Bonnie Raitt
November 10	Capitol	*Greatest Hits*	Anne Murray
November 14	Columbia	*Alive*	Kenny Loggins
November 25	Planet/Elektra	He's So Shy (S)	Pointer Sisters
November 25	Liberty	Lady (S)	Kenny Rogers
December 2	Capitol	*Greatest Hits*	Kenny Rogers
December 2	MCA	*I Believe In You*	Don Williams
December 5	Asylum	*Linda Ronstadt's Greatest Hits, Volume 2*	Linda Ronstadt

1980 (Platinum)

Date Awarded	Company	Title	Artist
January 16	United Artists	*Kenny*	Kenny Rogers
February 1	Asylum	*The Long Run*	The Eagles
February 1	RCA	*A Christmas Together*	John Denver & the Muppets
February 7	Warner Bros.	*Rust Never Sleeps*	Neil Young
February 7	Reprise	*Summertime Dream*	Gordon Lightfoot
March 6	Columbia	*Willie Nelson & Family Live*	Willie Nelson & Family
March 13	Epic	*Phoenix*	Dan Fogelberg
May 9	Columbia	*Slow Train Coming*	Bob Dylan
May 12	Asylum	*Mad Love*	Linda Ronstadt

Date Awarded	Company	Title	Artist
May 28	United Artists	*Gideon*	Kenny Rogers
July 24	Asylum	*Urban Cowboy* (Original Motion Picture Soundtrack	Various artists
August 19	MCA	*Xanadu* (From Original Motion Picture Soundtrack)	Olivia Newton-John & Electric Light Orchestra
September 15	Elektra	*Hold Out*	Jackson Browne
November 7	Epic	*Full Moon*	The Charlie Daniels Band
November 12	Columbia	*Music from the Original Soundtrack, Honeysuckle Rose*	Willie Nelson & Family
November 26	Capitol	*Greatest Hits*	Anne Murray
December 2	Capitol	*Greatest Hits*	Kenny Rogers
December 22	Columbia	*Celebrate Me Home*	Kenny Loggins

1981 (Gold)

Date Awarded	Company	Title	Artist
January 7	Asylum	*Eagles Live*	Eagles
January 26	MCA	*The Best of Barbara Mandrell*	Barbara Mandrell
February 4	MCA	*Oak Ridge Boys Greatest Hits*	Oak Ridge Boys
February 11	Warner Bros.	*Luxury Liner*	Emmylou Harris
February 12	RCA	*Greatest Hits*	Ronnie Milsap
February 18	Warner Bros.	*Blue Kentucky Girl*	Emmylou Harris
February 18	Warner Bros.	*Profile—Best of Emmylou Harris*	Emmylou Harris
February 19	RCA	*9 to 5* (S)	Dolly Parton
February 25	Mercury/Polygram	*The Best of the Statler Brothers Ride Again, Volume 2*	The Statler Brothers
March 4	Casablanca/Polygram	*It's Hard to be Humble*	Mac Davis
March 6	RCA	*9 to 5 and Odd Jobs*	Dolly Parton
March 10	Elektra	I Love a Rainy Night (S)	Eddie Rabbitt
March 25	Elektra	Drivin' My Life Away (S)	Eddie Rabbitt
April 1	Warner Bros.	*Roses in the Snow*	Emmylou Harris
May 5	Columbia	*Dad Loves His Work*	James Taylor
May 5	Columbia	*Somewhere Over the Rainbow*	Willie Nelson
May 27	RCA	*Feel So Right*	Alabama

Date Awarded	Company	Title	Artist
June 16	EMI-America	Bette Davis Eyes (S)	Kim Carnes
June 16	MCA	Elvira (S)	Oak Ridge Boys
June 26	Mercury/ Polygram	*The Originals*	The Statler Brothers
June 29	Capitol	*Where Do You Go When You Dream*	Anne Murray
July 1	Capitol	Angel of the Morning (S)	Juice Newton
July 14	RCA	*My Home's in Alabama*	Alabama
July 23	MCA	*Fancy Free*	Oak Ridge Boys
August 13	Capitol	*Juice*	Juice Newton
August 28	Liberty	*Share Your Love*	Kenny Rogers
September 2	Planet	Slowhand (S)	The Pointer Sisters
September 2	Capitol	Queen of Hearts (S)	Juice Newton
September 4	Epic	*Saddle Tramp*	The Charlie Daniels Band
September 9	Columbia	*Greatest Hits*	Larry Gatlin & the Gatlin Brothers Band
September 15	RCA	*Leather & Lace*	Waylon Jennings & Jessie Colter
September 16	Planet	*Black & White*	The Pointer Sisters
September 18	Epic	*I Am What I Am*	George Jones
October 5	Elektra	*Step by Step*	Eddie Rabbitt
October 9	Warner Bros.	*Evangeline*	Emmylou Harris
October 29	MCA	*Greatest Hits, Volume 2*	Loretta Lynn
October 29	MCA	*Lead Me On*	Loretta Lynn & Conway Twitty
October 29	MCA	*Greatest Hits, Volume 1*	Conway Twitty
November 2	Elektra/Curb	*Whiskey Bent & Hell Bound*	Hank Williams, Jr.
November 3	Columbia	*Willie Nelson's Greatest Hits (And Some That Will Be)*	Willie Nelson
November 3	Full Moon/Epic	*The Innocent Age*	Dan Fogelberg
December 8	RCA	*There's No Gettin' Over Me*	Ronnie Milsap
December 16	MCA	*Physical*	Olivia Newton-John
December 30	RCA	*Some Days Are Diamonds*	John Denver

Date Awarded	Company	Title	Artist
		1981 (Platinum)	
January 7	Elektra	*Eagles Live*	Eagles
February 23	Elektra	*Horizon*	Eddie Rabbitt
June 5	RCA	*John Denver's Greatest Hits, Volume 2*	John Denver
July 14	RCA	*Greatest Hits*	Ronnie Milsap
August 13	Columbia	*Somewhere Over the Rainbow*	Willie Nelson
August 28	Liberty	*Share Your Love*	Kenny Rogers
July 29	MCA	*Fancy Free*	Oak Ridge Boys
September 15	RCA	*Feel So Right*	Alabama
November 10	Full Moon/Epic	*The Innocent Age*	Dan Fogelberg
December 16	MCA	*Physical*	Olivia Newton-John
December 30	Columbia	*Best of Friends*	Loggins and Messina

BIBLIOGRAPHY

Aaron, John, "Gordon Lightfoot," *Guitar Player*, December 1973, p. 20.

Adamson, Dale, "John Conlee," *Houston Chronicle*, June 17, 1979.

———, "Guy Clark's got an album out—but he's not sure if it's his first," *ibid*, January 4, 1976.

———, "Roy Head thinks . . . 'My ship is coming in one of these days,'" *ibid*, May 3, 1976.

Albrecht, Jim, "Dottie West," *Country Style*, May 1981.

Allen, Bob, "Anne Murray, A New Kind of Feeling," *Country Music*, July 1979.

———, "Cheatin' Heart Special: Hank Williams Jr.," *Rolling Stone*, January 17, 1974, p. 20.

Anonymous, "Champion Country Picker" [Doc Watson], *Time*, August 25, 1967, pp. 40-41.

———, "Delaney Bramlett," *Village Voice*, February 12, 1970.

———, "James Taylor: One Man's Family of Rock," *Time*, March 1, 1971, pp. 45-53.

———, "John Wesley Ryles—A Comeback at 27," *Country Style*, February 1978.

———, "Latin Soul" [Jose Feliciano], *Time*, September 27, 1968.

———, "A Loose Federation" [Crosby, Stills, Nash, and Young], *Time*, March 30, 1970, p. 62.

———, "Montage of Loss" [Don McLean], *Time*, February 1972, p. 55.

———, "The Original Hippies, Homer and Jethro," *Gibson Gazette*, Volume 11, Number 1, 1971.

———, "Roy Acuff: After All These Years, Still Number One," *Country Song Roundup*, November 1978, pp. 15-17, 38.

———, "Tom Bresh," *Academy of Country Music Newsletter*, May 1975, p. 3.

———, "Scruggs Talks Through Banjo,"

Music City News, October 1969, p. 34A.

———, "Stu Philips," *Folk & Country*, Volume 1, Number 10.

———"Johnny Bond," CMA Close Up, March 1975, pp. 1, 7.

———, "Jim Ed Brown," *ibid*, October 1979, pp. 1, 3.

———, "Pee Wee King," *ibid*, May 1976, 1, 3.

———, "Charley Pride," *ibid*, March 1974, 1, 3.

———, "Porter Wagoner," *ibid*, August 1975, 1, 7.

Ansorge, Rick, "Goodman Leads His Flock From the Wilderness," [Steve Goodman], *Chicago Lakes Countryside*, March 16, 1978.

Anthony, Michael, "Twitty Remains Loyal to Country Music," *Minneapolis Tribune*, July 25, 1979.

Arnold, Christine, "Three Ex-Byrds Fly a New Course" [McGuinn, Clark and Hillman], *Miami Herald*, October 20, 1978.

Asch, Moses and Silber, Irwin, *900 Miles— The Ballads, Blues and Folksongs of Cisco Houston*, Oak Publications, New York, 1965.

Atkinson, Terry, "Western Rock: Son of the Sons of the Pioneers," *Los Angeles Times Calendar*, August 27, 1977, pp. 32, 34-35.

Axton, Mae Boren, "Hoyt Axton," *Picking Up the Tempo*, February/March 1976.

Ayres, Tom, "Gene Watson He Doesn't Cut Any 'B' Sides," *Country Style*, March 1978.

Bailey, Jerry, "Johnny Rodriguez 'Sometimes I Get Lonesome,'" *Country Music Beat*, January 1975.

Bane, Michael, "Eddie Rabbitt: Our New Entertainer of the Year," *Country Music*, January 1978.

Becker, Terry, "Politics Proved Final Note to Weavers' Brief Reign" [Lee Hays Obit],

Los Angeles Times, August 31, 1981, p. 22.

Billboard [weekly], Los Angeles, CA, Billboard Publications, various issues.

Blount, Roy Jr., "Wrasslin' with this Thing Called Willie Nelson," *Esquire*, August 1981, pp. 78-80, 83-87.

Blume, Mary, "The Rise of Leonard Cohen," *Los Angeles Times*, Part IV, August 28, 1970, p. 16.

Brand, Oscar, *The Ballad Mongers*, Funk & Wagnalls, New York, 1962.

Brokaw, Sanford, "Vern Gosdin—Success and the Grand Ole Opry the Second Time Around," *Country Song Roundup*, 1978.

Brooks, Michael, "David Bromberg," *Guitar Player*, March 1973, pp. 24-25, 36.

Broonzy, Big Bill, *Big Bill Blues* (as told to Yannick Bruynoghe), England, 1955; revised, with additional material, Oak Publications, New York, 1964.

Brown, Janes, "Other Things to Do—Phil Everly," *Los Angeles Times*, Part IV, January 3, 1974.

———, "That Old-Time Religion From the Old Cowboy" [Stuart Hamblen], *ibid* Calendar, April 4, 1976, p. 37.

Buchalter, Gail, "Tanya Tucker grows up into new music image," *Los Angeles Herald-Examiner*, November 20, 1978.

Burk, Bill E., "For Juice Press of Success Has Sweet Flavor" [Juice Newton], *Memphis Press—Scimitar*, May 22, 1981.

Cabot, Christopher, "Apostle of Nashville Sound" [Chet Atkins], *Los Angeles Times*, September 13, 1974.

Cackett, Alan, "Johnny Rodriguez," *Country Music People*, July 1974.

Caldwell, Carol, "Listen to Rosanne Cash," *Esquire*, July 1981.

Callahan, Kathy, "Fiddle champ credits classical music" [Jana Jae], *Tulsa Tribune*, Tempo, March 16, 1978.

Campbell, Bob, "The Oak Ridge Explosion" [Oak Ridge Boys], *Country Music*, June 1979.

Campbell, Mary, "The Joy Now Cooks Two Ways" [Joy of Cooking], *Associated Press*, January, 1978.

Carlisle, Dolly, "Gospel's Oak Ridge Boys Find a New Energy Source," *Country People*, May 28, 1979.

Carr, Patrick, "Johnny Cash's Freedom," *Country Music*, April 25, 1977.

Carrier, James, "Scruggs Plugs in to the New Sound," *Associated Press*, January 2, 1976.

Carter, Walter, "Moe & Joe Make 'Good Ol' Boy' Music," *Tennessean*, October 3, 1979.

Cash Box [weekly], New York, New York, Cash Box Publishing Co., various issues.

Charters, Samuel, *The Country Blues*, Rinehart, Winston & Co., New York, 1959.

———*The Bluesmen*, Oak Publications, New York, 1968.

Cherry, Hugh, "Johnny Cash—the Man Behind the Mask," *Family Weekly*, August 16, 1970.

Claypool, Bob, "Daniels Mirrors His Music" [Charlie Daniels], *Houston Post*, May 22, 1977, p. 42.

———. "Van Zandt—no average tourist on life's road," *ibid*, June 1, 1977.

Coats, Art and Leota, "Bryan Bowers," *Frets*, May 1979.

Coe, David Allan, *Just For the Record*, Dream Enterprises, Big Pine Key, Florida, 1978.

Cohen, John, "Fiddlin' Eck Robertson," *Sing Out!*, April-May 1964, pp. 55-59.

———"Joan Baez," *ibid*, Summer 1963, pp. 5-7.

——— "Roscoe Holcomb: First Person," *ibid*, April-May 1966, pp. 3-7.

Cohen, John and Seeger, Mike, eds. *The New Lost City Ramblers Song Book*, Oak Publications, New York, 1964.

Cohen, Norman, and Cohen, Anne, "The Legendary Jimmie Tarleton," *Sing Out!*, September 1966, pp. 16-19.

Cohn, Lawrence, "Mississippi John Hurt," *Sing Out!*, November 1964, pp. 16-21.

Corbin, Everett, "It's a Long Way From Chester County" [Eddy Arnold], *Music City News*, October 1969, p. 3B.

——— "Uncle Dave Macon, First Featured Star of the Grand Ole Opry," *ibid*, October 1973, pp. 24-C, 26-27-C.

——— "Mac Wiseman: Getting Back to Country Roots," *ibid*, October 1973, pp. 30-C, 31-C.

——— "Rouse Brothers Have Claim to Fame, Write 'Orange Blossom Special,'" *ibid*, October 1969, p. 38-B.

Crawford, Wayne, "There's much more now for Dion DiMucci," *Chicago Daily News*, February 28, 1970.

Cromelin, Richard, "De Shannon's Back on the Charts," *Los Angeles Times Calendar*, December 4, 1977, p. 80.

——— "Old School Folk From Eric Andersen," *Los Angeles Times*, June 1975.

Dane, Barbara, "Lone Cat Jesse Fuller," *Sing Out!*, December-January 1963-64, pp. 5-11.

Dane, Michael, "Roy Clark," *Country Music*, June 1978.

Deen, Dixie, "Bonnie Owens: a 'Capitol' Gain," *Music City News*, January 1968, pp. 3-4.

—— "Purely . . . Porter Wagoner," *ibid*, March 1967, pp. 3-4.

Deford, Frank, "To Conway Twitty, Who's Been a Star of Both, Country Is a Higher Art Than Rock'n'Roll," *People*, September 3, 1979.

Delaney, Kelly, "Ronnie Sessions: I've Been in Entertainment Since I Was Seven . . . And Still a Long Ways to Go," *Country Music*, January/February 1979.

Dew, Joan, "Freddie Hart: Pumping Out Great Music," *Country Music*, October 1976.

—— "Guess Who Lives Next Door to the Governor? Mrs. Sarah Ophelia Colley Cannon, That's Who" [Minnie Pearl], *ibid*, November 1974.

—— "Tammy Wynette: Heroine of Heartbreak," *Cosmopolitan*, April 1978.

Dorfman, Marilyn, "Lone Star sippin'. The country honkytonks are still home for Michael Murphey," *Unicorn Times*, August 1979.

Diehl, Digby, "Lightnin' Hopkins: Bolt From the Blue," *Los Angeles Times*, Part IV, July 12, 1968, p. 12.

Dylan, Bob, *The Freewheelin' Bob Dylan*, M. Witmark & Sons, New York, 1964.

Edwards, Joe, "Looks Like Kristofferson, Sounds Like Jim Reeves" [Johnny Duncan], *Chattanooga News Free Press*, September 11, 1976.

Ehler, Jay, "Waylon Jennings," *Country Life*, March/April 1973, pp. 4-5.

Eipper, Laura, "Conway Twitty—Making Changes These Days," *Tennessean*, May 13, 1979.

—— "Sharing Laughter with the Whole World" [Minnie Pearl], *Tennessean* Newspapers, 1978.

Epand, Len, "Country Joe" [McDonald], *City*, December 26, 1974, pp. 24-25.

Eskow, John, "Hank Williams Jr. The Son Also Rises," *New Times*, May 29, 1978.

Feather, Leonard, "Woody Guthrie, Noted Folk Singer, Dies at 55" [Obit], *Los Angeles Times*, October 4, 1967, p. 24.

Fein, Art, "Burnette: Salute to 'A Lovely Guy,' " *Los Angeles Times Calendar*, October 7, 1979, p. 66.

Fong-Torres, Ben, "Leon Russell," *Rolling Stone*, December 2. 1970, pp. 33-37.

Forrest, Rick, "The Kenny Rogers Touring Machine," *On Stage*, 1981.

Fulton, E. Kaye, "The New, Improved Anne Murray, Happier, Richer Than Ever," *Odyssey*, Volume 1, Number 2, 1979.

Gentry, Linnell, *History and Encyclopedia of Country, Western & Gospel Music*, McQuiddy Press, Nashville, Tennessee, 1961.

Graustark, Barbara and Abramson, Pamela, "Paganini of the Mandolin" [David Grisman], *Newsweek*, November 10, 1980, p. 81.

Green, Archie, "Dorsey Dixon: Minstrel of the Mills," *Sing Out!*, July 1966, pp. 10-12.

Green, Douglas B., "Barbara Mandrell, Picker/Singer," *Pickin'* September 1978.

Green, Douglas B., Notes for jacket of album *Roy Acuff Greatest Hits, Volume 1*, Elektra Records, September 1978.

Greenblatt, Mike, "Lacy J. Dalton's Ongoing Odyssey," *Aquarian*, April 16, 1980.

Guralnick, Peter, "Ernest Tubb: Still the Texas Troubadour," *Country Music*, 1977.

—— "James Talley Goes Home Again," *Village Voice*, New York, March 15, 1976.

—— "Mickey Gilley's Piano Roll Blues," *Country Music*.

Guthrie, Woody, *American Folksong/Woody Guthrie* (Ed. Moses Asch), Disc. Co. of America, New York, 1947; Oak Publications, New York, 1961.

—— *Born to Win*, Macmillan, New York, 1965.

Hackett, Vernell, "Gene Watson: A Lesson in Learning," *Country Song Roundup*, November 1977.

—— "Even Stevens Writes 'Em and Sings 'Em," *Music City News*.

Hardesty, Will, "The Pride of Paw Paw, West Virginia: Asleep at the Wheel," *Rocky Mountain Musical Express*, August 1977, p. 15.

Hedy, Judy, "Mel Tillis—It's a Long Way From Detroit City," *Country Song Roundup*, February 1977.

Henstell, Bruce, "How the King of Western Swing Reached the End of His Rope" [Spade Cooley], *Los Angeles Magazine*, June 1979, 126-136.

Hentoff, Nat, "Profile: Bob Dylan," *New Yorker*, October 24, 1964, pp. 61-62.

Hilburn, Robert, "Bob Dylan: Still Playing

Guitar and Singing His Songs," *Los Angeles Times Calendar*, May 28, 1978, p. 66.

——— "Bruised Orange: Prine Gets His Second Wind" [John Prine], *ibid*, May 21, 1978, pp. 64, 86.

——— "Dazzling Vegas Debut for Dolly Parton," *ibid*, February 23, 1981.

——— "George Jones—Back From the Brink," *ibid*, March 8, 1981, pp. 72, 74.

——— "Gram Parsons—Straight Home to Us," *ibid*, November 2, 1975, pp. 62-63.

——— "I Learned That Jesus Is Real and I Wanted That" [Bob Dylan], *ibid*, November 23, 1980, p. 1.

——— "The Legend of Jennings," *Los Angeles Times*, Part IV, May 20, 1975, p. 12.

——— "Nelson Avoids the Country Bland Wagon," *Los Angeles Times Calendar*, November 23, 1976, p. 68.

——— "Mickey Newbury——Leaving Despair Behind," *ibid*, April 1, 1973.

——— "Parton: The New Pop Sweetheart" [Dolly Parton], *ibid*, February 15, 1981, p. 66.

——— "Ray Charles: Q & A With a Genius," *ibid*, August 24, 1980, pp. 74, 78.

——— "Simon Without Garfunkel Makin' It As a Single," *ibid*, May 27, 1973.

——— "Tallying the Rents in the Fabric of a Dream" [James Talley], *ibid*, March 28, 1976, pp. 68, 71.

——— "A Texan Tries It As a Lone Star" [Doug Sahm], *ibid*, June 16, 1974, p. 58.

——— "Willie Nelson, Country Music With a Concept," *ibid*, March 17, 1974, p. 54.

Hinton, Sam, "Bess Hawes," *Sing Out!*, September 1965, pp. 26-30.

Hofen, Betty, " 'I'll Stick to My Guns,' Says Popular Diana Trask," *Music City News*, February 1970.

House, Son, "I Can Make My Own Songs," *Sing Out!*, July 1965, pp. 38-45.

Hume, Martha, "Crystal Gayle, at home in the middle of the road," *Rolling Stone*, May 19, 1977.

Humphrey, Mark, "Bert Jansch," *Frets*, March 1980, pp. 18-22.

Hunt, Dennis, "Alabama Loves Southern Rock," *Los Angeles Times Calendar*, June 4, 1981.

——— "Gatlin Goes for the Gusto," *Los Angeles Times*, November 30, 1980.

——— "Juice Newton? She's a Star on the Rise," *ibid*, April 8, 1981, pp. 1, 10.

——— "Judy Collins Nears 40," *ibid*, Part IV, February 16, 1979, p. 28.

——— "Olivia Newton-John Just Another Pretty Voice," *ibid*, Part IV, pp. 1, 12.

Hunter, Glenn, "Stoney Edwards, the Case of Country's Number Two Black Star," *Country Music*, March 1976.

Hunter, Mark, "Tony Rice," *Frets*, April 1980, pp. 26-30.

Hurst, Jack, "Barbara Mandrell Tries Not to Mix Music, Politics," *Chicago Tribune*, Section 4, January 3, 1979.

——— "Gene Watson: From auto body shops to a real smash on country record charts," *ibid*, June 28, 1978.

——— "Hank Williams Jr. is alive and well and that's very close to being a miracle," *ibid*, Magazine, February 12, 1978.

——— "Mandrell on the Move," *ibid*, Magazine, April 22, 1979.

——— "New dawn awaits 'Make It Through the Night' singer" [Sammi Smith], *ibid*, March 23, 1978.

——— "Thompson, echo from the past, still finds a place on the charts" [Hank Thompson], *ibid*, September 12, 1979.

——— "Willie Nelson: Country Music's Gentleman Outlaw," *ibid*, Magazine, November 18, 1979.

Ives, Burl, *Wayfaring Stranger*, Whittlesey House, New York, 1948.

Jackson, Bill, "La Costa: Country gal with homespun talent," *Valley News*, Van Nuys, CA, April 21, 1976.

Johnson, Jared, "Eddie Rabbitt Proves Country-Pop Crossover Capabilities," *Denver Post*, September 9, 1979.

Johnson, Tom, "Josh White Jr.," *Performance*, March 30, 1979, pp. 4-5.

Keil, Charles, *Urban Blues*, University of Chicago Press, 1966.

Keil, Karen, "A Touch of Pride" [Charley Pride], *Folk & Country*, Volume 1, Number 3, May 1968, p. 5.

King, Bill, "On the Road With the Oak Ridge Boys," *Atlanta Journal & Constitution Weekend*, February 16, 1980, pp. 34-36.

Kingsley, Michelle Pelick, "Wanted: Byron Berline," *Frets*, June 1979, pp. 34-36.

Klomar, William, "Laura Nyro: She's the Hippest—and Maybe the Hottest," *New York Times*, October 6, 1968.

Koppel, David, "Jessi Colter and her big grey bus," *Chicago Sun Times*, August 6, 1978.

Lawless, Ray McKinley, *Folksingers and Folksongs in America*, Duell, Sloan & Pearce, New York, 1960; revised ed., 1965.

Littleton, Bill, "T.G. Adjusts to Success" [T.G. Sheppard], *Music City News*, February 1976, p. 19.

Lloyd, Jack, "Asleep at the Wheel Plays More Than Western Swing," *Philadelphia Enquirer*, December 9, 1977.

Lomax, Alan, *The Folk Songs of North America*, Doubleday, Garden City, New York, 1960.

——, ed., *The Penguin Book of American Folk Songs*, Penguin Books, Baltimore, Maryland, 1965.

Lomax, John Avery, *Adventures of a Ballad Hunter*, Macmillan, New York, 1947.

Lomax, John A. and Alan, *Folksong, U.S.A.*, Duell, Sloan & Pearce, New York, 1947.

—— *Our Singing Country*, Macmillan, New York, 1941.

Mann, Roderick, "Kristofferson: A Star Is Reborn," *Los Angeles Times Calendar*, January 10, 1982, p. 18.

Mariani, John, "The Fighting Side of Merle Haggard," *Saga*, November 1979, p. 41.

Marsh, Dave and Swenson, John, *The Rolling Stone Record Guide*, Random House/Rolling Stone Press, New York, 1979.

Maslin, Janet, "There's Nothing I Like About It—But It May Be a Classic" [Leonard Cohen], *New York Times*, November 6, 1977.

McCollum, Charlie, "James Talley: Jimmie Rodgers in Mod Dress," *Washington Star*.

McGhee, Brownie, "Brownie McGhee On Playing the Blues," as told to Michael Brooks, *Guitar Player*.

McMahon, Regan, "Holly Near: Power in the Darkness," *BAM Magazine*, November 2, 1979.

—— "Rick Nelson," *ibid*, January 16, 1981, pp. 14-17.

Millar, Jeff, "Leadbelly—Music Man With a Mean Streak," *Los Angeles Times Calendar*, December 22, 1974, p. 44.

Millard, Bob, "Sonny Throckmorton: A 14 Year Overnight Success," *Country Scene*, April 1979.

Moon, Buck, "Tribute to a White Trash Saint" [Hank Williams Sr.], *Rocky Mountain Musical Express*, March 1977, p. 20.

Moore, Thurston, *Country Music Who's Who*, Heather Publications, Denver, Colorado, various editions.

Moore, Mary Ellen, "Watch This Face: Mel McDaniel," *Country Music*, January 1977.

Modderno, Craig, "Lady's Man" [Kenny Rogers], *US*, December 9, 1980.

Morthland, John, "Jerry Jeff Rides Again . . . Again" [Jerry Jeff Walker], *Country Music*.

—— "Jersey's Country Boy" [Eddie Rabbit], *Newsday*, September 18, 1977.

Mothner, I., "Big Folk-Singers on Campus: Peter, Paul & Mary," *Look*, July 2, 1963, pp. 59-62.

Music City News, Nashville, Tennessee, various issues.

Neff, James, "Freddy Fender Bares All," *Country Style*, August 11, 1977.

Nelson, Paul and Pankake, Jon, "Uncle Dave Macon—Country Immortal," *Sing Out!*, Summer 1963, pp. 19-21.

Niles, John Jacob, *The Ballad Book*, Houghton, Mifflin, New York, 1961.

O'Neal, Jim and Amy, "John Lee Hooker," *Living Blues*, Autumn 1979, pp. 14-22.

Pankake, Jon, "Mike Seeger: the Style of Tradition," *Sing Out!*, July 1964, pp. 6-11.

—— "Sam and Kirk McGee From Sunny Tennessee," *ibid*, November 1964, pp. 46-50.

Pierce, Michael, "Brewer & Shipley," *Guitar Player*, July/August 1973, p. 13.

Proffitt, Frank, "Good Memories for Me," *Sing Out!*, November 1965, pp. 34-37.

Pugh, John T., "Mel Tillis—From a Strawberry Patch to National Stardom," *Music City News*, May 1970, p. 22.

Ramsey, Frederic, Jr., "Leadbelly: A Great Long Time," *Sing Out!*, March 1965, pp. 7-24.

Rassenfoss, Joe, "A couple weeks, that's a long time" [Delbert McClinton], *Birmingham Post-Herald Kudzu*, October 31, 1980, p. 4.

Rea, Steven, "Melancholy Genius," [Eric Andersen], *Music World*, November 1973, p. 70.

Record World [weekly], Record World Publishing Co., New York, various issues.

Rector, Lee, "Oak Ridge Boys Set High Energy Levels for Career, Today and Tomorrow," *Music City News*, November 1979, pp. 14-15.

Reinert, Al, "King of Country" [Willie Nelson], *New York Times Magazine*, March 26, 1978.

Ritchie, Jean, *Singing Family of the Cumberlands*, Oak Publications, New York, 1963.

Roberts, Frank M., "Life's a Bed of Roses

for the Statler Brothers," *Charlotte News,* January 17, 1980.

Robinson, Lisa, "Rogers Is a Big Star" [Kenny Rogers], *New York Times Feature Syndicate,* September 14, 1981.

Rockwell, John, "Folk Music Is Back With a Twang," *New York Times,* Section 2, April 30, 1978, pp. 1, 22.

—— "Steve Forbert, New Folk Singer," *ibid,* December #, 1977.

Roden, Jim, "Bandy revives a new old sound," *Dallas Times Herald,* February 6, 1976.

Rowlett, Sharon, "Cal Smith," *Rocky Mountain Musical Express,* May 1978, p. 17.

—— "Life at the Top So Beautiful for Sensuous Craddock" [Billy "Crash" Craddock], *Country Style Monthly,* January 1978.

Sander, Ellen, "Paul Siebel: Homegrown Weed," *Saturday Review,* January 30, 1971.

—— "Crosby, Stills & Nash: Renaissance Fare," *ibid,* May 31, 1969.

Satterfield, La Wayne, " 'I Want to Be a Giver, Not a Taker,' Says Tommy Overstreet of Life, Career," *Music City News,* July 1971, p. 8.

—— "Johnny Rodriguez, New Heartthrob of Country Music," *ibid,* October 1973, p. 37-A.

—— "Melba Wraps Herself in Song" [Melba Montgomery], *ibid,* October 1973, p. 16-A.

—— "O.B. Doesn't Mind Being 'The Other One' " [O.B. McClinton], *ibid,* October 1973, pp. 3-C, 37-C.

—— "Sandy Posey Measures Success in Giving," *ibid,* December 1971, p. 13.

Schwann's Record and Tape Guide, W. Schwann, Inc., Boston, MA, various issues.

Scobey, Lola, "Buck Trent, 'The Banjo Bandit' Sidekick, Steps Out From Roy Clark's Shadow," *Country Music,* March 1979.

Scruggs, Louise, "A History of America's Favorite Folk Instrument," *Sing Out!,* December/January 1963-64, pp. 26-29.

Seder, Jennifer, "Buffy" [Buffy Sainte-Marie], *Los Angeles Times,* March 31, 1978.

Siegal, Eric, "Country or rock . . . Who Cares? Lacy J. Dalton's on her way up," *Baltimore Sun,* April 6, 1980.

Siminoff, Roger H., "Bill Keith," *Frets,* March 1980, pp. 32-37.

Smith, Hobart, "I Just Got the Music in My Head," *Sing Out!,* January 1964, pp. 10-13.

Stambler, Irwin, *Encyclopedia of Pop, Rock & Soul,* St. Martin's Press, New York, 1974, 1977.

Stambler, Irwin and Landon, Grelun, *Encyclopedia of Folk Country and Western Music,* First Edition, *ibid,* New York, 1969.

—— *Golden Guitars, The Story of Country Music,* Four Winds Press, New York, 1971.

Sullivan, Jerry, "Magic Fingers" [Doc Watson], *Chicago Sun Times,* October 3, 1977.

Thompson, Toby, *Positively Main Street: An Unorthodox View of Bob Dylan,* Coward McCann, New York, 1971.

Trubo, Richard, "Tim Can Almost Smell the Roses Now" [Tim Rose], *Los Angeles Times Calendar,* July 16, 1972, p. 78.

Underwood, Lee, "Tim Buckley Remembered," *downbeat,* June 16, 1977, pp. 25-27, 56.

Wakefield, Dan, "Joan Baez," *Redbook,* January 1967, p. 114.

Warner, Frank, "Traditional Singers #3: Frank Proffitt," *Sing Out!,* October/November 1963, pp. 6-11.

Watson, Doc, "Folksinging Is a Way of Life," *Sing Out!,* February/March 1964, pp. 8-12.

Weintraub, Boris, " 'Oak Ridge' in business to make music," *Washington Star,* Section B, March 24, 1979.

Welding, Pete, "B.B. King, the Mississippi Giant," *downbeat,* October 5, 1978, pp. 20-22, 64; October 19, 1978, pp. 17, 39-40.

Whitburn, Joel, *Top Country Records* [based on *Billboard* charts], Record Research, Menomenee Falls, WI, various editions.

Williams, Don, "The Private World of Don Williams" (as told to Kelly Delaney), *Country Style,* September 1980.

Williams, Roger Neville, "Jesse Winchester: the return of the native," *San Francisco Bay Guardian,* June 9, 1977.

Wilson, John S., "Newport Is His Just for a Song" [Arlo Guthrie], *New York Times,* July 18, 1967.

Winters, Audrey, "Buck Owens: A Career Built on Careful Planning," *Music City News,* October 1969, p. 40-A.

Yaryan, Bill, "Ramblin' Jack Elliott," *Sing Out!,* November 1965, pp. 25-28.

Young, Jon, "Charlie Daniels' million-dollar miles," *Rolling Stone,* November 1, 1979.